Great Britain

LEGEND
Freeway/Motorway
Major Rail Line
Airport
National Park/ Natural Wonder
Ruin, Museum, other Point of Interest
Mountain Peak
Castle/Monument/Palace
50 Km
50 Miles
SCOTLAND
HIGHLANDS
Outer Hebrides
The Minch
Sea of the Hebrides
Moray Firth
Firth of Forth
Firth of Lorn
North Sea
NETHERLANDS
BELGIUM
FRANCE
FLANDERS
EAST ANGLIA
KENT
SOUTH DOWNS
Channel
Isle of Lewis
Stornoway
Durness
Scourie
Scrabster
Thurso
Gills
John o'Groats
Wick
To Orkney Islands
Helmsdale
Ullapool
Harris
Tarbert
North Uist
Lochmaddy
South Uist
Uig
DUNVEGAN
Portree
Isle of Skye
Broadford
Lochboisdale
Barra
Tain
Ringwall
Nairn
Macduff
Inverness
CAWDOR
CULLODEN BATTLEFIELD
CLAVA CAIRNS
Kyle of Lochalsh
EILEAN DONAN
URQUART
Kyleakin
Armadale
Rhum
Mallaig
Loch Ness
Caledonian Canal
Fort Augustus
Aviemore
Aberdeen
BALMORAL
Fort William
BEN NEVIS
Coll
Tiree
Tobermory
Isle of Mull
Staffa
Craigmure
Iona
Kerrera
Seil
Colonsay
Jura
Islay
Loch Linnhe
Glencoe
BLAIR
Pitlochry
Crianlarich
Oban
Loch Awe
Inveraray
Loch Fyne
Loch Lomond
WALLACE MONUMENT
Stirling
Perth
Dundee
Leuchars
St. Andrews
Anstruther
East Neuk
M-90
M-9
M-8
Glasgow
Edinburgh
To Amsterdam, Neth.
dlesbrough
Staithes
Whitby
Pickering
Scarborough
CASTLE HOWARD
Bridlington
York
Kingston-upon-Hull
Grimsby
Lincoln
Skegness
Boston
AND
Cromer
King's Lynn
Norwich
Great Yarmouth
Stamford
Peterborough
Ely
Northampton
Cambridge
Ipswich
Harwich
Colchester
M-1
Luton
Stansted
Hertford
M-11
To Esbjerg, Denmark
London
Southend
Southend-on-Sea
Windsor
City
Greenwich
Heathrow
M-20
M-2
M-23
Gatwick
Ramsgate
Canterbury
Dover
Ashford
Folkestone
Rye
Hastings
Brighton
Eastbourne
BEACHY HEAD
Channel Tunnel
Dunkerque
Calais
To Ouistreham & Le Havre, France
Haarlem
Aalsmeer
The Hague
Delft
Hoek van Holland
Rotterdam
Zeebrugge
Ostende
Bruges
Antwerp
E313
E40
Ghent
E17
Brussels
WATERLOO
Lille
A16
A26
E42
To Paris
Namur

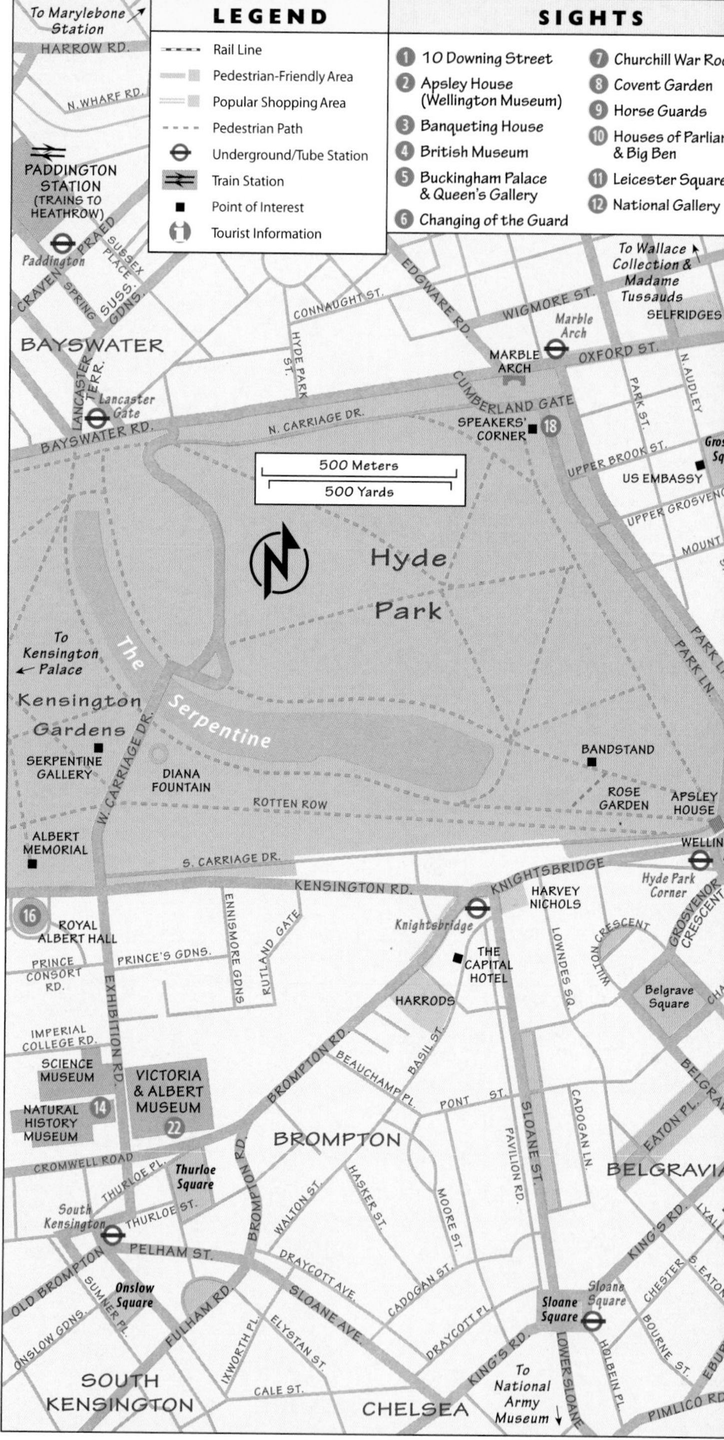

LEGEND
Rail Line
Pedestrian-Friendly Area
Popular Shopping Area
Pedestrian Path
Underground/Tube Station
Train Station
Point of Interest
Tourist Information
SIGHTS
1 10 Downing Street
2 Apsley House (Wellington Museum)
3 Banqueting House
4 British Museum
5 Buckingham Palace & Queen's Gallery
6 Changing of the Guard
7 Churchill War Roo
8 Covent Garden
9 Horse Guards
10 Houses of Parliam & Big Ben
11 Leicester Square
12 National Gallery
To Marylebone Station
HARROW RD.
N. WHARF RD.
PADDINGTON STATION (TRAINS TO HEATHROW)
Paddington
PRAED
SUSSEX PLACE
SUSS. GDNS.
CRAVEN
SPRING
BAYSWATER
LANCASTER TERR.
Lancaster Gate
BAYSWATER RD.
CONNAUGHT ST.
HYDE PARK ST.
EDGWARE RD.
WIGMORE ST.
Marble Arch
MARBLE ARCH
OXFORD ST.
To Wallace Collection & Madame Tussauds
SELFRIDGES
CUMBERLAND GATE
N. CARRIAGE DR.
SPEAKERS' CORNER
18
PARK ST.
N. AUDLEY
UPPER BROOK ST.
US EMBASSY
UPPER GROSVENO
MOUNT
500 Meters
500 Yards
Hyde Park
PARK LN.
PARK LN.
To Kensington Palace
Kensington Gardens
The Serpentine
SERPENTINE GALLERY
W. CARRIAGE DR.
DIANA FOUNTAIN
ROTTEN ROW
BANDSTAND
ROSE GARDEN
APSLEY HOUSE
ALBERT MEMORIAL
S. CARRIAGE DR.
WELLING
KENSINGTON RD.
KNIGHTSBRIDGE
HARVEY NICHOLS
Hyde Park Corner
16
ROYAL ALBERT HALL
Knightsbridge
GROSVENOR CRESCENT
WILTON CRESCENT
PRINCE CONSORT RD.
PRINCE'S GDNS.
ENNISMORE GDNS.
RUTLAND GATE
THE CAPITAL HOTEL
LOWNDES SQ.
Belgrave Square
HARRODS
IMPERIAL COLLEGE RD.
EXHIBITION RD.
BROMPTON RD.
BEAUCHAMP PL.
BASIL ST.
SCIENCE MUSEUM
VICTORIA & ALBERT MUSEUM
NATURAL HISTORY MUSEUM
14
22
PONT ST.
SLOANE ST.
CADOGAN LN.
PAVILION RD.
BELGRAVE
EATON PL.
BROMPTON
CROMWELL ROAD
THURLOE PL.
Thurloe Square
BROMPTON RD.
BELGRAVIA
South Kensington
THURLOE ST.
WALTON ST.
HASKER ST.
MOORE ST.
KING'S RD.
LYALL
PELHAM ST.
OLD BROMPTON
SUMNER PL.
Onslow Square
DRAYCOTT AVE.
SLOANE AVE.
CADOGAN ST.
Sloane Square
CHESTER
S. EATON
FULHAM RD.
ONSLOW GDNS.
IXWORTH PL.
ELYSTAN ST.
DRAYCOTT PL.
BOURNE ST.
SOUTH KENSINGTON
CALE ST.
KING'S RD.
To National Army Museum
LOWER SLOANE
HOLBEIN PL.
EBURY
PIMLICO RD.
CHELSEA

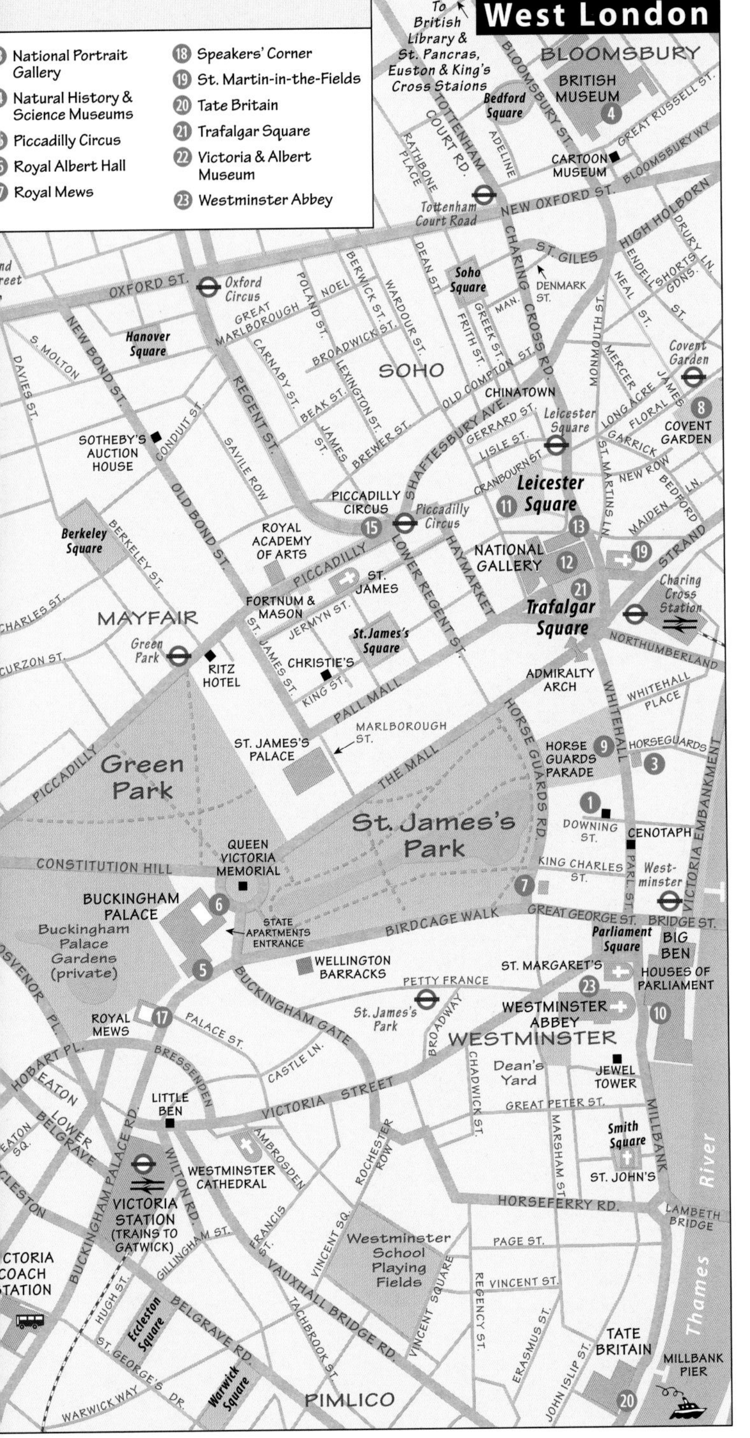
West London
National Portrait Gallery
Natural History & Science Museums
Piccadilly Circus
Royal Albert Hall
Royal Mews
18 Speakers' Corner
19 St. Martin-in-the-Fields
20 Tate Britain
21 Trafalgar Square
22 Victoria & Albert Museum
23 Westminster Abbey
To British Library & St. Pancras, Euston & King's Cross Staions
BLOOMSBURY
BRITISH MUSEUM
Bedford Square
CARTOON MUSEUM
SOHO
Soho Square
CHINATOWN
Leicester Square
COVENT GARDEN
Covent Garden
MAYFAIR
Hanover Square
Berkeley Square
SOTHEBY'S AUCTION HOUSE
ROYAL ACADEMY OF ARTS
PICCADILLY CIRCUS
FORTNUM & MASON
ST. JAMES
St. James's Square
CHRISTIE'S
RITZ HOTEL
NATIONAL GALLERY
Trafalgar Square
Charing Cross Station
ADMIRALTY ARCH
ST. JAMES'S PALACE
Green Park
St. James's Park
HORSE GUARDS PARADE
CENOTAPH
QUEEN VICTORIA MEMORIAL
BUCKINGHAM PALACE
Buckingham Palace Gardens (private)
STATE APARTMENTS ENTRANCE
WELLINGTON BARRACKS
Parliament Square
BIG BEN
HOUSES OF PARLIAMENT
ST. MARGARET'S
WESTMINSTER ABBEY
WESTMINSTER
Dean's Yard
JEWEL TOWER
ROYAL MEWS
LITTLE BEN
WESTMINSTER CATHEDRAL
VICTORIA STATION (TRAINS TO GATWICK)
VICTORIA COACH STATION
Smith Square
ST. JOHN'S
Westminster School Playing Fields
Eccleston Square
Warwick Square
PIMLICO
TATE BRITAIN
MILLBANK PIER
River Thames

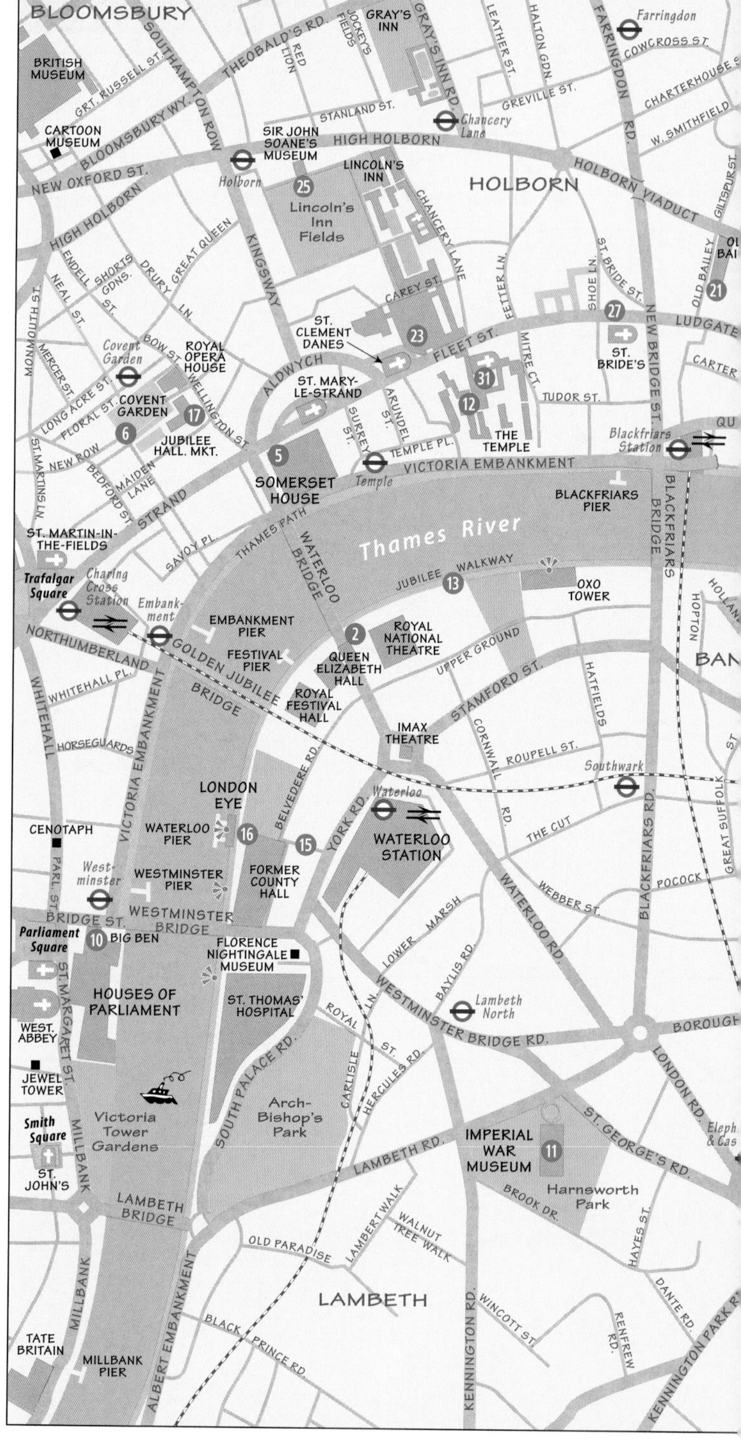

BLOOMSBURY
HOLBORN
LAMBETH
Thames River
BRITISH MUSEUM
CARTOON MUSEUM
SIR JOHN SOANE'S MUSEUM
GRAY'S INN
LINCOLN'S INN
Lincoln's Inn Fields
ROYAL OPERA HOUSE
COVENT GARDEN
JUBILEE HALL. MKT.
ST. CLEMENT DANES
ST. MARY-LE-STRAND
SOMERSET HOUSE
THE TEMPLE
ST. BRIDE'S
BLACKFRIARS PIER
ST. MARTIN-IN-THE-FIELDS
Trafalgar Square
EMBANKMENT PIER
FESTIVAL PIER
QUEEN ELIZABETH HALL
ROYAL NATIONAL THEATRE
ROYAL FESTIVAL HALL
OXO TOWER
IMAX THEATRE
LONDON EYE
WATERLOO PIER
FORMER COUNTY HALL
WATERLOO STATION
CENOTAPH
WESTMINSTER PIER
Parliament Square
BIG BEN
FLORENCE NIGHTINGALE MUSEUM
HOUSES OF PARLIAMENT
ST. THOMAS' HOSPITAL
WEST. ABBEY
JEWEL TOWER
Smith Square
ST. JOHN'S
Victoria Tower Gardens
Arch-Bishop's Park
IMPERIAL WAR MUSEUM
Harnsworth Park
TATE BRITAIN
MILLBANK PIER
Farringdon
Chancery Lane
Holborn
Covent Garden
Temple
Blackfriars Station
Charing Cross Station
Embankment
Southwark
Waterloo
Westminster
Lambeth North
25
23
27
21
31
12
17
6
5
13
2
16
15
10
11

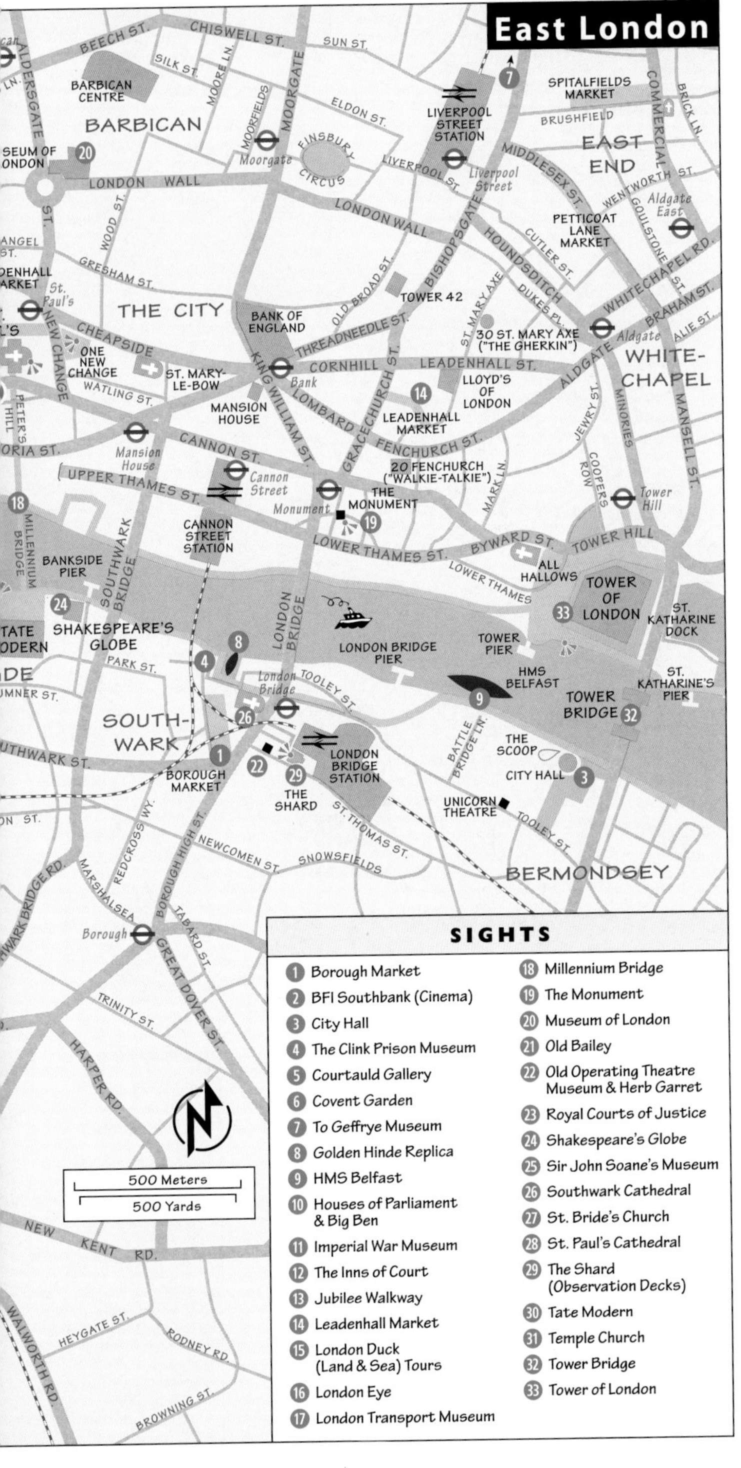
East London
SIGHTS
1 Borough Market
2 BFI Southbank (Cinema)
3 City Hall
4 The Clink Prison Museum
5 Courtauld Gallery
6 Covent Garden
7 To Geffrye Museum
8 Golden Hinde Replica
9 HMS Belfast
10 Houses of Parliament & Big Ben
11 Imperial War Museum
12 The Inns of Court
13 Jubilee Walkway
14 Leadenhall Market
15 London Duck (Land & Sea) Tours
16 London Eye
17 London Transport Museum
18 Millennium Bridge
19 The Monument
20 Museum of London
21 Old Bailey
22 Old Operating Theatre Museum & Herb Garret
23 Royal Courts of Justice
24 Shakespeare's Globe
25 Sir John Soane's Museum
26 Southwark Cathedral
27 St. Bride's Church
28 St. Paul's Cathedral
29 The Shard (Observation Decks)
30 Tate Modern
31 Temple Church
32 Tower Bridge
33 Tower of London
500 Meters
500 Yards
BARBICAN CENTRE
BARBICAN
THE CITY
BANK OF ENGLAND
MANSION HOUSE
ONE NEW CHANGE
ST. MARY-LE-BOW
TOWER 42
30 ST. MARY AXE ("THE GHERKIN")
LLOYD'S OF LONDON
LEADENHALL MARKET
20 FENCHURCH ("WALKIE-TALKIE")
THE MONUMENT
CANNON STREET STATION
LIVERPOOL STREET STATION
SPITALFIELDS MARKET
EAST END
PETTICOAT LANE MARKET
WHITE-CHAPEL
ALL HALLOWS
TOWER OF LONDON
ST. KATHARINE DOCK
ST. KATHARINE'S PIER
TOWER PIER
HMS BELFAST
TOWER BRIDGE
LONDON BRIDGE PIER
BANKSIDE PIER
SHAKESPEARE'S GLOBE
SOUTH-WARK
BOROUGH MARKET
THE SHARD
LONDON BRIDGE STATION
THE SCOOP
CITY HALL
UNICORN THEATRE
BERMONDSEY
Moorgate
Liverpool Street
Aldgate East
Aldgate
Bank
Mansion House
Cannon Street
Monument
Tower Hill
London Bridge
Borough
St. Paul's
CHISWELL ST.
BEECH ST.
SUN ST.
SILK ST.
MOORE LN.
MOORFIELDS
MOORGATE
ELDON ST.
FINSBURY CIRCUS
LIVERPOOL ST.
LONDON WALL
BRUSHFIELD
COMMERCIAL
BRICK LN.
MIDDLESEX ST.
WENTWORTH ST.
GOULSTONE ST.
WHITECHAPEL RD.
ALDERSGATE ST.
WOOD ST.
GRESHAM ST.
OLD BROAD ST.
BISHOPSGATE
HOUNDSDITCH
CUTLER ST.
DUKES PL.
ST. MARY AXE
BRAHAM ST.
ALIE ST.
CHEAPSIDE
NEW CHANGE
WATLING ST.
THREADNEEDLE ST.
CORNHILL
LEADENHALL ST.
ALDGATE
KING WILLIAM ST.
LOMBARD ST.
GRACECHURCH ST.
FENCHURCH ST.
JEWRY ST.
MINORIES
MANSELL ST.
CANNON ST.
UPPER THAMES ST.
MARK LN.
COOPERS ROW
LOWER THAMES ST.
BYWARD ST.
TOWER HILL
LOWER THAMES
MILLENNIUM BRIDGE
SOUTHWARK BRIDGE
LONDON BRIDGE
PARK ST.
TOOLEY ST.
BATTLE BRIDGE LN.
ST. THOMAS ST.
REDCROSS WY.
BOROUGH HIGH ST.
NEWCOMEN ST.
SNOWSFIELDS
MARSHALSEA RD.
TABARD ST.
GREAT DOVER ST.
TRINITY ST.
HARPER RD.
NEW KENT RD.
HEYGATE ST.
RODNEY RD.
BROWNING ST.
WALWORTH RD.

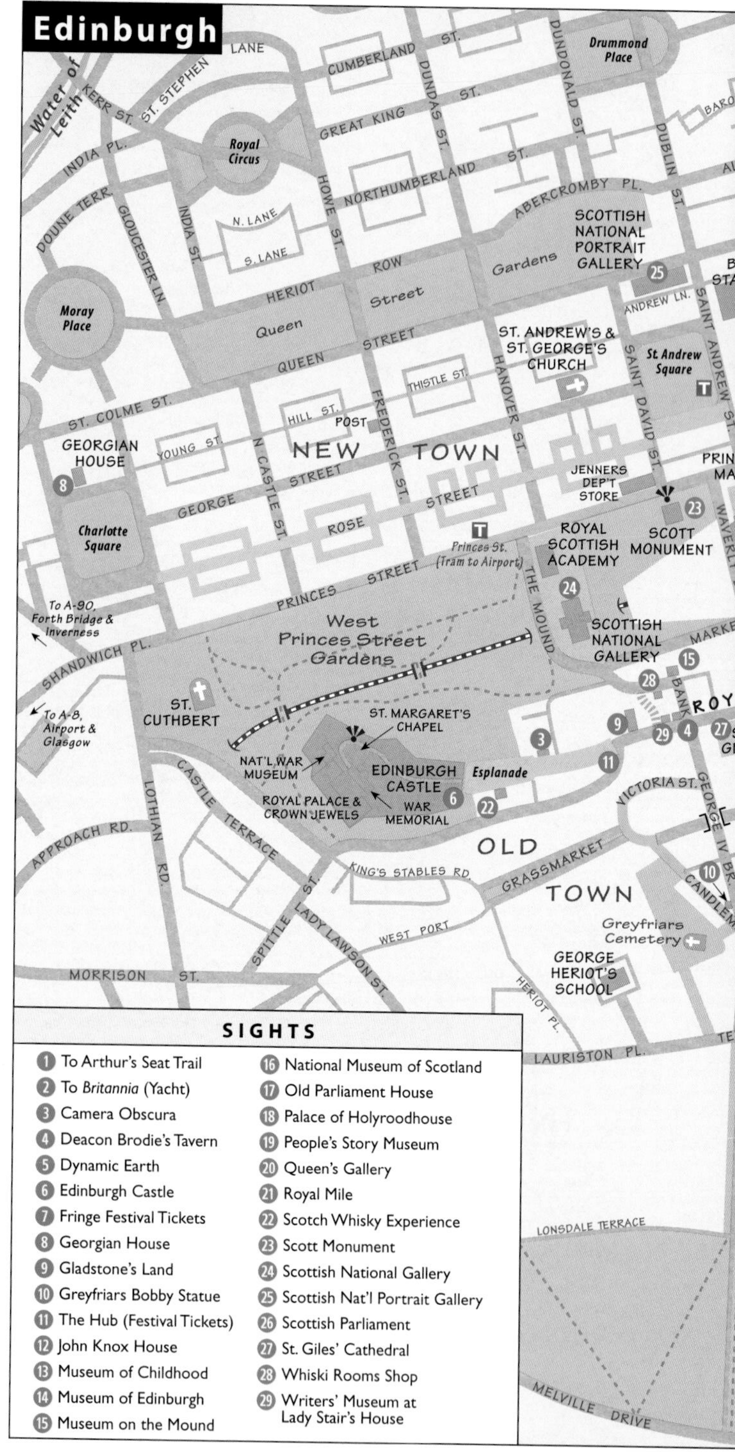
Edinburgh
NEW TOWN
OLD TOWN
Water of Leith
Drummond Place
Royal Circus
Moray Place
Charlotte Square
St Andrew Square
Queen Street Gardens
West Princes Street Gardens
Greyfriars Cemetery
SCOTTISH NATIONAL PORTRAIT GALLERY
ST. ANDREW'S & ST. GEORGE'S CHURCH
GEORGIAN HOUSE
POST
JENNERS DEP'T STORE
ROYAL SCOTTISH ACADEMY
SCOTT MONUMENT
SCOTTISH NATIONAL GALLERY
Princes St. (Tram to Airport)
ST. CUTHBERT
ST. MARGARET'S CHAPEL
NAT'L WAR MUSEUM
EDINBURGH CASTLE
ROYAL PALACE & CROWN JEWELS
WAR MEMORIAL
Esplanade
GEORGE HERIOT'S SCHOOL
To A-90, Forth Bridge & Inverness
To A-8, Airport & Glasgow
LANE
CUMBERLAND ST.
DUNDAS ST.
DUNDONALD ST.
ST. STEPHEN
KERR ST.
GREAT KING ST.
INDIA PL.
NORTHUMBERLAND ST.
DUBLIN ST.
ABERCROMBY PL.
DOUNE TERR.
GLOUCESTER LN.
INDIA ST.
N. LANE
S. LANE
HOWE ST.
HERIOT ROW
ANDREW LN.
SAINT ANDREW ST.
QUEEN STREET
THISTLE ST.
HANOVER ST.
SAINT DAVID ST.
ST. COLME ST.
HILL ST.
YOUNG ST.
N CASTLE ST.
FREDERICK ST.
GEORGE STREET
ROSE STREET
PRINCES STREET
THE MOUND
SHANDWICH PL.
BANK
CASTLE TERRACE
LOTHIAN RD.
APPROACH RD.
VICTORIA ST.
GEORGE IV BR.
KING'S STABLES RD.
GRASSMARKET
SPITTLE ST.
LADY LAWSON ST.
WEST PORT
MORRISON ST.
HERIOT PL.
LAURISTON PL.
LONSDALE TERRACE
MELVILLE DRIVE
SIGHTS
1 To Arthur's Seat Trail
2 To Britannia (Yacht)
3 Camera Obscura
4 Deacon Brodie's Tavern
5 Dynamic Earth
6 Edinburgh Castle
7 Fringe Festival Tickets
8 Georgian House
9 Gladstone's Land
10 Greyfriars Bobby Statue
11 The Hub (Festival Tickets)
12 John Knox House
13 Museum of Childhood
14 Museum of Edinburgh
15 Museum on the Mound
16 National Museum of Scotland
17 Old Parliament House
18 Palace of Holyroodhouse
19 People's Story Museum
20 Queen's Gallery
21 Royal Mile
22 Scotch Whisky Experience
23 Scott Monument
24 Scottish National Gallery
25 Scottish Nat'l Portrait Gallery
26 Scottish Parliament
27 St. Giles' Cathedral
28 Whiski Rooms Shop
29 Writers' Museum at Lady Stair's House

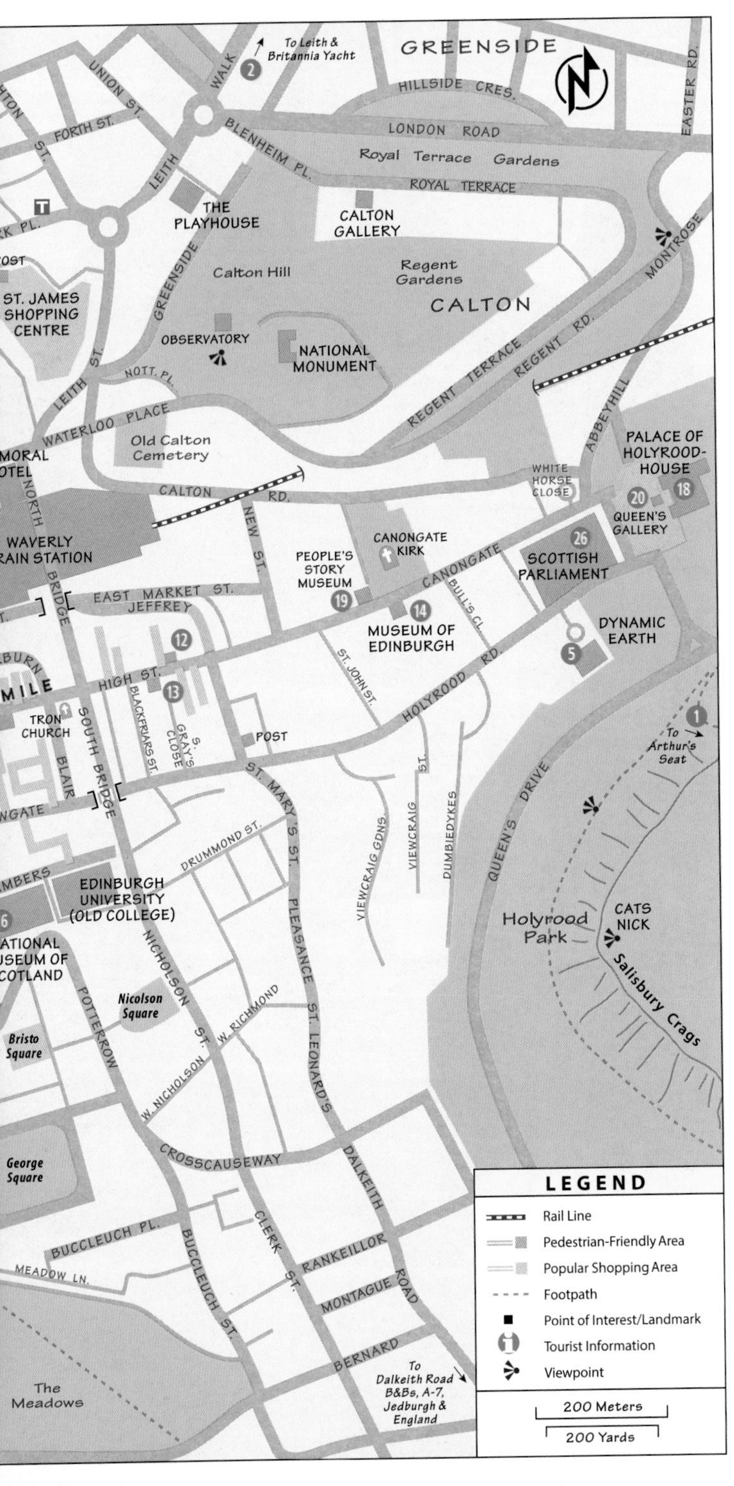

GREENSIDE
To Leith & Britannia Yacht
HILLSIDE CRES.
LONDON ROAD
Royal Terrace Gardens
ROYAL TERRACE
BLENHEIM PL.
UNION ST.
FORTH ST.
LEITH WALK
THE PLAYHOUSE
CALTON GALLERY
Calton Hill
Regent Gardens
CALTON
ST. JAMES SHOPPING CENTRE
OBSERVATORY
NATIONAL MONUMENT
GREENSIDE
LEITH ST.
NOTT. PL.
WATERLOO PLACE
Old Calton Cemetery
REGENT TERRACE
REGENT RD.
MONTROSE
EASTER RD.
ABBEYHILL
PALACE OF HOLYROOD-HOUSE
WHITE HORSE CLOSE
CALTON RD.
QUEEN'S GALLERY
WAVERLY TRAIN STATION
NORTH BRIDGE
NEW ST.
CANONGATE KIRK
PEOPLE'S STORY MUSEUM
CANONGATE
SCOTTISH PARLIAMENT
EAST MARKET ST.
JEFFREY
MUSEUM OF EDINBURGH
BULL'S CL.
DYNAMIC EARTH
HIGH ST.
MILE
TRON CHURCH
BLACKFRIARS ST.
S. GRAY'S CLOSE
ST. JOHN ST.
HOLYROOD RD.
POST
SOUTH BRIDGE
BLAIR
COWGATE
ST. MARY'S ST.
To Arthur's Seat
QUEEN'S DRIVE
VIEWCRAIG GDNS.
VIEWCRAIG ST.
DUMBIEDYKES
DRUMMOND ST.
EDINBURGH UNIVERSITY (OLD COLLEGE)
NATIONAL MUSEUM OF SCOTLAND
PLEASANCE
Holyrood Park
CATS NICK
Salisbury Crags
NICHOLSON ST.
Nicolson Square
POTTERROW
Bristo Square
W. RICHMOND
ST. LEONARD'S
W. NICHOLSON
CROSSCAUSEWAY
George Square
DALKEITH
CLERK ST.
BUCCLEUCH PL.
BUCCLEUCH ST.
RANKEILLOR
MEADOW LN.
MONTAGUE
ROAD
BERNARD
To Dalkeith Road B&Bs, A-7, Jedburgh & England
The Meadows
LEGEND
Rail Line
Pedestrian-Friendly Area
Popular Shopping Area
Footpath
Point of Interest/Landmark
Tourist Information
Viewpoint
200 Meters
200 Yards

Royal Mail

Great Britain

What's so great about Britain? Plenty. You can watch a world-class Shakespeare play, do the Beatles blitz in Liverpool, and walk along a windswept hill in the footsteps of Wordsworth. Climb cobblestone streets as you wander Edinburgh's Royal Mile, or take a ferry to a windswept isle. Ponder a moody glen, lonesome stone circle, or ruined abbey. Try getting your tongue around a few Welsh words, relax in a bath in Bath, and enjoy evensong at Westminster Abbey. Stroll through a cute-as-can-be Cotswold town, try to spot an underwater monster in a loch, and sail along the Thames past Big Ben. Great Britain has it all.

Regardless of the revolution we had 230-some years ago, many American travelers feel that they "go home" to Britain. This most popular tourist destination has a strange influence and power over us. The more you know of Britain's roots, the better you'll get in touch with your own.

The Isle of Britain is small (about the size of Idaho)—600 miles long and 300 miles at its widest point. Britain's highest mountain (Scotland's Ben Nevis) is 4,406 feet, a foothill by our standards. The population is a fifth that of the United States. At its peak in the mid-1800s, Britain owned one-fifth of the world and accounted for more than half the planet's industrial output. Today, the empire is down to the Isle of Britain itself and a few token scraps, such as Northern Ireland, Gibraltar, and the Falklands.

And yet, culturally, Britain remains a world leader. Her

heritage, culture, and people cannot be measured in traditional units of power. London is a major exporter of actors, movies, and theater; of rock and classical music; and of writers, painters, and sculptors.

On the other hand, when it comes to cuisine, Britain has given the world...fish-and-chips and haggis. Bad, bland British food is almost a universal joke, headed by dishes with funny names like "bubble and squeak" and "toad in the hole." Traditionally, Britain was known for heavy, no-nonsense meals. The day started with a hearty breakfast of eggs and bacon, followed by meat pies and beer for lunch, and finished with a filling dinner of red meat and thick sauces.

But the cuisine has improved. The British have added fresh fruits and vegetables to their diet, and many regions pride themselves on using locally grown foods to make lighter, more creative variations of old favorites. Foreign influences—especially Indian and Chinese imports—are especially popular, having been adapted to local tastes.

Thankfully, one distinctive British tradition remains popular: afternoon tea served with biscuits, cookies, or little sandwiches. This four o'clock break is part pick-me-up and part social ritual.

Ethnically, the British Isles are a mix of the descendants

of the early Celtic natives (in Scotland, Ireland, Wales, and Cornwall), the invading Anglo-Saxons who took southeast England in the Dark Ages, and the conquering Normans of the 11th century...not to mention more recent immigrants from around the world. Cynics call the United Kingdom an English Empire ruled by London, whose dominant Anglo-Saxon English (50 million) far outnumber their Celtic brothers and sisters (10 million).

It's easy to think that "Britain" and "England" are one and the same. But actually, three very different countries make up Great Britain: England, Wales, and Scotland. (Add Northern Ireland and you've got the United Kingdom—but you'll need a different guidebook.) Let's take a quick cultural tour through Great Britain's three nations.

ENGLAND

Even today, England remains a cultural and linguistic touchstone for the almost one billion humans who speak English.

It's the center of the United Kingdom in every way: home to four out of five UK citizens, the seat of government, the economic powerhouse, the center of higher learning, and the cultural heart. And, although it lacks some of the Celtic color of other parts of Britain, you'll find plenty of variety even in "plain vanilla" England.

North England tends to be hilly with poor soil, so the

Great Britain Almanac

Official Name: The United Kingdom of Great Britain and Northern Ireland (locals say "the UK" or "Britain").

Population: Britain's 64 million people include a sizable and growing minority of immigrants, largely from China, India, Pakistan, and Eastern Europe. Six in ten British call themselves Christian (half of those are Anglican), but in any given week, more Brits visit a mosque than an Anglican church.

Latitude and Longitude: 54°N and 2°W. The latitude is similar to Alberta, Canada.

Area: From "Britannia's" 19th-century peak of power, when it dominated much of the globe, the British Empire shrank to a quarter of its former size. Today, this nation is 95,000 square miles (about the size of Michigan). It's composed of one large island and a chunk of another large island.

Geography: Most of the British Isles consists of low hills and rolling plains, with a generally moderate climate. The country's highest point is 4,406-foot Ben Nevis in western Scotland. Britain's longest river, the Severn, loops 220 miles from the mountains of Wales east into England, then south to the Bristol Channel. The Thames River runs 215 miles east-west through the heart of southern England (including London).

Biggest Cities: London is the capital, with 8 million people. Industrial Birmingham has about 1 million, Glasgow 600,000, Edinburgh 500,000, and the port of Liverpool 870,000.

Economy: The Gross Domestic Product is $2.5 trillion and the GDP per capita is $39,500. Moneymakers include banking, insurance and business services, agriculture, shipping, and trade with the US

and Germany. Heavy industry—which once drove the Industrial Revolution—is now in decline.

Government: Queen Elizabeth II officially heads the country, but in practice it's the prime minister, who leads the majority party in Parliament. Since 2010, the British House of Commons has had 650 members. (The House of Lords is now a mere advisory body.) Britain's traditional two-party system—Labour and Conservatives ("Tories")—now has two other players, the Liberal Democrats ("Lib Dems") and the Scottish National Party. The current prime minister, Conservative leader David Cameron, came to power in a coalition in 2010, but after the 2015 elections his party rules alone. Britain is a member of the European Union (but not the euro system) and is one of five permanent members (with veto power) of the UN Security Council. In 1999, Scotland, Wales, and Northern Ireland were each granted their own Parliament—and, with that, more autonomy in their domestic affairs. However, independence movements still run strong, particularly in Scotland.

Flag: The "Union Jack" has three crosses on a field of blue: the English cross of St. George, the Irish cross of St. Patrick, and the Scottish cross of St. Andrew.

The Average Brit: Eats 35 pounds of pizza and 35 pounds of chocolate a year, and weighs 12 stone (170 pounds). He or she is 40 years old, has 1.9 children, and will live to age 80. He/she drinks 2.5 cups of tea a day and 2.5 glasses of wine a week (Americans drink less than half that). He/she has free health care, and gets 28 vacation days a year (versus 13 in the US). He/she sleeps 7.5 hours a night, speaks one language, loves soccer, and enjoys talking about the weather.

traditional economy was based on livestock (grazing cows and sheep). Today it has some of England's most beautiful landscapes, but in the 19th century it was dotted with belching smokestacks as its major cities and its heartland became centers of coal and iron mining and manufacturing. Now its working-class cities and ports (such as Liverpool) are experiencing a comeback, buoyed by higher employment, tourism, and vibrant arts scenes.

South England, including London, has always had more people and more money than the north. Blessed with rolling hills, wide plains, and the Thames River, in the past this area was rich with farms, its rivers flowed with trade, and high culture flourished around the epicenter in London. And today, even though London is a thriving metropolis of eight million people, much the same can still be said.

The English people have a worldwide reputation (or stereotype) for being cheerful, courteous, and well-mannered. Cutting in line is very gauche. On the other hand, English soccer fans can be notorious "hooligans." The English are not known for being touchy-feely or physically demonstrative (hugging and kissing), but they sure do love to talk. When times get tough, they persevere with a stiff upper lip. The understated English wit is legendary—when someone dies, it's "a bit of a drag" (but if the tea is cold, it's "ghastly"!).

For the tourist, England offers a little of everything we associate with Britain: castles, cathedrals, and ruined abbeys; chatty locals nursing beers in village pubs; mysterious prehistoric stone circles and Roman ruins; tea, scones, and clotted cream; hikes across unspoiled, sheep-speckled hillsides; and drivers who cheerfully wave from the "wrong" side of the

road. And then there's London, a world in itself, with monuments (Big Ben), museums (the British Museum), royalty (Buckingham Palace), theater, and nightlife, throbbing with the pulse of the global community.

You can trace England's illustrious history by roaming the countryside. Prehistoric peoples built the mysterious stone circles of Stonehenge and Avebury. Then came the Romans, who built Hadrian's Wall and baths at Bath. Viking invaders left their mark in York, and the Normans built the Tower of London. As England Christianized and unified, the grand cathedrals of Salisbury, Wells, and Durham arose. Next came the castles and palaces of the English monarchs (Windsor) and the Shakespeare sights from the era of Elizabeth I (Stratford-upon-Avon). In following centuries, tiny England became a maritime empire (the *Cutty Sark* at Greenwich) and the world's first industrial power (Ironbridge Gorge). England's Romantic poets were inspired by the unspoiled nature and time-

passed villages of the Lake District and the Cotswolds. In the 20th century, the gritty urban world of 1960s Liverpool gave the world the Beatles. Finally, end your journey through English history in London—on the cutting edge of 21st-century trends.

For a thousand years, England has been a major cultural center. Parliamentary democracy, science (Isaac Newton), technology (Michael Faraday), and education (Oxford and Cambridge) were nurtured here. In literature, England has few peers in any language, producing some of the greatest legends (King Arthur, *Beowulf,* and *The Lord of the Rings*), poems (by Chaucer, Wordsworth, and Byron), novels (by Dickens, Austen, and J. K. Rowling), and plays (by William Shakespeare, England's greatest writer). London rivals New York as the best scene for live theater. England is a major exporter of movies and movie actors—Laurence Olivier, Alec Guinness, Ian McKellen, Helen Mirren, Judi Dench, Kate Winslet, Keira Knightley, Ralph Fiennes, Hugh Grant, Ricky Gervais, and on and on.

In popular music, England remains neck and neck with America. It started in the 1960s with the "British invasion" of bands that reinfused rock and blues into America—the Beatles, the Rolling Stones, and the Who. Then came successive waves in the 1970s (Elton John, Led Zeppelin, David Bowie, Pink Floyd, Queen, Black Sabbath, the Clash, the Sex Pistols); the '80s (Dire Straits, Phil Collins and Genesis, Elvis Costello, the Cure, the Smiths, the Police, Depeche Mode, Duran Duran, Wham!); the Britpop '90s (Oasis, Blur, PJ Harvey, Spice Girls, the rave scene); and into the 21st century (Coldplay, Adele, M.I.A., Radiohead, the late Amy Winehouse).

WALES

Humble, charming little Wales is traditional and beautiful—it sometimes feels trapped in a time warp. When you first enter Wales, it may seem like you're still in England. But soon you'll awaken to the uniqueness and crusty yet poetic vitality of this small country and realize...you're not in Oxford anymore. And don't ask for an "English breakfast" at your Welsh B&B—they'll smile politely and remind you that it's a "Welsh breakfast," made with Welsh ingredients.

For the tourist, Wales is a land of stout castles (the best are at Conwy and Caernarfon), salty harbors, chummy community choirs, slate-roofed villages, and a landscape of mountains, moors, and lush green fields dotted with sheep. Snowdonia National Park is a hiker's paradise, with steep but manageable mountain trails, cute-as-a-hobbit villages (Beddgelert and Betws-y-Coed), and scenery more striking than most anything in England. Fascinating slate-mine museums (such as at Blaenau Ffestiniog), handy home-base towns (Conwy and Caernarfon), and enticing offbeat attractions round out Wales' appeal.

Perhaps Wales' best attraction is hearing the locals speak Welsh (or Cymraeg, pronounced kum-RAH-ig). The Welsh

people often use this tongue-twisting and fun-to-listen-to Celtic language when speaking with one another, smoothly switching to English when a visitor asks a question. With its sometimes harsh, sometimes melodic tones, Welsh transports listeners to another time and place.

Culturally, Wales is "a land of poets and singers"—or so says the national anthem. From the myths of Merlin and King Arthur to the poetry of Dylan Thomas (1914-1953), Wales has a long literary tradition. In music, the country nourishes its traditional Celtic folk music (especially the harp) and has exported popular singers such as Tom Jones, Charlotte Church, and Jem. Popular actors born in Wales include Richard Burton and Catherine Zeta-Jones.

SCOTLAND

Rugged, feisty, colorful Scotland is the yin to England's yang. Whether it's the looser, less-organized nature of the people, the stone and sandstone architecture, the unmanicured landscape, or simply the haggis, go-its-own-way Scotland still stands apart. The home of kilts, bagpipes, whisky, golf, lochs, and shortbread lives up to its clichéd image—and then some.

While the Scots are known for their telltale burr—and more than a few unique words (aye, just listen for a wee blether)—they're also trying to keep alive their own Celtic

tongue: Gaelic (pronounced "gallic"). While few Scots speak Gaelic in everyday life, legislation protects it, and it's beginning to be used on road signs.

That's just one small sign of the famously independent Scottish spirit. Since the days of William "Braveheart" Wallace, the Scots have chafed under English rule. Thanks to the relatively recent trend of "devolution," Scotland has become increasingly autonomous (even opening its own Parliament in 1999). However, Scotland opted to remain part of the United Kingdom in a 2014 referendum on Scottish independence, with 55 percent of voters saying they prefer things how they are.

Visitors divide their time between the two Scotlands: the Lowlands (the flatter southern area around Edinburgh and Glasgow, populated by yuppies) and the Highlands (the remote rugged northern area, where proudly traditional Scots eke out a living).

In the Lowlands, don't miss the impressive Scottish capital of Edinburgh, with its attraction-lined Royal Mile and stirring hilltop castle. Nearby, the rival city of Glasgow offers a grittier (but quickly gentrifying) urban ambience. And golfers can't miss the seaside town of St. Andrews, with its world-famous links, vast sandy beaches, colorful university life, and evocative ruined cathedral.

To commune with the traditional Scottish soul, head for the Highlands. Here you'll find hills, lochs (lakes), "sea lochs" (inlets), castles, and a feeling of remoteness. The "Weeping Glen" of Glencoe offers grand views and a sad tale of Scottish history. The provincial city of Inverness is a handy home base for venturing to uniquely Scottish sights (including the historic site of "Bonnie" Prince Charlie's disastrous Battle of Culloden). Ever-present whisky distilleries offer the chance to sample another uniquely Scottish "spirit," and viewing the engineering feat of the Caledonian Canal—not to mention famous Loch Ness—inspires awe (say hi to Nessie). Hardy souls can set sail for some of Scotland's islands: Iona, Mull, and Staffa (from Oban).

Whether going to England, Wales, Scotland, or (my choice) all three, you'll have a grand adventure—and a great experience—in Great Britain. Cheerio!

INTRODUCTION

This book breaks Great Britain into its top big-city, small-town, and rural destinations. It gives you all the information and opinions necessary to wring the maximum value out of your limited time and money in each of these locations. If you plan a month or less for Britain and have a normal appetite for information, this book is all you need. If you're a travel-info fiend, this book sorts through all the superlatives and provides a handy rack upon which to hang your supplemental information.

Note that this book covers the island of Great Britain, which comprises England, Wales, and Scotland. If your trip will focus on the southern two-thirds of Great Britain, pick up a copy of *Rick Steves England* instead. If you plan to spend considerable time in Scotland, my *Rick Steves Scotland* guidebook offers in-depth information on that country. (Northern Ireland—which is part of the UK, but not Great Britain—is covered in my book *Rick Steves Ireland.*)

Experiencing British culture, people, and natural wonders economically and hassle-free has been my goal for more than three decades of traveling, tour guiding, and travel writing. With this new edition, I pass on to you the lessons I've learned, updated for your trip.

While including the predictable biggies (such as Big Ben, Edinburgh, Stratford-upon-Avon, and Stonehenge), this book also mixes in a healthy dose of Back Door intimacy (windswept Roman lookouts, angelic boys' choirs, misty Scottish isles, and nearly edible Cotswold villages). This book is selective. For example, while Hadrian's Wall is more than 70 miles long, I recommend visiting just the best six-mile stretch.

The best is, of course, only my opinion. But after spending much of my life researching Europe, I've developed a sixth sense

Map Legend

Viewpoint	Prehistoric Sight	Tunnel
Entrance	Taxi Stand	Railway
Tourist Info	Tram	Mtn. Rail
Restroom	Bus Stop	Ferry/Boat Route
Castle, Manor House	Parking	Airport
Church	Tube	Stairs
Statue/Point of Interest	Pedestrian Zone	Walk/Tour Route
Pub	Park	Trail

Use this legend to help you navigate the maps in this book.

for what travelers enjoy. The places featured in this book will knock your spots off.

ABOUT THIS BOOK

Rick Steves Great Britain is a personal tour guide in your pocket. This book is organized by destinations. Each is a minivacation on its own, filled with exciting sights, strollable neighborhoods, affordable places to stay, and memorable places to eat. Within the destination chapters, you'll find these sections:

Planning Your Time suggests a schedule for how to best use your limited time.

Orientation has specifics on public transportation, helpful hints, local tour options, easy-to-read maps, and tourist information.

Sights describes the top attractions and includes their cost and hours.

Self-Guided Walks take you through interesting neighborhoods, pointing out sights and fun stops.

Sleeping describes my favorite hotels, from good-value deals to cushy splurges.

Eating serves up a buffet of options, from inexpensive pubs to fancy restaurants.

Connections outlines your options for traveling to destinations by train, bus, and plane, plus route tips for drivers.

The **Britain: Past and Present** chapter is a quick overview of British history and culture.

Practicalities is a traveler's tool kit, with my best tips about money, sightseeing, sleeping, eating, staying connected, and transportation (trains, buses, car rentals, driving, and flights).

The **appendix** has the nuts and bolts: useful phone numbers and websites, a holiday and festival list, recommended books and

Key to This Book

Updates

This book is updated regularly—but things change. For the latest, visit www.ricksteves.com/update.

Abbreviations and Times

I use the following symbols and abbreviations in this book:

Sights are rated:

▲▲▲	Don't miss
▲▲	Try hard to see
▲	Worthwhile if you can make it
No rating	Worth knowing about

Tourist information offices are abbreviated as **TI,** and bathrooms are **WC**s. To categorize accommodations, I use a **Sleep Code** (described on page 997).

Like Europe, this book uses the **24-hour clock** for schedules. It's the same through 12:00 noon, then keeps going: 13:00, 14:00, and so on. For anything over 12, subtract 12 and add p.m. (14:00 is 2:00 p.m.).

When giving **opening times,** I include both peak season and off-season hours if they differ. So, if a museum is listed as "May-Oct daily 9:00-16:00," it should be open from 9 a.m. until 4 p.m. from the first day of May until the last day of October (but expect exceptions).

A 🎧 symbol indicates that a free, downloadable self-guided Rick Steves audio tour is available.

For **transit** or **tour departures,** I first list the frequency, then the duration. So, a train connection listed as "2/hour, 1.5 hours" departs twice each hour, and the journey lasts an hour and a half.

films, a climate chart, a handy packing checklist, and a fun British-Yankee dictionary.

Browse through this book, choose your favorite destinations, and link them up. Then have a brilliant trip! Traveling like a temporary local, you'll get the absolute most out of every mile, minute, and dollar. And, as you visit places I know and love, I'm happy that you'll be meeting some of my favorite British people.

Planning

This section will help you get started on planning your trip—with advice on trip costs, when to go, and what you should know before you take off.

TRAVEL SMART

Your trip to Britain is like a complex play—it's easier to follow and really appreciate on a second viewing. While no one does the same trip twice to gain that advantage, reading this book in its entirety before your trip accomplishes much the same thing.

Design an itinerary that enables you to visit sights at the best possible times. Note festivals, holidays, specifics on sights, and days when sights are closed or most crowded (all covered in this book). To connect the dots smoothly, read the tips in the Practicalities chapter on taking trains and buses, or renting a car and driving. Designing a smart trip is a fun, doable, and worthwhile challenge.

Make your itinerary a mix of intense and relaxed stretches. To maximize rootedness, minimize one-night stands. It's worth a long drive after dinner (or a train ride with a dinner picnic) to be settled into a town for two nights. Hotels and B&Bs are more likely to give a better price to someone staying more than one night. Every trip (and every traveler) needs slack time (laundry, picnics, people-watching, and so on). Pace yourself. Assume you will return.

Reread this book as you travel, and visit local tourist information offices (abbreviated as TI in this book). Upon arrival in a new town, lay the groundwork for a smooth departure; confirm the train, bus, or road you'll take when you leave.

Even with the best-planned itinerary, you'll need to be flexible. Update your plans as you travel. Get online or call ahead to double-check tourist information, learn the latest on sights (special events, tour schedules, and so on), book tickets and tours, make reservations, reconfirm hotels, and research transportation connections.

Enjoy the friendliness of the British people. Connect with the culture. Set up your own quest for the best pub, cathedral, or chocolate bar. Slow down and be open to unexpected experiences. You speak the language—use it! Ask questions—most locals are eager to point you in their idea of the right direction. Keep a notepad in your pocket for noting directions, organizing your thoughts, and confirming prices. Wear your money belt, learn the currency, and figure out how to estimate prices in dollars. Those who expect to travel smart, do.

TRIP COSTS

Five components make up your trip costs: airfare, surface transportation, room and board, sightseeing and entertainment, and shopping and miscellany.

Airfare: A basic round-trip US-to-London flight can cost, on average, about $1,000-2,000 total, depending on where you fly from and when (cheaper in winter). If your trip extends beyond Britain, consider saving time and money by flying into one city and out of another—for instance, into London and out of Amsterdam.

Top Destinations in Great Britain

Great Britain at a Glance

England

▲▲▲London Thriving metropolis packed with world-class museums, monuments, churches, parks, palaces, theaters, pubs, Beefeaters, telephone boxes, double-decker buses, and all things British. Maritime Greenwich, with its famous observatory, is on the city's outskirts.

▲▲Windsor and Cambridge Easy side-trips from London to the Queen's impressive home-sweet-castle at Windsor and, for many, England's best university town, Cambridge.

▲▲▲Bath Genteel Georgian showcase city, built around the remains of an ancient Roman bath.

▲▲Near Bath England's mysterious heart, including the prehistoric-meets-New Age hill at Glastonbury, spine-tingling stone circles at Stonehenge and Avebury, enjoyable cathedral towns of Wells and Salisbury, and romantic ruins of South Wales.

▲▲The Cotswolds Remarkably quaint villages—including the cozy market town Chipping Campden, popular hamlet Stow-on-the-Wold, and handy transit hub Moreton-in-Marsh—scattered over a hilly countryside and near one of England's top palaces, Blenheim.

▲Stratford-upon-Avon Shakespeare's hometown and top venue for seeing his plays performed.

▲Ironbridge Gorge Birthplace of the Industrial Revolution, with sights and museums that tell the earth-changing story.

▲Liverpool Rejuvenated port city and the Beatles' hometown.

▲▲The Lake District Idyllic lakes-and-hills landscape, with enjoyable hikes and joyrides, time-passed valleys, William Wordsworth and Beatrix Potter sights, and the charming home-base town of Keswick.

▲▲▲York Walled medieval town with grand Gothic cathedral, excellent museums (Viking, Victorian, Railway), and atmospheric old center.

▲**Durham and Northeast England** Youthful working-class town with magnificent cathedral, plus (nearby) an open-air museum and the Roman remains of Hadrian's Wall.

Wales

▲▲**North Wales** Scenically rugged land with the castle towns of Conwy, Caernarfon, and Beaumaris; natural beauty of Snowdonia National Park; tourable slate mines at Blaenau Ffestiniog; colorful Welsh villages of Beddgelert and Llangollen; and charming locals who speak a tongue-twisting old language.

Scotland

▲▲▲**Edinburgh** Proud and endlessly entertaining Scottish capital, with an imposing castle, attractions-studded Royal Mile, excellent museums, and atmospheric neighborhoods.

▲▲**Glasgow** Scotland's gritty but gentrifying, cultural "second city," a hotbed of 20th-century architecture.

▲**Stirling and Nearby** One of Scotland's top castles (home of the Stuart kings) overlooking a historic plain, with great sights nearby—from giant horse heads to a Ferris wheel for boats.

▲▲**St. Andrews** Sandy beach town that gave birth to golf and hosts Scotland's top university.

▲▲**Oban and the Inner Hebrides** Handy home-base town of Oban, with boat trips to the isles of Mull, Iona, and Staffa.

▲**Glencoe and Fort William** Stirring "Weeping Glen" of Glencoe offering some of the Highlands' best scenery and hikes, plus the transit-hub town of Fort William.

▲▲**Inverness and Loch Ness** Regional capital with easy access to more Highland sights, including Culloden Battlefield (Scotland's Alamo) and monster-spotting at the famous Loch Ness.

Please Tear Up This Book!

There's no point in hauling around a big chapter on London for a day in Bath. That's why I hope you'll rip this book apart. Before your trip, attack this book with a utility knife to create an army of pocket-sized mini guidebooks—one for each area you visit.

I love the ritual of trimming down the size of guidebooks I'll be using: Fold the pages back until you break the spine, neatly slice apart the sections you want with a utility knife, then pull them out with the gummy edge intact. If you want, finish each one off with some clear, heavy-duty packing tape to smooth and reinforce the spine, and/or use a heavy-duty stapler along the edge to prevent the first and last pages from coming loose.

To make things even easier, I've created a line of laminated covers with slide-on binders (available at www.ricksteves.com). With every stop, you can make a ritual of swapping out the last chapter with the new one.

As you travel, throw out the chapters you're done with (or, much better, give them to a needy fellow traveler). While you may be tempted to keep this book intact as a souvenir of your travels, you'll appreciate even more the footloose freedom of traveling light.

Overall, Kayak.com is the best place to start searching for flights on a combination of mainstream and budget carriers.

Surface Transportation: For a three-week whirlwind trip of all my recommended British destinations, allow $600 per person for public transportation (train pass, key buses, and Tube fare in London). If you'll be renting a car, allow at least $230 per week, not including tolls, gas, and supplemental insurance. If you'll be keeping the car for three weeks or more, look into leasing, which can save you money on insurance and taxes for trips of this length. Car rentals and leases are cheapest when arranged from the US. Train passes, which normally must be purchased outside Europe, aren't necessarily your best option—you may save money by simply buying tickets as you go. Don't hesitate to consider flying, as budget airlines are often cheaper than taking the train (check Skyscanner.com for intra-European flights). For more details, see "Transportation" in the Practicalities chapter.

Room and Board: Outside of London, you can thrive in Britain on $120 per day per person for room and board. This allows $15 for lunch, $30 for dinner, and $75 for lodging (based on two people splitting the cost of a $150 double room that includes breakfast). Allow about 15 percent more for your days in London or other big cities. Students and tightwads can enjoy Britain for as little as $60 ($30 for a bed, $30 for meals and snacks).

Sightseeing and Entertainment: Figure about $20-40 per major sight (Stonehenge-$26, Shakespeare's Birthplace in Stratford-$24, Westminster Abbey-$31, Tower of London-$38, Edinburgh Castle-$25), $7 for minor ones (climbing church towers), and $35-50 for splurge experiences (e.g., bus tours, concerts, discounted tickets for plays). For information on various sightseeing passes, see page 993.

Fortunately, many of the best sights in London are free, including the British Museum, National Gallery, National Portrait Gallery, Tate Britain, Tate Modern, British Library, and the Victoria & Albert Museum. An overall average of $30 a day works in most cities (allow $50-60 for London). Don't skimp here. After all, this category is the driving force behind your trip—you came to sightsee, enjoy, and experience Britain.

Shopping and Miscellany: Figure roughly $2 per postcard, $3 for tea or an ice-cream cone, and $5 per pint of beer. Shopping can vary in cost from nearly nothing to a small fortune. Good budget travelers find that this has little to do with assembling a trip full of lifelong memories.

SIGHTSEEING PRIORITIES

Depending on the length of your trip, and taking geographic proximity into account, here are my recommended priorities:

3 days:	London
5 days, add:	Bath and the Cotswolds
7 days, add:	York
9 days, add:	Edinburgh
11 days, add:	Stratford, Blenheim
14 days, add:	North Wales, Wells/Glastonbury/Avebury
17 days, add:	Lake District, Hadrian's Wall, Durham
21 days, add:	Scottish Highlands, Liverpool, Ironbridge Gorge
24 days, add:	Choose two of the following—St. Andrews, Glasgow, Cambridge, South Wales

This list includes virtually everything on my "Britain's Best Three-Week Trip by Car" itinerary and map (see page 10).

Note: Instead of spending the first few days of your trip in busy London, consider a gentler small-town start in Bath (the ideal jet-lag pillow), and let London be the finale of your trip. You'll be more rested and ready to tackle Britain's greatest city. Heathrow Airport has direct bus connections to Bath and other cities. (Bristol Airport is also near Bath.)

Build your itinerary to match your interests. Nature lovers will likely put the lovely Lake District, the Scottish Highlands, and

Britain's Best Three-Week Trip by Car

Day	Plan	Sleep in
1	Arrive in London, connect to Bath	Bath
2	Bath	Bath
3	Pick up car, Avebury, Wells, Glastonbury	Bath
4	South Wales, Cardiff, Tintern	Chipping Campden
5	Explore the Cotswolds, Blenheim	Chipping Campden
6	Stratford	Ironbridge Gorge
7	Ironbridge Gorge to North Wales	Conwy
8	Highlights of North Wales	Conwy
9	Liverpool	Liverpool
10	South Lake District	Keswick area
11	North Lake District	Keswick area
12	Drive up west coast of Scotland	Oban
13	Explore the Highlands, Loch Ness	Edinburgh
14	Edinburgh	Edinburgh
15	Edinburgh	Edinburgh
16	Hadrian's Wall, Beamish Museum, Durham's Cathedral and evensong	Durham
17	York, turn in car	York
18	York	York
19	Early train to London	London
20	London	London
21	London	London
22	Whew!	

While this three-week itinerary is designed to be done by car, it can also be done by train and bus. For three weeks without a car, I'd cut back on the recommended sights with the most frustrating public transportation (South and North Wales, Ironbridge Gorge, and the Scottish Highlands). Lacing together the cities by train is very slick, and buses get you where the trains don't go. With more time, everything is workable without a car.

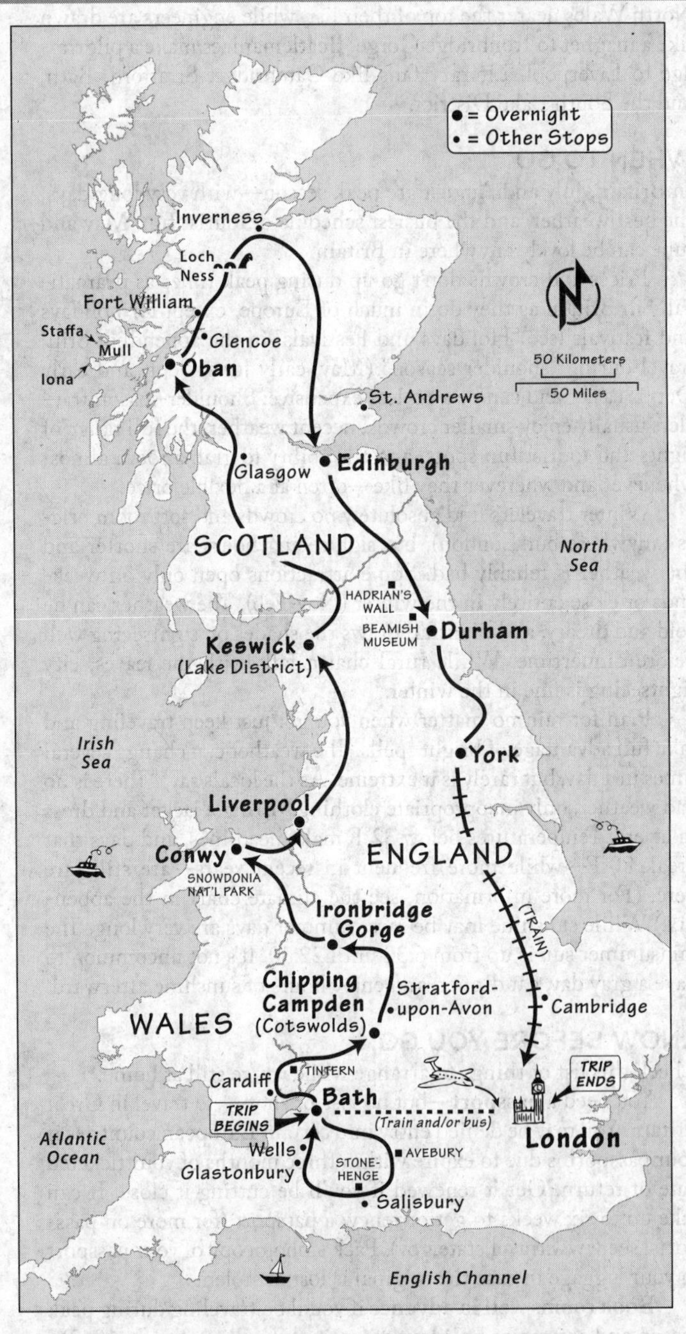

● = Overnight
• = Other Stops
50 Kilometers
50 Miles
Inverness
Loch Ness
Fort William
Staffa
Mull
Iona
Glencoe
Oban
St. Andrews
Glasgow
Edinburgh
SCOTLAND
North Sea
HADRIAN'S WALL
BEAMISH MUSEUM
Durham
Keswick
(Lake District)
Irish Sea
York
Liverpool
Conwy
SNOWDONIA NAT'L PARK
ENGLAND
(TRAIN)
Ironbridge Gorge
Chipping Campden
(Cotswolds)
Stratford-upon-Avon
Cambridge
WALES
TINTERN
Cardiff
Bath
TRIP BEGINS
TRIP ENDS
(Train and/or bus)
London
Atlantic Ocean
Wells
Glastonbury
AVEBURY
STONE-HENGE
Salisbury
English Channel

North Wales nearer the top of their list, while engineers are drawn like a magnet to Ironbridge Gorge. Beatlemaniacs make a pilgrimage to Liverpool. Literary fans like Cambridge, Stratford, Bath, and the South Lake District.

WHEN TO GO

In Britain, July and August are peak season—with very long days, the best weather, and the busiest schedule of tourist fun. May and June can be lovely anywhere in Britain.

Prices and crowds don't go up during peak times as dramatically in Britain as they do in much of Europe, except for holidays and festivals (see "Holidays and Festivals" in the appendix). Still, travel during "shoulder season" (May, early June, Sept, and early Oct) is easier and can be a bit less expensive. Shoulder-season travelers usually enjoy smaller crowds, decent weather, the full range of sights and tourist fun spots, and the ability to grab a room almost whenever and wherever they like—often at a flexible price.

Winter travelers find absolutely no crowds and soft room prices (anywhere but London), but sightseeing hours are shorter and the weather is reliably bad. Some attractions open only on weekends or close entirely in the winter (Nov-Feb). The weather can be cold and dreary, and nightfall draws the shades on sightseeing well before dinnertime. While rural charm falls with the leaves, city sightseeing is fine in the winter.

Plan for rain no matter when you go. Just keep traveling and take full advantage of bright spells. The weather can change several times in a day, but rarely is it extreme. As the locals say, "There is no bad weather, only inappropriate clothing." Bring a jacket and dress in layers. Temperatures below 32°F make headlines, and days that break 80°F—while more frequent in recent years—are still rare here. (For more information, see the climate chart in the appendix.) While sunshine may be rare, summer days are very long. The midsummer sun is up from 6:30 until 22:30. It's not uncommon to have a gray day, eat dinner, and enjoy hours of sunshine afterward.

KNOW BEFORE YOU GO

Check this list of things to arrange while you're still at home.

You need a **passport**—but no visa or shots—to travel in Great Britain. You may be denied entry into certain European countries if your passport is due to expire within three months of your ticketed date of return. Get it renewed if you'll be cutting it close. It can take up to six weeks to get or renew a passport (for more on passports, see www.travel.state.gov). Pack a photocopy of your passport in your luggage in case the original is lost or stolen.

Book rooms well in advance if you'll be traveling during peak season and any major **holidays** or **festivals** (see list on page 1042).

🎧 Rick Steves Audio Europe 🎧

My free **Rick Steves Audio Europe app** is a great tool for enjoying Europe. This app makes it easy to download my audio tours of top attractions, plus hours of travel interviews, all organized into destination-specific playlists.

My self-guided **audio tours** of major sights and neighborhoods are free, user-friendly, fun, and informative. Among the sights in this book, these audio tours include London's British Museum, British Library, St. Paul's Cathedral, my Westminster and Historic London: "The City" walks, and Edinburgh's Royal Mile. Sights covered by my audio tours are marked with this symbol: 🎧. These audio tours are hard to beat: Nobody will stand you up, the quality is reliable, you can take the tour exactly when you like, and the price is right.

The Rick Steves Audio Europe app also offers a far-reaching library of insightful **travel interviews** from my public radio show with experts from around the globe—including many of the places in this book.

This app and all of its content are entirely free. You can download Rick Steves Audio Europe via Apple's App Store, Google Play, or the Amazon Appstore. For more information, see www.ricksteves.com/audioeurope.

Call your **debit- and credit-card companies** to let them know the countries you'll be visiting, to ask about fees, to request your PIN code (it will be mailed to you), and more. See page 987 for details.

Do your homework if you want to buy **travel insurance.** Compare the cost of the insurance to the cost of your potential loss. Also, check whether your existing insurance (health, homeowners, or renters) covers you and your possessions overseas. For more tips, see www.ricksteves.com/insurance.

Consider buying a **rail pass** after researching your options (see page 1020 and www.ricksteves.com/rail for all the specifics). If traveling to continental Europe on the **Eurostar** train, you can order a ticket in advance or buy it in Britain; for details, see page 195.

If you'll be in London or Stratford and want to **see a play,** check theater schedules ahead of time. For simplicity, I book plays when I arrive, but if there's something you just have to see, consider buying tickets before you go. For a current schedule of London plays and musicals, visit www.officiallondontheatre.co.uk. Tickets to performances at Stratford's Royal Shakespeare Theatre are likely to sell out (see www.rsc.org.uk), but if it's just

How Was Your Trip?

Were your travels fun, smooth, and meaningful? If you'd like to share your tips, concerns, and discoveries, please fill out the survey at www.ricksteves.com/feedback. To check out readers' hotel and restaurant reviews—or leave one yourself—visit my travel forum at www.ricksteves.com/travel-forum. I value your feedback. Thanks in advance.

Shakespeare you're after—with or without Stratford—you can see his plays in London, too.

The only way to guarantee entrance to **Stonehenge** is by reserving in advance, and if you want to go inside the stone circle, book your visit as soon as you know the date you'll be there (see page 308). You can also reserve a tour of the **Lennon and McCartney homes in Liverpool** (figure on two weeks ahead in peak season, otherwise just a few days; see page 475).

Tickets to **Edinburgh's Military Tattoo** (Aug) sell out early—book as far ahead as possible (www.edintattoo.co.uk; for details, see page 756). If you'll be in **Edinburgh at festival time** (most of Aug), check the schedule for theater and music in advance (for tips, see page 756). To **golf at St. Andrews' famous Old Course,** you'll need to reserve the previous fall, or put your name in for the "ballot" two days before (see page 869).

If you plan to hire a **local guide,** reserve ahead by email. Popular guides can get booked up.

If you're bringing a **mobile device,** consider signing up for an international plan for cheaper calls, texts, and data (see page 1013). Download any apps you might want to use on the road, such as maps, transit schedules, and **Rick Steves Audio Europe** (see page 13).

Traveling as a Temporary Local

We travel all the way to Britain to enjoy differences—to become temporary locals. You'll experience frustrations. Certain truths that we find "God-given" or "self-evident," such as cold beer, ice in drinks, bottomless cups of coffee, "the customer is king," and bigger being better, are suddenly not so true. One of the benefits of travel is the eye-opening realization that there are logical, civil, and even better alternatives. A willingness to go local ensures that you'll enjoy a full dose of British hospitality.

Europeans generally like Americans. But if there is a negative aspect to the British image of Americans, it's that we are loud, wasteful, ethnocentric, too informal (which can seem disrespectful), and a bit naive.

The British (and Europeans in general) place a high value on speaking quietly in restaurants and on trains. Listen while on the bus or in a restaurant—the place can be packed, but the decibel level is low. Try to adjust your volume accordingly to show respect for their culture.

While the British look bemusedly at some of our Yankee excesses—and worriedly at others—they nearly always afford us individual travelers all the warmth we deserve.

Judging from all the happy feedback I receive from travelers who have used this book, it's safe to assume you'll enjoy a great, affordable vacation—with the finesse of an independent, experienced traveler.

Thanks, and have a brilliant holiday!

Rick Steves

Back Door Travel Philosophy

From *Rick Steves Europe Through the Back Door*

Travel is intensified living—maximum thrills per minute and one of the last great sources of legal adventure. Travel is freedom. It's recess, and we need it.

Experiencing the real Europe requires catching it by surprise, going casual..."through the Back Door."

Affording travel is a matter of priorities. (Make do with the old car.) You can eat and sleep—simply, safely, and enjoyably—anywhere in Europe for $100 a day plus transportation costs. In many ways, spending more money only builds a thicker wall between you and what you traveled so far to see. Europe is a cultural carnival, and time after time, you'll find that its best acts are free and the best seats are the cheap ones.

A tight budget forces you to travel close to the ground, meeting and communicating with the people. Never sacrifice sleep, nutrition, safety, or cleanliness to save money. Simply enjoy the local-style alternatives to expensive hotels and restaurants.

Connecting with people carbonates your experience. Extroverts have more fun. If your trip is low on magic moments, kick yourself and make things happen. If you don't enjoy a place, maybe you don't know enough about it. Seek the truth. Recognize tourist traps. Give a culture the benefit of your open mind. See things as different, but not better or worse. Any culture has plenty to share. When an opportunity presents itself, make it a habit to say "yes."

Of course, travel, like the world, is a series of hills and valleys. Be fanatically positive and militantly optimistic. If something's not to your liking, change your liking.

Travel can make you a happier American, as well as a citizen of the world. Our Earth is home to seven billion equally precious people. It's humbling to travel and find that other people don't have the "American Dream"—they have their own dreams. Europeans like us, but with all due respect, they wouldn't trade passports.

Thoughtful travel engages us with the world. It reminds us what is truly important. By broadening perspectives, travel teaches new ways to measure quality of life.

Globetrotting destroys ethnocentricity, helping us understand and appreciate other cultures. Rather than fear the diversity on this planet, celebrate it. Among your most prized souvenirs will be the strands of different cultures you choose to knit into your own character. The world is a cultural yarn shop, and Back Door travelers are weaving the ultimate tapestry. Join in!

ENGLAND

ENGLAND

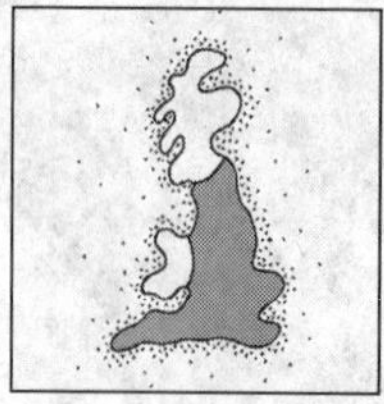

England (pop. 55 million) is a hilly country about the size of Louisiana (50,346 square miles) that occupies the lower two-thirds of the isle of Britain (with 80 percent of its population). Scotland is to the north and the English Channel to the south, with the North Sea to the east and Wales (and the Irish Sea) to the west. England's highest mountain (Scafell Pike in the Lake District) is 3,206 feet, a foothill by our standards. Fed by ocean air from the southwest, the climate is mild, with a chance of cloudy, rainy weather almost any day of the year.

England has an economy that can stand alongside many much larger nations. It boasts high-tech industries (software, chemicals, aviation), international banking, and textile manufacturing, and is a major exporter of beef. While farms and villages remain, England is now an urban, industrial, and post-industrial colossus.

England traditionally has been very class-conscious, with the wealthy landed aristocracy, the middle-class tradesmen, and the lower-class farmers and factory workers. While social stratification is fading with the new global economy, regional differences remain strong. Locals can often identify where someone is from by their dialect or local accent—Geordie, Cockney, or Queen's English.

One thing that sets England apart from its fellow UK countries (Scotland, Wales, and Northern

Ireland) is its ethnic makeup. Traditionally, those countries had Celtic roots, while the English mixed in Saxon and Norman blood. In the 20th century, England welcomed many Scots, Welsh, and Irish as low-wage workers. More recently, it's become home to immigrants from former colonies of its worldwide empire—particularly from India/Pakistan/Bangladesh, the Caribbean, and Africa—and to many workers from poorer Eastern European countries. These days it's not a given that every "English" person speaks English. Nearly one in three citizens does not profess the Christian faith. As the world becomes interconnected by communications technology, it's possible for many immigrants to physically inhabit the country while remaining closely linked to their home culture—rather than truly assimilating into England.

This is the current English paradox. England—the birthplace and center of the extended worldwide family of English speakers—is losing its traditional Englishness. Where Scotland, Wales, and

Northern Ireland have cultural movements to preserve their local languages and customs, England does not. Politically, there is no "English" party in the UK Parliament. While Scotland, Wales, and Northern Ireland have their own parliaments to decide local issues, England must depend on the decisions of the UK government at large. Except for the occasional display of an English flag (the red St. George's cross on a white background) at a football (soccer) match, many English people don't really think of themselves as "English"—more as "Brits," a part of the wider UK.

Today, England tries to preserve its rich past as it races forward as a leading global player. There are still hints of its legacy of farms, villages, Victorian lamplighters, and upper-crust dandies. But it's also a jostling world of unemployed factory workers, investment bankers, football matches, rowdy "stag parties," and faux-Tudor suburbs. Modern England is a culturally diverse land in transition. Catch it while you can.

LONDON

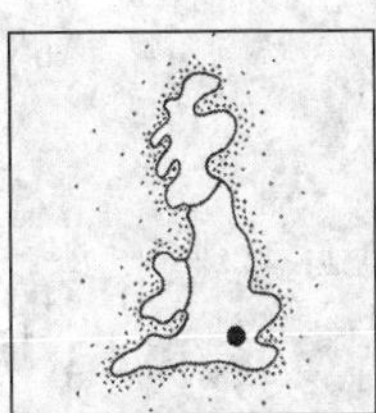

London is more than 600 square miles of urban jungle—a world in itself and a barrage on all the senses. On my first visit, I felt extremely small.

London is more than its museums and landmarks. It's the L.A., DC, and N.Y.C. of Britain—a living, breathing, thriving organism...a coral reef of humanity. The city has changed dramatically in recent years, and many visitors are surprised to find how "un-English" it is. ESL (English as a second language) seems like the city's first language, as white people are now a minority in major parts of the city that once symbolized white imperialism. Arabs have nearly bought out the area north of Hyde Park. Chinese takeouts outnumber fish-and-chips shops. Eastern Europeans pull pints in British pubs, and Italians express your espresso. Many hotels are run by people with foreign accents (who hire English chambermaids), while outlying suburbs are home to huge communities of Indians and Pakistanis. London is a city of eight million separate dreams, inhabiting a place that tolerates and encourages them. With the English Channel Tunnel and discount airlines making travel between Britain and the Continent easier than ever, London is learning—sometimes fitfully—to live as a microcosm of its formerly vast empire.

The city, which has long attracted tourists, seems perpetually at your service, with an impressive slate of sights, entertainment, and eateries, all linked by a great transit system. With just a few days here, you'll get no more than a quick splash in this teeming human tidal pool. But with a good orientation, you'll find London manageable and fun. You'll get a sampling of the city's top sights, history, and cultural entertainment, and a good look at its ever-changing human face.

Blow through the city on the open deck of a double-decker orientation tour bus, and take a pinch-me-I'm-in-London walk through the West End. Ogle the crown jewels at the Tower of London, hear the chimes of Big Ben, and see the Houses of Parliament in action. Cruise the Thames River, and take a spin on the London Eye. Hobnob with poets' tombstones in Westminster Abbey, and visit with Leonardo, Botticelli, and Rembrandt in the National Gallery. Enjoy Shakespeare in a replica of the Globe theater and marvel at a glitzy, fun musical at a modern-day theater. Whisper across the dome of St. Paul's Cathedral, then rummage through our civilization's attic at the British Museum. And sip your tea with pinky raised and clotted cream dribbling down your scone.

PLANNING YOUR TIME

The sights of London alone could easily fill a trip to England. It's a great one-week getaway. But on a three-week tour of England, I'd give London three busy days. You won't be able to see everything, so don't try. You'll keep coming back to London. After dozens of visits myself, I still enjoy a healthy list of excuses to return. If you're flying in to one of London's airports, consider starting your trip in Bath and making London your English finale. Especially if you hope to enjoy a play or concert, a night or two of jet lag is bad news.

Here's a suggested four-day schedule:

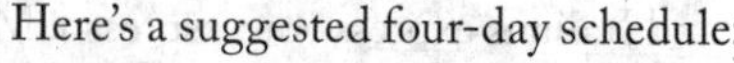

Day 1

Use my Westminster Walk to link the following sights:

9:00	Be in line at Westminster Abbey (opens at 9:30, closed Sun), to tour the place with fewer crowds.
11:00	Visit the Churchill War Rooms.
13:00	Eat lunch at the Churchill War Rooms café or nearby, or grab a later lunch near Trafalgar Square.
15:00	Visit the National Gallery and any nearby sights that interest you (National Portrait Gallery or St. Martin-in-the-Fields Church).
Evening	Dinner and a play in the West End.

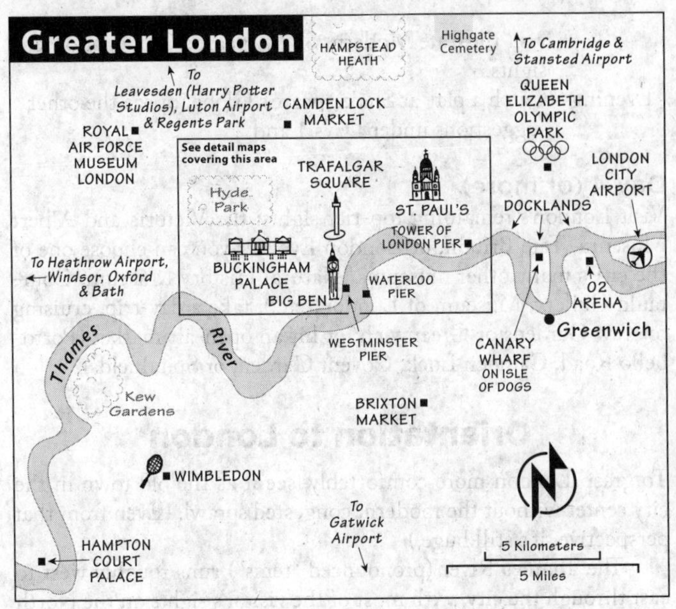

Day 2

8:30	Take a double-decker hop-on, hop-off London sightseeing bus tour (from Victoria Station or Green Park), and hop off for the Changing of the Guard.
11:00	Buckingham Palace (guards change most days May-July at 11:30, alternate days Aug-April—confirm online).
14:00	After lunch, tour the British Museum.
16:00	Tour the British Library.
Evening	Choose from a play, concert, or walking tour, or do some shopping at one of London's elegant department stores (Harrod's, Liberty, and Fortnum & Mason are open until 20:00 or 21:00 except on Sun).

Day 3

9:00	Tower of London (crown jewels first, then Beefeater tour and White Tower; note that on Sun-Mon, the Tower opens at 10:00).
12:00	Grab a picnic, catch a boat at Tower Pier, and have lunch on the Thames while cruising to Blackfriars Pier.
13:00	Tour St. Paul's Cathedral and climb its dome for views (cathedral closed Sun except for worship).
15:00	Walk across Millennium Bridge to the South Bank to

visit the Tate Modern, Shakespeare's Globe, or other sights.

Evening Catch a play at Shakespeare's Globe, or see the other suggestions under Days 1 and 2.

Day 4 (or more)

Visit London's remaining top-tier sights: the Victoria and Albert Museum, Tate Britain, or London Eye. Or you can choose one of the city's many other museums (Natural History Museum, Courtauld Gallery, Museum of London, etc.); take a day-trip, cruising to Kew Gardens or Greenwich; or hit an open-air market (Portobello Road, Camden Lock, Covent Garden, or Spitalfields).

Orientation to London

To grasp London more comfortably, see it as the old town in the city center without the modern, congested sprawl. (Even from that perspective, it's still huge.)

The Thames River (pronounced "tems") runs roughly west to east through the city, with most of the visitor's sights on the North Bank. Mentally, maybe even physically, trim down your map to include only the area between the Tower of London (to the east), Hyde Park (west), Regent's Park (north), and the South Bank (south). This is roughly the area bordered by the Tube's Circle Line. This four-mile stretch between the Tower and Hyde Park (about a 1.5-hour walk) looks like a milk bottle on its side (see map), and holds 80 percent of the sights mentioned in this chapter.

With a core focus and a good orientation, you'll get a sampling of London's top sights, history, and cultural entertainment, and a good look at its ever-changing human face.

The sprawling city becomes much more manageable if you think of it as a collection of neighborhoods.

Central London: This area contains Westminster and what Londoners call the West End. The Westminster district includes Big Ben, Parliament, Westminster Abbey, and Buckingham Palace—the grand government buildings from which Britain is ruled. Trafalgar Square, London's gathering place, has many major museums. The West End is the center of London's cultural life, with bustling squares: Piccadilly Circus and Leicester Square host cinemas, tourist traps, and nighttime glitz. Soho and Covent Garden are thriving people zones with theaters, restaurants, pubs, and boutiques. And Regent and Oxford streets are the city's main shopping zones.

North London: Neighborhoods in this part of town—including Bloomsbury, Fitzrovia, and Marylebone—contain such major sights as the British Museum and the overhyped Madame Tus-

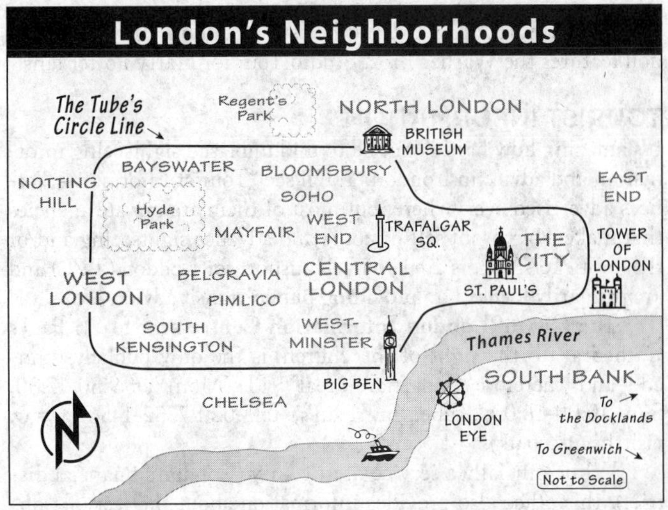

sauds Waxworks. Nearby, along busy Euston Road, is the British Library, plus a trio of train stations (one of them, St. Pancras International, is linked to Paris by the Eurostar "Chunnel" train).

The City: Today's modern financial district, called simply "The City," was a walled town in Roman times. Gleaming skyscrapers are interspersed with historical landmarks such as St. Paul's Cathedral, legal sights (Old Bailey), and the Museum of London. The Tower of London and Tower Bridge lie at The City's eastern border.

East London: Just east of The City is the East End—the increasingly gentrified former stomping ground of Cockney ragamuffins and Jack the Ripper.

The South Bank: The South Bank of the Thames River offers major sights (Tate Modern, Shakespeare's Globe, London Eye) linked by a riverside walkway. Within this area, Southwark (SUTH-uck) stretches from the Tate Modern to London Bridge. Pedestrian bridges connect the South Bank with The City and Trafalgar Square.

West London: This huge area contains neighborhoods such as Mayfair, Belgravia, Pimlico, Chelsea, South Kensington, and Notting Hill. It's home to London's wealthy and has many trendy shops and enticing restaurants. Here you'll find a range of museums (Victoria and Albert Museum, Tate Britain, and more), my top hotel recommendations, lively Victoria Station, and the vast green expanses of Hyde Park and Kensington Gardens.

Outside the Center: The Docklands, London's version of Manhattan, is farther east than the East End. Historic Greenwich is southeast of London and across the Thames. Kew Gardens and

Hampton Court Palace are southwest of London. North of London features the Warner Bros. Studio Tour for Harry Potter fans.

TOURIST INFORMATION

It's amazing how hard it can be to find unbiased sightseeing information and advice in London. You'll see "Tourist Information" offices advertised everywhere, but most of them are private agencies that make a big profit selling tours and advance sightseeing and/or theater tickets; others are run by Transport for London (TFL) and are primarily focused on providing public-transit advice.

The City of London Information Centre next to St. Paul's Cathedral (to the right of the church) is the only publicly funded—and therefore impartial—"real" TI (Mon-Sat 9:30-17:30, Sun 10:00-16:00; Tube: St. Paul's, tel. 020/7332-1456, www.visitthecity.co.uk).

While officially a service of The City (London's financial district), this office also provides information about the rest of London. It sells Oyster cards, London Passes, advance "Fast Track" sightseeing tickets (all described later), and some National Express bus tickets. It also stocks various free publications: *London Planner* (a free monthly that lists all the sights, events, and hours), some walking-tour brochures, the *Official London Theatre Guide,* a free Tube and bus map, the *Guide to River Thames Boat Services,* and brochures describing self-guided walks in The City (various themes, including Dickens, modern architecture, and film locations).

The TI gives out a free map of The City and sells several citywide maps; ask if they have yet another, free map with a coupon good for 20 percent off admission to St. Paul's. I'd skip their room-booking service (charges a commission) and theater box office (may charge a commission).

Visit London, which serves the greater London area, doesn't have an office you can visit in person—but does have an information-packed website (www.visitlondon.com).

Fast Track Tickets: To skip the ticket-buying queues at certain London sights, you can buy Fast Track tickets in advance—and they can be cheaper than tickets sold right at the sight. They're particularly smart for the Tower of London, the London Eye, and Madame Tussauds Waxworks, all of which get very busy in high season. They're available through various sales outlets around London (including the City of London TI, souvenir stands, and faux-TIs scattered throughout touristy areas).

London Pass: This pass, which covers many big sights and lets you skip some lines, is expensive but potentially worth the investment for extremely busy sightseers (£52/1 day, £71/2 days, £85/3 days, £159/6 days; days are calendar days rather than 24-hour periods; comes with 160-page guidebook, also sold at major train stations and airports, tel. 020/7293-0972, www.londonpass.com). Among the many sights it includes are the Tower of London, Westminster Abbey, Churchill War Rooms, and Windsor Castle, as well as many temporary exhibits and audioguides at otherwise "free" biggies. Think through your sightseeing plans, study their website to see what's covered, and do the math before you buy.

ARRIVAL IN LONDON

For more information on getting to or from London by train, bus, plane, and cruise ship, see "London Connections," at the end of this chapter.

By Train: London has nine major train stations, all connected by the Tube (subway). All have ATMs, and many of the larger stations also have shops, fast food, exchange offices, and luggage storage. From any station, you can ride the Tube or taxi to your hotel. For more info on train travel, see www.nationalrail.co.uk.

By Bus: The main intercity bus station is Victoria Coach Station, one block southwest of Victoria train/Tube station. For more on bus travel, see www.nationalexpress.com.

By Plane: London has six airports. Most tourists arrive at Heathrow or Gatwick airport, although flights from elsewhere in Europe may land at Stansted, Luton, Southend, or London City airport. For hotels near Heathrow and Gatwick, see page 165.

HELPFUL HINTS

Theft Alert: Wear your money belt. The Artful Dodger is alive and well in London. Be on guard, particularly on public transportation and in places crowded with tourists, who, considered naive and rich, are targeted. The Changing of the Guard scene is a favorite for thieves. And more than 7,500 purses are stolen annually at Covent Garden alone.

Pedestrian Safety: Cars drive on the left side of the road—which can be as confusing for foreign pedestrians as for foreign drivers. Before crossing a street, I always look right, look left, then look right again just to be sure. Most crosswalks are even painted with instructions, reminding foreign guests to "Look right" or "Look left." While locals are champion jaywalkers, you shouldn't try it; jaywalking is treacherous when you're disoriented about which direction traffic is coming from.

Medical Problems: Local hospitals have good-quality 24-hour-a-day emergency care centers, where any tourist who needs help can drop in and, after a wait, be seen by a doctor. Your hotel has details. St. Thomas' Hospital, immediately across the river from Big Ben, has a fine reputation.

Getting Your Bearings: London is well-signed for visitors. Through an initiative called Legible London, the city has erected thoughtfully designed, pedestrian-focused maps around town—especially handy when exiting Tube stations. In this sprawling city—where predictable grid-planned streets are relatively rare—it's also smart to buy and use a good map.

Maps: Bensons MapGuides' *London Street Map*, sold at many newsstands and bookstores, is my favorite for efficient sightseeing and might be the best £3 you'll spend. I also like *The Handy London Map & Guide*, which shows every little lane and all the sights, and comes with a transit map. Many Londoners, along with obsessive-compulsive tourists, rely on the highly detailed *London A-Z* map book (generally £5-7, called "A to Zed" by locals, available at newsstands).

Festivals: For one week in February and another in September, fashionistas descend on the city for **London Fashion Week** (www.londonfashionweek.co.uk). The famous **Chelsea Flower Show** blossoms in late May (book ahead for this popular event at www.rhs.org.uk/chelsea). During the annual **Trooping the Colour** in June, there are military bands and pageantry, and the Queen's birthday parade (www.trooping-the-colour.co.uk). Tennis fans pack the stands at the **Wimbledon Tennis Championship** in late June to early July (www.wimbledon.org), and partygoers head for the **Notting Hill Carnival** in late August.

Traveling in Winter: London dazzles year-round, so consider visiting in winter, when airfares and hotel rates are generally cheaper and there are fewer tourists. For ideas on what to do, see the "Winter Activities in London" article at www.ricksteves.com/winteracts.

Getting Online with a Mobile Device: In addition to the Wi-Fi that's likely available at your hotel, many major museums, sights, and even entire boroughs also offer free access. If that's still not enough, consider signing up for a free account with **The Cloud,** a Wi-Fi service found in many convenient spots around London, including most train stations and many museums, coffee shops, cafés, and shopping centers (though the connection can be slow). When you sign up at www.thecloud.net/free-wifi, you'll have to enter a street address and postal code; it doesn't matter which one (use your hotel's, or the Queen's: Buckingham Palace, SW1A 1AA).

Most **Tube stations** and trains have Wi-Fi, but it's free only to those with a British Virgin Media account. However, the Tube's Wi-Fi always lets you access Transport for London's "Journey Planner" (www.tfl.gov.uk), making it easy to look up your city transit options—and get real-time updates on delays—once you're in a station. To use the Tube's pay Wi-

Fi, you can spend £2 for a one-day pass, or £5 for a one-week pass (http://my.virginmedia.com/wifi).

Useful Apps: Tube travelers might want to download MX Apps' free **Tube Map London Underground** (www.mxapps.co.uk), which shows the easiest way to connect station A to station B. While you can always get Tube info on the Web (with Transport for London's "Journey Planner," www.tfl.gov.uk), the app works even when you're not online. When you are online, the app provides live updates about Tube delays and closures. (It doesn't, however, look up bus connections, and sometimes there are fake navigation buttons at the bottom of the screen which are actually ads. Unfortunately, MX Apps' "Bus London" map isn't very useful offline.) The handy **Citymapper** app for London covers every mode of public transit in the city. **City Maps 2Go** lets you download searchable offline maps; their London version is quite good. **Time Out London**'s free app has reviews and listings for theater, museums, movies, and more (download the "Make Your City Amazing" version, which is updated weekly, rather than the boilerplate "Travel Guide" version).

Travel Bookstores: Located between Covent Garden and Leicester Square, the very good **Stanfords Travel Bookstore** stocks a huge selection of guidebooks (including current editions of nearly all of mine), travel-related novels, maps, and gear (Mon-Sat 9:00-20:00, Sun 11:30-18:00, 12 Long Acre, second entrance on Floral Street, Tube: Leicester Square, tel. 020/7836-1321, www.stanfords.co.uk).

Two impressive **Waterstones** bookstores have the biggest collection of travel guides in town: on Piccadilly (Mon-Sat 9:00-22:00, Sun 12:00-18:30, café, great views from top-floor bar—see sidebar on page 100, 203 Piccadilly, tel. 0843-290-8549) and on Trafalgar Square (Mon-Sat 9:00-21:00, Sun 12:00-18:00, Costa Café on second floor, tel. 020/7839-4411).

Baggage Storage: Train stations have replaced lockers with more secure left-luggage counters. Each bag must go through a scanner (just like at the airport). Expect long waits in the morning to check in (up to 45 minutes) and in the afternoon to pick up (each item-£10/24 hours, most stations daily 7:00-23:00). You can also store bags at the airports (similar rates and hours, www.left-baggage.co.uk).

"Voluntary Donations": Some London sights automatically add a "voluntary donation" of about 10 percent to their admission fees. The prices posted and quoted in this chapter include the donation, though it's perfectly fine to pay the base price without the donation. Some of London's free museums also ask for donations as you enter, but again, it's completely optional.

London at a Glance

▲▲▲**Westminster Abbey** Britain's finest church and the site of royal coronations and burials since 1066. **Hours:** Mon-Fri 9:30-16:30, Wed until 19:00, Sat 9:30-14:30, closed Sun to sightseers except for worship. See page 58.

▲▲▲**Churchill War Rooms** Underground WWII headquarters of Churchill's war effort. **Hours:** Daily 9:30-18:00. See page 67.

▲▲▲**National Gallery** Remarkable collection of European paintings (1250-1900), including Leonardo, Botticelli, Velázquez, Rembrandt, Turner, Van Gogh, and the Impressionists. **Hours:** Daily 10:00-18:00, Fri until 21:00. See page 69.

▲▲▲**British Museum** The world's greatest collection of artifacts of Western civilization, including the Rosetta Stone and the Parthenon's Elgin Marbles. **Hours:** Daily 10:00-17:30, Fri until 20:30 (selected galleries only). See page 84.

▲▲▲**British Library** Fascinating collection of important literary treasures of the Western world. **Hours:** Mon-Fri 9:30-18:00, Tue until 20:00, Sat 9:30-17:00, Sun 11:00-17:00. See page 89.

▲▲▲**St. Paul's Cathedral** The main cathedral of the Anglican Church, designed by Christopher Wren, with a climbable dome and daily evensong services. **Hours:** Mon-Sat 8:30-16:30, closed Sun except for worship. See page 95.

▲▲▲**Tower of London** Historic castle, palace, and prison housing the crown jewels and a witty band of Beefeaters. **Hours:** Tue-Sat 9:00-17:30, Sun-Mon 10:00-17:30; Nov-Feb closes one hour earlier. See page 102.

▲▲▲**Victoria and Albert Museum** The best collection of decorative arts anywhere. **Hours:** Daily 10:00-17:45, Fri until 22:00 (selected galleries only). See page 124.

▲▲**Houses of Parliament** London landmark famous for Big Ben and occupied by the Houses of Lords and Commons. **Hours:** When Parliament is in session, generally open Mon-Thu, closed Fri-Sun and most of Aug-Sept. Guided tours offered year-round on Sat and most weekdays during Aug-Sept. See page 63.

▲▲**Trafalgar Square** The heart of London, where Westminster, The City, and the West End meet. **Hours:** Always open. See page 69.

▲▲**National Portrait Gallery** A *Who's Who* of British history, featuring portraits of this nation's most important historical figures. **Hours:** Daily 10:00-18:00, Thu-Fri until 21:00, first and second floors open Mon at 11:00. See page 74.

▲▲**Covent Garden** Vibrant people-watching zone with shops, cafés, street musicians, and an iron-and-glass arcade that once hosted a produce market. **Hours:** Always open. See page 76.

▲▲**Changing of the Guard at Buckingham Palace** Hour-long spectacle at Britain's royal residence. **Hours:** Generally May-July daily at 11:30, Aug-April every other day. See page 81.

▲▲**London Eye** Enormous observation wheel, dominating—and offering commanding views over—London's skyline. **Hours:** Daily 10:00-20:30, later in July and Aug. See page 109.

▲▲**Imperial War Museum** Exhibits examining the military history of the bloody 20th century. **Hours:** Daily 10:00-18:00. See page 110.

▲▲**Tate Modern** Works by Monet, Matisse, Dalí, Picasso, and Warhol displayed in a converted powerhouse. **Hours:** Daily 10:00-18:00, Fri-Sat until 22:00. See page 113.

▲▲**Shakespeare's Globe** Timbered, thatched-roofed reconstruction of the Bard's original "wooden O." **Hours:** Theater complex, museum, and actor-led tours generally daily 9:00-17:30; in summer, morning theater tours only. Plays are also staged here. See page 114.

▲▲**Tate Britain** Collection of British painting from the 16th century through modern times, including works by William Blake, the Pre-Raphaelites, and J. M. W. Turner. **Hours:** Daily 10:00-18:00. See page 119.

▲▲**Natural History Museum** A Darwinian delight, packed with stuffed creatures, engaging exhibits, and enthralled kids. **Hours:** Daily 10:00-18:00. See page 125.

▲▲**Greenwich** Seafaring borough just east of the city center, with *Cutty Sark* tea clipper, Royal Observatory, other maritime sights, and a pleasant market. **Hours:** Most sights open daily, typically 10:00-17:00; market closed Mon. See page 126.

▲**Wallace Collection** One of the finest private family art collections anywhere—free and open to the public—with paintings by such masters as Rembrandt, Rubens, and Velázquez. **Hours:** Daily 10:00-17:00. See page 91.

▲**Courtauld Gallery** Fine collection of paintings filling one wing of the Somerset House, a grand 18th-century palace. **Hours:** Daily 10:00-18:00. See page 77.

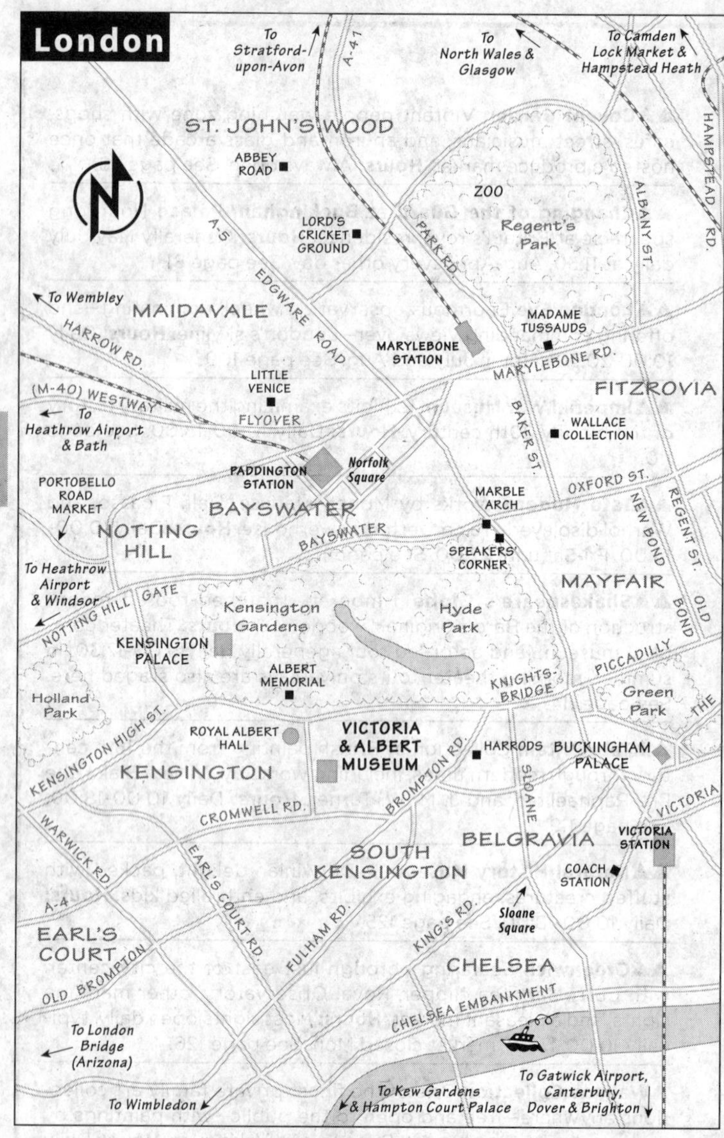

Updates to This Book: For the latest, see www.ricksteves.com/update.

GETTING AROUND LONDON

To travel smart in a city this size, you must get comfortable with public transportation. London's excellent taxis, buses, and subway (Tube) system can take you anywhere you need to go—a blessing for travelers' precious vacation time, not to mention their feet. It's

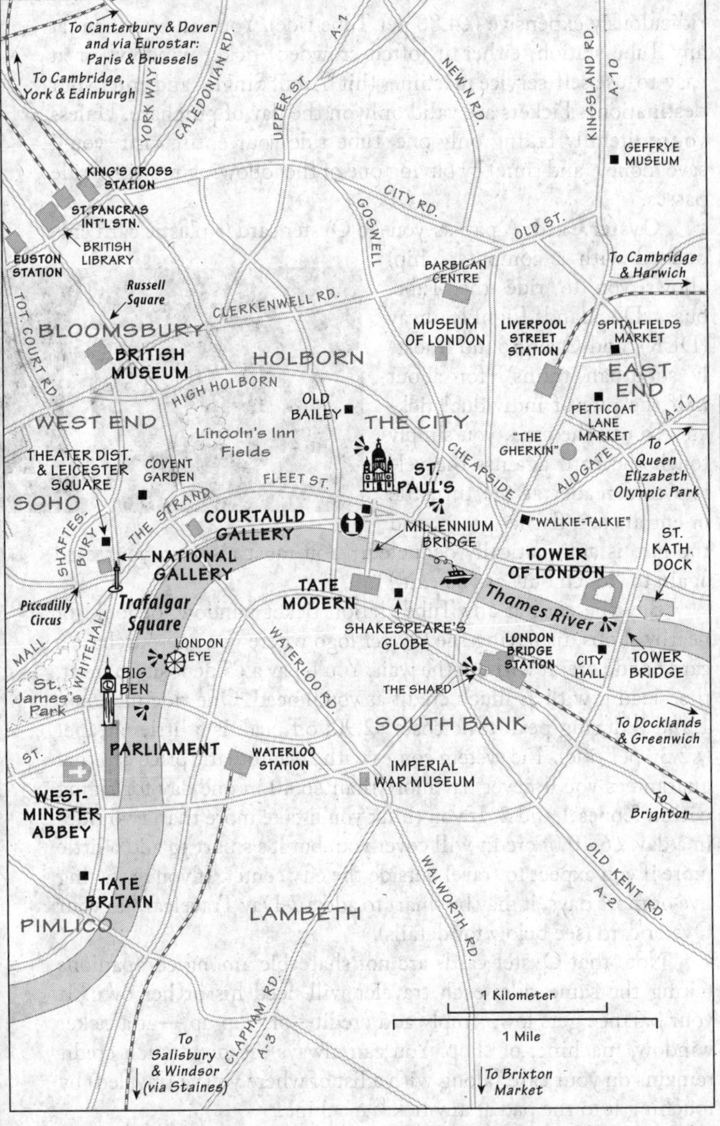

also the most expensive public transit in the world. While single-ride and paper tickets still exist, for most visitors the Oyster card is simply the only way to go—saving precious time and money.

Public Transit Tickets and Passes

While the transit system has six zones, almost all tourist sights are within Zones 1 and 2, so those are the prices I've listed.

Individual tickets: Individual paper tickets for the Tube are ridiculously expensive (£4.80 per Tube ride). You can buy them at any Tube station, either at (often-crowded) ticket windows or at easy-to-use self-service machines (hit "Adult Single" and enter your destination). Tickets are valid only on the day of purchase. Unless you're literally taking only one Tube ride your entire visit, you'll save money (and time) by buying one of the following multiple-ride passes.

Oyster Card: A pay-as-you-go Oyster card (a plastic card embedded with a computer chip) allows you to ride the Tube, buses, Docklands Light Railway (DLR), and Overground (mostly suburban trains), for about half the rate of individual tickets. To use the card, you simply touch the card against the yellow card reader at the turnstile or entrance, it flashes green, and the fare is automatically deducted. (You must also tap your card again to "touch out" as you exit.)

Buy the card at any Tube station ticket window, or look for nearby shops displaying the Oyster logo where you can purchase a card or add credit without the wait. You'll pay a £5 deposit up front, then load it with as much credit as you'll need. One ride in Zones 1 and 2 during peak time costs £2.90; off peak is a little cheaper (£2.30 per ride). The system comes with an automatic price cap that guarantees you'll never pay more than £6.40 in one day for riding within Zones 1 and 2. If you think you'll take more than two rides in a day, £6.40 of credit will cover you, but it's smart to add a little more if you expect to travel outside the city center. If you're staying five or more days, it may be smart to add a 7-Day Travelcard to your Oyster card (see below for details).

Note that Oyster cards are not shareable among companions taking the same ride; each traveler will need his or her own. If your balance gets low, simply add credit—or "top up"—at a ticket window, machine, or shop. You can always see how much credit remains on your card (along with a list of where you've traveled) by touching it to the pad at any ticket machine.

At the end of your trip, you can reclaim your deposit and unused balance (up to £5) by selecting "Pay as you go refund" on any ticket machine that gives change. This will deactivate your card. For balances of more than £5, you'll have to wait in line at a ticket window for your refund. If you do not deactivate your card, the credit never expires—you can use it again on your next trip.

Visitor Oyster Travel Cards, aimed specifically at tourists, have some advantages. But you must purchase them online in advance and have them delivered by mail before your trip, making them more expensive than a regular Oyster card. For more information, visit www.tfl.gov.uk/tickets.

Travelcards: Paper Travelcards let you ride as many times as you want within a one- or a seven-day period for one fixed price, but are only a good deal in limited instances. The card works like a traditional paper ticket: Buy it at any Tube station ticket window or machine, then feed it into a turnstile (and retrieve it) to enter and exit the Tube. On a bus, just show it to the driver when you get on.

Your options are the **Anytime Day Travelcard** (covers Zones 1-4, valid for one day of travel anytime, £12), **Off-Peak Day Travelcard** (covers Zones 1-6, valid for one day of travel after 9:30 on weekdays, anytime on weekends, £12), and **7-Day Travelcard** (£32.10 for Zones 1-2; £58.60 for Zones 1-6). Skip the Anytime or Off-Peak Travelcards unless you're taking full advantage of the discounts that come with them (see below); an Oyster card with its daily cap is almost always a better deal.

The 7-Day Travelcard, which can be added to an Oyster card, is the best option if you're staying five or more days and plan to use public transit a lot. For most travelers, the Zone 1-2 pass works best. Heathrow Airport is in Zone 6, but there's no need to buy the Zones 1-6 version if that's the only ride outside the city center you plan to take—instead you can pay a small supplement to cover the difference.

The Bottom Line

Wondering which pass works best for your trip? On a short visit (three days or fewer), consider purchasing an Oyster card and adding £20-25 of credit (£6.40 daily cap times three days, plus a little extra for any rides outside Zones 1-2). If you'll be taking fewer rides, £15 will be enough, and if not you can always top up. If you're in London for five days or longer, the 7-Day Travelcard—either the paper version or on an Oyster card—will likely pay for itself. Note that certain Travelcards come with sightseeing discounts (see below) that might make them a worthwhile option.

Discounts

Families: A paying adult can take up to four kids (ages 10 and under) for free on the Tube, Docklands Light Railway (DLR), Overground, and buses. Explore other child and student discounts at www.tfl.gov.uk/tickets or ask a clerk at a Tube ticket window which deal is best.

River Cruises: A Travelcard gives you a 33 percent discount on most Thames cruises (see page 50). The Oyster card gives you a 10 percent discount on Thames Clippers (including the Tate Boat museum ferry).

Sightseeing Deal: If you buy a paper Anytime Day or Off-

Peak Day Travelcard at a National Rail train station (not a Tube station), you get same-day, two-for-one discounts at some sights, including the pricey Tower of London (not valid July-Aug), Churchill War Rooms, and Madame Tussauds. For more information, visit www.daysoutguide.co.uk.

By Tube

London's subway system is called the Tube or Underground (but never "subway," which, in Britain, refers to a pedestrian underpass). The Tube is one of this planet's great people-movers and usually the fastest long-distance transport in town (runs Mon-Sat about 5:00-24:00, Sun about 7:00-23:00; Central, Jubilee, Northern, Piccadilly, and Victoria lines also run Fri-Sat 24 hours). Two other commuter rail lines are tied into the network and use the same tickets: the Docklands Light Railway (called DLR) and the Overground.

Get your bearings by studying a map of the system, free at any station (or download a transit app as described earlier).

Each line has a name (such as Circle, Northern, or Bakerloo) and two directions (indicated by the end-of-the-line stops). Find the line that will take you to your destination, and figure out roughly which direction (north, south, east, or west) you'll need to go to get there.

At the Tube station, there are two ways to pass through the turnstile. With a paper ticket or Travelcard, you'll feed it into the turnstile, reclaim it, and hang on to it—you'll need it later. With an Oyster card, touch it flat against the turnstile's yellow card reader, both when you enter and exit the station.

Find your train by following signs to your line and the (general) direction it's headed (such as Central Line: east). Since some tracks are shared by several lines, double-check before boarding a train—make sure your destination is one of the stops listed on the sign at the platform. Also, check the electronic signboards that announce which train is next, and make sure the destination (the end-of-the-line stop)

is the direction you want. Some trains, particularly on the Circle and District lines, split off for other directions, but each train has its final destination marked above its windshield.

Trains run about every 3-10 minutes. For a rough idea of how long it takes to get from point A to point B by Tube, estimate five minutes per stop (which includes time to walk into and out of stations, and to change trains). So a destination six stops away will take you about 30 minutes.

When you leave the system, "touch out" with your Oyster card at the electronic reader on the turnstile, or feed your paper ticket into the turnstile (it will eat your now-expired ticket). With a Travelcard, it will spit out your still-valid card. When leaving a station, save walking time by choosing the best street exit—check the maps on the walls or ask any station personnel.

The system can be fraught with construction delays and breakdowns. Pay attention to signs and announcements explaining necessary detours. Rush hours (8:00-10:00 and 16:00-19:00) can be packed and sweaty. If one train is stuffed—and another is coming in three minutes—wait to avoid the sardine routine. If you get confused, ask for advice from a local, a blue-vested staff person, or at the information window located before the turnstile entry. Online, get help from the "Journey Planner" at www.tfl.gov.uk, which is accessible (via free Wi-Fi) on any mobile device within most Tube stations before you go underground.

Tube Etiquette

- When your train arrives, stand off to the side and let riders exit before you try to board.
- Avoid using the hinged seats near the doors of some trains when the car is jammed; they take up valuable standing space.
- If you're blocking the door when the train stops, step out of the car and off to the side, let others off, then get back on.
- Talk softly in the cars. Listen to how quietly Londoners communicate and follow their lead.
- On escalators, stand on the right and pass on the left. But note that in some passageways or stairways, you might be directed to walk on the left (the direction Brits go when behind the wheel).
- Discreet eating and drinking are fine (nothing smelly); drinking alcohol and smoking are not.

By Bus

If you figure out the bus system, you'll swing like Tarzan through the urban jungle of London (see sidebar for a list of handy routes). Get in the habit of hopping buses for quick little straight shots, even just to get to a Tube stop. However, during bump-and-grind rush hours (8:00-10:00 and 16:00-19:00), you'll usually go faster by Tube.

You can't buy single-trip tickets for buses, and you can't use cash to pay for your fare when boarding. Instead, you must have an Oyster card, a Travelcard, or a one-day Bus and Tram Pass (£5, buy paper pass from the ticket machine or window in any Tube station). If you're using your Oyster card, any bus ride in downtown London costs £1.50 (with a cap of £4.40 per day).

The first step in mastering London's bus system is learning how to decipher the bus-stop signs. The accompanying photo shows a typical sign listing the various buses (the N91, N68, etc.) that come by here and the destinations they go to (Oakwood, Old Coulsdon, etc). In the first column, find your destination on the list—e.g., to Paddington (Tube and rail station). In the next column, find a bus that goes there—the #23 (routes marked "N" are night-only). In the final column, a letter within a circle (e.g., "H") tells you exactly which nearby bus stop is yours. Find where that stop is on the accompanying bus-stop map, then make your way to that stop—you'll know it's yours because it will have the same letter on its pole.

Nunhead Inverton Road	N343	
O		
Oakwood	N91	
Old Coulsdon	N68	Aldwych
Old Ford	N8	Oxford Circus
Old Kent Road Canal Bridge	53, N381	
	453	
	N21	
Old Street	243	Aldwych
Orpington	N47	
Oxford Circus	Any bus	
	N18	
P		
Paddington	23, N15	
Palmers Green	N29	
Park Langley	N3	
Peckham	12	
	N89, N343	
	N136	
	N381	
Penge Pawleyne Arms	176	
	N3	
Petts Wood	N47	
Pimlico Grosvenor Road	24	
Plaistow Greengate	N15	
Plumstead	53	
Plumstead Common	53	
Ponders End	N279	
Poplar All Saints	N15, N551	

When your bus approaches, it's wise to hold your arm out to let the driver know you want on. Hop on and confirm your destination with the driver (often friendly and helpful).

As you board, touch your Oyster card to the card reader, or show your paper Travelcard or Bus and Tram Pass to the driver. Unlike the Tube, there's no need to show or tap your card when you hop off. On the older heritage "Routemaster" buses without card-readers (used on the #15 route), you simply take a seat, and the conductor comes around to check cards and passes.

To alert the driver you want to get off, press one of the red buttons (on the poles between the seats) before your stop.

With a mobile phone, you can find out the arrival time of the next bus by texting your bus stop's five-digit code (posted at the stop, above the timetable) to 87287 (if you're using your US phone, text the code to 011-44-7797-800-287). Or try the helpful London Bus Checker app, with route maps and real-time bus info.

For more information about public transit (bus and Tube), the best single source is the helpful *Hello London* brochure, which includes both a Tube map and a handy schematic map of the best bus routes (available free at TIs, museums, hotels, and at www.tfl.gov.uk). For specific directions on how to get from point A to point B on London's transit, detailed bus maps, updated prices, and general information, check www.tfl.gov.uk or call the automated info line at 0843-222-1234.

By Taxi

London is the best taxi town in Europe. Big, black, carefully regulated cabs are everywhere—there are about 25,000 of them. (While

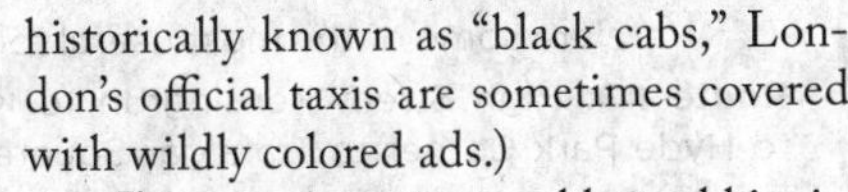

historically known as "black cabs," London's official taxis are sometimes covered with wildly colored ads.)

I've never met a crabby cabbie in London. They love to talk, and they know every nook and cranny in town. I ride in a taxi each day just to get my London questions answered. Drivers must pass a rigorous test on "The Knowledge" of London geography to earn their license.

If a cab's top light is on, just wave it down. Drivers flash lights when they see you wave. They have a tight turning radius, so you can hail cabs going in either direction. If waving doesn't work, ask someone where you can find a taxi stand. Telephoning a cab will get you one in a few minutes, but costs a little more.

Rides start at £2.40. The regular tariff #1 covers most of the day (Mon-Fri 6:00-20:00), tariff #2 is during "unsociable hours" (Mon-Fri 20:00-22:00 and Sat-Sun 6:00-22:00), and tariff #3 is for nighttime (22:00-6:00) and holidays. Rates go up about 20 percent with each higher tariff. All extra charges are explained in writing on the cab wall. Tip a cabbie by rounding up (maximum 10 percent).

Connecting downtown sights is quick and easy, and will cost you about £8-10 (for example, St. Paul's to the Tower of London, or between the two Tate museums). For a short ride, three adults in a cab generally travel at close to Tube prices—and groups of four or five adults should taxi everywhere. All cabs can carry five passengers, and some take six, for the same cost as a single traveler.

Don't worry about meter cheating. Licensed British cab meters come with a sealed computer chip and clock that ensures you'll get the correct tariff. The only way a cabbie can cheat you is by taking a needlessly long route. One serious pitfall, however, is taking a cab when traffic is bad to a destination efficiently served by the Tube. On one trip to London, I hopped in a taxi at South Kensington for Waterloo Station and hit bad traffic. Rather than spending 20 minutes and £2 on the Tube, I spent 40 minutes and £16 in a taxi.

Handy Bus Routes

Ever since London instituted a congestion charge for cars, the bus system has gotten faster, easier, and cheaper. Tube-oriented travelers need to get over their tunnel vision, learn the bus system, and get around fast and easy. The best views are upstairs on a double-decker.

Here are some of the most useful routes:

Route #9: High Street Kensington to Knightsbridge (Harrods) to Hyde Park Corner to Trafalgar Square to Aldwych (Somerset House).

Route #11: Victoria Station to Westminster Abbey to Trafalgar Square to St. Paul's and Liverpool Street Station and the East End.

Route #15: Trafalgar Square to St. Paul's to Tower of London (sometimes with heritage "Routemaster" old-style double-decker buses).

Routes #23 and #159: Paddington Station (#159 begins at Marble Arch) to Oxford Circus to Piccadilly Circus to Trafalgar Square; from there, #23 heads east to St. Paul's and Liverpool Street Station, while #159 heads to Westminster and the Imperial War Museum. In addition, several buses (including #6, #13, and #139) also

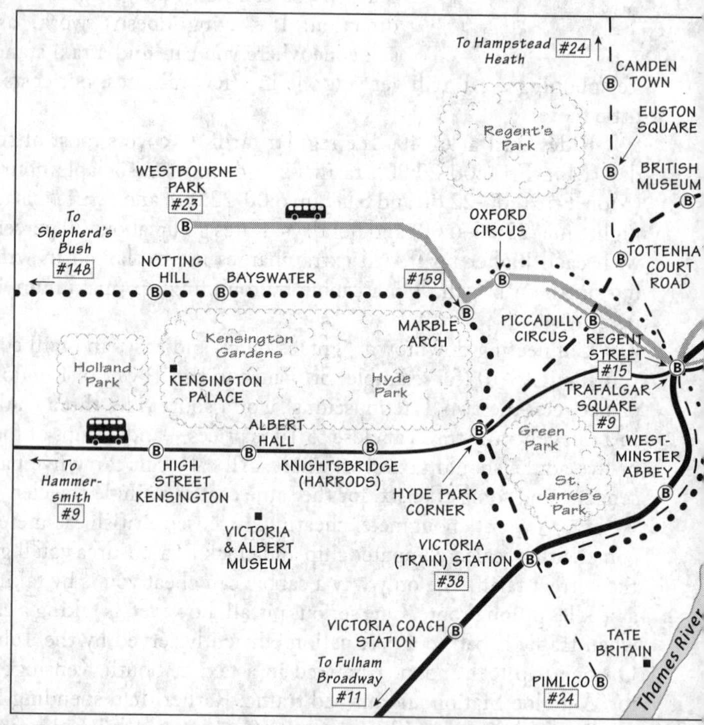

make the corridor run between Marble Arch, Oxford Circus, Piccadilly Circus, and Trafalgar Square.

Route #24: Pimlico to Victoria Station to Westminster Abbey to Trafalgar Square to Euston Square, then all the way north to Camden Town (Camden Lock Market).

Route #38: Victoria Station to Hyde Park Corner to Piccadilly Circus to British Museum.

Route #RV1 (a scenic South Bank joyride): Tower of London to Tower Bridge to Southwark Street (five-minute walk behind Tate Modern/Shakespeare's Globe) to London Eye/Waterloo Station, then over Waterloo Bridge to Aldwych and Covent Garden.

Route #148: Westminster Abbey to Victoria Station to Notting Hill and Bayswater (by way of the east end of Hyde Park and Marble Arch).

Check the bus stop closest to your hotel—it might be convenient to your sightseeing plans.

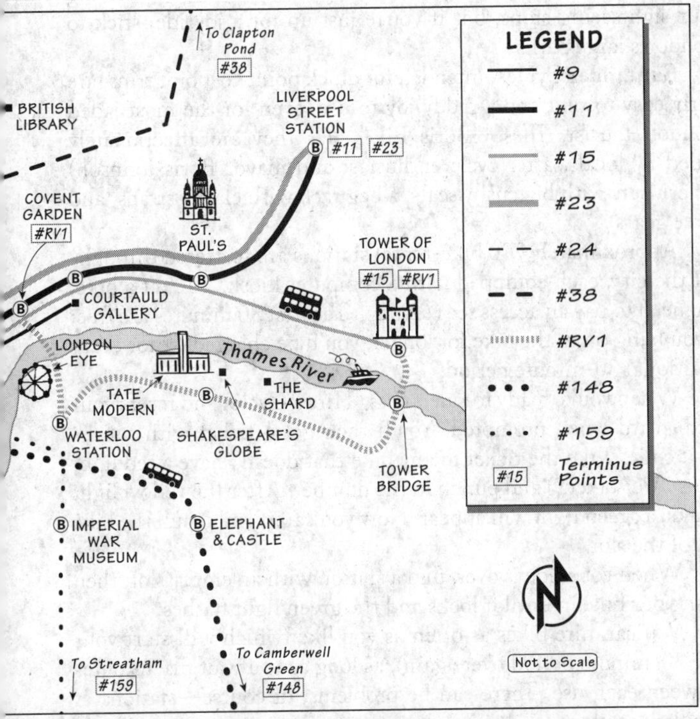

If you overdrink and ride in a taxi, be warned: Taxis charge £40 for "soiling" (a.k.a., pub puke). If you forget this book in a taxi, call the Lost Property office and hope for the best (tel. 0845-330-9882).

By Bike

London is keeping up its push to become more bike-friendly. It operates a citywide bike-rental program similar to ones in other major European cities, and new bike lanes are still cropping up around town.

Still, London isn't (yet) ideal for biking. Although the streets are relatively uncongested, the network of designated bike lanes is far from complete, and the city's many one-way streets (not to mention the need to bike on the "wrong" side) can make biking here a bit more challenging than it sounds. If you're accustomed to urban biking, it can be a good option for connecting your sightseeing stops, but if you're just up for a joyride, stick to London's large parks.

Santander Cycles, intended for quick point-to-point trips, are fairly easy to rent and a giddy joy to use, even for the most jaded London tourist. These "Boris Bikes" (as they are affectionately called by locals, after cycle enthusiast and mayor Boris Johnson) are cruisers with big cushy seats, a bag rack with elastic straps, and three gears.

Approximately 700 bike-rental stations are scattered throughout the city, each equipped with a computer kiosk. To rent a bike, you need to pay an access fee (£2/day). The first 30 minutes are free; if you hang on to the bike for longer, you'll be charged £2 for every additional 30-minute period.

When you're ready to ride, press "Hire a Cycle" and insert your credit card when prompted. You'll then get a ticket with a five-digit code. Take the ticket to any bike that doesn't have a red light (those are "taken") and punch in the number. After the yellow light blinks, a green light will appear: Now you can (firmly) pull the bike out of the slot.

When your ride is over, find a station with an empty slot, then push your bike in until it locks and the green light flashes.

You can hire bikes as often as you like (which will start your free 30-minute period over again), as long as you wait five minutes between each use. There can be problems, of course—stations at popular locations (such as entrances to parks) can temporarily run out of bikes, and you may have trouble finding a place to return a bike—but for the most part, this system works great. To make things easier, get a map of the docking stations—pick one up at any major Underground station. It's also available online at www.tfl.gov.uk (click on "Santander Cycles") and as a free smartphone app (http://cyclehireapp.com).

Helmets are not provided, so ride carefully. Stay to the far-left side of the road and watch closely at intersections for *left*-turning cars. Be aware that in most parks (including Hyde Park/Kensington Gardens) only certain paths are designated for bike use—you can't ride just anywhere. Maps posted at park entrances identify bike paths, and non-bike paths are generally clearly marked.

Some bike tour companies also rent bikes—for details, see page 49.

By Car

If you have a car, stow it—you don't want to drive in London. If you need convincing, here's one more reason: A £10 **congestion charge** is levied on any private car entering the city center during peak hours (Mon-Fri 7:00-18:00, no charge Sat-Sun and holidays, fee payable at gas stations, convenience stores, and self-service machines at public parking lots, or online at www.cclondon.com). There are painfully stiff penalties for late payments. The system has cut down traffic jams, bolstered London's public transit, and made buses cheaper and more user-friendly. Today, the vast majority of vehicles in the city center are buses, taxis, and service trucks.

Tours in London

🎧 To sightsee on your own, download my **free audio tours** that illuminate some of London's top sights and neighborhoods (see sidebar on page 13 for details).

▲▲▲HOP-ON, HOP-OFF DOUBLE-DECKER BUS TOURS

Two competitive companies (**Original** and **Big Bus**) offer essentially the same two tours of the city's sightseeing highlights, with nearly 30 stops on each route. Big Bus tours are a little more expensive (£32, cheaper if you book in advance online), while Original tours are cheaper (£26 with this book).

These two-to-three hour, once-over-lightly bus tours drive by all the famous sights, providing a stress-free way to get your bearings and see the biggies. They stop at the same core group of sights regardless of which overview tour you're on: Piccadilly Circus, Trafalgar Square, Big Ben, St. Paul's, the Tower of London, Marble Arch, Victoria Station, and elsewhere. With a good guide and nice

Combining a London Bus Tour and the Changing of the Guard

For a grand and efficient intro to London, consider catching an 8:30 departure of a hop-on, hop-off overview bus tour, riding 90 percent of the loop (which takes just over two hours, depending on traffic), and hopping off at Buckingham Palace in time to find a good spot to watch the Changing of the Guard ceremony at 11:30. If you miss the first bus, you could take the next one (generally about 20 minutes later), though it may get you to the ceremony late (check with the driver).

weather, I'd sit back and enjoy the entire tour. (If you don't like your guide, you can hop off and try your luck with the next departure.) On a recent trip, I had a livelier, more informative guide on the Original tour than the Big Bus tour, though guides can vary even within the same company.

Each company offers at least one route with live (English-only) guides, and a second (sometimes slightly different route) comes with recorded, dial-a-language narration. In addition to the overview tours, both Original and Big Bus include the Thames River boat trip by City Cruises (between Westminster and the Tower of London) and three 1.5-hour walking tours.

Pick up a map from any flier rack or from one of the countless salespeople, and study the color-coded system. Sunday morning—when the traffic is light and many museums are closed—is a fine time for a tour. Traffic is at its peak around lunch and during the evening rush hour (around 17:00). Unless you're using the bus tour mainly for hop-on, hop-off transportation, consider saving time and money by taking a night tour (described later).

Buses run daily about every 10-15 minutes in summer, every 10-20 minutes in winter. They start at about 8:00 or 8:30 and run until early evening in summer or late afternoon in winter. The last full loop usually leaves Victoria Station at about 19:00 in summer, and at about 17:00 in winter (confirm by checking the schedule or asking the driver).

You can buy tickets online in advance, or on the day of your trip from drivers or from staff at street kiosks (credit cards accepted at kiosks at major stops such as Victoria Station, ticket good for 24 hours, or 48 hours in winter).

Original London Sightseeing Bus Tour

They offer two versions of their basic highlights loop: **The Original Tour** (live guide, marked with a yellow triangle on the front of the bus) and the **City Sightseeing Tour** (essentially the same route but with recorded narration, a kids' soundtrack option, and a stop at

Madame Tussauds; bus marked with a red triangle). Other routes include the blue-triangle **Museum Tour** (connecting far-flung museums and major shopping stops), and green, black, and purple triangle routes (linking major train stations to the central route). All routes are covered by the same ticket. Keep it simple and just take one of the city highlights tours (£30, £4 less with this book, limit four discounts per book, they'll rip off the corner of this page—raise bloody hell if the staff or driver won't honor this discount; also online deals, info center at 17 Cockspur Street, tel. 020/8877-1722, www.theoriginaltour.com).

Big Bus London Tours

For £32 (up to 30 percent discount online—print tickets or have them delivered to your phone), you get the same basic overview tours: Red buses come with a live guide, while the blue route has a recorded narration and a one-hour longer path that goes around Hyde Park. These pricier Big Bus tours tend to have more departures—meaning shorter waits for those hopping on and off (tel. 020/7808-6753, www.bigbustours.com).

BUS OR CAR TOURS

London by Night Sightseeing Tour

This tour offers a 1.5-hour circuit, but after hours, with no extras (e.g., walks, river cruises), and at a lower price. While the narration can be pretty lame, the views at twilight are grand—though note that it stays light until late on summer nights, and London just doesn't do floodlighting as well as, say, Paris (£20, £15 online). June through September, open-top buses depart at 20:00 and 21:30 from Victoria Station (Jan-May and late Sept-late Dec departs at 19:00 and 21:00, only with closed-top bus, no tours between Christmas and New Year). Buses leave from near Victoria Station, in front of Grosvenor Hotel on Buckingham Palace Road (or you can board at any stop, such as Marble Arch, Trafalgar Square, London Eye, or Tower of London; tel. 020/8545-6110, www.london-by-night.net). For a memorable and economical evening, munch a scenic picnic dinner on the top deck. (There are plenty of take-away options within the train stations and near the various stops.)

Land and Sea Tours

A bright-yellow amphibious WWII-vintage vehicle (the model that ferried supplies and wounded soldiers on Normandy's beaches on D-Day) takes a gang of 30 tourists past some famous sights on land—Big Ben, Trafalgar Square, Piccadilly Circus—then splashes into the Thames for a cruise. All in all, it's good fun at a rather steep price. The live guide works hard, and it's kid-friendly to the point of goofiness. Beware: These book up in advance (£24, April-Sept daily, first tour 9:30 or 10:00, last tour usually 18:00, shorter hours Oct-March, 2-6/hour, 1.25 hours—45 minutes on land and 30 minutes in the river, £3 booking fee by phone or online, departs from Chicheley Street—you'll see the big, ugly vehicle parked 100 yards behind the London Eye, Tube: Waterloo or Westminster, tel. 020/7928-3132, www.londonducktours.co.uk).

Driver-Guides

These three guides have cars or a minibus (particularly helpful for travelers with limited mobility), and they also do walking-only tours: **Robina Brown** (£345/half-day, £515/day, £600 outside London, £40 more for groups of 4-6 people, also does overnight tours farther afield, tel. 020/8675-2810, www.driverguidetours.com, robina@driverguidetours.com), **Janine Barton** (£370/half-day, £490/day within London, £550 outside London, tel. 020/7402-4600, http://seeitinstyle.synthasite.com, jbsiis@aol.com), and **David Stubbs** (£195/half-day, £295/day, about £50 more for groups of 4-6 people, also does tours to the Cotswolds, Stonehenge, and Stratford, mobile 07775-888-534, www.londoncountrytours.co.uk, info@londoncountrytours.co.uk).

▲▲WALKING TOURS

Several times a day, top-notch local guides lead (sometimes big) groups through specific slices of London's past. Look for brochures at TIs or ask at hotels, although the latter usually push higher-priced bus tours. *Time Out,* the weekly entertainment guide, lists some, but not all, scheduled walks. Check with the various tour companies by phone or online to get their full picture.

To take a walking tour, simply show up at the announced location and pay the guide. Then enjoy two chatty hours of Dickens, Harry Potter, the Plague, Shakespeare, street art, the Beatles, Jack the Ripper, or whatever is on the agenda.

London Walks

This leading company lists its extensive and creative daily schedule on their amusing website, as well as in a beefy, plain *London Walks* brochure (available at hotels and in racks all over town, including one at St. Martin-in-the-Fields' Café in the Crypt on Trafalgar Square). Just perusing their fascinating lineup of tours opens me up to dimensions of the city I never considered and inspires me to stay longer in London. Their two-hour walks, led by top-quality professional guides (ranging from archaeologists to actors), cost £10 (cash only, walks offered year-round, private tours for groups-£140, tel. 020/7624-3978 for a live person, tel. 020/7624-9255 for a recording of today's or tomorrow's walks and the Tube station they depart from, www.walks.com).

London Walks also offers day trips into the countryside, a good option for those with limited time and transportation (£18 plus £36-59 for transportation and admission costs, cash only: Stonehenge/Salisbury, Oxford/Cotswolds, Cambridge, Bath, and so on). These are economical in part because everyone gets group discounts for transportation and admissions.

Sandemans New London "Free Royal London Tour"

This company employs students (rather than licensed guides) who recite three-hour spiels covering the basic London sights. While the youthful tours are light and irreverent, and can be both entertaining and fun, it's misleading to call the tours "free," as tips are expected (the guides actually pay the company for the privilege of asking for tips). You'll spend a lot of time at the start as they collect emails and take a group photo (not doing you a favor but establishing the size of the group so the guide can be charged accordingly). Given that London Walks offers daily tours at a reasonable price, taking this "free" tour makes no sense to me (daily at 10:00, 11:00, and 14:00; meet at Covent Garden Piazza by the Apple Store, Tube: Covent Garden). Sandemans also has other guided tours for a charge, including a Pub Crawl (£20, nightly at 19:30, meet at Slug and Lettuce Bar in Leicester Square, Tube: Leicester Square, www.newlondon-tours.com).

Beatles Walks

Fans of the still-Fab Four can take one of three Beatles walks (London Walks has two that run 5 days/week; for more on Beatles sights, see page 93).

Jack the Ripper Walks

Each walking tour company seems to make most of its money with "haunted" and Jack the Ripper tours. Many guides are historians and would rather not lead these lightweight tours—but, in tourism as in journalism, "if it bleeds, it leads" (which is why the juvenile London Dungeon is one of the city's busiest sights).

Two reliably good two-hour tours start every night at the Tower Hill Tube station exit. **London Walks** leaves nightly at 19:30 (£10, pay at the start, tel. 020/7624-3978, recorded info tel. 020/7624-9255, www.jacktheripperwalk.com). **Ripping Yarns,** which leaves earlier, is guided by off-duty Yeoman Warders—the Tower of London "Beefeaters" (£8, pay at end, nightly at 18:30, no tours between Christmas and New Year, mobile 07813-559-301, www.jack-the-ripper-tours.com). After taking both, I found the London Walks tour more entertaining, informative, and with a better route (along quieter, once hooker-friendly lanes, with less traffic), starting at Tower Hill and ending at Liverpool Street Station. Groups can be huge for both, and one group can be nearly on top of another, but there's always room—just show up.

Daily Reminder

Sunday: The Tower of London and British Museum are both especially crowded today. Speakers' Corner in Hyde Park rants from early afternoon until early evening. These places are closed: Sir John Soane's Museum and legal sights (Houses of Parliament, City Hall, and Old Bailey; the neighborhood called The City is dead). Westminster Abbey and St. Paul's are open during the day for worship but closed to sightseers. With all these closures, this morning is a good time to take a bus tour. Most big stores open late (around 11:30) and close early (18:00). Street markets are flourishing at Camden Lock, Spitalfields (at its best today), Petticoat Lane, Brick Lane, and Greenwich, but Portobello Road and Brixton markets are closed (though the Brixton farmers market is open 10:00-14:00). Because of all the market action, it's a good day to visit the East End. Theaters are quiet, as most actors take today off. (There are a few exceptions, such as Shakespeare's Globe, which offers Sunday performances in summer, and theaters with family-oriented fare, including *The Lion King,* offered year-round.)

Monday: Virtually all sights are open, except Apsley House, Sir John Soane's Museum, and a few others. The Houses of Parliament may be open as late as 22:30.

Tuesday: Virtually all sights are open, except Apsley House. The British Library is open until 20:00, and the Houses of Parliament may be open as late as 22:00. On the first Tuesday of the month, Sir John Soane's Museum is open until 21:00.

Wednesday: Virtually all sights are open. Houses of Parliament may be open as late as 22:00.

LONDON

Private Walks with Local Guides

Standard rates for London's registered Blue Badge guides are about £150-165 for four hours and £250 or more for nine hours (tel. 020/7611-2545, www.guidelondon.org.uk or www.britainsbestguides.org). I know and like five fine local guides: **Sean Kelleher** (tel. 020/8673-1624, mobile 07764-612-770, sean@seanlondonguide.com); **Britt Lonsdale** (£230/half-day, £330/day, great with families, tel. 020/7386-9907, mobile 07813-278-077, brittl@btinternet.com); **Joel Reid,** an imaginative guide who specializes in off-the-beaten-track London (mobile 07887-955-720, joelyreid@gmail.com); and two others who work in London when they're not on the road leading my Britain tours: **Tom Hooper** (mobile 07986-048-047, tomh@ricksteves.net), and **Gillian Chadwick** (mobile 07889-976-598, gillychad@hotmail.co.uk). If you have a particular interest, London Walks (see above) has a huge selection of guides and can book you one for your exact focus (£180/half-day).

Thursday: All sights are open, plus evening hours at the National Portrait Gallery (until 21:00).

Friday: All sights are open, except the Houses of Parliament. Sights open late include the British Museum (selected galleries until 20:30), National Gallery (until 21:00), National Portrait Gallery (until 21:00), Victoria and Albert Museum (selected galleries until 22:00), and Tate Modern (until 22:00).

Saturday: Most sights are open, except legal ones (Old Bailey, City Hall; skip The City). The Houses of Parliament are open only with a tour. Tate Modern is open until 22:00. The Tower of London is especially crowded today. Today's the day to hit the Portobello Road street market; the Camden Lock and Greenwich markets are also good.

Notes: St. Martin-in-the-Fields church offers concerts at lunchtime (Mon, Tue, and Fri at 13:00) and in the evening (several nights a week at 19:30, jazz Wed at 20:00).

Evensong occurs nearly daily at St. Paul's (Sun at 15:15 and Tue-Sat at 17:00), Westminster Abbey (Sun at 15:00, Mon-Tue and Thu-Sat at 17:00 except Sat at 15:00 Sept-April), and Southwark Cathedral (Sun at 15:00, Tue-Fri 17:30, Sat at 16:00).

London by Night Sightseeing Tour buses leave from Victoria Station each evening (two departures nightly 20:00 and 21:30 in summer, 19:00 and 21:00 in autumn and winter).

The London Eye spins nightly (last departure 20:30 or 21:30, or even later, depending on the season).

BIKE TOURS

London is committed to creating more bike paths, and many of its best sights can be laced together with a pleasant pedal through its parks. A bike tour is a fun way to see the sights and enjoy the city on two wheels.

London Bicycle Tour Company

Three tours covering London are offered daily from their base at Gabriel's Wharf on the South Bank of the Thames. Sunday is the best, as there is less car traffic (**Central Tour**—£24, daily at 10:30, 6 miles, 3 hours, includes Westminster, Buckingham Palace, Covent Garden, and St. Paul's; **West End Tour**—£24, April-Oct daily at 14:30, Nov-March daily at 12:00 as long as at least 4 people show up, 7 miles, 3 hours, includes Westminster, Buckingham Palace, Hyde Park, Soho, and Covent Garden; **East Tour**—£27.50, April-Oct Sat-Sun at 14:00, Nov-March Sat-Sun at 12:00, 9 miles, 3.5 hours, includes south side of the river to Tower Bridge, then The City to the East End; book ahead for off-season tours). They also rent bikes (£3.50/hour, £20/day; office open daily April-Oct 9:30-18:00, Nov-March 10:00-16:00, west of Blackfriars Bridge on the South Bank, 1 Gabriel's Wharf, tel. 020/7928-6838, www.londonbicycle.com).

Fat Tire Bike Tours

Nearly daily bike tours cover the highlights of downtown London, on two different itineraries (£2 discount with this book): **Royal London** (£22, April-Oct daily at 11:00, mid-May-mid-Sept also at 15:30, Nov-March Thu-Mon at 11:00, 7 miles, 4 hours, meet at Queensway Tube station; includes Parliament, Buckingham Palace, Hyde Park, and Trafalgar Square) and **River Thames** (£28, nearly daily in summer at 10:30, March-Nov Thu-Sat at 10:30, 4.5 hours, meet just outside Southwark Tube Station; includes London Eye, St. Paul's, Tower of London, and London Bridge). Their guiding style wears its learning lightly, mixing history with humor. Reservations are easy online, and required for River Thames tours and kids' bikes (off-season tours can be arranged, mobile 078-8233-8779, www.fattirebiketourslondon.com). Confirm the schedule online or by phone. They also offer a range of walking tours that include a fish-and-chips dinner, a beer-tasting pub tour, and theater packages (details online or by phone).

▲▲CRUISE BOAT TOURS

London offers many made-for-tourist cruises, most on slow-moving, open-top boats accompanied by entertaining commentary about passing sights. Several companies offer essentially the same trip. Generally speaking, you can either do a **short city-center cruise** by riding a boat 30 minutes from Westminster Pier to Tower Pier (particularly handy if you're interested in visiting the Tower of London anyway), or take a **longer cruise** that includes a peek at the East End, riding from Westminster all the way to Greenwich (save time by taking the Tube back).

Each company runs cruises daily, about twice hourly, from morning until dark; many reduce frequency off-season. Boats come and go from various docks in the city center (see sidebar). The most popular places to embark are Westminster Pier (at the base of Westminster Bridge across the street from Big Ben) and Waterloo Pier (at the London Eye, across the river).

A one-way trip within the city center costs about £10; going

Thames Boat Piers

While Westminster Pier is the most popular, it's not the only dock in town. Consider all the options (listed from west to east, as the Thames flows—see the color maps in the front of this book):

Millbank Pier (North Bank), at the Tate Britain Museum, is used primarily by the Tate Boat service (express connection to Tate Modern at Bankside Pier).

Westminster Pier (North Bank), near the base of Big Ben, offers round-trip sightseeing cruises and lots of departures in both directions (though the Thames Clippers boats don't stop here). Nearby sights include Parliament and Westminster Abbey.

Waterloo Pier (a.k.a. **London Eye Pier,** South Bank), right at the base of the London Eye, is a good, less-crowded alternative to Westminster, with many of the same cruise options (Waterloo Station is nearby).

Embankment Pier (North Bank) is near Covent Garden, Trafalgar Square, and Cleopatra's Needle (the obelisk on the Thames). This pier is used mostly for special boat trips (such as some RIB—rigid inflatable boat—trips, and lunch and dinner cruises).

Festival Pier (South Bank) is next to the Royal Festival Hall, just downstream from the London Eye.

Blackfriars Pier (North Bank) is in The City, not far from St. Paul's.

Bankside Pier (South Bank) is directly in front of the Tate Modern and Shakespeare's Globe.

London Bridge Pier (a.k.a. **London Bridge City Pier,** South Bank) is near the HMS *Belfast.*

Tower Pier (North Bank) is at the Tower of London, at the east edge of The City and near the East End.

St. Katharine's Pier (North Bank) is just downstream from the Tower of London.

Canary Wharf Pier (North Bank) is at the Docklands, London's new "downtown."

In outer London, you might also use the piers at **Greenwich, Kew Gardens,** and **Hampton Court.**

all the way to Greenwich costs about £2 more. Most companies charge around £3 more for a round-trip ticket, and others sell hop-on, hop-off day tickets (around £19). But I'd rather just savor one cruise, then zip home by Tube—making these return tickets not usually worthwhile.

You can buy tickets at kiosks on the docks. A Travelcard can snare you a 33 percent discount on most cruises (just show the card when you pay for the cruise); the pay-as-you-go Oyster card nets you a discount only on Thames Clippers. Because companies vary in the discounts they offer, always ask. Children and seniors

Affording London's Sights

London is one of Europe's most expensive cities, with the dubious distinction of having some of the world's steepest admission prices. Fortunately, many sights are free.

Free Museums: Free sights include the British Museum, British Library, National Gallery, National Portrait Gallery, Tate Britain, Tate Modern, Wallace Collection, Imperial War Museum, Victoria and Albert Museum, Natural History Museum, Science Museum, Sir John Soane's Museum, the Museum of London, the Geffrye Museum, and the Guildhall. About half of these museums request a donation of a few pounds, but whether you contribute or not is up to you. If you feel like supporting these museums, renting audioguides, using their café, and buying a few souvenirs all help.

Free Churches: Smaller churches let worshippers (and tourists) in free, although they may ask for a donation. The big sightseeing churches—Westminster Abbey and St. Paul's—charge higher admission fees, but offer free evensong services nearly daily (though you can't stick around afterward to sightsee). Westminster Abbey also offers free organ recitals most Sundays.

Other Freebies: London has plenty of free performances, such as lunch concerts at St. Martin-in-the-Fields (see page 74). For other freebies, check out www.whatsfreeinlondon.co.uk. There's no charge to enjoy the pageantry of the Changing of the Guard, rants at Speakers' Corner in Hyde Park (on Sun afternoon), displays at Harrods, the people-watching scene at Covent Garden, and the colorful streets of the East End. It's free to view the legal action at the Old Bailey and the legislature at work in the Houses of Parliament. And you can get into a bit of the Tower of London and Windsor Castle by attending Sunday services in each place's chapel (chapel access only). Greenwich makes for an inexpensive outing. Many of its sights are free, and the journey there is covered by a cheap Zones 1-2 Tube pass.

Sightseeing Deals: Certain One-Day Travelcards (for the Tube) come with discounts at some popular and pricey sights, such as the Churchill War Rooms, Tower of London, and Madame Tussauds. (There are many restrictions—must be purchased at a train station, see page 33 for details.)

Good-Value Tours: The London Walks tours with professional guides (£10) are one of the best deals going. (Note that the guides for the "free" walking tours are unpaid by their companies, and they expect tips—I'd pay up front for an expertly guided tour instead.) Hop-on, hop-off big-bus tours, while expensive (£26-32), provide a great overview and include free boat tours as well as city walks. (Or, for the price of a transit ticket, you could get similar views from the top of a double-decker public bus.) A one-hour Thames ride to Greenwich costs about £12 one-way, but most boats come with entertaining commentary. A three-hour bicycle tour is about £24.

Pricey...but Worth It? Big-ticket sights worth their hefty admission fees (£14-18) are Kew Gardens, Shakespeare's Globe, and the Churchill War Rooms.

The London Eye has become a London must-see—but you may feel differently when you see the prices (£21.50). St. Paul's Cathedral (£18) becomes more worthwhile if you climb the dome for the stunning view. While Hampton Court Palace is expensive (£19), it is well-presented and a reasonable value if you have an interest in royal history. The Queen charges royally for a peek inside Buckingham Palace (£21, open Aug-Sept only) and her fine art gallery and carriage museum (adjacent to the palace, £9-10 each). Madame Tussauds Waxworks is pricey but still hard for many to resist (£33, see page 92 for info on discounts). Harry Potter fans gladly pay the Hagrid-sized £33 fee to see the sets and props at the Warner Bros. Studio Tour (but those who wouldn't know a wizard from a Muggle needn't bother).

The Courtauld Gallery and the Wellington Museum at Apsley House are small but affordable (under £10).

Totally Pants (Brit-speak for Not Worth It): The London Dungeon, at £26, is gimmicky, overpriced, and a terrible value...despite the long line at the door.

Theater: Compared with Broadway's prices, London's theater is a bargain. Seek out the freestanding TKTS booth at Leicester Square to get discounts from 25 to 50 percent on good seats (and full-price tickets to the hottest shows with no service charges; see page 140). Buying direct at the theater box office can score you a great deal on same-day tickets, and even the most popular shows generally have some seats under £20 (possibly with obstructed views)—ask. A £5 "groundling" ticket for a play at Shakespeare's Globe is the best theater deal in town (see page 114). Tickets to the Open Air Theatre at north London's Regent's Park start at about £25 (see page 144).

London doesn't come cheap. But with its many free museums and affordable plays, this cosmopolitan, cultured city offers days of sightseeing thrills without requiring you to pinch your pennies (or your pounds).

generally get discounts. You can purchase drinks and scant over-priced snacks on board. Clever budget travelers pack a picnic and munch while they cruise.

The three dominant companies are **City Cruises** (handy 30-minute cruise from Westminster Pier to Tower Pier; www.citycruises.com), **Thames River Services** (fewer stops, classic boats, friendlier and more old-fashioned feel; www.thamesriverservices.co.uk), and **Circular Cruise** (full cruise takes about an hour, operated by Crown River Services, www.crownriver.com). I'd skip the **London Eye**'s River Cruise from Waterloo Pier—it's about the same price as Circular Cruise, but 20 minutes shorter. The speedy **Thames Clippers** (described later) are designed more for no-nonsense transport than lazy sightseeing.

For details—including prices, schedules, and exactly which piers each company uses—check their websites or look for ticket kiosks at the docks. If you'd like to compare all of your options in one spot, head to Westminster Pier, which has a row of kiosks for all of the big outfits.

Cruising Downstream, to Greenwich: Both **City Cruises** and **Thames River Services** head from Westminster Pier to Greenwich. The cruises are usually narrated by the captain, with most commentary given on the way to Greenwich. The companies' prices are the same, though their itineraries are slightly different (Thames River Services makes only one stop en route and takes just an hour, while City Cruises makes two stops and adds about 15 minutes). The **Thames Clippers** boats, described later, are cheaper and faster (about 20-45 minutes to Greenwich), but have no commentary and no seating up top. To maximize both efficiency and sightseeing, I'd take a narrated cruise to Greenwich one way, and go the other way on the DLR (Docklands Light Railway), with a stop in the Docklands (Canary Wharf station).

Cruising Upstream, to Kew Gardens and Hampton Court Palace: Boats operated by the Westminster Passenger Service Association leave for Kew Gardens from Westminster Pier (£12 one-way, £18 round-trip, cash only, discounts with Travelcard, 2-4/day depending on season, 1.5 hours, boats sail April-Oct, about half the trip is narrated, www.wpsa.co.uk). Most boats continue on to Hampton Court Palace for an additional £3 (and another 1.5 hours). Because of the river current, you can save 30 minutes cruising from Hampton Court back into town (depends on the tide—ask before you commit to the boat). Romantic as these rides sound, it can be a long trip...especially upstream.

Commuting by Clipper

The sleek 220-seat catamarans used by **Thames Clippers** are designed for commuters rather than sightseers. Think of the boats as express buses on the river—they zip through London every 20-30 minutes, stopping at most of the major docks en route (including Canary Wharf/Docklands and Greenwich). They're fast: roughly 20 minutes from Embankment to Tower, 10 more minutes to Docklands, and 10 more minutes to Greenwich. However, the boats are less pleasant for joyriding than the cruises described earlier, with no commentary and no open deck up top (the only outside access is on a crowded deck at the exhaust-choked back of the boat, where you're jostling for space to take photos). Any one-way ride costs £7.15, and a River Roamer all-day ticket costs £17.35 (discounts with Travelcard and Oyster card, www.thamesclippers.com).

Thames Clippers also offers two express trips. The **Tate Boat** ferry service, which directly connects the Tate Britain (Millbank Pier) and the Tate Modern (Bankside Pier), is made for art lovers (£7.15 one-way, covered by River Roamer day ticket; buy ticket at self-service machines before boarding or use Oyster Card; for frequency and times, see the Tate Britain and Tate Modern listings, later, or www.tate.org.uk/visit/tate-boat). The **O2 Express** runs only on nights when there are events at the O2 arena (departs from Waterloo Pier).

TOUR PACKAGES FOR STUDENTS

Andy Steves (my son) runs **Weekend Student Adventures (WSA Europe),** offering three-day and longer guided and unguided packages—including accommodations, sightseeing, and unique local experiences—for student travelers in 12 top European cities, including London (guided trips from €199, see www.wsaeurope.com).

Westminster Walk

Just about every visitor to London strolls along historic Whitehall from Big Ben to Trafalgar Square. This self-guided walk gives meaning to that touristy ramble (most of the sights you'll see are described in more detail later). Under London's modern traffic and big-city bustle lie 2,000 fascinating years of history. You'll get a whirlwind tour as well as a practical orientation to London. (You can download a 🎧 free, extended audio version of this walk to your mobile device; see page 13.)

Start halfway across ❶ **Westminster Bridge** for that "Wow, I'm really in London!" feeling. Get a close-up view of the **Houses of Parliament** and **Big Ben** (floodlit at night). Downstream you'll see the **London Eye.** Down the stairs to Westminster Pier are boats to the Tower of London and Greenwich (downstream) or Kew Gardens (upstream).

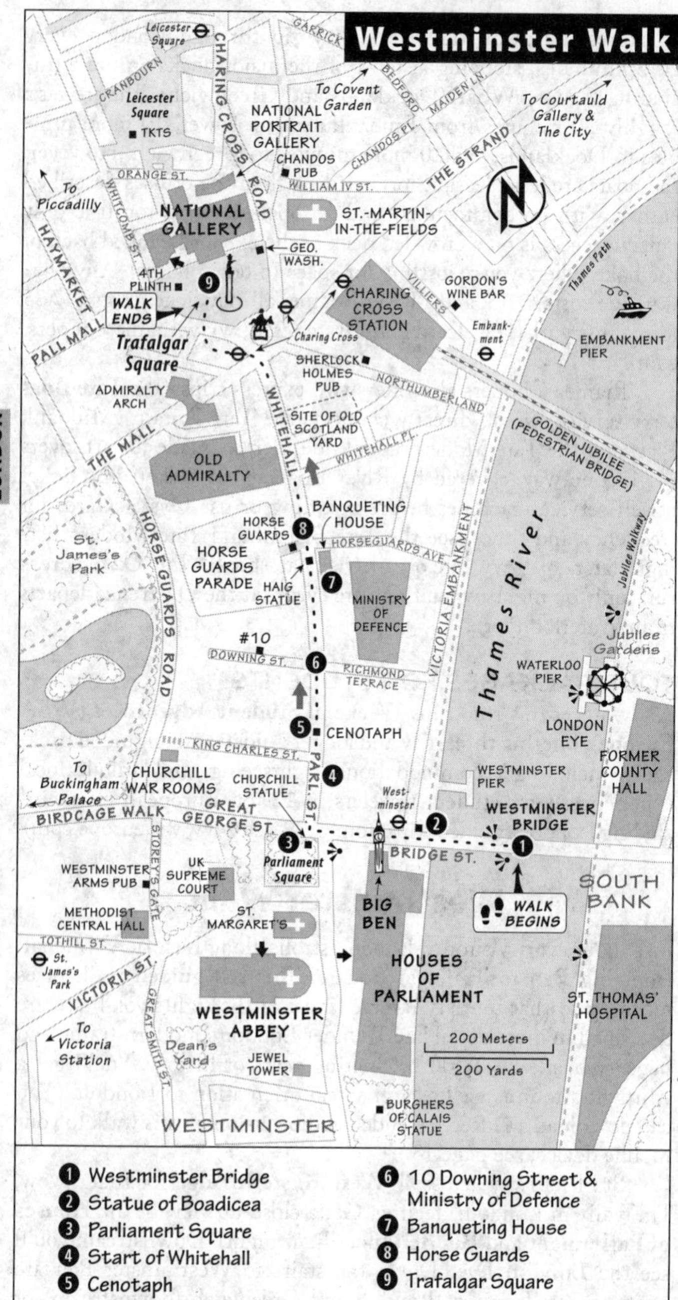
Westminster Walk
Leicester Square
CHARING CROSS ROAD
GARRICK
To Covent Garden
BEDFORD
MAIDEN LN.
To Courtauld Gallery & The City
CRANBOURN
Leicester Square
TKTS
NATIONAL PORTRAIT GALLERY
CHANDOS PL.
THE STRAND
CHANDOS PUB
ORANGE ST.
WILLIAM IV ST.
To Piccadilly
NATIONAL GALLERY
ST.-MARTIN-IN-THE-FIELDS
WHITCOMB ST.
HAYMARKET
GEO. WASH.
4TH PLINTH
WALK ENDS
Trafalgar Square
CHARING CROSS STATION
VILLIERS
GORDON'S WINE BAR
Thames Path
Charing Cross
Embankment
EMBANKMENT PIER
PALL MALL
SHERLOCK HOLMES PUB
ADMIRALTY ARCH
NORTHUMBERLAND
SITE OF OLD SCOTLAND YARD
WHITEHALL
WHITEHALL PL.
GOLDEN JUBILEE (PEDESTRIAN BRIDGE)
THE MALL
OLD ADMIRALTY
BANQUETING HOUSE
HORSE GUARDS
HORSEGUARDS AVE.
St. James's Park
HORSE GUARDS PARADE
HAIG STATUE
MINISTRY OF DEFENCE
VICTORIA EMBANKMENT
Thames River
Jubilee Walkway
Jubilee Gardens
#10
DOWNING ST.
RICHMOND TERRACE
WATERLOO PIER
HORSE GUARDS ROAD
CENOTAPH
LONDON EYE
KING CHARLES ST.
To Buckingham Palace
CHURCHILL WAR ROOMS
CHURCHILL STATUE
PARL. ST.
WESTMINSTER PIER
FORMER COUNTY HALL
BIRDCAGE WALK
GREAT GEORGE ST.
Westminster
WESTMINSTER BRIDGE
Parliament Square
BRIDGE ST.
WESTMINSTER ARMS PUB
STOREY'S GATE
UK SUPREME COURT
SOUTH BANK
METHODIST CENTRAL HALL
ST. MARGARET'S
BIG BEN
WALK BEGINS
TOTHILL ST.
St. James's Park
VICTORIA ST.
HOUSES OF PARLIAMENT
GREAT SMITH ST.
WESTMINSTER ABBEY
ST. THOMAS' HOSPITAL
To Victoria Station
Dean's Yard
200 Meters
200 Yards
JEWEL TOWER
BURGHERS OF CALAIS STATUE
WESTMINSTER
1 Westminster Bridge
2 Statue of Boadicea
3 Parliament Square
4 Start of Whitehall
5 Cenotaph
6 10 Downing Street & Ministry of Defence
7 Banqueting House
8 Horse Guards
9 Trafalgar Square

En route to Parliament Square, you'll pass a ❷ **statue of Boadicea,** the Celtic queen defeated by Roman invaders in A.D. 60.

For fun, call home from near Big Ben at about three minutes before the hour to let your loved one hear the bell ring. You'll find four red phone booths lining the north side of ❸ **Parliament Square** along Great George Street—also great for a phone-box-and-Big-Ben photo op.

Wave hello to Winston Churchill and Nelson Mandela in Parliament Square. To Churchill's right is **Westminster Abbey,** with its two stubby, elegant towers. The white building (flying the Union Jack) at the far end of the square houses Britain's **Supreme Court.**

Head north up Parliament Street, which turns into ❹ **Whitehall,** and walk toward Trafalgar Square. You'll see the thought-provoking ❺ **Cenotaph** in the middle of the boulevard, reminding passersby of the many Brits who died in the last century's world wars. To visit the **Churchill War Rooms,** take a left before the Cenotaph, on King Charles Street.

Continuing on Whitehall, stop at the barricaded and guarded ❻ **#10 Downing Street** to see the British "White House," home of the prime minister. Break the bobby's boredom and ask him a question. The huge building across Whitehall from Downing Street is the **Ministry of Defence** (MOD), the "British Pentagon."

Nearing Trafalgar Square, look for the 17th-century ❼ **Banqueting House** across the street and the ❽ **Horse Guards** behind the gated fence.

The column topped by Lord Nelson marks ❾ **Trafalgar Square.** The stately domed building on the far side of the square is the **National Gallery,** which has a classy café in the Sainsbury wing. To the right of the National Gallery is **St. Martin-in-the-Fields Church** and its Café in the Crypt.

To get to Piccadilly from Trafalgar Square, walk up Cockspur Street to Haymarket, then take a short left on Coventry Street to colorful **Piccadilly Circus** (see map on page 78).

Near Piccadilly, you'll find a number of theaters. **Leicester Square** (with its half-price "TKTS" booth for plays—see page 141) thrives just a few blocks away. Walk through seedy **Soho** (north of Shaftesbury Avenue) for its fun pubs. From Piccadilly or Oxford Circus, you can take a taxi, bus, or the Tube home.

Sights in Central London

WESTMINSTER

These sights are listed in roughly geographical order from Westminster Abbey to Trafalgar Square, and are linked in my self-guided Westminster Walk, above, and the 🎧 free Westminster Walk audio tour (see sidebar on page 13 for details).

LONDON

▲▲▲Westminster Abbey

The greatest church in the English-speaking world, Westminster Abbey is where the nation's royalty has been wedded, crowned, and buried since 1066. Indeed, the histories of Westminster Abbey and England are almost the same. A thousand years of English history—3,000 tombs, the remains of 29 kings and queens, and hundreds of memorials to poets, politicians, scientists, and warriors—lie within its stained-glass splendor and under its stone slabs.

Cost and Hours: £20, £40 family ticket (covers 2 adults and 1 child), includes audioguide and entry to cloisters and Abbey Museum; abbey—Mon-Fri 9:30-16:30, Wed until 19:00 (main church only), Sat 9:30-14:30, last entry one hour before closing, closed Sun to sightseers but open for services; museum—daily 10:30-16:00; cloisters—daily 8:00-18:00; no photos allowed, café in cellar, Tube: Westminster or St. James's Park, tel. 020/7222-5152, www.westminster-abbey.org. It's also free to enter just the cloisters and Abbey Museum (through Dean's Yard, around the right side as you face the main entrance), but if it's too crowded inside, the marshal at the cloister entrance may not let you in.

When to Go: The place is most crowded every day at midmorning and all day Saturdays and Mondays. Visit early, during lunch, or late to avoid tourist hordes. Weekdays after 14:30—especially Wed—are less congested; come after that time and stay for the 17:00 evensong (but keep in mind the Wed 17:00 evensong is generally spoken, not sung). The main entrance, on the Parliament Square side, often has a sizable line—skip it by booking tickets in advance via the Abbey's website.

Music and Church Services: Mon-Fri at 7:30 (prayer), 8:00 (communion), 12:30 (communion), 17:00 evensong (except on Wed, when the evening service is generally spoken—not sung); **Sat** at 8:00 (communion), 9:00 (prayer), 15:00 (evensong; May-Aug it's at 17:00); **Sun** services generally come with more music: at 8:00 (communion), 10:00 (sung Matins), 11:15 (sung Eucharist), 15:00 (evensong), 18:30 (evening service). Services are free to anyone, though visitors who haven't paid church admission aren't allowed to linger afterward. Free **organ recitals** are usually held Sun at 17:45 (30 minutes). For a schedule of services or recitals on a particular day, look for posted signs with schedules or check the Abbey's website.

Tours: The included **audioguide** is excellent, taking some of the sting out of the steep admission fee. To add to the experi-

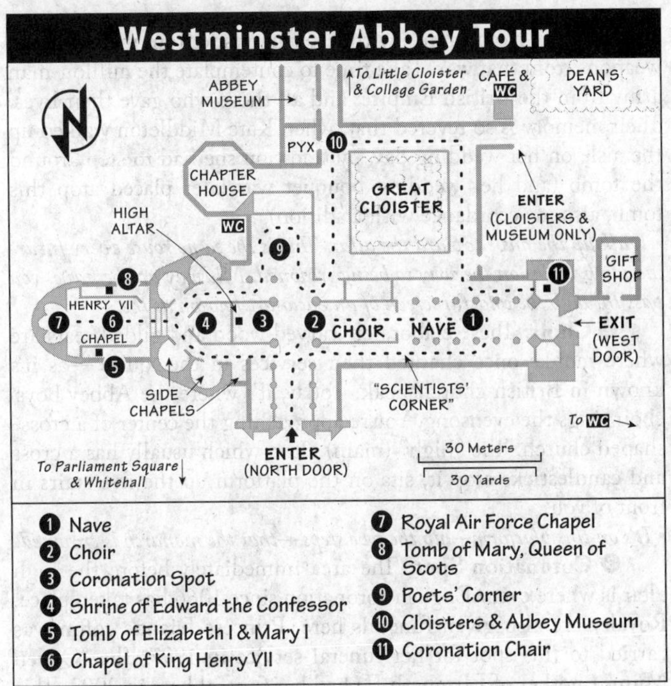

ence, you can take an entertaining **guided tour** from a verger—the church equivalent of a museum docent (£5, schedule posted both outside and inside entry, up to 5/day in summer, 4/day in winter, 1.5 hours).

➲ **Self-Guided Tour:** You'll have no choice but to follow the steady flow of tourists through the church, along the route laid out for the audioguide. My tour covers the Abbey's top stops.

• *Walk straight through the north transept. Follow the crowd flow to the right and enter the spacious...*

❶ **Nave:** Look down the long and narrow center aisle of the church. Lined with the praying hands of the Gothic arches, glowing with light from the stained glass, it's clear that this is more than a museum. With saints in stained glass, heroes in carved stone, and the bodies of England's greatest citizens under the floor stones, Westminster Abbey is the religious heart of England.

The king who built the Abbey was Edward the Confessor. Find him in the stained glass windows on the left side of the nave (as you face the altar). He's in the third bay from the end (marked *S: Edwardus rex...*), with his crown, scepter, and ring. The Abbey's 10-story nave is the tallest in England.

On the floor near the west entrance of the Abbey is the flower-lined Grave of the Unknown Warrior, one ordinary WWI soldier buried in soil from France with lettering made from melted-down weapons from that war. Take time to contemplate the million-man army from the British Empire, and all those who gave their lives. Their memory is so revered that, when Kate Middleton walked up the aisle on her wedding day, by tradition she had to step around the tomb (and her wedding bouquet was later placed atop this tomb, also in accordance with tradition).

• *Walk up the nave toward the altar. This is the same route every future monarch walks on the way to being crowned. Midway up the nave, you pass through the colorful screen of an enclosure known as the...*

❷ **Choir:** These elaborately carved wood and gilded seats are where monks once chanted their services in the "quire"—as it's known in British churchspeak. Today, it's where the Abbey boys' choir sings the evensong. You're approaching the center of a cross-shaped church. The "high" (main) altar, which usually has a cross and candlesticks atop it, sits on the platform up the five stairs in front of you.

• *It's on this platform—up the five steps—that the monarch is crowned.*

❸ **Coronation Spot:** The area immediately before the high altar is where every English coronation since 1066 has taken place. Royalty are also given funerals here. Princess Diana's coffin was carried to this spot for her funeral service in 1997. The "Queen Mum" (mother of Elizabeth II) had her funeral here in 2002. This is also where most of the last century's royal weddings have taken place, including the unions of Queen Elizabeth II and Prince Philip (1947), Prince Andrew and Sarah Ferguson (1986), and Prince William and Kate Middleton (2011).

• *Veer left and follow the crowd. Pause at the wooden staircase on your right.*

❹ **Shrine of Edward the Confessor:** Step back and peek over the dark coffin of Edward I to see the tippy-top of the green-and-gold wedding-cake tomb of King Edward the Confessor—the man who built Westminster Abbey.

God had told pious Edward to visit St. Peter's Basilica in Rome. But with the Normans thinking conquest, it was too dangerous for him to leave England. Instead, he built this grand church and dedicated it to St. Peter. It was finished just in time to bury Edward and to crown his foreign successor, William the Conqueror, in 1066. After Edward's death, people prayed at his tomb, and, after getting good results, Pope Alexander III canonized him. This elevated, central tomb—which lost some of its luster when Henry VIII melted down the gold coffin-case—is surrounded by the tombs of eight kings and queens.

• *At the top of the stone staircase, veer left into the private burial chapel of Queen Elizabeth I.*

❺ **Tomb of Queens Elizabeth I and Mary I:** Although

only one effigy is on the tomb (Elizabeth's), there are actually two queens buried beneath it, both daughters of Henry VIII (by different mothers). Bloody Mary—meek, pious, sickly, and Catholic—enforced Catholicism during her short reign (1553-1558) by burning "heretics" at the stake.

Elizabeth—strong, clever, and Protestant—steered England on an Anglican course. She holds a royal orb symbolizing that she's queen of the whole globe. When 26-year-old Elizabeth was crowned in the Abbey, her right to rule was questioned (especially by her Catholic subjects) because she was considered the bastard seed of Henry VIII's unsanctioned marriage to Anne Boleyn. But Elizabeth's long reign (1559-1603) was one of the greatest in English history, a time when England ruled the seas and Shakespeare explored human emotions. When she died, thousands turned out for her funeral in the Abbey. Elizabeth's face on the tomb, modeled after her death mask, is considered a very accurate take on this hook-nosed, imperious "Virgin Queen."

• *Continue into the ornate, flag-draped room up a few more stairs, directly behind the main altar.*

❻ **Chapel of King Henry VII (The Lady Chapel):** The light from the stained-glass windows, the colorful banners overhead, and the elaborate tracery in stone, wood, and glass give this room the festive air of a medieval tournament. The prestigious Knights of the Bath meet here, under the magnificent ceiling studded with gold pendants. The ceiling—of carved stone, not plaster (1519)—is the finest English Perpendicular Gothic and fan vaulting you'll see (unless you're going to King's College Chapel in Cambridge). The ceiling was sculpted on the floor in pieces, then jigsaw-puzzled into place. It capped the Gothic period and signaled the vitality of the coming Renaissance.

• *Go to the far end of the chapel and stand at the banister in front of the modern set of stained-glass windows.*

❼ **Royal Air Force Chapel:** Saints in robes and halos mingle with pilots in parachutes and bomber jackets. This tribute to WWII flyers is for those who earned their angel wings in the Battle of Britain (July-Oct 1940). A bit of bomb damage has been preserved—look for the little glassed-over hole in the wall below the windows in the lower left-hand corner.

• *Exit the Chapel of Henry VII. Turn left into a side chapel with the tomb (the central one of three in the chapel).*

❽ **Tomb of Mary, Queen of Scots:** The beautiful, French-educated queen (1542-1587) was held under house arrest for 19 years by Queen Elizabeth I, who considered her a threat to her sovereignty. Elizabeth got wind of an assassination plot, suspected Mary was behind it, and had her first cousin (once removed) beheaded. When Elizabeth—who was called the "Virgin Queen"—died heirless, Mary's son, James VI, King of Scots, also became King James I of England and Ireland. James buried his mum here (with her head sewn back on) in the Abbey's most sumptuous tomb.

• *Exit Mary's chapel. Continue on, until you emerge in the south transept. You're in...*

❾ **Poets' Corner:** England's greatest artistic contributions are in the written word. Here the masters of arguably the world's most complex and expressive language are remembered: Geoffrey Chaucer *(Canterbury Tales),* Lord Byron, Dylan Thomas, W. H. Auden, Lewis Carroll *(Alice's Adventures in Wonderland),* T. S. Eliot *(The Waste Land),* Alfred Tennyson, Robert Browning, and Charles Dickens. Many writers are honored with plaques and monuments; relatively few are actually buried here. Shakespeare is commemorated by a fine statue that stands near the end of the transept, overlooking the others.

• *Exit the church (temporarily) at the south door, which leads to the...*

❿ **Cloisters and Abbey Museum:** The buildings that adjoin the church housed the monks. Cloistered courtyards gave them a place to meditate on God's creations.

The small Abbey Museum, formerly the monks' lounge, is worth a peek for its fascinating and well-described exhibits. Look into the impressively realistic eyes of Elizabeth I, Charles II, Admiral Nelson, and a dozen others, part of a compelling series of wax-and-wood statues that, for three centuries, graced coffins during funeral processions. The once-exquisite, now-fragmented Westminster Retable, which decorated the high altar in 1270, is the oldest surviving altarpiece in England.

• *Go back into the church for the last stop.*

⓫ **Coronation Chair:** A gold-painted oak chair waits here

under a regal canopy for the next coronation. For every English coronation since 1308 (except two), it's been moved to its spot before the high altar to receive the royal buttocks. The chair's legs rest on lions, England's symbol.

▲▲Houses of Parliament (Palace of Westminster)

This Neo-Gothic icon of London, the site of the royal residence from 1042 to 1547, is now the meeting place of the legislative branch of government. Like the US Capitol in Washington, DC, the complex is open to visitors. You can view parliamentary sessions in either the bickering House of Commons or the sleepy House of Lords. Or you can simply wander on your own (through a few closely monitored rooms) to appreciate the historic building itself.

The Palace of Westminster has been the center of political power in England for nearly a thousand years. In 1834, a horrendous fire gutted the Palace. It was rebuilt in a retro, Neo-Gothic style that recalled England's medieval Christian roots—pointed arches, stained-glass windows, spires, and saint-like statues. At the same time, Britain was also retooling its government. Democracy was on the rise, the queen became a constitutional monarch, and Parliament emerged as the nation's ruling body. The Palace of Westminster became a symbol—a kind of cathedral—of democracy. A visit here offers a chance to tour a piece of living history and see the British government inaction.

Cost and Hours (Public Galleries): Free, open only when parliament is in session; House of Commons—Oct-July Mon 14:30-22:30, Tue-Wed 11:30-19:30, Thu 9:30-17:30; House of Lords—Oct-July Mon-Tue 14:30-22:00, Wed 15:00-22:00, Thu 11:00-19:30; last entry depends on the debates; get the exact schedule at www.parliament.uk.

Tours: Audioguide-£18.50, guided tour-£25.50, Saturdays year-round 9:00-16:30 and most weekdays during recess (Aug-Sept), 1.5 hours. Confirm the tour schedule and book ahead at www.parliament.uk or by calling 020/7219-4114. The ticket office sells tour tickets, but there's no guarantee there will be same-day spaces available (open weekdays 10:00-16:00, Sat 9:00-17:00, closed Sun, located in Portcullis House, entrance on Victoria Embankment).

Choosing a House: If you only visit one of the bicameral legislative bodies, I'd choose the House of Lords. Though less im-

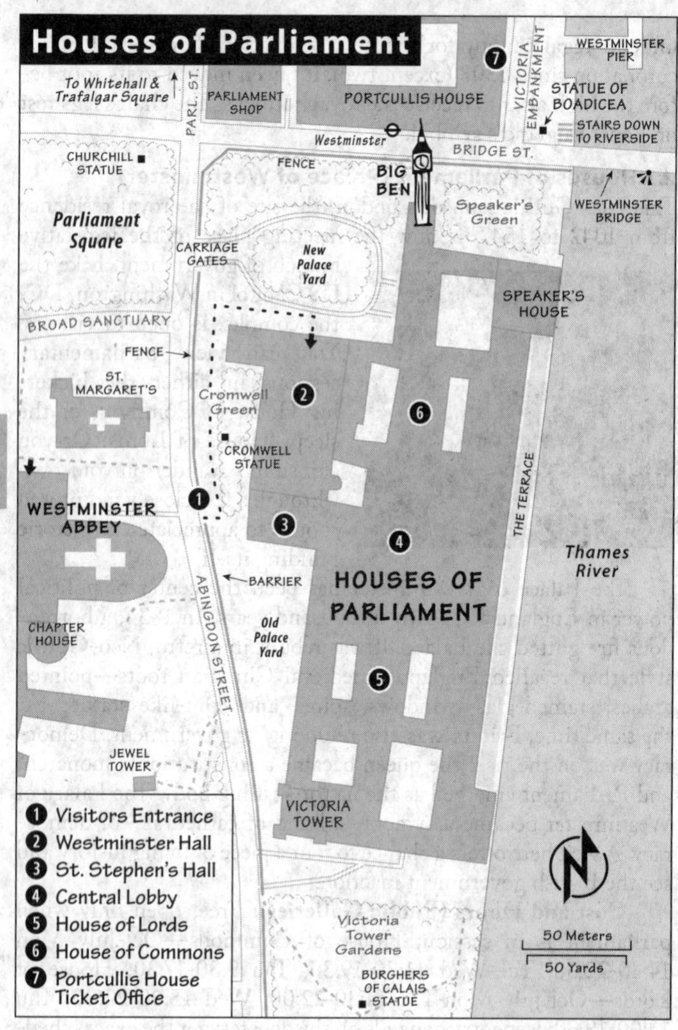

portant politically, the Lords meet in a more ornate room, and the wait time is shorter (likely less than 30 minutes). The House of Commons is where major policy is made, but the room is sparse, and wait times are longer (30-60 minutes or more).

Crowd-Beating Tips: For the public galleries, lines tend to be longest at the start of each session, particularly on Wednesdays; for the shortest wait, try to show up later in the afternoon (but don't push it, as things sometimes close down early).

➲ **Self-Guided Tour:** Enter midway along the west side of the building (across the street from Westminster Abbey), where a tourist ramp leads to the visitors entrance. Once inside, you'll be able to see all the public spaces described in this tour as you transit to the chamber you intend to visit.

• *First, take in the cavernous...*

Westminster Hall: This vast hall—covering 16,000 square feet—survived the 1834 fire, and is one of the oldest and most important buildings in England. England's vaunted legal system was invented in this hall, as this was the major court of the land for 700 years. King Charles I was sentenced to death here. Guy Fawkes was condemned for plotting to blow up the Halls of Parliament in 1605.

• *Walking through the hall and up the stairs, you'll enter the busy world of today's government. You soon reach...*

St. Stephen's Hall: This long, beautifully lit room was the original House of Commons for three centuries (from 1550 until the fire of 1834). MPs sat in church pews on either side of the hall—the ruling party on one side, the opposition on the other.

• *Next, you reach the...*

Central Lobby: This ornate, octagonal, high-vaulted room is often called the "heart of British government," because it sits midway between the House of Commons (to the left) and House of Lords (right). Video monitors list the schedule of meetings and events in this 1,100-room governmental hive. This is the best place to admire the Palace's carved wood, chandeliers, statues, and floor tiles.

• *This lobby marks the end of the public space where you can wander freely. To see the House of Lords or House of Commons you must wait in line and check your belongings.*

House of Lords: When you're called, you'll walk to the Lords Chamber by way of the long Peers' Corridor—referring to the House's 800 unelected members, called "Peers." Paintings on the corridor walls depict the antiauthoritarian spirit brewing under the reign of Charles I. When you reach the House of Lords Chamber, you'll watch the proceedings from the upper-level visitors gallery. Debate may occur among the few Lords who show up at any given time, but these days the Peers' role is largely advisory—they have no real power to pass laws on their own.

The Lords Chamber is church-like and impressive, with stained glass and intricately carved walls. At the far end is the Queen's gilded throne, where she sits once a year to give a speech to open Parliament. In front of the throne sits the woolsack—a cushion stuffed with wool. Here the Lord Speaker presides, with a ceremonial mace behind the backrest. To the Lord Speaker's right are the members of the ruling party (a.k.a. "government"), and to his left are the members of the opposition (the Labour Party). Unaffiliated Crossbenchers sit in between.

House of Commons: The Commons Chamber may be much less grandiose than the Lords', but this is where the sausage gets made. The House of Commons is as powerful as the Lords, prime minister, and Queen combined.

Of today's 650-plus MPs, only 450 can sit—the rest have to stand at the ends. As in the House of Lords, the ruling party sits on the right of the Speaker (in his canopied Speaker's Chair), and opposition sits on the left. Keep an eye out for two red lines on the floor, which cannot be crossed when debating the other side. (They're supposedly two sword-lengths apart, to prevent a literal clashing of swords.) The clerks sit at a central table that holds the ceremonial mace, a symbol of the power given Parliament by the monarch, who is not allowed in the Commons Chamber.

When the prime minister visits, his ministers (or cabinet) join him on the front bench, while lesser MPs (the "backbenchers") sit behind. It's often a fiery spectacle as the prime minister defends his policies while the opposition grumbles and harrumphs in displeasure. It's not unheard-of for MPs to get out of line and be escorted out by the Serjeant at Arms.

Nearby: Across the street from the Parliament building's St. Stephen's Gate, the **Jewel Tower** is a rare remnant of the old Palace of Westminster, used by kings until Henry VIII. The crude stone tower (1365-1366) was a guard tower in the palace wall, overlooking a moat. It contains a fine exhibit on the medieval Westminster Palace and the tower (£4.70, April-Sept daily 10:00-18:00; Oct daily 10:00-17:00; Nov-March Sat-Sun 10:00-16:00, closed Mon-Fri; tel. 020/7222-2219). Next to the tower (and free) is a quiet courtyard with picnic-friendly benches.

Big Ben, the 315-foot-high clock tower at the north end of the Palace of Westminster, is named for its 13-ton bell, Ben. The light above the clock is lit when Parliament is in session. The face of the clock is huge—you can actually see the minute hand moving. For a good view of it, walk halfway over Westminster Bridge.

▲▲▲Churchill War Rooms

This excellent sight offers a fascinating walk through the underground headquarters of the British government's fight against the Nazis in the darkest days of the Battle for Britain. It has two parts: the war rooms themselves, and a top-notch museum dedicated to the man who steered the war from here, Winston Churchill. For details on all the blood, sweat, toil, and tears, pick up the excellent, essential, and included audioguide at the entry, and dive in.

Advance reservations are not compulsory, but if you book ahead you can skip the line; otherwise on busy days you may find yourself waiting up to 30 minutes. Allow yourself 1-2 hours for this sight.

Cost and Hours: £18 includes audioguide, daily 9:30-18:00, last entry one hour before closing, guidebook-£5; on King Charles Street, 200 yards off Whitehall, follow the signs, Tube: Westminster, tel. 020/7930-6961, www.iwm.org.uk/churchill. The museum's gift shop is great for anyone nostalgic for the 1940s.

Cabinet War Rooms: The 27-room, heavily fortified nerve center of the British war effort was used from 1939 to 1945. Churchill's room, the map room, and other rooms are just as they were in 1945. As you follow the one-way route, be sure to take advantage of the audioguide, which explains each room and offers first-person accounts of wartime happenings here. Be patient—it's well worth it. While the rooms are spartan, you'll see how British gentility survived even as the city was bombarded—posted signs informed those working underground what the weather was like outside, and a cheery notice reminded them to turn off the light switch to conserve electricity.

Churchill Museum: Don't bypass this museum, which occupies a large hall amid the war rooms. It dissects every aspect of the man behind the famous cigar, bowler hat, and V-for-victory sign. It's extremely well-presented and engaging, using artifacts, quotes, political cartoons, clear explanations, and high-tech interactive exhibits to bring the colorful statesman to life. You'll get a taste of Winston's wit, irascibility, work ethic, passion for painting, American ties, writing talents, and drinking habits. The exhibit shows Winston's warts as well: It questions whether his party-switching was just political opportunism, examines the basis for his opposition to Indian self-rule, and reveals him to be an intense taskmaster who worked 18-hour days and was brutal to his staffers (who deeply respected him nevertheless).

A long touch-the-screen timeline lets you zero in on events in his life from birth (November 30, 1874) to his first appointment as prime minister in 1940. Many of the items on display—such as a European map divvied up in permanent marker, which Churchill brought to England from the postwar Potsdam Conference—drive home the remarkable span of history this man lived through. Imagine: Churchill began his military career riding horses in the cavalry and ended it speaking out against the proliferation of nuclear armaments. It's all the more amazing considering that, in the 1930s, the man who would become my vote for greatest statesman of the 20th century was considered a washed-up loony ranting about the growing threat of fascism.

Eating: Get your rations at the Switch Room café (until 17:00, in the museum), or for a nearby pub lunch, try Westminster Arms (food served downstairs, on Storey's Gate, a couple of blocks south of the museum).

Horse Guards

The Horse Guards change daily at 11:00 (10:00 on Sun), and a colorful dismounting ceremony takes place daily at 16:00. The rest of the day, they just stand there—terrible for video cameras (at Horse Guards Parade on Whitehall, directly across from the Banqueting House, between Trafalgar Square and 10 Downing Street, Tube: Westminster, www.royal.gov.uk—search "Changing the Guard"). Buckingham Palace pageantry is canceled when it rains, but the Horse Guards change regardless of the weather.

▲Banqueting House

England's first Renaissance building (1619-1622) is still standing. Designed by Inigo Jones, built by King James I, and decorated by his son Charles I, the Banqueting House came to symbolize the Stuart kings' "divine right" management style—the belief that God himself had anointed them to rule. The house is one of the few London landmarks spared by the 1698 fire and the only surviving part of the original Palace of Whitehall. Today it opens its doors to visitors, who enjoy a restful 10-minute audiovisual history, a 45-minute audioguide, and a look at the exquisite banqueting hall itself. As a tourist attraction, it's basically one big room, with sumptuous ceiling paintings by Peter Paul Rubens. At Charles I's request, these paintings drove home the doctrine of the legitimacy of the divine right of kings. Ironically, in 1649—divine right ignored—King Charles I was famously executed right here.

Cost and Hours: £6 includes audioguide, daily 10:00-17:00, may close for government functions—though it promises to stay open at least until 13:00 (call ahead for recorded information about closures), immediately across Whitehall from the Horse Guards, Tube: Westminster, tel. 020/3166-6155, www.hrp.org.uk.

ON TRAFALGAR SQUARE

Trafalgar Square, London's central square (worth ▲▲), is at the intersection of Westminster, The City, and the West End. It's the climax of most marches and demonstrations, and is a thrilling place to simply hang out. A remodeling of the square has rerouted car traffic, helping reclaim the area for London's citizens. At the top of Trafalgar Square (north) sits the domed National Gallery with its grand staircase, and to the right, the steeple of St. Martin-in-the-Fields, built in 1722, inspiring the steeple-over-the-entrance style of many town churches in New England. In the center of the square, Lord Horatio Nelson stands atop his 185-foot-tall fluted granite column, gazing out toward Trafalgar, where he lost his life but defeated the French fleet. Part of this 1842 memorial is made from his victims' melted-down cannons. He's surrounded by spraying fountains, giant lions, hordes of people, and—until recently—even more pigeons. A former London mayor decided that London's "flying rats" were a public nuisance and evicted Trafalgar Square's venerable seed salesmen (Tube: Charing Cross).

▲▲▲National Gallery

Displaying an unsurpassed collection of European paintings from 1250 to 1900—including works by Leonardo, Botticelli, Velázquez, Rembrandt, Turner, Van Gogh, and the Impressionists—this is one of Europe's great galleries. You'll peruse 700 years of art—from gold-backed Madonnas to Cubist bathers.

Cost and Hours: Free, but suggested donation of £5, special exhibits extra, daily 10:00-18:00, Fri until 21:00, last entry to special exhibits 45 minutes before closing, on Trafalgar Square, Tube: Charing Cross or Leicester Square.

Information: Helpful £1 floor plan available from information desk; free one-hour overview tours leave from Sainsbury Wing info desk daily at 11:30 and 14:30, plus Fri at 19:00; excellent £4 audioguides—choose from one-hour highlights tour, several theme tours, or tour option that lets you dial up info on any

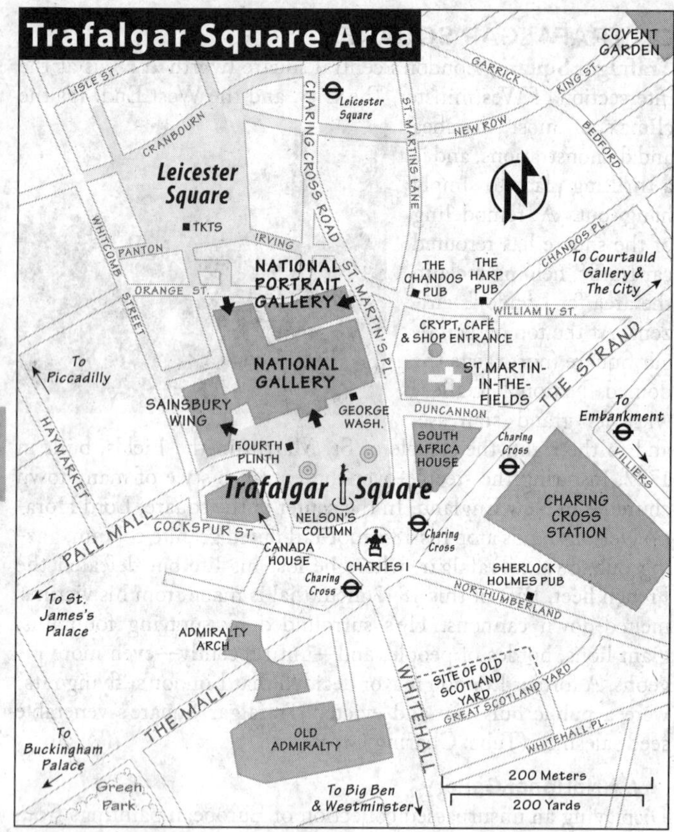

painting in the museum; tel. 020/7747-2885, www.nationalgallery.org.uk.

Eating: Consider splitting afternoon tea at the excellent-but-pricey National Dining Rooms, on the first floor of the Sainsbury Wing (see page 186). The National Café, located near the Getty Entrance, has a table-service restaurant and a café. Seek out the Espresso Bar, near the Portico and Getty entrances, for sandwiches, pastries, and soft couches.

Visiting the Museum: Go in through the Sainsbury Entrance (in the smaller building to the left of the main entrance), and approach the collection chronologically.

Medieval and Early Renaissance: In the first rooms, you see shiny paintings of saints, angels, Madonnas, and crucifixions floating in an ethereal gold never-never land.

After leaving this gold-leaf peace, you'll stumble into Uccello's *Battle of San Romano* and Van Eyck's *The Arnolfini Portrait,* called by some "The Shotgun Wedding." This painting—a masterpiece of

down-to-earth details—was once thought to depict a wedding ceremony forced by the lady's swelling belly. Today it's understood as a portrait of a solemn, well-dressed, well-heeled couple, the Arnolfinis of Bruges, Belgium (she likely was not pregnant—the fashion of the day was to gather up the folds of one's extremely full-skirted dress).

Italian Renaissance: In painting, the Renaissance meant realism. Artists rediscovered the beauty of nature and the human body, expressing the optimism and confidence of this new age. Look for Botticelli's *Venus and Mars,* Michelangelo's *The Entombment,* and Raphael's *Pope Julius II.*

In Leonardo's *The Virgin of the Rocks,* Mary plays with her son Jesus and little Johnny the Baptist (with cross, at left) while an androgynous angel looks on. Leonardo brings this holy scene right down to earth by setting it among rocks, stalactites, water, and flowering plants.

In *The Origin of the Milky Way* by Venetian Renaissance painter Tintoretto, the god Jupiter places his illegitimate son, baby Hercules, at his wife's breast. Juno says, "Wait a minute. That's not my baby!" Her milk spurts upward, becoming the Milky Way.

Northern Protestant: Greek gods and Virgin Marys are out, and hometown folks and hometown places are in. Highlights include Vermeer's *A Young Woman Standing at a Virginal* and Rembrandt's *Belshazzar's Feast.*

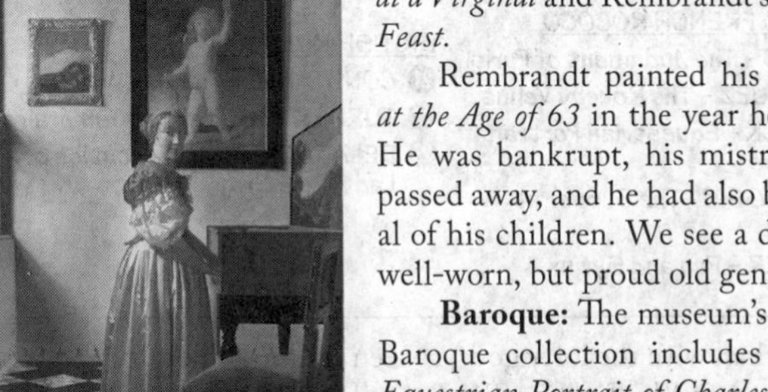

Rembrandt painted his *Self-Portrait at the Age of 63* in the year he would die. He was bankrupt, his mistress had just passed away, and he had also buried several of his children. We see a disillusioned, well-worn, but proud old genius.

Baroque: The museum's outstanding Baroque collection includes Van Dyck's *Equestrian Portrait of Charles I* and Caravaggio's *The Supper at Emmaus.* In Velázquez's *The Rokeby Venus,* Venus lounges diagonally across the canvas, admiring herself, with flaring red, white, and gray fabrics to highlight her rosy white skin and inflame our passion. This work by the king's personal court painter is a rare Spanish nude from that ultra-Catholic country.

British: The reserved British were more comfortable cavorting with nature than with the lofty gods, as seen in Constable's *The Hay Wain* and Turner's *The Fighting Téméraire*. Turner's messy, colorful style influenced the Impressionists and gives us our first glimpse into the modern art world.

Impressionism: At the end of the 19th century, a new breed of artists burst out of the stuffy confines of the studio. They donned scarves and berets and set up their canvases in farmers' fields or carried their notebooks into crowded cafés, dashing off quick sketches in order to catch a momentary...impression. Check out Impression-

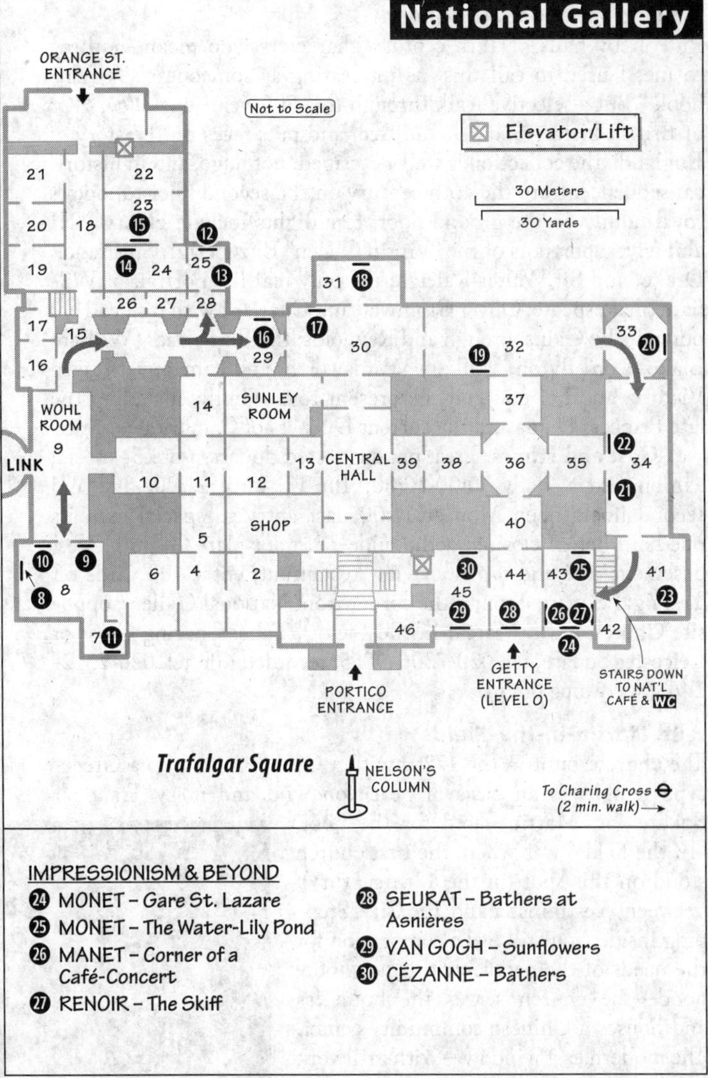

ist and Post-Impressionist masterpieces such as Monet's *Gare St. Lazare* and *The Water-Lily Pond,* Renoir's *The Skiff,* Seurat's *Bathers at Asnières,* and Van Gogh's *Sunflowers.*

Cézanne's *Bathers* are arranged in strict triangles. Cézanne uses the Impressionist technique of building a figure with dabs of paint (though his "dabs" are often larger-sized "cube" shapes) to make solid, 3-D geometrical figures in the style of the Renaissance. In the process, his cube shapes helped inspire a radical new style—Cubism—bringing art into the 20th century.

▲▲National Portrait Gallery

Put off by halls of 19th-century characters who meant nothing to me, I used to call this "as interesting as someone else's yearbook." But a selective walk through this 500-year-long *Who's Who* of British history is quick and free, and puts faces on the story of England. The collection is well-described, not huge, and in historical sequence, from the 16th century on the second floor to today's royal family on the ground floor. Highlights include Henry VIII and wives; portraits of the "Virgin Queen" Elizabeth I, Sir Francis Drake, and Sir Walter Raleigh; the only real-life portrait of William Shakespeare; Oliver Cromwell and Charles I with his head on; portraits by Gainsborough and Reynolds; the Romantics (William Blake, Lord Byron, William Wordsworth, and company); Queen Victoria and her era; and the present royal family, including the late Princess Diana and the current Duchess of Cambridge—Kate.

Cost and Hours: Free, but suggested donation of £5, special exhibits extra; daily 10:00-18:00, Thu-Fri until 21:00, first and second floors open Mon at 11:00, last entry to special exhibits one hour before closing; audioguide-£3, floor plan-£1, no photos, basement café and top-floor view restaurant; entry 100 yards off Trafalgar Square (around the corner from National Gallery, opposite Church of St. Martin-in-the-Fields), Tube: Charing Cross or Leicester Square, tel. 020/7306-0055, recorded info tel. 020/7312-2463, www.npg.org.uk.

▲St. Martin-in-the-Fields

The church, built in the 1720s with a Gothic spire atop a Greek-type temple, is an oasis of peace on wild and noisy Trafalgar Square. St. Martin cared for the poor. "In the fields" was where the first church stood on this spot (in the 13th century), between Westminster and The City. Stepping inside, you still feel a compassion for the needs of the people in this neighborhood—the church serves the homeless and houses a Chinese community center. The modern east window—with grillwork bent into the shape of a warped cross—was installed in 2008 to replace one damaged in World War II.

A freestanding glass pavilion to the left of the church serves as the entrance to the church's underground areas. There you'll find the concert ticket office, a gift shop, brass-rubbing center, and the recommended support-the-church Café in the Crypt.

Cost and Hours: Free, but donations welcome; hours vary but generally Mon-Fri 8:30-13:00 & 14:00-18:00, Sat 9:30-18:00, Sun 15:30-17:00; services listed at entrance; Tube: Charing Cross, tel. 020/7766-1100, www.smitf.org.

Music: The church is famous for its concerts. Consider a free lunchtime concert (suggested £3.50 donation; Mon, Tue, and Fri at 13:00), an evening concert (£8-28, several nights a week at 19:30), or Wednesday night jazz at the Café in the Crypt (£5.50-12 at 20:00). See the church's website for the concert schedule.

THE WEST END AND NEARBY

To explore this area during dinnertime, see my recommended restaurants on page 166.

▲Piccadilly Circus

Although this square is slathered with neon billboards and tacky attractions (think of it as the Times Square of London), the surrounding streets are packed with great shopping opportunities and swimming with youth on the rampage.

Nearby Shaftesbury Avenue and Leicester Square teem with fun-seekers, theaters, Chinese restaurants, and street singers. To the northeast is London's Chinatown and, beyond that, the funky Soho neighborhood (described next). And curling to the northwest from Piccadilly Circus is genteel Regent Street, lined with exclusive shops.

▲Soho

North of Piccadilly, seedy Soho has become trendy—with many recommended restaurants—and is well worth a gawk. It's the epicenter of London's thriving, colorful youth scene, a fun and funky *Sesame Street* of urban diversity.

Soho is also London's red light district (especially near Brewer and Berwick Streets), where "friendly models" wait in tiny rooms up dreary stairways, voluptuous con artists sell strip shows, and eager male tourists are frequently ripped off. But it's easy to avoid trouble if you're not looking for it. In fact, the sleazy joints share the block with respectable pubs and restaurants, and elderly couples stroll past neon signs that flash *Licensed Sex Shop in Basement*.

▲▲Covent Garden

This large square teems with people and street performers—jugglers, sword swallowers, and guitar players. London's buskers (including those in the Tube) are auditioned, licensed, and assigned times and places where they are allowed to perform.

LONDON

The square's centerpiece is a covered marketplace. A market has been here since medieval times, when it was the "convent" garden owned by Westminster Abbey. In the 1600s, it became a housing development with this courtyard as its center, done in the Palladian style by Inigo Jones. Today's fine iron-and-glass structure was built in 1830 (when such buildings were all the Industrial Age rage) to house the stalls of what became London's chief produce market. Covent Garden remained a produce market until 1973, when its venerable arcades were converted to boutiques, cafés, and antique shops. A tourist market thrives here today (for details, see page 138).

The "Actors' Church" of St. Paul, the Royal Opera House, and the London Transport Museum (described next) all border the square, and theaters are nearby. The area is a people-watcher's delight, with cigarette eaters, Punch-and-Judy acts, food that's good for you (but not your wallet), trendy crafts, and row after row of boutique shops and market stalls. For better Covent Garden lunch deals, walk a block or two away from the eye of this touristic hurricane (check out the places north of the Tube station, along Endell and Neal Streets).

▲London Transport Museum

This modern, well-presented museum, located right at Covent Garden, is fun for kids and thought-provoking for adults (if a bit overpriced). Whether you're cursing or marveling at the buses and Tube, the growth of Europe's third-biggest city (after Moscow and Istanbul) has been made possible by its public transit system.

After you enter, take the elevator up to the top floor...and the year 1800, when horse-drawn vehicles ruled the road. Next, you descend to the first floor and the world's first underground Metro system, which used steam-powered locomotives (the Circle Line, c. 1865). On the ground floor, horses and trains are replaced by motorized vehicles (cars, taxis, double-decker buses, streetcars), resulting in 20th-century congestion. How to deal with it? In 2003, car drivers in London were slapped with a congestion charge, and today, a half-billion people ride the Tube every year.

Cost and Hours: £16, ticket good for one year, kids under 18 free, Sat-Thu 10:00-18:00, Fri 11:00-18:00, last entry 45 minutes before closing; pleasant upstairs café with Covent Garden view; in southeast corner of Covent Garden courtyard, Tube: Covent Gar-

London for Early Birds and Night Owls

Most sightseeing in London is restricted to the hours between 10:00 and 18:00. Here are a few exceptions:

Sights Open Early

St. Paul's Cathedral: Mon-Sat at 8:30

Shakespeare's Globe: Daily at 9:00

Madame Tussauds Waxworks: Daily at 8:30 or 9:30

Tower of London: Tue-Sat at 9:00

Churchill War Rooms: Daily at 9:30

Westminster Abbey: Mon-Sat at 9:30

British Library: Mon-Sat at 9:30

Buckingham Palace: Aug-Sept daily at 9:30

Sights Open Late

Keep in mind that many of these sights stop admitting visitors well before their posted closing times.

Westminster Abbey: Wed until 19:00

Madame Tussauds: Daily until 19:30 or 20:00, and until 21:00 or later in July and August

London Eye: Last ascent daily at 20:30, later in July and Aug

Clink Prison Museum: July-Sept daily until 21:00, Oct-June Sat-Sun until 19:30

British Library: Tue until 20:00

British Museum (some galleries): Fri until 20:30

National Portrait Gallery: Thu-Fri until 21:00

National Gallery: Fri until 21:00

Victoria and Albert Museum (some galleries): Fri until 22:00

Tate Modern: Fri-Sat until 22:00

Houses of Parliament: House of Commons—Oct-July Mon until 22:30, Tue-Wed until 19:30; House of Lords—Oct-July Mon-Wed until 22:00, Thu until 19:30

LONDON

den, switchboard tel. 020/7379-6344, recorded info tel. 020/7565-7299, www.ltmuseum.co.uk.

▲Courtauld Gallery

This wonderful and compact collection of paintings is a joy. The gallery is part of the Courtauld Institute of Art, and the thoughtful description of each piece of art reminds visitors that the gallery is still used for teaching. You'll see medieval European paintings and works by Rubens, the Impressionists (Manet, Monet, and Degas), Post-Impressionists (Cézanne and an intense Van Gogh self-portrait), and more. Besides the permanent collection, a quality selection of loaners and special exhibits are often included in the entry fee. The gallery is

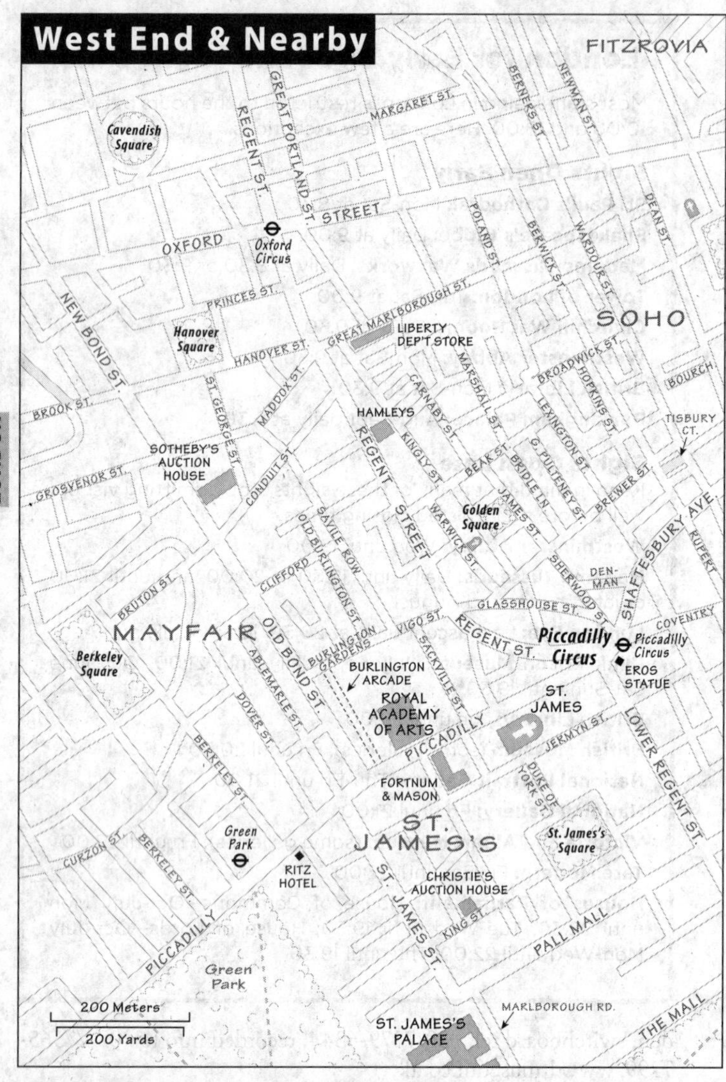

located within the grand Somerset House; enjoy the riverside eateries and the courtyard featuring a playful fountain.

Cost and Hours: £7 (£3 on Mon); open daily 10:00-18:00, occasionally open Thu until 21:00—check website; in Somerset House on the Strand, Tube: Temple or Covent Garden, recorded info tel. 020/7848-2526, www.courtauld.ac.uk.

BUCKINGHAM PALACE AREA

The working headquarters of the British monarchy, Buckingham Palace is where the Queen carries out her official duties as the head

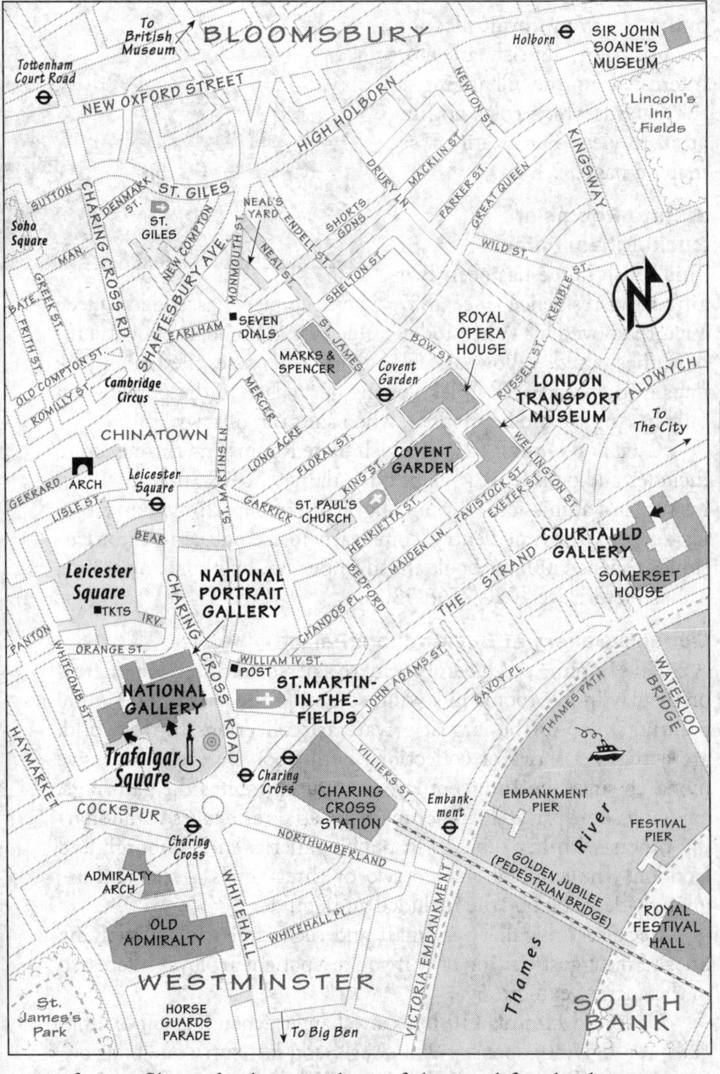

of state. She and other members of the royal family also maintain apartments here. The property hasn't always been this grand—James I (1603-1625) first brought the site under royal protection as a place for his mulberry plantation, for rearing silkworms.

Ticketing Options: Three palace sights require admission—the State Rooms (Aug-Sept only), Queen's Gallery, and Royal Mews. You can pay for each separately (prices below), or buy a **combo-ticket:** A £35.60 "Royal Day Out" combo-ticket admits you to all three sights; a £17.10 version covers the Queen's Gallery and Royal Mews. For more information or to book tickets online, see www.royalcollection.org.uk. Many tourists are more interested in the Changing of the Guard, which costs nothing at all to view. For locations, see map on page 82.

▲State Rooms at Buckingham Palace

This lavish home has been Britain's royal residence since 1837, when the newly ascended Queen Victoria moved in. When today's Queen is at home, the royal standard flies (a red, yellow, and blue flag); otherwise, the Union Jack flaps in the wind. The Queen opens her palace to the public—but only in August and September, when she's out of town.

Cost and Hours: £21 for lavish State Rooms and throne room, includes audioguide; Aug-Sept only, daily 9:30-18:30, until 19:00 in Aug, last admission 17:15 in Aug, 16:15 in Sept; limited to 8,000 visitors a day by timed entry; come early to the palace's Visitor Entrance (opens 9:00), or book ahead in person, by phone, or online; Tube: Victoria, tel. 020/7766-7300.

Queen's Gallery at Buckingham Palace

A small sampling of Queen Elizabeth's personal collection of art is on display in five rooms in a wing adjoining the palace. Her 7,000 paintings, one of the largest private art collections in the world, are actually a series of collections built upon by each successive monarch since the 16th century. The Queen rotates the paintings, enjoying some privately in her many palatial residences while sharing others with her subjects in public galleries in Edinburgh and London. The exhibits change two or three times a year and are lovingly described by the included audioguide.

Because the gallery is small and security is tight (involving lines), I'd suggest visiting only if you're a patient art lover interested in the current exhibit.

Cost and Hours: £10 but can change depending on exhibit, daily 10:00-17:30, opens at 9:30 Aug-Sept, last entry one hour before closing, Tube: Victoria, tel. 020/7766-7301—but Her Majesty rarely answers. Men shouldn't miss the mahogany-trimmed urinals.

Royal Mews

A visit to the Queen's working stables is likely to be disappointing unless you follow the included audioguide or the hourly guided tour (April-Oct only, 45 minutes), in which case it's fairly entertaining—especially if you're interested in horses and/or royalty. You'll see only a few of the Queen's 30 horses (most active between 10:00 and 12:00), a fancy car, and a bunch of old carriages, finishing with the Gold State Coach (c. 1760, 4 tons, 4 mph). Queen Victoria said absolutely no cars. When she died in 1901, the mews got its first Daimler. Today, along with the hay-eating transport, the stable is home to five Bentleys and Rolls-Royce Phantoms, with at least one on display.

Cost and Hours: £9, April-Oct daily 10:00-17:00, Nov-March Mon-Sat 10:00-16:00, closed Sun; last entry 45 minutes before closing, generally busiest immediately after changing of the guard, guided tours on the hour in summer; Buckingham Palace Road, Tube: Victoria, tel. 020/7766-7302.

▲▲Changing of the Guard at Buckingham Palace

This is the spectacle every visitor to London has to see at least once: stone-faced, red-coated (or in winter, gray-coated), bearskin-hatted guards changing posts with much fanfare, in an hour-long ceremony accompanied by a brass band.

It's 11:00 at Buckingham Palace, and the on-duty guards (the "Queen's Guard") are ready to finish their shift. Nearby at St. James's Palace (a half-mile northeast), a second set of guards is also ready for a break. Meanwhile, fresh replacement guards (the "New Guard") gather for a review and inspection at Wellington Barracks, 500 yards east of the palace (on Birdcage Walk).

At 11:13, the tired St. James's "Old Guard" heads out to the Mall, and then takes a right turn for Buckingham Palace. At 11:27, the "New Guard" replacement troops, led by the band, also head for Buckingham Palace from the Wellington Barracks. Meanwhile, a fourth group—the Horse Guard—passes by along the Mall on its way back to Hyde Park Corner from its own changing-of-the-guard ceremony on Whitehall (which just took place at Horse Guards Parade at 11:00, or 10:00 on Sun).

At 11:30, the tired and fresh guards converge on Buckingham Palace in a perfect storm of red-coat pageantry. Everyone parades around, the guard changes (passing the regimental flag, or "colour") with much shouting, the band plays a happy little concert, and then they march out. Just after noon, two bands escort two detachments of guards away: the tired "Old Guard" to Wellington Barracks and the fresh "New Guard" to St. James's Palace. As the fresh guards set up at St. James's Palace and the tired ones dress down at the barracks, the tourists disperse.

Cost and Hours: Free, daily May-July at 11:30, every other

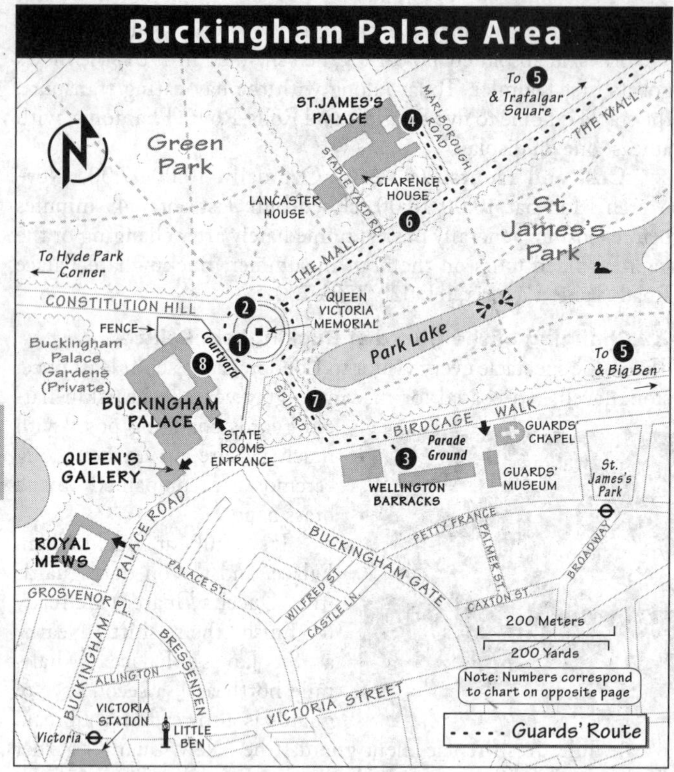

day Aug-April, no ceremony in very wet weather; exact schedule subject to change—call 020/7766-7300 for the day's plan, or check www.royal.gov.uk (search "Changing the Guard"); Buckingham Palace, Tube: Victoria, St. James's Park, or Green Park. Or hop into a big black taxi and say, "Buck House, please."

Sightseeing Strategies: Most tourists just show up and get lost in the crowds, but those who anticipate the action and know where to perch will enjoy the event more. The action takes place in stages over the course of an hour, at several different locations. There are several ways to experience the pageantry. Get out your map (or download the official app at www.royalcollection.org.uk) and strategize. Here are a few options to consider:

Watch from One Location: Pick one event and find a good unobstructed place from which to view it. The key is to get either right up front along the road or fence, or find some raised elevation to stand or sit on—a balustrade or a curb—so you can see over people's heads. The main event is in the forecourt right in front of Buckingham Palace (between Buckingham Palace and the fence)

Changing of the Guard Timeline

When	What
10:30	Tourists begin to gather; arrive now for a spot front and center by the ❶ fence outside Buckingham Palace.
11:00	❷ Victoria Memorial gets crowded.
11:00-11:15	"New Guard" gathers for inspection at ❸ Wellington Barracks. "Old Guard" gathers for inspection at ❹ St. James's Palace.
11:00 (10:00 Sun)	Changing of the Horse Guard at ❺ Horse Guards Parade, opposite end of St. James's Park.
11:13	Tired St. James's Palace guards march down ❻ the Mall, heading for Buckingham Palace.
11:27	Fresh replacement troops head from Wellington Barracks down ❼ Spur Road to Buckingham Palace.
11:30	All guards gradually converge around the Victoria Memorial in front of the palace.
11:30-12:00	Changing of the Guard ceremony takes place ❽ inside fenced courtyard of Buckingham Palace.
12:10	Tired "Old Guard" heads up Spur Road for Wellington Barracks. Fresh "New Guard" heads up the Mall for St. James's Palace.
12:15	Smaller changing of the guard ceremony takes place in front of St. James's Palace.

from 11:30 to 12:00. To see it close up, you'll need to get here no later than 10:30 to get a place front and center, next to the fence.

If you get there too late to score a premium spot right along the fence, head for the high ground on the circular Victoria Memorial, which provides the best overall view (come before 11:00 to get a place). From a high spot on the memorial, you have good (if more distant) views of the palace as well as the arriving and departing parades along The Mall and Spur Road. The actual Changing of the Guard in front of the palace is a nonevent. It is interesting, however, to see nearly every tourist in London gathered in one place at the same time.

If you arrive too late to get any good spot at all, or you just don't feel like jostling for a view, stroll down to St. James's Palace and wait near the corner for a great photo-op. At about 12:15, the parade marches up The Mall to the palace and performs a smaller changing ceremony—with almost no crowds. Afterward, stroll through nearby St. James's Park.

Follow the Procession: You won't get the closest views, but you'll get something even better—the thrill of participating in the action. Start with the "Old Guard" mobilizing in the courtyard of St. James's Palace (11:00). Arrive early, and grab a spot just across the road (otherwise you'll be asked to move when the inspection begins). Just before they prepare to leave (at 11:13), march ahead of them down Marlborough Street to The Mall. Pause here to watch them parade past, band and all, on their way to the Palace, then cut through the park and head to the Wellington Barracks—where the "New Guard" is getting ready to leave for Buckingham (11:27). March along with full military band and fresh guards from the barracks to the Palace. At 11:30 the two guard groups meet in the courtyard, the band plays a few songs, and soldiers parade and finally exchange compliments before returning to Wellington Barracks and St. James Palace (12:10). Use this time to snap a few photos of the guards—and the crowds—before making your way across the Mall to Clarence House (on Stable Yard Road), where you'll see the "New Guard" pass one last time on their way to St. James' Palace. On their way, the final piece of ceremony takes place—one member of the "Old Guard" and one member of the first-relief "New Guard" change places here.

Join a Tour: Local tour companies such as **Fun London Tours** more or less follow the self-guided route above but add in history and facts about the guards, bands, and royal family to their already entertaining march. These walks add color and good value to what can otherwise seem like a stressful mess of tourists (£15, Changing of the Guard tour starts at Piccadilly Circus at 10:00, must book online in advance, www.funlondontours.com).

Sights in North London

▲▲▲British Museum

Simply put, this is the greatest chronicle of civilization...anywhere. A visit here is like taking a long hike through *Encyclopedia Britannica* National Park. The vast British Museum wraps around its Great Court (the huge entrance hall), with the most popular sections filling the ground floor: Egyptian, Assyrian, and ancient Greek, with the famous frieze sculptures from the Parthenon in Athens. The museum's stately Read-

ing Room—famous as the place where Karl Marx hung out while formulating his ideas on communism and writing *Das Kapital*—sometimes hosts special exhibits.

Cost and Hours: Free but a £5 donation requested, special exhibits usually extra (and with timed ticket); daily 10:00-17:30, Fri until 20:30 (selected galleries only), least crowded weekday late afternoons; Great Russell Street, Tube: Tottenham Court Road.

Information: Information desks offer a basic map (£2 donation), but it's not essential; the *Visitor's Guide* (£3.50) offers 15 different tours and skimpy text. Free 30-minute **eyeOpener tours** are led by volunteers, who focus on select rooms (daily 11:00-15:45, generally every 15 minutes). Free 45-minute **gallery talks** on specific subjects are offered Tue-Sat at 13:15; a free 20-minute highlights tour is available on Friday evening. The £5 **multimedia guide** offers dial-up audio commentary and video on 200 objects, as well as several theme tours (must leave photo ID). There's also a fun children's multimedia guide (£3.50). Or ☊ download my free **audio tour**—see page 13. General info tel. 020/7323-8299, ticket desk tel. 020/7323-8181, www.britishmuseum.org.

➲ **Self-Guided Tour:** From the Great Court, doorways lead to all wings. To the left are the exhibits on Egypt, Assyria, and Greece—the highlights of your visit.

Egypt: Start with the Egyptian section. Egypt was one of the world's first "civilizations"—a group of people with a government, religion, art, free time, and a written language. The Egypt we think

British Museum Overview

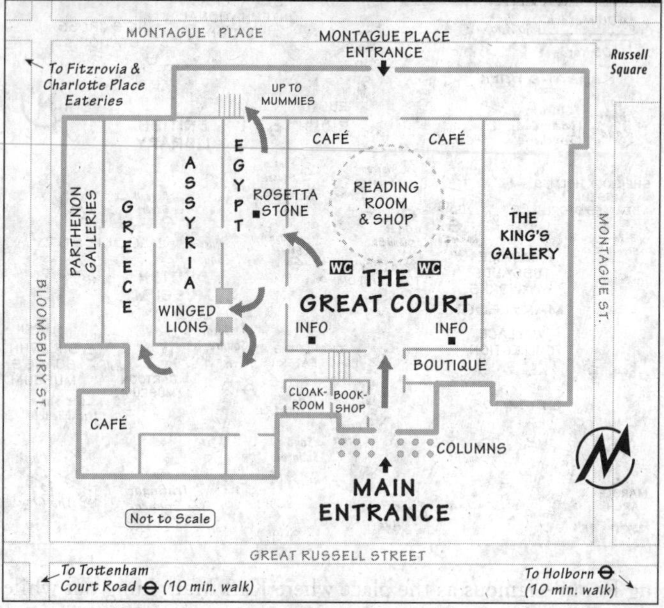

MONTAGUE PLACE
MONTAGUE PLACE ENTRANCE
Russell Square
To Fitzrovia & Charlotte Place Eateries
UP TO MUMMIES
CAFÉ
CAFÉ
PARTHENON GALLERIES
GREECE
ASSYRIA
EGYPT
ROSETTA STONE
READING ROOM & SHOP
THE KING'S GALLERY
MONTAGUE ST.
WC
WC
THE GREAT COURT
WINGED LIONS
INFO
INFO
BLOOMSBURY ST.
BOUTIQUE
CLOAK-ROOM
BOOK-SHOP
CAFÉ
COLUMNS
MAIN ENTRANCE
Not to Scale
GREAT RUSSELL STREET
To Tottenham Court Road (10 min. walk)
To Holborn (10 min. walk)

of—pyramids, mummies, pharaohs, and guys who walk funny—lasted from 3000 to 1000 B.C. with hardly any change in the government, religion, or arts. Imagine two millennia of Nixon.

The first thing you'll see in the Egypt section is the **Rosetta Stone.** When this rock was unearthed in the Egyptian desert in 1799, it was a sensation in Europe. This black slab, dating from 196 B.C., caused a quantum leap in the study of ancient history. Finally, Egyptian writing could be decoded. It contains a single inscription repeated in three languages. The bottom third is plain old Greek, while the middle is medieval Egyptian. By comparing the two known languages with the one they didn't know, translators figured out the hieroglyphics.

Next, wander past the many **statues,** including a seven-ton Ramesses, with the traditional features of a pharaoh (goatee, cloth headdress, and cobra diadem on his forehead). When Moses told the king of Egypt, "Let my people go!," this was the stony-faced look he got. You'll also see the Egyptian gods as animals—these include Amun, king of the gods, as a ram, and Horus, the god of the living, as a falcon.

At the end of the hall, climb the stairs to **mummy** land (use the elevator if it's running). To mummify a body, you first disembowel it (but leave the heart inside), then pack the cavities with pitch, and dry it with natron, a natural form of sodium carbonate (and, I believe, the active ingredient in Twinkies). Then carefully bandage it head to toe with hundreds of yards of linen strips. Let it sit 2,000 years, and...*voilà!* The mummy was placed in a wooden coffin, which was put in a stone coffin, which was placed in a tomb. The result is that we now have Egyptian bodies that are as well-preserved as Larry King. Many of the mummies here are from the time of the Roman occupation, when fine memorial portraits painted in wax became popular. X-ray photos in the display cases tell us more about these people. Don't miss the animal mummies. Cats were popular pets. They were also considered incarnations of the cat-headed goddess Bastet. Worshipped in life as the sun god's allies, preserved in death, and memorialized with statues, cats were given the adulation they've come to expect ever since.

Assyria: Long before Saddam Hussein, Iraq was home to other palace-building, iron-fisted rulers—the Assyrians, who conquered their southern neighbors and dominated the Middle East for 300 years (c. 900-600 B.C.). Their strength came from a superb army (chariots, mounted cavalry, and siege engines), a policy of terrorism against enemies ("I tied their heads to tree trunks all around the city," reads a royal inscription), ethnic cleansing and mass deportations of the vanquished, and efficient administration (roads and express postal service). They have been called the "Romans of the East."

The British Museum's valuable collection of Assyrian artifacts has become even more priceless since the recent destruction of ancient sites in Iraq by ISIS terrorists.

Standing guard over the Assyrian exhibit halls are two human-headed **winged lions.** These stone lions guarded an Assyrian palace (11th-8th century B.C.). With the strength of a lion, the wings of an eagle, the brain of a man, and the beard of ZZ Top, they protected the king from evil spirits and scared the heck out of foreign ambassadors and left-wing newspaper reporters. (What has five legs and flies? Take a close look. These winged quintupeds, which appear complete from both the front and the side, could guard both directions at once.)

Carved into the stone between the bearded lions' loins, you can see one of civilization's most impressive achievements—writing. This wedge-shaped **(cuneiform)** script is the world's first written language, invented 5,000 years ago by the Sumerians (of

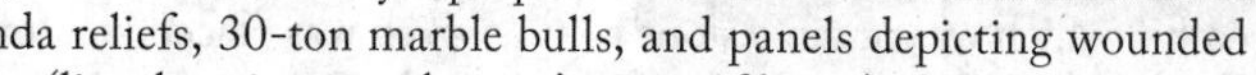

southern Iraq) and passed down to their less-civilized descendants, the Assyrians.

The **Nimrud Gallery** is a mini version of the throne room and royal apartments of King Ashurnasirpal II's Northwest Palace at Nimrud (9th century B.C.). It's filled with royal propaganda reliefs, 30-ton marble bulls, and panels depicting wounded lions (lion-hunting was Assyria's sport of kings).

Greece: During their civilization's Golden Age (500-430 B.C.), the ancient Greeks set the tone for all of Western civilization to follow. Democracy, theater, literature, mathematics, philosophy, science, gyros, art, and architecture, as we know them, were virtually all invented by a single generation of Greeks in a small town of maybe 80,000 citizens.

Your walk through Greek art history starts with pottery, usually painted red and black and a popular export product for the sea-trading Greeks. The earliest featured geometric patterns (eighth century B.C.), then a painted black silhouette on the natural orange clay, then a red figure on a black background. Later, painted vases show a culture really into partying.

The highlight is the **Parthenon Sculptures,** taken from the temple dedicated to Athena—the crowning glory of an enormous urban-renewal plan during Greece's Golden Age. The sculptures are also called the Elgin Marbles for the shrewd British ambassador who had his men hammer, chisel, and saw them off the Parthenon in the early 1800s. Though the Greek government complains about losing its marbles, the Brits feel they rescued and preserved the sculptures. These much-wrangled-over bits of the Parthenon (from about 450 B.C.) are indeed impressive. The marble panels you see lining the walls of this large hall are part of the frieze that originally ran around the exterior of the Parthenon, under the eaves. The statues at either end of the hall once filled the Parthenon's triangular-shaped pediments and showed the birth of Athena. The relief panels known as metopes tell the story of the struggle between the forces of human civilization and animal-like barbarism.

The Rest of the Museum: Be sure to venture upstairs to see artifacts from **Roman Britain** that surpass anything you'll see at

Hadrian's Wall or elsewhere in the country. Also look for the Sutton Hoo Ship Burial artifacts from a seventh-century royal burial on the east coast of England (Room 41). A rare Michelangelo cartoon (preliminary sketch) is in Room 90 (level 4).

▲▲▲British Library

Here, in just two rooms, are the literary treasures of Western civilization, from early Bibles, to Shakespeare's *Hamlet,* to Lewis Carroll's *Alice's Adventures in Wonderland.* You'll see the Lindisfarne Gospels transcribed on an illuminated manuscript, as well as Beatles lyrics scrawled on the back of a greeting card. You might even glimpse the *Magna Carta*—though after celebrating its 800th birthday it may be taking time off from public view during your visit. The British Empire built its greatest monuments out of paper; it's through literature that England made her most lasting and significant contribution to civilization and the arts.

Cost and Hours: Free, but £5 suggested donation, admission charged for some special exhibits; Mon-Fri 9:30-18:00, Tue until 20:00, Sat 9:30-17:00, Sun 11:00-17:00; 96 Euston Road, Tube: King's Cross St. Pancras or Euston, tel. 019/3754-6060 or 020/7412-7676, www.bl.uk.

Tours: There are no guided tours or audioguides for the permanent collection, but you can download my free British Library **audio tour** (see page 13). There are guided tours of the building itself—the archives and reading rooms. Touch-screen computers in the permanent collection let you page virtually through some of the rare books.

Self-Guided Tour: Everything that matters for your visit is in the delightful Sir John Ritblat Gallery and an adjacent room. We'll concentrate on a handful of documents—literary and historical—that changed the course of history. Note that exhibits change often, and many of the museum's old, fragile manuscripts need to "rest" periodically in order to stay well-preserved.

Upon entering the Ritblat Gallery, start at the far side of the room with the display case of historic ❶ **maps** showing how humans' perspective of the world expanded over the centuries. Next, move into the area dedicated to ❷ **sacred texts and early Bibles** from several cultures. This section includes the oldest complete Bibles in existence. In the display cases called ❸ **Art of the Book,** you'll find beautifully illustrated, or "illuminated," Bibles from the early medieval period, including the Lindisfarne Gospels (A.D 698). Look out for some of the first-ever English translations of the Bible.

In the glass cases featuring early ❹ **printing,** you'll see the Diamond Sutra (c. 868), the world's earliest complete printed book,

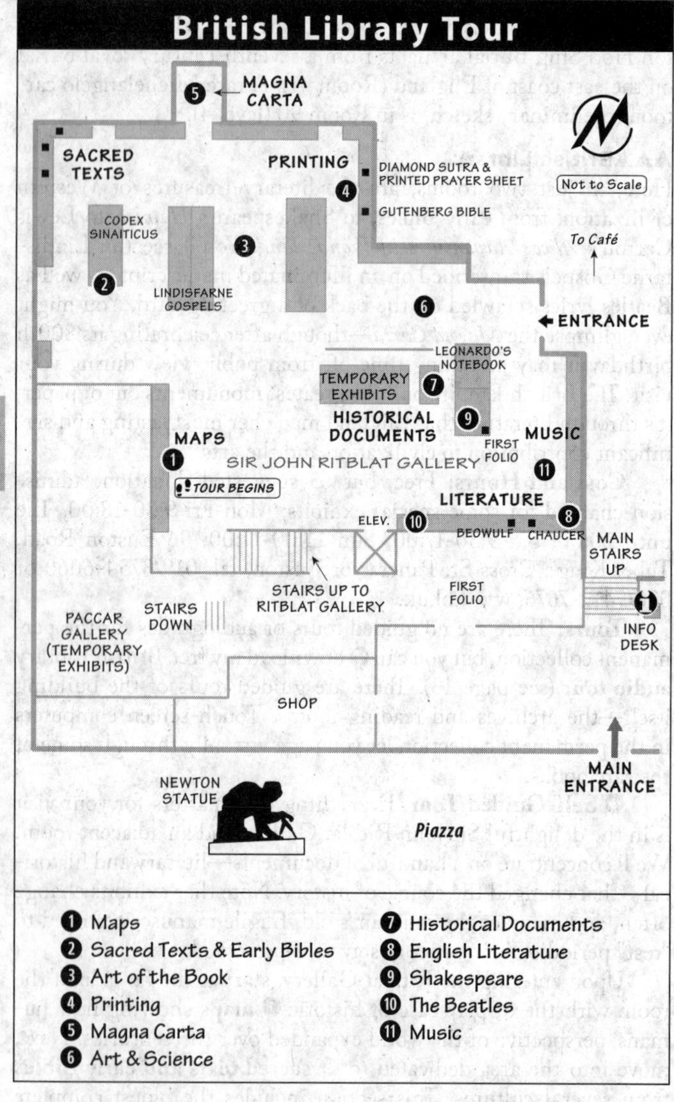

and the Gutenberg Bible, the first book printed in Europe using movable type (c. 1455)—a revolutionary document.

Through a nearby doorway is a small room that holds the ❺ **Magna Carta,** assuming it's not "resting." The basis for England's constitutional system of Government, this "Great Charter" listing rules about mundane administrative issues was radical because of the simple fact that the king had agreed to abide by them as law.

Return to the main room to find display cases featuring

❻ **art and science.** Pages from Leonardo da Vinci's notebook show his powerful curiosity, his genius for invention, and his famous backward and inside-out handwriting. Nearby are many more ❼ **historical documents.** The displays change frequently, but you may see letters by Henry VIII, Queen Elizabeth I, Darwin, Freud, Gandhi, and others.

Next, trace the evolution of ❽ **English literature.** Check out the A.D. 1000 manuscript of *Beowulf,* the first English literary masterpiece, and the *The Canterbury Tales* (c. 1410), Geoffrey Chaucer's bawdy collection of stories. The Literature wall is often a greatest-hits sampling of literature in English, from Brontë to Kipling to Woolf to Joyce to Dickens. The most famous of England's writers—❾ **Shakespeare**—generally gets his own display case. Look for the First Folio—one of the 700 copies of the first complete collection of his plays, published in 1623.

Now fast-forward a few centuries to ❿ **The Beatles.** Find photos of John Lennon, Paul McCartney, George Harrison, and Ringo Starr before and after their fame, as well as manuscripts of song lyrics written by Lennon and McCartney. In the ⓫ **music** section, there are manuscripts by Mozart, Beethoven, Schubert, and others (kind of an anticlimax after the Fab Four, I know). George Frideric Handel's famous oratorio, the *Messiah* (1741), is often on display and marks the end of our tour. Hallelujah.

▲Wallace Collection

Sir Richard Wallace's fine collection of 17th-century Dutch Masters, 18th-century French Rococo, medieval armor, and assorted aristocratic fancies fills the sumptuously furnished Hertford House on Manchester Square. From the rough and intimate Dutch lifescapes of Jan Steen to the pink-cheeked Rococo fantasies of François Boucher, a wander through this little-visited mansion makes you nostalgic for the days of the empire. This collection would be a big deal in a mid-sized city, but here in London it gets lost. It's thoroughly enjoyable and affords a classic old-time museum-going experience.

Cost and Hours: Free, daily 10:00-17:00, audioguide-£4

(consider the cost a donation to a great cause), free guided tours or lectures almost daily at 11:30, 13:00, and 14:30—call to confirm times, just north of Oxford Street on Manchester Square, Tube: Bond Street, tel. 020/7563-9500, www.wallacecollection.org.

▲Madame Tussauds Waxworks

This waxtravaganza is gimmicky, crass, and crazily expensive, but dang fun...a hit with the kind of tourists who skip the British Museum. The original Madame Tussaud did wax casts of heads lopped off during the French Revolution (such as Marie-Antoinette's). She took her show on the road and ended up in London in 1835. Now it's all about squeezing Leonardo DiCaprio's bum, singing with Lady Gaga, and partying with Brangelina, Benedict Cumberbatch, and the Beatles. In addition to posing with all the eerily realistic wax dummies—from Johnny Depp to Barack Obama—you'll have the chance to tour a hokey haunted-house exhibit; learn how they created this waxy army; hop on a people-mover and cruise through a kid-pleasing "Spirit of London" time trip; and visit with Spider-Man, the Hulk, and other Marvel superheroes. A nine-minute "4-D" show features a 3-D movie heightened by wind, "back ticklers," and other special effects.

Cost: £33, kids-£28.80 (kids under 5-free), family passes available; up to 25 percent discount and shorter lines if you buy tickets on their website (also consider a combo-deal with the London Eye), often even bigger discount—up to 50 percent—if you get "Late Saver" tickets at the door after 17:30, but be aware that some experiences close at 18:00; two-for-one rail vouchers accepted (see page 36).

Hours: July-Aug and school holidays daily 8:30-19:00, Sept-June Mon-Fri 9:30-17:30, Sat-Sun 9:00-18:00, these are last-entry times—place stays open roughly two hours later; Marylebone Road, Tube: Baker Street, tel. 0871-894-3000, www.madametussauds.com.

Crowd-Beating Tips: This popular attraction can be swamped. The ticket-buying line can be an hour or more (believe the posted signs about the wait). Once inside, there can be more waits for some popular exhibits. To avoid the ticket line, buy an Online Saver and reserve a time slot at least a day in advance. The place is less crowded (for both buying tickets at the door and for simply enjoying the place) if you arrive after 15:00.

▲Sir John Soane's Museum

Architects love this quirky place, as do fans of interior decor, eclectic knickknacks, and Back Door sights. Tour this furnished home on a bird-chirping square and see 19th-century chairs, lamps, wood-paneled nooks and crannies, sculptures, and stained-glass skylights. As professor of architecture at the Royal Academy, Soane created his home to be a place of learning, cramming it floor to ceiling with ancient relics, curios, and famous paintings, including several excellent Canalettos and Hogarth's series on *The Rake's Progress* (which is hidden behind a panel in the Picture Room and opened randomly at the museum's discretion, usually twice an hour). In 1833, just before his death, Soane established his house as a museum, stipulating that it be kept as nearly as possible in the state he left it. If he visited today, he'd be entirely satisfied by the diligence with which the staff safeguards his treasures. You'll leave wishing you'd known the man.

Cost and Hours: Free, but donations much appreciated; Tue-Sat 10:00-17:00, open and candlelit the first Tue of the month 18:00-21:00, closed Sun-Mon, long entry lines on Sat; guidebook-£5, guided tour-£10 Tue, Thu, Fri, and Sat at 12:00; 13 Lincoln's Inn Fields, quarter-mile southeast of British Museum, Tube: Holborn, tel. 020/7405-2107, www.soane.org.

Beatles Sights

London's city center is surprisingly devoid of sights associated with the famous '60s rock band. To see much of anything, consider taking a guided walk (see page 47).

For a photo op, go to **Abbey Road** and walk the famous crosswalk pictured on the *Abbey Road* album cover (Tube: St. John's Wood, get information and buy Beatles memorabilia at the small kiosk in the station). From the Tube station, it's a five-minute walk west down Grove End Road to the intersection with Abbey Road. The Abbey Road recording studio is the low-key, white building to the right of Abbey House (it's still a working studio, so you can't go inside). Ponder the graffiti on the low wall outside, and...imagine. To re-create the famous cover photo, shoot the crosswalk from the roundabout as you face north up Abbey Road. Shoes are optional.

Nearby is **Paul McCartney's current home** (7 Cavendish Avenue): Continue down Grove End Road, turn left on Circus Road, and then right on Cavendish. Please be discreet.

The **Beatles Store** is at 231 Baker Street (Tube: Baker Street). It's small—some Beatles-logo T-shirts, mugs, pins, and old vinyl like you might have in your closet—and has nothing of historic value (open eight days a week, 10:00-18:30, tel. 020/7935-4464, www.beatlesstorelondon.co.uk; another rock memorabilia store is across the street).

Sherlock Holmes Museum

A few doors down from the Beatles Store, this meticulous re-creation of the (fictional) apartment of the (fictional) detective sits at the (real) address of 221b Baker Street. The first-floor replica (so to speak) of Sherlock's study delights fans with the opportunity to play Holmes and Watson while sitting in authentic 18th-century chairs. The second and third floors offer fine exhibits on daily Victorian life, showing off furniture, clothes, pipes, paintings, and chamber pots; in other rooms, models are posed to enact key scenes from Sir Arthur Conan Doyle's famous books (but not the recently popular BBC series).

Cost and Hours: £15, daily 9:30-18:00, expect to wait 15 minutes or more—up to 2 hours in peak season; large gift shop for Holmes connoisseurs, including souvenirs from the BBC TV series; Tube: Baker Street, tel. 020/7935-8866, www.sherlock-holmes.co.uk.

Sights in The City

When Londoners say "The City," they mean the one-square-mile business center in East London that 2,000 years ago was Roman Londinium. The outline of the Roman city walls can still be seen in the arc of roads from Blackfriars Bridge to Tower Bridge. Within The City are 23 churches designed by Sir Christopher Wren, mostly just ornamentation around St. Paul's Cathedral. Today, while home to only 10,000 residents, The City thrives with around 400,000 office workers coming and going daily. It's a fascinating district to wander on weekdays, but since almost nobody actually lives there, it's dull in the evenings and on Saturday and Sunday.

You can 🎧 download my free audio tour of The City, which

peels back the many layers of history in this oldest part of London (see page 13).

▲▲▲St. Paul's Cathedral

Sir Christopher Wren's most famous church is the great St. Paul's, its elaborate interior capped by a 365-foot dome. There's been a church on this spot since 604. After the Great Fire of 1666 destroyed the old cathedral, Wren created this Baroque masterpiece. And since World War II, St. Paul's has been Britain's symbol of resilience. Despite 57 nights of bombing, the Nazis failed to destroy the cathedral, thanks to St. Paul's volunteer fire watchmen, who stayed on the dome.

Cost and Hours: £18, £15.50 if purchased in advance on the website, includes church entry, dome climb, crypt, tour, and audioguide; Mon-Sat 8:30-16:30 (dome opens at 9:30), closed Sun except for worship; book ahead online to skip the line or you might be waiting 15-30 minutes at busy times; Tube: St. Paul's.

Music and Church Services: If interested, check the website for worship times the day of your visit. Communion is generally Mon-Sat at 8:00 and 12:30. On Sunday, services are held at 8:00, 10:15 (Matins), 11:30 (sung Eucharist), 15:15 (evensong), and 18:00. The rest of the week, evensong is at 17:00 Tue-Sat (not Mon). For more on evensong, see page 145. If you come 20 minutes early for evensong worship (under the dome), you may be able to grab a big wooden stall in the choir, next to the singers. On some Sundays, there's a free organ recital at 16:45.

Information: Admission includes an **audioguide** (with video clips), as well as a 1.5-hour guided **tour** (Mon-Sat at 10:00, 11:00, 13:00, and 14:00; call 020/7246-8357 to confirm or ask at church). Free 20-minute **introductory talks** are offered throughout the day. You can also 🎧 download my free St. Paul's Cathedral **audio tour** (see page 13). Recorded info tel. 020/7246-8348, reception tel. 020/7246-8350, www.stpauls.co.uk.

➲ **Self-Guided Tour:** Even now, as skyscrapers encroach, the 365-foot-high dome of St. Paul's rises majestically above the rooftops of the neighborhood. The tall dome is set on classical columns, capped with a lantern, topped by a six-foot ball, and iced with a cross. As the first Anglican cathedral built in London after the Reformation, it is Baroque: St. Peter's in Rome filtered through

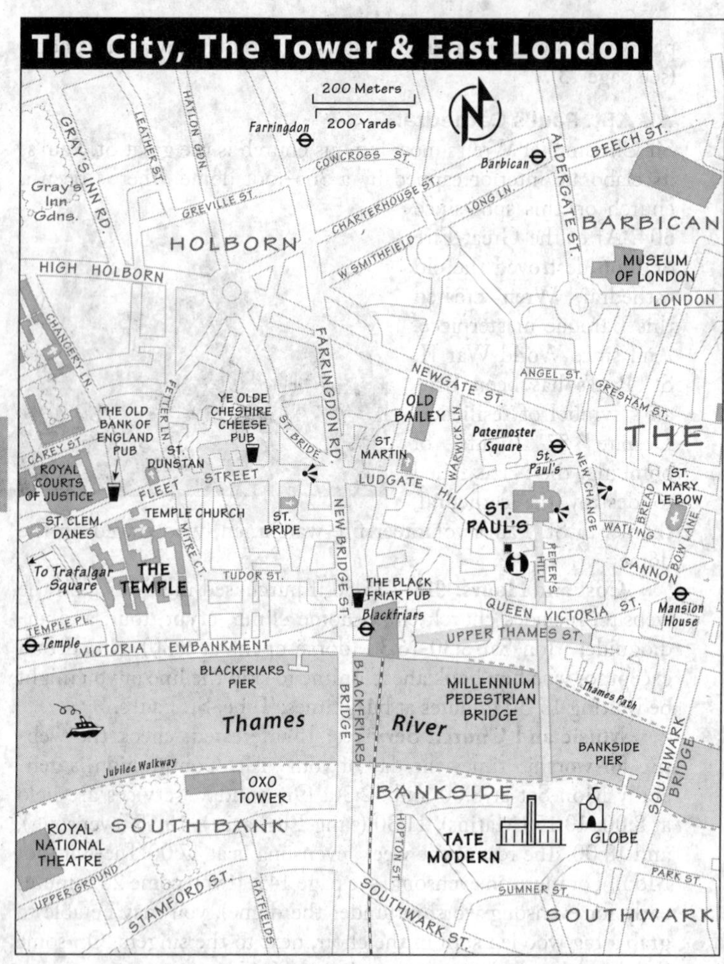

clear-eyed English reason. Though often the site of historic funerals (Queen Victoria and Winston Churchill), St. Paul's most famous ceremony was a wedding—when Prince Charles married Lady Diana Spencer in 1981.

Enter, buy your ticket, pick up the free visitor's map, and stand at the far back of the ❶ **nave,** behind the font. This big church feels big. At 515 feet long and 250 feet wide, it's Europe's fourth largest, after Rome (St. Peter's), Sevilla, and Milan. The spaciousness is accentuated by the relative lack of decoration. The simple, cream-colored ceiling and the clear glass in the windows light everything evenly. Wren wanted this: a simple, open church with nothing to hide. Unfortunately, only this entrance area keeps his original vision—the rest was encrusted with 19th-century Victorian ornamentation.

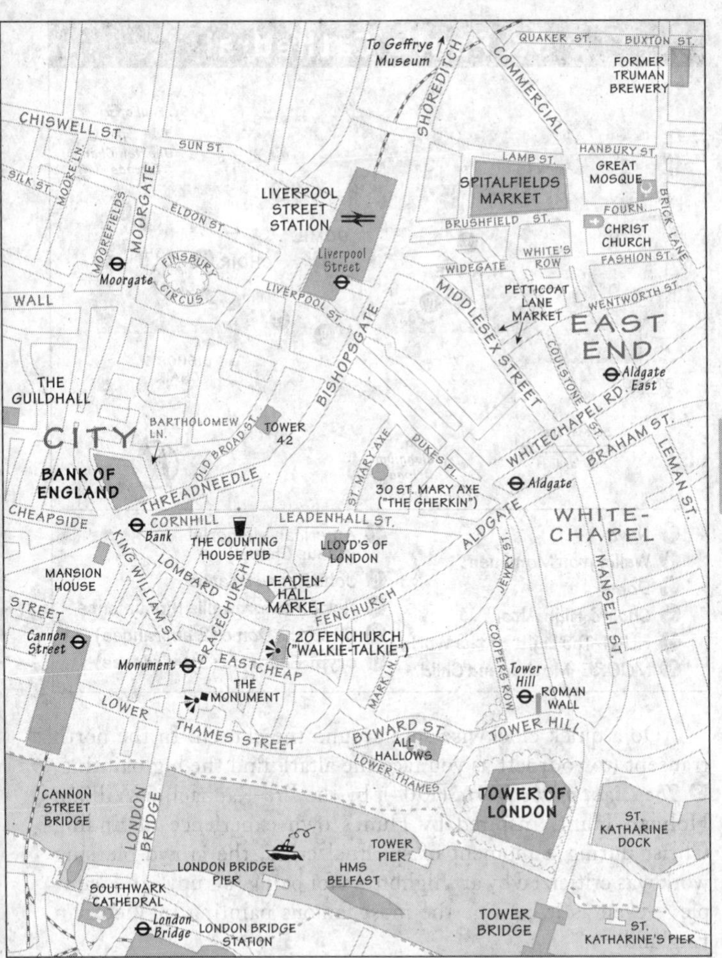

Ahead and on the left is the towering black-and-white ❷ **Wellington Monument.** Wren would have been appalled, but his church has become so central to England's soul that many national heroes are buried here (in the basement crypt).

The ❸ **dome** you see from here, painted with scenes from the life of St. Paul, is only the innermost of three. From the painted interior of the first dome, look up through the opening to see the light-filled lantern of the second dome. Finally, the whole thing is covered on the outside by the third and final dome, the shell of lead-covered wood that you see from the street. Wren's ingenious three-in-one design was psychological as well as functional—he wanted a low, shallow inner dome so worshippers wouldn't feel diminished. The ❹ **choir** area blocks your way, but you can see the **altar** at the far end under a golden canopy.

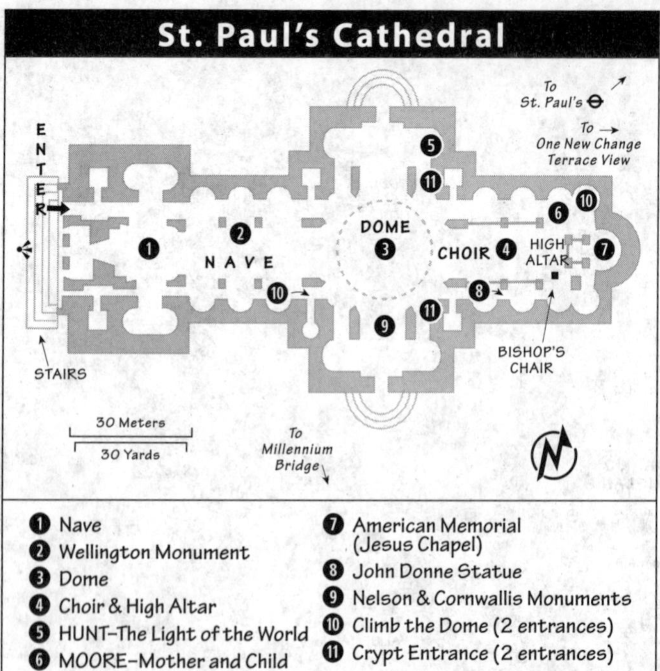

Do a quick clockwise spin around the church. In the north transept (to your left as you face the altar), find the big painting, ❺ ***The Light of the World*** (1904), by the Pre-Raphaelite William Holman Hunt. Inspired by Hunt's own experience of finding Christ during a moment of spiritual crisis, the crowd-pleasing work was criticized by art highbrows for being "syrupy" and "simple"—even as it became the most famous painting in Victorian England.

Along the left side of the choir is the modern statue ❻ ***Mother and Child,*** by the great modern sculptor Henry Moore. Typical of Moore's work, this Mary and Baby Jesus—inspired by the sight of British moms nursing babies in WWII bomb shelters—renders a traditional subject in an abstract, minimalist way.

The area behind the altar, with three bright and modern stained-glass windows, is the ❼ **American Memorial Chapel**—honoring the Americans who sacrificed their lives to save Britain in World War II. In colored panes that arch around the big windows, spot the American eagle (center window, to the left of Christ), George Washington (right window, upper-right corner), and symbols of all 50 states (find your state seal). In the carved wood beneath the windows, you'll see birds and foliage native to the US. The Roll of Honor (a 500-page book under glass, immediately behind the altar) lists the names of 28,000 US servicemen and women based in Britain who gave their lives during the war.

Around the other side of the choir is a shrouded statue honoring ❽ **John Donne** (1621–1631), a passionate preacher in old St. Paul's, as well as a great poet ("never wonder for whom the bell tolls—it tolls for thee"). In the south transept are monuments to military greats ❾ **Horatio Nelson,** who fought Napoleon, and **Charles Cornwallis,** who was finished off by George Washington at Yorktown.

Climbing the Dome: During your visit, you can climb 528 steps to reach the dome and great city views. Along the way, have some fun in the Whispering Gallery (257 steps up). Whisper sweet nothings into the wall, and your partner (and anyone else) standing far away can hear you. For best effects, try whispering (not talking) with your mouth close to the wall, while your partner stands a few dozen yards away with his or her ear to the wall.

Visiting the Crypt: The crypt is a world of historic bones and interesting cathedral models. Many legends are buried here—Horatio Nelson, who wore down Napoleon; the Duke of Wellington, who finished Napoleon off; and even Wren himself. Wren's actual tomb is marked by a simple black slab with no statue, though he considered this church to be his legacy. Back up in the nave, on the floor directly under the dome, is Christopher Wren's name and epitaph (written in Latin): "Reader, if you seek his monument, look around you."

LONDON

▲Old Bailey

To view the British legal system in action—lawyers in little blonde wigs speaking legalese with an upper-crust accent—spend a few minutes in the visitors' gallery at the Old Bailey courthouse, called the "Central Criminal Court." Don't enter under the dome; continue up the block about halfway to the modern part of the building—the entry is at Warwick Passage.

Cost and Hours: Free, generally Mon-Fri 10:00-13:00 & 14:00-17:00 depending on caseload, last entry at 12:40 and 15:40 but often closes an hour or so earlier, closed Sat-Sun, fewer cases in Aug; no kids under 14; 2 blocks northwest of St. Paul's on Old Bailey Street (down a tunnel called Warwick Passage, follow signs to public entrance), Tube: St. Paul's, tel. 020/7248-3277 www.cityoflondon.gov.uk.

Bag Check: Old Bailey has a strictly enforced policy of no bags, mobile phones, cameras, computers, or food. Small purses are OK (but no phones or cameras inside). You can check bags at the Capable Travel agency just down the street at 4 Old Bailey for

London's Best Views

Though London is a height-challenged city, you can get lofty perspectives on it from several high-flying places. For some viewpoints, you need to pay admission, and at the bars or restaurants, you'll need to buy a drink; the only truly free spots are Primrose Hill, the rooftop terrace of One New Change shopping mall (behind St. Paul's Cathedral), the Sky Garden at 20 Fenchurch, and the viewpoint in front of Greenwich's Royal Observatory.

London Eye: Ride the giant Ferris wheel for stunning London views. See page 109.

St. Paul's Dome: You'll earn a striking, unobstructed view by climbing hundreds of steps to the cramped balcony of the church's cupola. See page 99.

One New Change Rooftop Terrace: Get fine, free views of St. Paul's Cathedral and surroundings—nearly as good as those from St. Paul's Dome—from the rooftop terrace of the shopping mall just behind and east of the church.

Tate Modern: Take in a classic vista across the Thames from the restaurant/bar on the museum's sixth level. See page 113.

20 Fenchurch (a.k.a. "The Walkie-Talkie"): Get 360-degree views of London from the mostly enclosed Sky Garden, complete with a thoughtfully planned urban garden, bar, restaurants, and lots of locals. It's free to access but you'll need to make reservations in advance and bring photo ID (Mon-Fri 10:00-18:00, Sat-Sun 11:00-21:00, 20 Fenchurch Street, Tube: Monument, www.skygarden.london). If you can't get a reservation, try arriving before 10:00 (or 11:00 on weekends) and ask to go up. Once in, you can stay as long as you like.

National Portrait Gallery: A mod top-floor restaurant peers over Trafalgar Square and the Westminster neighborhood. See page 74.

£5/bag and £1/phone or camera; or at the nearby Museum of London for £1.

The Guildhall

Hiding out in The City six blocks northeast of St. Paul's on Gresham Street, the Guildhall offers visitors a grand medieval hall and a delightful painting gallery for free (Mon-Sat 10:00-17:00, Sun 12:00-16:00). This gathering place served as the meeting spot for guilds in medieval times and still hosts about 100 professional associations. The Guildhall Art Gallery gives insight into old London society with mostly Victorian paintings.

▲Museum of London

This museum tells the fascinating story of London, taking you on a walk from its pre-Roman beginnings to the present. It features London's distinguished citizens through history—from Nean-

Waterstones Bookstore: Its hip, low-key, top-floor café/bar has reasonable prices and sweeping views of the London Eye, Big Ben, and the Houses of Parliament (see page 29, on Sun bar closes one hour before bookstore, www.5thview.co.uk).

OXO Tower: Perched high over the Thames River, the building's upscale restaurant/bar boasts views over London and St. Paul's, with al fresco dining in good weather (Barge House Street, Tube: Blackfriars, tel. 020/7803-3888, www.harveynichols.com/restaurants/oxo-tower-london).

London Hilton, Park Lane: You'll spot Buckingham Palace, Hyde Park, and the London Eye from Galvin at Windows, a 28th-floor restaurant/bar in an otherwise nondescript hotel (22 Park Lane, Tube: Hyde Park Corner, tel. 020/7208-4021, www.galvinatwindows.com).

The Shard: The observation decks that cap this 1,020-foot-tall skyscraper offer London's most commanding views, but at an outrageously high price. See page 117.

Primrose Hill: For dramatic 360-degree city views, head to the huge grassy expanse at the summit of Primrose Hill, just north of Regent's Park (off Prince Albert Road, Tube: Chalk Farm or Camden Town, www.royalparks.org.uk/parks/the-regents-park).

The Thames River: Various companies run boat trips on the Thames, offering a unique vantage point and unobstructed, ever-changing views of great landmarks (see page 50).

Royal Observatory Greenwich: Enjoy sweeping views of Greenwich's grand buildings in the foreground, the Docklands' skyscrapers in the middle ground, and The City and central London in the distance. See page 128.

derthals, to Romans, to Elizabethans, to Victorians, to Mods, to today. The displays are chronological, spacious, and informative without being overwhelming. Scale models and costumes help you visualize everyday life in the city at different periods. In the last room, you'll see the museum's prized possession: the Lord Mayor's Coach, a golden carriage pulled by six white horses, looking as if it had pranced right out of the pages of *Cinderella*. There are enough whiz-bang multimedia displays (including the Plague and the Great Fire) to spice up otherwise humdrum artifacts. This regular stop for the local school kids gives the best overview of London history in town.

Cost and Hours: Free, daily 10:00-18:00, last admission an hour before closing, see the day's events board for special talks and tours, café, luggage lockers, 150 London Wall at Aldersgate Street,

LONDON

Tube: Barbican or St. Paul's plus a five-minute walk, tel. 020/7001-9844, www.museumoflondon.org.uk.

The Monument

Wren's recently-restored 202-foot-tall tribute to London's 1666 Great Fire is at the junction of Monument Street and Fish Street Hill. Climb the 311 steps inside the column for a monumental view of The City (£4, £10.50 combo-ticket with Tower Bridge, daily 9:30-18:00, until 17:30 Oct-March, Tube: Monument).

▲▲▲Tower of London

The Tower has served as a castle in wartime, a king's residence in peacetime, and, most notoriously, as the prison and execution site of rebels. You can see the crown jewels, take a witty Beefeater tour, and ponder the executioner's block that dispensed with Anne Boleyn, Sir Thomas More, and troublesome heirs to the throne.

Cost and Hours: £24.50, family-£61, entry fee includes Beefeater tour (described later); Tue-Sat 9:00-17:30, Sun-Mon 10:00-17:30; Nov-Feb closes one hour earlier; skippable audioguide-£4; Tube: Tower Hill, tel. 0844-482-7788, www.hrp.org.uk.

Advance Tickets: To avoid the long ticket-buying lines at the Tower, buy your ticket at the Trader's Gate gift shop, located down the steps from the Tower Hill Tube stop (tickets here are slightly cheaper than at the gate—they don't include the voluntary donation—and can be used any day). Tickets are also sold at various locations (such as travel agencies) throughout London. You can also try buying tickets, with credit card only, at the Tower Welcome Centre to the left of the normal ticket lines—though on busy days they may turn you away. It's easy to book online, but you must use your ticket within seven days of purchase (www.hrp.org.uk, 10 percent discount). You can also book by phone (tel. 0844-482-7799 within UK or tel. 011-44-20-3166-6000 from the US; £2 fee), then pick up your tickets at the Tower group ticket office.

More Crowd-Beating Tips: It's most crowded in summer, on weekends (especially Sundays), and during school holidays. Any time of year, the line for the crown jewels—the best on earth—can be just as long as the line for tickets. For fewer crowds, arrive before 10:00 and go straight for the jewels. Alternatively, arrive in the afternoon, tour the rest of the Tower first, and see the jewels an hour before closing time, when crowds die down.

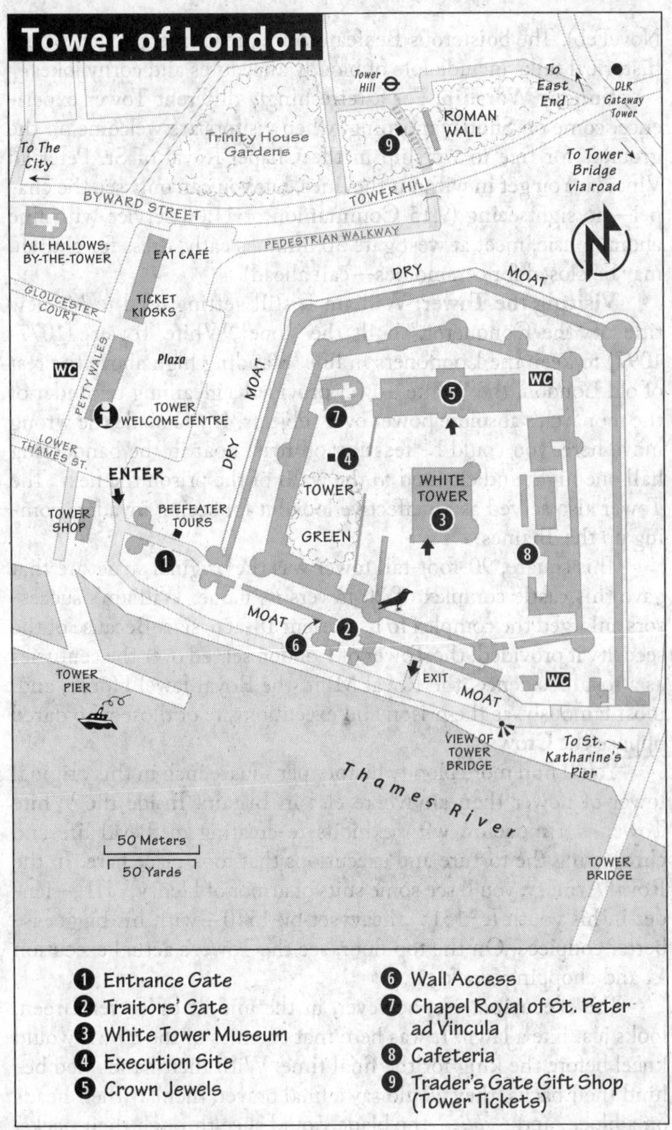

Yeoman Warder (Beefeater) Tours: Today, while the Tower's military purpose is history, it's still home to the Beefeaters—the 35 Yeoman Warders and their families. (The original duty of the Yeoman Warders was to guard the Tower, its prisoners, and the jewels.) The free, worthwhile, one-hour Beefeater tours leave every 30 minutes from just inside the entrance gate (first tour Tue-Sat at 10:00, Sun-Mon at 10:30, last one at 15:30—or 14:30 in

Nov-Feb). The boisterous Beefeaters are great entertainers, whose historical talks include lots of bloody anecdotes and corny jokes.

Sunday Worship: For a refreshingly different Tower experience, come on Sunday morning, when visitors are welcome on the grounds for free to worship in the Chapel Royal of St. Peter ad Vincula. You get in without the lines, but you can only see the chapel—no sightseeing (9:15 Communion or 11:00 service with fine choral music, meet at west gate 30 minutes early, dress for church, may be closed for ceremonies—call ahead).

Visiting the Tower: William I, still getting used to his new title of "the Conqueror," built the stone "White Tower" (1077-1097) to keep the Londoners in line. Standing high above the rest of old London, the White Tower provided a gleaming reminder of the monarch's absolute power over subjects. If you made the wrong move here, you could be feasting on roast boar in the banqueting hall one night and chained to the walls of the prison the next. The Tower also served as an effective lookout for seeing invaders coming up the Thames.

This square, 90-foot-tall tower was the original structure that gave this castle complex of 20 towers its name. William's successors enlarged the complex to its present 18-acre size. Because of the security it provided, the Tower of London served over the centuries as a royal residence, the Royal Mint, the Royal Jewel House, and, most famously, as the prison and execution site of those who dared oppose the Crown.

You'll find more bloody history per square inch in this original tower of power than anywhere else in Britain. Inside the White Tower is a **museum** with exhibits re-creating medieval life and chronicling the torture and executions that took place here. In the Royal Armory, you'll see some suits of armor of Henry VIII—slender in his youth (c. 1515), heavyset by 1540—with his bigger-is-better codpiece. On the top floor, see the Tower's actual execution ax and chopping block.

The **execution site,** however, in the middle of Tower Green, looks just like a lawn. It was here that enemies of the crown would kneel before the king for the final time. With their hands tied behind their backs, they would say a final prayer, then lay their heads on a block, and—*shlit*—the blade would slice through their necks, their heads tumbling to the ground. Tower Green was the most prestigious execution site at the Tower. Henry VIII axed a couple of his ex-wives here (divorced readers can insert their own joke), including Anne Boleyn and his fifth wife, teenage Catherine Howard (for more on Henry, see the sidebar on page 106).

The Tower's hard stone and glittering **crown jewels** represent the ultimate power of the monarch. The Sovereign's Scepter is encrusted with the world's largest cut diamond—the 530-carat Star of Africa, beefy as a quarter-pounder. The Crown of the Queen Mother (Elizabeth II's famous mum, who died in 2002) has the 106-carat Koh-I-Noor diamond glittering on the front (considered unlucky for male rulers, it only adorns the crown of the king's wife). The Imperial State Crown is what the Queen wears for official functions such as the State Opening of Parliament. Among its 3,733 jewels are Queen Elizabeth I's former earrings (the hanging pearls, top center), a stunning 13th-century ruby look-alike in the center, and Edward the Confessor's ring (the blue sapphire on top, in the center of the Maltese cross of diamonds).

The Tower was defended by state-of-the-art **walls** and fortifications in the 13th century. Walking along them offers a good look at the walls, along with a fine view of the famous Tower Bridge, with its twin towers and blue spans (described next).

After your visit, consider taking the boat to Greenwich from here (see cruise info on page 54).

Tower Bridge

The iconic Tower Bridge (often mistakenly called London Bridge) has been recently painted and restored. The hydraulically powered drawbridge was built in 1894 to accommodate the growing East End. While fully modern, its design was a retro Neo-Gothic look.

The bridge is most interesting when the drawbridge lifts to let ships pass, as it does a thousand times a year (best viewed from the Tower side of the Thames). For the bridge-lifting schedule, check the website or call.

You can tour the bridge at the **Tower Bridge Exhibition,** with a history display and a peek at the Victorian engine room that lifts the span. Included in your entrance is the chance to cross the bridge—138 feet above the road along a see-through glass walkway. As an exhibit, it's overpriced, though the adrenaline rush and spectacular city views from the walkways may help justify the cost.

Cost and Hours: £9, £10.50 combo-ticket with The Monument, daily 10:00-18:00 in summer, 9:30-17:30 in winter, enter at northwest tower, Tube: Tower Hill, tel. 020/7403-3761, www.towerbridge.org.uk.

Nearby: The best remaining bit of London's **Roman Wall** is just north of the Tower (at the Tower Hill Tube station). The chic **St. Katharine Dock,** just east of Tower Bridge, has private yachts and mod shops. Across the bridge, on the South Bank, is the upscale Butlers Wharf area, as well as City Hall, museums, the Jubilee Walkway, and, towering overhead, the Shard. Or you can head north to Liverpool Street Station and stroll London's East End (described next).

Henry VIII (1491-1547)

The notorious king who single-handedly transformed England was a true Renaissance Man—six feet tall, handsome, charismatic, well-educated, and brilliant. He spoke English, Latin, French, and Spanish. A legendary athlete, he hunted, played tennis, and jousted with knights and kings. He played the lute and wrote folk songs; his "Pastime with Good Company" is still being performed. When 17-year-old Henry, the second monarch of the House of Tudor, was crowned king in Westminster Abbey, all of England rejoiced.

Henry left affairs of state in the hands of others, and filled his days with sports, war, dice, women, and the arts. But in 1529, Henry's personal life became a political atom bomb, and it changed the course of history. Henry wanted a divorce, partly because his wife had become too old to bear him a son, and partly because he'd fallen in love with Anne Boleyn, a younger woman who stubbornly refused to be just the king's mistress. Henry begged the pope for an annulment, but—for political reasons, not moral ones—the pope refused. Henry went ahead and divorced his wife anyway, and he was excommunicated.

The event sparked the English Reformation. With his defiance, Henry rejected papal authority in England. He forced monasteries to close, sold off some church land, and confiscated everything else for himself and the Crown. Within a decade, monastic institutions that had operated for centuries were left empty and gutted (many ruined sites can be visited today, including the abbeys of Glastonbury, St. Mary's at York, Rievaulx, and Lindisfarne). Meanwhile, the Catholic Church was reorganized into the (Anglican) Church of England, with Henry as its head. Though Henry himself basically adhered to Catholic doctrine, he discouraged the veneration of saints and relics, and commissioned an English translation of the Bible. Hard-core Catholics had to assume a low profile. Many English welcomed this break from Italian religious influence, but others rebelled. For the next few generations, England would suffer through bitter Catholic-Protestant differences.

Henry famously had six wives. The issue was not his love life (which could have been satisfied by his numerous mistresses), but the politics of royal succession. To guarantee the Tudor family's dominance, he needed a male heir born by a recognized queen.

Henry's first marriage, to Catherine of Aragon, had been arranged to cement an alliance with her parents, Ferdinand and Isabel of Spain. Catherine bore Henry a daughter, but no sons. Next came Anne Boleyn, who also gave birth to a daughter. After a turbulent few years with Anne and several miscarriages, a frustrated Henry had her beheaded at the Tower of London. His next wife, Jane Seymour, finally had a son (but Jane died soon after giving birth). A blind marriage with Anne of Cleves ended quickly when she proved to be both politically useless and ugly—the "Flanders Mare." Next, teen bride Catherine Howard ended up cheating on Henry, so she was executed. Henry finally found comfort—but no children—in his later years with his final wife, Catherine Parr.

In 1536 Henry suffered a serious accident while jousting. His health would never be the same. Increasingly, he suffered from festering boils and violent mood swings, and he became morbidly obese, tipping the scales at 400 pounds with a 54-inch waist.

Henry's last years were marked by paranoia, sudden rages, and despotism. He gave his perceived enemies the pink slip in his signature way—charged with treason and beheaded. (Ironically, Henry's own heraldic motto was "Coeur Loyal"—true heart.) Once-wealthy England was becoming depleted, thanks to Henry's expensive habits, which included making war on France, building and acquiring palaces (he had 50), and collecting fine tapestries and archery bows.

Henry forged a large legacy. He expanded the power of the monarchy, making himself the focus of a rising modern nation-state. Simultaneously, he strengthened Parliament—largely because it agreed with his policies. He annexed Wales, and imposed English rule on Ireland (provoking centuries of resentment). He expanded the navy, paving the way for Britannia to soon rule the waves. And—thanks to Henry's marital woes—England would forever be a Protestant nation.

When Henry died at age 55, he was succeeded by his nine-year-old son by Jane Seymour, Edward VI. Weak and sickly, Edward died six years later. Next to rule was Mary, Henry's daughter from his first marriage. A staunch Catholic, she tried to brutally reverse England's Protestant Reformation, earning the nickname "Bloody Mary." Finally came Henry's daughter with Anne Boleyn—Queen Elizabeth I, who ruled a prosperous, expanding England, seeing her father's seeds blossom into the English Renaissance.

London abounds with "Henry" sights. He was born in Greenwich (at today's Old Royal Naval College) and was crowned in Westminster Abbey. He built a palace along Whitehall and enjoyed another at Hampton Court. At the National Portrait Gallery, you can see portraits of some of Henry's wives, and at the Tower you can see where he executed them. Henry is buried alongside his final wife at Windsor Castle.

Sights in East London

▲East End

The East End has a long history as London's poorer side of town—even in medieval times. These days, it still lacks the posh refinement of the West End—but the area just beyond Liverpool Street Station is now one of London's hippest, most fun spots. It boasts a colorful mix of bustling markets, late-night dance clubs, the Bangladeshi neighborhood (called "Banglatown"), and tenements of Jack the Ripper's London, all in the shadow of glittering new skyscrapers. Head up Brick Lane for a meal in "the curry capital of Europe," or check out the former Truman Brewery, which now houses a Sunday market, cool shops, and Café 1001 (good coffee). This neighborhood is best on Sunday afternoons, when the Spitalfields, Petticoat Lane, and Backyard markets thrive (for more on these markets, see page 135).

▲Geffrye Museum

This low-key but well-organized museum—housed in an 18th-century almshouse—is located north of Liverpool Street Station. It's a strip of 11 rooms, each furnished as a living room from a different age and each very well-described. It's an intimate peek at the middle class as its comforts evolved from 1600 to 2000. In summer, explore the fragrant herb garden.

Cost and Hours: Free, Tue-Sun 10:00-17:00, closed Mon, garden open April-Oct, 136 Kingsland Road, tel. 020/7739-9893, www.geffrye-museum.org.uk.

Getting There: Take the Tube to Liverpool Street, then ride the bus 10 minutes north (bus #149 or #242—leave station through Bishopsgate exit and head left a few steps to find stop; hop off at the Pearson Street stop, just after passing the brick museum on the right). Or take the East London line on the Overground to the Hoxton stop, which is right next to the museum (Tube tickets and Oyster cards also valid on Overground).

Sights on the South Bank

The South Bank of the Thames is a thriving arts and cultural center, tied together by the riverfront Jubilee Walkway.

▲Jubilee Walkway

This riverside path is a popular, pub-crawling pedestrian promenade that stretches all along the South Bank, offering grand views of the Houses of Parliament and St. Paul's. On a sunny day, this is the place to see Londoners out strolling. The Walkway hugs the river except just east of London Bridge, where it cuts inland for a couple of blocks. It has been expanded into a 60-mile "Greenway" circling the city, including the 2012 Olympics site.

▲▲London Eye

This giant Ferris wheel, towering above London opposite Big Ben, is one of the world's highest observational wheels and London's answer to the Eiffel Tower. Riding it is a memorable experience, even though London doesn't have much of a skyline, and the price is borderline outrageous. Whether you ride or not, the wheel is a sight to behold.

The experience starts with an engaging four-minute show combining a 3-D movie with wind and water effects. Then it's time to spin around the Eye. Designed like a giant bicycle wheel, it's a pan-European undertaking: British steel and Dutch engineering, with Czech, German, French, and Italian mechanical parts. It's also very "green," running extremely efficiently and virtually silently. Twenty-five people ride in each of its 32 air-conditioned capsules (representing the boroughs of London) for the 30-minute rotation (you go around only once). From the top of this 443-foot-high wheel—the second-highest public viewpoint in the city—even Big Ben looks small.

Cost: £21.50, family ticket available, about 10 percent cheaper if bought online. Combo-tickets save money if you plan on visiting Madame Tussauds. Buy tickets in advance at www.londoneye.com, by calling 0870-500-0600, or in person at the box office (in the corner of the County Hall building nearest the Eye).

Hours: Daily 10:00-20:30, until 21:30 or later in July and August, check the website for latest schedule, these are last-ascent times, closed Dec 25 and a few days in Jan for annual maintenance, Tube: Waterloo or Westminster. Thames boats come and go from Waterloo Pier at the foot of the wheel.

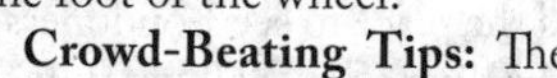

Crowd-Beating Tips: The London Eye is busiest between 11:00 and 17:00, especially on weekends year-round and every day in July and August. You might have to wait up to 30 minutes to buy your ticket, then another 30-45 minutes to board your capsule—it's best to call ahead or go online to prebook your ticket during these times. To retrieve your ticket at the sight, punch your confirmation code into the machine in the ticket office (or pick it up in the short "Groups and Ticket Collection" line at desks #15-16). Even if you prereserve, you still have to wait a bit to board the wheel. You can pay an extra £10 for a Fast Track ticket that lets you jump the queue, but it's probably not worth the expense.

By the Eye: The area next to the London Eye has developed a cotton-candy ambience of kitschy, kid-friendly attractions. There's a game arcade, an aquarium, and the Shrek's Adventure amusement ride.

▲▲Imperial War Museum

This impressive museum covers the wars of the last century—from World War I biplanes, to the rise of fascism, the Cold War, the Cuban Missile Crisis, the Troubles in Northern Ireland, the wars in Iraq and Afghanistan, and terrorism. Rather than glorify war, the museum encourages an understanding of the history of modern warfare and the wartime experience, including the effect it has on the everyday lives of people back home. The museum's coverage never neglects the human side of one of civilization's more uncivilized, persistent traits.

Allow plenty of time, as this powerful museum—with lots of artifacts and video clips—can be engrossing. The highlights are the new WWI galleries (renovated to commemorate the 100-year anniversary of that conflict) and the WWII area, the "Secret War" section, and the Holocaust exhibit. War wonks love the place, as do general history buffs who enjoy patiently reading displays. For the rest, there are enough interactive experiences and multimedia exhibits and submarines for the kids to climb in to keep it interesting.

The museum (which sits in an inviting park equipped with an equally inviting café) is housed in what had been the Royal Bethlam Hospital. Also known as "the Bedlam asylum," the place was so wild that it gave the world a new word for chaos. Back in Victorian times, locals—without reality shows and YouTube—paid admission to visit the asylum on weekends for entertainment.

Cost and Hours: Free, £5 suggested donation, daily 10:00-18:00, special exhibits extra, various free audioguides may be available—ask at the info desk, Tube: Lambeth North or Elephant and Castle; buses #3, #12, and #159 come here from Westminster area; tel. 020/7416-5000, www.iwm.org.uk.

Visiting the Museum: Start with the atrium to grasp the massive scale of warfare as you wander among and under notable battle machines, then head directly for the museum's latest pride and joy: the recently renovated **WWI galleries.** Here, firsthand accounts connect the blunt reality of a brutal war with the contributions, heartache, and efforts of a nation. Exhibits cover the various theaters and war at sea, as well as life on the home front.

As you escape unscathed, pause to ponder the irony of how different this museum would be if the war to end all wars had lived up to its name. Instead, the museum, much like history, builds on itself. Ascending to the first floor, you'll find the permanent **Turning Points** galleries progressing up to and through World War II and including sections explaining Blitzkrieg and its effects (see an actual Nazi parachute bomb like the ones that devastated London). For a deeper understanding of life during these decades, visit the **Family in Wartime** exhibit to see London through the eyes of an ordinary family.

The second floor houses the **Secret War** exhibit, which peeks into the intrigues of espionage in World Wars I and II through present-day security. You'll learn about MI5 (Britain's domestic spy corps), MI6 (their international spies—like the CIA), and the Special Operations Executive (SOE), who led espionage efforts during World War II. The exhibit features actual surveillance equipment and poses challenging questions about the role of secrecy in government.

The third floor houses various (and often rotating) temporary art and film exhibits speckled with military-themed works including **John Singer Sargent**'s *Gassed* (1919), showing besieged troops in World War I, and other giant canvases.

The fourth-floor section on the **Holocaust,** one of the best

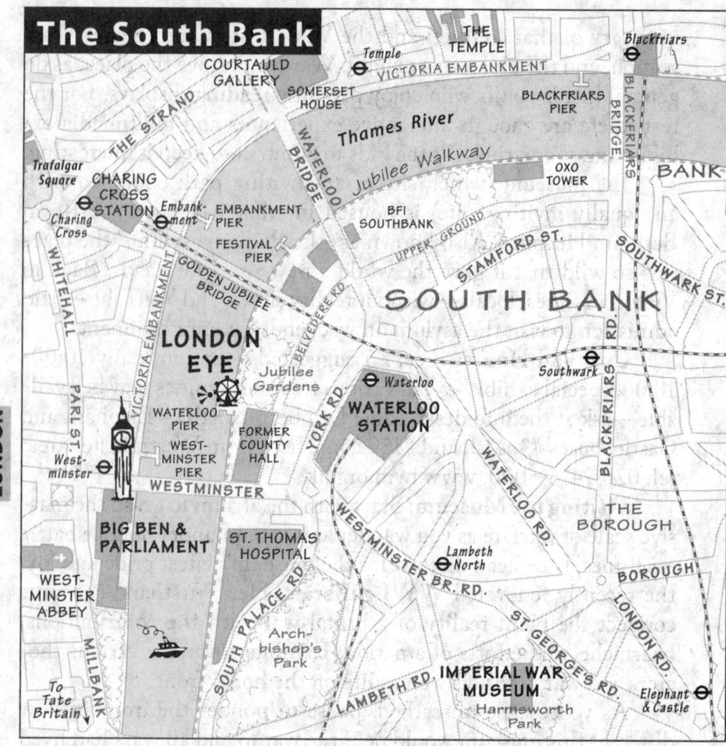

on the subject anywhere, tells the story with powerful videos, artifacts, and fine explanations. While it's not the same as actually being at one of Europe's many powerful Holocaust sites, the exhibits are compelling enough to evoke the same emotions.

Crowning the museum on the fifth floor is the Lord Ashcroft Gallery and the **Extraordinary Heroes** display. Here, more than 250 stories celebrate Britain's highest military award for bravery with the world's largest collection of Victoria Cross medals. Civilians who earned the George Cross medal for bravery are also honored.

FROM TATE MODERN TO CITY HALL

These sights are in Southwark (SUTH-uck), the core of the tourist's South Bank. Southwark was for centuries the place Londoners would go to escape the rules and decency of the city and let their hair down. Bearbaiting, brothels, rollicking pubs, and theater—you name the dream, and it could be fulfilled just across the Thames. A run-down warehouse district through the 20th century, it's been gentrified with classy restaurants, office parks, pedestrian promenades, major sights (such as the Tate Modern and Shakespeare's Globe), and a colorful collection of lesser sights. The area is easy on foot and a scenic—though circuitous—way to connect the Tower of London with St. Paul's.

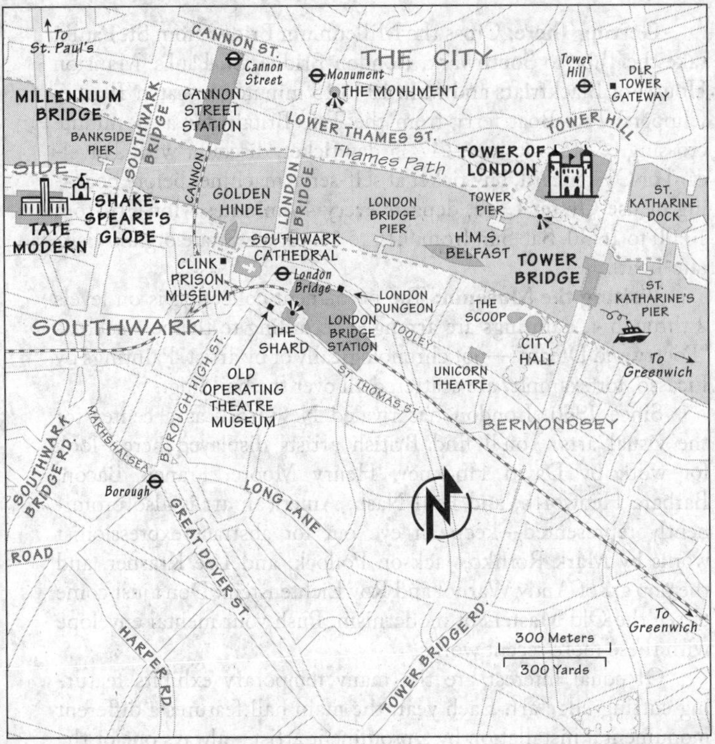

▲▲Tate Modern

Dedicated in the spring of 2000, the striking museum fills a derelict old power station across the river from St. Paul's—it opened the new century with art from the previous one. Its powerhouse collection includes Dalí, Picasso, Warhol, and much more.

Cost and Hours: Free, but £4 donation appreciated, fee for special exhibitions; open daily 10:00-18:00, Fri-Sat until 22:00, last entry to special exhibits 45 minutes before closing, especially crowded on weekend days (crowds thin out on Fri and Sat evenings); videoguide-£4.50, free 45-minute guided tours are offered about four times daily (ask for schedule at info desk), view restaurant on top floor, no photos beyond entrance hall; tel. 020/7887-8888, www.tate.org.uk.

Getting There: Cross the Millennium Bridge from St. Paul's; take the Tube to Southwark, London Bridge, St. Paul's, Mansion House, or Blackfriars and walk 10 to 15 minutes; or catch Thames Clippers' Tate Boat ferry from the Tate Britain for a 15-minute crossing (£7.15 one-way, £17.35 day ticket, discount with Travelcard or Oyster card, buy ticket at self-serve machines before boarding or use Oyster Card, departs every 40 minutes Mon-Fri from 10:00 to 16:30, Sat-Sun from 9:15 to 18:40, www.tate.org.uk/visit/tate-boat).

Visiting the Museum: The permanent collection is on levels 2 through 4. Paintings are arranged according to theme—such as "Poetry and Dream"—not chronologically or by artist. Paintings by Picasso, for example, are scattered all over the building.

Since 1960, London has rivaled New York as a center for the visual arts. You'll find British artists displayed here—look for work by David Hockney, Henry Moore, Francis Bacon, Barbara Hepworth, and Paul Nash. American art is also prominently represented—keep an eye out for abstract expressionist works by Mark Rothko, Jackson Pollock, and Lee Krasner, and the pop art of Andy Warhol and Roy Lichtenstein. Don't just come to see the Old Masters of modernism. Push your mental envelope with these more recent works.

Of equal interest are the many temporary exhibits featuring cutting-edge art. Each year, the main hall features a different monumental installation by a prominent artist—always one of the highlights of the art world. The Tate is constructing a new wing to the south, which will double the museum's exhibition space. The new wing is opening bit by bit and, once it's finished, the permanent exhibits will likely be rearranged, with some pieces moving to the new section.

▲Millennium Bridge

The pedestrian bridge links St. Paul's Cathedral and the Tate Modern across the Thames. This is London's first new bridge in a century. When it opened, the $25 million bridge wiggled when people walked on it, so it promptly closed for repairs; 20 months and $8 million later, it reopened. Nicknamed the "blade of light" for its sleek minimalist design (370 yards long, four yards wide, stainless steel with teak planks), its clever aerodynamic handrails deflect wind over the heads of pedestrians.

▲▲Shakespeare's Globe

This replica of the original Globe Theatre was built, half-timbered and thatched, as it was in Shakespeare's time. (This is the first thatched roof constructed in London since they were outlawed after the Great Fire of 1666.) The Globe originally accommodated 2,200 seated and another 1,000 standing. Today, slightly smaller and leaving space for reasonable aisles, the theater holds 800 seated and 600 groundlings. Its promoters brag that the theater melds "the three A's"—actors, audience, and architecture—with each contributing to the play. The working theater hosts authentic performances of Shakespeare's plays with actors in period costumes, modern interpretations of his works, and some works by other playwrights. For details on attending a play, see page 143.

The Globe complex has four parts: the Globe theater itself, the box office, a museum (called the Exhibition), and the Sam Wanamaker Playhouse (an indoor Jacobean theater around back). The Playhouse, which hosts performances through the winter, is horseshoe-shaped, intimate (seating fewer than 350), and sometimes uses authentic candle-lighting for period performances. The repertoire focuses less on Shakespeare and more on the work of his contemporaries (Jonson, Marlow, Fletcher), as well as concerts.

Cost: £13.50 ticket (good all day) includes Exhibition, audioguide, and 40-minute tour of the Globe; when theater is in use, you can tour the Exhibition only for £6.

Hours: The complex is open daily 9:00-17:30. Tours start every 30 minutes; during Globe theater season (late April-mid-Oct), last tour Mon at 17:00, Tue-Sat at 12:30, Sun at 11:30—it's safest to arrive for a tour before noon; located on the South Bank over the Millennium Bridge from St. Paul's, Tube: Mansion House or London Bridge plus a 10-minute walk; tel. 020/7902-1400, box office tel. 020/7401-9919, www.shakespearesglobe.com.

Visiting the Globe: You browse on your own in the **Exhibition** (with the included audioguide) through displays of Elizabethan-era costumes and makeup, music, script-printing, and special effects (the displays change). There are early folios and objects that were dug up on site. Videos and scale models help put Shakespearean theater within the context of the times. (The Globe opened one year after England mastered the seas by defeating the Spanish Armada. The debut play was Shakespeare's *Julius Caesar.*) You'll also learn how they built the replica in modern times, using Elizabethan materials

and techniques. Take advantage of the touch screens to delve into specific topics.

You must **tour the theater** at the time stamped on your ticket, but you can come back to the Exhibition museum afterward. A guide (usually an actor) leads you into the theater to see the stage and the various seating areas for the different classes of people. You take a seat and learn how the new Globe is similar to the old Globe (open-air performances, standing-room by the stage, no curtain) and how it's different (female actors today, lights for night performances, concrete floor). It's not a backstage tour—you don't see dressing rooms or costume shops or sit in on rehearsals—but the guides are energetic, theatrical, and knowledgeable, bringing the Elizabethan period to life.

Eating: The Swan at the Globe café offers a sit-down restaurant (for lunch and dinner, reservations recommended, tel. 020/7928-9444), a drinks-and-plates bar, and a sandwich-and-coffee cart (daily 9:00-closing, depending on performance times).

The Clink Prison Museum

Proudly the "original clink," this was, until 1780, where law-abiding citizens threw Southwark troublemakers. Today, it's a low-tech torture museum filling grotty old rooms with papier-mâché gore. There are storyboards about those unfortunate enough to be thrown in the Clink, but little that seriously deals with the fascinating problem of law and order in Southwark, where 18th-century Londoners went for a good time.

Cost and Hours: Overpriced at £7.50; July-Sept daily 10:00-21:00; Oct-June Mon-Fri 10:00-18:00, Sat-Sun until 19:30; 1 Clink Street, Tube: London Bridge, tel. 020/7403-0900, www.clink.co.uk.

Golden Hinde Replica

This is a full-size replica of the 16th-century warship in which Sir Francis Drake circumnavigated the globe from 1577 to 1580. Commanding the original ship (now long gone), Drake earned his reputation as history's most successful pirate. This replica, however, has logged more than 100,000 miles, including a voyage around the world. While the ship is fun to see, its interior is not worth touring.

Cost and Hours: £6, daily 10:00-17:00, Tube: London Bridge, ticket office just up Pickfords Wharf from the ship, tel. 020/7403-0123, www.goldenhinde.com.

▲Southwark Cathedral

While made a cathedral only in 1905, it's been the neighborhood church since the 13th century, and comes with some interesting history. The enthusiastic docents give impromptu tours if you ask.

Cost and Hours: Free, but £4 donation requested, Mon-Fri 8:00-18:00, Sat-Sun 8:30-18:00, guidebook-£4.50, Tube: London Bridge, tel. 020/7367-6700, http://cathedral.southwark.anglican.org.

Music: The cathedral hosts evensong Sun at 15:00, Tue-Fri 17:30, Sat at 16:00; they also host organ recitals Mon at 13:00 and music recitals Tue at 15:15 (call or check website to confirm times of evensong and recitals).

▲Old Operating Theatre Museum and Herb Garret

Climb a tight and creaky wooden spiral staircase to a church attic where you'll find a garret used to dry medicinal herbs, a fascinating exhibit on Victorian surgery, cases of well-described 19th-century medical paraphernalia, and a special look at "anesthesia, the defeat of pain." Then you stumble upon Britain's oldest operating theater, where limbs were sawed off way back in 1821.

Cost and Hours: £6.50, borrowable laminated descriptions, daily 10:30-17:00, closed Dec 15-Jan 5, 9a St. Thomas Street, Tube: London Bridge, tel. 020/7188-2679, www.thegarret.org.uk.

The Shard

Rocketing dramatically 1,020 feet above the south end of the London Bridge, this addition to London's skyline is by far the tallest building in Western Europe. Designed by Renzo Piano (best known as the co-architect of Paris' Pompidou Center), the glass-clad pyramid shimmers in the sun and its prickly top glows like the city's nightlight after dark. Its uppermost floors are set aside as public viewing galleries, but the ticket price is as outrageously high as the building itself, especially given that it's a bit far from London's most exciting landmarks. The Aqua Shard bar on the 31st floor offers views from half the height for the price of a fancy drink (free to ride up, but if they're at capacity they can turn you away, bar open 12:00-24:00; no sportswear, shorts, or flip-flops; access the bar from separate entrance on St. Thomas Street, www.aquashard.co.uk). For a list of cheaper view opportunities in London, see the sidebar on page 100.

Cost and Hours: £25 if booked at least a day in advance, £30 for same-day reservations; book as soon as you have reasonable chance of assuring decent weather, least crowded on weekday mornings, but perhaps better photo opportunities in the early evening (less haze); daily 10:00-22:00, last entry slot at 21:00; Tube: London Bridge—use London Bridge exit and follow signs, tel. 0844-499-7111, www.theviewfromtheshard.com.

Ascending the Tower: From the entrance on Joiner Street (just off St. Thomas Street), you'll take a two-part elevator ride up to the 68th floor, then climb up one story to the main observation platform. It's equipped with cool telescopes that label major landmarks, and even let you see how the view from here would appear at other times of the day. From here you've got great views of St. Paul's, the Tower of London, Southwark Cathedral (straight down), and, in the distance, the 2012 Olympic stadium in one direction, and the Houses of Parliament in the other (find Buckingham Palace, just left of the Eye). On the clearest days, you can see 40 miles out, and a few people say they've been able to make out ships on the North Sea. Even in bad weather it's mesmerizing to watch the constant movement of the city's transit system, which looks like a model-train set from this height. Ascending to the 72nd floor gets you to the open-air deck, where the wind roars over the glass enclosure. As you look up, try to picture Prince Andrew rappelling off the very top, which he and 40 others did in 2012 as a charity fundraising stunt.

HMS *Belfast*

The last big-gun armored warship of World War II clogs the Thames just upstream from the Tower Bridge. This huge vessel—now manned with wax sailors—thrills kids who always dreamed of sitting in a turret shooting off their imaginary guns. If you're into WWII warships, this is the ultimate. Otherwise, it's just lots of exercise with a nice view of the Tower Bridge.

Cost and Hours: Adult-£16, kids 5-15-£8, kids under 5-free, includes audioguide, daily March-Oct 10:00-18:00, Nov-Feb 10:00-17:00, last entry one hour before closing, Tube: London Bridge, tel. 020/7940-6300, www.iwm.org.uk/visits/hms-belfast.

City Hall

The glassy, egg-shaped building near the south end of Tower Bridge is London's City Hall, designed by Sir Norman Foster, the architect who worked on London's Millennium Bridge and Berlin's Reichstag. Nicknamed "the Armadillo," City Hall houses the office of London's mayor—it's here that the mayor consults with the Assembly representatives of the city's 25 districts. An interior spiral ramp allows visitors to watch and hear the action below in the Assembly Chamber—ride the lift to floor 2 (the highest visitors can go) and spiral down. On the lower ground floor is a large aerial photograph of London and a handy cafeteria. Next to City Hall is the outdoor amphitheater called The Scoop (see page 146).

Cost and Hours: Free, open to visitors Mon-Thu 8:30-18:00, Fri 8:30-17:30, closed Sat-Sun; Tube: London Bridge station plus

10-minute walk, or Tower Hill station plus 15-minute walk; tel. 020/7983-4000, www.london.gov.uk.

Sights in West London

▲▲Tate Britain

One of Europe's great art houses, Tate Britain specializes in British painting from the 16th century through modern times. This is people's art, with realistic paintings rooted in the people, landscape, and stories of the British Isles. The recently-renovated Tate shows off Hogarth's stage sets, Gainsborough's ladies, Blake's angels, Constable's clouds, Turner's tempests, the naturalistic realism of the Pre-Raphaelites, and the camera-eye portraits of Hockney and Freud.

Cost and Hours: Free but £4 donation requested, admission fee for special exhibits; daily 10:00-18:00, last entry 45 minutes before closing; map-£1 suggested donation; free tours generally daily (ask at the information desk or call ahead), or use the Tate's Wi-Fi to download their handy room-by-room audio tour or smartphone app; café and restaurant, tel. 020/7887-8888, www.tate.org.uk.

Getting There: It's on the Thames River, south of Big Ben and north of Vauxhall Bridge. Tube to Pimlico, then walk seven minutes. Or hop on the Tate Boat museum ferry from Tate Modern (for details, see page 55).

Visiting the Museum: Works from the early centuries are located in the west half of the building, 20th-century art is in the east half, and the works of J. M. W. Turner are in an adjacent wing (the Clore Gallery). Certain artists' work is placed in special rooms outside the chronological flow. Other rooms focus on a particular aspect of British art. The Tate's great strength is championing contemporary British art in special exhibitions—there are two exhibition spaces (one free, the other usually requiring separate admission).

1700s—Art Blossoms: With peace at home (under three King Georges), a strong overseas economy, and a growing urban center in London, England's artistic life began to bloom. As the English grew more sophisticated, so did their portraits. Painters branched out into other subjects, capturing slices of everyday life (find William Hogarth, with his unflinchingly honest portraits, and Thomas Gainsborough's elegant, educated women). The Royal

Academy added a veneer of classical Greece to even the simplest subjects.

1800-1850—The Industrial Revolution: Newfangled inventions were everywhere. Many artists rebelled against "progress" and the modern world. They escaped the dirty cities to commune with nature (Constable and the Romantics). Or they found a new spirituality in intense human emotions (dramatic scenes from history or literature). Or they left the modern world altogether.

William Blake, whose work hangs in a darkened room to protect his watercolors from deterioration, painted angels, not the dull material world. Blake turned his gaze inward, illustrating the glorious visions of the soul. His pen and watercolor sketches glow with an unearthly aura. In visions of the Christian heaven or Dante's hell, his figures have superhero musculature. The colors are almost translucent.

1837-1901—The Victorian Era: In the world's wealthiest nation, the prosperous middle class dictated taste in art. They admired paintings that were realistic (showcasing the artist's talent and work ethic), depicting Norman Rockwell-style slices of everyday life. We see families and ordinary people eating, working, and relaxing. Some paintings tug at the heartstrings, with scenes of parting couples, the grief of death, or the joy of families reuniting.

Overdosed with the gushy sentimentality of their day, a band of 20-year-old artists—including Sir John Everett Millais, Dante Gabriel Rossetti, and William Holman Hunt—said "Enough!" and dedicated themselves to creating less saccharine art (the Pre-Raphaelites). Like the Impressionists who followed them, they donned their scarves, barged out of the stuffy studio, and set up outdoors, painting trees, streams, and people, like scientists on a field trip. Still, they often captured nature with such a close-up clarity that it's downright unnatural.

British Impressionism: Realistic British art stood apart from the modernist trends in France, but some influences drifted across the Channel. John Singer Sargent (American-born) studied with Parisian Impressionists, learning the thick, messy brushwork and play of light at twilight. James Tissot used Degas' snapshot technique to capture a crowded scene from an odd angle. And James McNeill Whistler (born in America, trained in Paris, lived in London) composed his paintings like music—see some of his paintings' titles.

The Turner Collection: Walking through J. M. W. Turner's life's work, you can trace his progression from a painter of realistic historical scenes, through his wandering years, to Impressionist paintings of color-and-light patterns. As you explore the collection, you'll watch Turner's style evolve from clear-eyed realism to hazy proto-Impressionism. You'll also see how Turner dabbled in different subjects: landscapes, seascapes, Roman ruins, snapshots of Venice, and so on.

The corner room of the Clore Gallery is dedicated to Turner's great rival and contemporary, John Constable, who brought painting back into the real world. Although the Royal Academy thought Nature needed makeup, Constable thought she was just fine. He painted the English landscape as it was—realistically, without idealizing it.

1900-1950—World Wars: As two world wars whittled down the powerful British Empire, it still remained a major cultural force. British art mirrored many of the trends and "-isms" pioneered in Paris. You'll see Cubism like Picasso's, abstract art like Mondrian's, and so on. But British artists also continued the British tradition of realistic paintings of people and landscapes.

Henry Moore's statues—mostly female, mostly reclining—catch the primitive power of carved stone. He captured the human body in a few simple curves, with minimal changes to the rock itself.

With a stiff upper lip, Britain survived the Blitz, World War II, and the loss of hundreds of thousands of men—but at war's end, the bottled-up horror came rushing out. Francis Bacon's deformed half-humans/half-animals express the existential human predicament of being caught in a world not of your making, isolated and helpless to change it.

1950-2000—Modern World: No longer a world power, Britain in the Swinging '60s became a major exporter of pop culture. British art's traditional strengths—realism, portraits, landscapes, and slice-of-life scenes—were redone in the modern style. Look for works by David Hockney, Lucian Freud, Bridget Riley, and Gilbert and George.

HYDE PARK AND NEARBY

A number of worthwhile sights border this grand park, from Apsley House on the east to Kensington Palace on the west.

▲Apsley House (Wellington Museum)

Having beaten Napoleon at Waterloo, Arthur Wellesley, the First Duke of Wellington, was once the most famous man in Europe. He was given a huge fortune, with which he purchased London's ultimate address, Number One London. His refurbished mansion offers a nice interior, a handful of world-class paintings, and a glimpse at the life of the great soldier and two-time prime minister.

The highlight is the large ballroom, the Waterloo Gallery, decorated with Anthony van Dyck's *Charles I on Horseback* (over the main fireplace), Diego Velázquez's earthy *Water-Seller of Seville* (to the left of Van Dyck), and Jan Steen's playful *Dissolute Household* (to the right). Just outside the door, in the Portico Room, is a large portrait of the Duke of Wellington by Francisco Goya. The place is well-described by the included audioguide, which has sound bites from the current Duke of Wellington (who still lives at Apsley).

Cost and Hours: £9.20, Wed-Sun 11:00-17:00, closed Mon-Tue, no photos, 20 yards from Hyde Park Corner Tube station, tel. 020/7499-5676, www.english-heritage.org.uk.

Nearby: **Hyde Park**'s pleasant rose garden is picnic-friendly. **Wellington Arch,** which stands just across the street, is open to the public but not worth the £5.20 charge (or £10 combo-ticket with Apsley House; elevator up, lousy views and boring exhibits).

▲Hyde Park and Speakers' Corner

London's "Central Park," originally Henry VIII's hunting grounds, has more than 600 acres of lush greenery, Santander Cycles rental stations, the huge man-made Serpentine Lake (with rental boats and a lakeside swimming pool), the royal Kensington Palace (described later), and the ornate Neo-Gothic Albert Memorial across

from the Royal Albert Hall (for more about the park, see www.royalparks.org.uk/parks/hyde-park). The western half of the park is known as Kensington Gardens. The park is huge—study a Tube map to choose the stop nearest to your destination.

On Sundays, from just after noon until early evening, **Speakers' Corner** offers soapbox oratory at its best (northeast corner of the park, Tube: Marble Arch). Characters climb their stepladders, wave their flags, pound emphatically on their sandwich boards, and share what they are convinced is their wisdom. Regulars have resident hecklers who know their lines and are always ready with a verbal jab or barb. "The grass roots of democracy" is actually a holdover from when the gallows stood here and the criminal was allowed to say just about anything he wanted to before he swung. I dare you to raise your voice and gather a crowd—it's easy to do.

The **Princess Diana Memorial Fountain** honors the "People's Princess," who once lived in nearby Kensington Palace. The low-key circular stream, great for cooling off your feet on a hot day, is in the south-central part of the park, near the Albert Memorial and Serpentine Gallery (Tube: Knightsbridge). A similarly named but different sight, the **Diana, Princess of Wales Memorial Playground** in the park's northwest corner, is loads of fun for kids (Tube: Queensway).

Kensington Palace

For nearly 150 years (1689-1837), Kensington was the royal residence, before Buckingham Palace became the official home of the monarch. Sitting primly on its pleasant parkside grounds, the palace gives a glimpse into royal life, especially Queen Victoria, who was born and raised here.

After Queen Victoria moved the monarchy to Buckingham Palace, lesser royals bedded down at Kensington.

Princess Diana lived here both during and after her marriage to Prince Charles (1981-1997). More recently, Will and Kate moved into a thoroughly renovated Apartment 1A (the southern flank of the palace complex, with four stories and 20 rooms). And Prince Harry lives in their old digs, a "cottage" on the other side of the main building. However—as many disappointed visitors discover—none of these more recent apartments are open to the public.

The palace has three main exhibits. To see them chronologically, head to the right from the vestibule, starting with the **Queen's State Apartments** (with highly conceptual exhibits focusing on the later Stuart dynasty—William and Mary, and Mary's sister, Queen Anne). Then move on to the **King's State Apartments** (the grandest spaces, from Hanoverian times), and finish with the **Victoria Revealed** exhibit (telling the story, through quotes and artifacts, of Britain's longest-ruling monarch).

Cost and Hours: £17.50, daily 10:00-18:00, Nov-Feb until 17:00, last entry one hour before closing, least crowded in mornings; £5 guidebook but friendly and knowledgeable "explainers" will answer questions for free, cloakroom available for bags and luggage; a long 10-minute stroll through Kensington Gardens from either High Street Kensington or Queensway Tube stations, tel. 0844-482-7788, www.hrp.org.uk.

Nearby: Garden enthusiasts enjoy popping into the secluded Sunken Garden, 50 yards from the exit. Consider afternoon tea at the nearby Orangery (see page 185), built as a greenhouse for Queen Anne in 1704. On the south side of the palace are the golden gates that became famous in 1997 as the backdrop to the sea of flowers left here by Princess Diana's mourners.

▲▲▲Victoria and Albert Museum

The world's top collection of decorative arts encompasses 2,000 years of art and design (ceramics, stained glass, fine furniture, clothing, jewelry, carpets, and more). Known as "The V&A," this museum presents a surprisingly interesting and diverse assortment of crafts from the West, as well as Asian and Islamic cultures. There's much to see, including Raphael's tapestry cartoons, a cast of Trajan's Column that depicts the emperor's conquests, one of Leonardo da Vinci's notebooks, ladies' underwear through the ages, a life-size *David* with detachable fig leaf, and Mick Jagger's sequined jumpsuit. From the worlds of Islam and India there are stunning carpets, the ring of the man who built the Taj Mahal, and a mechanical tiger that eats Brits. Best of all, the objects are all quite beautiful. You could spend days in the place.

Cost and Hours: Free, but £4 donation requested, extra for some special exhibits; daily 10:00-17:45, some galleries open Fri until 22:00; £1 suggested donation for much-needed museum map, free tours daily, on Cromwell Road in South Kensington, Tube: South Kensington, from the Tube station a long tunnel leads directly to museum, tel. 020/7942-2000, www.vam.ac.uk.

Visiting the Museum: In the Grand Entrance lobby, look up to see the colorful **chandelier/sculpture** by American glass artist Dale Chihuly. This elaborate piece epitomizes the spirit of the V&A's collection—beautiful manufactured objects that demonstrate technical skill and innovation, wedding the old with the new, and blurring the line between arts and crafts.

The V&A has (arguably) the best collection of **Italian Renaissance sculpture** outside Italy. One prime example is *Samson Slaying a Philistine,* by Giambologna (c. 1562), carved from a single block of marble, which shows the testy Israelite warrior preparing to decapitate a man who'd insulted him. The statue's spiral-shaped pose is reminiscent of Michelangelo.

The museum's **Islamic art** reflects both religious influences and sophisticated secular culture. Many Islamic artists expressed themselves with beautiful but functional objects. Notice floral patterns (twining vines, flowers, arabesques) and geometric designs (stars, diamonds). But the most common pattern is calligraphy—elaborate lettering of an inscription in Arabic, the language of the Quran.

The **British Galleries** sweep chronologically through 400 years of British high-class living (1500-1900). Look for rare miniature portraits—a popular item of Queen Elizabeth I's day—including Hilliard's oft-reproduced *Young Man Among Roses* miniature, capturing the romance of a Shakespeare sonnet. A room dedicated to Henry VIII has a portrait of him, his writing box (with quill pens, ink, and sealing wax), and a whole roomful of the fancy furniture, tapestries, jewelry, and dinnerware that may have decorated his palaces.

▲▲Natural History Museum

Across the street from the Victoria and Albert, this mammoth museum is housed in a giant and wonderful Victorian Neo-Romanesque building. It was built in the 1870s specifically for the huge collection (50 million specimens). Exhibits are wonderfully explained, with lots of creative, interactive displays. It covers everything from life ("creepy crawlies," human biology, our place in evolution, and awe-inspiring dinosaurs) to earth science (meteors, volcanoes, and earthquakes).

Cost and Hours: Free, but £5 donation requested, fees for

(optional) special exhibits, daily 10:00-18:00, helpful £1 map, open later last Fri of the month, long tunnel leads directly from South Kensington Tube station to museum (follow signs), tel. 020/7942-5000, exhibit info and reservations tel. 020/7942-5011, www.nhm.ac.uk. Free visitor app available via the "Visit" section of the website.

▲Science Museum

Next door to the Natural History Museum, this sprawling wonderland for curious minds is kid-perfect, with themes such as measuring time, exploring space, climate change, and the evolution of modern medicine. It offers hands-on fun, from moonwalks to deep-sea exploration, with trendy technology exhibits, a state-of-the-art IMAX theater (shows-£11, £9 for kids, £27/£30 for families of 3 or 4), and the Garden, a cool play area for children up to age seven.

Cost and Hours: Free, daily 10:00-18:00, until 19:00 during school holidays, last entry 45 minutes before closing, Exhibition Road, Tube: South Kensington, tel. 0870-870-4868, www.sciencemuseum.org.uk.

Sights in Greater London

EAST OF LONDON

▲▲Greenwich

This borough of London—an easy boat trip or light-rail journey from downtown—combines majestic picnic-perfect parks, the stately trappings of Britain's proud nautical heritage, and the Royal Observatory Greenwich, with a fine museum on the evolution of seafaring and a chance to straddle the eastern and western hemispheres at the prime meridian. The map on page 127 shows a recommended walking route that links the sights; if you're in a rush, make a beeline to those that interest you. Note that Greenwich pairs perfectly with a quick visit to the Docklands, London's glittering skyscraper zone (just across the river from Greenwich, and described next).

Getting There: Ride a boat to Greenwich for the scenery and commentary, and take the Docklands Light Railway (DLR) back—especially if you want to stop at the Docklands on the way home. Various tour **boats** with commentary and open-deck seating up top (2/hour, 30-75 minutes), as well as faster Thames Clippers

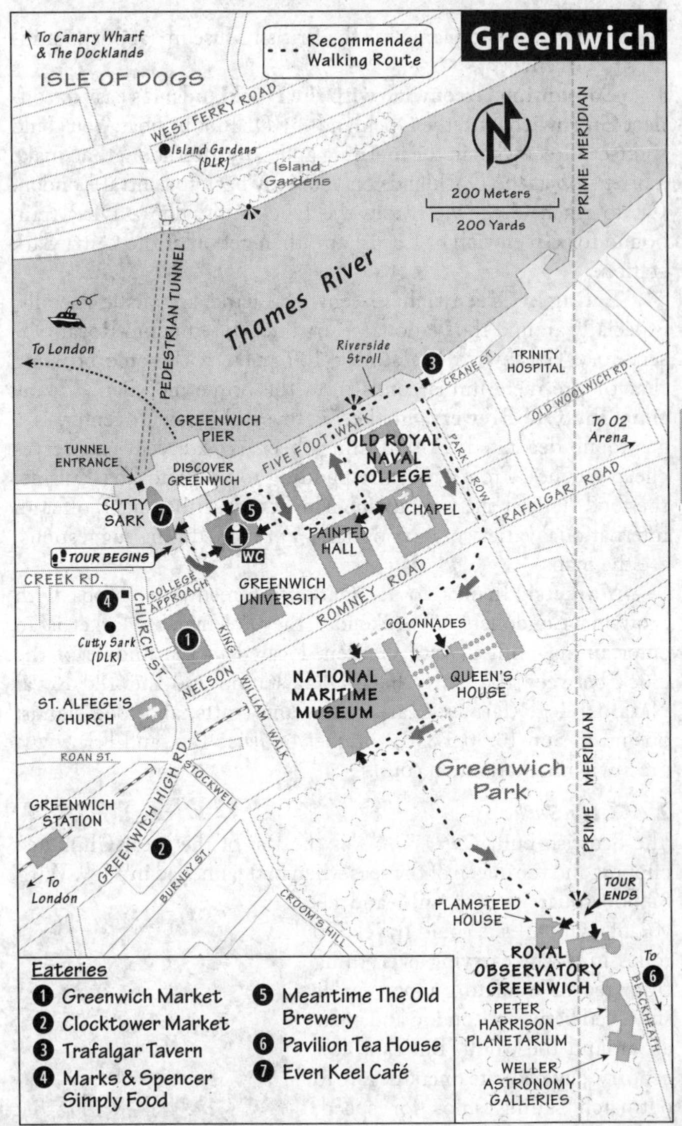

(2-3/hour, 20-45 minutes) leave from several piers in central London. Thames Clippers also connects Greenwich to the Docklands' Canary Wharf Pier (2-3/hour, 10 minutes). By **DLR,** ride from Bank Station in central London to Cutty Sark Station in central Greenwich; it's one stop before the main—but less central—Greenwich Station (departs at least every 10 minutes, 20 minutes, all in Zone 2, covered by any Tube pass). Alternately, catch **bus**

#188 from Russell Square near the British Museum (about 45 minutes to Greenwich).

Combining Greenwich with the Docklands: It's easy to connect Greenwich with the Docklands by DLR or by boat. You could sightsee Greenwich in the morning and early afternoon, then make a brief stop at the Docklands on your way back to central London. Or, to reach Greenwich from the Docklands, hop a DLR train bound for Greenwich or Lewisham, then get off at the Cutty Sark station.

Eating in Greenwich: Greenwich's parks are picnic-friendly, especially around the National Maritime Museum and Royal Observatory. Greenwich has almost 100 pubs, with some boasting that they're mere milliseconds from the prime meridian. **Meantime The Old Brewery,** in the Discover Greenwich center, is a gastropub decorated with all things beer. An adjacent café serves cheap lunches. From Yorkshire pudding to paella to Thai cuisine, the food stalls at the **Greenwich Market** (described next) offer an international variety of tasty options. For more dining suggestions, see the map.

Markets: Thanks to its markets, Greenwich throbs with browsing Londoners on weekends. The Greenwich Market is an entertaining mini-Covent Garden, located in the middle of the block between the Cutty Sark DLR station and the Old Royal Naval College (farmers market, arts and crafts, and food stands; open Tue-Sun 10:00-17:30; antiques on Tue, Thu, and Fri, www.greenwichmarketlondon.com).

▲▲*Cutty Sark*

The Scottish-built *Cutty Sark* was the last of the great China tea clippers and the queen of the seas when first launched in 1869. With 32,000 square feet of sail—and favorable winds—she could travel 300 miles in a day, carrying everything from tea to wool to gunpowder as she raced between London and ports all around the world. But as a new century dawned, steamers began to outmatch sailing ships for speed, and by the mid-1920s the *Cutty Sark* was the world's last operating clipper ship.

The first deck you'll visit is full of not-quite-gimmicky displays on the ship's history. Attempt to beat Captain Woodget's record voyage sailing a wool-laden *Sark* from Sydney to London. Sailing fans will like the gorgeously restored top deck best. Don't miss the video showing the rigger's-eye-view as he climbs high above the deck. Your visit ends down below, where you can take a coffee break directly under the ship's shiny hull.

Cost and Hours: £13.50, kids aged 5-15-£7, free for kids under age 5, family tickets available, combo-ticket with Royal Observatory-£18.50, kids combo-ticket-£8.50; daily 10:00-17:00, may stay open until 18:00 during school holidays, when it is wise to purchase tickets ahead online or by phone; last entry 45 minutes before closing; £5 guidebook available but hardly necessary, reservation tel. 020/8312-6608, www.rmg.co.uk.

▲Old Royal Naval College

The college was originally a hospital founded by Queen Mary II and King William III in 1692 as a charity to care for retired or injured naval officers (called pensioners). William and Mary spared no expense, hiring the great Christopher Wren to design the complex (though other architects completed it). Its days as a hospital ended in 1869, and it served as a college for training naval officers from 1873 to 1998. Now that the Royal Navy has moved out, the public is invited to view the college's elaborate Painted Hall and Chapel of Sts. Peter and Paul, which are in symmetrical buildings that face each other overlooking a broad riverfront park.

Each building sells a descriptive guide (50p-£1), or you can buy the fun *Nasty Naval College* brochure (made for children, but with entertaining offbeat facts about the place; £1). Volunteers are often standing by to answer questions. Visit the highlight—the Painted Hall—first, before touring the chapel.

Cost and Hours: Free, daily 10:00-17:00, sometimes closed for private events, service Sun at 11:00 in chapel—all are welcome, www.ornc.org.

▲National Maritime Museum

Great for anyone interested in the sea, this museum holds everything from a giant working paddlewheel to the uniform Admiral Horatio Nelson wore when he was killed at Trafalgar (look for the bullet hole, in the left shoulder). A big glass roof tops three levels of slick, modern, kid-friendly exhibits about all things seafaring.

The Explorers exhibit covers early expeditions and an ill-fated Arctic trip, complete with a soundtrack of creaking wooden ships and crashing waves. Kids like the All Hands and Bridge galleries, where they can send secret messages by Morse code and operate a miniature dockside crane. Along with displays of lighthouse technology and a whaling cannon, you'll see model ships, nautical paintings, and various salty odds and ends.

Cost and Hours: Free, daily 10:00-17:00, tel. 020/8858-4422, www.rmg.co.uk. The museum hosts frequent family-oriented events—singing, treasure hunts, and storytelling—particularly on weekends; ask at the desk. Inside, listen for announcements alerting visitors to free tours on various topics.

▲▲Royal Observatory Greenwich

Located on the prime meridian (0° longitude), the observatory is famous as the point from which all time is measured. The observatory was founded in 1675 by King Charles II for the purpose of improving navigation by more accurately charting the night sky.

A visit here gives you a taste of the sciences of astronomy, timekeeping, and seafaring—and how they all meld together—along with great views over Greenwich and the distant London skyline. The Royal Observatory grounds are made up of the observatory (with the prime meridian and three worthy exhibits), the **Weller Astronomy Galleries** (where interactive, kid-pleasing displays allow you to guide a space mission and touch a 4.5-billion-year-old meteorite), and the state-of-the-art, 120-seat **Peter Harrison Planetarium.**

If your only interest in the Royal Observatory is the famous prime meridian line, you can go through an unassuming iron gate just below the entrance for a free, more simplistic (and significantly less crowded) display of the prime meridian. Under the analog clock just outside the courtyard, see how your foot measures up to the foot where the public standards of length are cast in bronze.

Cost and Hours: Observatory—£9.50, includes free audioguide, combo-ticket with *Cutty Sark*—£18.50, combo-ticket with planetarium—£12.50, daily 10:00-17:00, later in summer; Astronomy Galleries—free, daily 10:00-17:00; Planetarium—£7.50, 30-minute shows generally run every hour Mon-Fri 13:00-16:00, Sat-Sun 11:00-16:00, fewer in winter, confirm times in advance and consider calling ahead to order tickets; tel. 020/8858-4422, www.rmg.co.uk.

▲▲The Docklands

Once the primary harbor for the Port of London, the Docklands has been transformed into a vibrant business center, with ultra-tall skyscrapers, subterranean supermalls, trendy pubs, and peaceful parks with pedestrian bridges looping over canals. It also boasts the very good Museum of London Docklands. While not full of the touristy sights that many are seeking in London, the Docklands offers a refresh-

ing look at the British version of a 21st-century city. It's best at the end of the workday, when it's lively with office workers. It's ideal to see on your way back from Greenwich, since both line up on the same train tracks.

Getting There: Coming from central London, take the Tube to a DLR stop (the Bank/Monument stops are the most central), then take the Lewisham line to South Quay. If you're coming from Greenwich, take any northbound DLR line to South Quay.

▲Museum of London Docklands

Illuminating the gritty and fascinating history of this site, this museum traces the story of what was London's primary harbor. You'll see fascinating models of Old London Bridge, crammed with little houses and shops; a reconstruction of a "Legal Quay," where cargo was processed; and a re-creation of the fuel pipeline that was laid under the English Channel to supply the Allies on the Continent during World War II. You'll also walk through gritty "Sailortown," listening to the salty voices of those who lived and worked in quarters like these.

Cost and Hours: Free, daily 10:00-18:00, last entry one hour before closing, www.museumoflondon.org.uk/docklands.

WEST OF LONDON

▲▲Kew Gardens

For a fine riverside park and a palatial greenhouse jungle to swing through, take the Tube or the boat to every botanist's favorite escape, Kew Gardens. While to most visitors the Royal Botanic Gardens of Kew are simply a delightful opportunity to wander among 33,000 different types of plants, to the hardworking organization that runs them, the gardens are a way to promote the understanding and preservation of the botanical diversity of our planet.

Garden lovers could spend days exploring Kew's 300 acres. For a quick visit, spend a fragrant hour wandering through three buildings: the Palm House, a humid Victorian world of iron, glass, and tropical plants that was built in 1844; a Waterlily House that Monet would swim for; and the Princess of Wales Conservatory, a meandering modern greenhouse with many different climate zones growing countless cacti, bug-munching carnivorous plants, and more. With extra time, check out the Xstrata Treetop Walkway, a 200-yard-long scenic steel walkway that puts you high in the canopy 60 feet above the ground. Young kids will love the Climbers and Creepers indoor/outdoor playground and little zip line, as well as a slow and easy ride on the hop-on, hop-off Kew Explorer tram (adults-£4.50, kids-£1.50 for narrated 40-minute ride, departs Victoria Gate, ask for schedule when you enter).

Cost and Hours: £16.50, June-Aug £11 after 16:00, kids 4-16-£3.50, kids under 4-free; April-Aug Mon-Fri 10:00-18:30, Sat-Sun 10:00-19:30, closes earlier Sept-March—check schedule online, glasshouses close at 17:30 in high season—earlier off-season, free one-hour walking tours daily at 11:00 and 13:30, tel. 020/8332-5000, www.kew.org.

Getting There: If taking the Tube, ride to Kew Gardens; from the Kew Tube station, cross the footbridge over the tracks, which drops you in a little community of plant-and-herb shops, a two-block walk from Victoria Gate (the main garden entrance). Another option is to take a boat, which runs April-Oct between Kew Gardens and Westminster Pier (see page 54).

Eating: For a sun-dappled lunch or snack, walk 10 minutes from the Palm House to the Orangery Cafeteria (£4 sandwiches, £8-12 lunches, Mon-Fri 10:00-18:30, Sat-Sun 10:00-19:30, until 16:15 in winter, closes early for events).

▲Hampton Court Palace

Fifteen miles up the Thames from downtown, the 500-year-old palace of Henry VIII is worth ▲▲ for palace aficionados. Actually, it was originally the palace of his minister, Cardinal Wolsey. When Wolsey, a clever man, realized Henry VIII was experiencing a little palace envy, he gave the mansion to his king. The Tudor palace was also home to Elizabeth I and Charles I. Sections were updated by Christopher Wren for William and Mary. The stately palace stands overlooking the Thames and includes some fine Tudor rooms, including a Great Hall with a magnificent hammer-beam ceiling. The industrial-strength Tudor kitchen was capable of keeping 600 schmoozing courtiers thoroughly—if not

well—fed. The sculpted garden features a rare Tudor tennis court and a popular maze.

The palace tries hard to please, but it doesn't quite sparkle. From the information center in the main courtyard, you can pick up audioguides for self-guided tours of various wings of the palace (free but slow, aimed mostly at school-aged children). For more in-depth information, strike up a conversation with the costumed characters or docents posted in each room. The Tudor portions of the castle, including the rooms dedicated to the young Henry, are most interesting; the Georgian rooms are pretty dull. The maze in the nearby garden is a curiosity some find fun (maze free with palace ticket, otherwise £4.40).

Cost and Hours: £19.30, family-£48.20; online discounts, daily April-Oct 10:00-18:00, Nov-March 10:00-16:30, last entry one hour before closing, café, tel. 0844-482-7777 or 020/3166-6000, www.hrp.org.uk.

Getting There: The train (2/hour, 35 minutes, Oyster cards OK) from London's Waterloo Station drops you across the river from the palace (just walk across the bridge). Consider arriving at or departing from the palace by boat (connections with London's Westminster Pier, see page 54); it's a relaxing and scenic three- to four-hour cruise past two locks and a fun new/old riverside mix.

Kew Gardens/Hampton Court Blitz: Because these two sights are in the same general direction (about £20 for a taxi between the two), you can visit both in one day. Here's a game plan: Start your morning at Hampton Court, tour the palace and garden, and have a Tudor-style lunch in the atmospheric dining hall. After lunch, take bus #R68 from Hampton Court Station to Richmond (40 minutes), then transfer to bus #65, which will drop you off at the Kew Gardens gate (5 minutes). After touring the gardens, have tea in the Orangery, then Tube or boat back to London.

NORTH OF LONDON

The Making of Harry Potter: Warner Bros. Studio Tour London

While you can visit several real-life locations in Britain where the Harry Potter movies were filmed, there's only one way to see imaginary places like Hogwarts' Great Hall, Diagon Alley, Dumbledore's office, and the interior of #4 Privet Drive: by visiting the Warner Bros. Studio in Leavesden, 20 miles northwest of London.

Attractions include the actual sets, costumes, and props used for the films, video interviews with the actors and filmmakers, and exhibits about how the films' special effects were created. The visit culminates with a stroll down Diagon Alley and a room-sized 1:24-scale model of Hogwarts that will bring young Potter fans to tears.

As this attraction is understandably popular, it's essential to reserve your visit online as far ahead as you can (entrance possible only with reserved time slot). Allowing about three hours for your time at the studio, plus nearly three hours to get there and back, this experience will eat up the better part of a day.

Cost and Hours: £33, kids ages 5 to 15-£25.50, family ticket for 2 adults and 2 kids-£101; opening hours flex with season—first tour at 9:00 or 10:00, last tour as early as 16:30 or as late as 18:30; audio/videoguide-£5, café, still photography allowed, tel. 0845-084-0900, www.wbstudiotour.co.uk.

Getting There: Take the frequent train from London Euston to Watford Junction (about 5/hour, 15-20 minutes), then catch the brightly painted Mullany's Coaches shuttle bus to the studio (2-4/hour, 15 minutes, £2 round-trip, buy ticket from driver). Alternately, book a Golden Tours **bus** trip (3-4/day, price includes round-trip bus and studio entrance: adults-£57, kids-£52; reserve ahead at www.goldentours.com).

Shopping in London

Most stores are open Monday through Saturday from roughly 9:00 or 10:00 until 17:00 or 18:00, with a late night on Wednesday or Thursday (usually until 19:00 or 20:00). Many close on Sundays. Large department stores stay open later during the week (until about 21:00 Mon-Sat) and are open shorter hours on Sundays. If you're looking for bargains, visit one of the city's many street markets.

SHOPPING STREETS

London is famous for its shopping. The best and most convenient shopping streets are in the West End and West London (roughly between Soho and Hyde Park). You'll find midrange shops along **Oxford Street** (running east from Tube: Marble Arch), and fancier shops along **Regent Street** (stretching south from Tube: Oxford Circus to Piccadilly Circus) and **Knightsbridge** (where you'll find Harrods and Harvey Nichols; Tube: Knightsbridge). Other streets are more specialized, such as **Jermyn Street** for old-fashioned men's clothing (just south of Piccadilly Street) and **Charing Cross Road** for books. **Floral Street,** connecting Leicester Square to Covent Garden, is lined with fashion boutiques.

FANCY DEPARTMENT STORES IN WEST LONDON

Harrods

Harrods is London's most famous and touristy department store. With more than four acres of retail space covering seven floors, it's a place where some shoppers could spend all day. (To me, it's still just a department store.) Big yet classy, Harrods has everything from elephants to toothbrushes (Mon-Sat 10:00-21:00, Sun 11:30-18:00; baggage check outside on Basil Street—follow *left luggage* signs at back of the store, £10/bag; Brompton Road, Tube: Knightsbridge, tel. 020/7730-1234, www.harrods.com).

Harvey Nichols

Once Princess Diana's favorite, "Harvey Nick's" remains the department store *du jour* (Mon-Sat 10:00-20:00, Sun 11:30-18:00, near Harrods, 109 Knightsbridge, Tube: Knightsbridge, tel. 020/7235-5000, www.harveynichols.com). Want to pick up a £20 scarf? You won't do it here, where they're more like £200. The store's fifth floor is a veritable food fest, with a gourmet grocery store, a fancy restaurant, a Yo! Sushi bar, and a lively café. Consider a takeaway tray of sushi to eat on a bench in the Hyde Park rose garden two blocks away.

Fortnum & Mason

The official department store of the Queen, Fortnum & Mason embodies old-fashioned British upper-class taste. While some feel it is too stuffy, you won't find another store with the same storybook atmosphere (Mon-Sat 10:00-21:00, Sun 11:30-18:00, elegant tea served in their Diamond Jubilee Tea Salon—see page 186, 181 Piccadilly, Tube: Green Park, tel. 020/7734-8040, www.fortnumandmason.com).

Liberty

Designed to make well-heeled shoppers feel at home, this half-timbered, mock-Tudor emporium is a 19th-century institution that thrives today. Known for its gorgeous floral fabrics and well-stocked crafts department, it's fun to stroll through just for a look at its hip, artful displays and castle-like interior, constructed of two decommissioned battleships (Mon-Sat 10:00-20:00, Sun 12:00-18:00, Great Marlborough Street, Tube: Oxford Circus, tel. 020/7734-1234, www.liberty.co.uk).

STREET MARKETS

Antiques buffs, people-watchers, and folks who brake for garage sales love London's street markets. There's good early-morning market activity somewhere any day of the week. The best markets—which combine lively stalls and a colorful neighborhood with cute and characteristic shops of their own—are Portobello

Road and Camden Lock Market. Any London TI has a complete up-to-date list. Hagglers will enjoy the no-holds-barred bargaining encouraged in London's street markets.

Warning: Markets attract two kinds of people—tourists and pickpockets.

In Notting Hill

Portobello Road Market

Arguably London's best street market, Portobello Road stretches for several blocks through the delightful, colorful, funky-yet-quaint Notting Hill neighborhood. Already-charming streets lined with pastel-painted houses and offbeat antique shops are enlivened on Fridays and Saturdays with 2,000 additional stalls (9:00-19:00), plus food, live music, and more. (The best strategy is to come on Friday; most stalls are open, with half the crowds of Saturday.) If you start at Notting Hill Gate and work your way north, you'll find these general sections: antiques, new goods, produce, vintage clothing, more new goods, a flea market, and more food. While Portobello Road is best on Fridays and Saturdays, it's enjoyable to stroll this street on most other days as well, since the quirky shops are fun to explore (Tube: Notting Hill Gate, near recommended accommodations, tel. 020/7727-7684, www.portobelloroad.co.uk).

In Camden Town

Camden Lock Market

This huge, trendy arts-and-crafts festival is divided into three areas, each with its own vibe. The main market, set alongside the picturesque canal, features a mix of shops and stalls selling boutique crafts and artisanal foods. The market on the opposite side of Chalk Farm Road is edgier, with cheap ethnic food stalls, lots of canalside seating, and punk crafts. The Stables, a sprawling, incense-scented complex, is decorated with fun statues of horses and squeezed into tunnels under the old rail bridge just behind the main market. It's a little lowbrow and wildly creative, with cheap clothes, junk jewelry, and loud music (daily 10:00-18:00, busiest on weekends, tel. 020/3763-9999, www.camdenlockmarket.com).

In the City

Leadenhall Market

One of London's oldest, Leadenhall Market stands on the original Roman center of town. Today, cheese and flower shops nestle between pubs, restaurants, and fashion boutiques, all beneath a beautiful Victorian arcade (Harry Potter fans may recognize it as Diagon Alley). This is not a "street market" in the true sense, but more a hidden gem in the midst of London's financial grind (Mon-Fri 10:00-18:00, closed Sat-Sun, tel. 020/7332-1523, Tube: Monument or Liverpool; off Gracechurch Street near Leadenhall Street and Fenchurch).

In the East End

Most of these East End markets are busiest and most interesting on Sundays; the Broadway Market is best on Saturdays.

Spitalfields Market

This huge, mod-feeling market hall (pronounced "spittle-fields") combines a shopping mall with old brick buildings and sleek modern ones, all covered by a giant glass roof. The shops, stalls, and a rainbow of restaurant options are open every day, tempting you with ethnic eateries, crafts, trendy clothes, bags, and an antiques-and-junk market (Mon-Fri 10:00-17:00, Sat 11:00-17:00, Sun 9:00-17:00, Tube: Liverpool Street; from the Tube stop, take Bishopsgate East exit, turn left, walk to Brushfield Street, and turn right; www.spitalfields.co.uk).

Petticoat Lane Market

Just a block from Spitalfields Market, this line of stalls sits on the otherwise dull, glass-skyscraper-filled Middlesex Street; adjoining Wentworth Street is grungier and more characteristic. Expect budget clothing, leather, shoes, watches, jewelry, and crowds (Sun 9:00-14:00, sometimes later; smaller market Mon-Fri on Wentworth Street only; closed Sat; Middlesex Street and Wentworth Street, Tube: Liverpool Street).

Truman Markets

Housed in the former Truman Brewery on Brick Lane, this cluster of markets is in the heart of the "Banglatown" Bangladeshi community. Of the East End market areas, these are the grittiest and most avant-garde, selling handmade clothes and home decor as well as ethnic street food. The markets are in full swing on Sundays (roughly 10:00-17:00), though you'll see some action on Saturdays (11:00-18:00). The Boiler House Food Hall and the Backyard Market (hipster arts and crafts) go all weekend—and the Vintage Market (clothes) even operates on Thursdays and Fridays (11:00-17:30). Surrounding shops and eateries are open all week (Tube:

Liverpool Street or Aldgate East, tel. 020/7770-6028, www.bricklanemarket.com).

Columbia Road Flower Market

From the Truman Brewery complex, Brick Lane is lined with Sunday market stalls all the way up to Bethnal Green Road, about a 10-minute walk. Continuing straight (north) about five more minutes takes you to Columbia Road, a colorful shopping street made even more so by the Sunday-morning commotion of shouting flower vendors. The prices are good (why not brighten up your hotel room with a bouquet?), and the sales pitches are entertaining (Sun 8:00-15:00, closed Mon-Sat, http://columbiaroad.info). Halfway up Columbia Road, be sure to loop left up little Ezra Street, with characteristic eateries, boutiques, and antiques vendors.

Broadway Market

While the other listed East End markets are best on Sundays, Saturdays are best for the festive market sprawling through this aptly named neighborhood—ground zero for London's hipsters. Several blocks are filled with foodie delights, along with a few arts and crafts (www.broadwaymarket.co.uk). On sunny days, the London Fields park just north of the market is filled with thousands of picnicking and sunbathing locals enjoying their little slice of the city. A bit farther out, this market can be trickier to reach; it's easiest to take the Overground from Liverpool Street Station three stops to London Fields, then walk through that park to the market.

In the West End

Covent Garden Market

Originally the convent garden for Westminster Abbey, the iron-and-glass market hall hosted a produce market until the 1970s (earning it the name "Apple Market"). Now it's a mix of fun shops, eateries, markets, and—thanks to Steve Jobs—a more modern-day Apple store. Mondays are for antiques, while arts and crafts dominate the rest of the week. Yesteryear's produce stalls are open daily 10:30-18:00, and on Thursdays a food market brightens up the square (Tube: Covent Garden, tel. 020/7395-1350, www.coventgardenlondonuk.com).

Jubilee Hall Market

Located on the south side of Covent Garden, this market features antiques on Mondays; a general market Tuesday through Friday; and arts and crafts on Saturdays and Sundays (Mon 5:00-17:00, Tue-Fri 10:30-19:00, Sat-Sun 10:00-18:00, tel. 020/7379-4242, www.jubileemarket.co.uk).

In South London

Borough Market

London's oldest fruit and vegetable market has been serving the Southwark community for over 800 years. These days there are as many people taking photos as buying fruit, cheese, and beautiful breads, but it's still a fun carnival atmosphere with fantastic stall food. For maximum market and minimum crowds, join the locals on Thursdays (full market open Wed-Thu 10:00-17:00, Fri 10:00-18:00, Sat 8:00-17:00, closed Sun; surrounding food stalls open daily; south of London Bridge, where Southwark Street meets Borough High Street; Tube: London Bridge, tel. 020/7407-1002, www.boroughmarket.org.uk).

Ropewalk (Maltby Street Market)

This short-but-sweet, completely untouristy food bazaar bustles on weekends under a nondescript rail bridge in the shadow of the Shard. Two dozen vendors fill the narrow passage with a festival of hipster/artisan food carts, offering everything from gourmet burgers to waffles to scotch eggs to ice-cream sandwiches. Come as hungry as possible and graze your way to a satisfying lunch (Sat 9:00-16:00, Sun 11:00-16:00, www.maltby.st). This area of South London—called Bermondsey—is a lowbrow but emerging neighborhood that's fun to explore for a slice of youthful, untrampled city. A short walk southeast of Tower Bridge, it has several rustic microbreweries tucked between self-storage shops and auto-repair garages.

Brixton Market

This seedy neighborhood south of the Thames features yet another thriving market. Here the food, clothing, records, and hair-braiding throb with an Afro-Caribbean beat (stalls open Mon-Sat 8:00-18:00, Wed until 15:00, farmers market Sun 10:00-14:00 but otherwise dead on Sun; Tube: Brixton, www.brixtonmarket.net).

In Greenwich

With several sightseeing treats just a quick DLR ride from central London, Greenwich has its share of great markets, especially lively on weekends. For details, see page 128.

Entertainment in London

For the best list of what's happening and a look at the latest London scene, check www.timeout.com/london. The free monthly *London Planner* covers sights, events, and plays, though generally not as well as the *Time Out* website.

THEATER (A.K.A. "THEATRE")

London's theater scene rivals Broadway's in quality and sometimes beats it in price. Choose from 200 offerings—Shakespeare, musicals, comedies, thrillers, sex farces, cutting-edge fringe, revivals starring movie celebs, and more. London does it all well.

If spending the time and money for a London play, I like a full-fledged high-energy musical; long-running shows like ***Mamma Mia!*** or ***Wicked*** are fun, seats are easily booked, and you'll likely find them on the discount list at the TKTS booth (described later). If you go for this year's hit, you'll need to book long in advance and pay top price.

Seating Terminology: Just like at home, London's theaters sell seats in a range of levels—but the Brits use different terms: stalls (ground floor), dress circle (first balcony), upper circle (second balcony), balcony (sky-high third balcony), and slips (cheap seats on the fringes). Discounted tickets are called "concessions" (abbreviated as "conc" or "s"). For floor plans of the various theaters, see www.theatremonkey.com.

Big West End Shows

Nearly all big-name shows are hosted in the theaters of the West End, clustering around Soho (especially along Shaftesbury Avenue) between Piccadilly and Covent Garden. With a centuries-old tradition of pleasing the masses, they present London theater at its grandest.

I prefer big, glitzy—even bombastic—musicals over serious chamber dramas, simply because London can deliver the lights, booming voices, dancers, and multimedia spectacle I rarely get back home. If that's not to your taste—or you already have access to similar spectacles at home—you might prefer some of London's more low-key offerings.

Well-known musicals may draw the biggest crowds, but the West End offers plenty of other crowd-pleasers, from revivals of classics to cutting-edge works by the hottest young playwrights. These productions tend to have shorter runs than famous musicals. Many productions star huge-name celebrities—London is a magnet for movie stars who want to stretch their acting chops.

You'll see the latest offerings advertised all over the Tube and elsewhere. The free *Official London Theatre Guide,* updated weekly, is a handy tool (find it at hotels, box offices, the City of London TI, and online at www.officiallondontheatre.co.uk). If you're picky, check the reviews at www.timeout.com/london.

Most performances are nightly except Sunday, usually with two or three matinees a week. The few shows that run on Sundays are mostly family fare (*Matilda, The Lion King,* and so on). Tickets range from about £25 to £120 for the best seats at big shows. Matinees are generally cheaper and rarely sell out.

Buying Tickets for West End Shows

For most visitors, it makes sense to simply buy tickets in London. Most shows have tickets available on short notice—likely at a discount. But if your time in London is limited—and you have your heart set on a particular show that's likely to sell out (usually the newest shows, and especially on weekends)—you can buy peace of mind by booking your tickets from home.

Advance Tickets: It's generally cheapest to buy your tickets directly from the theater, either through its website or by calling the theater box office. Often, a theater will reroute you to a third-party ticket vendor such as Ticketmaster. You'll pay with a credit card, and generally be charged a per-ticket booking fee (around £3). You can have your tickets emailed to you or pick them up before show time at the theater's Will Call window. Note that many third-party websites sell all kinds of London theater tickets, but these generally charge higher prices and fees. It's best to try the theater's website or box office first.

Discount Tickets from the TKTS Booth: This famous outlet at Leicester Square sells discounted tickets (25-30 percent off) for many shows (£3/ticket service charge, open Mon-Sat 10:00-19:00, Sun 11:00-16:30). TKTS offers a wide variety of shows on any given day, though they may not have the hottest shows in town. You must buy in person at the kiosk, and the best deals are same-day only.

The list of shows and prices is posted outside the booth and updated throughout the day. The same info is available on their constantly refreshed website (www.tkts.co.uk), which is worth checking before you head to Leicester Square. For the best choice and prices, come early in the day—the line starts forming even before the booth opens (it moves quickly). Have a second-choice show in mind, in case your first choice is sold out by the time you reach the ticket window. If you're less picky, come later in the day, when lines (and choices) diminish.

TKTS also sells advance tickets for some shows (but not as cheaply) and some regular-price tickets to extremely popular shows—convenient, but no savings. If TKTS runs out of its ticket allotment for a certain show, it doesn't necessarily mean the show is sold out—you can still try the theater's box office.

Is the TKTS booth right for you? If you're not committed to a particular show and just want a decent deal, this is a great option. You might snag a top-price seat for a popular-but-not-too-popular show (say, *Billy Elliot*) for about half-price through TKTS. But if you're committed to a particular show—especially a popular one—

or if you want the absolute cheapest seats, it's better to book directly at the theater—read on.

Take note: The real TKTS booth (with its prominent sign) is a freestanding kiosk at the south edge of Leicester Square. Several dishonest outfits nearby advertise "official half-price tickets"—avoid these, where you'll rarely pay anything close to half-price.

Tickets at the Theater Box Office: Even if a show is "sold out," there's usually a way to get a seat. Many theaters offer various discounts or "concessions": same-day tickets, cheap returned tickets, standing-room, matinee, senior or student standby deals, and more. Start by checking the show's website, call the box office, or simply drop by (many theaters are right in the tourist zone).

Same-day tickets (called "day seats") are generally available only in person at the box office starting at 10:00 (people start lining up well before then). These tickets (£20 or less) tend to be either in the nosebleed rows or have a restricted view (behind a pillar or extremely far to one side).

Another strategy is to show up at the box office shortly before show time (best on weekdays) and—before paying full price—ask about any cheaper options. Last-minute return tickets are often sold at great prices as curtain time approaches.

For a helpful guide to "day seats," consult www.theatremonkey.com/dayseatfinder.htm; for tips on getting cheap and last-minute tickets, visit www.londontheatretickets.org and www.timeout.com/london/theatre.

Booking Through Other Agencies: Although booking through a middleman such as your hotel or a ticket agency is quick and easy (and may be your last resort for a sold-out show), prices are greatly inflated. Ticket agencies and third-party websites are often just scalpers with an address. If you do buy from an agency, choose one who is a member of the Society of Ticket Agents and Retailers (look for the STAR logo—short for "secure tickets from authorized retailers"). These legitimate resellers normally add a maximum 25 percent booking fee to tickets.

Scalpers (or "Touts"): As at any event, you'll find scalpers hawking tickets outside theaters. And just like at home, those people may either be honest folk whose date just happened to cancel at the last minute...or they may be unscrupulous thieves selling forgeries. London has many of the latter.

THEATER BEYOND THE WEST END

Tickets for lesser-known shows tend to be cheaper (figure £15-30), in part because most of the smaller theaters are government-subsidized. Remember that plays don't need a familiar title or famous actor to be a worthwhile experience—read up on the latest offerings online; Time Out's website is a great place to start.

Major Noncommercial Theaters

One particularly good venue is the **National Theatre,** which has a range of impressive options, often starring recognizable names. While the building is ugly on the outside, the acts that play out upon its stage are beautiful—as are the deeply discounted tickets it commonly offers (looming on the South Bank by Waterloo Bridge, Tube: Waterloo, www.nationaltheatre.org.uk).

The **Barbican Centre** puts on high-quality, often experimental work (right by the Museum of London, just north of The City, Tube: Barbican, www.barbican.org.uk), as does the **Royal Court Theatre,** which has £10 tickets for its Monday shows (west of the West End in Sloane Square, Tube: Sloane Square, www.royalcourttheatre.com).

Menier Chocolate Factory is a small theater in Southwark gaining popularity for its impressive productions and intimate setting. Check their website to see what's on—they tend to have a mix of plays, musicals, and even an occasional comedian (behind the Tate Modern at 56 Southwark Street, Tube: Southwark, www.menierchocolatefactory.com).

Royal Shakespeare Company: If you'll ever enjoy Shakespeare, it'll be in Britain. The RSC performs at various theaters around London and in Stratford-upon-Avon year-round (for details, see page 425 in the Stratford-upon-Avon chapter). To get a schedule, contact the RSC (Royal Shakespeare Theatre, Stratford-upon-Avon, tel. 0844-800-1110, www.rsc.org.uk).

Shakespeare's Globe

To see Shakespeare in a replica of the theater for which he wrote his plays, attend a play at the Globe. In this round, thatch-roofed, open-air theater, the plays are performed much as Shakespeare intended—under the sky, with no amplification.

The play's the thing from late April through early October (usually Tue-Sat 14:00 and 19:30, Sun either 13:00 and/or 18:30, tickets can be sold out months in advance). You'll pay £5 to stand and £17-43 to sit, usually on a backless bench. Because only a few rows and the pricier Gentlemen's Rooms have seats with backs, £1 cushions and £3 add-on backrests are considered a good investment by many. Dress for the weather.

The £5 "groundling" tickets—which are open to rain—are most fun. Scurry in early to stake out a spot on the stage's edge, where the most interaction with the actors occurs. You're a crude peasant. You can lean your elbows on the stage, munch a picnic dinner (yes, you can bring in food), or walk around. I've never enjoyed Shakespeare as much as here, performed as it was meant to be in the "wooden O." If you can't get a ticket, consider waiting around. Plays can be long, and many groundlings leave before the end. Hang around outside and beg or buy a ticket from someone leaving early (groundlings are allowed to come and go). A few non-Shakespeare plays are also presented each year. If you can't attend a show, you can take a guided tour of the theater and museum by day (see page 114).

The new indoor Sam Wanamaker Playhouse allows Shakespearean-era plays and early-music concerts to be performed through the winter. Many of the productions in this intimate venue are one-offs and can be quite pricey.

To reserve tickets for plays at the Globe or Sam Wanamaker, call or drop by the box office (Mon-Sat 10:00-18:00, Sun 10:00-17:00, open one hour later on performance days, New Globe Walk entrance, no extra charge to book by phone, tel. 020/7401-9919). You can also reserve online (www.shakespearesglobe.com, £2.50 booking fee). If the tickets are sold out, don't despair; a few often free up at the last minute. Try calling around noon the day of the performance to see if the box office expects any returned tickets. If so, they'll advise you to show up a little more than an hour before the show, when these tickets are sold (first-come, first-served).

The theater is on the South Bank, directly across the Thames over the Millennium Bridge from St. Paul's Cathedral (Tube: Mansion House or London Bridge). The Globe is inconvenient for public transport, but during theater season, there's a regular supply of black cabs waiting nearby.

Outdoor and Fringe Theater

In summer, enjoy Shakespearean drama and other plays under the stars at the **Open Air Theatre,** in leafy Regent's Park in north London. You can bring your own picnic, order à la carte from the theater menu, or preorder a picnic supper from the theater at least 48 hours in advance (season runs late May-mid-Sept, tickets available beginning in mid-Jan; book at www.openairtheatre.org or—for an extra booking fee—by calling 0844-826-4242; grounds open 1.5 hours prior to evening performances, one hour prior to matinees; 10-minute walk north of Baker Street Tube, near Queen Mary's Gardens within Regent's Park; detailed directions and more info at www.openairtheatre.org).

London's rougher evening-entertainment scene is thriving. Choose from a wide range of **fringe theater** and comedy acts (generally £12).

CONCERTS AT CHURCHES

For easy, cheap, or free concerts in historic churches, attend a **lunch concert,** especially:

- St. Bride's Church, with free half-hour lunch concerts twice

Evensong

One of my favorite experiences in Britain is to attend evensong at a great church. Evensong is an evening worship service that is typically sung rather than said (though some parts—including scripture readings, a few prayers, and a homily—are spoken). It follows the traditional Anglican service in the Book of Common Prayer, including prayers, scripture readings, canticles (sung responses), and hymns that are appropriate for the early evening—traditionally the end of the working day and before the evening meal. In major churches with resident choirs, this service is filled with quality, professional musical elements. A singing or chanting priest leads the service, and a choir—usually made up of both men's and boys' voices (to sing the lower and higher parts, respectively)—sings the responses. The choir usually sings a cappella, or is accompanied by an organ. While regular attendees follow the service from memory, visitors—who are welcome—are given an order of service or a prayer book to help them follow along. (If you're not familiar with the order of service, watch the congregation to know when to stand, sit, and kneel.)

The most impressive places for evensong include London (Westminster Abbey, St. Paul's, Southwark Cathedral, or St. Bride's Church), Cambridge (King's College Chapel), York Minster, and Durham Cathedral. While this list includes many of the grandest churches in England, be aware that evensong typically takes place in the small choir area—which is far more intimate than the main nave. (To see the full church in action, a concert is a better choice.) Evensong generally occurs daily between 17:00 and 18:00 (often two hours earlier on Sundays)—check with individual churches for specifics. At smaller churches, evensong is sometimes spoken, not sung.

Note that evensong is not a performance—it's a somewhat somber worship service. If you enjoy worshipping in different churches, attending evensong can be a trip-capping highlight. But if regimented church services aren't your thing, consider getting a different music fix. Most major churches also offer organ or choral concerts—look for posted schedules or ask at the information desk or gift shop.

LONDON

a week at 13:15 (usually Tue and Fri—confirm in advance, church tel. 020/7427-0133, www.stbrides.com).

- St. James's at Piccadilly, with 50-minute concerts on Mon, Wed, and Fri at 13:10 (suggested £3.50 donation, info tel. 020/7734-4511, www.sjp.org.uk).
- St. Martin-in-the-Fields, offering concerts on Mon, Tue, and Fri at 13:00 (suggested £3.50 donation, church tel. 020/7766-1100, www.smitf.org).

St. Martin-in-the-Fields also hosts fine **evening concerts** by candlelight (£8-28, several nights a week at 19:30) and live jazz in its underground Café in the Crypt (£5.50-12, Wed at 20:00).

Evensong services are held at several churches, including St. Paul's Cathedral (see details on page 95), Westminster Abbey (see page 58), Southwark Cathedral (see page 116), and St. Bride's Church (Sun at 17:30).

Free **organ recitals** are usually held on Sunday at 17:45 in Westminster Abbey (30 minutes, tel. 020/7222-5152). Many other churches have free concerts; ask for the *London Organ Concerts Guide* at the City of London TI.

SUMMER EVENINGS ALONG THE SOUTH BANK

If you're visiting London in summer, consider hitting the South Bank neighborhood after hours.

Take a trip around the **London Eye** while the sun sets over the city (the wheel spins until late—last ascent at 20:30, later in July-Aug). Then cap your night with an evening walk along the pedestrian-only **Jubilee Walkway,** which runs east-west along the river. It's where Londoners go to escape the heat. This pleasant stretch of the walkway—lined with pubs and casual eateries—goes from the London Eye past Shakespeare's Globe to Tower Bridge (you can walk in either direction).

If you're in the mood for a movie, take in a flick at the **BFI Southbank,** located just across the river, alongside Waterloo Bridge. Run by the British Film Institute, the state-of-the-art theater shows mostly classic films, as well as art cinema (Tube: Waterloo or Embankment, check www.bfi.org.uk for schedules and prices).

Farther east along the South Bank is **The Scoop**—an outdoor amphitheater next to City Hall. It's a good spot for movies, concerts, dance, and theater productions throughout the summer—with Tower Bridge as a scenic backdrop. These events are free, nearly nightly, and family-friendly. For the latest event schedule, see www.morelondon.com and click on "Events" (next to City Hall, Riverside, The Queen's Walkway, Tube: London Bridge).

SPORTING EVENTS

London offers many sporting events. Tennis, cricket, rugby, football (soccer), and horse races all take place within an hour of the city. Each June Wimbledon draws a half-million spectators (www.wimbledon.com), while big-name English Premier League soccer clubs—including Chelsea, Arsenal, Tottenham Hotspurs, and West Ham United—take the pitch in London to sell-out crowds (www.premierleague.com). The two biggest horse races of the year take place in June: the Royal Ascot Races (www.ascot.co.uk) near

Windsor and the Epsom Derby (www.epsomderby.co.uk) in Surrey are both once-in-a-lifetime experiences.

Securing tickets to anything sporting in London can be difficult—and expensive—for travelers. Check the official team or event website several months in advance; tickets can sell out within minutes of going on sale to the general public. Third-party booking companies such as SportsEvents 365 (www.sportsevents365.com) and Ticketmaster (www.ticketmaster.co.uk) often have tickets to popular events at a premium price—a godsend for die-hard fans. Many teams also offer affordable, well-run stadium tours—check your favorite side's official website for details. Even if you can't attend a sports event in person, consider cheering on the action in a London pub.

Sleeping in London

London is an expensive city for lodging. Cheaper rooms are relatively dumpy. Don't expect £160 cheeriness in an £80 room. For £80, you'll get a double with breakfast in a safe, cramped, and dreary place with minimal service and the bathroom down the hall. For £100, you'll get a basic, reasonably cheery double with worn carpet and a private bath in a usually cramped, somewhat outdated, cracked-plaster building, or a soulless but comfortable room without breakfast in a huge Motel 6-type place. My London splurges, at £160-300, are spacious, thoughtfully appointed places good for entertaining or romancing.

Deals at Chain Hotels: Given London's high hotel prices, it's worth searching for a deal. Various websites list rooms in London in high-rise, three- and four-star business hotels. You'll give up the charm and warmth of a family-run establishment, and breakfast probably won't be included, but you might find that the price is right. Start by browsing the websites of several chains to get a sense of typical rates and online deals (see "Big, Good-Value, Modern Hotels," later).

Pricier London hotel chains include Millennium/Copthorne, Thistle, InterContinental/Holiday Inn, Radisson, Hilton, and Red Carnation. Auction-type sites (such as Priceline and Hotwire) match flexible travelers with empty hotel rooms, often at prices well below the hotel's normal rates. You can also browse these accommodation discount sites: www.londontown.com (an informative site with a discount booking service), athomeinlondon.co.uk and www.londonbb.com (both list central B&Bs), www.lastminute.com, www.visitlondon.com, and www.eurocheapo.com.

Book your accommodations well in advance if you'll be traveling during peak season or if your trip coincides with a major holi-

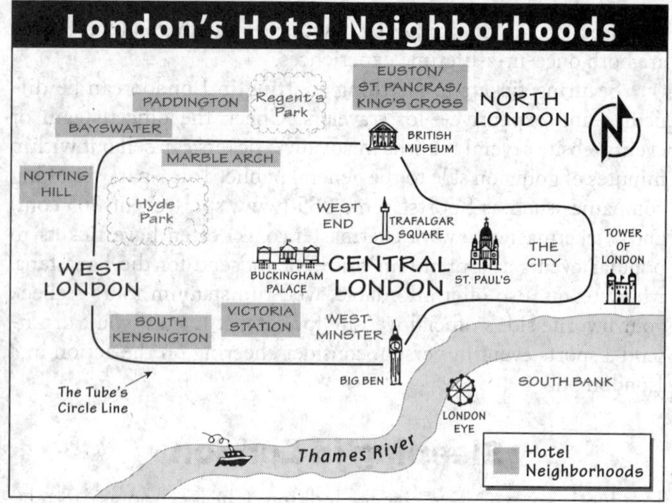

day or festival (see page 1042). For information and tips on pricing, getting deals, making reservations, and much more, see page 994.

VICTORIA STATION NEIGHBORHOOD

The streets behind Victoria Station teem with little, moderately-priced-for-London B&Bs. It's a safe, surprisingly tidy, and decent area without a hint of the trashy, touristy glitz of the streets in front of the station. I've divided these accommodations into two broad categories: Belgravia, west of the station, feels particularly posh, while Pimlico, to the east, is still upscale and dotted with colorful eateries. While I wouldn't go out of my way just to dine here, each area has plenty of good restaurants (see "Eating in London," later). All of my recommended hotels are within a five-minute walk of the Victoria Tube, bus, and train stations. On hot summer nights, request a quiet back room; most of these B&Bs lack air-conditioning and may front busy streets.

Laundry: The nearest laundry option is **Pimlico Launderette,** on the east—Pimlico—side about five blocks southwest of Warwick Square. Low prices and friendly George brighten your chore (£7.40 for small-load, same-day full service, £5-6 self-service, daily 8:00-19:00, last wash at 17:30; 3 Westmoreland Terrace—go down Clarendon Street, turn right on Sutherland, and look for the launderette on the left at the end of the street; tel. 020/7821-8692).

Parking: The 400-space Semley Place **NCP parking garage** is near the hotels on the west/Belgravia side (£42/day, possible discounts with hotel voucher, just west of Victoria Coach Station at Buckingham Palace Road and Semley Place, tel. 0845-050-7080, www.ncp.co.uk). **Victoria Station car park** is about half the price

Sleep Code

Abbreviations **(£1=about $1.60, country code: 44)**
S=Single, **D**=Double/Twin, **T**=Triple, **Q**=Quad, **b**=bathroom
Price Rankings
$$$ Higher Priced—Most rooms £125 or more
$$ Moderately Priced—Most rooms £75-125
$ Lower Priced—Most rooms £75 or less
Unless otherwise noted, breakfast is included, credit cards are accepted, and free Wi-Fi and/or a guest computer is generally available. For most places, the rates I list include the 20 percent VAT tax—but it's smart to ask when you book your room. Prices change; verify current rates online or by email. For the best prices, always book directly with the hotel.

and a quarter of the size, making it hard to find a spot here; check here first, but don't hold your breath (£24/day on weekdays, £12/day on weekends, entrance on Eccleston Bridge between Buckingham Palace Road and Bridge Place, tel. 0345-222-4224, www.apcoa.co.uk).

West of Victoria Station (Belgravia)

In Belgravia, the prices are a bit higher and your neighbors include some of the world's wealthiest people. These two places sit on tranquil Ebury Street, two blocks over from Victoria Station (or a slightly shorter walk from the Sloane Square Tube stop). You can cut the walk from Victoria Station to nearly nothing by taking a short ride on frequent bus #C1 (leaves from Buckingham Palace Road side of Victoria Station and drops you off on corner of Ebury and Elizabeth streets).

$$$ Lime Tree Hotel, enthusiastically run by Charlotte and Matt, is a gem, with 25 spacious, stylish, comfortable, thoughtfully decorated rooms, a helpful staff, and a fun-loving breakfast room (Sb-£115, Db-£175, larger superior Db-£205, Tb-£220, usually cheaper Jan-Feb, small lounge opens onto quiet garden, 135 Ebury Street, tel. 020/7730-8191, www.limetreehotel.co.uk, info@limetreehotel.co.uk, Laura manages the office).

$$$ B&B Belgravia, with its bright, airy rooms and traveler-chic style, feels more boutique but less like you've found your home—and family—away from home. Most of its 28 rooms come with closets, high ceilings, and larger-than-average space. If you're a light sleeper, ask for a room in the back (Sb-£140, Db-£160, family rooms-£179, 64 Ebury Street, tel. 020/7259-8570, www.bb-belgravia.com, info@bb-belgravia.com).

East of Victoria Station (Pimlico)

This area feels a bit less genteel than Belgravia, but it's still plenty inviting, with eateries and grocery stores. Most of these hotels are on or near Warwick Way, the main drag through this area. Generally the best Tube stop for this neighborhood is Victoria (though the Pimlico stop works equally well for the Luna Simone). Bus #24 runs right through the middle of Pimlico, connecting the Tate Britain to the south with Victoria Station, the Houses of Parlia-

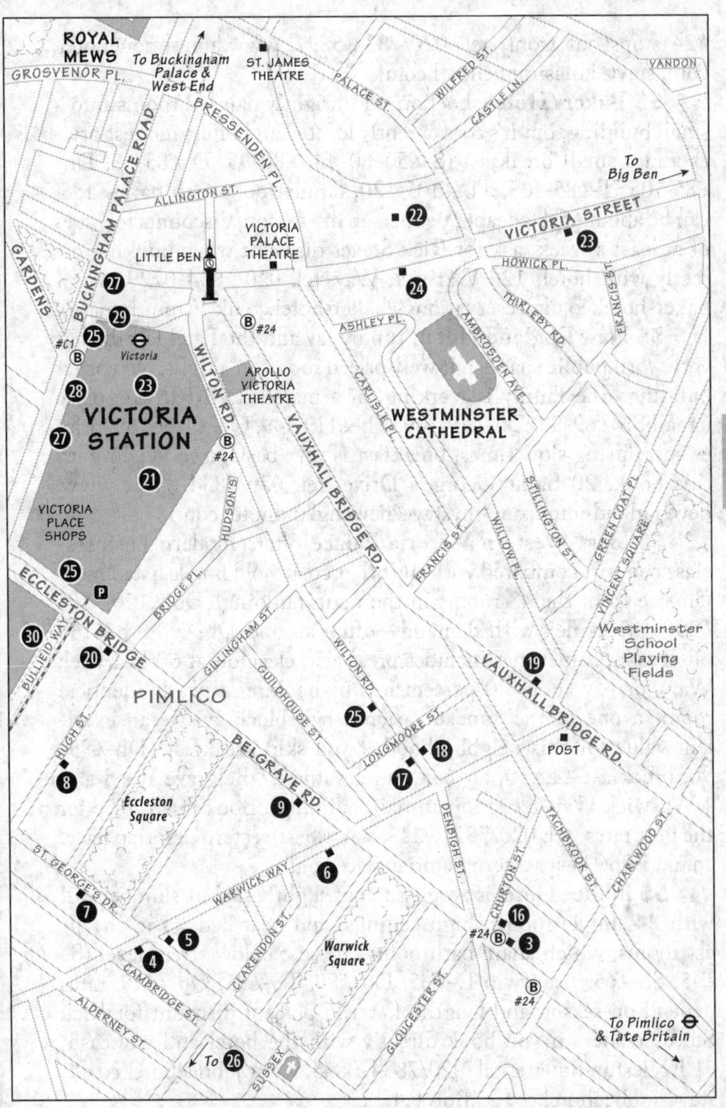

ment, Trafalgar Square, the British Museum, and much more to the north.

$$ Luna Simone Hotel rents 36 fresh, spacious, remodeled rooms with modern bathrooms. It's a smartly managed place, run for more than 40 years by twins Peter and Bernard—and Bernard's son Mark—and they still seem to enjoy their work (Sb-£85-90, Db-£115-140, Tb-£165-185, Qb-£180-210, prices vary with season, 10 percent discount when you book directly with the hotel, at 47 Belgrave Road near the corner of Charlwood Street, handy bus

#24 stops out front, tel. 020/7834-5897, www.lunasimonehotel.com, stay@lunasimonehotel.com).

$$ Bakers Hotel shoehorns 11 brightly painted rooms into a small building, but it's conveniently located and offers modest prices and a small breakfast (S-£50-60, Sb-£80-95, D-£85-95, Db-£85-105, T-£85-105, Tb-£105-120, family room with bath-£135, can be about £5-8 cheaper per person off-season, discounts for stays of at least a week, ask for Rick Steves discount when booking directly with hotel, 126 Warwick Way, tel. 020/7834-0729, www.bakershotel.co.uk, reservations@bakershotel.co.uk, Amin Jamani).

$$ New England Hotel, run by Jay and the Patel family, has very worn public spaces but well-priced rooms in a tight, old corner building. The family is working on a major facelift to the place (small Sb-£69-89, Db-£79-109, Tb-£119-149, Qb-£129-169, prices soft during slow times, breakfast is very basic, free Wi-Fi with this book, 20 Saint George's Drive, tel. 020/7834-8351, www.newenglandhotel.com, mystay@newenglandhotel.com).

$$ Best Western Victoria Palace offers modern business-class comfort compared with the other creaky old hotels listed here. Choose from the 43 rooms in the main building (Db-£120, Tb-£200, prices flex with demand—often around Db-£90/Tb-£160 off-season, sometimes includes breakfast, elevator, at 60 Warwick Way), or pay about 20 percent less by booking a nearly identical room in one of the annexes, each a half-block away—an excellent value for this neighborhood if you skip breakfast (Db-£85-90, breakfast-£12.50, air-con, no elevator, 17 Belgrave Road and 1 Warwick Way, reception at main building). Book in advance for the best rates (tel. 020/7821-7113, www.bestwesternvictoriapalace.co.uk, info@bestwesternvictoriapalace.co.uk).

$$ Jubilee Hotel is a well-run but slightly shabby slumbermill with 24 simple rooms, high ceilings, and neat beds. The cheapest rooms, which share bathrooms, are just below street level (S-£45, Sb-£65, tiny twin D-£65, Db-£89, Tb-£95, Qb-£119, rates depend on season and length of stay, 5 percent discount for Rick Steves readers if you book directly with the hotel and pay cash, 31 Eccleston Square, tel. 020/7834-0845, www.jubileehotel.co.uk, stay@jubileehotel.co.uk, Bob Patel).

$ Cherry Court Hotel, run by the friendly and industrious Patel family, rents 12 very small but bright and well-designed rooms with firm mattresses in a central location. Considering London's sky-high prices, this is a fine budget choice (Sb-£65, Db-£75, Tb-£110, Quint/b family room-£135, these prices with this book, 5 percent credit-card fee, fruit-basket breakfast in room, air-con, laundry, 23 Hugh Street, tel. 020/7828-2840, www.cherrycourthotel.co.uk, info@cherrycourthotel.co.uk, daughter Neha answers emails and offers informed restaurant advice).

$ easyHotel Victoria, at 36 Belgrave Road, is part of the budget chain described on page 163.

"SOUTH KENSINGTON," SHE SAID, LOOSENING HIS CUMMERBUND

To stay on a quiet street so classy it doesn't allow hotel signs, make "South Ken" your London home. The area has plenty of colorful restaurants, and shoppers like being a short walk from Harrods and the designer shops of King's Road and Chelsea. When I splurge, I splurge here. Sumner Place (where my first two listings are located) is just off Old Brompton Road, 200 yards from the handy South Kensington Tube station (on Circle Line, two stops from Victoria Station; and on Piccadilly Line, direct from Heathrow).

$$$ Aster House, well-run by friendly and accommodating Simon and Leonie Tan, has a cheerful lobby, lounge, and breakfast room. Its 13 rooms are comfy and quiet, with TV, phone, and air-conditioning. Enjoy breakfast or just lounging in the whisper-elegant Orangery, a glassy greenhouse. Simon and Leonie offer free loaner mobile phones to their guests (Sb-£180, Db-£240, bigger Db-from £270, more for garden room or superior twin; significant discount offered to readers of this book—up to 20 percent if you book three or more nights, up to 25 percent for five or more nights; additional 5 percent off when you pay with cash, check website for specials, 3 Sumner Place, tel. 020/7581-5888, www.asterhouse.com, asterhouse@gmail.com).

$$$ Number Sixteen, for well-heeled travelers, packs over-the-top class into its 41 artfully imagined rooms, plush designer-chic lounges, and tranquil garden. It's in a labyrinthine building, with boldly modern decor—perfect for an urban honeymoon (Sb-from £180, "superior" Db-from £276—but soft, ask for discounted "seasonal rates," especially on weekends and in Aug—subject to availability, larger "luxury" Db-£330, breakfast buffet in the conservatory-£19 continental or £24 full English, elevator, 16 Sumner Place, tel. 020/7589-5232, US tel. 1-888-559-5508, www.numbersixteenhotel.co.uk, sixteen@firmdale.com).

$$$ The Pelham Hotel, a 51-room business-class hotel with crisp service and a pricey mix of pretense and style, is genteel, with low lighting and a pleasant drawing room among the many perks (Db-£210-320, rate depends on room size and season, breakfast-£15 continental or £19.50 full English, slightly lower prices on weekends and in Aug, Web specials can include free breakfast; air-con, elevator, fitness room, 15 Cromwell Place, tel. 020/7589-8288, US tel. 1-888-757-5587, www.pelhamhotel.co.uk, reservations.thepelham@starhotels.co.uk, Jamie will take good care of you).

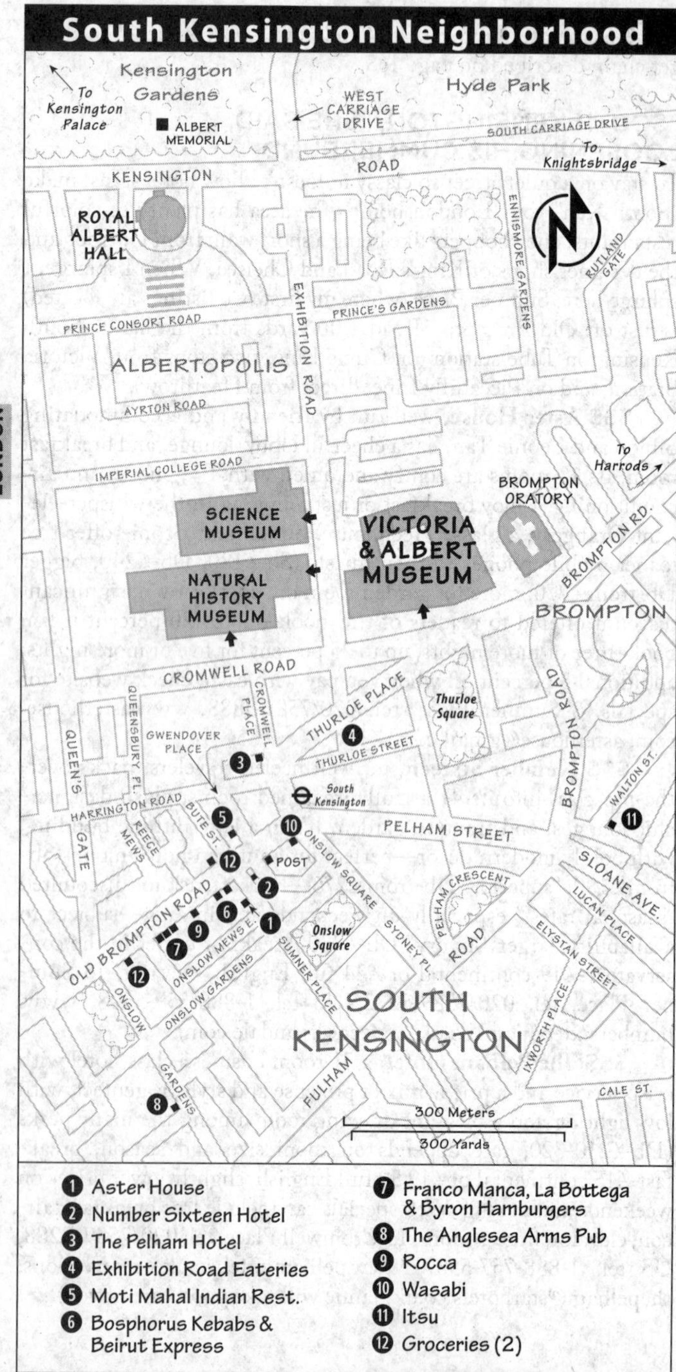

South Kensington Neighborhood
Kensington Gardens
To Kensington Palace
ALBERT MEMORIAL
Hyde Park
WEST CARRIAGE DRIVE
SOUTH CARRIAGE DRIVE
To Knightsbridge
KENSINGTON
ROAD
ROYAL ALBERT HALL
ENNISMORE GARDENS
RUTLAND GATE
EXHIBITION ROAD
PRINCE'S GARDENS
PRINCE CONSORT ROAD
ALBERTOPOLIS
AYRTON ROAD
IMPERIAL COLLEGE ROAD
To Harrods
BROMPTON ORATORY
SCIENCE MUSEUM
VICTORIA & ALBERT MUSEUM
BROMPTON RD.
NATURAL HISTORY MUSEUM
BROMPTON
CROMWELL ROAD
QUEENSBURY PL.
CROMWELL PLACE
THURLOE PLACE
Thurloe Square
BROMPTON ROAD
GWENDOVER PLACE
THURLOE STREET
QUEEN'S GATE
South Kensington
WALTON ST.
HARRINGTON ROAD
BUTE ST.
PELHAM STREET
REECE MEWS
POST
ONSLOW SQUARE
SLOANE AVE.
PELHAM CRESCENT
LUCAN PLACE
OLD BROMPTON ROAD
SYDNEY PL.
ROAD
ELYSTAN STREET
ONSLOW MEWS E.
Onslow Square
ONSLOW GARDENS
SUMNER PLACE
ONSLOW
SOUTH KENSINGTON
IXWORTH PLACE
GARDENS
FULHAM
CALE ST.
300 Meters
300 Yards
1 Aster House
2 Number Sixteen Hotel
3 The Pelham Hotel
4 Exhibition Road Eateries
5 Moti Mahal Indian Rest.
6 Bosphorus Kebabs & Beirut Express
7 Franco Manca, La Bottega & Byron Hamburgers
8 The Anglesea Arms Pub
9 Rocca
10 Wasabi
11 Itsu
12 Groceries (2)

NORTH OF KENSINGTON GARDENS

From the core of the tourist's London, the vast Hyde Park spreads west, eventually becoming Kensington Gardens. Three good accommodations neighborhoods line up side by side along the northern edge of the park: Bayswater (with the highest concentration of good hotels) anchors the area; it's bordered by Notting Hill to the west and Paddington to the east. This area has quick bus and Tube access to downtown and, for London, is very "homely" (Brit-speak for cozy).

Bayswater

Most of my Bayswater accommodations flank a tranquil, tidy park called Kensington Gardens Square (not to be confused with the much bigger Kensington Gardens adjacent to Hyde Park), a block west of bustling Queensway, north of Bayswater Tube station. These hotels are quiet for central London, but the area feels a bit sterile, and the hotels here tend to be impersonal. Popular with young international travelers, the Bayswater street called Queensway is a multicultural festival of commerce and eateries (see page 184).

$$$ Vancouver Studios offers one of the best values in this neighborhood. Its 45 modern, tastefully furnished rooms come with fully equipped kitchenettes (utensils, stove, microwave, and fridge) rather than breakfast. It's nestled between Kensington Gardens Square and Princes Square and has its own tranquil garden patio out back, which is refreshing if you land a somewhat-smoky room (Sb-£97, Db-£149, Tb-£189, extra bed-£20, 10 percent discount for seven or more nights, welcoming lounge, 30 Princes Square, tel. 020/7243-1270, www.vancouverstudios.co.uk, info@vancouverstudios.co.uk).

$$$ Garden Court Hotel is understated, with 40 simple, homey-but-tasteful rooms (prices vary seasonally with demand—these are normal/low-demand rates: Sb-£74, Db-£129, Tb-£149, Qb-£179, all rooms can be £20 more when demand is especially high, continental breakfast included or English breakfast-£3.50, elevator, 30 Kensington Gardens Square, tel. 020/7229-2553, www.gardencourthotel.co.uk, info@gardencourthotel.co.uk).

$$$ London House Hotel has 103 spiffy, modern, cookie-cutter rooms on Kensington Gardens Square. Its rates are great considering the quality and fine location (rates fluctuate, but generally Db-£105 weekdays and £130 on weekends, expect to pay more during busiest times and less in winter, smaller rooms not facing the square are about £10-20 cheaper, basement family rooms-£140, check online for specific rates and last-minute deals, continental breakfast-£7, elevator, 81 Kensington Gardens Square,

LONDON

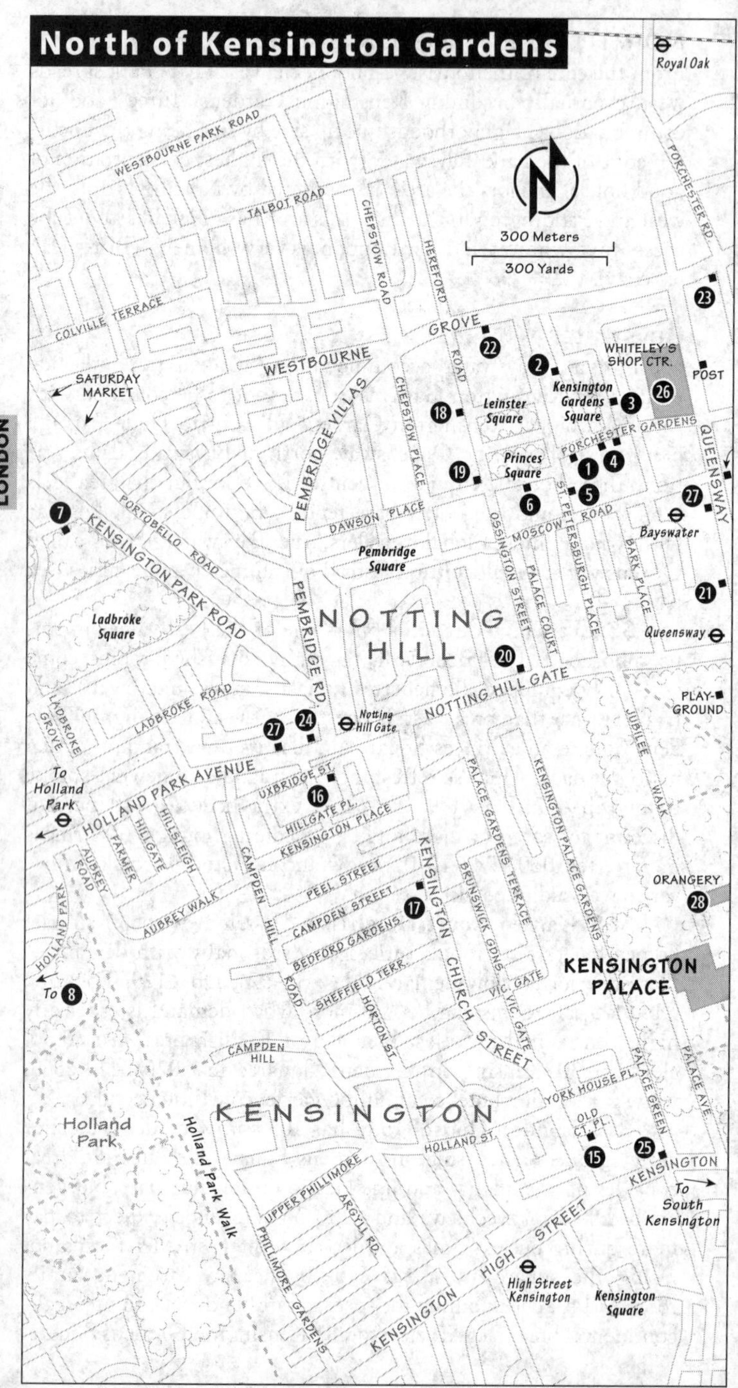
North of Kensington Gardens
Royal Oak
300 Meters
300 Yards
NOTTING HILL
KENSINGTON
KENSINGTON PALACE
WHITELEY'S SHOP. CTR.
POST
Leinster Square
Kensington Gardens Square
Princes Square
Pembridge Square
Ladbroke Square
Bayswater
Queensway
Notting Hill Gate
PLAY-GROUND
ORANGERY
SATURDAY MARKET
To Holland Park
To 8
Holland Park
Holland Park Walk
High Street Kensington
Kensington Square
To South Kensington
LONDON

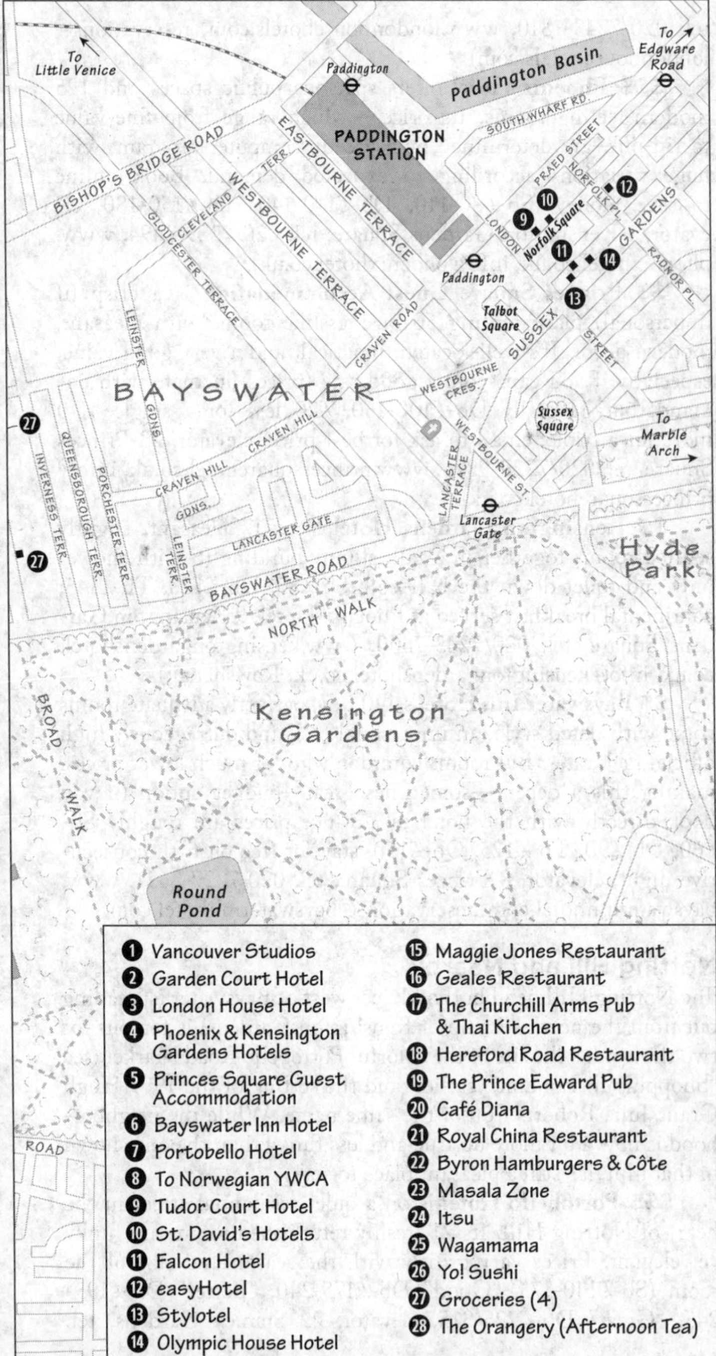

1 Vancouver Studios
2 Garden Court Hotel
3 London House Hotel
4 Phoenix & Kensington Gardens Hotels
5 Princes Square Guest Accommodation
6 Bayswater Inn Hotel
7 Portobello Hotel
8 To Norwegian YWCA
9 Tudor Court Hotel
10 St. David's Hotels
11 Falcon Hotel
12 easyHotel
13 Stylotel
14 Olympic House Hotel
15 Maggie Jones Restaurant
16 Geales Restaurant
17 The Churchill Arms Pub & Thai Kitchen
18 Hereford Road Restaurant
19 The Prince Edward Pub
20 Café Diana
21 Royal China Restaurant
22 Byron Hamburgers & Côte
23 Masala Zone
24 Itsu
25 Wagamama
26 Yo! Sushi
27 Groceries (4)
28 The Orangery (Afternoon Tea)

tel. 020/7243-1810, www.londonhousehotels.com, reservations@londonhousehotels.com).

$$$ Phoenix Hotel offers spacious public spaces and 125 modern-feeling rooms. Its prices—which range from fine-value to rip-off—are determined by a greedy computer program, with huge variations according to expected demand. Book online to save money (Sb-£80-110, Db-£110-140, Tb-£150-180, elevator, 1 Kensington Gardens Square, tel. 020/7229-2494, www.phoenixhotel.co.uk, info@phoenixhotel.co.uk).

$$ Princes Square Guest Accommodation is a crisp (if impersonal) place renting 50 businesslike rooms with pleasant, modern decor. It's well-located, practical, and a very good value, especially if you can score a good rate (prices fluctuate with demand, but generally Db-£100-160, £20 less for a single, £40 more for a triple; email to ask for best price, elevator, 23 Princes Square, tel. 020/7229-9876, www.princessquarehotel.co.uk, info@princessquarehotel.co.uk).

$$ Kensington Gardens Hotel laces 17 pleasant, slightly scuffed rooms together in a tall, skinny building (S with shower only and toilet down the hall-£68, Sb-£85, Db-£120, Tb-£145; continental breakfast served at Phoenix Hotel, 9 Kensington Gardens Square, tel. 020/7243-7600, www.kensingtongardenshotel.co.uk, info@kensingtongardenshotel.co.uk, Rowshanak).

$$ Bayswater Inn Hotel's 140 tidy, perfectly adequate rooms come with dated style, an impersonal feel, and outrageously high official rack rates. But rooms commonly go for much lower prices, making this a decent—sometimes great—budget option (if you book directly with the hotel in advance prices are roughly Sb-£60, Db-£90, Tb-£125, Qb-£150, stay for free on fifth consecutive night, elevator, 8 Princes Square, tel. 020/7727-8621, www.bayswaterinnhotel.com, reservations@bayswaterinnhotel.com).

Notting Hill and Nearby

The Notting Hill neighborhood, just west of Bayswater (spreading out from the northwest tip of Kensington Gardens) is famous for two things: It's the site of the colorful Portobello Road Market (see "Shopping in London," earlier) and the setting of the 1999 Hugh Grant/Julia Roberts film of the same name. While the neighborhood is now a bit more upscale and less funky than the one shown in that film, it's still a pleasant place to stay.

$$$ Portobello Hotel is on a quiet residential street in the heart of Notting Hill. Its 21 freshly refurbished rooms are funky yet elegant. Prices vary greatly with the season and size of the room (Sb-£140-175, "Good" Db-£175-240, "Better" Db-£195-245, "Great" Db-£225-315, elevator, 22 Stanley Gardens, tel.

020/7727-2777, www.portobellohotel.com, stay@portobellohotel.com, Hannah).

Near Holland Park: **$ Norwegian YWCA (Norsk K.F.U.K.)**—where English is definitely a second language—is open to any Norwegian woman and to non-Norwegian women under 30. (Men must be under 30 with a Norwegian passport.) Located on a quiet, stately street, it offers a study, TV room, piano lounge, and an open-face Norwegian ambience (goat cheese on Sundays!). They have mostly quads, so those willing to share with strangers are most likely to get a bed (S with shower only and toilet down the hall-£54, shared double-£46/bed, shared triple-£44/bed, shared quad-£42/bed, includes sheets and towels, includes breakfast year-round plus sack lunch and dinner Sept-June, £20 key deposit and £3 membership fee required, 52 Holland Park, Tube: Holland Park, tel. 020/7727-9346, www.kfukhjemmet.org.uk, kontor@kfukhjemmet.org.uk). With each visit, I wonder which is easier to get—a sex change or a Norwegian passport?

Paddington Station Neighborhood

Just to the east of Bayswater, the neighborhood around Paddington Station—while much less charming than the other areas I've recommended—is pleasant enough and very convenient to the Heathrow Express airport train. The area is flanked by the Paddington and Lancaster Gate Tube stops. Most of my recommendations circle Norfolk Square, just two blocks in front of Paddington Station, but are still quiet and comfortable. The main drag, London Street, is lined with handy eateries—pubs, Indian, Italian, Moroccan, Greek, Lebanese—plus convenience stores and more. (Better restaurants are a short stroll to the west, near Queensway and Notting Hill—see page 182.)

To reach this area, exit the station toward Praed Street (with your back to the tracks, it's to the left). Once outside, continue straight across Praed Street and down London Street; Norfolk Square is a block ahead on the left.

On Norfolk Square

These places (and many more on the same street) all offer small rooms at a reasonable price in tall buildings with lots of stairs and no elevator. I've chosen the ones that offer the most reasonable prices and the warmest welcome.

$$ Tudor Court Hotel has 38 colorful rooms and is conscientiously run by Connan and the Gupta family. While the tiny rooms are tight (with prefab plastic bathrooms and creaky plumbing) and the rates are a bit high, this place distinguishes itself with its warm welcome. If you smell a big batch of curry rice cooking, the Guptas are getting ready to take it to the homeless shelter, where they volunteer each week (S-£54-63, Sb-£95-108, "compact" Db-£99-129, larger "standard" Db-£135-165, Tb-£155-185, family room-£180-225, higher rates are for Fri-Sat and other busy times, 10 Norfolk Square, tel. 020/7723-5157, www.tudorcourtpaddington.co.uk, reservations@tudorcourtpaddington.co.uk).

$$ St. David's Hotels, run by the Neokleous family, has 60 rooms in several adjacent buildings. The rooms are small—as is typical for less-expensive hotels in London with minimal amenities—but the staff is friendly, and their non-en-suite rooms are a workable budget option (S-£50-60, Sb-£70-85, Db-£90-120, Tb-£100-130, pay Wi-Fi in rooms, 14 Norfolk Square, tel. 020/7723-3856, www.stdavidshotels.com, info@stdavidshotels.com).

$$ Falcon Hotel, a lesser value, has less personality and 19 simple, old-school, slightly dingy rooms (S-£64, Sb-£74, D-£94, Db-£99, Tb-£145, Qb-£155, rates flex with demand, free Wi-Fi if you book directly with the hotel, 11 Norfolk Square, tel. 020/7723-8603, www.falcon-hotel.com, info@falcon-hotel.com).

$ easyHotel, a budget chain described later, under "Big, Good-Value, Modern Hotels," has a branch at 10 Norfolk Place.

On Sussex Gardens

To reach these hotels, follow the directions to Norfolk Square (described earlier), but continue away from the station past the square to the big intersection with Sussex Gardens; you'll find them immediately to the left.

$$ Stylotel feels like the stylish, super-modern, aluminum-clad big sister of the easyHotel chain. Their tidy 39 rooms come with hard surfaces—hardwood floors, prefab plastic bathrooms, and metallic walls. While rooms can be a little cramped, the beds have space for luggage underneath. You may feel like an astronaut in a retro science-fiction film, but if you don't need ye olde doilies, this place offers a good value (Sb-£65, Db-£95, Tb-£115, Qb-£135, prices go up with demand—book early and directly with the hotel to get these rates, elevator, pay Wi-Fi, 160 Sussex Gardens, tel. 020/7723-1026, www.stylotel.com, info@stylotel.com, well-run by Andreas). They also have eight fancier, pricier, air-conditioned suites across the street (£180-220 for 2-4 people, kitchenettes, no breakfast).

$$ Olympic House Hotel has clean public spaces and a no-nonsense welcome, but its 38 business-class rooms offer predictable comfort and fewer old-timey quirks than many hotels in this price range (Sb-£75, Db-£105, Tb-£135, rates vary with demand, air-con in most rooms costs extra, elevator, pay Wi-Fi, 138 Sussex Gardens, tel. 020/7723-5935, www.olympichousehotel.co.uk, olympichousehotel@btinternet.com).

ELSEWHERE IN CENTRAL LONDON

$$$ The Sumner Hotel rents 19 rooms in a 19th-century Georgian townhouse sporting a lounge decorated with fancy modern Italian furniture and large contemporary rooms. This swanky place packs in all the amenities and is conveniently located north of Hyde Park and near Oxford Street, a busy shopping destination—close to Selfridges and a Marks & Spencer (queen Db-£193, king Db-£213, "deluxe" Db-£229, mention this book to get these Rick Steves rates, can be cheaper off-season, extra bed-£60, air-con, elevator, 54 Upper Berkeley Street, a block and a half off Edgware Road, Tube: Marble Arch, tel. 020/7723-2244, www.thesumner.com, reservations@thesumner.com).

$$$ The 22 York Street B&B offers a casual alternative in the city center, renting 10 traditional, hardwood, comfortable rooms, each named for a notable London landmark (Sb-£120, Db-£150, Tb-£180, inviting lounge; near Marylebone/Baker Street: from Baker Street Tube station, walk 2 blocks down Baker Street and take a right to 22 York Street—no sign, just look for #22; tel. 020/7224-2990, www.22yorkstreet.co.uk, mc@22yorkstreet.co.uk, energetically run by Liz and Michael Callis).

$$$ The Fielding Hotel is a simple and affordable little place lodged in the center of all the action—just steps from Covent Garden—on a quiet lane. They rent 25 basic rooms, serve no breakfast, and have almost no public spaces. Grace Langley, the manager, sticks with straight pricing (Sb-£108, Db-£168, family rooms for 3 or 4-£216, 12 percent more on Fri-Sat, air-con, 4 Broad Court off Bow Street, Tube: Covent Garden—for location see map on page 168, tel. 020/7836-8305, www.thefieldinghotel.co.uk, reservations@thefieldinghotel.co.uk).

$$ Seven Dials Hotel's 18 no-nonsense rooms are plain and fairly tight, but they're also clean, reasonably priced, and incredibly well-located. Since doubles here all cost the same, request one of their larger rooms when you book (Sb-£90, Db-£110 but £10 more for twin beds, Tb-£135, Qb-£150, 7 Monmouth Street, Tube: Leicester Square or Covent Garden—for location see map on page 168, tel. 020/7681-0791, www.sevendialshotel.co.uk, info@sevendialshotel.co.uk, run by friendly and hardworking Hanna).

OTHER SLEEPING OPTIONS

Big, Good-Value, Modern Hotels

If you can score a double for £90-100 (or less—often possible with promotional rates) and don't mind a modern, impersonal, American-style hotel, one of these can be a decent value in pricey London (for details on chain hotels, see page 1002).

I've listed a few of the dominant chains, along with a quick rundown on their more convenient London locations. Many of

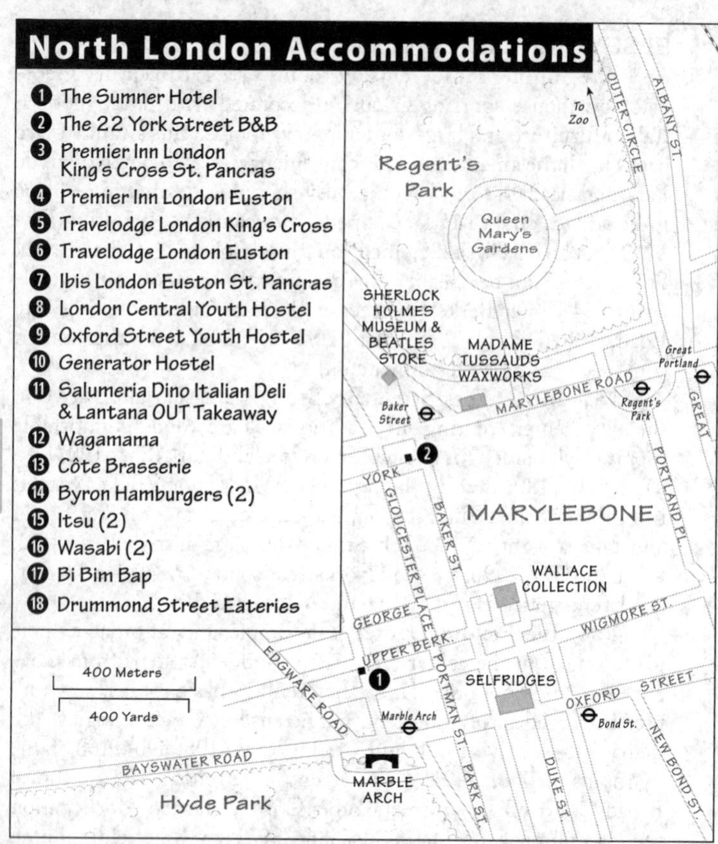

these hotels sit on busy streets in dreary train-station neighborhoods, so use common sense after dark and wear a money belt.

Premier Inn's locations include a branch inside **London County Hall** (next door to the London Eye), at **Southwark/Borough Market** (near Shakespeare's Globe on the South Bank, 34 Park Street, Tube: London Bridge), **Southwark/Tate Modern** (on Great Suffolk Street), **London King's Cross St. Pancras** (across the street from the east end of King's Cross Station and near the Eurostar terminus at St. Pancras), **London Euston** (handy but noisy location at corner of Euston Road and Dukes Road), **Kensington/Earl's Court** (11 Knaresborough Place, Tube: Earl's Court or Gloucester Road), **Victoria** (82 Eccleston Square, Tube: Victoria), **Leicester Square** (1 Leicester Place), and **Putney Bridge** (farther out, 3 Putney Bridge Approach). Avoid the **Tower Bridge** location, which is an inconvenient 15-minute walk from the nearest Tube stop. Book online at www.premierinn.com or call 0871-527-9222; from North America, dial 011-44-1582-567-890.

Travelodge has quite a few locations in London, including at

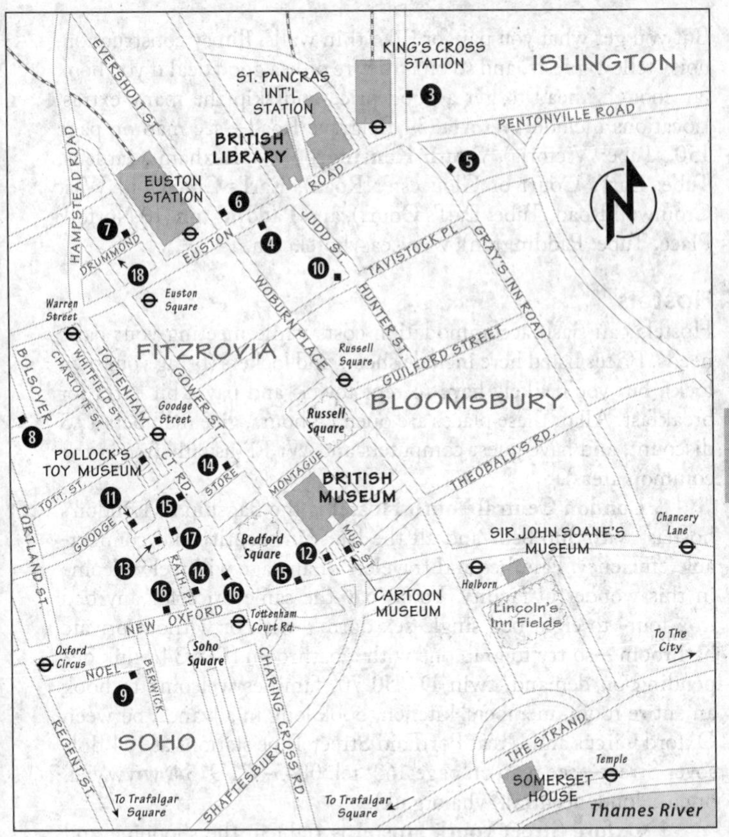

King's Cross (200 yards in front of King's Cross Station, Grays Inn Road, Tube: King's Cross St. Pancras), **Kings Cross Royal Scot, Euston, Marylebone, Covent Garden, Liverpool Street,** and **Farringdon** (www.travelodge.co.uk).

Ibis has only two locations that are convenient to London's center: **Euston St. Pancras** (on a quiet street a block west of Euston Station, 3 Cardington Street, Tube: Euston) and **The City** (5 Commercial Street, Tube: Aldgate East); book at www.ibishotel.com.

easyHotel, with several branches in good neighborhoods around London, has a unique business model inspired by its parent company, the easyJet budget airline. The generally tiny, super-efficient, no-frills rooms feel popped out of a plastic mold, down to the prefab ship's head-type "bathroom pod." Rates can be surprisingly low (with doubles as cheap as £30 if you book early enough)—but you'll be charged à la carte for expensive add-ons, such as TV use, Wi-Fi, luggage storage, fresh towels, and daily cleaning (breakfast, if available, comes from a vending machine). If you go with the base rate, it's like hosteling with privacy—a hard-to-beat value.

But you get what you pay for (like thin walls, flimsy construction, noisy fellow guests, and so on). They're only a good deal if you book far enough ahead to get a good price and skip the many extras. Locations include **Victoria** (34 Belgrave Road—see map on page 150, Tube: Victoria), **South Kensington** (14 Lexham Gardens, Tube: Earl's Court or Gloucester Road), **Earl's Court** (44 West Cromwell Road, Tube: Earl's Court), and **Paddington** (10 Norfolk Place, Tube: Paddington); www.easyhotel.com.

Hostels

Hostels can slash accommodation costs while meeting your basic needs. Prices listed here include sheets and lockers (bring your own lock), but you'll likely have to rent towels and pay a bit extra for breakfast. All of these places are open 24 hours, give members a £3 discount, and have guest computers and Wi-Fi (usually free in the common areas).

$ London Central Youth Hostel is the flagship of London's hostels, with 300 beds and all the latest in security and comfortable efficiency. Families and travelers of any age will feel welcome in this wonderful facility. You'll pay the same price for any bed in a four- to eight-bed single-sex dorm—with or without private bathroom—so try to grab one with a bathroom (£18-34/bunk depending on demand, twin D-£50-70, families welcome to book an entire room, members' kitchen, book long in advance, between Oxford Circus and Great Portland Street Tube stations at 104 Bolsover Street—see map on page 162, tel. 0845-371-9154, www.yha.org.uk, londoncentral@yha.org.uk).

$ Oxford Street Youth Hostel is right in the shopping and clubbing zone in Soho, with 90 beds (£20-30/bunk, twin D-£50-70, members' kitchen, 14 Noel Street, Tube: Oxford Street, tel. 0845-371-9133, www.yha.org.uk, oxfordst@yha.org.uk).

$ St. Paul's Youth Hostel, near St. Paul's Cathedral, is modern, friendly, well-run, and a bit scruffy. Most of the 213 beds are in shared, single-sex, 3- to 11-bunk rooms (£16-30/bunk depending on demand, twin D-£45-70, cheap meals, 36 Carter Lane, Tube: St. Paul's, tel. 020/7236-4965 or 0845-371-9012, www.yha.org.uk, stpauls@yha.org.uk).

$ Generator Hostel is a brightly colored, hip hostel with a café, a DJ spinning the hits, and 870 beds in 220 rooms, including doubles. It's in a renovated building tucked behind a busy street halfway between Kings Cross and the British Museum (£18-34/bunk depending on demand, twin Db-£70-120, breakfast-£5, 37 Tavistock Place, Tube: Russell Square, tel. 020/7388-7666, www.generatorhostels.com, london@generatorhostels.com).

$ A cluster of three **St. Christopher's Inn** hostels, south of the Thames near London Bridge, have cheap dorm beds; one branch (the Oasis) is for women only. All have loud and friendly bars attached (£22-36, higher price is for weekends, less in off-season, D-£70-80 or thereabouts, includes small breakfast, must be over 18 years old, 161 Borough High Street, Tube: Borough or London Bridge, reservations tel. 020/8600-7500, www.st-christophers.co.uk, bookings@st-christophers.co.uk).

Apartment Rentals

Consider this option if you're traveling as a family, in a group, or staying five days or longer. Websites such as Airbnb and VRBO let you correspond directly with European property owners or managers, or consider one of the sites listed below. Some specialize in London, while others also cover areas outside of London. For more information on renting apartments, see page 1003 in the Practicalities chapter.

LondonConnection.com is a Utah-based company that owns and rents several properties around London. The owner, Thomas, prides himself on providing personal service.

OneFineStay.com focuses on finding stylish, contemporary flats (most of them part-time residences) in desirable London neighborhoods. While pricey, it can be a good choice if you're seeking a hip, nicely decorated home away from home.

Other options include **Cross-Pollinate.com, Coach House Rentals** (rentals.chslondon.com), **APlaceLikeHome.co.uk, HomeFromHome.co.uk, London-House.com,** and **GoWithIt.co.uk.**

Staying near the Airports

It's so easy to get to Heathrow and Gatwick from central London, I see no reason to sleep at either one. But if you do, here are some options.

Heathrow: A **Yotel** is inside the airport (Terminal 4), while **easyHotel** and **Hotel Ibis London Heathrow** are a short bus or taxi ride away.

Gatwick: The South Terminal has a **Yotel,** while **Gatwick Airport Central Premier Inn** rents cheap rooms 350 yards away, and **Gatwick Airport Travelodge** has budget rooms about two miles from the airport.

Eating in London

Whether it's dining well with the upper crust, sharing hearty pub fare with the blokes, or joining young professionals at the sushi bar, eating out has become an essential part of the London experience. You could try a different cuisine for each meal and never eat "local" English food, even on a lengthy stay in London. The sheer variety of foods—from every corner of its former empire and beyond—is astonishing.

But the thought of a £50 meal in Britain generally ruins my appetite, so my London dining is limited mostly to easygoing, fun, moderately priced alternatives. I've listed places by neighborhood—handy to your sightseeing or hotel. Considering how expensive London can be, if there's any good place to cut corners to stretch your budget, it's by eating cheaply. Pub grub (at one of London's 7,000 pubs) and ethnic restaurants (especially Indian and Chinese) are good low-cost options. Of course, picnicking is the fastest and cheapest way to go. Good grocery stores and sandwich shops, fine park benches, and polite pigeons abound in Britain's most expensive city.

For advice on eating in London, including information on pubs, beer, ethnic eats, and good chain restaurants, plus details on tipping, eating on a budget, English breakfasts, and afternoon tea, see page 1004. Most London restaurants generally open daily no later than noon and close sometime between 22:00 and midnight.

CENTRAL LONDON

I've arranged these options by neighborhood, but they're all within about a 20-minute walk of each other. Survey your options before settling on a place.

Near Soho and Chinatown

London has a trendy scene that many Beefeater seekers miss. Foodies who want to eat well skip the more staid and touristy zones near Piccadilly and Trafalgar Square and head to Soho instead. Make it a point to dine in Soho at least once, to feel the pulse of London's eclectic urban melting pot of international flavors. These restaurants are scattered throughout a chic, creative, and borderline-seedy zone that teems with hipsters, theatergoers, and London's gay community. Even if you plan to have dinner elsewhere, it's a treat just to wander around Soho.

Note: While gentrification has mostly stripped this area of its former "red light district" vibe, a few pockets of sex for sale survive. Beware of the extremely welcoming women standing outside the strip clubs (especially on Great Windmill Street). Enjoy the sales pitch—but know that only fools fall for the "£5 drink and show" lure.

On and near Wardour Street, in the Heart of Soho

Running through the middle of Soho, rumbling past what's left of the strip-club zone, Wardour Street is ground zero for creative restaurateurs hoping to break into the big leagues. Strolling up this street—particularly from Brewer Street northward—you can take your pick from a world of options: Thai, Indonesian, Vietnamese, Italian, French, and even...English. Not yet tarnished by the corporatization creeping in from areas to the south, this drag still seems to hit the right balance between trendy and accessible. While I've listed several choices below (including some that are a block or two off Wardour Street), simply strolling the length of the street and following your appetite to the place that looks best is a great plan.

Princi is a vast, bright, efficient, wildly popular Italian deli/bakery with Milanese flair. Along one wall is a long counter with display cases offering a tempting array of pizza rustica, panini sandwiches, focaccia, a few pasta dishes, and desserts (look in the window from the street to see their wood-fired oven in action). Order your food at the counter, then find a space at a long shared table; or get it to go for an affordable and fast meal (£7-13 meals, daily 8:00-24:00, 135 Wardour Street, tel. 020/7478-8888).

Bi Bim Bap is a popular and muggy little diner named for what it sells: *bibimbap* (literally "mixed rice"), a scalding stone bowl of rice and thinly sliced veggies, topped with a fried egg. Flavor it to taste with the two sauces, then mix it up. You can pay a few pounds extra to add other toppings—including chicken, *bulgogi* (marinated beef strips), and mushrooms. Though the food is traditional Korean, the stylish, colorful interior reminds you you're in Soho (£7-10 meals, Mon-Sat 12:00-15:00 & 18:00-23:00, closed Sun, 11 Greek Street, second location near British Museum at 8 Charlotte Street, tel. 020/7287-3434).

The Gay Hussar, dressy and tight, squeezes several elegant tables into what the owners say is the only Hungarian restaurant in England. It's traditional fare: cabbage, sauerkraut, sausage, paprika, and pork, as well as duck and chicken. Wash down this Hungarian comfort food with a Hungarian wine (£15-18 meals, Mon-Sat 12:15-14:30 & 17:30-22:45, closed Sun, 2 Greek Street, tel. 020/7437-0973).

Bocca di Lupo, a stylish and popular option, serves half and full portions of classic regional Italian food. Dressy but with a fun

LONDON

Central London Eateries

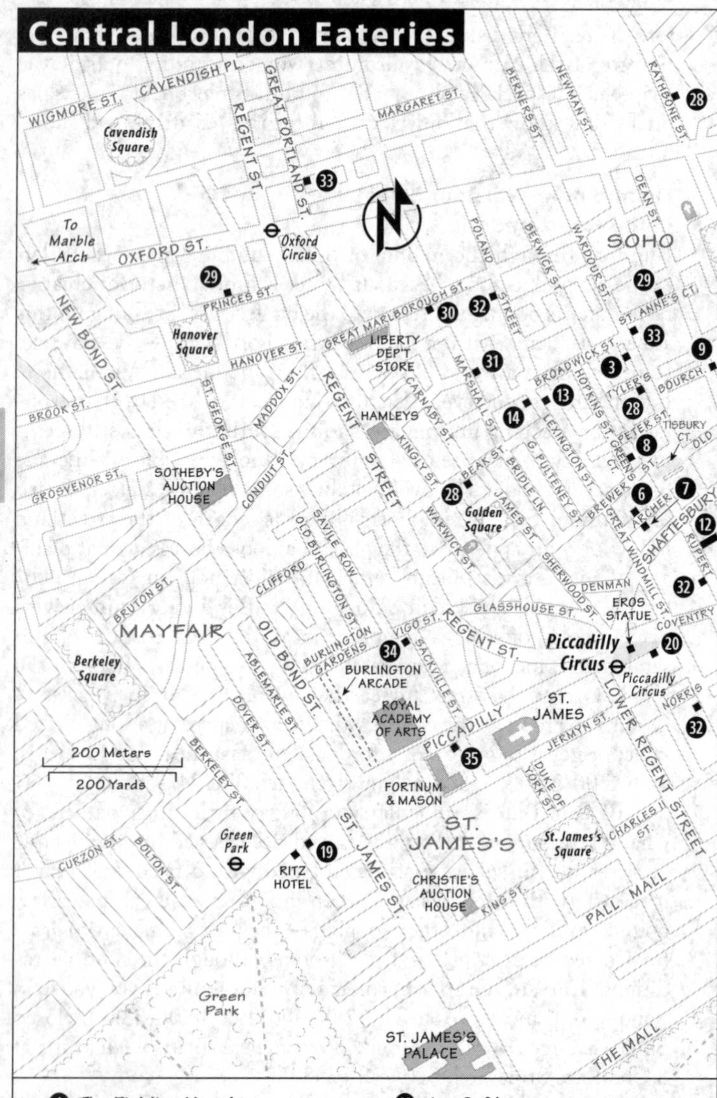

1. The Fielding Hotel
2. Seven Dials Hotel
3. Princi Italian Deli
4. Bi Bim Bap
5. The Gay Hussar
6. Bocca di Lupo
7. Gelupo Gelato
8. Yalla Yalla
9. Ducksoup
10. Y Ming Chinese Restaurant
11. Jen Café
12. Wong Kei
13. Andrew Edmunds Restaurant
14. Mildred's Vegetarian Rest.; Bao; Fernandez & Wells
15. St. Martin-in-the-Fields
16. The Chandos Pub
17. Gordon's Wine Bar
18. The Harp Pub
19. The Wolseley

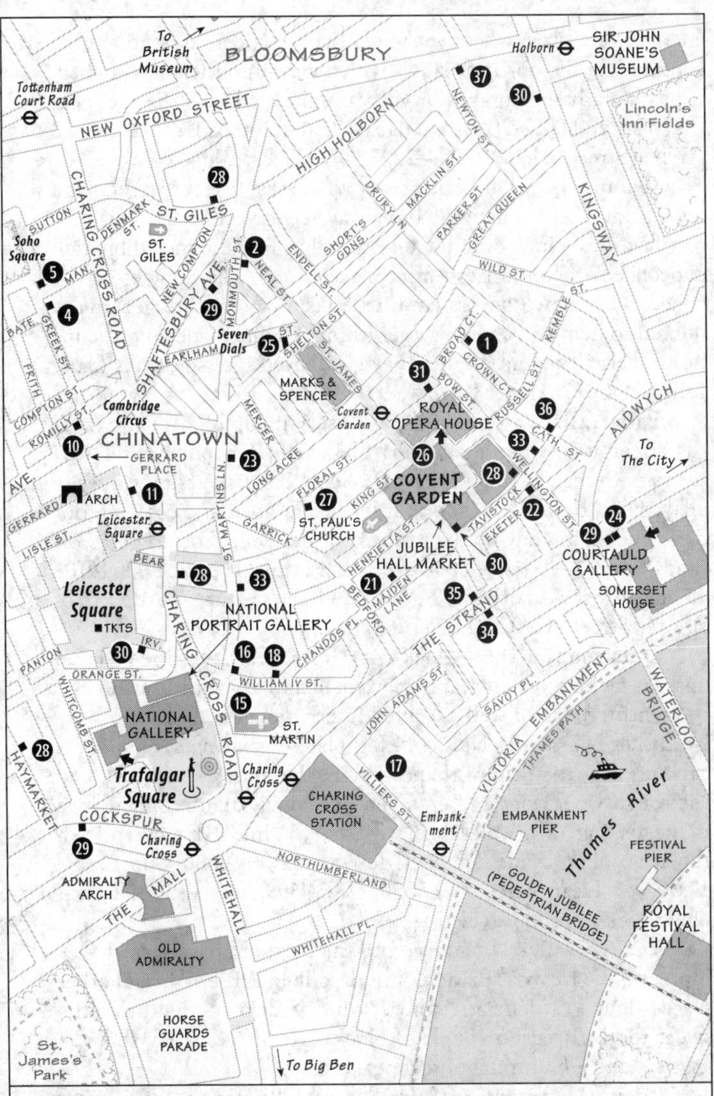

20 Criterion Restaurant
21 Rules Restaurant
22 Joe Allen
23 Dishoom
24 Sitar Indian Restaurant
25 Belgo Centraal
26 Union Jacks
27 Lamb & Flag Pub
28 Byron (7)
29 Thai Square (5)
30 Wagamama (4)
31 Masala Zone (2)
32 Yo! Sushi (3)
33 Côte (4)
34 Itsu (2)
35 Wasabi (2)
36 Loch Fyne Fish Restaurant
37 The Princess Louise Pub

energy, it's a place where you're glad you made a reservation. The counter seating, on cushy stools with a view into the open kitchen, is particularly memorable, or you can take a table in the snug, casual back end (£12-20 dishes, daily 12:30-15:00 & 17:30-23:00, 12 Archer Street, tel. 020/7734-2223, www.boccadilupo.com).

Gelupo, Bocca di Lupo's sister *gelateria* across the street, has a wide array of ever-changing but always creative and delicious dessert favorites—including popular standbys like the incredibly rich chocolate sorbet and fresh-mint *stracciatella.* A £4 sampler cup or cone gets you two flavors (and little taster spoons are generously offered to help you choose). Everything is homemade, and the interior feels clean and bright. They also have espresso drinks (daily 11:00-23:00, 7 Archer Street, tel. 020/7287-5555).

Yalla Yalla is a hole-in-the-wall serving up high-quality Beirut street food—hummus, baba ghanoush, tabbouleh, and *shawarmas.* Stylish as you'd expect for Soho, it's tucked down a seedy alley across from a sex shop. Eat in the cramped and cozy interior or at one of the few outdoor tables, or get your food to go (£3-4 sandwiches, £4-6 *meze,* £8 *mezes* platter available until 17:00, £10-15 bigger dishes, daily 10:00-23:00, 1 Green's Court—just north of Brewer Street, tel. 020/7287-7663).

Ducksoup, a short block over from Wardour Street, is an upscale-feeling yet cool and relaxed little bar, with a small but thoughtful menu of well-executed international and modern British dishes (£7 small plates, £14 big plates—sharing several items can add up). The menu is handwritten, the music is on vinyl, and the rough woodwork and cramped-but-convivial atmosphere give it the feeling of a well-loved wine bar. While a bit overpriced, the atmosphere is memorable (Mon-Sat 12:00-22:30, Sun 13:00-17:00, 41 Dean Street, tel. 020/7287-4599, reservations smart, www.ducksoupsoho.co.uk).

And for Dessert: In addition to the outstanding gelato at **Gelupo** and the treats at **Princi** (both described earlier), several other places along Wardour Street boast window displays that tickle the sweet tooth. In just a couple of blocks, you'll see pastry shops, a *crêperie,* and a Hummingbird cupcake shop.

Chain Restaurants in Soho: Some of Britain's most popular chain restaurants started out here in Soho, but in this fast-evolving neighborhood, they're now a little like stale sushi. While I wouldn't waste a Soho meal on one of these places, they're a convenient fallback. You'll find **Byron Hamburgers** (particularly appealing industrial-mod branch at 97 Wardour Street, also near Golden Square at 16 Beak Street and at 1A St. Giles High Street), **Thai Square** (27 St. Anne's Court, also at 5 Princes Street on Hanover Square), **Wagamama** (42 Great Marlborough Street), **Masala Zone** (9 Marshall Street), **Yo! Sushi** (52 Poland Street), and **Côte**

(124 Wardour Street and near Oxford Circus at 4 Great Portland Street). For descriptions, see page 1008 of the Practicalities chapter.

Authentic Chinese Food in and near Chinatown

The main drag of Chinatown (Gerrard Street, with the ornamental archways) is lined with touristy, interchangeable Chinese joints—but these places seem to have an edge.

Y Ming Chinese Restaurant—across Shaftesbury Avenue from the ornate gates, clatter, and dim sum of Chinatown—has dressy European decor, serious but helpful service, and authentic Northern Chinese cooking. London's food critics consider this well worth the short walk from the heart of Chinatown for food that's a notch above (good £12 meal deal offered 12:00-18:00, £8-12 plates, open Mon-Sat 12:00-23:45, closed Sun, turquoise corner shop at 35 Greek Street, tel. 020/7734-2721).

Jen Café, across the little square called Newport Place, is a humble Chinese corner eatery much loved for its homemade dumplings. It's just stools and simple seating, with fast service, a fun and inexpensive menu, and a devoted following (£6-8 plates, daily 10:30-20:30, until 21:30 Thu-Sun, cash only, 4 Newport Place, tel. 020/7287-9708).

Wong Kei Chinese restaurant, at the Wardour Street (west) end of the Chinatown drag, offers a bewildering variety of dishes served by notoriously brusque waiters in a setting that feels like a hospital cafeteria. Londoners put up with the abuse to enjoy one of the satisfying BBQ rice dishes or hot pots. Individuals and couples are usually seated at communal tables, while larger parties are briskly shuffled up or down stairs (£7-12 main dishes, £10-15 chef special combos, daily 11:30-23:30, cash only, 41 Wardour Street, tel. 020/7437-8408).

Sedate and Upscale Options on Lexington Street, in the Heart of Soho

Andrew Edmunds Restaurant is a tiny candlelit space where you'll want to hide your camera and guidebook and not act like a tourist. This little place—with a jealous and loyal clientele—is the closest I've found to Parisian quality in a cozy restaurant in London. The extensive wine list, modern European cooking, and creative seasonal menu are worth the splurge (£5-8 starters, £12-20 main dishes, Mon-Sat 12:00-15:30 & 17:30-22:45, Sun 13:00-16:00 & 18:00-22:30, these are last-order times, come early or call ahead, request ground floor rather than basement, 46 Lexington Street, tel. 020/7437-5708, www.andrewedmunds.com).

Mildred's Vegetarian Restaurant, across from Andrew Edmunds, has an enjoyable menu and a pleasant interior filled with happy eaters (£8-11 meals, £6-7 dishes from small takeaway menu,

Pub Appreciation

The pub is the heart of the people's England, where all manner of folks have, for generations, found their respite from work and a home away from home. England's classic pubs are national treasures, with great cultural value and rich history, not to mention good beer and grub (you'll find details on beer and pub food in the Practicalities chapter on pages 1011 and 1007).

Their odd names can go back hundreds of years. Because so many medieval pub-goers were illiterate, pubs were simply named for the picture hung outside (e.g., The Crooked Stick, The Queen's Arms—meaning her coat of arms).

The Golden Age for pub-building was in the late Victorian era (c. 1880-1905), when pubs were independently owned and land prices were high enough to make it worthwhile to invest in fixing them up. The politics were pro-pub as well: Conservatives, backed by Big Beer, were in, and temperance-minded Liberals were out.

Especially in class-conscious Victorian times, traditional pubs were divided into sections by elaborate screens (now mostly gone), allowing the wealthy to drink in a more refined setting, while commoners congregated on the pub's rougher side. These were really "public houses," featuring nooks (snugs) for groups and clubs to meet, friends and lovers to rendezvous, and families to get out of the house at night.

Historic pubs still dot the London cityscape. The only place to see the very oldest-style tavern in the "domestic tradition" is at **Ye Olde Cheshire Cheese,** which was rebuilt in 1667 (after the Great Fire) from a 16th-century tavern (£6-12 pub grub, £11-16 meals in the restaurant, open daily, 145 Fleet Street, Tube: Blackfriars, tel. 020/7353-6170). Imagine this mazelike place, with three separate bars, in the pre-Victorian era: With no bar, drinkers gathered around the fireplaces, while tap boys shuttled tankards up from the cellar. (This was long before barroom taps were connected to casks in the cellar. Oh, and don't say "keg"—that's a gassy modern thing.)

Late-Victorian pubs are more common, such as the lovingly restored 1897 **Princess Louise** (daily midday until 23:00, lunch and dinner served Mon-Sat 12:00-21:00 in less atmospheric upstairs lounge, no food Sun, 208 High Holborn, see map on page 168, Tube: Holborn, tel. 020/7405-8816). These places are fancy, often with heavy embossed wallpaper ceilings, decorative tile work, fine-etched glass, ornate carved stillions (the big central hutch for storing bottles and glass), and even urinals equipped with a place to set your glass.

London's best Art Nouveau pub is **The Black Friar** (c. 1900-1915), with fine carved capitals, lamp holders, and quirky phrases worked into the decor (£9-15 meals, Mon-Sat 9:00-23:00, Sun

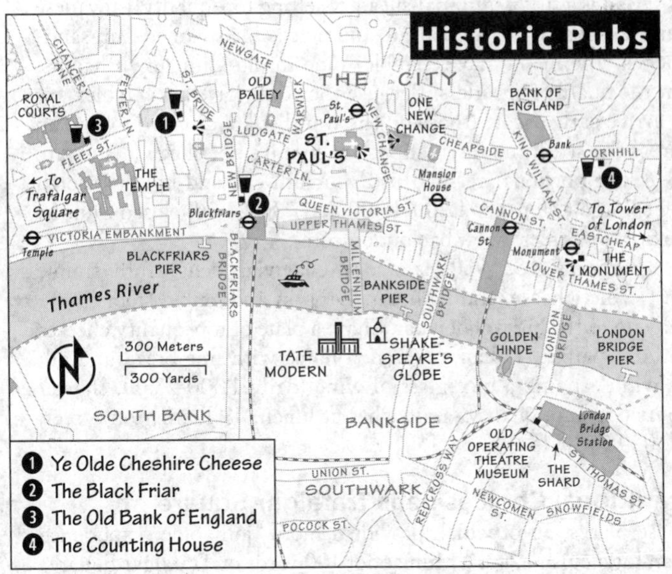

12:00-22:30, food daily until 22:00, outdoor seating, 174 Queen Victoria Street, Tube: Blackfriars, tel. 020/7236-5474).

The "former-bank pubs" represent a more modern trend in pub-building. As banks increasingly go electronic, they're moving out of lavish, high-rent old buildings. Many of these former banks are being refitted as pubs with elegant bars and freestanding stillions, which provide a fine centerpiece. Three such pubs are **The Old Bank of England** (£10-13 meals, Mon-Fri 11:00-23:00, food served 12:00-21:00, closed Sat-Sun, 194 Fleet Street, Tube: Temple, tel. 020/7430-2255), **The Jugged Hare** (open daily, 172 Vauxhall Bridge Road—see map on page 150, Tube: Victoria, tel. 020/7614-0134, also see listing on page 180), and **The Counting House** (Mon-Fri 11:00-23:00, closed Sat-Sun, 50 Cornhill, Tube: Bank, tel. 020/7283-7123, see listing on page 184).

Go pubbing in the evening for a lively time, or drop by during the quiet late morning (from 11:00), when the pub is empty and filled with memories.

Mon-Sat 12:00-23:00, closed Sun, vegan options, 45 Lexington Street, tel. 020/7494-1634).

Bao is a tight, minimalist eatery selling top-quality Taiwanese cuisine, specializing in delicate and delectable steamed-bun sandwiches. The menu may resemble some in old Chinatown haunts, but the quality is peerless. Because they only have a few tables, try to arrive early or late (those on the wait list are directed to line up across the street; no reservations). While it's not cheap (dishes are £3-6, but portions are small, so your bill can add up), it's worth the splurge (Mon-Sat 12:00-15:00 & 17:30-22:00, closed Sun, 53 Lexington Street, www.baolondon.com).

Fernandez & Wells is a cozy, convivial, delightfully simple little wine, cheese, and ham bar. Drop in and grab a stool as you belly up to the big wooden bar. Share a plate of top-quality cheeses and/or Spanish, Italian, or French hams with fine bread and oil, all while sipping a nice glass of wine (daily 11:00-23:00, shorter hours Sat-Sun, quality sandwiches at lunch, 43 Lexington Street, tel. 020/7734-1546).

Traditional Choices near Trafalgar Square

These places, all of which provide a more "jolly olde" experience than high cuisine, are within about 100 yards of Trafalgar Square.

St. Martin-in-the-Fields Café in the Crypt is just right for a tasty meal on a monk's budget—maybe even on a monk's tomb. You'll dine sitting on somebody's gravestone in an ancient crypt. Their enticing buffet line is kept stocked all day, serving breakfast, lunch, and dinner (£7-10 cafeteria plates, hearty traditional desserts, free jugs of water). They also serve a restful cream tea (£6.50, daily 14:00-18:00). You'll find the café directly under the St. Martin-in-the-Fields Church, facing Trafalgar Square—enter through the glass pavilion next to the church (generally about 8:00-20:00 daily, profits go to the church, Tube: Charing Cross, tel. 020/7766-1158 or 020/7766-1100). On Wednesday evenings you can dine to the music of a live jazz band at 20:00 (£5.50-12 tickets). While here, check out the concert schedule for the busy church upstairs (or visit www.smitf.org).

The Chandos Pub's Opera Room floats amazingly apart from the tacky crush of tourism around Trafalgar Square. Look for it opposite the National Portrait Gallery (corner of William IV Street and St. Martin's Lane) and climb the stairs—to the left or right of the pub entrance—to the Opera Room. This is a fine Trafalgar rendezvous point and wonderfully local pub. They serve £6 sandwiches and a better-than-average range of traditional pub meals for under £10—meat pies and fish-and-chips are their specialty. The ground-floor pub is stuffed with regulars and offers snugs (private booths) and more serious beer drinking. To eat on that level, you have to order upstairs and carry it down. Chandos proudly serves the local Samuel Smith beer at £3 a pint (kitchen open daily 11:30-21:00, Fri until 18:00, order and pay at the bar, 29 St. Martin's Lane, Tube: Leicester Square, tel. 020/7836-1401).

Gordon's Wine Bar is really a Back Door eatery—you have to enter through its leafy patio just past its locked street entrance. The candlelit 15th-century wine cellar is filled with dusty old bottles, faded British memorabilia, and nine-to-fivers. At the "English rustic" buffet, choose a hot meal or cold meat dish with a salad (figure around £7-10/dish); the £11 cheese plate comes with two cheeses, bread, and a pickle. Then step up to the wine bar and consider the many varieties of wine and port available by the glass (this place is passionate about port). The low carbon-crusted vaulting deeper in the back seems to intensify the Hogarth-painting atmosphere. Although it's crowded—downright packed on nice days—you can normally corral two chairs and grab the corner of a table. The crowd often spills out onto the tight, parkside patio, where on hot days a chef cooks at an outdoor cooktop for a long line of happy customers (arrive before 17:00 to get a seat, Mon-Sat 11:00-23:00, Sun 12:00-22:00, 2 blocks from Trafalgar Square, bottom of Villiers Street at #47, Tube: Embankment, tel. 020/7930-1408, manager Gerard Menan).

Ales: **The Harp,** clearly a local favorite, is a crowded and cluttered little pub just a block above Trafalgar Square. While they serve no food, this is a good central spot to nurse a fine ale and befriend one of the Londoners crowded around the coaster-coated bar. This is a top choice for an après-work pint among nine-to-fivers, who stand in the dozens out front after the workday, sipping their beers (Mon-Sat 10:30-23:30, Sun 12:00-22:30, 47 Chandos Place, tel. 020/7836-0291).

Near Piccadilly

The first few listings are upscale and snooty—but if you want something cheaper in this area, you'll find plenty of other options.

Swanky Splurges

The Wolseley is the grand 1920s showroom of a long-defunct British car. The last Wolseley drove out with the Great Depression, but today this old-time bistro bustles with formal waiters serving traditional Austrian and French dishes in an elegant black-marble-and-chandeliers setting fit for its location next to the Ritz. Although the food can be unexceptional, prices are reasonable, and the presentation and setting are grand. Reservations are a must (£13-30 main courses; cheaper soup, salad, and sandwich "café menu" available; both menus available in all areas of restaurant, daily 7:00-24:00, 160 Piccadilly, tel. 020/7499-6996, www.thewolseley.com).

They're popular for their fancy cream or afternoon tea (for details, see page 185).

The Criterion is a palatial dining hall offering grand-piano ambience beneath gilded tiles and chandeliers in a dreamy Byzantine church setting from 1880. It's right on Piccadilly Circus but a world away from the punk junk. It's a deal for the visual experience during lunch and if you order the £20-25 fixed-price meal (except on Sun, when you must order from the expensive à la carte menu). At any hour, the service couldn't care less. Anyone can drop in for coffee or a drink (daily 12:00-14:30 & 17:30-23:30, 224 Piccadilly, tel. 020/7930-0488, www.criterionrestaurant.com).

Rules Restaurant, established in 1798, is as traditional as can be—extremely British, classy yet comfortable. It's a big place where you'll eat in a plush Edwardian atmosphere with formal service and plenty of game on the menu. (A warning reads "Game birds may contain lead shot.") This is the place to splurge for classic English dishes (£15 starters, £30 main courses, daily 12:00-24:00, between the Strand and Covent Garden at 34 Maiden Lane, tel. 020/7836-5314, www.rules.co.uk).

Cheaper Options near Piccadilly

Hungry and broke in the theater district? Head for Panton Street (off Haymarket, two blocks southeast of Piccadilly Circus), where several hardworking little places compete, all seeming to offer a pretheater menu. Peruse the entire block (vegetarian, Pizza Express, Moroccan, Chinese, noodle houses, and diners) before making your choice.

Chain Restaurants near Piccadilly: **Wagamama** (in Leicester Square at 14 Irving Street), **Byron Hamburgers** (11 Haymarket, also at 24 Charing Cross near Leicester Square), **Thai Square** (near Trafalgar Square at 21 Cockspur Street), **Yo! Sushi** (57 Haymarket, also at Trocadero Center on Rupert Street), **Côte** (beyond Leicester Square at 50 St. Martin's Lane), **Itsu** (west of Regent Street at 27 Sackville Street), and **Wasabi** (also west of Regent at 42 Piccadilly).

Near Covent Garden

Covent Garden bustles with people and touristy eateries. The area feels overrun, but if you must eat around here, you have some good choices.

Joe Allen, tucked in a brick cellar a block away from the market, serves modern international and American cuisine with both style and hubbub. Downstairs off a quiet street with candles and white tablecloths, it's comfortably spacious and popular with the theater crowd. It feels a bit old-fashioned and cluttered, but in a welcoming way (£7 starters, £11-30 main courses, £15 two-course specials and £18 three-course specials available at lunch and for early birds, open daily 12:00-24:00, piano music after 19:00, 13 Exeter Street, tel. 020/7836-0651).

Dishoom is London's hotspot for upscale Indian cuisine, with top-quality ingredients and carefully executed recipes. The dishes seem familiar, but the flavors are a revelation. People line up early (starting around 17:30) for a seat, either in the bright, rollicking, brasserie-like ground floor or in the less appealing basement. If the line is long, you'll have to queue outside while waiting for a chance to head down to the bar to kill your remaining wait time—not a bad thing, as they offer a wide range of creative cocktails (£4-6 small plates, £8-12 main courses, daily 8:00-23:00, 12 Upper St. Martin's Lane, tel. 020/7420-9320, www.dishoom.com). They also have locations near King's Cross Station and in trendy Shoreditch.

Sitar Indian Restaurant is a well-respected Indian/Bangladeshi place serving dishes from many regions, fine fish, and a tasty £15 vegetarian *thali* (combo platter). It's small and dressy, with snappy service (£10-18 main dishes, Mon-Fri 12:00-14:30 & 17:30-23:30, Sat 15:00-23:30, closed Sun, next to Somerset House at 149 Strand, tel. 020/7836-3730, www.sitarstrand.co.uk).

Belgo Centraal serves hearty Belgian specialties in a vast 400-seat underground lair. It's a mussels, chips, and beer emporium dressed up as a mod-monastic refectory—with noisy acoustics and vibrant diners. The classy restaurant section is more comfortable and less rowdy, but it usually requires reservations. It's often more fun just to grab a spot in the boisterous beer hall, with its tight, communal benches (no reservations accepted). Both sides have the same menu and specials. Belgians claim they eat as well as the French and as heartily as the Germans. This place, which offers a stunning array of dark, blonde, and fruity Belgian beers, actually makes Belgian things trendy—a formidable feat (£10-14 main dishes, open daily 12:00-23:00; 1 kid eats free for each parent ordering a regular entrée; 1 block north of Covent Garden Tube station at 50 Earlham Street, tel. 020/7813-2233).

Union Jacks, a venture of British celebrity chef Jamie Oliver, fuses traditional British ingredients to make inventive modern dishes. Jamie's wood-fired pizzas are topped not with cheese and tomatoes, but roast pig shoulder or oxtail and brisket. While this sounds risky, he pulls it off with great flavors, plus fun "fizzy drinks" (£6-8 small plates are very small, £12-14 pizzas, £15 classic British dishes, daily 12:00-23:00, right inside Covent Garden market hall, tel. 020/3640-7086).

Lamb and Flag Pub is a survivor—a spit-and-sawdust pub serving traditional grub two blocks off Covent Garden, yet seemingly a world away. Here since 1772, this pub was a favorite of Charles Dickens. Once known for fights, it's now peaceful and a hit with local workers (long hours daily, 33 Rose Street, across from Stanfords bookstore entrance on Floral Street—find Lazenby Court, then duck and enter, tel. 020/7497-9504).

Chain Restaurants near Covent Garden: **Masala Zone** (particularly fun branch at top end of market with giant colorful marionettes suspended from the ceiling, 48 Floral Street), **Côte** (17 Tavistock Street), **Thai Square** (166 Shaftesbury Avenue, plus one next to Sitar Indian Restaurant at 148 The Strand), **Wagamama** (1 Tavistock Street), **Byron Hamburgers** (behind the London Transport Museum at 33 Wellington Street), **Wasabi** (two blocks down Southampton Street at 388 The Strand), **Itsu** (past Wasabi and across the street at 82 The Strand), and **Loch Fyne** (a couple of blocks behind the square at 2 Catherine Street). A **Marks & Spencer** with a good deli section is across from the Covent Garden Tube station.

Near the British Museum, in Fitzrovia

To avoid the touristy crush right around the museum (and just southwest, in Soho), Londoners head a few blocks west, to the Fitzrovia area. Here, tiny Charlotte Place is lined with small eateries (including the first two listed below); nearby, the much bigger Charlotte Street has several more good options. The higher street signs you'll notice on Charlotte Street are a holdover from a time when they needed to be visible to carriage drivers. This area is a short walk from the Goodge Street Tube station—convenient to the British Museum. See the map on page 162 for locations.

Salumeria Dino serves up hearty sandwiches, pasta, and Italian coffee. Dino, a native of Naples, has run his little shop for more than 30 years and has managed to create a classic Italian deli that's so authentic you'll walk out singing "O Sole Mio" (£4-5 sandwiches, £1 takeaway cappuccinos, Mon-Fri 9:00-18:00, closed Sat-Sun, 15 Charlotte Place, tel. 020/7580-3938).

Lantana OUT, next door to Salumeria Dino, is an Australian coffee shop that sells modern soups, sandwiches, and salads at their takeaway window (£3-8 meals, pricier sit-down café—**Lantana IN**—serves £9-12 meals next door, Mon-Fri 7:30-15:00, café also open Sat-Sun 9:00-17:00, 13 Charlotte Place, tel. 020/7637-3347).

Chain Restaurants near the British Museum: **Wagamama** (4 Streatham Street; another location near Holborn Tube stop at 123 Kingsway—see map on page 162), **Côte** (5 Charlotte Street),

Byron Hamburgers (6 Store Street, also at 6 Rathbone Place), **Itsu** (54 Tottenham Court Road, also at 74 New Oxford Street), and **Wasabi** (17 Tottenham Court Road, also at 58 Oxford Street). There's also another **Bi Bim Bap** here (8 Charlotte Street, see listing on page 167).

WEST LONDON

Near Victoria Station Accommodations

These restaurants are within a few blocks of Victoria Station—and all are places where I've enjoyed eating. As with the accommodations in this area, I've grouped them by location: east or west of the station (see the map on page 150).

Cheap Eats: For groceries, a handy **M&S Simply Food** is inside Victoria Station (daily 7:00-24:00, near the front, by the bus terminus), along with a **Sainsbury's Local** (daily 6:00-23:00, at rear entrance, on Eccleston Street). A larger Sainsbury's is on Wilton Road near Warwick Way, a couple of blocks southeast of the station (Mon-Sat 7:00-23:00, Sun 11:00-17:00). A string of good ethnic restaurants lines Wilton Road. For affordable if forgettable meals, try the row of cheap little eateries on Elizabeth Street.

Chain Restaurants near Victoria Station: **Yo! Sushi** and **Wasabi** are in the main concourse of Victoria Station (another Wasabi is at 131 Victoria Street). You'll also find **Wagamama** (at Cardinal Place off Victoria Street) and an **Itsu** (163 Victoria Street).

LONDON

West of Victoria Station (Belgravia)

Ebury Wine Bar, filled with young professionals, provides a cut-above atmosphere (rumor has it that Prince William held his bachelor party here). In the delightful back room, the fancy menu features modern European cuisine with a French accent, including delicious £16-22 main dishes and a £23 two-course or £29 three-course special (available Mon-Fri at lunch and daily 18:00-20:00; three-course meal includes a glass of Prosecco that you're welcome to swap for house wine). At the wine bar, find a cheaper bar menu that's better than your average pub grub (£9-15 meals). This is emphatically a "traditional wine bar," with no beers on tap (restaurant open daily 12:00-15:00 & 18:00-22:30, wine bar open all day long, reservations smart, at intersection of Ebury and Elizabeth Streets, 139 Ebury Street, tel. 020/7730-5447, www.eburyrestaurant.co.uk).

La Bottega is an Italian delicatessen that fits its upscale Belgravia neighborhood. It offers tasty freshly-cooked pastas (£6), lasagnas, and salads (£9 lasagna-and-salad meal), along with great sandwiches (£3-5) and a good coffee bar with Italian pastries. It's fast (order at the counter), and the ingredients would please an Italian grandmother. Grab your meal to go, or enjoy the Belgravia good life with locals, either sitting inside or on the sidewalk (Mon-Fri 8:00-19:00, Sat-Sun 9:00-18:00, on corner of Ebury and Eccleston Streets, tel. 020/7730-2730; second location in South Kensington at 97 Old Brompton Road).

The Thomas Cubitt pub, named for the urban planner who designed much of Belgravia, is a trendy neighborhood gastropub packed with young professionals. It's pricey and a pinch pretentious and prides itself on using sustainable ingredients in its modern English cooking. With a bright but slightly cramped interior and fine sidewalk seating, it's great for a drink or meal (£8 small plates, £14-18 main dishes, 44 Elizabeth Street). Upstairs is a more refined restaurant with the same kitchen, but an emphasis on finer technique and presentation (£8-12 starters, £18-22 main courses, reservations recommended, food served daily 12:00-22:00, tel. 020/7730-6060, thethomascubitt.co.uk).

The Duke of Wellington pub is a classic neighborhood place with forgettable grub, sidewalk seating, and an inviting interior. A bit more lowbrow than my other Belgravia listings, this may be your best shot at meeting a local (£5-7 sandwiches, £9-10 meals, food served Mon-Sat 12:00-15:00 & 18:00-21:00, Sun lunch only, 63 Eaton Terrace, tel. 020/7730-1782).

South End of Ebury Street: A five-minute walk down Ebury Street, where it intersects with Pimlico Road, you'll find a pretty square with a few more eateries to consider—including **The Orange,** a high-priced gastropub with the same owners and a similar menu to The Thomas Cubitt (described earlier); and **Daylesford,** the deli and café of an organic farm (£3-5 light meals to go—a good picnic option).

East of Victoria Station (Pimlico)

Grumbles brags it's been serving "good food and wine at nonscary prices since 1964." Offering a delicious mix of "modern eclectic French and traditional English," this unpretentious little place with cozy booths inside (on two levels, including a cellar) and four nice sidewalk tables is the best spot to eat well in this otherwise workaday neighborhood. Their traditional dishes are their forte (£11-18 plates, early-bird specials, open daily 12:00-14:30 & 18:00-23:00, reservations wise, half a block north of Belgrave Road at 35 Churton Street, tel. 020/7834-0149, www.grumblesrestaurant.co.uk).

Pimlico Fresh's breakfasts and lunches feature fresh, organic ingredients, served up with good coffee and/or fresh-squeezed juices. Choose from the dishes listed on the wall-sized chalkboard that lines the small eating area, then order at the counter. This place is heaven if you've slept through your hotel's breakfast hour, or if you just need a break from the bacon-eggs-beans routine (£5-10 meals, takeout lunches, plenty of vegetarian options; Mon-Fri 7:30-19:30, breakfast served until 15:00; Sat-Sun 9:00-18:00; 86 Wilton Road, tel. 020/7932-0030).

Seafresh Fish Restaurant is the neighborhood place for plaice—and classic and creative fish-and-chips cuisine. You can either take out on the cheap or eat in, enjoying a white-fish ambience. Though Mario's father started this place in 1965, it feels like the chippy of the 21st century (£5-8 meals to go, £13-17 to sit, Mon-Sat 12:00-15:00 & 17:00-22:30, closed Sun, 80 Wilton Road, tel. 020/7828-0747).

The Jugged Hare pub, a 10-minute walk from Victoria Station, sits in a lavish old bank building, with vaults replaced by tankards of beer and a kitchen. They have a traditional menu and a plush, vivid pub scene good for a meal or just a drink (£7 sandwiches, £10-12 meals, food served daily 12:00-21:30, 172 Vauxhall Bridge Road, tel. 020/7828-1543).

St. George's Tavern is the neighborhood's best pub for a full meal. They serve dinner from the same menu in three zones: on the sidewalk to catch the sun and enjoy some people-watching, in the ground-floor pub, and in a classier downstairs dining room with full table service. They're proud of their sausages. The scene is inviting for just a beer, too (£10-14 meals, food served daily 10:00-22:00, corner of Hugh Street and Belgrave Road, tel. 020/7630-1116).

South Kensington

These places are close to several recommended hotels and just a couple of blocks from the Victoria and Albert Museum and Natural History Museum (Tube: South Kensington; for locations see map on page 153).

Exhibition Road Food Circus, a one-block-long road (on the Victoria and Albert Museum side of the South Kensington Tube station), is a traffic-free pedestrian zone lined with enticing little eateries. There's a good amount of choices, including **Fernandez and Wells** (if you want wine, fine meats, and cheese), **Thai Square** (for good Thai), **Casa Brindisa** (for tapas and shared Mediterranean-style dishes), **Daquise** (a venerable Polish restaurant much loved by the local Polish community and the only nonchain mentioned here; at 20 Thurloe Street), and much more.

Moti Mahal Indian Restaurant, with minimalist-yet-upscale ambience and attentive service, serves delicious mostly-Bangladeshi cuisine. Consider chicken *jalfrezi* if you like spicy food, and buttery chicken if you don't (£9-15 main dishes, daily 12:00-14:30 & 17:30-23:30, Sat-Sun open all day, 3 Glendower Place, tel. 020/7584-8428).

Bosphorus Kebabs is the student favorite for a quick, fast, and hearty Turkish dinner. While mostly for takeaway, they have a few tight tables indoors and on the sidewalk (£5-7 meals, Turkish kebabs, daily 10:30-24:00, 59 Old Brompton Road, tel. 020/7584-4048).

Beirut Express has fresh, well-prepared Lebanese cuisine. In the front you'll find takeaway service as well as barstools for a quick bite (£4.50 sandwiches). In the back is a sit-down restaurant with £15-18 plates and £6-8 *mezes* (daily 12:00-24:00, 65 Old Brompton Road, tel. 020/7591-0123).

Franco Manca, a taverna-inspired pizzeria, is part of a chain serving Neapolitan-style pies using organic ingredients and boasting typical Italian charm. If you skip the pricey drinks you can feast like a king on a paisano's budget (£5-7 pizzas, daily 11:30-23:00, 97 Old Brompton Road, tel. 020/7584-9713).

La Bottega occupies a busy corner, with a similar menu to the one at its Belgravia location (daily 9:00-20:00, 97 Old Brompton Road, tel. 020/7581-6622, see listing on page 179).

The Anglesea Arms, with a great terrace surrounded by classy South Kensington buildings, is a destination pub that feels like the classic neighborhood favorite. It's a thriving and happy place, with a woody ambience and a mellow step-down back dining room a world away from any tourism. While the food is the main draw, this is also a fine place to just have a beer. Don't let the crowds here put you off. Behind all the drinkers is an elegant and more peaceful back dining room (£6-8 starters, £12-17 main dishes, meals served daily 12:00-15:00 & 18:00-22:00; from Old Brompton Road, turn left at Onslow Gardens and go down a few blocks to 15 Selwood Terrace; tel. 020/7373-7960).

Rocca is a bright and dressy Italian place with a heated terrace (£6-9 pizza, pasta, and salads; daily 11:30-23:30, 73 Old Brompton Road, tel. 020/7225-3413).

Supermarkets: **Tesco Express** (50 Old Brompton Road) and **Little Waitrose** (99 Old Brompton Road) are both open long hours daily.

Chain Restaurants in South Kensington: **Byron Hamburgers** (93 Old Brompton Road), **Wasabi** (21 Old Brompton Road), and **Itsu** (five-minute walk east of South Kensington Tube station at 118 Draycott Avenue).

Near Bayswater and Notting Hill Accommodations

For locations, see the map on page 156.

Maggie Jones's has been feeding locals for 40 years in a neighborhood where eateries come and go. Its countryside antique decor and candlelight make a visit a step back in time. It's a longer walk than most of my recommendations, but you'll get solid English cuisine. It's pricey, but the portions are huge (especially the meat-and-fish pies, their specialty). You're welcome to save lots by splitting your main course. The candlelit upstairs is the most romantic, while the basement is kept lively with the kitchen, tight seating, and lots of action. The staff is young and slightly aloof (lunch—£5 starters, £7-8 main dishes; dinner—£7-9 starters, £17-24 main dishes; daily 12:00-14:30 & 18:00-23:00, reservations recommended, 6 Old Court Place, just east of Kensington Church Street, near High Street Kensington Tube stop, tel. 020/7937-6462, www.maggie-jones.co.uk).

Geales, which opened its doors in 1939 as a fish-and-chips shop, has been serving Notting Hillbillies ever since. Today the menu is much more varied, but the emphasis is still on fish. The gingham-clad tables are casual, but the food is upscale. If you still want the crispy battered cod that put them on the map, it's the best around (lunch—£10 two-course express menu; dinner—£4-11 starters and salads, £14-23 main dishes; daily 12:00-15:00 & 18:00-22:30, reservations smart, 2 Farmer Street, just south of Notting Hill Gate Tube stop, tel. 020/7727-7528, www.geales.com).

The Churchill Arms pub and **Thai Kitchen** (same location) are local hangouts, with good beer and a thriving old-English ambience in front, and hearty £9 Thai plates in an enclosed patio in the back. You can eat the Thai food in the tropical hideaway (table service) or in the atmospheric pub section (order at the counter and they'll bring it to you). The place is festooned with Churchill memorabilia and chamber pots (including one with Hitler's mug on it—hanging from the ceiling farthest from Thai Kitchen—sure to cure the constipation of any Brit during World War II). Arrive by 18:00 or after 21:00 to avoid a line. During busy times, diners are limited to an hour at the table (food served daily 12:00-22:00, 119 Kensington Church Street, tel. 020/7727-4242 for the pub or 020/7792-1296 for restaurant reservations, www.churchillarmskensington.co.uk).

Hereford Road is a cozy, mod eatery tucked at the far end of Princes Square. It's stylish but not pretentious, serving heavy, meaty English cuisine made with modern panache. Cozy two-person booths face the open kitchen up top; the main dining room is down below. There are also a few sidewalk tables (£7-10 starters, £14-17 main dishes, reservations smart, daily 12:00-15:00 & 18:00-22:00, 3 Hereford Road, tel. 020/7727-1144, www.herefordroad.org).

The Prince Edward serves good grub in a comfy, upscale-pub setting and at its sidewalk tables (£10-15 meals, daily 10:30-23:00, family-friendly, 2 blocks north of Bayswater Road at the corner of Dawson Place and Hereford Road, 73 Princes Square, tel. 020/7727-2221).

Café Diana is a healthy little eatery serving sandwiches, salads, and Middle Eastern food. It's decorated—almost shrine-like—with photos of Princess Diana, who used to drop by for pita sandwiches. You can dine in the simple interior or order some food from the counter to go (£3-5 sandwiches, £6-10 meat dishes, daily 8:00-23:00, cash only, 5 Wellington Terrace, on Bayswater Road, opposite Kensington Palace Garden Gates, where Di once lived, tel. 020/7792-9606, Abdul).

On Queensway: The road called Queensway is a multiethnic food circus, lined with lively and inexpensive eateries—browse the options along here and choose your favorite. For a cut above, head for **Royal China Restaurant**—filled with London's Chinese, who consider this one of the city's best eateries. It's dressed up in black, white, and gold, with candles and brisk waiters. While it's pricier than most neighborhood Chinese restaurants, the food is noticeably better (£9-13 dim sum menu, served until 17:00, £10-14 main dishes, £25-40 special dishes, daily 12:00-23:00, 13 Queensway, tel. 020/7221-2535). For a lowbrow alternative, **Whiteleys Shopping Centre Food Court**—at the top end of Queensway—offers fast-food chain eateries among Corinthian columns, and a multiscreen theater in a mall that dates back to 1912 (most restaurants daily 12:00-22:00, some eateries open shorter hours; options include Yo! Sushi, good salads at Café Rouge, pizza, gelato, and Starbucks; third floor, corner of Porchester Gardens and Queensway).

Supermarkets: There are a handful of options, all of which open early and close late (except on Sundays). **Tesco** is a half-block from the Notting Hill Gate Tube stop (near intersection with Pembridge Road at 114 Notting Hill Gate). Queensway is home to several supermarkets, including **Sainsbury's Local** and **Tesco Express** (both next to Bayswater Tube stop), **Spar Market** (at #18), and **Marks & Spencer** (Whiteleys Shopping Centre).

Chain Restaurants in Bayswater and Notting Hill: **Byron Hamburgers** (103 Westbourne Grove), **Masala Zone** (75 Bishop's Bridge Road), **Yo! Sushi** (Whiteleys Shopping Centre), **Itsu** (100 Notting Hill Gate), and **Côte** (98 Westbourne Grove). To the south, past Kensington Palace, is **Wagamama** (26 Kensington High Street).

ELSEWHERE IN LONDON

Between St. Paul's and the Tower: **The Counting House,** formerly an elegant old bank, offers great £10-13 meals, nice homemade £11-13 meat pies, fish, and fresh vegetables. The fun "nibbles menu," with £3-7 snacks, is available starting in the early evening until 22:00 (open Mon-Fri 11:00-23:00, closed Sat-Sun; gets really busy with the buttoned-down 9-to-5 crowd after 12:15, especially Thu-Fri; near Mansion House in The City, 50 Cornhill—see map on page 173, tel. 020/7283-7123).

Near the British Library: Drummond Street (running just west of Euston Station—see map on page 162) is famous for cheap and good Indian vegetarian food (£5-10 dishes, £7 lunch buffets). For a good *thali* (combo platter) consider **Chutneys** (124 Drummond, tel. 020/7388-0604) and **Ravi Shankar** (133 Drummond, tel. 020/7388-6458, both open long hours daily).

Near the Tower of London: In **The Medieval Banquet**'s underground brick-arched room, costumed wenches bring you a tasty four-course medieval-themed meal (includes ale and red wine, juice for kids) as minstrels, knights, jesters, and contortionists perform. If you enjoy an act, pound on the table. Reserve in advance online or by phone (adult-£50, child-£30, family deal for 2 adults and 2 kids-£110—Wed, Thu, and Sun only, doors open Wed-Sat at 19:15, Sun at 17:15, show starts about 30 minutes later, closed Mon-Tue, veggie option possible, rentable medieval garb, The Medieval Banquet Ivory House, St. Katharine Docks, enter docks off East Smithfield Street, Tube: Tower Hill, tel. 020/7480-5353, www.medievalbanquet.com).

Near East End Street Markets: Brick Lane in "Banglatown" is where London's Bangladeshi community goes to dine at their favorite curry house. If you join them, be prepared for curbside hawkers pitching their eateries (Tube: Aldgate East, see page 108).

TAKING TEA IN LONDON

While visiting London, consider partaking in this most British of traditions. While some tearooms—such as the wallet-draining £50-a-head tea service at Claridges and the finicky Fortnum & Mason—still require a jacket and tie, most happily welcome tourists in jeans and sneakers. Most tearooms are usually open for lunch and close about 17:00. At all the places listed below, it's perfectly acceptable for two people to order one afternoon tea and one cream tea (at about £5) and share the afternoon tea's goodies. For details on afternoon tea, see page 1010.

Traditional Tea Experiences

The Wolseley serves a good afternoon tea between their meal service. Split one with your companion and enjoy two light meals at a great price in classic elegance (£11 cream tea, £24 afternoon tea, £34 champagne tea, generally served 15:00-18:30 daily, see full listing on page 175).

The Orangery at Kensington Palace serves a £26 "Orangery tea" and a £32-36 champagne tea in its bright white hall near William and Kate's residence. You can also order treats à la carte. The portions aren't huge, but who can argue with eating at a royal orangery or on the terrace? (Tea served 12:00-18:00, no reservations taken; a 10-minute walk through Kensington Gardens from either Queensway or High Street Kensington Tube stations to the orange brick building, about 100 yards from Kensington Palace—see map on page 156; tel. 020/3166-6113, www.hrp.org.uk.)

The Capital Hotel, a luxury hotel a half-block from Harrods, caters to weary shoppers with its intimate five-table, linen-tablecloth tearoom. It's where the ladies-who-lunch meet to decide whether to buy that Versace gown they've had their eye on. Even so, casual clothes, kids, and sharing plates are all OK (£30 afternoon tea, daily 14:00-17:30, call to book ahead—especially on weekends, 22 Basil Street—see color map on page VII, Tube: Knightsbridge, tel. 020/7591-1202, www.capitalhotel.co.uk).

The **Fortnum & Mason** department store offers tea at several different restaurants within its walls. You can "Take Tea in the Parlour" for £20 (including ice-cream cakes; Mon-Sat 10:00-19:30, Sun 11:30-17:00). The pièce de resistance is their Diamond Jubilee Tea Salon, named in honor of the Queen's 60th year on the throne (and, no doubt, to remind visitors of Her Majesty's visit for tea here in 2012 with Camilla and Kate). At these royal prices, consider it dinner (£40-44, daily 12:00-19:00, Sun until 18:00, dress up a bit—no shorts, "children must be behaved," 181 Piccadilly—see map on page 168, smart to reserve at least a week in advance, tel. 020/7734-8040, www.fortnumandmason.com).

Other Places to Sip Tea

Taking tea is not just for tourists and the wealthy—it's a true English tradition. If you want the teatime experience but are put off by the price, consider these options.

Teapod, a modern place near the Tower Bridge, serves cream tea for £6 and afternoon tea for £9 (daily until 18:00, 31 Shad Thames, tel. 020/7407-0000), but may be closing.

Museum Cafés: Many museum restaurants offer a fine inexpensive tea service. The **National Dining Rooms,** within the National Gallery on Trafalgar Square, serves a £7 cream tea and £17.50 afternoon tea with a great view (14:30-17:00, in Sainsbury Wing of National Gallery, Tube: Charing Cross or Leicester Square, tel. 020/7747-2525). The **Victoria and Albert Museum** café serves a classic cream tea in an elegant setting that won't break your budget.

Shop Cafés: You'll find good-value teas at various cafés in shops and bookstores across London. Most department stores on Oxford Street (including those between Oxford Circus and Bond Street Tube stations) offer an afternoon tea. **John Lewis**' mod third-floor brasserie serves a nice afternoon tea from 15:30 (£10, on Oxford Street one block west of Bond Street Tube station, tel. 020/7629-7711, www.johnlewis.com).

The Café at Sotheby's, on the ground floor of the auction giant's headquarters, gives shoppers a break from fashionable New Bond Street (£9-25, tea served Mon-Fri 15:00-16:45, reservations smart, 34 New Bond Street—see map on page 168, Tube: Bond Street or Oxford Circus, tel. 020/7293-5077, www.sothebys.com/cafe).

At **Waterstones** bookstore you can put together a spread for less than £10 in their fifth-floor view café (203 Piccadilly).

London Connections

BY PLANE

London has six airports; I've focused my coverage on the two most widely used—Heathrow and Gatwick—with a few tips for using the others (Stansted, Luton, London City, and Southend).

For accommodations at or near the major airports, see page 165. For more on flights within Europe, see page 1037.

Heathrow Airport

Heathrow Airport is one of the world's busiest airports. Think about it: 73 million passengers a year on 470,000 flights from 185 destinations riding 80 airlines, like some kind of global maypole dance. For Heathrow's airport, flight, and transfer information, call the switchboard at 0844-335-1801, or visit the helpful website at www.heathrowairport.com (airport code: LHR).

Heathrow's terminals are numbered T-1 through T-5. Though T-1 is now closed for arrivals and departures, it still supports other terminals with baggage, and the newly renovated T-2 ("Queen's Terminal") will likely eventually expand into the old T-1 digs. Each terminal is served by different airlines and alliances; for example, T-5 is exclusively for British Air and Iberia Air flights, while T-2 serves mostly Star Alliance flights, such as United and Lufthansa. Screens posted throughout the airport identify which terminal each airline uses; this information should also be printed on your ticket or boarding pass.

To navigate, read signs and ask questions. You can walk between T-2 and T-3. From this central hub (called "Heathrow Central"), T-4 and T-5 split off in opposite directions (and are not walkable). The easiest way to travel between the T-2/T-3 cluster and either T-4 or T-5 is by Heathrow Express train (free, departs every 15-20 minutes). You can also take a shuttle bus (free, serves all terminals), or the Tube (requires a ticket, serves all terminals).

If you're flying out of Heathrow, it's critical to confirm which terminal your flight will use (look carefully at your ticket/boarding

pass, check online, or call your airline in advance)—if it's T-4 or T-5, allow extra time. Taxi drivers generally know which terminal you'll need based on the airline, but bus drivers may not.

Services: Each terminal has an airport information desk (open long hours daily), car-rental agencies, exchange bureaus, ATMs, a pharmacy, a VAT refund desk (tel. 0845-872-7627, you must present the VAT claim form from the retailer here to get your tax rebate on purchased items—see page 990 for details), room-booking services, and baggage storage (£5/item up to 2 hours, £10/item for 2-24 hours, daily 5:00-23:00, www.left-baggage.co.uk). Heathrow offers both Wi-Fi (first 4 hours free) and pay Internet access points (in each terminal, check map for locations). You'll find a post office on the first floor of T-3 (departures area). Each terminal also has cheap eateries.

Heathrow's small **"TI"** (tourist info shop), even though it's a for-profit business, is worth a visit if you're nearby and want to pick up free information: a simple map, the *London Planner,* and brochures (long hours daily, 5-minute walk from T-3 in Tube station, follow signs to Underground; bypass queue for transit info to reach window for London questions).

LONDON

Getting Between Heathrow and Downtown London

You have five basic options for traveling the 14 miles between Heathrow Airport and downtown London: Tube (about £5-6/person), bus (£6-9/person), direct shuttle bus (£20/person), express train with connecting Tube or taxi (about £10/person for slower train, £21.50/person for faster train, price does not include connecting Tube fare), or taxi (about £75/group). The one that works best for you will depend on your arrival terminal, your destination in central London, and your budget.

By Tube (Subway): The Tube takes you from any Heathrow terminal to downtown London in 50-60 minutes on the Piccadilly Line (6/hour, buy ticket at Tube station ticket window or self-service machine). Depending on your destination in London, you may need to transfer (for example, if headed to the Victoria Station neighborhood, transfer at Hammersmith to the District line and ride six more stops). If you plan to use the Tube for transport in London, it makes sense to buy a Travelcard or pay-as-you-go Oyster card at the airport's Tube station ticket window. (For details on these passes, see page 32.) If your Travelcard covers only Zones 1-2, you'll need to pay a small supplement for the initial trip from Heathrow (Zone 6) to downtown.

If you're taking the Tube from downtown London *to* the airport, note that Piccadilly Line trains don't stop at every terminal. Trains either stop at T-4, then T-2/T-3 (also called Heathrow Central), in that order; or T-2/T-3, then T-5. When leaving central London on the Tube, allow extra time if going to T-4 or T-5, and check the reader board in the station to make sure that the train goes to the right terminal before you board.

By Bus: Most buses depart from the outdoor common area called the Central Bus Station, a five-minute walk from the T-2/T-3 complex. To connect between T-4 or T-5 and the Central Bus Station, ride the free Heathrow Express train or the shuttle buses.

National Express has regular service from Heathrow's Central Bus Station to Victoria Coach Station in downtown London, near several of my recommended hotels. While slow, the bus is affordable and convenient for those staying near Victoria Station (£6-9, 1-2/hour, less frequent from Victoria Station to Heathrow, 45-75 minutes depending on time of day, tel. 0871-781-8181, www.nationalexpress.com). A less-frequent National Express bus goes from T-5 directly to Victoria Coach Station.

By Shuttle: Heathrow Shuttle is an economical shuttle-bus service that goes to/from your hotel and your terminal at Heathrow. You'll share a minivan with other travelers who are also being picked up or dropped off, so it's not much of a time-savings over taking the Tube (£20/person, progressive discounts for groups of two or more, 1 child under age 10 travels free with 2 adults, runs daily 4:00-18:00, book at least 24 hours in advance, office open daily 7:00-20:00, tel. 020/309-2771, www.heathrowshuttle.com, info@heathrowshuttle.com). Another option is **Just Airports,** which offers a private car service between five London airports and the city center (from £32/car; see website for price quote, tel. 020/8900-1666, www.justairports.com).

By Train: Two different trains run between Heathrow Airport and London's Paddington Station. At Paddington Station, you're in the thick of the Tube system, with easy access to any of my recommended neighborhoods—my Paddington hotels are just outside the front door, and Notting Hill Gate is just two Tube stops away. The **Heathrow Connect** train is the slightly slower, much cheaper option, serving T-2/T-3 at a single station called Heathrow Central; use free transfers to get from either T-4 or T-5 to Heathrow Central (£10.10 one-way, £20.20 round-trip, 2/hour Mon-Sat, 1-2/hour Sun, 40 minutes, tel. 0345-604-1515, www.heathrowconnect.com).

The **Heathrow Express** train is fast and runs more frequently, but it's pricey (£21.50 one-way, £35 round-trip, £5 more if you buy your ticket on board, 4/hour; 15 minutes to downtown from Heathrow Central Station serving T-2/T-3, 21 minutes from T-5; for T-4 take free transfer to Heathrow Central; covered by BritRail pass, daily 5:10-23:48, tel. 0345-600-1515, www.heathrowexpress.co.uk). At the airport, you can use the Heathrow Express as a free transfer between terminals.

By Taxi: Taxis from the airport cost £45-75 to west and central London (one hour). For four people traveling together, this can be a reasonable option. Hotels can often line up a cab back to the airport for about £40.

Gatwick Airport

More and more flights land at Gatwick Airport, which is halfway between London and the south coast (airport code: LGW, tel. 0844-892-0322, www.gatwickairport.com). Gatwick has two terminals, North and South, which are easily connected by a free monorail (two-minute trip, runs 24 hours daily). Note that boarding passes say "Gatwick N" or "Gatwick S" to indicate your terminal. British Airways flights generally use Gatwick North. The Gatwick Express trains (described next) stop only at Gatwick South.

Schedules in each terminal show only arrivals and departures from that terminal.

Getting Between Gatwick and Downtown London: Gatwick Express trains are the best way into London from this airport. They shuttle conveniently between Gatwick South and London's Victoria Station, with many of my recommended hotels close by (£20 one-way, £35 round-trip, at least 10 percent cheaper if purchased online, 4/hour, 30 minutes, runs 5:00-24:00 daily, a few trains as early as 3:30, tel. 0345-850-1530, www.gatwickexpress.com). If you buy your tickets at the station before boarding, ask about possible group deals. (If you see others in the ticket line, suggest buying your tickets together.) When going *to* the airport, at Victoria Station note that Gatwick Express has its own ticket windows right by the platform (tracks 13 and 14).

A train also runs between Gatwick South and **St. Pancras International Station** (£10, 3-5/hour, 45-60 minutes, www.thetrainline.com)—useful for travelers taking the Eurostar train (to Paris or Brussels) or staying in the St. Pancras/King's Cross neighborhood.

Even slower, but cheap and handy to the Victoria Station neighborhood, you can take the **bus.** National Express runs a bus from Gatwick direct to Victoria Station (£10, at least hourly, 1.5 hours, tel. 0871-781-8181, www.nationalexpress.com); easyBus has one going to near the Earls Court Tube stop (£2-10 depending on how far ahead you book, 2-3/hour, www.easybus.co.uk).

London's Other Airports

Stansted Airport: From Stansted (airport code: STN, tel. 0844-335-1803, www.stanstedairport.com), you have several options for getting into or out of London. Two different **buses** connect the airport and London's Victoria Station neighborhood: National Express (£10-14, every 15 minutes, 2 hours, runs 24 hours a day, picks up and stops throughout London, ends at Victoria Coach Station or Liverpool Street Station, tel. 0871-781-8181, www.nationalexpress.com) and Terravision (£10, 2/hour, 1.5-2 hours, ends at Green Line Coach Station just south of Victoria Station). Or you can take the faster, pricier Stansted Express **train** (£19, connects to London's Tube system at Tottenham Hale or Liverpool Street, 4/hour, 45 minutes, 4:30-23:00, www.stanstedexpress.com). Stansted is expensive by **cab;** figure £100-120 one-way from central London.

Luton Airport: For Luton (airport code: LTN, airport tel. 01582/405-100, www.london-luton.co.uk), the fastest way to go into London is by **train** to St. Pancras International Station (£15.50 one-way, 1-5/hour, 25-45 minutes—check schedule to avoid slower trains, tel. 0345-712-5678, www.eastmidlandstrains.co.uk); catch the 10-minute shuttle bus (every 10 minutes, £1.60) from outside the terminal to the Luton Airport Parkway Station. The Green Line express **bus** #757 runs to Buckingham Palace Road, just south of Victoria Station, and stops en route near the Baker Street Tube station—best if you're staying near Paddington Station or in North London (£10 one-way, 2-4/hour, 1-1.5 hours, runs 24 hours, tel. 0344-800-4411, www.greenline.co.uk). If you're sleeping at Luton, consider easyHotel (see listing on page 163).

London City and Southend Airports: To get into the city center from London City Airport (airport code: LCY, tel. 020/7646-0088, www.londoncityairport.com), take the Docklands Light Railway (DLR) to the Bank Tube station, which is one stop east of St. Paul's on the Central Line (less than £5 one-way, covered by Travelcard, a bit cheaper with an Oyster card, 22 minutes, www.tfl.gov.uk/dlr). Some easyJet flights land farther out, at Southend Airport (airport code: SEN, tel. 01702/538-500, www.southendairport.com). Trains connect this airport to London's Liverpool Street Station (£16.70 one-way, 3-8/hour, 55 minutes, www.abelliogreateranglia.co.uk).

Connecting London's Airports by Bus

A handy **National Express bus** runs between Heathrow, Gatwick, Stansted, and Luton airports—easier than having to cut through the center of London—although traffic can be bad and can increase travel times (tel. 0871-781-8181, www.nationalexpress.com).

From Heathrow Airport to: Gatwick Airport (1-6/hour, about 1.5 hours—but allow at least three hours between flights, £25), **Stansted Airport** (1 direct bus every 2 hours, about 1.5 hours, £27), **Luton Airport** (roughly hourly, 1-1.5 hours, £23).

BY TRAIN

London, the country's major transportation hub, has a different train station for each region. There are nine main stations (see the map):

Euston—Serves northwest England, North Wales, and Scotland.

St. Pancras International—Serves north and south England, plus the Eurostar to Paris or Brussels (see "Crossing the Channel," later).

King's Cross—Serves northeast England and Scotland, including York and Edinburgh.

Liverpool Street—Serves east England, including Essex and Harwich.

London Bridge—Serves south England, including Brighton.

Waterloo—Serves south England, including Salisbury and Southampton.

Victoria—Serves Gatwick Airport, Canterbury, Dover, and Brighton.

Paddington—Serves south and southwest England, including Heathrow Airport, Windsor, Bath, South Wales, and the Cotswolds.

Marylebone—Serves southwest and central England, including Stratford-upon-Avon.

In addition, London has several smaller train stations that you're less likely to use, such as **Charing Cross** (serves southeast England, including Dover) and **Blackfriars** (serves Brighton).

Any train station has schedule information, can make reservations, and can sell tickets for any destination. Most stations offer a baggage-storage service (£10/bag for 24 hours, look for *left luggage* signs); because of long security lines, it can take a while to check or pick up your bag (www.left-baggage.co.uk). For more details on the services available at each station, see www.nationalrail.co.uk/stations. UK train and bus info is available at www.traveline.org.uk. For information on tickets and rail passes, see page 1020 of the Practicalities chapter.

Train Connections from London

To Points West

From Paddington Station to: Windsor (Windsor & Eton Central Station, 2-3/hour, 35 minutes, easy change at Slough), **Bath** (2/hour, 1.5 hours), and **Cardiff** (2/hour, 2 hours).

From Waterloo Station to: Windsor (to Windsor & Eton Riverside Station, 2/hour, 50 minutes) and **Salisbury** (2/hour, 1.5 hours).

To Points North

From King's Cross Station: Trains run at least hourly, stopping in **York** (2 hours), **Durham** (3 hours), and **Edinburgh** (4.5 hours). Trains to **Cambridge** also leave from here (2/hour, 45 minutes).

From Euston Station to: Conwy (nearly hourly, 3.5 hours, transfer in Chester), **Liverpool** (at least hourly, 2-2.5 hours, more with transfer), **Keswick** (hourly, 4 hours, transfer to bus at Penrith), and **Glasgow** (1-2/hour, 4.5-5 hours).

From Marylebone Station: Direct trains leave for **Stratford-upon-Avon** from this station located near the southwest corner of Regent's Park (3/day direct, more with transfers, 2-2.5 hours).

BY BUS

Buses are slower but considerably cheaper than trains for reaching destinations around Britain and beyond. Most depart from **Victoria Coach Station,** which is one long block south of Victoria Station (near many recommended accommodations, Tube: Victoria). Inside the station, you'll find basic eateries, kiosks, and a helpful information desk stocked with schedules and staff ready to point you to your bus or answer any questions. Watch your bags carefully—luggage thieves thrive at the station.

Ideally you'll buy your tickets online (for tips on buying tickets and taking buses, see page 1026 of the Practicalities chapter). But if you must buy one at the station, try to arrive an hour before the bus departs, or drop by the day before. Ticketing machines are scattered around the station (separate machines for National Express/Eurolines and Megabus; you can buy either for today or for tomorrow); there's also a ticket counter near gate 21. For UK train and bus info, check www.traveline.org.uk.

National Express buses go to: **Bath** (nearly hourly, 3-3.5 hours; also consider a guided Evan Evans tour by bus—see page 307), **Cambridge** (every 60-90 minutes, 2 hours), **Cardiff** (hourly, 3.5 hours), **Stratford-upon-Avon** (3/day, 3.5 hours), **Liverpool** (8/day direct, 5-6 hours, overnight available), **York** (4/day direct, 5.5 hours), **Durham** (3/day direct, 6-8 hours, train is better), **Glasgow** (2-4/day direct, 8-9 hours, train is much better), **Edinburgh** (2/day direct, 9 hours, go by train instead).

To Dublin, Ireland: This bus/boat journey, operated by Eurolines, takes 10-12 hours (£35-40, 1/day, departs Victoria Coach Station at 18:00, check in with passport one hour before). Consider a cheap 1-hour Ryanair flight instead.

To the Continent: Especially in summer, buses run to destinations all over Europe, including Paris, Amsterdam, Brussels, and Germany (sometimes crossing the Channel by ferry, other times through the Chunnel). For any international connection, you need to check in with your passport one hour before departure. For details, call 0871-781-8181 or visit www.eurolines.co.uk.

CROSSING THE CHANNEL

By Eurostar Train

The Eurostar zips you (and up to 800 others in 18 sleek cars) from downtown London to downtown Paris or Brussels at 190 mph in 2.5 hours (1-2/hour). The tunnel crossing is a 20-minute, silent, 100 mph nonevent. Your ears won't even pop.

More high-speed connections are coming: Eurostar already runs direct service to Lyon, Avignon, and Marseille (5/week in summer, less frequent off-season). Germany's national railroad is looking to run bullet trains between Frankfurt, Amsterdam, and

London, while Eurostar is hoping to expand into Amsterdam (with stops in Antwerp and at Amsterdam's airport) sometime in 2017.

Eurostar Tickets and Fares: The Eurostar is not covered by rail passes and requires a separate, reserved, nonrefundable train ticket. A one-way ticket between London and Paris or Brussels runs about $60-200 (Standard), $160-310 (Standard Premier), and $400 (Business Premier). Fares depend on how far ahead you reserve and whether you're eligible for any discounts—available for children (under age 12), youths (under 26), seniors (60 or older), round-trip travelers, and rail-pass holders. You can book tickets 4-9 months in advance. Tickets can be exchanged before the scheduled departure for a fee (about $45 plus the cost of any price increase), but only Business Premier class allows any refund.

You can buy tickets online using the print-at-home eticket option (see www.ricksteves.com/eurostar or www.eurostar.com). You can also order by phone through Rail Europe (US tel. 800-387-6782) for home delivery before you go, or through Eurostar (tel. 0843-218-6186, priced in euros) to pick up at the station. In Britain, tickets are issued only at the Eurostar office in St. Pancras International Station. In continental Europe, you can buy Eurostar tickets at any major train station in any country or at any travel agency that handles train tickets (expect a booking fee). Discount tickets for rail-pass holders (which can sell out) are available at Eurostar departure stations, through US agents, or by phone with Eurostar, but they may be harder to get at other train stations and travel agencies.

Eurostar Routes

Those traveling on short notice—when only the costliest Eurostar tickets are available—can consider an "unescorted tour" to Paris, Brussels, or Bruges that includes Eurostar fare (sold by a tour company called BritainShrinkers, about £129 for one-day Paris "tour," Mon-Sat, includes one-day Paris Visite travel card; tel. 020/7713-1311, www.britainshrinkers.com).

Taking the Eurostar: Eurostar trains depart from and arrive at London's St. Pancras International Station. Check in at least 30 minutes in advance (remember that times listed on tickets are local times; Britain's time zone is one hour earlier than France and Belgium's). Pass through airport-like security, show your passport to customs officials, and locate your departure gate (shown on a TV monitor). The waiting area has shops, newsstands, horrible snack bars, and cafés (bring food for the trip from elsewhere), free Wi-Fi, and a currency-exchange booth.

Crossing the Channel Without Eurostar

For speed and affordability, look into **cheap flights** (see page 1037). Or consider the following old-fashioned ways of crossing the Channel (cheaper but more complicated and time-consuming than the Eurostar).

By Train and Boat: To reach **Paris,** take a train from London's St. Pancras International Station to Dover's Priory Station (hourly, 1 hour), then catch a P&O ferry to Calais, France (1/hour, 1.5 hours, www.poferries.com). From Calais, take the TGV train to Paris.

For **Amsterdam,** consider Stena Line's Dutchflyer service, which combines train and ferry tickets. Trains go from London's Liverpool Street Station to the port of Harwich (hourly, 2 hours, most transfer in Manningtree). From Harwich, Stena Line ferries sail to Hoek van Holland (8 hours), where you can catch a train to Amsterdam (book ahead for best price, 13 hours total, www.stenaline.co.uk, Dutch train info at www.ns.nl). For additional European ferry info, visit www.aferry.to.

By Bus and Boat: The bus from London's Victoria Coach Station goes direct to **Paris** (4-5/day, 8-10 hours), **Brussels** (4/day, 9 hours), or **Amsterdam** (4/day, 12 hours) via ferry or Chunnel (day or overnight; around £60-70 one-way, cheaper in advance, tel. 0870-514-3219, www.eurolines.co.uk).

BY CRUISE SHIP

Many cruises begin, end, or call at one of several English ports offering easy access to London. Cruise lines favor two ports: Southampton, 80 miles southwest of London; and Dover, 80 miles southeast of London. If you don't want to bother with public transportation, most cruise lines offer transit-only excursion packages into London. For more details, see my *Rick Steves Northern European Cruise Ports* guidebook.

Southampton Cruise Port

Within Southampton's sprawling port (www.cruisesouthampton.com), cruises use two separate dock areas, each with two terminals.

To reach London, it's about a 1.5-hour train ride. To get to

Southampton Central Station from the cruise port, you can take a taxi or walk 10-15 minutes to the public ferry dock (Town Quay), where you can ride the Citylink bus to the train station. From there, trains depart at least every 30 minutes for London's Waterloo Station.

If you have time to kill in port, consider taking the train to Portsmouth (50 minutes), best known for its Historic Dockyard and many nautical sights, or stick around Southampton and visit the excellent SeaCity Museum, with a beautifully presented exhibit about the *Titanic,* which set sail from here on April 10, 1912.

Dover Cruise Port

Little Dover has a huge port. Cruises put in at the Western Docks, with two terminals.

Trains go from Dover Priory Station to London in 1-2 hours. From either cruise terminal, the best way into town (or to the train station) is by taxi or shuttle bus (take it to Market Square, then walk 15 minutes to the train station). From Dover's station, a fast train leaves for London's St. Pancras International Station (2/hour, 1 hour); slower trains go to either Victoria Station or Charing Cross Station (each 1-2/hour, 2 hours).

If you have extra time in port, Dover Castle, perched upon chalk cliffs, is well worth a visit for its WWII-era Secret Wartime Tunnels. Or take the train to Canterbury (2/hour, less than 30 minutes), notable for its important cathedral and fine historic core.

WINDSOR AND CAMBRIDGE

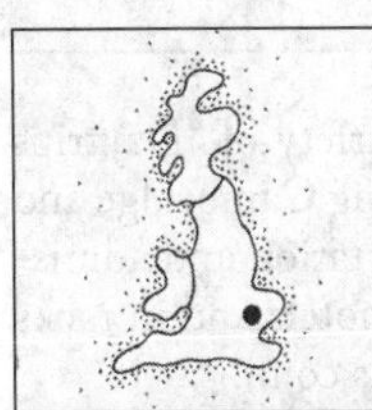

Windsor and Cambridge are a couple of great day-trip possibilities near London. Each destination is very different and yet equally enjoyable.

The primary residence of Her Majesty the Queen, **Windsor** hosts a castle that's regally lived-in, yet open to the public. This is simply a charming town to relax in—and its proximity to Heathrow Airport (60 minutes by train west of London) makes Windsor easy to combine with a flight into or out of London. Nearby is an oddball collection of intriguing sights, including Legoland Windsor, Eton College (Britain's most elite high school), Ascot Racecourse (for horse racing), and Highclere Castle, where the TV series *Downton Abbey* was filmed.

Britain's venerable Cambridge University is mixed into the delightful town of **Cambridge,** north of London, which offers a mellow, fun-to-explore townscape with a big-league university.

Other destinations that make for a practical day-trip from London include both Stonehenge and Salisbury—covered in the Near Bath chapter.

GETTING AROUND

By Train: If day-tripping from London, take advantage of British Rail's discounts. The "off-peak day return" ticket is a round-trip fare that costs virtually the same as one-way, provided you depart London outside rush hour (usually after 9:30 on weekdays and anytime Sat-Sun). Be sure to specifically ask for the "day return" ticket (round-trip within a single day) rather than the more expensive standard "return." You can also save a little money if you purchase tickets before 18:00 the day before your trip.

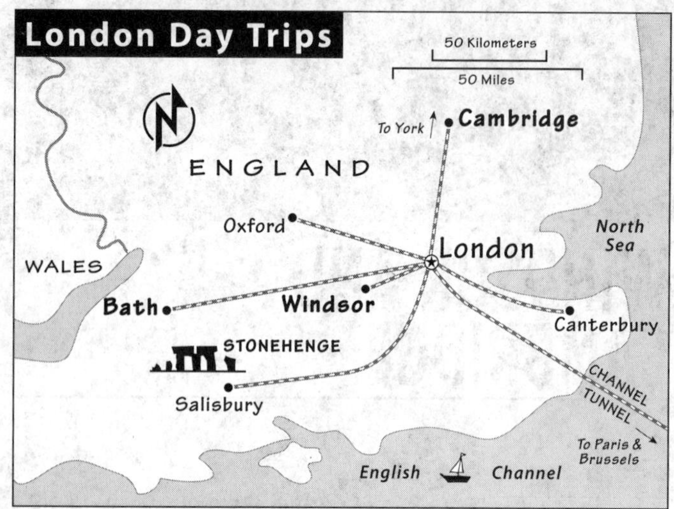

By Train Tour: London Walks offers a variety of "Daytrips from London" tours year-round by train, including Cambridge and Oxford itineraries (£18 plus £36-59 for transportation and admission costs, cash only; pick up their brochure at hotels and in racks all over London, tel. 020/7624-3978, www.walks.com).

Windsor

Windsor, a compact and easy walking town of about 30,000 people, originally grew up around the royal residence. In 1070, William the Conqueror continued his habit of kicking Saxons out of their various settlements, taking over what the locals called "Windlesora" (meaning "riverbank with a hoisting winch")—which eventually became "Windsor." William built the first fortified castle on a chalk hill above the Thames; later kings added on to his early designs, rebuilding and expanding the castle and surrounding gardens.

By setting up their primary residence here, modern monarchs increased Windsor's popularity and prosperity—most notably, Queen Victoria, whose stern statue glares at you as you approach the castle. After her death, Victoria rejoined her beloved husband, Albert, in the

Royal Mausoleum at Frogmore House, a mile south of the castle in a private section of the Home Park (house and mausoleum rarely open). The current Queen considers Windsor her primary residence, and the one where she feels most at home. She generally hangs her crown here on weekends, using it as an escape from her workaday grind at Buckingham Palace in the city. You can tell if Her Majesty is in residence by checking to see which flag is flying above the round tower: If it's the royal standard (a red, yellow, and blue flag) instead of the Union Jack, the Queen is at home.

While 99 percent of visitors just come to tour the castle and go, some enjoy spending the night. Daytime crowds trample Windsor's charm, which is most evident when the tourists are gone. Consider overnighting here—parking and access to Heathrow Airport are easy, and an evening at the horse races (on Mondays) is hoof-pounding, heart-thumping fun.

GETTING TO WINDSOR

By Train: Windsor has two train stations—Windsor & Eton Central and Windsor & Eton Riverside. London's Paddington Station connects with Windsor & Eton Central (2-3/hour, 35 minutes, easy change at Slough; £9.90 one-way standard class, £10-13 same-day return, www.firstgreatwestern.co.uk). London's Waterloo Station connects with Windsor & Eton Riverside (2/hour, no changes but slower—50 minutes; £10-13 one-way standard class, £16-20 same-day return, info tel. 0345-748-4950, www.nationalrail.co.uk).

If you're day-tripping into London *from* Windsor, ask at the train station about combining a same-day return train ticket with a Travelcard transit pass (£13-22, lower price for travel after 9:30, includes some London sightseeing discounts—ask or look for brochure at station, www.daysoutguide.co.uk).

By Bus: Green Line buses #701 and #702 run from London's Victoria Colonnades (between the Victoria train and coach stations) to the Parish Church stop on Windsor's High Street, before continuing on to Legoland (1-2/hour, 1.5 hours to Windsor, £5.50-9.50 one-way, £9-16 round-trip, prices vary depending on time of day, tel. 0871-200-2233, www.firstgroup.com).

By Car: Windsor is about 20 miles from London and just off Heathrow Airport's landing path. The town (and then the castle and Legoland) is well-signposted from the M-4 motorway. It's a convenient first stop if you're arriving at Heathrow and renting a car there and saving London until the end of your trip.

From Heathrow Airport: First Bus Company's buses #71 and #77 run between Terminal 5 and Windsor, dropping you in the center of town at the Parish Church stop on High Street (about £8, 1-3/hour, 50 minutes, tel. 01753/524-144, www.firstgroup.com). London black cabs can (and do) charge whatever they like from

Heathrow to Windsor; avoid them by calling a local cab company, such as Windsor Radio Cars (£26, includes 40 minutes waiting time—handy if you checked your luggage, tel. 01753/677-677, www.windsorcars.com).

Orientation to Windsor

Windsor's pleasant pedestrian shopping zone litters the approach to its famous palace with fun temptations. You'll find most shops and restaurants around the castle on High and Thames Streets, and down the pedestrian Peascod Street (PESS-cot), which runs perpendicular to High Street.

TOURIST INFORMATION

The TI is immediately adjacent to Windsor & Eton Central Station, in the Windsor Royal Shopping Centre's Old Booking Hall (June-Sept Mon-Sat 9:30-17:00, Sun 10:00-16:00; Oct-May Sun-Fri 10:00-16:00, Sat 10:00-17:00; tel. 01753/743-900, www.windsor.gov.uk). The TI sells discount tickets to Legoland and is extremely enthusiastic about their Royal Windsor Historical Tour.

ARRIVAL IN WINDSOR

By Train: Whichever train station you arrive at, you're only a five-minute walk to the castle. From Windsor & Eton Central, walk through the Windsor Royal Shopping Centre (which houses the TI), and up the hill to the castle. From Windsor & Eton Riverside, you'll see the castle as you exit—just follow the wall to the ticket office.

By Car: To get into town, follow signs from the M-4 motorway for pay-and-display parking in the center. River Street Car Park is closest to the castle, but it's pricey and often full. The cheaper, bigger Alexandra Car Park (near the riverside Alexandra Gardens) is farther west. To walk to the town center from the Alexandra Car Park, head east through the tour-bus parking lot toward the castle. At the souvenir shop, walk up the stairs (or take the elevator) and cross the overpass to Windsor & Eton Central Station. Just beyond the station, you'll find the TI in the Windsor Royal Shopping Centre.

The cheapest parking option is the King Edward VII Avenue car-park-and-ride, east of the castle on B-470 (£5 for 5 or more hours; includes shuttle bus into town).

HELPFUL HINTS

Internet Access: You'll find free Wi-Fi at the **library,** located on Bachelors' Acre, between Peascod and Victoria Streets (pay

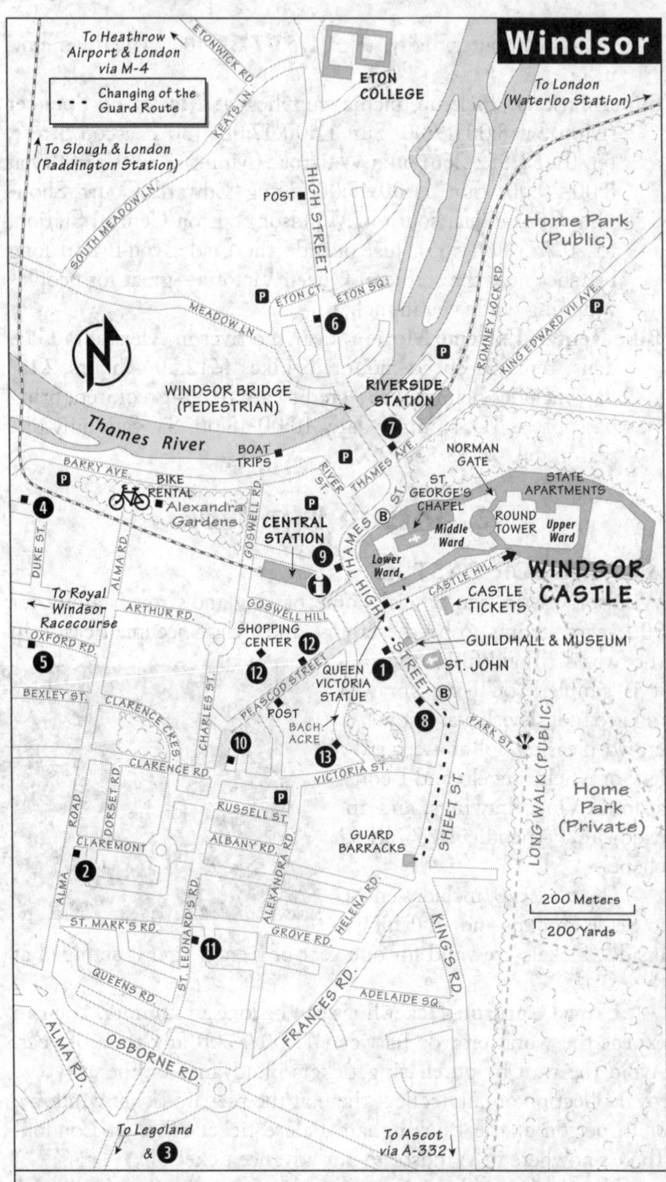

1. MGallery Windsor Castle Hotel
2. Langton House B&B
3. To Park Farm B&B
4. 76 Duke Street B&B
5. Dee & Steve's B&B
6. Crown & Cushion Rooms
7. Bel & The Dragon
8. Cornucopia Bistro
9. The Duchess of Cambridge Pub
10. Meimo Restaurant
11. Saffron Restaurant
12. Grocery Stores (2)
13. Library (Internet Access)

public computer, daily, tel. 01753/743-940, www.rbwm.gov.uk).

Supermarkets: Pick up picnic supplies at **Marks & Spencer** (Mon-Sat 8:00-19:00, Sun 11:00-17:00, 130 Peascod Street, tel. 01753/852-266) or at **Waitrose** (Mon-Fri 8:00-21:00, Sat 8:00-20:00, Sun 11:00-17:00, King Edward Court Shopping Centre, just south of Windsor & Eton Central Station, tel. 01753/860-565). Just outside the castle, you'll find long benches near the statue of Queen Victoria—great for people-watching while you munch.

Bike Rental: Extreme Motion, near the river in Alexandra Gardens, rents 21-speed mountain bikes (£12.50/4 hours, £18/day, includes helmet, £150 credit-card deposit required, bring passport as ID, summer daily 10:00-18:00, Sat-Sun only off-season, tel. 01753/830-220).

Sights in Windsor

▲▲WINDSOR CASTLE

Windsor Castle, the official home of England's royal family for 900 years, claims to be the largest and oldest occupied castle in the world. Thankfully, touring it is simple. You'll see sprawling grounds, lavish staterooms, a crowd-pleasing dollhouse, a gallery of Michelangelo and Leonardo da Vinci drawings, and an exquisite Perpendicular Gothic chapel.

Cost: £19.20, includes entry to castle grounds and all exhibits inside. Tickets are valid for one year of reentry (get it stamped at the exit).

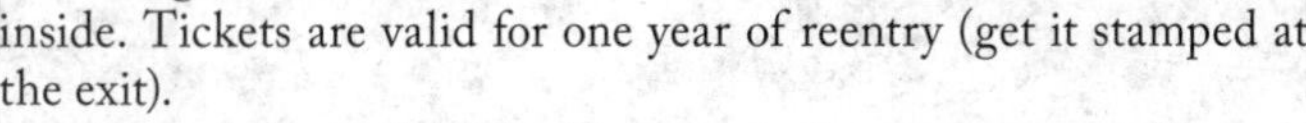

Crowd Control: Ticket lines can be long in summer. You can expect the worst crowds between 11:00-13:00 any time of year. Avoid the wait by purchasing tickets in advance online at www.royalcollection.org.uk (collect them at the prepaid ticket window), or in person at the Buckingham Palace ticket office in London. There's nowhere in Windsor to buy advance tickets.

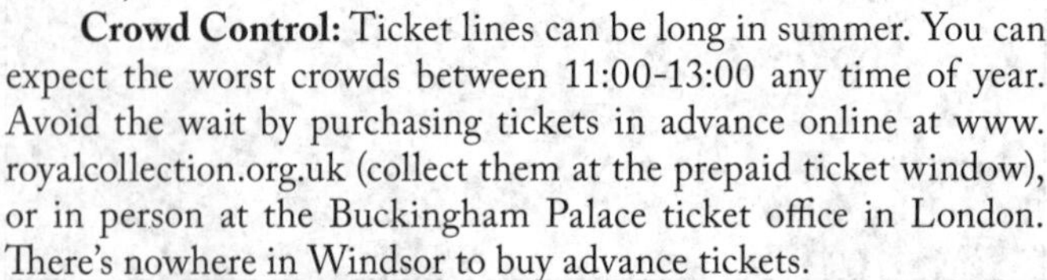

Hours: Grounds and most interiors open daily March-Oct 9:30-17:15, Nov-Feb 9:45-16:15, except St. George's Chapel, which is closed Sun to tourists (but open to worshippers; wait at the exit gate to be escorted in). Last entry to grounds and St. George's Chapel 75 minutes before closing. Last entry to State Apartments and Queen Mary's Dolls' House 45 minutes before closing.

Possible Closures: On rare occasions when the Queen is entertaining guests, the State Apartments close (and tickets are reduced to £10.40). Sometimes the entire castle closes. It's smart to call ahead or check the website (especially in mid-June) to make sure everything is open when you want to go. While you're at it, confirm the Changing of the Guard schedule.

Tours: An included audioguide (dry, reverent, informative) covers both the grounds and interiors. For a good overview—and an opportunity to ask questions—consider the free 30-minute guided walk around the grounds (usually 2/hour, schedule posted next to audioguide desk). The official £5 guidebook is full of gorgeous images and makes a fine souvenir, but the information within is covered by the audioguide and tour.

Photography: Taking photographs inside any of the buildings is strictly forbidden.

Information: Tel. 020/7766-7324, www.royalcollection.org.uk.

Changing of the Guard: The Changing of the Guard takes place Monday through Saturday at 11:00 (April-July) and on alternating days the rest of the year (check website to confirm schedule; get there by 10:30 or earlier if you expect a line for tickets). There is no Changing of the Guard on Sundays or in very wet weather. The fresh guards, led by a marching band, leave their barracks on Sheet Street and march up High Street, hanging a right at Victoria, then a left into the castle's Lower Ward, arriving at about 11:00. After about a half-hour, the tired guards march back the way the new ones came. To watch the actual ceremony inside the castle, you'll need to have already bought your ticket, entered the grounds, and staked out a spot. Alternatively, you could wait for them to march by on High Street or on the lower half of Castle Hill.

Evensong: An evensong takes place in the chapel nightly at 17:15 (free for worshippers, line up at exit gate to be admitted).

Best View: While you can get great views of the castle from any direction, the classic views are from the long, wooded walkway called the Long Walk, which stretches south of the palace and is open to the public.

Eating: There are no real eateries inside (other than shops selling gifty boxes of chocolates and bottled water), so consider bringing a snack with you.

The Order of the Garter

In addition to being the royal residence, Windsor is the home of the Most Noble Order of the Garter—Britain's most prestigious chivalrous order. The castle's history is inexorably tied to this order.

Founded in 1348 by King Edward III and his son (the "Black Prince"), the Order of the Garter was designed to honor returning Crusaders. This was a time when the legends of King Arthur and the Knights of the Round Table were sweeping England, and Edward III fantasized that Windsor could be a real-life Camelot. (He even built the Round Tower as an homage to the Round Table.)

The order's seal illustrates the story of the order's founding and unusual name: a cross of St. George encircled with a belt and a French motto loosely translated as "Shame be upon he who thinks evil of it." Supposedly while the king was dancing with a fair maiden, her garter slipped off onto the floor; in an act of great chivalry, he rescued her from embarrassment by picking it up and uttering those words.

The Order of the Garter continues to the present day as the single most prestigious honor in the United Kingdom. There can be only 24 knights at one time (perfect numbers for splitting into two 12-man jousting teams), plus the sitting monarch and the Prince of Wales. Aside from royals and the nobility, past Knights of the Garter have included Winston Churchill, Bernard "Monty" Montgomery, and Ethiopian Emperor Haile Selassie. In 2008, Prince William became only the 1,000th knight in the order's 660-year history. Other current members include various ex-military officers, former British Prime Minister John Major, and a member of the Colman's Mustard family.

The patron of the order is St. George—the namesake of the State Apartments' most sumptuous hall and of the castle's own chapel. Both of these spaces—the grandest in all of Windsor—are designed to celebrate and to honor the Order of the Garter.

➲ Self-Guided Tour

After buying your ticket and going through the security checkpoint, pick up your audioguide and start strolling along the path through...

The Grounds: Head up the hill, enjoying the first of many fine castle views you'll see today. The tower-topped, conical hill on your left represents the historical core of the castle. William the Conqueror built this motte (artificial mound) and bailey (fortified stockade around it) in 1080—his first castle in England. Among the later monarchs who spiffed up Windsor were Edward III (flush with French war booty, he made it a palace fit for a 14th-century king), Charles II (determined to restore the monarchy properly in the 1660s), and George IV (Britain's "Bling King," who financed many such vanity projects in the 1820s). On your right, the circular bandstand platform has a seal of the Order of the Garter, which has important ties to Windsor (see sidebar).

Passing through the small gate, you approach the stately St. George's Gate. Peek through here to the Upper Ward's **Quadrangle,** surrounded by the State Apartments (across the field) and the Queen's private apartments (to the right).

Turn left and follow the wall. On your right-hand side, you enjoy great views of the **Round Tower** atop that original motte; running around the base of this artificial hill is the delightful, peaceful garden of the castle governor. The unusual design of this castle has not one "bailey" (castle yard), but three, which today make up Windsor's Upper Ward (where the Queen lives, which we just saw), Middle Ward (the ecclesiastical heart of the complex, with St. George's Chapel, which you'll soon pass on the left), and Lower Ward (residences for castle workers).

Continue all the way around this mini moat to the **Norman Gate,** which once held a prison. Walking under the gate, look up to see the bottom of the portcullis that could be dropped to seal off the inner courtyard. Three big holes are strategically situated for dumping boiling goo or worse on whoever was outside the gate. Past the gate are even finer views of the Quadrangle we just saw from the other side.

Do a 180 and head back toward the Norman Gate, but before you reach it, go down the staircase on the right. You'll emerge onto a fine **terrace** overlooking the flat lands all around. It's easy to understand why this was a strategic place to build a castle. That's Eton College across the Thames. Imagine how handy it's been for royals to be able to ship off their teenagers to an elite prep school so close that they could easily keep an eye on them...literally. The power-plant cooling towers in the distance mark the workaday burg of Slough (rhymes with "plow," immortalized as the setting for Britain's original version of the television series *The Office*).

• *Turn right and wander along the terrace. You'll likely see two lines. The long one leads to Queen Mary's Dolls' House, then to the State Apartments. The short line skips the dollhouse and heads directly to the apartments. Read the following descriptions and decide if the dollhouse is worth waiting for (or try again later in the day, when the line sometimes eases up). You can see the Drawings Gallery and the China Museum either way.*

Queen Mary's Dolls' House: This palace in miniature (1:12 scale, from 1924) is "the most famous dollhouse in the world." It was a gift for Queen Mary (the wife of King George V, and the current Queen's grandmother), who greatly enjoyed miniatures, when she was already a fully-grown adult. It's basically one big, dimly-lit room with the large dollhouse in the middle, executed with an astonishing level of detail. Each fork, knife, and spoon on the expertly set banquet table is perfect and made of real silver—and the tiny pipes of its plumbing system actually have running water. But you're kept a few feet away by a glass wall, and are constantly jostled by fellow sightseers in this crowded space, making it difficult to fully appreciate. Unless you're a dollhouse devotee, it's probably not worth waiting half an hour for a five-minute peek at this, but if the line is short it's definitely worth a look.

Drawings Gallery and China Museum: Positioned at the exit of Queen Mary's Dolls' House, this gallery displays a changing array of pieces from the Queen's collection—usually including some big names, such as Michelangelo and Leonardo. The China Museum features items from the Queen's many exquisite settings for royal shindigs.

State Apartments: Dripping with chandeliers, finely furnished, and strewn with history and the art of a long line of kings and queens, they're the best I've seen in Britain. This is where Henry VIII and Charles I once lived, and where the current Queen wows visiting dignitaries. Take advantage of the talkative docents in each room, who are happy to answer your questions.

You'll climb the Grand Staircase up to the **Grand Vestibule,** decorated with exotic items seized by British troops during their missions to colonize various corners of the world. Ask a docent to help you find the bullet that killed Lord Nelson at Trafalgar (in one of the many glass cases). In the next room, the magnificent wood-ceilinged **Waterloo Chamber** is wallpapered with portraits of figures from the pan-European alliance that defeated Napoleon. Find General Wellington (high on the far wall, in red) who outmaneuvered him at Waterloo, and Pope Pius VII (right wall, in red and white) whom Napoleon befriended...then imprisoned. Next, you'll pass through a **series of living rooms**—bedchambers, dressing rooms, and drawing rooms of the king and queen (who traditionally maintained separate quarters). Many rooms are decorated with canvases by Rubens, Van Dyck, and Holbein. Finally you emerge into **St. George's Hall,** decorated with emblems representing the knights of the prestigious Order of the Garter (see sidebar). This is the site of some of the most elaborate royal banquets—imagine one long table stretching from one end of the hall to the other, seating 160 VIPs. From here, you'll proceed into the rooms that were restored after a fire in 1992, including the "Semi-State Apartments." The **Garter Throne Room** is where new members of the Order of the Garter are invested (ceremonially granted their titles).

• *Exiting the State Apartments, you have one more major sight to see. Get out your castle-issued map or follow signs to find...*

St. George's Chapel: This church is known for housing numerous royal tombs, and is an exquisite example of the Perpendicular Gothic style (dating from about 1500). Pick up a free map and circle the interior clockwise, finding these highlights:

Stand at the back and look down the **nave,** with its classic fan-vaulting spreading out from each slender pillar and nearly every joint capped with an elaborate and colorful roof boss. Most of these emblems are associated with the Knights of the Garter, who consider St. George's their "mother church." Under the upper stained-glass windows, notice the continuous frieze of 250 angels, lovingly carved with great detail, ringing the church.

In the corner (#4 on your church-issued map), take in the melodramatic monument to **Princess Charlotte of Wales,** the only child of King George IV. Heir to the throne, her death in 1817 (at 21, in childbirth) devastated the nation. Head up the left side of the nave and find the simple chapel (#6) containing the tombs of the current Queen's parents, **King George VI and "Queen Mum" Elizabeth;** the ashes of her younger sister, Princess Margaret, are also kept here (see the marble slab against the wall). It's speculated that the current Queen may choose this chapel for her final resting place. Farther up the aisle is the tomb of **Edward IV** (#8)**,** who expanded St. George's Chapel.

Stepping into the **choir area** (#12), you're immediately aware that you are in the inner sanctum of the Order of the Garter. The banners lining the nave represent the knights, as do the fancy helmets and half-drawn swords at the top of each wood-carved seat. These symbols honor only living knights; on the seats are some 800 golden panels memorializing departed knights. Under your feet lies the **Royal Vault** (#13), burial spot of Mad King George III (nemesis of American revolutionaries). Strolling farther up the aisle, notice the marker in the floor: You're walking over the burial site of **King Henry VIII** (#14) and Jane Seymour, Henry's favorite wife (perhaps because she was the only one who died before he could behead her). The body of King Charles I, who was beheaded by Oliver Cromwell's forces at the Banqueting House (see page 68), was also discovered here...with its head sewn back on.

On your way out, you can pause at the door of the sumptuous 13th-century **Albert Memorial Chapel** (#28), redecorated in 1861 after the death of Queen Victoria's husband, Prince Albert, and dedicated to his memory.

• *On exiting the chapel, you come into the castle's...*

Lower Ward: This area is a living town where some 160 people who work for the Queen reside; they include clergy, military, and castle administrators. Just below the chapel, you may be able to enter a tranquil little horseshoe-shaped courtyard ringed with residential doorways—all of them with a spectacular view of the chapel's grand entrance.

Back out in the yard, look for the guard posted at his pillbox. Like those at Buckingham Palace, he's been trained to be a ruthless killing machine...just so he can wind up as somebody's photo op. Click!

MORE SIGHTS IN WINDSOR

Legoland Windsor

Paradise for Legomaniacs under age 12, this huge, kid-pleasing park has dozens of tame but fun rides (often with very long lines) scattered throughout its 150 acres. The impressive Miniland has 40 million Lego pieces glued together to create 800 tiny buildings and a minitour of Europe; the Creation Centre boasts an 80 percent scale-model Boeing 747 cockpit, made of two million bricks. Several of the more exciting rides involve getting wet, so dress accordingly or buy a cheap disposable poncho in the gift shop. While you may be tempted to hop on the Hill Train at the entrance, it's faster and more convenient to walk down into the park. Food is available in the park, but you can save money by bringing a picnic.

Cost: Adults-£48, children-£43, 25 percent cheaper booked online at least seven days in advance, 10 percent discount at Windsor TI, free for ages 3 and under; optional Q-Bot ride-reservation gadget allows you to bypass lines (£15-75 depending on when you go and how much time you want to save).

Hours: Convoluted schedule, but generally late July-Aug daily 10:00-19:00; mid-March-late July and Sept-Oct Mon-Fri 10:00-17:00, Sat-Sun 10:00-18:00, often closed Tue-Wed; closed Nov-mid-March. Call or check website for exact schedule, tel. 0871-222-2001, www.legoland.co.uk.

Getting There: A £5 round-trip shuttle bus runs from opposite Windsor's Theatre Royal on Thames Street, and from the Parish Church stop on High Street (2/hour). If day-tripping from London, ask about rail/shuttle/park admission deals from Paddington or Waterloo train stations. For drivers, the park is on B-3022 Windsor/Ascot road, two miles southwest of Windsor and 25 miles west of London. Legoland is clearly signposted from the M-3, M-4, and M-25 motorways. Parking is easy (£4).

Eton College

Across the bridge from Windsor Castle is the most famous "public" (the equivalent of our "private") high school in Britain. Eton was founded in 1440 by King Henry VI; today it educates about 1,300 boys (ages 13-18), who live on campus. Eton has molded the characters of 19 prime ministers as well as members of the royal family, most recently princes William and Harry. Sparse on actual sights, the college is closed to visitors except via guided tour, where you may get a glimpse of the schoolyard, chapel, cloisters, and the Museum of Eton Life. For more information visit www.etoncollege.com or call 01753/671-000.

Eton High Street

Even if you're not touring the college, it's worth the few minutes it takes to cross the pedestrian bridge and wander straight up Eton's High Street. A bit more cutesy and authentic-feeling than Windsor (which is given over to shopping malls and chain stores), Eton has a charm that's fun to sample.

Windsor and Royal Borough Museum

Tucked into a small space beneath the Guildhall (where Prince Charles remarried), this little museum does its best to give some insight into the history of Windsor and the surrounding area. They also have lots of special activities for kids. Ask at the desk whether tours are running to the Guildhall itself (visits only possible with a guide); if not, it's probably not worth the admission.

Cost and Hours: £2, includes audioguide, Tue-Sat 10:00-16:00, Sun 12:00-16:00, closed Mon, located in the Guildhall on High Street, tel. 01628/685-686, www.rbwm.gov.uk.

Boat Trips

Cruise up and down the Thames River for classic views of the castle, the village of Eton, Eton College, and the Royal Windsor Racecourse. Choose from a 40-minute or two-hour tour, then relax onboard and nibble a picnic. Boats leave from the riverside promenade adjacent to Barry Avenue.

Cost and Hours: 40-minute tour-£7, family pass-about £19, mid-Feb-Oct 1-2/hour daily 10:00-17:00, fewer and Sat-Sun only in Nov; 2-hour tour—£11, family pass-about £30, late March-Oct only, 1-2/day; closed Dec-mid-Feb; online discounts, tel. 01753/851-900, www.frenchbrothers.co.uk.

Horse Racing

The horses race near Windsor every Monday at the Royal Windsor Racecourse (£21-25 entry, online discounts, under age 18 free with an adult, April-Aug and Oct, no races in Sept, sporadic in Aug, off the A-308 between Windsor and Maidenhead, tel. 01753/498-400, www.windsor-racecourse.co.uk). The romantic way to get there from Windsor is by a 10-minute shuttle boat (£6.50 round-trip, www.frenchbrothers.co.uk). The famous Ascot Racecourse (described next) is also nearby.

NEAR WINDSOR

Ascot Racecourse

Located seven miles southwest of Windsor and just north of the town of Ascot, this royally owned track is one of the most famous horse-racing venues in the world. The horses first ran here in 1711, and the course is best known for June's five-day Royal Ascot race meeting, attended by the Queen and 299,999 of her loyal subjects. For many, the outlandish hats worn on Ladies Day (Thu) are more interesting than the horses. Royal Ascot is usually the third week in June. The pricey tickets go on sale the preceding November; while the Friday and Saturday races tend to sell out far ahead, tickets for the other days are often available close to the date (check website). In addition to Royal Ascot, the racecourse runs the ponies year-round—funny hats strictly optional.

Cost: Regular tickets generally £18-40—may be available at a discount at TI; Royal Ascot £25-75, online discounts, kids ages 17 and under free; parking-free-£20, depending on event; dress code enforced in some areas and on certain days, tel. 0844-346-3000, www.ascot.co.uk.

Sleeping in Windsor

Most visitors stay in London and do Windsor as a day trip. But here are a few suggestions for those staying the night:

Sleep Code

Abbreviations **(£1=about $1.60, country code: 44)**

S=Single, **D**=Double/Twin, **T**=Triple, **Q**=Quad, **b**=bathroom

Price Rankings

$$$ Higher Priced—Most rooms £105 or more

$$ Moderately Priced—Most rooms £60-105

$ Lower Priced—Most rooms £60 or less

Unless otherwise noted, credit cards are accepted, breakfast is included, and free Wi-Fi and/or a guest computer is generally available. Prices change; verify the hotel's current rates online or by email. For the best prices, always book directly with the hotel.

$$$ MGallery Windsor Castle Hotel, part of the boutique division of Accor Hotels, offers 108 rooms and elegant public spaces in a location that's as central as can be, just down the street from Her Majesty's weekend retreat (Db-from £189, breakfast-£17, check for online deals, air-con, parking-£10/day, 18 High Street, tel. 01753/851-577, www.mercure.com, h6618@accor.com).

$$ Langton House B&B is a stately Victorian home with five spacious, well-appointed rooms lovingly maintained by Paul and Sonja Fogg (S-£71, Sb-£83, D/Db-£101, huge four-poster Db-£113, Tb-£129, Qb-£149, 5 percent extra if paying by credit card, includes continental breakfast, full English breakfast-£6, prices can be soft—especially off-season, family-friendly, guest kitchen, 46 Alma Road, tel. 01753/858-299, www.langtonhouse.co.uk, bookings@langtonhouse.co.uk).

$$ Park Farm B&B, bright and cheery, is most convenient for drivers. But even if you're not driving, this beautiful place is such a good value and the welcome is so warm that you're unlikely to mind the bus ride into town (Sb-£70, Db-£89-95, Tb-£115, Qb-£130, family room with bunk beds, cash only—credit card solely for reservations, shared fridge and microwave, free off-street parking, 1 mile from Legoland on St. Leonards Road near Imperial Road, 5-minute bus ride or 1-mile walk to castle, £5 taxi ride from station, tel. 01753/866-823, www.parkfarm.com, stay@parkfarm.com, Caroline and Drew Youds).

$$ 76 Duke Street has two nice rooms, but only hosts one set of guests at a time. While the bathroom is (just) outside your bedroom, you have it to yourself (Db-£85-90, rent both rooms for £170-180, 15-minute walk from station at—you guessed it—76 Duke Street, tel. 01753/620-636 or 07884/222-225, www.76dukestreet.co.uk, bandb@76dukestreet.co.uk, Julia).

$$ Dee and Steve's B&B is a friendly four-room place above a window shop on a quiet residential street about a 10-minute walk from the castle and station. The rooms are cozy, Dee and Steve are pleasant hosts, and breakfast is served in the contemporary kitchen/lounge (S-£50, Sb-£60-65, Db-£80, 169 Oxford Road, tel. 01753/854-489, www.deeandsteve.com, dee@deeandsteve.com).

$$ Crown and Cushion is a good option on Eton's High Street, just across the pedestrian bridge from Windsor's waterfront (a short uphill walk to the castle). While the pub it's situated over is worn and drab, you're right in the heart of charming Eton, and the eight creaky rooms—with uneven floors and old-beam ceilings—are nicely furnished (Sb-£70, Db-£80, free parking, 84 High Street in Eton, tel. 01753/861-531, www.thecrownandcushioneton.co.uk, info@thecrownandcushioneton.com).

Eating in Windsor

Elegant Spots with River Views: Several places flank Windsor Bridge, offering romantic dining after dark. The riverside promenade, with cheap takeaway stands scattered about, is a delightful place for a picnic lunch or dinner with the swans. If you don't see anything that appeals, continue up Eton's High Street, which is also lined with characteristic eateries.

In the Tourist Zone Around the Palace: Strolling the streets and lanes around the palace entrance—especially in the shopping zone near Windsor & Eton Station—you'll find countless trendy and inviting eateries. The central area also has a sampling of dependable British chains (including a Wagamama, Gourmet Burger Kitchen, and Thai Square). Residents enjoy a wide selection of unpretentious little eateries (including a fire station turned pub-and-cultural center) just past the end of pedestrian Peascod Street.

Bel & The Dragon is the place to splurge on high-quality classic British food in a charming half-timbered building with an upscale-rustic dining space (£6-9 starters, £14-21 main courses, food served daily 12:00-15:00 & 18:00-22:00, afternoon tea served between lunch and dinner, bar open longer hours, on Thames Street near the bridge to Eton, tel. 01753/866-056, http://belandthedragon.co.uk).

Cornucopia Bistro, with a cozy, woody atmosphere, serves tasty international dishes (£10 two-course and £13 three-course lunch meals, £13-16 main courses at dinner, open daily 12:00-14:30 & 18:00-21:30, Fri-Sat until 22:00, closed Sun night, 6 High Street, tel. 01753/833-009).

The Duchess of Cambridge's friendly staff serves up the normal grub in a pub that's right across from the castle walls, and with an open fireplace to boot (£10-14 meals, daily 10:00-22:30 or later, 3 Thames Street, tel. 01753/864-405). While the pub pre-

Visiting Highclere Castle

If you're a fan of *Downton Abbey,* consider a day trip from London to Highclere Castle, the stately house where much of the show was filmed. Though the hugely popular TV series is set in Yorkshire, the actual house is located in Hampshire, about an hour's train ride west of London. Highclere has been home to the Earls of Carnarvon since 1679 (and the current residents enjoy watching the TV show), but the present Jacobean-style house was rebuilt in the 1840s by Sir Charles Berry, who also designed London's Houses of Parliament. Noted landscape architect Capability Brown laid out the traditional gardens in the mid-18th century. The castle's Egyptian exhibit features artifacts collected by Highclere's fifth Earl, George Herbert, a keen amateur archaeologist. When Howard Carter discovered King Tut's tomb in 1922, he waited three weeks for his friend and patron Herbert to join him before looking inside. The Earl died unexpectedly a few months later, giving birth to the legend of a "mummy's curse."

Cost and Hours: Entrance is by timed entry, reserve well in advance online; £20 for castle, garden, and Egyptian exhibit; £13 for castle and garden only, or Egyptian exhibit and garden only; garden only—£5; open days sporadic but generally mid-April-Sept daily 10:30-17:30, last entry at 16:00; tickets available online several months ahead, sales begin as early as Feb for following summer, last-minute afternoon-entry tickets sometimes available—call ahead; no photos inside, 24-hour info tel. 01635/253-204, www.highclerecastle.co.uk.

Getting There: Highclere is six miles south of Newbury, about 70 miles west of London, off the A-34.

By Train and Taxi: First Great Western trains run from London's Paddington Station to Newbury (1-2/hour, 50-70 minutes, £24-54 same-day return, tel. 0345-026-5430, www.firstgreatwestern.co.uk). From Newbury train station, you can take a taxi (£15-22 one-way, higher price is for Sun, taxis wait outside station) or reserve a car and driver (must arrange in advance, £12.50/person round-trip; £25 minimum, WebAir, tel. 07818/430-095, mapeng@msn.com).

By Tour: Brit Movie Tours offers an all-day bus tour of *Downton Abbey* filming locations, including Highclere Castle and the fictional village of Downton (sells out early, £95, includes transport and castle/garden entry, £5 extra for Egyptian exhibit, 9 hours, depart London from outside Gloucester Road Tube Station, reservations required, tel. 0844-247-1007, from the US or Canada call 011-44-20-7118-1007, www.britmovietours.com).

dates Kate, it was named in her honor following a recent remodel, and has the photos to prove her endorsement.

Meimo offers "Mediterranean/Moroccan" cuisine in a nicely subdued dining room at the quieter end of the pedestrian zone (£10-15 main dishes, several fixed-price meal options, daily 10:00-22:00, 69 Peascod Street, tel. 01753/862-222).

Saffron Restaurant, while a fairly long walk from the castle, is the local choice for South Indian cuisine, with a modern interior and attentive waiters who struggle with English but are fluent at bringing out tasty dishes. Their vegetarian *thali* is a treat (£8-12 dishes, daily 12:00-14:30 & 17:30-23:30, 99 St. Leonards Road, tel. 01753/855-467).

Cambridge

Cambridge, 60 miles north of London, is world-famous for its prestigious university. Wordsworth, Isaac Newton, Tennyson, Darwin, and Prince Charles are a few of its illustrious alumni. The university dominates—and owns—most of Cambridge, a historic town of about 125,000 people. Cambridge is the epitome of a university town, with busy bikers, stately residence halls, plenty of bookshops, and proud locals who can point out where DNA was originally modeled, the atom first split, and electrons discovered.

In medieval Europe, higher education was the domain of the Church and was limited to ecclesiastical schools. Scholars lived in "halls" on campus. This academic community of residential halls, chapels, and lecture halls connected by peaceful garden courtyards survives today in the colleges that make up the universities of Cambridge and Oxford. By 1350 (Oxford is roughly 100 years older), Cambridge had eight colleges, each with a monastic-type courtyard, chapel, library, and lodgings. Today, Cambridge has 31 colleges, each with its own facilities, and about 12,000 undergrads. In the town center, these grand old halls date back centuries, with ornately decorated facades that try to one-up each other. While students' lives revolve around their independent colleges, the university organizes lectures, presents degrees, and promotes research.

The university schedule has three terms: Lent term from mid-January to mid-March, Easter term from mid-April to mid-June, and Michaelmas term from early October to early December. During exams (roughly the month of May), the colleges are closed to visitors, which can impede access to some of the town's picturesque little corners. But the main sights—King's College Chapel and the Wren Library at Trinity College—stay open, and Cambridge is never sleepy.

PLANNING YOUR TIME

Cambridge can easily be seen as a day trip from London. A good five-hour plan is to follow my self-guided walk, spend an hour on a punt ride, tour the Fitzwilliam Museum (closed Mon), and see the Wren Library at Trinity College (open Mon-Sat for only two hours a day, so plan ahead). For a little extra color, consider joining a walk through town with a local guide from the TI (2 hours, repeats much of my self-guided walk but splices in local flavor). The TI's town walk includes King's College Chapel, so don't do that on your own.

If you're in town for the evening, the evensong service at King's College Chapel (at 17:30) is a must. If you like plays and music, events are always happening in this thriving cultural hub.

GETTING TO CAMBRIDGE

By Train: It's an easy trip from London and less than an hour away. Catch the train from London's King's Cross Station (2/hour, trains leave King's Cross at :15 and :44 past the hour, 45 minutes, £23 one-way standard class, £24 same-day return after 9:30, tel. 0345-748-4950, www.nationalrail.co.uk). Cheaper direct trains also run from London's Liverpool Street Station, but take longer (2/hour, 1.5 hours).

By Bus: National Express coaches run from London's Victoria Coach Station to the Parkside stop in Cambridge (every 60-90 minutes, 2-2.5 hours, £12, discounted fares may be available in advance online, tel. 0871-781-8181, www.nationalexpress.co.uk).

Orientation to Cambridge

Cambridge is small. Everything is within a pleasant walk. The town has two main streets, separated from the Cam River by the most interesting colleges. The town center, brimming with tearooms, has a TI and a colorful open-air market square. The train station is about a mile to the southeast.

TOURIST INFORMATION

Cambridge's TI is well run and well signposted, just off Market Square in the town center. They book rooms for £5, offer walking tours (see "Tours in Cambridge," later), and sell bus tickets and a £2 map/guide (Mon-Sat 10:00-17:00, Easter-Sept also Sun 11:00-15:00—otherwise closed Sun, phones answered from 9:00, Peas Hill, tel. 0871-226-8006, room-booking tel. 01223/457-581, www.visitcambridge.org). In the same building as the TI, you can duck into a former courtroom to catch a free video overview of the town and its history.

ARRIVAL IN CAMBRIDGE

By Train: Cambridge's train station doesn't have baggage storage or a TI. You can pick up a free map at the small info desk on the platform and other brochures on an interior wall just before the turnstiles.

To get from the station to downtown Cambridge, you can **walk** for about 25 minutes (exit straight ahead on Station Road, bear right at the war memorial onto Hills Road, and follow it into town); take public **bus** #1, #3, #7, or #8 (referred to as "Citi 1," "Citi 3," and so on in schedules, but buses are marked only with the number; £1.60, pay driver, runs every 5-10 minutes, turn left when exiting station and walk half a block to find bus stands, get off when you see Lion's Yard shopping mall on the left); pay about £6 for a **taxi;** or take a City Sightseeing **bus tour** (described later).

By Car: To park in the middle of town, follow signs from the M-11 motorway to any of the central short-stay parking lots. Or leave your car at one of five park-and-ride lots outside the city, then take the shuttle into town (parking-£1/4 hours; shuttle-£2.70 round-trip).

HELPFUL HINTS

Live Theater and Entertainment: With all the smart and talented students in town, there is always something going on. Make a point of enjoying a play or concert. The ADC **(Cambridge University Amateur Dramatic Club)** is Britain's oldest university playhouse, offering a steady stream of performances since 1855. It's lots of fun and casual, with easy-to-get and inexpensive tickets. This is your chance to see a future Emma Thompson or Ian McKellen—alums who performed here as students—before they become stars (tel. 01223/300-085, www.adctheatre.com).

Cambridge Live Tickets is a very helpful service, offering event info and ticket sales in person and online (Mon-Fri 12:00-18:00, Sat from 10:00, Sun from 18:00 until 30 minutes before showtime, 2 Wheeler Street, tel. 01223/357-851

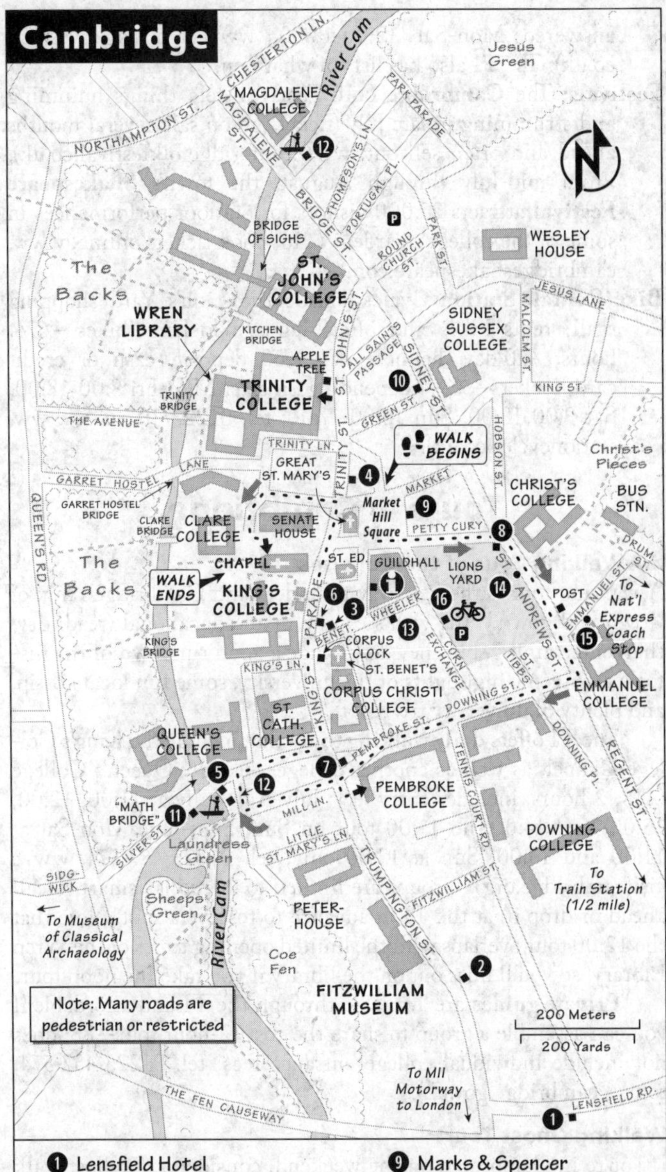

1. Lensfield Hotel
2. Hotel du Vin
3. The Eagle Pub; Bread & Meat
4. Michaelhouse Café
5. The Anchor Pub
6. Agora at The Copper Kettle
7. Fitzbillies
8. Healthy Fast Food Chains
9. Marks & Spencer
10. Sainsbury's
11. Cambridge Chauffeur Punts
12. Scudamore's Punts (2)
13. Cambridge Live Tickets
14. Bus from Train Station
15. Bus to Train Station
16. Bike Rental

answered Mon-Sat 12:00-18:00, www.cambridgelivetrust.co.uk). The TI also has lists of what's on.

Festivals: The **Cambridge Folk Festival** gets things humming and strumming in late July (tickets go on sale several months ahead and often sell out; www.cambridgefolkfestival.co.uk). From mid-July through August, the town's **Shakespeare Festival** attracts 25,000 visitors for outdoor performances in some of the college's gardens (£16, book tickets online, www.cambridgeshakespeare.com).

Bike Rental: Station Cycles, inside the Lion's Yard shopping mall, rents bikes and offers luggage lockers (bikes—£7/4 hours, £10/day, helmets—£1, £60 deposit, cash or credit card; lockers—£3-4 depending on size; Mon-Fri 8:00-18:00, Sat 9:00-18:00, Sun 10:00-17:00; tel. 01223/307-655, www.stationcycles.co.uk).

Tours in Cambridge

▲▲Walking Tour of the Colleges

A walking tour is the best way to understand Cambridge's mix of "town and gown." The walks can be more educational (read: dry) than entertaining, but they do provide a good rundown of the historic and scenic highlights of the university, some fun local gossip, and plenty of university trivia.

The TI offers **daily walking tours** that include the King's College Chapel, as well as another college—usually Queen's College (£18, 2 hours, includes entry fees; July-Aug daily at 11:00, 12:00, 13:00, and 14:00, no 11:00 tour on Sun; Sept-June Mon-Sat at 11:00 and 13:00, Sun at 13:00 only; tel. 01223/457-574, www.visitcambridge.org). Groups are limited to 20, so it's smart to call ahead or drop in at the TI in advance to reserve a spot. Note that the 12:00 tour overlaps with the limited opening times of the Wren Library, so you'll miss out on the library if you take the noon tour.

Private guides are available through the TI and affordable if you can assemble a group to share the cost (2-hour tour-£88; does not include individual college entrance fees, tel. 01223/457-574, tours@cambridge.gov.uk).

Walking Ghost Tour

If you're in Cambridge on the weekend, consider a £6 ghost walk to where spooky sightings have been reported (Fri-Sat at 18:00, organized by the TI, tel. 01223/457-574).

Bus Tours

City Sightseeing hop-on, hop-off bus tours are informative and cover the outskirts, including the American WWII Cemetery. But keep in mind that buses can't go where walking tours can—right

Cambridge Colleges 101

Colleges are central to life at Cambridge, and are where students spend most of their time. Cambridge has 31 colleges, which house, feed, and parent the students, while the university offers formal teaching and lectures. Each college has a "home professor" who coaches students as they navigate the higher education system.

Some colleges are free to visit and welcoming to the public, some are closed off and very private, and others are famous and make money by charging for visits. Most are open only in the afternoons, and all have a similar design and etiquette. At their historic front gates, you'll find a porter's lodge where the porter keeps an eye on things. He delivers mail, monitors who comes and goes, and keeps people off the grass. The exclusive putting-green quality of the courtyard lawns is a huge deal here: Only fellows (senior professors) can walk on the courts, which are the centerpiece of each college campus. Whether a college is open to visitors or private, you can usually at least pop in through the gate, chat with the porter, and enjoy the view of the grassy court.

The court is ringed by venerable buildings, always including a library, dormitories, a dining hall, and a chapel. The dining hall is easy to identify by its big bay windows marking the location of the "high table," where VIPs eat. A portrait of the college's founder usually hangs above the high table, and paintings of rectors and important alumni also decorate the walls. Students still eat in these halls, which is why they are rarely open to the public (but you can look in from the main door). A college's chapel is the building that most often allows visitors (including at evensong services, usually at 17:30 or 18:00). In the chapel, seating is usually arranged in several rows of pews that face each other to allow for antiphonal singing and chanting—where one side starts and the other responds. The chapels often contain memorials to students who died in World Wars I and II. Libraries are treasured and generally not open to the public. There's also a Senior Common Room (like a teachers' lounge but much fancier), where fellows share ideas in an exclusive social hall, creating a fertile intellectual garden. Students live on campus not along halls but in "staircases" (never open to the public). Their address includes their college, their staircase, and their room number.

into the center (£15, 80 minutes for full 19-stop circuit, buy ticket with credit card at the bus-stop kiosk—or pay cash to driver when you board, departs every 20 minutes in summer, every 40 minutes in winter, first bus leaves train station at 10:06, last bus around 17:30, recorded commentary, tel. 01223/433-250, www.city-sightseeing.com). If arriving by train, you can buy your ticket from the kiosk directly in front of the station, then ride the bus into town.

Cambridge Town Walk

Cambridge is built along its dreamy little river and around its 31 colleges (the first, Peterhouse, was founded in the 1280s). It's easy to sort out. There's a small and youthful commercial center—quiet and traffic free (except for lots of bikes), one important museum (the Fitzwilliam), and lots of minor museums (all free). The Cam River has boat tours, three public bridges, and a strip of six colleges whose gardens basically own the river through the center of town and make it feel like an exclusive park. The university includes two dominant colleges (Trinity with its famous Wren Library, and King's College with its famous chapel), but also plenty of minor ones, each with a grand front gate. The city is filled with students year-round—scholars throughout the regular terms and visiting students enjoying summer programs.

In the following self-guided walk, I cover the essential town sights (including two less-visited colleges), finishing at King's College Chapel. Trinity College and the Fitzwilliam Museum are covered in "Sights in Cambridge," later.

• *Start this self-guided walk on Market Hill Square (the TI is just half a block away). To find the square from the lively street called King's Parade—which feels like the center of town and is where this walk ends—go behind Great St. Mary's Church (with the tall tower).*

Market Hill Square

This square has been a center of commerce for more than a thousand years. Think of the history this place has seen: Romans first built a bridge over the Cam in 43 A.D., Anglo-Saxons and Danes established a market here in the Dark Ages, and Normans built a castle here (now gone) in the 11th century.

But the big year was 1209, when scholars and students first arrived. After scuffles in Oxford between its townsfolk and university (which is older than Cambridge), Oxford's students and professors fled here and settled. (The Oxford-Cambridge rivalry just seems natural.) Where's the university? Everywhere, mixed into the town, with the 31 individual colleges, university halls, and student dorms scattered about. Even on this square you can see dorms (the more modern, tasteless buildings around you). Cambridge suffered no bomb damage in World War II, so the older buildings you see are originals. As you walk, notice how peaceful the town is. Almost no cars, but bikes everywhere—be careful! They are silent and pack a punch.

The Guildhall facing this square (the seat of the city council today) overlooks market stalls. The big market is on Sunday (9:30-16:30) and features produce, arts, and crafts. On other days, you'll find mostly clothes and food (Mon-Sat generally 9:30-16:00).

• *Facing the Guildhall, exit the square to your left down Petty Curry Lane, a modern pedestrian shopping street. At its end (with my three favorite fast-food chains: Eat, Pret a Manger, and Wasabi) you hit St. Andrews Street. On the left is the fine 16th-century gatehouse of Christ's College. Step inside to enjoy the classic court, next to a bust of Charles Darwin (a notable alum). Although the college isn't open to the public, you can chat with the porter. Now continue down St. Andrews Street a long block to Emmanuel College.*

Emmanuel College

This college welcomes the public and offers a classic peek at a typical Cambridge college (free, open 9:00-18:00). Emmanuel was founded in 1584 as a Protestant college on land that had once been a Dominican friary. (Like many monasteries and convents in the 16th century, the friary had been dissolved by the English king in an epic power struggle that left England with its own version of Christianity and the government with lots of land once owned by the Catholic Church.)

Facing the court with the big clock is one of two chapels in town designed by Christopher Wren. Above the church is the Senior Common Room, a social hall for college fellows. On the left is the dining hall—marked by its big bay window.

At this point you could visit the church (find the portrait of John Harvard—the Emmanuel College student who went to America and founded another prestigious school—in the stained glass on the left), look through the doorway into the dining hall, enjoy the garden behind the chapel (typical of these colleges; the fish pond goes back to monastic days when the fish were part of the diet), or chat with the porter.

• *Leaving Emmanuel College, walk straight ahead, down Downing Street. You'll pass several museums that are owned by the university to support various fields of study (generally free to enter). Downing Street ends at King's Parade, with Pembroke College on the left and the recommended Fitzbillies Café on the right. (Fitzbillies is famous for its local cinnamon roll, the Chelsea Bun, and is a good place for a break).*

Pembroke College

Founded in 1347, Pembroke is the third-oldest college in Cambridge. Step into the court, past the porter's lodge—it's polite to say hello and ask whether you can wander around. Survey the court. Two chapels face it. The original chapel (on the left) was replaced by the bigger one on the right. Ahead of you is the medieval dining hall, and the fancy building with the pointed clock tower is the library (the statue in front is of alumnus William Pitt the Younger—a great 18th-century prime minister), with a charming garden beyond.

The highlight here is the chapel on the right. The chapel dates from about 1660 and is the first building that the famed architect Christopher Wren completed. Before stepping inside to enjoy the interior, pause for a moment at the somber WWI and WWII memorial.

• *From Pembroke College, cross King's Parade and follow Mill Lane directly down to the River Cam and its mill pond.*

River Cam, the Mill Pond, and Punting

From this perch you see the "harbor action" of Cambridge. The city was a sort of harbor in medieval times: Trading vessels from the North Sea could navigate to here. Today a weir divides the River Cam from the River Granta (on the left), which leads through idyllic countryside to the town of Grantchester (note that punts cannot cross the weir). Filling the actual mill pond is a commotion of the iconic Cambridge boats called *punts.* Students hustle to take visitors on a 45-minute trip along the parklike "backs" of the colleges that line the river from here to the far side of town (about £15, see page 231). You can share a boat with others and enjoy a colorful narration as you're poled past fine college architecture. Skilled residents rent boats for themselves, as do not-so-skilled tourists—much to the amusement of locals who sip their beer while watching clumsy visitors fumble with the boats (which are tougher to maneuver than they look).

Walk along the harbor past the recommended Anchor Pub (with waterfront tables and fancier seating upstairs) to the Silver Street Bridge. From here you can watch more punt action and check out the famous "Mathematical Bridge," which links the old and new buildings of Queens' College. This wooden bridge, although curved, is made of straight boards. (It was not designed by Isaac Newton, as a popular fable would have it—Newton died before the bridge was constructed.)

Gazing upstream past the wooden bridge, you see the start of the stretch of six colleges, each with a bridge that connects their campus complexes with the garden-like "backs."

• *Walk up Silver Street, back to King's Parade, and turn left toward this walk's finale—King's College. On the first corner, find the fancy gilded clock.*

The Corpus Clock, Benet Street, and Eagle Pub

Designed and commissioned by Corpus Christi College alum John Taylor, this clock was unveiled by Cambridge physicist Stephen Hawking in a 2008 ceremony. Perched on top is the Chronophage—the "time eater"—a grotesque giant grasshopper that keeps the clock moving and periodically winks at passersby. The message? Time is passing, so live every moment to the fullest.

The Eagle Pub, a venerable joint, is just down Benet Street on the left. This is Cambridge's oldest pub and a sight in itself. Poke into the courtyard and atmospheric rooms even if you don't eat or drink here.

From the courtyard outside, look up at the balcony of second-floor guest rooms that date back to when this was a coachmen's inn as well as a pub. (It's said that in Shakespeare's time, plays were performed from this perch to entertain guests below.) The faded *Bath* sign indicates that this was a posh place—you could even wash. Notice that the window on the right end is open; any local will love to tell you why.

Step past the "glancing stones" that protected the corner from careening coaches. During World War II, US Army Air Corps pilots famously hung out here before missions over Germany. The fun interior is plastered with stickers of air crews and WWII memorabilia. Next to the fireplace a photo and plaque remember two esteemed regulars—Francis Crick and James Watson—the scientists who first described the structure of DNA. They announced their finding here in 1953, and if you'd like to drink to that, there's a beer on tap for you—a bitter called DNA.

St. Benet's Church, across the street from the pub, is the oldest surviving building in Cambridgeshire. The Saxons who built the church in the 11th century included circular holes in its bell tower to encourage owls to roost there and keep the mouse population under control.

• *Return to the creepy grasshopper clock and turn right, continuing down King's Parade past the regal front facade of King's College Chapel (we'll return here shortly) to the...*

Senate House

This stately classical building with triangular pediments is the ceremonial and administrative heart of Cambridge University and the meeting place of the university's governing body. In June, you might notice green boxes lining the front of this house. Traditionally at the end of the term, students came to these boxes to see whether they earned their degree; those not listed knew they had flunked. Amazingly, until 2010 this was the only notification students received about their status. (Now they first get an email.)

Looming across the street from the Senate House is **Great St. Mary's Church** (a.k.a. the University Church), with a climbable bell tower (£4, Mon-Sat 9:30-16:30, Sun 12:30-16:00, 123 stairs). On the corner nearby is **Ryder and Amies** (22 King's Parade), which has been the official university outfitter for 150 years. It's a great shop for college gear: sweaters, ties, and so on. Upstairs, if you ask, you can try on an undergraduate gown and mortar board.

• *Just after the Senate House, take the first left possible (on Senate House passage); at the end, bear left on Trinity Lane to reach the gate where you pay to enter...*

▲▲King's College Chapel

Built from 1446 to 1515 by Henrys VI through VIII, England's best example of Perpendicular Gothic architecture is the single most impressive building in Cambridge.

Cost and Hours: £8, erratic hours depending on school events; during academic term usually Mon-Fri 9:30-15:30, Sat 9:30-15:15, Sun 13:15-14:30; during breaks (see page 216) usually daily 9:30-16:30; recorded info tel. 01223/331-1212.

Evensong: When school's in session, you're welcome to enjoy an evensong service in this glorious space, with a famous choir made up of men and boys (free, Mon-Sat at 17:30, Sun at 15:30; for more on evensong, see page 145). Line up at the front entrance (on King's Parade) by 17:00 if you want prime seats in the choir.

Visiting the Chapel: Stand inside, look up, and marvel, as Christopher Wren did, at what was then the largest single span of **vaulted roof** anywhere. Built between 1512 and 1515, its 2,000 tons of incredible fan vaulting—held in place by the force of gravity—are a careful balancing act resting delicately on the buttresses visible outside the building.

While Henry VI—who began work on the chapel—wanted it to be austere, his successors on the throne decided it should glorify the House of Tudor (of which Henry VI's half-nephew, Henry VII, was the first king). Lining the walls are giant **Tudor coats-of-arms.** The shield is supported by symbolism for each branch of the family: the fleur-de-lis is there because an earlier ancestor, Edward III, woke up one day and somewhat arbitrarily declared himself

king of France; a rose and the dragon of Wales represent the family of Henry VII's father, Edmund Tudor; and the greyhound holding the shield and the portcullis (the iron grate) symbolize the family of Henry VII's mother, Lady Margaret Beaufort.

The 26 **stained-glass windows** date from the 16th century. It's the most Renaissance stained glass anywhere in one spot. (Most of the stained glass in English churches dates from Victorian times, but this glass is three centuries older.) The lower panes show scenes from the New Testament, while the upper panes feature corresponding stories from the Old Testament. Considering England's turbulent history, it's miraculous that these windows have survived for nearly half a millennium in such a pristine state. After Henry VIII separated from the Catholic Church in 1534, many such windows and other Catholic features around England were destroyed. (Think of all those ruined abbeys dotting the English countryside.) However, since Henry had just paid for these windows, he couldn't bear to destroy them. A century later, in the days of Oliver Cromwell, another wave of iconoclasm destroyed more windows around England. Though these windows were slated for removal, they stayed put. (Historians speculate that Cromwell's troops, who were garrisoned in this building, didn't want the windows removed in the chilly wintertime.) Finally, during World War II, the windows were taken out and hidden away for safekeeping, then painstakingly replaced after the war ended. The only nonmedieval windows are on the west wall (opposite the altar). These are in the Romantic style from the 1880s; when Nazi bombs threatened the church, all agreed they should be left in place.

The **choir screen** that bisects the church was commissioned by King Henry VIII to commemorate his marriage to Anne Boleyn. By the time it was finished, so was she (beheaded). But it was too late to remove her initials, which were carved into the screen (look on the far left and right for *R.A.*, for *Regina Anna*—"Queen Anne"). Behind the screen is the **choir** area, where the King's College Choir performs a daily evensong (during school terms). On Christmas Eve, a special service is held here and broadcast around the world on the BBC—a tradition near and dear to British hearts.

Walk to the altar and admire Rubens' masterful ***Adoration of the Magi*** (1634). It's actually a family portrait: The admirer in the front (wearing red) is a self-portrait of Rubens, Mary looks an awful lot like his much-younger wife, and the Baby Jesus resembles their own newborn at the time. The chapel to the right of the altar is a moving memorial to those who died in the World Wars.

Finally, check out the long and fascinating series of rooms that run the length of the nave on the left. Dedicated to the history and art of the church, these are a great little King's College Chapel museum (including a model showing how the fan vaults were constructed).

• *Exit the church opposite where you entered, into the college court. From here you can stroll the rich grounds all the way to the River Cam and then back, passing through the grand entry gate and onto King's Parade.*

Sights in Cambridge

My self-guided walk takes you to most of the main sights in Cambridge, but not all. Visiting the following places in and near town is also worthwhile

▲▲Trinity College and Wren Library

More than a third of Cambridge's 83 Nobel Prize winners have come from this richest and biggest of the town's colleges, founded in 1546 by Henry VIII. The college has three sights to see: the entrance gate, the grounds, and the magnificent Wren Library.

Cost and Hours: Grounds—£2, often free off-season, daily 10:00-17:00; library—free, Mon-Fri 12:00-14:00, during full term also Sat 10:30-12:30, closed Sun year-round; only 20 people allowed in at a time, tel. 01223/338-400, www.trin.cam.ac.uk.

Visiting the College: To see the Wren Library without paying for the grounds, access it from the riverside entrance (a long walk around the college via the Garret Hostel Bridge).

Trinity Gate: You'll notice gates like these adorning facades of colleges around town. Above the door is a statue of **King Henry VIII,** who founded Trinity because he feared that Cambridge's existing colleges were too cozy with the Church. Notice Henry's right hand holding a chair leg instead of the traditional crown jewels scepter. This is courtesy of Cambridge's Night Climbers, who first replaced the scepter a century ago, and continue to periodically switch it out for other items. According to campus legend, decades ago some of the world's most talented mountaineers enrolled at Cambridge...in one of the flattest parts of England. (Cambridge was actually a seaport until Dutch engineers drained the surrounding swamps.) Lack-

ing opportunities to practice their skill, they began scaling the frilly facades of Cambridge's college buildings under cover of darkness (if caught, they'd have been expelled). In the 1960s, climbers actually managed to haul an entire automobile onto the roof of the Senate House. The university had to bring in the army to cut it into pieces and remove it. Only 50 years later, at a class reunion, did the guilty parties finally fess up.

In the little park to the right, notice the lone **apple tree.** Supposedly, this tree is a descendant of the very one that once stood in the garden of Sir Isaac Newton (who spent 30 years at Trinity). According to legend, Newton was inspired to investigate gravity when an apple fell from the tree onto his head. This tree stopped bearing fruit long ago; if you do see apples, they've been tied on by mischievous students.

Beyond the gate are the Trinity grounds. Note that there's often a fine and free view of Trinity College courtyard—if the gate is open—from Trinity Lane (leading, under a uniform row of old chimneys, around the school to the Wren Library).

Trinity Grounds: The grounds are enjoyable to explore. Inside the **Great Court,** the clock (on the tower on the right) double-rings at the top of each hour. It's a college tradition to take off running from the clock when the high noon bells begin (it takes 43 seconds to clang 24 times), race around the courtyard, touching each of the four corners without setting foot on the cobbles, and try to return to the same spot before the ringing ends. Supposedly only one student (a young lord) ever managed the feat—a scene featured in *Chariots of Fire* (but filmed elsewhere).

The **chapel** (entrance to the right of the clock tower)—which pales in comparison to the stunning King's College Chapel—feels like a shrine to thinking, with statues honoring great Trinity minds both familiar (Isaac Newton, Alfred Lord Tennyson, Francis Bacon) and unfamiliar. Who's missing? The poet Lord Byron, who was such a hell-raiser during his time at Trinity that a statue of him was deemed unfit for Church property; his statue stands in the library instead.

Wren Library: Don't miss the 1695 Christopher Wren-designed library, with its wonderful carving and fascinating original manuscripts. Just outside the library entrance, Sir Isaac Newton clapped his hands and timed the echo to measure the speed of sound as it raced down the side of the cloister and back. In the library's 12 display cases (covered with cloth that you flip back), you'll see handwritten works by Sir Isaac Newton and John Milton, alongside A. A. Milne's original *Winnie the Pooh* (the real Christopher Robin attended Trinity College). Unlike the other libraries at Cambridge, Wren designed his to be used from the first floor up—instead of the damp, dark ground floor. As a result, Wren's library is flooded with light rather than water (and it's also brimming with students during exam times).

▲▲Fitzwilliam Museum

Britain's best museum of antiquities and art outside London is the Fitzwilliam. Housed in a grand Neoclassical building, a 10-minute walk south of Market Square, it's a palatial celebration of beauty and humankind's ability to create it.

Cost and Hours: Free but £5 donation suggested, Tue-Sat 10:00-17:00, Sun 12:00-17:00, closed Mon, photos allowed without flash, lockers, Trumpington Street, tel. 01223/332-900, www.fitzmuseum.cam.ac.uk.

Visiting the Museum: The Fitzwilliam's broad collection is like a mini British Museum and National Gallery rolled into one; you're bound to find something you like. Helpful docents—many with degrees or doctorates in art history—are more than willing to answer questions about the collection. The ground floor features an extensive range of antiquities and applied arts—everything from Greek vases, Mesopotamian artifacts, and Egyptian sarcophagi to Roman statues, fine porcelain, and suits of armor.

Upstairs is the painting gallery, with works that span art history: Italian Venetian masters (such as Titian and Canaletto), a worthy English section (featuring Gainsborough, Reynolds, Hogarth, and others), and a notable array of French Impressionist art (including Monet, Renoir, Pissarro, Degas, and Sisley). Rounding out the collection are old manuscripts, including some musical compositions from Handel.

Museum of Classical Archaeology

Although this museum contains no originals, it offers a unique chance to study accurate copies (19th-century casts) of virtually every famous ancient Greek and Roman statue. More than 450 statues are on display. If you've seen the real things in Greece, Istanbul, Rome, and elsewhere, touring this collection is like a high school reunion..."Hey, I know you!" But since it takes some time to get here, this museum is best left to devotees of classical sculpture.

Cost and Hours: Free, Mon-Fri 10:00-17:00, Sat 10:00-13:00 during term, closed Sun year-round, Sidgwick Avenue, tel. 01223/330-402, www.classics.cam.ac.uk/museum.

Getting There: The museum is a five-minute walk west of Silver Street Bridge; after crossing the bridge, continue straight until you reach a sign reading *Sidgwick Site*.

▲Punting on the Cam

For a little levity and probably more exercise than you really want, try renting one of the traditional flat-bottom punts at the river and pole yourself up and down (or around and around, more likely) the lazy Cam. This is one of the best memories the town has to offer, and once you get the hang of it, it's a fine way to enjoy the scenic side of Cambridge. It's less crowded in late afternoon (and less embarrassing).

Several companies rent punts and also offer punting tours with entertaining narration. Hawkers try to snare passengers in the thriving people zone in front of King's College. Prices are soft in slow times—try talking them down a bit before committing.

Scudamore's has two locations: on Mill Lane, just south of the central Silver Street Bridge, and at the less convenient Quayside at Magdalene Bridge, at the north end of town (£25/hour, credit-card deposit required; 45-minute tours-£18/person, ask for discount; open daily 9:00-dusk, tel. 01223/359-750, www.scudamores.com).

Cambridge Chauffeur Punts, just under the Silver Street Bridge, also rents punts. Take yourself and up to five friends for a spin, or they will chauffeur (£22/hour; passport, credit card, or £60 cash deposit required; 45-minute shared tours-£14/person; open daily March-Nov 9:00-dusk, tel. 01223/354-164, www.punting-in-cambridge.co.uk).

NEAR CAMBRIDGE

Imperial War Museum Duxford

This former airfield, nine miles south of Cambridge, is popular with aviation fans and WWII buffs. Wander through seven exhibition halls housing 200 vintage aircraft (including Spitfires, B-17 Flying Fortresses, a Concorde, and a Blackbird) as well as military land vehicles and special displays on Normandy and the Battle of Britain. On many weekends, the museum holds special events, such as air shows (extra fee)—check the website for details.

Cost and Hours: £17.50, show local bus ticket for discount, daily 10:00-18:00, off-season until 16:00, last entry one hour before closing; tel. 01223/835-000, www.iwm.org.uk/visits/iwm-duxford.

Getting There: The museum is located off the A-505 in Duxford. On Sundays, direct Myalls bus #132 runs to the museum from the train station (4/day, 30 minutes, www.travelineeastanglia.org.uk). On other days of the week, it's best to take a taxi from Cambridge. (Other buses do stop in Duxford, but too far from the museum to walk.)

Sleeping in Cambridge

While Cambridge is an easy side-trip from London (and you can enjoy an evening here before catching a late train back), its subtle charms might convince you to spend a night or two. Cambridge has few accommodations in the city center, and none in the tight maze of colleges and shops where you'll spend most of your time. These recommendations (each just past the Fitzwilliam Museum) are about a 10-minute walk south of the town center, toward the train station. (Though weak in hotel offerings, Cambridge does have plenty of B&Bs, which you can research and book online.)

$$$ Lensfield Hotel, popular with visiting professors, has 40 comfortable old-fashioned rooms (Sb-£75, Db-£114, newer "deluxe" Db-£155, Tb-£139, spa and fitness room, 53 Lensfield Road, tel. 01223/355-017, www.lensfieldhotel.co.uk, enquiries@lensfieldhotel.co.uk).

$$$ Hotel du Vin is a pretentious place that rents 41 decent rooms at a high price. It has duck-your-head character and a good location (Db-£150-225, check online for special offers, breakfast-£14, Trumpington Street 15, tel. 01223/227-330 or 0844-736-4253, www.hotelduvin.com, reception.cambridge@hotelduvin.com).

Eating in Cambridge

The Eagle, near the TI and described earlier in my town walk, is the oldest pub in town. While the food is mediocre, the pub is a Cambridge institution with a history so rich that a visit here practically qualifies as sightseeing (£10-18 lunches and dinners, food served daily 11:00-22:00, 8 Benet Street, tel. 01223/505-020).

Michaelhouse Café is a heavenly respite from the crowds, tucked into the repurposed St. Michael's Church, just north of Great St. Mary's Church. At lunch, choose from salads and sandwiches, as well as a few hot dishes and a variety of tasty baked goods (£6-10 lunches, Mon-Sat 8:00-17:00, breakfast served 8:00-11:30, lunch served 12:00-15:30, closed Sun, Trinity Street, tel. 01223/309-147). Between 14:30 and 15:30 you can pay £4.50 to fill your plate with whatever they have left.

The Anchor Pub's claim to fame is as the setting of Pink Floyd's first gig. Today it's known for the best people-watching—and some locals say best food—in Cambridge. Choose from its outdoor riverside terrace, inside bar, or more romantic upstairs restaurant (all seating areas serve the same menu, but the upstairs menu has a few added specials; £6-8 starters, £13-16 main dishes, daily 12:00-21:30, on the riverfront at Silver Street, tel. 01224/353-554).

Bread & Meat serves simple soups and hearty sandwiches. Grab a signature *porchetta* sandwich to take away or snag a rustic table in the small dining room (£2 soups, £7 sandwiches, £2-3 sides, daily 9:00-21:00, Sun-Mon until 17:00, 4 Benet Street, tel. 0791/808-3057).

Agora at The Copper Kettle is a popular place for Greek and Turkish *meze,* beautifully situated facing King's College on King's Parade (£10-12 dishes, also fish-and-chips at lunch, open for lunch and dinner, 4 King's Parade, tel. 01223/308-448).

Fitzbillies, long a favorite for cakes (Chelsea Buns) and coffee, offers an inviting lunch menu (£8-10) and a fancier one for dinner (£8 first courses, £17 main dishes, daily, 51 Trumpington Street).

Fast Food: For healthy fast-food chains, the corner of Petty Curry Lane and Sidney Street (a long block off Market Hill Square) has three good places: **Eat, Pret a Manger,** and **Wasabi.**

Supermarkets: There's a **Marks & Spencer Simply Food** at the train station (daily 7:00-23:00) and a larger Marks & Spencer department store on Market Hill Square (Mon-Tue 8:00-18:00, later Wed-Sat, Sun 11:00-17:00). **Sainsbury's** supermarket has longer hours (Mon-Sat 7:30-23:30, Sun 11:00-17:00, 44 Sidney Street, at the corner of Green Street).

A good picnic spot is Laundress Green, a grassy park on the river, at the end of Mill Lane near the Silver Street Bridge punts. There are no benches, so bring something to sit on. Remember, the college lawns are private property, so walking or picnicking on the grass is generally not allowed. When in doubt, ask at the college's entrance.

Cambridge Connections

From Cambridge by Train to: York (hourly, 2.5 hours, transfer in Peterborough), **London** (King's Cross Station: 2/hour, 45 minutes; Liverpool Street Station: 2/hour, 1.5 hours). Train info: Tel. 0345-748-4950, www.nationalrail.co.uk.

By Bus to: London (every 60-90 minutes, 2 hours), **Heathrow Airport** (1-2/hour, 2-3 hours). Bus info: Tel. 0871-781-8181, www.nationalexpress.com.

BATH

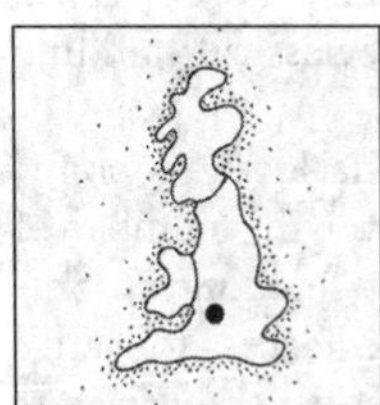

The best city to visit within easy striking distance of London is Bath—just a 1.5-hour train ride away. Two hundred years ago, this city of 90,000 was the trendsetting Tinseltown of Britain. If ever a city enjoyed looking in the mirror, Bath's the one. It has more "government-listed" or protected historic buildings per capita than any other town in England. Built of the creamy warm-tone limestone called "Bath stone," it beams in its cover-girl complexion. An architectural chorus line, it's a triumph of the Neoclassical style of the Georgian era—named for the four Georges who sat as England's kings from 1714 to 1830. Proud locals remind visitors that the town is routinely banned from the "Britain in Bloom" contest to give other towns a chance to win. Bath's narcissism is justified. Even with its mobs of tourists (2 million per year) and greedy prices, Bath is a joy to visit.

Bath's fame began with the allure of its (supposedly) healing hot springs. Long before the Romans arrived in the first century, Bath was known for its curative waters. Romans named the popular spa town Aquae Sulis, after a local Celtic goddess. The town's importance carried through Saxon times, when it had a huge church on the site of the present-day abbey and was considered the religious capital of Britain. Its influence peaked in 973 with King Edgar's sumptuous coronation in the abbey. Later, Bath prospered as a wool town.

Bath then declined until the mid-1600s, wasting away to just a huddle of huts around the abbey, with hot, smelly mud and 3,000 residents, oblivious to the Roman ruins 18 feet below their dirt floors. In fact, with its own walls built upon ancient ones, Bath was no bigger than that Roman town. Then, in 1687, Queen Mary, fighting infertility, bathed here. Within 10 months, she gave birth to a son...and a new age of popularity for Bath.

The revitalized town boomed as a spa resort. Ninety percent of the buildings you'll see today are from the 18th century. The classical revivalism of Italian architect Andrea Palladio inspired a local father-and-son team—both named John Wood (the Elder and the Younger)—to build a "new Rome." The town bloomed in the Neoclassical style, and streets were lined not with scrawny sidewalks but with wide "parades," upon which women in their stylishly wide dresses could spread their fashionable tails.

Beau Nash (1673-1762) was Bath's "master of ceremonies." He organized the daily social regimen of aristocratic visitors, and he made the city more appealing by lighting the streets, improving security, banning swords, and opening the Pump Room. Under his fashionable baton, Bath became a city of balls, gaming, and concerts—the place to see and be seen in England. This most civilized place became even more so with the great Neoclassical building spree that followed.

These days, modern tourism has stoked the local economy, as has the fast morning train to London. (A growing number of Bath-based professionals catch the 7:13 train to Paddington Station every weekday morning.) And, with renewed access to Bath's soothing hot springs at the Thermae Bath Spa, the venerable waters are in the spotlight again, attracting a new generation of visitors in need of a cure or a soak.

PLANNING YOUR TIME

Bath deserves two nights even on a quick trip. On a three-week England getaway, spend three nights in Bath, with one day for the city and one day for side-trips (see next chapter). Ideally, use Bath as your jet-lag recovery pillow (easy access from Heathrow Airport), and do London at the end of your trip.

Consider starting your English vacation this way:

Day 1: Land at Heathrow. Connect to Bath either by train via London Paddington, direct bus, or bus/train combination via Reading (for details, see page 275). You can also consider flying into Bristol, which has easy bus connections with Bath. While you don't need or want a car in Bath, those who land early and pick up their cars at the airport can visit Windsor Castle (near Heathrow) on their way to Bath. If you have the evening free in Bath, take a walking tour.

Day 2: 9:00—Tour the Roman Baths; 10:30—Catch the free city walking tour; 12:30—Picnic on the open deck of a tour bus; 14:00—Visit the abbey, then free time in the shopping center of old Bath; 15:30—Tour the No. 1 Royal Crescent Georgian house and Fashion Museum or Museum of Bath at Work. At night, consider seeing a play, take the evening walking tour (unless you did last night), enjoy the Bizarre Bath comedy walk, or go for an evening soak in the Thermae Bath Spa.

Day 3 (and possibly 4): By car, explore nearby sights. Without a car, consider a one-day Avebury/Stonehenge/cute-towns minibus tour from Bath (Mad Max tours are best; see "Tours in and near Bath," later).

Orientation to Bath

Bath's town square, three blocks in front of the bus and train station, is a cluster of tourist landmarks, including the abbey, Roman Baths, and the Pump Room. Bath is hilly. In general, you'll gain elevation as you head north from the town center.

TOURIST INFORMATION

The TI is in the abbey churchyard (Mon-Sat 9:30-17:30, Sun 10:00-16:00, tel. 0844-847-5256, www.visitbath.co.uk). It sells tickets for the Roman Baths, allowing you to skip the (often long) line, stocks visitor guides and maps (survey your options before buying one, £2), books rooms with no extra fee, and posts event listings on the bulletin board.

ARRIVAL IN BATH

The Bath Spa **train station** has a staffed ticket desk and ticket machines. Directly in front of the train station is the SouthGate Bath shopping center. To get from the train station to the TI, exit straight ahead and continue up Manvers Street for about five minutes, then turn left at the triangular "square" overlooking the riverfront park, following the small TI arrow on a signpost. The **bus station** is immediately west of the train station, along Dorchester Street. There is a handy luggage-check service a half block away (see "Helpful Hints," next).

HELPFUL HINTS

Getting to Bath and Stonehenge by Tour: Several companies offer guided bus tours from London to Stonehenge, Salisbury, and Bath; you can abandon the tour in Bath, essentially using the tour as one-way transport; see page 307.

Festivals: The **Bath Literature Festival** is an open book in early March (www.bathlitfest.org.uk). The **Bath International Music Festival** bursts into song in late May (classical, folk,

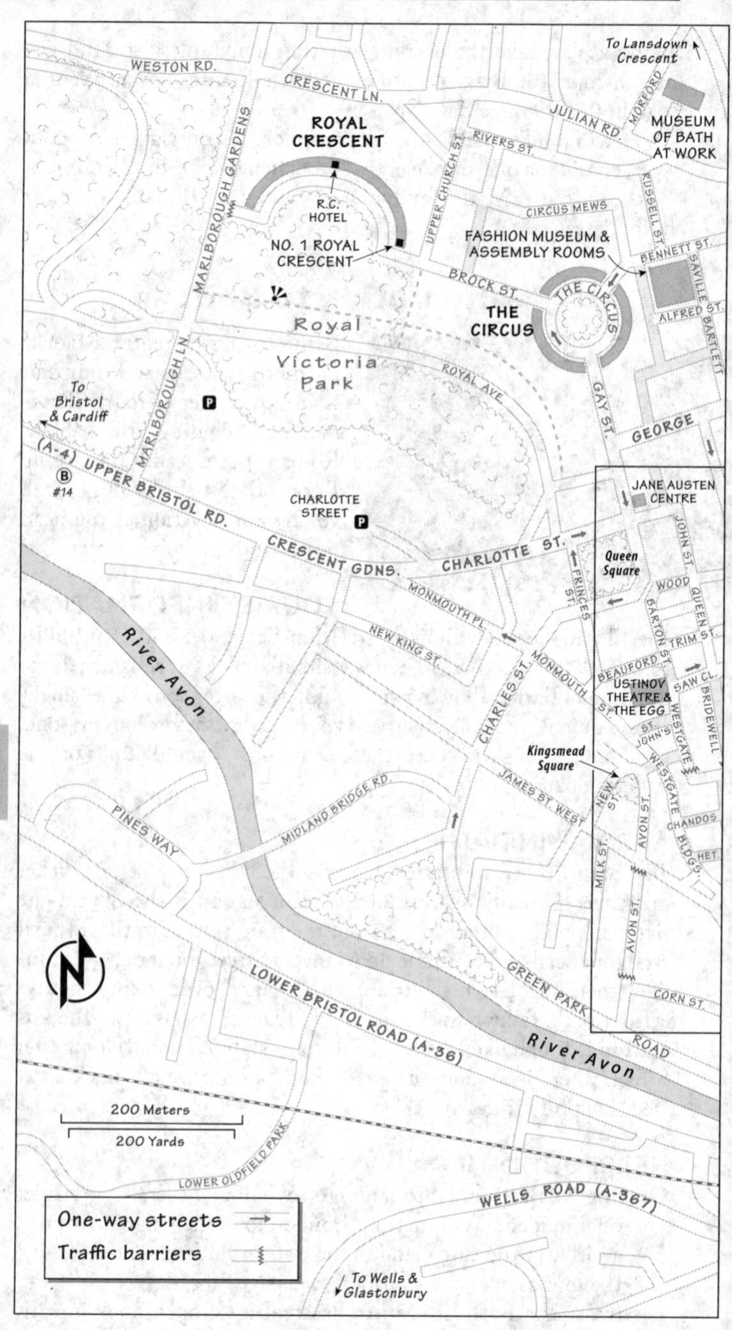
To Lansdown Crescent
WESTON RD.
CRESCENT LN.
ROYAL CRESCENT
JULIAN RD.
MORFORD
MUSEUM OF BATH AT WORK
RIVERS ST.
MARLBOROUGH GARDENS
R.C. HOTEL
UPPER CHURCH ST.
CIRCUS MEWS
RUSSELL ST.
NO. 1 ROYAL CRESCENT
FASHION MUSEUM & ASSEMBLY ROOMS
BENNETT ST.
SAVILLE
BROCK ST.
THE CIRCUS
THE CIRCUS
ALFRED ST.
BARTLETT
Royal Victoria Park
MARLBOROUGH LN.
ROYAL AVE.
To Bristol & Cardiff
GAY ST.
GEORGE
(A-4) UPPER BRISTOL RD.
#14
JANE AUSTEN CENTRE
CHARLOTTE STREET
JOHN ST.
CRESCENT GDNS.
CHARLOTTE ST.
Queen Square
PRINCES ST.
WOOD
MONMOUTH PL.
QUEEN
BARTON ST.
NEW KING ST.
TRIM ST.
River Avon
MONMOUTH ST.
BEAUFORD SQ.
CHARLES ST.
USTINOV THEATRE & THE EGG
SAW CL.
BRIDEWELL
ST. JOHN'S
WESTGATE
Kingsmead Square
JAMES ST. WEST
NEW ST.
MIDLAND BRIDGE RD.
PINES WAY
AVON ST.
CHANDOS
BLDGS.
MILK ST.
AVON ST.
GREEN PARK ROAD
LOWER BRISTOL ROAD (A-36)
CORN ST.
River Avon
200 Meters
200 Yards
LOWER OLDFIELD PARK
WELLS ROAD (A-367)
One-way streets
Traffic barriers
To Wells & Glastonbury

BATH

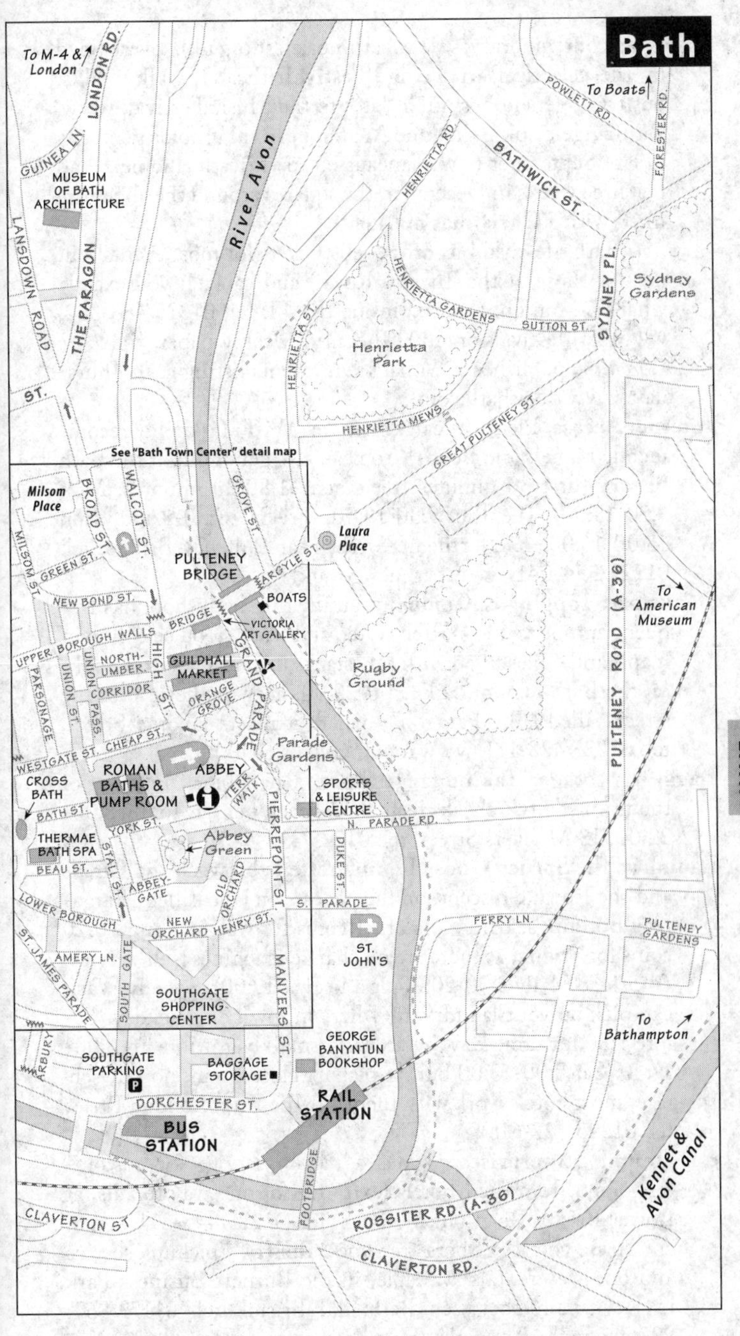

Bath
To M-4 & London
LONDON RD.
GUINEA LN.
MUSEUM OF BATH ARCHITECTURE
LANSDOWN ROAD
THE PARAGON
ST.
River Avon
To Boats
POWLETT RD.
FORESTER RD.
HENRIETTA RD.
BATHWICK ST.
SYDNEY PL.
Sydney Gardens
HENRIETTA GARDENS
SUTTON ST.
HENRIETTA ST.
Henrietta Park
HENRIETTA MEWS
GREAT PULTENEY ST.
See "Bath Town Center" detail map
Milsom Place
BROAD ST.
WALCOT ST.
GROVE ST.
Laura Place
MILSOM ST.
GREEN ST.
PULTENEY BRIDGE
ARGYLE ST.
NEW BOND ST.
BOATS
BRIDGE
VICTORIA ART GALLERY
UPPER BOROUGH WALLS
HIGH ST.
NORTH-UMBER.
GUILDHALL MARKET
GRAND PARADE
Rugby Ground
PULTENEY ROAD (A-36)
To American Museum
PARSONAGE
UNION ST.
UNION PASS.
CORRIDOR
ORANGE GROVE
WESTGATE ST.
CHEAP ST.
Parade Gardens
ROMAN BATHS & PUMP ROOM
ABBEY
CROSS BATH
TERR. WALK
SPORTS & LEISURE CENTRE
BATH ST.
YORK ST.
PIERREPONT ST.
N. PARADE RD.
THERMAE BATH SPA
Abbey Green
BEAU ST.
DUKE ST.
STALL ST.
ABBEY-GATE
OLD ORCHARD
S. PARADE
LOWER BOROUGH
NEW ORCHARD
HENRY ST.
FERRY LN.
PULTENEY GARDENS
ST. JAMES PARADE
AMERY LN.
SOUTH GATE
MANVERS ST.
ST. JOHN'S
SOUTHGATE SHOPPING CENTER
To Bathampton
ARBURY
SOUTHGATE PARKING
BAGGAGE STORAGE
GEORGE BANYNTUN BOOKSHOP
RAIL STATION
DORCHESTER ST.
BUS STATION
Kennet & Avon Canal
FOOTBRIDGE
CLAVERTON ST
ROSSITER RD. (A-36)
CLAVERTON RD.
BATH

jazz, contemporary; www.bathmusicfest.org.uk), overlapped by the eclectic **Bath Fringe Festival** (theater, walks, talks, bus trips; generally similar dates to the Music Festival, www.bathfringe.co.uk). The **Jane Austen Festival** unfolds genteelly in late September (www.janeausten.co.uk/festivalhome). And for three weeks in December, the squares around the abbey are filled with a **Christmas market.**

Bath's festival **box office** sells tickets for most events (but not for those at the Theatre Royal) and can tell you exactly what's on tonight (housed inside the TI, tel. 01225/463-362, www.bathfestivals.org.uk). The city's weekly paper, the *Bath Chronicle,* publishes a "What's On" events listing each Thursday (www.thisisbath.com).

Internet Access: Plenty of cafés offer free Wi-Fi (as do my recommended hotels and B&Bs). You can also get online at the Bath **library** (first 30 minutes free, then £1.80/30 minutes, Mon 9:30-18:00, Tue-Thu 9:30-19:00, Fri-Sat 9:30-17:00, Sun 13:00-16:00, 19 Northgate Street near Pulteney Bridge, tel. 01225/394-041, www.bathnes.gov.uk).

Bookstore: Topping & Company, an inviting bookshop, has frequent author readings, free coffee and tea, a good selection of maps, and tables filled with tidy stacks, including lots of books on the Bath region (daily 9:00-20:00, near the bottom of the street called "The Paragon"—where it meets George Street, tel. 01225/428-111, www.toppingbooks.co.uk).

Baggage Storage: The Luggage Store, a half block in front of the train station, checks bags for £4 each per day (daily 8:00-22:00, 13 Manvers Street, tel. 01225/312-685).

Laundry: The **Spruce Goose Launderette** is between the Circus and the Royal Crescent, on the pedestrian lane called Margaret's Buildings. Bring lots of £1 coins for washing and £0.20 coins for drying, as there are no change machines (self-service, £4-5/load, daily 8:00-20:00, last load at 19:00). **Speedy Wash** can pick up your laundry anywhere in town on weekdays before 9:30 for same-day service (£14/small bag, Mon-Fri 8:00-17:30, Sat 8:00-13:00 but no pickup, closed Sun, no self-service, most hotels work with them, 4 Mile End, London Road, tel. 01225/427-616).

Car Rental: Enterprise provides a pickup service for customers to and from their hotels (extra fee for one-way rentals, at Lower Bristol Road outside Bath, tel. 01225/443-311, www.enterprise.com). Others include **Thrifty** (pickup service and one-way rentals available, in the Burnett Business Park in Keynsham—between Bath and Bristol, tel. 01179/867-997, www.thrifty.co.uk), **Hertz** (one-way rentals possible, at Windsor Bridge, tel. 0843-309-3004, www.hertz.co.uk), and

National/Europcar (one-way rentals available, £7 by taxi from the train station, at Brassmill Lane—go west on Upper Bristol Road, tel. 0871-384-9985, www.europcar.co.uk). Skip **Avis**—it's a mile from the Bristol train station; you'd need to rent a car to get there. Most offices close Saturday afternoon and all day Sunday, which complicates weekend pickups. Ideally, take the train or bus from downtown London to Bath, and rent a car as you leave Bath.

Parking: As Bath becomes increasingly pedestrian-friendly, street parking in the city center is disappearing. **Park & Ride** service is a stress-free, no-hassle option to save time and money. Shuttles from Newbridge, Lansdown, and Odd Down (all just outside of Bath) offer free parking and 10-minute shuttle buses into town (daily every 15 minutes, £3 round-trip).

If you drive into town, be aware that short-term lots fill up fast (£1.60/hour, 2-4-hour maximum). You'll find more spots in long-stay lots for about the same cost. The SouthGate Bath shopping center lot on the corner of Southgate and Dorchester streets is a five-minute walk from the abbey (£5/up to 3 hours, £14/24 hours, cash or credit card, open 24/7); the Charlotte Street car park is the most convenient. For more info on parking (including Park & Ride service), visit the "Travel and Maps" section of http://visitbath.co.uk.

Updates to This Book: For the latest, see www.ricksteves.com/update.

Tours in and near Bath

IN THE CITY

▲▲▲Free City Walking Tours

Free two-hour tours are led by **The Mayor's Corps of Honorary Guides,** volunteers who want to share their love of Bath with its many visitors (as the city's mayor first did when he took a group on a guided walk back in the 1930s). These chatty, historical, and gossip-filled walks are essential for your understanding of this town's amazing Georgian social scene. How else would you learn that the old "chair ho" call for your sedan chair evolved into today's "cheerio" farewell? Tours leave from outside the Pump Room in the abbey churchyard (free, no tips, year-round Sun-Fri at 10:30 and 14:00, Sat at 10:30 only; additional evening walks May-Sept Tue and Thu at 19:00; tel. 01225/477-411, www.bathguides.org.uk). Tip for theatergoers: When your guide stops to talk outside the Theatre Royal, skip out for a moment, pop into the box office, and see about snaring a great deal on a play for tonight.

The Honorary Guides also lead free two-hour Pulteney Estate

Bath at a Glance

▲▲▲Free City Walking Tours Top-notch tours helping you make the most of your visit, led by The Mayor's Corps of Honorary Guides. **Hours:** Sun-Fri at 10:30 and 14:00, Sat at 10:30 only; additional evening walks offered May-Sept Tue and Thu at 19:00. See page 241.

▲▲▲Roman Baths Ancient baths that gave the city its name, tourable with good audioguide. **Hours:** Daily July-Aug 9:00-22:00, March-June and Sept-Oct 9:00-18:00, Nov-Feb 9:30-17:30 except Sat until 18:00. See page 245.

▲▲Bath Abbey 500-year-old Perpendicular Gothic church graced with beautiful fan vaulting and stained glass. **Hours:** Mon-Sat 9:00-18:00 except Nov-March until 16:30, Sun 13:00-14:30 & 16:30-17:30. See page 250.

▲▲The Circus and the Royal Crescent Stately Georgian (Neoclassical) buildings from Bath's 18th-century glory days. **Hours:** Always viewable. See page 252.

▲▲No. 1 Royal Crescent Your best look at the interior of one of Bath's high-rent Georgian beauties. **Hours:** Mon 12:00-17:30, Tue-Sun 10:30-17:30. See page 253.

▲Pump Room Swanky Georgian hall, ideal for a spot of tea or a taste of unforgettably "healthy" spa water. **Hours:** Daily 9:30-12:00 for coffee and breakfast, 12:00-14:30 for lunch, 14:30-17:00 for afternoon tea (open 18:00-21:00 for dinner July-Aug and Christmas holidays only). See page 249.

walks, including Pulteney Street and Sydney Gardens (May-Sept, Tue and Thu at 11:00).

Private Tours

For a private tour, call the local guides' bureau, **Bath Parade Guides** (£90/2 hours, tel. 01225/337-111, www.bathparadeguides.co.uk, bathparadeguides@yahoo.com). For **Ghost Walks** and **Bizarre Bath** tours, see "Nightlife in Bath," later.

▲▲City Bus Tours

City Sightseeing's hop-on, hop-off bus tours zip through Bath. Jump on a bus anytime at one of 17 signposted pickup points, pay the driver, climb upstairs, and hear recorded commentary about Bath. City Sightseeing has two 45-minute routes: a city tour and

▲**Pulteney Bridge and Parade Gardens** Shop-strewn bridge and relaxing riverside gardens. **Hours:** Bridge—always open; gardens—Easter-Sept daily 10:00-17:00, shorter hours off-season. See page 251.

▲**Victoria Art Gallery** Paintings from the late 17th century to today. **Hours:** Tue-Sat 10:00-17:00, Sun 13:30-17:00, closed Mon. See page 251.

▲**Fashion Museum** 400 years of clothing under one roof, plus the opulent Assembly Rooms. **Hours:** Daily March-Oct 10:30-18:00, Nov-Feb 10:30-17:00. See page 254.

▲**Museum of Bath at Work** Gadget-ridden circa-1900 engineer's shop, foundry, factory, and office. **Hours:** April-Oct daily 10:30-17:00, Nov and Jan-March weekends only, closed in Dec. See page 255.

▲**American Museum** Insightful look primarily at colonial/early American lifestyles, with 18 furnished rooms and eager-to-talk guides. **Hours:** Mid-March-Oct Tue-Sun 12:00-17:00, late Nov-mid-Dec Tue-Sun 12:00-16:30, closed Mon except in Aug, closed most of Nov and late Dec-mid-March. See page 257.

▲**Thermae Bath Spa** Relaxation center that put the bath back in Bath. **Hours:** Daily 9:00-21:30. See page 258.

Jane Austen Centre Exhibit on 19th-century Bath-based novelist, best for her fans. **Hours:** April-Oct daily 9:45-17:30, July-Aug until 18:00; Nov-March Sun-Fri 11:00-16:30, Sat 9:45-17:30. See page 256.

a "Skyline" route outside town. Try to get one with a live guide (June-Sept usually at :12 and :24 past the hour for the city tour, and on the hour for the Skyline route—confirm with driver); otherwise, bring your own earbuds if you've got 'em (the audio recording on the other buses is barely intelligible with the headsets provided). On a sunny day, this is a multitasking tourist's dream come true: You can munch a sandwich, work on a tan, snap great photos, and learn a lot, all at the same time. Save money by doing the bus tour first—ticket stubs get you minor discounts at many sights (£14, ticket valid for 24 hours and both tour routes, generally 4/hour daily in summer 9:30-17:30, in winter 10:00-15:00, tel. 01225/330-444, www.city-sightseeing.com).

Taxi Tours

Local taxis, driven by good talkers, go where big buses can't. A group of up to four can rent a cab for an hour (about £40; try to negotiate) and enjoy a fine, informative, and—with the right cabbie—entertaining private joyride. It's probably cheaper to let the meter run than to pay for an hourly rate, but ask the cabbie for advice.

NEARBY SIGHTS

Bath is a good launchpad for visiting nearby Wells, Avebury, Stonehenge, and more.

Mad Max Minibus Tours

Operating daily from Bath, Maddy offers thoughtfully organized, informative tours run with entertaining guides and limited to 16 people per group. Check their website for the latest offerings and book ahead—as far ahead as possible in summer. The **Stonehenge, Avebury, and Villages** full-day tour, by far their most popular, covers 110 miles and visits Stonehenge; the Avebury Stone Circles; photogenic Lacock (LAY-cock); and Castle Combe, the southernmost Cotswold village (£38 plus Stonehenge entry fee, tours depart daily at 8:30 and return at 17:30). Three additional all-day itineraries do a good job covering other areas surrounding Bath: **Avebury & Cotswold Villages** tour (includes Avebury Stone Circles, Lacock, and Castle Combe; £35, May-Aug Tue and Fri, departs at 11:00); **Cotswolds Discovery** (visits a handful of villages; check their website for details, £38, April-Sept Mon, Wed, and Sat, departs at 9:00); **Wells and Glastonbury** (includes scenic drive through Cheddar Gorge, £38, May-Aug Tue and Thu, departs at 9:00).

BATH

All tours depart from outside the Abbey Hotel on Terrace Walk in Bath, a one-minute walk from the abbey. Arrive 15 minutes before your departure time and bring cash (or book online with a credit card at least 48 hours in advance, Rick Steves readers get £10 cash rebate from guide with online purchase of two full-day tours if requested at time of booking; mobile 07990-505-970, phone answered daily 8:00-18:00, www.madmaxtours.co.uk, maddy@madmaxtours.co.uk).

Lion Tours

This well-run outfit gets you to Stonehenge on their half-day **Stonehenge and Lacock** tour (£22 transportation only, £34 including Stonehenge entry fee; leaves daily at 12:15 and returns at 17:30, in summer this tour also leaves at 8:30 and returns at 12:00). They also run full-day tours of **Cotswold Villages** and **King Arthur's Realm** (info on website). If you ask in advance, you can bring your luggage along and use this tour to get to Stow. Or, for £10 extra per person or group, you can hop off in Moreton-in-Marsh for easy train connections to Oxford and bus connections to Chipping Campden. Lion's tours depart from the same stop as Mad Max Tours—see earlier (mobile 07769-668-668, book online at www.liontours.co.uk).

Other Tour Options

Scarper Tours runs four-hour narrated minibus tours to Stonehenge—giving you two hours at the site (£19 transportation only, £32 including Stonehenge entry fee, departs from behind the abbey on Terrace Walk; daily mid-March-mid-Oct at 9:30 and 14:00; mid-Oct-mid-March at 13:00; tel. 07739/644-155, www.scarpertours.com).

Celtic Horizons offers tours from Bath to a variety of destinations, such as Stonehenge, Avebury, and Wells. They can provide a convenient transfer service (to or from London, Heathrow, Bristol Airport, the Cotswolds, and so on), with or without a tour itinerary en route. Allow about £35/hour for a group (comfortable minivans seat 4, 6, or 8 people) and £150 for Heathrow-Bath transfers (1-4 persons). Make arrangements and get pricing information by email at info@celtichorizons.com (tel. 01373/800-500, US tel. 855-895-0165, www.celtichorizons.com).

BATH

Sights in Bath

IN THE TOWN CENTER

▲▲▲Roman Baths

In ancient Roman times, high society enjoyed the mineral springs at Bath. From Londinium, Romans traveled so often to Aquae Sulis, as the city was called, to "take a bath" that finally it became known simply as Bath. Today, a fine museum surrounds the ancient bath. With the help of a great audioguide, you'll wander past well-documented displays, Roman artifacts, a temple pediment with an evocative bearded face, a bronze head of the goddess Sulis Minerva, excavated ancient foundations, and the actual mouth of the health-giving spring. At the end, you'll have a chance to walk around the big pool itself, where Romans once lounged, splished, splashed, and thanked the gods for the gift of therapeutic hot water.

Cost and Hours: £14, includes audioguide, £20 combo-ticket

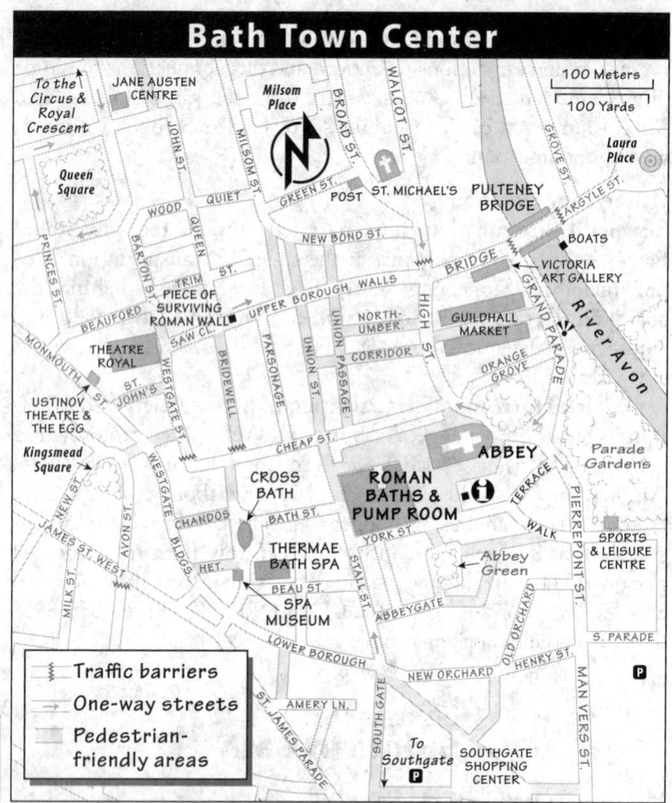

includes Fashion Museum and Victoria Art Gallery temporary exhibits, family ticket available, daily July-Aug 9:00-22:00, March-June and Sept-Oct 9:00-18:00, Nov-Feb 9:30-17:30 except Sat until 18:00, last entry one hour before closing, tel. 01225/477-785, www.romanbaths.co.uk.

Crowd-Beating Tips: Long ticket lines are typical in the summer. You can avoid them by purchasing a combo-ticket at the Fashion Museum or by buying a ticket at the nearby TI. With voucher or combo-ticket in hand, enter through the "fast track" lane, to the left of the general admission line. On any day, try to visit early or late; peak time is between 13:00 and 15:00. If you're here in July or August, the best time is after 19:00, when the baths are romantic, gas-lit, and all yours.

Tours: Take advantage of the included, essential **audioguide,** which makes your visit easy and informative. In addition to the basic commentary, look for posted numbers to key into your audioguide for specialty topics—including a kid-friendly tour and musings from American expat writer Bill Bryson. For those with a big appetite for Roman history, in-depth **guided tours** leave from the end of the museum at the edge of the actual bath (included with ticket, on the hour, a poolside clock is set for the next departure time, 20-40 minutes depending on the guide). You can revisit the museum after the tour.

➲ **Self-Guided Tour:** Follow the one-way route through the bath and museum complex. This self-guided tour offers a basic overview; for more in-depth commentary, make ample use of the audioguide.

Begin by walking around the upper **terrace,** overlooking the Great Bath. This terrace—lined with sculptures of VIRs (Very Important Romans)—evokes ancient times but was built in the 1890s. The ruins of the bath complex sat undisturbed for centuries before finally being excavated and turned into a museum in the late 19th century.

Head inside to the **museum,** where exhibits explain the dual purpose of the buildings that stood here in Roman times: a bath complex for relaxation and for healing; and a temple dedicated to the goddess Sulis Minerva, who was believed to be responsible for the mysterious and much-appreciated thermal springs. Cut-away diagrams and models resurrect both parts of this complex and help establish your bearings among the remaining fragments and foundations—including the original entrance (just off the main suspended walkway, on your right, as you pass through the temple courtyard and Minerva section).

Peer down into the **spring,** where little air bubbles remind you that 240,000 gallons of water a day emerge from the earth—magically, it must have seemed to Romans—at a constant 115°F. The water you see now, heated more than a mile below the earth's surface, first fell to earth as rain onto nearby hills about 10,000 years ago...making the Romans seem relatively recent.

Go downstairs to get to know the Romans who built and enjoyed these baths. The fragments of the **temple pediment**—carved by indigenous Celtic craftsmen but with

Roman themes—represent a remarkable cultural synthesis. Sit and watch for a while, as a slide projection fills in historians' best guesses as to what once occupied the missing bits. The identity of the circular face in the middle puzzles researchers. (God? Santa Claus?) It could be the head of the Gorgon monster after it was slain by Perseus—are those snakes peeking through its hair and beard? And yet, the Gorgon was traditionally depicted as female. Perhaps instead it's Neptune, the god of the sea—appropriate for this aquatic site.

The next exhibits examine the importance of Aquae Sulis (the settlement here) in antiquity. Much like the pilgrimage sites of the Middle Ages, this spot exerted a powerful pull on people from all over the realm, who were eager to partake in its healing waters and to worship at the religious site. A display of the **Beau Street Hoard**—over 17,500 Roman coins dating from 32 B.C.-A.D. 274 that were found near the Baths—emphasizes just how well-visited this area was.

You'll also see some of the small but extremely heavy carved-stone tables that pilgrims hauled here as an offering to the gods. Take time to read some of the requests (inscribed on sheets of pewter or iron) that visitors made of the goddess—many are comically spiteful and petty, offering a warts-and-all glimpse into day-to-day Roman culture.

As you walk through the temple's original foundations, keep an eye out for the sacrificial altar. The gilded-bronze head of the goddess **Sulis Minerva** (in the display case) once overlooked a flaming cauldron inside the temple, where only priests were allowed to enter. Similar to the Greek goddess Athena, Sulis Minerva was considered to be a life-giving mother goddess.

Engineers enjoy a close-up look at the spring overflow and the original **drain system**—built two millennia ago—that still carries excess water to the River Avon. Marvel at the cleverness and durability of Roman engineering, created in (what we usually imagine to be) a "primitive" time. A nearby exhibit on pulleys and fasteners lets you play with these inventions.

Head outside to the **Great Bath** itself (where you can join one of the included guided tours for a much more extensive visit—look for the clock with the next start time). Take a slow lap (by foot) around the perimeter, imagining the frolicking Romans who once immersed themselves up to their necks in this five-foot-deep pool. The water is greenish because of algae—don't drink it. The best views are from the west end, looking back toward the abbey. Nearby is a giant chunk of roof span, from a time when this was a cavernous covered swimming hall. At the corner, you'll step over a small canal where hot water still trickles into the main pool. Nearby, find a length of original lead pipe, remarkably well preserved since antiquity.

Symmetrical bath complexes branch off at opposite ends of the Great Bath (perhaps dating from a conservative period when the Romans maintained separate facilities for men and women). The **East Baths** show off changing rooms and various bathing rooms, each one designed for a special therapy or recreational purpose (immersion therapy tub, sauna-like heated floor, and so on), as described in detail by the audioguide.

When you're ready to leave, head for the **West Baths** (including a sweat bath and a *frigidarium,* or "cold plunge" pool) and take another look at the spring and more foundations. After returning your audioguide, pop over to the fountain for a free taste of the spa water. Then pass through the gift shop, past the convenient public WCs (which use plain old tap water), and exit through the **Pump Room**—or stay for a spot of tea.

▲Pump Room

For centuries, Bath was forgotten as a spa. Then, in 1687, the previously barren Queen Mary bathed here, became pregnant, and bore a male heir to the throne. A few years later, Queen Anne found the water eased her painful gout. Word of its miraculously curative waters spread, and Bath earned its way back on the aristocratic map. High society soon turned the place into one big pleasure palace. The Pump Room, an elegant Georgian hall just above the Roman Baths, offers visitors their best chance to raise a pinky in Chippendale grandeur. Above the clock, a statue of Beau Nash himself sniffles down at you. Come for a light meal, or to try a famous (but forgettable) "Bath bun" with your spa water (the same water that's in the fountain at the end of the baths tour; also free in the Pump Rooms if you present your ticket). The spa water is served by an appropriately attired waiter, who will tell you the water is pumped up from nearly 100 yards deep and marinated in 43 wonderful minerals. Or for just the price of a coffee, drop in anytime—except during lunch—to enjoy live music and the atmosphere. Even

if you don't eat here, you're welcome to enter the foyer for a view of the baths and dining room.

Cost and Hours: Daily 9:30-12:00 for coffee and £6-15 breakfast, 12:00-14:30 for £12-20 lunches, 14:30-17:00 for £21 traditional afternoon tea (last orders at 16:00), tea/coffee and pastries also available in the afternoons; open 18:00-21:00 for dinner July-Aug and Christmas holidays only; live music daily—string trio or piano, times vary; tel. 01225/444-477.

▲▲Bath Abbey

The town of Bath wasn't much in the Middle Ages, but an important church has stood on this spot since Anglo-Saxon times. King Edgar I was crowned here in 973, when the church was much bigger (before the bishop packed up and moved to Wells). Dominating the town center, today's abbey—the last great church built in medieval England—is 500 years old and a fine example of the Late Perpendicular Gothic style, with breezy fan vaulting and enough stained glass to earn it the nickname "Lantern of the West."

Cost and Hours: £2.50 suggested donation; Mon-Sat 9:00-18:00 except Nov-March until 16:30, Sun 13:00-14:30 & 16:30-17:30, last entry 45 minutes before closing; handy flier narrates a self-guided 19-stop tour, ask about schedule of events—including concerts, services, and evensong—also posted on the door and online, tel. 01225/422-462, www.bathabbey.org.

Evensong: Though the evensong service is spoken, not sung, on Monday through Saturday, it's still a beautiful 20 minutes of worship (nightly at 17:30, choral evensong on Sun only).

Visiting the Abbey: Take a moment to appreciate the abbey's architecture from the square. The facade (c. 1500, but mostly restored) is interesting for some of its carvings. Look for the angels going down the ladder. The statue of Peter (to the left of the door) lost its head to mean-spirited iconoclasts; it was recarved out of Peter's once supersized beard.

Going inside is worth the small suggested contribution. The glass, red-iron gas-powered lamps, and the heating grates on the floor are all remnants of the 19th century. The window behind the altar shows 52 scenes from the life of Christ. A window to the left of the altar shows Edgar's coronation. Note that a WWII bomb blast destroyed the medieval glass; what you see today is from the 1950s.

Climbing the Tower: You can reach the top of the tower only with a worthwhile, 50-minute guided tour. You'll hike up 212 steps for views across the rooftops of Bath and a peek down into the Roman Baths. In the rafters, you walk right up behind the clock face on the north transept, and get an inside-out look at the fan vaulting. Along the way, you'll hear a brief town history as you learn all about the tower's bells. If you've always wanted to clang a huge church bell for all the town to hear, this is your chance—it's oddly satisfying (£6, sporadic schedule but generally at the top of each hour when abbey is open, more often during busy times; Mon-Sat April-Oct 10:00-16:00, Nov-March 11:00-15:00, these are last tour-departure times; today's tour times usually posted outside abbey entrance, no tours Sun, buy tickets in abbey gift shop).

▲Pulteney Bridge and Parade Gardens

Bath is inclined to compare its shop-lined Pulteney Bridge to Florence's Ponte Vecchio. That's pushing it. But to best enjoy a sunny day, pack a picnic lunch and pay £1.50 to enter the Parade Gardens below the bridge (Easter-Sept daily 10:00-17:00, shorter hours off-season, includes deck chairs, ask about concerts held some Sun at 15:00 in summer, entrance a block south of bridge). Relaxing peacefully at the riverside provides a wonderful break (and memory). Across the bridge at Pulteney Weir, tour boat companies run **cruises**—see "Activities in Bath," later.

Note that one of the free city walking tours covers Pulteney Bridge, Pulteney Street, and Sydney Gardens (see "Tours in and near Bath," earlier).

Guildhall Market

The little old-school shopping mall located across from Pulteney Bridge is a frumpy time warp in this affluent town. It's fun for browsing and picnic shopping, and its recommended Market Café is a cheap place for a bite.

▲Victoria Art Gallery

This small gallery, next to Pulteney Bridge, has two parts: The ground floor houses temporary exhibits, while the upstairs is filled with paintings from the late 17th century to the present, along with a small collection of decorative arts.

The permanent painting collection presents an intimate world of portraiture and Bath-scapes. On the back wall, find Thomas Gainsborough's portrait of *Thomas Rumbold and Son*. During the

18th century, members of high society flocked to Bath and employed Gainsborough to paint their portraits as a souvenir. Thanks to this fad, Gainsborough found steady employment in this city.

Scan the wall on the left to find *Bath from the East*—just below eye level—for a look at preindustrial Bath. Riffle through the chest of drawers nearby to find even more scenes of Bath throughout the years. As you exit the museum, a clever donation box on the staircase invites you to watch an artist at work; it's worth a small coin to see him in action.

Cost and Hours: Free, temporary exhibits-£3.50 or covered by combo-ticket to the Roman Baths and Fashion Museum, combo-ticket not sold at the Victoria Art Gallery—only the other locations; Tue-Sat 10:00-17:00, Sun 13:30-17:00, closed Mon, tel. 01225/477-233, www.victoriagal.org.uk.

NORTHWEST OF THE TOWN CENTER

Several worthwhile public spaces and museums can be found a slightly uphill 10-minute walk away.

▲▲The Circus and the Royal Crescent

If Bath is an architectural cancan, these are its knickers. These first Georgian "condos"—built in the mid-18th century by the father-and-son John Woods (the Circus by the Elder, the Royal Crescent by the Younger)—are well explained by the city walking tours. "Georgian" is British for "Neoclassical." These two building complexes, conveniently located a block apart from each other, are quintessential Georgian and quintessential Bath.

Circus: True to its name, this is a circular housing complex. Picture it as a coliseum turned inside out. Its Doric, Ionic, and Corinthian capital decorations pay homage to its Greco-Roman origin and are a reminder that Bath (with its seven hills) aspired to be "the Rome of England." The frieze above the first row of columns has hundreds of different panels representing the arts, sciences, and crafts. The ground-floor entrances were made large enough that aristocrats could be carried right through the door in their sedan chairs, and women could enter without disturbing their sky-high hairdos. The tiny round windows on the top floors were the servants' quarters. While the building fronts are uniform, the backs are higgledy-piggledy, infamous for their "hanging loos" (bathrooms added years later). Stand in the middle of the Circus among the grand plane trees, on the capped old well. Imagine the days when there was no indoor plumbing, and the servant girls gathered here to fetch water—this was gossip central. If you stand on the well, your clap echoes three times around the circle (try it).

Royal Crescent: A long, graceful arc of buildings—impossible to see in one glance unless you step way back to the edge of the

big park in front—evokes the wealth and gentility of Bath's glory days. As you cruise the Crescent, pretend you're rich. Then pretend you're poor. Notice the "ha ha fence," a drop-off in the front yard that acted as a barrier, invisible from the windows, for keeping out sheep and peasants. The refined and stylish **Royal Crescent Hotel** sits virtually unmarked in the center of the Crescent (with the giant rhododendron growing over the door). You're welcome to (politely) drop in to explore its fine ground-floor public spaces and back garden, where a gracious and traditional tea is served (£14.50 cream tea, £32 afternoon tea, daily 13:30-17:00, sharing is OK, reserve a day in advance, tel. 01225/823-333, www.royalcrescent.co.uk).

▲▲No. 1 Royal Crescent

This museum (corner of Brock Street and Royal Crescent) takes visitors behind one of those classy Georgian facades, offering your best look into a period house—and how the wealthy lived in 18th-century Bath. Docents in each room hand out placards, but take the time to talk with them to learn many more fascinating details of Georgian life...such as how high-class women shaved their eyebrows and pasted on carefully trimmed strips of mouse fur in their place.

Start with the **parlor,** the main room of the house used for breakfast in the mornings, business affairs in the afternoon, and various other everyday activities throughout the evening. The bookcase was a status symbol of knowledge and literacy. In the **gentleman's retreat,** find a machine with a hand crank. This "modern" device was thought to cure ailments by shocking them out of you—give it a spin and feel for yourself. Shops in town charged for these electrifying cures; only the wealthiest citizens had in-home shock machines. Upstairs in the **lady's bedroom** are trinkets befitting a Georgian socialite; look for a framed love letter, wig scratcher, and hidden doorway (next to the bed) providing direct access to the servants' staircase. The **gentleman's bedroom** upstairs is the masculine equivalent of the lady's room—rich colors, scenes of Bath, and manly decor. The back staircase leads directly to the **servants' hall.** Look up to find Fido, who spent his days on the treadmill powering the rotisserie.

Finally, you'll end in the **kitchen.** Notice the wooden rack hanging from the ceiling—it kept the bread, herbs, and ham away from the mice. The scattered tools here helped servants create the upper-crust lifestyle overhead.

Cost and Hours: £9, £11.50 combo-ticket with Museum of Bath Architecture, Mon 12:00-17:30, Tue-Sun 10:30-17:30, last entry at 16:30, tel. 01225/428-126, www.bath-preservation-trust.org.uk.

▲Fashion Museum

Housed underneath Bath's Assembly Rooms, this museum displays four centuries of fashion on one floor. It's small, but the fact-filled, included audioguide can stretch a visit to an informative and enjoyable hour. Like fashion itself, the exhibits change all the time. A major feature is the "Dress of the Year" display, for which a fashion expert anoints a new frock each year. Ongoing since 1963, it's a chance to view a half-century of fashion trends in one sweep of the head. (The menswear version—awarded sporadically—shows a bit less variation, but has flashes of creativity.) Many of the exhibits are organized by theme (bags, shoes, underwear, wedding dresses). You'll see how fashion evolved—just like architecture and other arts—from one historical period to the next: Georgian, Regency, Victorian, the Swinging '60s, and so on. If you're intrigued by all those historic garments, go ahead and lace up your own trainer corset (which looks more like a life jacket) and try on a hoop underdress.

Cost and Hours: £8.25, includes audioguide; £20 combo-ticket also covers Roman Baths and Victoria Art Gallery temporary exhibits, family ticket available; daily March-Oct 10:30-18:00, Nov-Feb 10:30-17:00, last entry one hour before closing, free 30-minute guided tour most days at 12:00 and 16:00; self-service café, Bennett Street, tel. 01225/477-789, www.fashionmuseum.co.uk.

Assembly Rooms

Above the Fashion Museum, these grand, empty rooms—where card games, concerts, tea, and dances were held in the 18th century (before the advent of fancy hotels with grand public spaces made them obsolete)—evoke images of dashing young gentlemen mingling with elegant ladies in a who's who of high society. Note the extreme symmetry (pleasing to the aristocratic eye) and the high windows (assuring privacy). After the Allies bombed the historic and well-preserved German city of Lübeck, the Germans picked up a Baedeker guide and chose a similarly lovely city to bomb:

Bath. The Assembly Rooms—gutted in this wartime tit-for-tat by WWII bombs—have since been restored to their original splendor. (Only the chandeliers are original.)

Cost and Hours: Free, same hours and contact information as Fashion Museum.

Nearby: Below the Assembly Rooms and Fashion Museum (to the left as you exit, 20 yards away at the door marked *14* and *Alfred House*) is one of the few surviving sets of **iron house hardware.** "Link boys" carried torches through the dark streets, lighting the way for big shots in their sedan chairs as they traveled from one affair to the next. The link boys extinguished their torches in the black conical "snuffers." The lamp above was once gas-lit. The crank on the left was used to hoist bulky things to various windows (see the hooks). Few of these sets survived the dark days of the WWII Blitz, when most were collected and melted down, purportedly to make weapons to feed the British war machine. (Not long ago, these well-meaning Brits finally found out that all of their patriotic extra commitment to the national struggle had been for naught, since the metal ended up in junk heaps.)

Shoppers head down **Bartlett Street,** just below the Fashion Museum, to browse the boutique shops.

▲Museum of Bath at Work

This modest but lovable place explains the industrial history of Bath. The museum is a vivid reminder that there's always been a grimy, workaday side to this spa town. The core of the museum is the well-preserved, circa-1900 fizzy-drink business of one Mr. Bowler. It includes a Dickensian office, engineer's shop, brass foundry, essence room lined with bottled scents (see photo), and factory floor. It's just a pile of meaningless old gadgets—until the included audioguide resurrects Mr. Bowler's creative genius. Each item has its own story to tell.

Upstairs are display cases featuring other Bath creations through the years, including a 1914 Horstmann car, wheeled sedan chairs (this *is* Bath, after all), and versatile plasticine (colorful proto-Play-Doh—still the preferred medium of Aardman Studios, creators of the stop-motion animated Wallace & Gromit movies). At the snack bar, you can buy your own historic fizzy drink (a descendant of the ones once made here). On your way out, don't miss the intriguing collection of small exhibits on the ground floor, featuring cabinetmaking, the traditional methods for cutting the local "Bath stone," a locally produced six-stroke engine, and more.

Cost and Hours: £5, includes audioguide, April-Oct daily 10:30-17:00, Nov and Jan-March weekends only, closed Dec, last entry one hour before closing, Julian Road, 2 steep blocks up Russell Street from Assembly Rooms, tel. 01225/318-348, www.bath-at-work.org.uk.

Sightseeing Tip: Notice the proximity of this museum to the Fashion Museum (described earlier). Museum attendants told me that—while open-minded spouses appreciate both places—it's standard for husbands to visit the Museum of Bath at Work while their wives tour the Fashion Museum. Maybe it's time to divide and conquer?

Jane Austen Centre

This exhibition focuses on Jane Austen's tumultuous, sometimes-troubled five years in Bath (circa 1800, during which time her father died) and the influence the city had on her writing. There's little of historic substance here. You'll walk through a Georgian townhouse that she didn't live in (one of her real addresses in Bath was a few houses up the road, at 25 Gay Street), and you'll see mostly enlarged reproductions of things associated with her writing as well as her overhyped waxwork likeness, but none of that seems to bother the steady stream of happy Austen fans touring through the house.

The exhibit does describe various places from two novels set in Bath (*Persuasion* and *Northanger Abbey*). Costumed guides give an intro talk (on the first floor, 15 minutes, 3/hour, on the hour and at :20 and :40 past the hour) about the romantic but down-to-earth Austen, who skewered the silly, shallow, and arrogant aristocrats' world, where "the doing of nothing all day prevents one from doing anything." They also show a 15-minute video; after that, you're free to wander through the rest of the exhibit. The well-stocked gift shop—with "I love Mr. Darcy" tote bags and Colin Firth's visage emblazoned on teacups, postcards, and more—is a shopping spree in the making for Austen fans.

Cost and Hours: £9; April-Oct daily 9:45-17:30, July-Aug until 18:00; Nov-March Sun-Fri 11:00-16:30, Sat 9:45-17:30; last entry one hour before closing, between Queen's Square and the Circus at 40 Gay Street, tel. 01225/443-000, www.janeausten.co.uk.

Tea: Upstairs, the award-winning **Regency Tea Rooms** (free entrance) hits the spot for Austen-ites with costumed waitstaff and themed teas (£8-10), including the all-out "Tea with Mr. Darcy" for £16.50 (also £6 sandwiches, opens at 11:00, closes same time as the center, last order taken one hour before closing).

Museum of Bath Architecture

This unique collection offers a geographic introduction to Bath and an intriguing behind-the-scenes look at how the Georgian city was actually built. Near the entrance, an aerial map outlines Bath's expansion from its 17th century origins to today's neighborhoods. In the back of the museum, an interactive model highlights town sights. Compare the 1694 Gilmore map, one of Bath's first tourist maps, with the one you're using today.

Cost and Hours: £5.50, £11.50 combo-ticket with No. 1 Royal Crescent, mid-Feb-Nov Tue-Fri 14:00-17:00, Sat-Sun 10:30-17:00, closed Mon and Dec-mid-Feb, 10-minute intro film runs on a loop, a short walk north of the city center on a street called "The Paragon," tel. 01225/333-895, www.museumofbatharchitecture.org.uk.

George Bayntun Bindery and Bookshop

This high-end bookshop and working bindery is worth a peek. While the workshop is not open to the public, their bookshop—with a reverent, Oxford-library feel—welcomes visitors to browse through an impressive back-room collection of rare editions and old prints for sale (Mon-Fri 9:00-17:30, Sat 9:30-13:00, closed Sun, Manvers Street near the train station, tel. 01225/466-000).

OUTER BATH

▲American Museum

I know, you need this in Bath like you need a Big Mac. The UK's sole museum dedicated to American history, this may be the only place that combines Geronimo and Groucho Marx. It has thoughtful exhibits on the history of Native Americans and the Civil War, but the museum's heart is with the decorative arts and cultural artifacts that reveal how Americans lived from colonial times to the mid-19th century. Each of the 18 completely furnished rooms (from a plain 1600s Massachusetts dining/living room to a Rococo Revival explosion in a New Orleans bedroom) is hosted by eager guides waiting to fill you in on the everyday items that make domestic Yankee history surprisingly interesting. (In the Lee Room, look for the original mouse holes, strategically backlit in the floorboards.) One room is a quilter's nirvana. It's interesting to see your own country through British eyes—but on a nice day, the surrounding gardens and view of the hills might be the best reasons to visit. You could easily spend an afternoon here, enjoying the gardens, arboretum, and trails.

Cost and Hours: £10, mid-March-Oct Tue-Sun 12:00-17:00, late Nov-mid-Dec Tue-Sun 12:00-16:30, closed Mon except in Aug, closed most of Nov and late Dec-mid-March, at Claverton Manor, tel. 01225/460-503, www.americanmuseum.org.

Getting There: The museum is outside of town, but a free hourly shuttle from Terrace Walk just behind the abbey gets you there in 15 minutes (5/day, call or check their website for times; keep your eye out for a white van with the museum's name on it—or hop a taxi for about £10).

Activities in Bath

▲Thermae Bath Spa

After simmering unused for a quarter-century, Bath's natural thermal springs once again offer R&R for the masses. The state-of-the-art spa is housed in a complex of three buildings that combine historic structures with new glass-and-steel architecture.

Is the Thermae Bath Spa worth the time and money? The experience is pretty pricey and humble compared to similar German and Hungarian spas. The tall modern building in the city center lacks a certain old-time elegance. Jets in the pools are very limited, and the only water toys are big foam noodles. There's no cold plunge—the only way to cool off between steam rooms is to step onto a small, unglamorous balcony. The Royal Bath's two pools are essentially the same, and the water isn't particularly hot in either—in fact, the main attraction is the rooftop view from the top one (best with a partner or as a social experience).

All that said, this is the only natural thermal spa in the UK and your one chance to actually bathe in Bath. Bring your swimsuit and come for a couple of hours (Fri night and all day Sat-Sun are most crowded). Consider an evening visit, when—on a chilly day—Bath's twilight glows through the steam from the rooftop pool.

Cost: The cheapest spa pass is £32 for two hours (£35 on weekends), which includes towel, robe, and slippers and gains you access to the Royal Bath's large, ground-floor "Minerva Bath"; four steam rooms and a waterfall shower; and the view-filled, open-air, rooftop thermal pool. Longer stays are £10 for each additional hour. If you arrived in Bath by train, your used rail ticket will score you a four-hour session for the price of two hours. The much-hyped £45 Twilight Package includes three hours and a meal (one plate, drink, robe, towel, and slippers). The appeal of this package is not the mediocre meal, but being on top of the building at a magical hour (which you can do for less money at the regular rate).

Thermae has all the "pamper thyself" extras: massages, mud wraps, and various healing-type treatments, including "watsu"—water shiatsu (£40-90 extra). Book treatments in advance by phone.

Hours: Daily 9:00-21:30, last entry at 19:00, pools close at 21:00. No kids under age 16.

Information: It's 100 yards from the Roman Baths, on Beau Street (tel. 01225/331-234, www.thermaebathspa.com). There's a salad-and-smoothies café for guests.

The Cross Bath: Operated by Thermae Bath Spa, this renovated circular Georgian structure across the street from the main spa provides a simpler and less-expensive bathing option. It has a hot-water fountain that taps directly into the spring, making its water hotter than the spa's (£18-20/1.5 hours, daily 10:00-20:00, last entry at 18:00, check in at Thermae Bath Spa's main entrance across the street and you'll be escorted to the Cross Bath, changing rooms, no access to Royal Bath, no kids under 12).

Spa Visitor Center: Also across the street, in the Hetling Pump Room, this free one-room exhibit explains the story of the spa (Mon-Sat 10:00-17:00, Sun 11:00-16:00, audioguide-£2).

Walking

The Bath Skyline Walk is a six-mile wander around the hills surrounding Bath (leaflet at TI). Another option—with scenic access to the Kennet and Avon Canal—is a walk through the park behind the Holburne Museum—any local can point the way on a city map. Plenty of other scenic paths are described in the TI's literature. For additional options, get *Country Walks around Bath* by Tim Mowl (£4.50 at TI or bookstores).

Hiking the Canal to Bathampton

An idyllic towpath leads three miles from the Bath Spa train station, along the Kennet and Avon Canal, to the sleepy village of Bathampton. Immediately behind the station in Bath, cross the footbridge, turn left, and find where the canal hits the River Avon. Head northeast along the small canal, noticing the series of Industrial Age locks and giving thanks that you're not a horse pulling a barge. After the path crisscrosses the canal a few times, you'll mostly walk with the water on your right. You'll be in Bathampton in about an hour, where The George, a classic pub, awaits with a nice meal and beer (reservations smart, tel. 01225/425-079, www.chefandbrewer.com), or try The Bathampton Mill pub, with garden tables overlooking the waterway (tel. 01225/469-758).

Slow Cruise to Bathampton

The *Pulteney Princess* cruises to the neighboring village of Bathampton about hourly from Pulteney Weir. It's a sleepy float with sporadic commentary, but it's certainly relaxing, and boats come with picnic-friendly sundecks. The good news: The fine Bathampton Mill pub awaits at the dock in Bathampton (see previous listing). Consider combining the cruise with a walk along the riverside trail back into town as described earlier (£4 each way, up to 12/day in good weather, one hour to Bathampton and back, WCs on board, mobile 07791-910-650, £10 taxi back to Bath if dining late).

Boating

The Bath Boating Station, in an old Victorian boathouse, rents rowboats, canoes, and punts (£7/person for first hour, then £4/hour; all day for £18; Easter-Sept daily 10:00-18:00, closed off-season, intersection of Forester and Rockcliffe roads, one mile northeast of center, tel. 01225/312-900, www.bathboating.co.uk).

Swimming and Kids' Activities

The Bath Sports and Leisure Centre has a fine pool for laps as well as lots of waterslides. Kids will also enjoy the "Zany Zone" indoor playground (swimming-£4/adult, £3/kid, family discounts, Mon-Fri 6:30-22:00, Sat 10:30-19:00, Sun 8:00-20:00, kids' hours limited, call for open-swim times, just across the bridge on North Parade Road, tel. 01225/486-905, www.aquaterra.org).

Shopping

There's great browsing between the abbey and the Assembly Rooms. Shops close at about 17:30, and many are open on Sunday (11:00-16:00). Explore the antique shops around Bartlett Street, below the Fashion Museum.

Nightlife in Bath

For an up-to-date list of events, pick up the local weekly newspaper, the *Bath Chronicle,* which includes a "What's On" schedule (www.thisisbath.com).

▲▲Bizarre Bath Street Theater

For an entertaining walking-tour comedy act "with absolutely no history or culture," follow Toby or Noel on their creative and lively Bizarre Bath walk. This 1.5-hour "tour," which combines stand-up comedy with cleverly executed magic tricks, plays off unsuspecting passersby as well as tour members. It's a belly laugh a minute.

Cost and Hours: £10, £8 if you show this book, April-Oct nightly at 20:00, smaller groups Mon-Thu, promises to insult all nationalities and sensitivities, just racy enough but still good family fun, leaves from The Huntsman Inn near the abbey (confirm at TI or call 01225/335-124, www.bizarrebath.co.uk).

▲Theatre Royal Performance

The 18th-century, 800-seat Theatre Royal, restored in 2010 and one of England's loveliest, offers a busy schedule of London West End-type plays, including many "pre-London" dress-rehearsal runs. The Theatre Royal also oversees performances at two other theaters around the corner from the main box office: Ustinov Studio (edgier, more obscure titles, many of which are premier runs in the UK) and "the egg" (for children, young people, and families).

Cost and Hours: £20-40 plus small booking fee; shows generally start at 19:30 or 20:00, matinees at 14:30, box office open Mon-Sat 10:00-20:00, Sun 12:00-20:00 if there's a show, book in person, online, or by phone; on Saw Close, tel. 01225/448-844, www.theatreroyal.org.uk.

Ticket Deals: Forty nosebleed spots on a bench (misnamed "standbys") go on sale at noon Monday through Saturday for that day's evening performance in the main theater (£6, 2 tickets maximum). If the show is sold out, same-day "standing places" go on sale at 18:00 (12:00 for matinees) for £4 (cash only). Also at the box office, you can snatch up any "last minute" seats for £15-20 a half-hour before "curtain up" (cash only). Shows in the Ustinov Theatre go for around £20, with no cheap-seat deals.

Sightseeing Tip: During the free Bath walking tour, your guide stops here. Pop into the box office, ask what's playing, and see if there are many seats left for that night. If the play sounds good and plenty of seats remain unsold, you're fairly safe to come back 30 minutes before curtain time to buy a ticket at the cheaper price. Oh...and if you smell jasmine, it's the ghost of Lady Grey, a mistress of Beau Nash.

Evening Walks

Take your choice: comedy (Bizarre Bath, described earlier), history, or ghost tour. The **free city walking tours** (a daily standard described on page 241) are offered on some summer evenings (2 hours, May-Sept Tue and Thu at 19:00, leave from Pump Room). **Ghost Walks** are a popular way to pass the after-dark hours (£8, cash only, 1.5 hours, year-round Thu-Sat at 20:00, leave from The Garrick's Head pub—to the left and behind Theatre Royal as you face it, tel. 01225/350-512, www.ghostwalksofbath.co.uk). The cities of York and Edinburgh—which have houses thought to be actually haunted—are better for ghost walks.

Pubs

Most pubs in the center are very noisy, catering to a rowdy twentysomething crowd. But on the top end of town, you can still find some classic old places with inviting ambience and live music. See the map on page 270 for locations.

The Old Green Tree, conveniently right in the town center, is a rare traditional pub offering a warm welcome (locally brewed real ales, no TVs, 12 Green Street, tel. 01225/448-259).

The Star Inn is much appreciated by local beerlovers for its fine ale and "no machines or music to distract from the chat." It's a spit-and-sawdust place, and its long bench, nicknamed "death row," still comes with a complimentary pinch of snuff from tins on the ledge. Try the Bellringer Ale, made just up the road (daily 12:00-late, no food served, 23 The Vineyards, top of The Paragon/A-4 Roman Road, tel. 01225/425-072, generous and friendly welcome from Paul, who runs the place).

The Bell has a jazzy, pierced-and-tattooed, bohemian feel, but with a mellow older crowd. After learning the much-beloved bar would be sold to an outsider, 536 locals—plus a few well-known celebrities—banded together to save it. Thanks to their efforts, some kind of activity continues to brew nearly nightly, usually involving live music (daily 11:30-23:00, 103 Walcot Street, tel. 01225/460-426, www.thebellinnbath.co.uk).

Summer Nights at the Baths

In July and August, you can stretch your sightseeing day at the Roman Baths, open nightly until 22:00 (last entry 21:00), when the gas lamps flame and the baths are far less crowded and more atmospheric. To take a dip yourself, consider popping over to the Thermae Bath Spa (last entry at 19:00).

Sleeping in Bath

Bath is a busy tourist town. Reserve in advance, and keep in mind B&Bs favor those lingering longer. Accommodations are expensive, and low-cost alternatives are rare. By far the best budget option is the YMCA—it's central, safe, simple, very well-run, and has plenty of twin rooms available. At B&Bs, it's worth asking for a weekday, three-nights-in-a-row, or off-season deal. Friday and Saturday nights are tightest (with many rates going up by about 25 percent)—especially if you're staying only one night. If you're driving to Bath, stowing your car near the center will cost you (though some less-central B&Bs have parking)—see "Parking" on page 241, or ask your hotelier.

NEAR THE ROYAL CRESCENT

These listings are all a 5- to 10-minute walk from the town center, and an easy 15-minute walk from the train station. With bags in tow you may want to either catch a taxi (£5-7) or (except for Brocks Guest House) hop on bus #14 or #14A (direction: Weston, catch bus inside bus station, pay driver £2.20, get off at the Comfort-

Sleep Code

Abbreviations **(£1=about $1.60, country code: 44)**
S=Single, **D**=Double/Twin, **T**=Triple, **Q**=Quad, **b**=bathroom
Price Rankings
$$$ Higher Priced—Most rooms £100 or more
$$ Moderately Priced—Most rooms £60-100
$ Lower Priced—Most rooms £60 or less
Unless otherwise noted, credit cards are accepted, breakfast is included, and free Wi-Fi and/or a guest computer is generally available. Prices change; verify current rates online or by email. For the best prices, always book directly with the hotel.

able Place stop—just after the car shop on the left, cross street and backtrack 100 yards).

Marlborough, Brooks, and Cornerways all face a busy arterial street; while the noise is minimal by urban standards and these B&Bs have well-insulated windows, those sensitive to traffic noise should request a rear- or side-facing room.

$$$ Marlborough House, exuberantly run by hands-on owner Peter, mixes modern style with antique furnishings and features a welcoming breakfast room with an open kitchen. Each of the six rooms comes with a sip of sherry (Sb-£85-115, Db-£105-155, Tb-£115-165, rates can vary with demand, must mention this book in your initial request for Rick Steves discount, £5 additional discount when you pay cash, air-con, minifridges, free parking, 1 Marlborough Lane, tel. 01225/318-175, www.marlborough-house.net, mars@manque.dircon.co.uk).

$$$ Brooks Guesthouse is the biggest and most polished of the bunch, albeit the least personal, with 22 modern rooms and classy public spaces, including an exceptionally pleasant breakfast room (Sb-£60-90, Db/Tb-£85-120, rates vary with room size and season/demand, shared guest fridge, limited parking-£8/day, 1 Crescent Gardens, Upper Bristol Road, tel. 01225/425-543, www.brooksguesthouse.com, info@brooksguesthouse.com).

$$ Brocks Guest House rents six rooms in a Georgian townhouse built by John Wood in 1765. Located between the prestigious Royal Crescent and the courtly Circus, it's been redone in a way that would make the great architect proud. Each room has its own Bath-related theme (Db-£99, Db with fireplace-£109, larger Db-£119, Db suite-£129, little top-floor library, 32 Brock Street, tel. 01225/338-374, www.brocksguesthouse.co.uk, brocks@brocksguesthouse.co.uk, Marta and Rafal).

$$ Parkside Guest House rents five large, thoughtfully-appointed Edwardian rooms. It's tidy, clean, homey, and well-priced—and has a spacious back garden (Sb-£70, Db-£90, these

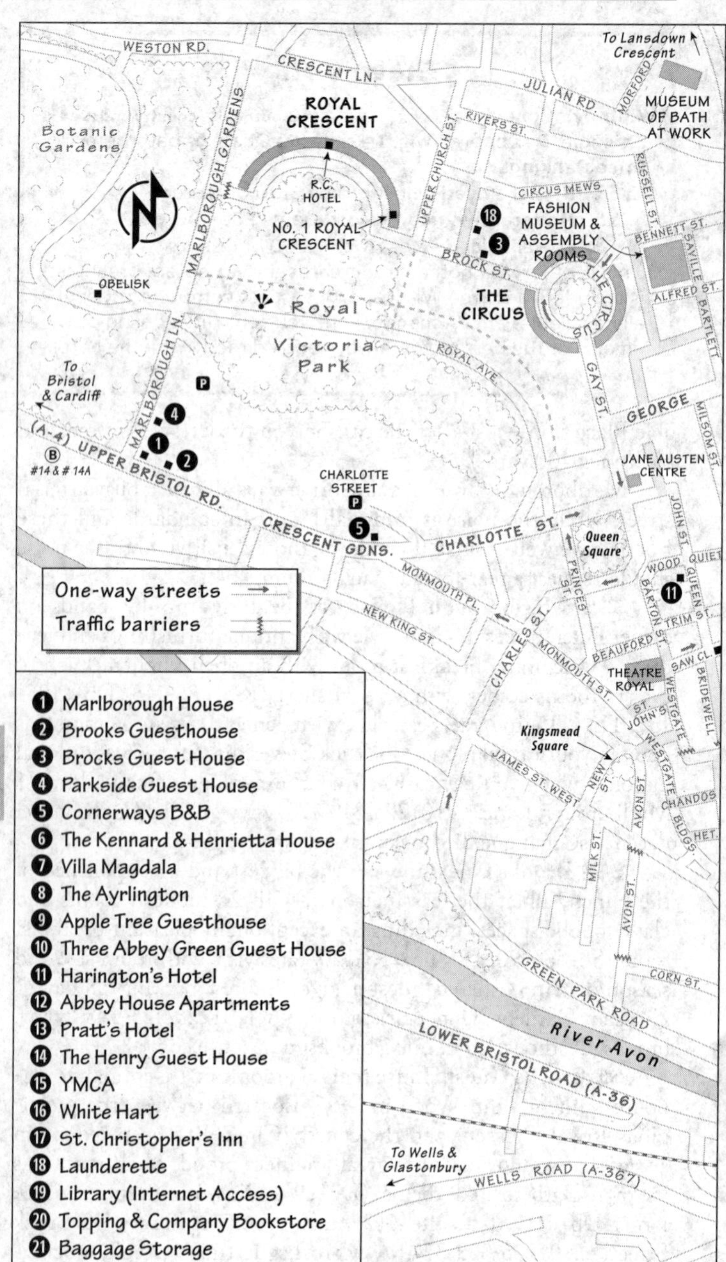

1. Marlborough House
2. Brooks Guesthouse
3. Brocks Guest House
4. Parkside Guest House
5. Cornerways B&B
6. The Kennard & Henrietta House
7. Villa Magdala
8. The Ayrlington
9. Apple Tree Guesthouse
10. Three Abbey Green Guest House
11. Harington's Hotel
12. Abbey House Apartments
13. Pratt's Hotel
14. The Henry Guest House
15. YMCA
16. White Hart
17. St. Christopher's Inn
18. Launderette
19. Library (Internet Access)
20. Topping & Company Bookstore
21. Baggage Storage

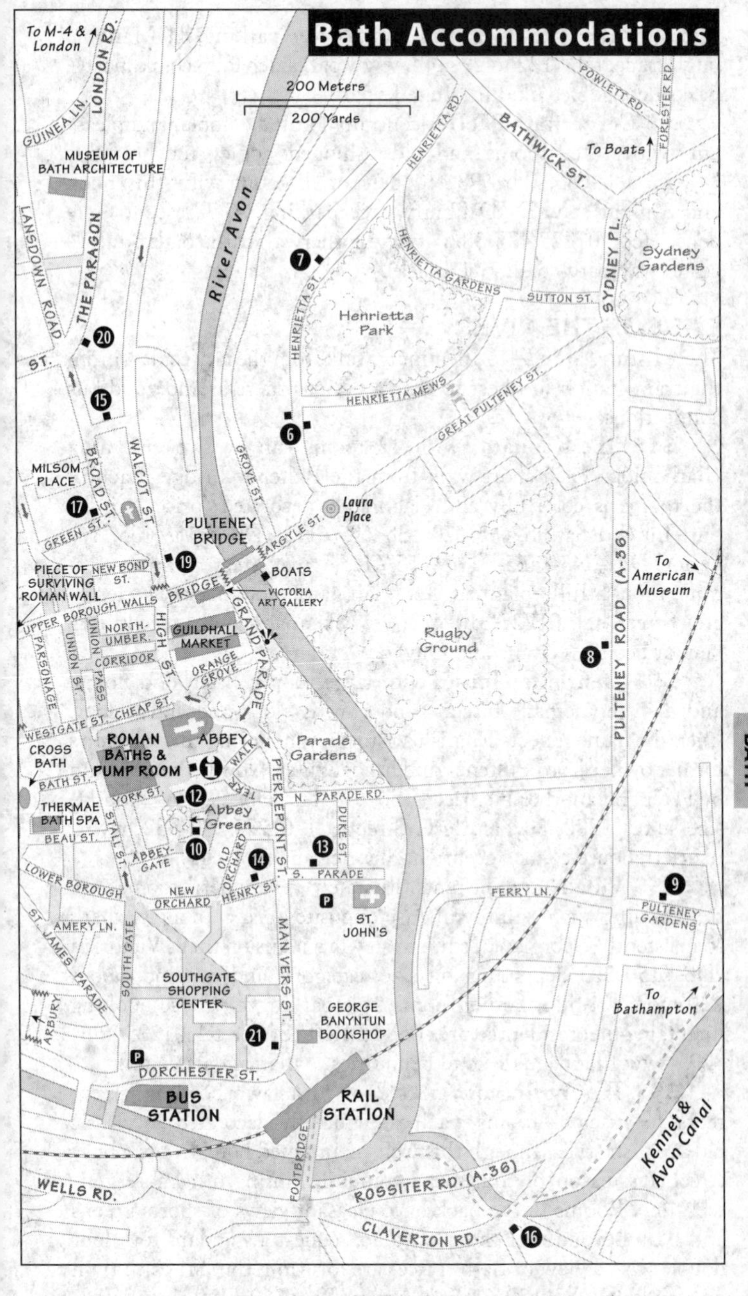
Bath Accommodations
To M-4 & London
LONDON RD.
GUINEA LN.
200 Meters
200 Yards
MUSEUM OF BATH ARCHITECTURE
LANSDOWN ROAD
THE PARAGON
River Avon
HENRIETTA RD.
POWLETT RD.
FORESTER RD.
BATHWICK ST.
To Boats
HENRIETTA ST.
HENRIETTA GARDENS
SUTTON ST.
SYDNEY PL.
Sydney Gardens
Henrietta Park
HENRIETTA MEWS
GREAT PULTENEY ST.
ST.
BROAD ST.
WALCOT ST.
MILSOM PLACE
GREEN ST.
GROVE ST.
ARGYLE ST.
Laura Place
PULTENEY BRIDGE
PIECE OF SURVIVING ROMAN WALL
NEW BOND ST.
BRIDGE
BOATS
VICTORIA ART GALLERY
UPPER BOROUGH WALLS
HIGH ST.
NORTH-UMBER.
UNION ST.
UNION PASS.
PARSONAGE
CORRIDOR
GUILDHALL MARKET
GRAND PARADE
ORANGE GROVE
Rugby Ground
PULTENEY ROAD (A-36)
To American Museum
WESTGATE ST.
CHEAP ST.
ABBEY
ROMAN BATHS & PUMP ROOM
WALK
Parade Gardens
CROSS BATH
BATH ST.
YORK ST.
TERR.
PIERREPONT ST.
N. PARADE RD.
THERMAE BATH SPA
Abbey Green
DUKE ST.
BEAU ST.
STALL ST.
ABBEY-GATE
OLD ORCHARD
S. PARADE
LOWER BOROUGH
NEW ORCHARD
HENRY ST.
MAN VERS ST.
ST. JOHN'S
FERRY LN.
PULTENEY GARDENS
AMERY LN.
ST. JAMES PARADE
SOUTH GATE
SOUTHGATE SHOPPING CENTER
GEORGE BANYNTUN BOOKSHOP
ARBURY
To Bathampton
DORCHESTER ST.
BUS STATION
RAIL STATION
FOOTBRIDGE
Kennet & Avon Canal
WELLS RD.
ROSSITER RD. (A-36)
CLAVERTON RD.
BATH

prices for Rick Steves readers, limited free parking, 11 Marlborough Lane, tel. 01225/429-444, www.parksidebandb.co.uk, post@parksidebandb.co.uk, kind Inge Lynall).

$$ Cornerways B&B is centrally located, simple, and pleasant, with three rooms and old-fashioned homey touches (Sb-£48-55, Db-£85, Tb-£98, 10 percent discount with this book and 3-night stay, DVD library, free parking, 47 Crescent Gardens, tel. 01225/422-382, www.cornerwaysbath.co.uk, info@cornerwaysbath.co.uk, Sue Black).

EAST OF THE RIVER

These listings are a 5- to 10-minute walk from the city center. From the train station, it's best to take a taxi, as there are no good bus connections.

$$$ The Kennard, with 12 rooms run by two charming "Bathonions," is a short walk from the Pulteney Bridge. Each of the rooms is colorfully and elaborately decorated (prices are for Sun-Thu/Fri-Sat: S-£65/£70, Sb-£95/£115, Db-£115/£135, superior Db-£145/£165, Tb-£155/£175, free street parking permits, thoughtfully-planned Georgian garden out back, 11 Henrietta Street, tel. 01225/310-472, www.kennard.co.uk, reception@kennard.co.uk, Natalie and Guy).

$$$ Henrietta House, with large rooms, hardwood floors, and daily homemade biscuits and jam, is cloak-and-cravat cozy. Even the name reflects English aristocracy, honoring the mansion's former owner Lord Pulteney and his daughter. Now it's smartly run by Peter and another Henrietta (Sb-£95-115, Db-£95-165, family-size suites-£280, 33 Henrietta Street, tel. 01225/632-632, www.henriettahouse.co.uk, reception@henriettahouse.co.uk).

BATH

$$$ Villa Magdala rents 20 stately yet modern rooms in a freestanding Victorian townhouse opposite a park. In a city that's so insistently Georgian, it's fun to stay in a mansion that's Victorian (Db-£150-225 depending on size, category, and demand, about £20 more Fri-Sun, family rooms, free parking for those booking direct, in quiet residential area on Henrietta Street, tel. 01225/466-329, www.villamagdala.co.uk, enquiries@villamagdala.co.uk).

$$$ The Ayrlington, next door to a lawn-bowling green, rents 16 spacious rooms, each thoughtfully decorated in classic old-English style. Though this well-maintained hotel fronts a busy street, it's reasonably quiet and tranquil, hinting of a more genteel time. Rooms in the back have pleasant views of sports greens and Bath beyond. For the best value, request a standard top-floor double with a view of Bath (prices are for Mon-Thu/Fri-Sun: twin or standard Db-£120/£135, superior Db-£150/£170, big deluxe Db-£160/£190, larger and fancier rooms also available, extra person-£35, fine garden, free and easy parking, 24 Pulteney Road, tel.

01225/425-495, www.ayrlington.com, theayrlington@gmail.com, Ling Roper).

$$ At **Apple Tree Guesthouse,** near a shady canal, hostess Ling rents four comfortable rooms sprinkled with Asian decor (Sb-£80-150, Db-£90-160, family/Tb-£120-190, 2-night minimum Fri-Sat nights, free parking, 7 Pulteney Gardens, tel. 01225/337-642, www.appletreebath.com, enquiries@appletreebath.co.uk).

IN THE TOWN CENTER

You'll pay a premium to sleep right in the center. And since Bath is so pleasant and manageable by foot, a downtown location isn't essential. Still, these are particularly well-located.

$$$ Three Abbey Green Guest House, renting 10 spacious rooms, is bright, cheery, and located in a quiet, traffic-free courtyard only 50 yards from the abbey and the Roman Baths (Db-£100-160, four-poster Db-£140-200, family rooms-£160-240, price depends on season and size of room, 2-night minimum on weekends, limited free parking, 2 ground-floor rooms work well for those with limited mobility, tel. 01225/428-558, www.threeabbeygreen.com, stay@threeabbeygreen.com, Sue, Derek, daughter Nicola, and son-in-law Alan). They also rent self-catering apartments (Db-£140-180, 2-night minimum).

$$$ Harington's Hotel rents 13 fresh, modern rooms on a quiet street. This stylish place feels like a boutique hotel, but with a friendlier, laid-back vibe (Sb-£78-155, Db-£98-170, large superior Db-£108-170, Tb-£130-200, prices vary substantially with demand—always highest on weekends, ask for a Rick Steves discount, parking-£11/day, 8 Queen Street, tel. 01225/461-728, www.haringtonshotel.co.uk, post@haringtonshotel.co.uk, manager Julian). Owners Melissa and Peter also rent three self-catering apartments down the street—one can sleep up to three and the others can sleep up to eight (prices on request; 2-night minimum on weekdays, 3-night minimum on weekends).

$$$ At **Abbey House Apartments,** Laura rents five flats on Abbey Green and several others scattered around town. The apartments called Abbey Green (which comes with a washer and dryer), Abbey View, and Abbey Studio have views of the abbey from their nicely equipped kitchens. Laura provides everything you need for simple breakfasts, and it's fun and cheap to stock the fridge. When Laura meets you to give you the keys, you become a local (Sb-£90, Db-£100-175, price depends on size, 2-night minimum, rooms can sleep four with Murphy and sofa beds, apartments clearly described on website, Abbey Green, tel. 01225/464-238, www.laurastownhouseapartments.co.uk, bookings@laurastownhouseapartments.co.uk).

$$$ Pratt's Hotel rents 46 worn but comfy and proper olde-

English rooms. It's recently been taken over by a hotel franchise that intends to expand into the building next door, turning its aristocratic creaks and frays into something more modern. Since it's near a busy street, request a quiet room (Sb-£60-100, Db-£80-150, price depends on size and demand, breakfast-£10, check website for current rates and specials, children under 15 free with 2 adults, elevator, attached restaurant-bar, 4 South Parade, tel. 01225/460-441, www.sjhotels.co.uk/pratts, reservations.pratts@sjhotels.co.uk).

$$ The Henry Guest House is a simple vertical place, renting seven clean rooms. It's friendly, well-run, and just two blocks from the train station (Sb-£75-85, Db-£80-105, premier Db-£95-120, extra bed-£20, family/Tb-£145-205, 2-night minimum on weekends, 6 Henry Street, tel. 01225/424-052, www.thehenry.com, stay@thehenry.com, Tonia and Guido).

BARGAIN ACCOMMODATIONS

$ The **YMCA,** centrally located on a leafy square, has 210 beds in industrial-strength rooms—all with sinks and basic furnishings. Although it smells a little like a gym, this place is a godsend for budget travelers—safe, secure, quiet, and efficiently run. With lots of twin rooms and a few double beds, this is the only easily accessible budget option in downtown Bath (rates for Sun-Thu/Fri-Sat: S-£32/£36, twin D-£50/£60, D-£60/£64, T-£69/£75, Q-£88/£96, bunk in dorm room-£14/£16, WCs and showers down the hall, includes continental breakfast, free linens, rental towels, lockers, laundry facilities, down a tiny alley off Broad Street on Broad Street Place, tel. 01225/325-900, www.bathymca.co.uk, stay@bathymca.co.uk).

$ White Hart is a friendly and colorful place in need of a little updating, but offering good, cheap stays in four private rooms or a dorm (bunk in dorm room-£15, S-£25, D-£40, Db-£50-70, fine garden out back, 5-minute walk behind the train station at Widcombe—where Widcombe Hill hits Claverton Street, tel. 01225/313-985; if no one answers, ring the bar at tel. 01225/338-053, www.whitehartbath.co.uk). The White Hart also has a pub with a reputation for good food.

$ St. Christopher's Inn, in a prime central location, is part of a chain of low-priced, high-energy hubs for backpackers looking for beds and brews. Their beds are so cheap because they know you'll spend money on their beer. The inn sits above the lively, youthful Belushi's pub, which is where you'll find the reception (bunk in dorm room-£15-25, D-£70-118, higher prices are for weekends and walk-ins—it's always cheaper to book online, check website for specials, no guests under 18, laundry facilities, lounge, 9 Green Street, tel. 01225/481-444, www.st-christophers.co.uk).

Eating in Bath

Bath is bursting with eateries. There's something for every appetite and budget—just stroll around the center of town. A picnic dinner of deli food or take-out fish-and-chips in the Royal Crescent Park or down by the river is ideal for aristocratic hoboes. The restaurants I recommend are small and popular—reserve a table for dinner—especially on Friday and Saturday. Most pricey little bistros offer big savings with their two- and three-course lunches and "pre-theatre" specials. Look for early-bird specials: As long as you order within the time window, you're in for a less-expensive meal.

ROMANTIC, UPSCALE FRENCH AND ENGLISH

Clayton's Kitchen is fine for a modern English splurge in a woody, romantic, candlelit atmosphere, where Michelin-star chef Rob Clayton aims to offer affordable British cuisine without pretense. The food is artfully prepared and presented—and they love their scallops (£15 two-course lunch deal, £10 starters, £20-30 main courses, daily from noon and from 18:00, a few outside tables, live jazz on Sundays, 15 George Street, tel. 01225/585-100, http://theporter.co.uk/claytons-kitchen).

The Circus Restaurant is a relaxing little eatery serving well-executed English cuisine with European flair. Choose between the modern interior—with seating on the main floor or in the less-charming cellar—and the four tables on the peaceful street connecting the Circus and the Royal Crescent (£9-14 lunches; £8 starters and £18-23 main courses at dinner, open Mon-Sat 10:00-24:00, closed Sun, 34 Brock Street, tel. 01225/466-020, www.thecircuscafeandrestaurant.co.uk).

Casanis French Bistro-Restaurant is an intimate place where Chef Laurent, who hails from Nice, cooks "authentic Provençal cuisine," while his wife, Jill, serves. The decor matches the cuisine—informal, relaxed, simple, and top quality (lunch and early dinner specials: £20 for two courses, £24 for three courses; open Tue-Sat 12:00-14:00 & 18:00-22:00, closed Sun-Mon, behind the Assembly Rooms at 4 Saville Row, tel. 01225/780-055, www.casanis.co.uk).

PUBS

Bath is not a great pub-grub town, and with so many other tempting options, pub dining isn't as appealing as it is elsewhere. Among my listings, The Garrick's Head is a "gastropub," The Raven is for meat pies, and Crystal Palace is a fun, basic place. See "Nightlife in Bath," earlier, for other pubs I recommend—but not for their food.

The Garrick's Head is an elegantly simple gastropub around the corner from the Theatre Royal, with a pricey restaurant on one

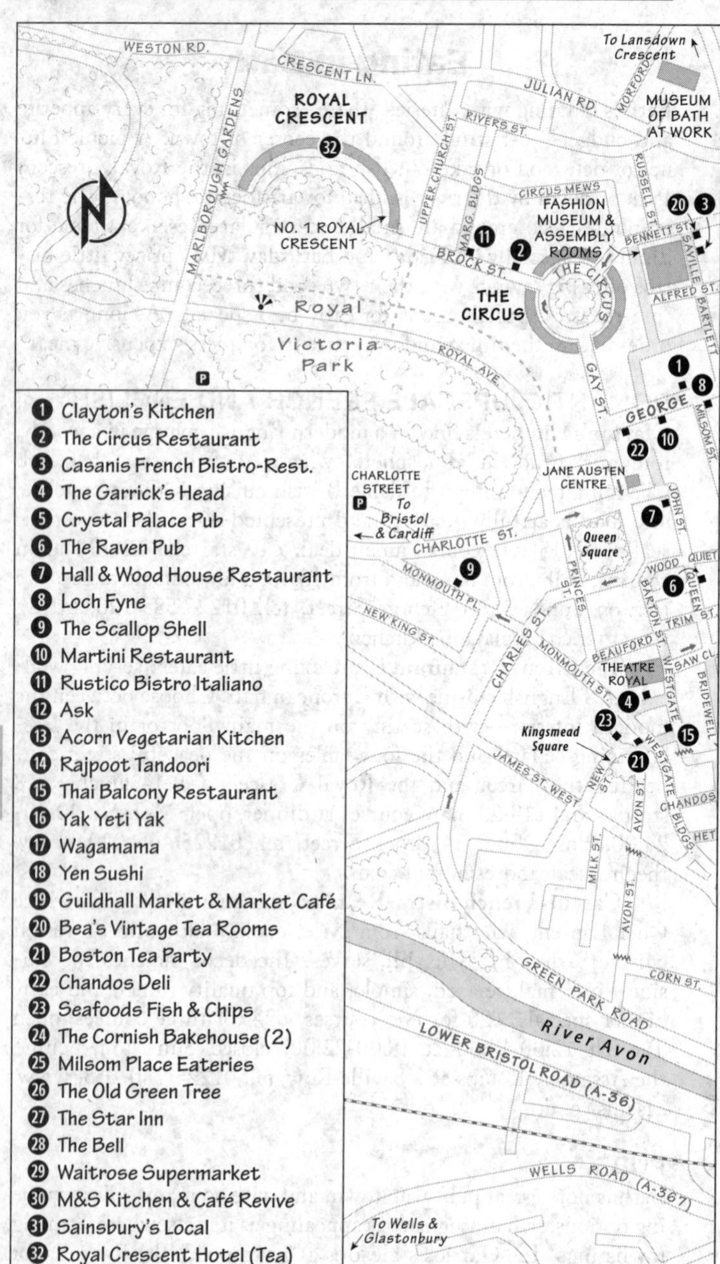

WESTON RD.
CRESCENT LN.
ROYAL CRESCENT
JULIAN RD.
To Lansdown Crescent
MORFORD
MUSEUM OF BATH AT WORK
RIVERS ST.
UPPER CHURCH ST.
MARLBOROUGH GARDENS
MARG. BLDGS.
CIRCUS MEWS
FASHION MUSEUM & ASSEMBLY ROOMS
RUSSELL ST.
BENNETT ST.
SAVILLE
NO. 1 ROYAL CRESCENT
BROCK ST.
THE CIRCUS
ALFRED ST.
BARTLETT
Royal
Victoria
Park
ROYAL AVE.
GAY ST.
GEORGE
MILSOM ST.
JANE AUSTEN CENTRE
CHARLOTTE STREET
To Bristol & Cardiff
CHARLOTTE ST.
JOHN ST.
Queen Square
WOOD
QUIET
QUEEN
MONMOUTH PL.
PRINCES ST.
BARTON ST.
TRIM ST.
NEW KING ST.
CHARLES ST.
MONMOUTH ST.
BEAUFORD
THEATRE ROYAL
SAW CL.
WESTGATE
BRIDEWELL
Kingsmead Square
JAMES ST. WEST
NEW ST.
AVON ST.
WESTGATE BLDGS.
CHANDOS
HET
MILK ST.
AVON ST.
CORN ST.
GREEN PARK ROAD
River Avon
LOWER BRISTOL ROAD (A-36)
WELLS ROAD (A-367)
To Wells & Glastonbury
1 Clayton's Kitchen
2 The Circus Restaurant
3 Casanis French Bistro-Rest.
4 The Garrick's Head
5 Crystal Palace Pub
6 The Raven Pub
7 Hall & Wood House Restaurant
8 Loch Fyne
9 The Scallop Shell
10 Martini Restaurant
11 Rustico Bistro Italiano
12 Ask
13 Acorn Vegetarian Kitchen
14 Rajpoot Tandoori
15 Thai Balcony Restaurant
16 Yak Yeti Yak
17 Wagamama
18 Yen Sushi
19 Guildhall Market & Market Café
20 Bea's Vintage Tea Rooms
21 Boston Tea Party
22 Chandos Deli
23 Seafoods Fish & Chips
24 The Cornish Bakehouse (2)
25 Milsom Place Eateries
26 The Old Green Tree
27 The Star Inn
28 The Bell
29 Waitrose Supermarket
30 M&S Kitchen & Café Revive
31 Sainsbury's Local
32 Royal Crescent Hotel (Tea)

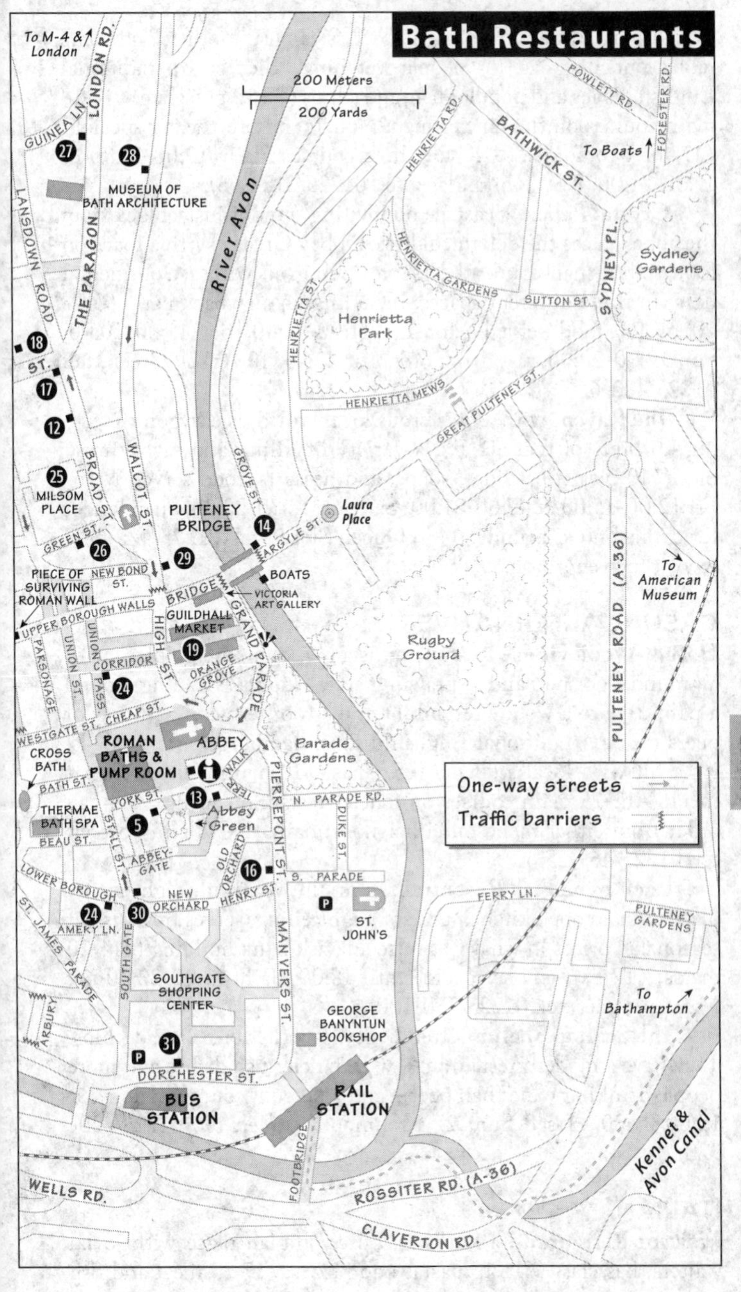
Bath Restaurants
To M-4 & London
200 Meters
200 Yards
GUINEA LN.
LONDON RD.
MUSEUM OF BATH ARCHITECTURE
LANSDOWN ROAD
THE PARAGON
River Avon
HENRIETTA RD.
POWLETT RD.
FORESTER RD.
BATHWICK ST.
To Boats
HENRIETTA GARDENS
HENRIETTA ST.
Henrietta Park
SUTTON ST.
SYDNEY PL.
Sydney Gardens
HENRIETTA MEWS
GREAT PULTENEY ST.
ST.
BROAD ST.
WALCOT ST.
MILSOM PLACE
PULTENEY BRIDGE
GROVE ST.
Laura Place
ARGYLE ST.
GREEN ST.
PIECE OF SURVIVING ROMAN WALL
NEW BOND ST.
BOATS
BRIDGE
VICTORIA ART GALLERY
To American Museum
UPPER BOROUGH WALLS
HIGH ST.
GUILDHALL MARKET
GRAND PARADE
Rugby Ground
PULTENEY ROAD (A-36)
PARSONAGE
UNION ST.
UNION PASS
CORRIDOR
ORANGE GROVE
WESTGATE ST.
CHEAP ST.
CROSS BATH
ROMAN BATHS & PUMP ROOM
ABBEY
TERR. WALK
Parade Gardens
BATH ST.
YORK ST.
N. PARADE RD.
One-way streets
Traffic barriers
THERMAE BATH SPA
Abbey Green
PIERREPONT ST.
DUKE ST.
BEAU ST.
STALL ST.
ABBEY-GATE
OLD ORCHARD
S. PARADE
LOWER BOROUGH
NEW ORCHARD
HENRY ST.
FERRY LN.
ST. JOHN'S
PULTENEY GARDENS
ST. JAMES PARADE
AMERY LN.
SOUTH GATE
MANVERS ST.
SOUTHGATE SHOPPING CENTER
To Bathampton
ARBURY
GEORGE BANYNTUN BOOKSHOP
DORCHESTER ST.
BUS STATION
RAIL STATION
Kennet & Avon Canal
FOOTBRIDGE
WELLS RD.
ROSSITER RD. (A-36)
CLAVERTON RD.
BATH

side, a bar serving affordable pub classics on the other, and some tables outside great for people-watching. They serve traditional English dishes and popular fish-and-chips (£7-12 pub grub, £14-18 main courses on the fancier menu; lunch and pre-theater specials: £17 for two courses, £20 for three courses; daily 12:00-14:30 & 17:30-21:00, 8 St. John's Place, tel. 01225/318-368).

Crystal Palace, a casual and inviting standby just a block from the abbey, faces the delightful little Abbey Green. With a focus on food rather than drink, they serve "pub grub with a Continental flair" in three different spaces, including an airy back patio (£12-20 meals, food served Mon-Fri 11:00-21:00, Sat 11:00-20:00, Sun 12:00-20:00, last drink orders at 22:45, 10 Abbey Green, tel. 01225/482-666).

The Raven, with a boisterous local crowd, is easygoing, serving up pints of real ale and a variety of filling and savory meat pies (£10 pies; £3-9 sides, soups, and desserts; food served Mon-Fri 12:00-15:00 & 17:00-21:00, Sat-Sun 12:30-20:30, open longer for drinks; no kids under 14, 6 Queen Street, tel. 01225/425-045, www.theravenofbath.co.uk).

CASUAL ALTERNATIVES

Hall & Wood House Restaurant is a big, high-energy place with a ground-floor pub and a sprawling spiral staircase leading around a palm tree to a woody restaurant and a roof terrace. With lots of beers on tap, traditional English dishes, hamburgers, and salads, it's a hit with local students (£5 tapas, £10 main courses on bar menu; £12-15 main courses on fancier restaurant menu—but can order from either menu on either floor; daily, 1 Old King Street, tel. 01225/469-259).

Loch Fyne Fish Restaurant, a bright, youthful, high-energy place with an open kitchen under a high ceiling, serves fresh fish at reasonable prices in what was once a lavish bank building (£14-20 meals, £12 two-course special until 18:00, daily 12:00-22:00, 24 Milsom Street, tel. 01225/750-120).

The Scallop Shell is a trendy new favorite for fish-and-chips. They have a modern restaurant—with fancier fish dishes and more people drinking wine than beer—and a takeout counter (Mon-Sat 12:00-21:30, closed Sun, 27 Monmouth Street, tel. 01225/420-928).

ITALIAN

Martini Restaurant, a hopping, purely Italian place with jovial waiters, has class (£11-13 pastas and pizzas, £17-23 meat and fish main courses, lunch and early dinner specials: £10 for two courses, £12 for three courses; open daily 12:00-14:30 & 18:00-22:30, veggie options, daily fish specials, extensive wine list, 9 George Street, tel. 01225/460-818; Nunzio, Franco, and chef Luigi).

Rustico Bistro Italiano, nestled between the Circus and the Royal Crescent, is precisely what its name implies. Franco and his staff are kept busy by a local crowd (£10 pastas, £15-19 main courses, no pizza, check chalkboard for specials, Tue-Sun 12:00-14:30 & 18:00-22:00, closed Mon, just off Brock Street at 2 Margaret's Buildings, tel. 01225/310-064).

Ask Italian is a big, bright, fresh chain dishing up reliable Italian food in an inviting atmosphere (£8-13 pizzas and pastas, good salads, daily 11:30-23:00, entrance on Broad Street, tel. 01225/789-997).

VEGETARIAN AND ETHNIC

Acorn Vegetarian Kitchen is highly rated and ideal for the well-heeled vegetarian. Its tight, understated interior comes with a vegan vibe (£6-12 lunches, £8 starters, and £17 main courses at dinner; lunch and early dinner specials: £17 for two courses, £20 for three courses; daily 12:00-15:00 & 17:30-21:30, 2 North Parade Passage, tel. 01225/446-059).

Rajpoot Tandoori serves reliably good Indian food. You'll hike down deep into a sprawling cellar, where the plush atmosphere and award-winning cooking make paying the extra pounds palatable. The seating is tight and the ceilings low, but it's air-conditioned (£9 three-course lunch, £9-16 main courses; figure £20 per person with rice, naan, and drink; daily 12:00-14:30 & 18:00-23:00, 4 Argyle Street, tel. 01225/466-833, Ali).

Thai Balcony Restaurant's open, spacious interior is so plush, it'll have you wondering, "Where's the Thai wedding?" While residents debate which of Bath's handful of Thai restaurants serves the best food or offers the lowest prices, there's no doubt that Thai Balcony's fun and elegant atmosphere makes for a memorable and enjoyable dinner (£10 two-course lunch special, £8-13 plates, daily 12:00-14:00 & 18:00-22:00, Saw Close, tel. 01225/444-450).

Yak Yeti Yak is a fun Nepalese restaurant with both Western and sit-on-the-floor seating. Sera and his wife Sarah, along with their cheerful, hardworking Nepali team, cook up great traditional food (including plenty of vegetarian plates) at prices that would delight a sherpa (£7-9 lunches, £7 veggie plates, £9 meat plates; daily 12:00-14:00 & 18:00-22:00; downstairs at 12 Pierrepont Street, tel. 01225/442-299).

Wagamama Noodle Restaurant is a big, sleek, pan-Asian slurp-a-thon with a modern flair and healthy, hearty, and tasty dishes (£10-13 meals, daily 11:30-23:00, 1 York Buildings, corner of George and Broad streets, tel. 01225/337-314).

Yen Sushi is your basic little Japanese sushi bar—plain and sterile, with stools facing a conveyor belt that constantly tempts you with a variety of freshly made delights on color-coded plates (£2-5 plates, daily 12:00-15:00 & 17:30-22:30, 11 Bartlett Street, tel. 01225/333-313).

SIMPLE LUNCH OPTIONS

Market Café, in the Guildhall Market across from Pulteney Bridge, is where you can munch really cheaply on a homemade meat pie or sip tea while surrounded by stacks of used books, bananas on the push list, and honest-to-goodness old-time locals (£3-6 traditional English meals including fried breakfasts all day, Mon-Sat 8:00-17:00, closed Sun, tel. 01225/461-593 a block north of the abbey, on High Street).

Bea's Vintage Tea Rooms, just behind the Assembly Rooms and Fashion Museum, is a charming trip back to the 1940s, with light lunches, teas, and cakes—just right for a break from the crowds of Bath (daily 10:00-17:00, 6 Saville Row, tel. 01225/464-552).

Boston Tea Party is what Starbucks aspires to be—the neighborhood coffeehouse and hangout. Its extensive breakfasts, light lunches, and salads are fresh and healthy. The outdoor seating overlooks a busy square. Their walls are decorated with works by local artists (£4-7 breakfasts, £5-7 lunches, Mon-Sat 7:30-19:30, Sun 9:00-19:00, 19 Kingsmead Square, tel. 01225/319-901).

Chandos Deli has good coffee, breakfast pastries, and tasty £3-5 sandwiches made on artisan breads plus meats, cheese, baguettes, and wine for assembling a gourmet picnic. Upscale yet casual, this place satisfies dedicated foodies who don't want to pay too much (Mon-Fri 8:00-18:00, Sat 9:00-19:00, Sun 9:00-17:00, 12 George Street, tel. 01225/314-418).

Seafoods Fish & Chips is respected by lovers of greasy fried fish. There's diner-style and outdoor seating, or you can get your food to go (£5-7 takeaway meals, Mon-Wed 11:30-21:00, Thu-Sat 11:30-22:00, Sun 12:00-19:00, 38 Kingsmead Square, tel. 01225/465-190).

The Cornish Bakehouse has freshly-baked £3 takeaway pasties (Mon-Sat 8:30-17:30, Sun 10:00-17:00, kitty-corner from Marks & Spencer at 1 Lower Borough Walls, second location off High Street at 11A The Corridor, tel. 01225/426-635).

Chain Eateries at Milsom Place: A pleasant hidden courtyard holds several dependable chain eateries: **Yo! Sushi, Jamie's Italian,** and French-themed **Côte Brasserie.**

Supermarkets: **Waitrose** is great for picnics and has a good salad bar (Mon-Sat 7:30-21:00, Sun 11:00-17:00, just west of Pulteney Bridge and across from post office on High Street). **Marks & Spencer,** near the bottom end of town, has a grocery at the back of its department store and two eateries: **M&S Kitchen** on the ground floor and the pleasant, inexpensive **Café Revive** on the top floor (Mon-Sat 8:00-19:00, Sun 11:00-17:00, 16 Stall Street). **Sainsbury's Local,** across the street from the bus station, has the longest hours (daily 7:00-23:00, 2 Dorchester Street).

Bath Connections

Bath's train station is called Bath Spa (tel. 0345-748-4959). The National Express bus station is just west of the train station (bus info tel. 0871-781-8181, www.nationalexpress.com). For all public bus services in southwestern England, see www.travelinesw.com.

From Bath to London: You can catch a **train** to London's Paddington Station (2/hour, 1.5 hours, best deals for travel after 9:30 and when purchased in advance, www.firstgreatwestern.co.uk), or save money—but not time—by taking the National Express **bus** to Victoria Coach Station (direct buses nearly hourly, 3.5 hours, avoid those with layover in Bristol, one-way-£5-12, round-trip-£10-18, cheapest to purchase online several days in advance).

Connecting Bath with London's Airports: To get to or from **Heathrow,** it's fastest and most pleasant to take the **train via London;** with a Britrail pass it's also the cheapest option, as the whole trip is covered. Without a rail pass, it's the most expensive way to go (£60 total for off-peak travel without rail pass, £10-20 cheaper bought in advance, up to £60 more for full-fare peak-time ticket; 2/hour, 2.25 hours depending on airport terminal, easy change between First Great Western train and Heathrow Express at London's Paddington Station). The **National Express bus** is direct, and often much cheaper for those without a rail pass, but it's relatively infrequent, and can take nearly twice as long as the train (nearly hourly, 3-3.5 hours, £24-40 one-way depending on time of day, tel. 0871-781-8181, www.nationalexpress.com). Doing a **train-and-bus combination** via the town of Reading can make sense for travelers without a rail pass, as it's more frequent, can take less time than the direct bus—allow 2.5 hours total—and can be much cheaper than the train via London (RailAir Link shuttle bus to Reading: 2-3/hour, 45 minutes; train from Reading to Bath: 2/hour, 1 hour; £31-41 for off-peak, nonrefundable travel booked in advance—but up to double for peak-time trains; tel. 0118-957-9425, buy bus ticket from www.railair.com, train ticket from www.firstgreatwestern.co.uk). Another option is the **minibus** operated by recommended tour company Celtic Horizons (see page 245).

You can get to **Gatwick** by train with a transfer in Reading (hourly, 3 hours, £55-75 one-way depending on time of day, cheaper in advance; avoid transfer in London, where you'll have to change stations; www.firstgreatwestern.co.uk) or by bus with a transfer at Heathrow (6/day, 4 hours, about £30 one-way, transfer at Heathrow Airport, www.nationalexpress.com).

Connecting Bath and Bristol Airport: Located about 20 miles west of Bath, this airport is closer than Heathrow and has good connections by bus. From Bristol Airport, your most convenient option is the Bristol Air Decker bus #A4 (£14, 2/hour, 1.25 hours, www.airdecker.com). Otherwise, you can take a taxi (£40) or call Celtic Horizons (see page 245).

From Bath by Train to: Salisbury (1-2/hour, 1 hour), **Moreton-in-Marsh** (hourly, 3 hours, 1-2 transfers), **York** (hourly with transfer in Bristol, 4.5 hours, more with additional transfers), **Cardiff** (hourly, 1-1.5 hours), and **points north** (via Birmingham, a major transportation hub, trains depart for Scotland and North Wales; use a train/bus combination to reach Ironbridge Gorge and the Lake District).

From Bath by Bus to: Salisbury (hourly, 3 hours; or National Express #300 at 17:05, 1.5 hours), **Stratford-upon-Avon** (1/day, 4 hours, transfer in Bristol). For bus connections to **Glastonbury, Avebury,** and **Wells,** see the next chapter.

NEAR BATH

Glastonbury • Wells • Avebury • Stonehenge • Salisbury • South Wales

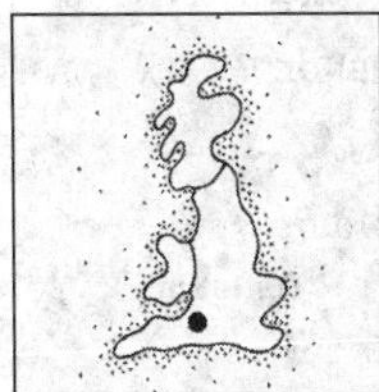

Ooooh, mystery, history. The countryside surrounding Bath holds some of England's most goose-pimply prehistoric sites, as well as two particularly fine cathedral towns. Glastonbury (perhaps a.k.a. Avalon) is the ancient resting place of King Arthur, and home (maybe) to the Holy Grail. Nearby, medieval Wells gathers around its grand cathedral, where you can enjoy an evensong service. Then get Neolithic at every druid's favorite stone circles, Avebury and Stonehenge. Salisbury is known for its colorful markets and soaring cathedral.

An hour west of Bath, Cardiff (Wales' capital) has polished off its former rust-belt vibe to become a bustling, people-friendly city. At the nearby St. Fagans National History Museum, you'll find South Wales' story vividly told in a park full of restored houses. Relish the romantic ruins and poetic wax of Tintern Abbey and the lush Wye River Valley.

PLANNING YOUR TIME

In England: Avebury, Glastonbury, and Wells make a wonderful day out from Bath. With a car, you can do all three in a day if you're selective with your sightseeing in each town (no lingering). If you want to squeeze a little less into each day, choose either the sights to the west (Wells and Glastonbury), or those to the east (Avebury, Stonehenge, and Salisbury).

Everybody needs to see

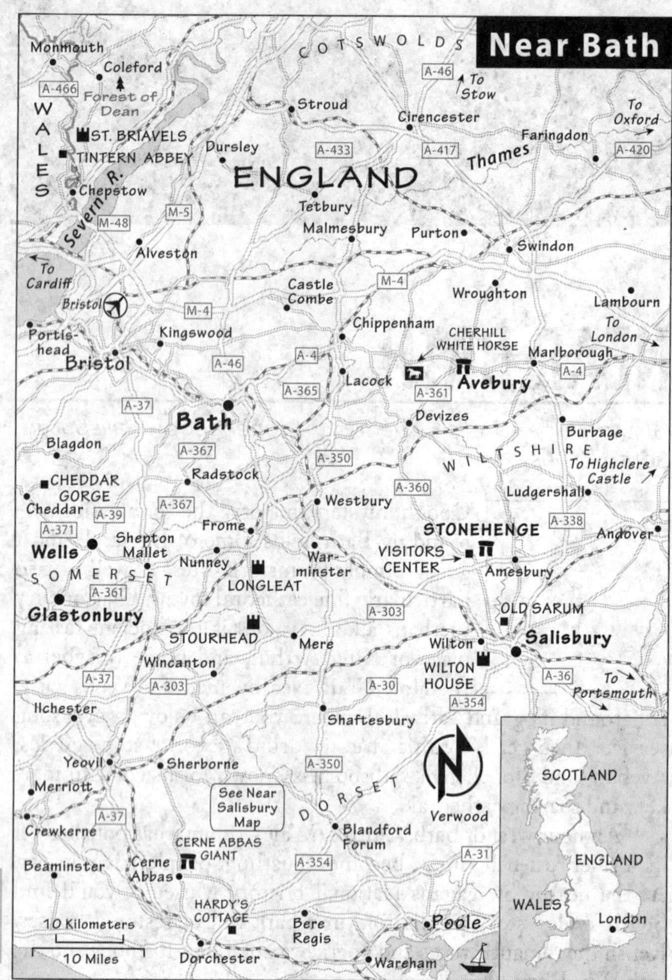

Stonehenge, but I'll tell you now: It looks just like it looks. You'll know what I mean when you pay to get in and rub up against the rope fence that keeps tourists at a distance. **Avebury** is the connoisseur's stone circle: more subtle and welcoming.

Wells is simply a cute small town, much smaller and more medieval than Bath, with a uniquely beautiful cathedral that's best experienced at the 17:15 evensong service (Sun at 15:00)—though the service isn't usually held in July and August.

Glastonbury can be covered well in two to three hours: See the abbey, climb the tor, and ponder your hippie past (and where you are now).

Just an hour from Bath, **Salisbury** makes a pleasant stop, particularly on a market day (Tue, Sat, every other Wed, plus more), though its cathedral is striking any time. Salisbury is also the logical launchpad for visiting nearby Stonehenge (particularly if you lack a car).

In Wales: Think of the South Wales sights as a different grouping. Ideally, they fill the day you leave Bath for the Cotswolds. Anyone interested in Welsh culture can spend four hours in St. Fagans National History Museum. Or for an urban Welsh experience, visit Cardiff. Castle lovers and romantics will want to consider seeing Tintern Abbey and the castles of Caerphilly and Chepstow (Caerphilly is best).

For a great day in South Wales, consider this schedule:

9:00 Leave Bath for South Wales.
10:30 Tour St. Fagans or visit Cardiff.
14:30 Leave for Tintern Abbey and/or a castle of your choice, then drive to the Cotswolds.
18:00 Set up in your Cotswolds home base.

GETTING AROUND THE REGION

By Car: Drivers can do a 133-mile loop, from Bath to Avebury (25 miles) to Stonehenge (30 miles) to Glastonbury (50 miles) to Wells (6 miles) and back to Bath (22 miles). A loop from Bath to South Wales is 100 miles, mostly on the 70-mph motorway. Each of the Welsh sights is just off the motorway.

By Bus and Train: Wells and Glastonbury are both easily accessible by bus from Bath. Bus #173 goes direct from Bath to **Wells** (nearly hourly, less frequent on Sun, 1.5 hours), where you can continue on to **Glastonbury** by catching a bus (#375/#376/#377, #29, or #37, 3-4/hour, 25 minutes, drops off directly in front of abbey entrance on Magdalene Street). Note that there are no direct buses between Bath and Glastonbury. First Bus Company offers a £7 day pass that covers all their routes—a good deal if you plan on connecting Glastonbury and Wells from your Bath home base. Wells and Glastonbury are also connected to each other by a 10-mile foot and bike path (unfortunately neither town offers bike rental).

Many different buses run between Bath and **Avebury,** all requiring one or two transfers (hourly, 2.5 hours, transfer at Trowbridge or Devizes). There is no bus between Avebury and Stonehenge.

A one-hour train trip connects Bath to **Salisbury** (1-2/hour). With the best public transportation of all these towns, Salisbury is a good jumping-off point for Stonehenge or Avebury by bus or car. The Stonehenge Tour runs buses between Salisbury, Old Sarum, and Stonehenge (see page 317). Buses also run from Salisbury to Avebury (hourly, 2-2.5 hours; transfer in Devizes or Marlborough).

Various bus companies run these routes, including Stage-

Near Bath at a Glance

Glastonbury

▲▲Glastonbury Abbey Once a leading Christian pilgrimage destination, now a lush park with some of England's finest abbey ruins—along with the purported gravesite of Arthur and Guinevere. **Hours:** Daily June-Aug 9:00-20:00, Sept-Nov and March-May 9:00-18:00, Dec-Feb 9:00-16:00. See page 285.

▲Glastonbury Tor Holy hill topped with the remnants of a church tower and worth climbing for its sweeping views. **Hours:** Always open. See page 288.

Wells

▲▲Wells Cathedral England's first wholly Gothic cathedral, with an ornate facade and heavenly evensong service (except July-Aug). **Hours:** Daily Easter-Sept 7:00-19:00, Oct-Easter 7:00-18:00. See page 292.

▲Bishop's Palace Home of the Bishop of Bath and Wells, with spectacular gardens. **Hours:** Daily April-Oct 10:00-18:00, Nov-March 10:00-16:00, often closed on Sat for special events. See page 297.

Avebury

▲▲Avebury Stone Circle Giant stone circle, 16 times the size of Stonehenge—but with a fraction of the tourists. **Hours:** Always open. See page 301.

▲Ritual Procession Way Double line of stones that once served as a route for ritual processions. **Hours:** Always open. See page 304.

▲Silbury Hill Pyramid-shaped chalk mound—and the largest man-made object from prehistoric Europe. **Hours:** Always viewable. See page 304.

Stonehenge and Salisbury

▲▲Stonehenge England's most famous stone circle, unique for

coach, Bodmans Coaches, the First Bus Company, and Wilts & Dorset. To find fare information, check with Traveline South West, which combines all the information from these companies into an easy-to-use website that covers all the southwest routes (www.travelinesw.com, tel. 0871-200-2233). Buses run much less frequently on Sundays.

its horizontal stones. **Hours:** Daily June-Aug 9:00-20:00, mid-March-May and Sept-mid-Oct 9:30-19:00, mid-Oct-mid-March 9:30-17:00. See page 313.

▲▲Salisbury Cathedral Architecturally harmonious Gothic cathedral, boasting the tallest spire in England, surrounded by a huge, peaceful green. **Hours:** Mon-Sat 9:00-17:00, Sun 12:00-16:00. See page 317.

▲The Salisbury Museum Random collection of costumes, art, ceramics, and other historical items, plus a fine exhibit about Stonehenge. **Hours:** Mon-Sat 10:00-17:00, Sun 12:00-17:00 except closed Sun Oct-May. See page 320.

South Wales

▲Cardiff Castle Sumptuous castle with a fanciful Victorian-era makeover, plus WWII tunnels, museum, and expansive walled grounds. **Hours:** Daily March-Oct 9:00-18:00, Nov-Feb 9:00-17:00. See page 329.

▲▲Cardiff Bay People-friendly, rejuvenated harborfront brimming with major attractions, striking architecture, entertainment, and dining options. **Hours:** Public areas always open. See page 335.

▲▲St. Fagans National History Museum One hundred acres dedicated to Welsh folk life, including a museum, castle, and more than 40 reconstructed houses demonstrating bygone Welsh ways. **Hours:** Daily 10:00-17:00. See page 339.

▲▲Caerphilly Castle Britain's second-largest castle, featuring a leaning tower inhabited by a heartbroken ghost. **Hours:** March-Oct daily 9:30-17:00, July-Aug until 18:00; Nov-Feb Mon-Sat 10:00-16:00, Sun 11:00-16:00. See page 342.

▲▲Tintern Abbey Remains of a Cistercian abbey that once inspired William Wordsworth and J. M. W. Turner. **Hours:** March-Oct daily 9:30-17:00, July-Aug until 18:00; Nov-Feb Mon-Sat 10:00-16:00, Sun 11:00-16:00. See page 347.

To get to **South Wales** from Bath, take a train to Cardiff, then connect by bus (or train) to the sights.

By Tour: From Bath, if you don't have a car, the most convenient and quickest way to see Avebury and Stonehenge is to take an all-day bus tour or a half-day tour just to Stonehenge. Mad

Max is the liveliest of the tours leaving from Bath (see "Tours in and near Bath" on page 244).

Glastonbury

Marked by its hill, or "tor," and located on England's most powerful line of prehistoric sites, the town of Glastonbury gurgles with history and mystery.

In A.D. 37, Joseph of Arimathea—Jesus' wealthy uncle—reputedly brought vessels containing the blood of Jesus to Glastonbury, and with him, Christianity came to England. (Joseph's visit is plausible—long before Christ, locals traded lead and tin to merchants from the Levant.)

While this story is "proven" by fourth-century writings and accepted by the Church, the King-Arthur-and-the-Holy-Grail legends it inspired are not. Those medieval tales came when England needed a morale-boosting folk hero for inspiration during a war with France. They pointed to the ancient Celtic sanctuary at Glastonbury as proof enough of the greatness of the fifth-century warlord Arthur. In 1191, after a huge fire, Arthur's supposed remains (along with those of Queen Guinevere) were dug up from the abbey garden. Reburied in the abbey choir, Arthur and Guinevere's gravesite is a shrine today. Many think the Grail trail ends at the bottom of the Chalice Well, a natural spring at the base of the Glastonbury Tor.

By the 10th century, Glastonbury Abbey was England's most powerful and wealthy, and was part of a nationwide network of monasteries that by 1500 owned one-quarter of all English land and had four times the income of the Crown. Then Henry VIII dissolved the abbeys in 1536. He was particularly harsh on Glastonbury—he not only destroyed the abbey but also hung and quartered the abbot, sending the parts of his body on four different national tours...at the same time. This was meant as a warning to other religious clerics, and it worked.

But Glastonbury rebounded. In an 18th-century tourism campaign, thousands signed affidavits stating that they'd been healed by water from the Chalice Well, and once again Glastonbury was on the tourist map. Today, Glastonbury and its tor are a center for "searchers"—too creepy for the mainstream Church but

just right for those looking for a place to recharge their crystals. Glastonbury is also synonymous with its music and arts festival, an annual long-hair-and-mud Woodstock re-creation that's a rite of passage for young music lovers in Britain.

Part of the fun of a visit to Glastonbury is just being in a town where every other shop and eatery is a New Age place. Locals who are not into this complain that on High Street, you can buy any kind of magic crystal or incense—but not a roll of TP. But, as this counterculture is their town's bread and butter, they do their best to sit in their pubs and go "Ommmmm."

Orientation to Glastonbury

TOURIST INFORMATION

The TI is on High Street—as are many of the dreadlocked folks who walk it. It occupies a fine 15th-century townhouse called The Tribunal (Mon-Sat 10:00-16:00, closed Sun, shorter hours in winter, 9 High Street, tel. 01458/832-954, www.glastonburytic.co.uk). The TI sells several booklets about cycling and walking in the area, including the *Glastonbury and Street Guide*, with local listings and a map (£1); and the *Glastonbury Millennium Trail* pamphlet, which sends visitors on a historical scavenger hunt, following 20 numbered marble plaques embedded in the pavement throughout the town (£1).

Above the TI is the marginally interesting **Lake Village Museum,** with two humble rooms featuring tools made of stones, bones, and antlers. Preserved in and excavated from the local peat bogs, these tools offer a look at the lives of marshland people. In pre-Roman times, these ancients chose to live in the shadow of a mystical hill crossed by two equally mystical "ley lines"—supposed energy paths that circle the globe (£3.50, extensive descriptions, same hours as TI, tel. 01458/832-954).

HELPFUL HINTS

Market Day: Tuesday is market day for crafts, knickknacks, and local produce on the main street. There's also a country market Tuesday mornings in the Town Hall.

Glastonbury Festival: Nearly every summer (around the June solstice), the gigantic Glastonbury Festival—billing itself as the "largest music and performing arts festival in the world"—

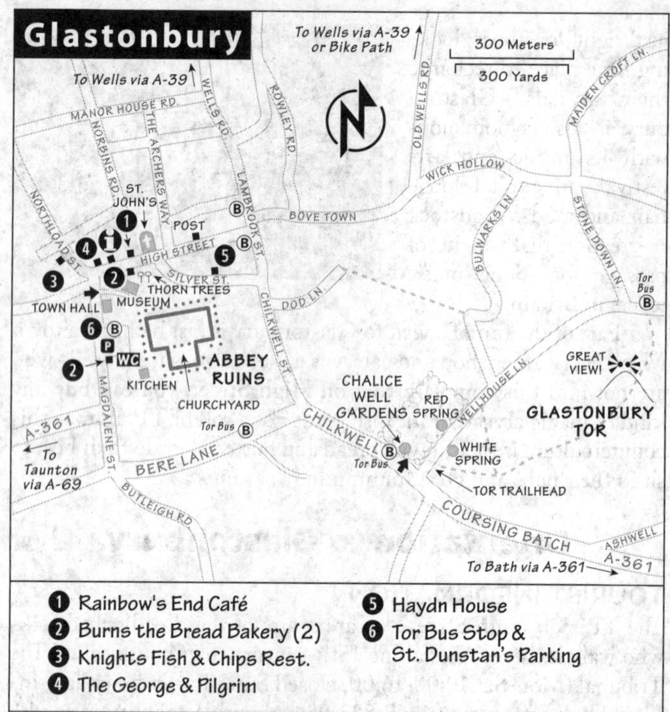

brings all manner of postmodern flower children to its notoriously muddy "Healing Fields." Music fans and London's beautiful people make the trek to see the hottest British and American bands. If you're near Glastonbury during the festival, anticipate increased traffic and crowds (especially on public transportation; more than 165,000 tickets generally sell out), even though the actual music venue—practically a temporary city of its own—is six miles east of town (www.glastonburyfestivals.co.uk).

Sights in Glastonbury

I've listed these sights in the order you'll reach them, moving from the town center to the tor.

Glastonbury Town

The tiny town itself is worth a pleasant stroll. The abbey came first, and Glastonbury grew up to serve it. For example, the George and Pilgrim Hotel was originally a freestanding structure built in the 15th century to house pilgrims. And St. John's Church, which dates from the same century, was constructed to give townsfolk a place to worship, as they weren't allowed in the abbey. The Market Cross at the base of High Street dates from around 1800.

Though Glastonbury is much older, its character dates to 1970, when the town hosted its first rock festival. Like Woodstock, it was held on a farm. Unlike Woodstock, the Glastonbury Festival had legs—it's held annually on the same farm. Perhaps the most "authentic" hippie or New Age shop in town is the Gothic Image bookshop, which also dates back to the 1970s (7 High Street, next to the George and Pilgrim Hotel).

▲▲Glastonbury Abbey

The massive and evocative ruins of the first Christian sanctuary in the British Isles stand mysteriously alive in a lush 36-acre park.

Because it comes with a small museum, a dramatic history, and enthusiastic guides dressed in period costumes, this is one of the most engaging to visit of England's many ruined abbeys.

Cost and Hours: £7.60, daily June-Aug 9:00-20:00, Sept-Nov and March-May 9:00-18:00, Dec-Feb 9:00-16:00.

Getting There: Enter the abbey from Magdalene Street (around the corner from High Street, near the St. Dunstan's parking lot). Pay parking is nearby.

Information: Tel. 01458/832-267, www.glastonburyabbey.com.

Tours and Demonstrations: Costumed guides offer 30-minute tours (generally daily March-Oct on the hour from 10:00). As you enter, confirm these times, and ask about other tour and show times.

Eating: Picnicking is encouraged—bring something from one of the shops in town (see "Eating in Glastonbury," later), or buy food at the small café on site (open May-Sept).

Background: The space that these ruins occupy has been sacred ground for centuries. The druids used it as a pagan holy site, and during Joseph of Arimathea's supposed visit here, he built a simple place of worship. In the 12th century—because of that legendary connection—Glastonbury was the leading Christian pilgrimage site in all of Britain. The popular abbey grew powerful and very wealthy, employing a thousand people to serve the needs of the pilgrims.

In 1184, there was a devastating fire in the monastery, and in 1191, the abbot here "discovered"—with the help of a divine dream—the tomb and bodies of King Arthur and Queen Guinevere. Of course, this discovery boosted the pilgrim trade in Glastonbury, and the new revenues helped to rebuild the abbey.

Then, in 1539, King Henry VIII ordered the abbey's destruction. When Glastonbury Abbot Richard Whiting questioned the king's decision, he was branded a traitor, hung at the top of Glastonbury Tor (after carrying up the plank that would support his noose), and his body cut into four pieces. His head was stuck over the gateway to the former abbey precinct. After this harsh example, the other abbots accepted the king's dissolution of England's abbeys, with many returning to monastic centers in France. Glastonbury Abbey was destroyed. With the roof removed, it fell into ruin and was used as a quarry.

Today, the abbey attracts both the curious and pious. Tie-dyed, starry-eyed pilgrims seem to float through the grounds, naturally high. Others lie on the grave of King Arthur, whose burial site is marked off in the center of the abbey ruins.

➲ **Self-Guided Tour:** After buying your ticket, pick up a map and tour the informative **museum** at the entrance building. A model shows the abbey in its pre-Henry VIII splendor, and exhibits tell the story of a place "grandly constructed to entice the dullest minds to prayer." Knowledgeable costumed guides are eager to share the site's story and might even offer an impromptu tour.

Next, head out to explore the green park, dotted with bits of the **ruined abbey.** You come face-to-face with the abbey's Lady Chapel, the site of first wattle-and-daub church, possibly dating to the first century. Today, the crypt is dug out and exposed; posted information helps you imagine its 12th-century splendor.

The Lady Chapel became the abbey's west entry when the church expanded. The abbey was long and skinny, but vast. Measuring 580 feet, it was the longest in Britain (larger than York Minster is today) and Europe's largest building north of the Alps.

Before poking around the ruins, circle to the left behind the entrance building to find the two **thorn trees.** According to legend, when Joseph of Arimathea came here, he climbed nearby Wearyall Hill and stuck his staff into the soil. A thorn tree sprouted, and its descendant still stands there today; the trees here in the abbey are its offspring. In 2010, vandals hacked off the branches of the original tree on Wearyall Hill, but miraculously, the stump put out small green shoots the following spring. The trees inside the abbey grounds bloom twice a year, at Easter and at Christmas. If the story seems far-fetched to you, don't tell the Queen—a blossom from the abbey's trees sits proudly on her breakfast table every Christmas morning.

Ahead and to the left of the trees, inside what was the north wall, look for two trap doors in the ground. Lift up the doors to see surviving fragments of the abbey's original tiled floor.

Now hike through the remains of the ruined complex to the far end of the abbey. You can stand and, from what was the altar, look down at what was the gangly nave. Envision the longest church nave in England. In this area, you'll find the tombstone (formerly in the floor of the church's choir) marking the spot where the supposed relics of **Arthur and Guinevere** were interred.

Continue around the far side of the abbey ruins, feeling free to poke around the park.

Head for the only surviving intact building on the grounds—the abbot's conical **kitchen,** with a humble exhibit about life in the abbey.

NEAR GLASTONBURY TOR

These sights are about a 15-minute walk from the town center, toward the tor (see "Getting There," on page 288).

Chalice Well Gardens

According to tradition, Joseph of Arimathea brought the chalice from the Last Supper to Glastonbury in A.D. 37. Supposedly it ended up in the bottom of a well, which is now the centerpiece of a peaceful and inviting garden. Even if the chalice is not in the bottom of the well (another legend says it made the trip to Wales), and the water is red from iron ore and not Jesus' blood, the tranquil setting is one where nature's harmony is a joy to ponder. To find the well itself, follow the well-marked path uphill alongside the gurgling stream, passing several places to drink from or wade in the healing water, as well as areas designated for silent reflection. The stones of the well shaft date from the 12th century and are believed to have come from the church in Glastonbury Abbey (which was destroyed by fire). During the 18th century, pilgrims flocked to Glastonbury for the well's healing powers. Have a drink or take some of the precious water home—they sell empty bottles to fill.

Cost and Hours: £4, daily April-Oct 10:00-18:00, Nov-

March 10:00-16:30, on Chilkwell Street/A-361, tel. 01458/831-154, www.chalicewell.org.uk.

Red and White Spring Waters

Two waterspouts with free, cool, refreshing water are just around the corner from the Chalice Well Gardens entrance (just beyond the trailhead to the tor, where the bus drops off). The spout on the Chalice Well side comes from the Red Spring; the other spout's source is the White Spring. Try both and see which you prefer.

▲Glastonbury Tor

Seen by many as a Mother Goddess symbol, the Glastonbury Tor—a natural plug of sandstone on clay—has an undeniable geological charisma. Climbing the tor is the essential activity on a visit to Glastonbury. A fine Somerset view rewards those who hike to its 520-foot summit.

Getting There: The tor is a steep hill at the southeastern edge of the town (it's visible from just about everywhere). The base of the tor is a 20-minute **walk** from the TI and town center. From the base, a trail leads up to the top (figure another 15-20 uphill minutes, if you keep a brisk pace). While you can hike up the tor from either end, the less-steep approach (which most people take) starts next to the Chalice Well.

If you're without a car and don't want to walk to the tor trailhead, you have two options: The **Tor Bus** shuttles visitors from the town center to the base of the tor, stopping at the Chalice Well en route (£3 round-trip, 2/hour, departs from St. Dunstan's parking lot next to the abbey on the half-hour, Easter-Sept daily 10:00-12:30 & 14:00-17:00, doesn't run Oct-Easter). If you have a **car,** you won't find any parking nearby so expect a bit of a hike. A **taxi** to the tor trailhead costs about £5 one-way—an easier and more economical choice for couples or groups. Remember, these take you only to the bottom of the tor; to reach the top, you have to hike.

A good plan is to ride the shuttle bus to the tor, climb to the top, hike down, drop by Chalice Well Gardens, and stroll back into town from there.

Climbing the Tor: Hiking up to the top of the tor, you can survey the surrounding land—a former swamp, inhabited for 12,000 years, which is still below sea level at high tide. Up until the 11th century you could actually sail to the tower. The ribbon-like man-made drainage canals that glisten as they slice through the farmland are the work of Dutch engineers—Huguenot refugees imported centuries ago to turn the marshy wasteland into something arable.

Looking out, find Glastonbury (at the base of the hill) and Wells (marked by its cathedral) to the right. Above Wells, a TV tower marks the 996-foot high point of the Mendip Hills. It was lead from these hills that attracted the ancient Romans (and, perhaps, Jesus' uncle Joe) so long ago. Stretching to the left, the Mendip Hills define what was the coastline before those Dutch engineers arrived.

The tor-top tower is the remnant of a chapel dedicated to St. Michael. Early Christians often employed St. Michael, the warrior angel, to combat pagan gods. When a church was built upon a pagan holy ground like this, it was frequently dedicated to Michael. But apparently those pagan gods fought back: St. Michael's Church was destroyed by an earthquake in 1275.

Eating in Glastonbury

These restaurants are on or near High Street.

Rainbow's End is one of several fine, healthy, vegetarian lunch cafés for hot meals (different every day), salads, herbal teas, soups, yummy homemade sweets, and New Age people-watching. If you're looking for a midwife or a male-bonding tribal meeting, check their notice board (£6-8 meals, cheaper salads sold by the portion, vegan and gluten-free options, counter service, daily 10:00-16:00, a few doors up from the TI, 17 High Street, tel. 01458/833-896).

Burns the Bread has two locations in town, making hearty pasties (savory meat pies) as well as fresh pies, sandwiches, delicious cookies, and pastries. Ask for a sample of the Torsy Moorsy Cake (a type of fruitcake made with cheddar), or try a gingerbread man made with real ginger. Grab a pasty and picnic with the ghosts of Arthur and Guinevere in the abbey ruins (£1-2 pasties and pastries, £2-3 sandwiches, Mon-Sat 6:00-17:00, Sun 11:00-17:00, main location at 14 High Street; smaller shop in St. Dunstan's parking lot next to the abbey, tel. 01458/831-532).

Knights Fish and Chips Restaurant has been in the same family since 1909 and is the town's top chippy. It's another fine option for a picnic at the abbey (£6 to go, about £1 more for table service, Mon-Sat 12:00-21:30, Sun 12:00-19:30, closed Sun off-season, 5 Northload Street, tel. 01458/831-882, Kevin and Charlotte).

The George & Pilgrim Hotel's wonderfully Old World pub might be exactly what the doctor ordered for visitors suffering a New Age overdose. The local owners serve up a traditional pub-grub menu (£5-6 sandwiches, £8-12 meals, food served daily 12:00-14:45 & 18:00-20:45, 1 High Street, tel. 01458/831-146). They also rent rooms (Db-£80-90, family rooms-£85-95).

Sleeping in Glastonbury: **$ Haydn House** rents several rooms in a centrally located 19th-century red-brick house (D-£65, Db-£70-85, Tb-£120, 13a Silver Street, tel. 01458/834-771, www.hhglastonbury.com, haydnhouseglastonbury@gmail.com, Sharon and Jon).

Glastonbury Connections

The nearest train station is in Bath. Local buses are run by First Bus Company (tel. 0845-602-0156, www.firstgroup.com).

From Glastonbury by Bus to: Wells (3-4/hour, 25 minutes, bus #375/#376/#377, #29, or #37), **Bath** (nearly hourly, allow 2 hours, take bus Wells, transfer to bus #173 to Bath, 1.5 hours between Wells and Bath). Buses are sparse on Sundays (generally one bus every other hour). If you're heading to points west, you'll likely connect through **Taunton** (which is a transfer point for westbound buses from Bristol).

Wells

Because this well-preserved little town has a cathedral, it can be called a city. It's England's smallest cathedral city (pop. just under 12,000), with one of its most interesting cathedrals and a wonderful evensong service (generally not offered July-Aug). Wells has more medieval buildings still doing what they were originally built to do than any town you'll visit, and you can still spot a number of the wells, water, and springs that helped give the town its name. Market day fills the town square on Wednesday (farmers' market) and Saturday (general goods).

Orientation to Wells

TOURIST INFORMATION

The TI is in the lobby of the Wells Museum, across the green from the cathedral. Consider purchasing their town map for £0.50, or the £1 *Wells City Trail* booklet (April-Oct Mon-Sat 10:00-17:00, Nov-March Mon-Sat 11:00-16:00, closed Sun year-round, 8 Cathedral Green, tel. 01749/671-770, www.wellssomerset.com). Ask TI staff about one-hour walking tours of town for £6 on Wednesdays at 11:00 (www.wellswalkingtours.co.uk). The TI's attached museum houses displays on the archaeology and geology of nearby

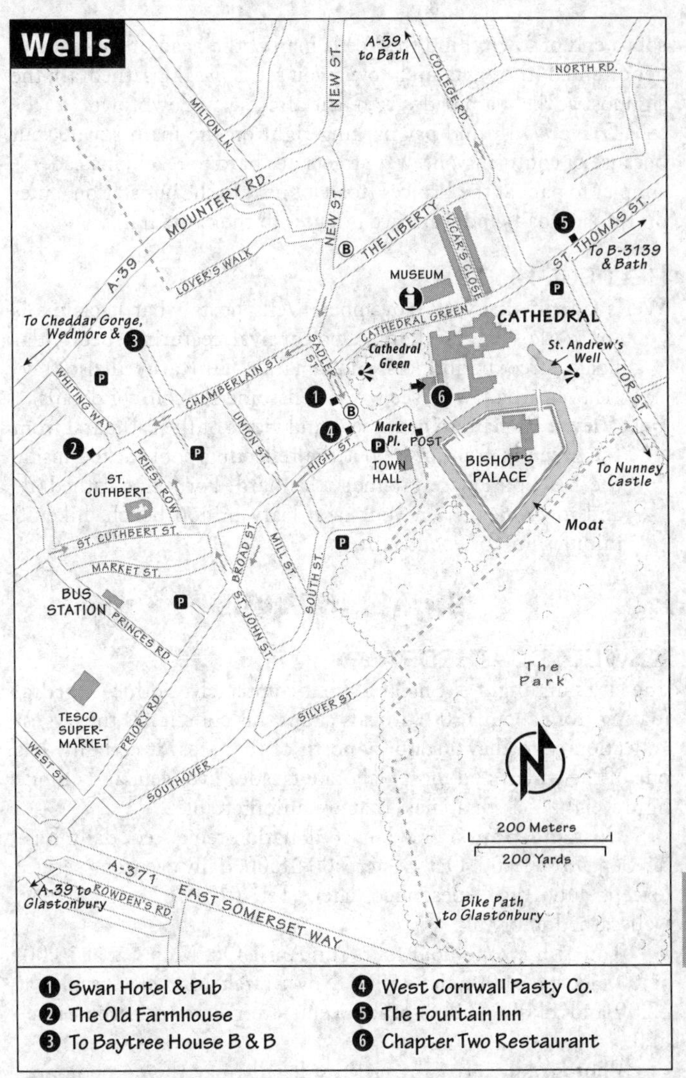

Mendip Hills and Wookey Caves, along with an exhibit on World War I (£3, same hours as TI).

ARRIVAL IN WELLS

If you're coming by **bus,** you can get off in the city center at the Sadler Street stop, around the corner from the cathedral (tell the driver that's your stop). Or you can disembark at the big, well-organized bus station/parking lot (staffed Mon-Fri 9:30-13:30, closed Sat-Sun), about a five-minute walk from the town center at the south end of town. Find the Wells map at the head of the stalls to get oriented (the big church tower you see is *not* the cathedral); the signpost at the main pedestrian exit directs you downtown.

Drivers will find pay parking right on the main square, but because of confusing one-way streets, it's hard to reach; instead, it's simpler to park at the Princes Road lot next to the bus station (enter on Priory Road) and walk five minutes to the cathedral.

HELPFUL HINTS

Wells Carnival: Every November Wells hosts what it claims is the world's biggest illuminated carnival, featuring spectacular floats, street performers, and a market fair (carnival also travels to nearby towns; see www.wellssomerset.com for details).

Best Views: It's hard to beat the grand views of the cathedral from the green in front of it...but the reflecting pool tucked inside the Bishop's Palace grounds tries hard. For a fine cathedral-and-town view from your own leafy hilltop bench, hike 10 minutes up Torwoods Hill.

Sights in Wells

▲▲WELLS CATHEDRAL

The city's highlight is England's first completely Gothic cathedral (dating from about 1200). Locals claim this church has the largest collection of medieval statuary north of the Alps. It certainly has one of the widest and most elaborate facades I've seen, and unique figure-eight "scissor arches" that are unforgettable.

Cost and Hours: Free but £6 donation requested, daily Easter-Sept 7:00-19:00, Oct-Easter 7:00-18:00, daily evensong service (except July-Aug)—described later. Tel. 01749/674-483, www.wellscathedral.org.uk.

Tours: Free one-hour tours run April-Oct Mon-Sat at 10:00, 11:00, 13:00, 14:00, and 15:00; Nov-March Mon-Sat usually at 12:00 and 14:00—unless other events are going on in the cathedral.

Photography: To take pictures legally, pay the £4 photography fee at the info desk. No flash is allowed in the choir.

Eating: The handy Chapter Two restaurant is right by the entrance (described in "Eating in Wells," later).

➲ Self-Guided Tour:

Begin on the vast inviting **green** in front of the cathedral. In the Middle Ages, the cathedral was enclosed within "The Liberty," an area free from civil jurisdiction until the 1800s. The Liberty included the green on the west side of the cathedral, which, from the 13th to the 17th century, was a burial place for common folk, including 17th-century plague victims. The green became a cricket pitch, then a field for grazing animals and picnicking people. Today, it's the perfect spot to marvel at an impressive cathedral.

Peer up at the magnificent **facade.** The west front displays almost 300 original 13th-century carvings of kings and the Last Judgment. The bottom row of niches is empty, too easily reached by Cromwell's men, who were hell-bent on destroying "graven images." Stand back and imagine it as a grand Palm Sunday welcome with a cast of hundreds—all gaily painted back then, choristers singing boldly from holes above the doors and trumpets tooting through the holes up by the 12 apostles.

Now head **inside.** Visitors enter by going to the right, through the door under the small spire, into the lobby and welcome center.

At the **welcome center,** you'll be warmly greeted and reminded how expensive it is to maintain the cathedral. Pay the donation, buy a photo-permission sticker (if you want to take photos), and pick up a map of the cathedral's highlights. Then head through the cloister and into the cathedral.

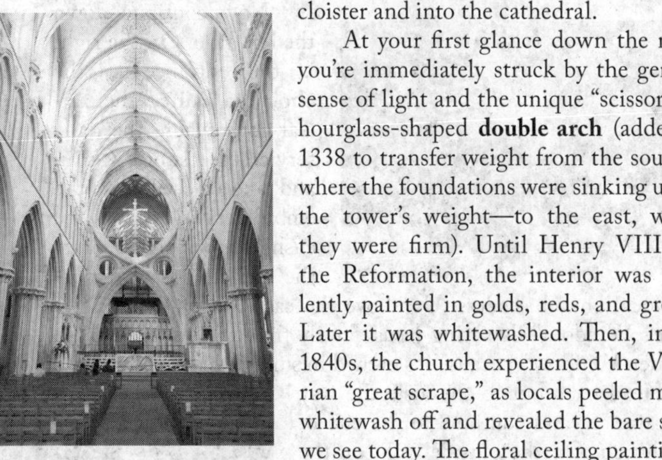

At your first glance down the nave, you're immediately struck by the general sense of light and the unique "scissors" or hourglass-shaped **double arch** (added in 1338 to transfer weight from the south—where the foundations were sinking under the tower's weight—to the east, where they were firm). Until Henry VIII and the Reformation, the interior was opulently painted in golds, reds, and greens. Later it was whitewashed. Then, in the 1840s, the church experienced the Victorian "great scrape," as locals peeled moldy whitewash off and revealed the bare stone we see today. The floral ceiling painting is based on the original medieval design: A single pattern was discovered under the 17th-century whitewash and repeated throughout.

Small, ornate, 15th-century pavilion-like chapels flank the altar, carved in lacy Gothic for church VIPs. The **pulpit** features a post-Reformation, circa-1540 English script—rather than the standard Latin (see where the stonemason ran out of space when carving the inscription—we've all been there). Since this was not a monastery church, the Reformation didn't destroy it as it did the Glastonbury Abbey church.

We'll do a quick clockwise spin around the cathedral's interior. First walk down the left aisle until you reach the north transept. The medieval **clock** does a silly but much-loved joust on the quarter-hour. If you get to watch the show, notice how—like clock-

work—the same rider gets clobbered, as he has for hundreds of years. The clock's face, which depicts the earth at the center of the universe, dates from 1390. The outer ring shows hours, the middle ring shows minutes, and the inner ring shows the dates of the month and phases of the moon. Up above in the right corner is Jack Blandiver, a chap carved out of wood in the 14th century. Beneath the clock, the fine **crucifix** (1947) was carved out of a yew tree. Also in the north transept is the door with well-worn steps leading up to the grand, fan-vaulted **Chapter House**—an inspiring architectural achievement and intimate place for the theological equivalent of a huddle among church officials.

Now continue down the left aisle. On the right is the entrance to the **choir** (or "quire," the central zone where the daily services are sung). Go in and take a close look at the embroidery work on the cushions, which celebrate the hometowns of important local church leaders. Up above the east end of the choir is "Jesse's Window," depicting Jesus' family tree. It's also called the "Golden Window," because it's bathed in sunlight each morning.

Head back out to the aisle the way you came in, and continue to the end of the church. On the outside wall, on the left, is the entry to the undercroft, now a cathedral history exhibit worth a look. In the apse you'll find the **Lady Chapel.** Examine the medieval stained-glass windows. Do they look jumbled? In the 17th century, Puritan troops trashed the precious original glass. Much was repaired, but many of the broken panes were like a puzzle that was never figured out. That's why today many of the windows are simply kaleidoscopes of colored glass.

Next to the chapel is the oldest piece of wooden furniture in England: a **"cope**

chest," which is still used to store the clergy's garments. It is so large it can't be moved out through any of the cathedral's doors. Historians theorize the chest is older than the existing building, and was originally installed around A.D. 800, in the Saxon church that predated the cathedral.

Now circle around and head up the other aisle. As you walk, notice that many of the black **tombstones** set in the floor have decorative recesses that aren't filled with brass (as they once were). After the Reformation in the 1530s, the church was short on cash, so they sold the brass lettering to raise money for roof repairs.

Once you reach the south transept, you'll find several items of interest. The **old Saxon font** survives from the previous church (A.D. 705) and has been the site of Wells baptisms for more than a thousand years. (Its carved arches were added by Normans in the 12th century, and the cover is from the 17th century.) In the far end of this transept (in the shade of the fancy chapels), a little of the original green and red wall painting, which wasn't whitewashed, survives.

Nearby, notice the **carvings** in the capitals of the freestanding pillars, with whimsical depictions of medieval life. On the first pillar, notice the man with a toothache and another man with a thorn in his foot. The second pillar tells a story of medieval justice: On the left, we see thieves stealing grapes; on the right, the woodcutter (with an axe) is warning the farmer (with the pitchfork) what's happening. Circle around to the back of the pillar for the rest of the story: On the left, the farmer chases one of the thieves, grabbing him by the ear. On the right, he clobbers the thief over the head with his pitchfork—so hard the farmer's hat falls off.

Also in the south transept, you'll find the entrance to the cathedral **Reading Room** (free, April-Oct Mon-Sat 11:00-13:00 & 14:30-16:30 only; it's often possible to step in for a quick look on weekday mornings and afternoons). Housing a few old manuscripts, it offers a peek into a real 15th-century library. At the back of the Reading Room, peer through the doors and notice the irons chaining the books to the shelves—a reflection perhaps of the trust in the clergy at that time.

Head out into the cloister, then cross the courtyard back to the welcome center, shop, Chapter Two restaurant, and exit. Go in peace.

MORE CATHEDRAL SIGHTS

▲▲Cathedral Evensong Service

The cathedral choir takes full advantage of heavenly acoustics with a nightly 45-minute evensong service. You'll sit right in the old "quire" as you listen to a great pipe organ and the world-famous Wells Cathedral choir.

Cost and Hours: Free, Mon-Sat at 17:15, Sun at 15:00, generally no service when school is out July-Aug unless a visiting choir performs, to check call 01749/674-483 or visit www.wellscathedral.org.uk. At 17:05 (Sun at 14:50), the verger ushers visitors to their seats. There's usually plenty of room.

Returning to Bath After the Evensong: Confirm the departure time for the last direct bus to Bath in advance—it's usually 18:45. If you need to catch the 17:40 bus instead, request a seat on the north side of the presbytery, so you can slip out the side door without disturbing the service (10-minute walk from cathedral to station, bus may also depart from The Liberty stop—a 4-minute walk away; your other option is a bus and train connection via Bristol—explained later, under "Wells Connections").

Other Cathedral Concerts: The cathedral also hosts several evening concerts each month (most about £20, generally Thu-Sat at 19:00 or 19:30, buy tickets by phone or at box office in cathedral gift shop; Mon-Sat 10:00-16:30, Sun 11:00-16:30; tel. 01749/672-773). Concert tickets are also sometimes available at the TI, along with pamphlets listing what's on.

Vicars' Close

Lined with perfectly pickled 14th-century houses, this is the oldest continuously occupied complete street in Europe (since 1348; just a block north of the cathedral—go under the big arch and look left). It was built to house the vicar's choir, and it still houses church officials and choristers. These dwellings were bachelor pads until the Reformation allowed clerics to marry; they were then redesigned to accommodate families. Notice how the

close gets narrower at the top, creating the illusion that it is a longer lane than it is. Notice also the elevated passageway connecting these choristers' quarters with the church.

▲Bishop's Palace

Next to the cathedral stands the moated Bishop's Palace, built in the 13th century and still in use today as the residence of the bishop of Bath and Wells. While the interior of the palace itself is dull, the grounds and gardens surrounding it are the most tranquil and scenic spot in Wells, with wonderful views of the cathedral. It's just the place for a relaxing walk in the park. Watch the swans ring the bell—hanging over the water just left of the entry gate—when they have an attack of the munchies.

Cost and Hours: £8; daily April-Oct 10:00-18:00, Nov-March 10:00-16:00, often closed on Sat for special events—call to confirm; multimedia guide £1; tel. 01749/988-111, www.bishopspalace.org.uk.

Visiting the Palace and Gardens: The palace's spring-fed moat was built in the 14th century to protect the bishop during squabbles with the borough. Bishops would generously release this potable water into the town during local festivals. Now the moat serves primarily as a pool for mute swans. The bridge was last drawn in 1831. Crossing that bridge, you'll buy your ticket and enter the grounds (past the old-timers playing a proper game of croquet—several times a week after 13:30). On your right, pass through the evocative ruins of the Great Hall (which was deserted and left to gradually deteriorate), and stroll through the chirpy south lawn. If you're feeling energetic, hike up to the top of the ramparts that encircle the property.

Circling around the far side of the mansion, walk through a door in the rampart wall, cross the wooden bridge, and follow a path to a smaller bridge and the wells (springs) that gave the city its name. Surrounding a reflecting pool with the cathedral towering overhead, these flower-bedecked pathways are idyllic. Nearby are an arboretum, picnic area, and sweet little pea-patch gardens.

After touring the gardens, the mansion's interior is a letdown—despite the borrowable descriptions that struggle to make the dusty old place meaningful. Have a spot of tea in the café (with outdoor garden seating—free access), or climb the creaky wooden staircase to wander long halls lined with portraits of bishops past.

NEAR WELLS

The following stops are best for drivers.

Cheddar Cheese

If you're in the mood for a picnic, drop by any local aromatic cheese shop for a great selection of tasty Somerset cheeses. Real farmhouse cheddar puts Velveeta to shame. The **Cheddar Gorge Cheese Company,** eight miles west of Wells, gives guests a chance to see the cheese-making process and enjoy a sample (£2, daily 10:00-15:30; take the A-39, then the A-371 to Cheddar Gorge; tel. 01934/742-810, www.cheddargorgecheeseco.co.uk).

Scrumpy Farms

Scrumpy is the wonderfully dangerous hard cider brewed in this part of England. You don't find it served in many pubs because of the unruly crowd it attracts. Scrumpy, at 8 percent alcohol, will rot your socks—this is potent stuff. "Scrumpy Jack," carbonated mass-produced cider, is not real scrumpy. The real stuff is "rough farmhouse cider." It's said some farmers throw a side of beef into the vat, and when fermentation is done only the teeth remain. (Some use a pair of old boots, for the tannin from the leather.)

TIs list cider farms open to the public, such as **Mr. Wilkins' Land's End Cider Farm,** a great Back Door travel experience (free, Mon-Sat 10:00-20:00, Sun 10:00-13:00; west of Wells in Mudgley, take the B-3139 from Wells to Wedmore, then the B-3151 south for 2 miles, farm is a quarter-mile off the B-3151—tough to find, get close and ask locals; tel. 01934/712-385, www.wilkinscider.com).

Apples are pressed from August through December. Hard cider, while not quite scrumpy, is also typical of the West Country, but more fashionable, "decent," and accessible. You can get a pint of hard cider at nearly any pub, drawn straight from the barrel—dry, medium, or sweet.

Nunney Castle

The centerpiece of the charming and quintessentially English village of Nunney (between Bath and Glastonbury, off the A-361) is a striking 14th-century castle surrounded by a fairy-tale moat. Its rare, French-style design brings to mind the Paris Bastille. The year 1644 was a tumultuous one for Nunney. Its noble family was royalist (and likely closet Catholics). They defied Parliament, so

Sleep Code

Abbreviations **(£1=about $1.60, country code: 44)**
S=Single, **D**=Double/Twin, **T**=Triple, **Q**=Quad, **b**=bathroom
Price Rankings
$$ Higher Priced—Most rooms £90 or more
$ Lower Priced—Most rooms less than £90
Unless otherwise noted, credit cards are accepted, breakfast is included, and free Wi-Fi and/or a guest computer is generally available. Prices change; verify current rates online or by email. For the best prices, always book directly with the hotel.

Parliament ordered their castle "slighted" (deliberately destroyed) to ensure that it would threaten the order of the land no more. Looking at this castle, so daunting in the age of bows and arrows, you can see how it was no match for the modern cannon. The pretty Mendip village of Nunney, with its little brook, is also worth a wander.

Cost and Hours: Free, visitable at "any reasonable time," tel. 0370/333-181, www.english-heritage.org.uk.

Sleeping in Wells

Wells is a pleasant overnight stop, with a handful of agreeable B&Bs.

$$ Swan Hotel, a Best Western Plus facing the cathedral, is a big, comfortable, 48-room hotel. Prices for their Tudor-style rooms vary based on whether you want extras like a four-poster bed or a cathedral view. They also rent five apartments in the village (Sb-£110-124, Db-£144-160, superior Db-£169-179, deluxe Db-£190-207, apartments-£119-155, ask about weekend deals, Sadler Street, tel. 01749/836-300, www.swanhotelwells.co.uk, info@swanhotelwells.co.uk).

$$ The Old Farmhouse, a five-minute walk from the town center, welcomes you with a secluded front garden and two tastefully decorated rooms (Db-£85-90, 2-night minimum, secure parking, next to the gas station at 62 Chamberlain Street, tel. 01749/675-058, www.wellssomerset.com, theoldfarmhousewells@hotmail.com, charming owners Felicity and Christopher Wilkes).

$ Baytree House B&B is a modern and practical home at the edge of town with lovely views (on a big road, a 10-minute walk to the bus station) renting three fresh, bright, and comfy rooms. Amanda runs the place with kindness and enthusiasm (Db-£64-85, Tb-£75-120, free parking, near where Strawberry Way hits the A-39 road to Cheddar at 85 Portway, tel. 01749/677-933, mobile

07745-287-194, www.baytree-house.co.uk, stay@baytree-house.co.uk).

Eating in Wells

Downtown Wells is tiny. A fine variety of eating options are within a block or two of its market square, including classic pubs; little delis and bakeries serving light meals; and a branch of **West Cornwall Pasty Company,** selling good savory pasties to eat in or take away (£5, daily 9:00-17:00, 1a Sadler Street, tel. 01749/671-616).

The Fountain Inn, on a quiet street 50 yards behind the cathedral, serves good pub grub (£7-14 lunches, £10-15 dinners, daily 12:00-14:00 & 18:00-21:00, no lunch on Mon, pub open until later, St. Thomas Street, tel. 01749/672-317).

Chapter Two, the modern restaurant in the cathedral welcome center, offers a handy if not heavenly lunch (£5-7 lunches, Mon-Sat 10:00-17:00, Sun 11:00-16:30, may close earlier in winter, tel. 01749/676-543).

The **Swan Hotel** has a pub that serves lunches in their garden across the street with a view over the green and cathedral (£8-10 main courses, Sadler Street, tel. 01749/836-300).

Wells Connections

The nearest train station is in Bath. The bus station in Wells is at a well-organized bus parking lot at the intersection of Priory and Princes roads. Local buses are run by First Bus Company (for Wells, tel. 0845-602-0156, www.firstgroup.com), while buses to and from London are run by National Express (tel. 0871-781-8181, www.nationalexpress.com).

From Wells by Bus to: Bath (nearly hourly, less frequent on Sun, 1.5 hours; if you miss the last direct bus to Bath, catch the bus to Bristol—runs hourly and takes one hour, then a 15-minute train ride to Bath), **Glastonbury** (3-4/hour, 25 minutes, bus #375/#376/#377, #29, or #37), **London**'s Victoria Coach Station (£21-30, 1/day direct, 4 hours; otherwise hourly with a change in Bristol).

Avebury

Avebury is a prehistoric open-air museum, with a complex of fascinating Neolithic sites all gathered around the great stone henge (circle). Because the area sports only a thin skin of topsoil over chalk, it is naturally treeless (similar to the area around Stonehenge). Perhaps this unique landscape—where the land connects with the big sky—made it the choice of prehistoric societies for their religious monuments. Whatever the case, Avebury dates to 2800 B.C.—six centuries older than Stonehenge. This complex, the St. Peter's Basilica of Neolithic civilization, makes for a fascinating visit. Many enjoy it more than Stonehenge.

Orientation to Avebury

Avebury, just a little village with a big stone circle, is easy to reach by car, but difficult by public transportation (see "Getting Around the Region," page 279).

Tourist Information: While there is no TI in Avebury, the National Trust hands out maps and answers questions from a trailer in their parking lot (daily April-Oct 10:30-16:30). For more information on the Avebury sights, see the websites of the English Heritage (www.english-heritage.org.uk) and the National Trust (www.nationaltrust.org.uk).

Arrival by Car: You must pay to park in Avebury, and your only real option is the flat-fee National Trust parking lot, a three-minute walk from the village (£7, £4 after 15:00, £3 in winter; open summer 9:30-18:30, off-season 9:30-16:30). No other public parking is available in the village.

Sights in Avebury

All of Avebury's prehistoric sights are free to visit and always open. The National Trust offers a 60-minute guided tour of the stone circle daily (£3, check schedule at trailer in their parking lot or in the Alexander Keiller Museum's Barn Gallery).

▲▲Avebury Stone Circle

The stone circle at Avebury is bigger (16 times the size), less touristy, and for many, more interesting than Stonehenge. You're free to wander among 100 stones, ditches, mounds, and curious patterns

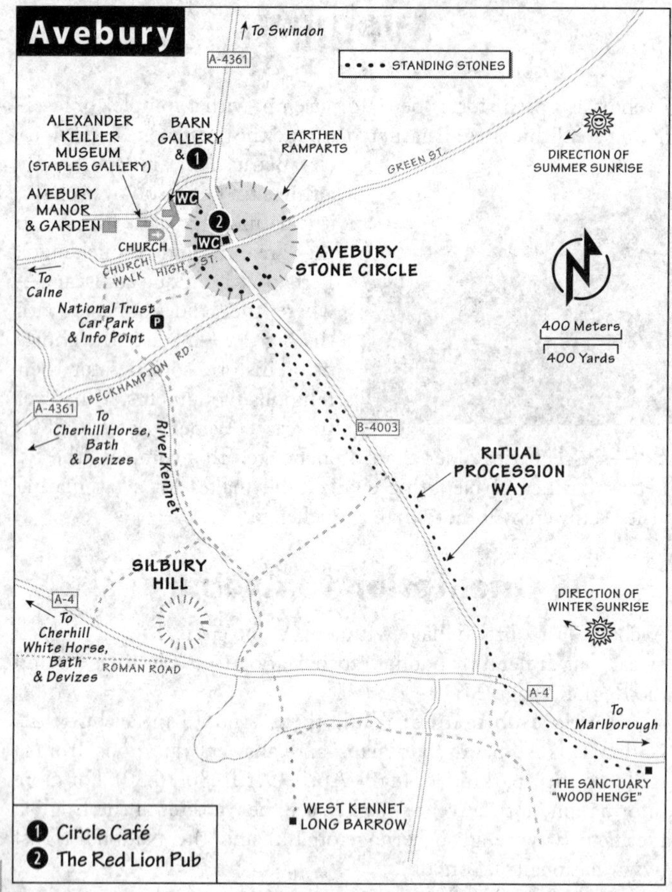

from the past, as well as the village of Avebury, which grew up in the middle of this fascinating 1,400-foot-wide Neolithic circle.

In the 14th century, in a frenzy of ignorance and religious paranoia, Avebury villagers buried many of these mysterious pagan stones. Their 18th-century descendants hosted social events in which they broke up the remaining pagan stones (topple, heat up, douse with cold water, and scavenge broken stones as building blocks). In modern times, the buried stones were dug up and re-erected. Concrete markers show where the missing broken-up stones once stood.

To make the roughly half-mile walk around the circle, you'll hike along an impressive earthwork henge—a 30-foot-high outer bank surrounding a ditch 30 feet deep, making a 60-foot-high rampart. (To pass through a gate, slide the handle sideways rather than lifting it.) This earthen rampart once had stones standing around

Stone Circles: The Riddle of the Rocks

Britain is home to roughly 800 stone circles, most of them rudimentary, jaggedly sparse boulder rings that lack the iconic upright-and-lintel form of Stonehenge. But their misty, mossy settings provide curious travelers with an intimate and accessible glimpse of the mysterious people who lived in prehistoric Britain.

Bronze Age Britain (2000-600 B.C.) was populated by farming folk who had mastered the craft of smelting heated tin and copper together to produce bronze, which was used to make more durable tools and weapons. Late in the Bronze Age, many of these primitive clannish communities also chose to put considerable time and effort into gathering huge rocks and arranging them into ceremonial circles for use in rituals with long-forgotten meanings. Some scholars believe that these circles may have been used as solar observatories, to calculate solstices and equinoxes as they planned life-sustaining seasonal crop-planting cycles. Archaeologists have discovered a few ancient remains in the center of some circles, but their primary use seems to have been ceremonial rather than as burial sites. And without any written records, we can only make educated guesses as to their exact purpose.

The superstitious people of the Middle Ages, who hadn't quite perfected their carbon-dating techniques, came up with colorful explanations for the circles. Stonehenge, for example, was believed to have been arranged by giants (makes sense to me). Later, several circles were thought to be petrified partiers who had dared to dance on the Sabbath; nearby standing stones were supposedly the frozen figures of the pipers who had been playing the dance tunes.

Britain's stone circles generally lie in Scotland, Wales, and at the fringes of England, clustering mostly in the southwest (particularly on the Cornwall peninsula), in the hills north of Manchester, and on the east side of Scotland (near Aberdeen). Dedicated travelers seeking stone circles will find them marked in the Ordnance Survey atlas and signposted along rural roads. Ask a local farmer for directions—and savor the experience (wear shoes impervious to grass dew and sheep doo). I've highlighted my favorites in this book: **Stonehenge** and **Avebury** (both described in this chapter), **Castlerigg** (in the Lake District, near Keswick—see page 500), and Scotland's **Clava Cairns** (just outside Inverness—see page 953).

the perimeter, placed about every 30 feet, and four grand causeway entries. Originally, two smaller circles made of about 200 stones stood within the henge.

▲Ritual Procession Way

Also known as West Kennet Avenue (one of four streets leaving the circle), this double line of stones provided a ritual procession way leading from Avebury to a long-gone wooden circle dubbed "The Sanctuary." This "wood henge," thought to have been 1,000 years older than everything else in the area, is considered to have been the genesis of Avebury and its big stone circle. Most of the stones standing along the procession way today were reconstructed in modern times.

▲Silbury Hill

This pyramid-shaped hill (reminiscent of Glastonbury Tor) is a 130-foot-high, yet-to-be-explained mound of chalk just outside of Avebury. More than 4,000 years old, this mound is considered the largest man-made object in prehistoric Europe (with the surface area of London's Trafalgar Square and the height of the Nelson Column). It's a reminder that we've only just scratched the surface of England's mysterious and ancient religious landscape.

Inspired by a legend that the hill hid a gold statue in its center, locals tunneled through Silbury Hill in 1830, undermining the structure. Work is currently underway to restore the hill, which remains closed to the public. Archaeologists (who date things like this by carbon-dating snails and other little critters killed in its construction) figure Silbury Hill took only 60 years to build, in about 2200 B.C. This makes Silbury Hill the last element built at Avebury and contemporaneous with Stonehenge. Some think it may have been an observation point for all the other bits of the Avebury site. You can still see evidence of a spiral path leading up the hill and a moat at its base.

The Roman road detoured around Silbury Hill. (Roman engineers often used features of the landscape as visual reference points when building roads. Their roads would commonly kink at the crest of hills or other landmarks, where they realigned with a new visual point.) Later, the hill sported a wooden Saxon fort, which likely acted as a lookout for marauding Vikings. And in World War II, the Royal Observer Corps stationed men up here to count and report Nazi bombers on raids.

West Kennet Long Barrow

A pullout on the road just past Silbury Hill marks the West Kennet Long Barrow (a 15-minute walk from Silbury Hill). This burial chamber, the best-preserved Stone Age chamber tomb in the UK, stands intact on a ridge. It lines up with the rising sun on the summer solstice. You can walk inside the barrow, or sit on its roof and survey the Neolithic landscape around you.

Cherhill Horse

Heading west from Avebury on the A-4 (toward Bath), you'll see an obelisk (a monument to some important earl) above you on the downs, or chalk hills, near the village of Cherhill. You'll also see a white horse carved into the chalk hillside. Above it are the remains of an Iron Age hill fort known as Oldbury Castle—described on an information board at the roadside pullout. There is one genuinely prehistoric white horse in England (the Uffington White Horse); the Cherhill Horse, like all the others, is just an 18th-century creation. Prehistoric discoveries were all the rage in the 1700s, and it was a fad to make your own fake ones. Throughout southern England, you can cut into the thin layer of topsoil and find chalk. Now, so they don't have to weed, horses like this are cemented and painted white.

Alexander Keiller Museum

This museum, named for the archaeologist who led excavations at Avebury in the late 1930s, is housed in two buildings. The 17th-century Barn Gallery has an interactive exhibit, while the Stables Gallery, across the farmyard, holds artifacts from past digs.

Cost and Hours: £5, daily April-Oct 10:00-18:00, Nov-March 10:00-16:00, tel. 01672/539-250.

Avebury Manor and Garden

Archaeologist Alexander Keiller's former home, a 500-year-old estate, was restored by a team of historians and craftspeople in collaboration with the BBC (for their 2001 documentary *The Manor Reborn*). Nine rooms were decorated in five different period styles showing the progression of design, from a Tudor wedding chapel to a Queen Anne-era bedroom to an early-20th-century billiards room. The grounds were also spruced up with a topiary and a Victorian kitchen garden.

Cost and Hours: £10, limited number of timed tickets sold per day, April-Oct daily 11:00-17:00, shorter hours off-season; closed Jan-mid-Feb and Mon-Wed in Nov-Dec, last entry one hour before closing, buy tickets at Alexander Keiller Museum's Barn Gallery (listed earlier), tel. 01672/539-250, www.nationaltrust.org.uk.

Eating in Avebury

The pleasant **Circle Café** serves healthy, hearty lunches, including vegan and gluten-free dishes, and cream teas on most days (daily April-Oct 10:00-17:30, Nov-March 10:00-16:00, no hot food after 14:30, next to National Trust store and the Alexander Keiller Museum, tel. 01672/539-250).

The Red Lion has inexpensive traditional pub grub; a creaky, well-worn, dart-throwing ambience; and a medieval well in its dining room (£6-12 meals, Mon-Sat 12:00-21:00, Sun 12:00-20:00, High Street, tel. 01672/539-266).

Stonehenge

As old as the pyramids, and older than the Acropolis and the Colosseum, this iconic stone circle amazed medieval Europeans, who figured it was built by a race of giants. And it still impresses visitors today. As one of Europe's most famous sights, Stonehenge, worth ▲▲, does a valiant job of retaining an air of mystery and majesty (partly because cordons, which keep hordes of tourists from trampling all over it, foster the illusion that it stands alone in a field). Although some people are underwhelmed by Stonehenge, most of its almost one million annual visitors find that it's worth the trip. And the ancient site continues to reveal its mysteries: In 2010, within sight of Stonehenge, archaeologists discovered another 5,000-year-old henge, which they believe once encircled a wooden "twin" of the famous circle. Recent excavations revealed that people had been living on the site since around 3,000 B.C.—about five centuries earlier than anyone had realized.

GETTING TO STONEHENGE

Stonehenge is about 90 miles southwest of central London. To reach it from London, you can take a bus tour; go on a guided tour that uses public transportation; or do it on your own using public transit, connecting via Salisbury. It's not worth the hassle or expense to rent a car just for a Stonehenge day trip.

By Bus Tour from London: Several companies offer big-bus day trips to Stonehenge from London, often with stops in Bath, Windsor, Salisbury, and/or Avebury. These generally cost about

£45-85 (including admission to Stonehenge), last 8-12 hours, and pack a 45-seat bus. Some include hotel pickup, admission fees, and meals; understand what's included before you book. The more destinations listed for a tour, the less time you'll have at any one stop. Well-known companies are **Evan Evans** (their bare-bones Stonehenge Express gets you there and back for £44, tel. 020/7950-1777 or US tel. 866-382-6868, www.evanevanstours.co.uk) and **Golden Tours** (£44, tel. 020/7630-2028 or US toll-free tel. 800-509-2507, www.goldentours.com). **International Friends** runs pricier but smaller 16-person tours that include Windsor and Bath (£119, tel. 01223/244-555, www.internationalfriends.co.uk).

By Bus Tour from Bath: For tours of Stonehenge from Bath (Mad Max is best), see page 244.

By Guided Tour on Public Transport: London Walks offers a guided "Stonehenge and Salisbury Tour" from London by train and bus on Tuesdays from May through October (£60, includes all transportation, Salisbury walking tour, entry fees, and guided tours of Stonehenge and Salisbury Cathedral; buy all tickets from guide; cash only, Tue at 8:45, meet at Waterloo Station's main ticket office, opposite Platform 16, verify price and schedule by phone or online, advance booking not required, tel. 020/7624-3978, recorded info tel. 020/7624-9255, www.walks.com).

On Your Own on Public Transport: From **London,** you can catch a train to Salisbury, then go by bus or taxi to Stonehenge. Trains to Salisbury run from London's Waterloo Station (around £38 for same-day return leaving weekdays after 9:30, 2/hour, 1.5 hours, tel. 0871-200-4950 or 0345-748-4950, www.southwesttrains.co.uk or www.nationalrail.co.uk).

From **Salisbury,** you can take **The Stonehenge Tour** bus to the site. Their distinctive double-decker buses leave from the Salisbury train station (also stops at bus station) and make a circuit to Stonehenge and Old Sarum, with lovely scenery and a decent light commentary along the way (£14, £27 with Stonehenge and Old Sarum admission; tickets good all day; buy ticket from driver; daily June-Aug 10:00-18:00, 2/hour; may not run June 21 because of solstice crowds, shorter hours and hourly departures off-season; 30 minutes from station to Stonehenge, tel. 01202/338-420, timetable at www.thestonehengetour.info).

A **taxi** from Salisbury to Stonehenge can make sense for groups (about £40-50). Try Value Cars Taxis (tel. 01722/505-050, www.salisbury-valuecars.co.uk) or a local cabbie named Brian (tel. 01722/339-781, briantwort@ntlworld.com).

By Car: Stonehenge is well-signed just off the A-303, about 15 minutes north of Salisbury, an hour southeast of Bath, an hour east of Glastonbury, and an hour south of Avebury.

Stonehenge is about 70 miles and 1.5 hours west of **London**

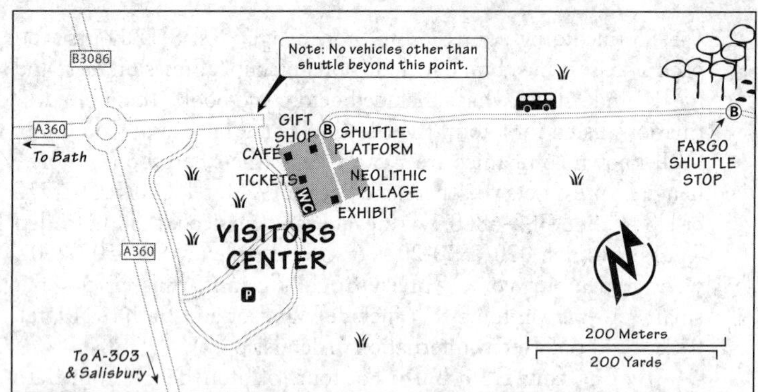

Heathrow (barring traffic). From the M-25 ring road, connect with the M-3 toward Southampton. Past Basingstoke, exit to the A-303. Continue west past Andover to Amesbury. In 3.5 miles, turn onto northbound A-360 at the roundabout, and follow "From Salisbury" directions from that point (see next).

From **Salisbury,** head north on A-360 (at the St. Paul's roundabout, take the second exit, direction: Devizes). Continue for eight miles, crossing the A-303 roundabout. In one more mile you'll encounter another roundabout; follow it around to the exit for the visitors center.

ORIENTATION TO STONEHENGE

Cost: £17.20, best to buy in advance online (see next), covered by English Heritage Pass (see page 993), includes shuttle-bus ride to the stone circle. In summer, there's a £5 refundable parking fee for drivers.

Hours: Daily June-Aug 9:00-20:00, mid-March-May and Sept-mid-Oct 9:30-19:00, mid-Oct-mid-March 9:30-17:00. Note that last entry is two hours before closing. Expect shorter hours and possible closures June 20-22 due to huge, raucous solstice crowds.

Advance Tickets: Prebooking a timed-entry ticket at least 24 hours in advance is the only way to assure you'll actually get in to the site, which caps the number of visitors per day at 7,000. (Some same-day tickets may be available at the ticket window, but in high season, it's risky to count on this.) Purchase your ticket online at www.english-heritage.org.uk/stonehenge. After booking a 30-minute arrival window, you'll receive a confirmation email with your e-ticket. Either print your ticket to present at the site, or bring your booking reference number with you.

If tickets are sold out for the day you planned to visit,

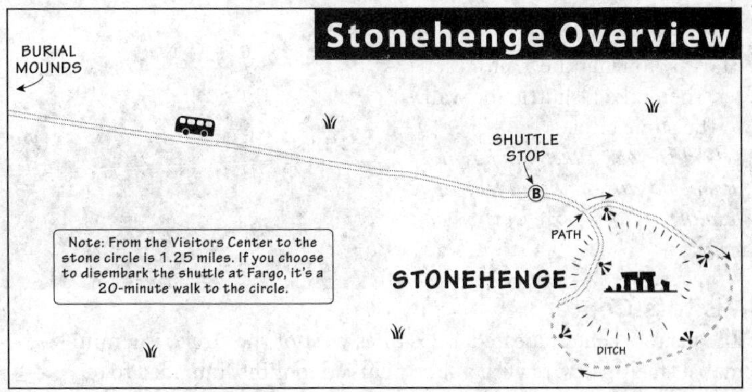

consider a guided tour that includes entry (see various options under "Getting to Stonehenge," earlier).

Information: Tel. 0870-333-1181, www.english-heritage.org.uk/stonehenge.

Tours: Audioguides are available behind the ticket counter (included with Heritage Pass, otherwise £2); the same audio content can be downloaded for free to your mobile device from the English Heritage website using the visitors center's free Wi-Fi (download before boarding the shuttle bus).

Visiting the Inner Stones: For the true Stonehenge fan, special one-hour access to the stones' inner circle is available early in the morning (times vary depending on sunrise, but the earliest is 5:00 in June and July) or after closing to the general public. Touching the stones is not allowed. Only 30 people are allowed at a time, so reservations must be made well in advance (£30, allows you to revisit the site the same day at no extra charge, tel. 0370-333-0605). Details are on the English Heritage website (under "Visit Stonehenge," click "Prices and Opening Times," then "Stone Circle Access Application Form"—depending on the time of year, it may be under "Group Tours").

Length of this Tour: Allow at least two hours to see everything.

Services: The visitors center has WCs, a large gift shop, and free Wi-Fi. Services at the circle itself are limited to emergency WCs. Even in summer, carry a jacket, as there are no trees to act as a wind-break and there's a reason the Salisbury plains are so green.

Eating: A large café within the visitors center serves hot drinks, soup, sandwiches, and salads along with hot light bites (£4-7).

➲ SELF-GUIDED TOUR

Whether you're using the audioguide or downloading the audio tour to your mobile device, this commentary will help make your visit even more meaningful. Start by touring the visitors center, then take a shuttle (or walk) to the stone circle.

• *Collect your ticket (and rent or download the audioguide) before heading to the excellent exhibit space.*

Visitors Center

The visitors center, located 1.25 miles west of the circle, is a minimalist steel structure with a subtly curved roofline, intended to replicate the Salisbury plains.

The **permanent exhibit** uses an artful combination of high-tech multimedia displays and prehistoric bones, tools, and pottery shards to explore the history of the people who built Stonehenge, how they lived, and why they might have built the stone circle.

Stand in the virtual center of Stonehenge, as 5,000 years pass by around you. Find the forensic reconstruction of a Neolithic man, based on a skeleton unearthed in 1863. Then step outside and visit his ancient neighborhood—a village of **Neolithic huts** modeled after the traces of a village discovered just northeast of Stonehenge.

If nature calls, be sure to use the WCs within the visitors center, as there are only emergency WCs at the circle itself.

• *Shuttle buses to the stone circle depart every 5-10 minutes from the platform behind the gift shop. The trip takes six minutes. If you'd prefer, you can walk 1.25 miles through the fields to the site (use the map you receive with your ticket, or ask a staff member for directions).*

Along the way, you have the option of stopping at ***Fargo Plantation,*** *where you can see several burial mounds (tell the shuttle attendant if you want to disembark here). After wandering through the burial mounds, you'll need to walk the rest of the way to the stone circle (about 20 minutes).*

Stone Circle

As you approach the massive structure, walk right up to the knee-high cordon and let your fellow 21st-century tourists melt away. It's just you and the druids...

England has hundreds of stone circles, but Stonehenge—which literally means "hanging stones"—is unique. It's the only one that has horizontal cross-pieces (called lintels) spanning the vertical monoliths, and the only one with stones that have been made smooth and uniform. What you see here is a bit more than half the original structure—the rest was quarried centuries ago for other buildings.

Now do a slow **clockwise spin** around the monument, and

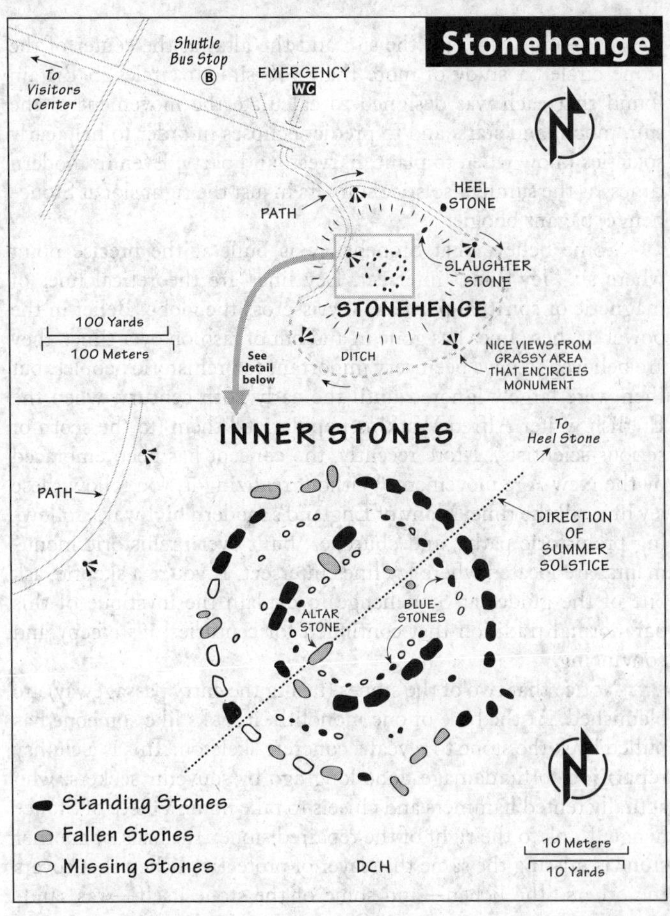

ponder the following points. As you walk, mentally flesh out the missing pieces and re-erect the rubble. Knowledgeable guides posted around the site are happy to answer your questions.

It's now believed that Stonehenge, which was built in phases between 3000 and 1500 B.C., was originally used as a cremation **cemetery.** But that's not the end of the story, as the monument was expanded over the millennia. This was a hugely significant location to prehistoric peoples. There are several hundred burial mounds within a three-mile radius of Stonehenge—some likely belonging to kings or chieftains. Some of the human remains are of people from far away, and others show signs of injuries—evidence that Stonehenge may have been used as a place of **medicine** or healing.

Whatever its original purpose, Stonehenge still functions as a celestial **calendar.** As the sun rises on the summer solstice (June 21), the **"heel stone"**—the one set apart from the rest, near the road—lines up with the sun and the altar at the center of the stone circle. A study of more than 300 similar circles in Britain found that each was designed to calculate the movement of the sun, moon, and stars, and to predict eclipses in order to help early societies know when to plant, harvest, and party. Even in modern times, as the summer solstice sun sets in just the right slot at Stonehenge, pagans boogie.

Some believe that Stonehenge is built at the precise point where six **"ley lines"** intersect. Ley lines are theoretical lines of magnetic or spiritual power that crisscross the globe. Belief in the power of these lines has gone in and out of fashion over time. They are believed to have been very important to prehistoric peoples, but then were largely ignored until the early 20th century, when the English writer Alfred Watkins popularized them (to the scorn of serious scientists). More recently, the concept has been embraced by the New Age movement. Without realizing it, you follow these ley lines all the time: Many of England's modern highways, following prehistoric paths, and churches, built over prehistoric monuments, are located where ley lines intersect. If you're a skeptic, ask one of the guides at Stonehenge to explain the mystique of this paranormal tradition that continued for centuries; it's creepy and convincing.

Notice that two of the stones (facing the entry passageway) are blemished. At the base of one monolith, it looks like someone has pulled back the stone to reveal a concrete skeleton. This is a clumsy **repair job** to fix damage done long ago by souvenir seekers, who actually rented hammers and chisels to take home a piece of Stonehenge. Look to the right of the repaired stone: The back of another stone is missing the same thin layer of protective lichen that covers the others. The lichen—and some of the stone itself—was sandblasted off to remove graffiti. (No wonder they've got Stonehenge roped off now.) The repairs were intentionally done in a different color, so as not to appear like the original stone.

Stonehenge's builders used two different types of stone. The tall, stout monoliths and lintels are sandstone blocks called **sarsen stones.** Most of the monoliths weigh about 25 tons (the largest is 45 tons), and the lintels are about 7 tons apiece. These sarsen stones were brought from "only" 20 miles away. The shorter stones in the middle, called **bluestones,** came from the south coast of Wales—240 miles away (close if you're taking a train, but far if you're packing a megalith). Imagine the logistical puzzle of floating six-ton stones across Wales' Severn Estuary and up the River Avon, then rolling them on logs about 20 miles to this position...an impressive feat, even in our era of skyscrapers. We know the stones came from Wales because geologists have chemically matched the bluestones to specific outcrops there.

Why didn't the builders of Stonehenge use what seem like perfectly adequate stones nearby? This, like many other questions about Stonehenge, remains shrouded in mystery. Think again about the ley lines. Ponder the fact that many experts accept none of the explanations of how these giant stones were transported. Then imagine congregations gathering here 5,000 years ago, raising thought levels, creating a powerful life force transmitted along the ley lines. Maybe a particular kind of stone was essential for maximum energy transmission. Maybe the stones were levitated here. Maybe psychics really do create powerful vibes. Maybe not. It's as unbelievable as electricity used to be.

Salisbury

Salisbury, set in the middle of the expansive Salisbury Plain, is a favorite stop for its striking cathedral and intriguing history. Salisbury was originally settled during the Bronze Age, possibly as early as 600 B.C., and later became a Roman town called Sarum. The modern city of Salisbury developed when the old settlement outgrew its boundaries, prompting the townspeople to move the city from a hill to the river valley below. Most of today's visitors come to marvel at the famous Salisbury Cathedral, featuring England's tallest spire and largest cathedral green. Collectors, bargain-hunters, and foodies will savor Salisbury's colorful market days. And archaeologists will dig the region around Salisbury, with England's highest concentration of ancient sites. The town itself is pleasant and walkable, and is a convenient base camp for visiting the ancient sites of Stonehenge and Avebury, or for exploring the countryside. It also makes a pleasant day trip from London.

Orientation to Salisbury

Salisbury (pop. 45,000) stretches along the River Avon in the shadow of its huge landmark cathedral. The heart of the city clusters around Market Place, a pedestrian square buzzing with action. High Street, a block to the west, leads to the medieval North Gate of the Cathedral Close. Shoppers can explore the quirkily named

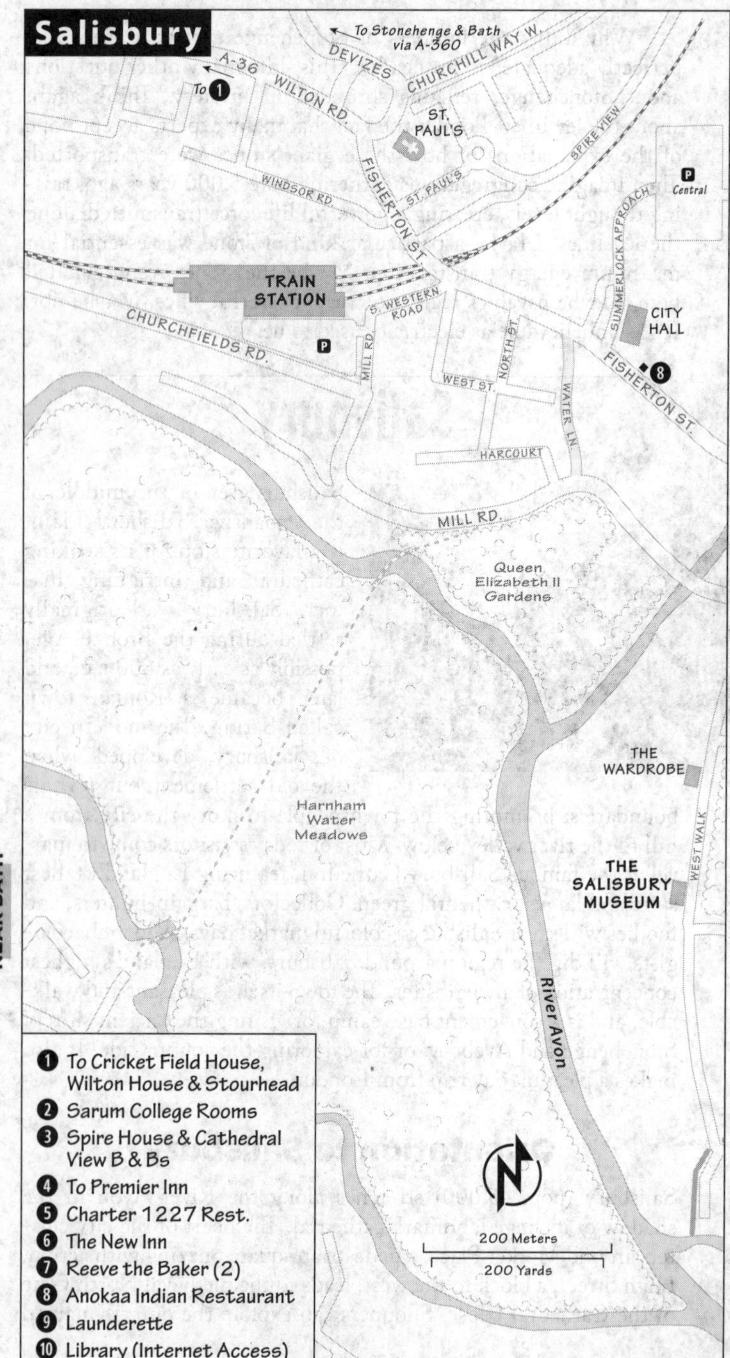

Salisbury
To Stonehenge & Bath via A-360
A-36
To 1
DEVIZES
CHURCHILL WAY W.
WILTON RD.
ST. PAUL'S
SPIRE VIEW
WINDSOR RD
ST. PAUL'S
FISHERTON ST.
SUMMERLOCK APPROACH
P Central
TRAIN STATION
S. WESTERN ROAD
CHURCHFIELDS RD.
P
MILL RD.
NORTH ST.
WEST ST.
CITY HALL
8
FISHERTON ST.
WATER LN
HARCOURT
MILL RD.
Queen Elizabeth II Gardens
THE WARDROBE
Harnham Water Meadows
WEST WALK
THE SALISBURY MUSEUM
River Avon
200 Meters
200 Yards
1 To Cricket Field House, Wilton House & Stourhead
2 Sarum College Rooms
3 Spire House & Cathedral View B & Bs
4 To Premier Inn
5 Charter 1227 Rest.
6 The New Inn
7 Reeve the Baker (2)
8 Anokaa Indian Restaurant
9 Launderette
10 Library (Internet Access)

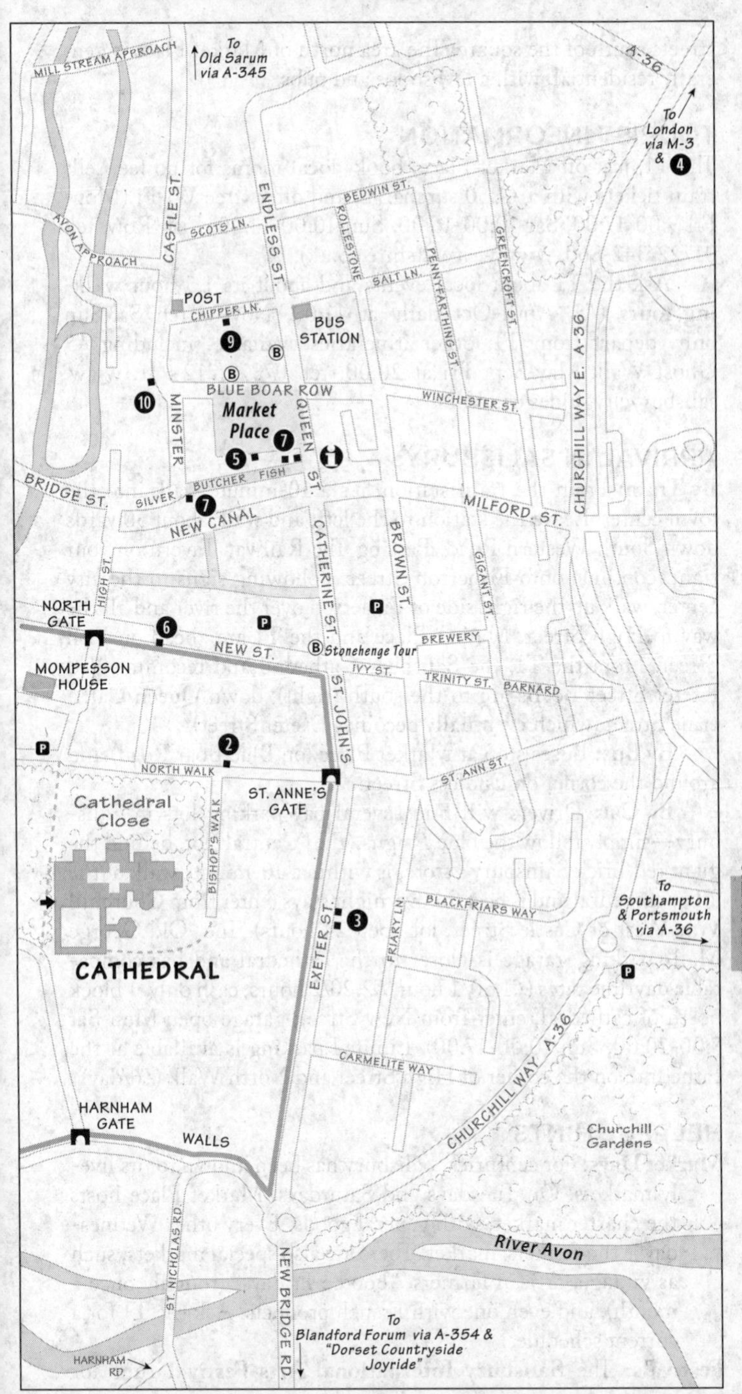
To
Old Sarum
via A-345
MILL STREAM APPROACH
A-36
To
London
via M-3
& 4
BEDWIN ST.
SCOTS LN.
CASTLE ST.
ENDLESS ST.
ROLLESTONE
PENNYFARTHING ST.
GREENCROFT ST.
AVON APPROACH
SALT LN.
POST
CHIPPER LN.
BUS
STATION
9
B
B
BLUE BOAR ROW
10
MINSTER
Market
Place
QUEEN
ST.
WINCHESTER ST.
CHURCHILL WAY E. A-36
7
5
BRIDGE ST.
SILVER
BUTCHER
FISH
7
NEW CANAL
MILFORD ST.
CATHERINE ST.
BROWN ST.
GIGANT ST.
HIGH ST.
NORTH
GATE
6
P
P
NEW ST.
B Stonehenge Tour
BREWERY
IVY ST.
TRINITY ST.
BARNARD
MOMPESSON
HOUSE
ST. JOHN'S
2
P
NORTH WALK
ST. ANNE'S
GATE
ST. ANN ST.
Cathedral
Close
BISHOP'S WALK
To
Southampton
& Portsmouth
via A-36
BLACKFRIARS WAY
EXETER ST.
3
FRIARY LN.
P
CATHEDRAL
CARMELITE WAY
CHURCHILL WAY A-36
HARNHAM
GATE
WALLS
Churchill
Gardens
River Avon
ST. NICHOLAS RD.
NEW BRIDGE RD.
To
Blandford Forum via A-354 &
"Dorset Countryside
Joyride"
HARNHAM
RD.

NEAR BATH

streets south of the square. The area north of Market Place is generally residential, with a few shops and pubs.

TOURIST INFORMATION

The TI, just off Market Place, books local rooms for no fee, sells train tickets with a £1.50 surcharge, and offers free Wi-Fi (Mon-Fri 9:00-17:00, Sat 10:00-16:00, Sun 10:00-14:00; Fish Row, tel. 01722/342-860, www.visitwiltshire.co.uk).

Ask the TI about local events and about its 1.5-hour **walking tours** (£5, April-Oct daily at 11:00, Nov-March Sat-Sun only, depart from TI; other itineraries available, including £5 Ghost Walk May-Sept Fri at 20:00; tel. 07873/212-941, www.salisburycityguides.co.uk).

ARRIVAL IN SALISBURY

By Train: From the train station, it's a 10-minute walk into the town center. Leave the station to the left, and walk about 50 yards down South Western Road. Passing The Railway Tavern on your right, continue onto Fisherton Street. Following signs to the city center, walk up the right side of Fisherton over the river and all the way to High Street. Market Place and the TI are ahead on Fish Street. From the TI, the Salisbury Cathedral and recommended Exeter Street B&Bs are to the south (right), down Queen/Catherine Street (which eventually becomes Exeter Street).

By Bus: Buses stop at Market Place (on Blue Boar Road) and around the corner on Endless Street.

By Car: Drivers will find several pay parking lots in Salisbury—simply follow the blue *P* signs. The "Central" lot, behind the giant red-brick Sainsbury's store, is within a 10-minute walk of the TI or cathedral and is best for overnight stays (enter from Churchill Way West or Castle Street, lot open 24 hours). The "Old George Mall" parking garage is closer to the cathedral and has comparable daytime rates (£1.50/1 hour, £2.20/2 hours, cash only, 1 block north of cathedral, enter from New Street; garage open Mon-Sat 7:00-20:00, Sun 10:00-17:00). Limited parking is available at the cathedral, on the corner of High Street and North Walk (£6/day).

HELPFUL HINTS

Market Days: For centuries, Salisbury has been known for its lively markets. On Tuesdays and Saturdays, Market Place hosts the charter market, with general goods. Every other Wednesday is the farmers' market. There are also special markets, such as vintage, artisan farmers, "Foodie Fridays" (roughly once a month), and even one with French products. Ask the TI for a current schedule.

Festivals: The **Salisbury International Arts Festival** runs for just over two weeks at the end of May and beginning of June (www.salisburyfestival.co.uk).

Internet Access: The library has free Wi-Fi along with terminals on the first floor for visitors (terminals £1/hour, Mon 10:00-19:00, Tue and Fri 9:00-19:00, Wed-Thu and Sat 9:00-17:00, closed Sun, show ID at desk to sign in for access number, Market Place, tel. 01722/324-145).

Laundry: Washing Well has full-service (£9-16/load depending on size, 2-hour service, Mon-Sat 8:30-17:00) as well as self-service (Mon-Sat 15:30-21:00, Sun 7:00-21:00, last self-service wash one hour before closing; 28 Chipper Lane, tel. 01722/421-874).

Getting to the Stone Circles: You can get to Stonehenge from Salisbury on **The Stonehenge Tour** double-decker bus in summer or by **taxi,** which can make sense if you're traveling with a group (see page 307).

For buses to Avebury's stone circle, see "Salisbury Connections," later.

Sights in Salisbury

▲▲Salisbury Cathedral

This magnificent cathedral, visible for miles around because of its huge spire (the tallest in England at 404 feet), is a wonder to behold. The surrounding enormous grassy field (called a "close") makes the Gothic masterpiece look even larger. What's more impressive is that all this was built in a mere 38 years—astonishingly fast for the Middle Ages. When the old hill town of Sarum was moved down to the valley, its cathedral had to be replaced in a hurry. So, in 1220, the townspeople began building, and in 1258 their sparkling-new cathedral was ready for ribbon-cutting. Since the structure was built in just a few decades, its style is uniform, rather than the patchwork of styles common in cathedrals of the time (which often took centuries to construct).

Cost and Hours: £7.50 suggested donation; Mon-Sat 9:00-17:00, Sun 12:00-16:00; Chapter House usually open Mon-Sat 9:30-16:30, Sun 12:30-15:45, closes entirely for special events; choral evensong Mon-Sat at 17:30, Sun at 16:30. This working cathedral opens early for services: Be respectful if you arrive when one is in session. Tel. 01722/555-156, www.salisburycathedral.org.uk.

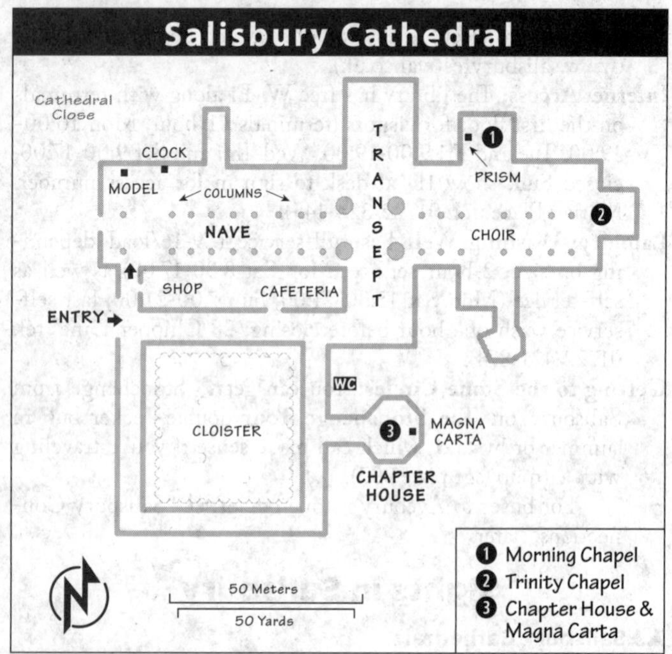

Tower Tours: Imagine building a cathedral on this scale before the invention of cranes, bulldozers, or modern scaffolding. An excellent tower tour (1.5-2 hours) helps visitors understand how it was done. You'll climb in between the stone arches and the roof to inspect the vaulting and trussing; see a medieval winch that was used in the construction; and finish with the 332-step climb up the narrow tower for a sweeping view of the Wiltshire countryside (£12.50; early April-Sept Mon-Sat at 11:15, 12:15, 13:15, 14:15, and 15:15, Sun at 13:15 and 14:15; fewer off-season but usually one at 13:15, no tours in Dec except Christmas week; maximum 12 people, can reserve by calling 01722/555-156).

Eating: The cathedral's cafeteria is excellent.

➲ **Self-Guided Tour:** Entering the church, you'll instantly feel the architectural harmony. Volunteer guides posted strategically throughout the church stand ready to answer your questions. (Free guided tours of the cathedral nave are offered every hour or so, when enough people assemble.)

As you look down the **nave,** notice how the stone columns march identically down the aisle, like a thick gray forest of tree trunks. The arches overhead soar to grand heights, helping churchgoers appreciate the vast and amazing heavens. Now imagine the interior surfaces painted in red, blue, green, and gold, as they would have been prior to the English Reformation.

From the entrance, head to the far wall (the back-left corner). You'll find an interesting **model** showing how this cathedral was built so quickly in the 13th century. Next to that is the "oldest working clock in existence," dating from the 14th century (the hourly bell has been removed, so as not to interrupt worship services). On the wall by the clock is a bell from the decommissioned ship HMS *Salisbury*. Look closely inside the bell to see the engraved names of crew members' children who were baptized on the ship.

Wander down the aisle past monuments and knights' tombs, as well as tombstones set into the floor. When you get to the transept, examine the **columns** where the arms of the church cross. These posts were supposed to support a more modest bell tower, but when a heavy tower was added 100 years later, the columns bent under the enormous weight, causing the tower to lean sideways. Although the posts were later reinforced, the tower still tilts about two and a half feet.

Continue down the left side of the choir and dip into the **Morning Chapel.** At the back of this chapel, find the spectacular glass prism engraved with images of Salisbury—donated to the church in memory of a soldier who died at the D-Day landing at Normandy.

The oldest part of the church is at the apse (far end), where construction began in 1220: the **Trinity Chapel.** The giant, modern stained-glass window ponders the theme "prisoners of conscience."

After you leave the nave, pace the cloister and follow signs to the medieval **Chapter House.** All English cathedrals have a chapter house, so called because it's where the daily Bible verse, or chapter, is read. These spaces often served as gathering places for conducting church or town business. Here you can see a modest display of cathedral items, plus one must-see: an exhibit centering on the best preserved of the four original copies of the Magna Carta. This document is as important to the English as the Constitution is to Americans. This "Great Charter," dating from 1215, settled a dispute between the slimy King John and some powerful barons. Revolutionary for limiting the monarch's power, the Magna Carta constitutionally guaranteed that the monarch was not above the law. This was one of the first major victories in the long tug-of-war between monarchs and nobles.

▲Cathedral Close

The enormous green surrounding the cathedral is the largest in England, and one of the loveliest. It's cradled in the elbow of the River Avon and ringed by row houses, cottages, and grand mansions. The church owns the houses on the green and rents them to lucky people with holy connections. A former prime minister,

Edward Heath, lived on the green, not because of his political influence, but because he was once the church organist.

The benches scattered around the green are an excellent place for having a romantic moonlit picnic or for gazing thoughtfully at the leaning spire. Although you may be tempted to linger until it's late, don't—this is still private church property... and the heavy medieval gates of the close shut at about 23:00.

A few houses are open to the public, such as the overpriced Mompesson House and the medieval Wardrobe. The most interesting attraction is...

▲The Salisbury Museum

Occupying the building just opposite the cathedral entry, this eclectic and sprawling collection was heralded by American expat travel writer Bill Bryson as one of England's best. While that's a stretch, the museum does offer a little something for everyone, including exhibits on local archaeology and social history, a costume gallery, the true-to-its-name "Salisbury Giant" puppet once used by the tailors' guilds during parades, some J. M. W. Turner paintings of the cathedral interior, and a collection of exquisite Wedgwood china and other ceramics. The highlight is the Wessex Gallery, with informative and interactive exhibits explaining Stonehenge and related prehistoric discoveries.

Cost and Hours: £8 (includes small donation), Mon-Sat 10:00-17:00, Sun 12:00-17:00 except closed Sun Oct-May, check with desk about occasional tours, 65 The Close, tel. 01722/332-151, www.salisburymuseum.org.uk.

Sleeping in Salisbury

Salisbury's town center has very few affordable accommodations, and I've listed them below—plus a couple of good choices a little farther out. Drivers should ask about parking when reserving. The town gets particularly crowded during the arts festival (late May through early June).

$$ Cricket Field House, outside of town on the A-36 toward Wilton, overlooks a cricket pitch and golf course. It has 10 large, comfortable rooms, its own gorgeous garden, and plenty of parking (Db-£95-160, price depends on season, Wilton Road, tel. 01722/322-595, www.cricketfieldhouse.co.uk, cricketfieldcottage@btinternet.com; Brian, Margaret, and Andrew

James). While this place works best for drivers, it's a 20-minute walk from the train station or a five-minute bus ride from the city center.

$$ Sarum College is a theological college that rents 40 rooms in its building right on the peaceful Cathedral Close. Much of the year, it houses visitors to the college, but it usually has rooms for tourists as well—except the week after Christmas, when it closes. The slightly institutional but clean rooms share hallways with libraries, bookstores, and offices, and the five attic rooms come with grand cathedral views (Sb-£65, Db-£100 depending on size, meals available at additional cost, elevator, 19 The Close, tel. 01722/424-800, www.sarum.ac.uk, hospitality@sarum.ac.uk).

$$ Cathedral View B&B, with four rooms, offers a good value in an outstanding location just off the Cathedral Close (Db-£95, Tb-£90-135, cash only, 2-night minimum on weekends, no kids under age 10, 83 Exeter Street, tel. 01722/502-254, www.cathedral-viewbandb.co.uk, info@cathedral-viewbandb.co.uk, Wenda and Steve).

$ Spire House B&B, next door, is similar. The four bright, surprisingly quiet rooms come with quirky themes, and three have canopied beds (Db-£80-90, Tb-£100-120, no kids under age 8, optional breakfast-£5, 84 Exeter Street, tel. 01722/339-213, www.salisbury-bedandbreakfast.com, spire.enquiries@btinternet.com, friendly Lois and John).

$ Premier Inn, two miles from the city center, offers dozens of prefab and predictable rooms ideal for drivers and families (Db-£70-85, more during special events, 2 kids ages 15 and under sleep free, breakfast-£5-8, pay Wi-Fi, possible noise from nearby trains, off roundabout at A-30 and Pearce Way, tel. 0871-527-8956, www.premierinn.com).

Eating in Salisbury

There are plenty of atmospheric pubs all over town. For the best variety of restaurants, head to the Market Place area. Many places offer great "early bird" specials before 20:00.

Charter 1227, an upstairs eatery overlooking Market Place, is a handy choice for a nice meal (£10 lunches, open Tue-Sat 12:00-14:30 & 18:00-21:30, closed Sun-Mon, dinner reservations smart, 6 Ox Row, enter from Market Place, tel. 01722/333-118, www.charter1227.co.uk).

Reeve the Baker crafts an array of high-calorie delights and handy pick-me-ups for a fast and affordable lunch. The long cases of pastries and savory treats will make you drool (Mon-Sat 7:00-17:00, Sun 10:00-16:00, one location is next to the TI at 2 Butcher

Row, another much smaller one is at the corner of Market and Bridge streets at 61 Silver Street, tel. 01722/320-367.

Anokaa is a classy splurge that's highly acclaimed for its updated Indian cuisine. You won't find the same old chicken *tikka* here, but clever newfangled variations on Indian themes, dished up in a dressy contemporary setting (£13-20 main courses, £9 lunch buffet, daily 12:00-14:00 & 17:30-23:00, 60 Fisherton Street, tel. 01722/414-142, www.anokaa.com).

The New Inn serves inventive, game-centered dishes and classic pub fare in a 13th-century house rumored to have a tunnel leading directly into the cathedral—perhaps dug while the building housed a brothel? (£5 starters, £6-9 sandwiches, £8-10 main courses, daily 11:00-24:00, food served 12:00-15:00 & 18:00-21:00, 41 New Street, tel. 01722/326-662).

Salisbury Connections

From Salisbury by Train to: London's Waterloo Station (2/hour, 1.5 hours), **Bath** (1-2/hour, 1 hour). Train info: tel. 0345-748-4950, www.nationalrail.co.uk.

By Bus to: Bath (hourly, 3 hours, www.travelinesw.com; or National Express #300 at 10:35, 1.5 hours, tel. 0871-781-8181, www.nationalexpress.com), **Avebury** (hourly, 2-2.5 hours, transfer in Devizes or Marlborough, www.travelinesw.com). Many of Salisbury's long-distance buses are run by Wilts & Dorset (tel. 01722/336-855 or 01202/338-420, www.salisburyreds.co.uk).

Near Salisbury

OLD SARUM

Right here, on a hill overlooking the plain below, is where the original town of Salisbury was founded many centuries ago. While little remains of the old town, the view of the valley is amazing... and a little imagination can transport you back to *very* olde England. This is one of the most historically important sites in southern England. Uniquely, it combined both a castle and a cathedral within an Iron Age fortification.

Human settlement in this area stretches back to the Bronze Age, and the Romans, Saxons, and Normans all called this hilltop home. From about 500 B.C. through A.D. 1220, Old Sarum flourished, giving rise to a motte-and-bailey castle, a cathedral, and scores of wooden homes along the town's outer ring. The town grew so quickly that by the Middle Ages, it had outgrown its spot on the

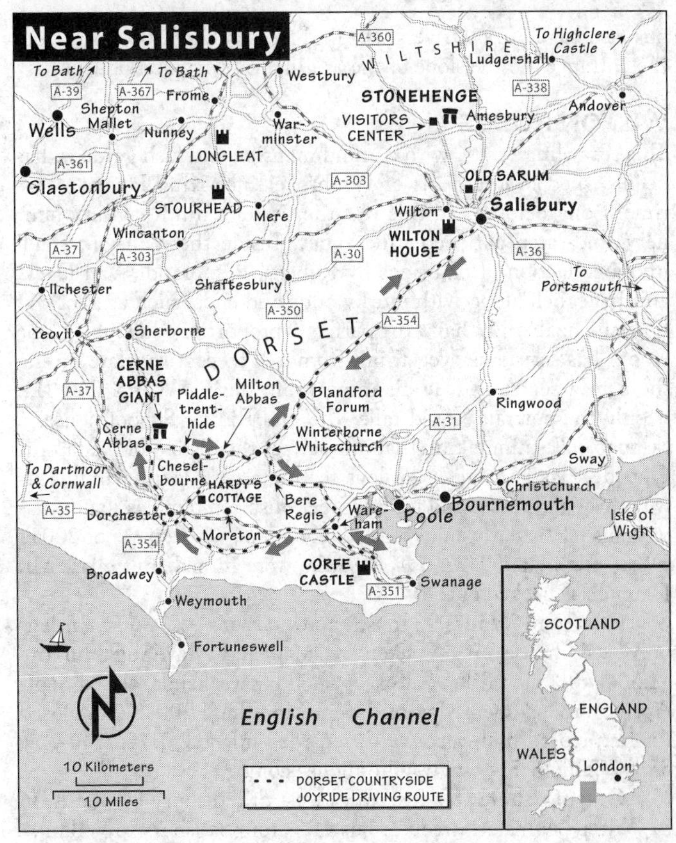

hill. In 1220, the local bishop successfully petitioned to move the entire city to the valley below, where space and water was plentiful. So, stone by stone, Old Sarum was packed up and shipped to New Sarum, where builders used nearly all the rubble from the old city to create a brand-new town with a magnificent cathedral.

Old Sarum was eventually abandoned altogether, leaving only a few stone foundations. The grand views of Salisbury from here have in-"spired" painters for ages and provided countless picnickers with a scenic backdrop: Grab a sandwich or snacks from one of the grocery stores in Salisbury or at the excellent Waitrose supermarket at the north end of town—just west of where the A-36 meets the A-345.

Cost and Hours: £5, daily April-Sept 10:00-18:00, Oct 10:00-17:00, Nov-March 10:00-16:00, tel. 01722/335-398, www.english-heritage.org.uk.

Getting There: It's two miles north of Salisbury off the A-345, accessible by Wilts & Dorset bus #X5 or via The Stonehenge Tour bus (see page 307). Drivers will find free parking 200 yards from the entrance (on the slope of the original castle's outer bailey).

WILTON HOUSE

This sprawling estate, with a grand mansion and lush gardens, has been owned by the Earls of Pembroke since King Henry VIII's time. Long before that, this was the site of a ninth-century nunnery, and later, a Benedictine abbey. Inside the mansion, you'll find a collection of paintings by Rubens, Rembrandt, Van Dyck, and Brueghel, along with quirky odds and ends, such as a lock of Queen Elizabeth I's hair. The perfectly proportioned Double Cube Room has served as everything from a 17th-century state dining room to a secret D-Day planning room during World War II... if only the portraits could talk. The Old Riding School houses a skippable 20-minute film that dramatizes the history of the family. Outside, classic English gardens feature a river lazily winding its way through grasses and under Greek-inspired temples. Jane Austen fans particularly enjoy this stately home, where parts of 2005's Oscar-nominated *Pride and Prejudice* were filmed. But, alas, Mr. Darcy has checked out.

Cost and Hours: House and gardens—£14.50, gardens only—£6; house open Easter weekend and May-Aug Sun-Thu 11:30-17:00, closed Fri-Sat except holiday weekends, closed Sept-April; gardens open May-mid-Sept Sun-Thu 11:00-17:30, closed Fri-Sat, closed mid-Sept-April; recorded info tel. 01722/746-729, tel. 01722/746-714, www.wiltonhouse.com.

Getting There: It's five miles west of Salisbury via the A-36 to Wilton's Minster Street; or bus #R3 from Salisbury to Wilton.

STOURHEAD

For a serious taste of a traditional English landscape and miles of footpaths, don't miss this 2,650-acre delight. Stourhead, designed by owner Henry Hoare II in the mid-18th century, is a wonderland of rolling hills, meandering paths, placid lakes, and colorful trees, punctuated by classically-inspired bridges and monuments. It's what every other English estate aspires to be—like nature, but better.

Cost and Hours: House and garden—£15, or £9 to see just one; house open March-Oct daily 11:00-17:00, garden open year-round daily 9:00-18:00; tel. 01747/841-152, www.nationaltrust.org.uk.

Getting There: It's 28 miles (40 minutes) west of Salisbury off the B-3092 in the town of Stourton (3 miles northwest of Mere).

Nearby: Drivers or ambitious walkers can visit nearby **King Alfred's Tower** and climb its 205 steps for glorious views of the estate and surrounding countryside (£4 to climb tower, same opening times as house, 2.5 miles northwest of Stourhead, off Tower Road).

DORSET COUNTRYSIDE JOYRIDE

The region of Dorset, just southwest of Salisbury, is full of rolling fields, winding country lanes, footpaths, quaint cottages, and villages stuffed with tea shops. Anywhere you go in the area will take you someplace charming, so consider this tour only a suggestion and feel free to get pleasantly lost in the English countryside. You'll be taking some less-traveled roads, so bring along a good map.

Starting in Salisbury, take the A-354 through Blandford Forum to Winterborne Whitechurch. From here, follow signs and small back roads to the village of **Bere Regis,** where you'll find some lovely 15th-century buildings, including one with angels carved on the roof. Follow the A-35 and the B-3075 to Wareham, where T. E. Lawrence (a.k.a. Lawrence of Arabia) lived; he's buried in nearby Moreton. Continue south on the A-351 to the dramatic and romantic **Corfe Castle.** This was a favorite residence for medieval kings until it was destroyed by a massive gunpowder blast during a 17th-century siege (£8, April-Sept daily 10:00-18:00, closes earlier off-season, tel. 01929/481-294, www.nationaltrust.org.uk). Retrace the A-351 to Wareham, and then take the A-352 to Dorchester.

Just northeast of Dorchester on the A-35, near the village of Stinsford, novelist Thomas Hardy was born in 1840; you'll find **Hardy's family's cottage** nearby, in Higher Bockhampton (£6, March-Oct Wed-Sun 11:00-17:00, closed Mon-Tue and Nov-Feb, tel. 01305/262-366, www.nationaltrust.org.uk). While Hardy's heart is buried in Stinsford with his first wife, Emma, the rest of him is in Westminster Abbey's Poets' Corner. Take the A-35 back to Dorchester. Just west of Dorchester, stay on the A-35 until it connects to the A-37; then follow the A-352 north toward Sherborne.

About eight miles north of Dorchester, on the way to Sherborne, you'll find the little town of **Cerne Abbas** (surn AB-iss), named for an abbey in the center of town. There are only two streets to wander down, so take this opportunity to recharge with a cup of tea and a scone. Abbots Tea Room has a nice cream tea (pot of tea, scone, jam, and clotted cream, 7 Long Street, tel. 01300/341-349). Up the street, you can visit the abbey and its well, reputed to have healing powers.

Just outside of town, a large chalk figure, the **Cerne Abbas Giant,** is carved into the green hillside. Chalk figures such as this one can be found in many parts of the region. Because the soil is only a few inches deep, the overlying grass and dirt can easily be removed to expose the bright white chalk bedrock beneath, creating the outlines. While nobody is sure exactly how old this figure is, or what its original purpose was, the giant is faithfully maintained by the locals, who mow and clear the fields at least once a year. This particular figure, possibly a fertility god, looks friendly... maybe a little too friendly. Locals claim that if a woman who's having trouble getting pregnant sleeps on the giant for one night, she will soon be able to conceive a child. (A few years back, controversy surrounded this giant, as a 180-foot-tall, donut-hoisting Homer Simpson was painted onto the adjacent hillside. No kidding.)

Leaving Cerne Abbas on country roads toward Piddletrenthide (on the aptly named River Piddle), continue through Cheselbourne to **Milton Abbas.** (This area, by the way, has some of the best town names in the country, such as Droop, Plush, Pleck, Folly, and of course, Piddle.) The village of Milton Abbas looks overly perfect. In the 18th century, a wealthy man bought up the town's large abbey and estate. His new place was great...except for the neighbors, a bunch of vulgar villagers with houses that cluttered his view from the garden. So, he had the town demolished and rebuilt a mile away. What you see now is probably the first planned community, with identical houses, a pub, and a church. The estate is now a "public school," which is what the English call an expensive private school. From Milton Abbas, signs lead you back to Winterborne Whitechurch, and the A-354 to Salisbury.

South Wales

South Wales, just an hour from Bath and the Cotswolds, feels much farther away. While the dramatic castles and scenery that many find quintessentially Welsh are in the north (see the North Wales chapter), a day or more in South Wales leaves you with great memories.

The capital of Wales, Cardiff—like so many Industrial-Age giants—became a run-down rust-belt city, but has now reemerged with fresh vigor. Its castle has medieval intrigue as well as Victorian bling, its downtown is ruddy yet vibrant, and its port—which around 1900 shipped 20 percent of the world's fuel when coal was king—is now a delightful people zone.

Just outside Cardiff, St. Fagans open-air museum celebrates the unheralded Welsh culture. The towns of Chepstow and Caerphilly both have stout castles designed by the British to keep the natives of this feisty little country in line. And the beloved Tintern Abbey, frequently immortalized in verse and on canvas, is the most spectacular of Britain's many ruined abbeys.

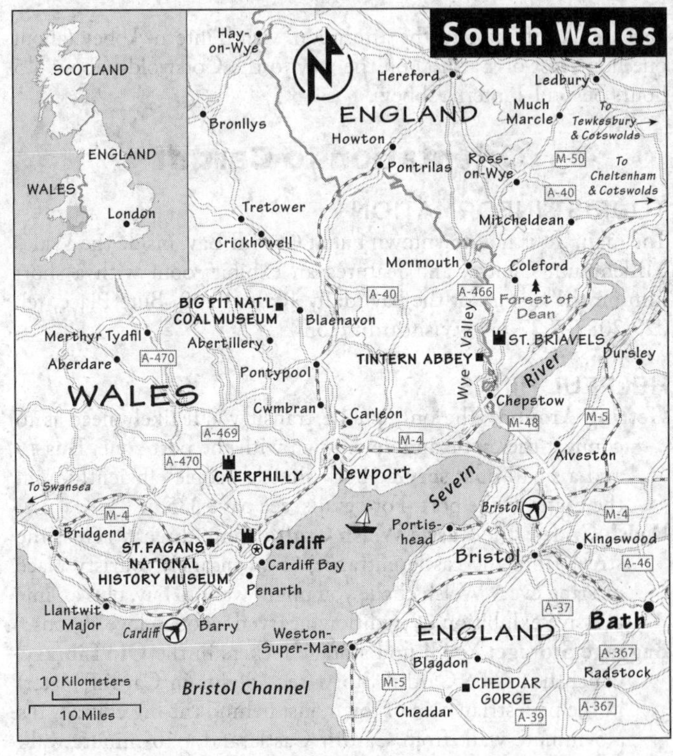

Cardiff

The Welsh capital of Cardiff (pop. 350,000) comes with a fine castle, a freshly revitalized pedestrian core, a smattering of museums, and an impressively modern waterfront. While rugby and soccer fans know Cardiff as the home of Millennium Stadium, and sci-fi fans know it as the place where *Doctor Who* is filmed, the Welsh proudly view the city as their political and cultural capital. You'll notice immediately that this place just feels different from England.

PLANNING YOUR TIME

Unless you're a Welsh patriot, Cardiff isn't worth an overnight stay. Its best sights—the castle and Cardiff Bay waterfront zone—can easily be seen in a few hours. Just outside Cardiff are two sights well worth visiting: St. Fagans National History Museum (open-air folk museum) to the west, and Caerphilly (with its sturdy castle) to the north.

Drivers connecting Bath to the Cotswolds via Cardiff can try this long-but-rewarding day: Get an early start, and go directly to St. Fagans. Then head into Cardiff for a tour of the castle and quick

NEAR BATH

visit to Cardiff Bay. In the afternoon, visit Tintern Abbey (about one hour east of Cardiff) on the way to the Cotswolds (about 1.5 hours beyond Tintern Abbey).

Orientation to Cardiff

TOURIST INFORMATION

The main TI is not downtown but at Cardiff Bay, inside the Wales Millennium Centre, and features an exhibit room with a short film on the history of the bay (daily 10:00-18:00, Bute Place, tel. 029/2087-7927, www.visitcardiff.com).

HELPFUL HINTS

Getting Around: The only public transit you'll likely need is to connect the castle and downtown with the port zone. **Bus #6** and a small **boat service** both shuttle people efficiently from the castle to the port. For details, see page 335.

Welsh Crafts: The **Castle Welsh Crafts Shop** (directly across the street from the castle entrance) is an insanely touristy place offering every Welsh cliché you might want to buy, plus an impressive exhibition of traditional carved wooden love spoons.

Baggage Storage: You'll find storage lockers in the **Old Library,** which hosts the Cardiff Story (see "Sights in Cardiff," later) in the pedestrian core of town, just behind the big church. It's a 5-minute walk from Cardiff Castle and a 10-minute walk from the train station (lockers open Mon-Sat 9:30-17:30, closed Sun).

Walking Tours: Bill O'Keefe and friends lead town walks about every other day at 11:00 (£7/person, 2 hours, covers the city but not the castle, leaves from the Castle Welsh Crafts Shop across from the castle entrance, schedule posted in window, call to confirm dates and time, mobile 07849-067-449).

Local Guide: Bill O'Keefe—a blue-badge guide and walking encyclopedia well versed in the history of Cardiff and South Wales—is a passionate, nonstop teacher. While he leads public walks daily (see above), you can also book him for a private tour (£100/half-day, £200/day, £250/day with car for up to 4 people, www.planetwales.co.uk, tours@planetwales.co.uk).

Sights in Cardiff

Many of Cardiff's main sights are within a five-minute walk of the castle. With your back to the castle's front door, Bute Park (with a shuttle boat to the port) is behind you on the right; the civic center with the national museum is behind on the left; and High Street,

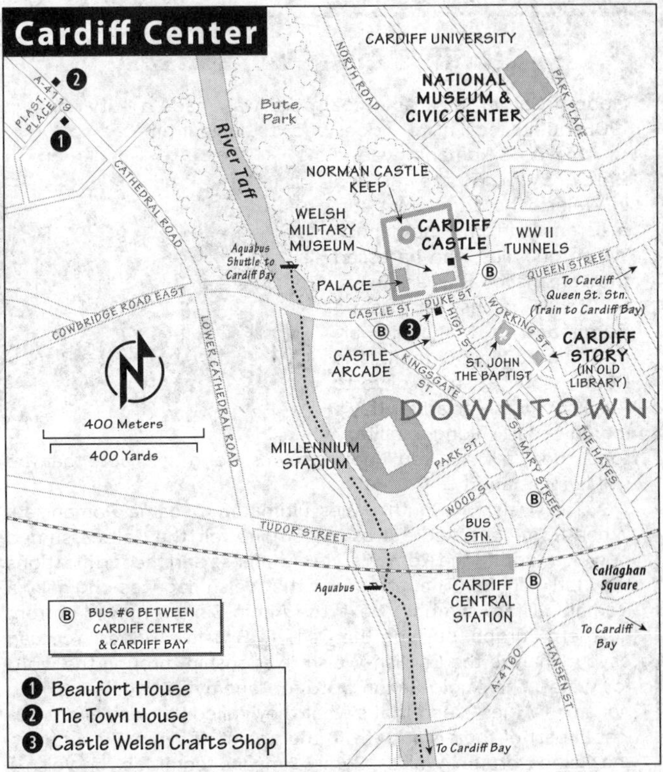

Cardiff Center

CARDIFF UNIVERSITY
NATIONAL MUSEUM & CIVIC CENTER
NORMAN CASTLE KEEP
WELSH MILITARY MUSEUM
CARDIFF CASTLE
WW II TUNNELS
PALACE
CASTLE ARCADE
ST. JOHN THE BAPTIST
CARDIFF STORY (IN OLD LIBRARY)
DOWNTOWN
MILLENNIUM STADIUM
BUS STN.
CARDIFF CENTRAL STATION
Callaghan Square
Bute Park
River Taff
Aquabus Shuttle to Cardiff Bay
Aquabus
To Cardiff Queen St. Stn. (Train to Cardiff Bay)
To Cardiff Bay
400 Meters
400 Yards
B BUS #6 BETWEEN CARDIFF CENTER & CARDIFF BAY

1. Beaufort House
2. The Town House
3. Castle Welsh Crafts Shop

the arcades, and the city's main church are directly in front of you. The port district is a quick taxi, bus, or boat ride away.

CARDIFF CASTLE AND BUTE PARK

▲Cardiff Castle

Cardiff Castle (Castell Caerdydd in Welsh) is one of the town's top sights—a fun complex that contains within its big medieval wall bits of several fortresses erected here since Roman times. You'll ramble its ramparts, climb an impressive Norman keep built on a man-made mound, see a WWII bomb shelter, visit an impressive Welsh military museum, and tour a romantically rebuilt Victorian-era palace that is less than historic but dazzling just the same.

Cost and Hours: £12, includes audioguide; daily March-Oct

Cardiff's Rise, Fall, and Rise

Modern Cardiff, built as a coal port, was made a "city" only in 1905, but its local history goes back to ancient times.

In A.D. 43 Romans invaded Britain. By A.D. 50 they arrived in Wales, where they met stiff resistance from indigenous Welsh guerillas who harassed the Romans for 30 years. In A.D. 55, the Romans established Cardiff as a fort that could garrison up to 6,000 men. The Romans built a string of forts (each 12 miles—or a half-day's march—apart) along a military road, today's A-48. You'll notice towns along this route that are still 12 miles apart.

The Welsh in South Wales ultimately became Romanized. When Rome checked out as the Empire fell, the Celts assumed power, adopting the Roman style of defense and the fortifications they left behind. (The dragon on the Welsh flag was originally a Roman military symbol.) Next, the Anglo-Saxons moved in from northern Europe, pushing the Celts to Britain's fringes. You can psychoanalyze the English-Welsh relationship through the word for Wales. The Anglo-Saxon word for "enemy" is "wealas" (which became "Wales"), and that's what they called this wild and unruleable part of their island (from their point of view). By contrast, the Celtic word for Wales, "Cymru," means "comrade" in Welsh—the opposite of what eventually became the English name for this region.

A fixed border dividing England and Wales was established in about A.D. 780. Behind that border, Wales was a mosaic of small independent kingdoms. When the Normans beat the English at the Battle of Hastings in 1066, they moved rapidly to consolidate greater Norman rule, and Wales sank into three centuries of war with generations of Norman warlords.

This was the age of castles—man-made earthen mounds crowned by wooden forts, eventually becoming the evocative stone wonders we climb through today. The big castles you can see throughout Wales were generally Norman-built and designed to keep the angry Welsh locals under control. Just as the Normans built the Tower of London in their capital, they built Cardiff's castle to protect their foothold in Wales. English settlers were imported to live within the walls of the garrison town (with gardens behind their houses) and to give the place a tax base. The indigenous Welsh people, outside the walls, were called "piss poor"—back then, very poor people sold their own urine (used to soak leather in Norman tanneries) to earn a few pennies.

In 1800 Cardiff had fewer than 2,000 residents (two dozen other Welsh towns were bigger). That all changed when the steam-powered Industrial Revolution hit and fuel-hungry factories recognized Welsh coal as the world's finest. (Welsh coal provided more heat per ton with less smoke and ash.) Coal-mining valleys led to Cardiff, which built a suitable port to export the mainstay of Wales' new economy. By 1900 Cardiff was nicknamed "Coal-opolis," and the old town was obliterated by the sudden industrialization. (There's little for the modern visitor to see that predates this building boom.) Wales became the first country on earth with the majority of its people working in industry. That's why the Welsh didn't emigrate to North America in droves like the Scottish and Irish. The big people movement here was from the villages and farms to the mining valleys and seaports.

But eventually, Britain began looking east for coal. The rise of modern container ports on England's east coast (facing the continent), coupled with a Europe-wide emphasis on free trade, prompted Britain to begin importing its coal rather than using coal from Wales. Today the port of Hull in eastern England imports nearly the same tonnage of coal as Cardiff exported in 1900.

In 1964, the last shipment of coal left Cardiff, marking the end of its industrial port. Like many blue-collar British towns, Cardiff's economy slumped severely in the 1970s and 1980s with the closure of steelworks and other heavy industry. But, also like similar towns, it experienced a rebounding effect through the 1990s and 2000s, sharing in the prosperity of Britain's new economic model.

Once a gloomy industrial wasteland, Cardiff's docklands have been revitalized with state-of-the-art facilities (such as the impressive Wales Millennium Centre for the performing arts) that sit side by side with restored historic buildings and futuristic government centers. The formerly traffic-choked downtown streets have been largely pedestrianized and are today filled with modern shopping centers.

Cardiff's recent transformation is yet another on a long list of "second cities" in Britain and beyond that have emerged from dark economic times to a brighter future. And here, on the south coast of Wales, it comes with a lilting Welsh accent.

9:00-18:00, Nov-Feb 9:00-17:00, last entry one hour before closing, café, tel. 029/2087-8100, www.cardiffcastle.com.

Tours: For a 45-minute tour of the 19th-century palace, pay £3 extra as you enter and reserve a time. Tours depart at the top of each hour and cover the rooms you can see on your own plus a handful of otherwise inaccessible rooms (the nursery, bedroom, and rooftop garden).

Visiting the Castle: Your visit includes the following stops—all well explained in the included audioguide.

In the **Neo-Gothic Fantasy Palace** you'll find the castle apartments, rebuilt by John Crichton-Stuart, third marquess of Bute, whose income from the thriving coal trade flowing through his docklands made him one of Europe's wealthiest men in the late 1860s. He spared no expense. With his funds and architect William Burges' know-how, the castle was turned into a whimsical, fantastical take on the Middle Ages. It's the Welsh equivalent of "Mad" King Ludwig's fairy-tale castles in Bavaria (built in the same romantic decade). In 1947, the family donated it to the city of Cardiff.

The highlight of the complex is the Great Hall, with every surface covered in the highly detailed, gilded imagery of medieval symbolism. The glittering **Arab Room** is slathered in gold, including a gold-leaf stalactite ceiling. The breathtaking **Banqueting Hall** evokes the age of chivalry, right down to the raised minstrel's gallery (where musicians could perform overhead but remain unseen). The small **dining room** has a table designed for a grapevine to grow up through a hole in the middle—so that guests could pick their own dessert. The **library** boasts rows of leather-bound books and desks that double as radiators.

In the building with the ticket office and shop is the **Welsh Military Museum.** Here you'll find a short video (upstairs), a remaining bit of the Roman castle wall (downstairs), and a fine exhibition on Welsh military history called "The Firing Line."

Dominating the castle grounds is the **keep,** a classic Norman motte-and-bailey construction, with a stout fortress on top of a man-made hill. The original structure, made of wood, was built by William the Conqueror in 1081. He was returning from what he called a "pilgrimage" to St. David's—a cathedral town in western Wales—which clearly included a little scouting for future military action as well.

Along the right wall is a long, two-level stretch of passageways—the **battlements and WWII tunnels.** The old battlements are above, and underneath them is a tunnel that was used during WWII air-raids as a bomb shelter. Cardiff was an important military port (20 percent of all American GIs who fought in Europe landed here), which made it a target of Nazi bombers. While the port was hit hard, the city got off pretty lightly.

Bute Park

Bute Park runs from the castle to the open valley beyond Cardiff and is the largest urban park in Britain (as big as New York's Central Park). Just as you might imagine, it offers a world of escapes for relaxing locals—formal gardens, rugby and cricket pitches, and a riverside path that leads through natural surroundings from the castle into the hills. On the River Taff, at the southeast end of the park (nearest the castle), you'll find the dock for the shuttle boats to the port. For more about the shuttle boat, see "Getting to Cardiff Bay" on page 335.

HIGH STREET AND NEARBY

Cardiff was a garrison town when Wales was an English-ruled apartheid society. The English lived within the walls, and the indigenous Welsh who lived beyond made the English thankful they had those walls. Today the walls are long gone, and the city was mostly built over in the Victorian boom times. Pedestrianized High Street is the spine, running from the castle's entrance through the center. Branching off of High Street are several Victorian shopping arcades and more-modern shopping centers, including the enormous St. David's shopping mall (which locals say gives women something to do when men fill the stadium for soccer or rugby games).

Castle Arcade

The most impressive of the Victorian arcades is Castle Arcade. It has two entrances: one across the street from the castle entrance—about two o'clock with your back to the gate—and another half a block down High Street on the right. During the late 1800s, when Cardiff was booming, there was suddenly a class of wealthy women who needed climate-controlled, London-quality shopping. The city developed several Victorian-era arcades with glass roofs to make sure that the ladies stayed warm in the winter and didn't get a "working-class" tan in the summer. (The term "blue blooded" refers to the fact that their wrists were so lily white that the blue of the veins popped.) These long, narrow Victorian arcades—echoing the shape of farm plats from the days when people lived and farmed within the town's protective walls—were state-of-the-art when first constructed, with some of the first elec-

tric lighting anywhere. Today the joy of visiting these arcades lies in their characteristic shops and little cafés, the majority of which are unique and family-run rather than chain stores.

St. John the Baptist Church

This Anglican church, a block off High Street, is the most important church in the city's center. Built in 1180 then rebuilt in the 15th century after damage sustained during a rebellion against English rule, St. John the Baptist is one of the oldest buildings in Cardiff. Step inside to enjoy the Victorian stained glass and the Herbert family tomb. (The Herberts ran the town in the 16th century like gangster Medicis.) In the graveyard is a medieval preaching cross. Originally standing on High Street, this cross marked the site of official announcements and special preaching (e.g., "Join in on the newest crusade!").

The Cardiff Story

This engaging exhibit is in a big room on the ground floor of the Old Library building—a fine late-Victorian structure built so that the general public would have access to good books. The exhibit explores the city's history during its 19th-century coal-fired boom time.

Cost and Hours: Free, Mon-Sat 10:00-16:00, closed Sun, The Hayes, tel. 029/2034-6214.

National Museum and Civic Center

These imposing buildings were erected just before Cardiff reached the end of its boom. A leading citizen sold the city some prime land at a great price on one condition: Grand London-class structures made of Portland stone must be built here and remain forever open to the public. So, in 1910 the city built its Edwardian city hall, law courts, national museum, and the University of Wales just north of the castle on North Road. The **National Museum** focuses not on Welsh culture and history—that's at St. Fagans (see "Near Cardiff," later)—but on art (with a particularly strong Impressionist collection), natural history (dinosaurs and mammoths), and archaeology (scant fragments of prehistoric Wales).

Cost and Hours: Free, Tue-Sun 10:00-17:00, closed Mon, Cathays Park, tel. 0300-111-2333, www.museumwales.ac.uk/cardiff.

Millennium Stadium

This is the big sports venue for all of Wales. Located just a couple of blocks south of the castle and High Street, it seems to dwarf the city, with its modern construction towering above the Victorian skyline. Nicknamed "The Dragon's Den" (after the symbol and mascot of Wales), it serves as the home pitch of the Welsh national rugby (WRU) and soccer teams, hosted soccer matches during the

2012 London Summer Olympics, and is *the* place for big rock concerts in Wales. The stadium boasts the largest retractable roof in Europe. Even if you don't join 74,500 screaming spectators for a rugby or soccer match, you can pay for a guided tour of the building.

Cost and Hours: Guided tour—£10.50, offered Mon-Sat 10:00-17:00, Sun until 16:00, check website for availability on game days, www.millenniumstadium.com.

CARDIFF BAY

Locals here love to brag that in its heyday the port of Cardiff shipped almost a quarter of the world's coal. Valleys rich with the best coal deposits anywhere funneled the black gold of the 19th century right into Cardiff. Capitalizing on the Industrial Revolution demand for steam power, the city built a massive port, ultimately with about 200 miles of train tracks lining its shipping piers. (You'll notice that there are none of the vast brick warehouses you'd expect in a 19th-century port, because rather than being warehoused, the coal was just piled next to the tracks and shipped almost immediately upon arrival.)

But with the coming of imported coal and oil, Cardiff's port declined. A generation ago Cardiff's port was derelict—a place no tourist would dream of visiting. But in the late 1980s, city leaders hatched a scheme for the "Cardiff Bay Barrage," designed to seal off the mouth of the port and create a permanent high-tide waterline. Their goal was to attract developers with the promise of an inviting new people zone on the waterfront. It worked, and today, as with rusty old ports all over Europe, Cardiff Bay is thriving—packed with sparkling, bold architecture, major sightseeing attractions, and fun entertainment. It's worth ▲▲ and a short bus ride from downtown to see how a once-flailing city can right the ship.

Getting to Cardiff Bay: Catch bus #6—also known as the "Baycar"—from either end of High Street (direction: Porth Teigr). It stops at the bottom, just past Starbucks; at the Kingsway stop on St. Mary Street; and at the top, in front of the Hilton Hotel, across the street from the side wall of Cardiff Castle (£1.80, exact change only; about every 10 minutes, trip takes 10-15 minutes, www.cardiffbus.com). Hop off at the East Bute Street stop, just behind the Wales Millennium Centre. For the return trip, you can catch the bus at the more convenient Millennium Centre stop, facing Roald Dahl Plass.

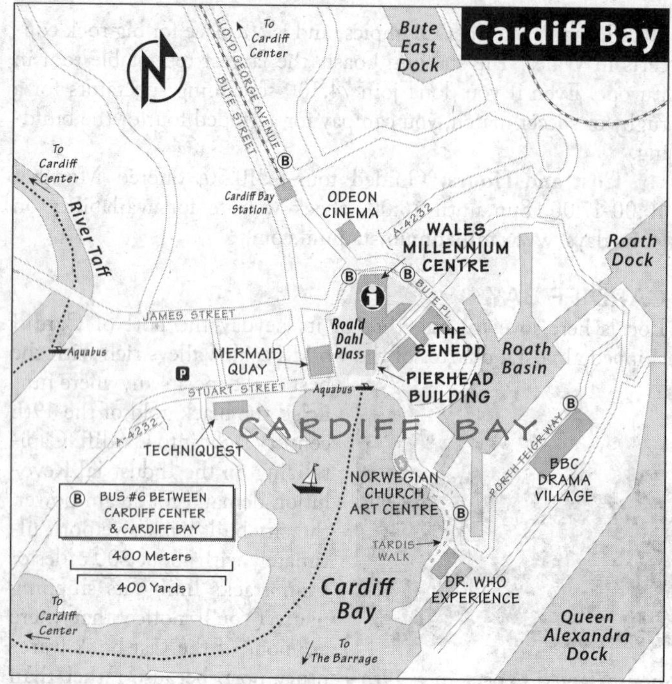

To ride the Aquabus shuttle boat from near the castle to the bay, look for the tiny riverside pier in Bute Park (see earlier), beyond the trees to the left of the castle as you face it (£4, 2/hour, 20 minutes, www.cardiffboat.com).

Visiting Cardiff Bay: For an orientation, belly up to the railing on Roald Dahl Plass (in front of the copper-and-steel opera house) and look out over the bay. In this spin tour, you can locate the sights I describe in detail later.

Before 2002, one of biggest tides in the world literally emptied this bay twice a day. Now the mouth of the harbor is dammed by "The Barrage" (a high-tech dam marked by the grassy slope in the distance). While locks let in boats and a fish ladder lets in fish, the tide is kept out, and Cardiff Bay has become an inviting people zone.

Standing here, turn clockwise. Along the harborfront to your right is **Mermaid Quay,** with shops and restaurants. At the pier, you can catch a boat back to the city center (details earlier, under "Getting to Cardiff Bay"). Just beyond the old-time carousel is an artificial **beach** (summer only) and fun zone for families, and the Roald Dahl Plass entertainment area. The big modern opera house is the **Wales Millennium Centre.**

Now find the historic red-brick **Pierhead Building** and the sleek **Senedd Building** (home to the Welsh National Assembly) with its shade-giving porch. In front of that is a big metal head decorating the sidewalk. The giant head is the **Merchant Marine Memorial,** built to remember the sailors who died keeping Britain supplied during the WWII Battle of the Atlantic.

The rotting **wooden pilings** in the harbor nearby are called "dolphins," and were used to brace ships caught here by falling tides before the construction of the Barrage. (Captains would tie their boats to a dolphin and gently settle onto mud without toppling.)

Next, find the white **Norwegian Church** (now a center for the arts) and the **Dr. Who Experience** (in a blue-gray building) beyond that. At the far end of the bay is the **Barrage** itself, a bluff called **Penarth Head,** and the hills of **West England** in the far distance.

While these are the main landmarks, there's much more to see and do around this bay: bikes and boats for rent, harbor boat tours, a hands-on science museum (Techniquest), fake-yet-thrilling whitewater rafting, an open-air exhibit of boats from around the world, a multiplex (with Wales' only IMAX screen), and the nearby International Sports Village (with an ice arena and swimming pool).

Roald Dahl Plass and Mermaid Quay

Visitors congregate on the expansive bowl-shaped main plaza named for **Roald Dahl,** the Cardiff-born children's author with many fans worldwide. (The Norwegian term *plass*—"square"—honors Dahl's Norwegian ancestry.) As this area was once a coal port, it angles down to the water. The pillars are illuminated with a light show after dark, and the 70-foot-tall silver water tower is always trickling. Mermaid Quay, across the square, is an inviting outdoor-dining zone loaded with mostly chain restaurants.

Wales Millennium Centre

Wales, a land famous for its love of music, had no national opera house until 2004. They fixed that with gusto by building the 2,000-seat Wales Millennium Centre. It's a cutting-edge venue for opera, theater, and other performances (funded mostly by lottery money—a regressive tax levied on less-educated people). The enormous opera house overlooks Roald Dahl Plass and anchors the entire Cardiff Bay district. Its facade, dominated by slate and steel (two important Welsh resources that have kept this small country humming), is carved with the words of one-time Welsh national poet Gwyneth Lewis: the English phrase "In these stones horizons sing," and the Welsh phrase *Creu gwir fel gwydr o ffwrnais awen* ("Creating truth like glass from the furnace of inspiration"). In its expansive lobby are shops, an enticing food court, the Cardiff **TI,** and lots of activities, including regular free concerts at lunch (tours-£6, daily at 11:00 and 14:30, check website for info on free performances, Bute Place, tel. 029/2063-6464, www.wmc.org.uk).

Pierhead Building

This stately red-brick building, one of the few historic structures remaining here, looks out over the port. Sometimes called the "Welsh Big Ben," this landmark is a symbol of the city. Note its evocative relief celebrating steamships and trains with the Welsh phrase "by water and fire." A history exhibit inside shows a free and interesting video (tel. 0845-010-5500, www.pierhead.org).

Senedd, The National Assembly of Wales

Just behind the Pierhead Building is the Senedd (with the huge overhanging roof), home of the National Assembly and essentially the Welsh capitol. While Wales—like Scotland and Northern Ireland—has a degree of autonomy from the United Kingdom, many matters are still decided in London. The National Assembly was created in 1999, moved into these new digs in 2006, and gained more authority in 2007. The building, with vast walls of glass symbolizing the ideal of an open and transparent government, was designed by prominent architect Richard Rogers (best known for London's Millennium Dome and Lloyd's Building, and—with frequent collaborator Renzo Piano—Paris' Pompidou Centre).

Norwegian Church Art Centre

This shiplap church seems like it would be more at home on a fjord. It was built as a seamen's mission by the Norwegian merchant marines, in properly austere Lutheran style, during Cardiff's Industrial-Age boom. Originally, it sat where the Wales Millennium Centre is today, but in the 1970s and 1980s—when the docklands were a dangerous, derelict no-man's land—the church was literally disassembled and mothballed for future use. Over the last couple of decades, it has been reassembled, reconsecrated, refurbished, and repurposed as a successful arts center (free, daily 11:00-16:00, café, www.norwegianchurchcardiff.com).

Doctor Who Experience

Beyond the Norwegian Church is the blue-gray curve of the giant Doctor Who Experience. Honoring the astoundingly long-running BBC science-fiction series—which celebrated its 50th anniversary in 2013—this interactive exhibit is a must for fans...but totally lost on those who don't know a Dalek from a Sontaran (admission price varies—generally £14-16, book tickets online for small discount, daily 10:00-17:00 in summer, Sept-June closed Tue, Nov-Feb also closed Mon, tel. 020/8433-3162, www.doctorwhoexperience.com).

Doctor Who is just one of many BBC shows filmed in Cardiff. Behind the museum, on Roath Lock, sprawls the **BBC Drama Village,** a studio lot where many popular series—including *Torchwood, Casualty,* and the 2010-12 version of *Upstairs Downstairs*—were filmed.

NEAR CARDIFF

▲▲St. Fagans National History Museum

The best look anywhere at traditional Welsh folk life, St. Fagans is a 100-acre open-air museum with more than 40 carefully reconstructed and fully furnished historic buildings from all corners of Wales, as well as a "castle" (actually a Tudor-era manor house) that offers a glimpse of how the other half lived. Also known as Amgueddfa Werin Cymru (Museum of Welsh Life), its workshops feature busy craftsmen eager to demonstrate their skills. Each house comes equipped with a local expert warming up beside a toasty fire, happy to tell you anything you want to know about life in this old cottage. Ask questions.

Cost and Hours: Free, parking-£4, daily 10:00-17:00, tel. 030/0111-2333, www.museumwales.ac.uk/en/stfagans.

Information: Be sure to pick up the essential £0.30 map, which helps you navigate your way through the park. Plaques by each building do an exceptional job of succinctly explaining where the building came from, its role in Welsh culture, and how it came to be here, all illustrated by a helpful timeline. Docents posted throughout can tell you more. And if you want more detail, buy the £4 museum guidebook.

Expect Changes: The main entrance building (which usually houses the indoor part of the museum) is closed for renovation until 2017. When it reopens, its much-expanded exhibit will offer more to keep visitors occupied on not-uncommon rainy days, covering such topics as traditional dress, social history, and agriculture. In the meantime, the services usually housed inside (ticket desk, WCs, café, restaurant, gift shop) have been relocated to other areas. If you're looking for something, ask one of the docents. Don't be surprised if the changes displace some of the exhibits mentioned next.

Getting There: To get from the Cardiff train station to the museum, catch bus #32A (which stops right at the museum entrance; bus #320 takes you to St. Fagans village, a 5-minute walk to the museum; buses run hourly, 25 minutes, tel. 0871-200-2233, www.traveline-cymru.info). Drivers leave the M-4 at Junction 33 and follow the brown signs to *Museum of Welsh Life*. Leaving the museum, jog left on the freeway, take the first exit, and circle back, following signs to the M-4.

Getting Around: While large, the sprawling grounds are walkable. But if you want to take it easy, a small train trundles among the exhibits from Easter to October (five stops, £0.50/stop, whole circuit takes 30 minutes).

Eating at St. Fagans: Within the park are plenty of snack stands, as well as two bigger eateries: the Gwalia Tea Room in the heart of the traditional building zone, and The Buttery inside the castle. Derwen Bakehouse sells snacks and traditional fruit-studded bread, which is tasty and warm out of the oven. Back in the real world, The Plymouth Arms pub, just outside the museum, serves the best food.

Visiting the Museum: Buy the map and pick up the list of today's activities. Once in the park, you'll find most of the traditional buildings to your left, while to the right are the castle and its surrounding gardens. Here's a rough framework for seeing the highlights:

First, head left and do a clockwise spin around the traditional buildings, starting with the circa-1800, red-and-white **Kennixton Farmhouse.** Then swing left, go down past the mill, and hook left again down the path to the fine **Lywyn-yr-eos Farmhouse.** Along with the castle, this is the only building at the museum that stands in its original location. It's furnished as it would have been at the end of World War I—complete with "welcome home" banner and patriotic portraits of stiff-upper-lip injured troops. From here you can side-trip five minutes to two Celtic **round houses,** which were farmhouses back in the Iron Age.

Head back up the main path and continue deeper into the park, turning left at the fork (toward *Church* and *Y Garieg Fawr*). Passing another farmhouse, then a small mill (used for grinding gorse—similar to scotch broom—into animal feed) and a Tudor-era trader's house, continue through the woods to **St. Teilos' Church,** surrounded by a white-washed stone fence. The interior has been restored to the way it looked around 1520—including vibrantly colorful illustrations of Bible stories on all the walls.

Leaving the church, turn left and continue ahead to the **Oakdale Workmen's Institute**—basically a leisure club and community center for hardworking miners and their families. Poking around the building—from the library, reading room, and meeting hall downstairs to the concert hall upstairs—you can imagine how a space like this provided a humble community with a much-needed social space.

Next up, just past the tall red box (a **telephone booth** from the 20th century, where people would make "telephonic" calls) are the **Gwalia Stores,** a village general store where you could buy just about anything imaginable (poke around to see what locals may have shopped for). One section of the store still sells canned goods, local cheeses, sweets, and ice cream; upstairs is a full-service tearoom.

Pass the olde-tyme portrait studio on your way up to the museum's highlight, the **Rhyd-y-Car** terrace of row houses, which displays ironworker cottages as they might have looked in 1805, 1855, 1895, 1925, 1955, and 1985—offering a fascinating zip through Welsh domestic life from hearths to microwaves. Notice the pea patches in front, the outhouse, and the chicken coops in the back.

Just past the row houses is a large grassy expanse (with a penny arcade and period rides on the far side). Turn right and step into the one-room **St. Mary's Board Schoolhouse,** where the docent can explain the various items used to punish ill-behaved kids in the late 19th century. What looks like a wooden version of brass knuckles was used to force lefties to write right. The "Welsh not" was worn as a badge of shame by any student heard speaking Welsh rather than the required English. Students could pass it on to other kids they heard speaking Welsh, and whoever was wearing it at day's end was caned (spanked with a stick). On the day of my visit, I overheard a present-day schoolkid loudly complaining that his teachers force him to speak *Welsh* instead of English.

After exiting the schoolhouse, take a hard right at the tollhouse to reach the **bakery.** This is a fine place to break for coffee and cake—they sell *bara brith* (speckled bread), a kind of fruit bread, hot out of the oven. Sitting on the picnic benches, you can enjoy all the family fun around you. Listen for parents talking to their kids in Welsh.

Head back past the entrance area and continue to the castle and gardens. You'll dip down past a series of terraced ponds, then climb steeply up to the misnamed **"castle"**—so-called because it was built on the remains of a real, Norman-era castle that once stood here. This circa-1580 Elizabethan manor house boasts a stately interior decorated with antique, period furnishing. It feels like the perfect setting for a murder mystery or a ghost tale. Pick up the information paddles in each room, and ask the docents questions. Entering, you'll walk through The Hall (a reception room for visitors), The Study (where the master of the house carried out his business), and The Drawing Room (where the ladies would convene for a post-dinner chat, à la *Downton Abbey*). Climb the funhouse stairs up to the long gallery, where you can dip into a series of bedrooms.

Leaving the castle, if it's nice out, turn left and explore the expansive manicured **gardens** that stretch out across the grounds. Near the far end is a woolen mill.

▲▲Caerphilly Castle

This impressive but gutted old castle—evocative but with no actual artifacts—is surrounded by lakes, gently rolling hills, and the town of Caerphilly. It's the most visit-worthy I've seen in South Wales.

Cost and Hours: £5.50; March-Oct daily 9:30-17:00, July-Aug until 18:00; Nov-Feb Mon-Sat 10:00-16:00, Sun 11:00-16:00; tel. 029/2088-3143, www.cadw.wales.gov.uk.

Information: Scant explanations are offered by a few posted plaques; if you want the full story, invest in the £4 guidebook. Across the moat, Caerphilly's helpful town **TI** happily answers questions. It also has free Wi-Fi with comfortable seating overlooking the castle, and sells a variety of locally-sourced, nontacky Welsh souvenirs, from hand-carved heart spoons to gifty edibles (daily 10:00-17:30, tel. 029/2088-0011, www.visitcaerphilly.com).

Getting There: The castle is located right in the center of the town of Caerphilly, nine miles north of Cardiff. To get there, take the train from Cardiff to Caerphilly (4/hour Mon-Sat, every 2 hours Sun, 20 minutes) and walk five minutes. It's 20 minutes by car from St. Fagans (exit 32, following signs from the M-4). Once in town, follow signs to park in the pay lot right next to the TI (described above), facing the castle.

Background: Spread over 30 acres, Caerphilly is the second-largest castle in Britain after Windsor. English Earl Gilbert de Clare erected this squat behemoth to try to establish a stronghold in Wales. With two concentric walls, it was considered to be a brilliant arrangement of defensive walls and moats. Attackers had to negotiate three drawbridges and four sets of doors and portcullises just to reach the main entrance. For the record, there were no known successful enemy forays beyond the current castle's inner walls. Later, this castle understandably became a favorite of Romantics, who often painted it in the shimmering Welsh mist. And in modern times, during the Great Depression of the 1930s, the castle's owner undertook a restoration of the then-mostly ruined structure (as a sort of private stimulus package), restoring it at least partway to its previous glory. Today it's surrounded by a picturesque, picnic-perfect park.

Visiting the Castle: Cross the first moat and enter the outer gate to buy your ticket. Then head across the second moat to reach the central keep of the castle.

You'll enter through the **Inner East Gatehouse,** with a short introductory video on the ground floor, and unfurnished but still stately residential halls upstairs. The top-floor terrace offers great views between the crenellations of the castle complex and the town. On the way up and down, look for the little bathrooms. No need to flush—the chute beneath the hole drops several stories directly into the moat below. (Just one more disincentive for would-be attackers thinking of crossing that moat.)

From there, head into the **Inner Ward**—the central yard (or "bailey") that's ringed by thick walls and stout towers. The tower across the Inner Ward to the right features another short video about the castle. To the left as you enter the Inner Ward is the restored, cavernous **Great Hall,** with thick stony walls, a wood-beam ceiling, and a man-sized fireplace. This space helps you imagine a great medieval feast. (If you'd like to do more than imagine, you can rent out the hall for a banquet of your own.)

Hiding behind the Great Hall is the icon of the castle—a half-destroyed listing **tower** (which, they like to brag, "out-leans Pisa's"). Following the English Civil War, the Parliament decreed that many castles like this one be destroyed as a preventive measure; this tower was a victim. Some believe that the adjacent **Braose Gallery** has a resident ghost: Legend has it that de Clare, after learning of his wife Alice's infidelity, exiled her back to France and had her lover killed. Upon discovering her paramour's fate, Alice died of a broken heart. Since then, the "Green Lady," named for her husband's jealousy, has reportedly roamed the ramparts.

Before leaving, be sure to visit the strip of yard that stretches out in front of the ticket office (along the inner moat). The first tower has a replica (complete with sound effects) of the **latrines** that were used by the soldiers—again, these dumped right into the moat. Just beyond that tower is a collection of life-size replica **siege engines**—ingenious catapult-like devices and oversized crossbows designed to deter attackers (each one is well described).

Big Pit National Coal Museum

To learn just how important the coal industry was to the economic development of South Wales, venture 30 miles north of Cardiff to a former coal mine in Blaenavon. Now part of the National Museum of Wales, the mine operated from 1860 to 1980. You can wander the grounds to see machinery and visit old buildings and exhibits. The highlight is the hour-long miner-guided tour 300 feet underground (hard hats and headlamps provided).

Cost and Hours: Free, parking-£3, daily 9:30-17:00, underground tours run 10:00-15:30, shorter hours off-season, last entry one hour before closing, café and coffee shop; in Blaenavon on the A-4043, tel. 0300-111-2333 or 029/2057-3650, www.museumwales.ac.uk/bigpit.

Sleeping in Cardiff

To overnight here, the basic choice is between a chain hotel downtown (which can be deeply discounted when it's not busy—check hotel-booking sites for deals) or a more characteristic B&B, most of which line Cathedral Road, a one-mile walk or quick bus ride from the city center. Parking along Cathedral Road is free but tight; some places offer private parking. Here are just a few of the seemingly dozens of choices along Cathedral Road.

$$ Beaufort House, with 10 rooms, boasts abundant decoration, a palatial breakfast room, and an inviting winter-garden lounge (Sb-£55-80, Db-£82-105, price depends on demand, private parking, 65 Cathedral Road, tel. 029/2023-7003, www.beauforthousecardiff.co.uk, paul@beauforthousecardiff.co.uk, Paul).

$ The Town House has eight nondescript rooms in a classy old townhouse with a big shared breakfast table (Sb-£50, Db-£70, 70 Cathedral Road, tel. 029/2023-9399, www.thetownhousecardiff.co.uk, thetownhouse@msn.com, Charles and Paula).

Cardiff Connections

From Cardiff by Train to: Caerphilly (2-4/hour, 20 minutes), **Bath** (hourly, 1-1.5 hours), **Birmingham** (1/hour direct, more with change in Bristol, 2 hours), **London**'s Paddington Station (2/hour, 2 hours), **Chepstow** (2/hour, 35 minutes; then bus #69 to **Tintern**—runs every 1-2 hours, 20 minutes). Train info: tel. 0871-200-2233, www.traveline-cymru.info.

By Car: For driving directions from Bath to Cardiff, see "Route Tips for Drivers" at the end of this chapter.

The Wye Valley

From Chepstow, on the mouth of the River Severn, the River Wye cuts north, marking the border between Wales (Monmouthshire, on the west bank) and England (Gloucestershire, on the east bank).

While everything covered here is in Wales, it's all within sight of England—just over the river.

This land is lush, mellow, and historic. Local tourist brochures explain the area's special dialect, its strange political autonomy, and its oaken ties to Trafalgar and Admiral Nelson (who harvested timbers for his ships in the Forest of Dean). The valley is home to the legendary Tintern Abbey, the ruined skeleton of a glorious church that's well worth a quick stop. The abbey sits partway between two pleasant, workaday towns with interesting sights of their own: Chepstow (with a fine castle) and Monmouth (a market town with some quirky sights). Just to the east of the river, in England, is the romantic-sounding but disappointing Forest of Dean.

If you've always dreamed of visiting Tintern Abbey—and wouldn't mind a quick taste of a stout castle and a couple of charming Welsh towns—the riverside A-466 traces the Wye and makes a detour between Bath and the Cotswolds that's worth considering (adding about an hour of driving compared with the less scenic, more direct route). I've listed these sights in the order you'll reach them as you move north up the Wye.

Chepstow

This historic burg enjoys a strategic location, for the same reason it may be your first stop in Wales: It marks the natural boundary between England and Wales. Driving into town, you'll pass through the town gate where, in medieval times, folks arriving to sell goods or livestock were hit up for tolls.

Park in the pay 'n' display lot just below the castle, which is also conveniently close to the TI, museum, and free WCs. Everything worth seeing is within a short walk. To explore more of the town, buy the *Chepstow Town Trail* guide at the TI or Chepstow Museum; basic walking instructions can also be found on the TI website (go to www.chepstowtowncrier.org.uk and click on "Things to Do," then "Walking"). St. Mary's Street is lined with appealing little lunch spots (try the Lime Tree Café).

The **TI** is helpful, with an inviting seating area in the back where you can access their free Wi-Fi and plan your River Wye day (Easter-early Oct daily 9:30-17:00, off-season until 15:30, Bridge Street, tel. 01291/623-772, www.chepstowtowncrier.org.uk).

Chepstow Castle

Perched on a riverside ridge overlooking the pleasant village of Chepstow on one side and the River Wye on the other, this castle is worth a short stop for drivers heading for Tintern Abbey, or it's a 10-minute walk from the Chepstow train station (follow signs; uphill going back). The stone-built Great Tower, dating from 1066, was among the first castles the Normans plunked down to

secure their turf in Wales, and it remained in use through 1690. While many castles of the time were built first in wood, Chepstow, then a key foothold on the England-Wales border, was built from stone from the start for durability. You'll work your way up through various towers and baileys (inner yards); a few posted plaques provide details, but you're mostly on your own. As you clamber along the battlements (with great views to town and over the river to England), you'll find architectural evidence of military renovations through the centuries, from Norman to Tudor right up through Cromwellian additions. You can tell which parts date from Norman days—they're the ones built from yellow sandstone instead of the grayish limestone that makes up the rest of the castle. While the castle would benefit from more exhibits (it's basically an empty shell), with a little imagination you can resurrect the skeletons of buildings and appreciate how formidable and strategic it must have been in its heyday.

Cost and Hours: £4.50; March-Oct daily 9:30-17:00, July-Aug until 18:00; Nov-Feb Mon-Sat 10:00-16:00, Sun 11:00-16:00; guidebook-£4.50, in Chepstow village a half-mile from train station, tel. 01291/624-065, www.cadw.wales.gov.uk.

▲Chepstow Museum

Highlighting Chepstow's history, this museum is in an 18th-century townhouse across the street from the castle. Endearingly earnest, jammed with artifacts, and well presented, it says just about everything that could possibly be said about this small town. Upstairs, the 1940 machine for giving women permanents will be etched in your memory forever.

Cost and Hours: Free; July-Sept daily 10:30-17:30; March-June and Oct Mon-Sat 11:00-17:00, Sun 14:00-17:00; Nov-Feb daily 11:00-16:00; tel. 01291/625-981.

Riverfront Park

From the TI and parking lot, walk one block down Bridge Street to the River Wye. The river is spanned by a graceful, white cast-iron bridge. If you walk across it to the ornate decorations in the middle (at the *Gloucester/Monmouth* sign), you can stand with one foot in Wales and the other in England (notice the *Gloucestershire* sign across the bridge). From the bridge, you'll also have great views back to the castle. Beneath your feet, the River Wye's banks and water are muddy because this is a tidal river, which can rise and fall about 20 feet twice a day.

Back in Wales, stroll 100 yards along the riverside park (with the river on your left), noticing that the English bank sits on a chalk cliff—into which has been painted a Union Jack (to celebrate King George V's Silver Jubilee in 1935). Near the standing stones is a large circular plaque marking the beginning of the Welsh Coast Path; from here, you can walk 870 miles all the way along the coast of Wales. Nearby is the 176-mile Offa's Dyke Path, which roughly traces the border between Wales and England. Together, these two paths go almost all the way around the country.

▲▲Tintern Abbey

Inspiring monks to prayer, William Wordsworth to poetry, J. M. W. Turner to a famous painting, and rushed tourists to a thoughtful moment, this verse-worthy ruined-castle-of-an-abbey merits a five-mile detour off the motorway. Founded in 1131 on a site chosen by Norman monks for its tranquility, it functioned as an austere Cistercian abbey until its dissolution in 1536. The monks followed a strict schedule. They rose several hours after midnight for the first of eight daily prayer sessions and spent the rest of their time studying, working the surrounding farmlands, and meditating. Dissolved under Henry VIII's Act of Suppression in 1536, the magnificent church moldered in relative obscurity until tourists in the Romantic era (late-18th century) discovered the wooded Wye Valley and abbey ruins. J. M. W. Turner made his first sketches in 1792, and William Wordsworth penned "Lines Composed a Few Miles Above Tintern Abbey..." in 1798.

With all the evocative ruined abbeys dotting the British landscape, why all the fuss about this one? Because few are as big, as remarkably intact, and as picturesquely situated. Most of the external walls of the 250-foot-long, 150-foot-wide church still stand, along with the exquisite window tracery and outlines of the sacristy, chapter house, and dining hall. The daylight that floods through the roofless ruins highlights the Gothic decorated arches—in those days a bold departure from Cistercian simplicity. While the guidebook (described next) narrates a very detailed, architecture-oriented tour, the best visit is to simply stroll the cavernous interior and let your imagination roam, like the generations of Romantics before you.

In summer, the abbey is flooded with tourists, so visit early or late to miss the biggest crowds. The shop sells Celtic jewelry and other gifts. Take an easy 15-minute walk up to St. Mary's Church (on the hill above town) for a view of the abbey, River Wye, and England just beyond.

Cost and Hours: £5.50; March-Oct daily 9:30-17:00, July-Aug until 18:00; Nov-Feb Mon-Sat 10:00-16:00, Sun 11:00-16:00; occasional summertime concerts in the cloisters (check website for schedule or ask at the TI), tel. 01291/689-251, www.cadw.wales.gov.uk.

Information: Sparse informational plaques clearly identify and explain each part of the complex. The dry, extensive £4.50 guidebook may be too much information—but if you're looking to redeem your £3 parking fee (see next), it brings the cost down to just £1.50, and makes the guidebook a fine souvenir.

Getting There: Drivers park in the pricey pay lot right next to the abbey (£3, refundable if you buy anything in the official shop or at The Anchor restaurant). By public transportation from Cardiff, catch a 35-minute train to Chepstow; from there, hop on bus #69 (runs every 1-2 hours, 20 minutes) or take a taxi to the abbey (figure about £10 one-way).

Near Tintern Abbey: The villages of **Tintern** and **Tintern Parva** cluster in wide spots along the main riverside road, just north of the abbey. A couple of miles north, just beyond the last of the inns, you'll find the **Old Station**—a converted train station with old rail cars that house a regional TI, gift shop, and an exhibit on the local railway (closed Nov-March, pay parking lot, tel. 01291/689-566, www.visitmonmouthshire.com). Surrounding the train cars are a fine riverside park, a café, and a few low-key, kid-friendly attractions.

Monmouth

Another bustling market town—bookending the valley of the River Wye with Chepstow—Monmouth has a pleasant square, a few offbeat museums, and an impressive roster of past residents. The main square is called **Agincourt Square,** after the famous battle won by a king who was born right here: Henry V (you'll see a statue of him in the niche on the big building). The stately building on that square, which houses the TI, is **Shire Hall,** the historic home of the courts and town council. This was the site of a famous 1840 trial of John Frost, a leader of the Chartist movement (championing the rights of the working class in Victorian Britain).

Standing in front of Shire Hall is a statue of **Charles Rolls** (1877-1910), contemplating a model airplane. This descendant of a noble Monmouth family was a pioneer of ballooning and aviation, and—together with his business partner, Frederick Royce—revolutionized motoring with the creation of their company, Rolls-Royce. The airplane he's holding, which he purchased from the Wright Brothers, helped him become the first person to fly over the English Channel and back, in 1910. (Just over a month later, he also became the first British person to die in a plane crash, when that same Wright Flyer lost its tail midflight.)

Across the street from Shire Hall, angle right up the lane to the Regimental Museum and the scant ruins of **Monmouth Castle,** where Henry V was born in 1386. While there's not much to see, the site may wring out a few goose bumps for historians.

A block up Priory Street is the endearing **Nelson Museum** (a.k.a. Monmouth Museum). Admiral Horatio Nelson, who was considered in Victorian times (and, by many, still today) to be the savior of England for his naval victories in the Napoleonic Wars, was a frequent visitor to Monmouth.

This remarkable collection of Nelson-worship began as the personal collection of local noblewoman Lady Georgiana Llangattock, who was also the mother of Charles Rolls. You'll see several of Nelson's personal effects, a replica of his uniform, the actual sword he wore in the Battle of Trafalgar (as well as the two swords surrendered by the French and Spanish commanders), and some 800 letters by or to him (pull out the drawers to see them). There are also a few small exhibits about other aspects of town history, including the Rolls family (www.monmouthshire.gov.uk).

A few blocks downhill in the opposite direction (down Monnow Street from Agincourt Square) is the picturesque, 13th-century **Monnow Bridge,** with its graceful arches and stout defensive tower in the middle.

Forest of Dean

East of Monmouth and the River Wye is this heavily promoted, 43-square-mile patch of rare "ancient woodland" (what Americans call "old-growth forest"). While the name alone is enough to conjure fantasies of primeval forests, King Arthur, and Robin Hood, the reality is underwhelming if you come from a region with a forested area of any significant size.

You could drive to the visitors center at Beechenhurst Lodge to pay too much for parking and get advice for a local hike, but I'd rather skip this forest entirely. Both England and Wales have far more interesting natural areas that are deserving of your time.

Sleeping in the Wye Valley

If you're seduced into spending the night in this charming area, you'll find plenty of B&Bs near Tintern Abbey or in the castle-crowned town of Chepstow, located just down the road (a one-hour drive from Bath). I've listed a few accommodations that are near the abbey.

$ The Florence is snuggled in the lower Wye Valley north of Tintern on the way to Monmouth. Four rooms are in the 17th-century main hotel building, with four more in the former gardener's cottage. All of the rooms are nicely maintained and a great value. On a nice day, hotel guests can eat on the garden terrace and share the scenery with the cows lazing along the riverbanks (Sb-£40, Db-£80, all with river view, no kids under 10, tel. 01594/530-830, www.florencehotel.co.uk, enquiries@florencehotel.co.uk, kind owners Dennis and Kathy). The B&B is along the main road between Tintern Abbey and Monmouth, about a 12-minute drive north of the abbey (just after the St. Briavels turnoff).

$ Parva Farmhouse, a lesser value, has eight old-fashioned rooms in a 400-year-old building right along the main road through Tintern. While a bit dated, it comes with Welsh charm and is within walking distance of the abbey, village, and local pubs (Sb-£60-70, Db-£78-85, a few pounds more on weekends, Monmouth Road, tel. 01291/689-411, www.parvafarmhouse.co.uk, Peter and Angela).

$ St. Briavels Castle Youth Hostel is housed in an 800-year-old Norman castle used by King John in 1215 (the year he signed the Magna Carta). The hostel is comfortable (as castles go), friendly, and in the center of the quiet village of St. Briavels just north of Tintern Abbey. Nonguests are welcome to poke around the courtyard; if you're in town and the gates are open, step inside (70 beds, bed in dorm room-£23-25, members-£3 less, breakfast-£5, private 4- to 8-bed rooms available, Nov-March open to groups only, reception open daily 8:00-10:00 & 17:00-23:00, curfew at 23:30, modern kitchen and medieval banquet hall, brown-bag lunches and evening meals available, tel. 0845-371-9042, www.yha.org.uk, stbriavels@yha.org.uk). The village of St. Briavels sits in a forest high above the river. From Tintern, head north on the A-466, watch for the St. Briavels turnoff on the right, and switchback up the steep road into town.

South Wales Connections

ROUTE TIPS FOR DRIVERS

Bath to Cardiff and St. Fagans: Leave Bath following signs for the A-4, then the M-4. It's 10 miles north (on the A-46 past a village called Pennsylvania) to the M-4 freeway. Zip westward, crossing a huge suspension bridge over the Severn, into Wales (£6.50 toll westbound only). Stay on the M-4 (not the M-48) past Cardiff, take exit 33, and follow the brown signs south to *St. Fagans National History Museum/Amgueddfa Werin Cymru/Museum of Welsh Life.*

Bath to Tintern Abbey: Follow the directions above to the M-4. Take the M-4 to exit 21 and get on the M-48. The abbey is six miles (up the A-466, follow signs to *Chepstow,* then *Tintern*) off the M-48 at exit 2, right where the northern bridge (£6.50 toll) across the Severn hits Wales.

Cardiff to the Cotswolds via Forest of Dean: On the Welsh side of the big suspension bridge, take the Chepstow exit and follow signs up the A-466 to *Tintern Abbey* and the *Wye River Valley.* Carry on to Monmouth, and follow the A-40 and the M-50 to the Tewkesbury exit, where small roads lead to the Cotswolds.

THE COTSWOLDS

Chipping Campden • Stow-on-the-Wold • Moreton-in-Marsh • Blenheim Palace

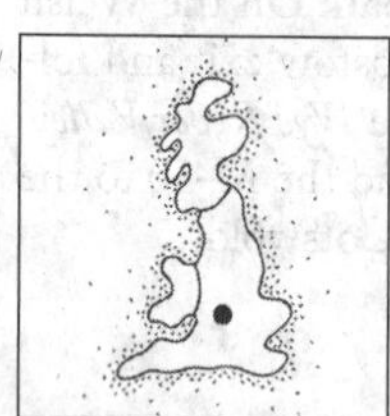

The Cotswold Hills, a 25-by-90-mile chunk of Gloucestershire, are dotted with enchanting villages and graced with England's greatest countryside palace, Blenheim. As with many fairy-tale regions of Europe, the present-day beauty of the Cotswolds was the result of an economic disaster. Wool was a huge industry in medieval England, and Cotswold sheep grew the best wool. A 12th-century saying bragged, "In Europe the best wool is English. In England the best wool is Cotswold." The region prospered. Wool money built fine towns and houses. Local "wool" churches are called "cathedrals" for their scale and wealth. Stained-glass slogans say things like "I thank my God and ever shall, it is the sheep hath paid for all."

With the rise of cotton and the Industrial Revolution, the woolen industry collapsed. Ba-a-a-ad news. The wealthy Cotswold towns fell into a depressed time warp; the homes of impoverished nobility became gracefully dilapidated. Today, visitors enjoy a harmonious blend of man and nature—the most pristine of English countrysides decorated with time-passed villages, rich wool churches, tell-me-a-story stone fences, and "kissing gates" you wouldn't want to experience alone. Appreciated by throngs of 21st-century Romantics, the Cotswolds are enjoying new prosperity.

The north Cotswolds are best. Two of the region's coziest towns, Chipping Campden and Stow-on-the-Wold, are eight and four miles, respectively, from Moreton-in-Marsh, which has the best public transportation connections. Any of these three towns makes a fine home base for your exploration of the thatch-happiest of Cotswold villages and walks.

PLANNING YOUR TIME

The Cotswolds are an absolute delight by car and, with a well-organized plan—and patience—are enjoyable even without one. Do your homework in advance; read this chapter carefully but don't get too hung up on the details. Then decide if you want to rent a car, rely on public transportation (budgeting for an inevitable taxi ride), or reserve a day with a tour company or private driver. Whatever you choose, on a three-week countrywide trip, I'd spend at least two nights and a day in the Cotswolds. The Cotswolds' charm has a softening effect on many uptight itineraries. You could enjoy days of walking from a home base here.

Home Bases: Chipping Campden and **Stow-on-the-Wold** are quaint without being overrun, and both have good accommodations. Stow has a bit more character for an overnight stay and offers the widest range of choices. The plain town of **Moreton-in-Marsh** is the only one of the three with a train station, and only worth visiting as a transit hub. While Moreton has the most convenient connections, nondrivers can also make it work to home-base in Chipping Campden or Stow—especially if you don't mind sorting through bus schedules or springing for the occasional taxi to connect towns. (This becomes even more challenging on Sundays, when there is essentially no bus service.) With a car, consider really getting away from it all by staying in one of the smaller villages.

Nearby Sights: England's top countryside palace, **Blenheim,** is located at the eastern edge of the Cotswolds, between Moreton and Oxford (see the end of this chapter); for drivers, Blenheim fits well on the way into or out of the region. If you want to take in some Shakespeare, note that Stow, Chipping Campden, and Moreton are only a 30-minute drive from **Stratford,** which offers a great evening of world-class entertainment (see next chapter).

One-Day Driver's Cotswold Blitz: Use a good map and reshuffle this plan to fit your home base:

- 9:00 Browse through Chipping Campden, following my self-guided walk.
- 10:30 Joyride through Snowshill, Stanway, and Stanton.
- 12:30 Have lunch in Stow-on-the-Wold, then follow my self-guided walk there.
- 15:00 Drive to the Slaughters, Bourton-on-the-Water, and Bibury; or, if you're up for a hike instead of a drive, walk from Stow to the Slaughters to Bourton, then catch the bus back to Stow.

Cotswold Appreciation 101

History can be read into the names of the area. *Cotswold* could come from the Saxon phrase meaning "hills of sheep's cotes" (shelters for sheep). Or it could mean shelter ("cot" like cottage) on the open upland ("wold").

In the Cotswolds, a town's main street (called High Street) needed to be wide to accommodate the sheep and cattle being marched to market (and today, to park tour buses). Some of the most picturesque cottages were once humble row houses of weavers' cottages, usually located along a stream for their waterwheels (good examples in Bibury and Lower Slaughter). The towns run on slow clocks and yellowed calendars. An entire village might not have a phone booth.

Fields of yellow (rapeseed) and pale blue (linseed) separate pastures dotted with black and white sheep. In just about any B&B, when you open your window in the morning you'll hear sheep baa-ing. The decorative "toadstool" stones dotting front yards throughout the region are medieval staddle stones, which buildings were set upon to keep the rodents out.

Cotswold walls and roofs are made of the local limestone. The limestone roof tiles hang by pegs. To make the weight more bearable, smaller and lighter tiles are higher up. An extremely

18:00 Have dinner at a countryside gastropub (reserve in advance by phone), then head home; or drive 30 minutes to Stratford-upon-Avon for a Shakespeare play.

Two-Day Plan by Public Transportation: This plan is best for any day except Sunday—when virtually no buses run—and assumes you're home-basing in Moreton-in-Marsh.

Day 1: Take the morning bus to Chipping Campden (likely departing around 9:30) to explore that town. Hike up Dover's Hill and back (about 1-hour round-trip), or take the bus to Mickleton and walk (uphill, 45 minutes) to Hidcote Manor Garden for a visit there. Eat lunch in Chipping Campden, then squeeze in either Broad Campden or Broadway before returning directly from either town to Moreton by bus #21 or #22.

Day 2: Take a day trip to Blenheim Palace via Oxford (train to Oxford, bus to palace—explained on page 407). Or take a morn-

strict building code keeps towns looking what many locals call "overly quaint."

While you'll still see lots of sheep, the commercial wool industry is essentially dead. It costs more to shear a sheep than the 50 pence the wool will fetch. In the old days, sheep lived long lives, producing lots of wool. When they were finally slaughtered, the meat was tough and eaten as "mutton." Today, you don't find mutton much because the sheep are raised primarily for their meat, and slaughtered younger. When it comes to Cotswold sheep these days, it's lamb (not mutton) for dinner (not sweaters).

Towns are small, and everyone seems to know everyone. The area is provincial yet ever-so-polite, and people commonly rescue themselves from a gossipy tangent by saying, "It's all very... mmm...yaaa."

In contrast to the village ambience are the giant manors and mansions whose private gated driveways you'll drive past. Many of these now belong to A-list celebrities, who have country homes here. If you live in the Cotswolds, you can call Madonna, Elizabeth Hurley, and Kate Moss your neighbors.

This is walking country. The English love their walks and vigorously defend their age-old right to free passage. Once a year the Ramblers, Britain's largest walking club, organizes a "Mass Trespass," when each of the country's 50,000 miles of public footpaths is walked. By assuring that each path is used at least once a year, they stop landlords from putting up fences. Any paths found blocked are unceremoniously unblocked.

Questions to ask locals: Do you think foxhunting should have been banned? Who are the Morris men? What's a kissing gate?

ing bus to Stow. After poking around the town, hike from Stow through the Slaughters to Bourton-on-the-Water (about 3 hours at a relaxed pace), then return by bus or taxi to Moreton for dinner.

TOURIST INFORMATION

Local TIs stock a wide array of helpful resources and can tell you about any local events during your stay. Ask for the *Cotswold Lion*, the biannual newspaper, which includes suggestions for walks and hikes (spring/summer); bus schedules for the routes you'll be using; and the *Attractions and Events Guide* (with updated prices and hours for Cotswold sights). Each village also has its own assortment of brochures, often for a small fee (£0.50-1). While paying for these items seems chintzy, realize that Cotswold TIs have lost much of their funding and are struggling to make ends meet (some are run by volunteers).

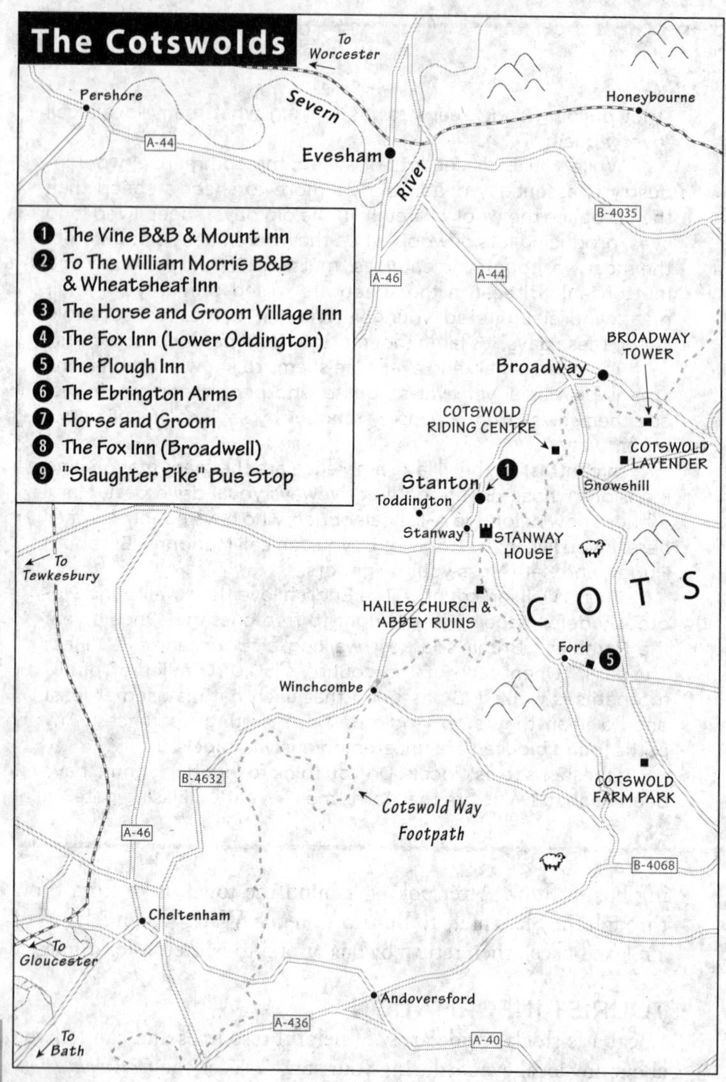

GETTING AROUND THE COTSWOLDS

By Bus

The Cotswolds are so well-preserved, in part, because public transportation to and within this area has long been miserable. Fortunately, larger towns are linked by trains, and a few key buses connect the more interesting villages. Centrally located Moreton-in-Marsh is the region's transit hub—with the only train station and several bus lines.

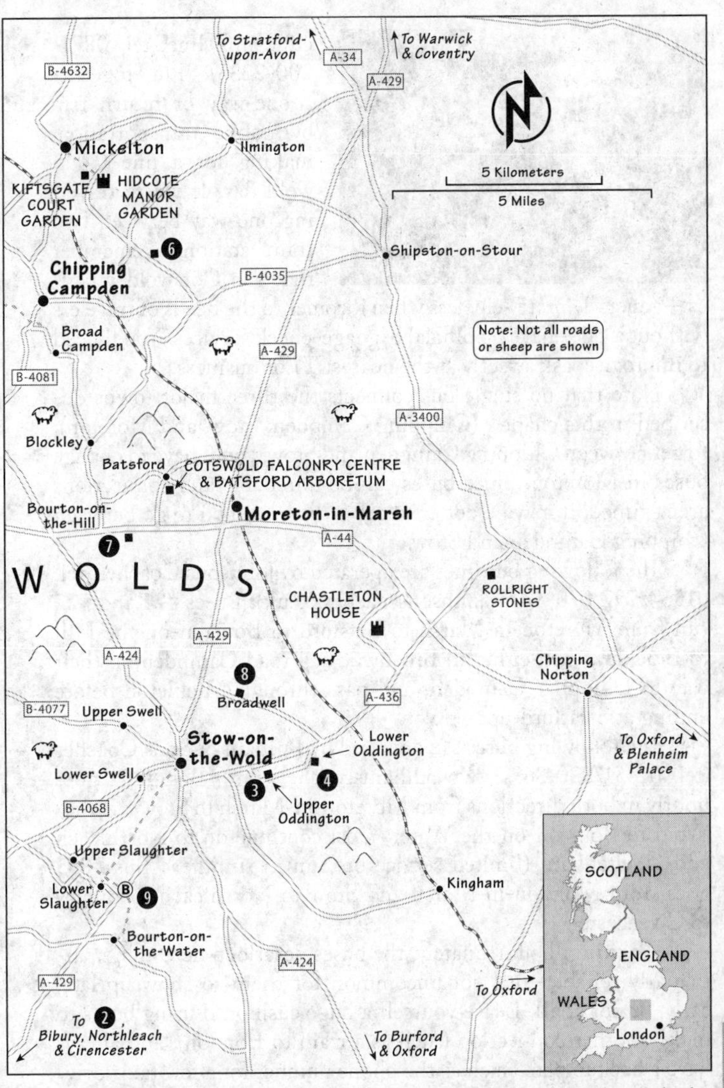

To explore the towns, use the bus routes that hop through the Cotswolds about every 1.5 hours, lacing together main stops and ending at rail stations. In each case, the entire trip takes about an hour. Individual fares are around £4. If you plan on taking more than two rides in a day, consider the Cotswolds Discoverer pass, which offers unlimited travel on most buses including those listed below (£10/day, £25/3 days, www.escapetothecotswolds.org.uk/discoverer).

The TI hands out easy-to-read bus schedules for the key lines described below (or check www.traveline.org.uk, or call the Trav-

eline info line, tel. 0871-200-2233). Put together a one-way or return trip by public transportation, making for a fine Cotswold day. If you're traveling one-way between two train stations, remember that the Cotswold villages—generally pretty clueless when it comes to the needs of travelers without a car—have no official baggage-check services. You'll need to improvise; ask sweetly at the nearest TI or business.

Note that no single bus connects the three major towns described in this chapter (Chipping Campden, Stow, and Moreton); to get between Chipping Campden and Stow, you'll have to change buses in Moreton. Since buses can be unreliable and connections aren't timed, it may be better to call a driver or taxi to go between Chipping Campden and Stow.

The following bus lines are operated by Johnsons Coaches (tel. 01564/797-070, www.johnsonscoaches.co.uk): Buses **#21** and **#22** run from Moreton-in-Marsh to Batsford to Bourton-on-the-Hill to Blockley, then either to Broadway or Broad Campden on their way to Chipping Campden, and pass through Mickleton before ending at Stratford-upon-Avon.

The following buses are operated by Pulham & Sons Coaches (tel. 01451/820-369, www.pulhamscoaches.com): Bus **#801** goes hourly in both directions from Moreton-in-Marsh to Stow-on-the-Wold to Bourton-on-the-Water; most continue on to Northleach and Cheltenham (limited service on Sun in summer). Bus **#855** goes from Moreton-in-Marsh and Stow to Northleach to Bibury to Cirencester.

Warning: Unfortunately, the buses described here aren't particularly reliable—it's not uncommon for them to show up late, early, or not at all. Leave yourself a huge cushion if using buses to make another connection (such as a train to London), and always have a backup plan (such as the phone number for a few taxis/drivers or for your hotel, who can try calling someone for you). Remember that bus service is essentially nonexistent on Sundays.

By Bike

Despite narrow roads, high hedgerows (blocking some views), and even higher hills, bikers enjoy the Cotswolds free from the constraints of bus schedules. For each area, TIs have fine route planners that indicate which peaceful, paved lanes are particularly scenic for biking. In summer, it's smart to book your rental bike a couple of days ahead—but note that only Chipping Campden and Bourton-on-the-Water have shops that rent out bikes.

In **Chipping Campden** your only choice is **Cycle Cotswolds,** at the Volunteer Inn pub (£12/day, daily 7:00-dusk, Lower High Street, mobile 07549-620-597, www.cyclecotswolds.co.uk). If you make it to **Bourton-on-the-Water,** you can rent bicycles through **Hartwells** on High Street (£10/3 hours, £14/day, includes helmet, route map, and locks; Mon-Sat 9:00-18:00, Sun 10:00-18:00; tel. 01451/820-405, www.hartwells.supanet.com).

If you're interested in a biking vacation, **Cotswold Country Cycles** offers self-led bike tours of the Cotswolds and surrounding areas (tours last 2-7 days and include accommodations and luggage transfer, see www.cotswoldcountrycycles.com).

By Foot

Walking guidebooks and leaflets abound, giving you a world of choices for each of my recommended stops (choose a book with clear maps). If you're doing any hiking whatsoever, get the excellent Ordnance Survey Explorer OL #45 map, which shows every road, trail, and ridgeline (£8 at local TIs). Nearly every hotel and B&B has a box or shelf of local walking guides and maps, including Ordnance Survey #45. Don't hesitate to ask for a loaner. For a quick circular hike from a particular village, peruse the books and brochures offered by that village's TI. Villages are generally no more than three miles apart, and most have pubs that would love to feed and water you. For a list of guided walks, ask at any TI for the free *Cotswold Lion* newspaper. The walks range from 2 to 12 miles, and often involve a stop at a pub or tearoom (*Lion* newspaper also online at www.cotswoldsaonb.org.uk—click on "Publications").

Another option is to leave the planning to a company such as **Cotswold Walking Holidays,** which can help you design a walking vacation, provide route instructions and maps, transfer your bags, and even arrange lodging. They also offer five- to six-night walking tours that come with a local guide. Walking through the towns allows you to slow down and enjoy the Cotswolds at their very best—experiencing open fields during the day and arriving into towns just as the day-trippers depart (www.cotswoldwalks.com).

There are many options for hikers, ranging from the "Cotswold Way" path that leads 100 miles from Chipping Campden all the way to Bath, to easy loop trips to the next village. Serious hikers enjoy doing a several-day loop, walking for several hours each day and sleeping in a different village each night. One popular route is the **"Cotswold Ring":** Day 1—Moreton-in-Marsh to Stow-on-the-Wold to the Slaughters to Bourton-on-the-Water (12 miles);

The Cotswolds at a Glance

Chipping Campden and Nearby

▲▲Chipping Campden Picturesque market town with finest High Street in England, accented by a 17th-century Market Hall, wool-tycoon manors, and a characteristic Gothic church. See page 365.

▲▲Stanway House Grand aristocratic home of the Earl of Wemyss, with the tallest fountain in Britain and a 14th-century tithe barn. **Hours:** June-Aug Tue and Thu only 14:00-17:00, closed Sept-May. See page 376.

▲Stanton Classic Cotswold village with flower-filled exteriors and 15th-century church. See page 378.

▲Snowshill Manor Eerie mansion packed to the rafters with eclectic curiosities collected over a lifetime. **Hours:** July-Aug Wed-Mon 11:30-16:30, closed Tue; April-June and Sept-Oct Wed-Sun 12:00-17:00, closed Mon-Tue; closed Nov-March. See page 380.

▲Hidcote Manor Garden Fragrant garden organized into color-themed "outdoor rooms" that set a trend in 20th-century garden design. **Hours:** March-Sept daily 10:00-18:00; Oct daily 10:00-17:00; Nov-Dec Sat-Sun 11:00-16:00, closed Mon-Fri; closed Jan-Feb. See page 381.

▲Broad Campden, Blockley, and Bourton-on-the-Hill Trio of villages with sweeping views and quaint homes, far from the madding crowds. See page 382.

Stow-on-the-Wold and Nearby

▲▲Stow-on-the-Wold Convenient Cotswold home base with charming shops and pubs clustered around town square, plus popular day hikes. See page 383.

▲Lower and Upper Slaughter Inaptly named historic villages—home to a working waterwheel, peaceful churches, and a folksy museum. See page 394.

Day 2—Bourton-on-the-Water to Winchcombe (13 miles); Day 3—Winchcombe to Stanway to Stanton (7 miles), or all the way to Broadway (10.5 miles total); Day 4—On to Chipping Campden (just 5.5 miles, but steeply uphill); Day 5—Chipping Campden to Broad Campden, Blockley, Bourton-on-the-Hill, or Batsford, and back to Moreton (7 miles).

Realistically, on a short visit, you won't have time for that

▲Bourton-on-the-Water The "Venice of the Cotswolds," touristy yet undeniably striking, with petite canals and impressive Motor Museum. See page 395.

▲Cotswold Farm Park Kid-friendly park with endangered breeds of native British animals, farm demonstrations, and tractor rides. **Hours:** Daily Feb-Oct 10:30-17:00, Nov-Dec 10:30-16:00, closed Jan. See page 397.

▲Mechanical Music Museum Tiny museum brimming with self-playing musical instruments, demonstrations, and Victorian music boxes. **Hours:** Daily 10:00-17:00. See page 398.

▲Bibury Village of antique weavers' cottages, ideal for outdoor activities like fishing and picnicking. See page 399.

▲Cirencester Ancient 2,000-year-old city noteworthy for its crafts center and museum, showcasing artifacts from Roman and Saxon times. See page 400.

Moreton-in-Marsh and Nearby

▲Moreton-in-Marsh Relatively flat and functional home base with the best transportation links in the Cotswolds and a bustling Tuesday market. See page 401.

▲Chastleton House Lofty Jacobean-era home with a rich family history. **Hours:** April-Sept Wed-Sun 13:00-17:00; late March and Oct closes at 16:00; closed Nov-mid-March and Mon-Tue year-round. See page 405.

▲▲▲Blenheim Palace Fascinating, sumptuous, still-occupied aristocratic abode—one of Britain's best. **Hours:** Mid-Feb-Oct daily 10:30-17:30, Nov-mid-Dec at least Wed-Sun 10:30-17:30, park open but palace closed mid-Dec-mid-Feb. See page 407.

much hiking. But if you have a few hours to spare, consider venturing across the pretty hills and meadows of the Cotswolds. Each of the home-base villages I recommend has several options. Stow-on-the-Wold, immersed in pleasant but not-too-hilly terrain, is within easy walking distance of several interesting spots and is probably the best starting point. Chipping Campden sits along a ridge, which means that hikes from there are extremely scenic, but also more strenuous. Moreton—true to its name—sits on a marsh, offering flatter and less picturesque hikes.

Here are a few hikes to consider, in order of difficulty (easiest first). I've selected these for their convenience to the home-base towns and because the start and/or end points are on bus lines, allowing you to hitch a ride back to where you started (or on to the next town) rather than backtracking by foot.

Stow, the Slaughters, and Bourton-on-the-Water: Walk from Stow to Upper and Lower Slaughter, then on to Bourton-on-the-Water (which has bus service back to Stow on #801). One big advantage of this walk is that it's mostly downhill (4 miles, about 2-3 hours one-way). For details, see page 388.

Chipping Campden, Broad Campden, Blockley, and Bourton-on-the-Hill: From Chipping Campden, it's an easy mile walk into charming Broad Campden, and from there, a more strenuous hike to Blockley and Bourton-on-the-Hill (which are both connected by buses #21 and #22 to Chipping Campden and Moreton). For more details, see page 365.

Winchcombe, Stanway, Stanton, and Broadway: You can reach the charming villages of Stanway and Stanton by foot, but it's tough going—lots of up and down. The start and end points (Winchcombe and Broadway) have decent bus connections, and in a pinch some buses do serve Stanton (but carefully check schedules before you set out).

Broadway to Chipping Campden: The hardiest hike of those I list here, this takes you along the Cotswold Ridge. Attempt it only if you're a serious hiker (5.5 miles).

Bibury and the Coln Valley are pretty, but limited bus access makes hiking there less appealing.

By Car

Joyriding here truly is a joy. Winding country roads seem designed to spring bucolic village-and-countryside scenes on the driver at every turn. Distances here are wonderfully short—but only if you invest in the Ordnance Survey map of the Cotswolds, sold locally at TIs and newsstands (the £8 Explorer OL #45 map is excellent but almost too detailed for drivers; a £5 tour map covers a wider area in less detail). Here are driving distances from Moreton: **Stow-on-the-Wold** (4 miles), **Chipping Campden** (8 miles), **Broadway** (10 miles), **Stratford-upon-Avon** (17 miles), **Warwick** (23 miles), **Blenheim Palace** (20 miles).

Car hiking is great. In this chapter, I cover the postcard-perfect (but discovered) villages. With a car and the local Ordnance Survey map, you can easily ramble about and find your own gems. The problem with having a car is that you are less likely to walk.

Consider taking a taxi or bus somewhere, so that you can walk back to your car and enjoy the scenery (see suggestions earlier).

Car Rental: Two places near Moreton-in-Marsh rent cars by the day—reserve yours in advance. **Value Self Drive,** based in Shipston-on-Stour (about six miles north of Moreton) and run by Steve Bradley, has affordable rates (£32-49/day plus tax, includes insurance, discount rates available for longer rentals; open Mon-Sat 8:15-17:30, Sun by appointment only; call ahead to arrange, mobile 07974-805-485, stevebradleycars@aol.com). Conveniently, Steve will pick you up in Moreton (£18) or Stratford-upon-Avon (£20), and bring you back to Shipston to get your car. **Robinson Goss Self Drive,** also six miles north of Moreton-in-Marsh, is a bit more expensive and won't bring the car to you in Moreton (£31-61/day plus extras like navigation and gas, Mon-Fri 8:30-17:00, Sat 8:30-12:00, closed Sun, tel. 01608/663-322, www.robgos.co.uk).

By Taxi or Private Driver

Two or three town-to-town taxi trips can make more sense than renting a car. While taking a cab cross-country seems extravagant, the distances are short (Stow to Moreton is 4 miles, Stow to Chipping Campden is 10), and one-way walks are lovely. If you call a cab, confirm that the meter will start only when you are actually picked up. Consider hiring a private driver at the hourly "touring rate" (generally around £35), rather than the meter rate. For a few more bucks than taking a taxi, you can have a joyride peppered with commentary. Whether you book a taxi or a private driver, expect to pay about £25 between Chipping Campden and Stow and about £20 between Chipping Campden and Moreton.

Note that the drivers listed here are not typical city taxi services (with many drivers on call), but are mostly individuals—it's smart to call ahead if you're arriving in high season, since they can be booked in advance on weekends.

To scare up a taxi in Moreton, try Stuart and Stephen at **ETC,** "Everything Taken Care of" (tel. 01608/650-343 or toll-free 0800/955-8584, cotswoldtravel.co.uk) or **Iain Taxis** (mobile 07836-374-491, iaintaxis@btinternet.com); see also the taxi phone numbers posted outside the Moreton train station office. In Stow, try Iain (above) or **Tony Knight** (mobile 07887-714-047, anthonyknight205@btinternet.com). In Chipping Campden, call Iain (above), Paul at **Cotswold Private Hire** (mobile 07980-857-833), Barry Roberts at **Chipping Campden Private Hire** (also does tours, mobile 07774-224-684, www.cotswoldpersonaltours.com), or **Les Proctor,** who offers village tours and station pick-ups (mobile 07580-993-492, Les also co-runs Cornerways B&B—see page 372). Tim Harrison at **Tour the Cotswolds** specializes in tours of the Cotswolds and its gardens, but will also do tours outside the area (mobile 07779-030-820, www.tourthecotswolds.co.uk).

By Tour

Departing from Bath, **Lion Tours** offers a Cotswold Discovery full-day tour, and can drop you and your luggage off in Stow at no extra charge or in Moreton-in-Marsh for £5/person (minimum £10). If you want to get back to London in time for a show, ask to be dropped off at Kemble Station; it's best to arrange these drop-offs in advance (see page 244 of the Bath chapter).

Cotswold Tour offers a smartly arranged day of sightseeing for people with limited time and transportation. Reserve your spot online, then meet Becky at Moreton-in-Marsh's train station at 10:15 (10:30 on Sundays). The tour follows a set route that includes a buffet lunch and cream tea served in her cottage and returns to the station by 16:30—good timing for day-trippers to return to London for the evening (£85/person, Mon-Sat departs Moreton-in-Marsh station at 10:15, Sun at 10:30, must reserve ahead online, no luggage allowed—if you're traveling with bags you'll have to find somewhere in Moreton to store them for the day, tel. 01608/674-700, www.cotswoldtourismtours.co.uk).

While none of the Cotswold towns offer regularly scheduled walks, many have voluntary **warden groups** who love to meet visitors and give walks for a small donation (see specific contact information later for Chipping Campden).

Chipping Campden

Just touristy enough to be convenient, the north Cotswold town of Chipping Campden (CAM-den) is a ▲▲ sight. This market town, once the home of the richest Cotswold wool merchants, has some incredibly beautiful thatched roofs. Both the great British historian G. M. Trevelyan and I call Chipping Campden's High Street the finest in England.

Orientation to Chipping Campden

TOURIST INFORMATION

Chipping Campden's TI is tucked away in the old police station on High Street. Get the £1.50 town guide with map, or the local *Footpath Guide* for £2.25 (April-Oct daily 9:30-17:00; Nov-March Mon-Thu 9:30-13:00, Fri-Sun 9:30-16:00; tel. 01386/841-206, www.chippingcampdenonline.org).

HELPFUL HINTS

Festivals: Chipping Campden's biggest festival is the **Cotswold Olimpicks,** a series of tongue-in-cheek countryside games (such as competitive shin-kicking) atop Dover's Hill, just above town (first Fri-Sat after Late May Bank Holiday, www.olimpickgames.co.uk). They also have a **music festival** in May and an **open gardens festival** the third weekend in June.

Internet Access: Try the occasionally open **library** (closed Thu and Sun; High Street, tel. 08452/305-420) or **Butty's at the Old Bakehouse,** a casual eatery with free Wi-Fi (see page 374 for hours, Lower High Street, tel. 01386/840-401).

Bike Rental: Call **Cycle Cotswolds** (see page 358).

Taxi: Try **Cotswold Private Hire, Chipping Campden Private Hire,** or **Tour the Cotswolds** (see page 363).

Parking: Find a spot anywhere along High Street and park for free with no time limit. There's also a pay-and-display lot on High Street, across from the TI (1.5-hour maximum). If those are full, there is free parking on the street called Back Ends. On weekends, you can also park for free at the school (see map).

Tours: The local members of the **Cotswold Voluntary Wardens**

would be happy to show you around town for a small donation to their conservation society (suggested donation-£3/person, 1-hour walk, walks June-Sept Tue at 14:30 and Thu at 10:00, meet at Market Hall). Tour guide and coordinator Ann Colcomb can help arrange for a walk on other days as well (tel. 01386/832-131).

Walks and Hikes from Chipping Campden: Since this is a particularly hilly area, long-distance hikes are challenging. The easiest and most rewarding stroll is to the thatch-happy hobbit village of **Broad Campden** (about a mile, mostly level). From there, you can walk or take the bus (#22) back to Chipping Campden.

Or, if you have more energy, continue from Broad Campden up over the ridge and into picturesque **Blockley**—and, if your stamina holds out, all the way to **Bourton-on-the-Hill** (Blockley and Bourton-on-the-Hill are also connected by buses #21 and #22 to Chipping Campden and Moreton).

Alternatively, you can hike up to **Dover's Hill,** just north of the village. Ask locally about this easy circular one-hour walk that takes you on the first mile of the 100-mile-long Cotswold Way (which goes from here to Bath).

For more about hiking, see "Getting Around the Cotswolds—By Foot" on page 359.

Chipping Campden Walk

This self-guided stroll through "Campden" (as locals call their town) takes you from the Market Hall west to the old silk mill, and then back east the length of High Street to the church. It takes about an hour.

Market Hall: Begin at Campden's most famous monument—the Market Hall. It stands in front of the TI, marking the town center. The Market Hall was built in 1627 by the 17th-century Lord of the Manor, Sir Baptist Hicks. (Look for the Hicks family coat of arms on the east end of the building's facade.) Back then, it was an elegant—even over-the-top—shopping hall for the townsfolk who'd come here to buy their produce. In the 1940s, it was almost sold to an American, but the townspeople heroically raised money to buy it first, then gave it to the National Trust for its preservation.

The timbers inside are true to the original. Study the classic

Cotswold stone roof, still held together with wooden pegs nailed in from underneath. (Tiles were cut and sold with peg holes, and stacked like waterproof scales.) Buildings all over the region still use these stone shingles. Today, the hall, which is rarely used, stands as a testimony to the importance of trade to medieval Campden.

Adjacent to the Market Hall is the sober WWI monument—a reminder of the huge price paid by nearly every little town. Walk around it, noticing how 1918 brought the greatest losses.

Between the Market Hall and the WWI monument, you'll find a limestone disc embedded in the ground marking the ceremonial start of the Cotswold Way (you'll find its partner in front of the abbey in Bath—100 miles away—marking the southern end).

The TI is just across the street, in the old police courthouse. If it's open, you're welcome to climb the stairs and peek into the **Magistrate's Court** (free, same hours as TI, ask at TI to go up). Under the open-beamed courtroom, you'll find a humble little exhibit on the town's history.

• *Walk west, passing the town hall and the parking lot that was originally the sheep market, until you reach the Red Lion Inn. Across High Street (and a bit to the right), look for the house with a sundial and sign over the door reading...*

"Green Dragons": The house's decorative black cast-iron fixtures (originally in the stables) once held hay and functioned much like salad bowls for horses. Fine-cut stones define the door, but "rubble stones" make up the rest of the wall. The pink stones are the same limestone but have been heated, and likely were scavenged from a house that burned down.

• *At the Red Lion, leave High Street and walk a block down Sheep Street. At the little creek just past the public WC, a 30-yard-long lane on the right leads to an old Industrial-Age silk mill (and the Hart silversmith shop).*

Silk Mill: The tiny Cam River powered a mill here since about 1790. Today it houses the handicraft workers guild and some interesting history. In 1902, Charles Robert Ashbee (1863-1942) revitalized this sleepy hamlet of 2,500 by bringing a troupe of London artisans and their families (160 people in all) to town. Ashbee was a leader in the romantic Arts and Crafts movement—craftspeople repulsed by the Industrial Revolution who idealized the handmade crafts and preindustrial ways. Ashbee's idealistic craftsmen's guild lasted only until 1908, when most of his men grew bored with their small-town, back-to-nature ideals. Today, the only shop surviving

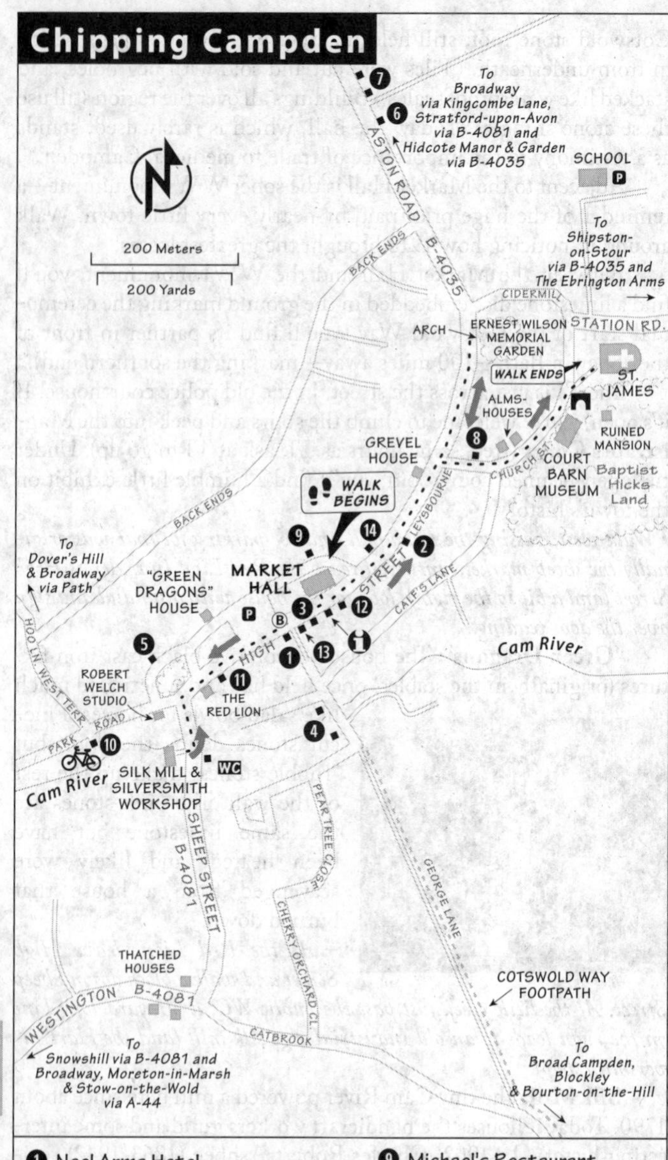

1 Noel Arms Hotel
2 The Lygon Arms Hotel & Pub
3 Badgers Hall Tea Room/B&B
4 Cornerways & Stonecroft B&Bs
5 The Old Bakehouse & Butty's
6 Cherry Trees B&B
7 The Chance B&B & Bramley House
8 Eight Bells Pub
9 Michael's Restaurant
10 Maharaja Indian Restaurant & Cycle Cotswolds
11 La Tradition Bakery
12 Bantam Tea Rooms
13 Co-op Grocery
14 Tokes Grocery

from the originals is that of **silversmith David Hart.** His grandfather came to town with Ashbee, and the workshop (upstairs in the mill building) is an amazing time warp—little-changed since 1902. Hart is a gracious man as well as a fine silversmith, and he, his son William, and nephew Julian welcome browsers six days a week (Mon-Fri 9:00-17:00, Sat 9:00-12:00, closed Sun, tel. 01386/841-100). They're proud that everything they make is a "one-off." (While you could continue 200 yards farther to see some fine thatched houses, this walk doesn't.)

• *Return to High Street. On the corner is the studio shop of Robert Welsh, a local industrial designer who worked in the spirit of the Arts and Crafts movement. His son and daughter carry on his legacy in the fine shop (with a little museum case in the back). Turn right, and walk through town.*

High Street: Chipping Campden's High Street has changed little architecturally since 1840. (The town's street plan and property lines survive from the 12th century.) As you now walk the length of England's finest surviving High Street, study the skyline, see the dates on the buildings, and count the sundials. Notice the harmony of the long rows of buildings. While the street comprises different styles through the centuries, everything you see was made of the same Cotswold stone—the only stone allowed today.

To remain level, High Street arcs with the contour of the hillside. Because it's so wide, you know this was a market town. In past centuries, livestock and packhorses laden with piles of freshly shorn fleece would fill the streets. Campden was a sales and distribution center for the wool industry, and merchants from as far away as Italy would come here for the prized raw wool.

High Street has no house numbers: Locals know the houses by their names. In the distance, you'll see the town church (where this walk ends). Notice that the power lines are buried underground, making the scene delightfully uncluttered.

As you stroll High Street, you'll find the finest houses on the uphill side—which gets more sun. Decorative features (like the Ionic capitals near the TI) are added for nonstructural touches of class. Most High Street buildings are half-timbered, but with cosmetic stone facades. You may see some exposed half-timbered walls. Study the crudely beautiful framing, made of hand-hewn oak (you can see the adze marks) and held together by wooden pegs.

Peeking down alleys, you'll notice how the lots are narrow but very deep. Called "burgage plots," this platting goes back to 1170. In medieval times, rooms were lined up long and skinny like train cars: Each building had a small storefront, followed by a workshop, living quarters, staff quarters, stables, and a garden at the very back. Now the private alleys that still define many of these old lots lead to comfy gardens. While some of today's buildings are wider, virtually all the widths are exact multiples of that basic first unit (for example, a modern building may be three times wider than its medieval counterpart).

• *Hike the length of High Street toward the church, to just before the first intersection, to find a house on the left with gargoyles hanging out above. This is the....*

Grevel House: In 1367, William Grevel built what's considered Campden's first stone house. Sheep tycoons had big homes. Imagine back then, when this fine building was surrounded by humble wattle-and-daub huts. It had newfangled chimneys, rather than a crude hole in the roof. (No more rain inside!) Originally a "hall house" with just one big, tall room, it got its upper floor in the 16th century. The finely carved central bay window is a good early example of the Perpendicular Gothic style. The gargoyles scared away bad spirits—and served as rain spouts. The boot scrapers outside each door were fixtures in that muddy age—especially in market towns, where the streets were filled with animal dung.

• *Continue up High Street for about 100 yards. Go past Church Street (which we'll walk up later). On the right, at a big tree behind a low stone wall, you'll find a small Gothic arch leading into a garden.*

Ernest Wilson Memorial Garden: Once the church's vegetable patch, this small and secluded garden is a botanist's delight today. Pop inside if it's open. The garden is filled with well-labeled plants that the Victorian botanist Ernest Wilson brought back to England from his extensive travels in Asia. There's a complete history of the garden on the board to the left of the entry.

• *Backtrack to Church Street. Turn left, walk past the recommended Eight Bells pub, and hook left with the street. Along your right-hand side stretches...*

Baptist Hicks Land: Sprawling adjacent to the town church, the area known as Baptist Hicks Land held Hicks' huge estate and manor house. This influential Lord of the Manor was from "a family of substance," who were merchants of silk and fine clothing as well as moneylenders. Beyond the ornate gate (which you'll see ahead, near the church), only a few outbuildings and the charred corner of his **mansion** survive. The mansion was burned by royalists in 1645 during the Civil War—notice how Cotswold stone turns red when burned. Hicks housed the poor, making a show of his generosity, adding a long row of almshouses (with his family coat of arms) for neighbors to see as they walked to church.

These almshouses (lining Church Street on the left) house pensioners today, as they have since the 17th century. Across the street is a ditch built as a "cart wash"—it was filled with water to soak old cart wheels so they'd swell up and stop rattling.

On the right, filling the old **Court Barn,** is a museum about crafts and designs from the Arts and Crafts movement, with works by Ashbee and his craftsmen (overpriced at £5, April-Sept Tue-Sun 10:00-17:00, Oct-March Tue-Sun 10:00-16:00, closed Mon year-round, tel. 01386/841-951, www.courtbarn.org.uk).

• *Next to the Hicks gate, a scenic, tree-lined lane leads to the front door of the church. On the way, notice the 12 lime trees, one for each of the apostles, that were planted in about 1760 (sorry, no limes).*

St. James Church: One of the finest churches in the Cotswolds, St. James Church graces one of its leading towns. Both the town and the church were built by wool wealth. Go inside. The church is Perpendicular Gothic, with lots of light and strong verticality. Notice the fine vestments and altar hangings (intricate c. 1460 embroidery) behind protective blue curtains (near the back of the church). Tombstones pave the floor in the chancel (often under protective red carpeting)—memorializing great wool merchants through the ages.

At the altar is a brass relief of William Grevel, the first owner of the Grevel House (described earlier), and his wife. But it is Sir Baptist Hicks who dominates the church. His huge canopied tomb is the ornate final resting place for Hicks and his wife, Elizabeth. Study their faces, framed by fancy lace ruffs (trendy in the 1620s). Adjacent—as if in a closet—is a statue of their daughter, Lady Juliana, and her husband, Lutheran Yokels. Juliana commissioned the statue in 1642, when her husband died, but had it closed up until *she* died in 1680. Then the doors were opened, revealing these two people holding hands and living happily ever after—at least in marble. The hinges were likely used only once.

As you leave the church, look immediately around the corner to the right of the door. A small tombstone reads "Thank you Lord for Simon, a dearly loved cat who greeted everyone who entered this church. RIP 1980."

Sleeping in Chipping Campden

In Chipping Campden—as in any town in the Cotswolds—B&Bs offer a better value than hotels. Try to book well in advance, as rooms are snapped up early in the spring and summer by happy hikers heading for the nearby Cotswold Way. Rooms are also generally tight on Saturdays (when many charge a bit more and are reluctant to rent to one-nighters) and in September, another peak month. Parking is never a problem. Always ask for a discount if staying longer than one or two nights.

ON OR NEAR HIGH STREET

Located on the main street (or just off of it), these places couldn't be more central.

$$$ Noel Arms Hotel, the characteristic old hotel on the main square, has welcomed guests for 600 years. Its lobby was remodeled in a medieval-meets-modern style, and its 28 rooms are well-furnished with antiques (standard Db-£120, bigger Db-£140, fancier four-poster Db-£160-180, deluxe king Db-£180, £10 less for singles, prices are lower midweek or off-season, some ground-floor doubles, attached restaurant/bar and café, free parking, High Street, tel. 01386/840-317, www.noelarmshotel.com, reception@noelarmshotel.com).

$$$ The Lygon Arms Hotel (pronounced "lig-un"), attached to the popular pub of the same name, has small public areas and 10 cheery, open-beamed rooms (huge "superior" Db-£115-120, lovely courtyard Db-£145-165, lower prices are for midweek or multi-night stays, family deals, free parking, High Street, go through archway and look for hotel reception on the left, tel. 01386/840-318, www.lygonarms.co.uk, sandra@lygonarms.co.uk, Sandra Davenport).

$$$ Badgers Hall Tea Room, also listed later under "Eating in Chipping Campden," rents four pricey rooms (small low-ceilinged Db-£95, larger Db-£110-120, 2-night minimum, includes breakfast, no kids under age 10, High Street, tel. 01386/840-839, www.badgershall.com, badgershall@talk21.com, Karen).

$$ Cornerways B&B is a fresh, bright, and comfy home (not "oldie worldie") a block off High Street. It's run by the delightful Carole Proctor, who can "look out the window and see the church where we were married." The two huge, light, airy loft rooms are great for families. If you're happy to exchange breakfast for more space, ask about the cottage across the street (Db-£90, Tb-£120, Qb-£150, 2-night minimum; cottage Db-£85, 3-night minimum; cash only, off-street parking, George Lane, just walk through the arch beside Noel Arms Hotel, tel. 01386/841-307, www.

Sleep Code

Abbreviations **(£1=about $1.60, country code: 44)**
S=Single, **D**=Double/Twin, **T**=Triple, **Q**=Quad, **b**=bathroom
Price Rankings
$$$ Higher Priced—Most rooms £100 or more
$$ Moderately Priced—Most rooms £75-100
$ Lower Priced—Most rooms £75 or less
Unless otherwise noted, credit cards are accepted, breakfast is included, and free Wi-Fi and/or a guest computer is generally available. Prices change; verify current rates online or by email. For the best prices, always book directly with the hotel.

cornerways.info, carole@cornerways.info). For a fee, Les can pick you up from the train station, or take you on village tours.

$$ Stonecroft B&B, next to Cornerways, has three polished, well-maintained rooms (one with low slanted ceilings—unfriendly to tall people). The lovely garden with a patio and small stream is a tranquil place for meals or an early-evening drink (Sb-£70, Db-£80, Tb-£120, Qb-£160, no kids under 12, George Lane, tel. 01386/840-486, www.stonecroft-chippingcampden.co.uk, info@stonecroft-chippingcampden.co.uk, Roger and Lesley Yates).

$$ The Old Bakehouse, run by energetic young mom Zoe, rents two small but pleasant twin-bedded rooms in a 600-year-old home with exposed beams and cottage charm (Sb-£75, Db-£85, prices higher in peak season, discount for multiple nights, cash only, Lower High Street, near intersection with Sheep Street, tel. 01386/840-979, mobile 07717-330-838, www.theoldbakehouse.org.uk, zoegabb@yahoo.co.uk).

A SHORT WALK FROM TOWN ON ASTON ROAD

The B&Bs below are a 10-minute walk from Market Hall. They are listed in the order you would find them when strolling from town (if arriving by bus, ask to be dropped off at Aston Road).

$$ Cherry Trees B&B, set well off the road, is bubbly Angie's spacious, modern home, with three king rooms and one superior king room with balcony (Sb-£70, Db-£90-115, discount for multiple nights, free parking, Aston Road, tel. 01386/840-873, www.cherrytreescampden.com, sclrksn7@tiscali.co.uk).

$$ The Chance B&B—a modern home with Cotswold charm—has two tastefully decorated rooms with king beds (which can also be twins if requested) and a breakfast room that opens onto a patio. They also offer two self-catering cottages in town, next to the silk mill (Db-£100, call for cottage prices, discounts for stays of 5 nights or longer, cash only, free parking, 1 Aston

Road, tel. 01386/849-079, www.the-chance.co.uk, enquiries@the-chance.co.uk, Sally and Paul).

$$ Bramley House, which backs up to a farm, has a spacious garden suite with a private outdoor patio and lounge area (bathroom downstairs from bedroom) and a superior king double. Crisp white linens and simple country decor give the place a light and airy feel (king Db-£90, garden suite Db-£97, 2-night minimum, homemade cake with tea or coffee on arrival, locally sourced/organic breakfast, 6 Aston Road, tel. 01386/840-066, www.bramleyhouse.co.uk, dppovey@btinternet.com, Jane and David Povey).

Eating in Chipping Campden

This town—filled with wealthy residents and tourists—comes with many choices. I've listed some local favorites below. If you have a car, consider driving to one of the excellent countryside pubs mentioned in the sidebar on page 392.

Eight Bells pub is a charming 14th-century inn on Leysbourne with a classy and woody restaurant and a more rustic pub. Neil and Julie keep their seasonal menu as locally sourced as possible. They serve a daily special and always have a good vegetarian dish. As this is the best deal going in town for top-end pub dining with warm service, reservations are smart (£8-12 lunches, £13-22 dinners, daily 12:00-14:00 & 18:30-21:00, tel. 01386/840-371, www.eightbellsinn.co.uk).

The Lygon Arms pub is cozy and inviting, with a good basic bar menu. You can order from the same menu in the colorful pub or the more elegant dining room across the passage (£6-8 sandwiches, £8-15 meals, daily 11:30-14:30 & 18:00-22:00, tel. 01386/840-318).

Michael's, a fun Mediterranean restaurant on High Street, serves hearty portions and breaks plates at closing every Saturday night. Michael, who runs his place with a contagious love of life, is from Cyprus: The forte here is Greek, with plenty of *mezes*—small dishes for £6-10 (also £15-21 larger dishes, £7 *meze* lunch platter, Tue-Sun 11:00-14:30 & 19:00-22:00, closed Mon, tel. 01386/840-826).

Maharaja Indian Restaurant in the Volunteer Inn, while forgettable, is the only Indian place in town (£10-15 meals, daily 18:00-22:30, grassy courtyard out back, Lower High Street, tel. 01386/849-281).

LIGHT MEALS

If you want a quick takeaway sandwich, consider these options. Munch your lunch on the benches on the little green near the Market Hall.

Butty's at the Old Bakehouse offers tasty £3-4 sandwiches and wraps made to order (Mon-Sat 7:30-14:30, closed Sun, free Wi-Fi, Lower High Street, tel. 01386/840-401).

La Tradition is a hardworking French bakery that serves sausage rolls, quiches, filled croissants, and Cornish pasties (takeaway only, Tue-Sat 8:30-17:00, closed Sun-Mon, 6 High Street, tel. 01386/840-766).

Picnic: The **Co-op** grocery is the town's small "supermarket" (Mon-Sat 7:00-22:00, Sun 8:00-22:00, next to TI on High Street). **Tokes,** on the opposite end of High Street, has a tempting selection of cheeses, meats, and wine for a make-your-own ploughman's lunch (Mon-Fri 9:00-18:00, Sat 10:00-17:00, Sun 10:00-16:00, just past the Market Hall, tel. 01386/849-345).

TEAROOMS

To visit a cute tearoom, try one of these places, located in the town center.

Badgers Hall Tea Room is pricey but good, with a wide selection of savory dishes and desserts. A tempting table of homemade cakes, crumbles, and scones just inside the door lures passersby into its delightful half-timbered dining room and a patio out back. Along with light lunches, they serve a generous afternoon tea—a tall and ritualistic tray of dainty sandwiches, pastries, and scones with tea—for £31 for two—much less than the London price. Simpler and still fun is their Crumpet Platter—£12 for two (£8-13 lunches, daily 10:00-16:30, possibly later in summer, afternoon tea 14:30-16:00, High Street).

Bantam Tea Rooms, near the Market Hall, is also a good value (£8 teas, £6 sandwiches, daily 10:00-16:00, High Street, tel. 01386/840-386).

Near Chipping Campden

Because the countryside around Chipping Campden is particularly hilly, it's also especially scenic. This is a very rewarding area to poke around and discover little thatched villages.

WEST OF CHIPPING CAMPDEN

Due west of Chipping Campden lies the famous and touristy town of Broadway. Just south of that, you'll find my nominations for the cutest Cotswold villages. Like marshmallows in hot chocolate, Stanway, Stanton, and Snowshill nestle side by side, awaiting your arrival. (Note the Stanway House's limited hours when planning your visit.)

Broadway

This postcard-pretty town, a couple of miles west of Chipping Campden, is filled with inviting shops and fancy teahouses. With a "broad way" indeed running through its middle, it's one of the bigger towns in the area. This means you'll likely pass through at some point if you're driving—but, since all the big bus tours seem to stop here, I usually give Broadway a miss. However, with a new road that allows traffic to skirt the town, Broadway has gotten cuter than ever. Broadway has good bus connections with Chipping Campden.

Just outside Broadway, on the road to Chipping Campden, you might spot signs for the **Broadway Tower,** which looks like a turreted castle fortification stranded in the countryside without a castle in sight. This 55-foot-tall observation tower is a "folly"—a uniquely English term for a quirky, outlandish novelty erected as a giant lawn ornament by some aristocrat with more money than taste. If you're also weighted down with too many pounds, you can relieve yourself of £5 to climb to its top for a view over the pastures. But the view from the tower's parklike perch is free, and almost as impressive (daily 10:00-17:00).

Stanway

More of a humble crossroads community than a true village, sleepy Stanway is worth a visit mostly for its manor house, which offers an intriguing insight into the English aristocracy today. If you're in the area when it's open, it's well worth visiting.

▲▲Stanway House

The Earl of Wemyss (pronounced "Weemz"), whose family tree charts relatives back to 1202, opens his melancholy home and grounds to visitors just two days a week in the summer. Walking through his house offers a unique glimpse into the lifestyles of England's eccentric and fading nobility.

Cost and Hours: £7 ticket covers house and fountain, £9 ticket also includes watermill; both tickets include a wonderful and intimate audioguide, narrated by the lordship himself; June-Aug Tue and Thu only 14:00-17:00, closed Sept-May, tel. 01386/584-469, www.stanwayfountain.co.uk.

Getting There: By car, leave B-4077 at a statue of (the Christian) George slaying the dragon (of pagan superstition); you'll round the corner and see the manor's fine 17th-century Jacobean gatehouse. Park in the lot across the street. There's no public transportation to Stanway.

Visiting the Manor: The bitchin' **Tithe Barn** (near where you enter the grounds) dates to the 14th century, and predates the manor. It was originally where monks—in the days before money—would accept one-tenth of whatever the peasants produced. Peek inside: This is a great hall for village hoedowns. While the Tithe Barn is no longer used to greet motley peasants and collect their feudal "rents," the lord still gets rent from his vast landholdings, and hosts community fêtes in his barn.

Stepping into the obviously very lived-in **manor,** you're free to wander around pretty much as you like, but keep in mind that a family does live here. His lordship is often roaming about as well. The place feels like a time warp. Ask a staff member to demonstrate the spinning rent-collection table. In the great hall, marvel at the one-piece oak shuffleboard table and the 1780 Chippendale exercise chair (half an hour of bouncing on this was considered good for the liver).

The manor dogs have their own cutely painted "family tree," but the Earl admits that his last dog, C. J., was "all character and no breeding." Poke into the office. You can psychoanalyze the lord by the books that fill his library, the DVDs stacked in front of his bed (with the mink bedspread), and whatever's next to his toilet.

The place has a story to tell. And so do the docents stationed in each room—modern-day peasants who, even without family trees, probably have relatives going back just as far in this village. Talk to these people. Probe. Learn what you can about this side of England.

Wandering through the expansive back yard you'll see the earl's pet project: restoring "the tallest **fountain** in Britain"—300 feet tall, gravity-powered, and running for 30 minutes at 14:45 and 16:00.

Signs lead to a working **watermill,** which produces flour from wheat grown on the estate (about 100 yards from the house, requires higher-priced ticket to enter).

COTSWOLDS

Hailes Church and Abbey

A three-mile drive or pleasant two-and-a-half-mile walk from Stanway House along the Cotswold Way leads you to a fine Norman church and abbey ruins. Richard, Earl of Cornwall (and younger brother of King Henry III) founded the abbey after surviving a shipwreck, but it was his son Edmund who turned it into a pilgrimage site after buying a vial of holy blood and bringing the relic to Hailes around 1270. Thanks to Henry VIII's dissolution of monasteries in the 16th century, not much remains of the abbey today. However, the church—which predates the abbey by about a century—houses some of its original tiles and medieval stained glass. It's worth a look inside the humble church for its 800-year-old baptismal font and cave-like surviving murals (including St. Christopher, patron saint of travelers, and a hunting scene attributed to a local knight). Check out the wooden screen added long after the original construction—look closely and you'll see how the arch had to be cut away in order for the screen to fit.

From Stanway to Stanton

These towns are separated by a row of oak trees and grazing land, with parallel waves echoing the furrows plowed by medieval farmers. Centuries ago, farmers were allotted long strips of land called "furlongs." The idea was to dole out good and bad land equitably. (One square furlong equals 10 acres.) Over centuries of plowing these, furrows were formed. Let someone else drive, so you can hang out the window under a canopy of oaks, passing stone walls and sheep. Leaving Stanway on the road to Stanton, the first building you'll see (on the left, just outside Stanway) is a thatched cricket pavilion overlooking the village cricket green. Originally built for *Peter Pan* author J. M. Barrie, it dates from 1930 and is raised up (as medieval buildings were) on rodent-resistant staddle stones. Stanton is just ahead; follow the signs.

▲Stanton

Pristine Cotswold charm cheers you as you head up the main street of the village of Stanton. Go on a photo safari for flower-bedecked doorways and windows. (A scant few buses serve Stanton.)

Stanton's **Church of St. Michael** (with the pointy spire) betrays a pagan past. It's safe to assume any church dedicated to St. Michael (the archangel who fought the devil) sits upon a sacred pagan site. Stanton is actually at the intersection of two ley lines (a line connecting prehistoric or ancient sights). You'll see St. Michael's well-worn figure (and, above that, a sundial) over the

door as you enter. Inside, above the capitals in the nave, find the pagan symbols for the sun and the moon (see photo). While the church probably dates back to the 9th century, today's building is mostly from the 15th century, with 13th-century transepts. On the north transept (far side from entry), medieval frescoes show faintly through the 17th-century whitewash. (Once upon a time, these frescoes were considered too "papist.") Imagine the church interior colorfully decorated throughout. Original medieval glass is behind the altar. The list of rectors (at the very back of the church, under the organ loft) goes back to 1269. Finger the grooves in the back pews, worn away by sheepdog leashes. (A man's sheepdog accompanied him everywhere.)

Horse Riding: Anyone can enjoy the Cotswolds from the saddle. Jill Carenza's **Cotswolds Riding Centre,** set just outside Stanton village, is in the most scenic corner of the region. The facility's horses can take anyone from rank beginners to more experienced riders on a scenic "hack" through the village and into the high country (per-hour prices: £30/person for a group hack, £40/person for a semi-private hack, £50 for a private one-person hack; lessons, longer rides, rides for experts, and pub tours available; tel. 01386/584-250, www.cotswoldsriding.co.uk, info@cotswoldsriding.co.uk). From Stanton, head toward Broadway and watch for the riding center on your right after about a third of a mile.

Sleeping in Stanton: **$$ The Vine B&B** has five rooms in a characteristic old Cotswold house near the center of town, next to the cricket pitch (ask if any matches are on if you're there on a Saturday in summer). It's owned by no-nonsense Jill, whose daughter, Sarah Jane, welcomes you to their large lovingly-worn family home. While it suffers from absentee management, the Vine is convenient if you want to ride all day (S with shower in room and WC down the hall-£65-85, twin D with shower in room and WC down the hall-£85, Db-£85, most rooms with four-poster beds, some stairs; for contact info, see listing for riding center, above).

Eating in Stanton: High on a hill at the far end of Stanton's main drag, nearest to Broadway, the aptly named **Mount Inn**

serves up pricey upscale meals on its big inviting terrace with grand views of Stanton rooftops and the Cotswold hills (£14-17 meals, food served daily 12:00-14:00 & 18:00-21:00, may be closed Mon off-season, Old Snowshill Road, tel. 01386/584-316).

Snowshill

Another nearly edible little bundle of cuteness, the village of Snowshill (SNOWS-hill) has a photogenic triangular square with a characteristic pub at its base.

▲Snowshill Manor

Dark and mysterious, this old palace is filled with the lifetime collection of Charles Paget Wade. It's one big musty celebration of craftsmanship, from finely carved spinning wheels to frightening samurai armor to tiny elaborate figurines carved by prisoners from the bones of meat served at dinner. Taking seriously his family motto, "Let Nothing Perish," Wade dedicated his life and fortune to preserving things finely crafted. The house (whose management made me promise not to promote it as an eccentric collector's pile of curiosities) really shows off Wade's ability to recognize and acquire fine examples of craftsmanship. It's all very...mmm...yaaa.

Cost and Hours: £11.30; manor house open July-Aug Wed-Mon 11:30-16:30, closed Tue; April-June and Sept-Oct Wed-Sun 12:00-17:00, closed Mon-Tue; closed Nov-March; gardens and ticket window open at 11:00, last entry one hour before closing, restaurant, tel. 01386/852-410, www.nationaltrust.org.uk/snowshillmanor.

Getting There: The manor overlooks the town square, but there's no direct access from the square; instead, the entrance and parking lot are about a half-mile up the road toward Broadway. Park there and follow the long walkway through the garden to get to the house. A golf-cart-type shuttle to the house is available for those who need assistance.

Getting In: This popular sight strictly limits the number of entering visitors by doling out entry times. No reservations are possible; to get a slot, you must report to the ticket desk. It can be up to an hour's wait—even more on busy days, especially weekends (when they can sell out for the day as early as 14:00). Tickets go on sale and the gardens open at 11:00. Therefore, a good strategy is to arrive close to the opening time, and if there's a wait, enjoy the gardens (it's a 10-minute walk to the manor). If you have more time to kill, head into the village of Snowshill itself (a half-mile away) to wander and explore—or get a time slot for later in the day, and return in the afternoon.

Cotswold Lavender

In 2000, farmer Charlie Byrd realized that tourists love lavender. He planted his farm with 250,000 plants, and now visitors come to wander among his 53 acres, which burst with gorgeous lavender blossoms from mid-June through late August. His fragrant fantasy peaks late each July. Lavender—so famous in France's Provence—is not indigenous to this region, but it fits the climate and soil just fine. A free flier in the shop explains the variations of blooming flowers. Farmer Byrd produces lavender oil (an herbal product valued since ancient times for its healing, calming, and fragrant qualities) and sells it in a delightful shop, along with many other lavender-themed items. In the café, enjoy a pot of lavender-flavored tea with a lavender scone.

Cost and Hours: Free to enter shop and café, £2.50 to walk through the fields and the distillery; generally open June-Aug daily 10:00-17:00; closed Sept-May; schedule changes annually depending on when the lavender blooms—call ahead or check their website, tel. 01386/854-821, www.cotswoldlavender.co.uk.

Getting There: It's a half-mile out of Snowshill on the road toward Chipping Campden (easy parking). Entering Snowshill from the road to the manor (described earlier), take the left fork, then turn left again at the end of the village.

EAST OF CHIPPING CAMPDEN

Hidcote Manor Garden is just northeast of Chipping Campden, while Broad Campden, Blockley, and Bourton-on-the-Hill lie roughly between Chipping Campden and Stow (or Moreton)—handy if you're connecting those towns.

▲Hidcote Manor Garden

This is less "on the way" between towns than the other sights in this section—but the grounds around this manor house are well worth a detour if you like gardens. Hidcote is where garden designers pioneered the notion of creating a series of outdoor "rooms," each with a unique theme (such as maple room, red room, and so on) and separated by a yew-tree hedge. The garden's design, mostly inspired by the Arts and Crafts movement, is most formal near the house and becomes more pastoral as it approaches the countryside. Ogle the gigantic, 350-year-old cedar tree, then follow your nose through a clever series of small gardens that lead delightfully from one to the next. Among the best in England, Hidcote Gardens are at their fragrant peak from May through August. But don't expect much indoors—the manor house has only a few rooms open to the public.

Cost and Hours: £10.50; March-Sept daily 10:00-18:00; Oct daily 10:00-17:00; Nov-Dec Sat-Sun 11:00-16:00, closed Mon-Fri; closed Jan-Feb; last entry one hour before closing, café, restaurant, tel. 01386/438-333, www.nationaltrust.org.uk/hidcote.

Getting There: If you're driving, it's four miles northeast of Chipping Campden—roughly toward Ilmington. The gardens are accessible by bus and a 45-minute country walk. Buses #21 and #22 take you to Mickleton (one stop past Chipping Campden), where a footpath begins next to the churchyard. Continuing more or less straight, the path leads uphill through sheep pastures and ends at Hidcote's driveway.

Nearby: Gardening enthusiasts will want to also stop at **Kiftsgate Court Garden,** just across the road from Hidcote. While not as impressive, these private gardens are a fun contrast since they were designed at the same time and influenced by Hidcote (£8; May-July Sat-Wed 12:00-18:00, Aug opens at 14:00, closed Thu-Fri; April and Sept Sun-Mon and Wed only 14:00-18:00; closed Oct-March; tel. 01386/438-777, www.kiftsgate.co.uk).

▲Broad Campden, Blockley, and Bourton-on-the-Hill

COTSWOLDS

This trio of pleasant villages lines up along an off-the-beaten-path road between Chipping Campden and Moreton or Stow. **Broad Campden,** just on the outskirts of Chipping Campden, has some of the cutest thatched-roof houses I've seen. **Blockley,** nestled higher in the picturesque hills, is a popular setting for films. The same road continues on to **Bourton-on-the-Hill** (pictured), with fine views looking down into a valley and an excellent gastropub (Horse and

Groom, described on page 392). All three of these towns are connected to Chipping Campden by bus #21 and #22, or you can walk (easy to Broad Campden, more challenging to the other two—see page 359).

Stow-on-the-Wold

Located 10 miles south of Chipping Campden, Stow-on-the-Wold—with a name that means "meeting place on the uplands"—is the highest point of the Cotswolds. Despite its crowds, it retains its charm, and it merits ▲▲. Most of the tourists are day-trippers, so nights—even in the peak of summer—are peaceful. Stow has no real sights other than the town itself, some good pubs, antique stores, and cute shops draped seductively around a big town square. Visit the church, with its evocative old door guarded by ancient yew trees and the tombs of wool tycoons. A visit to Stow is not complete until you've locked your partner in the stocks on the village green.

Orientation to Stow-on-the-Wold

TOURIST INFORMATION

A small TI staffed by volunteers is run out of the library in St. Edwards Hall on the main square (hours erratic, generally Mon-Sat 10:00-14:00, sometimes as late as 17:00, closed Sun, tel. 08452-305-420). Aside from the meager rack of brochures, don't expect much information—get your serious questions answered in Moreton-in-Marsh instead (see page 401).

HELPFUL HINTS

Internet Access: The TI offers free Wi-Fi and a few public computers.

Taxi: See "Getting Around the Cotswolds—By Taxi or Private Driver" (page 363).

Parking: Park anywhere on Market Square free for two hours, and overnight between 18:00 and 9:00 (combining overnight plus daily 2-hour allowances means you can park free 16:00-11:00—they note your license, so you can't just move to another spot after your time is up; £50 tickets for offenders). You can also park for free on some streets farther from the center (such as Park Street and Well Lane) for an unlimited amount of time. Alternately, a convenient pay-and-display lot is at the bottom of town (toward the Oddingtons), and there's a free lot at Tesco Supermarket—an easy five-minute walk north of town (follow the signs).

Stow-on-the-Wold Walk

This four-stop self-guided walk covers about 500 yards and takes about 45 minutes.

Start at the **Stocks on the Market Square.** Imagine this village during the era when people were publicly ridiculed here as a punishment. Stow was born in pre-Roman times; it's where three trade routes crossed at a high point in the region (altitude: 800 feet). This square was the site of an Iron Age fort, and then a Roman garrison town. This main square hosted an international fair starting in 1107, and people came from as far away as Italy for the wool fleeces. This grand square was a vast, grassy expanse. Picture it in the Middle Ages (before the buildings in the center were added): a public commons and grazing ground, paths worn through the grass, and no well. Until the late 1800s, Stow had no running water; women fetched water from the "Roman Well" a quarter-mile away.

With as many as 20,000 sheep sold in a single day, this square was a thriving scene. And Stow was filled with inns and pubs to keep everyone housed, fed, and watered. A thin skin of topsoil covers the Cotswold limestone, from which these buildings were made. The **Stow Lodge** (next to the church) lies a little lower than the church; the lodge sits on the spot where locals quarried stones for the church. That building, originally the rectory, is now a hotel. The church (where we'll end this little walk) is made of Cotswold stone, and marks the summit of the hill upon which the town was built. The stocks are a great photo op (lock dad up for a great family Christmas card).

• *Walk past The White Hart Inn to the market, and cross to the other part of the square. Notice how locals seem to be part of a tight-knit little community. Enjoy the stonework and the crazy rooflines. Notice the cheap signage and think how shops have been coming and going for centuries in buildings that never change.*

For 500 years, the **Market Cross** stood in the market reminding all Christian merchants to "trade fairly under the sight of God."

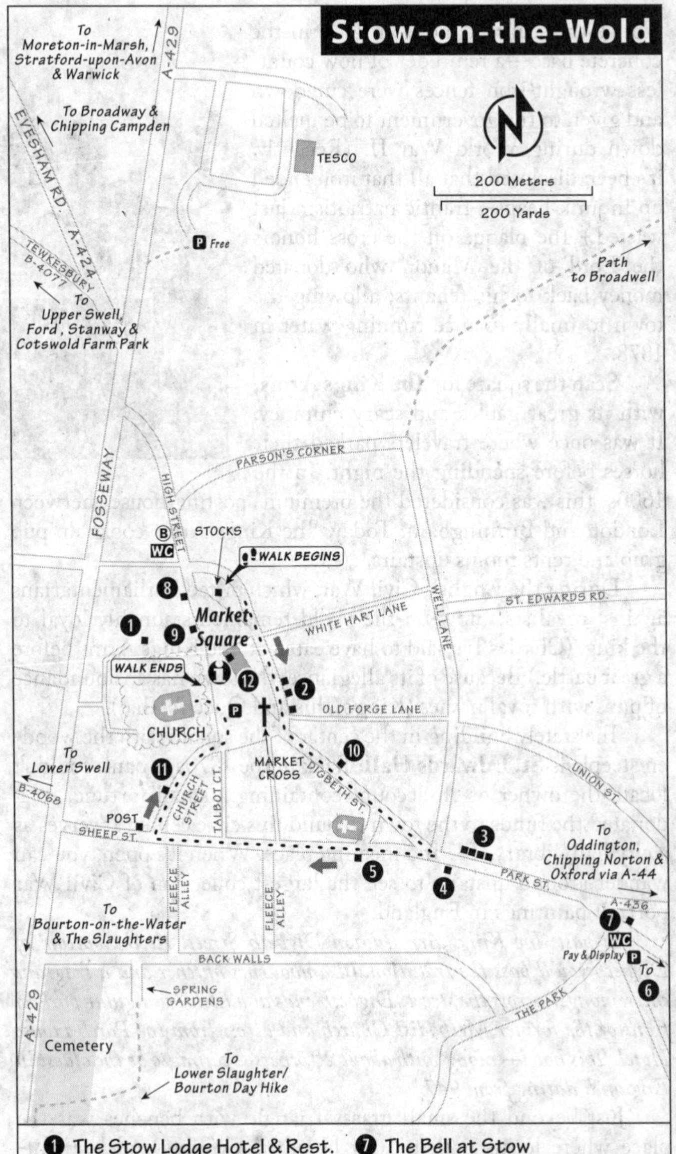

1. The Stow Lodge Hotel & Rest.
2. The Kings Arms Hotel & Pub, Co-op Grocery & Cotswold Chocolate Factory
3. Number Nine B&B; Park Street Eateries
4. Cross Keys Cottage
5. The Pound B&B
6. To Little Broom B&B
7. The Bell at Stow
8. The Queen's Head Pub
9. Huffkins Bakery & Tea Rooms
10. The Old Bakery Tearoom
11. The Coffee House
12. St. Edwards Hall, TI & Library (Internet)

Notice the stubs of the iron fence in the concrete base—a reminder of how countless wrought-iron fences were cut down and given to the government to be melted down during World War II. (Recently, it's been disclosed that all that iron ended up in junk heaps—frantic patriotism just wasted.) The plaque on the cross honors the Lord of the Manor, who donated money back to his tenants, allowing the town to finally finance running water in 1878.

Scan the square for **The Kings Arms,** with its great gables and scary chimney. It was once where travelers parked their horses before spending the night. In the 1600s, this was considered the premium "posting house" between London and Birmingham. Today, The Kings Arms cooks up pub grub and rents rooms upstairs.

During the English Civil War, which pitted Parliamentarians against royalists, Stow-on-the-Wold remained staunchly loyal to the king. (Charles I is said to have eaten at The Kings Arms before a great battle.) Because of its allegiance, the town has an abundance of pubs with royal names (King's This and Queen's That).

The stately building in the center of the square with the wooden steeple is **St. Edwards Hall.** Back in the 1870s, a bank couldn't locate the owner of an account containing a small fortune, so it donated the funds to the town to build this civic center. It serves as a city hall, library, TI, and meeting place. When it's open, you can wander around upstairs to see the largest collection of Civil War portrait paintings in England.

• *Walk past The Kings Arms down Digbeth Street. At the bottom of Digbeth you'll pass the traditional Lambournes butcher and a fragrant cheesemonger across the street. Digbeth ends at a little triangular park in front of the former Methodist Church and across from the Porch House Hotel. This hotel—along with about 20 others—claims to be the oldest in England, dating from 947.*

Just beyond the small grassy triangle with benches was the place where locals gathered for bloody cockfights and bearbaiting (watching packs of hungry dogs tear at bears). Today this is where—twice a year, in May and October—the Stow Horse Fair attracts nomadic Roma (Gypsies) and Irish Travellers from far and wide. They congregate down the street on the Maugersbury Road. Locals paint a colorful picture of the Roma, Travellers, and horses inundating the town. The young women dress up because the fair also functions as a marriage market.

• *Hook right and hike up the wide street.*

As you head up **Sheep Street,** you'll pass a boutique-filled former brewery yard (on the left). Notice its fancy street-front office, with a striking flint facade. Sheep Street was originally not a street, but a staging place for medieval sheep markets. The sheep would be gathered here, then paraded into the Market Square down narrow alleys—just wide enough for a single file of sheep to walk down, making it easier to count them. You'll see several of these so-called "fleece alleys" as you walk up the street.

• *Walk a couple blocks until about 50 yards before the streetlight and the highway, then make a right onto Church Street, which leads to the church.*

Before entering the **church,** circle it. On the back side, a door is flanked by two ancient yew trees. While many view it as the Christian "Behold, I stand at the door and knock" door, J. R. R. Tolkien fans see something quite different. Tolkien hiked the Cotswolds and had a passion for sketching evocative trees such as this. *Lord of the Rings* enthusiasts are convinced this must be the inspiration for the door into Moria.

While the church (open daily 9:00-18:00, except during services) dates from Saxon times, today's structure is from the 15th century. Its history is played up in leaflets and plaques just inside the door. The floor is paved with the tombs of big shots who made their money from wool and are still boastful in death. (Find the tombs crowned with the bales of wool.) Most of the windows are traditional Victorian (19th century) designs, but the two sets high up in the clerestory are from the dreamier Pre-Raphaelite school.

On the right wall as you approach the altar, a monument remembers the many boys from this small town who were lost in World War I (50 out of a population of 2,000). There were far fewer in World War II. The biscuit-shaped plaque remembers an admiral from Stow who lost four sons defending the realm. It's sliced from an ancient fluted column (which locals believe is from Ephesus, Turkey).

During the English Civil War (1615), the church was ransacked, and more than 1,000 soldiers were imprisoned here. The tombstone in front of the altar remembers the royalist Captain Francis Keyt. His long hair, lace, and sash indicate he was a "cavalier," and true-blue to the king (Cromwellians were called "round heads"—named for their short hair). Study the crude provincial art—childlike skulls and (in the upper corners) symbols of his service to the king (armor, weapons).

Finally, don't miss the kneelers tucked in the pews. These are made by a committed band of women known as "the Kneeler Group." They meet most Tuesday mornings (except sometimes in summer) at 10:30 in the Church Room to needlepoint, sip coffee, and enjoy a good chat. (The vicar assured me that any tourist wanting to join them would be more than welcome. The help would be appreciated and the company would be excellent.) If you'd rather sing, the choir practices on the first and third Fridays of the month at 18:00, and visitors are encouraged to join in. And with Reverend Martin Short for the pastor, the services could be pretty lively.

Hiking from Stow

STOW/LOWER SLAUGHTER/BOURTON DAY HIKE

Stow is made to order for day hikes. The most popular is the downhill stroll to Lower Slaughter (3 miles), then on to Bourton-on-the-Water (about 1.5 miles more). It's a two-hour walk if you keep up a brisk pace and don't stop, but dawdlers should allow three to four hours. At the end, from Bourton-on-the-Water, a bus can bring you back to Stow. While those with keen eyes can follow this walk by spotting trail signs, it can't hurt to bring a map (ask to borrow one at your B&B). Note that these three towns are described in more detail starting on page 394.

To reach the trail, find the cemetery (from the main square, head down Church Street, turn left on Sheep Street, right into Fleece Alley, right onto Back Walls, and left onto Spring Gardens). Walk past the community's big pea patch, then duck right through the cemetery to the far end. Here, go through the gate and walk down the footpath that runs alongside the big A-429 road for about 200 yards, then cross the road and catch the well-marked trail (gravel road with green sign noting *Public Footpath/Gloucestershire Way*, next to Quarwood Cottage). Follow this trail for a delightful hour across farms, through romantic gates, across a fancy driveway, and past Gainsborough-painting vistas. You'll enjoy an intimate backyard look at local farm life. Although it seems like you might lose the trail, tiny easy-to-miss signs (yellow *Public Footpath* arrows—sometimes also marked *Gloucestershire Way* or *The Monarch's Way*—usually embedded in fence posts) keep you on target—watch for these very carefully to avoid getting lost.

Finally, passing a cricket pitch, you reach **Lower Slaughter,** with its fine church and a mill creek leading up to its mill.

Hiking from Lower Slaughter up to **Upper Slaughter** is a worthwhile one-mile detour each way, if you have the time and energy.

From Lower Slaughter, it's a less-scenic 25-minute walk into the bigger town of **Bourton-on-the-Water.** Leave Lower Slaughter along its mill creek, then follow a bridle path back to A-429 and into Bourton. Walking through Bourton's burbs, you'll pass two different bus stops for the ride back to Stow; better yet, to enjoy some time in Bourton itself, continue all the way into town and—when ready—catch the bus from in front of the Edinburgh Woolen Mill shop (bus #801 departs roughly hourly, none on Sun except May-Aug when it runs about 2/day, 10-minute ride).

Sleeping in Stow

$$$ The Stow Lodge Hotel fills the historic church rectory with lots of old English charm. Facing the town square, with its own sprawling and peaceful garden, this lavish old place offers 21 large, thoughtfully appointed rooms with soft beds, stately public spaces, and a cushy-chair lounge (slippery rates but generally Db-£130, £10 extra on Sat, cheaper Nov-April, closed Jan, free parking, The Square, tel. 01451/830-485, www.stowlodge.co.uk, enquiries@stowlodge.co.uk, helpful Hartley family).

$$$ The Kings Arms, with 10 rooms above a pub, manages to keep its historic Cotswold character while still feeling fresh and modern in all the right ways (standard Db-£100, superior Db-£120, steep stairs, three "cottages" out back, free parking, Market Square, tel. 01451/830-364, www.kingsarmsstow.co.uk, info@kingsarmsstow.co.uk, Lucinda and Felicity).

$$ Number Nine has three large, bright, refurbished, and tastefully decorated rooms. This 200-year-old home comes with watch-your-head beamed ceilings and beautiful old wooden doors (Sb-£50-60, Db-£80-85, 9 Park Street, tel. 01451/870-333, mobile 07779-006-539, www.number-nine.info, enquiries@number-nine.info, friendly James and Carol Brown and their dog Snoop).

$$ Cross Keys Cottage offers four smallish but smartly updated rooms—some bright and floral, others classy white—with modern bathrooms. Kindly Margaret and Roger Welton take care of their guests in this 370-year-old beamed cottage (Sb-£55-70, Db-£80-90, 5 percent Rick Steves cash discount, call ahead to confirm arrival time, Park Street, tel. 01451/831-128, www.crosskeyscottage.co.uk, rogxmag@hotmail.com).

$ The Pound is the quaint, 500-year-old, slanty, cozy, and low-beamed home of Patricia Whitehead. She offers two bright, inviting, rooms and a classic old fireplace lounge (S-£55, D-£70, T-£95, Q-£110, cash only, downtown on Sheep Street next to the Grapevine Hotel, tel. 01451/830-229, patwhitehead1@live.co.uk).

NEAR STOW

$ Little Broom B&B hides out in the neighboring hamlet of Maugersbury, which enjoys the peace Stow once had. It rents three cozy rooms that share a lush garden and pool (S-£30, Sb-£45-65, Db-£60-75, apartment Db-£85 for two people plus £15 for each extra person, cash only, tel. 01451/830-510, www.cotswolds.info/webpage/little-broom.htm, brendarussell1@hotmail.co.uk). Brenda has racehorses, and her greenhouse keeps the pool warm throughout the summer (guests welcome). It's an easy eight-minute walk from Stow: Head east on Park Street and stay right toward Maugersbury. Turn right into Chapel Street and take the first right uphill to the B&B.

Eating in and near Stow

While Stow has several good dining options, consider venturing out of town for a meal. You can walk to the pub in nearby Broadwell, or—better yet—drive to one of several enticing gastropubs in the surrounding villages (see sidebar on page 392).

IN STOW

These places are all within a five-minute walk of each other, either on the main square or downhill on Queen and Park streets. For dessert, consider munching a locally-made chocolate treat under the trees on the square's benches and watching the sky darken, the lamps come on, and visitors having their photo fun in the stocks.

Restaurants and Pubs

The Stow Lodge is the choice of the town's proper ladies. There are two parts: The formal but friendly bar serves fine pub grub (hearty £9-12 lunches and dinners, daily 12:00-14:00 & 19:00-20:30). The restaurant serves a popular £30 three-course dinner (nightly, veggie options, good wines, just off main square, tel. 01451/830-485, Val). On a sunny day, the pub serves lunch in the well-manicured garden, where you'll feel quite aristocratic.

The Bell at Stow, at the end of Park Street (on the edge of town), has a great scene and a fun pub energy for a drink or for a full meal. They serve up classic English dishes with a lighter, sometimes-Asian twist. Produce and fish are locally sourced (£7-15 lunches, £12-15 dinners, veggies extra, daily 12:00-21:00, reservations recommended, tel. 01451/870-916, www.thebellatstow.com). Enjoy live music on Sunday evenings.

The Queen's Head faces the Market Square, near the Stow Lodge. With a classic pub vibe, it's a great place to bring your dog and watch the eccentrics while you eat pub grub and drink the local Cotswold brew, Donnington Ale. They have a meat pie of the day, good fish-and-chips, and live music on Saturdays (£5-7 sandwiches, £8-10 lunches, £9-13 dinners, beer garden out back, daily 12:00-14:30 & 18:30-21:00, tel. 01451/830-563, Johnny).

Huffkins Bakery and Tea Rooms is a cute, old-school institution overlooking the center of the market square with to-go lunches and a well-worn tea room for bakery-fresh meals—soups, sandwiches, all-day breakfast, tea and scones, gluten-free options (£7-10 plates, daily 9:00-17:00, tel. 01451/832-870).

Cheaper Options and Ethnic Food

Head to the grassy triangle where Digbeth hits Sheep Street; there you'll find takeout fish-and-chips, Chinese, and Indian food. You can picnic at the triangle or on the benches by the stocks on Market Street.

Greedy's Fish and Chips, on Park Street, is the go-to place for takeout. There's no seating, but they do have benches in front (£5 fish-and-chips, Mon-Sat 12:00-14:00 & 16:30-21:00, closed Sun, tel. 01451/870-821). For good sit-down fish-and-chips, go zto either pub on the main square: The Queen's Head or The Kings Arms.

Jade Garden Chinese Take-Away is appreciated by locals who don't want to cook (£3-6 dishes, Wed-Mon 17:00-23:00, closed Tue, 15 Park Street, tel. 01451/870-288).

The Prince of India offers good Indian food to take out or eat in (£9-13 main dishes, nightly 18:00-23:30, 5 Park Street, tel. 01451/830-099).

The Old Bakery Tearoom is a local favorite hidden away in a tiny mall at the bottom of Digbeth Street with traditional cakes and light lunches (Mon-Wed & Fri-Sat 10:00-16:00, closed Thu and Sun, Digbeth Street, Alan and Jackie).

The Coffee House provides a nice break from the horses-and-hounds traditional cuisine found elsewhere. You can get your food to go, or eat here—there's pleasant garden seating out back (£5 soups, £9-10 salads and sandwiches, good coffee; April-Sept Mon-Sat 9:00-17:00, Sun 10:00-16:30; Church Street, tel. 01451/870-802).

The **Cotswold Chocolate Factory** creates handmade choco-

Great Country Gastropubs

These places—known for their high-quality meals and fine settings—are very popular. Arrive early or phone in a reservation. (If you show up at 20:00, it's unlikely that they'll be able to seat you for dinner if you haven't called first.) These pubs allow "well-behaved children," and are practical only for those with a car. If you have wheels, make a point to dine at one (or more) of these—no matter where you're sleeping. In addition to these fine choices, other pubs serving worth-a-trip food are **Eight Bells** in Chipping Camden (described on page 374) and **The Wheatsheaf Inn** in Northleach (see page 398).

Near Stow

The first two (in Oddington, about three miles from Stow) are more trendy and fresh, yet still in a traditional pub setting. The Plough (in Ford, a few miles farther away) is your jolly olde dark pub.

The Fox Inn, a different Fox Inn than the one in Broadwell (see "Pub Dinner Hike from Stow"), has a long history but a fresh approach. It's a popular choice among local foodies for its delicately prepared, borderline-pretentious but still reasonably priced updated pub classics and more-creative dishes. They've perfected their upmarket rustic-chic vibe, with a genteelly Old World interior that's fresh and candle-lit and a delightful back terrace and garden (£15-21 main courses, extensive wine list, daily 12:00-14:00 & 18:30-21:30, in Lower Oddington, tel. 01451/870-555). They also rent three rooms (Db-£85-105, www.foxinn.net).

The Horse and Groom Village Inn in Upper Oddington is a smart place in a 16th-century inn, serving modern English and Continental food with a good wine list (38 wines by the glass) and top honors as pub of the year for its serious attention to beer. Owners Simon and Sally boast the best fireplace you'll see and lots of game (lunch: £7-10 sandwiches, £10-15 main courses; dinner: £16-20 main courses; daily 12:00-14:00; 18:30-21:00, tel. 01451/830-584, www.horseandgroom.uk.com).

Between Stow and Chipping Campden

The Plough Inn, in the hamlet of Ford, fills a fascinating old building—once an old coaching inn, later a courthouse, and now a tribute to all things horse racing (it sits across from the Jackdaws

Castle racehorse training facility). Ask the bar staff for some fun history—like what "you're barred" means. Eat from the same traditional English menu in the restaurant, bar, or garden. They are serious about their beer, and serve up heaping portions of stick-to-your-ribs pub-grub classics—a bit more traditional and less refined than others listed here (£11-19 meals, food served daily 12:00-14:00 & 18:00-21:00, all day long Fri-Sun and June-Aug, 6 miles from Stow on the road to Tewkesbury, reservations smart, tel. 01386/584-215, www.theploughinnford.co.uk).

Near Chipping Campden

The Ebrington Arms is a quintessential neighborhood pub with 21st-century amenities: modern British cuisine, home-brewed beer, an extensive wine list, and friendly service. Rub elbows with locals in the crowded bar—energetic any day of the week. The restaurant and rotating menu are classy without being pretentious, and owners Jim and Claire make you feel welcomed but not smothered (£7-8 starters, £18-22 main courses, food served daily 12:00-14:30 & 18:00-21:00, Sun until 15:30 and 20:30, 3 miles from Chipping Campden, reservations smart, tel. 01386/593-223, www.theebringtonarms.co.uk).

Near Moreton-in-Marsh, in Bourton-on-the-Hill

The hill-capping Bourton—about a five-minute drive (or two-mile uphill walk) above Moreton—offers sweeping views over the Cotswold countryside. Perched at the top of this steep picturesque burg is an enticing destination pub.

Horse and Groom melds a warm welcome with a tempting menu of delicious modern English fare. Of the pubs listed here, they seem to hit the best balance of old and new, combining unassumingly delicious food with a convivial spit-and-sawdust spirit. Choose between the lively, light, spacious interior or—in good weather—the terraced picnic-table garden out back (£13-19 meals, food served Mon-Thu 12:00-14:00 & 19:00-21:00, Fri-Sat 12:00-14:00 & 19:00-21:30, Sun 12:00-14:30 only, tel. 01386/700-413). They also rent five rooms (Db-£120-170 depending on size, www.horseandgroom.info, greenstocks@horseandgroom.info). Don't confuse this with The Horse and Groom Village Inn in Upper Oddington, near Stow (described earlier).

late bars, bon-bons, truffles, and more. Pop in to watch Tony working through a window in the back of the shop (his wife, Heidi, does the decorating after he's done). The friendly shopkeepers are happy to offer suggestions. If you're struggling to decide, try the fruit-and-chili bar or the chocolate-covered...anything (daily 10:00-17:30, Digbeth Street, tel. 01451/798-082).

Even Cheaper: Small grocery stores face the main square (the **Co-op** is open daily 7:00-22:00; next to The Kings Arms), and a big **Tesco** supermarket is 400 yards north of town.

PUB DINNER HIKE FROM STOW

From Stow, consider taking a half-hour countryside walk to the village of Broadwell, where you'll find a traditional old pub serving good basic grub in a convivial atmosphere. **The Fox Inn** serves pub dinners and draws traditional ales—including the local Donnington ales (£8-10 meals, food served Mon-Sat 11:30-14:00 & 18:30-21:00, Sun 12:00-14:00 only, outdoor tables in garden out back, on the village green, reservations smart, tel. 01451/870-909, www.foxbroadwell.co.uk, Mike and Carol).

Getting There: If you walk briskly, it's just 20 minutes downhill from Stow. While the walk is not particularly scenic (it's one-third paved lane, and the rest on an arrow-straight bridle path), it is peaceful, and the exercise is a nice way to start and finish your meal. The trail is poorly marked, but it's hard to get lost: Leave Stow at Parson's Corner, continue downhill, pass the town well, follow the bridle path straight until you hit the next road, then turn right at the road and walk downhill into the village of Broadwell. You can often hitch a ride with someone from the pub back to Stow after you eat.

Near Stow-on-the-Wold

These sights are all south of Stow: Some are within walking distance (the Slaughters and Bourton-on-the-Water), and one is 20 miles away (Cirencester). The Slaughters and Bourton are tied together by the countryside walk described on page 388.

▲LOWER AND UPPER SLAUGHTER

"Slaughter" has nothing to do with lamb chops. It likely derives from an Old English word, perhaps meaning sloe tree (the one used to make sloe gin).

Lower Slaughter is a classic village, with ducks, a charming little church, a working water mill, and usually an artist busy at her easel somewhere. The Old Mill Museum is a folksy ensemble with a tiny museum, shop, and café complete with a delightful terrace overlooking the mill pond, enthusiastically run by Gerald and his daughter Laura, who just can't resist giving generous tastes of their homemade ice cream (£2.50 for museum, March-Oct daily 10:00-18:00, Nov-Feb daily 10:00-dusk, tel. 01451/822-127, www.oldmill-lowerslaughter.com). Just behind the Old Mill, two kissing gates lead to the path that goes to nearby Upper Slaughter, a 15-minute walk or 2-minute drive away (leaving the Old Mill, take two lefts, then follow sign for *Wardens Way*). And if you follow the mill creek downstream, a bridle path leads to Bourton-on-the-Water (described next).

In **Upper Slaughter,** walk through the yew trees (sacred in pagan days) down a lane through the raised graveyard (a buildup of centuries of graves) to the peaceful church. In the back of the fine graveyard, the statue of a wistful woman looks over the tomb of an 18th-century rector (sculpted by his son). Notice the town is missing a war memorial—that's because every soldier who left Upper Slaughter for World War I and World War II survived the wars. As a so-called "Doubly Thankful Village" (one of only 13 in England and Wales), the town instead honors those who served in war with a simple wood plaque in the town hall.

Getting There: Though the stop is not listed on schedules, you should be able to reach these towns on bus #801 (from Moreton or Stow) by requesting the "Slaughter Pike" stop (along the main road, near the villages). Confirm with the driver before getting on. If driving, the small roads from Upper Slaughter to Ford and Kineton (and the Cotswold Farm Park, described later) are some of England's most scenic. Roll your window down and joyride slowly.

▲BOURTON-ON-THE-WATER

I can't figure out whether they call this "the Venice of the Cotswolds" because of its quaint canals or its miserable crowds. Either way, this town—four miles south of Stow and a mile from Lower Slaughter—is very pretty. But it can be mobbed with tour groups during the day: Sidewalks become jammed with disoriented tourists wearing nametags. Perhaps the most touristy town in Britain, Bourton-on-the-Water charges 20 pence to pee and has a turnstile to be sure it gets the coin.

If you can avoid the crowds, it's worth a drive-through and maybe a short stop. It's pleasantly empty in the early evening and after dark.

Bourton's attractions are tacky tourist traps, but the three listed below might be worth considering. All are on High Street in the town center. In addition to these, consider Bourton's **leisure center** (big pool and sauna, a five-minute walk from town center off Station Road; Mon-Fri 6:30-22:00, Sat-Sun 8:00-20:00; shared with the school—which gets priority for use, tel. 01451/824-024).

Getting There: It's conveniently connected to Stow and Moreton by bus #801.

Parking: Finding a spot here can be tough. Even during the busy business day, rather than park in the pay-and-display parking lot a five-minute walk from the center, drive right into town and wait for a spot on High Street just past the village green (where the road swings left, turn right to go down High Street; there's a long row of free two-hour spots in front of the Edinburgh Woolen Mills shop, on the right).

Tourist Information: The TI is tucked across the stream a short block off the main drag, on Victoria Street, behind Village Hall (Mon-Fri 9:30-17:00, Sat 9:30-17:30, Sun 10:00-14:00 except closed Sun Oct-April, closes one hour earlier Nov-March, tel. 01451/820-211).

Bike Rental: Hartwells on High Street rents bikes by the hour or day and includes a helmet, map, and lock (£10/3 hours; £14/day, Mon-Sat 9:00-18:00, Sun opens at 10:00, tel. 01451/820-405, www.hartwells.supanet.com).

▲Motor Museum

Lovingly presented, this good, jumbled museum shows off a lifetime's accumulation of vintage cars, old lacquered signs, threadbare toys, and prewar memorabilia. If you appreciate old cars, this is nirvana. Wander the car-and-driver displays, which range from the automobile's early days to the stylish James Bond era, including period music to add mood. Talk to an elderly Brit who's touring the place for some personal memories.

Cost and Hours: £5.25, mid-Feb-early Dec daily 10:00-18:00, closed off-season, in the mill facing the town center, tel. 01451/821-255, www.cotswoldmotormuseum.co.uk.

Model Railway Exhibition

This exhibit of three model railway layouts is impressive only to train buffs.

Cost and Hours: £2.75, June-Aug daily 11:00-17:00; closed Jan and Mon-Fri off-season; located in the back of a hobby shop in the center of town.

Model Village

This light but fun display re-creates the town on a 1:9 scale in a tiny outdoor park, and has an attached room full of tiny models showing off various bits of British domestic life.

Cost and Hours: £3.60 for the park; daily 10:00-18:00, until 16:00 in winter; at the edge of town, behind The Old New Inn.

Walk to the Slaughters

From Bourton-on-the-Water, it's about a 30-minute walk (or a two-minute drive) to Upper and Lower Slaughter (described previously); taken together, they make for an easy two-hour round-trip walk from Bourton. (You could also walk from Stow through the Slaughters to Bourton—hike described on page 388.)

▲COTSWOLD FARM PARK

Here's a delight for young and old alike. This park is the private venture of the Henson family, who are passionate about preserving rare and endangered breeds of native British animals. While it feels like a kids' zone (with all the family-friendly facilities you can imagine), it's actually a fascinating chance for anyone to get up close and (very) personal with piles of mostly cute animals, including the sheep that made this region famous—the big and woolly Cotswold Lion. The "listening posts" deliver audio information on each rare breed.

A busy schedule of demonstrations gives you a look at local farm life—check the events board as you enter for times for the milking, "farm safari," shearing, and well-done "sheep show." Join the included 20-minute tractor ride, with live narration. Buy a bag of seed upon arrival, or have your map eaten by munchy goats as I did. Tykes love the little tractor rides, maze, and zip line, but the "touch barn" is where it's at for little kids.

Cost and Hours: £9.25, kids-£8.40, family ticket for 2 adults and 2 kids-£31.50, daily Feb-Oct 10:30-17:00, Nov-Dec 10:30-16:00, closed Jan, good guidebook (small fee), decent cafeteria, tel. 01451/850-307, www.cotswoldfarmpark.co.uk.

Getting There: It's well-signposted about halfway between Stow and Stanway (15 minutes from either), just off Tewkesbury Road (B-4077, toward Ford from Stow). A visit here makes sense if you're traveling from Stow to Chipping Campden.

NORTHLEACH

One of the "untouched and untouristed" Cotswold villages, Northleach is worth a short stop. The town's impressive main square and church attest to its position as a major wool center in the Middle Ages. Park in the square called The Green or the adjoining Market Place. The town has no TI, but you can pick up a free town map and visitor guide at the Mechanical Music Museum (described next) or at the post office on the Market Place (Mon-Fri 9:00-13:00 & 14:00-17:30, Sat 9:00-12:30, closed Sun) and at other nearby shops. Information: www.northleach.gov.uk.

Getting There: Northleach is nine miles south of Stow, down A-429. Bus #801 connects it to Stow and Moreton.

▲Mechanical Music Museum

This delightful little one-room place offers a unique opportunity to listen to 300 years of amazing self-playing musical instruments. It's run by people who are passionate about the restoration work they do on these musical marvels. The curators delight in demonstrating about 20 of the museum's machines with each hour-long tour. You'll hear Victorian music boxes and the earliest polyphones (record players) playing cylinders and then discs—all from an age when music was made mechanically, without the help of electricity. The admission fee includes an essential hour-long tour.

Cost and Hours: £8, daily 10:00-17:00, last entry at 16:00, tours go constantly—join one in progress, High Street, Northleach, tel. 01451/860-181, www.mechanicalmusic.co.uk.

Church of Saints Peter and Paul

This fine Perpendicular Gothic church has been called the "cathedral of the Cotswolds." It's one of the Cotswolds' two finest "wool" churches (along with Chipping Campden's), paid for by 15th-century wool tycoons. Find the oldest tombstone. The brass plaques on the floor me-

morialize big shots, showing sheep and sacks of wool at their long-dead feet, and inscriptions mixing Latin and Old English (daily 9:00-17:00 or until dusk, tel. 01451/861-132).

Eating in Northleach: Tucked along unassuming Northleach's main drag is a foodies' favorite, **The Wheatsheaf Inn.** With a pleasantly traditional dining room and a gorgeous sprawling garden, it serves up an intriguing eclectic menu of modern English cuisine. They pride themselves on offering a warm welcome, relaxed service, and a take-your-time approach to top-quality food. Reservations are smart (£17-22 meals, daily, on West End, tel. 01451/860-244, www.cotswoldswheatsheaf.com).

▲BIBURY

Six miles northeast of Cirencester, this village is a favorite with British picnickers fond of strolling and fishing. Bibury (BYE-bree) offers some relaxing sights, including a row of very old weavers' cottages, a trout farm, a stream teeming with fat fish and proud ducks, and a church surrounded by rosebushes, each tended by a volunteer of the parish. A protected wetlands area on the far side of the stream hosts newts and water voles. Walk up the main street, then turn right along the old weavers' Arlington Row and back on the far side of the marsh, peeking into the rushes for wildlife.

For a closer look at the fish, cross the little bridge to the 15-acre **Trout Farm,** where you can feed them—or catch your own (£4 to walk the grounds, fish food-£0.50; daily April-Sept 8:00-18:00, Oct and March 8:00-17:00, Nov-Feb 8:00-16:00; catch-your-own only on weekends March-Oct 10:00-17:00, no fishing in winter, call or email to confirm fishing schedule, tel. 01285/740-215, www.biburytroutfarm.co.uk).

Drivers will enjoy exploring the scenic **Coln Valley** from A-429 to Bibury through the enigmatic villages of Coln St. Dennis, Coln Rogers, Coln Powell, and Winson.

Getting There: Bus #855 goes direct from Moreton-in-Marsh and Stow to Bibury (3/day, 1 hour).

Sleeping in Bibury: If you'd like to spend the night in tiny Bibury, consider **$$ The William Morris B&B,** named for the 19th-century designer and writer (small Db-£100, big Db-£110, 2 rooms, tearoom, 200 yards from the bridge toward the church at 11 The Street, tel. 01285/740-555, www.thewilliammorris.com, ian@ianhowards.wanadoo.co.uk).

▲CIRENCESTER

Almost 2,000 years ago, Cirencester (SIGH-ren-ses-ter) was the ancient Roman city of Corinium. It's 20 miles from Stow down A-429, which was called Fosse Way in Roman times. The **TI,** in the shop at the Corinium Museum (described later), answers questions and sells a £0.50 town map and a £1.50 town walking-tour brochure (same hours as museum, tel. 01285/654-180).

Getting There: If traveling by bus, take #855 from Moreton-in-Marsh or Stow direct to Cirencester (3/day, 1.5 hours). Drivers follow *Town Centre* signs and find parking right on the market square; if it's parked up, retreat to the Waterloo pay-and-display lot (a five-minute walk away).

Sights: In Cirencester, stop by the impressive **Corinium Museum** to find out why they say, "If you scratch Gloucestershire, you'll find Rome." The museum chronologically displays well-explained artifacts from the town's rich history, with a focus on Roman times—when Corinium was the second-biggest city in the British Isles (after Londinium). You'll see column capitals and fine mosaics, before moving on to the Anglo-Saxon and Middle Ages exhibits (£5, Mon-Sat 10:00-17:00, Sun 14:00-17:00, Park Street, tel. 01285/655-611, www.coriniummuseum.org).

Cirencester's **church** is the largest of the Cotswold "wool" churches. The cutesy **New Brewery Arts** crafts center entertains visitors with traditional weaving and potting, workshops, an interesting gallery, and a good coffee shop (www.newbreweryarts.org.uk). Monday and Friday are general-**market** days, Friday features an antique market, and a crafts market is held on the second and fourth Saturdays of the month.

Moreton-in-Marsh

This workaday town—worth ▲—is like Stow or Chipping Campden without the touristy sugar. Rather than gift and antique shops, you'll find streets lined with real shops: ironmongers selling cottage nameplates and carpet shops strewn with the remarkable patterns that decorate B&B floors. A traditional market of 100-plus stalls fills High Street each Tuesday, as it has for the last 400 years (8:00-15:30, handicrafts, farm produce, clothing, books, and people-watching; best if you go early). The Cotswolds has an economy aside from tourism, and you'll feel it here.

Orientation to Moreton-in-Marsh

Moreton has a tiny sleepy train station two blocks from High Street, lots of bus connections, and the best **TI** in the region. The TI offers a room-booking service and discounted tickets for major sights (such as Blenheim Palace and Warwick Castle). Peruse the racks of fliers, confirm rail and bus schedules, and consider the £0.50 *Town Trail* self-guided walking tour leaflet (Mon 8:45-16:00, Tue-Thu 8:45-17:15, Fri 8:45-16:45, Sat 10:00-13:00—or until 12:30 in winter, closed Sun, good public WC, tel. 01608/650-881).

HELPFUL HINTS

Internet Access: Free Wi-Fi is available at the TI and the library (erratic hours, down High Street where it becomes Stow Road, tel. 0845-230-5420).

Baggage Storage: While there is no formal baggage storage in town, the **Black Bear Inn** (next to the TI) might let you leave bags there—especially if you buy a drink.

Laundry: The handy launderette is a block in front of the train station on New Road (daily 7:00-19:00, last wash at 18:00, £4-5 self-service wash, £2-3 self-service dry, or drop off Mon-Fri 8:00-11:00 for £3 extra and same-day service—pick up by 17:00, tel. 01608/650-888).

Bike Rental, Taxis, and Car Rental: See "Getting Around the Cotswolds" (page 356).

Parking: It's easy—anywhere on High Street is fine any time, as long as you want, for free (though there is a 2-hour parking limit for the small lot in the middle of the street). On Tuesdays, when the market makes parking tricky, you can park at the **Budgens** supermarket for £3—refundable if you spend at least £5 in the store (2-hour limit).

Hikes and Walks from Moreton-in-Marsh: As its name implies, Moreton-in-Marsh sits on a flat boggy landscape, making it a bit less appealing for hikes; I'd bus to Chipping Campden or to Stow, both described earlier, for a better hike (this is easy, since Moreton is a transit hub). If you do have just a bit of time to kill in Moreton, consider taking a fun and easy walk a mile out to the arboretum and falconry center in **Batsford** (described later).

Sleeping in Moreton-in-Marsh

$$$ Manor House Hotel is Moreton's big old hotel, dating from 1545 but sporting such modern amenities as toilets and electricity. Its 35 classy-for-the-Cotswolds rooms and its garden invite relaxation (Sb-£150, standard Db-£170, superior Db-£200, four-poster Db-£210-230, family suite-£250, £40 more for Sat night, rates are soft—often a bit less, elevator, log fire in winter, attached restaurants, free parking, on far end of High Street away from train station, tel. 01608/650-501, www.cotswold-inns-hotels.co.uk, info@manorhousehotel.info).

$$ The Swan Inn is wonderfully perched on the main drag, with eight en suite rooms. Though the halls look a bit worn and you enter through a bar/restaurant (that can be noisy on weekends), the renovated rooms themselves are classy and the bathrooms modern (Sb-£60, standard Db-£70-115, four-poster Db-£105-130, free parking, restaurant gives guests 10 percent discount, High Street, tel. 01608/650-711, www.swanmoreton.co.uk, info@swanmoreton.co.uk, Sara and Terry Todd and their two sons). Terry can pick up guests from the train station and is willing to drive carless guests to various destinations within 20 miles if no public transport is available.

$ Treetops B&B is plush, with seven spacious, attractive rooms, a sun lounge, and a three-quarter-acre backyard. Liz and Ben (the family dog) will make you feel right at home—if you meet the two-night minimum on weekends (Sb-£50, large Db-£75, gigantic Db-£85, two wheelchair-accessible ground-floor rooms have patios, set far back from the busy road, London Road, tel. 01608/651-036, www.treetopscotswolds.co.uk, treetops1@talk21.com, Liz and Brian Dean). It's an eight-minute walk from town and the train station (exit station, keep left, go left on bridge over train tracks, look for sign, then long driveway).

$ Acacia B&B, on the short road connecting the train station to the town center, is a convenient budget option. Dorothy has four

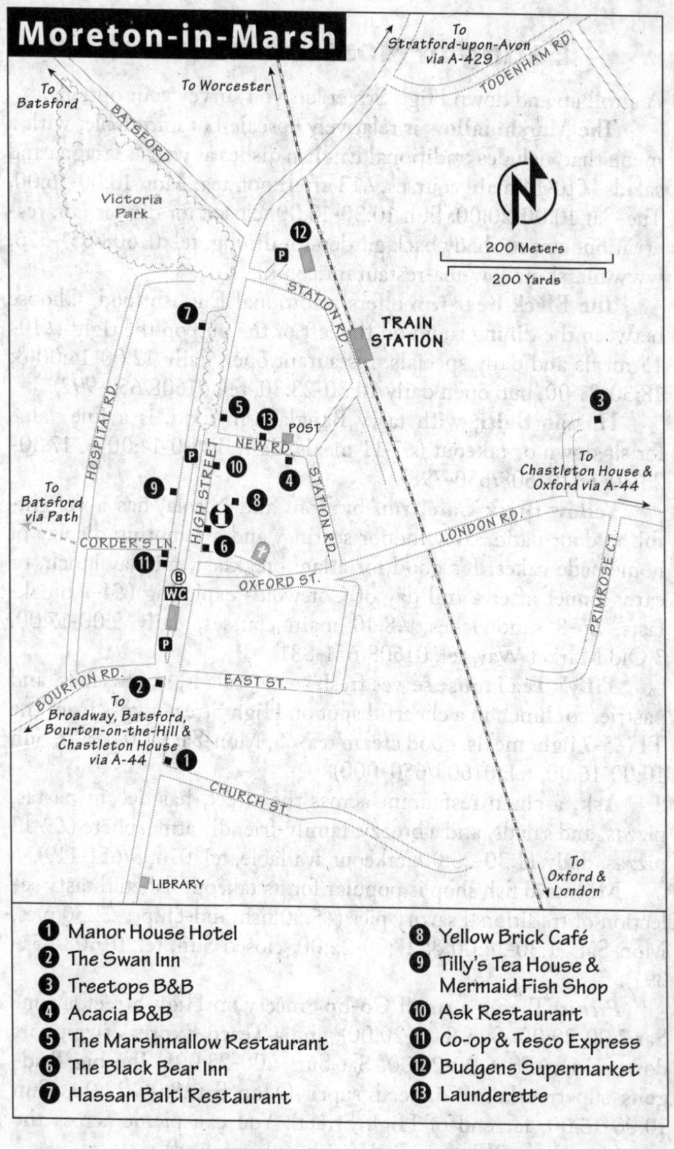

small rooms: one is en suite, the other three share one bathroom. The public spaces are a bit tired, but the rooms are bright and tidy, and most overlook a lovely garden (S-£45, D-£60, Db-£65, tel. 01608/650-130, 2 New Road, www.acaciainthecotswolds.co.uk, acacia.guesthouse@tiscali.co.uk).

Eating in Moreton-in-Marsh

A stroll up and down High Street lets you survey your options.

The Marshmallow is relatively upscale but affordable, with a menu that includes traditional English dishes as well as lasagna and salads (£10-14 main courses, £13 afternoon tea, Mon 10:00-16:00, Tue-Sat 10:00-20:00, Sun 10:30-18:00, closed for dinner Jan, reservations smart, shady back garden for dining, tel. 01608/651-536, www.marshmallow-tea-restaurant.co.uk).

The Black Bear Inn offers traditional English food. Choose between the dining room on the left or the pub on the right (£10-15 meals and daily specials, restaurant open daily 12:00-14:00 & 18:30-21:00, pub open daily 10:30-23:30, tel. 01608/652-992).

Hassan Balti, with tasty Bangladeshi food, is a fine value for sit-down or takeout (£7-11 meals, daily 12:00-14:00 & 17:30-23:30, tel. 01608/650-798).

Yellow Brick Café, run by Tom and Nicola, has a delightful outdoor patio, cozy indoor seating, and a tempting display of homemade cakes. It's good for a late breakfast, midday lunch, or early dinner after a full day of Cotswolds exploring (£4-7 breakfasts, £6-8 sandwiches, £8-10 main courses, daily 9:00-17:00, 3 Old Market Way, tel. 01608/651-881).

Tilly's Tea House serves fresh soups, salads, sandwiches, and pastries for lunch in a cheerful spot on High Street across from the TI (£5-7 light meals, good cream tea-£5, Mon-Sat 9:00-17:00, Sun 10:00-16:00, tel. 01608/650-000).

Ask, a chain restaurant across the street, has decent pastas, pizzas, and salads, and a breezy, family-friendly atmosphere (£9-13 pizzas, daily 11:30-23:00, takeout available, tel. 01608/651-119).

Mermaid fish shop is popular for its takeout fish and tasty selection of traditional savory pies (£5.50 fish-and-chips, £2.50 pies, Mon-Sat 11:30-14:00 & 17:00-22:00, closed Sun, tel. 01608/651-391).

Picnic: There's a small **Co-op** grocery on High Street (Mon-Sat 7:00-20:00, Sun 8:00-20:00), and a **Tesco Express** two doors down (Mon-Fri 6:00-23:00, Sat-Sun 7:00-23:00). The big **Budgens** supermarket is indeed super (Mon-Sat 8:00-22:00, Sun 10:00-16:00, far end of High Street). You can picnic across the street in pleasant Victoria Park (with a playground).

Nearby: The excellent **Horse and Groom** gastropub in Bourton-on-the-Hill is a quick drive or uphill two-mile walk away (see page 393).

Moreton-in-Marsh Connections

Moreton, the only Cotswold town with a train station, is also the best base for exploring the region by bus (see "Getting Around the Cotswolds," page 356).

From Moreton by Train to: London's Paddington Station (every 1-2 hours, 1.5-2 hours), **Bath** (hourly, 3 hours, 1-2 transfers), **Oxford** (every 1-2 hours, 40 minutes), **Ironbridge Gorge** (hourly, 2.5-3 hours, 2 transfers; arrive Telford, then catch bus or cab 7 miles to Ironbridge Gorge—see page 438), **Stratford-upon-Avon** (almost hourly, 2.5-3 hours, 2-3 transfers, slow and expensive, better by bus). Train info: Tel. 0345-748-4950, www.nationalrail.co.uk.

From Moreton by Bus to: Stratford-upon-Avon (#21 and #22 go via Chipping Campden: Mon-Sat 8/day, none on Sun, 1-1.5 hours, Johnsons Coaches, tel. 01564/797-070, www.johnsonscoaches.co.uk).

Near Moreton-in-Marsh

▲CHASTLETON HOUSE

This stately home, located about five miles southeast of Moreton-in-Marsh, was actually lived in by the same family from 1607 until 1991. It offers a rare peek into a Jacobean gentry house. (Jacobean, which comes from the Latin for "James," indicates the style from the time of King James I—the early 1600s.) Built, like most Cotswold palaces, with wool money, it gradually declined with the fortunes of its aristocratic family until, according to the last lady of the house, it was "held together by cobwebs." It came to the National Trust on condition that they would maintain its musty Jacobean ambience. It's so authentic that the BBC used it to film scenes from its adaptation of *Wolf Hall* (a best-seller about Henry VIII's chief minister, Thomas Cromwell, who masterminded Henry's divorce, marriage to Anne Boleyn, and break with Rome). Wander on creaky floorboards, many of them original, and chat with volunteer guides stationed in each room. It's an uppity place that doesn't encourage spontaneity. The docents are proud to play on one of the best croquet teams in the region (the rules of croquet were formalized in this house in 1868—if you fancy a round, the ticket counter rents

sets for a £10 deposit). Page through the early 20th-century family photo albums in the room just off the entry.

Cost and Hours: £9.50; April-Sept Wed-Sun 13:00-17:00; late March and Oct closes at 16:00; closed Nov-mid-March and Mon-Tue year-round; ticket office opens at 12:30, last entry one hour before closing; recorded info tel. 01494/755-560, www.nationaltrust.org.uk/chastleton.

Getting In: Only 180 visitors a day are allowed into the home (25 people every 30 minutes), and reservations are not possible—it's first-come, first served. At the busiest times, you might have to wait a bit to enter the house. Fridays are the quietest days, with the shortest wait times.

Getting There: Chastleton House is well-signposted (be sure you follow signs to the house, not the town), about a 10-minute drive southeast of Moreton-in-Marsh off A-44. It's a five-minute hike to the house from the free parking lot.

BATSFORD

This village has two side-by-side attractions that might appeal if you have a special interest or time to kill.

Getting There: Batsford is an easy 45-minute, one-mile country walk west of Moreton-in-Marsh. It's also connected to Moreton by buses #21 and #22.

Cotswold Falconry Centre

Along with the Cotswolds' hunting heritage comes falconry—and this place, with dozens of specimens of eagles, falcons, owls, and other birds, gives a sample of what these deadly birds of prey can do. You can peruse the cages to see all the different birds, but the demonstration, with vultures or falcons swooping inches over your head, is what makes it fun.

Cost and Hours: £10, ticket good for 10 percent discount at Batsford Arboretum; daily mid-Feb-mid-Nov 10:30-17:30, closed mid-Nov-mid-Feb; flying displays at 11:30, 13:30, and 15:00, plus in summer at 16:30; Batsford Park, tel. 01386/701-043, www.cotswold-falconry.co.uk.

Batsford Arboretum

This sleepy grove, with 2,800 trees from around the world, pales in comparison to some of the Cotswolds' genteel manor gardens. But it's next door to the Falconry Centre, and handy to visit if you'd enjoy strolling through a diverse wood. The arboretum's café serves lunch and tea on a terrace with sweeping views of the Gloucestershire countryside.

Cost and Hours: £8, ticket good for 10 percent discount at Falconry Centre, daily 9:00-18:00, last entry at 16:45, tel. 01386/701-441, www.batsarb.co.uk.

Blenheim Palace

Conveniently located halfway between the Cotswolds and Oxford, Blenheim Palace is one of Britain's best—worth ▲▲▲. Too many palaces can send you into a furniture-wax coma, but as a sightseeing experience and in simple visual grandeur, this palace is among Europe's finest. The Duke of Marlborough's home—the largest in England—is still lived in, which is wonderfully obvious as you prowl through it. The 2,000-acre yard, well-designed by Lancelot "Capability" Brown, is as majestic to some as the palace itself. Note: Americans who pronounce the place "blen-HEIM" are the butt of jokes. It's "BLEN-em."

John Churchill, first duke of Marlborough, defeated Louis XIV's French forces at the Battle of Blenheim in 1704. This pivotal event marked a turning point in the centuries-long struggle between the English and the French, and some historians claim that if not for his victory, we'd all be speaking French today. A thankful Queen Anne rewarded Churchill by building him this nice home, perhaps the finest Baroque building in England. Eleven dukes of Marlborough later, the palace is as impressive as ever. In 1874, a later John Churchill's American daughter-in-law, Jennie Jerome, gave birth at Blenheim to another historic baby in that line...and named him Winston.

GETTING TO BLENHEIM PALACE

Blenheim Palace sits at the edge of the cute cobbled town of Woodstock. The train station nearest the palace (Hanborough, 1.5 miles away) has no taxi or bus service.

If you're coming from the **Cotswolds,** your easiest train connection is from Moreton-in-Marsh to Oxford, where you can catch the bus to Blenheim (explained next; note that bus #S3 doesn't always stop at the Oxford train station—you may have to walk five minutes to the bus station).

From **Oxford,** take bus #S3 (2/hour, 30 minutes; bus tel. 01865/772-250, www.stagecoachbus.com). Catch it from the bus station at Gloucester Green (may also pick up in the center on George Street—ask). It stops twice near Blenheim Palace: the "Blenheim Palace Gates" stop is along the main road about a half-mile walk to the palace itself; the "Woodstock/Marlborough Arms" stop puts you right in the heart of the village of Woodstock (handy if you want to poke around town before heading to the palace; this adds just a few more minutes' walking than the other bus stop). The Woodstock gate also offers the most spectacular view of the palace and lake.

Drivers head for Woodstock (from the Cotswolds, follow signs for *Oxford* on A-44); the palace is well-signposted once in town, just off the main road. Buy your ticket at the gate, then drive up the long driveway to park near the palace.

ORIENTATION TO BLENHEIM PALACE

Cost and Hours: £22.50, park and gardens only—£14, discount palace tickets that save £3 are available at TIs in surrounding towns—including Oxford and Moreton-in-Marsh—or on the #S3 bus from Oxford; family ticket for two adults and two kids-£59, £5.50 guidebook; open mid-Feb-Oct daily 10:30-17:30; Nov-mid-Dec at least Wed-Sun 10:30-17:30; park open but palace closed mid-Dec-mid-Feb. Doors to the palace close at 16:45, it's "everyone out" at 17:30, and the park closes at 18:00. Late in the afternoon the palace is relaxed and quiet (even on the busiest of days).

Information: The interactive map on their website gives a good visual orientation; recorded info toll-free tel. 0800-849-6500, www.blenheimpalace.com.

Tours: Guided tours are available for the state rooms (included in admission, 2/hour, 45 minutes, last tour 16:45, daily except Sunday), the private apartments (£5, 2/hour, 30 minutes, generally daily 11:00-16:30, most likely to be running in summer, tickets are limited—16 per group), and the gardens (included in admission).

Eating and Sleeping near the Palace: The delightful Water Terraces Café sits at the garden exit for basic lunch and teatime treats. The pleasant town of Woodstock is just outside the palace gates. If you need a bed, consider a room in the characteristic old half-timbered **$$ Blenheim Buttery** (Db-£95-135, 7 Market Place, tel. 01865/811-950, www.theblenheimbuttery.co.uk, info@theblenheimbuttery.co.uk).

VISITING THE PALACE

From the parking lot, you'll enter through the Visitors Center (shop, café, and WCs). Pick up a free map and daily tour program, consider signing up for tours of the private apartments and the gardens, and head through the small courtyard. You'll emerge into a grand courtyard in front of the palace's columned yellow facade.

Facing the palace, review your six options: the state rooms, the Winston Churchill Exhibition, a skippable multimedia exhibit called The Untold Story, the private apartments tour, the gardens, and the Churchills' Destiny exhibit. The first three of these depart from the Great Hall, directly ahead. The palace tour and Winston Churchill Exhibition are substantial and most important (allow a total of 90 minutes for both). The private apartment tour, an excellent behind-the-scenes peek at the palace, requires a special ticket and meets in the corner of the courtyard to the left. The gardens, through the wing on the right, are simply delightful. And the Churchills' Destiny exhibit, worth a 15-minute walk-through, is in the stables farther to the right.

State Rooms: Enter into the truly great Great Hall, where you'll be greeted and have your options explained. While you can go "free flow" (reading info plaques and talking with docents in each room), you'll get much more out of your visit by taking the included guided tour of the state rooms.

The state rooms are the fancy halls the dukes use to impress visiting dignitaries. These most sumptuous rooms in the palace are ornamented with fine porcelain, gilded ceilings, portraits of past dukes, photos of the present duke's family, and "chaperone" sofas designed to give courting couples just enough privacy...but not *too* much.

Enjoy the series of 10 Brussels tapestries that commemorate military victories of the First Duke of Marlborough, including the Battle of Blenheim. After winning that pivotal conflict, he scrawled a quick note on the back of a tavern bill notifying the queen of his victory (you'll see a replica). The tour offers insights into the quirky ways of England's fading nobility—for example, in exchange for this fine palace, the duke still pays "rent" to the Queen in the form of one ornamental flag per year.

Finish with the remarkable "long library"—with its tiers of books and stuccoed ceilings—before exiting through the chapel, near the entrance to the gardens.

Winston Churchill Exhibition: This is a fascinating display of letters, paintings, and other artifacts of the great statesman who was born here. You'll either be instructed to see this before touring the main state rooms or be directed into this exhibition from the library—the last room of the state rooms tour—before leaving the palace.

A highlight of your visit, the exhibit gives you an appreciation for this amazing leader and how blessed Britain was to have him when it did. Along with lots of intimate artifacts from his life, you'll see the bed in which Sir Winston was born in 1874 (prematurely...his mother went into labor suddenly while attending a party here).

The Untold Story: Upstairs, to the left as you enter the Great Hall, is a modern, 45-minute, multimedia "visitors' experience" in a series of eight rooms (15 people go in every 5 minutes, included in your ticket). You'll travel from room to room—as doors open and close behind you every five minutes or so—guided through 300 years of history by a maid named Grace Ridley. (If you have limited time to spend at the palace, this is skippable.) If bored (which is likely), you can quietly push open the next door and fast-track your experience.

Private Apartments: For a more extensive visit, book a spot as soon as you arrive for a 30-minute guided walk through the private apartments of the duke. Tours leave at the top and bottom of each hour—when His Grace is not in; enter in the corner of courtyard to left of grand palace entry.

You'll see the chummy billiards room, luxurious china, the servants quarters with 47 bells—one for each room to call the servants, private rooms, 18th-century Flemish tapestries, family photos, and so on.

Churchills' Destiny: In the "stables block" (under the gateway to the right, as you face the main palace entrance) is an exhibit that traces the military leadership of two great men who shared the name Churchill: John, who defeated Louis XIV at the Battle of Blenheim in the 18th century and in whose honor this palace was built; and Winston, who was born in this palace and who won the Battle of Britain and helped defeat Hitler in the 20th century. It's remarkable that arguably two of the most important military victories in the nation's history were overseen by distant cousins. (Winston Churchill fans can visit his tomb, just over a mile away to the south in the Bladon town churchyard—the church is faintly visible from inside the palace. Look for the footpath across from the White House pub.)

Gardens: The palace's expansive gardens stretch nearly as far as the eye can see in every direction. Access them from the main courtyard by following signs through a little door (as you face the main palace entrance, it's to the right). You'll emerge into the **Water Terraces;** from there, you can loop around to the left, behind the palace, to see (but not enter) the Italian Garden. Or, head down to the lake to walk along the waterfront trail; going left takes you to the rose gardens and arboretum, while turning right brings you to the Grand Bridge. You can explore on your own (using the map and good signposting), or join a free tour.

On the way out of the palace

complex, stop in at the **kid-friendly pleasure garden,** where a lush and humid greenhouse flutters with butterflies. A kid zone includes a few second-rate games and the "world's largest symbolic hedge maze." The maze is worth a look if you haven't seen one and want some exercise. If you have a car, you'll pass these gardens as you drive down the road toward the exit; otherwise, you can take the tiny train from the palace parking lot to the garden (2/hour).

STRATFORD-UPON-AVON

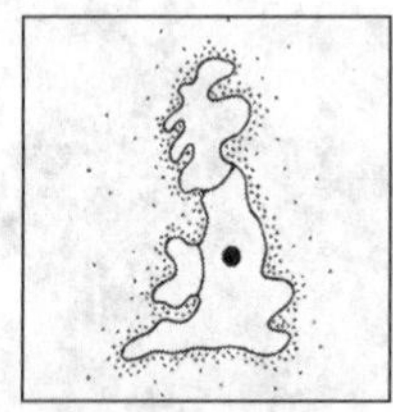

Stratford is Shakespeare's hometown. To see or not to see? Stratford is a must for every big bus tour in England, and one of the most popular side-trips from London. English majors and actors are in seventh heaven here. Sure, it's touristy, and nonliterary types might find it's much ado about nothing. But nobody back home would understand if you skipped Shakespeare's house.

Shakespeare connection aside, the town's riverside and half-timbered charm, coupled with its hardworking tourist industry, make Stratford a fun stop. But the play's the thing to bring the Bard to life—and you've arrived just in time to see the Royal Shakespeare Company (the world's best Shakespeare ensemble) making the most of their state-of-the-art theater complex. If you'll ever enjoy a Shakespeare performance, it'll be here...even if you flunked English Lit.

PLANNING YOUR TIME

If you're just passing through Stratford, it's worth a half-day—stroll the charming core, visit your choice of Shakespeare sights (Shakespeare's Birthplace is best and easiest), and watch the swans along the river. But if you can squeeze it in, it's worth it to stick around to see a play; in this case, you'll need to spend the night here or drive in from the nearby Cotswolds (doable—just 30 minutes away; see previous chapter).

By Train or Bus: It's easy to stop in Stratford for a wander or an overnight. Stratford is well-connected by train to London and Oxford, and linked by bus and train to nearby towns (Warwick and Coventry to the north, and Moreton in the Cotswolds to the south).

By Car: Stratford, conveniently located at the northern edge of the Cotswolds, is made to order for drivers connecting the Cotswolds with points north (such as Ironbridge Gorge or North Wales).

Orientation to Stratford

Stratford, with around 30,000 people, has a compact old town, with the TI and theater along the riverbank, and Shakespeare's Birthplace a few blocks inland; you can easily walk to everything except Mary Arden's place. The core of the town is lined with half-timbered houses. The River Avon has an idyllic yet playful feel, with a park along both banks, paddleboats, hungry swans, and a fun old crank-powered ferry.

TOURIST INFORMATION

The TI is in a small brick building on Bridgefoot, where the main street hits the river (Mon-Sat 9:00-17:30, Sun 10:00-16:00, tel. 01789/264-293, www.discover-stratford.com).

Combo-Tickets: The TI sells the Shakespeare Birthplace Trust Five House combo-ticket at a discount, as well as a special any-three combo-ticket, which gives you entry into your pick of three of the five trust sights (see "Shakespearean Sights," later, for details).

ARRIVAL IN STRATFORD

By Train: Don't get off at the Stratford Parkway train station—you want Stratford-upon-Avon. Once there, exit straight ahead from the train station, bear right up the stairs, then turn left and follow the main drag straight to the river. (For the Grove Road B&Bs, turn right at the first big intersection.)

By Car: If you're sleeping in Stratford, ask your B&B for arrival and parking details (many have a few free parking spaces, but it's best to reserve ahead). If you're just here for the day, you'll find plenty of lots scattered around town. The Bridgefoot garage is big, easy, and cheap—coming from the south (i.e., the Cotswolds), cross the big bridge and veer right, following *Through Traffic, P,* and *Wark* (Warwick Road) signs. Go around the block—turning right and right and right—and enter the multistory garage; first hour free, £6/9 hours, £10/24 hours. The City Sightseeing bus stop and the TI are a block away. Parking is free at the park-and-ride near

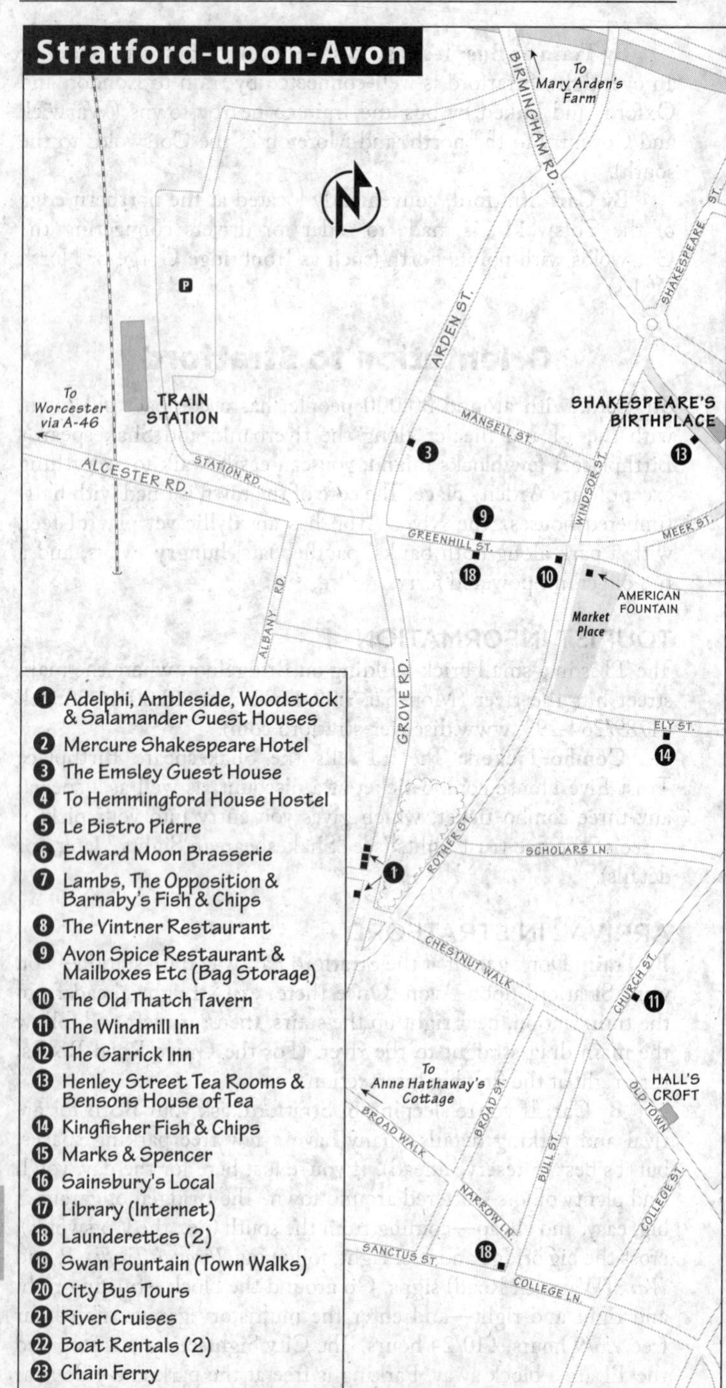
Stratford-upon-Avon
To Mary Arden's Farm
BIRMINGHAM RD.
SHAKESPEARE ST.
ARDEN ST.
To Worcester via A-46
TRAIN STATION
SHAKESPEARE'S BIRTHPLACE
MANSELL ST.
STATION RD.
ALCESTER RD.
WINDSOR ST.
MEER ST.
GREENHILL ST.
AMERICAN FOUNTAIN
Market Place
ALBANY RD.
GROVE RD.
ELY ST.
ROTHER ST.
SCHOLARS LN.
CHESTNUT WALK
CHURCH ST.
To Anne Hathaway's Cottage
BROAD WALK
BROAD ST.
HALL'S CROFT
OLD TOWN
BULL ST.
NARROW LN.
COLLEGE ST.
SANCTUS ST.
COLLEGE LN.
1 Adelphi, Ambleside, Woodstock & Salamander Guest Houses
2 Mercure Shakespeare Hotel
3 The Emsley Guest House
4 To Hemmingford House Hostel
5 Le Bistro Pierre
6 Edward Moon Brasserie
7 Lambs, The Opposition & Barnaby's Fish & Chips
8 The Vintner Restaurant
9 Avon Spice Restaurant & Mailboxes Etc (Bag Storage)
10 The Old Thatch Tavern
11 The Windmill Inn
12 The Garrick Inn
13 Henley Street Tea Rooms & Bensons House of Tea
14 Kingfisher Fish & Chips
15 Marks & Spencer
16 Sainsbury's Local
17 Library (Internet)
18 Launderettes (2)
19 Swan Fountain (Town Walks)
20 City Bus Tours
21 River Cruises
22 Boat Rentals (2)
23 Chain Ferry

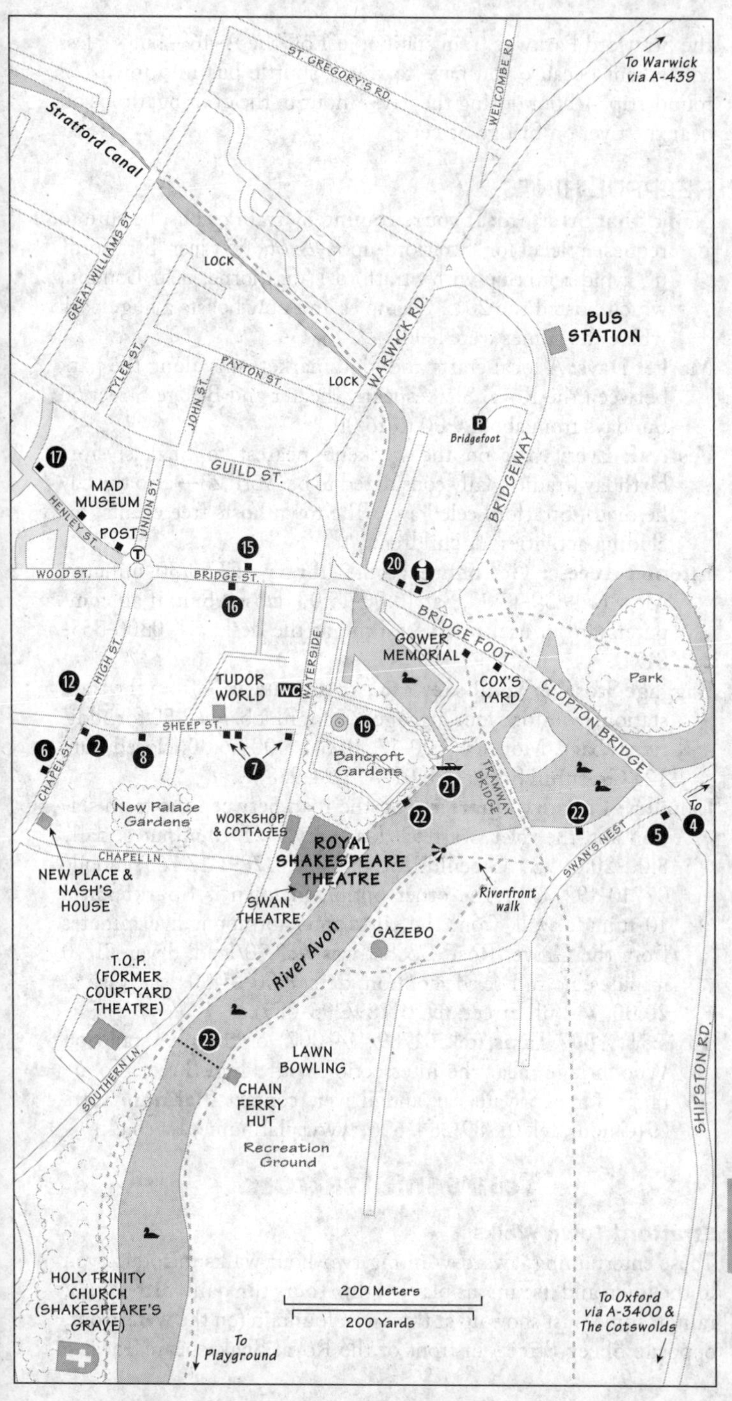
To Warwick via A-439
St. Gregory's Rd.
Welcombe Rd.
Stratford Canal
Great Williams St.
Lock
Warwick Rd.
Bus Station
Tyler St.
Payton St.
Lock
John St.
P
Bridgefoot
Guild St.
Bridgeway
17
Mad Museum
Henley St.
Post
Union St.
T
15
20
Wood St.
Bridge St.
16
Bridge Foot
Gower Memorial
High St.
Waterside
12
Tudor World
WC
Cox's Yard
Clopton Bridge
Park
Sheep St.
19
6
2
8
7
Bancroft Gardens
21
Tramway Bridge
Chapel St.
22
22
To
5
4
New Palace Gardens
Workshop & Cottages
Royal Shakespeare Theatre
Swan's Nest
Chapel Ln.
New Place & Nash's House
Swan Theatre
Riverfront walk
River Avon
Gazebo
T.O.P. (Former Courtyard Theatre)
23
Lawn Bowling
Southern Ln.
Chain Ferry Hut
Shipston Rd.
Recreation Ground
Holy Trinity Church (Shakespeare's Grave)
200 Meters
200 Yards
To Oxford via A-3400 & The Cotswolds
To Playground

the Stratford Parkway train station, just off the A-46—but it's less convenient because you have to ride a shuttle bus into town (£2 round-trip, 4/hour during the day, 2/hour in the evening, drops off near the river on Bridge Street).

HELPFUL HINTS

Name That Stratford: If you're coming by train or bus, be sure to request a ticket for "Stratford-upon-Avon," not just "Stratford" (to avoid a mix-up with Stratford Langthorne, near London, which hosted the 2012 Olympics and now boasts a huge park where the games were held).

Market Days: A local crafts and food market runs along the park between the Royal Shakespeare Theater and Bridge Street on Sundays from about 9:00 to 16:00.

Festival: Every year on the weekend nearest to Shakespeare's birthday (traditionally considered to be April 23—also the day he died), Stratford celebrates. The town hosts free events, including activities for children.

Internet Access: Get online at the **library** (£2.50/30 minutes; Mon-Fri 9:30-17:00, Sat 10:00-15:00, closed Sun; if all computers are in use, reserve a time at the desk; tel. 0300-555-8171).

Baggage Storage: Mailboxes Etc., a 5-minute walk from the train station, can store your luggage (£5 for first bag, £2.50 for additional bags, Mon-Fri 9:00-17:30, Sat 9:00-16:00, closed Sun, 12a Greenhill Street, tel. 01789/294-968).

Laundry: Laundry Quarter is on the road between the train station and the river (wash-£4/load, dryer-£1/10 minutes, daily 8:00-20:00, 34 Greenhill Street, tel. 01789/417-766, mobile 07710-192-704). The other option in town is **Sparklean,** a 10-minute walk from the city center, or about five minutes from the Grover Road B&Bs (wash-£3.70/load, dryer-£1/10 minutes, no full-service option, daily 8:00-21:00, last wash at 20:00, 74 Bull Street, tel. 01789/296-075).

Taxis: Try **007 Taxis** (tel. 01789/414-007) or the taxi stand on Woodbridge, near the intersection with High Street. To arrange for a private car and driver, contact **Platinum Cars** (£40/hour, tel. 01789/264-626, www.platinum-cars.co.uk).

Tours in Stratford

Stratford Town Walks

These entertaining, award-winning two-hour walks introduce you to the town and its famous playwright. Tours run daily year-round, rain or shine. Just show up at the Swan fountain (on the waterfront, opposite Sheep Street) in front of the Royal Shakespeare Theatre

and pay the guide (£6, kids-£3, ticket stub offers discounts to some sights and shops, daily at 11:00, Sat-Sun also at 14:00, mobile 07855/760-377, www.stratfordtownwalk.co.uk). They also run an evening ghost walk led by a professional magician (£6, kids-£4, Mon and Thu-Sat at 19:30, 1.5 hours, must book in advance).

City Sightseeing Bus Tours

Open-top buses constantly make the rounds, allowing visitors to hop on and hop off at all the Shakespeare sights. Given the far-flung nature of two of the Shakespeare sights, and the value of the fun commentary provided, this tour makes the town more manageable. The full 11-stop circuit takes about an hour and comes with a steady and informative commentary (£13.50, discount with town walk ticket stub, buy tickets on bus or as you board, ticket good for 24 hours, buses leave from the TI every 20 minutes in high season from about 9:30-17:00, every 30 minutes and shorter hours off-season; buses alternate between recorded commentary and live guides—for the best tour, wait for a live guide; tel. 01789/412-680, www.citysightseeing-stratford.com).

Shakespearean Sights

Stratford's five biggest Shakespeare sights are run by the same organization, the Shakespeare Birthplace Trust (www.shakespeare.org.uk). While these sights are promoted as if they were tacky tourist attractions—and are designed to be crowd-pleasers rather than to tickle academics—they're well-run and genuinely interesting. Shakespeare's Birthplace, New Place & Nash's House, and Hall's Croft are in town; Mary Arden's Farm and Anne Hathaway's Cottage are just outside Stratford. Each has a tranquil garden and helpful, eager docents who love to tell a story; and yet each is quite different, so visiting all five gives you a well-rounded look at the Bard.

If you're here for Shakespeare sightseeing—and have time to venture to the countryside sights—you might as well buy the "Five House" combo-ticket and drop into them all. If your time is more limited, visit only Shakespeare's Birthplace, which is the most convenient to reach (right in the town center) and offers the best historical introduction to the playwright.

Combo-Tickets: Admission to the three Shakespeare Birth-

William Shakespeare (1564-1616)

To many, William Shakespeare is the greatest author, in any language, period. In one fell swoop, he expanded and helped define modern English—the unrefined tongue of everyday people—and granted it a beauty and legitimacy that put it on par with Latin. In the process, he gave us phrases like "one fell swoop," which we quote without knowing that no one ever said it before Shakespeare wrote it.

Shakespeare was born in Stratford-upon-Avon in 1564 to John Shakespeare and Mary Arden. Though his parents were probably illiterate, Shakespeare is thought to have attended Stratford's grammar school, finishing his education at age 14. When he was 18, he married a 26-year-old local girl, Anne Hathaway (she was three months pregnant with their daughter Susanna).

The very beginnings of Shakespeare's writing career are shrouded in mystery: Historians have been unable to unearth any record of what he was up to in his early 20s. We only know that seven years after his marriage, Shakespeare was living in London as a budding poet, playwright, and actor. He soon hit the big time, writing and performing for royalty, founding (along with his troupe) the Globe Theatre (a functioning replica of which now stands along the Thames' South Bank—see page 114), and raking in enough dough to buy New Place, a swanky mansion back in his hometown. Around 1611, the rich-and-famous playwright retired from the theater, moving back to Stratford, where he died at the age of 52.

With plots that entertained both the highest and the lowest minds, Shakespeare taught the play-going public about human nature. His tool was an unrivaled linguistic mastery of English. Using borrowed plots, outrageous puns, and poetic language, Shakespeare wrote comedies (c. 1590—*Taming of the Shrew, As You Like It*), tragedies (c. 1600—*Hamlet, Othello, Macbeth, King*

place Trust sights in town—Shakespeare's Birthplace, Hall's Croft, and New Place & Nash's House—requires a combo-ticket; no individual tickets are sold. To visit only these three sights, get the £15.90 **Shakespeare Birthplace combo-ticket,** which is sold at the participating sights. To add Anne Hathaway's Cottage and Mary Arden's Farm, you can buy the £23.90 **Shakespeare Five House combo-ticket** (sold at participating sights, good for one year; also available at a discount—£21.50—at the TI). You can also buy in-

Lear), and fanciful combinations (c. 1610—*The Tempest*), exploring the full range of human emotions and reinventing the English language.

Perhaps as important was his insight into humanity. His father was a glove-maker and wool merchant, and his mother was the daughter of a landowner from a Catholic family. Some scholars speculate that Shakespeare's parents were closet Catholics, practicing their faith during the rise of Protestantism. It is this tug-of-war between two worlds, some think that helped enlighten Shakespeare's humanism. Think of his stock of great characters and great lines: Hamlet ("To be or not to be, that is the question"), Othello and his jealousy ("It is the green-eyed monster"), ambitious Mark Antony ("Friends, Romans, countrymen, lend me your ears"), rowdy Falstaff ("The better part of valor is discretion"), and the star-crossed lovers Romeo and Juliet ("But soft, what light through yonder window breaks"). Shakespeare probed the psychology of human beings 300 years before Freud. Even today, his characters strike a familiar chord.

Mr. WILLIAM
SHAKESPEARES
COMEDIES,
HISTORIES, &
TRAGEDIES.
Published according to the True Originall Copies.

LONDON
Printed by Isaac Iaggard, and Ed. Blount. 1623

The scope of his brilliant work, his humble beginnings, and the fact that no original Shakespeare manuscripts survive raise a few scholarly eyebrows. Some have wondered if Shakespeare had help on several of his plays. After all, they reasoned, how could a journeyman actor with little education have written so many masterpieces? And he was surrounded by other great writers, such as his friend and fellow poet, Ben Jonson. Most modern scholars, though, agree that Shakespeare did indeed write the plays and sonnets attributed to him.

His contemporaries had no doubts about Shakespeare—or his legacy. As Jonson wrote in the preface to the First Folio, "He was not of an age, but for all time!"

dividual tickets for Anne Hathaway's Cottage and Mary Arden's Farm (see "Just Outside Stratford," later). Both tickets also include Holy Trinity Church, with Shakespeare's grave, which usually requests a £2 donation.

Another option is the £15.50 **any-three combo-ticket,** sold only at the TI. This ticket lets you choose which trio of sights you want to see—for instance, the birthplace, Anne Hathaway's Cottage, and Mary Arden's Farm (buy at TI; you'll get a receipt, then show it at the first sight you visit to receive your three-sight card).

Discounts: If you've taken a Stratford town walk (described under "Tours in Stratford," earlier), show your ticket stub to receive a 50 percent discount off any combo-ticket you buy at the sights. Also, ask your B&B owner if they have any discount vouchers—they often do.

Closing Times: What the Shakespeare sights list as their "closing time" is actually their last-entry time. If you show up at the closing time I've noted below, you'll still be able to get in, but with limited time to enjoy the sight (since they start closing things down soon after).

IN STRATFORD

▲▲Shakespeare's Birthplace

Touring this sight, you'll experience a modern exhibit before seeing Shakespeare's actual place of birth. While the birthplace itself is a bit underwhelming, the exhibit, helpful docents, and sense that Shakespeare's ghost still haunts these halls make it a good introduction to the Bard.

Cost and Hours: Covered by combo-tickets, daily April-Oct 9:00-17:00, July-Aug until 18:00, Nov-March 10:00-16:00, café, in town center on Henley Street, tel. 01789/204-016.

Visiting Shakespeare's Birthplace: You'll begin by touring an exhibit that provides an entertaining and easily digestible introduction (or, for some, review) about what made the Bard so great. The exhibit includes a timeline of his plays, movie clips of his works, and information about his upbringing in Stratford, his family life, and his career in London. Historical artifacts, including an original 1623 First Folio of Shakespeare's work, and less-significant pieces like a 19th-century visitors' book, are also on display.

You'll exit the exhibit into the garden, where you can follow signs to the **birthplace,** a half-timbered Elizabethan building where young William grew up. I find the old house a bit disappointing, as if millions of visitors have rubbed it clean of anything authentic. It was restored in the 1800s, and, while the furnishings seem tacky and modern, they're supposed to be true to 1575, when William was 11. To liven up the otherwise dead-feeling house, chat up the well-versed, often-costumed attendants posted in many of the rooms, eager to engage with travelers and answer questions.

You'll be greeted by a guide who offers an introductory talk, then set free to explore on your own. Look for the window etched with the names of decades of important visitors, from Water Scott to actor Henry Irving.

Shakespeare's father, John—who came from humble beginnings, but bettered himself by pursuing a career in glove-making (you'll see the window where he sold them to customers on the street)—provided his family with a comfortable, upper-middle-class existence. The guest bed in the parlor was a major status symbol: They must have been rich to afford such a nice bed that wasn't even used every day. This is also the house where Shakespeare and his bride, Anne Hathaway, began their married life together. Upstairs are the rooms where young Will, his siblings, and his parents slept (along with their servants). After Shakespeare's father died and William inherited the building, the thrifty playwright converted it into a pub to make a little money.

Exit into the fine **garden** where Shakespearean **actors** often perform brief scenes (they may even take requests). Pull up a bench and listen, imagining the playwright as a young boy stretching his imagination in this very place.

New Place & Nash's House

Set to open as a newly configured site by the time of your visit, New Place & Nash's House provides an atmospheric stop on a tour of the Bard's life. About 400 years after his death, visitors can finally stroll the former foundation and gardens of the mansion Shakespeare called home after he made it big. While nothing remains of the house purchased in 1597 (it was demolished in the 18th century), the grounds still manage to seduce many visitors. At the least, they have nostalgic value—especially for fans who can picture him writing *The Tempest* on this very spot. Next door, Nash's House (Nash was the first husband of Shakespeare's granddaughter...not exactly a close connection) features items related to its recent excavation and Shakespeare's 19 years living in New Place before he died there in 1616.

Cost and Hours: Covered by combo-ticket; daily April-Oct 10:00-17:00, Nov-March 11:00-16:00; Chapel Street, tel. 01789/292-325.

Hall's Croft

This former home of Shakespeare's eldest daughter, Susanna, is in Stratford town center. A fine old Jacobean house, it's the fanciest of the group. Since she married a doctor, the exhibits here are focused on

17th-century medicine. If you have time

to spare and one of the combo-tickets, it's worth a quick pop-in. To make the exhibits interesting, ask the docent for the 15- to 20-minute introduction, or one of the large laminated self-guides, both of which help bring the plague—and some of the bizarre remedies of the time—to life.

Cost and Hours: Covered by combo-ticket, same hours as New Place & Nash's House, on-site tearoom, between Church Street and the river on Old Town Street, tel. 01789/338-533.

Shakespeare's Grave

To see his final resting place, head to the riverside Holy Trinity Church. Shakespeare was a rector for this church when he died. While the church is surrounded by an evocative graveyard, the Bard is entombed in a place of honor, right in front of the altar inside. The church marks the ninth-century birthplace of the town, which was once a religious settlement.

Cost and Hours: £2 donation, covered by combo-ticket (but not included in individual tickets to Anne Hathaway's Cottage or Mary Arden's Farm), April-Sept Mon-Sat 8:30-17:40, Sun 12:30-16:40; Oct-March until 16:40 or 15:40, 10-minute walk past the theater—see its graceful spire as you gaze down the river, tel. 01789/266-316, www.stratford-upon-avon.org.

JUST OUTSIDE STRATFORD

To reach either of these sights, it's best to drive or take the hop-on, hop-off bus tour (see "Tours in Stratford," earlier)—unless you're staying at one of the Grove Road B&Bs, which are an easy 20-minute walk from Anne Hathaway's Cottage. Both sights are well-signposted (with brown signs) from the major streets and ring roads around Stratford. If driving between the sights, ask for directions at the sight you're leaving.

▲▲Mary Arden's Farm

Along with Shakespeare's Birthplace, this is my favorite of the Shakespearean sights. Famous as the girlhood home of William's mom, this homestead is in Wilmcote (about three miles from Stratford). Built around two historic farmhouses, it's an open-air folk museum depicting 16th-century farm life...which happens to have ties to Shakespeare. The Bard is basically an afterthought here.

Cost and Hours: £12.50, also covered by certain combo-tickets—see page 417, daily mid-March-Oct 10:00-17:00, visitors must leave by 17:30, closed Nov-mid-March, tel. 01789/293-455.

Getting There: The most convenient way to get here is by car (free parking) or the hop-on, hop-off bus tour, but it's also easy to reach by train. The Wilmcote train station is up the street, about a five-minute walk from Mary Arden's Farm (two stops from Stratford-upon-Avon on Birmingham- and London-bound trains, 1-2/hour, 5-minute trip, call London Midland to confirm departure time—tel. 0844-811-0133, www.londonmidland.com).

Visiting Mary Arden's Farm: The museum hosts many special **events,** including the falconry show described below. The day's events are listed on a chalkboard by the entry, or you can call ahead to find out what's on. There are always plenty of activities to engage kids: It's an active, hands-on place.

Pick up a map at the entrance and wander from building to building, through farmhouses with good displays about farm life. Throughout the complex, you'll see period interpreters in Tudor costumes. They'll likely be going through the day's chores as people back then would have done—activities such as milking the sheep and cutting wood to do repairs on the house. They're there to answer questions and provide fun, gossipy insight into what life was like at the time.

The first building, **Palmer's farm** (mistaken for Mary Arden's home for hundreds of years, and correctly identified in 2000), is furnished as it would have been in Shakespeare's day. Step into the kitchen to see food being prepared over an open fire—at 13:00 each day the "servants" (employees) sit down in the adjacent dining room for a traditional dinner.

Mary Arden actually lived in the neighboring **farmhouse,** covered in brick facade and seemingly less impressive. The house is filled with kid-oriented activities, including period dress-up clothes, board games from Shakespeare's day, and a Tudor alphabet so kids can write their names in fancy lettering.

Of the many events here, the most enjoyable is the **falconry demonstration,** with lots of mean-footed birds (daily, usually at 11:15, 12:15, 13:00 and 16:00). Chat with the falconers about their methods for earning the birds' trust. The birds'

Stratford Thanks America

Residents of Stratford are thankful for the many contributions Americans have made to their city and its heritage. Along with pumping up the economy day in and day out with tourist visits, Americans paid for half the rebuilding of the Royal Shakespeare Theatre after it burned down in 1926. The Swan Theatre renovation was funded entirely by American aid. Harvard University inherited—you guessed it—the Harvard House, and it maintains the house today. London's much-loved theater, Shakespeare's Globe, was the dream (and gift) of an American. And there's even an odd but prominent "American Fountain" overlooking Stratford's market square on Rother Street, which was given in 1887 to celebrate the Golden Jubilee of the rule of Queen Victoria.

hunger sets them to flight (a round-trip earns the bird a bit of food; the birds fly when hungry—but don't have the energy if they're *too* hungry). Like Katherine, the wife described as "my falcon" in *The Taming of the Shrew,* these birds are tamed and trained with food as a reward. If things are slow, ask if you can feed one.

▲Anne Hathaway's Cottage

Located 1.5 miles out of Stratford (in Shottery), this home is a 12-room farmhouse where the Bard's wife grew up. William courted Anne here—she was 26, he was only 18—and his tactics proved successful. (Maybe a little too much, as she was several months pregnant at their wedding.) Their 34-year marriage produced two more children, and lasted until his death in 1616 at age 52. The Hathaway family lived here for 400 years, until 1911, and much of the family's 92-acre farm remains part of the sight.

Cost and Hours: £9.50, also covered by certain combo-tickets—see page 417, daily mid-March-Oct 9:00-17:00, Nov-mid-March 10:00-16:00, tel. 01789/338-532.

Getting There: It's a 30-minute walk from central Stratford (20 minutes from the Grove Road B&Bs), a stop on the hop-on, hop-off tour bus, or a quick taxi ride from downtown Stratford (around £5). Drivers will find it well-signposted entering Stratford from any direction, with easy £1 parking.

Visiting Anne Hathaway's Cottage: After buying your ticket, turn right and head down through the garden to the thatch-roofed **cottage,** which looks cute enough to eat. The house offers an intimate peek at life in Shakespeare's day. In some ways, it feels even more authentic than his birthplace, and it's fun to imagine the writer of some of the world's greatest romances wooing his favorite girl right here during his formative years. Docents are posted in the first and last rooms to provide meaning and answer questions; while most tourists just stampede through, you'll have a more informative visit if you pause to listen to their introduction in the parlor and commentary throughout the house. (If the place shakes, a tourist has thunked his or her head on the low beams.)

Maybe even more interesting than the cottage are the **gardens,** which have several parts (including a prizewinning "traditional cottage garden"). Follow the signs to the "Woodland Walk" (look for the Singing Tree on your way), along with a fun sculpture garden littered with modern interpretations of Shakespearean characters (such as Falstaff's mead gut, and a great photo-op statue of the British Isles sliced out of steel). From April through June, the gardens are at their best, with birds chirping, bulbs in bloom, and a large sweet-pea display. You'll also find a music trail, a butterfly trail, and—likely—rotating exhibits, generally on a gardening theme.

THE ROYAL SHAKESPEARE COMPANY

The Royal Shakespeare Company (RSC), undoubtedly the best Shakespeare company on earth, performs year-round in Stratford and in London. Seeing a play here in the Bard's birthplace is a must for Shakespeare fans, and a memorable experience for anybody. Between its excellent acting and remarkable staging, the RSC makes Shakespeare as accessible and enjoyable as it gets.

The RSC makes it easy to take in a play, thanks to their very user-friendly website, painless ticket-booking system, and chock-a-block schedule that fills the summer with mostly big-name Shakespeare plays (plus a few more obscure titles to please the die-hard aficionados). Except in January and February, there's almost always something playing.

The RSC is enjoying renewed popularity this decade after the 2011 opening of its cutting-edge Royal Shakespeare Theatre. Even if you're not seeing a play, exploring this cleverly designed theater building is well worth your time. The smaller, attached Swan Theatre hosts plays on a more intimate scale, with only about 400 seats.

▲▲▲Seeing a Play

Performances take place most days (Mon-Sat generally at 19:15 at the Royal Shakespeare Theatre or 19:30 at the Swan, matinees around 13:15 at the RST or 13:30 at the Swan, sporadic Sun shows). Shows generally last three hours or more, with one intermission; for an evening show, don't count on getting back to your B&B

The Look of Stratford

There's much more to Stratford than Shakespeare sights. Take time to appreciate the look of the town itself. While the main street goes back to Roman times, the key date for the city was 1196, when the king gave the town "market privileges." Stratford was shaped by its marketplace years. The market's many "departments" were located on logically-named streets, whose names still remain: Sheep Street, Corn Street, and so on. Today's street plan—and even the 57' 9" width of the lots—survives from the 12th century. (Some of the modern storefronts in the town center are still that exact width.)

Starting in about 1600, three great fires gutted the town, leaving very few buildings older than that era. After those fires, tinderbox thatch roofs were prohibited—the Old Thatch Tavern on Greenhill Street is the only remaining thatch roof in town, predating the law and grandfathered in.

The town's main drag, Bridge Street, is the oldest street in town, but looks the youngest. It was built in the Regency style—a result of a rough little middle row of wattle-and-daub houses being torn down in the 1820s to double the street's width. Today's Bridge Street buildings retain that early 19th-century style: Regency.

Throughout Stratford, you'll see striking black-and-white, half-timbered buildings, as well as half-timbered structures that were partially plastered over and covered up in the 19th century. During Victorian times, the half-timbered style was considered low-class, but in the 20th century—just as tourists came, preferring ye olde style—timbers came back into vogue, and the plaster was removed on many old buildings. But any black and white you see is likely to be modern paint. The original coloring was "biscuit yellow" and brown.

much before 23:00. There's no strict dress code—and people dress casually (nice jeans and short-sleeve shirts are fine)—but shorts are discouraged. You can buy a program for £4. If you're feeling bold, buy a £5 standing ticket and then slip into an open seat as the lights dim—if nothing is available during the play's first half, something might open up after intermission.

Getting Tickets: Tickets range from £5 (standing) to £60, with most around £40. Saturday evening shows—the most popular—are most expensive. You can book tickets as you like it: online (www.rsc.org.uk), by phone (tel. 01789/403-493), or in person at the box office (Mon-Sat 10:00-20:00, Sun 10:00-17:00). Pay by credit card, get a confirmation number, then pick up your tickets at the theater 30 minutes before "curtain up." Because it's so easy to get tickets online or by phone, it makes absolutely no sense to pay extra to book tickets through any other source.

Tickets go on sale months in advance. Saturdays and very famous plays (such as *Romeo and Juliet* or *Hamlet*)—or any play with a well-known actor—sell out the fastest; the earlier in the week the performance is, the longer it takes to sell out (Thursdays sell out faster than Mondays, for example). Before your trip, check the schedule on their website, and consider buying tickets if something strikes your fancy. But demand is difficult to predict, and some tickets do go unsold. On a past visit, on a sunny Friday in June, the riverbank was crawling with tourists. I stepped into the RSC on a lark to see if they had any tickets. An hour later, I was watching King Lear lose his marbles.

Even if there aren't any seats available, you may be able to buy a returned ticket on the same day of an otherwise sold-out show. Also, the few standing-room tickets in the main theater are sold only on the day of the show. While you can check at the box office anytime during the day, it's best to go either when it opens at 10:00 (daily) or between 17:30 and 18:00 (Mon-Sat). Be prepared to wait.

Visiting the Theaters

▲▲The Royal Shakespeare Theatre

The RSC's main venue reopened in 2011 after it was updated head to toe, with both a respect for tradition and a sensitivity to the needs of contemporary theatergoers. You need to take a guided tour (explained later) to see the backstage areas, but you're welcome to wander the theater's public areas anytime the building is open. Interesting tidbits of theater history and easy-to-miss special exhibits make this one of Stratford's most fascinating sights. If you're seeing a play here, come early to poke around the building. Even if you're not, step inside and explore.

Cost and Hours: Free entry, Mon-Sat 10:00-23:00, Sun 10:00-17:00.

Guided Tours: Well-informed RSC volunteers lead entertaining, one-hour building tours. Some cover the main theater while others take you into behind-the-scenes spaces, such as the space-age control room (try for an £8.50 behind-the-scenes tour, but if those aren't running, consider a £6.50 front-of-the-house tour—which skips the backstage areas; tour schedule varies by day, depending on performances, but there's often one at 9:15—call, check online, or go to box office to confirm schedule; best to book ahead, tel. 01789/403-493, www.rsc.org.uk).

Background: The flagship theater of the RSC has an interesting past. The original, Victorian-style theater was built in 1879 to honor the Bard, but it burned down in 1926. The big Art Deco-style building you see today was erected in 1932 and outfitted with a stodgy Edwardian "picture frame"-style stage, even though a more dynamic "thrust"-style stage—better for engaging the audience—was the actors' choice. (It would also have been closer in design to Shakespeare's original Globe stage, which jutted into the crowd.)

The latest renovation addressed this ill-conceived design, adding an updated, thrust-style stage. They've left the shell of the 1930s theater, but given it an unconventional deconstructed-industrial style, with the seats stacked at an extreme vertical pitch. Though smaller, the redesigned theater can seat about the same size audience as before (1,048 seats), and now there's not a bad seat in the house—no matter what, you're no more than 50 feet from the stage (the cheapest "gallery" seats look down right onto Othello's bald spot). Productions are staged to play to all of the seats throughout the show. Those sitting up high appreciate different details from those at stage level, and vice versa.

Visiting the Theater: From the main lobby and box office/gift shop area, there's plenty to see. First head left. In the circular **atrium** between the brick wall of the modern theater and fragments of the previous theater, notice the ratty old floorboards. These were pried up from the 1932 stage and laid down here—so as you wait for your play, you're treading on theater history. Upstairs on level 2, find the **Paccar Room,** with generally excellent temporary exhibits assembled from the RSC's substantial collection of historic costumes, props, manuscripts, and other theater memorabilia. Continue upstairs to level 3 to the Rooftop Restaurant (described later). High on the partition that runs through the restaurant, facing the brick theater wall, notice the four **chairs** affixed to the wall. These are original seats from the earlier theater, situated where the back row used to be (90 feet from the stage)—illustrating how much more audience-friendly the new design is.

Back downstairs, pass through the box office/gift shop area to find the **Swan Gallery**—an old, Gothic-style Victorian space that survives from the original 1879 Memorial Theatre and hosts rotating exhibitions.

Back outside, across the street from the theater, notice the building with the steep gable and huge door (marked *CFE 1887*). This was built as a **workshop** for building sets, which could be moved in large pieces to the main theater. To this day, all of the sets, costumes, and props are made here in Stratford. The row of **cottages** to the right is housing for actors. The RSC's reputation exerts enough pull to attract serious actors from all over the UK and beyond, who live here for the entire season. The RSC uses a repertory company approach, where the same actors appear in multiple shows concurrently. Today's Lady Macbeth may be tomorrow's Rosalind.

Tower View: For a God's-eye view of all of Shakespeare's houses, ride the elevator to the top of the RSC's **tower** (£2.50, buy ticket at box office, closes 30 minutes before the theater). Aside from a few sparse exhibits, the main attraction here is the 360-degree view over the theater building, the Avon, and the lanes of Stratford.

The Food's the Thing: The main theater has a casual café with a terrace overlooking the river (£3-5 sandwiches, daily 10:00-21:00), as well as the fancier Rooftop Restaurant, which counts the Queen as a patron (£5-15 lunch menu; dinner-£20 two-course meal, £24 three-course meal; Mon-Sat 11:30 until late, Sun 12:00-18:00, dinner reservations smart, tel. 01789/403-449, www.rsc-rooftop-restaurant.co.uk).

The Swan Theatre

Adjacent to the RSC Theatre is the smaller (about 400 seats), Elizabethan-style Swan Theatre, named not for the birds that fill the park out front, but for the Bard's nickname—the "sweet swan of Avon." This galleried playhouse opened in 1986, thanks to an extremely generous donation from an American theater lover. It has a vertical layout and a thrust stage similar to the RSC Theatre, but its wood trim and railings give it a cozier, more traditional feel. The Swan is used for lesser-known Shakespeare plays and alternative works. Occasionally, the lowest level of seats is removed to accommodate "groundling" (standing-only) tickets, much like at the Globe Theatre in London.

The Other Place (TOP)

A two-minute walk down Southern Lane from the original Royal Shakespeare Theatre, the former Courtyard Theatre (affectionately called the "rusty shed" by locals) was built as a replacement venue while the RST was being renovated. It was used as a prototype for the main theater—a testing ground for the lights, seats, and structure of its big brother. Now it's being converted into an alternative, studio theater-type venue called The Other Place (TOP), which will showcase new writing and experimental works. Part of the building is also used for rehearsal space and a costume shop. The theater should be open by the time of your visit, with plays, tours, and yet another opportunity to appreciate the legacy of Stratford's most famous native son.

Other Stratford Sights

Avon Riverfront

The River Avon is a playground of swans and canal boats. The swans have been the mascots of Stratford since 1623, when, seven years after the Bard's death, Ben Jonson's poem in the First Folio dubbed him "the sweet swan of Avon." Join in the bird-scene fun and buy **swan food** to feed swans and ducks (sold at the TI for £1, and possibly by other vendors—ask around). Don't feed the Canada geese, which locals disdain (they say the geese are vicious and have been messing up the eco-balance since they were imported by a king in 1665).

For a nice **riverfront walk,** consider crossing over the Tramway Footbridge and following the trail to the right (west) along the south bank of the Avon. From here, you'll get a great view of the Royal Shakespeare Theater across the river. Continuing down the path, you'll pass the local lawn bowling club (guest players welcome, £3, Tue and Thu 14:00-16:00) and Lucy's Mill Weir, an area popular with fishers and kayakers, where you can turn around. On the way back, cross the river by chain ferry (described next) and return to the town center via the north bank for a full loop.

In the water you'll see colorful **canal boats.** These boats saw their workhorse days during the short window of time between the start of the Industrial Revolution and the establishment of the railways. Today, they're mostly pleasure boats. The boats are long and narrow, so two can pass in the slim canals. There are 2,000 miles of canals in England's Midlands, built to connect centers of industry with seaports and provide vital transportation during the early days of the Industrial Revolution. Stratford was as far inland as you could sail on natural rivers from Bristol; it was the terminus of the man-made Birmingham Canal, built in 1816. Even today, you can motor your canal boat all the way to London from here. Along the embankment, look for the signs indicating how many hours it'll take—and how many locks you'll traverse—to go by boat to various English cities.

For a little bit of mellow river action, rent a **rowboat** (£5/hour per person) or, for more of a challenge, pole yourself around on a Cambridge-style **punt** (canal is poleable—only 4 or 5 feet deep; same price as the rowboat and more memorable/embarrassing if you do the punting—don't pay £10/30 minutes per person for a waterman to do the punting for you). You can rent these boats at the Swan's Nest Boathouse across the Tramway Footbridge; another rental station, along the river, next to the theater, has higher prices but is more conveniently located.

You can also try a sleepy 40-minute **river cruise** (£5.50, includes commentary, Avon Boating, board boat in Bancroft Gardens near the RSC theater, tel. 01789/267-073, www.avon-boating.co.uk), or jump on the oldest surviving **chain ferry** (c. 1937) in Britain (£0.50), which shuttles people across the river just beyond the theater.

The old **Cox's Yard,** a riverside timber yard until the 1990s, is a rare physical remnant of the days when Stratford was an industrial port. Today, Cox's has been taken over by a pricey sprawling restaurant complex, with a steakhouse, a burger stand, a milkshake shop, lots of outdoor seating, and occasional live music. Upstairs is the Attic Theatre, which puts on fringe theater acts (www.treadtheboardstheatre.co.uk).

In the riverfront park, roughly between Cox's Yard and the TI, the **Gower Memorial** honors the Bard and his creations. Named for Lord Ronald Gower, the man who paid for and sculpted the memorial, this 1888 work shows Shakespeare up top ringed by four of his most indelible creations, each representing a human pursuit: Hamlet (philosophy), Lady Macbeth (tragedy), Falstaff (comedy), and Prince Hal (history). Originally located next to the theater, it was moved here after the 1932 fire.

▲MAD Museum

A refreshing change of pace in Bard-bonkers Stratford, this museum's name stands for "Mechanical Art and Design." It celebrates machines as art, showcasing a changing collection of skillfully constructed robots, gizmos, and Rube-Goldberg machines that spring to entertaining life with the push of a button. Engaging for kids, riveting for engineers, and enjoyable to anybody, it's pricey but conveniently located near Shakespeare's Birthplace.

Cost and Hours: £6.80, daily 10:30-17:30, off-season until

17:00, last entry 45 minutes before closing, 45 Hanley Street, tel. 01789/269-356, www.themadmuseum.co.uk.

Tudor World at the Falstaff Experience

This attraction is tacky, gimmicky, and more about entertainment than education. (And, while it's named for a Shakespeare character, the exhibit isn't about the Bard.) Filling Shrieve's House Barn with mostly kid-oriented exhibits (mannequins and descriptions, but few real artifacts), it sweeps through Tudor history from the plague to Henry VIII's privy chamber to a replica 16th-century tavern. If you're into ghost-spotting, their nightly ghost tours may be your best shot.

Cost and Hours: Museum—£5.50, daily 10:30-17:30; ghost tours—£7.50, daily at 18:00, additional tours may be available Fri-Sat; Sheep Street, tel. 01789/298-070, www.tudorworld.com.

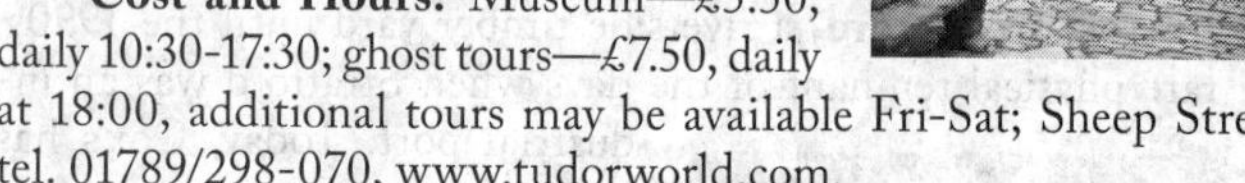

Sleeping in Stratford

If you want to spend the night after you catch a show, options abound. Ye olde timbered hotels are scattered through the city center. Most B&Bs are a short walk away on the fringes of town, right on the busy ring roads that route traffic away from the center. (The recommended places below generally have double-paned windows for rooms in the front, but still get some traffic noise.)

In general, the weekend on or near Shakespeare's birthday (April 23) is particularly tight, but Fridays and Saturdays are busy throughout the season. This town is so reliant upon the theater for its business that some B&Bs have secondary insurance covering their loss if the Royal Shakespeare Company ever stops performing in Stratford.

On Grove Road

These accommodations are at the edge of town on busy Grove Road, across from a grassy square, and come with free parking when booked in advance. From here, it's about a 10-minute walk either to the town center or to the train station (opposite directions).

Sleep Code

Abbreviations **(£1=about $1.60, country code: 44)**
S=Single, **D**=Double/Twin, **T**=Triple, **Q**=Quad, **b**=bathroom
Price Rankings
$$$ Higher Priced—Most rooms £90 or more
$$ Moderately Priced—Most rooms £60-90
$ Lower Priced—Most rooms £60 or less
Unless otherwise noted, credit cards are accepted, breakfast is included, and free Wi-Fi and/or a guest computer is generally available. Prices change; verify current rates online or by email. For the best prices, always book directly with the hotel.

$$$ Adelphi Guest House is run by Shakespeare buffs Sue and Simon, who pride themselves on providing a warm welcome, homemade gingerbread, and original art in every room (S-£45-55, Db-£85-100, Tb-£130, Qb-£160, 2 percent surcharge on credit cards, 10 percent discount off these prices if you stay at least 2 nights—mention this book when you reserve, 39 Grove Road, tel. 01789/204-469, www.adelphi-guesthouse.com, info@adelphi-guesthouse.com).

$$ Ambleside Guest House is run with quiet efficiency and attentiveness by owners Peter and Ruth. Each of the seven rooms has been completely renovated, including the small but tidy bathrooms. The place has a homey, airy feel, with no B&B clutter (S-£35-40, Db-£60-80, Tb-£85-115, Qb-£100-140, ground-floor rooms, 41 Grove Road, tel. 01789/297-239, www.amblesideguesthouse.com, peter@amblesideguesthouse.com—include your phone number in your request, since they like to call you back to confirm with a personal touch).

$$ Woodstock Guest House is a friendly, frilly, family-run, and flowery place with five comfortable rooms (Sb-£35-48, Db-£60-85, Tb-£90-120, can accommodate 4 people—ask, get Rick Steves discount if you stay 2 or more nights—mention this book when you reserve, 5 percent surcharge on credit cards, ground-floor room, 30 Grove Road, tel. 01789/299-881, www.woodstock-house.co.uk, jackie@woodstock-house.co.uk, owners Denis and bubbly Jackie).

$ Salamander Guest House, run by gregarious Frenchman Pascal and his wife, Anna, rents eight simple rooms that are a bit cheaper than their neighbors (S-£39-42, Db-£50-65, Tb-£70-93, Qb-£80-100, suite-£95-115, 40 Grove Road, tel. 01789/205-728, www.salamanderguesthouse.co.uk, p.delin@btinternet.com).

Elsewhere in Stratford

$$$ Mercure Shakespeare Hotel, centrally located in a black-

and-white building just up the street from New Place & Nash's House, has 78 business-class rooms, each one named for a Shakespearean play or character. Some of the rooms are old-style Elizabethan higgledy-piggledy (with modern finishes), while others are contemporary style—note your preference when you reserve (Sb-£80-100, standard Db-£110-140, deluxe Db-£140-170, prices soft depending on demand, breakfast-£10-15, parking-£10/day, Chapel Street, tel. 01789/294-997, www.mercure.com, h6630-re@accor.com).

$$ The Emsley Guest House holds five bright modern rooms named after different counties in England. It's conscientiously run by Melanie and Ray Coulson, who give it a homey and inviting atmosphere (Db-£70-90, Qb or Quint/b-£105-130, 5-person family room with extra bathroom, no kids under 5, free off-street parking, 5 minutes from station at 4 Arden Street, tel. 01789/299-557, www.theemsley.co.uk, mel@theemsley.co.uk).

$ ***Hostel:*** **Hemmingford House,** with 134 beds in 2- to 6-bed rooms (half of them en suite), is a 10-minute bus ride from town (bunk in dorm room-£17-28, breakfast-£5; take bus #15, #18, or #18A two miles to Alveston; tel. 01789/297-093 or 0845-371-9661, www.yha.org.uk/hostel/stratford-upon-avon, stratford@yha.org.uk).

Eating in Stratford

RESTAURANTS

Stratford's numerous restaurants vie for your pre-theater business, with special hours and meal deals. (Most offer light two- and three-course menus before 19:00.) You'll find many hardworking places on Sheep Street and Waterside. Unfortunately, post-theater dinners are more challenging, as most places close early.

Le Bistro Pierre, across the river near the boating station, is a French eatery that's been impressing Stratford residents. They have indoor or outdoor seating and slow service (£11 two-course lunches; £15 two-course meals before 18:45, otherwise £13-17 main courses; Mon-Fri 12:00-15:00 & 17:00-22:30, Sat 12:00-16:00 & 17:00-23:00, Sun 12:30-16:30 & 18:00-22:00, Swan's Nest, Bridgefoot, tel. 01789/264-804). The pub next door, **Bear Free House,** is owned by the same people and shares the same kitchen, but offers a different menu.

Edward Moon is an upscale English brasserie serving signature dishes like steak-and-ale pies and roasted lamb shank in a setting reminiscent of *Casablanca* (£6-7 starters, £12-18 main courses, Mon-Thu 12:00-14:30 & 17:00-21:30, Fri 12:00-15:00 & 17:00-20:00, Sun 12:00-15:00 & 17:00-21:00, closed Sat, 9 Chapel Street, tel. 01789/267-069, www.moonsrestaurants.com).

Sheep Street Eateries: The next three places, part of the same chain, line up along Sheep Street, offering trendy ambience and modern English cuisine at relatively high prices (all three have pre-theater menus before 19:00—£14 two-course meal, £18 for three courses): **Lambs** is intimate and serves meat, fish, and veggie dishes with panache. The upstairs feels dressy, under low, half-timbered beams (£13-20 main courses, Mon-Fri 17:00-21:00, Sat 16:30-21:30, Sun 18:00-21:00, lunch served Tue-Sun, 12 Sheep Street, tel. 01789/292-554). **The Opposition,** next door, has a less formal "bistro" ambience (£9-11 light meals, £14-20 main courses; Mon-Sat 12:00-14:00 & 17:00-21:00, Fri-Sat until 22:30, closed Sun, tel. 01789/269-980; book in advance if you want to have a post-theater dinner here on Fri or Sat). **The Vintner,** just up the street, has the best reputation and feels even trendier than its siblings, but still with old style. They're known for their £12 burgers (£9-11 light meals, £12-18 main courses, daily 9:30-22:00, until 21:30 Sun, 4 Sheep Street, tel. 01789/297-259).

Indian: **Avon Spice** has a good reputation and good prices (£7-10 main courses, daily 17:00-23:30, until later Fri-Sat, 7 Greenhill Street, tel. 01789/267-067).

PUBS

The Old Thatch Tavern is, according to natives, the best place in town for beer, serving up London-based Fuller's brews. The atmosphere is cozy, and the food is a cut above what you'll get in the other pubs; enjoy it either in the bar, in the tight candlelit restaurant, or out on the quiet patio (£10-12 main courses, food served Mon-Sat 12:00-21:00, Sun 12:00-15:00 & 17:00-21:00, on Greenhill Street overlooking the market square, tel. 01789/295-216).

The Windmill Inn serves decent, modestly-priced fare in a 17th-century inn. It combines old and new styles, and—since it's a few steps beyond the heart of the tourist zone—actually attracts some locals as well. Order drinks and food at the bar, settle into a comfy chair or head out to the half-timbered courtyard, and wait for your meal (£8-10 pub grub, food served daily 11:00-22:00, Church Street, tel. 01789/297-687).

The Garrick Inn bills itself as the oldest pub in town, and comes with a cozy, dimly-lit restaurant vibe. Choose between the pub or table-service section; either way, you'll dine on bland, pricey pub grub (£9-16 dishes, food served daily 11:00-22:00, 25 High Street, tel. 01789/292-186).

PICNICS

With its sprawling and inviting riverfront park, Stratford is a particularly pleasant place to picnic. Choose a bench with views of the river or vacation houseboats, and munch your meal while tossing a few scraps into the river to attract swans. It's a fine way to spend a midsummer night's eve. For groceries or prepared foods, find **Marks & Spencer** on Bridge Street (Mon-Sat 8:00-18:00, Sun 10:30-16:30, small coffee-and-sandwiches café upstairs, tel. 01789/292-430). Across the street, **Sainsbury's Local** stays open later than other supermarkets in town (daily 7:00-22:00).

For fish-and-chips, you have a couple of options: **Barnaby's** is a greasy fast-food joint near the waterfront—but it's convenient if you want to get takeout for the riverside park just across the street (£5-8 fish-and-chips, daily 11:00-19:30, at Sheep Street and Waterside). For better food (but a less convenient location—closer to my recommended B&Bs than to the park), queue up with the locals at **Kingfisher,** then ask for the freshly battered haddock (£6-7 fish-and-chips, Mon-Sat 11:30-13:45 & 17:00-22:00, closed Sun, a long block up at 13 Ely Street, tel. 01789/292-513).

TEAROOM

Henley Street Tea Rooms, across the street from Shakespeare's Birthplace, has indoor seating, outdoor tables right on the main pedestrian mall, and friendly service (£4.50 cream tea, £13 afternoon tea, teas available all day, daily 9:00-17:30, Sept-March until 17:00, 40 Henley Street, tel. 01789/415-572). The same people run Bensons House of Tea & Gift Shop, just down the street (at #33).

Stratford Connections

Remember: When buying tickets or checking schedules, ask for "Stratford-upon-Avon," not just "Stratford." Notice that a single train (running about every 2 hours) connects most of these destinations: Warwick, Leamington Spa (change for Coventry or Oxford), then London.

From Stratford-upon-Avon by Train to: London (3/day direct, more with transfers, 2-2.5 hours, to Marylebone Station), **Moreton-in-Marsh** (almost hourly, 2.5-3 hours, 2-3 transfers, slow and expensive, better by bus). Train info: tel. 0345-748-4950, www.nationalrail.co.uk.

By Bus to: Cotswolds towns (bus #21 or #22, Mon-Sat 8/day, none on Sun, 35 minutes to **Chipping Campden,** 1-1.5 hours to **Moreton-in-Marsh;** some also stop at Broadway, Broad Campden, Blockley, and/or Bourton-on-the-Hill; Johnsons Coaches, tel. 01564/797-070, www.johnsonscoaches.co.uk). Most intercity buses stop on Stratford's Bridge Street (a block up from the TI). For bus info that covers all the region's companies, call Traveline at tel. 0871-200-2233 (www.travelinemidlands.co.uk).

By Car: Driving is easy and distances are short: **Chipping Campden** (12 miles), **Stow-on-the-Wold** (22 miles).

ROUTE TIPS FOR DRIVERS

These tips assume you're heading north from Stratford.

Leaving the Bridgefoot garage in downtown Stratford (see map on page 414), circle to the right around the same block, but stay on "the Wark" (Warwick Road, A-439).

To the Northeast: Heading toward York, Durham, and other destinations northeast of Stratford, take the Wark to the A-46. Just past Coventry, it merges into the M-69 toward Leicester, which intersects with a major north-south route, the M-1.

To the Northwest: When heading toward Ironbridge Gorge, North Wales, Liverpool, or the Lake District, take A-46 toward Warwick, then exit onto the M-40 north toward Birmingham. You want to avoid driving through Birmingham. After Warwick, take the M-42 to the west; the sign will read *The Southwest (M5), Birmingham (S & W), Redditch.* When the M-42 ends at the M-5, follow M-5 north, the sign will read *The Northwest, B'ham, Stourbridge.*

After Birmingham, for Ironbridge Gorge, take the M-54 toward Telford. For specifics on getting to Ironbridge Gorge, see page 449. For other destinations, take the M-6.

IRONBRIDGE GORGE

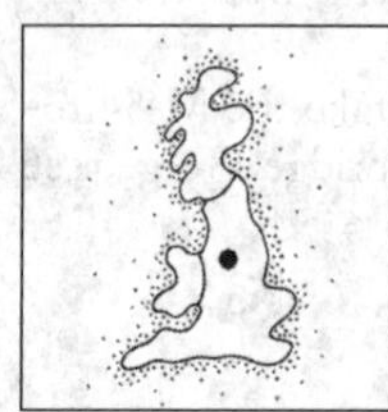

The Industrial Revolution was born in the Severn River Valley. In its glory days, this valley (blessed with abundant deposits of iron ore and coal, and a river for transport) gave the world its first iron wheels, steam-powered locomotive, and cast-iron bridge (begun in 1779). The museums in Ironbridge Gorge, which capture the flavor of the Victorian Age, take you back into the days when Britain was racing into the modern era and pulling the rest of the West with her.

Near the end of the 20th century, the valley went through a second transformation: Photos taken just 30 years ago show an industrial wasteland. Today the Severn River Valley is lush and lined with walks and parkland. Even its bricks, while still smoke-stained, seem warmer and more inviting.

PLANNING YOUR TIME

Without a car, Ironbridge Gorge isn't worth the headache. Drivers can slip it in between the Cotswolds/Stratford and points north (such as the Lake District or North Wales). Speed demons zip in for a midday tour of the Blists Hill Victorian Town, look at the famous Iron Bridge and quaint Industrial Age town that sprawls around it, and head out. For an overnight visit, arrive in the early evening to browse the town, see the bridge, and walk along the river. Spend the morning touring the Blists Hill Victorian Town, have lunch there, and head to your next destination.

With more time—say, a full month in Britain—I'd spend two nights and a leisurely day: 9:30-Iron Bridge and the town; 10:30-Museum of the Gorge; 11:30-Coalbrookdale Museum of

Iron; 14:30-Blists Hill Victorian Town; then dinner at one of my recommended restaurants.

Orientation to Ironbridge Gorge

The town is just a few blocks gathered around the Iron Bridge, which spans the peaceful, tree-lined Severn River. While the smoke-belching bustle is long gone, knowing that this wooded sleepy river valley was the "Silicon Valley" of the 19th century makes wandering its brick streets almost a pilgrimage. The actual museum sites are scattered over three miles. The modern cooling towers (for coal, not nuclear energy) that loom ominously over these red-brick remnants seem strangely appropriate.

TOURIST INFORMATION

The TI is in the Museum of the Gorge, just west of the town center. It has lots of booklets for sale, including pamphlets describing nearby walks (daily 10:00-17:00, tel. 01952/433-424, www.ironbridge.org.uk or www.ironbridgeguide.info). In summer, volunteers sporadically staff an info desk inside the Iron Bridge tollbooth.

GETTING AROUND IRONBRIDGE GORGE

By Bus: Gorge Connect buses link the various museums, running every 30 minutes on weekends and Bank Holidays from Easter through October—and every day in late July and August (£1.65/ride, £2.20 day ticket, £1 with Passport Ticket—described on page 442; runs 9:30-17:00, no buses Nov-Easter; see schedule at www.telford.gov.uk—search site for "Gorge Connect"; tel. 01952/200-005).

If you're waiting for the Gorge Connect bus on the main road by the bridge, or at a stop for one of the less-popular museums, make sure the driver sees you or the bus may not stop. For connections from the Telford train or bus stations to the sights, see the end of this chapter.

Bus **#9,** operated by Arriva, connects the Museum of Iron (stop: Coalbrookdale School Road) and the TI in Ironbridge, but it runs infrequently (roughly hourly).

By Car: Routes to the attractions are well-signed, so driving should be a snap (museum parking described later).

By Taxi: Taxis will pick up at the museums, making this a

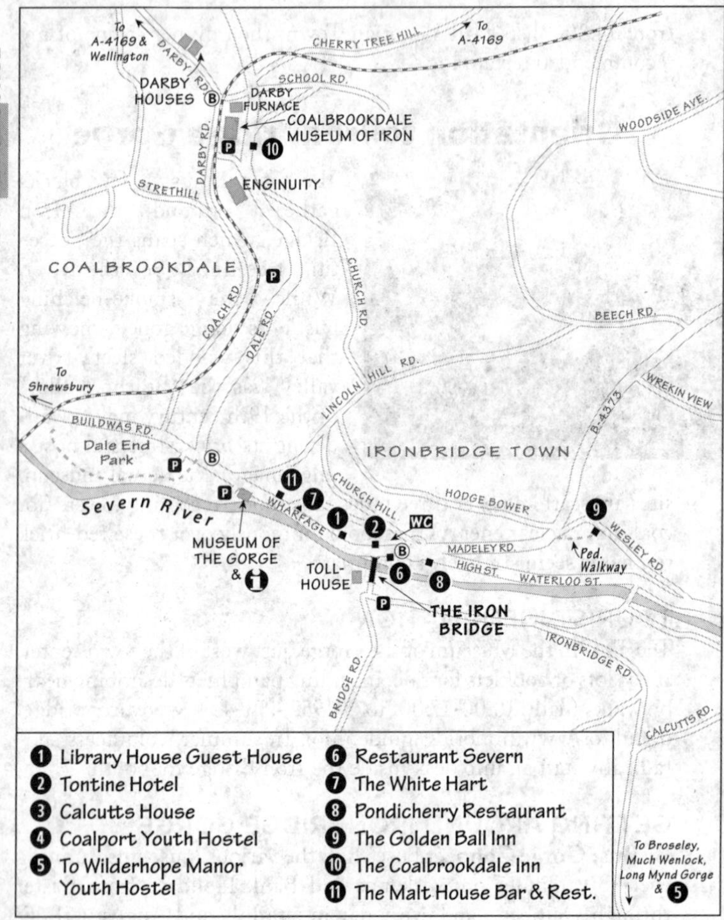

good option if you don't have a car and the bus is not convenient. Call Central Taxis at tel. 01952/501-050.

Sights in Ironbridge Gorge

▲▲Iron Bridge

While England was at war with her American colonies, this first cast-iron bridge was built in 1779 to show off a wonderful new building material. Lacking experience with cast iron, the builders erred on the side of sturdiness and constructed it as if it were made out of wood. Notice that the original construction used traditional timber-jointing techniques rather than rivets. (Any rivets are from later repairs.) The valley's centerpiece is free, open all the time, and thought-provoking...cars still used it into the 1960s. Walk across

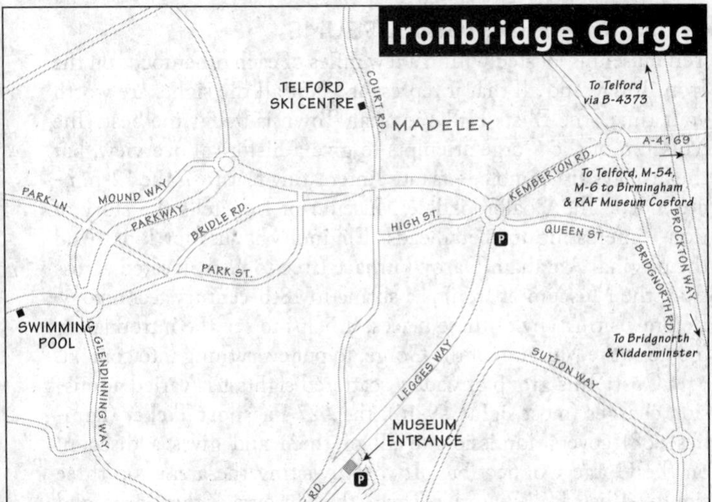

Ironbridge Gorge

TELFORD SKI CENTRE
COURT RD.
MADELEY
To Telford via B-4373
A-4169
To Telford, M-54, M-6 to Birmingham & RAF Museum Cosford
KEMBERTON RD.
PARK LN.
MOUND WAY
PARKWAY
BRIDLE RD.
HIGH ST.
QUEEN ST.
BROCKTON WAY
BRIDGNORTH RD.
PARK ST.
SWIMMING POOL
GLENDINNING WAY
To Bridgnorth & Kidderminster
SUTTON WAY
LEGGES WAY
MUSEUM ENTRANCE
COALPORT RD.
BLISTS HILL VICTORIAN TOWN
GREAT HAY DR.
THE LLOYDS
Old Canal
1/2 Kilometer
1/2 Mile
JACKFIELD TILE MUSEUM
SALTHOUSE RD.
JACKFIELD
COALPORT
COALPORT CHINA MUSEUM
COALPORT HIGH ST.

the bridge to the tollhouse. Inside, read the fee schedule and notice the subtle slam against royalty. (England was not immune to the revolutionary sentiment inhabiting the colonies at this time.) Pedestrians paid half a penny to cross; poor people crossed cheaper by coracle—a crude tub-like wood-and-canvas shuttle ferry. Cross back to the town and enjoy a pleasant walk downstream along the towpath. Where horses once dragged boats laden with Industrial Age cargo, locals now walk their dogs.

IRONBRIDGE GORGE MUSEUMS

Ten museums located within a few miles of each other focus on the Iron Bridge and all that it represents. Not all the sights are worth your time. The Blists Hill Victorian Town is by far the best. The Museum of the Gorge attempts to give a historical overview, but the displays are humble—its most interesting feature is the 12-minute video. The Coalbrookdale Museum of Iron tells the story of iron—interesting to metalheads. Enginuity is just for kids. And the original Abraham Darby Furnace (free to view, located across from the Museum of Iron) is a shrine to 18th-century technology. Before visiting any of these places, it helps to see the introductory movie at the Museum of the Gorge, to put everything into context.

Cost: This group of widely scattered sights has varied admission charges (most sights £9-16); the £27 **Passport Ticket** (families-£68) covers admission to all of them and gives a discount on the Gorge Connect bus. If you're visiting the area's top three sights—Blists Hill Victorian Town, the Museum of the Gorge, and the Coalbrookdale Museum of Iron—you'll save about £1 with the Passport Ticket.

Hours: Unless otherwise noted, the sights share the same opening hours: daily 10:00-17:00.

Parking: To see the most significant sights by car, you'll park three times: once in town (either in the pay-and-display lot just over the bridge or at the Museum of the Gorge—the Iron Bridge and Gorge Museum are connected by an easy, flat walk); once at the Blists Hill parking lot; and once outside the Coalbrookdale Museum of Iron (Enginuity is across the lot, and the Darby Houses are a three-minute uphill hike away). While you'll pay separately to park at the Museum of the Gorge, a single ticket is good for both pay-and-display lots at the Coalbrookdale Museum and Blists Hill.

Information: Tel. 01952/433-424, www.ironbridge.org.uk.

Museum of the Gorge

Orient yourself to the valley here in the Old Severn Warehouse. The 12-minute introductory movie (on a continuous loop) lays the groundwork for what you'll see in the other museums. Check out the exhibit and the model of the gorge in its heyday. There are also panels explaining the geology and ecology of the valley. Farther upstream from the museum parking lot is the fine riverside Dale End Park, with picnic areas and a playground.

Cost: £4.50, 500 yards upstream from the bridge, parking-£2.80 (3-hour maximum).

▲▲Blists Hill Victorian Town

Save most of your time and energy for this wonderful town—an immersive, open-air folk museum. You'll wander through 50 acres of Victorian industry, factories, and a re-created community from the 1890s. Pick up the Blists Hill guidebook for a good step-by-step rundown.

Cost and Hours: £15.40, closes at 16:00 Nov-March.

Eating in Blists Hill: Several places serve lunch: a café near the entrance, the New Inn Pub for beer and pub snacks, a traditional fish-and-chips joint, and the cafeteria near the children's old-time rides.

Visiting Blists Hill: The map you're given when entering is very important—it shows which stops in the big park are staffed with lively docents in Victorian dress. Pop in to say hello to the banker, the lady in the post office, the blacksmith, and the girl in the candy shop. Maybe the boys are singing in the pub. It's fine to take photos. Asking questions and chatting with the villagers is encouraged. What's a shilling? How was the pay? What about health care in the 1800s?

Stop by the pharmacy and check out the squirm-inducing setup of the dentist's chair—it'll make you appreciate the marvel of modern dental care. Check the hands-on activities in the barn across the way. Down the street, kids like watching a costumed candlemaker at work, as he explains the process and tells how candles were used back in the day.

Just as it would've had in Victorian days, the village has a working pub, a greengrocer's shop, a fascinating squatter's cottage, and a snorty, slippery pigsty. Don't miss the explanation of the "winding engine" at the Blists Hill Mine (demos throughout the day).

At the back of the park, you can hop aboard a train and enter a clay mine, complete with a sound and light show illustrating the dangers of working in this type of environment (£2, 10 minutes). Nearby, the Hay Inclined Plane was used to haul loaded tub boats between the river and the upper canal. Today, a passenger-operated lift hauls visitors instead (just press the button to call for it). At the top, you can walk along the canal back to the town.

▲Coalbrookdale Museum of Iron and Abraham Darby's Old Furnace

The Coalbrookdale neighborhood is the birthplace of modern technology—the place where locals like to claim that mass production was invented. The museum and furnace are located on either side of a parking lot.

Cost: Museum—£8.10, £8.60 combo-ticket includes the Darby

Houses; Furnace—free, volunteer tour guides sometimes lead free guided walks to the furnace (ask at museum info desk for times).

Museum: While old-school, this museum does a fine job of explaining the original iron-smelting process and how iron (which makes up 95 percent of all industrial metal) changed our world. But compared to the fun and frolicking Blists Hill village, this museum is sleepy. There's a café inside the museum.

Abraham Darby Furnace: Across from the museum, standing like a shrine to the Industrial Revolution, is Darby's blast furnace, sitting inside a big glass pyramid and surrounded by evocative Industrial Age ruins (info sheets on the furnace available at museum). It was here that, in 1709, Darby first smelted iron, using coke as fuel. To me, "coke" is a drink, and "smelt" is the past tense of smell...but around here, these words recall the event that kicked off the modern Industrial Age.

All the ingredients of the recipe for big industry were here in abundance—iron ore, top-grade coal, and water for power and shipping. Wander around Abraham Darby's furnace. Before this furnace was built, iron ore was laboriously melted by charcoal—they couldn't use coal because sulfur made the iron brittle. Darby experimented with coke instead. With huge waterwheel-powered bellows, Darby burned coke at super-hot temperatures and dumped iron ore into the furnace. Impurities floated to the top, while the pure iron sank to the bottom of a clay tub in the bottom of the furnace. Twice a day, the plugs were knocked off, allowing the "slag" to drain away on the top and the molten iron to drain out on the bottom. The low-grade slag was used locally on walls and paths. The high-grade iron trickled into molds formed in the sand below the furnace. It cooled into pig iron (named because the molds look like piglets suckling their mother). The pig-iron "planks" were broken off by sledgehammers and shipped away. The Severn River became one of Europe's busiest, shipping pig iron to distant foundries, where it was melted again and made into cast iron (for projects such as the Iron Bridge), or to forges, where it was worked like toffee into wrought iron.

Enginuity

Enginuity is a hands-on funfest for kids. Riffing on Ironbridge's engineering roots, this converted 1709 foundry is full of entertaining-to-kids water contraptions, pumps, magnets, and laser games.

Build a dam, try your hand at earthquake-proof construction, navigate a water maze, operate a remote-controlled robot, or power a turbine with your own steam.

Cost: £8.10, across the parking lot from the Coalbrookdale Museum of Iron.

Darby Houses

The Darby family, Quakers who were the area's richest residents by far, lived in these two homes located just above the Coalbrookdale Museum.

The 18th-century Darby mansion, **Rosehill House,** features a collection of fine china, furniture, and trinkets from various family members. It's decorated in the way the family home would have been in 1850. If the gilt-framed mirrors and fancy china seem a little ostentatious for the normally wealth-shunning Quakers, keep in mind that these folks were rich beyond reason, and—as docents will assure you—considering their vast wealth, this was relatively modest. At the end of the tour is a collection of period clothes—you're welcome to dress up as a modest Quaker or a fashionable dandy.

Skip the adjacent **Dale House.** Dating from the 1780s, it's older than Rosehill, but almost completely devoid of interior furniture, and its exhibits are rarely open.

Cost and Hours: £5, £8.60 combo-ticket includes Coalbrookdale Museum of Iron, closed Nov-March for lack of light.

Coalport China Museum, Jackfield Tile Museum, and Broseley Pipeworks

Housed in their original factories, these showcase the region's porcelain, decorated tiles, and clay tobacco pipes. These industries were developed to pick up the slack when the iron industry shifted away from the Severn Valley in the 1850s. Each museum features finely decorated pieces, and the china and tile museums offer low-energy workshops.

Cost and Hours: £5-8.10 each; Broseley Pipeworks open afternoons only in summer (mid-May-mid-Sept 13:00-17:00, closed mid-Sept-mid-May).

NEAR IRONBRIDGE

Skiing and Swimming

There's a small, brush-covered **ski and snowboarding slope** with two Poma lifts at Telford Snowboard and Ski Centre in Madeley, two miles from Ironbridge Gorge; you'll see signs for it as you drive into Ironbridge Gorge (£13.25/hour including gear, less for kids, open practice times vary by day—schedule posted online, tel. 01952/382-688, www.telfordandwrekinleisure.co.uk). A public **swimming pool** is in Madeley (5-minute drive from town on Ironbridge Road, Abraham Darby Sports and Leisure Centre, tel. 01952/382-770).

Royal Air Force (RAF) Museum Cosford

This Red Baron magnet displays more than 80 aircraft, from warplanes to rockets. Get the background on ejection seats and a primer on the principles of propulsion.

Cost and Hours: Free, daily March-Oct 10:00-18:00, Nov-Feb 10:00-17:00, last entry one hour before closing, parking-£2.50/3 hours, Shifnal, Shropshire, on the A-41 near junction with the M-54, tel. 01902/376-200, www.rafmuseum.org.uk/cosford.

More Sights

If you're looking for reasons to linger in Ironbridge Gorge, these sights are all within a short drive: the medieval town of Shrewsbury, the abbey village of Much Wenlock, the scenic Long Mynd gorge at Church Stretton, the castle at Ludlow, and the steam railway at the river town of Bridgnorth. Shoppers like Chester (en route to points north).

Sleeping in Ironbridge Gorge

$$$ Library House Guesthouse is *Town and Country*-elegant. Located in the town center, a half-block downhill from the bridge, it's a classy, friendly gem that actually used to be the village library. Each of its four rooms is a delight, with extra touches such as bathrobes and coffeemakers. The Chaucer Room, which includes a small garden, is the smallest and least expensive. Tim and Sarah offer a complimentary beverage upon arrival; they'll make you feel right at home (small Db-£95, larger Db-£110, twin Db-£90, take £10 off these prices for Sb, DVD library, free parking just up the road, 11 Severn Bank, Ironbridge Gorge, tel. 01952/432-299, www.libraryhouse.com, info@libraryhouse.com).

$$ Tontine Hotel is the town's big, 12-room, musty, Georgian-era hotel—royalty stayed here when visiting the bridge. Check out the historic photos in the bar (S-£30, Sb-£49, D-£50, Db-£69, Qb-£89, ask about discount with this book if you reserve direct, restaurant, The Square, tel. 01952/432-127, www.thetontinehotel.com, tontinehotel@tiscali.co.uk).

Sleep Code

Abbreviations **(£1=about $1.60, country code: 44)**
S=Single, **D**=Double/Twin, **T**=Triple, **Q**=Quad, **b**=bathroom
Price Rankings
$$$ Higher Priced—Most rooms £70 or more
$$ Moderately Priced—Most rooms £50-70
$ Lower Priced—Most rooms £50 or less
Unless otherwise noted, credit cards are accepted, breakfast is included, and free Wi-Fi and/or a guest computer is generally available. Prices change; verify current rates online or by email. For the best prices, always book directly with the hotel.

OUTSIDE OF TOWN

$$$ Calcutts House rents seven rooms in their 18th-century ironmaster's home and adjacent coach house. Rooms in the main house are elegant, while the coach-house rooms are bright, modern, and less expensive. Their inviting garden is a plus. Ask the owners, James and Sarah Pittam, how the rooms were named (Db-£63-100, price depends on room size, free parking, Calcutts Road, tel. 01952/882-631, www.calcuttshouse.co.uk, info@calcuttshouse.co.uk). From Calcutts House, it's a delightful 15-minute stroll down a former train track into town.

$ Coalport Youth Hostel, plush for a hostel, fills an old factory at the China Museum in Coalport (£15-24 bunks in mostly 4-bed dorms, bunk-bed Db-£70, £3 less for members, includes sheets, reception open 7:30-23:00, no lockout, kitchen, restaurant, self-service laundry, High Street, tel. 01952/588-755 or 0845-371-9325, www.yha.org.uk, coalport@yha.org.uk). Don't confuse this hostel with another area hostel, Coalbrookdale, which is only available for groups.

$ Wilderhope Manor Youth Hostel, a beautifully remote Elizabethan manor house from 1586, is one of Europe's best hostels—and recently refurbished (it even has a bridal suite). On Wednesday and Sunday afternoons, tourists actually pay to see what hostelers get to sleep in (£18.50-25 bunks, £3 less for members, single-sex dorms, family rooms available, reservations recommended, reception closed 10:00-15:00, restaurant open 18:00-20:30, laundry, kitchen, tel. 01694/771-363 or 0845-371-9149, www.yha.org.uk, wilderhope@yha.org.uk). It's in Longville-in-the-Dale, six miles from Much Wenlock, down the B-4371 toward Church Stretton.

Eating in Ironbridge Gorge

Restaurant Severn is the local favorite for a place with style that serves contemporary dishes. Choose from a £26-28 two-course fixed-price meal or a £28-30 three-course offering (evenings Wed-Sat, lunch only on Sun, closed Mon-Tue, across from the Iron Bridge in the town center, reservations smart—especially on weekends, 33 High Street, tel. 01952/432-233, www.restaurantseven.co.uk).

The White Hart has a split personality—the woody pub section is Brit-rustic, while the two-level restaurant is white-tablecloth chic. Prices make this a splurge, but the food is creative and tasty—try the beef with "ox cheek marmalade" (£7 starters, £14-22 main dishes, £27 three-course fixed-price meal, daily 11:00-22:00, food served until 21:00, reservations smart on weekends, 10 Wharfage, tel. 01952/432-901, www.whitehartironbridge.com).

Pondicherry, in a renovated former police station, serves delicious Indian curries and a few British dishes to keep the less adventurous happy. The mixed vegetarian sampler is popular even with meat eaters. The basement holding cells are now little plush lounges—a great option if you'd like your predinner drink "in prison" (£10-16 plates, daily 17:00-23:00 except Sun until 20:30, starts hopping after 19:00, 57 Waterloo Street, tel. 01952/433-055).

The Golden Ball Inn, a brewery back in the 18th century, is a popular pub known for its quality food and great atmosphere. You can dine with the friendly local crowd in the "bar," eat in back with the brewing gear in the more quiet—and formal—dining room, or munch out on the lush garden patio. This place is serious about their beer, listing featured ales daily (£10-15 meals, food served Mon-Sat 12:00-21:00, Sun 12:00-19:00, reservations smart on weekends, 10-minute hike up Madeley Road from the town roundabout, look for sign to pedestrian shortcut, 1 Newbridge Road, tel. 01952/432-179, www.goldenballironbridge.co.uk).

The Coalbrookdale Inn is filled with locals enjoying excellent ales and simple pub grub—nothing fancy. This former "best pub in Britain" has a tradition of offering free samples from a lineup of featured beers. Ask which real ales are available (Sun-Thu 16:00-23:00, Fri-Sat 12:00-23:00, lively ladies' loo, across street from Coalbrookdale Museum of Iron, 1 mile from Ironbridge, 12 Wellington Road, tel. 01952/432-166).

The Malt House, located in an 18th-century beer house, is a very popular scene with the local twentysomething gang (£9-20 main courses, bar menu at their Rock Bar, food served daily 11:30-22:00, near Museum of the Gorge, 5-minute walk from center, The Wharfage, tel. 01952/433-712). For nighttime action, The Malt

House is *the* vibrant spot in town, with live rock music and a fun crowd (generally Fri-Sat).

Ironbridge Gorge Connections

Ironbridge Gorge is five miles southwest of Telford, which has the nearest train station.

Getting Between Telford and Ironbridge Gorge: To go by **bus** from Telford's train station to the center of Ironbridge Gorge, you'll first have to zip over to the Telford bus station—any northbound bus that stops at the train station will take you there (every 5-10 minutes; some buses drive by without stopping—don't be alarmed—just wait for one that stops). From the Telford bus station, take bus #9, #18, or #96 into Ironbridge (roughly hourly, takes 30 minutes, none on Sun). The Telford bus station is attached to a large modern mall, making it an easy place to wait—ask at the info office when the next bus is leaving and from which door. The bus drops you off in Ironbridge at the TI or the bridge—tell the driver which stop you want (pay per leg or buy "Day Saver" pass—only cost-effective if you take the bus at least three times). Buses are run by Arriva (www.arrivabus.co.uk), but you can also call Traveline for departure times and other information (tel. 0871-200-2233, www.traveline.org.uk).

If the Gorge Connect bus is running (generally April-Oct on weekends and Bank Holidays, plus some weeks in summer; see page 439) you can take bus #4 (2-5/hour) direct from the Telford train station to High Street in the town of Madeley. This is where the Gorge Connect bus originates and ends. Hop on it to ride to one of the museums, the TI, or the bridge.

A **taxi** from Telford train station to Ironbridge costs about £10.

By Train from Telford to: Birmingham (2/hour, 30-50 minutes), **Stratford-upon-Avon** (roughly hourly, 2.5 hours, 1-2 changes), **Moreton-in-Marsh** (hourly, 2.5-3 hours, 2 transfers), **Conwy** in North Wales (10/day, 2.5-3 hours, some change in Chester or Shrewsbury), **Keswick/Lake District** (hourly, 4 hours total; 3 hours to Penrith with 1-2 changes, then catch a bus to Keswick—see page 517), **Edinburgh** (hourly, 4-5 hours, 1-2 changes). **Train info:** Tel. 0345-748-4950, www.nationalrail.co.uk.

ROUTE TIPS FOR DRIVERS

From the South to Ironbridge Gorge: From the Cotswolds and Stratford, you want to avoid going through Birmingham; see page 437 for the best route. After Birmingham, follow signs to *Telford* via the M-54. Leave the M-54 at the Telford/Ironbridge exit (Junction 4). Follow the brown *Ironbridge* signs through several roundabouts to Ironbridge Gorge. (Note: On maps, Ironbridge Gorge is often referred to as "Iron Bridge" or "Iron-Bridge.")

From Ironbridge Gorge to North Wales: The drive is fairly easy, with clear signs and good roads all the way. From Ironbridge Gorge, follow signs to the M-54. Get on the M-54 in the direction of Telford, and then Shrewsbury, as the M-54 becomes the A-5; then follow signs to North Wales. In Wales, the A-483 (direction Wrexham, then Chester) takes you to the A-55, which leads to Conwy.

LIVERPOOL

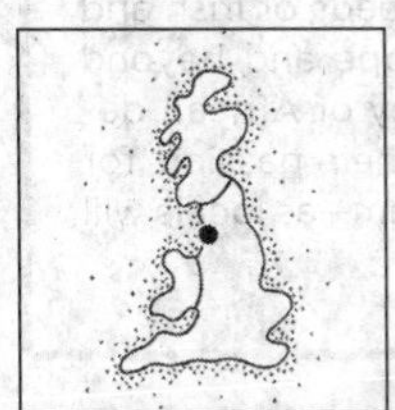

Wedged between serene North Wales and the even-more-serene Lake District, Liverpool provides an opportunity to sample the "real" England. It's the best look at urban England outside London.

Beatles fans flock to Liverpool to learn about the Fab Four's early days, but the city has much more to offer—most notably, a wealth of free and good museums, a pair of striking cathedrals, a dramatic skyline mingling old red-brick maritime buildings and glassy new skyscrapers, and—most of all—the charm of the Liverpudlians.

Sitting at the mouth of the River Mersey in the metropolitan county of Merseyside, Liverpool has long been a major shipping center. Its port played a key role in several centuries of world history—as a point in the "triangular trade" of African slaves, a gateway for millions of New World-bound European emigrants, and a staging ground for the British Navy's Battle of the Atlantic against the Nazi's U-boat fleet. But Liverpool was devastated physically by WWII bombs, then economically by the advent of container shipping in the 1960s. Liverpudlians looked on helplessly as postwar recovery resources were steered elsewhere, the city's substantial wartime contributions seemingly ignored.

Despite the pride and attention garnered in the 1960s by a certain quartet of favorite sons, Liverpool continued to decline through the 1970s and '80s. The Toxteth Riots of 1981, sparked by the city's dizzyingly high unemployment, brought worldwide attention to Liverpool's troubles.

But finally, things started looking up. The city's status as the 2008 European Capital of Culture spurred major gentrification, EU funding, and a cultural renaissance. And, with some 50,000

On the Scouse

Nicknamed "Scousers" (after a traditional local stew, originally brought here by Norwegian immigrants), the people of Liverpool have a reputation for being relaxed, easygoing, and welcoming to visitors. The Scouse dialect comes with a distinctive lilt and quick wit (the latter likely a means of coping with long-term hardship)—think of the Beatles' familiar accents, and all their famously sarcastic off-the-cuff remarks, and you get the picture. Many Liverpudlians attribute these qualities to the Celtic influence here: Liverpool is a melting pot of not only English culture, but also loads of Irish and Welsh, as well as arrivals from all over Europe and beyond (Liverpool's diverse population includes many of African descent). Liverpudlians are also famous for their passion for football (i.e., soccer), and the Liverpool FC team—as locals will be quick to tell you—is one of England's best.

students attending three universities in town, Liverpool is also a youthful city, with a pub or nightclub on every corner. Anyone who still thinks of Liverpool as a depressed industrial center is behind the times.

PLANNING YOUR TIME

Liverpool deserves at least a few hours, but those willing to give it a full day or more won't be disappointed.

For the quickest visit, focus your time at the Albert Dock, home to The Beatles Story, Merseyside Maritime Museum, Tate Gallery (for contemporary art lovers), and Museum of Liverpool. If time allows, consider a Beatles bus tour (departs from the Albert Dock).

A full day buys you time either to delve into the rest of the city (the rejuvenated urban core, the cathedrals, and the Walker Art Gallery near the train station), to binge on more Beatles sights (the boyhood homes of John and Paul), or a bit of both.

If you're here just for the Beatles, you can easily fill a day with Fab Four sights: Do the tour of John's and Paul's homes in the morning, then return to the Albert Dock to visit The Beatles Story. Take an afternoon bus tour from the Albert Dock to the other Beatles sights in town, winding up at the Cavern Quarter to enjoy a Beatles cover band in the reconstructed Cavern Club. (Beatles bus tours zip past the John and Paul houses from the outside, but visiting the interiors takes more time and should be reserved well in advance.)

International Beatles Week, celebrated in late August, is a very busy time in Liverpool, with lots of live musical performances.

Orientation to Liverpool

With nearly half a million people, Liverpool is Britain's fifth-biggest city. But for visitors, most points of interest are concentrated in the generally pedestrian-friendly downtown area. You can walk from one end of this zone to the other in about 25 minutes. Since interesting sights and colorful neighborhoods are scattered throughout this area, it's enjoyable to connect your sightseeing on foot. (Beatles sights, however, are spread far and wide—it's much easier to connect them with a tour.)

TOURIST INFORMATION

Liverpool's TI is at the **Albert Dock** (daily April-Oct 10:00-17:30, Nov-March 10:00-17:00, just inland from The Beatles Story, tel. 0151/707-0729, www.visitliverpool.com). Pick up the free, good city map and the comprehensive *Liverpool Visitor Guide,* crammed with updated lists of museums, hotels, restaurants, shops, and more.

ARRIVAL IN LIVERPOOL

By Train: Most trains use the main **Lime Street train station.** The station has eateries, shops, and baggage storage (per item: £6/3 hours, £8/24 hours, Mon-Thu 7:00-21:00, Fri-Sun 7:00-23:00, tel. 0151/909-3697, www.left-baggage.co.uk; most bus tours and private minivan/car tours are able to accommodate people with luggage). Note that regional trains also arrive at the much smaller, confusingly named **Central Station,** located just a few blocks south.

Getting to the Albert Dock: From Lime Street Station to the

Liverpool
Hotels
1 Hope Street Hotel
2 Hard Day's Night Hotel
3 Aachen Guest Accommodations
4 Best Western Feathers Hotel
5 Sir Thomas Hotel
6 Premier Inns (3)
7 Holiday Inn Express
8 International Inn Hostel
Restaurants & Pubs
9 The Quarter Restaurant
10 HOST
11 Jenever
12 60 Hope Street
13 Yuet Ben
14 Tokyou
15 The Philharmonic Dining Rooms Pub
16 The Fly in the Loaf Pub
17 Alma de Cuba
18 Liverpool One Bridewell
19 Bold Street Eateries
20 Duke Street Eateries
21 Delifonseca
22 Liverpool One Eateries
23 The Ship and Mitre Pub
24 Thomas Rigby's Pub
25 Ye Hole in Ye Wall Pub
26 The Globe Pub
To Southport
LEEDS ST.
VAUXHALL RD.
MIDGHALL ST.
MARYBONE
HIGHFIELD ST.
COCKSPUR ST.
EAST ST.
PALL MALL
HATTON GARDEN
TITHEBARN ST.
CHEAPSIDE
CUNLIFFE ST.
VERNON ST.
EDMUND
BIXTETH ST.
OLD HALL ST.
GEORGE
FAZAKERLEY ST.
MOORFIELDS
Moorfields
CUMBERLAND
NEW QUAY
PRINCES PARADE
PRINCES DOCK
EXCHANGE
HACKINS HEY
CHAPEL ST.
RUMFORD
JOHN ST.
PRINCES ST.
TEMPLE
VICTORIA ST.
STANLEY
DALE ST.
CASTLE ST.
COOK ST.
MATHEW ST.
HARRINGTON ST.
ROYAL LIVER BLDG.
WATER ST.
BRUNSWICK ST.
CANADA BLVD
MERSEY FERRIES DOCK
PIER HEAD FERRY TERMINAL & BEATLES STORY ANNEX
CUNARD BLDG.
James Street
JAMES ST.
LORD ST.
LIVERPOOL ONE MALL
PORT BLDG.
RED CROSS
STRAND ST.
JOHN ST.
PARADISE ST.
Chavasse Park
200 Meters
200 Yards
QUEENSWAY
MUSEUM OF LIVERPOOL
MARITIME & SLAVERY MUSEUMS
CANNING
CANNING
PARK LN.
HARTLEY QUAY
SALTHOUSE QUAY
ALBERT DOCK
LIVER ST.
TATE GALLERY LIVERPOOL
THE BEATLES STORY
WAPPING
GOWER ST.
ARENA & CONVENTION CENTRE
KEEL WHARF
KINGS DOCK
River Mersey
KINGS PARADE
QUEENS WHARF
HALFTIDE WHARF
Pedestrian Shopping Zone

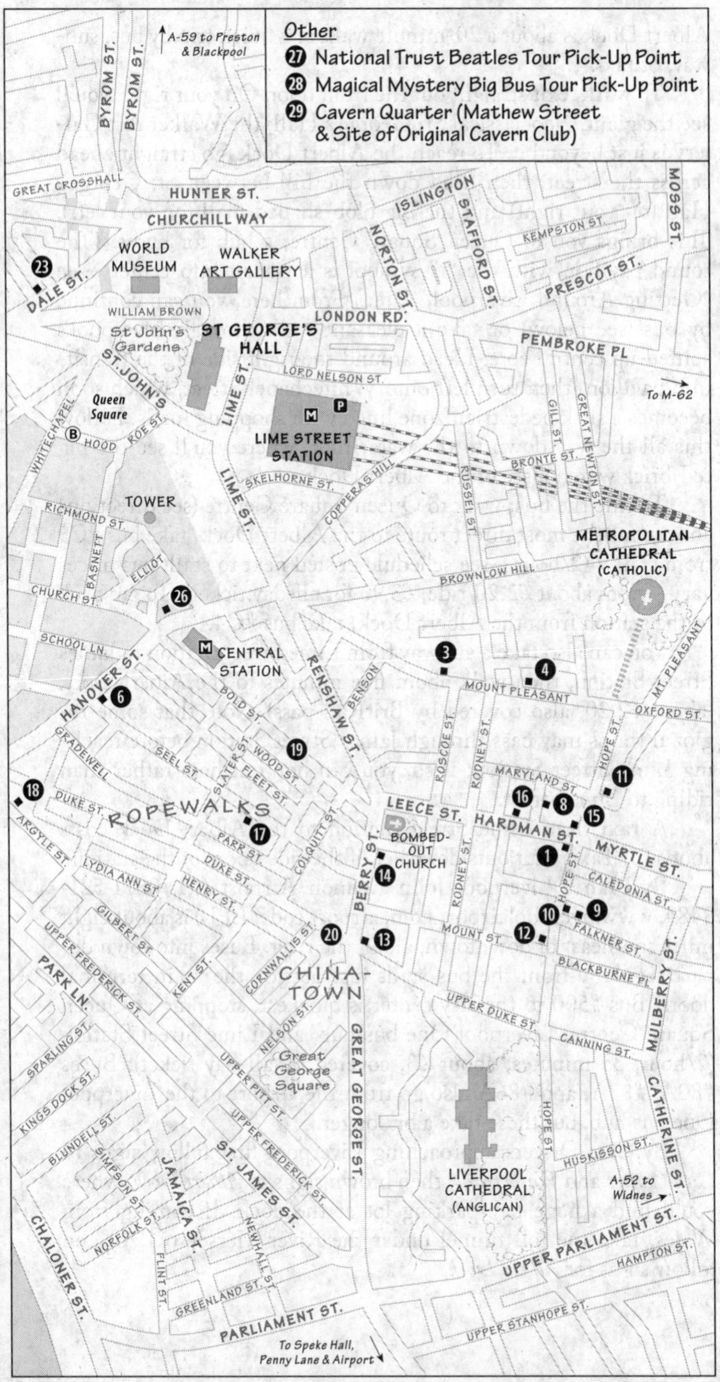

Other
27 National Trust Beatles Tour Pick-Up Point
28 Magical Mystery Big Bus Tour Pick-Up Point
29 Cavern Quarter (Mathew Street & Site of Original Cavern Club)
A-59 to Preston & Blackpool
To M-62
A-52 to Widnes
To Speke Hall, Penny Lane & Airport
WORLD MUSEUM
WALKER ART GALLERY
ST GEORGE'S HALL
St John's Gardens
Queen Square
LIME STREET STATION
TOWER
CENTRAL STATION
METROPOLITAN CATHEDRAL (CATHOLIC)
ROPEWALKS
BOMBED-OUT CHURCH
CHINA-TOWN
Great George Square
LIVERPOOL CATHEDRAL (ANGLICAN)

Albert Dock is about a 20-minute walk or a quick trip by bus, subway, or taxi.

To **walk,** exit straight out the front door. On your right, you'll see the giant, Neoclassical St. George's Hall; the Walker Art Gallery is just beyond it. To reach the Albert Dock, go straight ahead across the street, then head down the hill between St. George's Hall (on your right) and the big blob-shaped mall (on your left). This brings you to Queen Square Centre, a hub for buses. (The round pavilion with the "i" symbol is a transit info center—see "Getting Around Liverpool," later.) From here, you can continue by bus (see below) or take a pleasant walk through Liverpool's spiffed-up central core: Head around the right side of the transit-info pavilion, then turn left onto Whitechapel Street, which soon becomes a slick pedestrian zone lined with shopping malls. Follow this all the way down to the waterfront, where you'll see the big red-brick warehouses of the Albert Dock.

To ride the **bus,** walk to Queen Square Centre (see directions above); for the most direct route to the Albert Dock, take bus #C5 from stall 9 (2/hour—see schedule posted next to stall, bus prices vary—from about £2.20/ride, £3.90 for all-day ticket). To get back to the station from the Albert Dock, take bus #C4.

You can also take a **subway** from Lime Street Station to James Street Station, then walk about five minutes to the Albert Dock (about £2.20, also covered by BritRail pass). Note that some regional trains may pass through James Street Station before reaching Lime Street Station; if so, you can hop out here rather than riding to Lime Street.

A **taxi** from Lime Street Station to the Albert Dock costs about £5. Taxis wait outside either of the side doors of the station.

By Plane: Liverpool John Lennon Airport (tel. 0871-521-8484, www.liverpoolairport.com, airport code: LPL) is about eight miles southeast of downtown, along the river. Buses into town depart regularly from the bus stalls just outside the main terminal doors. Bus #500 to the city center is quickest, stopping at Queen Square Centre, Liverpool One bus hub, and Lime Street Station (2/hour, 35 minutes, about £3, covered by all-day ticket). Buses #80A, #82A, and #86A also go from the airport to the Liverpool One bus hub, but these take a bit longer.

By Car: Drivers approaching Liverpool first follow signs to *City Centre* and *Waterfront,* then brown signs to *Albert Dock,* where you'll find a huge pay parking lot at the dock. If coming from Wales, take the toll tunnel under the River Mersey (£1.70) and follow signs for *Albert Dock.*

GETTING AROUND LIVERPOOL

The city is walkable (and fun to explore), so you may not need to take advantage of the local bus network. But if you're near the Lime Street Station and Queen Square Centre bus hub and need to get to the Cavern sights, Liverpool One mall, or the Albert Dock, you can take public bus #C5 (#C4 visits the same stops in the opposite direction). For more public-transit information, visit a Merseytravel center—there's one at the main bus hub on Queen Square Centre and another at the Liverpool One bus station (1 Canning Place), across the busy street from the Albert Dock (open Mon-Sat 8:30-18:00, Sun 10:00-17:00, except Liverpool One closed Sun; tel. 0871-200-2233, www.merseytravel.gov.uk).

Tours in Liverpool

BEATLES BUS TOURS

If you want to see as many Beatles-related sights as possible in a short time, these tours are the way to go. Each drives by the houses where the Fab Four grew up (exteriors only), places they performed, and spots made famous by the lyrics of their hits ("Penny Lane," "Strawberry Fields," the Eleanor Rigby graveyard, and so on). Even lukewarm fans will enjoy the commentary and seeing the shelter on the roundabout, the barber who shaves another customer, and the banker who never wears a mack in the pouring rain. (Very strange.)

Magical Mystery Big Bus Tour

Beatles fans enjoy loading onto this old, psychedelically-painted bus for a spin past Liverpool's main Beatles landmarks, with a few photo ops off the bus. With an enthusiastic live commentary and Beatles tunes cued to famous landmarks, it leaves people happy (£17, 5-7/day, fewer on Sun and in off-season, 2 hours, buses depart from the Albert Dock near The Beatles Story and TI, tel. 0151/703-9100, www.cavernclub.org). As these tours often fill up, you'd be wise to book at least a day ahead by phone or online.

Phil Hughes Minibus Beatles and Liverpool Tours

For something more extensive, fun, and intimate, consider a four-hour minibus Beatles tour from Phil Hughes. It's longer because it includes information on historic Liverpool, along with the Beatles stuff and a couple of *Titanic* and *Lusitania* sights. Phil organizes his tour to fit your schedule and will do his best to accommodate you (£22/person, private group tour with 5-person minimum, can coordinate tour to include pickup from end of National Trust tour of Lennon and McCartney homes or drop-off for late-day tour starting at Speke Hall, also does door-to-door service from your hotel or train station, 8-seat minibus, tel. 0151/228-4565, mobile 07961-511-223, www.tourliverpool.co.uk, tourliverpool@hotmail.com).

Jackie Spencer Private Tours

To tailor a visit to your schedule and interests, Jackie Spencer is at your service...just say when and where you want to go (up to 5 people in her chauffeur-driven minivan-£210, 3 hours, longer tours available, will pick you up at hotel or train station, mobile 0799-076-1478, www.beatleguides.com, jackie@beatleguides.com).

OTHER TOURS

City Bus Tour

Two different hop-on, hop-off bus tours cruise around town, offering a quick way to get an overview that links all the major sights. The options are **Liverpool City Tours** (£10, buy ticket from driver, valid 24 hours, recorded commentary, 16 stops, April-Oct Mon-Sat 10:00-17:00, 3/hour, less frequent Sun and Nov-March, tel. 0151/298-1253, www.sightseeingliverpool.co.uk) and **City Explorer** (£9, buy ticket from driver, valid 24 hours, live guides, 13 stops; April-Aug daily 10:00-16:30, 2/hour; Sept-March generally daily 10:00 until 15:00 or 16:00, 1-2/hour; tel. 0151/933-2324, www.cityexplorerliverpool.co.uk).

Ferry Cruise

Mersey Ferries offers narrated cruises that depart from the Pier Head ferry terminal, a five-minute walk north of the Albert Dock. The 50-minute cruise makes two brief stops on the other side of the river; you can hop off and catch the next boat back (£10 round-trip, runs year-round, Mon-Fri 10:00-15:00, Sat-Sun 10:00-18:00, leaves Pier Head at top of hour, café, WCs onboard, tel. 0151/330-1000, www.merseyferries.co.uk).

Sights in Liverpool

ON THE WATERFRONT

In its day, Liverpool was England's greatest seaport, but trade declined after 1890, as the port wasn't deep enough for the big new ships. The advent of mega container ships in the 1960s put the final nail in the port's coffin, and by 1972 it was closed entirely.

But over the last couple of decades, this formerly derelict and dangerous area has been the focus of the city's rejuvenation efforts.

Liverpool at a Glance

▲▲**Museum of Liverpool** Three floors of intriguing exhibits, historical artifacts, and fun interactive displays tracing the port city's history, culture, and contributions to the world. **Hours:** Daily 10:00-17:00. See page 465.

▲▲**Liverpool Cathedral** Huge Anglican house of worship—the largest cathedral in Great Britain—with cavernous interior and tower climb. **Hours:** Daily 8:00-18:00. See page 472.

▲**Lennon and McCartney Homes** The 1950s boyhood homes of Beatles John Lennon and Paul McCartney, with restored interiors viewable on a National Trust minibus tour. Advance reservations smart. **Hours:** Tours run mid-March-Oct daily 4/day, mid-Feb-mid-March and Nov Wed-Sun 3/day. See page 475.

▲**The Beatles Story** Well-done if overpriced exhibit about the Fab Four, with a great audioguide narrated by John Lennon's sister, Julia Baird. **Hours:** Daily May-Sept 9:00-19:00, Oct-April 10:00-18:00. See page 460.

▲**Merseyside Maritime Museum and International Slavery Museum** Duo of thought-provoking museums exploring Liverpool's seafaring heritage and the city's role in the African slave trade. **Hours:** Daily 10:00-17:00. See page 461.

▲**Walker Art Gallery** Enjoyable, easy-to-appreciate collection of European paintings, sculptures, and decorative arts. **Hours:** Daily 10:00-17:00. See page 469.

▲**Metropolitan Cathedral of Christ the King** Striking, daringly-modern Catholic cathedral with a story as fascinating as the building itself. **Hours:** Daily 7:30-18:00, until 17:00 on Sun in winter; after 17:15 (during Mass), you can't walk around. See page 471.

Tate Gallery Liverpool Prestigious modern art gallery with a rotating collection of 20th-century statues and paintings. **Hours:** Daily 10:00-18:00. See page 465.

World Museum Family-oriented museum with five floors of kid-friendly exhibits, including dinosaurs and an aquarium. **Hours:** Daily 10:00-17:00. See page 470.

Liverpool's waterfront is now a venue for some of the city's top attractions. Three zones interest tourists (from south to north): the Wapping Dock area, with Liverpool's futuristic new arena, conference center, and adjacent Ferris wheel; the red-brick Albert Dock complex, with some of the city's top museums and lively restaurants and nightlife; and Pier Head, with the Museum of Liverpool, ferries across the River Mersey, and buildings both old/stately and new/glassy. Below are descriptions of the main sights at the Albert Dock and Pier Head.

At the Albert Dock

Opened in 1852 by Prince Albert, and enclosing seven acres of water, the Albert Dock is surrounded by five-story brick warehouses. A half-dozen trendy eateries are lined up here, protected from the rain by arcades and padded by lots of shopping mall-type distractions. There's plenty of pay parking.

▲The Beatles Story

It's sad to think the Beatles are stuck in a museum. Still, this exhibit—while overpriced and a bit small—is well-done, the story's a fascinating one, and even an avid fan will pick up some new information. The Beatles Story has two parts: the original main exhibit at the south end of the Albert Dock; and a much smaller branch in the Pier Head ferry terminal, near the Museum of Liverpool, just to the north. A free shuttle runs between the two locations every 30 minutes.

Cost and Hours: £15 covers both parts, tickets good for 48 hours, includes audioguide, daily May-Sept 9:00-19:00, Oct-April 10:00-18:00, last entry one hour before closing, tel. 0151/709-1963, www.beatlesstory.com.

Visiting the Museum: Start in the **main exhibit** with a chronological stroll through the evolution of the Beatles, focusing on their Liverpool years: meeting as schoolboys, performing at (and helping decorate) the Casbah Coffee Club, making a name for themselves in Hamburg's red light district, meeting their manager Brian Epstein, and the advent of worldwide Beatlemania (with some help from Ed Sullivan). There are many actual artifacts (from George Harrison's first boyhood guitar to John Lennon's orange-tinted "Imagine" glasses), as well as large dioramas celebrating landmarks in Beatles lore (a reconstruction of the Cavern Club, a life-size re-creation of the *Sgt. Pepper* album cover, and a walk-through yellow submarine). The last rooms trace the members' solo careers, and the final few steps are reserved for reverence about John's peace work, including a replica of the white room he used while writing "Imagine." Rounding out the exhibits are a "Discovery Zone" for kids and (of course) the "Fab 4 Store," with an impressive pile of Beatles buyables.

The great audioguide, narrated by Julia Baird (John Lennon's little sister), captures the Beatles' charm and cheekiness in a way the stiff wax mannequins can't. You'll hear clips of interviews from the actual participants in the Beatles' story—their families, friends, and collaborators. Cynthia Lennon, John's first wife, still marvels at the manic power of Beatlemania, while producer George Martin explains why he wanted their original drummer dumped for Ringo.

While this is a fairly sanitized look at the Fab Four (LSD and Yoko-related conflicts are glossed over), the exhibits remind listeners of all that made the group earth-shattering—and even a little edgy—at the time. For example, performing before the Queen Mother, John Lennon famously quips: "Will the people in the cheaper seats clap your hands? And the rest of you, if you'll just rattle your jewelry." Surprisingly, there are no clips from Beatles movies or performances—not even the epic *Ed Sullivan Show* broadcast. You'll find that it's strong on Beatles' history, but you'll have to go elsewhere to understand why Beatlemania happened.

The **Pier Head exhibit** is less interesting, but since it's included with the ticket, it's worth dropping into if you have the time. You'll find it upstairs in the Pier Head ferry terminal—10-minute walk north (at the opposite end of the Albert Dock, then another 5-minute walk across the bridge and past the Museum of Liverpool). The main attraction here is a corny "Fab 4D Experience," an animated movie that strings together Beatles tunes into something resembling a plot while mainly offering an excuse to play around with 3-D effects and other surprises (such as the smell of strawberries when you hear "Strawberry Fields Forever"). There are also rotating temporary exhibits here.

▲Merseyside Maritime Museum and International Slavery Museum

These museums tell the story of Liverpool, once the second city of the British Empire. The third floor covers slavery, while the first, second, and basement handle other maritime topics.

The Beatles in Liverpool

The most iconic rock-and-roll band of all time was made up of four Liverpudlians who spent their formative years amid the bombed-out shell of WWII-era Liverpool. The city has become a pilgrimage site for Beatlemaniacs, but even those with just a passing interest in the Fab Four are likely to find themselves humming their favorite tunes around town. Most Beatles sights in Liverpool relate to their early days, before the psychedelia, transcendental meditation, Yoko, and solo careers. Because these sights are so spread out, the easiest way to connect all of them in one go is by tour (see "Tours in Liverpool").

All four of the Beatles were born in Liverpool, and any tour of town glides by the **home** most identified with each one's childhood: John Lennon at "Mendips," Paul McCartney at 20 Forthlin Road, George Harrison at 12 Arnold Grove, and Ringo Starr (a.k.a. Richard Starkey) at 10 Admiral Grove.

Behind John's house at Mendips is a wooded area called **Strawberry Field** (he added the "s" for the song). This surrounds a Victorian mansion that was, at various times, a Salvation Army home and an orphanage. John enjoyed sneaking into the trees around the mansion to play. Today visitors pose in front of Strawberry Field's red gate (a replica of the original).

During the Beatles' formative years in the mid-1950s, skiffle music (American-inspired rockabilly/folk) swept through Liverpool. As a teenager, John formed a skiffle band called the Quarrymen. Paul met John for the first time when he saw the Quarrymen on July 6, 1957 at **St. Peter's Church** in Woolton. After the show, in the social hall across the street, Paul noted that John played only banjo chords (his mother had taught him to play on a banjo rather than a guitar—he didn't even know how to tune a guitar), and improvised many lyrics. John, two years older, realized he was a better improviser than a musician, so he was impressed when Paul borrowed a guitar, tuned it effortlessly, and played a note-perfect rendition of Eddie Cochran's "Twenty Flight Rock." Before long, Paul had joined the band.

In the St. Peter's Church graveyard is a headstone for a woman named **Eleanor Rigby.** But to this day, Paul swears that he never saw it, and made up the name for that famous song. Either he's lying, the name crept into his subconscious, or it's a truly remarkable coincidence.

The boys went to school on **Mount Street** in the center of Liverpool (near Hope Street, between the two cathedrals). John and his friend Stuart Sutcliffe attended the Liverpool College of Art, and Paul and his pal George Harrison went to Liverpool Institute High School for Boys. (When Paul introduced George to John as a possible new member for the band, John dismissed him as being too young...until he heard George play. He immediately became the lead guitarist.) Paul later bought his old school building and turned it into the Liverpool Institute for Performing Arts (LIPA)—nicknamed the "Fame Academy" for the similar school on the American TV series.

As young men, the boys rode the bus together to school—waiting at a bus stop in the **Penny Lane** neighborhood. Later they wrote a nostalgic song about the things they would observe while waiting there: the shelter by the roundabout, the barbershop, and so on. (While they also sing about the fireman with the clean machine, the firehouse itself is not actually on Penny Lane, but around the corner.)

After a series of lineup shuffles, by 1960 the group had officially become The Beatles: John Lennon, Paul McCartney, George Harrison, and...Pete Best and Stu Sutcliffe. The quintet gradually built a name for themselves in Liverpool's "Merseybeat" scene, performing at local clubs. While the famous **Cavern Club** is gone (the one you see advertised is a reconstruction, but does offer similar ambience and good cover bands), the original **Casbah Coffee Club**—which the group felt more attached to—still exists and is open for tours (3.5 miles northwest of downtown in Pete Best's former basement, prebook by calling the TI at tel. 0151/707-0729 or online at www.petebest.com).

The group went to Hamburg, Germany, to cut their teeth in the thriving music scene there. They wound up performing as the backing band for Tony Sheridan's single "My Bonny." When this caught on back in Liverpool, promoter Brian Epstein took note, and signed the act. His shrewd management would eventually propel the Beatles to superstardom.

Many different people could be considered the "Fifth Beatle." John's friend Stu, who performed with the group in Hamburg, left to pursue his own artistic interests. Pete Best was the band's original drummer, but he was a loner and producers questioned his musical chops, so he was replaced with Ringo Starr. (John later said, "Pete Best was a great drummer, but Ringo was a Beatle.") Brian Epstein, the manager who marketed the Beatles brilliantly before his untimely death, is another candidate. But—in terms of long-term musical influence—it's hard to ignore the case for George Martin, who produced all the Beatles' albums except *Let It Be,* and was instrumental in both forging and developing the Beatles sound.

By early 1964, the Beatles were already world famous—but, as evidenced by their songs about Penny Lane and Strawberry Fields, they never forgot their Merseyside home.

Cost and Hours: Free, donations accepted, daily 10:00-17:00, café, tel. 0151/478-4499, www.liverpoolmuseums.org.uk.

Background: Liverpool's port prospered in the 18th century as one corner of a commerce triangle with Africa and America. British shippers profited greatly through exploitation: About 1.5 million enslaved African people were taken to the Americas on Liverpool's ships (that's 10 percent of all African slaves). From Liverpool, the British exported manufactured goods to Africa in exchange for enslaved Africans; the slaves were then shipped to the Americas, where they were traded for raw material (cotton, sugar, and tobacco); and the goods were then brought back to Britain. While the merchants on all three sides made money, the big profit came home to England (which enjoyed substantial income from customs, duties, and a thriving smugglers' market). As Britain's economy boomed, so did Liverpool's.

After participation in the slave trade was outlawed in Britain in the early 1800s, Liverpool kept its port busy as a transfer point for emigrants. If your ancestors came from Scandinavia, Ukraine, or Ireland, they likely left Europe from this port. Between 1830 and 1930, nine million emigrants sailed from Liverpool to find their dreams in the New World.

Visiting the Museums: Begin by riding the elevator up to floor 3—we'll work our way back down.

On floor 3, three galleries make up the **International Slavery Museum.** First is a description of life in West Africa, which re-creates traditional domestic architecture and displays actual artifacts. Then comes a harrowing exhibit about enslavement and the Middle Passage. The tools of the enslavers—chains, muzzles, and a branding iron—and the intense film about the Middle Passage sea voyage to the Americas drive home the horrifying experience of being abducted from your home and taken in life-threatening conditions thousands of miles away to toil for a wealthy stranger. The exhibits don't shy away from how Liverpool profited from slavery; you can turn local street signs around to find out how they were named after slave traders—even Penny Lane has slavery connections. Finally, the museum examines the legacy of slavery—both the persistence of racism in contemporary society and the substantial positive impact that people of African descent have had on European and American cultures. Walls of photos celebrate important people of African descent, and a music station lets you sample songs from a variety of African-influenced genres.

Continue down the stairs to the **Maritime Museum,** on floor 2. This celebrates Liverpool's shipbuilding heritage and displays actual ship components, model boats, and a gallery of nautical paintings. Part of that heritage is covered in an extensive exhibit on the ***Titanic.*** The shipping line and its captain were based in Liverpool, and 89 of the crew members who died were from the city. The informative panels allow you to follow real people as they set off on the voyage and debunk many *Titanic* myths (no one ever said it was unsinkable).

Floor 1 shows footage and artifacts from another maritime disaster—the 1915 sinking of the ***Lusitania***, which was torpedoed by a German U-boat. She sank off the coast of Ireland in under 20 minutes; 1,191 people died in the tragedy, including 405 crew members from Liverpool. The attack on an unarmed passenger ship sparked riots in Liverpool and almost thrust the US into the war. Also on this floor, an extensive exhibit traces the **Battle of the Atlantic** (during World War II, Nazi U-boats attacked merchant ships bringing supplies to Britain, in an attempt to cripple this island nation). You'll see how crew members lived aboard merchant ships. The **Hello Sailor!** exhibit explains how gay culture flourished at sea at a time when it was taboo in almost every other walk of British life.

Make your way to the basement, where exhibits describe the tremendous wave of **emigration** through Liverpool's port. And the **Seized!** exhibit looks at the legal and illegal movement of goods through that same port, including thought-provoking displays on customs, taxation, and smuggling.

Tate Gallery Liverpool

This prestigious gallery of modern art is near the Maritime Museum. It won't entertain you as well as its London sister, the Tate Modern, but if you're into modern art, any Tate's great. Its two airy floors dedicated to the rotating collection of statues and paintings from the 20th century are free; the top and ground floors are devoted to special exhibits. The Tate also has an inexpensive recommended café.

Cost and Hours: Free, donations accepted, £7-13 for special exhibits, daily 10:00-18:00, tel. 0151/702-7400, www.tate.org.uk/visit/tate-liverpool.

At Pier Head, North of the Albert Dock

A five-minute walk across the bridge north of the Albert Dock takes you to the Pier Head area, with the following sights.

▲▲Museum of Liverpool

This museum, which opened in 2011 in the blocky white building just across the bridge north of the Albert Dock, does a good job of fulfilling its goal to "capture Liverpool's vibrant character and demonstrate the city's unique contribution to the world." The museum is full of interesting items, fun interactive displays (great for kids), and fascinating facts that bring a whole new depth to your Liverpool experience.

Cost and Hours: Free, donations accepted, daily 10:00-17:00, guidebook-£1, café, Mann Island, Pier Head, tel. 0151/478-4545, www.liverpoolmuseums.org.uk/mol.

Visiting the Museum: First, stop by the information desk to check on the show times for the museum's various videos. If you have kids age six and under, you can also get a free timed-entry ticket for the hands-on Little Liverpool exhibit on the ground floor.

Ground Floor: On this level, **The Great Port** details the story of Liverpool's defining industry and how it developed through the Industrial Revolution. On display is an 1838 steam locomotive that was originally built for the Liverpool and Manchester Railway. The **Global City** exhibit focuses on how Liverpool's status as a major British shipping center made it the gateway to a global empire and features a 20-minute video, *Power and the Glory,* about Liverpool's role within the British Empire.

First Floor: Don't miss the **Liverpool Overhead Railway** exhibit, which features the only surviving car from this 19th-century elevated railway. You can actually jump aboard and take a seat to watch 1897 movie footage shot from the train line. A huge interactive model shows the railway's route. Also on this floor is the **History Detectives** exhibit, which covers Liverpool's history and archaeology.

Second Floor: If you're short on time, spend most of it here. The **People's Republic** exhibit examines what it means to be a Liverpudlian (a.k.a. "Scouser") and covers everything from housing and health issues to military and religious topics. As industrialized Liverpool has long been a hotbed of the labor movement, exhibits here also detail the political side of the city, including child labor issues and women's suffrage.

One fascinating display is the re-creation of Liverpool's 19th-century court housing, which consisted of a series of tiny dwellings bunched around a narrow courtyard. With more than 60 people sharing two toilets, this was some of the most overcrowded and unsanitary housing in Britain at the time.

Next, the exhibit skips to religion and the centerpiece of this room: a 10-foot-tall model of Liverpool's Catholic cathedral that was never built. In 1932, Archbishop Richard Downey and architect Sir Edwin Lutyens commissioned this model to showcase their grandiose plans for constructing the world's second-largest cathedral. Their vision never came to fruition, and the Metropolitan Cathedral was built instead (for more on what happened, see page 471).

On the other side of the floor, the **Wondrous Place** exhibit celebrates the arts, cultural, and sporting side of Liverpool. An exhibit on the city's famous passion for soccer features memorabilia and the 17-minute video *Kicking and Screaming,* about the rivalry between the Everton and Liverpool football teams and the sometimes tragic history of the sport (such as when 96 fans were crushed to death at a Liverpool match).

Music is the other big focus here, with plenty of fun interactive stops that include music quizzes, a karaoke booth, and listening stations featuring artists with ties to Liverpool (from Elvis Costello to Echo & the Bunnymen). And of course you'll see plenty of Beatles mania, including their famous suits, the original stage from St. Peter's Church (where John Lennon was performing the first time Paul McCartney laid eyes on him; located in the theater), and an eight-minute film on the band.

Finally, in the **Skylight Gallery,** look for Ben Johnson's painting *The Liverpool Cityscape, 2008,* a remarkable and fun-to-examine melding of old and new art styles. At first glance, it's a typical skyline painting, but Johnson used computer models to create perfect depictions of each building before he put brush to canvas. This method allows for a photorealistic, highly detailed, but completely sanitized portrait of a city. Notice there are no cars or people.

The Three Graces

Three towering buildings near the Museum of Liverpool, remnants of a time of great seafaring prosperity, are known collectively as Liverpool's Three Graces: the double-clock-towered **Royal Liver Building,** with spires topped by the city's mythical mascot, the "Liver birds"; the relatively dull and boxy **Cunard Building;** and the domed **Port of Liverpool Building,** which strains to evoke memories of St. Paul's Cathedral in London. A 2002 plan to create a Fourth Grace—a metallic, glassy, and yellow blob called The Cloud—never panned out, and that site is now home to the Museum of Liverpool (described previously). While you can see the Three Graces from along the embankment—which is also lined with monuments to important Liverpudlians—the best views are from across the River Mersey (see page 484 for details on riding the ferry; note that the Pier Head ferry terminal also hosts some exhibits from The Beatles Story).

DOWNTOWN

Beatles Sights in the Cavern Quarter

The narrow, bar-lined Mathew Street, right in the heart of downtown, is ground zero for Beatles fans. The Beatles frequently performed in their early days together at the original Cavern Club, deep in a cellar along this street. While that's long gone, a mock-up of the historic nightspot (built with many of the original bricks) lives on a few doors down. Still billed as "the **Cavern Club,**" this is worth a visit to see the reconstructed cellar that's often filled by Beatles cover bands. While touristy, dropping by in the afternoon for a live Beatles tribute act in the Cavern Club somehow just feels right. You'll have Beatles songs stuck in your head all day anyway, so you might as well see a wannabe John and Paul strumming and harmonizing a close approximation of the original (open daily 10:00-24:00; live music daily from 14:00, Sat from 13:00, cover charge Thu-Fri after 20:00 and Sat-Sun after 14:00, tel. 0151/236-9091, www.cavernclub.org).

Across the street and run by the same owners, the **Cavern Pub** lacks its sibling's troglodyte aura, but makes up for it with walls lined with old photos and memorabilia from the Beatles and other bands who've performed here. Like the Cavern Club, the pub features frequent performances by Beatles cover bands and other acts (no cover, Mon-Wed 11:00-24:00, later Thu-Sun, tel. 0151/236-4041).

Out front is the Cavern's **Wall of Fame,** with a too-cool-for-school bronze John Lennon leaning up against a wall of bricks engraved with the names of musical acts that have graced the Cavern stage.

At the corner is the recommended **Hard Day's Night Hotel,** decorated inside and out to honor the Fab Four. Notice the statues of John, Paul, George, and Ringo on the second-story corners, and the Beatles gift shop (one of many in town) on the ground floor.

Museums near the Train Station

Both of these museums are just a five-minute walk from the Lime Street train station.

▲Walker Art Gallery

Though it has few recognizable works, Liverpool's main art gallery offers an enjoyable walk through an easy-to-digest collection of European (mostly British) paintings, sculpture, and decorative arts. There's no audioguide, but many of the works are well-explained by posted descriptions.

Cost and Hours: Free, donations accepted, daily 10:00-17:00, William Brown Street, tel. 0151/478-4199, www.liverpoolmuseums.org.uk.

Visiting the Museum: The ground floor has an information desk, café, children's area, small decorative arts collection, and sculpture gallery focusing on British Neoclassical works from the 19th century. The sculpture gallery has many works by John Gibson, a Welshman who grew up in Liverpool and later studied under the Italian master Antonio Canova. Gibson's *Tinted Venus* (in the case in the middle) was considered scandalous to Victorian mores because of the nude sculpture's lifelike pinkish tint.

Upstairs is a concise 15-room painting gallery. For a general chronological spin, from the top of the stairs head straight back to find Room 1. Because of various special exhibits that rotate in and out, the following paintings may be located in other rooms or not on display.

Room 1 (actually two adjoining rooms) has a famous Nicholas Hilliard portrait of Queen Elizabeth I (nicknamed "The Pelican," for her brooch) and a well-known royal portrait of Henry VIII by Hans Holbein. Room 3 has bombastic Baroque works by Rubens and Murillo, Room 4 features a Rembrandt self-portrait, while Room 5 focuses on 18th-century English painting, including canvases by Gainsborough, Hogarth (find the painting of the great actor David Garrick in the role of Richard III), and lots of George Stubbs. Rooms 6-8 showcase a delightful array of Pre-Raphaelite works, among them

Millias' evocative portrait of Isabella (Room 6). You'll find some Turners (a mushy landscape and a more sharp-focus Linlithgow Castle) in Room 7.

For a counterpoint to the lyrical, mystical Pre-Raphaelite works, step into Room 9, with very literal Victorian narrative paintings depicting slices of English life, such as Sadler's *Friday* (showing Dominican monks feasting on fish) and Yeams' *And When Did You Last See Your Father?* On this chilling canvas, showing a scene from the English Civil War, authorities are slyly interrogating a naive, cherubic boy while his family watches from behind, terrified that the child will reveal where his father is hiding.

Room 10 makes the transition to the 20th century and Impressionism, while modern British art dominates the rest of the gallery. In Room 11, Bernard Fleetwood-Walker's *Amity* shows a pair of chaste but (apparently) sexually charged teenagers relaxing in the grass.

World Museum

This catchall family museum offers five floors of kid-oriented exhibits. You'll see dinosaurs, an aquarium, artifacts from the ancient world, a planetarium and theater (get free tickets at the info desk in the lobby for these), and more.

Cost and Hours: Free, donations accepted, daily 10:00-17:00, William Brown Street, tel. 0151/478-4393, www.liverpoolmuseums.org.uk.

Cathedrals

Liverpool has not one but two notable cathedrals—one Anglican, the other Catholic. (As the Spinners song puts it, "If you want a cathedral, we've got one to spare.") Both are huge, architecturally significant, and well worth visiting. Near the eastern edge of downtown, they're connected by a 10-minute, half-mile walk on pleasant Hope Street, which is lined with theaters and good restaurants (see "Eating in Liverpool," later).

Liverpudlians enjoy pointing out that they have not only the world's only Catholic cathedral designed by a Protestant architect, but also the only Protestant one designed by a Catholic. With its large Irish-immigrant population, Liverpool suffered from tension between its Catholic and Protestant communities for much of its history. But during the city's darkest stretch of the depressed 1970s, the bishops of each church—Anglican Bishop David Sheppard and Catholic Archbishop Derek Worlock—came together and worked hard to reconcile the two communities for the betterment of Liverpool. (Liverpudlians nicknamed this dynamic duo "fish and chips" because they were "always together, and always in the newspaper.") It worked: Liverpool is a bold new cultural center, and relations between the two faiths remain healthy here. Join in this ecumenical spirit by visiting both of their main churches.

▲Metropolitan Cathedral of Christ the King (Catholic)

This daringly modern building, a cone topped with a crowned cylinder, seems almost out of place in its workaday Liverpool neighborhood. But the cathedral you see today bears no resemblance to Sir Edwin Lutyens' original 1930s plans for a stately Neo-Byzantine cathedral, which was to take 200 years to build and rival St. Peter's Basilica in Vatican City. (Lutyens was desperate to one-up the grandiose plans of Sir Giles Gilbert Scott, who was building the Anglican Cathedral down the street.) The crypt for the ambitious church was excavated in the 1930s, but World War II (during which the crypt was used as an air-raid shelter) stalled progress for decades. In the 1960s, the plans were scaled back, and this smaller (but still impressive) house of worship was completed in 1967.

Cost and Hours: Cathedral—free entry but donations accepted, daily 7:30-18:00 (until 17:00 on Sun in winter)—but after 17:15 (during Mass), you won't be able to walk around; crypt—£3, Mon-Sat 10:00-16:00, closed Sun, last entry 45 minutes before closing, enter from inside church near organ; visitors center and café, Mount Pleasant, tel. 0151/709-9222, www.liverpoolmetrocathedral.org.uk.

Visiting the Cathedral: On the stepped plaza in front of the church, you'll see the entrance to the cathedral's visitors center and café (on your right). You're standing on a big concrete slab that provides a roof to the humongous Lutyens Crypt, underfoot. The existing cathedral occupies only a small part of the would-be cathedral's footprint. Imagine what might have been—"the greatest building never built." Because of the cathedral's tent-like appearance and ties to the local Irish community, some Liverpudlians dubbed it "Paddy's Wigwam."

Climb up the stairs to the main doors, step inside, and let your eyes adjust to this magnificent, dimly-lit space. Unlike a typical nave-plus-transept cross-shaped church, this cathedral has a round footprint, with seating for a congregation of 3,000 fully surrounding the white marble altar. Like a theater in the round, it was designed to involve worshippers in the service. Suspended above the altar is a stylized crown of thorns.

Spinning off from the round central sanctuary are 13 smaller chapels, many of them representing different stages of Jesus' life. Each chapel is different. Explore, tuning into the symbolic details in each one. Also keep an eye out for the 14 exquisite bronze Stations of the Cross by local artist Sean Rice (on the wall).

The massive **Lutyens Crypt** (named for the ambitious original architect)—the only part of the originally planned cathedral to be completed—is massive, with huge vaults and vast halls lined with six million bricks. The crypt contains a chapel—with windows by Lutyens—that's still used for Sunday Mass, the tombs of three archbishops, a treasury, and an exhibit about the cathedral's construction.

Hope Street

The street connecting the cathedrals is the main artery of Liverpool's "uptown," a lively and fun-to-explore district loaded with dining and entertainment options. In addition to well-respected theaters, this street is home to the Philharmonic and its namesake pub (see "Eating in Liverpool," later). At the intersection with Mount Street is a monument consisting of concrete suitcases; just down this street are the high schools that Paul, George, and John attended (for details, see "The Beatles in Liverpool" sidebar, earlier).

▲▲Liverpool Cathedral (Anglican)

The largest cathedral in Great Britain, this gigantic house of worship hovers at the south end of downtown. Tour its cavernous interior and consider scaling its tower.

Cost and Hours: Free, £3 suggested donation, daily 8:00-18:00; £5 ticket includes tower climb (2 elevators and 108 steps), audioguide, and 10-minute *Great Space* film; tower—Mon-Fri 10:00-16:30 (last ascent), Thu until sunset March-

Oct, Sat 9:00-16:30, Sun 12:00-15:30 (changes possible depending on bell-ringing schedule); St. James Mount, tel. 0151/709-6271, www.liverpoolcathedral.org.uk.

Visiting the Cathedral: Over the main door is a modern *Risen Christ* statue by Elisabeth Frink. Liverpudlians, not thrilled with the featureless statue and always quick with a joke, have dubbed it **"Frinkenstein."**

Stepping inside, pick up a floor plan at the information desk, go into the main hall, and take in the size of the place. When Liverpool was officially designated a "city" (seat of a bishop), they wanted to build a huge house of worship as a symbol of Liverpudlian pride. Built in bold Neo-Gothic style (like London's Parliament), it seems to trumpet with modern bombast the importance of this city on the Mersey. Begun in 1904, the cathedral's construction was interrupted by the tumultuous 20th century and not completed until 1973.

Go to the big circular tile in the very center of the cathedral, under the highest tower. This is a plaque for the building's architect, **Sir Giles Gilbert Scott** (1880-1960). While the church you're surrounded by may seem like his biggest legacy, he also designed an icon that's synonymous with Britain: the classic red telephone box. Flanking this aisle, notice the highly detailed sandstone carvings.

Take a counterclockwise spin around the church interior. Head up the right aisle until you find the **model** of the original plan for the cathedral (press the button to light it up). Scott was a very young architect and received the commission with the agreement that he work closely under the wing of his more established mentor, George Bodley. These two architects' visions clashed, and Bodley usually won...until he died early in the planning stages, leaving Scott to pursue his own muse. If Bodley had survived, the cathedral would probably look more like this model. As it was, only one corner of the complex (the Lady Chapel, which we're about to see) was completed before Giles changed plans to create the version you see today.

Nearby, the **"whispering arch"** spanning the sarcophagus has remarkable acoustics, carrying voices from one end to the other. Try it.

Continuing down the church, notice the very colorful modern painting of ***The Good Samaritan*** (by Adrian Wiszniewski, 1995), high above on the right. The naked crime victim (who has been stabbed in his side, like the Crucifixion wound of Jesus) has been ignored by the well-dressed yuppies in the foreground, but the female Samaritan is finally taking notice. The canvas is packed with symbolism (for example, the Swiss Army knife, in a pool of blood in the left foreground, is open in the 3 o'clock position—the time that Jesus was crucified). This contemporary work of art demonstrates that this is a new, living church. But the congregation has its limits. This painting used to hang closer to the front of the church, but now they've moved it here, out of sight.

Proceeding to the corner, you'll reach the entrance to the oldest part of the church (1910): the **Lady Chapel,** with stained-glass windows celebrating important women. (Sadly, the original windows were destroyed in World War II; these are replicas.)

Back up in the main part of the church, continue behind the main altar to the **Education Centre,** with a fun, sped-up video showing all of the daily work it takes to make this cathedral run.

Circling around the far corner of the church, you'll pass the children's chapel and chapterhouse, and then pass under another modern Wiszniewski painting *(The House Built on Rock).* Across from that painting, go into the choir to get a good look at the Last Supper altarpiece above the **main altar.**

Continuing back up the aisle, you'll come to the **war chapel.** At its entrance is a book listing Liverpudlians lost in war. Battle flags fly high on the wall above.

You'll wind up at the gift shop, where you can buy a ticket to climb up to the top of the tower. The cathedral's café is up the stairs, above the gift shop.

AWAY FROM THE CENTER

▲Lennon and McCartney Homes

John's and Paul's boyhood homes are now owned by the National Trust and have both been restored to how they looked during the lads' 1950s childhoods. While some Beatles bus tours stop here for photo ops, only the National Trust minibus tour gets you inside the homes. This isn't Graceland—you won't find an over-the-top rock-and-roll extravaganza here. If you don't know the difference between John and Paul, you'll likely be bored. But for die-hard Beatles fans who want to get a glimpse into the time and place that created these musical masterminds, the National Trust tour is worth ▲▲▲.

Famous musicians who perform in Liverpool often make the pilgrimage to these homes—Bob Dylan turned up on one tour disguised in a hoodie—and Paul himself occasionally drops by. Ask the guides about recent memorable visitors.

Because the houses are in residential neighborhoods—and still share walls with neighbors—the National Trust runs only a few tours per day, limited to 15 or so Beatlemaniacs each.

Cost and Reservations: Tickets are £23. Because so few people are allowed on each tour, it's strongly advised to make a reservation ahead of time, especially in summer and on weekends or holidays. It's a good idea to book as soon as you know your Liverpool plans (or at least two weeks ahead)—though at times, you may be able to get tickets a couple of days in advance. (On the flip side, tours can be booked up months in advance, such as during Beatles week in August.) You can reserve online (www.nationaltrust.org.uk/beatles) or by calling 0151/427-7231. If you haven't reserved ahead, you can try to book a same-day tour (for the morning tours, call 0151/707-0729). The last tour is less likely to be full because it takes 30 minutes (by car or taxi) to reach the tour's starting point from central Liverpool—see below.

Tour Options: A minibus takes you to the homes of John and Paul, with about 45 minutes inside each. From mid-March-Oct, tours run daily from the Albert Dock at 10:00, 11:00, and 14:15; mid-Feb-mid-March and Nov Wed-Sun only (no tours Dec-mid-Feb). They depart from the Jurys Inn (south across the bridge from The Beatles Story, near the Ferris wheel) and follow a route that includes a quick pass by Penny Lane.

From mid-March-Oct, an additional tour leaves at 15:00 from Speke Hall, an out-of-the-way National Trust property located eight miles southeast of Liverpool. Drivers should allow 30 minutes from the city center to Speke Hall—follow the brown *Speke Hall* signs through dozens of roundabouts, heading in the general direction of the airport. If you don't have a car, hop in a taxi.

From either starting point, the entire visit takes about 2.5 hours. No photos are allowed inside either home.

Visiting the Homes: Each home has a caretaker who acts as your guide. These folks give an entertaining, insightful-to-fans 20- to 30-minute talk. You then have about 10-15 minutes to wander through the house on your own. Ask lots of questions if their spiel peters out early—these docents are a wealth of information.

Mendips (John Lennon's Home): Even though he sang about being a working-class hero, John grew up in the suburbs of Liverpool, surrounded by doctors, lawyers, and—beyond the back fence—Strawberry Field.

This was the home of John's Aunt Mimi, who raised him in this house from the time he was five years old and once told him, "A guitar's all right, John, but you'll never earn a living by it." (John later bought Mimi a country cottage with those fateful words etched over the fireplace.) John moved out at age 23, but his first wife, Cynthia, bunked here for a while when John made his famous first trip to America. Yoko Ono bought the house in 2002 and gave it as a gift to the National Trust (generating controversy among the neighbors). The house's stewards make this place come to life.

On the surface, it's just a 1930s house carefully restored to how it would have been in the past. But delve deeper. It's been lovingly cared for—restored to be the tidy, well-kept place Mimi would have recognized (down to dishtowels hanging in the kitchen). It's a lucky quirk of fate that the house's interior remained mostly unchanged after the Lennons left: The bachelor who owned it decades after them didn't upgrade much, so even the light switches are true to the time.

If you're a John Lennon fan, it's fun to picture him as a young boy drawing and imagining at his dining room table. His bedroom, with an Elvis poster and his favorite boyhood books, offers tantalizing hints at his later musical genius. Sing a song to yourself in the enclosed porch—John and Paul did this when they wanted an echo-chamber effect.

20 Forthlin Road (Paul McCartney's Home): In comparison to Aunt Mimi's house, the home where Paul grew up is simpler, much less "posh," and even a little ratty around the edges. Michael, Paul's brother, wanted it that way—their mother, Mary (famously mentioned in "Let It Be"), died when the boys were young, and it never had the tidiness of a woman's touch. It's been intentionally scuffed up around the edges to preserve the historical accuracy. Notice the differences—Paul has said that John's house was vastly different and more clearly middle class; at Mendips, there were books on the bookshelves—but Paul's father had an upright piano. He also rigged up wires and headphones that connected the boys' bedrooms to the living room radio so they could listen to rock 'n' roll on Radio Luxembourg.

More than a hundred Beatles songs were written in this house (including "I Saw Her Standing There") during days Paul and John spent skipping school. The photos from Michael, taken in this house, help make the scene of what's mostly a barren interior much more interesting. Ask your guide how Paul would sneak into the house late at night without waking up his dad.

Nightlife in Liverpool

Liverpool hops after hours, especially on weekends. The most happening zone is the area called **Ropewalks,** just east of the downtown shopping district and Albert Dock. Part of the protected historic area of Liverpool's docklands, the redeveloped Ropewalks area is now filled with trendy pubs, nightclubs, and lounges—some of them rough around the edges, others posh and sleek. While this area is aimed primarily at the college-age crowd, it's still worth a stroll, and has a few eateries worth considering.

Liverpool also has a wide range of watering holes. The ones listed here are all in the city center and are best for serious drinkers and beer aficionados—the food is an afterthought. **The Ship and Mitre,** overlooking an off-ramp at the edge of downtown, has perhaps Liverpool's best selection of beers—with 30-plus types on tap—as well as frequent beer festivals; it can get very crowded (133 Dale Street, tel. 0151/236-0859, see festival schedule at www.theshipandmitre.com). **Thomas Rigby's** has hard-used wooden floors that spill out into a rollicking garden courtyard (21 Dale

Street). Around the corner and much more sedate, **Ye Hole in Ye Wall** brags that it's Liverpool's oldest pub, from 1726. Notice the men's room on the ground floor—the women's room, required by law to be added in the 1970s, is upstairs (just off Dale Street on Hackins Hey). A few blocks over, right in the heart of downtown and surrounded by modern mega-malls, is **The Globe**—a tight, cozy, local-feeling pub with five real ales and sloping floors (17 Cases Street).

Sleeping in Liverpool

Your best budget options in this thriving city are the boring, predictable, and central chain hotels—though I've listed a couple of more colorful options also worth considering. Many hotels, including the ones listed below, charge more on weekends (particularly Sat), especially when the Liverpool FC soccer team plays a home game. Rates shoot up even higher two weekends a year: during the Grand National horse race (long weekend in April) and during Beatles Week in late August—avoid these times if you can. Prices plummet on Sunday nights.

$$$ Hope Street Hotel is a class act that sets the bar for Liverpool's hotels. Located across from the Philharmonic on Hope Street (midway between the cathedrals, in an enticing dining neighborhood), this stylish and contemporary hotel has 89 luxurious rooms with lots of hardwood, exposed brick, and elegant little extras. You won't hear Beatles music in the lobby (standard Db-officially £200, but often £120-160 Fri-Sat and £90-120 Sun-Thu; fancier and pricier deluxe rooms and suites available, breakfast-£12.50 if you prebook, elevator, some rooms handicap accessible, parking-£10, 40 Hope Street, tel. 0151/709-3000, www.hopestreethotel.co.uk, sleep@hopestreethotel.co.uk).

$$$ Hard Day's Night Hotel is the ideal splurge for Beatles pilgrims. Located in a carefully restored old building smack in the heart of the Cavern Quarter, its decor is purely Beatles, from its public spaces (lobby, lounge, bar, restaurant) to its 110 rooms, each with a different original Beatles portrait by New York artist Shannon. There's often live music in the afternoons in the lobby bar—and it's not all Beatles covers. What could have been a tacky travesty is instead tasteful, with a largely black-and-white color scheme and subtle nods to the Fab Four (standard Db-£90-150, deluxe Db-£20 more, prices can spike dramati-

Sleep Code

Abbreviations **(£1=about $1.60, country code: 44)**
S=Single, **D**=Double/Twin, **T**=Triple, **Q**=Quad, **b**=bathroom
Price Rankings
$$$ Higher Priced—Most rooms £90 or more
$$ Moderately Priced—Most rooms £45-90
$ Lower Priced—Most rooms £45 or less
Unless noted otherwise, credit cards are accepted, and free Wi-Fi and/or a guest computer is generally available. Prices change; verify current rates online or by email. For the best prices, always book directly with the hotel.

cally during peak times, especially busy for Sat weddings in their own wedding chapel/reception hall, breakfast-£16, £10 if you prebook, air-con, elevator, Internet-enabled TVs with music playlists, parking-£10.50/day, Central Building, North John Street, tel. 0151/236-1964, www.harddaysnighthotel.com, enquiries@harddaysnighthotel.com).

$$ Aachen Guest Accommodations has 15 modern, straightforward rooms in an old Georgian townhouse on a pleasant street just uphill from the heart of downtown (Sb-£45-65, D-£49-85, Db-£59-95, Tb-£95-130, rates depend on demand—higher price is usually for weekends, includes breakfast, 89-91 Mount Pleasant, tel. 0151/709-3477, www.aachenhotel.co.uk, enquiries@aachenhotel.co.uk).

$$ Best Western Feathers Hotel, nearly next door in a stately old Georgian building, has tight hallways and 82 small rooms with mod decor and amenities (Db-generally around £69-79 Sun-Thu, £99-109 Fri, £149-159 Sat, breakfast-£10 if you prebook, no elevator and six floors, parking-£10, 115 Mount Pleasant, tel. 0151/709-9655, www.feathers.uk.com, feathersreception@feathers.uk.com).

$$ Sir Thomas Hotel is a centrally located hotel that was once a bank. The lobby has been redone in trendy style, and the 39 rooms are comfortable. As windows are thin and it's a busy neighborhood, ask for a quieter room (Db-£69-85 Sun-Thu, £91-151 Fri-Sat, little difference between "standard" and "superior" rooms, one stately "luxury" room with heavy decor available, some rates include breakfast—otherwise £10, elevator, parking-£8.50/day, 10-minute walk from station, 24 Sir Thomas Street at the corner of Victoria Street, tel. 0151/236-1366, www.sirthomashotel.co.uk, reservations@sirthomashotel.co.uk).

$$ Premier Inn, which has 186 pleasant, American-style rooms and a friendly staff, is inside the giant converted warehouses on the Albert Dock; many rooms have exposed brick from the original structure (Db-£68-140, averages £70-80 on weekdays, check website for specific rates and special deals, breakfast-£8.75, elevator, pay Wi-Fi, discounted parking in nearby garage-£8.50/day, next to The Beatles Story, tel. 0151/702-6320, www.premierinn.com). There's also a second, downtown **$$ Premier Inn** with 165 rooms. While it's farther from the Albert Dock sights, it's just a 10-minute walk from the Lime Street train station and handy to downtown (Db-£55-145, Vernon Street, just off Dale Street, tel. 0151/242-7650). A third location is on Hanover Street, near the Liverpool One mall. These places can fill up quickly on weekends.

$$ Holiday Inn Express has a branch at the Albert Dock, next door and nearly identical to the Premier Inn described above. Its 135 rooms are a smidge more basic than the Premier Inn's; you might as well check both hotels' websites to see which has the better deal going (Db-generally around £70-100 Sun-Thu, £125-135 Fri-Sat, includes buffet breakfast, nearby parking-£7.50/day, beyond The Beatles Story at the Albert Dock, tel. 0844-875-7575, www.holidayinnexpressliverpool.com, enquiries@exliverpool.com).

$ International Inn Hostel, run by the daughter of the Beatles' first manager, rents 100 budget beds in a former Victorian warehouse (Db-£38-47, bed in 2- to 10-bed room-£17-22, includes sheets, all rooms have bathrooms, guest kitchen with free toast and tea/coffee available 24 hours, laundry room, game room/TV lounge, video library, 24-hour reception, 4 South Hunter Street, tel. 0151/709-8135, www.internationalinn.co.uk, info@internationalinn.co.uk). From the Lime Street Station, the hostel is an easy 15-minute walk; if taking a taxi, tell them it's on South Hunter Street near Hardman Street.

Eating in Liverpool

Liverpool has an exciting and quickly evolving culinary scene; as a rollicking, youthful city, it's a magnet for creative chefs as well as upscale chain restaurants. I've arranged my listings by neighborhood. Consider my suggestions, but also browse the surrounding streets. This is a city where restaurant-finding is a joy rather than a chore. Note that many places tend to close down a bit earlier on Sundays.

ON AND NEAR HOPE STREET

Hope Street, which connects the two cathedrals, is also home to several excellent restaurants. The Quarter, HOST, and 60 Hope Street—which cluster near the corner of Hope and Falkner streets—are owned by brothers.

The Quarter serves up Mediterranean food at rustic tables that sprawl through several connected houses. It's trendy but cozy. They also serve breakfast and have carryout coffee, cakes, pasta, and sandwiches in their attached deli (£4-7 starters, £8-11 pizzas and pastas, chalkboard specials, daily 9:00-23:00, 7 Falkner Street, tel. 0151/707-1965).

HOST (short for "Hope Street") features Asian fusion dishes in a casual, colorful, modern atmosphere. There are gluten-free and vegan options here (£4-6 small plates, £10-13 big plates, daily 11:00-23:00, 31 Hope Street, tel. 0151/708-5831).

Jenever is a little one-room bistro specializing in tapas and 65 varieties of gin. While there's also beer and wine, you can't help but try one of their gin cocktails or splurge on a four-flight gin tasting menu (£8 for two tapas, £10 for three, £5 lunch special, kitchen open Mon-Sat 12:00-21:00, Sun until 20:00, bar open later, 29a Hope Street, tel. 0151/707-7888).

60 Hope Street has modern English cuisine made with "as locally sourced as possible" ingredients in an upscale atmosphere. While the prices are high (£9-11 starters, £19-30 main dishes), their fixed-price meals are a good deal (£20/two courses, £25/three courses, £15 afternoon tea, open Mon-Sat 12:00-14:30 & 17:00-22:30, Sun 12:00-20:00, reservations smart—especially on weekends, 60 Hope Street, tel. 0151/707-6060, www.60hopestreet.com).

Chinatown: A few blocks southwest of Hope Street is Liverpool's thriving Chinatown neighborhood, with the world's biggest Chinese arch. Lots of enticing options dishing up Chinese grub line up along Berry Street in front of the arch and Cornwallis Street behind it. Among these, **Yuet Ben** is one of the most established (Tue-Sun 17:00-23:00, closed Mon, facing the arch at 1 Upper Duke Street, tel. 0151/709-5772). Or you can line up with the Liverpudlians at **Tokyou,** featuring tasty £5 noodle and rice dishes (Cantonese, Japanese, Malaysian, etc.), with service that's fast and furious (daily 12:30-23:30, 7 Berry Street, tel. 0151/445-1023).

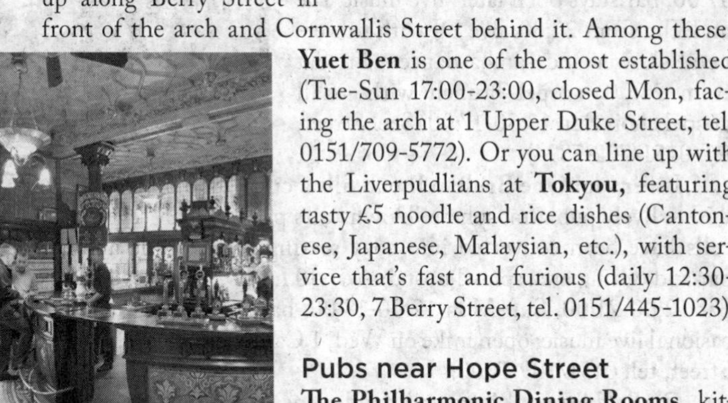

Pubs near Hope Street

The Philharmonic Dining Rooms, kitty-corner from the actual Philharmonic, is actually a pub—but what a pub. This place wins the "atmosphere award" for its old-time elegance. The bar is a work of art, the marble urinals are downright genteel, and the three sitting areas on the ground floor (including the giant hall) are an enticing place to sip a pint. This is a better place to drink than to eat, as food is usually served in the less-atmospheric upstairs. John Lennon once said that his biggest regret about fame was "not being able to go to the Phil for a drink" (£8-15 pub grub, food served daily 11:00-22:00, bar open until late, corner of Hope and Hardman streets, tel. 0151/707-2837).

The Fly in the Loaf has a classic pub exterior and interior, with efficient service, eight hand pulls for real ales, and good food (£3-5 sandwiches, £7-9 meals, food served daily 12:00-18:45, bar open until late, 13 Hardman Street, tel. 0151/708-0817).

ROPEWALKS

While primarily a nightlife zone, this gentrified area also has a smattering of unique restaurants—including one in a former church, and another in a former police station.

Alma de Cuba is housed in the former Polish Catholic Church of St. Peter's with a trendy bar (downstairs, in the nave and altar area) and restaurant (upstairs, looking down into the nave). While the food (an eclectic international mix) is an afterthought, the "hedonists' church" atmosphere is nothing short of remarkable—at least to those who don't find it all a bit sacrilegious. To keep out the stag parties, no male groups of five or more are allowed to enter (£5-9 starters, £14-20 main dishes; food served daily 12:00-22:00, tapas until 17:00, bar stays open later; live music Tue and Thu from 22:30, live DJ with flower-petal shower and samba dancers Fri-Sat from 23:00, gospel brunch with small gospel choir Sun 13:30-17:00; Seel Street, tel. 0151/702-7394).

Liverpool One Bridewell pub fills a circa-1850 police station with a lively pub atmosphere. Downstairs past the bar, several jail cells have been converted into cozy seating areas, while another bar and dining area sprawl upstairs (£7-10 meals; food served Tue-Sat 12:00-21:00, Sun-Mon 12:00-18:00, bar stays open later; occasional live music, open mike on Wed, 1 Campbell Square, Argyle Street, tel. 0151/709-7000).

On Bold Street: Liverpool's food scene is starting to percolate on this street between the pedestrian shopping zone and the Hope Street neighborhood. Look for trendy tapas, Middle Eastern, and Italian eateries. Check out **Leaf,** which started as a teahouse and now offers a range of inventive breakfast, lunch, and dinner menus (£4-6 starters and sandwiches, £9-12 main dishes, vegetarian options, daily 9:00-22:00, 65 Bold Street, tel. 0151/707-7747, www.thisisleaf.co.uk).

On Duke Street: A few big, modern, popular, chain-feeling restaurants—Japanese, Mexican, Italian, and more—line up along Duke Street in the heart of the Ropewalks area (concentrated on the block between Kent Street and the Chinatown arch). While not high cuisine, these crowd-pleasers are close to the nightlife action.

DOWNTOWN

Delifonseca is a trendy eatery with two parts. In the cellar is a small deli counter and large bar, with prepared salads sold by weight, a range of meats and cheeses, and made-to-order £3 sandwiches. Upstairs is a casual bistro serving British, Mediterranean, and international cuisine (£7-10 sandwiches and salads, £10-16 chalkboard main dishes). While not cheap, the food here is high quality (food served Tue-Sat 12:00-21:00, bar open until late, closed Sun-Mon, 12 Stanley Street, tel. 0151/255-0808).

Liverpool One: This shopping center, right in the heart of town, is nirvana for British chain restaurants. The upper Leisure Terrace has a row of some popular chains—including **Café Rouge** (French), **Wagamama Noodle Bar, Gourmet Burger Company, Pizza Express,** and more—all with outdoor seating. If you want to dine on predictable mass-produced food, you'll have a wide selection here.

AT THE ALBERT DOCK

The eateries at the Albert Dock aren't high cuisine, but they're handy to your sightseeing. A slew of trendy restaurants come alive with club energy at night, but are sedate and pleasant in the afternoon and early evening. For lunch near the sights, consider the café in the **Tate Gallery** (£3-4 sandwiches and soups, £6-9 main dishes, daily 10:00-16:30).

Liverpool Connections

BY TRAIN

Note that many connections from Liverpool transfer at the Wigan North Western Station, which is on a major north-south train line.

From Liverpool by Train to: Keswick/Lake District (train to Penrith—roughly hourly with change in Wigan and possibly elsewhere, 2.5 hours; then bus to Keswick), **York** (1/hour direct, 2.5 hours, more with transfer), **Edinburgh** (1-2/hour, 4-4.5 hours, most change in Wigan or Manchester), **Glasgow** (1-2/hour, 3.5-

4.5 hours, change in Wigan and possibly elsewhere), **London**'s Euston Station (at least hourly, 2-2.5 hours, more with changes), **Crewe** (3/hour, 45 minutes), **Chester** (3/hour, 45 minutes). Train info: Tel. 0345-748-4950, www.nationalrail.co.uk.

BY FERRY

By Ferry to Dublin, Republic of Ireland: P&O Irish Sea Ferries runs a car ferry only—no foot passengers (1-3/day, 7.5-hour trip, prices vary widely—roughly £150 for car and 2 passengers, overnight ferry includes berth and meals, 20-minute drive north of the city center at Liverpool Freeport—Gladstone dock, check in 1-2 hours before departure, tel. 0871-664-4777, www.poirishsea.com). Those without cars can take a ferry to Dublin via the Isle of Man (runs mid-June-Aug, www.steam-packet.com), or ride the train to North Wales and catch the Dublin ferry from Holyhead (www.stenaline.co.uk).

By Ferry to Belfast, Northern Ireland: Ferries sail from nearby Birkenhead roughly twice a day (8.5 hours, fares vary widely, tel. 0871-230-0330, www.stenaline.co.uk). Birkenhead's dock is a 15-minute walk from Hamilton Square Station on Merseyrail's Wirral Line.

THE LAKE DISTRICT

Keswick • North Lake District • Ullswater Lake • South Lake District

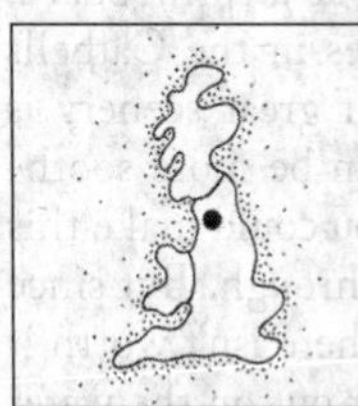

In the pristine Lake District, William Wordsworth's poems still shiver in trees and ripple on ponds. Nature rules this land, and humanity keeps a wide-eyed but low profile. Relax, recharge, take a cruise or a hike, and maybe even write a poem. Renew your poetic license at Wordsworth's famous Dove Cottage.

The Lake District, about 30 miles long and 30 miles wide, is nature's lush, green playground. Explore it by foot, bike, bus, or car. While not impressive in sheer height (Scafell Pike, the tallest peak in England, is only 3,206 feet), there's a walking-stick charm about the way nature and culture mix here. Locals are fond of declaring that their mountains are older than the Himalayas and were once as tall, but have been worn down by the ages. Walking along a windblown ridge or climbing over a rock fence to look into the eyes of a ragamuffin sheep, even tenderfeet get a chance to feel very outdoorsy. The tradition of staying close to the land remains true—albeit in an updated form—in the 21st century; you'll see restaurants serving organic food as well as stickers advocating for environmental causes in the windows of homes.

Dress in layers, and expect rain mixed with brilliant "bright spells" (pubs offer atmospheric shelter at every turn). Drizzly days can be followed by delightful evenings.

Plan to spend the majority of your time in the unspoiled North Lake District. In this chapter, I focus on the town of Keswick, the lake called Derwentwater, and the vast, time-passed Newlands Valley. The North Lake District works great by car or by bus (with easy train access via Penrith), delights nature lovers, and has good accommodations to boot.

The South Lake District—slightly closer to London—is

famous primarily for its Wordsworth and Beatrix Potter sights, and gets the promotion, the tour crowds, and the tackiness that comes with them. While the slate-colored towns (Ambleside, Windermere, Bowness-on-Windermere, and so on) are cute, they're also touristy—which means crowded and overpriced. I strongly recommend that you buck the trend and focus on the north. Ideally, enter the region from the north, via Penrith. Make your home base in or near Keswick, and side-trip from here into the South Lake District only if you're interested in the Wordsworth and Beatrix Potter sights. Dipping into the South Lake District also works well en route if you're driving between Keswick and points south.

PLANNING YOUR TIME

I'd suggest spending two days and two nights in this area. Penrith is the nearest train station, just 45 minutes by bus or car from Keswick. Those without a car will use Keswick as a springboard: Cruise the lake and take one of the many hikes in the Catbells area. Nonhikers can hop on a minibus tour. If great scenery is commonplace in your life, the Lake District can be more soothing (and rainy) than exciting. If you're rushed, you could make this area a one-night stand—or even a quick drive-through. But since the towns themselves are unexceptional, a visit here isn't worth it unless you have time to head up into the hills or out on the water at least once.

Two-Day Driving Plan: Here's the most exciting way for drivers coming from the south—who'd like to visit South Lake District sights en route to the North Lake District—to max out their time here:

Day 1: Get an early start, aiming to leave the motorway at Kendal by 10:30; drive along Windermere, the lake, and through the town of Ambleside.

11:30 Tour Dove Cottage and the Wordsworth Museum.

13:00 Backtrack to Ambleside, where a small road leads up and over the dramatic Kirkstone Pass (far more scenic northbound than southbound—get out and bite the wind) and down to Glenridding on Lake Ullswater.

15:00 Catch the next Ullswater boat and ride to Howtown. Hike six miles (3-4 hours) from Howtown back to Glenridding. Or, for a shorter Ullswater experience, hike up to the Aira Force waterfall (1 hour) or up and around Lanty's Tarn (2-2.5 hours).

19:00 Drive to your Keswick hotel or farmhouse B&B near Keswick, with a stop as the sun sets at Castlerigg Stone Circle.

Day 2: Spend the morning (3-4 hours) splicing the Catbells high-ridge hike into a circular boat trip around Derwentwater. In the afternoon, make the circular drive from Keswick through the Newlands Valley, Buttermere, Honister Pass, and Borrowdale. You could tour the Honister Slate Mine en route (last tour at 15:30) and/or pitch-and-putt nine holes in Keswick before a late dinner.

GETTING AROUND THE LAKE DISTRICT

By Car

Nothing is very far from Keswick and Derwentwater. Pick up a good map (any hotel can loan you one), get off the big roads, and leave the car, at least occasionally, for some walking. In summer, the Keswick-Ambleside-Windermere-Bowness corridor (A-591) suffers from congestion. Back lanes are far less trampled and lead you through forgotten villages, where sheep outnumber people and stone churchyards are filled with happily permanent residents.

To **rent a car** here, try Enterprise in Penrith. They'll pick you up in Keswick and drive you back to their office to get the car, and also drive you back to Keswick after you've dropped it off (Mon-Fri 8:00-18:00, Sat 9:00-12:00, closed Sun, requires drivers license and second form of ID, reserve a day in advance, located at the David Hayton Peugeot dealer, Haweswater Road, tel. 01768/893-840). Larger outfits are more likely to have a branch in Carlisle, which is a bit to the north but well-served by train (on the same Glasgow-Birmingham line as Penrith) and only a few minutes farther from the Keswick area.

Parking is tight throughout the region. It's easiest to park in the pay-and-display lots (generally about £3/2-3 hours, £5/4-5 hours, and £7/12 hours; have coins on hand, as most machines don't make change or won't take credit cards without a chip). If you're parking for free on the roadside, don't block vital turnouts. Never park on double yellow lines.

Without a Car

Those based in Keswick without a car manage fine. Because of the region's efforts to "green up" travel and cut down on car traffic, the bus service is quite efficient for hiking and sightseeing. (Consider leaving your car in town and using the bus for many sightseeing and hiking agendas.)

By Bus: Keswick has no real bus station; buses stop at a turnout in front of the Booths Supermarket. Local buses take you quickly and easily (if not always frequently) to all nearby points of interest.

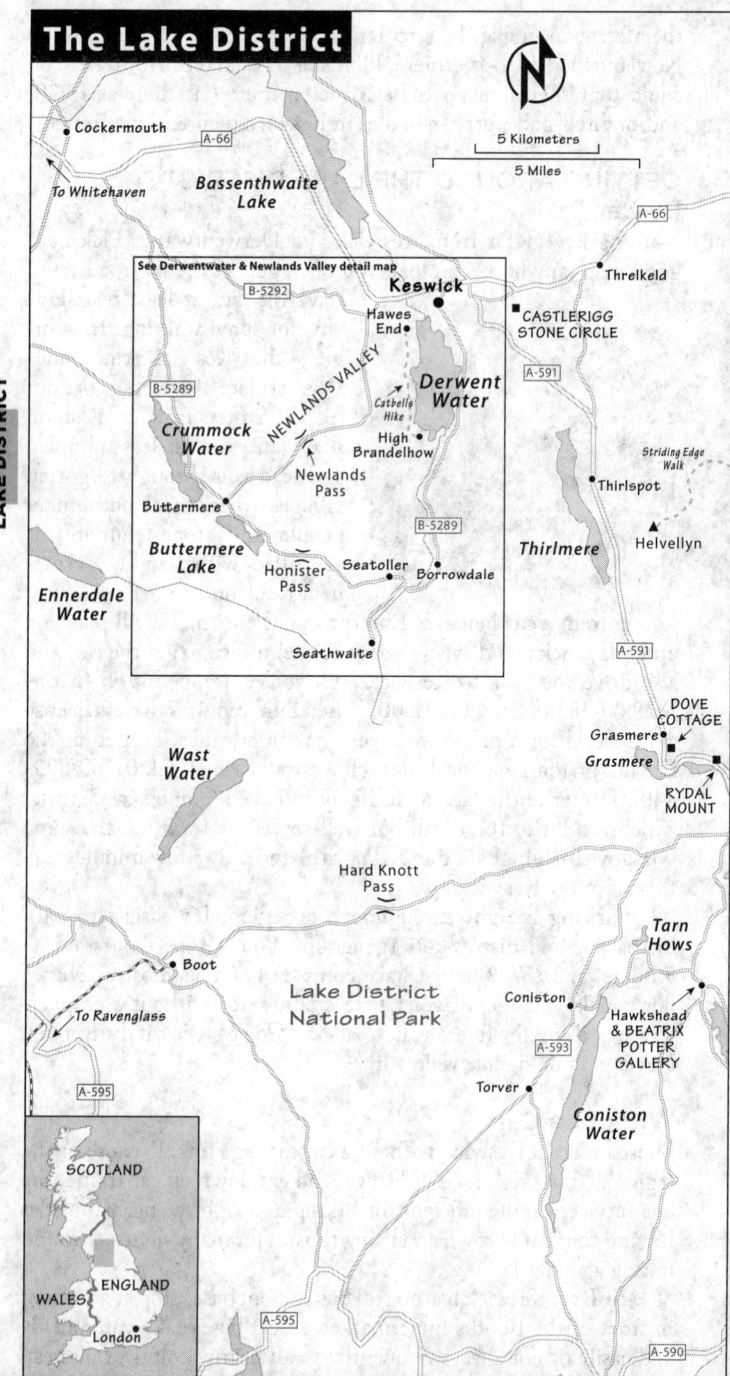

The Lake District
5 Kilometers
5 Miles
Cockermouth
To Whitehaven
A-66
Bassenthwaite Lake
A-66
Threlkeld
See Derwentwater & Newlands Valley detail map
B-5292
Keswick
Hawes End
CASTLERIGG STONE CIRCLE
NEWLANDS VALLEY
A-591
B-5289
Derwent Water
Catbells Hike
Crummock Water
High Brandelhow
Newlands Pass
Striding Edge Walk
Thirlspot
Buttermere
B-5289
Helvellyn
Buttermere Lake
Honister Pass
Seatoller
Borrowdale
Thirlmere
Ennerdale Water
Seathwaite
A-591
DOVE COTTAGE
Grasmere
Grasmere
Wast Water
RYDAL MOUNT
Hard Knott Pass
Tarn Hows
Boot
Lake District National Park
Coniston
Hawkshead & BEATRIX POTTER GALLERY
To Ravenglass
A-593
Torver
A-595
Coniston Water
SCOTLAND
ENGLAND
WALES
London
A-595
A-590

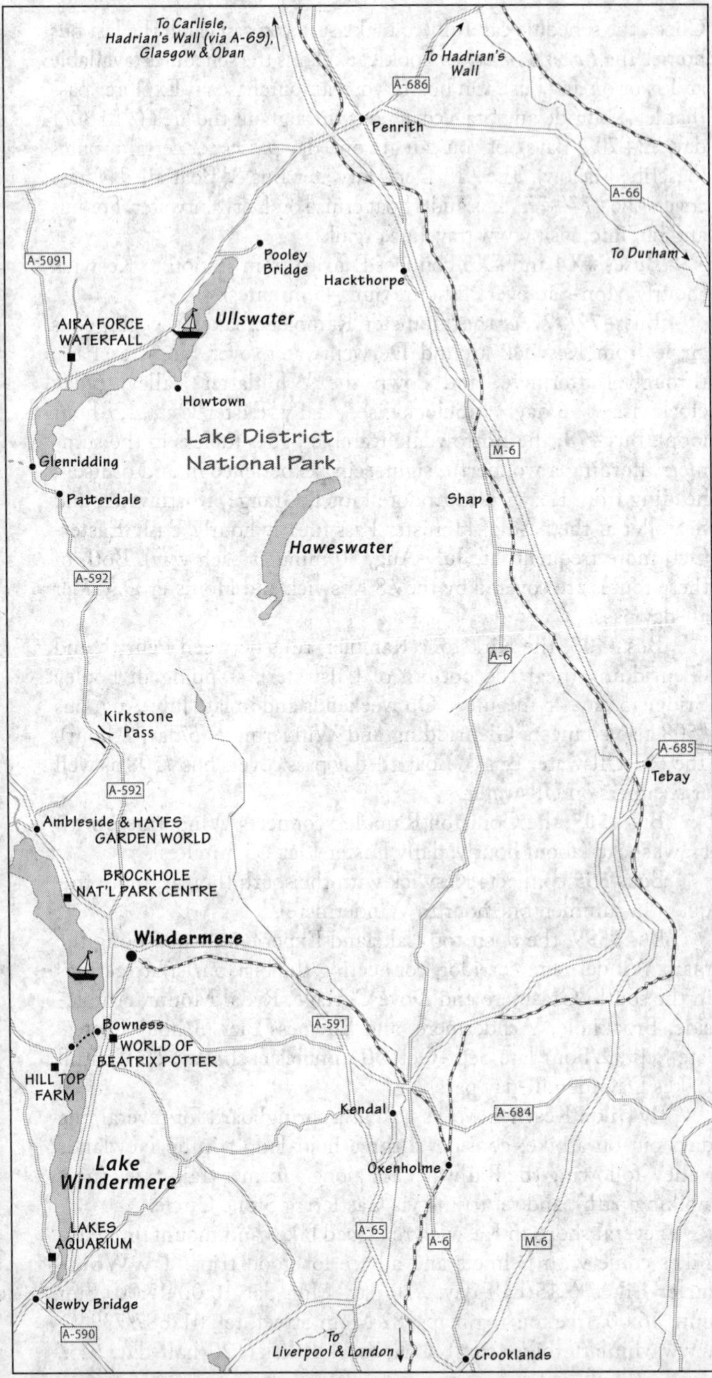

To Carlisle, Hadrian's Wall (via A-69), Glasgow & Oban
To Hadrian's Wall
A-686
Penrith
A-66
To Durham
A-5091
Pooley Bridge
Hackthorpe
AIRA FORCE WATERFALL
Ullswater
Howtown
Lake District National Park
Glenridding
M-6
Patterdale
Shap
Haweswater
A-592
A-6
Kirkstone Pass
A-685
Tebay
A-592
Ambleside & HAYES GARDEN WORLD
BROCKHOLE NAT'L PARK CENTRE
Windermere
Bowness
A-591
WORLD OF BEATRIX POTTER
HILL TOP FARM
Kendal
A-684
Oxenholme
Lake Windermere
A-65
A-6
M-6
LAKES AQUARIUM
Newby Bridge
A-590
To Liverpool & London
Crooklands

Check the schedule carefully to make sure you can catch the last bus home. The *Lakes Connection* booklet explains the schedules (available at TIs or on any bus). On board, you can purchase an Explorer pass that lets you ride any Stagecoach bus throughout the area (£10.80/1 day, £24.70/3 days), or you can get one-day passes for certain routes (described below). The £13 Derwentwater Bus & Boat all-day pass covers the #77/#77A bus and a boat cruise on Derwentwater. For bus and rail info, visit www.traveline.org.uk.

Buses **#X4** and **#X5** connect Penrith train station to Keswick (hourly Mon-Sat, every 2 hours Sun, 45 minutes).

Bus **#77/#77A,** the Honister Rambler, makes the gorgeous circle from Keswick around Derwentwater, over Honister Pass, through Buttermere, and down the Whinlatter Valley (6/day clockwise, 5-6/day "anticlockwise," daily Easter-Oct, 1.5-hour loop). Bus **#78,** the Borrowdale Rambler, goes topless in the summer, affording a wonderful sightseeing experience in and of itself, heading from Keswick to Lodore Hotel, Grange, Rosthwaite, and Seatoller at the base of Honister Pass (nearly hourly, daily Easter-Oct, more frequent late July-Aug, 30 minutes each way). Both of these routes are covered by the £8 Keswick and Honister Dayrider all-day pass.

Bus **#508,** the Kirkstone Rambler, runs between Penrith and Glenridding (near the bottom of Ullswater), stopping in Pooley Bridge (5/day, 45 minutes). On weekends and in late July-Aug, bus #508 also connects Glenridding and Windermere (5/day, 1 hour). The £15 Ullswater Bus & Boat all-day pass covers bus #508 as well as steamers on Ullswater.

Bus **#505,** the Coniston Rambler, connects Windermere with Hawkshead (about hourly, daily Easter-Oct, 35 minutes).

Bus **#555** connects Keswick with the south (hourly, more frequent in summer, one hour to Windermere).

Bus **#599,** the open-top Lakeland Experience, runs along the main Windermere corridor, connecting the big tourist attractions in the south: Grasmere and Dove Cottage, Rydal Mount, Ambleside, Brockhole, Windermere, and Bowness Pier (3/hour Easter-late Sept, 2/hour late Sept-Oct, 50 minutes each way, £8 Central Lakes Dayrider all-day pass).

By Bike: Keswick works well as a springboard for several fine days out on a bike; consider a three-hour loop trip up Newlands Valley, following the Railway Path along a former train track (now a biking path), and returning via Castlerigg Stone Circle.

Several shops in Keswick rent road bikes and mountain bikes. Bikes come with helmets and advice for good trips. Try **Whinlatter Bikes** (£15/half-day, £20/day, Mon-Sat 10:00-17:00, Sun until 16:00, free touring maps, 82 Main Street, tel. 017687/73940, www.whinlatterbikes.com) or **Keswick Bikes** (£20/half-day, £25/

day, daily 9:00-17:30, 133 Main Street, tel. 017687/73355, www.keswickbikes.co.uk).

By Boat: A circular boat service glides you around Derwentwater, with several hiker-aiding stops along the way (for a cruise/hike option, see "Derwentwater Lakeside Walk" on page 499).

By Foot: Hiking information is available everywhere. Don't hike without a good, detailed map (wide selection at Keswick TI and at the many outdoor gear stores, or borrow one from your B&B). Helpful fliers at TIs and B&Bs describe the most popular routes. For an up-to-date weather report, ask at a TI or call 0844-846-2444. Wear suitable clothing and footwear (you can rent boots in town; B&Bs can likely loan you a good coat or an umbrella if weather looks threatening). Plan for rain. Watch your footing. Injuries are common. Every year, several people die while hiking in the area (some from overexertion; others are blown off ridges).

By Tour: For organized bus tours that run the roads of the Lake District, see "Tours in Keswick," later.

Keswick and the North Lake District

As far as touristy Lake District towns go, Keswick (KEZ-ick, population 5,000) is far more enjoyable than Windermere, Bowness, or Ambleside. Many of the place names around Keswick have Norse origins, inherited from the region's 10th-century settlers. Notice that most lakes in the region end in either *water* (e.g., Derwentwater) or *mere* (e.g., Windermere), which is related to the German word for lake, *Meer.*

An important mining center for slate, copper, and lead through the Middle Ages, Keswick became a resort in the 19th century. Its fine Victorian buildings recall those Romantic days when city slickers first learned about "communing with nature." Today, the compact town is lined with tearooms, pubs, gift shops, and hiking-gear shops. The lake called Derwentwater is a pleasant 10-minute walk from the town center.

The Lake District at a Glance

North Lake District

In Keswick

▲▲Theatre by the Lake Top-notch theater a pleasant stroll from Keswick's main square. **Hours:** Shows generally at 20:00 in summer, possibly earlier fall through spring; box office open daily 9:30-20:00. See page 508.

▲Derwentwater Lake immediately south of Keswick, with good boat service and trails. See page 498.

▲Pencil Museum Paean to graphite-filled wooden sticks. **Hours:** Daily 9:30-17:00. See page 499.

▲Pitch-and-Putt Golf Cheap, easygoing nine-hole course in Keswick's Hope Park. **Hours:** Daily from 10:00, last start at 18:00 but possibly later in summer, closed Nov-Feb. See page 500.

Near Keswick

▲▲▲Scenic Circle Drive South of Keswick Hour-long drive through the best of the Lake District's scenery, with plenty of fun stops (including the fascinating Honister Slate Mine) and short side-trip options. See page 504.

▲▲Castlerigg Stone Circle Evocative and extremely old (even by British standards) ring of Neolithic stones. See page 500.

▲▲Catbells High Ridge Hike Two-hour hike along dramatic ridge southwest of Keswick. See page 501.

▲▲Buttermere Hike Four-mile, low-impact lakeside loop in a gorgeous setting. See page 503.

▲Honister Slate Mine Tour A 1.5-hour guided hike through a 19th-century mine at the top of Honister Pass. **Hours:** Daily at

Orientation to Keswick

Keswick is an ideal home base, with plenty of good B&Bs, an easy bus connection to the nearest train station at Penrith, and a prime location near the best lake in the area, Derwentwater. In Keswick, everything is within a 10-minute walk of everything else: the pedestrian town square, the TI, recommended B&Bs, grocery stores, the wonderful municipal pitch-and-putt golf course, the main bus stop, a lakeside boat dock, and a central parking lot. Thursdays and

10:30, 12:30, and 15:30; also at 14:00 in summer; Dec-Jan 12:30 tour only. See page 506.

Ullswater Lake Area

▲▲Ullswater Hike and Boat Ride Long lake best enjoyed via steamer boat and seven-mile walk. **Hours:** Boats generally daily 9:45-16:45, 6-9/day April-Oct, fewer off-season. See page 518.

▲▲Lanty's Tarn and Keldas Hill Moderately challenging 2.5-mile loop hike from Glenridding with sweeping views of Ullswater.

▲Aira Force Waterfall Easy uphill hike to thundering waterfall. See page 519.

South Lake District

▲▲Dove Cottage and Wordsworth Museum The poet's humble home, with a museum that tells the story of his remarkable life. **Hours:** Daily March-Oct 9:30-17:30, Nov-Feb 9:30-16:30 except closed Jan. See page 520.

▲Rydal Mount Wordsworth's later, more upscale home. **Hours:** March-Oct daily 9:30-17:00; Nov-Dec and Feb Wed-Sun 11:00-16:00, closed Mon-Tue; closed Jan. See page 523.

▲Hill Top Farm Beatrix Potter's painstakingly preserved cottage. **Hours:** June-Aug Sat-Thu 10:00-17:30, April-May and Sept-Oct Sat-Thu 10:30-16:30, mid-Feb-March Sat-Thu 10:30-15:30, closed Nov-mid-Feb and Fri year-round, often a long wait to visit—call ahead. See page 524.

▲Beatrix Potter Gallery Collection of artwork by and background on the creator of Peter Rabbit. **Hours:** April-Oct Sat-Thu 10:30-17:00, mid-Feb-March Sat-Thu 10:30-15:30, closed Fri (except possibly in summer) and Nov-mid-Feb. See page 526.

Saturdays are market days in the town square, but the square is lively every day throughout the summer.

Keswick town is a delight for wandering. Its centerpiece, Moot Hall (meaning "meeting hall"), was a 16th-century copper warehouse upstairs with an arcade below (closed after World War II; most Lake District towns and villages have similar meeting halls). "Keswick" means "cheese farm"—a legacy from the time when the town square was the spot to sell cheese. When the town square went pedestrian-only, locals were all abuzz about people tripping over the curbs. (The English, seemingly thrilled by ever-present danger, are endlessly warning visitors to "watch your head," "duck or grouse," "watch the step," and "mind the gap.")

Keswick and the Lake District are popular with English holidaymakers who prefer to bring their dogs with them on vacation. The town square in Keswick can look like the Westminster Dog Show, and the recommended Dog and Gun pub, where "well-behaved dogs are welcomed," is always full of patient pups. If you are shy about connecting with people, pal up to an English pooch—you'll often find they're happy to introduce you to their owners.

TOURIST INFORMATION

The National Park Visitors Centre/TI is in Moot Hall, right in the middle of the town square (daily Easter-Oct 9:30-17:30, Nov-Easter 9:30-16:30, tel. 017687/72645, www.lakedistrict.gov.uk and www.keswick.org). Staffers are pros at advising you about hiking routes. They can also help you figure out public transportation to outlying sights and tell you about the region's various adventure activities.

The TI sells theater tickets, Keswick Launch tickets (at a £1 discount), fishing licenses, and brochures and maps that outline nearby hikes (£1-2, including a very simple and driver-friendly *Lap Map* featuring sights, walks, and a mileage chart). The TI also has books and maps for hikers, cyclists, and drivers (more books are sold at shops all over town).

Check the boards inside the TI's foyer for information about walks, talks, and entertainment. You can also pick up the *Events and Guided Walks* guide. The daily weather forecast is posted just outside the front door (weather tel. 0844-846-2444). For information about the TI's guided walks, see "Tours in Keswick," later.

HELPFUL HINTS

Book in Advance: Keswick hosts a variety of festivals and conventions, especially during the summer, so it's smart to book ahead. Please honor your bookings—the B&B proprietors here lose out on much-needed business if you don't show up.

A sampling of events: The Keswick Jazz Festival mellows out the town in early May (www.keswickjazzfestival.co.uk), followed immediately by the Mountain Festival (www.keswickmountainfestival.co.uk), then a beer festival in early June (www.keswickbeerfestival.co.uk). The Keswick Convention packs the town with 4,000 evangelical Christians for three weeks each summer (sometime in July-Aug, www.keswickministries.org).

Several Bank Holiday Mondays in spring and summer (May 2, May 30, and Aug 29 in 2016; May 1, May 29, and Aug 28 in 2017) draw vacationers from all over the island for three-day weekends.

If you have trouble finding a room (or a B&B that accepts small children), try www.keswick.org to search for available rooms.

Internet Access: U-Compute, located between the post office and a pub, provides computer terminals and Wi-Fi (same price no matter how you connect—£2/30 minutes, £3/hour, Mon-Sat 9:00-17:30, closed Sun, Bank Street, tel. 017687/75127). The **launderette** listed next also has pay Wi-Fi.

Laundry: The town's launderette is on Bank Street, just up the side street from the post office (self-service Mon-Fri 8:00-19:00, Sat-Sun 9:00-18:00, about £8/load wash and dry, coin-op soap dispenser; full-service for a reasonable additional £1.40-2.80 fee depending on load size; pay Wi-Fi, see map on page 496, tel. 017687/75448).

Midges: Tiny biting insects called midges—similar to no-see-ums—might bug you in this region from late May through September, particularly at dawn and dusk. The severity depends on the weather since wind and sunshine can deter them, and insect repellant fends them off: Ask the locals what works if you'll be hiking.

Local Candy: Kendal mint cakes are advertised throughout this area. Basically a big, flat, mint-flavored sugar cube, these sweet, refreshing treats are worth sampling.

Tours in Keswick

BY FOOT

KR Guided Walks offers private guided hikes of varying levels of difficulty. The local guides also provide transportation from Keswick to the trailhead (£80/day, Easter-Oct, wear suitable clothing and footwear, bring lunch and water, must book in advance, tel. 017687/71302, mobile 0709-176-5860, www.keswickrambles.org.uk, booking@keswickrambles.org.uk).

TIs throughout the region also offer **free walks** led by "Voluntary Rangers" several times a month in summer (depart from Keswick TI; check schedule in the *Events and Guided Walks* guide, optional contribution welcome at end of walk).

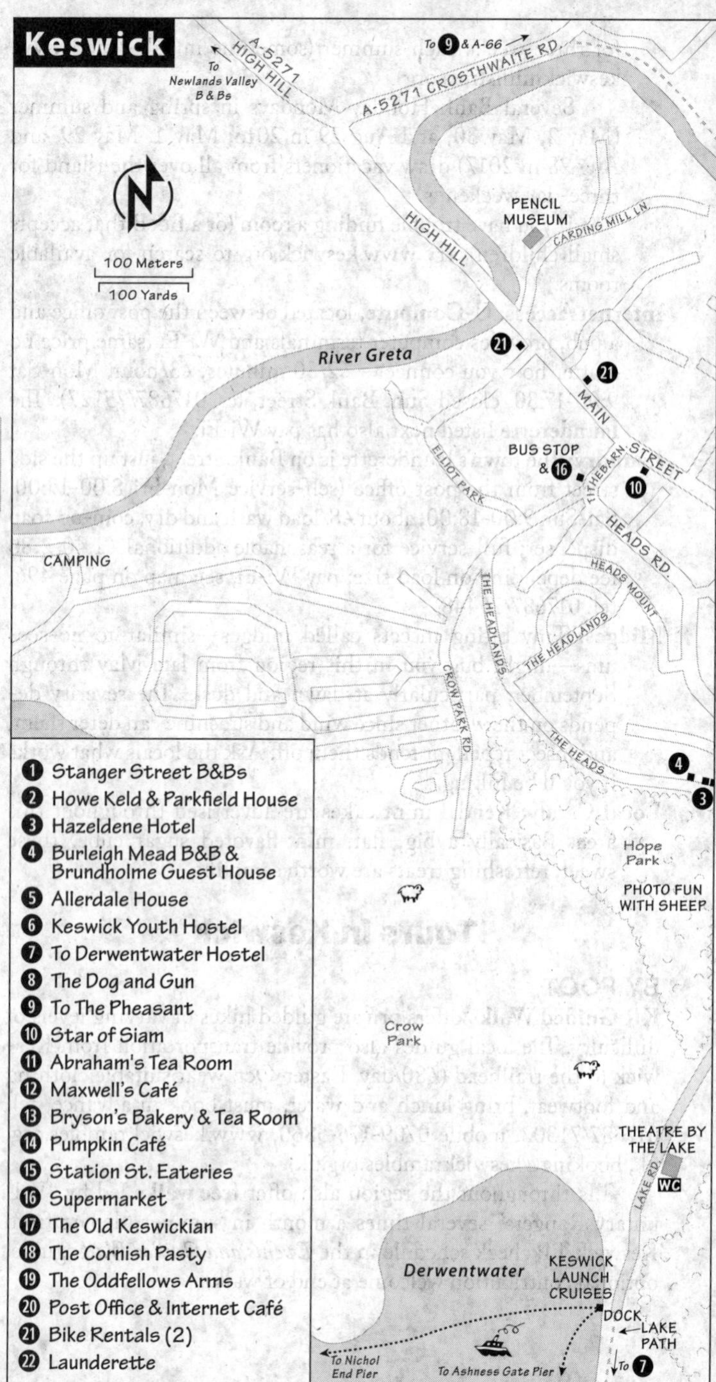

LAKE DISTRICT

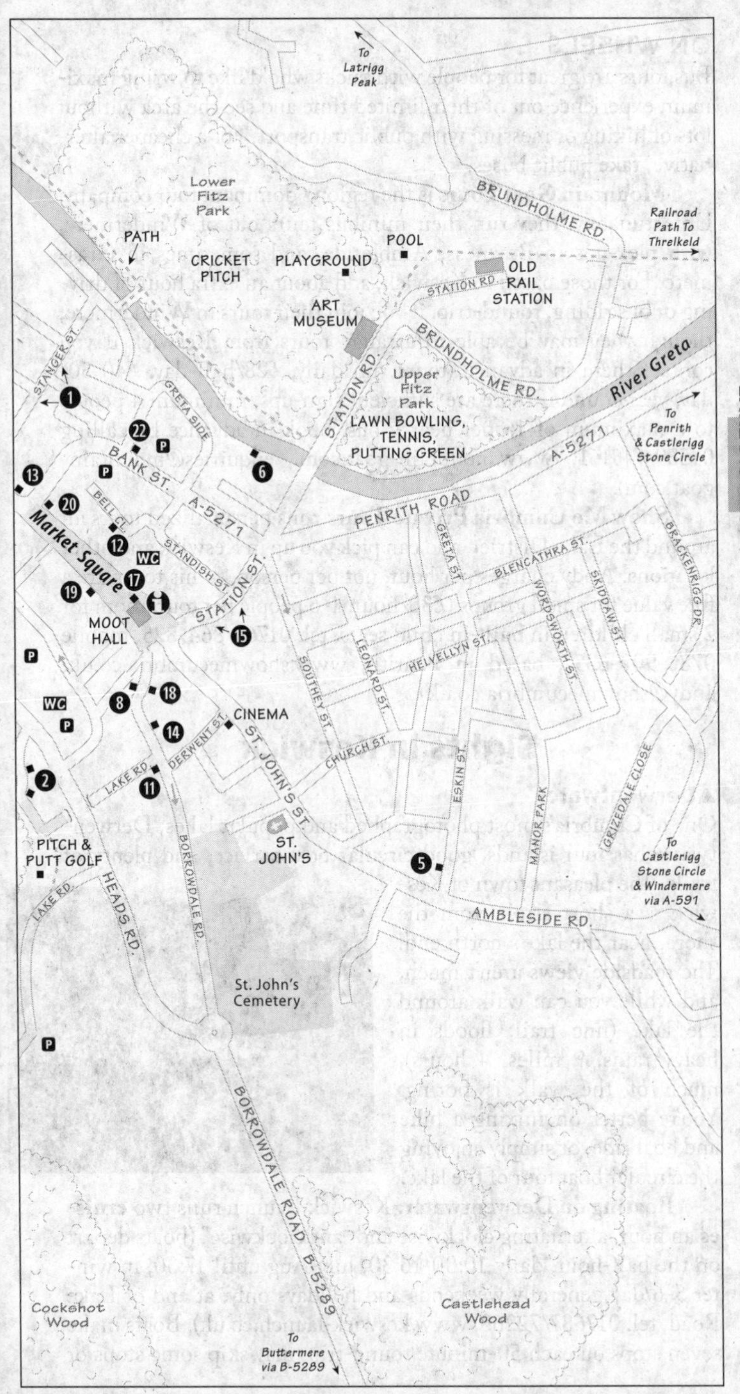
To Latrigg Peak
Lower Fitz Park
PATH
CRICKET PITCH
PLAYGROUND
POOL
BRUNDHOLME RD.
Railroad Path To Threlkeld
OLD RAIL STATION
STATION RD.
ART MUSEUM
BRUNDHOLME RD.
River Greta
STANGER ST.
GRETA SIDE
STATION RD.
Upper Fitz Park
LAWN BOWLING, TENNIS, PUTTING GREEN
To Penrith & Castlerigg Stone Circle
A-5271
BANK ST.
PENRITH ROAD
A-5271
BELL CL.
Market Square
STANDISH ST.
STATION ST.
GRETA ST.
BLENCATHRA ST.
WORDSWORTH ST.
SKIDDAW ST.
BRACKENRIGG DR.
WC
MOOT HALL
HELVELLYN ST.
LEONARD ST.
SOUTHEY ST.
WC
CINEMA
DERWENT ST.
ST. JOHN'S ST.
CHURCH ST.
LAKE RD.
ESKIN ST.
MANOR PARK
GRIZEDALE CLOSE
To Castlerigg Stone Circle & Windermere via A-591
PITCH & PUTT GOLF
ST. JOHN'S
AMBLESIDE RD.
LAKE RD.
HEADS RD.
BORROWDALE RD.
St. John's Cemetery
BORROWDALE ROAD B-5289
Cockshot Wood
Castlehead Wood
To Buttermere via B-5289
LAKE DISTRICT

ON WHEELS

Bus tours are great for people with bucks who'd like to wring maximum experience out of their limited time and see the area without lots of hiking or messing with public transport. For a cheaper alternative, take public buses.

Mountain Goat Tours is the region's dominant tour company. Unfortunately, they run their minibus tours out of Windermere, with pick-ups in Bowness, Ambleside, and sometimes in Grasmere. For those based in Keswick, add about an extra hour of driving or bus riding, round-trip, if you join their tours in Windermere, though they may be able to arrange tours from Keswick if you contact them in advance (tours run daily, £28/half-day, £40-50/day, year-round if there are sufficient sign-ups, minimum 4 people to a maximum of 16 per hearty bus, book in advance by calling 015394/45161, www.mountain-goat.com, enquiries@mountain-goat.com).

Show Me Cumbria Private Tours runs personalized tours all around the Lake District, and can pick you up in Keswick and other locations. Andy charges per hour, not per person, so his tours are a fine value for small groups (£30/hour, 1-6 people per tour, room for 2 small children in built-in child seats, tel. 01768/864-825, mobile 0780-902-6357, based in Penrith, www.showmecumbria.co.uk, andy@showmecumbria.co.uk).

Sights in Keswick

▲Derwentwater

One of Cumbria's most photographed and popular lakes, Derwentwater has four islands, good circular boat service, and plenty of trails. The pleasant town of Keswick is a short stroll from the shore, near the lake's north end. The roadside views aren't much, and while you can walk around the lake (fine trail, floods in heavy rains, 9 miles, 4 hours), much of the walk is boring. You're better off mixing a hike and boat ride, or simply enjoying the circular boat tour of the lake.

Boating on Derwentwater: Keswick Launch runs two **cruises** an hour, alternating clockwise and "anticlockwise" (boats depart on the half-hour, daily 10:00-16:30, July-Aug until 17:30, in winter 5-6/day generally weekends and holidays only, at end of Lake Road, tel. 017687/72263, www.keswick-launch.co.uk). Boats make seven stops on each 50-minute round-trip (may skip some stops or not run at all if the water level is very high—such as after a heavy rain). The boat trip costs about £2 per segment (cheaper the more segments you buy) or £10 per circle (£1 less if you book through TI) with free stopovers; you can get on and off all you want, but tickets are collected on the boat's last leg to Keswick, marking the end of your ride. If you want to hop on a #77/#77A bus and also cruise Derwentwater, the £13 Derwentwater Bus & Boat all-day pass covers both. To be picked up at a certain stop, stand at the end of the pier Gilligan-style, or the boat may not stop. See the map on page 504 for an overview of all the boat stops.

Keswick Launch also has a delightful **evening cruise** (see page 508) and rents **rowboats** for up to three people (£8/30 minutes, £12/hour, open Easter-Oct, larger rowboats and motor boats available).

Derwentwater Lakeside Walk: A trail runs all along Derwentwater, but much of it (especially the Keswick-to-Hawes End stretch) is not that interesting. The best hour-long section is the 1.5-mile path between the docks at High Brandelhow and Hawes End, where you'll stroll a level trail through peaceful trees. This walk works best in conjunction with the lake boat described above.

▲Pencil Museum

Graphite was first discovered centuries ago in Keswick. A hunk of the stuff proved great for marking sheep in the 15th century. In 1832, the first crude Keswick pencil factory opened, and the rest is history (which is what you'll learn about here). While you can't actually tour the 150-year-old factory where the famous Derwent pencils were made, you can enjoy the smell of thousands of pencils getting sharpened for the first time. The adjacent charming and kid-friendly museum is a good way to pass a rainy hour; you may even catch an artist's demonstration. Take a look at the exhibit on "war pencils," which were made for WWII bomber crews (filled with tiny maps and compasses). Relax in the theater with a 10-minute video on the pencil-manufacturing process, followed by a sleepy animated-snowman short (drawn with Rexel Cumberland pencils).

Cost and Hours: £4.75, daily 9:30-17:00, last entry one hour before closing, humble café, 3-minute walk from the town center, signposted off Main Street, tel. 017687/73626, www.pencilmuseum.co.uk.

Fitz Park

An inviting grassy park stretches alongside Keswick's tree-lined, duck-filled River Greta. There's plenty of room and a playground for kids to burn off energy. Consider an after-dinner stroll on the footpath. You may catch men in white (or frisky schoolboys in uniform) playing a game of cricket. There's the serious bowling green (where you're welcome to watch the experts play and enjoy the cheapest cuppa—i.e., tea—in town), and the public one where tourists are welcome to give lawn bowling a go. You can try tennis on a grass court or enjoy the putting green. Find the rental pavilion across the road from the art gallery (open daily Easter-Sept 10:00-17:30, longer hours July-Aug, mobile 07976-573-785).

▲Golf

A lush nine-hole pitch-and-putt golf course near the gardens in Hope Park separates the town from the lake and offers a classy, cheap, and convenient chance to golf near the birthplace of the sport. This is a great, fun, and inexpensive experience—just right after a day of touring and before dinner (£4.50 for pitch-and-putt, £3 for putting, £3.25 for 18 tame holes of "obstacle golf," daily from 10:00, last round starts around 18:00, possibly later in summer, closed Nov-Feb, café, tel. 017687/73445).

Swimming

While the leisure center doesn't have a serious adult pool, it does have an indoor pool kids love, with a huge waterslide and wave machine (swim times vary by day and by season—call or check website, no towels or suits for rent, lockers-£1 deposit, 10-minute walk from town center, follow Station Road past Fitz Park and veer left, tel. 017687/72760, www.carlisleleisure.com).

NEAR KESWICK

▲▲Castlerigg Stone Circle

For some reason, 70 percent of England's stone circles are here in Cumbria. Castlerigg is one of the best and oldest in Britain, and an easy stop for drivers. The circle—90 feet across and 5,000 years old—has 38 stones mysteriously laid out on a line between the two tallest peaks on the horizon. They served as a celestial calendar for ritual celebrations. Imagine the ambience here as ancient people filled this clearing in spring to celebrate fertility, in late summer to commemorate the harvest, and in the winter to celebrate the winter solstice and the coming renewal of light. Festival dates were dictated by how the sun rose and set in relation to the stones. The more that modern academics study this circle, the more meaning they find in the placement of the stones. The two front stones face due north, toward a cut in the mountains. The rare-for-stone-circles "sanctuary" lines

up with its center stone to mark where the sun rises on May Day. (Party!) For maximum "goose pimples" (as they say here), show up at sunset (free, open all the time, 1-mile hike from town; by car it's a 3-mile drive east of Keswick—follow brown signs, 3 minutes off the A-66, easy parking; see map on page 504).

Hikes and Drives in the North Lake District

FROM KESWICK

For an easy, flat stroll, consider the trail that runs alongside Derwentwater (see page 499). More involved options are described below.

▲▲Catbells High Ridge Hike

For a great "king of the mountain" feeling, 360-degree views, and a close-up look at the weather blowing over the ridge, hike above Derwentwater about two hours from Hawes End up along the ridge to Catbells (1,480 feet) and down to High Brandelhow. Because the mountaintop is basically treeless, you're treated to dramatic panoramas the entire way up. From High Brandelhow, you can catch the boat back to Keswick or take the easy path along the shore of Derwentwater to your Hawes End starting point. (Extending the hike farther around the lake to Lodore takes you to a waterfall, rock climbers, a fine café, and another boat dock for a convenient return to Keswick—see page 504). Note: When the water level is very high (for example, after a heavy rain), boats can't stop at Hawes End—ask at the TI or boat dock before setting out.

Catbells is probably the most dramatic family walk in the area (but wear sturdy shoes, bring a raincoat, and watch your footing). From Keswick, the lake, or your farmhouse B&B, you can see silhouetted figures hiking along this ridge.

Getting There: To reach the trailhead from Keswick, catch the "anticlockwise" boat (see "Boating on Derwentwater," earlier) and ride for 10 minutes to the second stop, Hawes End. (You can also ride to High Brandelhow and take this walk in the other direction, but I don't recommend it—two rocky scrambles along the way are easier and safer to navigate going uphill from Hawes End.) Note the schedule for your return boat ride. Drivers can park free at Hawes End, but parking is limited and the road can be hard to find—get very clear directions in town before heading out. (Hard-core hikers can walk to the foot of Catbells from Keswick via Portinscale, which takes about 40 minutes—ask your B&B or the TI for directions). The Keswick TI sells a *Catbells* brochure about the hike (£1).

The Route: The path is not signposted, but it's easy to follow, and you'll see plenty of other walkers. From Hawes End, walk away from the lake, through a kissing gate to the turn just before the car park. Then turn left and go up, up, up. After about 20 minutes, you'll hit the first of two short scrambles (where the trail vanishes into a cluster of steep rocks), which leads to a bluff. From the first little summit (great for a picnic break) and then along the ridge, you'll enjoy sweeping views of the lake on one side and of Newlands Valley on the other. The bald peak in the distance is Catbells. Broken stones crunch under each step, wind buffets your ears, clouds prowl overhead, and the sheep baa comically. To anyone looking up from the distant farmhouse B&Bs, you are but a stick figure on the ridge. Just below the summit, the trail disintegrates into another short, steep scramble. Your reward is just beyond: a magnificent hilltop perch.

After the Catbells summit, descend along the ridge to a saddle ahead. The ridge continues much higher, and while it may look like your only option, at its base a small unmarked lane with comfortable steps leads left. Unless you're up for extending the hike (see "Longer Catbells Options," next), take this path down to the lake. To get to High Brandelhow Pier, take the first left fork you come across down through a forest to the lake. When you reach Abbot's Bay, go left through a swinging gate, following a lakeside trail around a gravelly bluff to the idyllic High Brandelhow Pier, a peaceful place to wait for your boat back to Keswick. (You can pay your fare when you board.)

Longer Catbells Options: Catbells is just the first of a series of peaks, all connected by a fine ridge trail. Hardier hikers continue up to nine miles along this same ridge, enjoying valley and lake views as they arc around the Newlands Valley toward (and even down to) Buttermere. After High Spy, you can descend an easy path into Newlands Valley. The ultimate, very full day-plan would be to take a bus to Buttermere, climb Robinson, and follow the ridge around to Catbells and back to Keswick.

Latrigg Peak

For the easiest mountain-climbing sensation around, take the short drive to the Latrigg Peak parking lot just north of Keswick, and hike 15 minutes to the top of the 1,200-foot-high hill, where you'll be rewarded with a commanding view of the town, lake, and valley, all the way to the next lake over (Bassenthwaite). At the traffic circle just outside Keswick, take the A-591 Carlisle exit, then an immediate right (direction: Ormathwaite/Underscar). Take the next right, a hard right, at the *Skiddaw* sign, where a long, steep, one-lane road leads to the Latrigg car park at the end of the lane. With more time, you can walk all the way from your Keswick B&B to Latrigg and back (it's a popular evening walk for locals).

Railway Path

Right from downtown Keswick, this flat, easy, four-mile trail follows an old train track and the river to the village of Threlkeld (with two pubs). You can either walk back along the same path or loop back via the Castlerigg Stone Circle (described earlier, roughly seven miles total). The Railway Path starts behind the leisure center (as you face the center, head right and around back; pick up £1 map/guide from TI).

Walla Crag

From your Keswick B&B, a fine two-hour walk to Walla Crag offers great fell (mountain) walking and a ridge-walk experience without the necessity of a bus or car. Start by strolling along the lake to the Great Wood parking lot (or drive to this lot), and head up Cat Ghyl (where "fell runners"—trail-running enthusiasts—practice) to Walla Crag. You'll be treated to great panoramic views over Derwentwater and surrounding peaks. You can do a shorter version of this walk from the parking lot at Ashness Packhorse Bridge.

HIKES OUTSIDE KESWICK

▲▲Buttermere Hike

The ideal little lake with a lovely circular four-mile stroll offers nonstop, no-sweat Lake District beauty. If you're not a hiker (but kind of wish you were), take this walk. If you're very short on time, at least stop here and get your shoes dirty.

Buttermere is connected with Borrowdale and Derwentwater by a great road that runs over rugged Honister Pass. Buses #77/#77A make a 1.5-hour round-trip loop between Keswick and Buttermere that includes a trip over this pass. The two-pub hamlet of Buttermere has a pay-and-display parking lot, but many drivers park for free along the side of the road. There's also a pay parking lot at the Honister Pass end of the lake (at Gatesgarth Farm). The

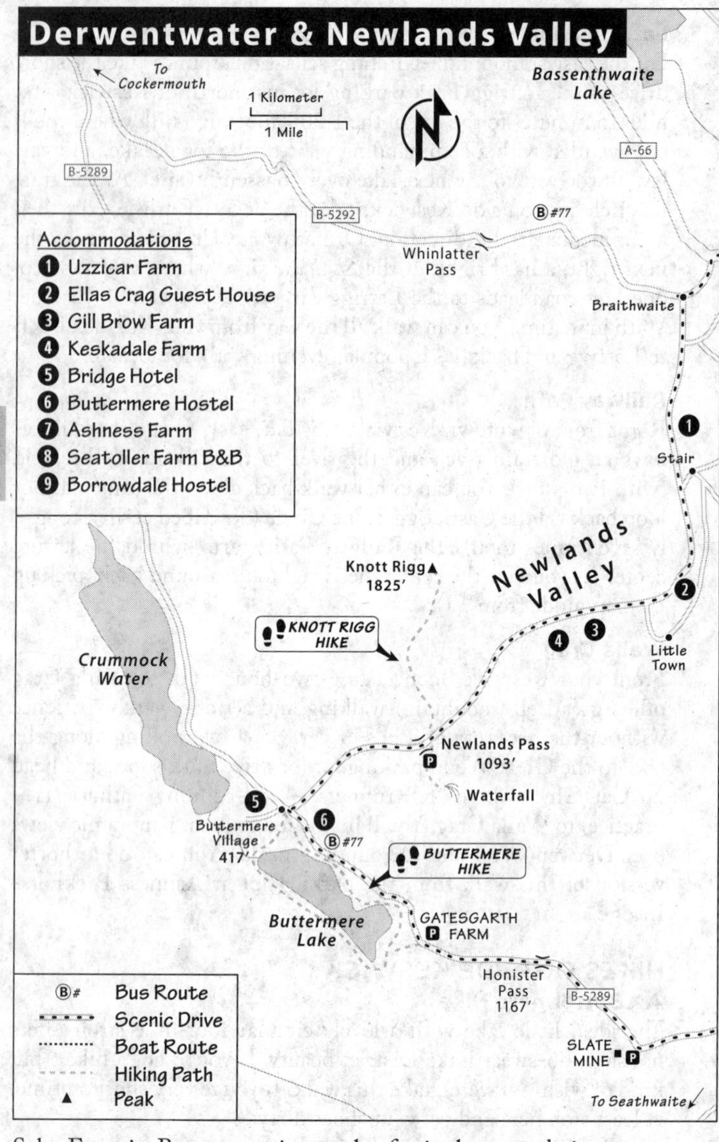

Syke Farm in Buttermere is popular for its homemade ice cream (tel. 017687/70277).

CAR HIKING

▲▲▲Scenic Circle Drive South of Keswick

This hour-long drive, which includes Newlands Valley, Buttermere, Honister Pass, and Borrowdale, gives you the best scenery you'll find in the North Lake District. (To do a similar route without a

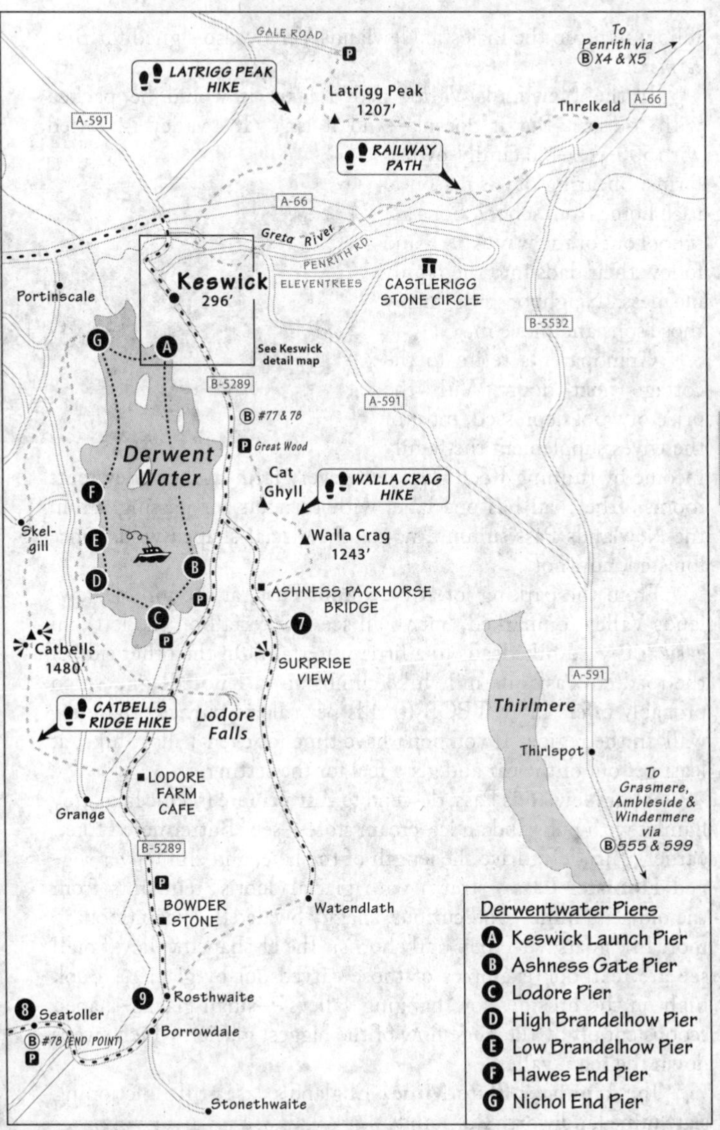

car from Keswick, take loop bus #77/#77A.) Distances are short, roads are narrow and have turnouts, and views are rewarding. Get a good map and ask your B&B host for advice. (For an overview of the route, see map above).

From Keswick, leave town on Crosthwaite Road, then, at the roundabout, head west on Cockermouth Road (A-66, following *Cockermouth* and *Workington* signs). Don't take the first Newlands Valley exit, but do take the second one (through Braithwaite), and

LAKE DISTRICT

follow signs up the majestic Newlands Valley (also signed for *Buttermere*).

If the **Newlands Valley** had a lake, it would be packed with tourists. But it doesn't—and it isn't. The valley is dotted with 500-year-old family-owned farms. Shearing day is reason to rush home from school. Sons get school out of the way ASAP and follow their dads into the family business. Neighbor girls marry those sons and move in.

Grandparents retire to the cottage next door. With the price of wool depressed, most of the wives supplement the family income by running B&Bs (virtually every farm in the valley rents rooms). The road has one lane, with turnouts for passing. From the Newlands Pass summit, notice the glacial-shaped wilds, once forested, now not.

From the parking lot at **Newlands Pass,** at the top of Newlands Valley (unmarked, but you'll see a waterfall on the left), an easy 300-yard hike leads to a little waterfall. On the other side of the road, an easy one-mile hike climbs up to **Knott Rigg,** which probably offers more TPCB (thrills per calorie burned) than any walk in the region. If you don't have time for even a short hike, at least get out of the car and get a feel for the setting.

After Newlands Pass, descend to **Buttermere** (scenic lake, tiny hamlet with pubs and an ice-cream store—see "Buttermere Hike," earlier), turn left, drive the length of the lake, and climb over rugged **Honister Pass**—strewn with glacial debris, remnants from the old slate mines, and curious, shaggy Swaledale sheep (looking more like goats with their curly horns). The U-shaped valleys you'll see are textbook examples of those carved out by glaciers. Look high on the hillsides for "hanging valleys"—small glacial-shaped scoops cut off by the huge flow of the biggest glacier, which swept down the main valley.

The **Honister Slate Mine,** England's last still-functioning slate mine (and worth ▲), stands at the summit of Honister Pass. The youth hostel next to it was originally built to house miners in the 1920s. The mine offers worthwhile tours (perfect for when it's pouring outside): You'll put on a hard hat, load onto a bus for a short climb, then hike

into a shaft to learn about the region's slate industry. It's a long, stooped hike into the mountain, made interesting by the guide and punctuated by the sound of your helmet scraping against low bits of the shaft. Standing deep in the mountain, surrounded by slate scrap and the beams of 30 headlamps fluttering around like fireflies, you'll learn of the hardships of miners' lives and how "green gold" is trendy once again, making the mine viable. Even if you don't have time to take the tour, stop here for its slate-filled shop (£12.50, 1.5-hour tour; departs daily at 10:30, 12:30, and 15:30; additional tour at 14:00 in summer; Dec-Jan 12:30 tour only; call ahead to confirm times and to book a spot, helmets and lamps provided, wear good walking shoes and bring warm clothing—even in summer, café and nice WCs, tel. 017687/77230, www.honister.com).

After stark and lonely Honister Pass, drop into sweet and homey **Borrowdale,** with a few lonely hamlets and fine hikes from Seathwaite. Circling back to Keswick past Borrowdale, the B-5289 (a.k.a., the Borrowdale Valley Road) takes you past the following popular attractions.

A set of stairs leads to the top of the house-size **Bowder Stone** (signposted, a few minutes' walk off the main road). For a great lunch or snack, including tea and homemade quiche and cakes, drop into the much-loved **High Lodore Farm Café** (Easter-Oct daily 9:00-18:00, closed Nov-Easter, short drive uphill from the main road and over a tiny bridge, tel. 017687/77221). Farther along, **Lodore Falls** is a short walk from the road, behind Lodore Hotel (a nice place to stop for tea and beautiful views). **Shepherds Crag,** a cliff overlooking Lodore, was made famous by pioneer rock climbers. (Their descendants hang from little ridges on its face today.) This is serious climbing, with several fatalities a year.

A very hard right off the B-5289 (signposted *Ashness Bridge, Watendlath*) and a steep half-mile climb on a narrow lane takes you to the postcard-pretty **Ashness Packhorse Bridge,** a quintessential Lake District scene (parking lot just above on right). A half-mile farther up, park the car and hop out (parking lot on left, no sign). You'll be startled by the "surprise view" of Derwentwater—great for a lakes photo op. Continuing from here, the road gets extremely narrow en route to the hamlet of **Watendlath,** which has a tiny lake and lazy farm animals.

Return to the B-5289 and head back to Keswick. If you have

yet to see it, cap your drive with a short detour from Keswick to the Castlerigg Stone Circle (described earlier).

Nightlife in Keswick

For a small and remote town, Keswick has lots going on in the evening. Remember, at this latitude it's light until 22:00 in midsummer.

▲▲Theatre by the Lake

Keswickians brag that they enjoy "London theater quality at Keswick prices." Their theater offers events year-round and a wonderful rotation of six plays from late May through October (plays vary throughout the week, with music concerts on Sun in summer). There are two stages: The main one seats 400, and the smaller "studio" theater seats 100 (and features edgier plays that may involve rough language and/or nudity). Attending a play here is a fine opportunity to enjoy a classy night out.

Cost and Hours: £10-32, discounts for old and young, shows generally at 20:00, possibly earlier fall through spring, café, restaurant (pretheater dinners start at 17:30 and must be booked 24 hours ahead by calling 017687/81102), parking at the adjacent lot is free after 19:00. It's smart to buy tickets in advance—book at box office (daily 9:30-20:00), by phone (tel. 017687/74411), at TI, or at www.theatrebythelake.com.

Hope Park

Along with the Theatre by the Lake (described above), you can do some early evening **golfing** (fine course, pitch-and-putt, goofy golf, or just enjoy the putting green—see page 500) or **walk** among the grazing sheep as the sun gets ready to set (between the lake and the golf course, access from just above the beach, great photo ops on balmy evenings).

Keswick Launch's **evening lake cruise** comes with a glass of wine and a midlake stop for a short commentary. You're welcome to bring a picnic dinner and munch scenically as you cruise (£10.50, £24 family ticket, 1 hour, daily mid-July-Aug at 18:30 and 19:30—weather permitting and if enough people show up).

Pub Events

To socialize with locals, head to a pub for one of their special evenings: There's **quiz night** at The Dog and Gun (21:30 on most Thu; £1, proceeds go to Keswick's Mountain Rescue team, which rescues hikers and the occasional sheep). At a quiz night, tourists are more than welcome. Drop in, say you want to join a team, and you're in. If you like trivia, it's a great way to get to know people here.

The Oddfellows Arms has free **live music** (often classic rock) just about every night in summer (April-Oct, from 21:30).

Keswick Street Theatre

This theatrical walk through Keswick and its history takes place on Tuesday evenings in summer (£3, 1.5 hours, usually starts at 19:30, weekly late May-early July, details at TI).

Movies

The Lonsdale Alhambra Cinema is a restored old-fashioned movie theater a few minutes' walk from the town center (St. Johns Street, tel. 017687/72195, www.keswick-alhambra.co.uk).

Sleeping in Keswick

The Lake District abounds with attractive B&Bs, guesthouses, and hostels. It needs them all when the summer hordes threaten the serenity of this Romantic mecca.

Reserve your room in advance in high season. From November through March, you should have no trouble finding a room. But to get a particular place (especially on Saturdays), call ahead. If you're using public transportation, you should sleep in Keswick. If you're driving, staying outside Keswick is your best chance for a remote farmhouse experience. Lakeland hostels offer inexpensive beds and come with an interesting crowd of all ages.

For Keswick, I've featured B&Bs and small hotels mainly on two streets, each within three blocks of the bus station and town square. Stanger Street, a bit humbler but quiet and handy, has smaller homes and more moderately priced rooms. "The Heads" is a classier area lined with proud Victorian houses, close to the lake and theater, overlooking the golf course. In addition to these two streets, Keswick abounds with many other options that are equally good; for example, the southeast area of the town center (around Eskin, Blencathra, and Helvellyn streets) is a few minutes' walk farther out, but has several B&Bs with easier parking.

Many of my Keswick listings charge extra for a one-night stay. Most won't book one-night stays on weekends (but if you show up and they have a bed free, it's yours) and don't welcome young children (generally ages 8-12). None have elevators and all have lots of stairs—look for listings with ground-floor units if steps are a problem. Owners are enthusiastic about offering plenty of advice to get you on the right walking trail. Most accommodations have inviting lounges with libraries of books on the region and loaner maps. Take advantage of these lounges to transform your tight B&B room into a suite.

This is still the countryside—expect huge breakfasts (often with a wide selection, including vegetarian options) and shower

Sleep Code

Abbreviations **(£1=about $1.60, country code: 44)**
S=Single, **D**=Double/Twin, **T**=Triple, **Q**=Quad, **b**=bathroom
Price Rankings
$$$ Higher Priced—Most rooms £90 or more
$$ Moderately Priced—Most rooms £70-90
$ Lower Priced—Most rooms £70 or less
Unless otherwise noted, credit cards are accepted, breakfast is included, and free Wi-Fi and/or a guest computer is generally available. Prices change; verify current rates online or by email. For the best prices, always book directly with the hotel.

systems that might need to be switched on to get hot water. Parking is pretty easy (each place has a line on parking).

ON STANGER STREET

This street, quiet but just a block from Keswick's town center, is lined with B&Bs situated in Victorian slate townhouses. Each of these places is small and family-run. They are all good, offering comfortably sized rooms, free parking, and a friendly welcome.

$$ Ellergill Guest House has four spic-and-span rooms with an airy, contemporary feel—several with views (Db-£70-90 depending on room size, 2 percent surcharge for credit cards, 2-night minimum, no children under age 10, 22 Stanger Street, tel. 017687/73347, www.ellergill.co.uk, stay@ellergill.co.uk, Clare and Robin Pinkney).

$$ Badgers Wood B&B, at the top of the street, has six modern, bright, unfrilly view rooms, each named after a different tree (Sb-£43, Db-£78-83, 3 percent surcharge for credit cards, 2-night minimum, no children under age 10, special diets accommodated, 30 Stanger Street, tel. 017687/72621, www.badgers-wood.co.uk, enquiries@badgers-wood.co.uk, chatty Scotsman Andrew and his charming wife Anne).

$$ Abacourt House, with a daisy-fresh breakfast room, has five pleasant doubles (Db-£76-84, 3 percent surcharge for credit cards, no children, £5 sack lunches available, 26 Stanger Street, tel. 017687/72967, www.abacourt.co.uk, abacourt.keswick@btinternet.com, John and Heather).

$$ Dunsford Guest House rents four recently updated rooms at bargain prices. Stained glass and wooden pews give the blue-and-cream breakfast room a country-chapel vibe (Db-£70, this price promised with this book when you book direct, cash only, 16 Stanger Street, tel. 017687/75059, www.dunsford.net, enquiries@dunsford.net, Deb and Keith).

ON THE HEADS

These B&Bs are in an area known as The Heads. This area is classier, with bigger and grander Victorian architecture and great views overlooking the pitch-and-putt range and out into the hilly distance. The golf-course side of The Heads has free parking, if you can snare a spot (easy at night). A single yellow line on the curb means you're allowed to park there for free, but only overnight (16:00-10:00).

$$$ Howe Keld has the polished feel of a boutique hotel, but offers all the friendliness of a B&B. Its 12 contemporary-posh rooms are spacious and tastefully decked out in native woods and slate. It's warm, welcoming, and family-run, with one of the best breakfasts I've had anywhere in England (Sb-£55-75, standard Db-£100-110, superior Db-£110-120, cash and 2-night minimum preferred, discount for 2 or more nights, family deals, tel. 017687/72417 or toll-free 0800-783-0212, www.howekeld.co.uk, david@howekeld.co.uk, run with care by David and Valerie Fisher).

$$$ Parkfield House, thoughtfully run and decorated by John and Susan Berry, is a big Victorian house with a homey lounge. Its six rooms, some with fine views, are bright and classy (Sb-£70, Db-£85, superior king Db-£115, ask for discount with this book but you must reserve direct, 2-night minimum, no children under age 16, free parking, tel. 017687/72328, www.parkfield-keswick.co.uk, parkfieldkeswick@hotmail.co.uk).

$$$ Burleigh Mead B&B is a slate mansion from 1892 with wild carpeting. Gill (pronounced "Jill," short for Gillian) rents seven lovely rooms and offers a friendly welcome, as well as a lounge and peaceful front-yard sitting area that's perfect for enjoying the view (north-facing Db with lesser views-£80-90, south-facing Db with grander views-£84-94, Db suite-£100-110, rate depends on length of stay, cash only, no children under age 8, tel. 017687/75935, www.burleighmead.co.uk, info@burleighmead.co.uk).

$$$ Hazeldene Hotel, on the corner of The Heads, rents 10 spacious rooms, many with commanding views. There's even a "boot room" that doubles as a guest rec room with a ping-pong table. It's run with care by delightful Helen and Howard (Db-£75-100 depending on view, one ground-floor unit available, free parking, tel. 017687/72106, www.hazeldene-hotel.co.uk, info@hazeldene-hotel.co.uk).

$$ Brundholme Guest House has four bright and comfy rooms, most with sweeping views at no extra charge—especially from the front side—and a friendly and welcoming atmosphere (Db-£80, minifridge, free parking, tel. 017687/73305, mobile 0773-943-5401, www.brundholme.co.uk, bazaly@hotmail.co.uk, Barry and Allison Thompson).

ON ESKIN STREET

The area just southeast of the town center has several streets lined with good B&Bs and is still within easy walking distance of downtown and the lake.

$$ Allerdale House, a classy, nicely-decorated stone mansion, holds six rooms and is well-run by Barbara and Paul (standard Db-£80, superior Db-£94, these prices promised if you reserve direct and mention this book, 3 percent surcharge for credit cards, free parking, 1 Eskin Street, tel. 017687/73891, www.allerdale-house.co.uk, reception@allerdale-house.co.uk).

HOSTELS IN AND NEAR KESWICK

The Lake District's inexpensive hostels, mostly located in great old buildings, are handy sources of information and social fun.

$ Keswick Youth Hostel, with 85 beds in a converted old mill that overlooks the river, has a big lounge and great riverside balcony. Travelers of all ages feel at home here, but book ahead—family rooms can be especially hard to come by from July through September (bunk in dorm room-£13-22, can go as high as £30, members pay £3 less, breakfast extra, family rooms, includes sheets, pay guest computer, free Wi-Fi, kitchen, laundry, café, bar, office open 7:00-23:00, center of town just off Station Road before river, tel. 017687/72484, www.yha.org.uk, keswick@yha.org.uk).

$ Derwentwater Hostel, in a 220-year-old mansion on the shore of Derwentwater, is two miles south of Keswick and has 88 beds (bed in dorm room-£19-22, family rooms, breakfast extra, kitchen, laundry, 23:00 curfew; follow B-5289 from Keswick—entrance is 2 miles along the Borrowdale Valley Road about 150 yards after Ashness exit—look for cottage and bus stop at bottom of the drive; tel. 017687/77246, www.derwentwater.org, contact@derwentwater.org).

WEST OF KESWICK, IN THE NEWLANDS VALLEY

If you have a car, drive 10 minutes past Keswick down the majestic Newlands Valley (described earlier, under "Scenic Circle Drive South of Keswick"). This valley is studded with 500-year-old farms that have been in the same family for centuries and now rent rooms to supplement the family income. Each place offers easy parking, grand views, and perfect tranquility. Most of these rooms tend to be plainer and generally more dated than the B&Bs in town, and come with steep and gravelly roads, plenty of dogs, and an earthy charm. Don't expect to get mobile phone service, and even satellite Wi-Fi provided by your B&B can be spotty—but living off the grid is why you came here. Traditionally, farmhouses lacked central heating, and while they are now heated, you can still request a hot-water bottle to warm up your bed.

Getting to the Newlands Valley: Leave Keswick via the roundabout at the end of Crosthwaite Road, and then head west on Cockermouth Road (A-66). Take the second Newlands Valley exit through Braithwaite, and follow signs through Newlands Valley (drive toward Buttermere). All of my recommended B&Bs are on this road: Uzzicar Farm (under the shale field, which local kids love hiking up to glissade down; a 10-minute drive from Keswick), Ellas Crag Guest House, then Gill Brow Farm, and finally—the last house before the stark summit—Keskadale Farm (about four miles before Buttermere at the top of the valley—about a 15-minute drive from Keswick). The one-lane road can be intimidating, but it has turnouts for passing.

$$$ Ellas Crag Guest House, with three rooms—each with a great view—is a comfortable stone house with a contemporary feel and tranquil terrace overlooking the valley. This homey B&B offers a good mix of modern and traditional decor, including beautifully tiled bathrooms (Sb-£65-75, Db-£90-105; 10 percent discount if you reserve directly with the B&B, mention this book, and pay in cash; singles available Mon-Thu only, 2-night minimum, local free-range meats and eggs for breakfast, sack lunches available, huge DVD library, laundry-£15/load, tel. 017687/78217, www.ellascrag.co.uk, info@ellascrag.co.uk, Jane and Ed Ma and their teenagers).

$$ Keskadale Farm is another good farmhouse experience, with Ponderosa hospitality. One of the valley's oldest, the house—with two guest rooms and a cozy lounge—is made from 500-year-old ship beams. This working farm is an authentic slice of Lake District life and is your chance to get to know lots of curly-horned sheep and the dogs that herd them. While her husband and sons work in the fields, Margaret Harryman runs the B&B (Db-£70-80, £2 extra for one-night stays, cash only, closed Dec-Feb, tel. 017687/78544, www.keskadalefarm.co.uk, info@keskadalefarm.co.uk). They also rent a two-bedroom apartment (£450/week).

$ Uzzicar Farm is a big rustic place with two comfy guest rooms in a low-ceilinged, 16th-century farmhouse—watch out for ducks. It's a particularly intimate and homey setting where you'll feel like part of the family (Db-£60, family rooms, cash or check only, continental breakfast only, tel. 017687/78026, www.uzzicarfarm.co.uk, stay@uzzicarfarm.co.uk, Helen, David, and three daughters).

$ Gill Brow Farm is a rough-hewn, working farmhouse more than 300 years old where Anne Wilson rents two simple but fine rooms, one with an en-suite bathroom, the other with a private bathroom down the hall (Db-£64, discount with 3-night stay, self-catering cottage that sleeps up to 6 also available, tel. 017687/78270, www.gillbrow-keswick.co.uk, info@gillbrow-keswick.co.uk).

SOUTHWEST OF KESWICK, IN BUTTERMERE

$$$ Bridge Hotel, just beyond Newlands Valley at Buttermere, offers 21 beautiful rooms—most of them quite spacious—and a classic Old World countryside-hotel experience. On Fridays and Saturdays, dinner is required (standard Db-£150 Sun-Thu, £170 Fri-Sat with dinner, fancier rooms for £10-20 more, apartments available, check website for specials, minimum 2-night stay on weekends, free Wi-Fi in lobby, tel. 017687/70252, www.bridge-hotel.com, enquiries@bridge-hotel.com). There are no shops within 10 miles—only peace and quiet a stone's throw from one of the region's most beautiful lakes. The hotel has a dark-wood pub/restaurant on the ground floor.

$ Buttermere Hostel, a quarter-mile south of Buttermere village on Honister Pass Road, has good food, 70 beds, family rooms, and a peacefully rural setting (bed in dorm room-£15-22, members pay £3 less, breakfast extra, inexpensive dinners and packed lunches, laundry, office open 8:30-10:00 & 17:00-22:30, 23:00 curfew, reservation tel. 0845-371-9508, hostel tel. 017687/70245, www.yha.org.uk, buttermere@yha.org.uk).

SOUTH OF KESWICK, NEAR BORROWDALE

$$$ Ashness Farm sits alone, ruling its valley high above Derwentwater. If you want to be immersed in farm sounds and lakeland beauty, this is the place. On this 750-acre working farm, now owned by the National Trust, people have raised sheep and cattle for centuries. Today Anne and her family are "tenant farmers," keeping this farm operating and renting five rooms to boot (Sb-£58-60, Db-£84-99, discount with stays of 2 or more nights, cozy lounge, eggs and sausage literally fresh off the farm for breakfast, sack lunches available, just above Ashness Packhorse Bridge, tel. 017687/77361, www.ashnessfarm.co.uk, enquiries@ashnessfarm.co.uk).

$$ Seatoller Farm B&B is a rustic 16th-century house on another working farm owned by the National Trust. Christine Simpson rents three rooms in her B&B, one of five buildings in this hamlet. The old windows are small, but the abundant flower boxes keep things bright (Db-£85, discount with stays of 2 or more nights, cottage available, closed Dec-mid-Jan, tel. 017687/77232, www.seatollerfarm.co.uk, info@seatollerfarm.co.uk).

$ Borrowdale Hostel, in secluded Borrowdale Valley just south of Rosthwaite, is a well-run place surrounded by many ways to immerse yourself in nature. The hostel offers cheap dinners and sack lunches (86 beds—mostly bunks, bed in dorm room-£18-23, D-£50-60, members pay £3 less, family rooms, breakfast extra, pay guest computer, free Wi-Fi, laundry, office open 7:00-23:00, 23:00 curfew, reservation tel. 0845-371-9624, hostel tel. 017687/77257, www.yha.org.uk, borrowdale@yha.org.uk). To reach this hostel from Keswick by bus, take #78, the Borrowdale Rambler. Note that the last bus from Keswick departs around 17:00-17:30 most of year (see page 487 for bus details).

Eating in Keswick

Keswick has a huge variety of eateries catering to its many visitors, but I've found nothing particularly enticing at the top end; the places listed here are just good, basic values. Most stop serving by 21:00.

The Dog and Gun serves good pub food (I love their rump of lamb) with great pub ambience. Upon arrival, muscle up to the bar to order your beer and/or meal. Then snag a table as soon as one opens up. Mind your head, and tread carefully: Low ceilings and wooden beams loom overhead, while paws poke out from under tables below, as Keswick's canines wait patiently for their masters to finish their beer (£6-10 meals, food served daily 12:00-21:00, famous goulash, dog treats, 2 Lake Road, tel. 017687/73463).

The Pheasant is a walk outside town, but locals trek here regularly for the food. The menu offers Lake District pub standards (fish pie, Cumbrian sausage, guinea fowl), as well as more inventive choices. Check the walls for caricatures of pub regulars, sketched at these tables by a Keswick artist. While they have a small restaurant section, I much prefer eating in the bar (£10-15 meals, kitchen open daily 12:00-14:00 & 18:00-21:00, bar open until 23:00, Crosthwaite Road, tel. 017687/72219). From the town square, walk past the Pencil Museum, hang a right onto Crosthwaite Road, and walk 10 minutes. For a more scenic route, cross the river into Fitz Park, go left along the riverside path until it ends at the gate to Crosthwaite Road, turn right, and walk five minutes.

Star of Siam serves authentic Thai dishes in a tasteful dining room (£8-11 plates, £10 lunch specials, daily 12:00-14:30 & 17:30-22:30, 89 Main Street, tel. 017687/71444).

Abraham's Tea Room, popular with townspeople, is a fine value for lunch. It's tucked away on the upper floor of the giant George Fisher outdoor store (£5-9 soups, salads, and sandwiches, gluten-free options; Mon-Sat 10:00-17:00, Sun 10:30-16:30, on the corner where Lake Road turns right, tel. 017687/71811).

Maxwell's Café serves burgers, tapas, and sandwiches during the day and has cocktails in the evening. Outside tables face a big parking lot (£8 meals, Hendersons Yard, find the narrow walkway off Market Street between pink Johnson's sweet shop and The Golden Lion, tel. 017687/74492).

Bryson's Bakery and Tea Room has an enticing ground-floor bakery, with sandwiches and light lunches. The upstairs is a popular tearoom. Order lunch to go from the bakery, or for a few pence more, eat there, either sitting on stools or at a couple of sidewalk tables. Consider their £22.50 two-person Cumberland Cream Tea, which is like afternoon tea in London, but cheaper and made with local products. Sandwiches, scones, and little cakes are served on a three-tiered platter with tea (£4-8 meals, daily 9:00-17:00, 42 Main Street, tel. 017687/72257).

Pumpkin has a small café space but a huge following, and is known for its fresh ingredients. Stop by for a light snack of homemade muffins and an espresso, or try a hot salmon salad (prices higher if you eat in, daily 9:00-16:30, 19 Lake Road, tel. 017687/75973).

Eateries on Station Street: The street leading from the town square to the leisure center has several restaurants, including **Casa Bella,** a popular and packed Italian place that's good for families—reserve ahead (£8-11 pizzas and pastas, daily 12:00-15:30 & 17:00-21:00, 24 Station Street, tel. 017687/75575, www.casabellakeswick.co.uk). Across the street is **Lakes Bar & Bistro,** with burgers, meat pies, and good fixed-price meal deals (£4-7 starters, £10-13 main dishes, £14 two-course and £17 three-course meals, daily 10:00-23:00, 25 Station Street, tel. 017687/74088).

Picnic: The fine **Booths supermarket** is right where all the buses arrive (Mon-Sat 8:00-21:00, Sun 9:30-16:00, The Headlands). The recommended **Bryson's Bakery** does good sandwiches to go (described earlier). **The Old Keswickian,** on the town square, serves up old-fashioned fish-and-chips to go (Sun-Thu 11:00-22:30, Fri-Sat 11:00-23:30, closes earlier in winter). Just around the corner, **The Cornish Pasty** offers an enticing variety of fresh meat pies to go (£3-4 pies, daily 9:00-17:00 or until the pasties are all gone, across from The Dog and Gun on Borrowdale Road, tel. 017687/72205).

IN THE NEWLANDS VALLEY

The farmhouse B&Bs of Newlands Valley don't serve dinner, so their guests have two good options: Go into Keswick, or take the lovely 10-minute drive to Buttermere for an evening meal at **The Fish Inn** pub, which has fine indoor and outdoor seating, but takes no reservations (£8-10 meals, food served daily 12:00-14:00 & 18:00-21:00, family-friendly, good fish and daily specials with fresh vegetables, tel. 017687/70253). The neighboring **Bridge Hotel Pub** is a bit cozier and serves "modern-day nibbles and good classic pub grub" (£10-12 meals, food served daily 9:30-21:30, tel. 017687/70252). For lunch also consider the **Croft House Farm Café,** which serves freshly-made soups and sandwiches (£3-5) to eat on their sunny deck or to take away (daily 10:00-17:00, tel. 017687/70235).

Keswick Connections

The nearest train station to Keswick is in Penrith (no lockers). For train and bus info, check at a TI, visit www.traveline.org.uk, or call 0345-748-4950 (for train) or 0871-200-2233. Most routes run less frequently on Sundays.

From Keswick by Bus: For connections, see page 487.

From Penrith by Bus to: Keswick (hourly Mon-Sat, every 2 hours on Sun, 45 minutes, pay driver, Stagecoach bus #X4 or #X5), **Ullswater** and **Glenridding** (5/day, 45 minutes, bus #508). The Penrith bus stop is just outside the train station (bus schedules posted inside and outside station).

From Penrith by Train to: Liverpool (nearly hourly, 2.5 hours, change in Wigan or Preston), **Durham** (hourly, 3 hours, change in Carlisle and Newcastle), **York** (roughly 2/hour, 3.5-4 hours, 1-2 transfers), **London**'s Euston Station (hourly, 4 hours), **Edinburgh** (9/day direct, 2 hours), **Glasgow** (roughly hourly, 1.5 hours), **Oban** (2/day, 6 hours, transfer in Glasgow).

ROUTE TIPS FOR DRIVERS

From Points South (such as Liverpool and North Wales) to the Lake District: The direct, easy way to Keswick is to leave the M-6 at Penrith and take the A-66 motorway for 16 miles to Keswick. For a scenic sightseeing drive through the south lakes to Keswick, exit the M-6 on the A-590/A-591 through the towns of Kendal and Windermere to reach Brockhole National Park Visitors Centre. From Brockhole, the A road to Keswick is fastest, but the high road—the tiny road over Kirkstone Pass to Glenridding and lovely Ullswater—is much more dramatic.

Coming from (or Going to) the West: Only 1,300 feet above sea level, Hard Knott Pass is still a thriller, with a narrow, winding, steeply graded road. Just over the pass are the scant but evocative remains of the Hard Knott Roman fortress. The great views can come with miserable rainstorms, and it can be very slow and frustrating when the one-lane road with turnouts is clogged by traffic. Avoid it on summer weekends.

Ullswater Lake Area

For advice on the Ullswater area, visit the **TI** at the pay parking lot in the heart of the lakefront village of Glenridding (daily 9:30-17:30, tel. 017684/82414, www.visiteden.co.uk).

▲▲Ullswater Hike and Boat Ride

Long, narrow Ullswater, which some consider the loveliest lake in the area, offers eight miles of diverse and grand Lake District scenery. While you can drive it or cruise it, I'd ride the boat from the south tip halfway up (to Howtown—which is nothing more than a dock) and hike back. Or walk first, then enjoy an easy ride back.

An old-fashioned **"steamer" boat** (actually diesel-powered) leaves Glenridding regularly for Howtown (departs daily generally 9:45-16:45, 6-9/day April-Oct, fewer off-season, 40 minutes; £6.40 one-way, £10.20 round-trip, £13.60 round-the-lake ticket lets you hop on and off, covered by £15 Ullswater Bus & Boat day pass, family rates, drivers can use safe pay-and-display parking lot, by public transit take bus #508 from Penrith, café at dock, £4 walking route map, tel. 017684/82229, www.ullswater-steamers.co.uk).

From Howtown, spend three to four hours hiking and dawdling along the well-marked path by the lake south to Patterdale, and then along the road back to Glenridding. This is a serious seven-mile walk with good views, varied terrain, and a few bridges and farms along the way. For a shorter hike from Howtown Pier, consider a three-mile loop around Hallin Fell. A rainy-day plan is to ride the covered boat up and down the lake to Howtown and Pooley Bridge at the northern tip of the lake (£13.60, 2 hours). Boats don't run in really bad weather—call ahead if it looks iffy.

▲▲Lanty's Tarn and Keldas Hill

If you like the idea of an Ullswater-area hike, but aren't up for the long huff from Howtown, consider this shorter (but still moderately challenging and plenty scenic) loop that leaves right from the TI's pay parking lot in Glenridding (about 2.5 miles, allow 2-2.5 hours; before embarking, buy the well-described leaflet for this walk in the TI).

From the parking lot, head to the main road, turn right to cross the river, then turn right again immediately and follow the river up into the hills. After passing a row of cottages, turn left, cross the wooden bridge, and proceed up the hill through the swing gate. Just before the next swing gate, turn left (following *Grisedale* signs) and head to yet another gate. From here you can see the small lake called Lanty's Tarn.

While you'll eventually go through this gate and walk along the lake to finish the loop, first you can detour to the top of the adjacent hill, called Keldas, for sweeping views over the near side of Ullswater (to reach the summit, climb over the step gate and follow the faint path up the hill). Returning to—and passing through—the swing gate, you'll walk along Lanty's Tarn, then begin your slow, steep, and scenic descent into the Grisedale Valley. Reaching the valley floor (and passing a noisy dog breeder's farm), cross the stone bridge, then turn left and follow the road all the way back to the lakefront, where a left turn returns you to Glenridding.

▲Aira Force Waterfall

At Ullswater, there's a delightful little park with parking, a ranger trailer, and easy trails leading half a mile uphill to a powerful 60-foot-tall waterfall. You'll read about how Wordsworth was inspired to write three poems here...and after taking this little walk, you'll know why. The pay-and-display car park is just where the Troutbeck road from the A-66 hits the lake, on the A-592 between Pooley Bridge and Glenridding.

Helvellyn

Considered by many the best high-mountain hike in the Lake District, this breathtaking round-trip route from Glenridding includes the spectacular Striding Edge—about a half-mile along the ridge. Be careful; do this six-hour hike only in good weather, since the wind can be fierce. While it's not the shortest route, the Glenridding ascent is best. Get advice from the Ullswater TI in Glenridding or look for various books on this hike at any area TI.

South Lake District

The South Lake District has a cheesiness that's similar to other popular English resort destinations. Here, piles of low-end vacationers suffer through terrible traffic, slurp ice cream, and get candy floss caught in their hair. The area around Windermere is worth a drive-through if you're a fan of Wordsworth or Beatrix Potter, but you'll still want to spend the majority of your Lake District time (and book your accommodations) up north.

GETTING AROUND THE SOUTH LAKE DISTRICT

By Car: Driving is your best option to see the small towns and sights clustered in the South Lake District; consider combining your drive with the bus trip mentioned below. If you're coming to or leaving the South Lake District from the west, you could take the Hard Knott Pass for a scenic introduction to the area.

By Bus: Buses are a fine and stress-free way to lace together this gauntlet of sights in the congested Lake Windermere neighborhood. The open-top Lakeland Experience bus #599 stops at Bowness Pier (lake cruises), Windermere (train station), Brockhole (National Park Visitors Centre), Ambleside, Rydal Mount, and Grasmere (Dove Cottage). Consider leaving your car at Grasmere and enjoying the breezy and extremely scenic ride, hopping off and on as you like (3/hour Easter-late Sept, 2/hour late Sept-Oct, 50 minutes each way, £8 Central Lakes Dayrider all-day pass). Bus #555 runs between Windermere and Keswick.

Sights in the South Lake District

WORDSWORTH SIGHTS

William Wordsworth was one of the first writers to reject fast-paced city life. During England's Industrial Age, hearts were muzzled and brains ruled. Science was in, machines were taming nature, and factory hours were taming humans. In reaction to these brainy ideals, a rare few—dubbed Romantics—began to embrace untamed nature and undomesticated emotions.

Back then, nobody climbed a mountain just because it was there—but Wordsworth did. He'd "wander lonely as a cloud" through the countryside, finding inspiration in "plain living and high thinking." He soon attracted a circle of like-minded creative friends.

The emotional highs the Romantics felt weren't all natural. Wordsworth and his poet friends Samuel Taylor Coleridge and Thomas de Quincey got stoned on opium and wrote poetry, combining their generation's standard painkiller drug with their tree-hugging passions (Coleridge's opium scale is on view in Dove Cottage). Today, opium is out of vogue, but the Romantic movement thrives as visitors continue to inundate the region.

▲▲Dove Cottage and Wordsworth Museum

For poets, this two-part visit is the top sight of the Lake District. Take a short tour of William Wordsworth's humble

Wordsworth at Dove Cottage

William Wordsworth (1770-1850) was a Lake District home-boy. Born in Cockermouth (in a house now open to the public), he was schooled in Hawkshead. In adulthood, he married a local girl, settled down in Grasmere and Ambleside, and was buried in Grasmere's St. Oswald's churchyard.

But the 30-year-old man who moved into Dove Cottage in 1799 was not the carefree lad who'd once roamed the district's lakes and fields. At Cambridge University, he'd been a C student, graduating with no job skills and no interest in a nine-to-five career. Instead, he and a buddy hiked through Europe, where Wordsworth had an epiphany of the "sublime" atop Switzerland's Alps. He lived a year in France, watching the Revolution rage. It stirred his soul. He fell in love with a Frenchwoman who bore his daughter, Caroline. But lack of money forced him to return to England, and the outbreak of war with France kept them apart.

Pining away in London, William hung out in the pubs and coffeehouses with fellow radicals, where he met poet Samuel Taylor Coleridge. They inspired each other to write, edited each other's work, and jointly published a groundbreaking book of poetry.

In 1799, his head buzzing with words and ideas, William and his sister (and soul mate) Dorothy moved into the white-washed, slate-tiled former inn now known as Dove Cottage. He came into a small inheritance, and dedicated himself to poetry full time. In 1802, with the war temporarily over, William returned to France to finally meet his daughter. (He wrote of the rich experience: "It is a beauteous evening, calm and free... / Dear child! Dear Girl! that walkest with me here, / If thou appear untouched by solemn thought, / Thy nature is not therefore less divine.")

Having achieved closure, Wordsworth returned home to marry a former kindergarten classmate, Mary. She moved into Dove Cottage, along with an initially jealous Dorothy. Three of their five children were born here, and the cottage was also home to Mary's sister, the family dog Pepper (a gift from Sir Walter Scott; see Pepper's portrait), and frequent house-guests who bedded down in the pantry: Scott, Coleridge, and Thomas de Quincey, the Timothy Leary of opium.

The time at Dove Cottage was Wordsworth's "Golden Decade," when he penned his masterpieces. But after almost nine years here, Wordsworth's family and social status had outgrown the humble cottage. They moved first to a house in Grasmere before settling down in Rydal Hall. Wordsworth was changing. After the Dove years, he would write less, settle into a regular government job, quarrel with Coleridge, drift to the right politically, and endure criticism from old friends who branded him a sellout. Still, his poetry—most of it written at Dove—became increasingly famous, and he died honored as England's Poet Laureate.

Wordsworth's Poetry at Dove

At Dove Cottage, Wordsworth was immersed in the beauty of nature and the simple joy of his young, growing family. It was here that he reflected on both his idyllic childhood and his troubled twenties. The following are select lines from two well-known poems from this fertile time.

Ode: Intimations of Immortality

There was a time when meadow, grove, and stream,
The earth, and every common sight, to me did seem
Apparelled in celestial light, the glory and the freshness of a dream.
It is not now as it hath been of yore; turn wheresoe'er I may, by night or day,
The things which I have seen I now can see no more.
Now while the birds thus sing a joyous song...
To me alone there came a thought of grief...
Whither is fled the visionary gleam?
Where is it now, the glory and the dream?
Our birth is but a sleep and a forgetting:
The Soul...cometh from afar...
Trailing clouds of glory do we come
From God, who is our home.

I Wandered Lonely as a Cloud

I wandered lonely as a cloud
That floats on high o'er vales and hills,
When all at once I saw a crowd,
A host, of golden daffodils;
Beside the lake, beneath the trees,
Fluttering and dancing in the breeze...
For oft, when on my couch I lie
In vacant or in pensive mood,
They flash upon that inward eye
Which is the bliss of solitude;
And then my heart with pleasure fills,
And dances with the daffodils.

cottage and be inspired in its excellent museum, which displays original writings, sketches, personal items, and fine paintings.

The poet whose appreciation of nature and a back-to-basics lifestyle put this area on the map spent his most productive years (1799-1808) in this well-preserved stone cottage on the edge of Grasmere. After functioning as the Dove and Olive Bow pub for almost 200 years, it was bought by his family. This is where Wordsworth got married, had kids, and wrote much of his best poetry. Still owned by the Wordsworth family, the furniture was his, and the place comes with some amazing artifacts, including the poet's passport and suitcase (he packed light). Even during his lifetime,

Wordsworth was famous, and Dove Cottage was turned into a museum in 1891—it's now protected by the Wordsworth Trust.

Cost and Hours: £7.75, daily March-Oct 9:30-17:30, Nov-Feb 9:30-16:30 except closed Jan, café, bus #555 from Keswick, bus #555 or #599 from Windermere, tel. 015394/35544, www.wordsworth.org.uk. Parking costs £1 in the Dove Cottage lot off the main road (A-591), 50 yards from the site.

Visiting the Cottage and Museum: Even if you're not a fan, Wordsworth's appreciation of nature, his Romanticism, and the ways his friends unleashed their creative talents with such abandon are appealing. The 25-minute cottage tour (which departs regularly—you shouldn't have to wait more than 30 minutes) and adjoining museum, with lots of actual manuscripts handwritten by Wordsworth and his illustrious friends, are both excellent. In dry weather, the garden where the poet was much inspired is worth a wander. (Visit this after leaving the cottage tour, and pick up the description at the back door. The garden is closed when wet.) Allow 1.5 hours for this visit.

Poetry Readings: On the second Tuesday of the month, the Wordsworth Trust puts on shared poetry readings of Wordsworth's works written at Dove Cottage. Readings are held in the library at the museum in a relaxed and friendly setting (£5, every second Tue at 18:30, generally April-Oct, confirm schedule in advance, same contact info as above).

▲Rydal Mount

Located just down the road from Dove Cottage, this sight is worthwhile for Wordsworth fans. The poet's final, higher-class home, with a lovely garden and view, lacks the humble charm of Dove Cottage, but still evokes the time and creative spirit of the literary giant who lived here for 37 years. His family repurchased it in 1969 (after a 100-year gap), and his great-great-great-granddaughter still calls it home on occasion, as shown by recent family photos sprinkled throughout the house. After a short intro by the attendant, you'll be given an explanatory flier and are welcome to roam. Wander

through the garden William himself designed, which has changed little since then. Surrounded by his nature, you can imagine the poet enjoying them with you. "O happy garden! Whose seclusion deep hath been so friendly to industrious hours; and to soft slumbers, that did gently steep our spirits, carrying with them dreams of flowers, and wild notes warbled among leafy bowers."

Cost and Hours: £7.25; March-Oct daily 9:30-17:00; Nov-Dec and Feb Wed-Sun 11:00-16:00, closed Mon-Tue; closed Jan, occasionally closed for private functions—check website, tearoom, 1.5 miles north of Ambleside, well-signed, free and easy parking, bus #555 from Keswick, tel. 015394/33002, www.rydalmount.co.uk.

BEATRIX POTTER SIGHTS

Of the many Beatrix Potter commercial ventures in the Lake District, there are two serious Beatrix Potter sights: her farm (Hill Top Farm) and her husband's former office, which is now the Beatrix Potter Gallery, filled with her sketches and paintings. The sights are two miles apart, in or near Hawkshead, a 20-minute drive south of Ambleside. If you're coming from Windermere, take bus #505 to Hawkshead or catch the little 15-car ferry from Bowness (runs constantly except when it's extremely windy, 10-minute trip, £4.50 car fare includes all passengers, £3.80 if you buy ticket at TI). If you have questions, visit the Hawkshead TI inside the Ooh-La-La gift shop right across from the parking lot (tel. 015394/36946). Note that both of the major sights are closed on Friday (though the Beatrix Potter Gallery may be open on Fridays in summer—call ahead).

On busy summer days, the wait to get into Hill Top Farm can last several hours (only 8 people are allowed in every 5 minutes, and the timed-entry tickets must be bought in person). If you like cutesy tourist towns (Hawkshead), this can be a blessing. Otherwise, you'll wish you were in the woods somewhere with Wordsworth.

▲Hill Top Farm

A hit with Beatrix Potter fans (and skippable for others), this dark and intimate cottage, swallowed up in the inspirational and rough nature around it, provides an enjoyable if quick experience. The six-room farm was left just as it was when she died in 1943. At her request, the house is set as if she had just stepped out—flowers on the tables, fire on, low lights. While there's no printed

Beatrix Potter (1866-1943)

As a girl growing up in London, Beatrix Potter vacationed in the Lake District, where she became inspired to write her popular children's books. Unable to get a publisher, she self-published the first two editions of *The Tale of Peter Rabbit* in 1901 and 1902. When she finally landed a publisher, sales of her books were phenomenal. With the money she made, she bought Hill Top Farm, a 17th-century cottage, and fixed it up, living there sporadically from 1905 until she married in 1913. Potter was more than a children's book writer; she was a fine artist, an avid gardener, and a successful farmer. She married a lawyer and put her knack for business to use, amassing a 4,000-acre estate. An early conservationist, she used the garden-cradled cottage as a place to study nature. She willed it—along with the rest of her vast estate—to the National Trust, which she enthusiastically supported.

information here, guides in each room are eager to explain things. Fans of her classic *The Tale of Samuel Whiskers* will recognize the home's rooms, furniture, and views—the book and its illustrations were inspired by an invasion of rats when she bought this place.

Cost and Hours: Farmhouse—£9.50, tickets often sell out by 14:00 or even earlier during busy times; gardens—free; June-Aug Sat-Thu 10:00-17:30, April-May and Sept-Oct Sat-Thu 10:30-16:30, mid-Feb-March Sat-Thu 10:30-15:30, closed Nov-mid-Feb and Fri year-round, tel. 015394/36269, www.nationaltrust.org.uk/hill-top.

Avoiding Crowds: You must buy tickets in person. To beat the lines, get to the ticket office when it opens—15 minutes before Hill Top starts its first tour. If you can't make it early, call the farm for the current wait times (if no one answers, leave a message for the administrator; someone will call you back).

Getting There: The farm is located in Near Sawrey village, 2 miles south of Hawkshead. Mountain Goat Tours runs a shuttle bus from across the Hawkshead TI to the farm every 40 minutes (tel. 015394/45161). Drivers can take the B-5286 and B-5285 from Ambleside or the B-5285 from Coniston—be prepared for extremely narrow roads with no shoulders that are often lined with stone walls. Park and buy tickets 150 yards down the road, and walk back to tour the place.

▲Beatrix Potter Gallery

Located in the cute but extremely touristy town of Hawkshead, this gallery fills Beatrix's husband's former law office with the wonderful and intimate drawings and watercolors that she did to illustrate her books. Each year the museum highlights a new theme and brings out a different set of her paintings, drawings, and other items. Unlike Hill Top, the gallery has plenty of explanation about her life and work, including touchscreen displays and information panels. Even non-Potter fans will find this museum rather charming and her art surprisingly interesting.

Cost and Hours: £5.50, April-Oct Sat-Thu 10:30-17:00, mid-Feb-March Sat-Thu 10:30-15:30, closed Fri except possibly in summer (June-Aug; call or check online), closed Nov-mid-Feb, Main Street, drivers use the nearby pay-and-display lot and walk 200 yards to the town center, tel. 015394/36355, www.nationaltrust.org.uk/beatrix-potter-gallery.

Hawkshead Grammar School Museum

The town of Hawkshead is engulfed in Potter tourism, and the extreme quaintness of it all is off-putting. Just across from the pay-and-display parking lot is the interesting Hawkshead Grammar School Museum, founded in 1585, where William Wordsworth studied from 1779 to 1787. It shows off old school benches and desks whittled with penknife graffiti.

Cost and Hours: £2.50 includes guided tour; April-Sept Mon-Sat 10:00-12:30 & 13:30-17:00, Oct until 16:30, closed Sun and Nov-March, tel. 015394/36735, www.hawksheadgrammar.org.uk.

The World of Beatrix Potter

This tour, a hit with children, is a gimmicky exhibit with all the historical value of a Disney ride. The 45-minute experience features a four-minute video trip into the world of Mrs. Tiggywinkle and company, a series of Lake District tableaux starring the same imaginary gang, and an all-about-Beatrix section, with an eight-minute video biography.

Cost and Hours: £7, kids-£3.65, daily April-Sept 10:00-17:30, Oct-March 10:00-16:30, tearoom, on Crag Brow in Bowness-on-Windermere, tel. 08445-041-233, www.hop-skip-jump.com.

MORE SIGHTS AT LAKE WINDERMERE

Brockhole National Park Visitors Centre

Look for a stately old lakeside mansion between Ambleside and Windermere on the A-591. Set in a nicely groomed lakeside park, the center offers a free video on life in the Lake District, an information desk, organized walks (see the park's free *Visitor Guide*), exhibits, a shop (excellent selection of maps and guidebooks), a cafeteria, gardens, and nature walks. It's also a great place to bring kids for its free indoor play space and fun adventure playground with slides, swings, nets, and swinging bridges. Other family activities, including an aerial treetop trek, a zip line, minigolf, and pony rides, have a fee. Boat and bike rentals are also available.

Cost and Hours: Free, pay-when-you-leave parking (coins only); daily April-Oct 10:00-17:00, Nov-March 10:00-16:00, bus #555 from Keswick, bus #599 from Windermere, tel. 015394/46601, www.lakedistrict.gov.uk.

Cruise: For a joyride around famous Lake Windermere, you can catch the Brockhole "Green" cruise here (£7.70, runs daily 10:00-16:00, 2/hour mid-July-Aug, hourly April-mid-July and Sept-Oct, 45-minute circle, scant narration, passengers can hop on and off on one ticket, tel. 015394/43360, www.windermere-lakecruises.co.uk).

Lakes Aquarium

This aquarium gives a glimpse of the natural history of Cumbria. Exhibits describe the local wildlife living in lake and coastal environments, including otters, eels, pike, and sharks. A rainforest exhibit features reptiles and marmoset monkeys. Experts give various talks throughout the day.

Cost and Hours: £9, £6 for kids under age 16, cheaper online, family deals, daily 9:00-18:00, until 17:00 in winter, last entry one hour before closing, in Lakeside, one mile north of Newby Bridge, at south end of Lake Windermere, tel. 015395/30153, www.lakesaquarium.co.uk.

Hayes Garden World

This extensive gardening center, a popular weekend excursion for locals, offers garden supplies, a bookstore, a playground, and gorgeous grounds. Gardeners could wander this place all afternoon. Upstairs is a fine cafeteria-style restaurant (open Mon-Sat 9:00-18:00, Sun 11:00-17:00, at south end of Ambleside on main drag, see *Garden Centre* signs, located at north end of Lake Windermere, tel. 015394/33434, www.hayesgardenworld.co.uk).

YORK

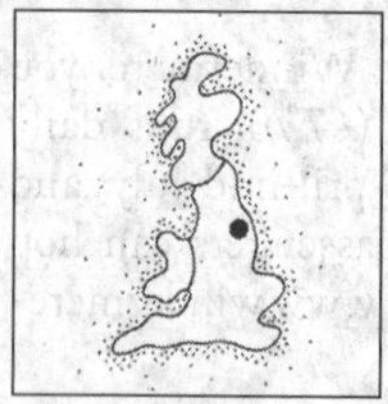

Historic York is loaded with world-class sights. Marvel at the York Minster, England's finest Gothic church. Ramble The Shambles, York's wonderfully preserved medieval quarter. Enjoy a walking tour led by an old Yorker. Hop a train at one of the world's greatest railway museums, travel to the 1800s in the York Castle Museum, head back 1,000 years to Viking times at the Jorvik Viking Centre, or dig into the city's buried past at the Yorkshire Museum.

York has a rich history. In A.D. 71, it was Eboracum, a Roman provincial capital—the northernmost city in the empire. Constantine was proclaimed emperor here in A.D. 306. In the fifth century, as Rome was toppling, the Roman emperor sent a letter telling England it was on its own, and York—now called Eoforwic—became the capital of the Anglo-Saxon kingdom of Northumbria.

The city's first church was built in 627, and the town became an early Christian center of learning. The Vikings later took the town, and from the 9th through the 11th century, it was a Danish trading center called Jorvik. The invading and conquering Normans destroyed, then rebuilt the city, fortifying it with a castle and the walls you see today.

Medieval York, with 9,000 inhabitants, grew rich on the wool trade and became England's second city. Henry VIII used the city's fine Minster as the northern capital of his Anglican Church. (In today's Anglican Church, the Archbishop of York is second only to the Archbishop of Canterbury.)

In the Industrial Age, York was the railway hub of northern England. When it was built, York's train station was the world's largest. During World War II, Hitler chose to bomb York by picking the city out of a travel guidebook (not this one).

Today, York's leading industry is tourism. It seems like everything that's great about Britain finds its best expression in this manageable town. While the city has no single claim to fame, York is more than the sum of its parts. With its strollable cobbles and half-timbered buildings, grand cathedral and excellent museums, thriving restaurant scene and welcoming locals, York delights.

PLANNING YOUR TIME

After London, York is the best sightseeing city in England. On even a 10-day trip through Britain, it deserves two nights and a day. For the best 36 hours, follow this plan: Arrive early enough to catch the 17:15 evensong service at the Minster, then take the free city walking tour at 18:45 (evening tours offered June-Aug only). Splurge on dinner at one of the city's bistros. The next morning at 9:00, take my self-guided walk, interrupting it midway with a tour of the Minster. Finish the walk and grab lunch. To fill your afternoon, choose among the town's many important sights (such as the York Castle Museum—open until 17:00; or the Railway Museum—open until 18:00). Spend the evening enjoying a ghost walk of your choice (they depart at different times between 18:45 and 20:00) and another memorable dinner.

This is a packed day; as you review this chapter, you'll see that there are easily two days of sightseeing fun in York.

Orientation to York

There are roughly 200,000 people in York and its surrounding area; about one in ten is a student. But despite the city's size, the sightseer's York is small. Virtually everything is within a few minutes' walk: sights, train station, TI, and B&Bs. The longest walk a visitor might take (from a B&B across the old town to the York Castle Museum) is about 25 minutes.

Bootham Bar, a gate in the medieval town wall, is the hub of your York visit. (In York, a "bar" is a gate and a "gate" is a street. Blame the Vikings.) At Bootham Bar and on Exhibition Square, you'll find the starting points for most walking tours and bus tours, handy access to the medieval town wall, a public WC, and Bootham Street (which leads to my recommended B&Bs). To find your way around York, use the Minster's towers as a navigational land-

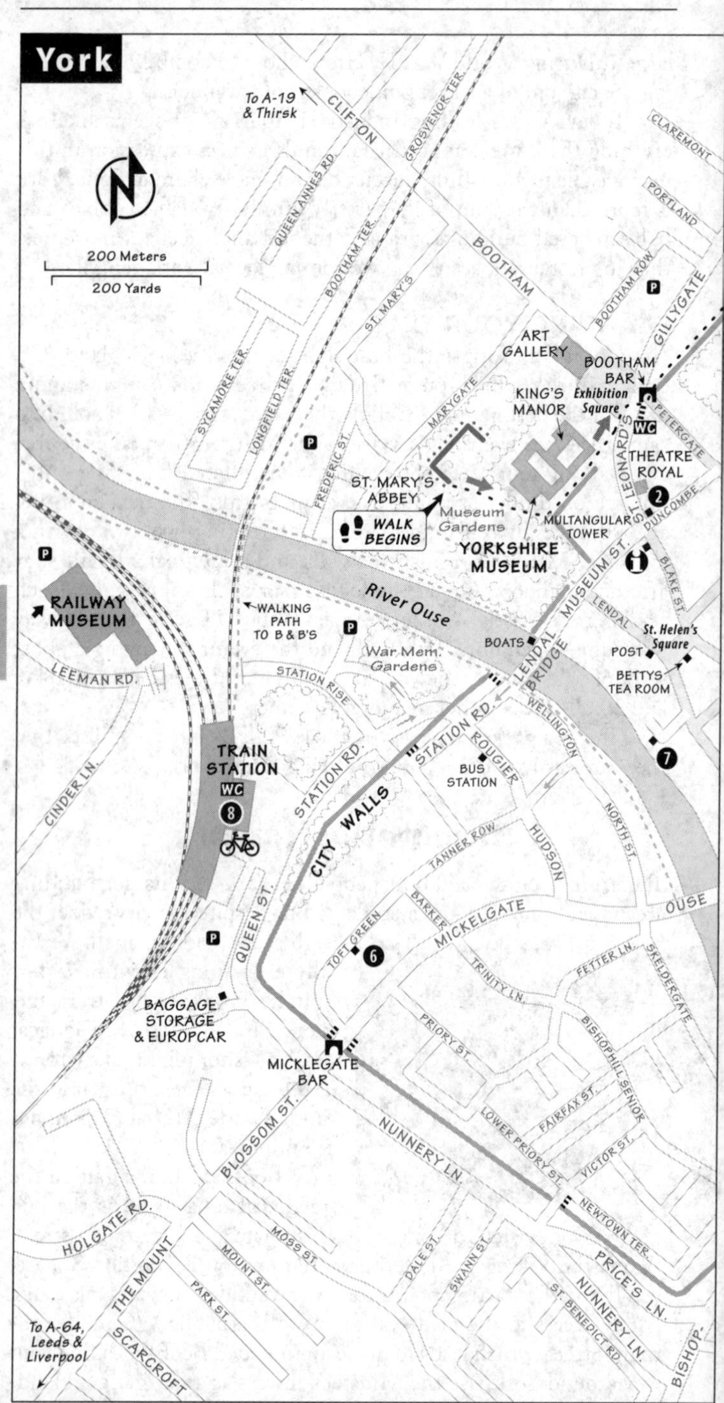
York
To A-19 & Thirsk
CLIFTON
GROSVENOR TER.
CLAREMONT
PORTLAND
QUEEN ANNES RD.
BOOTHAM TER.
BOOTHAM
200 Meters
200 Yards
ST. MARY'S
BOOTHAM ROW
GILLYGATE
ART GALLERY
BOOTHAM BAR
SYCAMORE TER.
LONGFIELD TER.
MARYGATE
KING'S MANOR
Exhibition Square
PETERGATE
WC
FREDERIC ST.
ST. LEONARD'S
THEATRE ROYAL
ST. MARY'S ABBEY
2
DUNCOMBE
WALK BEGINS
Museum Gardens
MULTANGULAR TOWER
YORKSHIRE MUSEUM
MUSEUM ST.
BLAKE ST.
RAILWAY MUSEUM
WALKING PATH TO B & B'S
River Ouse
LENDAL
St. Helen's Square
BOATS
LENDAL BRIDGE
POST
BETTYS TEA ROOM
War Mem. Gardens
LEEMAN RD.
STATION RISE
STATION RD.
WELLINGTON
ROUGIER
7
TRAIN STATION
WC
8
STATION RD.
BUS STATION
CINDER LN.
CITY WALLS
NORTH ST.
TANNER ROW
HUDSON
QUEEN ST.
BARKER
MICKELGATE
OUSE
TOFT GREEN
6
TRINITY LN.
FETTER LN.
SKELDERGATE
BAGGAGE STORAGE & EUROPCAR
PRIORY ST.
BISHOPHILL SENIOR
MICKLEGATE BAR
BLOSSOM ST.
FAIRFAX ST.
NUNNERY LN.
LOWER PRIORY ST.
VICTOR ST.
HOLGATE RD.
NEWTOWN TER.
MOSS ST.
THE MOUNT
MOUNT ST.
DALE ST.
SWANN ST.
PRICE'S LN.
PARK ST.
NUNNERY LN.
ST. BENEDICT RD.
To A-64, Leeds & Liverpool
SCARCROFT
BISHOP-

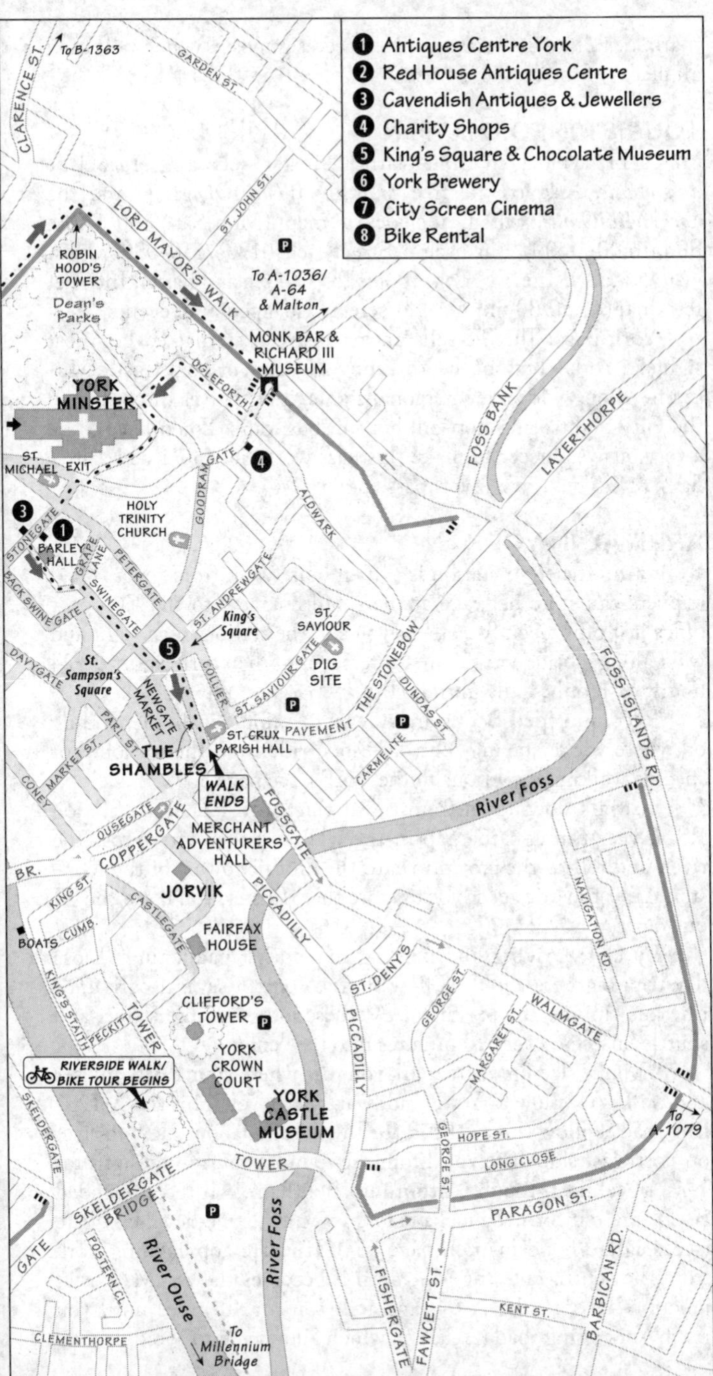

1 Antiques Centre York
2 Red House Antiques Centre
3 Cavendish Antiques & Jewellers
4 Charity Shops
5 King's Square & Chocolate Museum
6 York Brewery
7 City Screen Cinema
8 Bike Rental
To B-1363
CLARENCE ST.
GARDEN ST.
ST. JOHN ST.
LORD MAYOR'S WALK
ROBIN HOOD'S TOWER
Dean's Parks
To A-1036/ A-64 & Malton
MONK BAR & RICHARD III MUSEUM
OGLEFORTH
YORK MINSTER
FOSS BANK
LAYERTHORPE
ST. MICHAEL
EXIT
GOODRAMGATE
HOLY TRINITY CHURCH
ALDWARK
STONEGATE
BARLEY HALL
GRAPE LANE
PETERGATE
BACK SWINEGATE
SWINEGATE
ST. ANDREWGATE
King's Square
ST. SAVIOUR
DIG SITE
ST. SAVIOURGATE
THE STONEBOW
DUNDAS ST.
FOSS ISLANDS RD.
DAVYGATE
St. Sampson's Square
NEWGATE MARKET
COLLIER
PARL. ST.
MARKET ST.
PAVEMENT
CARMELITE
ST. CRUX PARISH HALL
THE SHAMBLES
WALK ENDS
CONEY
OUSEGATE
COPPERGATE
FOSSGATE
MERCHANT ADVENTURERS' HALL
River Foss
BR.
KING ST.
CASTLEGATE
JORVIK
PICCADILLY
NAVIGATION RD.
BOATS
CUMB.
FAIRFAX HOUSE
ST. DENY'S
GEORGE ST.
KING'S STAITH
CLIFFORD'S TOWER
PECKITT
TOWER
MARGARET ST.
WALMGATE
YORK CROWN COURT
RIVERSIDE WALK/ BIKE TOUR BEGINS
PICCADILLY
YORK CASTLE MUSEUM
To A-1079
SKELDERGATE
HOPE ST.
GEORGE ST.
LONG CLOSE
TOWER
SKELDERGATE BRIDGE
PARAGON ST.
GATE
River Ouse
River Foss
POSTERN CL.
FISHERGATE
FAWCETT ST.
BARBICAN RD.
KENT ST.
CLEMENTHORPE
To Millennium Bridge

mark, or follow the strategically-placed signposts, which point out all places of interest to tourists.

TOURIST INFORMATION

York's TI, a block in front of the Minster, sells a £1 *York Map and Guide.* Ask for the free monthly *What's On* guide and the *York MiniGuide,* which includes a map (Mon-Sat 9:00-17:00, Sun 10:00-16:00, 1 Museum Street, tel. 01904/550-099, www.visityork.org). The TI books rooms for a £4 fee and has an Internet terminal (£1.50/30 minutes). A screen lists upcoming events.

York Pass: The TI sells an expensive pass that covers most sights in York—but not the Yorkshire Museum or York Castle Museum—along with a few regional sights; it also gives discounts on the City Sightseeing hop-on, hop-off bus tours. You'd have to be a very busy sightseer to make this pass worth it (£36/1 day, £48/2 days, £58/3 days, www.yorkpass.com).

ARRIVAL IN YORK

By Train: The train station is a 10-minute walk from town. Day-trippers can store baggage at the small hut next to the Europcar office just off Queen Street—as you exit the station, turn right and walk along a bridge to the first intersection, then turn right (£6/24 hours, cash only, daily until 20:00).

Recommended B&Bs are a 5- to 15-minute walk (depending on where you're staying) or a £6-8 taxi ride from the station. For specific walking directions to the B&Bs, see page 562.

To walk downtown from the station, turn left down Station Road, veer through the gap in the wall and then left across the river, and follow the crowd toward the Gothic towers of the Minster. After the bridge, a block before the Minster, you'll see the TI on your right.

By Car: Driving and parking in York is maddening. Those day-tripping here should follow signs to one of several park-and-ride lots ringing the perimeter. At these lots, parking is free, and shuttle buses go every 10 minutes into the center.

If you're sleeping here, park your car where your B&B advises and walk. As you near York (and your B&B), you'll hit the A-1237 ring road. Follow this to the A-19/Thirsk roundabout (next to river on northeast side of town). From the roundabout, follow signs for *York,* traveling through Clifton into Bootham. All recommended B&Bs are four or five blocks before you hit the medieval city gate (see neighborhood map on page 564). If you're approaching York from the south, take the M-1 until it becomes the A-1M, exit at junction 45 onto the A-64, and follow it for 10 miles until you reach York's ring road (A-1237), which allows you to avoid driving through the city center. If you have more time, the A-19 from Selby is a slower and more scenic route into York.

HELPFUL HINTS

Festivals: Book a room well in advance during festival times and on weekends any time of year. The **Viking Festival** features *lur* horn-blowing, warrior drills, and re-created battles in mid-February (www.jorvik-viking-centre.co.uk). The **Early Music Festival** (medieval minstrels, Renaissance dance, and so on) zings its strings in early July (www.ncem.co.uk/yemf.shtml). York claims to be the "Ascot of the North," and the town fills up on horse-race weekends (once a month May-Oct, check schedules at www.yorkracecourse.co.uk); it's especially busy during the **Ebor Races** in mid-August. (Many avoid York during this period, as prices go up and the streets are filled with drunken revelers. Others find that attractive.) The **York Food and Drink Festival** takes a bite out of late September (www.yorkfoodfestival.com). And the St. Nicholas Fayre Christmas market jingles its bells in late November. For a complete list of festivals, see www.yorkfestivals.com.

Internet Access: You'll find public computers at the following spots: the **TI** (see "Tourist Information," earlier), the **Evil Eye Lounge** (£1/30 minutes, free Wi-Fi, daily 10:00-24:00, upstairs at 42 Stonegate, tel. 01904/640-002), and the **York Public Library** (£1/2 hours, free Wi-Fi, Mon-Thu 9:00-20:00, closes earlier Fri-Sun, Museum Street, tel. 01904/552-828).

Laundry: Some B&Bs will do laundry for a reasonable charge. Otherwise the nearest place is **Haxby Road Launderette,** a long 15-minute walk north of the town center (or you can take a bus—ask your B&B for directions, 124 Haxby Road, call ahead for prices and hours—tel. 01904/623-379).

Bike Rental: With the exception of the pedestrian center, the town's not great for biking. But there are several fine countryside rides from York, and the riverside New Walk bike path is pleasant. **Cycle Heaven** is at the train station (£10/2 hours, £15/5 hours, £20/24 hours, Mon-Sat 9:00-17:30, Sun 11:00-16:00, closed Sun off-season, to the left as you face the main station entrance from outside, tel. 01904/622-701). For location, see map on page 530.

Taxi: From the train station, taxis zip new arrivals to their B&Bs for £6-8. Queue up at the taxi stand, or call 01904/638-833 or 01904/659-659; cabbies don't start the meter until you get in.

Car Rental: If you're nearing the end of your trip, consider dropping your car upon arrival in York. The money saved by turning it in early just about pays for the train ticket that whisks you effortlessly to London. In York, you'll find these agencies:

Avis (3 Layerthorpe, tel. 0844-544-6117); **Hertz** (at train station, tel. 0843-309-3082); **Budget** (near the National Railway Museum behind the train station at 75 Leeman Road, tel. 01904/644-919); and **Europcar** (off Queen Street near train station, tel. 0844-846-4003). Beware: Car-rental agencies close early on Saturday afternoons and all day Sunday—when dropping off it's OK, but picking up is only possible by prior arrangement (and for an extra fee).

Updates to This Book: For the latest, see ricksteves.com/update.

Tours in York

▲▲▲WALKING TOURS

Free Walks with Volunteer Guides

Charming locals give energetic, entertaining, and free two-hour walks through York (April-Oct daily at 10:15 and 14:15, June-Aug also at 18:15; Nov-March daily at 10:15 and also at 13:15 on weekends; depart from Exhibition Square in front of the art gallery, tel. 01904/550-098, www.avgyork.co.uk). These tours often go long because the guides love to teach and tell stories. You're welcome to cut out early—but let them know, or they'll worry, thinking they've lost you.

Yorkwalk Tours

These are more serious 1.5- to 2-hour walks with a history focus. They do four different walks—Essential York, Roman York, Secret York, and The Snickelways of York—as well as a variety of "special walks" on more specific topics (£6, Feb-Nov daily at 10:30 and 14:15, Dec-Jan weekends only, depart from Museum Gardens Gate, just show up, tel. 01904/622-303, www.yorkwalk.co.uk—check website, ask TI, or call for schedule). Tours go rain or shine, with as few as two participants.

Ghost Walks

Each evening, the old center of York is crawling with creepy ghost walks. These are generally 1.5 hours long, cost £5, and go every evening, rain or shine. There are no reservations (you simply show up) and no tickets (just pay at the start). At the advertised time and place, your black-clad guide appears, and you follow him or her to the first stop. Your guide gives a sample of the entertainment you have in store, humorously collects the "toll," and you're off.

You'll see fliers and signboards all over town advertising the many ghost walks. Companies come and go, but I find there are three general styles of walks: historic, street theater, and storytelling. You will find three reliably good walks on page 536, one for each style. Each gives a £1 discount (limit two "victims" per book) off full price for Rick Steves readers with this book.

York at a Glance

▲▲▲**York Minster** York's pride and joy, and one of England's finest churches, with stunning stained-glass windows, textbook Decorated Gothic design, and glorious evensong services. **Hours:** Mon-Sat 9:00-18:30, Sun 12:30-18:30; shorter hours for tower and undercroft; evensong services Tue-Sat and some Mon at 17:15, Sun at 16:00. See page 542.

▲▲▲**Walking Tours** Variety of guided town walks and evening ghost walks covering York's history. **Hours:** Various times daily; fewer off-season. See page 534.

▲▲**Yorkshire Museum** Sophisticated archaeology and natural history museum with York's best Viking exhibit, plus Roman, Saxon, Norman, and Gothic artifacts. **Hours:** Daily 10:00-17:00. See page 550.

▲▲**Jorvik Viking Centre** Entertaining and informative Disney-style exhibit/ride exploring Viking lifestyles and artifacts. **Hours:** Daily April-Oct 10:00-17:00, Nov-March until 16:00. See page 553.

▲▲**York Castle Museum** Far-ranging collection displaying everyday objects from Victorian times to the present. **Hours:** Daily 9:30-17:00. See page 555.

▲▲**National Railway Museum** Train buff's nirvana, tracing the history of all manner of rail-bound transport. **Hours:** Daily 10:00-18:00. See page 557.

▲**The Shambles** Atmospheric old butchers' quarter, with colorful, tipsy medieval buildings. **Hours:** Always open. See page 541.

▲**Ouse Riverside Walk** Bucolic path along river to a mod pedestrian bridge. **Hours:** Always open. See page 559.

▲**York Brewery** Honest, casual tour through an award-winning microbrewery with the guy who makes the beer. **Hours:** Mon-Sat at 12:30, 14:00, 15:30, and 17:00. See page 558.

▲**Fairfax House** Glimpse into an 18th-century Georgian family house, with enjoyably chatty docents. **Hours:** Tue-Sat 10:00-16:30, Sun 11:00-15:30, Mon by tour only at 11:00 and 14:00, closed Jan-mid-Feb. See page 554.

The **Terror Trail Walk** is more historic, "all true," and a bit more intellectual (18:45, meet at The Golden Fleece at bottom of The Shambles, www.yorkterrortrail.co.uk).

The **Ghost Hunt** is comedic street theater produced and usually performed by Andy Dextrous, who introduces himself by saying, "My name is...unimportant" (19:30, meet at the bottom of The Shambles, www.ghosthunt.co.uk).

The **Original Ghost Walk** was the first of its kind, dating back to the 1970s, and is more classic spooky storytelling rather than comedy (20:00, meet at The Kings Arms at Ouse Bridge, www.theoriginalghostwalkofyork.co.uk).

HOP-ON, HOP-OFF BUS TOUR

City Sightseeing's half-enclosed, double-decker, hop-on, hop-off buses circle York, taking tourists past secondary sights that the city walking tours skip—the mundane perimeter of town. While you can hop on and off all day, York is so compact that these have no real transportation value. If taking a bus tour, I'd catch either one at Exhibition Square (near Bootham Bar) and ride it for an orientation all the way around. Consider getting off at the National Railway Museum, skipping the last five minutes. Once or twice an hour, they run a "Heritage Tour" route with a live guide (£12, ticket good for £3 off York Boat cruise—described next, pay driver, cash only, ticket valid 24 hours, Easter-Oct departs every 10-15 minutes, daily 9:00-17:30, less frequent off-season, about 1 hour, tel. 01904/633-990, www.yorkbus.co.uk).

BOAT CRUISE

York Boat does a lazy, narrated 45-minute lap along the River Ouse (£8, ticket good for £3 off City Sightseeing bus tours—see above, April-Sept runs every 30 minutes, daily 10:30-15:00, off-season 4/day, no cruises Dec-Jan; leaves from Lendal Bridge and King's Staith landings, near Skeldergate Bridge; also 1.5-hour evening cruise at 21:15 for £9.50, leaves from King's Staith; tel. 01904/628-324, www.yorkboat.co.uk).

York Walk

Get a taste of Roman and medieval York on this easy, self-guided stroll. The walk begins in the gardens just in front of the Yorkshire Museum, covers a stretch of the medieval city walls, and then cuts through the middle of the old town. Start at the ruins of St. Mary's Abbey in the Museum Gardens.

St. Mary's Abbey: This abbey dates to the age of William the Conqueror—whose harsh policies (called the "Harrowing of the North") consisted of massacres and destruction, including the burning of York's main church. His son Rufus, who tried to improve relations in the 11th century, established a great church here. The church became an abbey that thrived from the 13th century until the Dissolution of the Monasteries in the 16th century. The Dissolution, which accompanied the Protestant Reformation and break with Rome, was a power play by Henry VIII. The king wanted much more than just a divorce: He wanted the land and riches of the monasteries. Upset with the pope, he demanded that his subjects pay him taxes rather than give the Church tithes. (For more information, see the sidebar on page 545.)

As you gaze at this ruin, imagine magnificent abbeys like this scattered throughout the realm. Henry VIII destroyed most of them, taking the lead from their roofs and leaving the stones to scavenging townsfolk. Scant as they are today, these ruins still evoke a time of immense monastic power. The one surviving wall was the west half of a very long, skinny nave. The tall arch marked the start of the transept. Stand on the plaque that reads *Crossing beneath central tower,* and look up at the air that now fills the space where a huge tower once stood. (Fine carved stonework from the ruined abbey is on display in a basement room of the adjacent Yorkshire Museum.)

Beyond the abbey, laid out like a dozen stone eggs, are 12 ancient **Roman sarcophagi** that were excavated at the train station. You'll also see a bowling green and the abbey's original wall (not part of the city walls).

- *With your back to the abbey, see the fine Neoclassical building housing* *the **Yorkshire Museum** (well worth a visit and described later, under "Sights in York"). Walk past this about 30 yards to a corner of the city's **Roman wall.** A tiny lane through the garden (past a yew tree) leads through a small gated arch (may be locked), giving a peek into the ruined tower.*

Multangular Tower: This 12-sided tower (c. A.D. 300) was likely a catapult station built to protect the town from enemy river traffic. The red ribbon of bricks was a Roman trademark—both structural and decorative. The lower stones are Roman, while the bigger upper stones are medieval. After Rome fell, York suffered through two centuries of a dark age. Then, in the ninth century, the Vikings ruled. They built with wood, so almost nothing from that period remains. The Normans came in 1066 and built in stone, generally atop Roman structures (like this wall). The wall that defined the ancient Roman garrison town worked for the Norman town, too. But after the English Civil War in the 1600s and Jacobite rebellions in the 1700s, fortified walls were no longer needed in England's interior.

• *Now, return 10 steps down the lane and turn right, walking between the museum and the Roman wall. Continuing straight, the lane goes between the abbot's palace and the town wall. This is a "snickelway"—a small characteristic York lane or footpath. The snickelway pops out on...*

Exhibition Square: With Henry VIII's Dissolution of the Monasteries, the abbey was destroyed and the Abbot's Palace became the **King's Manor** (from the snickelway, make a U-turn to the left and through the gate). Enter the building under the coat of arms of Charles I, who stayed here during the English Civil War in the 1640s. Today, the building is part of the University of York. Because the northerners were slow to embrace the king's reforms, Henry VIII came here to enforce the Dissolution. He stayed 17 days in this mansion and brought along 1,000 troops to make his determination clear. You can wander into the grounds and building. The Refectory Café serves cheap cakes, soup, and sandwiches to students, professors, and visitors like you (Mon-Fri 9:30-15:00, closed Sat-Sun).

Exhibition Square is the departure point for various walking and bus tours. You can see the towers of the Minster in the distance. Travelers in the Middle Ages could see the Minster from miles away as they approached the city. Across the street is a pay

WC and **Bootham Bar**—one of the fourth-century Roman gates in York's wall—with access to the best part of the city walls (free, walls open 8:00-dusk).

• *Climb up the bar.*

Walk the Wall: Hike along the top of the wall behind the Minster to the first corner. Just because you see a padlock on an entry gate, don't think it's locked—give it a push, and you'll probably find it's open. York's 13th-century walls are three miles long. This stretch follows the original Roman wall. Norman kings built the walls to assert control over northern England. Notice the pivots in the crenellations (square notches at the top of a medieval wall), which once held wooden hatches to provide cover for archers. The wall was extensively renovated in the 19th century (Victorians added Romantic arrow slits).

At the corner with the benches—**Robin Hood's Tower**—you can lean out and see the moat outside. This was originally the Roman ditch that surrounded the fortified garrison town. Continue walking for a fine view of the Minster, with its truncated main tower and the pointy rooftop of its chapter house.

• *Continue on to the next gate.*

Monk Bar: This fine medieval gatehouse is the home of the overly-slick **Richard III Museum** (described later, under "Sights in York").

• *Descend the wall at Monk Bar, and step past the portcullis (last lowered in 1953 for the Queen's coronation) to emerge outside the city's protective wall. Take 10 paces and gaze up at the tower. Imagine 10 archers behind the arrow slits. Keep an eye on the 17th-century guards, with their stones raised and primed to protect the town.*

Return through the city wall. After a short block, turn right on Ogleforth. ("Ogle" is the Norse word for owl, hence our word "ogle"—to look at something fiercely.)

York's Old Town: Walking down Ogleforth, ogle (on your left) a charming little brick house called the **Dutch House.** Designed by an apprentice architect who was trying to show off for his master, it's from the 17th century. It was the first entirely brick house in town, a sign of opulence. Next, also of brick, is a former brewery, with a 19th-century industrial feel.

Ogleforth jogs left and becomes **Chapter House Street,** passing the Treasurer's House to the back side of the Minster. Circle around the left side of the church, past the stonemasons' lodge (where craftsmen are chiseling local limestone for the church, as has been done here since the 13th century), to the statue of Roman Emperor Constantine and an ancient Roman column.

Step up to lounging **Constantine.** Five emperors visited York when it was the Roman city of Eboracum. Constantine was here when his father died. The troops declared him the Roman emperor in A.D. 306 at this site, and six years later, he went to Rome to claim his throne. In A.D. 312, Constantine legalized Christianity, and in A.D. 314, York got its first bishop. The thought-provoking plaque reads: "His recognition of the civil liberty of his Christian subjects and his personal conversion established the religious foundation of Western Christendom."

The **ancient column,** across the street from Constantine, is a reminder that the Minster sits upon the site of the Roman headquarters, or *principia.* The city placed this column here in 1971, just before celebrating the 1,900th anniversary of the founding of Eboracum—a.k.a. York.

• *If you want to visit the* ***York Minster*** *now, find the entrance on its west side (see description on page 542). Otherwise, head into the town center. From opposite the Minster's south transept door (by Constantine), take a narrow pedestrian walkway—which becomes Stonegate—into the tangled commercial center of medieval York. Walk straight down Stonegate, a street lined with fun and inviting cafés, pubs, and restaurants. Just before the* Ye Olde Starre Inne *banner hanging over the street, turn left down the snickelway called Coffee Yard. (It's marked by a red devil.) Enjoy strolling York's...*

"Snickelways": This is a made-up York word combining "snicket" (a passageway between walls or fences), "ginnel" (a narrow passageway between buildings), and "alleyway" (any narrow passage)—snickelway. York—with its population packed densely inside its protective walls—has about 50 of these public passages. In general, when exploring the city, you should duck into these—both for the adventure and to take a shortcut. While some of York's history has been bulldozed by modernity, bits of it hide and survive in the snickelways.

Coffee Yard leads past Barley Hall, popping out at the corner of Grape Lane and Swinegate. Medieval towns named streets for the business done there. Swinegate, a lane of pig farmers, leads to the market. Grape Lane is a polite version of that street's original crude name, Gropec*nt Lane. If you were here a thousand years ago, you'd find it lined by brothels. Throughout England, streets for prostitutes were called by this graphic name. Today, if you see a street named Grape Lane, that's usually its heritage.

Skip Grape Lane and turn right down Swinegate to a market (which you can see in the distance). The frumpy **Newgate Market,** popular for cheap produce and clothing, was created in the 1960s with the demolition of a bunch of colorful medieval lanes.

• *In the center of the market, tiny "Little Shambles" lane (on the left) dead-ends into the most famous lane in York.*

The Shambles: This colorful old street (rated ▲) was once the "street of the butchers." The name is derived from "shammell"—a butcher's bench upon which he'd cut and display his meat. In the 16th century, this lane was dripping with red meat. Look for the hooks under the eaves; these were once used to hang rabbit, pheasant, beef, lamb, and pigs' heads. Fresh slabs were displayed on the fat sills, while people lived above the shops. All the garbage and sewage flushed down the street to a mucky pond at the end—a favorite hangout for the town's cats and dogs. Tourist shops now fill these fine, half-timbered Tudor buildings. Look above the modern crowds and storefronts to appreciate the classic old English architecture. Unfortunately, the soil here isn't great for building; notice how the structures have settled in the absence of a solid foundation.

Turn right and slalom down The Shambles. At the Mr. Sandwich shop, pop into the snickelway and look for very old **woodwork.** Study the 16th-century carpentry—mortise-and-tenon joints with wooden plugs rather than nails.

Next door (on The Shambles) is the **shrine of St. Margaret Clitherow,** a 16th-century Catholic crushed by Protestants under her own door (as was the humiliating custom when a city wanted to teach someone a lesson). She was killed for hiding priests in her home here. Step into the tiny shrine for a peaceful moment to ponder Margaret, who in 1970 was sainted for her faith.

At the bottom of The Shambles is the cute, tiny **St. Crux Parish Hall,** which charities use to raise funds by selling light meals (see "Eating in York," later). Take some time to chat with the volunteers.

With blood and guts from The Shambles' 20 butchers all draining down the lane, it's no wonder The Golden Fleece, just below, is considered the most haunted pub in town.

• *Your town walk is finished. From here, you're just a few minutes from plenty of fun: street entertainment and lots of cheap eating options on King's Square, good restaurants on Fossgate, the York Castle Museum (a few blocks farther downhill), and the starting point for my Ouse Riverside Walk.*

Sights in York

▲▲▲YORK MINSTER

The pride of York, this largest Gothic church north of the Alps (540 feet long, 200 feet tall) brilliantly shows that the High Middle Ages were far from dark. The word "minster" means an important church chartered with a mission to evangelize. As it's the seat of a bishop, York Minster is also a cathedral. While Henry VIII destroyed England's great abbeys, this was not part of a monastery and was therefore left standing. It seats 2,000 comfortably; on Christmas and Easter at least 4,000 worshippers pack the place. Today, more than 250 employees and 500 volunteers work to preserve its heritage and welcome 1.3 million visitors each year.

Cost: Cathedral—£10, includes guided tour, undercroft museum, and crypt; free for kids under age 16; tower climb—£5.

Hours: The cathedral is open for sightseeing Mon-Sat 9:00-18:30, Sun 12:30-18:30. It opens for worship daily at 7:30. Closing time flexes with activities, but last entry is generally at 17:30—call or look online to confirm. Sights within the Minster have shorter hours (listed below). The Minster may close for special events (check calendar on website).

Information: You'll get a free map with your ticket. For more information, pick up the *York Minster Short Guide* for £2.50. Helpful Minster guides stationed throughout are happy to answer your questions. Tel. 01904/557-217 or 0844-393-0011, www.yorkminster.org.

Tower Climb: It costs £5 for 30 minutes of exercise (275 steps) and forgettable views. The tower opens at 10:00 (later on Sun), with

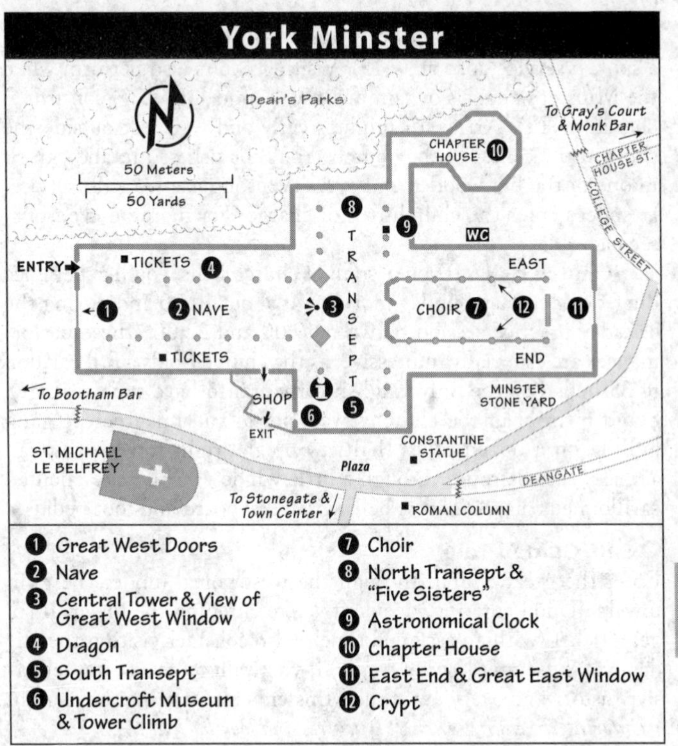

ascents every 45 minutes; the last ascent is generally at 17:30—later in peak season and earlier in winter (no children under 8, not good for acrophobes, closes in extreme weather). Be sure to get your ticket upon arrival, as only 50 visitors are allowed up at once; you'll be assigned an entry time. It's a tight, spiraling, claustrophobic staircase with an iron handrail. You'll climb about 150 steps to the top of the transept, step outside to cross a narrow walkway, then go back inside for more than 100 steps to the top of the central tower. From here (while caged in), you can enjoy views of rooftops and the flat countryside.

Undercroft Museum: This museum focuses on the history of the site and its origins as a Roman fortress (Mon-Sat 10:00-17:00, Sun 12:30-16:00).

Tours: Free guided tours depart from the ticket desk every hour on the hour (Mon-Sat 10:00-15:00, can be more frequent during busy times, none on Sun, one hour, they go even with just one or two people). You can join a tour in progress, or if none is scheduled, request a departure.

Evensong: To experience the cathedral in musical and spiritual action, attend an evensong (Tue-Sat at 17:15, Sun at 16:00). On

Mondays, visiting choirs fill in about half the time (otherwise it's a spoken service, also at 17:15). Visiting choirs also perform when the Minster's choir is on summer break (mid-July-Aug, confirm at church or TI). Arrive 15 minutes early and wait just outside the choir in the center of the church. You'll be ushered in and can sit in one of the big wooden stalls. As evensong is a worship service, attendees enter the church free of charge. For more on evensong, see page 145.

Church Bells: If you're a fan of church bells, you'll experience ding-dong ecstasy Sunday morning at about 10:00 and during the Tuesday practice session between 19:00 and 22:00. These performances are especially impressive, as the church holds a full carillon of 35 bells (it's the only English cathedral to have such a range). Stand in front of the church's west portal and imagine the gang pulling on a dozen ropes (halfway up the right tower—you can actually see the ropes through a little window) while one talented carillonneur plays 22 more bells with a keyboard and foot pedals.

➲ Self-Guided Tour

Enter the great church through the west portal (under the twin towers). Upon entering, decide if you're climbing the tower. If so, get a ticket (with an assigned time). Also consider visiting the undercroft museum (described later) if you want to get a comprehensive history and overview of the Minster before touring the church.

• *Entering the church, turn 180 degrees and look back at the...*

❶ **Great West Doors:** These are used only on special occasions. Flanking the doors is a list of archbishops (and other church officials) that goes unbroken back to the 600s. The statue of Peter with the key and Bible is a reminder that the church is dedicated to St. Peter, and the key to heaven is found through the word of God. While the Minster sits on the remains of a Romanesque church (c. 1100), today's church was begun in 1220 and took 250 years to complete. Up above, look for the female headless "semaphore saints," using semaphore flag code to spell out a message with golden discs: "Christ is here."

• *Grab a chair and enjoy the view down the...*

❷ **Nave:** Your first impression might be of its spaciousness and brightness. One of the widest Gothic naves in Europe, it was built between 1280 and 1360—the middle period of the Gothic style, called "Decorated Gothic." Rather than risk a stone roof, builders spanned the space with wood. Colorful shields on the arcades are

England's Anglican Church

The Anglican Church (a.k.a. the Church of England) came into existence in 1534 when Henry VIII declared that he, and not Pope Clement VII, was the head of England's Catholics. The pope had refused to allow Henry to divorce his wife to marry his mistress Anne Boleyn (which Henry did anyway, resulting in the birth of Elizabeth I). Still, Henry regarded himself as a faithful Catholic—just not a *Roman* Catholic—and made relatively few changes in how and what Anglicans worshipped.

Henry's son, Edward VI, later instituted many of the changes that Reformation Protestants were bringing about in continental Europe: an emphasis on preaching, people in the pews actually reading the Bible, clergy being allowed to marry, and a more "Protestant" liturgy in English from the revised Book of Common Prayer (1549). The next monarch, Edward's sister Mary I, returned England to the Roman Catholic Church (1553), earning the nickname "Bloody Mary" for her brutal suppression of Protestant elements. When Elizabeth I succeeded Mary (1558), she soon broke from Rome again. Today, many regard the Anglican Church as a compromise between the Catholic and Protestant traditions. In the US, Anglicans split off from the Church in England after the American Revolution, creating the Episcopal Church that still thrives today.

Ever since Henry VIII's time, the York Minster has held a special status within the Anglican hierarchy. After a long feud over which was the leading church, the archbishops of Canterbury and York agreed that York's bishop would have the title "Primate of England" and Canterbury's would be the "Primate of All England," directing Anglicans on the national level.

the coats of arms of nobles who helped tall and formidable Edward I, known as "Longshanks," fight the Scots in the 13th century.

The coats of arms in the clerestory (upper-level) glass represent the nobles who helped his son, Edward II, in the same fight. There's more medieval glass in this building than in the rest of England combined. This precious glass survived World War II—hidden in stately homes throughout Yorkshire.

Walk to the very center of the church, under the ❸ **central tower.** Look up. An exhibit in the undercroft explains how gifts and skill saved this 197-foot tower from collapse. Use the neck-saving mirror to marvel at it.

Look back at the west end to marvel at the **Great West Win-**

dow, especially the stone tracery. While its nickname is the "Heart of Yorkshire," it represents the sacred heart of Christ, meant to remind people of his love for the world.

Find the ❹ **dragon** on the right of the nave (two-thirds of the way up the wall). While no one is sure of its purpose, it pivots and has a hole through its neck—so it was likely a mechanism designed to raise a lid on a baptismal font.

• *Facing the altar, turn right and head into the...*

❺ **South Transept:** Look up. The new "bosses" (carved medallions decorating the point where the ribs meet on the ceiling) are a reminder that the roof of this wing of the church was destroyed by fire in 1984, caused when lightning hit an electricity box. Some believe the lightning was God's angry response to a new bishop, David Jenkins, who questioned the literal truth of Jesus' miracles. (Jenkins had been interviewed at a nearby TV studio the night before, leading locals to joke that the lightning occurred "12 hours too late, and 17 miles off-target.") Regardless, the entire country came to York's aid. *Blue Peter* (England's top kids' show) conducted a competition among their young viewers to design new bosses. Out of 30,000 entries, there were six winners (the blue ones—e.g., man on the moon, feed the children, save the whales).

Two other sights can be accessed through the south transept: the ❻ **Undercroft Museum** (explained later) and the **tower climb** (explained earlier). But for now, stick with this tour; we'll circle back to the south transept at the end, before exiting the church.

• *Head back into the middle of the nave and face the front of the church. You're looking at the...*

❼ **Choir:** Examine the choir screen—the ornate wall of carvings separating the nave from the choir. It's lined with all the English kings from William I (the Conqueror) to Henry VI (during whose reign it was carved, in 1461). Numbers indicate the years each reigned. It is indeed "slathered in gold leaf," which sounds impressive, but the gold is very thin...a nugget the size of a sugar cube is pounded into a sheet the size of a driveway.

Step into the choir, where a service is held daily. All the carving was redone after an 1829 fire, but its tradition of glorious evensong services (sung by choristers from the Minster School) goes all the way back to the eighth century.

• *To the left as you face the choir is the...*

❽ **North Transept:** In this transept, the grisaille windows—dubbed the **"Five Sisters"**—are dedicated to British servicewomen

who died in wars. Made in 1260, before colored glass was produced in England, these contain more than 100,000 pieces of glass.

The 18th-century ❾ **astronomical clock** is worth a look (the sign helps you make sense of it). It's dedicated to the heroic Allied aircrews from bases here in northern England who died in World War II (as Britain kept the Nazis from invading in its "darkest hour"). The Book of Remembrance below the clock contains 18,000 names.

• *A corridor leads to the Gothic, octagonal...*

❿ **Chapter House:** This was the traditional meeting place of the governing body (or chapter) of the Minster. On the pillar in the middle of the doorway, the Virgin holds Baby Jesus while standing on the devilish serpent. The Chapter House, without an interior support, is remarkable (almost frightening) for its breadth. The fanciful carvings decorating the canopies above the stalls date from 1280 (80 percent are originals) and are some of the Minster's finest. Stroll slowly around the entire room and imagine that the tiny sculpted heads are a 14th-century parade—a fun glimpse of medieval society. Grates still send hot air up robes of attendees on cold winter mornings. A model of the wooden construction illustrates the impressive 1285 engineering.

The Chapter House was the site of an important moment in England's parliamentary history. Fighting the Scots in 1295, Edward I (the "Longshanks" we met earlier) convened the "Model Parliament" here, rather than down south in London. (The Model Parliament is the name for its early version, back before the legislature was split into the Houses of Commons and Lords.) The government met here through the 20-year reign of Edward II, before moving to London during Edward III's rule in the 14th century.

• *Go back out into the main part of the church, turn left, and continue all the way down the nave (behind the choir) to the...*

⓫ **East End:** This part of the church is square, lacking a semicircular apse, typical of England's Perpendicular Gothic style (15th century). Monuments (almost no graves) were once strewn throughout the church, but in the Victorian Age they were gathered into the east end, where you see them today.

The **Great East Window,** the size of a tennis court, is currently under restoration. Under it, two exhibits—"Stone by Stone" and "Let There Be Light"—give an intimate look at Gothic stone and glasswork. Curators hope that this grand window might finally come out from its scaffolding for unveiling sometime in 2017.

"Let There Be Light" explains the significance of the window and the scope of the conservation project. It illustrates the painstaking process of removing, dismantling, cleaning, and restoring each of the 311 panels. Interactive computers let you zoom in on each panel, read about the stories depicted in them, and explore the codes and symbols that are hidden in the window.

Because of the Great East Window's immense size, the east end has an extra layer of supportive stonework, parts of it wide enough to walk along. In fact, for special occasions, the choir has been known to actually sing from the walkway halfway up the window. But just as the window has deteriorated over time, so too has the stone. Nearly 3,500 stones need to be replaced or restored (as explained in the "Stone by Stone" exhibit). On some days, you may even see masons in action in the stone yard behind the Minster.

• *Below the choir (on either side), steps lead down to the...*

⓬ **Crypt:** Here you can view the boundary of the much smaller, but still huge, Norman church from 1100 that stood on this spot (look for the red dots, marking where the Norman church ended, and note how thick the wall was). You can also see some of the old columns and additional remains from the Roman fortress that once stood here, the tomb of St. William of York (actually a Roman sarcophagus that was reused), and the modern concrete save-the-church foundations (much of this church history is covered in the undercroft museum).

• *You'll exit the church through the gift shop in the south transept. If you've yet to climb the* ***tower****, the entrance is in the south transept before the exit. Also before leaving, look for the entrance to the...*

Undercroft Museum: Well-described exhibits follow the history of the site from its origins as a Roman fortress to the founding of an Anglo-Saxon/Viking church, the shift to a Norman place of worship, and finally the construction of the Gothic structure that stands today. Videos re-create how the fortress and Norman structure would have been laid out, and various artifacts and remains provide an insight into each period. The museum fills a space that was excavated following the near collapse of the central tower in 1967.

Highlights include the actual remains of the Roman fort's basilica, which are viewable through a see-through floor. There are also patches of Roman frescoes from what was the basilica's anteroom. One remarkable artifact is the Horn of Ulf, an intricately carved elephant's tusk presented to the Minster in 1030 by Ulf, a Viking nobleman, as a symbol that he was dedicating his land to God and the Church. Also on view is the York Gospels manuscript, a thousand-year-old text containing the four gospels. Made by Anglo-Saxon monks at Canterbury, it's the only book in the Minster's collection that dates prior to the Norman Conquest. It is still used to this day to swear in archbishops. Your last stop in the undercroft is a small and comfortable theater where you can enjoy three short videos (10 minutes total) showing the Minster in action. One is about Roman Emperor Constantine and the rise of Christianity, another covers a day in the life of the cathedral (skippable), and the final video explores hidden treasures of the Minster. • *This finishes your visit. Before leaving, take a moment to just be in this amazing building. Then, go in peace.*

Nearby: As you leave through the south transept, notice the people-friendly plaza created here and how effectively it ties the church in with the city that stretches before you. To your left are the Roman column from the ancient headquarters, which stood where the Minster stands today (and from where Rome administered the northern reaches of Britannia 1,800 years ago); a statue of Emperor Constantine (for more details, see page 539); and the covered York Minster Stone Yard, where masons are chiseling stone—as they have for centuries—to keep the religious pride and joy of York looking good.

OTHER SIGHTS INSIDE YORK'S WALLS

I've listed these roughly in geographical order, from near the Minster at the northwest end of town to the York Castle Museum at the southeast end.

Note that several of York's glitzier and most heavily promoted sights (including Jorvik Viking Centre, Dig, and Barley Hall) are run by the York Archaeological Trust (YAT). While rooted in real history, YAT attractions are geared primarily for kids and work hard (some say too hard) to make the history entertaining. If you like their approach and plan to visit several, ask about the various combo-ticket options.

▲▲Yorkshire Museum

Located in a lush, picnic-perfect park next to the stately ruins of St. Mary's Abbey (described in my "York Walk," earlier), the Yorkshire Museum is the city's serious "archaeology of York" museum. You can't dig a hole in York without hitting some remnant of the city's long past, and most of what's found ends up here. While the hordes line up at Jorvik Viking Centre, this museum has no crowds and provides a broader historical context, with more real artifacts. The three main collections—Roman, medieval, and natural history—are well-described, bright, and kid-friendly.

Cost and Hours: £7.50, kids under 16 free with paying adult, daily 10:00-17:00, within Museum Gardens, tel. 01904/687-687, www.yorkshiremuseum.org.uk.

Visiting the Museum: At the entrance, you're greeted by an original, early fourth-century A.D. Roman statue of the god Mars. If he could talk, he'd say, "Hear me, mortals. There are three sections here: Roman (on this floor), medieval (downstairs), and natural history (a kid-friendly wing on this floor). Start first with the 10-minute video for a sweeping history of the city."

The **Roman** collection surrounds a large map of the Roman Empire, set on the floor. You'll see slice-of-life exhibits about Roman baths, a huge floor mosaic, and skulls accompanied by artists' renderings of how the people originally looked. (One man was apparently killed by a sword blow to the head—making it graphically clear that the struggle between Romans and barbarians was a violent one.) These artifacts are particularly interesting when you consider that you're standing in one of the farthest reaches of the Roman Empire.

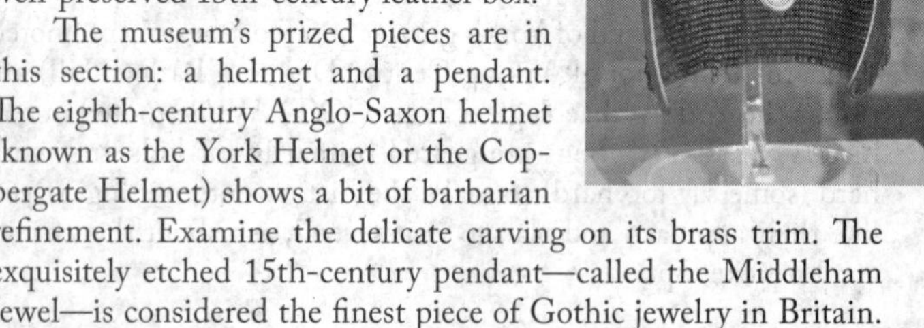

The **medieval** collection is in the basement. During the Middle Ages, York was England's second city. One large room is dominated by ruins of the St. Mary's Abbey complex (described on page 537; one wall still stands just out front—be sure to see it before leaving). You'll also see old weapons, glazed vessels, and a well-preserved 13th-century leather box.

The museum's prized pieces are in this section: a helmet and a pendant. The eighth-century Anglo-Saxon helmet (known as the York Helmet or the Coppergate Helmet) shows a bit of barbarian refinement. Examine the delicate carving on its brass trim. The exquisitely etched 15th-century pendant—called the Middleham Jewel—is considered the finest piece of Gothic jewelry in Britain. The noble lady who wore this on a necklace believed that it helped

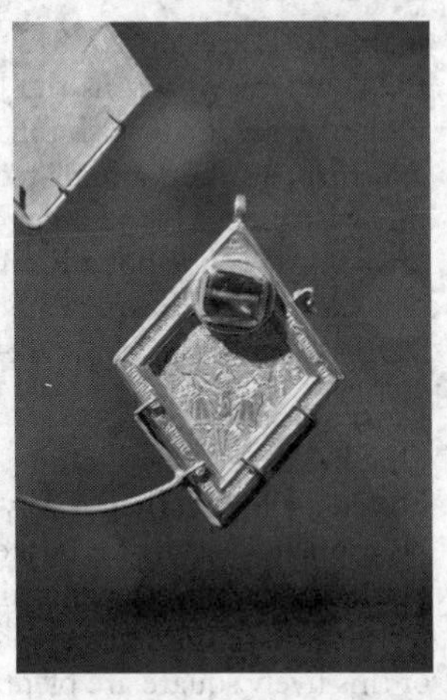

her worship and protected her from illness. The back of the pendant, which rested near her heart, shows the Nativity. The front shows the Holy Trinity crowned by a sapphire (which people believed put their prayers at the top of God's to-do list).

In addition to the Anglo-Saxon pieces, the Viking collection is one of the best in England. Looking over the artifacts, you'll find that the Vikings (who conquered most of the Anglo-Saxon lands) wore some pretty decent shoes and actually combed their hair. The Cawood Sword, nearly 1,000 years old, is one of the finest surviving swords from that era.

The **natural history** exhibit (titled "Extinct") is back upstairs, showing off skeletons of the extinct dodo and ostrich-like moa birds, as well as an ichthyosaurus.

Barley Hall

Uncovered behind a derelict office block in the 1980s, this medieval house has been restored to replicate a 1483 dwelling. It's designed to resurrect the Tudor age for visiting school groups, but feels soulless to adults.

Cost and Hours: £6, includes audioguide, kids under 5-free, combo-tickets with Jorvik Viking Centre and/or Dig, daily April-Oct 10:00-17:00, Nov-March 10:00-16:00, 2 Coffee Yard off Stonegate, tel. 01904/615-505, www.barleyhall.org.uk.

Holy Trinity Church

Built in the late Perpendicular Gothic style, this church has windows made of precious clear and stained glass from the 13th to 15th century. It holds rare box pews, which rest atop a floor that is sinking as bodies rot and coffins collapse. Enjoy its peaceful picnic-friendly gardens.

Cost and Hours: Free, Tue-Sat 10:00-16:00, Sun-Mon 12:00-16:00, 70 Goodramgate, www.holytrinityyork.org, info@holytrinityyork.org.

Richard III Museum

The last king of England's Plantagenet dynasty got a bad rap from Shakespeare (the Tudors took over after Richard was killed in 1485, so Shakespeare followed the party line and demonized him as a hunchbacked monster). With the discovery of Richard's remains in Leicester in 2013, interest in him has skyrocketed, and the company who runs the Jorvik Viking Centre (described later) took over an amateurish museum inside the Monk Bar's gatehouse and turned it into a high-tech extravaganza. It tries to excite visitors with all the blood and gore of that era, but it lacks any historic artifacts. If you're not a Richard III groupie, skip it.

Cost and Hours: £3.50, daily 10:00-17:00, Monk Bar, tel. 01904/615-505, www.jorvik-viking-centre.co.uk.

King's Square

This lively people-watching zone, with its inviting benches, once hosted a church. Then it was the site for the town's gallows. Today, it's prime real estate for buskers and street performers. Just hanging out here can be very entertaining. Just beyond is the most characteristic and touristy street in old York: The Shambles. Within sight of this lively square are plenty of cheap eating options (for tips, see "Eating in York," later).

Chocolate: York's Sweet Story

Though known mainly for its Roman, Viking, and medieval past, York also has a rich history in chocolate-making. Throughout the 1800s and 1900s, York was home to three major confectionaries—including Rowntree's, originators of the venerable Kit Kat. However, this chocolate "museum" is childish and overpriced. The building has no significance, and there are almost no historic artifacts. If you come, the visits are by tour only; your guide gives you lots of chocolate as you learn of York's confectionary past and watch brief videos.

Cost and Hours: £10.50, cheaper online, 30-minute tours run every 15 minutes daily starting at 10:00, last tour at 17:00, King's Square, tel. 0845-498-9411, www.yorksweetstory.com.

Dig

This hands-on, kid-oriented archaeological site gives young visitors an idea of what York looked like during Roman, Viking, medieval, and Victorian eras. Sift through "dirt" (actually shredded tires), dig up reconstructed Roman wall plaster, and take a look at what archaeologists have found recently. Entry is possible only with a one-hour guided tour (departures every 30 minutes); pass any waiting time by looking at the exhibits near the entry. The exhibits fill the haunted old St. Saviour's Church.

Cost and Hours: £6.50, kids under 5-free, combo-tickets with Jorvik Viking Centre and/or Barley Hall, daily 10:00-17:00, last tour departs one hour before closing, Saviourgate, tel. 01904/615-505, www.digyork.com.

Merchant Adventurers' Hall

Claiming to be the finest surviving medieval guildhall in Britain (from 1357-1361), this vast half-timbered building with marvelous exposed beams contains about 15 minutes' worth of interesting displays about life and commerce in the Middle Ages. You'll see three original, large rooms that are still intact: the great hall itself, where meetings took place; the undercroft, which housed a hospital and almshouse; and a chapel. Several smaller rooms are filled with exhibits about old York. Sitting by itself in its own little park, this classic old building is worth a stop even just to see it from the outside. Remarkably, the hall is still owned by the same Merchant Adventurers society that built it 650 years ago (now a modern charitable organization).

Cost and Hours: £6, includes audioguide, March-Oct Mon-Thu 9:00-17:00, Fri-Sat 9:00-15:30, Sun 11:00-16:00, shorter hours and closed Sun off-season, south of The Shambles between Fossgate and Piccadilly, tel. 01904/654-818, www.theyorkcompany.co.uk.

▲▲Jorvik Viking Centre

Take the "Pirates of the Caribbean," sail them northeast and back in time 1,000 years, sprinkle in some real artifacts, and you get Jorvik (YOR-vik)—as much a ride as a museum. Between 1976 and 1981, more than 40,000 artifacts were dug out of the peat bog right here in downtown York—the UK's largest archaeological dig of Viking-era artifacts. When the archaeologists were finished, the dig site was converted into this attraction. Innovative in 1984, the commercial success of Jorvik inspired copycat ride/museums all over England. Some love Jorvik, while others call it gimmicky and overpriced. If you think of it as Disneyland with a splash of history, Jorvik's fun. To me, Jorvik is a commercial venture designed for kids, with too much emphasis on its gift shop. But it's also undeniably entertaining, and—if you take the time to peruse its exhibits—it can be quite informative.

Cost and Hours: £10.25, various combo-tickets with Dig and/or Barley Hall, daily April-Oct 10:00-17:00, Nov-March until 16:00, these are last-entry times, tel. 01904/615-505, www.jorvik-viking-centre.co.uk.

Crowd-Beating Tips: This popular attraction can come with long lines. At the busiest times (roughly 11:00-15:00), you may have to wait an hour or more—especially on school holidays. For £1 extra, you can book a slot in advance, either over the phone or on their website. Or you can avoid the worst lines by coming early or late in the day (when you'll more likely wait just 10-15 minutes).

Visiting Jorvik: First you'll walk down stairs (marked with the layers of history you're passing) and explore a small **museum.** Under the glass floor is a re-creation of the archaeological dig that took place right here. Surrounding that are a few actual artifacts (such as a knife, comb, shoe, and cup) and engaging videos detailing the Viking invasions, longships, and explorers and the history of the excavations. Next to where you board your people-mover is the largest Viking timber found in the UK (from a wooden building on Coppergate). Don't rush through this area: These exhibits offer historical context to your upcoming journey back in time. Viking-costumed docents are happy to explain what you're seeing.

When ready, board a theme-park-esque **people-mover** for a 12-minute trip through the re-created Viking street of Coppergate. It's the year 975, and you're in the village of Jorvik. You'll glide past reconstructed houses and streets that sit atop the actual excavation site, while the recorded commentary tells you about everyday life in Viking times. Animatronic characters jabber at you in Old Norse, as you experience the sights, sounds, and smells of yore. Everything is true to the original dig—the face of one of the mannequins was computer-modeled from a skull dug up here.

Finally, you'll disembark at the **hands-on area,** where you can actually touch original Viking artifacts. You'll see several skeletons, carefully laid out and labeled to point out diseases and injuries, along with a big gob of coprolite (fossilized feces that offer archaeologists invaluable clues about long-gone lifestyles). Next, a gallery of everyday items (metal, glass, leather, wood, and so on) provides intimate glimpses into that redheaded culture. Take advantage of the informative touchscreens. The final section is devoted to swords, spears, axes, and shields. You'll also see bashed-in skulls (with injuries possibly sustained in battle) and a replica of the famous Coppergate Helmet (the original is in the Yorkshire Museum).

▲Fairfax House

This well-furnished home, supposedly the "first Georgian townhouse in England," is perfectly Neoclassical inside. Each room is staffed by wonderfully pleasant docents eager to talk with you. They'll explain how the circa-1760 home was built as the dowry for an aristocrat's daughter. The house is compact and bursting with stunning period furniture (the personal collection of a local chocolate magnate), gorgeously restored woodwork, and lavish stucco ceilings that offer clues as to each room's purpose. For example, stuccoed philosophers look down on the library, while the goddess of friendship presides over the drawing room. Taken together, this house provides fine insights into aristocratic life in 18th-century England.

Cost and Hours: £6, Tue-Sat 10:00-16:30, Sun 11:00-15:30, Mon by guided tour only at 11:00 and 14:00—the one-hour tours are worthwhile, closed Jan-mid-Feb, near Jorvik Viking Centre at 29 Castlegate, tel. 01904/655-543, www.fairfaxhouse.co.uk.

Clifford's Tower

Perched high on a knoll across from the York Castle Museum, this ruin is all that's left of York's 13th-century castle—the site of the gruesome 1190 mass-suicide of local Jews (they locked themselves inside and set the castle afire rather than face death at the hands of the bloodthirsty townspeople; read the whole story on the sign at the base of the hill). If you go inside, you'll see a model of the original castle complex as it looked in the Middle Ages, and you can climb up to enjoy fine city views from the top of the ramparts—but neither is worth the cost of admission.

Cost and Hours: £4.50, daily April-Sept 10:00-18:00, closes earlier off-season, tel. 01904/646-940.

▲▲York Castle Museum

This fascinating social-history museum is a Victorian home show, possibly the closest thing to a time-tunnel experience England has to offer. The one-way plan ensures that you'll see everything, including remakes of rooms from the 17th to 20th century, a re-creation of a Victorian street, a heartfelt WWI exhibit, and some eerie prison cells.

Cost and Hours: £10, kids under 16 free with paying adult, £13 combo-ticket with Yorkshire Museum, daily 9:30-17:00, cafeteria at entrance, tel. 01904/687-687, www.yorkcastlemuseum.org.uk. It's at the bottom of the hop-on, hop-off bus route. The museum can call you a taxi (worthwhile if you're hurrying to the National Railway Museum, across town).

Information: The museum's £4 guidebook isn't necessary, but it makes a fine souvenir. The museum proudly offers no audioguides, as its roaming guides are enthusiastic about talking—engage them.

Visiting the Museum: The exhibits are divided between two wings: the North Building (to the left as you enter) and the South Building (to the right).

Follow the one-way route through the complex, starting in the **North Building.** You'll first visit the Period Rooms, illuminating Yorkshire lifestyles during different time periods (1600s-1950s) and among various walks of life, and Toy Story—an enchanting review of toys through the ages from dollhouses to Transformers. Next is the "Shaping the Body" exhibit, detailing diet and fashion trends over the last 400 years. Check out the codpieces, bustles, and corsets that used to "enhance" the human form, and wonder over some of the odd diet fads that make today's paleo diet seem normal. For foodies and chefs, the exhibit showcasing fireplaces and kitchens from the 1600s to the 1980s is especially tasty.

Next, stroll down the museum's re-created Kirkgate, a street from the Victorian era, when Britain was at the peak of its power. It features old-time shops and storefronts, including a pharmacist, sweet shop, school, and grocer for the working class, along with roaming live guides in period dress. Around the back is a slum area depicting how the poor lived in those times.

Circle back to the entry and cross over to the **South Building.** In the WWI exhibit, erected to mark the war's centennial, you can follow the lives of five York citizens as they experience the horrors and triumphs of the war years. One room plunges you into the gruesome world of trench warfare, where the average life expectancy was six weeks (and if you fell asleep during sentry duty, you'd be shot). A display about the home front notes that York suffered from Zeppelin attacks in which six died. At the end you're encouraged to share your thoughts in a room lined with chalkboards.

Exit outside and cross through the castle yard. A detour to

the left leads to a flour mill (open sporadically). Otherwise, your tour continues through the door on the right, where you'll find another reconstructed historical street, this one capturing the spirit of the swinging 1960s—"a time when the cultural changes were massive but the cars and skirts were mini." Slathered with DayGlo colors, this street scene examines fashion, music, and television (including clips of beloved kids' shows and period news reports).

Finally, head into the York Castle Prison, which recounts the experiences of actual people who were thrown into the clink here. Videos, eerily projected onto the walls of individual cells, show actors telling tragic stories about the cells' one-time inhabitants.

ACROSS THE RIVER

▲▲National Railway Museum

If you like model railways, this is train-car heaven. The thunderous museum shows 200 illustrious years of British railroad history. This biggest and best railroad museum anywhere is interesting even to people who think "Pullman" means "don't push."

Cost and Hours: Free but £3 suggested donation, daily 10:00-18:00, café, restaurant, tel. 0844-815-3139, www.nrm.org.uk.

Getting There: It's about a 15-minute walk from the Minster (southwest of town, up the hill behind the train station). From the train station itself, the fastest approach is to go all the way to the back of the station (using the overpass to cross the tracks), exit out the back door, and turn right up the hill. To skip the walk, a cute little "road train" shuttles you more quickly between the Minster and the Railway Museum (£2 one-way, £3 round-trip, runs daily Easter-Oct, leaves museum every 30 minutes 11:00-16:00 at :00 and :30 past each hour; leaves town—from Duncombe Place, 100 yards in front of the Minster—at :15 and :45 past each hour).

Visiting the Museum: Pick up the floor plan to locate the various exhibits, which sprawl through several gigantic buildings on both sides of the street. Throughout the complex, red-shirted "explainers" are eager to talk trains.

The museum's most impressive room is the **Great Hall** (head right from the entrance area and take the stairs to the underground passage). Fanning out from this grand roundhouse is an array of historic cars and engines, starting with the very first "stagecoaches on rails," with a crude steam engine from 1830. You'll trace the evolution of steam-powered transportation, from a replica of the Rocket (one of the first successful steam locomotives), to the Flying Scotsman (the first London-Edinburgh express rail service), to the era of the aerodynamic Mallard (famous as the first train to travel at a startling two miles per minute—a marvel back in 1938) and the striking Art Deco-style Duchess of Hamilton. (The Flying Scotsman and other trains may not be on display, as they are sometimes on loan or under maintenance—ask an explainer if you can't find something.) The collection spans to the present day, with a replica of the Eurostar (Chunnel) train and the Shinkansen Japanese bullet train. Other exhibits include a steam engine that's been sliced open to show its cylinders, driving wheels, and smoke box, as well as a working turntable that's put into action twice a day. The Mallard Experience simulates a ride on the Mallard.

The Works is an actual workshop where engineers scurry about, fixing old trains. Live train switchboards show real-time rail traffic on the East Coast Main Line. Next to the diagrammed screens, you can look out to see the actual trains moving up and down the line. **The Warehouse** is loaded with more than 10,000 items relating to train travel (including dinnerware, signage, and actual trains). Exhibits feature dining cars, post cars, sleeping cars, train posters, and more info on the Flying Scotsman.

Crossing back to the entrance side, continue to the **Station Hall,** with a collection of older trains, including ones that the royals have used to ride the rails (including Queen Victoria's lavish royal car and a WWII royal carriage reinforced with armor). Behind that are the South Yard and the Depot, with actual working trains in storage.

▲York Brewery

This intimate, tactile, and informative 45-minute-long tour gives an enjoyable look at how this charming little microbrewery produces 5,500 pints per batch. Their award-winning Ghost Ale is strong, dark, and chocolaty. You can drink their beer throughout town, but to get it as fresh as possible, drink it where it's birthed, in their cozy Tap Room.

Cost and Hours: £8, includes four tasters of the best beer—ale not lager—in town; tours Mon-Sat at 12:30, 14:00, 15:30, and 17:00—just show up; cross the river on Lendal Bridge and walk 5 minutes to Toft Green just below Micklegate, tel. 01904/621-162, www.york-brewery.co.uk.

OUTSIDE OF TOWN

▲Ouse Riverside Walk or Bike Ride

The New Walk is a mile-long, tree-lined riverside lane created in the 1730s as a promenade for York's dandy class to stroll, see, and be seen—and is a fine place for today's visitors to walk or bike. This hour-long walk is a delightful way to enjoy a dose of countryside away from York. It's paved, illuminated in the evening, and a popular jogging route any time of day.

Start from the riverside under Skeldergate Bridge (near the York Castle Museum), and walk south away from town for a mile. Notice modern buildings across the river, with their floodwalls. Shortly afterwards, you cross the tiny Foss River on Blue Bridge, originally built in 1738. The easily-defended confluence of the Foss and the Ouse is the reason the Romans founded York in A.D. 71. Look back to see the modern floodgate (built after a flood in 1979) designed to stop the flooding Ouse from oozing up the Foss. At the bridge, a history panel describes this walk to the Millennium Bridge.

Stroll until you hit the striking, modern **Millennium Bridge.** Sit a bit on its reclining-lounge-chair fence and enjoy the vibrations of bikes and joggers as they pass. There's a strong biking trend in Britain these days. In recent Olympics, the British have won most of the gold medals in cycling. In 2012, Bradley Wiggins became Sir Bradley Wiggins by winning the Tour de France; his countryman, Chris Froome, won it in 2013 and 2015. You'll see lots of locals riding fancy bikes and wearing high-tech gear while getting into better shape. (Energetic bikers can continue past the Millennium Bridge 14 miles to the market town of Selby.)

Cross the river and walk back home, passing **Rowntree Park.** After the skateboard court, enter the park through its fine old gate. This park was financed by Joseph Rowntree, a wealthy chocolate baron with a Quaker ethic of contributing to his community. In the 19th century, life for the poor was a Charles Dickens-like struggle. A rich man building a park for the working class, which even had a swimming pool, was quite progressive. Victorian England had a laissez-faire approach to social issues. Then, like now, many wealthy people believed things would work out for the poor if the government just stayed out of it. However, others, such as the

Rowntree family, felt differently. Their altruism contributed to the establishment of a society that now takes care of its workers and poor much better.

Walk directly into the park toward the evocative Industrial Age housing complex capping the hill beyond the central fountain. In the park's brick gazebo are touching memorial plaques to WWI and WWII deaths. Rowntree gave this park to York to remember those lost in the "Great War." Stroll along the delightful, duck-filled pond near the Rowntree Park Café, return to the riverside lane, and continue back into York. You're almost home.

Shopping in York

With its medieval lanes lined with classy as well as tacky little shops, York is a hit with shoppers. I find two kinds of shopping in York particularly interesting: antique malls and charity shops.

Antique Malls: Three places within a few blocks of each other are filled with stalls and cases owned by antique dealers from the countryside (all open daily). The malls, a warren of rooms on three floors with cafés buried deep inside, sell the dealers' bygones on commission. Serious shoppers do better heading for the country, but York's shops are a fun browse: The **Antiques Centre York** (41 Stonegate, www.theantiquescentreyork.co.uk), the **Red House Antiques Centre** (a block from the Minster at Duncombe Place, www.redhouseyork.co.uk), and **Cavendish Antiques and Jewellers** (44 Stonegate, www.cavendishjewellers.co.uk).

Charity Shops: In towns all over Britain, it seems one low-rent street is lined with charity shops, allowing locals to both donate their junk and buy the junk of others in the name of a good cause. (Talk about a win-win.) It's great for random shopping. And, as the people working there are often volunteers involved in that cause, it can lead to some interesting conversations. In York, on Goodramgate (stretching a block or so in from the town wall), you'll find "thrift shops" run by the British Heart Foundation, Save the Children, Mind, and Oxfam. Good deals abound on clothing, purses, accessories, children's toys, books, CDs, and maybe even a guitar. If you buy something, you're getting a bargain and at the same time helping the poor, mentally ill, elderly, or even a pet in need of a vet (stores generally open between 9:00 and 10:00 and close between 16:00 and 17:00, with shorter hours on Sun).

Nightlife in York

PUBS

Even more than chocolate, York likes its beer. It has its own award-winning microbrewery, the York Brewery (which offers fine tours daily—see page 558), along with countless atmospheric pubs for memorable and convivial eating or drinking. Many pubs serve inexpensive plates at lunch, then focus on selling beer in the evening. Others offer lunch and early dinner. You can tell by their marketing how enthusiastic they are about cooking versus drawing pints.

The York Brewery Tap Room, a private club, feels like a fraternity of older men. But if you drop in, you can be an honorary guest. It's right at the microbrewery, with five beloved varieties on tap as fresh as you'll find anywhere (14 Toft Green, just below Micklegate, tel. 01904/621-162, www.york-brewery.co.uk).

The Maltings, just over Lendal Bridge, has classic pub ambience and serves good meals at lunch only. Local beer purists swear by this place (£6-7 pub lunches, open for drinks nightly, cross the bridge and look down and left to Tanners Moat, tel. 01904/655-387).

The Blue Bell is one of my favorites for old-school York vibes. This tiny traditional establishment with a time-warp Edwardian interior is the smallest pub in York. It has two distinct and inviting little rooms (limited food served at lunch only, east end of town at 53 Fossgate, tel. 01904/654-904).

The House of the Trembling Madness is another fine watering hole with a cozy atmosphere; it sits above a "bottle shop" that sells a stunning variety of beers by the bottle to go (48 Stonegate; also described later, under "Eating in York").

Evil Eye Lounge, a hit with York's young crowd, is a creaky, funky, hip space famous for its strong cocktails and edgy ambience. There are even beds to drink in. You can order downstairs at the bar (with a small terrace out back) or head upstairs (42 Stonegate; also a restaurant—described later, under "Eating in York").

The Golden Fleece is a sloppy, dingy place with tilty floors that make you feel drunk even if you aren't. Its wooden frame has survived without foundations for 500 years. Originally owned by wool traders, it's considered the oldest and most haunted coaching inn in York (16 Pavement, across the street from the southern end of The Shambles, tel. 01904/625-171).

The Last Drop is a solid basic pub—no music, no game machines, no children. It's owned by the York Brewery, so it always has their ales on tap (27 Colliergate facing King's Square, tel. 01904/621-951).

Student Pub Crawl: The **"Micklegate Run"** is a ritual for students all over Yorkshire. As this pub crawl starts just below the train station, students ride the train into York and then have a pint in each pub or club along Micklegate. You'll pass at least eight pubs as the street runs downhill from Micklegate Bar to the river. It can be lowbrow and sloppy. You'll see lots of hen-party and stag-party spectacles, and what local guys rudely call "mutton dressed as lamb"—older women trying to look young.

Riverside Eating and Drinking: On sunny days, there are several pubs with riverside tables just below Ouse Bridge, starting with **The Kings Arms,** which boasts flood marks inside its door and has a rougher local crowd than other recommended pubs. For a cheap thrill, grab a pint indoors and sit outside at their rustic picnic tables (3 King's Staith, tel. 01904/659-435).

ENTERTAINMENT

Theatre Royal

Recently reopened after a £4-million renovation, this spiffed-up theater offers a full variety of dramas, comedies, and works by Shakespeare. The locals are proud of the high-tech main theater and little 100-seat theater-in-the-round (£10-22 tickets, shows usually Tue-Sun at 19:30, tickets easy to get, on St. Leonard's Place near Bootham Bar and a 5- to 10-minute walk from recommended B&Bs, booking tel. 01904/623-568, www.yorktheatreroyal.co.uk). Those under 25 and students of any age can get tickets for £8-10.

Ghost Tours

You'll see fliers, signs, and promoters hawking a variety of entertaining after-dark tours. For a rundown on this scene, see page 534.

Movies

The centrally located **City Screen Cinema,** right on the river, plays both art-house and mainstream flicks. They also have an enticing café/bar overlooking the river that serves good food (13 Coney Street, tel. 0871-902-5726).

Sleeping in York

I've listed peak-season, book-direct prices; July through October are the busiest (and usually most expensive) months. B&Bs often charge more for weekends and sometimes turn away one-night bookings, particularly for peak-season Saturdays. (York is worth two nights anyway.) Prices may spike up for horse races and Bank Holidays (about 20 nights a season). Remember to book ahead during festival times (see "Helpful Hints," page 533) and weekends year-round.

B&Bs AND SMALL HOTELS

These B&Bs are all small and family-run. They come with plenty of steep stairs (and no elevators) but no traffic noise. Rooms can be tight; if maneuverability is important to you, say so when booking. For a good selection, contact them well in advance. B&B owners

Sleep Code

Abbreviations **(£1 = about $1.60, country code: 44)**
S=Single, **D**=Double/Twin, **T**=Triple, **Q**=Quad, **b**=bathroom
Price Rankings
$$$ Higher Priced—Most rooms £100 or more
$$ Moderately Priced—Most rooms £75-100
$ Lower Priced—Most rooms £75 or less
Unless otherwise noted, credit cards are accepted, breakfast is included, and free Wi-Fi and/or a guest computer is generally available. Prices change; verify current rates online or by email. For the best prices, always book directly with the hotel.

will generally hold a room with a credit-card number even if they want payment in cash. They work hard to help their guests sightsee and eat smartly. Most have permits to lend for street parking. Please honor your bookings—the B&B proprietors will have to charge you even if you don't show up.

The handiest B&B neighborhood is the quiet residential area just outside the old town wall's Bootham gate, along the road called Bootham. All of these are within a 10-minute walk of the Minster and TI, and a 5- to 15-minute walk or £6-8 taxi ride from the station. If driving, head for the cathedral and follow the medieval wall to the gate called Bootham Bar. The street called Bootham leads away from Bootham Bar.

Getting There: Here's the most direct way to walk to this B&B area from the train station: Head to the north end of the station, to the area between platforms 2 and 4. Shoot through the gap between the men's WC and the York Tap pub, past some racks of bicycles, and into the short-stay parking lot. Walk to the end of the lot to a pedestrian ramp, and zigzag your way down. At the bottom, head left, following the sign for the riverside route. When you reach the river, cross over on the footbridge—you'll have to carry your bags up and down some steps. At the far end of the bridge, the Abbey Guest House is a few yards to your right, facing the river. To reach The Hazelwood (closer to the town wall), walk from the bridge along the river until just before the short ruined tower, then turn inland up onto Marygate. For other B&Bs, at the bottom of the footbridge, turn left immediately onto a path that skirts the big parking lot (parallel to the train tracks). At the end of the parking lot, you'll turn depending on your B&B: for the places on or near Bootham Terrace, turn left and go under the tracks; for B&Bs on St. Mary's Street, take the short stairway on your right.

On or near Bootham Terrace

$$$ Hedley House Hotel, well-run by a wonderful family, has 30

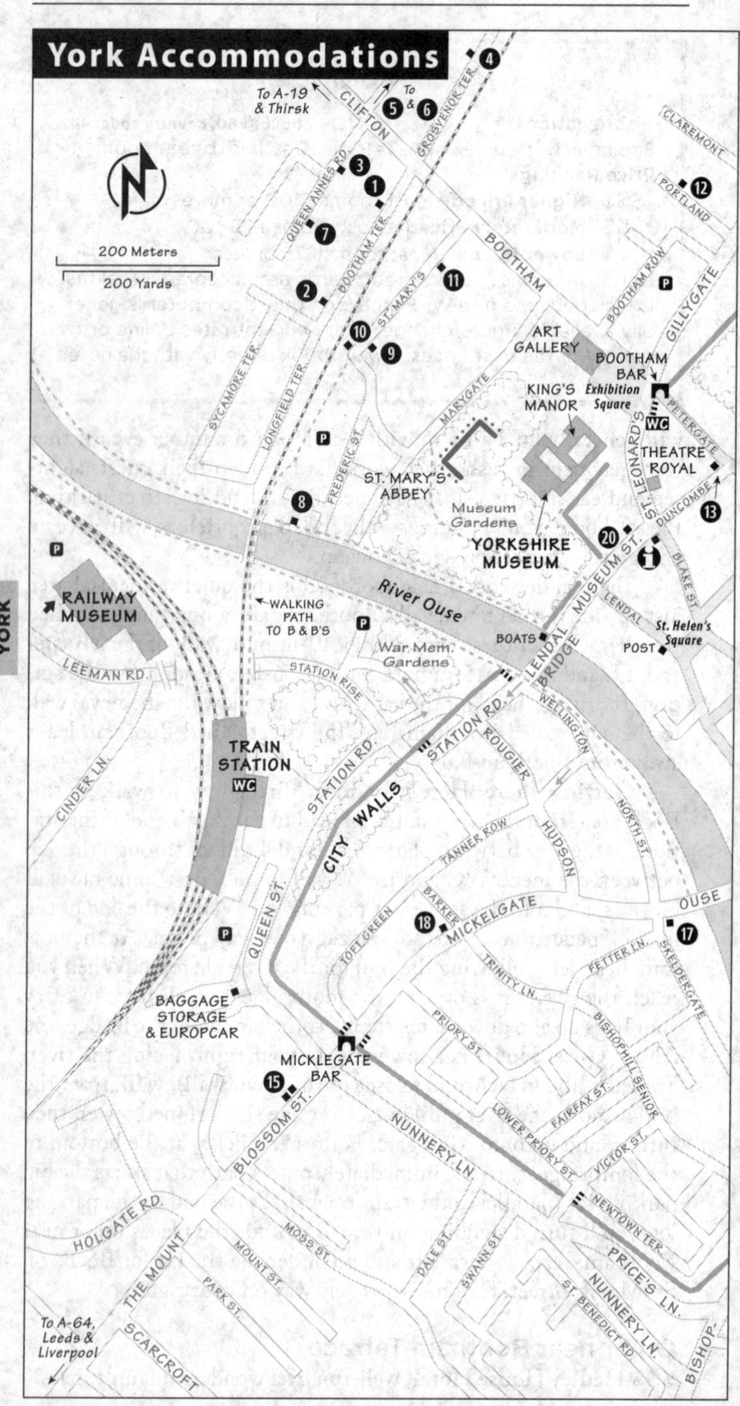
York Accommodations
To A-19 & Thirsk
To 5 & 6
CLIFTON
GROSVENOR TER.
QUEEN ANNE'S RD.
BOOTHAM TER.
BOOTHAM
ST. MARY'S
200 Meters
200 Yards
CLAREMONT
PORTLAND
BOOTHAM ROW
GILLYGATE
ART GALLERY
BOOTHAM BAR
Exhibition Square
KING'S MANOR
PETERGATE
WC
THEATRE ROYAL
ST. LEONARD'S
DUNCOMBE
SYCAMORE TER.
LONGFIELD TER.
FREDERIC ST.
MARYGATE
ST. MARY'S ABBEY
Museum Gardens
YORKSHIRE MUSEUM
MUSEUM ST.
BLAKE ST.
LENDAL
St. Helen's Square
POST
BOATS
River Ouse
RAILWAY MUSEUM
WALKING PATH TO B & B'S
War Mem. Gardens
STATION RISE
LENDAL BRIDGE
STATION RD.
WELLINGTON
LEEMAN RD.
ROUGIER
TRAIN STATION
WC
CINDER LN.
STATION RD.
CITY WALLS
NORTH ST.
HUDSON
TANNER ROW
QUEEN ST.
BARKER
MICKLEGATE
OUSE
TOFT GREEN
TRINITY LN.
FETTER LN.
SKELDERGATE
BAGGAGE STORAGE & EUROPCAR
PRIORY ST.
BISHOPHILL SENIOR
MICKLEGATE BAR
FAIRFAX ST.
BLOSSOM ST.
NUNNERY LN.
LOWER PRIORY ST.
VICTOR ST.
NEWTOWN TER.
HOLGATE RD.
MOSS ST.
MOUNT ST.
DALE ST.
SWANN ST.
PRICE'S LN.
THE MOUNT
PARK ST.
ST. BENEDICT RD.
NUNNERY LN.
To A-64, Leeds & Liverpool
SCARCROFT
BISHOP.
YORK

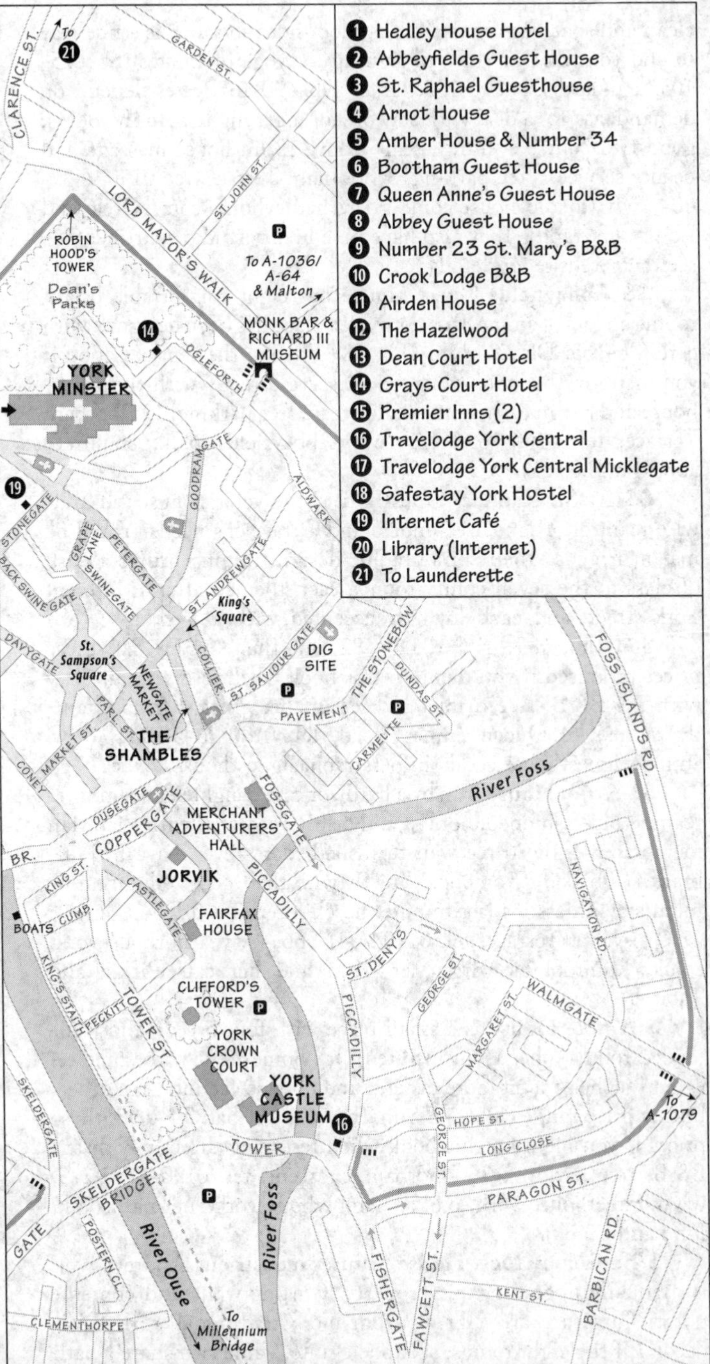

1 Hedley House Hotel
2 Abbeyfields Guest House
3 St. Raphael Guesthouse
4 Arnot House
5 Amber House & Number 34
6 Bootham Guest House
7 Queen Anne's Guest House
8 Abbey Guest House
9 Number 23 St. Mary's B&B
10 Crook Lodge B&B
11 Airden House
12 The Hazelwood
13 Dean Court Hotel
14 Grays Court Hotel
15 Premier Inns (2)
16 Travelodge York Central
17 Travelodge York Central Micklegate
18 Safestay York Hostel
19 Internet Café
20 Library (Internet)
21 To Launderette
YORK MINSTER
ROBIN HOOD'S TOWER
Dean's Parks
LORD MAYOR'S WALK
MONK BAR & RICHARD III MUSEUM
To A-1036/ A-64 & Malton
THE SHAMBLES
MERCHANT ADVENTURERS' HALL
JORVIK
FAIRFAX HOUSE
CLIFFORD'S TOWER
YORK CROWN COURT
YORK CASTLE MUSEUM
DIG SITE
River Foss
River Ouse
To Millennium Bridge
To A-1079
King's Square
St. Sampson's Square
BOATS

clean and spacious rooms. The outdoor hot tub/sauna is a fine way to end your day, or you can sign up for yoga or Pilates (Sb-£75-105, standard Db-£90-135, larger Db-£90-165, rates depend on demand, ask for a deal with stay of 3 or more nights, family rooms, good two-course evening meals from £18, in-house massage and beauty services, free parking, 3 Bootham Terrace, tel. 01904/637-404, www.hedleyhouse.com, greg@hedleyhouse.com, Greg and Louise Harrand). They also have nine luxury studio apartments—see their website for details.

$$ Abbeyfields Guest House has eight comfortable bright rooms up lots of stairs. This doily-free place has been designed with care (Sb-£55; Db-£84 Sun-Thu, £89 Fri-Sat; these prices good if you mention this book when you reserve directly with the guesthouse and pay in cash; homemade bread, free parking, 19 Bootham Terrace, tel. 01904/636-471, www.abbeyfields.co.uk, enquire@abbeyfields.co.uk).

$$ At **St. Raphael Guesthouse,** the veteran husband-and-wife team of Al and Les understand a traveler's needs. You'll be instant friends. Their son's graphic design training brings a dash of class to the seven comfy rooms, each themed after a different York street, and each lovingly accented with a fresh rose (Sb-£75 Sun-Thu, £85 Fri-Sat; Db-£82 Sun-Thu, £94 Fri-Sat; these prices promised if you mention this book when reserving directly with the B&B, free drinks and ice in their guests' fridge, family rooms, 44 Queen Annes Road, tel. 01904/645-028, www.straphaelguesthouse.co.uk, info@straphaelguesthouse.co.uk).

$$ Arnot House, run by a hardworking daughter-and-mother team, is old-fashioned, homey, and lushly decorated with Victorian memorabilia. The three well-furnished rooms even have little libraries (Db-£83 if you book directly with the B&B, 2-night minimum stay unless it's last-minute, no children, huge DVD library, 17 Grosvenor Terrace, tel. 01904/641-966, www.arnothouseyork.co.uk, kim.robbins@virgin.net, Kim and her cats Pickle and Tabitha).

$ Amber House is a small place with four breezy and well-tended rooms (one Asian-inspired). It's homey, but with some elegant touches—a bit more tasteful and upscale-feeling than others in this price range (Db-£66 Sun-Thu, £74 Fri-Sat; Tb-£93; these prices if you mention this book when reserving directly with the B&B, free parking, 36 Bootham Crescent, tel. 01904/620-275, www.amberhouse-york.co.uk, amberhouseyork@hotmail.co.uk, John and Linda).

$ Bootham Guest House features industrious Andrew, who is gradually upgrading his property. Creamy walls and contemporary furniture are a break from more traditional York B&B decor. Of the eight rooms, six are en-suite, while two share a bath

(S-£40-45, Sb-£45-50, D-£50-60, Db-£60-70, Tb-£90-105, higher in July-Aug, these prices if you mention this book when reserving directly with the B&B, 56 Bootham Crescent, tel. 01904/672-123, www.boothamguesthouse.co.uk, boothamguesthouse1@hotmail.com).

$ Number 34, run by hardworking Amy and Jason, has five simple, light, and airy rooms at fair prices. It has a clean, uncluttered feeling, with modern decor (Sb-£35-45, Db-£60-66, Tb-£85-90, 5-person apartment also available next door, price depends on season and day of week, mention Rick Steves when reserving to get best rates, ground-floor room, 34 Bootham Crescent, tel. 01904/645-818, www.number34york.co.uk, enquiries@number34york.co.uk).

$ Queen Annes Guest House has nine basic rooms in two adjacent houses. While it doesn't have the plushest beds or richest decor, this is a respectable, affordable, and clean place to sleep (S-£45, Db-£80, Tb-generally £100, 10 percent discount if you mention this book and reserve directly with the B&B, family room, lounge, 24 and 26 Queen Annes Road, tel. 01904/629-389, www.queen-annes-guesthouse.co.uk, info@queen-annes-guesthouse.co.uk, Phil).

On the River

$$ Abbey Guest House is a peaceful refuge overlooking the River Ouse, with five cheerful, beautifully updated, contemporary-style rooms and a cute little garden. The riverview rooms will ramp up your romance with York (Db-£80-90, ask for Rick Steves discount when you book directly with the B&B, free parking, £10 laundry service, 13 Earlsborough Terrace, tel. 01904/627-782, www.abbeyghyork.co.uk, info@abbeyghyork.co.uk, welcoming couple Jane and Kingley).

On St. Mary's Street

$$ Number 23 St. Mary's B&B is extravagantly decorated. Chris and Julie Simpson have done everything just right and offer nine spacious and tastefully comfy rooms, a classy lounge, and all the doily touches (Sb-£50-60, Db-£80-100 depending on room size and season, discount for longer stays, family room, honesty box for drinks and snacks, lots of stairs, 23 St. Mary's, tel. 01904/622-738, www.23stmarys.co.uk, stmarys23@hotmail.com).

$$ Crook Lodge B&B, with seven tight but elegantly charming rooms, serves breakfast in an old Victorian kitchen. The 21st-century style somehow fits this old house (Db-£75-85, cheaper off-season, check for online specials, one ground-floor room, free parking, quiet, 26 St. Mary's, tel. 01904/655-614, www.crooklodgeguesthouseyork.co.uk, crooklodge@hotmail.com, Brian and Louise Aiken).

$$ Airden House rents 10 nice, mostly-traditional rooms, though the two basement-level rooms are more mod—one has a space-age-looking Jacuzzi and a separate room with twin bed (standard Db-£76-80, traditional Db-£80-90, Jacuzzi Db-£100, 10 percent discount with 2-night minimum if you mention this book when reserving directly with the B&B, higher prices are for weekends, lounge, free parking, 1 St. Mary's, tel. 01904/638-915, www.airdenhouse.co.uk, info@airdenhouse.co.uk, Emma and Heather).

Closer to the Town Wall

$$$ The Hazelwood, more formal than a B&B, rents 14 rooms. The "standard" rooms have bright, cheery decor and small bathrooms, while the bigger "superior" rooms come with newer bathrooms and handcrafted furniture. Ask about their bright top-floor, two-bedroom apartment good for families (Sb-£70, standard Db-£80-100, superior Db-£100-130, price depends on season and day of week, homemade biscuits on arrival, free laundry service for Rick Steves readers if you book directly with the B&B, free parking, garden patio; fridge, ice, and travel library in pleasant basement lounge; 24 Portland Street, tel. 01904/626-548, www.thehazelwoodyork.com, reservations@thehazelwoodyork.com; Ian and Carolyn, along with Sharon and Emma).

LARGE HOTELS

$$$ Dean Court Hotel, a Best Western facing the Minster, is a big stately hotel with classy lounges and 37 comfortable rooms. It has a great location and friendly vibe for a business-class establishment. A few rooms have views for no extra charge—try requesting one (Sb-£115, small Db-£150, standard Db-£180, superior Db-£210, spacious deluxe Db-£230; cheaper midweek, off-season, and on Sun—check specific rates online; elevator, bistro, restaurant, Duncombe Place, tel. 01904/625-082, www.deancourt-york.co.uk, sales@deancourt-york.co.uk).

$$$ Grays Court Hotel is a historic mansion—the home of dukes and archbishops since 1091—that now rents nine rooms to tourists. While its public spaces and gardens are lavish, its rooms are elegant yet modest. The creaky, historic nature of the place makes for a memorable stay. If it's too pricey for lodging, consider coming here for its tearoom—described later, under "Eating in York" (Db-£165-280, cheaper on weekdays and off-season, Chapter House Street, tel. 01904/612-613, www.grayscourtyork.com).

$$$ Premier Inn offers 200 rooms in two side-by-side hotels that I hate to recommend, but it's a workable option if York's

B&Bs have filled up, or if you can score a deep advance discount. They have little character (at one, you enter through a coffee shop), but they offer industrial-strength efficiency and a decent value if you can get a deal (Db-£75-145, usually £80-95 Sun-Thu, £90-145 Fri-Sat; check for specials online; up to 2 kids stay free, continental breakfast-£5.75, full breakfast-£8.75, elevator in one building, pay guest computer, pay Wi-Fi, parking-£8.50/24 hours, 5-minute walk to train station, 20 and 28 Blossom Street, tel. 0871-527-9194 and 0871-527-9196, www.premierinn.com).

$$ Travelodge York Central offers 93 affordable rooms near the York Castle Museum. If you book long in advance on their website, this can be amazingly cheap. River views make some rooms slightly less boring—after booking online, call the front desk to try to arrange a view (rates vary wildly depending on demand—as cheap as £30 for a fully prepaid "saver rate" 21 days ahead; for best rates, book online; cheapest rates are first-come, first-served; continental breakfast-£5, elevator, pay Wi-Fi, parking-£7/24 hours and a 5-minute walk away, 90 Piccadilly, central reservations tel. 0871-984-8484, front desk tel. 0203-195-4978, www.travelodge.co.uk). A second location, **Travelodge York Central Micklegate,** has 104 rooms at the train station end of the Ouse Bridge (similar rates, Micklegate, tel. 0203-195-4976).

HOSTEL

$ Safestay York is a boutique hostel on a rowdy street, which can be very noisy late at night on Fridays and Saturdays. It's in a big old Georgian house that provides a much-needed option for backpackers. They rent 158 beds in 4- to 12-bed rooms, with great views, private prefab "pod" bathrooms, and reading lights for each bed. They also offer fancier, hotel-quality doubles (£18-32/bed in dorms, twin Db-£90-100, king Db-£120, family room for up to four-£192, rates depend on day and size of room, includes sheets, continental breakfast-£4, four floors, no elevator, air-con, free Wi-Fi in public areas only, self-service laundry, TV lounge, game room, bar, lockers, no curfew, 5-minute walk from train station at 88 Micklegate, tel. 01904/627-720, www.safestay.com/ss-york-micklegate.html, bookings@safestay.com).

Eating in York

York is touting its new reputation as a foodie city. It claims to be rated "#5 in Europe" by some social media—but that's a stretch. Still, the local high-tech industry and university—combined with all the tourists—build a demand that sustains lots of creative and fun eateries. There's also a wide range of ethnic food (including several good choices for Indian, Thai, Italian, Spanish tapas, and

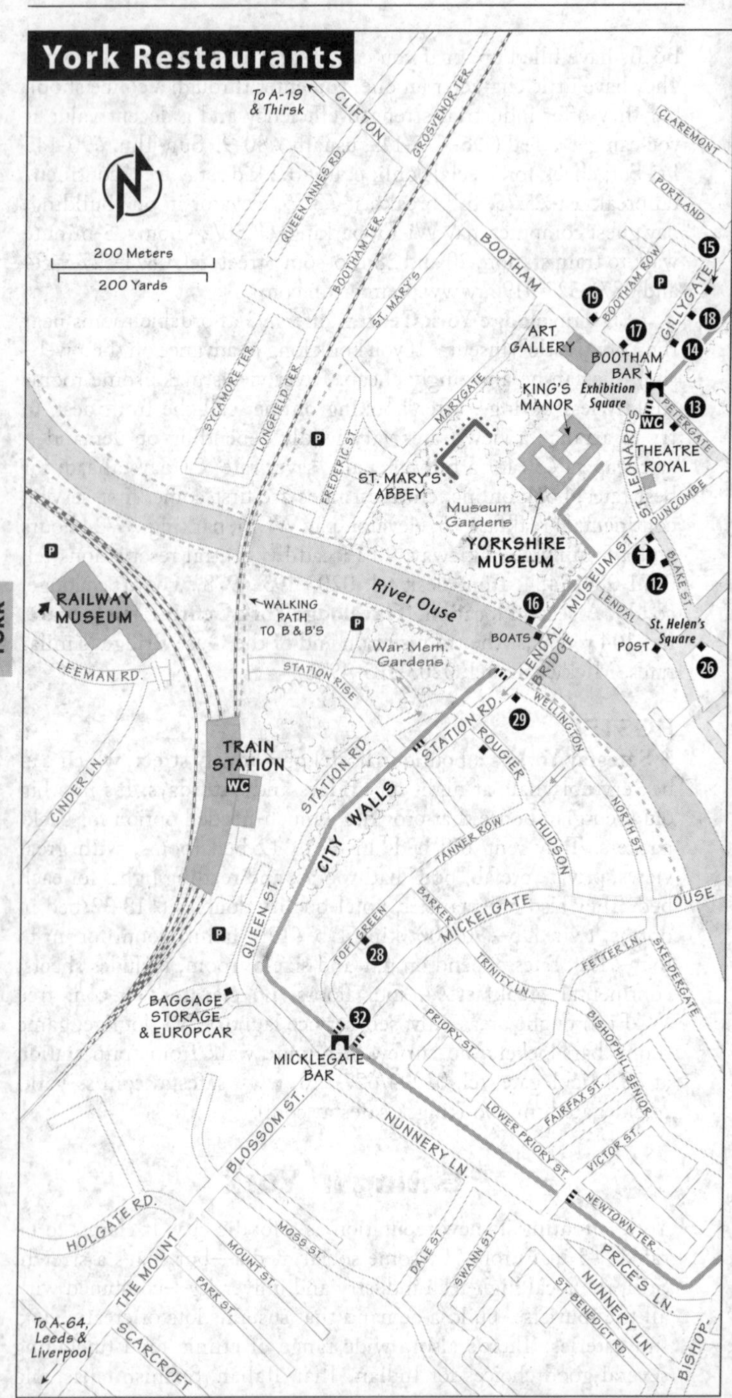
York Restaurants
To A-19 & Thirsk
200 Meters
200 Yards
CLIFTON
GROSVENOR TER.
QUEEN ANNES RD.
BOOTHAM TER.
BOOTHAM
BOOTHAM ROW
CLAREMONT
PORTLAND
GILLYGATE
ST. MARY'S
SYCAMORE TER.
LONGFIELD TER.
FREDERIC ST.
MARYGATE
ART GALLERY
BOOTHAM BAR
Exhibition Square
KING'S MANOR
PETERGATE
WC
THEATRE ROYAL
ST. LEONARD'S
DUNCOMBE
ST. MARY'S ABBEY
Museum Gardens
YORKSHIRE MUSEUM
MUSEUM ST.
BLAKE ST.
LENDAL
St. Helen's Square
POST
BOATS
LENDAL BRIDGE
River Ouse
RAILWAY MUSEUM
WALKING PATH TO B & B'S
War Mem. Gardens
STATION RISE
LEEMAN RD.
STATION RD.
WELLINGTON
ROUGIER
TRAIN STATION
WC
CINDER LN.
CITY WALLS
TANNER ROW
HUDSON
NORTH ST.
OUSE
BARKER
MICKELGATE
TOFT GREEN
QUEEN ST.
TRINITY LN.
FETTER LN.
SKELDERGATE
BAGGAGE STORAGE & EUROPCAR
MICKLEGATE BAR
PRIORY ST.
BISHOPHILL SENIOR
FAIRFAX ST.
LOWER PRIORY ST.
VICTOR ST.
BLOSSOM ST.
NUNNERY LN.
NEWTOWN TER.
PRICE'S LN.
HOLGATE RD.
THE MOUNT
MOSS ST.
MOUNT ST.
PARK ST.
DALE ST.
SWANN ST.
ST. BENEDICT RD.
NUNNERY LN.
BISHOP-
SCARCROFT
To A-64, Leeds & Liverpool
12
13
14
15
16
17
18
19
26
28
29
32
YORK

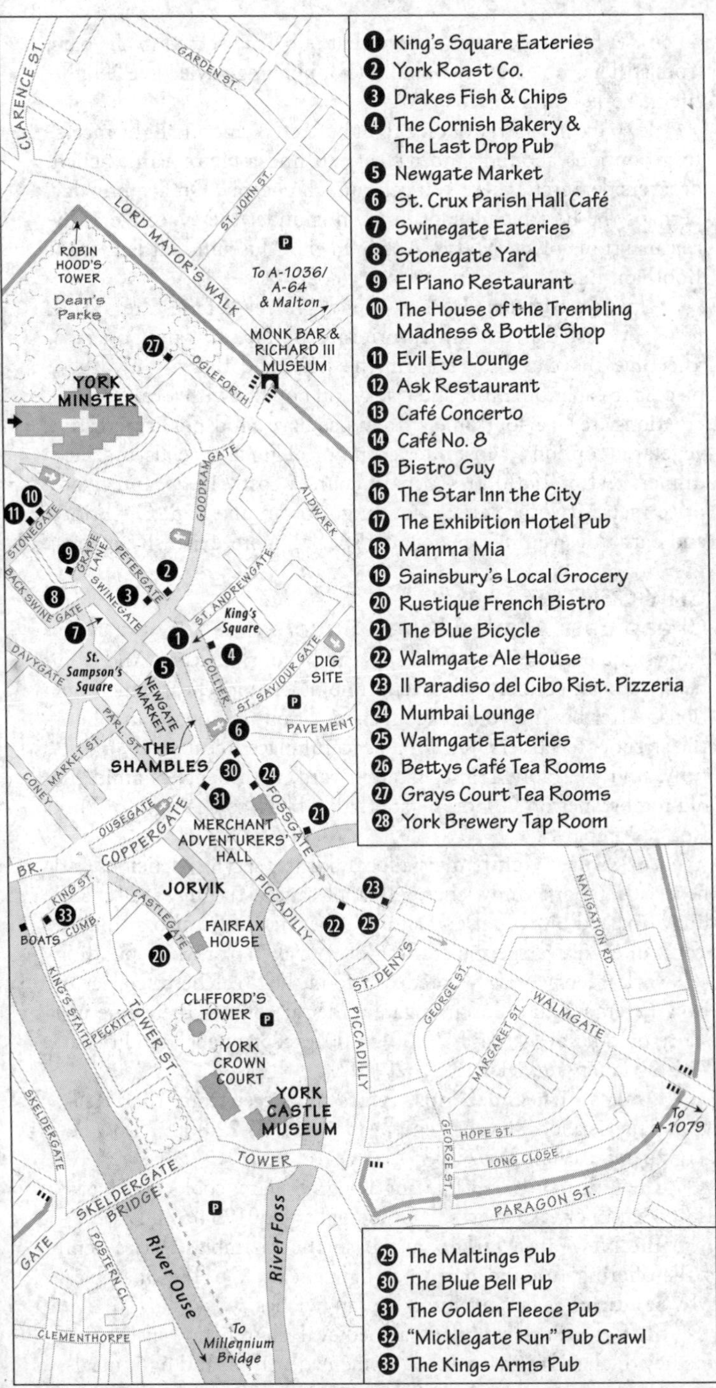

1 King's Square Eateries
2 York Roast Co.
3 Drakes Fish & Chips
4 The Cornish Bakery & The Last Drop Pub
5 Newgate Market
6 St. Crux Parish Hall Café
7 Swinegate Eateries
8 Stonegate Yard
9 El Piano Restaurant
10 The House of the Trembling Madness & Bottle Shop
11 Evil Eye Lounge
12 Ask Restaurant
13 Café Concerto
14 Café No. 8
15 Bistro Guy
16 The Star Inn the City
17 The Exhibition Hotel Pub
18 Mamma Mia
19 Sainsbury's Local Grocery
20 Rustique French Bistro
21 The Blue Bicycle
22 Walmgate Ale House
23 Il Paradiso del Cibo Rist. Pizzeria
24 Mumbai Lounge
25 Walmgate Eateries
26 Bettys Café Tea Rooms
27 Grays Court Tea Rooms
28 York Brewery Tap Room
29 The Maltings Pub
30 The Blue Bell Pub
31 The Golden Fleece Pub
32 "Micklegate Run" Pub Crawl
33 The Kings Arms Pub
CLARENCE ST.
GARDEN ST.
LORD MAYOR'S WALK
ST. JOHN ST.
ROBIN HOOD'S TOWER
Dean's Parks
To A-1036/ A-64 & Malton
MONK BAR & RICHARD III MUSEUM
OGLEFORTH
YORK MINSTER
GOODRAMGATE
ALDWARK
STONEGATE
GRAPE LANE
PETERGATE
BACK SWINE GATE
SWINEGATE
ST. ANDREWGATE
King's Square
DAVYGATE
St. Sampson's Square
NEWGATE MARKET
COLLIER
ST. SAVIOUR GATE
DIG SITE
PAVEMENT
PARL. ST.
MARKET ST.
THE SHAMBLES
CONEY
OUSEGATE
COPPERGATE
FOSSGATE
MERCHANT ADVENTURERS' HALL
BR.
KING ST.
JORVIK
CASTLEGATE
PICCADILLY
FAIRFAX HOUSE
BOATS
CUMB.
NAVIGATION RD.
ST. DENY'S
KING'S STAITH
PECKITT
TOWER ST.
CLIFFORD'S TOWER
YORK CROWN COURT
GEORGE ST.
MARGARET ST.
WALMGATE
YORK CASTLE MUSEUM
To A-1079
HOPE ST.
LONG CLOSE
SKELDERGATE
TOWER
SKELDERGATE BRIDGE
PARAGON ST.
GATE
FOSTERN CL.
River Ouse
River Foss
CLEMENTHORPE
To Millennium Bridge
YORK

so on). While there's plenty of decent pub grub served in the bars, York still has no great gastropubs. (For pubbing advice, see "Nightlife in York," earlier.)

If you're in a hurry or on a tight budget, picnic and light-meals-to-go options abound, and it's easy to find a churchyard, bench, or riverside perch where you can munch cheaply. On a sunny day, perhaps the best picnic spot in town is under the evocative 12th-century ruins of St. Mary's Abbey in the Museum Gardens (near Bootham Bar).

Upscale Bistros: As these trendy, pricey eateries are a York forte, I've listed five of my favorites: Café No. 8, Café Concerto, The Blue Bicycle, The Star Inn the City, and Bistro Guy. These places are each romantic, laid-back, and popular with locals (so reservations are wise for dinner). They also have good-quality, creative vegetarian options. Most offer economical lunch specials and early dinners. After 19:00 or so, main courses cost £15-25 and fixed-price meals (two or three courses) go for around £25. On Friday and Saturday evenings, many offer special, more-expensive menus.

CITY CENTER

Cheap Eats Around King's Square

King's Square is about as central as can be for sightseers. And from here, you can actually see several fine quick-and-cheap lunch options. After buying your takeout food, sit on the square and enjoy the street entertainers. Or, for a peaceful place to eat more prayerfully, find the Holy Trinity Church yard, with benches amid the old tombstones on Goodramgate (half a block to the right of York Roast Company).

York Roast Company is a local fixture, serving delicious and hearty £4-6 pork sandwiches with applesauce, stuffing, and "crackling" (roasted bits of fat and skin). Other meats are also available. You can even oversee the stuffing of your own Yorkshire pudding (£7-8). If Henry VIII wanted fast food, he'd eat here (corner of Low Petergate and Goodramgate, order at counter then dine upstairs or take away, daily 10:00-23:00 except open later Fri-Sat, 74 Low Petergate, tel. 01904/629-197).

Drakes Fish-and-Chips, across the street from York Roast Company, is a local favorite chippy (daily 11:00-22:30, 97 Low Petergate, tel. 01904/624-788).

The Cornish Bakery, facing King's Square, cooks up £3 pasties to eat in or take away (30 Colliergate, tel. 01904/671-177).

The Newgate Market, just past The Shambles, has several stalls offering fun and nutritious light meals. On The Shambles, **Mr. Sandwich** is famous for its £1 sandwiches.

St. Crux Parish Hall is a medieval church now used by a medley of charities that sell tea, homemade cakes, and light meals.

They each book the church for a day, often a year in advance (usually open Tue-Sat 10:00-16:00, closed Sun-Mon, at bottom of The Shambles at its intersection with Pavement, tel. 01904/621-756).

For a nice finish, consider the **Harlequin Café,** a charming place loved by locals for its good coffee and homemade cakes, as well as its light meals. It's up a creaky staircase overlooking the square (Mon-Sat 10:00-16:00, Sun 11:00-15:00, 2 King's Square, tel. 01904/630-631).

On or near Swinegate

Strolling this street, you can just take your pick of the various tempting bars and eateries. Some are trendy, with thumping music, while others are tranquil; some have elaborately decorated dining rooms, while others emphasize heated courtyards. This corner of town has two similar American-style bar/brasserie/lounges (both open daily and serving £8-12 meals): **Oscar's,** right on Swinegate, has a mod interior and good burgers; **Stonegate Yard,** around the corner on Little Stonegate, is in a delightful ivy-covered courtyard. Others enjoy the courtyard and Mediterranean food at **Lucia** (£4 small plates, £10-15 meals, daily, 12 Swinegate).

Vegetarian: **El Piano Restaurant,** just off Swinegate on charming Grape Lane, is a popular place serving only vegan, gluten-free, and low-sodium dishes. Their meals are made with locally sourced ingredients and Indian/Asian/Middle Eastern/East African flavors. The inside ambience is bubble gum with blinking lights. If you don't want to feel that you're eating inside a sombrero, they also have a pleasant patio out back (£4 starters, £12 meals, £30 2-or-3-person sampler, Mon-Sat 11:00-23:00, Sun 12:00-21:00, between Low Petergate and Swinegate at 15 Grape Lane, tel. 01904/610-676). Save money at the takeaway window (£5 boxes).

On or near Stonegate

The House of the Trembling Madness, considered by some to be the best pub in town, is easy to miss. Enter through The Bottle, a ground-floor shop selling an astonishing number of different takeaway beers (called a "bottle shop" in England). Climb the stairs to find a small but cozy pub beneath a high, airy timbered ceiling. It's youthful and a bit fashion-forward, yet still accessible to all ages—come early since seating can be tight. The food tries to be locally sourced and is far more creative than standard York pub grub (£3-6 snacks, £8-10 meals, daily 10:30-24:00, 48 Stonegate, tel. 01904/640-009).

Evil Eye Lounge serves large portions of delicious, authentic Southeast Asian cuisine. But the hipster space may be a bit too much for some, and it's best to avoid the Saturday afternoon party scene. There's food and drinks on several levels (£8 meals, food served Mon-Fri 12:00-21:00, Sat-Sun 12:00-18:00, 42 Stonegate, tel. 01904/640-002).

Italian: **Ask Restaurant** is a cheap and cheery Italian chain, similar to those found in historic buildings all over Britain. But York's version lets you dine in the majestic Neoclassical yellow hall of its Grand Assembly Rooms, lined with Corinthian marble columns. The food may be Italian-chain dull—but the atmsosphere is 18th-century deluxe (£9-12 pizza, pastas, and salads; daily 11:00-22:00, weekends until 23:00; Blake Street, tel. 01904/637-254). Even if you're just walking past, peek inside to gape at the interior.

NEAR BOOTHAM BAR AND RECOMMENDED B&Bs

Café Concerto, a casual and cozy bistro with wholesome food and a charming musical theme, has an understandably loyal following. The fun menu features updated English favorites with some international options (£4-8 starters; £9-12 soups, sandwiches, and salads; £12-17 main dishes; vegetarian and gluten-free options; daily 9:00-21:00, weekends until 22:00, smart to reserve for dinner—try for a window seat, also offers takeaway, facing the Minster at 21 High Petergate, tel. 01904/610-478, http://cafeconcerto.biz).

Café No. 8 feels like Café Concerto but is more romantic, with jazz, modern art, candles, and hardworking headwaiter Christopher bringing it all together. Grab one of the tables in front or in the sunroom, or enjoy a shaded little garden out back if the weather's good. Chef Chris Pragnell uses what's fresh in the market to shape his menu. The food—mod cuisine with veggie options—is simple, elegant, and creative (£6-10 lunches, £13-16 main dishes; daily 12:00-22:00 except opens at 9:00 Sat-Sun, 8 Gillygate, tel. 01904/653-074, www.cafeno8.co.uk).

Bistro Guy serves modern English and international dishes with seven cute tables in front. You can also dine in its delightful garden under the town wall out back. Chef Guy Whapples serves breakfast and lunch daily and dinners—with a fancier "bistro" menu—only three nights a week (£5-9 breakfast and lunch plates, Tue-Sun 9:00-17:00, closed Mon; £21 two-course and £25 three-course dinners, a bit less if you come before 19:00, dinner served Thu-Sat only 18:00-21:00—deposit required for dinner reservation; 40 Gillygate, tel. 01904/652-500, www.bistroguy.co.uk).

The Star Inn the City is an offshoot of Chef Andrew Pern's

Michelin-star-rated restaurant in the Yorkshire countryside—The Star Inn. He excels in showing off local meats and produce, creating memorable combinations such as chicken breasts in a beet-vegetable broth or duck with Asian spices in a Muscovado sauce. Dine outside along the river or in the mod eatery that looks out over the Museum Gardens (£8-12 starters, £16-24 main dishes, breakfast and lunch specials, kids menu, daily 8:30-22:00, reservations smart, next to the river in Lendal Engine House, Museum Street, tel. 01904/619-208, www.starinnthecity.co.uk).

The Exhibition Hotel pub has a classic pub interior, as well as a glassed-in conservatory and beer garden out back that's great for kids. While the food is nothing special, it's conveniently located near my recommended B&Bs (£9-12 pub grub, food served daily 12:00-21:00, bar open late, facing Bootham Bar at 19 Bootham Street, tel. 01904/641-105).

Italian: **Mamma Mia** is a popular choice for functional, affordable Italian. The casual, garlicky eating area features a tempting gelato bar, and in nice weather the back patio is *molto bello* (£8-10 pizza and pasta, daily 11:30-14:00 & 17:30-23:00, 20 Gillygate, tel. 01904/622-020).

Supermarket: **Sainsbury's Local** grocery store is handy and open late (long hours daily, 50 yards outside Bootham Bar, on Bootham).

AT THE EAST END OF TOWN

This neighborhood is across town from my recommended B&Bs, but still central (and a short walk from the York Castle Museum). These places are all hits with local foodies; reservations are smart for all.

Rustique French Bistro has one big room of tight tables and walls decorated with simple posters. The place has good prices and is straight French—right down to the welcome (£6 starters, £15 main dishes, £15 two-course and £17 three-course meals available except after 19:00 Fri-Sat, daily 12:00-22:00, across from Fairfax House at 28 Castlegate, tel. 01904/612-744, www.rustiqueyork.co.uk).

The Blue Bicycle is no longer a brothel (but if you explore downstairs, you can still imagine when the tiny privacy-snugs needed their curtains). Today, it is passionate about fish. The energy of its happy eaters, its charming canalside setting, and its tasty Anglo-French cuisine make it worth the splurge. It's a velvety, hardwood scene, a little sultry but fresh...like its fish. The basement, while *très romantique,* may be a bit hot and stuffy (£6-12 starters, £16-24 main dishes, vegetarian and meat options, daily 18:00-21:30, also open for lunch Thu-Sun 12:00-14:30, 34 Fossgate, tel. 01904/673-990, www.thebluebicycle.com).

Walmgate Ale House is a fun and casual place to eat. This homey, spacious, youthful restaurant (combining old timbers and mod tables) serves up elegantly simple traditional and international meals, all with a focus on local ingredients. The seating sprawls on several floors: ground-floor pub, upstairs bistro, and top-floor loft (£7 lunches, £11-15 dinners, £13.50 two-course and £15.50 three-course meals; Mon-Fri 12:00-22:30, Sat-Sun 9:30-22:30, just past Fossgate at 25 Walmgate, tel. 01904/629-222).

Italian: **Il Paradiso del Cibo Ristorante Pizzeria** just feels special. It's a small place with tight seating, no tourists, and a fun bustle, run by a Sardinian with attitude (£7 pastas and pizzas, £15-19 main dishes, £8.50 lunch/early dinner special Mon-Fri only, cash only, daily 12:00-15:00 & 18:00-22:00, 40 Walmgate, tel. 01904/611-444).

Indian: **Mumbai Lounge** (named for its top-floor lounge) is considered the best place in town for Indian food, so it's very popular. The space is big and high-energy, with a hardworking team of waiters in black T-shirts. I'd call to reserve a table on the ground floor—but avoid the basement (£11 plates, £7 lunch special, daily 12:00-14:00 & 17:30-23:30, 47 Fossgate, tel. 01904/654-155, www.mumbailoungeyork.co.uk).

YORK

Ethnic on Walmgate: The emerging bohemian-chic street called Walmgate has several quality restaurants within a few steps of one another. Each is small, feels real, and has a local, untouristy energy: **Il Paradiso del Cibo Ristorante Pizzeria** (described above), **Khao San Thai Bistro** (52 Walmgate, tel. 01904/635-599), and **The Barbakan Polish Restaurant** (58 Walmgate, tel. 01904/672-474).

TEAROOMS

York is famous for its elegant teahouses. These two places serve traditional afternoon tea as well as light meals in memorable settings. In both cases, the food is pricey and comes in small portions—I'd come here at 16:00 for tea and cakes, but dine elsewhere. It's permissible for travel partners on a budget to enjoy the experience for about half the price by having one person order "full tea" (with enough little sandwiches and sweets for two to share) and the other a simple cup of tea.

Bettys Café Tea Rooms is a destination restaurant for many ladies. You pay £10 for a Yorkshire Cream Tea (tea and scones with clotted Yorkshire cream and strawberry jam) or £19 for a full traditional English afternoon tea (tea, delicate sandwiches, scones, and sweets). Your table is so full of doily niceties that the food is served on a little three-tray tower. While you'll pay a little extra here (and the food's nothing special), the ambience and people-watching are hard to beat. When there's a line, it moves quickly (except at dinnertime). They'll offer to seat you sooner in the bigger and less atmospheric basement, but I'd be patient and wait for a place upstairs—ideally by the window (daily 9:00-21:00, "afternoon tea" served all day; on weekends the special £33 afternoon tea includes fresh-from-the-oven scones served 12:30-17:00 in upstairs room with pianist—smart to reserve ahead; piano music nightly 18:00-21:00 and Sun 10:00-13:00, tel. 01904/659-142, www.bettys.co.uk, St. Helen's Square, fine view of street scene from a window seat on the main floor). Near the WC downstairs is a mirror signed by WWII bomber pilots—read the story. For those just wanting to buy a pastry to go, it's fine to skip the lines and go directly to the bakery counter.

Grays Court, tucked away behind the Minster, holds court over its own delightful garden just inside the town wall. (You'll look down into its inviting oasis as you walk along the top of the wall.) For centuries, this was the residence of the Norman Treasurers of York Minster. Today it's home to a pleasant tearoom, small hotel, and bar. In summer, you can sit outside at tables scattered in the pleasant garden, or inside in their elegant dining room or Jacobean gallery—a long wood-paneled hall with comfy sofas (£37 for 2-person "afternoon tea" served all day, £6 sandwiches, £6-11 light meals, also serves dinner, daily 11:00-21:00, Chapter House Street, tel. 01904/612-613, www.grayscourtyork.com).

York Connections

From York by Train to: Durham (3-4/hour, 45 minutes), **London**'s King's Cross Station (2/hour, 2 hours), **Bath** (hourly with change in Bristol, 4.5 hours, more with additional transfers), **Cambridge** (hourly, 2.5 hours, transfer in Peterborough), **Keswick/Lake District** (train to Penrith: roughly 2/hour, 3.5-4 hours, 1-2 transfers; then bus, allow about 4.5 hours total), **Manchester Airport** (2/hour, 2 hours), **Edinburgh** (2/hour, 2.5 hours). Train info: Tel. 0345-748-4950, www.nationalrail.co.uk.

Connections with London's Airports: Heathrow (allow 3 hours minimum; from airport take Heathrow Express train to London's Paddington Station, transfer by Tube to King's Cross, then take train to York; for details on cheaper but slower Tube or bus option from airport to London King's Cross, see page 189), **Gatwick** (allow 3 hours minimum; from Gatwick South, catch First Capital Connect train to London's St. Pancras International Station; from there, walk to neighboring King's Cross Station, and catch train to York).

DURHAM AND NORTHEAST ENGLAND

Durham • Beamish Museum • Hadrian's Wall

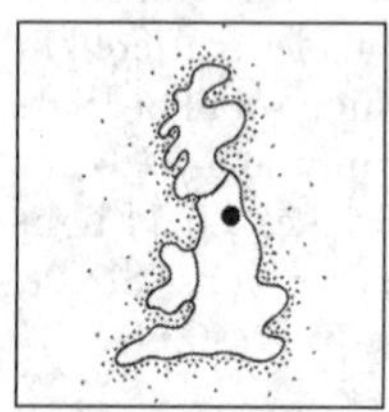

Northeast England harbors some of the country's best historical sights. Go for a Roman ramble at Hadrian's Wall, a reminder that Britain was an important Roman colony 2,000 years ago. Marvel at England's greatest Norman church—Durham's cathedral—and enjoy an evensong service there. And at the excellent Beamish Museum, travel back in time to the 19th and early 20th centuries.

PLANNING YOUR TIME

For **train** travelers, Durham is the most convenient overnight stop in this region. But it's problematic to see en route to another destination since there's no baggage storage in Durham: Either stay overnight, or do Durham as a day trip from York. If you like Roman ruins, visit Hadrian's Wall (tricky but doable by public transportation). The Beamish Museum is an easy day trip from Durham (less than an hour by bus).

By **car,** you can easily visit everything in this chapter. Spend a night in Durham and a night near Hadrian's Wall, stopping at the Beamish Museum on your way to Hadrian's Wall.

For the best quick visit to Durham, arrive by midafternoon, in time to tour the cathedral and enjoy the evensong service (Tue-Sat at 17:15, Sun at 15:30; limited access and no tours during June graduation ceremonies). Sleep in Durham. Visit Beamish the next morning before continuing on to your next destination.

Durham

Without its cathedral, Durham would hardly be noticed. But this magnificently-situated structure is hard to miss (even if you're zooming by on the train). Seemingly happy to go nowhere, Durham sits along the tight curve of its river, snug below its castle and famous church. It has a medieval, cobbled atmosphere and a scraggly peasant's indoor market just off the main square. Durham is home to England's third-oldest university, with a student vibe jostling against its lingering working-class mining-town feel. You'll see tattooed and pierced people in search of job security and a good karaoke bar. Yet Durham has a youthful liveliness and a small-town warmth that shines—especially on sunny days, when most everyone is out licking ice cream cones.

Orientation to Durham

As it has for a thousand years, tidy little Durham (pop. 50,000) clusters everything safely under its castle, within the protective hairpin bend of the River Wear. Because of the town's hilly topography, going just about anywhere involves a lot of up and down...and back up again. The main spine through the middle of town (Framwellgate Bridge, Silver Street, and Market Place) is level to moderately steep, but walking in any direction from that area involves some serious uphill climbing. Take advantage of the handy Cathedral Bus to avoid the tiring elevation changes—especially up to the cathedral and castle area, or to the train station (perched high on a separate hill).

TOURIST INFORMATION

Durham does not have a physical TI, but the town does maintain a call center and website (calls answered Mon-Sat 9:30-17:30, Sun 11:00-16:00, tel. 03000-262-626, www.thisisdurham.com, visitor@thisisdurham.com).

During the summer, a group of 60 volunteers called **Durham Pointers** staff a tourist information cart in Market Place near the equestrian statue. They hand out free maps of the city and offer unbiased advice on Durham attractions—tell them Rick Steves sent you (late May-early Oct Mon-Sat 9:30-15:30, Sun 11:00-15:00, mobile 0758-233-2621, www.durhampointers.co.uk).

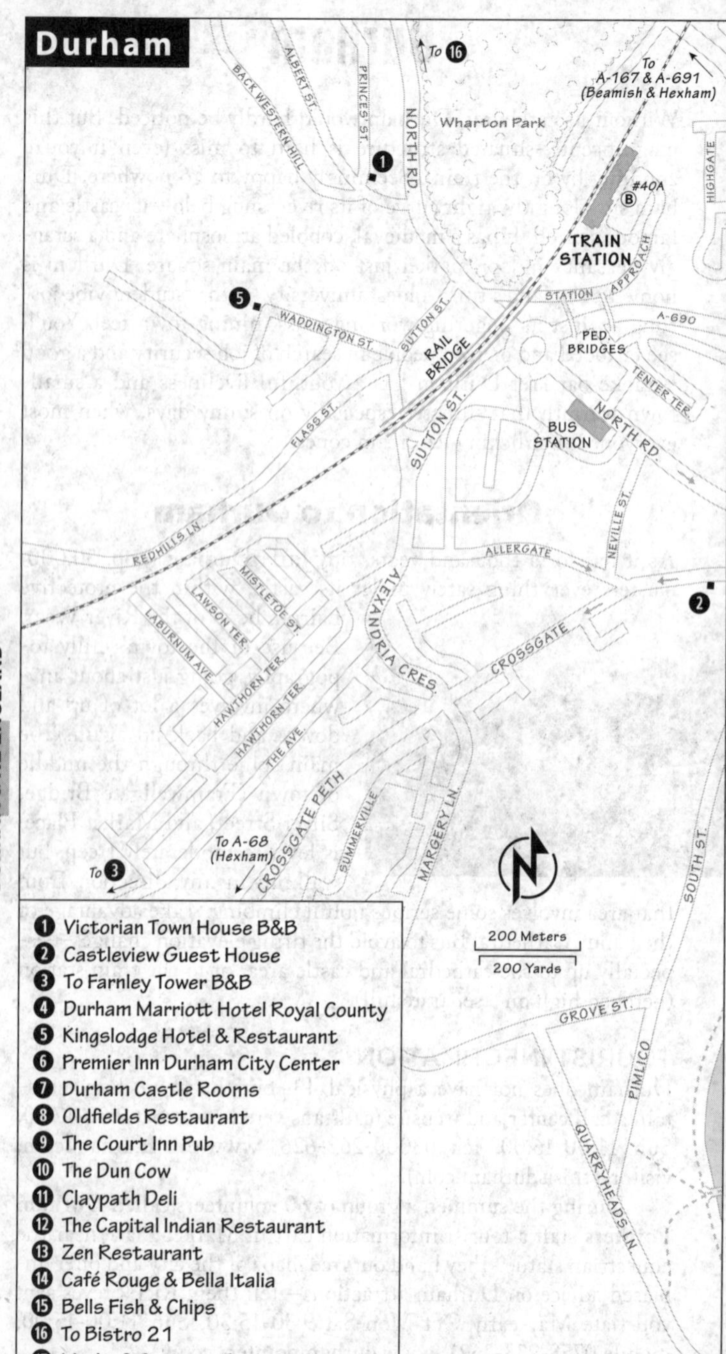
Durham
To 16
To A-167 & A-691 (Beamish & Hexham)
BACK WESTERN HILL
ALBERT ST.
PRINCES ST.
NORTH RD.
Wharton Park
HIGHGATE
#40A
B
TRAIN STATION
STATION APPROACH
A-690
WADDINGTON ST.
SUTTON ST.
RAIL BRIDGE
PED. BRIDGES
TENTER TER.
FLASS ST.
SUTTON ST.
BUS STATION
NORTH RD.
NEVILLE ST.
REDHILLS LN.
ALLERGATE
MISTLETOE ST.
LAWSON TER.
LABURNUM AVE.
ALEXANDRIA CRES.
CROSSGATE
HAWTHORN TER.
HAWTHORN TER.
THE AVE.
CROSSGATE PETH
SUMMERVILLE
MARGERY LN.
To A-68 (Hexham)
To 3
SOUTH ST.
N
200 Meters
200 Yards
GROVE ST.
PIMLICO
QUARRYHEADS LN.
1 Victorian Town House B&B
2 Castleview Guest House
3 To Farnley Tower B&B
4 Durham Marriott Hotel Royal County
5 Kingslodge Hotel & Restaurant
6 Premier Inn Durham City Center
7 Durham Castle Rooms
8 Oldfields Restaurant
9 The Court Inn Pub
10 The Dun Cow
11 Claypath Deli
12 The Capital Indian Restaurant
13 Zen Restaurant
14 Café Rouge & Bella Italia
15 Bells Fish & Chips
16 To Bistro 21
17 Marks & Spencer; Tesco Metro

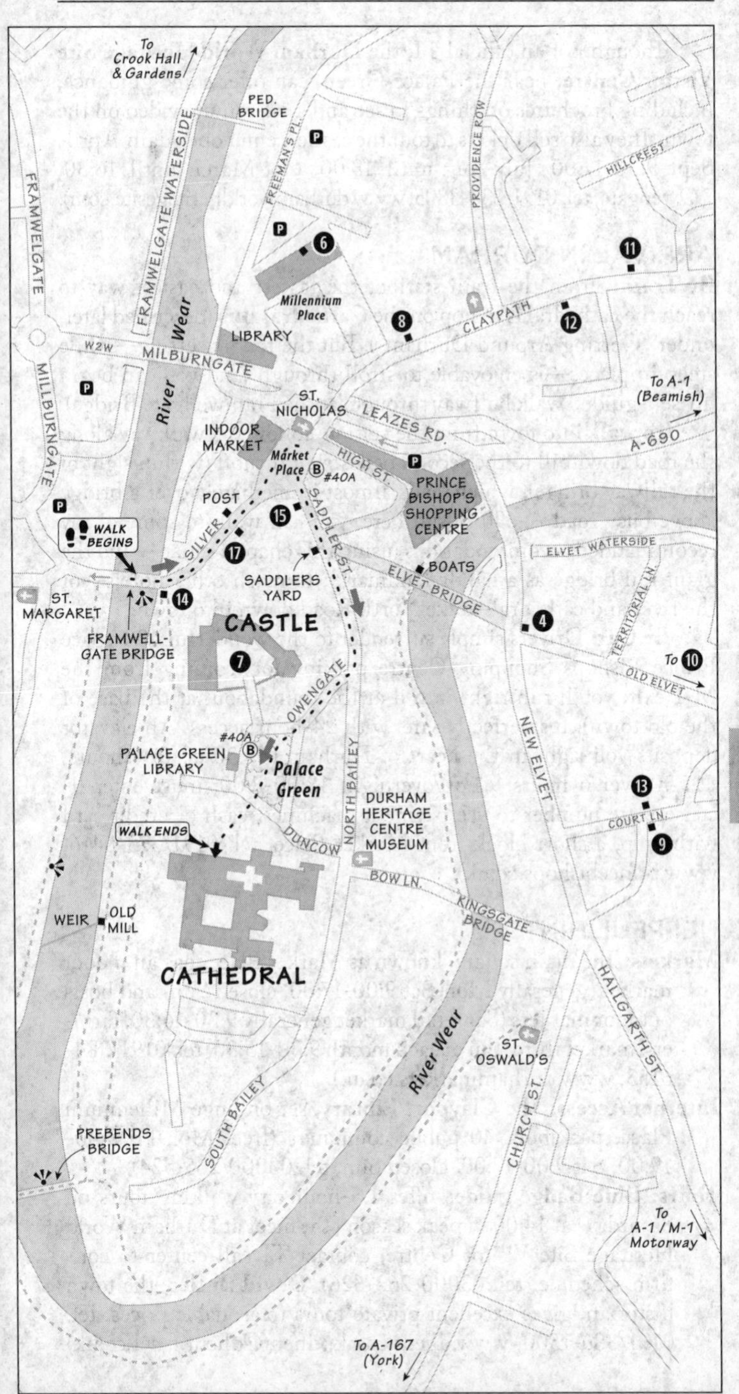
To Crook Hall & Gardens
PED. BRIDGE
FREEMAN'S PL.
PROVIDENCE ROW
HILLCREST
FRAMWELGATE
FRAMWELGATE WATERSIDE
River Wear
Millennium Place
CLAYPATH
LIBRARY
W2W
MILBURNGATE
MILLBURNGATE
To A-1 (Beamish)
A-690
River
ST. NICHOLAS
LEAZES RD.
INDOOR MARKET
Market Place
#40A
HIGH ST.
PRINCE BISHOP'S SHOPPING CENTRE
POST
SADDLER ST.
SILVER
WALK BEGINS
ELVET WATERSIDE
TERRITORIAL LN.
BOATS
ELVET BRIDGE
SADDLERS YARD
ST. MARGARET
FRAMWELL-GATE BRIDGE
CASTLE
OWENGATE
To
OLD ELVET
#40A
PALACE GREEN LIBRARY
Palace Green
NEW ELVET
NORTH BAILEY
DURHAM HERITAGE CENTRE MUSEUM
COURT LN.
WALK ENDS
DUNCOW
BOW LN.
KINGSGATE BRIDGE
WEIR
OLD MILL
CATHEDRAL
HALLGARTH ST.
River Wear
ST. OSWALD'S
SOUTH BAILEY
CHURCH ST.
PREBENDS BRIDGE
To A-1 / M-1 Motorway
To A-167 (York)

Though not an official TI, the **Durham World Heritage Site Visitor Centre,** near the Palace Green, can offer some guidance, including brochures on things to see and a 12-minute video on the town. They also sell tickets to tour the castle (center open daily April-Sept 9:30-17:00, July-Aug until 18:00, Oct-March until 16:30, 7 Owengate, tel. 0191/334-3805, www.durhamworldheritagesite.com).

ARRIVAL IN DURHAM

By Train: From the train station, the fastest and easiest way to reach the cathedral is to hop on the **Cathedral Bus** (described later, under "Getting Around Durham"). But the town's setting—while steep in places—is enjoyable to stroll through (and you can begin my self-guided walk halfway through, at the Framwellgate Bridge).

To **walk** into town from the station, follow the walkway along the road downhill to the second pedestrian turnoff (within sight of the railway bridge), which leads almost immediately over a bridge above busy road A-690. From here, you can walk to some of my recommended accommodations (using this chapter's map—and the giant rail bridge as a handy landmark); to reach other hotels—or the river and cathedral—take North Road down into town.

By Car: Drivers simply surrender to the wonderful 400-space Prince Bishops Shopping Centre parking lot (coming from the M-1 exit, you'll run right into it at the roundabout at the base of the old town). It's perfectly safe, with 24-hour access. An elevator deposits you right in the heart of Durham (£3.30/up to 4 hours, £11.50/over 6 hours, £1.50/overnight 18:00-8:00, must enter license plate number to use payment machines, cash or credit card with chip, a short block from Market Place, tel. 0191/375-0416, www.princebishops.co.uk).

HELPFUL HINTS

Markets: The main square, known as Market Place, has an indoor market (generally Mon-Sat 9:00-17:00, closed Sun) and hosts outdoor markets (Sat retail market generally 9:30-16:30, farmers' market third Thu of each month 9:30-15:30, tel. 0191/384-6153, www.durhammarkets.co.uk).

Internet Access: The **Clayport Library,** set on huge Millennium Place, has about 40 public computers (free, Mon-Fri 9:30-19:00, Sat 9:00-17:00, closed Sun, tel. 03000/265-524).

Tours: Blue Badge guides offer 1.5-hour city walking tours on Saturdays at 14:00 in peak season (£4, meet at Durham World Heritage Site Visitor Centre, contact TI call center to confirm schedule, tel. 03000-262-626). **David Butler,** the town historian, gives excellent private tours (reasonable prices, tel. 0191/386-1500, www.dhent.co.uk, dhent@dhent.fsnet.co.uk) as well as a weekly Durham Ghost Tour in summer (£5, July-Sept Mon at 19:00).

GETTING AROUND DURHAM

While all my recommended hotels, eateries, and sights are doable by foot, if you don't feel like walking Durham's hills, hop on the convenient **Cathedral Bus.** Bus #40A runs between the train station, Market Place, and the Palace Green (£1 all-day ticket, 3/hour Mon-Sat about 9:00-17:00, none on Sun; tel. 0191/372-5386, www.thisisdurham.com). A different bus #40A goes from Freeman's Place (near the Premier Inn) to Market Place and the Palace Green (2/hour Mon-Sat about 10:00-15:45). Confirm the route when you board.

Taxis zip tired tourists to their B&Bs or back up to the train station (about £5 from city center, wait on west side of Framwellgate Bridge at the bottom of North Road or on the east side of Elvet Bridge). If you need to call a taxi, try Polly's Taxis, mobile 07910-179-397.

Durham Walk

• Begin this self-guided walk at Framwellgate Bridge (down in the center of town, halfway between the train station and the cathedral).

Framwellgate Bridge was a wonder when it was built in the 12th century—much longer than the river is wide and higher than seemingly necessary. It was designed to connect stretches of solid high ground and to avoid steep descents toward the marshy river. Note how elegantly today's Silver Street (which leads toward town) slopes into the Framwellgate Bridge. (Imagine that until the 1970s, this people-friendly lane was congested with traffic and buses.)

• Follow Silver Street up the hill to the town's main square.

Durham's **Market Place** retains the same plotting the prince bishop gave it when he moved villagers here in about 1100. Each long and skinny plot of land was the same width (about eight yards), maximizing the number of shops that could have a piece of the Market Place action. Find today's distinctly narrow buildings (Thomas Cook, Whittard, and Thomson)—they still fit the 900-year-old plan. The widths of the other buildings fronting the square are multiples of that original shop width.

Examine the square's **statues.** Coal has long been the basis of this region's economy. The statue of Neptune was part of an ill-fated attempt by a coal baron to bribe the townsfolk into embracing a canal project that would make the shipment of his coal more efficient. The statue of the fancy guy on the horse is of Charles Stewart Vane, the Third Marquess of Londonderry. He was an Irish aristocrat and a general in Wellington's army who married a local coal heiress. A clever and aggressive businessman, he managed to create a vast business empire by controlling every link in the coal business chain—mines, railroads, boats, harbors, and so on.

In the 1850s throughout England, towns were moving their markets off squares and into Industrial Age iron-and-glass market halls. Durham was no exception, and today its funky 19th-century **indoor market** (which faces Market Place) is a delight to explore (closed Sun). There are also outdoor markets here on Saturdays and the third Thursday of each month.

Do you enjoy the sparse traffic in Durham's old town? It was the first city in England to institute a "congestion fee." When drivers enter the town Monday through Saturday, a camera snaps a photo of their car's license plate, and the driver receives a bill by mail for £2. This has cut downtown traffic by more than 50 percent. Locals brag that London (which now has a similar congestion fee) was inspired by their success.

• *Head up the hill on Saddler Street toward the cathedral, stopping where you reach the chunk of wall at the top of a stairway. On the left, you'll see a bridge.*

A 12th-century construction, **Elvet Bridge** led to a town market over the river. Like Framwellgate, it's very long (17 arches) and designed to avoid riverside muck and steep inclines. Even today, Elvet Bridge leads to an unusually wide road—once swollen to accommodate the market action. Shops lined the right-hand side of Elvet Bridge in the 12th century, as they do today. An alley separated the bridge from the buildings on the left. When the bridge was widened, it met the upper stories of the buildings on the left, which became "street level."

Turn back to look at the chunk of **wall** by the top of the stairs—a reminder of a once-formidable fortification. The Scots, living just 50 miles from here, were on the rampage in the 14th century. After their victory at Bannockburn in 1314, they pushed farther south and actually burned part of Durham. Wary of this new threat, Durham built thick city walls. As people settled within the walls, the population density soared. Soon, open lanes were covered by residences and became tunnels (called "vennels"). A classic vennel leads to Saddlers Yard, a fine little 16th-century courtyard (opposite the wall, look for the yellow Vennels Café sign). While the vennels are cute today, centuries ago they were Dickensian nightmares—the filthiest of hovels.

• *Continue up Saddler Street. Just before the fork at the top of the street, duck through the purple door below the* Georgian Window *sign. You'll see a bit of the medieval wall incorporated into the brickwork of a newer building and a turret from an earlier wall. Back on Saddler Street, you can see the ghost of the old wall. (It's exactly the width of the building now housing the Salvation Army.) Veer right at Owengate as you continue uphill to the Palace Green. (The Durham World Heritage Site Visitor Centre is near the top of the hill, on the left.)*

The **Palace Green** was the site of the original 11th-century Saxon town, filling this green between the castle and an earlier church. Later, the town made way for 12th-century Durham's defenses, which now enclose the green. With the threat presented by the Vikings, it's no wonder people found comfort in a spot like this.

The **castle** still stands—as it has for a thousand years—on its motte (man-made mound). Like Oxford and Cambridge, Durham University is a collection of colleges scattered throughout the town, and even this castle is now part of the school. Look into the old courtyard from the castle gate. It traces the very first and smallest bailey (protected area). As future bishops expanded the castle, they left their coats of arms as a way of "signing" the wing they built. Because the Norman kings appointed prince bishops here to rule this part of their realm, Durham was the seat of power for much of northern England. The bishops had their own

Durham's Early Years

Durham's location, tucked inside a tight bend in the River Wear, was practically custom-made for easy fortifications. But it wasn't settled until A.D. 995, with the arrival of St. Cuthbert's body (buried in Durham Cathedral). Shortly after that, a small church and fortification were built upon the site of today's castle and church to house the relic. The castle was a classic "motte-and-bailey" design (with the "motte," or mound, providing a lookout tower for the stockade encircling the protected area, or "bailey"). By 1100, the prince bishop's bailey was filled with villagers—and he wanted everyone out. This was *his* place! He provided a wider protective wall, and had the town resettle below (around today's Market Place). But this displaced the townsfolk's cows, so the prince bishop constructed a fine stone bridge (today's Framwellgate) to connect the new town to grazing land he established across the river. The bridge had a defensive gate, with a wall circling the peninsula and the river serving as a moat.

army and even minted their own coins. The castle is accessible with a 45-minute guided tour, which includes the courtyard, kitchens, great hall, and chapel (£5, open most days when school is in session—but schedule varies so call ahead, buy tickets at Durham World Heritage Site Visitor Centre or Palace Green Library—described next, ask about possible self-guided tour, tel. 0191/334-2932, www.dur.ac.uk/durham.castle).

• *Turning your back to the castle and facing the cathedral, on the right is the university's Palace Green Library.*

The **Palace Green Library** has a free permanent exhibit—*Living on the Hills*—that chronicles 10,000 years of human history on the site of Durham. It also hosts temporary exhibits in its Wolfson Gallery and Dunelm Gallery on everything from rare books to robots. Pop in or check online for current exhibits (temporary exhibits—generally £4.50, Tue-Sun 10:00-16:45, Mon 12:00-16:45, Palace Green, tel. 0191/334-2932, www.dur.ac.uk/library/asc).

• *This walk ends at Durham's stunning **cathedral**, described next.*

Sights in Durham

▲▲▲DURHAM'S CATHEDRAL

Built to house the much-venerated bones of St. Cuthbert from Lindisfarne (known today as Holy Island), Durham's cathedral offers the best look at

Durham's Cathedral

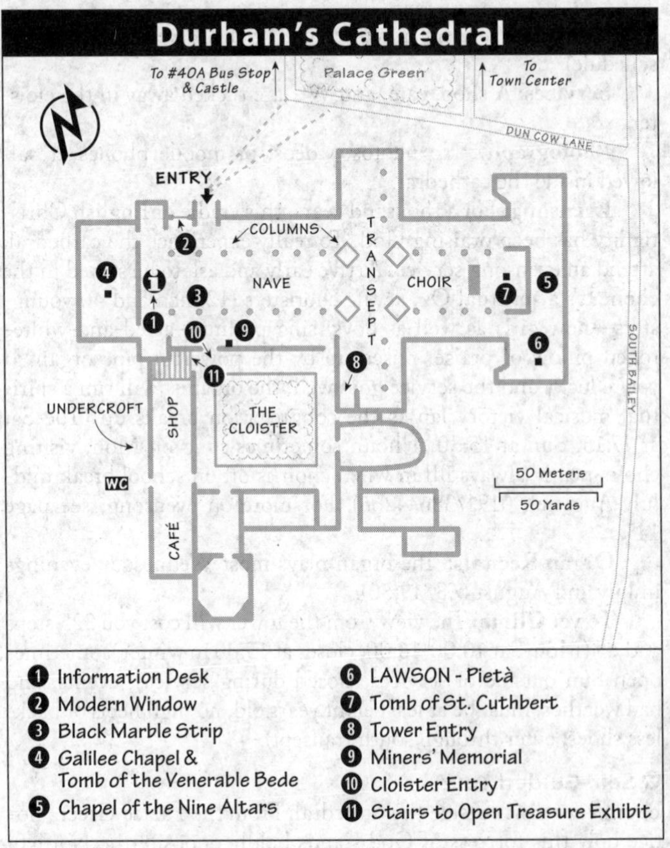

1. Information Desk
2. Modern Window
3. Black Marble Strip
4. Galilee Chapel & Tomb of the Venerable Bede
5. Chapel of the Nine Altars
6. LAWSON - Pietà
7. Tomb of St. Cuthbert
8. Tower Entry
9. Miners' Memorial
10. Cloister Entry
11. Stairs to Open Treasure Exhibit

Norman architecture in England. ("Norman" is British for "Romanesque.") In addition to touring the cathedral, try to fit in an evensong service.

Cost: Entry to the cathedral itself is free, though a donation is requested, and you must pay to climb the tower and to enter the new *Open Treasure* exhibit.

Hours: The cathedral is open to visitors Mon-Sat 9:30-18:00, Sun 12:30-18:00, daily until 20:00 mid-July-Aug, sometimes closes for special services, opens daily at 7:15 for worship and prayer. Access is limited for a few days in June, when the cathedral is used for graduation ceremonies (check online).

Information: The £1 pamphlet, *A Short Guide to Durham Cathedral,* is informative but dull. Tel. 0191/386-4266, www.durhamcathedral.co.uk.

Tours: Regular tours run Monday through Saturday. If one is already in session, you're welcome to join (£5; tours start at 10:30,

11:00, and 14:00; fewer in winter, call or check website to confirm schedule).

Services: A shop, café, and WC are tucked away in the cloister.

Photography: No photos, videos, or mobile phones are allowed inside the cathedral.

Evensong: For a thousand years, this cradle of English Christianity has been praising God. To really experience the cathedral, attend an evensong service. Arrive early and ask to be seated in the choir. It's a spiritual Oz, as the choristers (12 men and 40 youngsters—now girls as well as boys) sing psalms—a red-and-white-robed pillow of praise, raised up by the powerful pipe organ. If you're lucky and the service goes well, the organist will run a spiritual musical victory lap as the congregation breaks up (Tue-Sat at 17:15, Sun at 15:30, 1 hour, sometimes sung on Mon; visiting choirs nearly always fill in when choir is off on school break mid-July-Aug; tel. 0191/386-4266). For more on evensong, see page 145.

Organ Recitals: The organ plays most Wednesday evenings in July and August (£8, 19:30).

Tower Climb: The view from the tower will cost you 325 steps and £5 (Mon-Sat 10:00-16:00, closes at 15:00 in winter, sometimes open Sun outside of services; closed during services, events, and bad weather; must be at least eight years old, no high heels or backless shoes; enter through south transept).

➲ Self-Guided Tour

Begin your visit outside the cathedral. From the Palace Green, notice how this fortress of God stands boldly opposite the Norman keep of Durham's fortress of man.

Look closely: The **exterior** of this awe-inspiring cathedral has a serious skin problem. In the 1770s, as the stone was crumbling, they crudely peeled it back a few inches. The scrape marks give the cathedral a bad complexion to this day. For proof of this odd "restoration," study the masonry 10 yards to the right of the door. The L-shaped stones in the corner would normally never be found in a church like this—they only became L-shaped when the surface was cut back.

At the cathedral **door,** check out the big bronze lion-faced knocker (this is a replica of the 12th-century original, which is in the Open Treasure exhibit). The knocker was used by criminals seeking sanctuary (read the explanation).

Inside, purple-robed church attendants are standing by to happily answer questions. Ideally, follow a church tour. A handy ❶ **information desk** is at the back (right) end of the nave.

Notice the ❷ **modern window** with the novel depiction of the Last Supper (above and to the left of the entry door). It was given to the church by the local Marks & Spencer department store in 1984. The shapes of the apostles represent worlds and persons of every kind, from the shadowy Judas to the brightness of Jesus. This window is a good reminder that the cathedral remains a living part of the community.

Spanning the nave (toward the altar from the info desk), the ❸ **black marble strip** on the floor was as close to the altar as women were allowed in the days when this was a Benedictine church (until 1540). Sit down (ignoring the black line) and let the fine proportions of England's best Norman nave—and arguably Europe's best Romanesque nave—stir you. All the frilly woodwork and stonework were added in later centuries.

The architecture of the **nave** is particularly harmonious because it was built in a mere 40 years (1093-1133). The round arches and zigzag-carved decorations are textbook Norman. The church was also proto-Gothic, built by well-traveled French masons and architects who knew the latest innovations from Europe. Its stone and ribbed roof, pointed arches, and flying buttresses were revolutionary in England. Notice the clean lines and simplicity. It's not as cluttered as other churches for several reasons: For centuries—out of respect for St. Cuthbert—no one else was buried here (so it's not filled with tombs). During Reformation times, sumptuous Catholic decor was removed. Subsequent fires and wars destroyed what Protestants didn't.

Head to the back of the nave and enter the ❹ **Galilee Chapel** (late Norman, from 1175). Find the smaller altar just to the left of the main altar. The paintings of St. Cuthbert and St. Oswald (seventh-century king of Northumbria) on the side walls of the niche are rare examples of Romanesque (Norman) paintings. Facing this altar, look above to your right to see more faint paintings on the upper walls above the columns. On the right side of the chapel, the upraised tomb topped with a black slab contains the remains of the **Venerable Bede,** an eighth-century

Christian scholar who wrote the first history of England. The Latin reads, "In this tomb are the bones of the Venerable Bede."

Back in the main church, stroll down the nave to the center, under the highest **bell tower** in Europe (218 feet). Gaze up. The ropes turn wheels upon which bells are mounted. If you're stirred by the cheery ringing of church bells, tune in to the cathedral on Sunday (9:15-10:00 & 14:30-15:30) or Thursday (19:30-21:00 practice, trained bell ringers welcome, www.durhambellringers.org.uk) when the resounding notes tumble merrily through the entire town.

Continuing east (all medieval churches faced east), enter the **choir.** Monks worshipped many times a day, and the choir in the center of the church provided a cozy place to gather in this vast, dark, and chilly building. Mass has been said daily here in the heart of the cathedral for 900 years. The fancy wooden benches are from the 17th century. Behind the altar is the delicately-carved Neville Screen from 1380 (made of Normandy stone in London, shipped to Newcastle by sea, then brought here by wagon). Until the Reformation, the niches contained statues of 107 saints. Exit the choir from the far right side (south). Look for the stained-glass window (to your right) that commemorates the church's 1,000th anniversary in 1995. The colorful scenes depict England's history, from coal miners to cows to computers.

Step down behind the high altar into the east end of the church, which contains the 13th-century ❺ **Chapel of the Nine Altars.** Built later than the rest of the church, this is Gothic—taller, lighter, and relatively more extravagant than the Norman nave. On the right, see the powerful modern ❻ ***pietà*** made of driftwood, with brass accents by local sculptor Fenwick Lawson.

Climb a few steps to the ❼ **tomb of St. Cuthbert.** An inspirational leader of the early Christian Church in north England, St. Cuthbert lived in the Lindisfarne monastery (100 miles north of Durham, today called Holy Island). He died in 687. Eleven years later, his body was exhumed and found to be miraculously preserved. This stoked the popularity of his shrine, and pilgrims came in growing numbers. When Vikings raided Lindisfarne in 875, the monks fled with his body (and the famous illuminated Lindisfarne Gospels, now in the British Library in London). In 995, after 120 years of roaming, the monks settled in Durham on an easy-to-defend tight bend in the River Wear. This cathedral was built over Cuthbert's tomb.

Throughout the Middle Ages, a shrine stood here and was visited by countless pilgrims. In 1539, during the Reformation—whose proponents advocated focusing on God rather than saints—the shrine was destroyed. But pilgrims still come, especially on St. Cuthbert's feast day (March 20).

Turn around and walk back the way you came. In the **south**

transept (to your left) is the ❽ **tower entry** (described on page 588), as well as an astronomical clock and the Chapel of the Durham Light Infantry, a regiment of the British Army (1881-1968). The old flags and banners hanging above were actually carried into battle.

Return along the left side of the nave toward the entrance. Across from the entry is the door to the cloister. Along the wall by the door to the cloister, notice the ❾ **memorial honoring coal miners** who died, and those who "work in darkness and danger in those pits today." (This message is a bit dated—Durham's coal mines closed down in the 1980s.) The nearby book of remembrance lists mine victims. As an ecclesiastical center, a major university town, and a gritty, blue-collar coal-mining town, Durham's population has long been a complicated mix: priests, academics, and the working class.

After exiting the church, act like a monk and make a circuit of the Gothic ❿ **cloister** (made briefly famous in a scene from the Harry Potter film *The Sorcerer's Stone,* in which Harry walks with his owl through a snowy courtyard). This area provides a fine view back up to the church towers.

The new £9-million ⓫ **Open Treasure exhibit** may be open by the time you visit. You'll enter from the cloister, going up some stairs to the Monks' Dormitory, a long, impressive room that stretches out under an original 14th-century timber roof. Formerly the monks' sleeping quarters, the room now holds artifacts from the cathedral treasury and monks' library. The new space allows the cathedral to display more of its treasures in a climate-controlled environment—including a copy of the *Magna Carta* from 1216—as well as items from the Norman/medieval period (when the monks of Durham busily copied manuscripts), the Reformation, and the 17th century. The exhibit ends in the cloister's Great Kitchen, where the actual relics from St. Cuthbert's tomb are on view—his coffin, vestments, and cross (check exhibit status, prices, and times at info desk or by calling the cathedral).

In the undercroft, you'll find a **shop** and a **café.**

MORE SIGHTS IN DURHAM

There's little to see in Durham beyond its cathedral, but it's a pleasant place to go for a stroll and enjoy its riverside setting.

Durham Heritage Centre Museum

Situated in the old Church of St. Mary-le-Bow near the cathedral, this modest, somewhat-hokey little museum does its best to illuminate the city's history, but it's worthwhile only on a rainy day. The exhibits, which are scattered willy-nilly throughout the old nave, include a reconstructed Victorian-era prison cell; a look at Durham industries past and present, especially coal mining (in Victorian times, the river was literally black from coal); and a 10-minute movie about 20th-century Durham. In the garden on the side of the church are two modern sculptures by local artist Fenwick Lawson, whose work is also in the cathedral.

Cost and Hours: £2.50; July-Sept daily 11:00-16:30, weekend afternoons only in off-season, closed Nov-March; corner of North Bailey and Bow Lane, tel. 0191/384-5589, www.durhamheritagecentre.org.uk.

Riverside Path

For a 20-minute woodsy escape, walk Durham's riverside path from busy Framwellgate Bridge to sleepy Prebends Bridge.

Boat Cruise and Rental

Hop on the *Prince Bishop* for a relaxing one-hour narrated cruise of the river that nearly surrounds Durham (£8, Easter-Oct; for schedule, call 24-hour info line at 0191/386-9525, check their website, or go down to the dock at Brown's Boat House at Elvet Bridge, just east of old town; www.princebishoprc.co.uk). Sailings vary based on weather and tides. For some exercise with identical scenery, you can rent a rowboat at the same pier (£5/hour per person, £10 deposit, late-March-Oct daily 10:00-18:00, last rental at 17:00, tel. 0191/386-3779).

Crook Hall and Gardens

While most English gardens are in the countryside, Crook Hall is only a 10-minute walk from the city center, making it a convenient sight for travelers without a car. It has all the elements you'd expect in a classic English garden—walled "secret" gardens, a maze, a pool, and plenty of moss-covered statues. A map and witty signs take you on a self-guided tour.

Cost and Hours: £7, £5 off-season, April-Sept Sun-Wed 10:00-17:00, shorter hours off-season, closed Thu-Sat; café open daily 9:00-17:00, pay parking; from the city center, walk across the river and head north along the riverside path—it's just past the Radisson Hotel on Frankland Lane; tel. 0191/384-8028, www.crookhallgardens.co.uk.

Sleep Code

Abbreviations **(£1=about $1.60, country code: 44)**
S=Single, **D**=Double/Twin, **T**=Triple, **Q**=Quad, **b**=bathroom
Price Rankings
$$$ Higher Priced—Most rooms £95 or more
$$ Moderately Priced—Most rooms £70-95
$ Lower Priced—Most rooms £70 or less
Unless otherwise noted, credit cards are accepted, breakfast is included, and free Wi-Fi and/or a guest computer is generally available. Prices change; verify current rates online or by email. For the best prices, always book directly with the hotel.

Sleeping in Durham

Close-in pickings are slim in Durham. Because much of the housing is rented to students, there are only a handful of B&Bs. Otherwise, there are a few hotels within easy walking distance of the town center. During graduation (typically the last two weeks of June), everything books up well in advance and prices increase dramatically. Rooms can be tight on weekends any time of year. If the B&Bs are full, Durham could be a good place to resort to a bigger chain hotel (Premier Inn or Marriott).

B&Bs

$$$ Victorian Town House B&B offers three spacious boutique-like rooms in an 1853 townhouse. It's in a nice residential area just down the hill from the train station and is handy to the town center. This is your best B&B option in Durham (Sb-£55-65, Db-£95-105, family room for up to 4 people-£105-135, cash only, 2-night minimum preferred April-Oct, some view rooms, check-in 16:00-19:00 or by prior arrangement, 2 Victoria Terrace, 10-minute walk from train or bus station, tel. 0191/370-9963, www.durhambedandbreakfast.com, stay@durhambedandbreakfast.com, friendly Jill and Andy).

$$$ Castleview Guest House rents five airy, restful rooms in a well-located 250-year-old guesthouse next door to a little church. If it's sunny, guests relax in the Eden-like backyard. Located on a charming cobbled street, it's just above Silver Street and the Framwellgate Bridge (Sb-£80, Db-£100, cash preferred, free street-parking permit, 4 Crossgate, tel. 0191/386-8852, www.castle-view.co.uk, info@guesthousesdurham.co.uk, Anne and Mike Williams).

$$ Farnley Tower, a decent but impersonal B&B, has 13 large rooms and a quirky staff. On a quiet street at the top of a hill, it's a 15-minute hike up from the town center. Though you won't find the standard B&B warmth and service, this is a suitable alternative when the central hotels are booked (Sb-£65, Db-£90—some with cathedral view, family room-£120, 2 percent fee for credit cards, easy free parking, inviting yard, The Avenue—hike up this steep street and look for the sign on the right, tel. 0191/375-0011, www.farnley-tower.co.uk, enquiries@farnley-tower.co.uk, Raj and Roopal Naik). The Naiks also run the inventive Gourmet Spot fine-dining restaurant in the same building.

HOTELS

$$$ Durham Marriott Hotel Royal County scatters its 150 posh, four-star, but slightly-scruffy rooms among several buildings sprawling across the river from the city center. The Leisure Club has a pool, sauna, Jacuzzi, spa, and fitness equipment (prices vary, standard Db-about £94-114, supreme Db with separate seating area-about £119-129, check website for exact prices and deals, breakfast included in some rates but otherwise £16.50 extra, elevator, pay guest computer, free Wi-Fi in public areas, pay Wi-Fi in rooms, restaurant, bar, parking-£5/overnight, Old Elvet, tel. 0191/386-6821 or tel. 0870-400-7286, www.marriott.co.uk).

$$ Kingslodge Hotel & Restaurant is a slightly worn but comfortable 21-room place with charming terraces, an attached restaurant, and a pub. Located in a pleasantly wooded setting, it's convenient for train travelers (Sb-£60-67, Db-£75-89, family room-£109-115, free parking, Waddington Street, Flass Vale, tel. 0191/370-9977, www.kingslodge.info, kingslodgehotel@yahoo.co.uk).

$$ Premier Inn Durham City Center, squeezed between Clayport Library and the river, has 103 cookie-cutter purple rooms in a very convenient central location (Sb/Db-generally around £70-95, check online for prepaid deals as low as £29, continental breakfast-£6.25, full English breakfast-£8.75, air-con, elevator, validated parking for guests at Walkergate car park behind hotel-£7.70/24 hours, Freemans Place, tel. 0871-527-8338 or 0191/374-4400, www.premierinn.com).

STUDENT HOUSING OPEN TO ANYONE

$$$ Durham Castle, a student residence actually on the castle grounds facing the cathedral, rents rooms during the summer break (generally July-Sept). Request a room in the stylish main building, which is more appealing than the modern dorm rooms (S-£40, Sb-£65, Db-£98, fancier Db-£150-200, includes breakfast in an elegant dining hall, Palace Green, tel. 0191/334-4106, www.dur.ac.uk/university.college, durham.castle@durham.ac.uk). Note that the same office also rents rooms in other university buildings, but most are far less convenient to the city center—make sure to request the Durham Castle location when booking.

Eating in Durham

Durham is a university town with plenty of lively inexpensive eateries, but except for Bistro 21, there's not much to get excited about. Especially on weekends, the places downtown are crowded with noisy college kids and rowdy townies. Stroll down North Road, across Framwellgate Bridge, up through Market Place, and up Saddler Street, and consider the options suggested below. The better choices are about a five-minute walk from this main artery—or a long hike to the suburbs—and worth the trek.

Updated British Food: **Oldfields** serves pricey, updated British classics made from locally-sourced ingredients. The inviting dining room feels upscale but not snooty, and there's another more traditional dining room upstairs. While the service can be spotty and some locals wonder if this place is resting on its laurels, it remains one of the best options in the town center (£6.50 starters, £17.50 main dishes; lunch and early bird specials—£13.50/two courses, £15.50/three courses; Mon-Sat 12:00-22:00, Sun 12:00-21:00, 18 Claypath, tel. 0191/370-9595).

Pubs Across the Elvet Bridge: Two good options are within a five-minute walk of the Elvet Bridge (just east of the old town). **The Court Inn** offers an eclectic menu of pub grub and an open, lively atmosphere (£4-6 sandwiches, £8-12 meals, Spanish-style tapas, food served daily 11:00-22:00; cross the Elvet Bridge, turn right, walk several blocks, and then look left; Court Lane, tel. 0191/384-7350). For beer and ales, locals favor **The Dun Cow.** There's a cozy "snug bar" up front and a more spacious lounge in the back. Read the legend behind the pub's name on the wall along the outside corridor. More sedate than the student-oriented places in the town center, this pub serves only snacks and light meals—come here to drink and nibble, not to feast (daily 11:00-23:00; from the Elvet Bridge, walk five minutes straight ahead to Old Elvet 37; tel. 0191/386-9219).

Deli Lunch: **Claypath Delicatessen** is worth the five-minute uphill walk above Market Place. Not just any old sandwich shop, this creative place assembles fresh ingredients into tasty sandwiches, salads, sampler platters, and more. They pride themselves on their killer espresso. While carryout is possible, most people eat in the casual, comfortable café setting (£4-6 light meals, Tue-Fri 9:30-17:30, Sat 10:00-16:00, closed Sun-Mon; from Market Place, cross the bridge and walk up Claypath to #57; tel. 0191/340-7209).

Indian: **The Capital,** a five-minute uphill walk above Market Place (and across the street from Claypath Deli), has well-executed Indian food in a contemporary setting (£8-14 meals, daily 18:00-23:30, 69 Claypath, tel. 0191/386-8803).

Thai: **Zen** is a trendy, modern, dark-wood place serving curries, noodles, fried rice, and other Asian fare. It's popular with students, so it's best to book a table or go early and sit in the bar (£9-11 meals, daily 12:00-22:00, Court Lane, tel. 0191/384-9588, www.zendurham.co.uk).

Chain Restaurants with a Bridge View: Two chain places (that you'll find in every British city) are worth considering in Durham only because of their delightful setting right at the old-town end of the picturesque Framwellgate Bridge. **Café Rouge** has French-bistro food and decor (£5-9 starters and light meals, £11-14 main dishes, daily 9:00-22:30, 21 Silver Street, tel. 0191/384-3429). **Bella Italia,** next door and down the stairs, has a terrace overlooking the river and surprisingly good food (£5-7 starters, £7-11 pizzas and pastas, daily 9:00-22:30, reservations recommended, 20 Silver Street, tel. 0191/386-1060).

Fish-and-Chips: **Bells,** just off Market Place toward the cathedral, is a standby for carryout fish-and-chips. I'd skip their fancier dining room (£5-7, hours vary but likely Mon-Thu 11:00-21:00, Fri-Sat 11:00-24:00, Sun 12:00-16:00).

Splurge Outside the Town Center: **Bistro 21,** an untouristy splurge serving modern French/Mediterranean fare and good seafood, is one of Durham's top restaurants. You'll find inventive twists on regional standards—such as roasted venison or pork belly—and daily fish selections. More than a mile from the city center, it's practical only for drivers or hardy walkers staying near the train station who don't mind a 20-minute hike. The early evening specials are one of the best deals in town (£8-11 starters, £16-25 main dishes; dinner special available Mon-Sat 17:30-19:00—£16/two courses, £19/three courses; open Mon-Sat 12:00-14:00 & 17:30-22:00, Sun 12:00-15:00, reservations smart on weekends, northwest of town, Aykley Heads, tel. 0191/384-4354, www.bistrotwentyone.co.uk).

Supermarket: **Marks & Spencer** is in the old town, just off Market Place (Mon-Sat 8:00-18:00, Sun 11:00-17:00, 4 Silver Street, across from post office). Next door is a **Tesco Metro** (Mon-Sat 7:00-22:00, Sun 11:00-17:00). You can **picnic** on Market Place, or on the benches and grass outside the cathedral entrance (but not on the Palace Green, unless the park police have gone home).

Durham Connections

From Durham by Train to: York (3-4/hour, 45 minutes), **Keswick/Lake District** (train to Penrith—hourly, 3 hours, change in Newcastle and Carlisle; then bus to Keswick), **London** (1/hour direct, 3 hours, more with changes), **Hadrian's Wall** (take train to Newcastle—4/hour, 15 minutes, then a bus or a train/bus combination to near Hadrian's Wall—see "Getting Around Hadrian's Wall" on page 603), **Edinburgh** (hourly direct, 2 hours, more with changes, less frequent in winter). **Train info:** Tel. 0345-748-4950, www.nationalrail.co.uk.

ROUTE TIPS FOR DRIVERS

As you head north from Durham on the A-1 motorway, you'll pass a famous bit of public art: **The Angel of the North,** a modern rusted-metal angel standing 65 feet tall with a wingspan of 175 feet (wider than a Boeing 757). While initially controversial when it was erected in 1998, it has since become synonymous with Northeast England, and is a beloved local fixture.

Beamish Museum

This huge 300-acre open-air museum, which re-creates life in northeast England during the 1820s, 1900s, and 1940s, is England's best museum of its type. It takes at least three hours to explore its four sections: Pit Village (a coal-mining settlement with an actual mine), The Town (a 1913 street lined with actual shops), Pockerley Old Hall (a "gentleman farmer's" manor house), and Home Farm (a preserved farm and farmhouse). This isn't a wax museum. If you touch the exhibits, they may smack you. Attendants at each stop happily explain everything. In fact, the place is only really interesting if you talk to the attendants—who make it worth ▲▲▲.

GETTING TO BEAMISH MUSEUM

By **car,** the museum is five minutes off the A-1/M-1 motorway (one exit north of Durham at Chester-le-Street/Junction 63, well-signposted, 12 miles, 25-minute drive northwest of Durham).

Getting to Beamish from Durham by **bus** is a snap on peak-

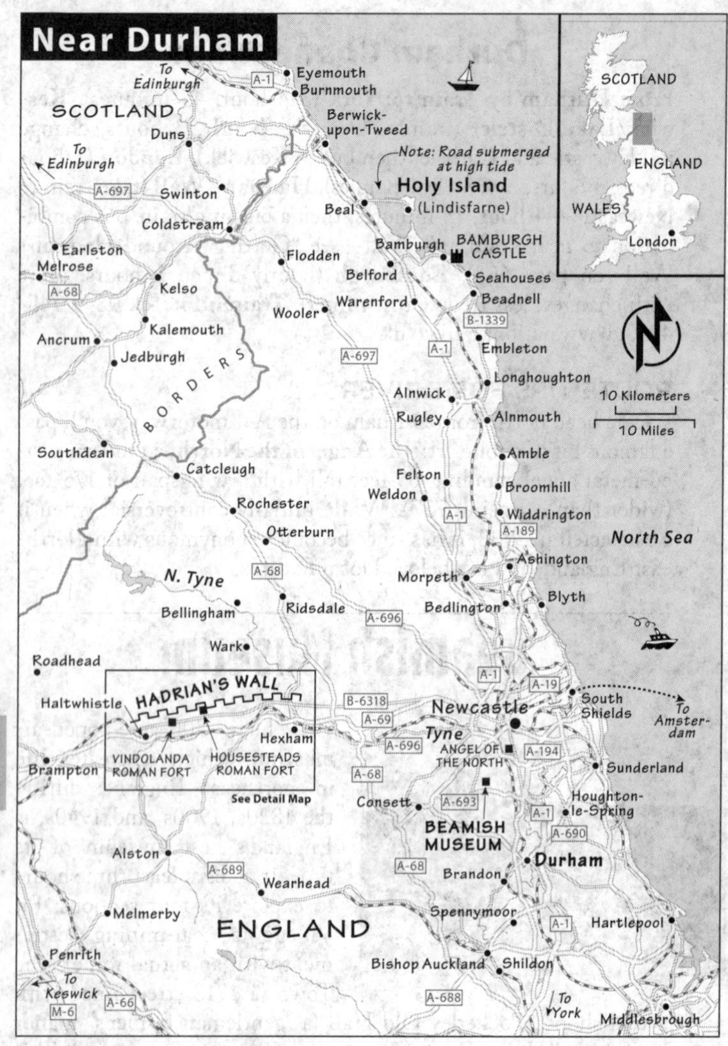

season Saturdays via direct bus #128 (8/day, 30 minutes, runs April-Oct only, stops at Durham train and bus stations). Otherwise, catch bus #21, #X21, or #50 from the Durham bus station (3-4/hour, 25 minutes) and transfer at Chester-le-Street to bus #8 or #8A, which takes you right to the museum entrance (2/hour Mon-Sat, hourly Sun, 15 minutes, leaves from central bus kiosk a half-block away, tel. 0845-606-0260, www.simplygo.com). Show your bus ticket for a 25 percent museum discount.

DURHAM & NE ENGLAND

ORIENTATION TO BEAMISH MUSEUM

Cost and Hours: £18.50, children 5-16-£10.50, under 5-free; open Easter-Oct daily 10:00-17:00; off-season until 16:00, weekends only Dec-mid-Feb, and only The Town and Pit Village are open with vintage trams still running; check events schedule on chalkboard as you enter, last tickets sold at 15:00 year-round, tel. 0191/370-4000, www.beamish.org.uk.

Getting Around the Museum: Pick up a free map at the entry to help navigate the four zones; while some are side by side, others are up to a 15-minute walk apart. Vintage trams and cool circa-1910 double-decker buses shuttle visitors around the grounds, and their attendants are helpful and knowledgeable. Signs on the trams advertise a variety of 19th-century products, from "Borax, for washing everything" to "Murton's Reliable Travelling Trunks."

Eating: Several eateries are scattered around Beamish, including a pub and tearooms (in The Town), a fish-and-chips stand (in the Pit Village), and various cafeterias and snack stands. Or bring a picnic.

VISITING THE MUSEUM

I've described the four areas in counterclockwise order from the entrance.

From the entrance building, bear left along the road, then watch for the turnoff on the right to the **Pit Village.** This is a company town built around a coal mine, with a schoolhouse, a Methodist chapel, and a row of miners' homes with long, skinny pea-patch gardens out front. Poke into some of the homes to see their modest interiors. In the Board School, explore the different classrooms, and look for the interesting poster with instructions for avoiding consumption (a.k.a. tuberculosis, a huge public-health crisis back then).

Next, cross to the adjacent **Colliery** (coal mine) where you can take a fascinating—if claustrophobic—20-minute tour into the drift mine (check in at the "lamp camp"—tours depart when enough people gather, generally every 5-10 minutes). Your guide will tell you stories about beams collapsing, gas exploding, and flooding; after that cheerful speech, you'll don a hard hat as you're led into the mine. Nearby (across the tram tracks) is the fascinating **engine works,** where you can see the actual steam-powered winding engine used to operate the mine elevator. The "winderman" demonstrates how he skillfully eases both coal and miners up and down the tight shaft of the mine. This delicate, high-stakes job was one of the most sought-after at the entire Colliery—passed down from father to son—and the winderman had to stay in this building for his entire shift (the seat of his chair flips up to reveal a built-in WC).

A path leads through the woods to Georgian-era **Pockerley,** which has two parts. First you'll see the **Waggonway,** a big barn filled with steam engines, including the re-created first-ever passenger train from 1825. (Occasionally this train takes modern-day visitors for a spin on 1825 tracks—a hit with railway buffs.)

Then, climb the hill to **Pockerley Old Hall,** the manor house of a gentleman farmer and his family. The house dates from the 1820s, and—along with the farmhouse described later—is Beamish's only vintage building still on its original site (other buildings at Beamish were relocated from elsewhere and reconstructed here). While not extremely wealthy, the farmer who lived here owned large tracts of land and could afford to hire help to farm it for him. This rustic home is no palace, but it was comfortable for the period. Costumed docents in the kitchen often bake delicious cookies from old recipes...and hand out samples.

The small garden terrace out front provides beautiful views across the pastures. From the garden, turn left and locate the narrow stairs up to the "old house." Actually under the same roof as the gentleman farmer's home, this space consists of a few small rooms that were rented by some of the higher-up workers to shelter their entire families of up to 15 children (young boys worked on the farm, while girls were married off early). While the parents had their own bedroom, the children all slept in the loft up above (notice the ladder in the hall).

From the manor house, hop on a vintage tram or bus or walk 10 minutes to the Edwardian-era **The Town** (c. 1913). This bustling street features several working shops and other buildings that are a delight to explore. In the Masonic Hall, ogle the grand high-ceilinged meeting room, and check out the fun old metal signs inside the garage. Across the street, poke into the courtyard to find the stables, which are full of carriages. The heavenly-smelling candy store sells old-timey sweets and has an actual workshop in back with trays of free samples. The newsagent sells stationery, cards, and old toys, while in the grocery, you can see old packaging and the scales used for weighing out products. Other buildings include a clothing store, a working pub (The Sun Inn, don't expect 1913 prices), Barclays Bank, and a hardware store featuring a variety of "toilet sets" (not what you think).

For lunch, try the Tea Rooms cafeteria (upstairs). Or, if the weather is good, picnic in the grassy park with the gazebo next to the tram stop. The row of townhouses includes both homes and offices (if the dentist is in, chat with him to hear some harrowing stories about pre-Novocain tooth extraction). At the circa-1913 railway station at the far end of The Town, you can stand on the bridge over the tracks to watch old steam engines go back and forth—along with a carousel of "steam gallopers." Nearby, look for the "Westoe netty," a circa-1890 men's public urinal. This loo became famous in 1972 as the subject in a nostalgic Norman Rockwell-style painting of six miners and a young boy doing their business while they read the graffiti.

Finally, walk or ride a tram or bus to the **Home Farm.** (This is the least interesting section—if you're running short on time, it's skippable.) Here you'll get to experience a petting zoo and see a "horse gin" (a.k.a. "gin gan")—where a horse walking in a circle turned a crank on a gear to amplify its "horsepower," helping to replace human hand labor. Near the cafeteria, you can cross a busy road (carefully) to the old farmhouse, still on its original site, where attendants sometimes bake goodies on a coal fire.

Hadrian's Wall

Cutting across the width of the isle of Britain, this ruined Roman wall is one of England's most thought-provoking sights. Once a towering 20-foot-tall fortification, these days "Hadrian's Shelf," as some cynics call it, is only about three feet wide and three to six feet high. (The conveniently precut stones of the wall were carried away by peasants during the post-Rome Dark Ages and now form the foundations of many local churches, farmhouses, and other structures.) In most places, what's left of the wall has been covered over by centuries of sod...making it effectively disappear into the landscape. But for those intrigued by Roman history, Hadrian's Wall provides a fine excuse to take your imagination for a stroll. These are the most impressive Roman ruins in Britain. Pretend you're a legionnaire on patrol in dangerous and distant Britannia, at the empire's northernmost frontier...with nothing but this wall protecting you from the terrifying bloodthirsty Picts just to the north.

Today, several restored chunks of the wall, ruined forts, and museums thrill history buffs. While a dozen Roman sights cling along the wall's route, I've focused my coverage on an easily-digestible six-mile stretch right in the middle, where you'll find the best museums and some of the most enjoyable-to-hike stretches of the wall. Three top sights are worth visiting: Housesteads Roman Fort shows you where the Romans lived; Vindolanda's museum shows you how they lived; and the Roman Army Museum explains the empire-wide military organization that brought them here.

A breeze for drivers, this area can also be seen fairly easily in summer by bus for those good at studying timetables (see "Getting Around Hadrian's Wall," later).

Hadrian's Wall is in vogue as a destination for multiday hikes through the pastoral English countryside. The Hadrian's Wall National Trail runs 84 miles, following the wall's route from coast to coast (for details, go to www.nationaltrail.co.uk/HadriansWall). Through-hikers (mostly British) can walk the wall's entire length in four to ten days. You'll see them bobbing along the ridgeline, drying out their socks in your B&B's mudroom, and recharging at local pubs in the evening. For those with less time, the brief ridge walk next to the wall from Steel Rigg to Sycamore Gap to

Housesteads Roman Fort gives you a perfect taste of the scenery and history.

Orientation to Hadrian's Wall

The area described in this section is roughly between the midsize towns of Bardon Mill and Haltwhistle, which are located along the busy A-69 highway. Each town has a train station and some handy B&Bs, restaurants, and services. However, to get right up close to the wall, you'll need to head a couple of miles north to the adjacent villages of Once Brewed and Twice Brewed (along the B-6318 road).

TOURIST INFORMATION

Portions of the wall are in Northumberland National Park. The **Walltown Visitor Centre** lies along the Hadrian's Wall bus #AD122 route and has information on the area, including walking guides to the wall (Easter-Oct daily 9:30-17:00, closed Nov-Easter, parking-£4/day, just off B-6318 next to the Roman Army Museum, follow signs to *Walltown Quarry,* tel. 01697/747-151 or 01434/344-396, www.northumberlandnationalpark.org.uk, tic.oncebrewed@nnpa.org.uk). Note that an additional visitor center based in the Twice Brewed Inn (described later) may be operating when you visit.

The helpful **TI** in Haltwhistle, a block from the train station inside the library, has a good selection of maps and guidebooks and schedule information for Hadrian's Wall bus #AD122 (Easter-Oct Mon-Sat 10:00-16:30, closed Sun and Nov-Easter, The Library, Westgate, tel. 01434/322-002, www.hadrians-wall.org).

GETTING AROUND HADRIAN'S WALL

Hadrian's Wall is anchored by the big cities of Newcastle to the east and Carlisle to the west. Driving is the most convenient way to see Hadrian's Wall. If you're coming by train, consider renting a car for the day at either Newcastle or Carlisle; otherwise, you'll need to rely on trains and a bus to connect the sights, or hire a private guide with a car. If you're just passing through for the day using public transportation, it's challenging to stop and see more than just one or two of the sights—study the schedules carefully and prioritize. Nondrivers who want to see everything—or even hike part of the wall—will need to stay one or two nights along the bus route.

By Car

Zip to this "best of Hadrian's Wall" zone on the speedy A-69; when you get close, head a few miles north and follow the B-6318, which parallels the wall and passes several viewpoints, minor sights, and

The History of Hadrian's Wall

In about A.D. 122, during the reign of Emperor Hadrian, the Romans constructed this great stone wall. Stretching 73 miles coast to coast across the narrowest stretch of northern England, it was built and defended by some 20,000 troops. Not just a wall, it was a military complex with forts, ditches, settlements, and roads. At every mile of the wall, a castle guarded a gate, and two turrets stood between each castle. The milecastles are numbered (80 covering 73 miles, because a Roman mile was slightly shorter than our mile).

In cross-section, Hadrian's Wall consisted of a stone wall—around 15 to 20 feet tall—with a ditch on either side. The flat-bottomed ditch on the south side of the wall, called the vallum, was flanked by earthen ramparts and likely demarcated the "no-man's land" beyond which civilians were not allowed to pass. Between the vallum and the wall ran a service road called the Military Way. Another less-elaborate ditch ran along the north side of the wall. In some areas—including the region that I describe—the wall was built upon a volcanic ridgeline that provided a natural fortification.

The wall's actual purpose is still debated. While Rome ruled Britain for 400 years, it never quite ruled its people. The wall may have been used for any number of reasons: to protect Roman Britain from invading Pict tribes from the north (or at least cut down on pesky border raids); to monitor the movement of people as a show of Roman strength and superiority; or to simply give an otherwise bored army something to do. (Emperors understood that nothing was more dangerous than a bored army.) Or perhaps the wall represented Hadrian's tacit admission that the empire had reached its maximum extent; Hadrian was known for consolidating his territory, in some cases giving up chunks of land that had been conquered by his predecessor, Trajan, to create an easier-to-defend (if slightly smaller) empire. His philosophy of "defense before expansion" is embodied by the impressive wall that still bears his name.

"severe dips." (These road signs add a lot to a photo portrait.) Buy a good local map to help you explore this interesting area more easily and thoroughly. Official Hadrian's Wall parking lots (including at the Walltown Visitor Centre, Housesteads Roman Fort, and the trailhead at Steel Rigg) are covered by a single one-day £4 parking pass (coin-op pay-and-display machines at all lots).

Without a Car

To reach the Roman sights without a car, take the made-for-tourists Hadrian's Wall **bus #AD122** (named for the year the wall was built; runs only in peak season—see below). Essential resources for navigating the wall by public transit include the *Hadrian's Wall Country Map,* the bus #AD122 schedule, and a local train timetable for Northern Line #4—all available at local visitors centers and train stations (also see www.visithadrianswall.co.uk). If you arrive by train during the off-season, you'll need to rely on taxis, a private guide, or long walks to visit the wall (see "Off-Season Options," later).

By Bus: Bus #AD122 connects the Roman sights (and several recommended accommodations) with train stations in **Haltwhistle** and **Hexham** (from £2/ride, £12 unlimited Day Rover ticket, buy tickets on board, tel. 01434/322-002).

The bus runs between Haltwhistle and Hexham (8/day in each direction Easter-Sept, no service Oct-Easter). If you're coming from Carlisle or Newcastle, you'll need to take the train to Haltwhistle or Hexham and pick up the bus there. (The bus used to run between Carlisle and Newcastle, and there's talk of restoring extended service in 2016.) If you're planning to take this bus, it's smart to confirm online whether it'll be running during your visit (www.visithadrianswall.co.uk).

By Train: Northern Line's train route #4 runs parallel to and a few miles south of the wall much more frequently than the bus. While the train stops at stations in larger towns—including (west to east) **Carlisle, Haltwhistle, Hexham,** and **Newcastle**—it doesn't take you near the actual Roman sights. You can catch bus #AD122 at Hexham and Haltwhistle (no bus service off-season; train runs daily 1/hour; Carlisle to Haltwhistle—30 minutes; Haltwhistle to Hexham—20 minutes; Hexham to Newcastle—40 minutes; www.northernrail.org). Note: To get to or from Newcastle on this line, you must transfer in Hexham.

By Taxi: These Haltwhistle-based taxi companies can help you connect the dots: Sprouls (tel. 01434/321-064, mobile 07712-321-064) or Diamond (mobile 07597-641-222). It costs about £11 one-way from Haltwhistle to Housesteads Roman Fort (arrange for return pickup or have museum staff call a taxi). Note that on school days, all of these taxis are busy shuttling rural kids to class in the morning (about 8:00-10:00) and afternoon (about 14:30-16:30), so you may have to wait.

By Private Tour: Peter Carney, a former history teacher who waxes eloquently on all things Roman, offers tours with his car and also leads guided walks around Hadrian's Wall, including an all-day seven-mile hike that starts at the Roman Army Museum and connects Vindolanda and Housesteads. He can also custom-

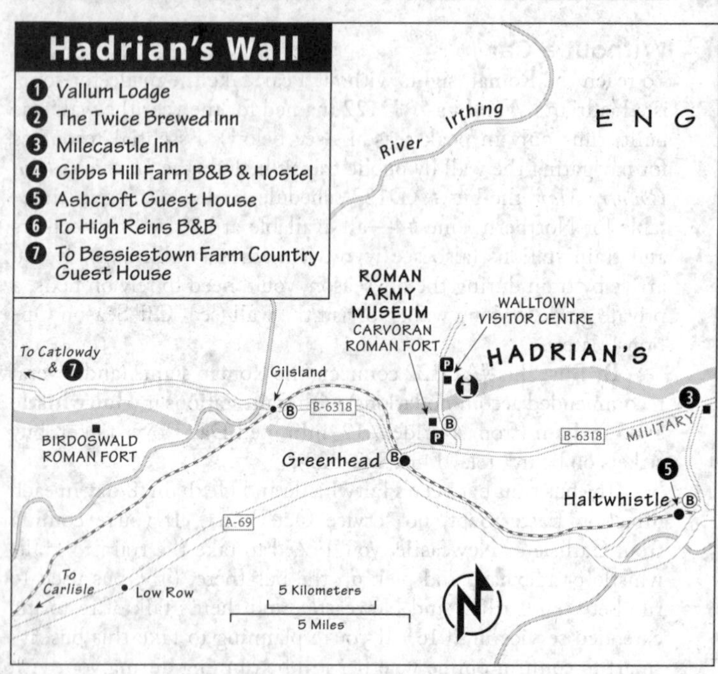

ize tours to suit your time frame and interests and is happy to pick you up from your B&B or the train station (£125/day for up to 5 people, £70/half-day, does not include museum admission, £25 extra for pick-up at Carlisle or Newcastle train stations, mobile 07585-139-016 or 07810-665-733, www.hadrianswall-walk.com, petercarney@hadrianswall-walk.com). Peter also offers tours of medieval Durham.

Off-Season Options: Bus #AD122 doesn't run off-season (Oct-Easter), so you can only get as far as the train will take you (i.e., Haltwhistle)—from there, you'll have to take a taxi or hire a local guide to take you to the sights. Or, if you're a hardy hiker, take the Northern Line train to Bardon Mill, then walk about two miles to Vindolanda and another 2.5 miles to Housesteads Roman Fort.

Baggage Storage: It's difficult to bring your luggage along with you. If you're day-tripping, you can store your luggage in **Carlisle** (across the street from the train station at Bar Solo, call for price and hours, tel. 01228/631-600) or in **Newcastle** at the Eldon Square Shopping Center, a five-minute walk north of the train station (tel. 01912/611-891, www.intu.co.uk/eldonsquare). If you must travel with luggage, Housesteads Roman Fort and Vindolanda will most likely let you leave your bags at the sight entrance while you're inside. If you want to walk the wall, various baggage-courier services will send your luggage ahead to your next B&B in the region for about £5 per bag (contact Hadrian's Haul, mobile

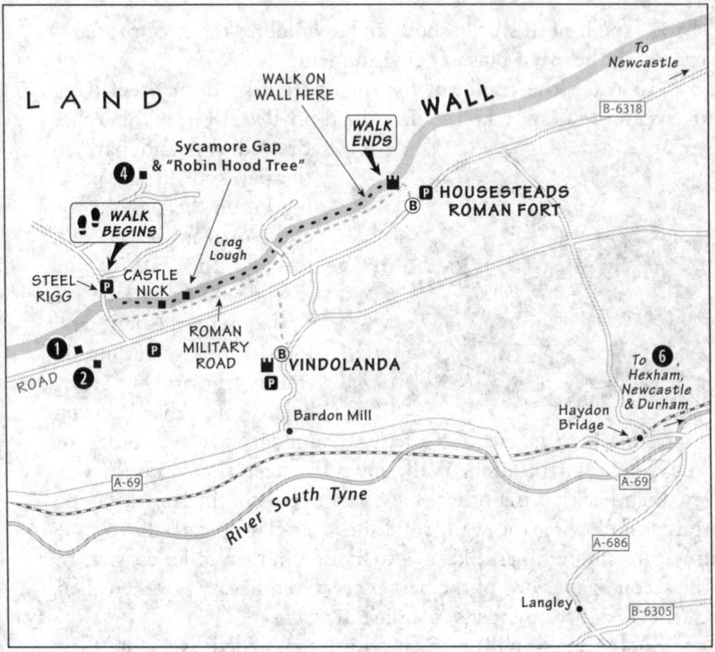

07967-564-823, www.hadrianshaul.com; or Walkers', tel. 0871-423-8803, www.walkersbags.co.uk).

Sights at Hadrian's Wall

▲▲Hiking the Wall

It's enjoyable to hike along the wall speaking Latin, even if only for a short stretch. Note that park rangers forbid anyone from actually walking on top of the wall, except along a very short stretch at Housesteads. On the following hike, you'll walk alongside the wall.

For a good, craggy, three-mile, one-way, up-and-down walk along the wall, hike between Steel Rigg and Housesteads Roman Fort. For a shorter stretch, begin at Steel Rigg (where there's a handy parking lot) and walk a mile to Sycamore Gap, then back again (described next; the Walltown Visitor Centre hands out a free sheet outlining this walk). These hikes are moderately strenuous and are best for those in good shape. You'll need sturdy shoes and a windbreaker to comfortably overcome the often-blustery environment.

To reach the trailhead for the short hike from **Steel Rigg to Sycamore Gap,** take the little road off B-6318 near the Twice Brewed Inn and park in the pay-and-display parking lot on the right at the crest of the hill. Walk through the gate to the shoulder-high stretch of wall, go to the left, and follow the wall running steeply down the valley below you. Ahead of you are dramatic cliffs, creating a natural boundary made-to-order for this Roman fortification. Walk down the steep slope into the valley, then back up the other side (watch your footing on the stone stairs). Following the wall, you'll do a similar up-and-down routine three more times, like a slow-motion human roller coaster. In the second gap is one of the best-preserved milecastles, #39 (called Castle Nick because it sits in a nick in a crag).

Soon after, you'll reach the third gap, called Sycamore Gap for the large symmetrical tree in the middle. (Do you remember the 1991 Kevin Costner movie *Robin Hood: Prince of Thieves*? Locals certainly do—this tree was featured in it, and tourists frequently ask for directions to the "Robin Hood Tree.") You can either hike back the way you came or cut down toward the main road to find the less strenuous Roman Military Way path, which skirts the bottom of the ridge (rather than following the wall); this leads back to the base of the Steel Rigg hill, where you can huff back up to your car.

If you continue on to Housesteads, you'll pass a traditional Northumbrian sheep farm, windswept lakes, and more ups and downs. The farther you go, the fewer people you'll encounter, making this hike even more magical. As you close in on Housesteads, you'll be able to actually walk on top of the wall.

▲▲Housesteads Roman Fort

With its respectable museum, powerful scenery, and the best-preserved segment of the wall, this is your best single stop at Hadrian's Wall. It requires a steep hike up from the parking lot, but once

there it's just you, the bleating sheep, and memories of ancient Rome.

Cost and Hours: £6.60 for site and museum; daily April-Sept 10:00-18:00, Oct 10:00-17:00, Nov-March 10:00-16:00; last entry 45 minutes before closing, parking-£4/day, same parking ticket also good for the Walltown Visitor Centre and Steel Rigg parking lots, bus #AD122 stops here.

Services and Information: At the car park is a visitors center with WCs, a snack bar, and a gift shop. They sell a £3.50 guidebook about the fort or a £5 guidebook covering the entire wall. If you're traveling by bus and want to leave your luggage, ask at the visitors center if they'll stow it for a bit. Museum tel. 01434/344-363, info tel. 0870-333-1181, gift shop tel. 01434/344-525, www.english-heritage.org.uk/housesteads.

Visiting the Museum and Fort: From the visitors center, head outside and hike about a half-mile uphill to the fort. At the top of the hill, duck into the **museum** (on the left) before touring the site. While smaller and housing fewer artifacts than the museum at Vindolanda, it's interesting nonetheless. Look for the giant Victory statue, which once adorned the fort's East Gate; her foot is stepping on a globe, serving as an intimidating reminder to outsiders of the Romans' success in battle. A good seven-minute film shows how Housesteads (known back then as Vercovicium) would have operated.

Artifacts offer more insights into those who lived here. A cooking pot from Frisia (Northern Holland) indicates the presence of women, showing that soldiers came with their families in tow. A tweezer, probe, spoons, and votive foot (that would have been offered to the gods in exchange for a cure for a foot ailment) reveal the type of medical care you could expect. And a weighted die and a coin mold—perhaps used to make counterfeit money—show what may have been the less-than-savory side of life at the fort.

After exploring the museum, head out to the sprawling ruins of the **fort.** Interpretive signs and illustrations explain what you're seeing. All Roman forts were the same rectangular shape and design, containing a commander's headquarters, barracks, and latrines (Housesteads has the best-preserved Roman toilets found anywhere—look for them at the lower-right corner). This fort even had a hospital. The fort was built right up to the wall, which runs along its upper end. Even if you're not a hiker, take some time to walk the wall here. (This is the one place along the wall where you're actually allowed to get up and walk on top of it for a photo op.) Visually trace the wall to the left to see how it disappears into a bank of overgrown turf.

▲▲Vindolanda

This larger Roman fort (which actually predates the wall by 40 years) and museum are just south of the wall. Although Housesteads has better ruins and the wall, Vindolanda has the more impressive museum, packed with artifacts that reveal intimate details of Roman life.

Cost and Hours: £6.75, £10.50 combo-ticket includes Roman Army Museum, daily April-Sept 10:00-18:00, mid-Feb-March and Oct 10:00-17:00, Nov 10:00-16:00, may be open on weekends Dec-mid-Feb, last entry 45 minutes before closing, call first during bad weather, free parking with entry, bus #AD122 stops here, café.

Information: A guidebook is available for £4; tel. 01434/344-277, www.vindolanda.com.

Tours: Guided tours run twice daily on weekends only (typically at 10:45 and 14:00); in high season, archaeological talks and tours may be offered on weekdays as well. Both are included in your ticket.

Archaeological Dig: The Vindolanda site is an active dig—from Easter through September, you'll see the excavation work in progress (usually Mon-Fri, weather permitting). Much of the work is done by volunteers, including armchair archaeologists from the US.

Visiting the Site and Museum: After entering, stop at the model of the entire site as it was in Roman times (c. A.D. 213-276). Notice that the site had two parts: the fort itself, and the town just outside that helped to supply it.

Head out to the **site,** walking through 500 yards of grassy parkland decorated by the foundation stones of the Roman fort and a full-size replica chunk of the wall. Over the course of 400 years, at least nine forts were built on this spot. The Romans, by lazily sealing the foundations from each successive fort, left modern-day archaeologists with a 20-foot-deep treasure trove of remarkably well-preserved artifacts: keys, coins, brooches, scales, pottery, glass, tools, leather shoes, bits of cloth, and even a wig. Many of these are now displayed in the museum, well-described in English, German, French, and...Latin.

At the far side of the site, pass through the pleasant riverside garden area on the way to the museum. The well-presented **mu-**

seum pairs actual artifacts with insightful explanations—such as a collection of Roman shoes with a description about what each one tells us about its wearer. The weapons (including arrowheads and spearheads) and fragments of armor are a reminder that Vindolanda was an important outpost on Rome's northern boundary—look for the Scottish skull stuck on a pike to discourage rebellion.

Thanks to Vindolanda's boggy grounds, trash tossed away by the Romans was preserved in an airless environment. You'll see the world's largest collection of Roman leather; tools that were used for building and expanding the fort; locks and keys (the fort had a password that changed daily—jotting it on a Post-It note wasn't allowed); a large coin collection; items imported here from the far corners of the vast empire (such as fragments of French pottery and amphora jugs from the Mediterranean); beauty aids such as combs, tools for applying makeup, and hairpins; and religious pillars and steles.

But the museum's main attraction is its collection of writing tablets. A good video explains how these impressively well-preserved examples of early Roman cursive were discovered here in 1973. Displays show some of the actual letters—written on thin pieces of wood—alongside the translations. These letters bring Romans to life in a way that ruins alone can't. The most famous piece (described but not displayed here) is the first known example of a woman writing to a woman (an invitation to a birthday party).

Finally, you'll pass through an exhibit about the history of the excavations, including a case featuring the latest discoveries, on your way to the shop and cafeteria.

▲▲Roman Army Museum

This museum, a few miles farther west at Greenhead (near the site of the Carvoran Roman fort), has cutting-edge interactive exhibits illustrating the structure of the Roman Army that built and monitored this wall, with a focus on the everyday lifestyles of the Roman soldiers stationed here. Bombastic displays, life-size figures, and several different films—but few actual artifacts—make this entertaining museum a good complement to the archaeological emphasis of Vindolanda. If you're visiting all three Roman sights, this is a good one to start at, as it sets the stage for what you're about to see.

Cost and Hours: £5.50, £10.50 combo-ticket includes Vindolanda, daily April-Sept 10:00-18:00, mid-Feb-March and Oct-mid-Nov 10:00-17:00, may be open on weekends mid-Nov-mid-Feb, free parking with entry, bus #AD122 stops here.

Information: Tel. 01697/747-485; if no answer, call Vindolanda tel. 01434/344-277; www.vindolanda.com.

Visiting the Museum: In the first room, a video explains the complicated structure of the Roman Army—legions, cohorts, centuries, and so on. While a "legionnaire" was a Roman citizen, an "auxiliary" was a noncitizen specialist recruited for their unique skills (such as horsemen and archers). A video of an army-recruiting officer delivers an "Uncle Caesar wants YOU!" speech to prospective soldiers. A timeline traces the history of the Roman Empire, especially as it related to the British Isles.

The good 20-minute *Edge of Empire* 3-D movie offers an evocative look at what life was like for a Roman soldier marking time on the wall, and digital models show reconstructions of the wall and forts. In the exhibit on weapons, shields, and armor (mostly replicas), you'll learn how Roman soldiers trained with lead-filled wooden swords, so that when they went into battle, their steel swords felt light by comparison. Another exhibit explains the story of Hadrian, the man behind the wall, who stopped the expansion of the Roman Empire, declaring the age of conquest was over.

Sleeping and Eating near Hadrian's Wall

If you want to spend the night in this area, set your sights on the adjacent villages of Once Brewed and Twice Brewed, with a few accommodations options, a good pub, and easy access to the most important sights. I've also listed some other accommodations scattered around the region.

IN AND NEAR ONCE BREWED AND TWICE BREWED

These two side-by-side villages, each with a handful of houses, sit at the base of the volcanic ridge along the B-6318 road. (While the mailing address for these hamlets is "Bardon Mill," that town is actually about 2.5 miles away, across the busy A-69 highway.) The Twice Brewed Inn and Milecastle Inn are reachable with Hadrian's Wall bus #AD122. Bus drivers can drop you off at Vallum Lodge by request (but they won't pick up).

$$ Vallum Lodge is a cushy, comfortable, nicely-renovated base situated near the vallum (the ditch that forms part of the fortification a half-mile from the wall itself). Its six cheery rooms are all on the ground floor, and a separate guesthouse called the Snug has one bedroom and a kitchen. It's just up the road from The Twice Brewed Inn—a handy dinner option (Sb-£75, Db-£90, Db in Snug-£110, laundry-£12/load, lounge, Military Road, tel. 01434/344-248, www.vallum-lodge.co.uk, stay@vallum-lodge.co.uk, Clare and Michael).

$$ The Twice Brewed Inn, two miles west of Housesteads and a half-mile from the wall, rents 16 basic workable rooms; all are en-suite and most have been recently renovated (Sb-£50, Db-£70-80, ask for a room away from the road, Military Road, tel. 01434/344-534, www.twicebrewedinn.co.uk, info@twicebrewedinn.co.uk). The inn's friendly **pub** serves as the community gathering place (free Wi-Fi) and is a hangout for hikers and the archaeologists digging at the nearby sites. It serves real ales and large portions of good pub grub (£9-12 meals, vegetarian options, fancier restaurant in back with same menu, food served daily 12:00-21:00, Sun until 20:00).

Rural and Remote, North of the Wall: **$$ Gibbs Hill Farm B&B and Hostel** is a friendly working sheep-and-cattle farm set on 700 acres in the stunning valley on the far side of the wall (only practical for drivers). The B&B offers three big, airy double en-suite rooms in the main house, while the three 6-bed dorm rooms are in a restored hay barn (hostel bed/bedding-£18, Sb-£60, Db-£80, packed lunch-£6, coin-op laundry facilities, 5-minute drive from Twice Brewed Inn or 30-minute walk from Steel Rigg trailhead, tel. 01434/344-030, www.gibbshillfarm.co.uk, val@gibbshillfarm.co.uk, warm Val). They also rent several cottages for two to six people by the week or occasionally shorter periods (£280-600).

Eating West of Once/Twice Brewed: **Milecastle Inn,** two miles to the west, cooks up all sorts of exotic game and offers the best dinner around, according to hungry national park rangers. You can order food at the counter and sit in the pub, or take a seat in the table-service area (£9-13 meals, food served daily Easter-Sept 12:00-20:45, Oct-Easter 12:00-14:30 & 18:00-20:30, smart to reserve in summer, North Road, tel. 01434/321-372, www.milecastle-inn.co.uk).

IN HALTWHISTLE

The larger town of Haltwhistle has a train station, along with stops for Hadrian's Wall bus #AD122 (at the train station and a few blocks east, at Market Place). It also has a helpful TI (see "Tourist Information," on page 603), a launderette, several eateries, and a handful of B&Bs, including this one.

$$ Ashcroft Guest House, a large Victorian former vicarage, is 400 yards from the Haltwhistle train station and 200 yards from the Market Place bus stop. It has seven big luxurious rooms, huge terraced gardens, and views from the comfy lounge, along with a two-bedroom apartment with kitchen. If you want to indulge yourself after hiking the wall, this is the place (Sb-£69, Db-£89, super king or four-poster Db-£99, ask about family deals, 2-night minimum for apartment, 1.5 miles from the wall, Lanty's Lonnen, tel. 01434/320-213, www.ashcroftguesthouse.co.uk, info@ashcroftguesthouse.co.uk, helpful Geoff and Christine James).

NEAR HEXHAM

$$ High Reins offers four rooms in a stone house built by a shipping tycoon in the 1920s. The rooms are cushy and comfortable—there's a cozy feeling all over the place (Sb-£48, Db-£75, cash only, 2-bedroom apartment also available in the house, lounge, 1 mile south of train station on the western outskirts of Hexham, Leazes Lane, tel. 01434/603-590, pwalton@highreins.co.uk, Jan and Peter Walton). They also rent an apartment in the town center; ask for details.

NEAR CARLISLE

$$ Bessiestown Farm Country Guest House, located far northwest of the Hadrian sights, is convenient for drivers connecting the Lake District and Scotland. It's a quiet and soothing stop in the middle of sheep pastures, with four bedrooms in the main house and two 2-bedroom apartments in the former stables. One apartment is on the ground floor and has a handicapped-accessible bath (Sb-£59, Db-£90, Tb-£120, honeymoon suite-£130, discount with 3-night stay, honesty bar; in Catlowdy, midway between Gretna Green and Hadrian's Wall, 14-mile 20-minute drive north of Carlisle; tel. 01228/577-219, www.bessiestown.co.uk, info@bessiestown.co.uk, gracious Margaret and John Sisson).

WALES

WALES

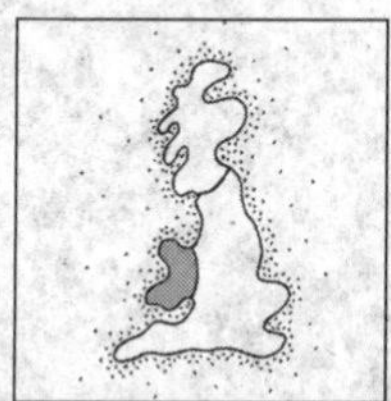

Wales, a country the size of Massachusetts, is located on a peninsula on the west coast of the Isle of Britain, facing the Irish Sea. Longer than it is wide (170 miles by 60 miles), it's shaped somewhat like a miniature Britain. The north is mountainous, rural, and sparsely populated. The south, with a less-rugged topography, is where two-thirds of the people live (including 350,000 in the capital of Cardiff). The country has 750 miles of scenic, windswept coastline and is capped by Mount Snowdon, which, at 3,560 feet, is taller than any mountain in England.

Despite centuries of English imperialism, the Welsh language (a.k.a. Cymraeg, pronounced kum-RAH-ig) remains alive and well—more so than its nearly-dead Celtic cousin in Scotland, Gaelic. Though everyone in Wales speaks English, one in five can also speak the native tongue. In the northwest, well over half the population is fluent in Welsh and uses it in everyday life. Listen in.

Most certainly *not* a dialect of English, the Celtic Welsh tongue sounds to foreign ears like it might be Elvish from *The Lord of the Rings*. One of Europe's oldest languages, Welsh has been written down since about A.D. 600, and it was spoken 300 years before French or German. Today, the Welsh language is protected by law from complete English encroachment—the country is officially bilingual, and signs always display both languages (e.g., *Cardiff/Caerdydd*). In schools, it's either the first or the required second language; in many areas, English isn't used in classes at all until middle school.

Though English has been the dominant language in Wales for many years (and most newspapers and media are in English), the Welsh people cherish their linguistic heritage as something that

Speaking Welsh

Welsh pronunciation is tricky. The common "ll" combination sounds roughly like "thl" (pronounced as if you were ready to

make an "l" sound and then blew it out). As in Scotland, "ch" is a soft, guttural k, pronounced in the back of the throat. The Welsh "dd" sounds like the English "th," f = v, ff = f, w = the "u" in "push," y = i. Non-Welsh people often make the mistake of trying to say a long Welsh name too fast, and inevitably trip themselves up. A local tipped me off: Slow down and say each syllable separately, and it'll come out right. For example, Llangollen is thang-GOTH-lehn. But it gets harder. Some words are a real mouthful, like Llanfairpwllgwyngyllgogerychwyrndrobwllllantysiliogogogoch, a small town on the island of Angelsey that is (not surprisingly) the longest place name in the UK.

Although there's no need to learn any Welsh (because everyone also speaks English), without too much effort you can make friends and impress the locals by learning a few polite phrases.

English	Welsh
Hello	**Helo** (hee-LOH)
Good-bye	**Hwyl** (hoo-il)
Please	**Os gwelwch yn dda** (os GWELL-uck UN thah)
Thank you	**Diolch** (dee-olkh)
Wales	**Cymru** (KUM-ree)
England	**Lloegr** (THLOY-ger)

In a pub, toast the guy who just bought your drink with Diolch and Yeach-hid dah (YECH-id dah, "Good health to you").

sets them apart. In fact, a line of the Welsh national anthem goes, "Oh, may the old language survive!"

Wales has some traditional foods worth looking for, particularly lamb dishes and leek soup *(cawl)*. In fact, the national symbol is the leek, ever since medieval warriors—who wore the vegetable on their helmets in battle—saved the land from Saxon invaders.

Cheese on toast is known as "Welsh rarebit" (or "Welsh rabbit"; the name is a throwback to a time when the poor Welsh couldn't afford much meat in their diet). At breakfast, you might get some "Welsh cakes," basically a small squashed scone. Cockles and seaweed bread were once common breakfast items—but don't expect your hotel to serve them.

Wales' three million people are mostly white and Christian (Presbyterian, Anglican, or Catholic). Like their English and Scottish counterparts, they enjoy football (soccer), but rugby is the unofficial Welsh sport, more popular in Wales than in any country outside of New Zealand. Other big sports are cricket and snooker (similar to billiards).

The Welsh flag features a red dragon on a field of green and white. The dragon has been a symbol of Wales since at least the ninth century (maybe even from Roman days). According to legend, King Arthur's men carried the dragon flag to battle.

Welsh history stretches back into the mists of prehistoric Britain. When Roman armies arrived on the island of Britain, they conquered the Celtic tribes here, built forts and cities, and (later) introduced Christianity. As Rome fell, Saxon (Germanic) tribes like the Angles stepped into the power vacuum, conquering what they renamed "Angle-land"—but they failed to penetrate Wales. Brave Welsh warriors, mountainous terrain, and the 177-mile manmade ditch-and-wall known as Offa's Dyke helped preserve the country's unique Celtic/Roman heritage. In 1216, Wales' medieval kingdoms unified under Llywelyn Fawr ("the Great").

But just a few decades later, in 1282, King Edward I of England invaded and conquered, putting an end to Wales' one era as a unified, sovereign nation. To solidify his hold on the country, Edward built a string of castles (at Caernarfon, Conwy, and many other places—see sidebar on page 634). He then named his son and successor the "Prince of Wales," starting the tradition of granting that ceremonial title to the heir to the English throne. Despite an unsuccessful rebellion in 1400, led by Owen Glendower (Owain Glyndwr), Wales has remained under English rule ever since Edward's invasion. In 1535, the annexation was formalized under Henry VIII.

By the 19th century, Welsh coal and iron stoked the engines of Britain's Industrial Revolution, and its slate was exported to shingle roofs throughout Europe. The stereotype of the Welsh as poor, grimy-faced miners continued into the 20th century. Their econo-

Singing the Praises of Welsh Choirs

The Welsh love their choirs. Every town has a choir (men's or mixed) that practices weekly. Visitors are usually welcome to observe the session (lasting about 1.5-2 hours), and sometimes the choir heads to the pub afterward for a good old-fashioned, beer-lubricated sing-along that you can join.

As these choir rehearsals have become something of a tourist attraction, many choirs ask attendees for a small donation—fair enough. Note that some towns have more than one choir, and schedules are subject to change; confirm the schedule with a TI or your B&B before making the trip. Additionally, many choirs regularly perform concerts—inquire for the latest schedule.

Here are choir practices that occur in or near towns I recommend visiting: **Llandudno Junction,** near **Conwy** (men's choir Mon at 19:30 except Aug, tel. 01248/681-159, www.cormaelgwn.cymru); **Caernarfon** (men's choir Tue at 19:45, arrive by 19:30 in summer to guarantee a seat, no practice in Aug, in the Galeri Creative Enterprise Centre at Victoria Dock, tel. 01286/677-404, www.cormeibioncaernarfon.org/eng); **Ruthin** (mixed choir Thu at 20:00 except Aug at Pwllglas Village Hall, three miles south of Ruthin in Pwllglas, mobile tel. 07724/112-984, www.corrhuthun.co.uk); and **Llangollen** (men's choir Fri at 19:30 at Hand Hotel, 21:30 pub singsong afterward, hotel tel. 01978/860-303).

my has been slow to transition from mining, factories, and sheep farming to the service-and-software model of the global world.

In recent decades, the Welsh have consciously tried to preserve their local traditions and language. In 1999, Wales was granted its own parliament, the National Assembly, with powers to distribute the national budget. Though still ruled by the UK government in London, Wales now has a measure of independence and self-rule.

Less urbanized and less wealthy than England, Wales consists of miles of green land where sheep graze (because the soil is too poor for crops). It makes for wonderful hillwalking, but hikers should beware of midges. From late May through September, these tiny biting insects are very interested in dawn, dusk, dampness, and you—bring insect repellent along on any hike.

Because Wales is an affordable weekend destination for many English, the country is popular among avid English drinkers, who pour over the border on Friday nights for cheap beer before stumbling home on Sunday. Expect otherwise-sleepy Welsh border towns to be rowdy on Saturday nights.

I've focused my coverage of Wales on the north, which has the highest concentration of castles, natural beauty, and attractions. A few South Wales sights that are convenient to visit from Bath are covered in the Near Bath chapter.

Try to connect with Welsh culture in your itinerary. Clamber over a castle, eat a leek, count sheep in a field, catch a rugby match, or share a pint of bitter with a baritone. Open your ears to the sound of words as old as the legendary King Arthur. "May the old language survive!"

NORTH WALES

Conwy • Caernarfon • Snowdonia National Park • Blaenau Ffestiniog • Northeast Wales

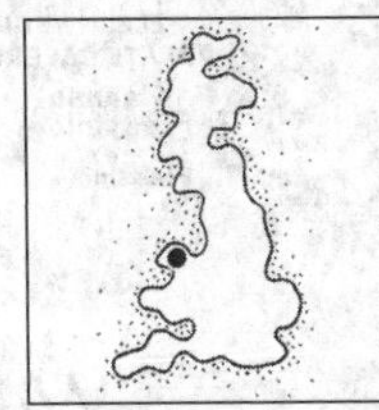

Wales' top historical, cultural, and natural wonders are found in its north. From towering Mount Snowdon to lush forests to desolate moor country, North Wales is a poem written in landscape. For sightseeing thrills and diversity, North Wales is Britain's most interesting slice of the Celtic crescent.

Wales is wonderful, but smart travelers sort through their options carefully. The region's economy is poor, and the Welsh tourism industry keeps busy trying to wring every possible pound out of the tourist trade—be careful not to be waylaid by the many gimmicky sights and bogus "best of" lists.

This chapter covers only my favorite Welsh stopovers. Conwy and Caernarfon offer two of Wales' top castles, which hover in the mist as mysterious reminders of the country's hard-fought history. Each castle adjoins a pleasant town; Conwy, the more charming of the two, makes the region's best home base, with appealing B&Bs and restaurants, a fun-to-explore townscape within mighty walls, and manageable connections to many nearby sights. Close by, Snowdonia National Park plunges you into some of Wales' top scenery—you can ride a train from Llanberis to the top of Mount Snowdon, learn more about the local industry at Llanberis' National Slate Museum, and explore the huggable villages of Beddgelert and Betws-y-Coed. The tongue-twisting industrial town of Blaenau Ffestiniog invites you to tour an actual slate mine. On the way back to England are the appealing towns of Ruthin, with a relaxing market-town vibe, and Llangollen, which straddles a canal. Rounding out your options are the sumptuous Bodnant Garden and the interesting Trefriw Woolen Mills (both south of Conwy), and plenty more imposing castles (I particularly like Beaumaris).

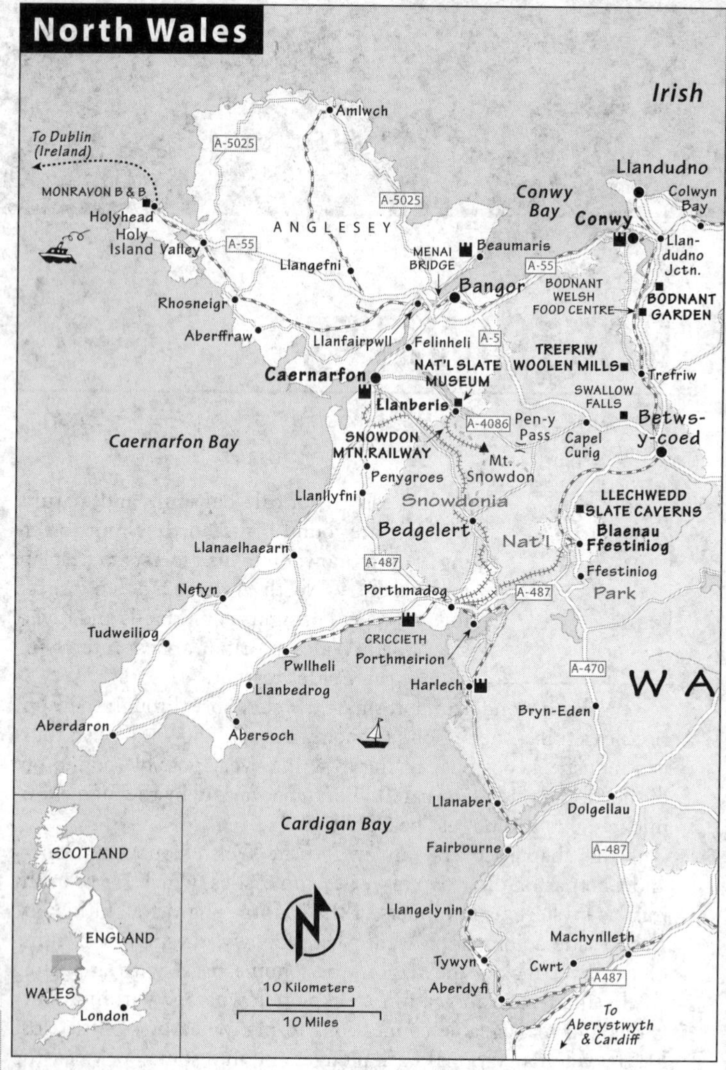

NORTH WALES

PLANNING YOUR TIME

On a three-week Britain trip, give North Wales two nights and a day. It'll give you mighty castles, a giant slate mine, and some of Britain's most beautiful scenery. Many visitors are charmed and decide to stay an extra day...or longer.

Drivers staying in Conwy who have just one day can follow this ambitious plan:

9:30 Leave after breakfast.
10:00 Visit Bodnant Garden.

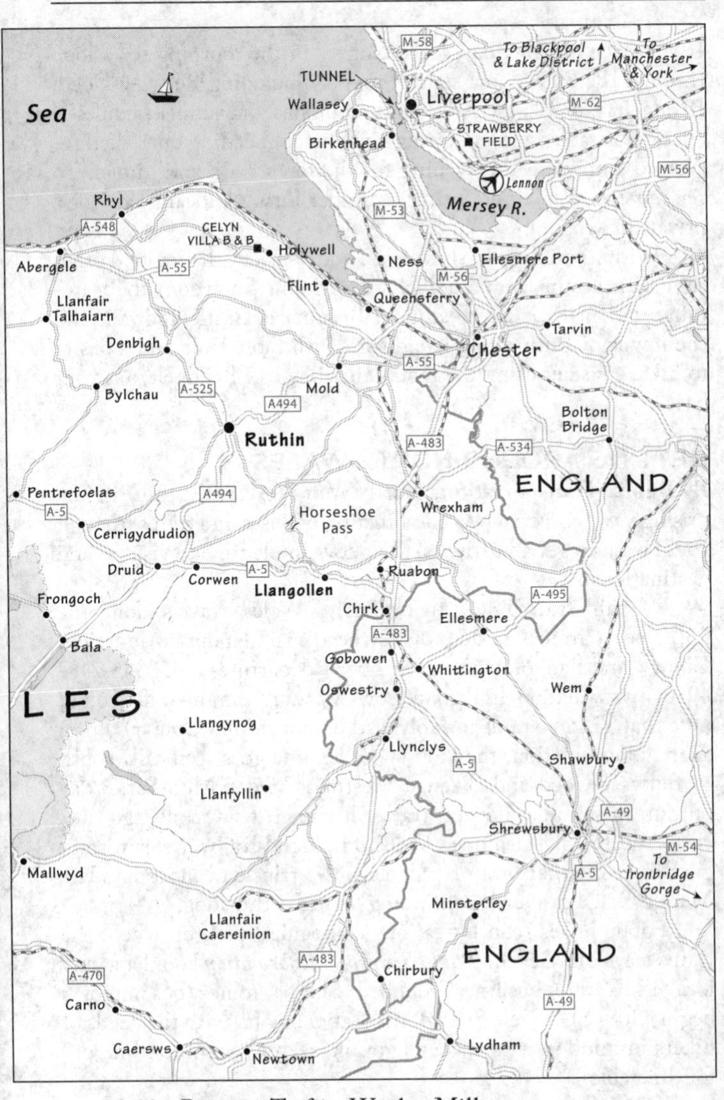

12:00 Pop into Trefriw Woolen Mills.
13:00 Lunch in Llanberis and tour the National Slate Museum, then drive to Caernarfon.
16:00 Catch the 16:00 Caernarfon Castle tour (castle open until 18:00 July-Aug).
18:00 Browse the town of Caernarfon.
19:00 Drive back to Conwy to follow my self-guided town walk and have dinner.

For those relying on **public transportation,** Conwy is a good home base, as it's a hub for many of the area's buses and trains.

If you have just one day, leave Conwy in the morning for a loop through the Snowdonia sights (possibly including Betws-y-Coed, Beddgelert, or Llanberis, depending on bus and train schedules—check timetables and plan your route before heading out), then return to Conwy in the evening for the town walk and dinner. To see more in your limited time, consider hiring a local guide for a private driving tour.

With a second day, slow down and consider the region's other sights: the train from Llanberis up Mount Snowdon, the slate-mine tour in Blaenau Ffestiniog, Beaumaris Castle and jail, and the towns of Ruthin or Llangollen. With more time and a desire to hike, consider using the mountain village of Beddgelert as your base.

GETTING AROUND NORTH WALES

By Public Transportation: North Wales (except Ruthin) is surprisingly well covered by a combination of buses and trains (though you'll want to get an early start to allow ample time to visit several destinations).

A main **train** line, run by Arriva Wales, travels along the north coast from Chester to Holyhead via Llandudno Junction, Conwy, and Bangor, with nearly hourly departures (tel. 0345-748-4950, www.nationalrail.co.uk or www.arrivatrainswales.co.uk; note that Virgin Trains to Holyhead do not stop in Conwy). From Llandudno Junction, the Conwy Valley line goes scenically south to Betws-y-Coed and Blaenau Ffestiniog (5/day Mon-Sat, 3/day on Sun in summer, no Sun trains in winter, www.conwy.gov.uk/cvr). And the old-fashioned Welsh Highland Railway steam train goes from Caernarfon to Beddgelert (2-3 trips/day, most days late March-Oct, 1.5 hours), continuing on to Porthmadog.

Public **buses** (run by various companies) pick up where the trains leave off. Get the *Public Transport Information* booklet at any local TI. Certain bus lines—dubbed "Sherpa" routes (bus numbers begin with #S)—circle Snowdonia National Park with the needs of hikers in mind (www.gwynedd.gov.uk, search "Snowdon Sherpa" for timetables).

Schedules get sparse late in the afternoon and on Sundays; plan ahead and confirm times carefully at local TIs and bus and train stations. For any questions about public transportation, call the Wales Travel Line at tel. 0871-200-2233, or check www.traveline-cymru.info.

Your choices for money-saving public-transportation **passes** are confusing. The Red Rover Ticket—the simplest and probably the best bet for most travelers—covers all buses west of Llandudno, including Sherpa buses (£6.80/day, buy from driver). The North Wales Rover Ticket covers trains and certain buses within a complex zone system (£12-36/day, depending on how many zones you need; buy on bus or train, www.taith.gov.uk).

By Private Tour: Mari Roberts, a Welsh guide based in Ruthin, leads driving tours of the area tailored to your interests. Tours in her car are generally out of Conwy, but she will happily pick you up in Ruthin or Holyhead (£20/hour, 4-hour minimum, £160/day, tel. 01824/702-713, marihr@talktalk.net). **Donna Goodman** leads private day trips of North Wales and walking tours of Conwy, Caernarfon, or Beaumaris, including the castles (from £180/day, book in advance, tel. 01286/677-059, mobile 07946-163-906, www.turnstone-tours.co.uk, info@turnstone-tours.co.uk).

By Car: Driving and parking throughout North Wales is easy and allows you to cover more ground. If you need to rent a car after your arrival, see "Helpful Hints," later.

Conwy

Along with Conwy Castle, this garrison town was built in the 1280s to give Edward I a toehold in Wales. As there were no real cities in 13th-century Wales, this was an English town, planted with settlers for the king's political purposes. What's left today are the best medieval walls in Britain, surrounding a humble town crowned by the bleak and barren hulk of a castle that was awesome in its day (and still is). Conwy's charming High Street leads down to a fishy harbor that permitted Edward to restock his castle safely. Because the highway was tunneled under the town, Conwy has a strolling ambience.

Orientation to Conwy

Conwy is an enjoyably small community of 4,000 people. The walled old town center is compact and manageable. Lancaster Square marks the center, where you'll find the bus "station" (a blue-and-white bus shelter), the unstaffed train kiosk (the little white hut at the end of a sunken parking lot), and the start of the main drag, High Street—and my self-guided walk.

TOURIST INFORMATION

Conwy's TI is located across from the castle's short-stay parking lot on Rosehill Street (Mon-Sat 9:30-17:00, Sun 9:30-16:30, tel. 01492/577-566, www.visitllandudno.org.uk). Because Conwy's train and bus "stations" are unstaffed, ask at the TI about train or bus schedules for your departure. Don't confuse the TI with the uninformative Conwy Visitors Centre, a big gift shop near the station.

ARRIVAL IN CONWY

Whether taking the bus or train, you need to tell the driver or conductor you want to stop at Conwy. Milk-run trains stop here only upon request; major trains don't stop here at all (instead, they stop at nearby Llandudno Junction—see below). Consider getting train times and connections for your onward journey at a bigger station before you come here. In Conwy, train schedules are posted at street level before you descend to the platforms. If you're leaving Conwy by train, you can buy your ticket on board with no penalty. For train info in town, ask at the TI, call tel. 0871-200-2233, or see www.traveline-cymru.info.

For more frequent trains, use **Llandudno Junction,** visible a mile away beyond the bridges (from Conwy, catch the bus, take a £5 taxi, or simply walk a mile). Make sure to ask for trains that stop at Llandudno Junction, not Llandudno proper, which is a seaside resort farther from Conwy.

HELPFUL HINTS

Festivals: The town is eager to emphasize its medieval history, with several events and festivals annually. These are some popular ones: the pirate festival (May, www.conwypirates.co.uk), the bluegrass festival (early July, www.northwalesbluegrass.co.uk), the River Festival (a week in Aug, www.conwyriverfestival.org), and a food festival, which includes a laser light show projected onto the castle (a weekend in Oct, www.conwyfeast.co.uk). Ask at the TI or at your B&B to see what's going on during your visit.

Internet Access: Get online at the **library** at the intersection of High and Castle streets (free guest computers and Wi-Fi, closed Wed and Sun, tel. 01492/596-242). The **TI** also has free Wi-Fi.

Car Rental: A dozen car-rental agencies in the city of Llandudno (a mile north of Llandudno Junction) offer cars and can generally deliver to you in Conwy; the Conwy TI has a list. The closest ones, in Llandudno Junction, are **Avis,** a 10-minute walk from Conwy (113a Conwy Road, tel. 0844-544-6075) and **Enterprise** (tel. 01492/593-380). Both close early on Saturday and all day Sunday.

Bike Rental: Veloconwy rents British-built bikes that come with helmets, locks, and maps covering flat coastal routes or hilly rides into the countryside (£20/half-day, £30/day, ID required for deposit, best to call ahead, daily 9:30-17:00, 39 Conwy Road, Llandudno Junction, mobile 07936-745-045, www.veloconwy.com).

Harbor Cruise: Two tour boats depart nearly hourly from the Conwy harborfront (£6.50 for 30 minutes, £8.50 for 1 hour, pay on boat, runs early Feb-Oct daily 10:30-17:00 or 18:00 depending on tides, longer trips available, mobile 07917-343-058, www.sightseeingcruises.co.uk).

Conwy Walk

This brief self-guided orientation walk introduces you to the essential Conwy in about an hour. As the town walls are open late, you can do this walk at any time—evening is a fine time. If you want a shorter stroll, skip ahead to the harborfront's promenade, which is perfect for a peaceful half-mile shoreline walk (start at the Smallest House in Great Britain—listed later, under "Harborfront").

• *Start at the top of High Street on the main square.*

Lancaster Square: The square's centerpiece is a **column** honoring the town's founder, the Welsh prince Llywelyn the Great. Looking downhill, past the blue-and-white bus stop, find the cute pointed archway built into the medieval wall so the train could get through. Looking uphill, you can see Bangor Gate, built by the British engineer Thomas Telford in 1826 to accommodate traffic from his suspension bridge.

• *Walk uphill past Alfredo Restaurant to the end of the lane.*

Slate Memorials: This wall of memorials recalls the 1937 coronation of King George VI (the father of today's Queen Elizabeth II). Notice the Welsh-language lesson here, given to the town by a citizen who never learned to read and wanted to inspire others to avoid his fate. It lists, in Welsh, the counties (shires, or *sir*), months (a few are vaguely recognizable), days, numbers, and alphabet with its different letters. Much has changed since this memorial was posted. Today more people are speaking Welsh, and all children are taught Welsh in school until age 12.

• *Turn left and walk uphill all the way to the wall, where steps lead to the ramparts. At the top of the stairs, head left and continue climbing to the very top of the town's tallest turret.*

Tallest Tower and Walls: You're standing atop the most complete set of medieval town walls in Britain. In 1283, workers started to build them in conjunction with the castle. Four years later, they

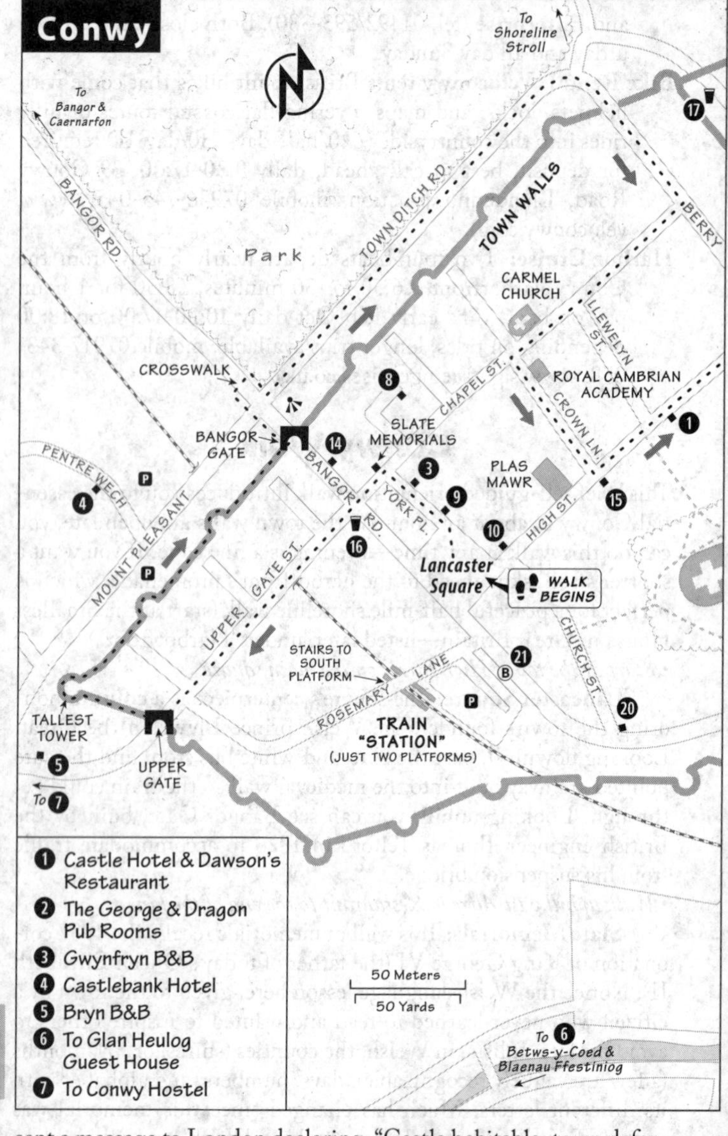

sent a message to London declaring, "Castle habitable, town defensible." Edward then sent in English settlers. Enjoy the view from the top. From here, guards could spot ships approaching by sea.

• *Heading left, walk two turrets downhill along the ramparts.*

The turrets were positioned about every 50 yards, connected by ramparts, and each one had a drawbridge that could be raised to bottle up any breach. Passing the second turret, notice that its wall is cracked. When they tunneled underneath this turret for the

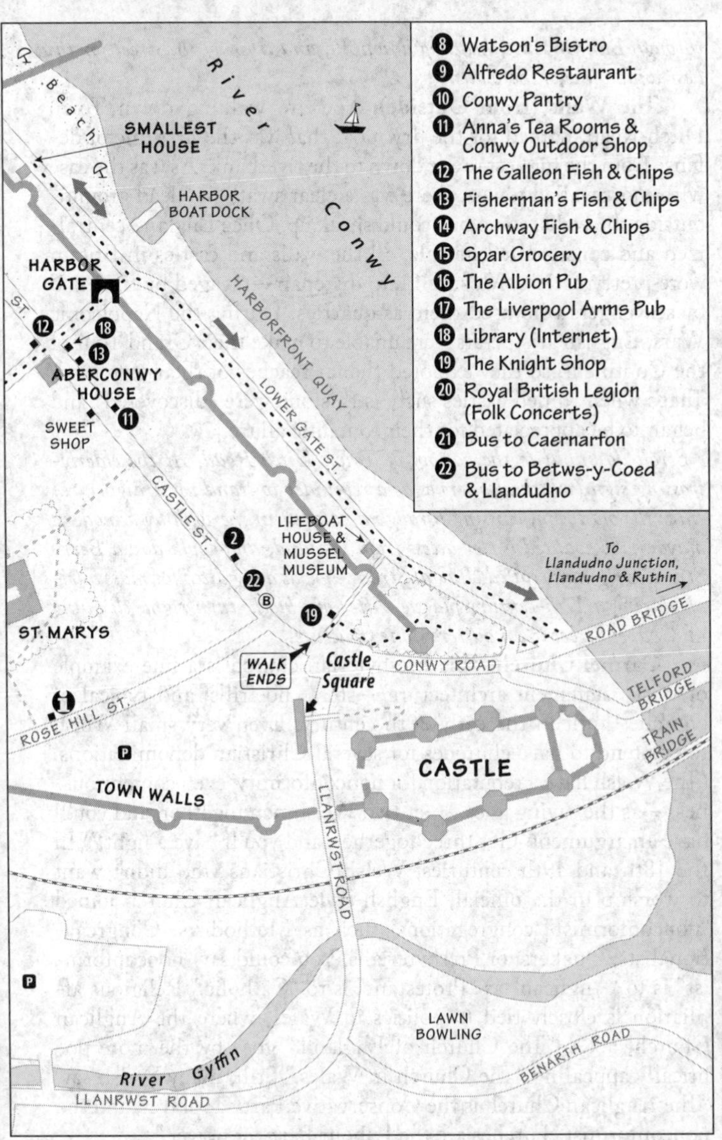

train, the construction accidentally undermined the foundation, effectively taking the same tactic that invading armies would have. The huge crack makes plain why undermining was such a popular technique in medieval warfare. (Unlike the town walls, Conwy Castle was built upon solid rock, so it couldn't be undermined.)

• *At the first opportunity (just after walking above Bangor Gate), take the steps back down to street level. Then leave the old town by passing through Bangor Gate, heading downhill, and crossing the street for the best wide view of the walls.*

The Walls (from Outside): You are walking down Town Ditch Road, named for the dry moat that was the first line of defense from the highest tower down to the riverbank. As was the case with most walled towns, there was a clear swath of "dead ground" outside the walls, so no one could sneak up. Once England centralized and consolidated its rule, all the walls and castles in Britain were pretty useless. Most fell into disrepair—ravaged by time and by scavengers who used them as quarries. During the Napoleonic Wars, English aristocrats were unable to make their Grand Tour of the Continent, so they explored the far reaches of their own land. That's when ruined castles such as this one were "discovered" and began to be appreciated for their romantic allure.

• *Stroll downhill to the bottom of Town Ditch Road. At the elderly-crossing sign (which also serves as a reminder to stand up straight), re-enter the old town, crossing through a hole cut in the wall by a modern mayor who wanted better access from his land, and walk down Berry Street. Originally called "Burial Street," it was a big ditch for mass burials during a 17th-century plague. After one block, turn right, climbing up Chapel Street to an austere stone structure.*

Carmel Church: This Presbyterian church is a fine example of stark "statement architecture"—stern, no-frills, and typical of churches built in the early 20th century. Even very small Welsh towns tend to have churches for several Christian denominations. (The Welsh have a reputation for nonconformity, even contentiousness—as the saying goes, "Get two Welshmen together, and you'll have an argument. Get three together, and you'll have a fight.") In the 18th and 19th centuries, Welsh Christians who didn't want to worship in the official, English-style Anglican Church joined "nonconformist" congregations, such as Methodists, Congregationalists, Quakers, or Presbyterians. You could say "nonconformist" is to "Anglican" as "Protestant" is to "Catholic." Religious affiliation is closely tied to politics in Wales, where the Anglican Church, a.k.a. "The Church of England," goes by the more politically appealing "The Church in Wales." Still, many Welsh say, "The Anglican Church is the Conservative Party at prayer, and the nonconformist churches are the Labour Party at prayer."

• *Just beyond the church (on the left, just past Seaview Terrace), in a modern building, is...*

The Royal Cambrian Academy: This art academy, showing off two floors of contemporary Welsh painting, gives a good glimpse into the region and its people through art (free, most paintings are for sale; Tue-Sat 11:00-17:00, closed Sun-Mon and for one week before each exhibition, shorter hours and closed Tue off-season; on Crown Lane just above Plas Mawr, tel. 01492/593-413, www.rcaconwy.org).

• *Continue on Crown Lane downhill past* ***Plas Mawr.*** *The first Welsh house built within the town walls, it dates from the time of Henry VIII (well worth touring, and described later, under "Sights in Conwy").*

Turn left onto...

High Street: Wander downhill, enjoying this slice-of-Welsh-life scene—tearooms, bakery, butcher, newsstand, and old timers. All the colorful flags you see have no meaning—merchants are flying them simply to pump up the town's medieval feel. **Aberconwy House** marks the bottom of High Street. One of the oldest houses in town, it's a museum (not worth touring). Conwy was once a garrison town filled with half-timbered buildings just like this one. At end of High Street, 20 yards to the right at 4 Castle Street, is the **Penny Farthing Sweet Shop**—filled with old-fashioned candy.

• *Follow High Street through the gate and to the harbor.*

Harborfront: The Harbor Gate, one of three original gates in the town walls, leads to the waterfront. The harbor dates from the 13th century, when it served Edward's castle and town. (The harborfront street is still called King's Quay.) Conwy was once a busy slate port. Slate, barged downstream to here, was loaded onto big three-masted ships and transported to the Continent. Back when much of Europe was roofed with Welsh slate, Conwy was a boomtown. All the mud is new—the modern bridge caused this part of the river to silt up.

The actions of the European Union have had a mixed effect on this waterfront. EU money helped pay for the recently built promenade, but hygiene laws have forced Conwy's fishermen out: Now that fish must be transported in refrigerated vehicles, the fishermen had to set up shop a few miles away (refrigerator trucks can't fit through the stone gate).

Conwy's harbor is now a laid-back area that locals treat like a town square. On summer evenings, the action is on the quay (pronounced "key"). The scene is mellow, multigenerational, and perfectly Welsh. It's a small town, and everyone is here enjoying the local cuisine—"chips," ice cream, and beer—and savoring that great British pastime: torturing little crabs. (If you want to do more than photograph the action, rent gear from the nearby lifeboat house. Mooch some bacon from others for bait, and join in. It's catch-and-release.)

The Liverpool Arms pub was built by a captain who ran a ferry service to Liverpool in the 19th century. Today it remains a salty and characteristic hangout—one of the few thriving pubs in town. In 1900, Conwy had about 40 pubs. Back when this harbor was busy with quarrymen shipping their slate, mussel men carting their catch, and small farmers with their goods, Conwy's pubs were all thriving. Today, times are tough on the pubs, and this one depends on tourism.

• *Facing the harbor in front of The Liverpool Arms, turn left and walk along the promenade.*

It's easy to miss the **Smallest House in Great Britain.** It's red, 72 inches wide, 122 inches high, and worth £1 to pop in and listen to the short audioguide tour. No WC—but it did have a bedpan (April-Oct daily 10:00-16:00, closed Nov-March, mobile 07925-049-786).

• *Turn around and walk along the promenade toward the bridges and castle. On your right, you'll find a processing plant.*

Mussels, historically a big "crop" for Conwy, are processed "in the months with an R" at the **Conwy Mussel Museum.** In the other months, it's open to visitors (free, Easter-Aug generally daily 10:30-16:30, tel. 01492-592-689).

The nearby **lifeboat house** also welcomes visitors. Each coastal town has a house like this one, outfitted with a rescue boat suited to the area—in the shallow waters around Conwy, inflatable boats work best. You'll see *Lifeboats* stickers around town, marking homes of people who donate to the valuable cause of the Royal National Lifeboat Institution (RNLI)—Britain's all-volunteer and totally donation-funded answer to the Coast Guard.

Check out the striking **sculpture** on the quay—a giant clump of mussels carved from dark-gray limestone. The benches are great for a picnic (two recommended fish-and-chips shops are back through the gate) or a visit with the noisy gulls.

• *Walk past the sculpture and a giant red-and-white buoy, and head up the stairs to the big street for a view of the castle and bridges. You can cross the road for a closer look at the...*

Bridges: Three bridges cross the river, side by side. Behind the modern 1958 highway bridge is the historic 1826 Telford Suspension Bridge. This was an engineering marvel in its day, part of a big infrastructure project to better connect Ireland with the rest of the realm (and, as a result, have more control over Ireland). In those days, Dublin was the number-two city in all of Britain. These two major landmarks—the castle and 19th-century bridge—are both symbols of English imperialism. Just beyond that is Robert Stephenson's tube bridge for the train line (built in 1848). These days, 90 percent of traffic passes Conwy underground, unseen and unheard, in a modern tunnel.

• *On the town side of the big road, follow the sidewalk away from the water, past the ivy and through an arch, to a tiny park around a well. Facing that square is...*

The Knight Shop: If you're in the market for a battle-axe or perhaps some chainmail, pop into The Knight Shop. Even if you're not, it's a fun place to browse. The manager, Toby, is evangelical about mead, an ancient drink made from honey. Most travelers just get the cheap stuff at tourist shops, but Toby offers free tastes so you can appreciate quality mead (daily 10:00-17:00, Castle Square, tel. 01492/596-142, www.theknightshop.co.uk).

• *Now, with a belly full of mead, set your bleary eyes on the...*

View of Conwy Castle: Imagine this when it was newly built. Its eight mighty drum towers were brightly whitewashed, a statement of power from the English king to the Welsh—who had no cities and little more than bows and arrows to fight with. The castle is built upon solid rock—making it impossible for invaders to tunnel underneath the walls. The English paid dearly for its construction, through heavy taxes. And today, with the Welsh flag proudly flying from its top, the English pay again just to visit. Notice the remains of the castle entry, which was within the town walls. There was once a steep set of stairs (designed so no horse could approach) up to the drawbridge. The castle is by far the town's top sight (described next).

Sights in Conwy

▲▲Conwy Castle

Dramatically situated on a rock overlooking the sea with eight linebacker towers, this castle has an interesting story to tell. Finished in just four years, it had a water gate that allowed safe entry for English boats in a land of hostile Welsh subjects. At the back, beyond the 91-foot-deep spring-fed well, is a tower containing the chapel (with reconstructed stained-glass windows) and the king's "watching chamber" (for observing chapel services by himself—complete with toilet).

King Edward's Castles

In the 13th century, the Welsh, unified by two great princes named Llywelyn, created a united and independent Wales. The English king Edward I fought hard to end this Welsh sovereignty. In 1282, Llywelyn the Last was killed (and went to "where everyone speaks Welsh"). King Edward spent the next 20 years building or rebuilding 17 great castles to consolidate his English foothold in troublesome North Wales. The greatest of these (such as Conwy Castle) were masterpieces of medieval engineering, with round towers (tough to undermine), castle-within-a-castle defenses (giving defenders a place to retreat and wreak havoc on the advancing enemy...or just wait for reinforcements), and sea access (safe to restock from England).

These castles were English islands in the middle of angry Wales. Most were built with a fortified grid-plan town attached and then filled with English settlers. (With this blatant abuse of Wales, you have to wonder, where was Greenpeace 700 years ago?) Edward I was arguably England's best monarch. By establishing and consolidating his realm (adding Wales to England), he made his kingdom big enough to compete with the other rising European powers.

In one of the towers, you'll also find a scale model of the town as it might have looked around the year 1312.

Cost and Hours: £6.75, £8.50 combo-ticket with Plas Mawr; March-Oct daily 9:30-17:00, July-Aug until 18:00; Nov-Feb Mon-Sat 10:00-16:00, Sun 11:00-16:00; guidebook-£4.50, tel. 01492/592-358, www.cadw.wales.gov.uk.

▲City Walls

Most of the walls, with 22 towers and castle and harbor views, can be walked for free. Start at Upper Gate (the highest point) or Berry Street (the lowest), or you can do the small section at the castle entrance. (My favorite stretch is described on my "Conwy Walk," earlier.) In the evening, most of the walkways stay open, though the section located near the castle closes 30 minutes before the castle does.

▲Plas Mawr

A rare house from 1580, built during the reign of Elizabeth I, Plas Mawr was the first Welsh home to be built within Conwy's walls.

Castle lovers will want to visit each of Edward's five greatest castles (see map on page 622). With a car and two days, this makes one of Europe's best castle tours (all the castles except for Criccieth—listed below—have the same opening hours: March-Oct daily 9:30-17:00, July-Aug until 18:00; Nov-Feb Mon-Sat 10:00-16:00, Sun 11:00-16:00). I'd rate them in this order:

Conwy is attached to the cutest medieval town and has the best public transport (see page 625).

Caernarfon is the most entertaining and best presented (see page 646).

Harlech is the most dramatically situated, on a hilltop (£5.25, tel. 01766/780-552, TI open March-Oct, www.harlech.com).

Beaumaris, surrounded by a moat, is the last, largest, and most romantic (see page 644).

Criccieth (KRICK-ith), built in 1230 by Llywelyn and later renovated by Edward, is also dramatic and remote (£3.50, April-Oct daily 10:00-17:00, Nov-March Fri-Sat 9:30-16:00, Sun 11:00-16:00, closed Mon-Thu, tel. 01766/522-227).

Cadw, the Welsh version of England's National Trust, sells a three-day Explorer Pass that covers many sights in Wales. If you're planning to visit at least three of the above castles, the pass will probably save you money (3-day pass: £17.50 for 1 person, £27 for 2 people, £37 for a family; 7-day pass also available; buy at castle ticket desks). For photos and more information on the castles, as well as information on Welsh historic monuments in general, check www.cadw.wales.gov.uk.

(The Tudor family had Welsh roots—and therefore relations between Wales and England warmed.) Billed as "the oldest house in Wales," it offers a delightful look at 16th-century domestic life. Historically accurate household items bring the rooms to life, as does the refreshing lack of velvet ropes—you're free to wander as you imagine life in this house. Unlike at the austere Welsh castles, here you'll feel that you are visiting a home where the 16th-century owner has just stepped out for a minute.

Cost and Hours: £5.75, £8.50 combo-ticket with Conwy Castle, includes audioguide; daily April-Sept 9:00-17:00, Oct 9:30-16:00, closed Nov-March; last entry 45 minutes before closing, tel. 01492/580-167, www.cadw.wales.gov.uk.

Visiting the House: At the entry, pick up the included audioguide or an info sheet. Docents, who are posted in some rooms, are happy to answer your questions—take advantage of their enthusiasm.

Guests stepping into the house in the 16th century were wowed by the heraldry over the fireplace. This symbol, now repainted in its original bright colors, proclaimed the family's rich lineage and princely stock. The kitchen came with all the circa-1600 conveniences: hay on the floor to add a little warmth and soak up spills; a hanging bread cage to keep food safe from wandering critters; and a good supply of fresh meat in the pantry (take a whiff). Inside the parlor, an interactive display lets you take a closer virtual look at the different parts of the house.

Upstairs, the lady of the house's bedroom doubled as a sitting room—with a finely carved four-poster bed and a foot warmer by the chair. At night, the bedroom's curtains were drawn to keep in warmth. In the great chamber next door, hearty evening feasting was followed by boisterous gaming, dancing, and music. And fixed above all of this extravagant entertainment was...more heraldry, pronouncing those important—if unproven—family connections and leaving a powerful impact on impressed guests. On the same floor is a well-done exhibit on health and hygiene in medieval Britain—you'll be grateful you were born a few centuries later.

St. Mary's Parish Church

Sitting lonely in the town center, Conwy's church was the centerpiece of a Cistercian abbey that stood here a century before the town or castle. The Cistercians were French monks who built their abbeys in places "far from the haunts of man." Popular here because they were French—that is, not English—the Cistercians taught locals farming and mussel-gathering techniques. Edward moved the monks 12 miles upstream but kept the church for his town. Find the tombstone of a survivor of the 1805 Battle of Trafalgar who died in 1860 (two feet left of the north transept). On the other side of the church, a tomb containing seven brothers and sisters is marked "We Are Seven." It inspired William Wordsworth to write his poem of the same name. The slate tombstones look new even though many are hundreds of years old; slate weathers better than marble.

Cost and Hours: Free, church generally open May-Sept Mon-Fri 10:00-12:00 & 14:00-16:00, closed Sat-Sun though you can try visiting before or after the Sunday services at 11:00, tel. 01492/593-402, www.stmarysconwy.org.uk.

NEAR CONWY

Llandudno

This genteel Victorian beach resort, a few miles away, is bigger and better known than Conwy. It was built after the advent of railroads, which made the Welsh seacoast easily accessible to the English industrial heartland. In the 1800s, the notion that bathing in seawater was good for your health was trendy, and the bracing sea air was just what the doctor ordered. These days, Llandudno remains popular with the English, but you won't see many other foreigners strolling its long pier and line of old-time hotels.

Hill Climb

For lovely views across the bay to Llandudno, take a pleasant walk (40 minutes one-way) along the footpath up Conwy Mount (follow Sychnant Pass Road past the Bryn B&B, look for fields on the right and a sign with a stick figure of a walker).

Nightlife in Conwy

No one goes to Conwy for wild nightlife. But you will find some typically Welsh diversions here.

In Town: The **Conwy Folk Music Club** plays at the Royal British Legion Club off Church Street Mondays at 20:30 (free, doors open at 20:00, www.conwyfolkclub.org.uk).

To sample local brews, including some made in Conwy, head to the **Albion.** Managed by a coalition of four local breweries, the Albion has real ales and a fun communal pub atmosphere (Sun-Thu 12:00-23:00, Fri-Sat 12:00-24:00, Upper Gate Street, tel. 01492/582-484, www.conwybrewery.co.uk).

Near Conwy: For an authentic Welsh experience, catch a performance of the **local choir.** The Maelgwn men's choir from nearby Llandudno Junction rehearses weekly, and visitors are welcome to watch (free, Mon 19:30-21:00 except Aug, at Maelgwn School, Broad Street, Llandudno Junction, tel. 01248/681-159, www.cormaelgwn.cymru).

Several churches in Llandudno hold regular **choir concerts** each summer. The concerts at St. John's Church feature a rotation of visiting choirs (£6, May-Oct Tue and Thu at 20:00, between the two Marks & Spencer stores at 53 Mostyn Street, tel. 01492/860-439, www.stjohnsllandudno.org). The Llanddulas Choir performs weekly concerts at Gloddaeth Church (£5, April-Sept most Tue at 20:00, corner of Chapel Street and Gloddaeth Street, www.llanddulaschoir.co.uk).

Llandudno also has the **beach fun** you'd expect at a Coney-Island-type coastal resort.

Sleeping in Conwy

Conwy's hotels are overpriced, but its B&Bs include some good-value gems. Nearly all have free parking (ask when booking), and most are happy to accommodate dietary needs in their breakfast offers (the local butcher, who supplies many of these B&Bs, even makes gluten-free sausages). There's no launderette in town.

Sleep Code

Abbreviations **(£1=about $1.60, country code: 44)**
S=Single, **D**=Double/Twin, **T**=Triple, **Q**=Quad, **b**=bathroom
Price Rankings
$$$ Higher Priced—Most rooms £85 or more
$$ Moderately Priced—Most rooms £55-85
$ Lower Priced—Most rooms £55 or less
Unless otherwise noted, credit cards are accepted, breakfast is included, and free Wi-Fi and/or a guest computer is generally available. Prices change; verify current rates online or by email. For the best prices, always book directly with the hotel.

INSIDE CONWY'S WALLED OLD TOWN

$$$ Castle Hotel, along the main drag, rents 28 elegant rooms where Old World antique furnishings mingle with modern amenities. Peter and Bobbi Lavin, along with sons Joe and Gareth, are eager to make your stay comfortable (Sb-£85-95, Db-£140-180, rates vary depending on room size and day of the week, prices lower in off-season—check website, 10 percent discount if you reserve direct and show this book at check-in, High Street, tel. 01492/582-800, www.castlewales.co.uk, mail@castlewales.co.uk). The hotel has a recommended restaurant and a bar.

$$$ The George and Dragon is a historic pub with seven remodeled rooms in the center. It's right along the town wall, within spitting distance of the castle, but is overpriced and can be noisy thanks to the pub action below—ask for a seaside room. Consider this if everything else in town is booked up (Db-£120, may be cheaper off-season, 21 Castle Street, tel. 01492/330-630, www.georgeanddragonconwy.com).

$$ Gwynfryn B&B rents five bright, airy rooms, each with eclectic decor, a DVD player, and access to a DVD library. The location is dead center in Conwy. It has a plush lounge, and out back there's a small patio for pleasant breakfasts in good weather (D with private bath across the hall-£73-78, standard Db-£75-83, king-size Db-£85-95, price depends on season, £10 extra for 1-night stays, no children under 15, fridges in rooms, self-catering cottage for 4 also available, 4 York Place, on the lane off Lancaster Square, tel. 01492/576-733, mobile 07947-272-821, www.bedandbreakfastconwy.co.uk, info@gwynfrynbandb.co.uk, energetic Monica and Colin). This B&B recently acquired an adjacent former chapel; additional accommodations may be open by the time you visit.

JUST OUTSIDE THE WALL

These options are just a few paces from Conwy's old town wall.

$$$ Castlebank Hotel is a cozy hotel with nine immaculate rooms—some quite spacious—a small bar, and an inviting lounge with a wood-burning fireplace that makes the Welsh winter warmer. Owners Jo and Henrique have done a heroic job of rehabilitating a formerly dumpy hotel into a dolled-up and comfortable home-away-from-home—and Jo cooks up a smashing Welsh breakfast (S with private bath down the hall-£40, Sb-£55-85, Db-£75-95, Tb-£95, price depends on season, 10 percent discount for 2 or more nights if you book directly with the hotel and mention this book when reserving—offer not valid on Bank Holiday and festival weekends, check website for deals, family rooms, DVD library, easy parking, closed first 3 weeks in Jan, just outside town wall at Mount Pleasant, tel. 01492/593-888, www.castlebankhotel.co.uk, bookings@castlebankhotel.co.uk).

$$ Bryn B&B offers four large, clutter-free rooms (and one small one) with castle or mountain views in a big 19th-century house with the city wall literally in the backyard. Owner Alison Archard runs the place with style and energy, providing all the thoughtful touches—a library of regional guides and maps, a glorious garden, granny's Welsh cakes for breakfast, and a very warm welcome (small Sb-£50, Sb-£60-65, Db-£80-85, Tb-£100-105, ground-floor room available, private parking in back, B&B located on the right just outside upper gate of wall on Sychnant Pass Road, tel. 01492/592-449, www.bryn.org.uk, stay@bryn.org.uk).

BEYOND THE OLD TOWN

$$ Glan Heulog Guest House offers six fresh, bright rooms and a pleasant, enclosed sun porch (Sb-£40-45, D-£60-65, standard Db-£63-70, superior Db-£70-80, Tb-£90-95, family suite possible, will pick up from train station, a 10-minute walk from town on Llanrwst Road on the way to Betws-y-Coed, tel. 01492/593-845, www.conwy-bedandbreakfast.co.uk, glanheulog@no1guesthouse.freeserve.co.uk, Richard and Jenny Nash).

$ Conwy Hostel, welcoming travelers of any age, has super views from all 24 of its rooms and a spacious garden. Rooms are equipped with bunk beds, sleep two to four people, and have a full bathroom. The airy dining hall and glorious rooftop lounge and deck make you feel like you're in the majestic midst of Wales (beds in 4-bed rooms-£16-24/person, Db-£35-38, Qb family room-£55-58, price depends on season, members pay £3 less, breakfast-£5.25, laundry, lockers, sack lunches, dinners, bar, elevator, parking, no lock-out times but office closed 10:30-14:00, check-in at 15:00, Sychnant Pass Road in Larkhill, tel. 01492/593-571, www.yha.org.uk, conwy@yha.org.uk). It's a 10-minute uphill walk from the upper gate of Conwy's wall.

Eating in Conwy

All of these places are inside Conwy's walled old town. For dinner, consider strolling down High Street, comparing the cute teahouses and workaday eateries. Most pubs serve food, but none in town is currently worth recommending for a meal.

Watson's Bistro, tucked away on Chapel Street, serves freshly prepared modern and traditional Welsh cuisine in a warm wood-floor-and-exposed-beam setting. Dishes on the inventive menu are made from locally sourced ingredients and well worth the splurge (£9-13 lunches, £17-22 dinners; Tue 17:30-20:00, Wed-Sun 12:00-14:00 & 17:30-20:00, later on Thu-Sat, closed Mon; reservations smart, tel. 01492/596-326, www.watsonsbistroconwy.co.uk).

Dawson's Restaurant, in the recommended Castle Hotel, is a hit with locals. The hotel bar has the same menu with a cozier and less formal ambience. They specialize in fish and seafood, and there are vegetarian and gluten-free options (£6-10 starters, £19-21 main courses, food served daily in the bar 12:00-21:30, restaurant open for lunch Sat-Sun 12:00-15:30 and daily for dinner 18:30-21:30, reservations smart for both bar and restaurant—especially on weekends, High Street, tel. 01492/582-800, www.castlewales.co.uk/dining.html).

Alfredo Restaurant, a thriving and family-friendly place right on Lancaster Square, serves solid, reasonably priced Italian food (£8-10 pizzas and pastas, £15-20 main courses, daily 18:00-22:00, reservations recommended on weekends, York Place, tel. 01492/592-381, Christine).

Conwy Pantry dishes up cheap, hearty daily specials, salads, and homemade sweets in a cheery setting (£4-7 lunches, daily 9:00-17:00, until 16:30 in winter, 26 High Street, tel. 01492/596-445).

Anna's Tea Rooms, a frilly, doily, very feminine-feeling eatery located upstairs in the masculine-feeling Conwy Outdoor Shop, is popular with locals (£5-8 lunches, daily 10:00-17:00, 9 Castle Street, tel. 01492/580-908).

Fish-and-Chips: At the bottom of High Street, on the intersecting Castle Street, are two chippies—**The Galleon** (daily 12:00-19:00 in summer, until 15:00 on off-season weekdays, closed Nov-mid-March, mobile 07899-901-637) and **Fisherman's** (May-Nov daily 11:30-20:00, closes earlier in off-season, tel. 01492/593-792). **Archway Fish & Chips,** at the top of town just inside Bangor Gate, is open later and has both a restaurant and a to-go operation (takeout open daily 11:30-22:00, restaurant open daily until 20:00, 10 Bangor Road, tel. 01492/592-458). Consider taking your fish-and-chips down to the harbor and sharing it with the noisy seagulls.

Picnics: The **Spar** grocery is conveniently located and well-stocked (daily 7:00-22:00, middle of High Street). Several other shops on High Street—including the bakery and the butcher nearby—sell meat pies and other microwaveables that can quickly flesh out a sparse picnic.

Conwy Connections

If you want to leave Conwy by train, be sure the schedule indicates the train can stop there, and then wave as it approaches; for more frequent trains, go to Llandudno Junction (see "Arrival in Conwy," earlier). There is no ticket machine on the Conwy platform; buy your ticket from the conductor. For train info, call 0871-200-2233, or see www.traveline-cymru.info. If hopping around by bus, simply buy the £6.80 Red Rover Ticket from the driver, and you're covered for the entire day on buses running west of Llandudno. Remember, all connections are less frequent on Sundays.

From Conwy by Bus to: Llandudno Junction (4/hour, 5 minutes), **Caernarfon** (2-4/hour, some may require transfer, 1.5 hours), **Betws-y-Coed** (hourly, 45 minutes, fewer on Sun), **Blaenau Ffestiniog** (8/day, none on Sun, 1 hour, transfer in Llandudno Junction to bus #X1, also stops in Betws-y-Coed; train is better—see below), **Beddgelert** (6/day Mon-Sat, none on Sun, 2 hours total, transfer in Caernarfon), **Llangollen** (2/day, 2 hours, take bus to Llandudno Junction, then transfer to bus #X6 to Llangollen).

From Conwy by Train to: Llandudno Junction (nearly hourly, 5 minutes), **Chester** (nearly hourly, 1 hour), **Holyhead** (nearly hourly, 1 hour), **Llangollen** (5/day, 2 hours; take train to Ruabon, then change to bus), **London's Euston Station** (nearly hourly, 3.5 hours, transfer in Chester).

From Llandudno Junction by Train to the Conwy Valley: Take the train to Llandudno Junction, where you'll board the scenic little Conwy Valley line, which runs up the pretty Conwy Valley to **Betws-y-Coed** and **Blaenau Ffestiniog** (5/day Mon-Sat, 3/day on Sun in summer, no Sun trains in winter, 30 minutes to Betws-y-Coed, 1 hour to Blaenau Ffestiniog, www.conwy.gov.uk/cvr). If your train from Conwy to Llandudno Junction is late and you miss the Conwy Valley connection, tell a station employee at Llandudno Junction, who can arrange a taxi for you. Your taxi is free, as long as the missed connection is the Conwy train's fault *and* the next train doesn't leave for more than an hour (common on the infrequent Conwy Valley line).

From Llandudno Junction by Train to: Chester (2-3/hour, 1 hour), **Birmingham** (1-2/hour, 2.5-3 hours, 1-2 transfers), **London**'s Euston Station (4/day direct, 3 hours, many more with changes in Chester and/or Crewe).

Near Conwy

SOUTH OF CONWY

These two attractions are south of Conwy, on the route to Betws-y-Coed and Snowdonia National Park. Note that Bodnant Garden is on the east side of the River Conwy, on the A-470, and Trefriw is on the west side, along the B-5106. To see them both, you'll drive about 20 minutes and cross the river at Tal-y-Cafn.

▲Bodnant Garden

This sumptuous 80-acre display of floral color six miles south of Conwy is one of Britain's best gardens—it's worth ▲▲▲ for gardeners and nature lovers. Originally the private garden of the stately Bodnant Hall, this lush landscape was donated by the Aberconway family (who still live in the house) to the National Trust in 1949. The map you receive upon entering suggests a handy walking route. The highlight for many is the famous Laburnum Arch—a 180-foot-long canopy made of bright-yellow laburnum, hanging like stalactites over the heads of garden lovers who stroll beneath it (just inside the entry, blooms late May through early June). The garden is also famous for its magnolias, rhododendrons, camellias, and roses—and for the way that the buildings of the estate complement the carefully planned landscaping. The wild English-style plots seem to spar playfully with the more formal rose gardens along the terrace. Victorian explorers donated rare species to the owners—try to find an American redwood tree and Himalayan poppies. Consider your visit an extravagantly beautiful nature hike, and walk all the way to the old mill and waterfall.

Cost and Hours: £10.50, March-Oct daily 10:00-17:00, possibly open later on some summer days, tickets are cheaper and hours are shorter off-season, café, WCs in parking lot and inside garden, best in spring, check online to see what's blooming and a schedule of guided walks, tel. 01492/650-460, www.nationaltrust.org.uk/bodnant-garden.

Getting There: To reach the garden by public transportation from Conwy, first take a bus or train to Llandudno Junction, then catch bus #25 (6/day Mon-Sat, 30 minutes, direction: Eglwysbach; on Sun take bus #X19, 4/day, 20 minutes, direction: Betws-y-Coed or Dolwyddelan).

Nearby: About 1.5 miles south of Bodnant Garden off the A-470, the **Bodnant Welsh Food Centre** is a fun stop for foodies, with a farm shop selling mostly food produced in Wales, a restaurant, a tearoom, and a cooking school (Mon-Sat 9:30-17:00, shorter hours on Sun, tel. 01492/651-100, www.bodnant-welshfood.co.uk). It's also the home of the National Beekeeping Centre, which features an interesting exhibit on bees and honey production and offers paid tours of its beehives in nice weather (closed Mon, tel. 01492/651-106, www.beeswales.co.uk).

Trefriw Woolen Mills

At Trefriw (TREV-roo), five miles north of Betws-y-Coed, you can peek into a working woolen mill. It's surprisingly interesting and rated ▲ if the machines are running (weekdays Easter-Oct).

Cost and Hours: Free, variable hours for different parts of mill (see below), tel. 01492/640-462, www.t-w-m.co.uk.

Getting There: Bus #19 goes from Conwy and Llandudno Junction right to Trefriw (hourly Mon-Sat, fewer on Sun, 30 minutes).

Visiting the Mill: This mill uses British wool (and some from New Zealand) and turns it into bedspreads, rugs, and tweeds. You can peruse the finished products in the **shop** (April-Oct daily 9:30-17:30, Nov-March Mon-Sat 10:00-17:00, closed Sun). The whole complex creates its own hydroelectric power; the **"turbine house"** in the cellar lets you glance at the enormous fiercely-spinning turbines dating from the 1930s and 1940s, powered by streams that flow down the hillside above the mill (same hours as shop). Watch the **weaving looms,** with bobbin-loaded shuttles flying to and fro, to see a bedspread being created (mid-Feb-mid-Dec Mon-Fri 10:00-13:00 & 14:00-17:00).

The highlight is the **mill museum,** which follows the 11 stages of wool transformation: blending, carding, spinning, doubling, hanking, spanking, warping, weaving, and so on. Follow a matted glob of fleece on its journey to becoming a fashionable cap or scarf. It's impressive that this Rube Goldberg-type process was so ingeniously designed and coordinated in an age before computers (mostly the 1950s and 1960s)—each machine seems to "know" how to do its rattling, clattering duty with amazing precision (some but not all machines are likely running at any one time; Easter-

Oct Mon-Fri 10:00-13:00 & 14:00-17:00, closed Sat-Sun, closed Nov-Easter because they don't heat it in winter). In the summer, the **rug-making and hand-spinning house** (next to the WC) has a charming spinster and yarn and knitted goods for sale (only open Tue-Thu in summer).

Nearby: The grade school next door is busy with rambunctious Welsh-speaking kids—fun to listen to at recess.

WEST OF CONWY

Beaumaris

Charming little Beaumaris is on the Isle of Anglesey ("Ynys Môn" in Welsh), about a 40-minute drive west from Conwy, and a short detour from the route to Caernarfon. On your way, you'll drive through the town of Llanfairpwllgwyngyllgogerychwyrndrobwllllantysiliogogogoch—(no kidding) the second-longest place name in the world. On the maps and road signs it's called by its nickname "Llanfairpwll." It's where the modern A-55 bridge crosses the strait—you can have your passport stamped with the official name if you stop at the James Pringle Weavers shop at the old train station.

Otherwise, head straight to the town of Beaumaris. It originated, like other castle towns, as an English "green zone" in the 13th century, surrounded by Welsh guerrillas. Today, it feels workaday Welsh, with a fine harborfront, lots of colorful shops and eateries, a fascinating Victorian prison (now a museum), and the remains of an idyllic castle. Around the castle are putt-putt-type amusements for the family and a moat.

Beaumaris has no official tourist information center, but you may find volunteers staffing a small **TI** office in the town hall on Castle Street—it's next to the Buckeley Hotel. The office is full of maps and brochures even if no one's there to answer questions. If the office is closed, the reception desk at the hotel can help you (tel. 01248/713-177, www.visitanglesey.co.uk).

Getting There: If driving, simply follow signs toward *Holyhead,* and immediately after crossing the big bridge onto the island, take the small coastal A-545 highway for 10 minutes into Beaumaris.

Beaumaris Gaol

The jail opened in 1829 as a result of new laws designed to give prisoners more humane treatment; it remained in use until 1878. Under this "modern" ethic, inmates had their own cells, women prisoners were kept separate and attended by female guards, and prisoners worked to pay for their keep rather than suffer from jailers bilking their families for favors. This new standard of incarceration is the subject of this fascinating museum, where you'll see the prisoners' quarters, work yard, punishment cells, whipping rack, treadmill, and chapel.

Cost and Hours: £5, includes audioguide, Easter-Sept Sat-Thu 10:30-17:00, closed Fri, weekends only in Oct, closed most days in off-season, last entry one hour before closing; it's on Bunkers Hill—coming down the main street from the castle, go right on Steeple Lane then left on Bunkers Hill; tel. 01248/810-921.

▲Beaumaris Castle

Begun in 1295, Beaumaris was the last link in King Edward's "Iron Chain" of castles to enclose Gwynedd, the rebellious former kingdom of North Wales. The site has no natural geological constraints like those that encumbered the castle designers at Caernarfon and Conwy, so its wall-within-a-wall design is almost perfectly concentric. The result is one of Britain's most beautiful castles. While Beaumaris shows medieval castle engineering at its best—four rings of defense, a moat, and a fortified dock—problems in Scotland changed the king's priorities. Construction stopped in 1330, and the castle was never finished. It looks ruined (and rather squat), but it was never ransacked or destroyed—it's simply unfinished. The site was overgrown until the last century, yet today it's like a park, with pristine lawns and a classic moat. Because it's harder to get here, it's less crowded, making your visit feel more authentic. Look for information boards explaining the architect's vision and an exhibit on the history of the castle.

Cost and Hours: £5.25; March-Oct daily 9:30-17:00, July-Aug until 18:00; Nov-Feb Mon-Sat 10:00-16:00, Sun 11:00-16:00; tel. 01248/810-361, www.beaumaris.com.

Menai Suspension Bridge

The Isle of Anglesey is connected to the mainland by one of the engineering marvels of its day, the Menai Suspension Bridge. Designed by Thomas Telford and finished in 1826, at 580 feet it was the longest bridge of its day. It was built to be 100 feet above sea level at high tide—high enough to let Royal Navy ships sail beneath. With the Act of Union of 1800, London needed to be better connected to Dublin. And, as the economy of the island of Anglesey was mainly cattle farming (cows had to literally swim the Straits of Menai to get to market), there was a local need for this bridge. When it opened, the bridge cut the travel time from London to Holyhead from 36 to 27 hours. Most drivers today take the modern A-55 highway bridge, but the historic bridge still handles local traffic.

Caernarfon

The small, lively little town of Caernarfon (kah-NAR-von) is famous for its striking castle—the place where the Prince of Wales is "invested" (given his title). Like Conwy, it has an Edward I garrison town marching out from the castle; it still follows the original medieval grid plan laid within its well-preserved ramparts.

Caernarfon is mostly a 19th-century town. At that time, the most important thing in town wasn't the castle but the area that sprawls below the castle (now a parking lot). This was once a booming slate port, shipping tidy bundles of slate from North Wales mining towns to roofs all over Europe.

The statue of local boy David Lloyd George looks over the town square. A member of Parliament from 1890 to 1945, he was the most important politician Wales ever sent to London, and ultimately became Britain's prime minister during the last years of World War I. Young Lloyd George began his career as a noisy nonconformist Liberal advocating Welsh rights. He ended up an eloquent spokesperson for the nation of Great Britain, convincing his slate-mining constituents that only as part of the Union would their industry boom.

Caernarfon bustles with shops, cafés, and people. Market-day activities fill its main square on Saturdays year-round; a smaller, sleepier market yawns on Monday from late May to September. The charming town is worth a wander.

Orientation to Caernarfon

The small walled old town of Caernarfon spreads out from its waterfront castle, its outer flanks fringed with modern sprawl (pop. 10,000). The main square, called Castle Square ("Y Maes" in Welsh), is fronted by the castle (with the TI across from its entry on Castle Street) and a post office. Public WCs are off the main square, on the road down to the riverfront and parking lot, where you'll find a bike-rental shop.

Conwy or Caernarfon?

Trying to decide between these two walled towns and their castles?

The town of Conwy is more quaint, with a higgledy-piggledy medieval vibe and a modern workaday heart and soul—both of which feel diluted in busier, although more Welsh-feeling, Caernarfon. Conwy also has more accommodations and good eateries than Caernarfon. All this makes Conwy the better home base, which also means its castle is more convenient to see. Conwy's castle is a bit more ruined and less slickly presented than Caernarfon's—with fewer fancy exhibits—but some think that makes it more evocative. While Caernarfon's castle is the most famous in Wales, I find Conwy's to be more exciting.

TOURIST INFORMATION

The TI, facing the castle entrance, has a wonderful free town map/guide (with a good self-guided town walk) and train and bus schedules. The staff dispenses tips about all the North Wales attractions, sells hiking books and maps, and books rooms here and elsewhere for a £2 fee (April-Oct daily 9:30-16:30; Nov-March Mon-Sat 10:00-15:30, closed Sun; tel. 01286/672-232, www.visitsnowdonia.info).

ARRIVAL IN CAERNARFON

If you arrive by **bus,** walk straight ahead up to the corner at Bridge Street, turn left, and walk two short blocks until you hit the main square and the castle. **Drivers** can park in the lot along the riverfront quay below the castle (£4/day) or follow signs as you enter town to a covered garage. The big lot under the Morrisons Supermarket (near Victoria Dock) has free parking.

HELPFUL HINTS

Internet Access: Get wired at the public **library** (pay terminals, free Wi-Fi, closed Sun, just around the corner from Bridge Street—between the castle and the recommended Celtic Royal Hotel, tel. 01286/679-463, www.gwynedd.gov.uk/library).

Laundry: Pete's Launderette hides at the end of Skinner Street, a narrow lane branching off the main square (same-day full-service-£8/load, Mon-Thu 9:00-18:00, Fri-Sat 9:00-17:30, Sun 11:00-16:00, tel. 01286/678-395, Pete, Monica, and their Newfoundland mix Yogi).

Bike Rental: Beics Menai Cycles rents good bikes on the riverfront, near the start of a handy bike path (£10/half-day, £15/day; includes helmet, lock, and map of suggested routes; daily

9:00-17:00, closed off-season Sun-Mon, 1 Slate Quay—across the parking lot from the lot's payment booth, tel. 01286/676-804, mobile 07770-951-007, www.beicsmenai.co.uk). One of their suggested routes is 12 miles down an old train track—now a bike path—through five villages to Bryncir and back (figure 4 hours for the 24-mile round-trip).

Harbor Cruise: Narrated cruises on the **Queen of the Sea** run daily in summer (£7; runs May-Oct 11:30-17:30 or 18:30—depending on weather, tides, and demand; 40 minutes, castle views, tel. 01286/672-772, mobile 07979-593-483, www.menaicruises.co.uk).

Welsh Choir: If you're spending a Tuesday night here, drop by the weekly practice of the local men's choir (Tue at 19:45 in Galeri Creative Enterprise Centre at Victoria Dock, no practice in Aug, arrive by 19:30 in summer since practices can be crowded, just outside the old town walls, tel. 01286/677-404, www.cormeibioncaernarfon.org/eng; best to call ahead or complete web form if you want to attend).

A Taste of Wales: For a store selling all things Welsh—books, movies, music, and more—check out **Na-Nog** on the main square (Mon-Sat 9:00-17:00, closed Sun, 16 Castle Square, tel. 01286/676-946).

Crabs on the Quay: As is the case in neighboring harbor towns, a popular family activity is capturing, toying with, then releasing little crabs (under the castle, along the harbor).

Sights in Caernarfon

▲▲Caernarfon Castle

Edward I built this impressive castle 700 years ago to establish English rule over North Wales. Rather than being purely defensive, it also had elements of a palace—where Edward and his family could stay on visits to Wales. Modeled after the striped angular walls of ancient Constantinople, the castle, though impressive, was never finished and never really used. From the inner courtyard, you can see the notched walls ready for more walls—which were never built.

The castle's fame derives from its physical grandeur and its association with the Prince of Wales. Edward got the angry Welsh to agree that if he presented them with "a prince, born in Wales, who spoke not a word of English," they would

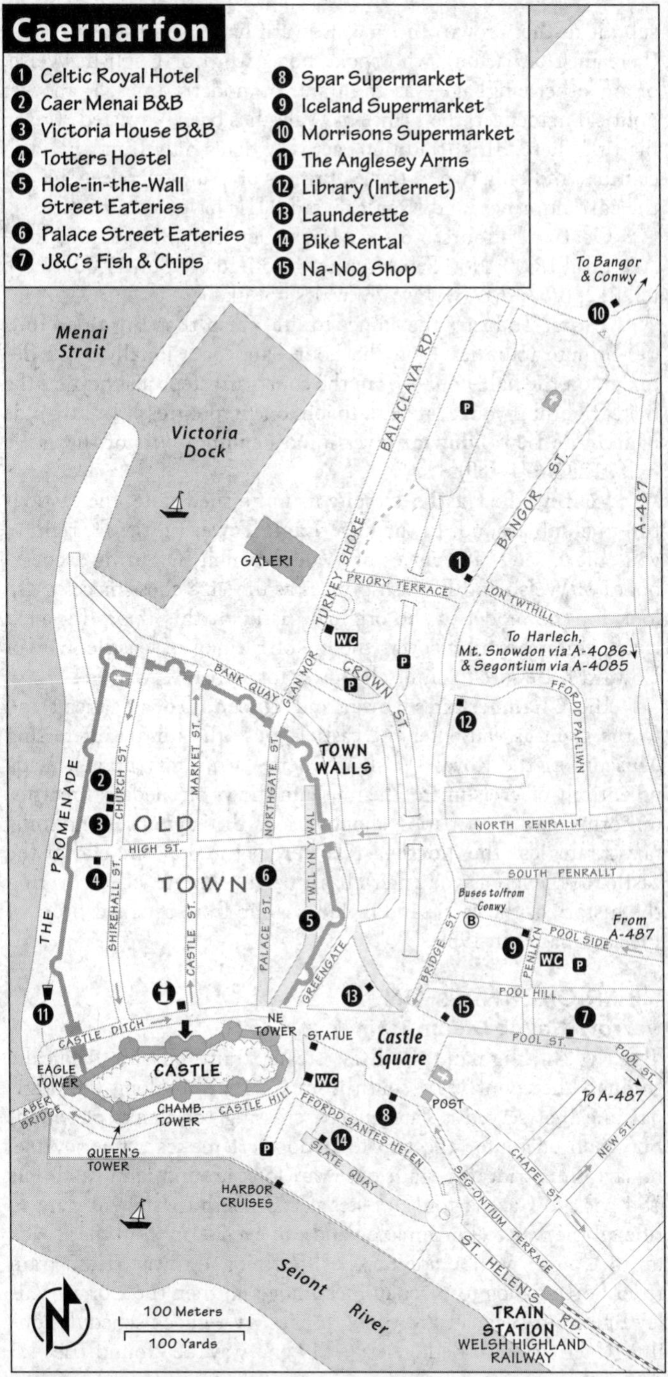

Caernarfon

1. Celtic Royal Hotel
2. Caer Menai B&B
3. Victoria House B&B
4. Totters Hostel
5. Hole-in-the-Wall Street Eateries
6. Palace Street Eateries
7. J&C's Fish & Chips
8. Spar Supermarket
9. Iceland Supermarket
10. Morrisons Supermarket
11. The Anglesey Arms
12. Library (Internet)
13. Launderette
14. Bike Rental
15. Na-Nog Shop

To Bangor & Conwy
Menai Strait
Victoria Dock
Balaclava Rd.
Bangor St.
A-487
Galeri
Turkey Shore
Priory Terrace
Lon Twthill
To Harlech, Mt. Snowdon via A-4086 & Segontium via A-4085
WC
Bank Quay
Glan Mor
Crown St.
Ffordd Pafliwn
Town Walls
Church St.
Market St.
Northgate St.
Twll yn y Wal
Old Town
High St.
North Penrallt
South Penrallt
The Promenade
Shirehall St.
Castle St.
Palace St.
Greengate
Bridge St.
Buses to/from Conwy
Pool Side
Penllyn
From A-487
Pool Hill
Castle Ditch
NE Tower
Statue
Castle Square
Pool St.
Eagle Tower
Castle
To A-487
Aber Bridge
Chamb. Tower
Castle Hill
Ffordd Santes Helen
Post
Queen's Tower
Slate Quay
Chapel St.
New St.
Harbor Cruises
Seg-ontium Terrace
St. Helen's Rd.
Seiont River
100 Meters
100 Yards
Train Station
Welsh Highland Railway

North Wales

submit to the Crown. In time, Edward had a son born in Wales (here in Caernarfon), who spoke not a word of English, Welsh, or any other language—as an infant. In modern times, as another political maneuver, the Prince of Wales has been "invested" (given his title) here. This "tradition" actually dates only from the 20th century, and only two of the 21 Princes of Wales (Prince Charles, the current prince, and King Edward VIII) have taken part.

Cost and Hours: £6.75; March-Oct daily 9:30-17:00, July-Aug until 18:00; Nov-Feb Mon-Sat 10:00-16:00, Sun 11:00-16:00; tel. 01286/677-617, www.cadw.wales.gov.uk.

Tours: To bring the stones to life, catch the £3 **guided tour** (50-minute tours leave on the hour—and occasionally, with demand, on the half-hour—from the courtyard steps just beyond the ticket booth; if you're late, ask to join one in progress). Local guide **Martin de Lewandowicz** gives mind-bending tours of the castle (tel. 01286/674-369).

Visiting the Castle: Despite its unfinished state, the castle is fun to climb around. In the huge **Eagle Tower** (to the far right as you enter), see the "Princes of Wales" exhibit, featuring a chessboard of Welsh and English princes as life-size chess pieces. Also look for the model of the original castle on this floor. The next level's skimpy exhibit covers the life of Eleanor of Castile, wife of Edward I. Be sure to climb the tower for a great view.

The **Chamberlain's Tower** and **Queen's Tower** (ahead and to the right as you enter the castle) house the mildly interesting Museum of the Royal Welsh Fusiliers—a military branch made up entirely of Welshmen. The museum shows off medals, firearms, uniforms, and information about various British battles and military strategies. The **Northeast Tower,** at the opposite end of the castle (to the left as you enter), has an eight-minute video covering the history of the castle and includes a clip from the investiture of Prince Charles in 1969.

NEAR CAERNARFON

Narrow-Gauge Steam Train

The Welsh Highland Railway steam train billows scenically through the countryside south from Caernarfon along the original line that served a slate quarry, crossing the flanks of Mount Snowdon en route. The trip to Beddgelert makes a fine joyride; to save time, ride the train one-way, look around, and catch bus #S4 back to Caernarfon. But steam-train enthusiasts will want to ride all the way to Porthmadog and can even loop from there back up to Conwy with a ride on the Ffestiniog Railway steam train from Porthmadog to Blaenau Ffestiniog and then the Conwy Valley line from Blaenau Ffestiniog to Conwy—check schedules online (Caernarfon to Beddgelert—£19 one-way, £28 round-trip, 1.5

hours; Caernarfon to Porthmadog—£24 one-way, £36 round-trip, 2.5 hours; trains run 2-3 times per day on most days late March-Oct, tel. 01766/516-000, www.festrail.co.uk).

Segontium Roman Fort

Dating from A.D. 77, this ruin is the westernmost Roman fort in Britain. It was manned for more than 300 years to keep the Welsh and the coast quiet. Little is left but foundations (the stone was plundered to help build Edward I's castle at Caernarfon), and any artifacts that are found end up in Cardiff.

Cost and Hours: Free, gate generally unlocked daily 12:30-16:30, 20-minute walk from town, atop a hill on the A-4085, drivers follow signs to Beddgelert, www.cadw.wales.gov.uk.

Horseback Riding

To ride a pony or horse, try **Snowdonia Riding Stables** (£22/hour, £48/half-day mountain ride, cash only, must book in advance, daily 8:00-18:00, 3 miles from Caernarfon, off the road to Beddgelert, bus #S4 from Caernarfon, tel. 01286/479-435, www.snowdoniaridingstables.co.uk, info@snowdoniaridingstables.co.uk).

Sleeping in Caernarfon

My listings favor traditional hotels and B&Bs, but if you're looking for a big hotel with cheap rooms, consider Caernarfon's branches of Premier Inn (www.premierinn.com) and Travelodge (www.travelodge.co.uk).

$$$ Celtic Royal Hotel rents 110 large, comfortable rooms and includes a restaurant, gym, pool, Jacuzzi, and sauna; some top-floor rooms have castle views. Its grand old-fashioned look comes with modern-day conveniences—but it's still overpriced (Sb-£86, Db-£120, extra bed-£20, discounts for 2 or more nights, bar, restaurant, on Bangor Street, tel. 01286/674-477, www.celtic-royal.co.uk, reservations@celtic-royal.co.uk).

$$ Caer Menai B&B ("Fort of the Menai Strait") rents seven classy rooms one block from the harbor (Sb-£35-48, Db-£55-74, Tb-£78-85, ask for seaview room, 15 Church Street, tel. 01286/672-612, www.caermenai.co.uk, info@caermenai.co.uk, Karen and Mark). Church Street is two blocks from the castle and the TI; with your back to the TI, turn right at the nearest corner and walk down Shirehall Street, which becomes Church Street after one block.

$$ Victoria House B&B, next door to the Caer Menai, rents four airy, fresh, large-for-Britain rooms with nice natural-stone bathrooms. Generous breakfasts are served in a pleasant woody room, and the lounge has a fridge stocked with free soft drinks. Stairs from the courtyard lead to the top of the castle wall for a fine view (Db-£75-85, Db suite with terrace-£80-100, 13 Church Street, tel. 01286/678-263, mobile 07748-098-928, www.thevictoriahouse.co.uk, jan@thevictoriahouse.co.uk, friendly Jan Baker). For directions, see previous listing.

$ Totters Hostel is a creative and sparkling clean little hostel well-run by Bob and Henryette (28 beds in 5 dorm rooms, £18.50/bed with sheets, includes continental breakfast, cash only, couples can have their own twin room when available-£44, beautiful and large top-floor Db-£50, open all day, lockers, welcoming cellar game room, inviting living room, DVD library, kitchen, a block from castle and sea at 2 High Street, tel. 01286/672-963, www.totters.co.uk, totters.hostel@googlemail.com). They also own a three-bedroom apartment across the street (generally £100/4 people, £120/6 people—perfect for families, 2-night minimum).

Eating in Caernarfon

The streets near Caernarfon's castle teem with inviting eateries. Rather than recommending a bunch of them, I'll point you in the direction of several good streets with reasonable options.

"Hole-in-the-Wall Street" (between Castle Square and TI) is lined with several charming cafés and bistros, with the expensive-but-trendy **Blas** heading the list (£15-20 main dishes, closed Mon, reservations smart, tel. 01286/677-707, www.blascaernarfon.co.uk). Nearby, on **Palace Street,** you'll find plenty of casual eateries. The pedestrianized but grubby **Pool Street** offers several budget options, including the popular **J&C's** fish-and-chips joint. In nice weather, several places on the **main square** have outside tables from which you can watch the people scene while munching your toasted sandwich.

Picnics: For groceries, you'll find a small **Spar** supermarket on the main square, an **Iceland** supermarket near the bus stop, and a huge **Morrisons** supermarket a five-minute walk from the city center on Bangor Street.

Pub Grub and Fun: **The Anglesey Arms** is a rough, old, characteristic pub serving basic lunches; it has picnic benches on the harborfront. The place is lively in the evening with darts and well-lubricated locals; they host live folk music on some Fridays from about 21:00 (Harbour Front, tel. 01286/672-158).

Caernarfon Connections

Caernarfon is a handy hub for buses into Snowdonia National Park (such as to Llanberis, Beddgelert, and Betws-y-Coed). Bus info: tel. 0871-200-2233, www.gwynedd.gov.uk/bwsgwynedd. And the narrow-gauge steam train provides both sightseeing and transport from Caernarfon to **Beddgelert** (described earlier).

From Caernarfon by Bus to: Conwy (2-4/hour, some may require transfer, 1.5 hours), **Llanberis** (2/hour, 20 minutes, bus #88), **Beddgelert** (7/day Mon-Sat, 2/day on Sun, 30 minutes, bus #S4), **Betws-y-Coed** (hourly, 1-1.5 hours, 1 transfer), **Blaenau Ffestiniog** (hourly, 1.5 hours, change in Porthmadog).

Snowdonia National Park

This is Britain's second-largest national park, and its centerpiece—the tallest mountain in Wales or England—is Mount Snowdon (www.eryri-npa.gov.uk). Each year, half a million people ascend one of seven different paths to the top of the 3,560-foot mountain. Hikes take from five to seven hours; if you're fit and the weather's good, it's an exciting day. Trail info abounds (local TIs sell maps and guidebooks, including the small £3 book *The Ascent of Snowdon,* by E. G. Bowland, which describes the routes). As you explore, notice the slate roofs—the local specialty.

Towns and Sights in Snowdonia National Park

Betws-y-Coed

The resort center of Snowdonia National Park, Betws-y-Coed (BET-oos-uh-coyd), bursts with tour buses and souvenir shops. This picturesque town is cuddled by wooded hills, made cozy by generous trees, and situated along a striking waterfall-rippled stretch of the River Conwy. It verges on feeling overly manicured, with uniform checkerboard-stone houses yawning at each other from across a broad central green.

There's little to do here except wander along the waterfalls (don't miss the old stone bridge—just up the river from the green—with the best waterfall views), have a snack or meal, and go for a walk in the woods.

Trains and buses arrive at the village green; with your back to the station, the TI is to the right of the green. If arriving by car, follow signs for *National Park* and *i* to find the main parking lot by the TI.

Betws-y-Coed's good **National Park Centre/TI** books rooms for a £2 fee and sells the handy £3 *Forest Walks* map, outlining five different hikes you can do from here. They show a free 13-minute video with bird's-eye views of the park (daily Easter-Oct 9:30-17:00, Nov-Easter 9:30-12:30 & 13:30-16:30, tel. 01690/710-426, www.snowdonia-npa.gov.uk). If you have an iPhone, you can download a free audioguide tour of the park from their website (with maps and navigational aids). In summer, you might be able to catch some live entertainment in the TI's courtyard.

Nearby: If you drive west out of town on the A-5 (toward Beddgelert or Llanberis), after two miles you'll see the parking lot for scenic **Swallow Falls,** a pleasant five-minute walk from the road (£1.50 entry). A half-mile past the falls on the right is **The Ugly House** (with a café), built overnight to take advantage of a 15th-century law that let any quickie building avoid fees and taxes.

Betws-y-Coed Connections: Betws-y-Coed is connected by the Conwy Valley train line to **Llandudno Junction** near Conwy (north, 30 minutes) and **Blaenau Ffestiniog** (south, 30 minutes; 5/day Mon-Sat, 3/day Sun in summer, no Sun trains in winter). Buses connect Betws-y-Coed with **Conwy** (hourly, 45 minutes, fewer on Sun), **Llanberis** (7/day, more in summer, 40 minutes), **Beddgelert** (4/day, 1-1.5 hours, 1 transfer), **Blaenau Ffestiniog** (8/day, none on Sun, 20 minutes; usually bus #X1), and **Caernarfon** (hourly, 1-1.5 hours, 1 transfer).

▲▲Beddgelert

This quintessential Snowdon village, 17 miles from Betws-y-Coed, packs a scenic mountain punch without the tourist crowds. Beddgelert (BETH-geh-lert) is a cluster of stone

houses lining a babbling brook in the shadow of Mount Snowdon and her sisters. Cute as a hobbit, Beddgelert will have you looking for The Shire around the next bend. Thanks to the fine variety of hikes from its doorstep and its decent bus service, Beddgelert makes a good stop for those wanting to experience the peace of Snowdonia.

The village doesn't have real "sights," but it's a starting place for some great walks—ask locals for tips, or stop at the **National Park Centre/TI** at the far end of town (daily 9:30-17:00, closed Thu in off-season; pay Internet access available; from the bridge, it's several blocks up, on your right; tel. 01766/890-615, www.snowdonia-npa.gov.uk). For info on the town, see www.beddgelerttourism.com.

Here are several **hikes** to consider: You can follow the lane along the river (3 miles round-trip); trek along the cycle path that goes from the center of Beddgelert, through the forest to the village of Rhyd-Ddu (4.5 miles); walk down the river and around the hill (3 hours, 6 miles, 900-foot gain, via Cwm Bycham); hike along (or around) Llyn Gwynant Lake and four miles back to Beddgelert (ride the bus to the lake); or try the dramatic ridge walks on Moel Hebog (Hawk Hill).

For **mountain-bike rentals,** try Beddgelert Bikes (directly under Welsh Highland Railway station, tel. 01766/890-434, www.beddgelertbikes.co.uk).

Getting There: The Welsh Highland Railway train serves Beddgelert. This narrow-gauge joyride (12 miles and 1.5 hours to or from Caernarfon) is a popular excursion (for details, see page 650). Most people ride the train one-way and return by bus (see bus connections on next page).

Sleeping in Beddgelert: My recommended B&Bs line up in a row at the bridge. They're quite different from each other—each seems to fill its own niche. The larger inn (listed first) is across the river.

$$$ Tanronnen Inn has seven hotelesque rooms above a pub that's been nicely renovated from its interior medieval timbers to its exterior stone walls (Sb-£58, Db-£110, discount for 2 or more nights, tel. 01766/890-347, www.tanronnen.co.uk, guestservice@tanronnen.co.uk, Alan and Gill).

$$ Plas Gwyn Guest House rents six rooms in a cozy, cheery, 19th-century townhouse with a comfy lounge (S-£40, Db-£80, 10 percent discount with this book if you stay 2 or more nights, cash only, packed lunch-£6, tel. 01766/890-215, mobile 07815-549-708, www.plas-gwyn.com, stay@plas-gwyn.com).

$$ Colwyn Guest House has five tight but slick and new-feeling rooms (S with private bath next door-£37.50, Db-£75, 2-night minimum on weekends, 10 percent discount with this book, cash only, tel. 01766/890-276, mobile 07774-002-637, www.beddgelertguesthouse.co.uk, colwynguesthouse@tiscali.co.uk, Colleen).

Sleeping near Beddgelert: Mountaineers appreciate that Sir Edmund Hillary and Sherpa Tenzing Norgay practiced here before the first successful ascent of Mount Everest. They slept at **$$$ Pen-y-Gwryd Hotel,** at the base of the road leading up to the Pen-y-Pass by Mount Snowdon, and today the bar is strewn with fascinating memorabilia from Hillary's 1953 climb. The 16 rooms, with dingy old furnishings and crampon ambience, are a poor value—aside from the impressive history (S-£45, Sb-£70, D-£86, Db-£110-150, old-time-elegant public rooms, some double rooms share museum-piece Victorian tubs and showers, natural pool and sauna for guests, £25 three-course dinners, £30 grand five-course dinners, closed Jan-Feb, tel. 01286/870-211, www.pyg.co.uk, escape@pyg.co.uk).

Eating in Beddgelert: **Caffi Colwyn,** just across the bridge from the B&Bs, serves nicely-done home cookin' at good prices in a cozy one-room bistro (£3-7 lunches, £9-15 dinners, daily Easter-mid-Sept 9:00-20:30, mid-Sept-Easter 10:00-18:00, closed Jan, tel. 01766/890-374).

The **Tanronnen Inn** serves up tasty food in an inviting pub setting, with several cozy, atmospheric rooms (£5-7 sandwiches, £9-14 meals, tel. 01766/890-347).

The **Glaslyn Homemade Ice Cream** shop (up the road from the Tanronnen Inn) offers good quality and selection.

Beddgelert Connections: Beddgelert is connected to **Caernarfon** by the scenic Welsh Highland Railway (2-3/day on most days late March-Oct, 1.5 hours) and handy bus #S4 (7/day Mon-Sat, 2/day Sun, 30 minutes). Bus connections to **Betws-y-Coed** are much less convenient (4/day, 1-1.5 hours, 1 transfer). To reach **Conwy,** it's generally easiest to transfer in Caernarfon (6/day Mon-Sat, none on Sun, 2 hours total). Buses to **Blaenau Ffestiniog** involve one or two transfers (7/day Mon-Sat, fewer on Sun, 1-2.5 hours).

Llanberis

Llanberis (THLAN-beh-ris) is a long, skinny, rugged, and functional town that feels like a frontier village. With 2,000 people and just as many tourists on a sunny day, Llanberis is a popular base for Snowdon activities. Most people prefer to take the train from here to the summit, but Llanberis is also loaded with hikers, as it's the launchpad for the longest (five miles) but least strenuous hiking route to the

Snowdon summit. (Routes from the nearby Pen-y-Pass, between here and Beddgelert, are steeper and even more scenic.)

Drivers approaching Llanberis will find pay parking lots throughout town, including one next to the Electric Mountain/TI and another along the lake (prices vary but generally are £2/2-4 hours and £4/4 hours-full day).

The **TI**, located in the Electric Mountain, sells maps and offers tips for ascending Snowdon (Easter-Sept Fri-Tue 10:00-16:00, closed Wed-Thu and Oct-Easter, tel. 01286/870-765, www.visitsnowdonia.info).

Getting There: Llanberis is easiest to reach from Caernarfon (2/hour, 20 minutes, bus #88) or Betws-y-Coed (7/day, more in summer, 40 minutes); from Conwy, transfer in one of these towns (Caernarfon is generally best). While it's a quick 30-minute drive from Beddgelert to Llanberis, the bus connection is more complicated, requiring a transfer at Caernarfon or Pen-y-Pass, on the high road around Mount Snowdon (9/day, 1-1.5 hours).

▲▲Snowdon Mountain Railway

This is the easiest and most popular ascent of Mount Snowdon. You'll travel five miles from Llanberis to the summit on Britain's only rack-and-pinion railway (from 1896), climbing a total of 3,500 feet. Along with the views, there's a mountaintop visitors' center and a café. You can take a diesel or steam train: The diesel-powered train with a 70-person car takes 2.5 hours, including a 30-minute stop at the top, while the steam train, carrying 34 passengers in a rebuilt Victorian carriage, takes 3 hours with a full hour at the summit.

Don't confuse this with the Welsh Highland Railway (described on page 650) or the Llanberis Lake Railway, a different (and far less appealing) "Thomas the Tank Engine"-type steam train that fascinates kids and runs to the end of Padarn Lake and back.

Cost and Hours: Diesel train—£27 round-trip, £21 early-bird special for 9:00 departure (must book in advance); steam train—£35 round-trip. The first departure is often at 9:00, and the last trip can be as late as 17:30 during peak season (July-Aug). While the schedule flexes with weather and demand, they try to run several trips each day late-March through October and up to 10/day in peak season (steam train 1-2/day). Until May (or in bad weather), the train may not run all the way to the summit. In that case, tickets are partially refunded or sold at a reduced rate.

Buying Tickets: On sunny summer days—especially in July and August—trains fill up fast. Originally designed for Victorian gentry, these days the train is overrun with commoners, and it's smart to reserve ahead. You can buy tickets in advance either online or by calling the booking line after 13:00 (£3.50 reservation fee per party, tel. 0844-493-8120, www.snowdonrailway.co.uk). If you're trying to buy same-day tickets, you can buy them only in person. Show up early—the office opens at 8:30, and on very busy days, tickets can be sold out by midmorning; even if you get one, you may have to wait until afternoon for your scheduled departure time.

Getting There: The train departs from Llanberis Station, along the main road at the south end of Llanberis' town center. The closest parking lots are the pay-and-display lot located behind the station (off Victoria Terrace) or the pricier car park at Royal Victoria Hotel (across the street from the station). You can also park at one of the other pay lots in town (cheaper, about a 10-minute walk).

▲▲National Slate Museum

Across the lake from Llanberis yawns a giant slate quarry. To learn more, venture across to this free museum. The well-presented exhibit, displayed around the 19th-century workshop that was used until 1969 to support the giant slate mine above, explains various aspects of this local industry. In addition to a giant waterwheel and the slate-splitting demo (lasts 30 minutes, starts at :15 past each hour), the museum has a little row of modest quarrymen's houses from different eras, offering a thought-provoking glimpse into their hardy lifestyle. The big 50-foot-high waterwheel turns a shaft that runs throughout the workshop, powering all the various belt-driven machinery. Galleries with historic photos and a 12-minute video re-create what was—until the last generation—a thriving industry employing 3,000 workers. While not as in-depth (literally) as the Llechwedd Slate Caverns in Blaenau Ffestiniog, this is as interesting and more convenient.

Cost and Hours: Free, Easter-Oct daily 10:00-17:00; Nov-Easter Sun-Fri 10:00-16:00, closed Sat; last entry one hour before closing, pay-and-display parking, tel. 02920/573-700, www.museumwales.ac.uk/en/slate.

Electric Mountain

This attraction offers tours into a power plant burrowed into Elidir Mountain, across the lake from town. After a 10-minute video, you'll board a bus and venture underground into Europe's biggest hydroelectric power station for a one-hour guided tour.

Cost and Hours: Visitors center-free, tour-£8.50, daily June-Aug 9:30-17:30, Sept-May 10:00-16:30, tours run Easter-Oct about hourly (every 30 minutes when busy), 3-5 tours/day off-season—call or check online for times, wear warm clothes and sturdy shoes, make advance reservations online, no children under 4, no photos, café, tel. 01286/870-636, www.electricmountain.co.uk.

Blaenau Ffestiniog

Blaenau Ffestiniog (BLEH-nigh FES-tin-yog) is a quintessential Welsh slate-mining town, notable for its slate-mine tour and its old steam train. The town seems to struggle on, oblivious to the tourists who nip in and out. Though it's tucked amidst a pastoral Welsh landscape, Blaenau Ffestiniog is surrounded by a gunmetal-gray wasteland of "tips," huge mountain-like piles of excess slate.

Take a walk. The shops are right out of the 1950s. Long rows of humble "two-up and two-down" houses (four rooms) feel a bit grim. The train station, bus stop, and parking lot all cluster along a one-block stretch in the heart of town. There's no TI.

Getting There: Blaenau Ffestiniog is conveniently connected by the Conwy Valley train to Betws-y-Coed and Conwy (5/day Mon-Sat, 3/day Sun in summer, no Sun trains in winter, 30 minutes to Betws-y-Coed, 1 hour to Conwy via Llandudno Junction) and by bus #X1 (8/day, none on Sun, 20 minutes to Betws-y-Coed, 1 hour to Llandudno Junction near Conwy). By bus, it's possible to connect with Beddgelert (7/day Mon-Sat, fewer on Sun, 1-2.5 hours, 1-2 transfers) or Caernarfon (hourly, 1.5 hours, transfer in Porthmadog).

Sights in Blaenau Ffestiniog

▲▲Llechwedd Slate Caverns

Slate mining played a blockbuster role in Welsh heritage, and this working slate mine on the northern edge of Blaenau Ffestiniog does a fine job of explaining the mining culture of Victorian Wales. The Welsh mined and split most of the slate roofs of Europe. For every ton of usable slate found, 10 tons were mined. You can wander around its re-created mining town or join a guided tour. Dress warmly—I mean it. You'll freeze underground without a sweater. Lines are longer when rain drives in the hikers.

Cost and Hours: Tour-£15.45, free entry to mining town, daily 9:00-17:30; in peak season (July-Aug), mine tours may run as often as every 15 minutes, depends on demand, first tour usually at 9:30, last tour generally at 17:00; cafeteria, pub, tel. 01766/830-306, www.llechwedd-slate-caverns.co.uk.

Getting There: The slate mine is about a mile from the town center. Bus #X1 leaves from the Blaenau Ffestiniog rail station and drops you off near the mine (8/day Mon-Sat, none on Sun, Express Motors). If you don't want to wait for a bus, you can walk 30 minutes to the mine or take a taxi (about £5, reserve in advance, tel. 01766/762-465).

Visiting the Mine: The one-hour tour takes you into the mine with a live guide. You'll descend on a cable railway about 400 feet into the mountain for an audiovisual dramatization, set in the 1860s and centered around a young boy who works in the mine with his dad. The tour requires a half-mile of walking through tunnels and caves with 60-plus stairs and some uneven footing.

The re-created Victorian mining town, with a pub, bank, candy shop, and other stops, is free and open for anyone to explore. A highlight is the interesting slate-splitting demonstration. While the demonstration is generally timed to coincide with the end of the tour, anyone is welcome to watch. Don't miss this—ask when the next one is scheduled.

NEAR BLAENAU FFESTINIOG

▲Ffestiniog Railway

This 13-mile narrow-gauge train line was built in 1836 for small horse-drawn wagons to transport the slate from the Ffestiniog mines to the port of Porthmadog. In the 1860s, horses gave way to steam trains. Today, hikers and tourists enjoy these tiny titans (tel. 01766/516-000, www.festrail.co.uk). This line connects to the narrow-gauge Welsh Highland Railway from Caernarfon via Porthmadog (see page 650). This is a novel steam-train experience, but the full-size Conwy Valley line from Llandudno to Blaenau Ffestiniog is more scenic and works a little better for hikers (see page 641).

Portmeirion

Ten miles southwest of Blaenau Ffestiniog, this "Italian Village" was the life's work of a rich local architect who began building it in 1925. Set idyllically on the coast just beyond the poverty of the slate-mine towns, this flower-filled fantasy is extravagant. Surrounded by lush Welsh greenery and a windswept mudflat at low tide, the village is an artistic glob of palazzo arches,

fountains, gardens, and promenades filled with cafés, tacky shops, a hotel, and local tourists who always wanted to go to Italy. Fans of the cultish British 1960s TV series *The Prisoner*, which was filmed here, will recognize the place.

Cost and Hours: £10, cheaper if you buy online, daily 9:30-19:30, tel. 01766/770-000, www.portmeirion-village.com.

Northeast Wales

If you're driving between North Wales and England, these two towns are worth a stop. Neither is particularly convenient by public transportation (Llangollen is two-plus hours to Conwy, and Ruthin has poor transportation connections to just about everywhere), so skip these unless you have a car.

Ruthin

Ruthin (RITH-in; "Rhuthun" in Welsh) is a low-key market town whose charm is in its ordinary Welshness. The town (pop. 5,000) is situated atop a gentle hill surrounded by undulating meadows. Simple streets branch out from the central roundabout (at the former medieval marketplace, St. Peter's Square) like spokes on a wheel. It's so untouristy that it has no TI. The market square, jail, museum, bus station, and in-town accommodations are all within five blocks of one another. To tweak visitors' interest, the city has installed 10 "spy holes" into walls across the city center; look inside to see 3-D images of historic events or people (www.ruthinarttrail.co.uk). Ruthin is as Welsh as can be, making it a distinctive stopover on your way to northern England. The people are the sights, and admission is free if you start the conversation.

▲Ruthin Gaol

Get a glimpse into crime and punishment in 17th- to early-20th-century Wales in this 100-cell prison. Explore the "dark" and condemned cells, give the dreaded hand-crank a whirl, and learn about the men, women, and children who did time here before the prison closed in 1916. The audioguide—partly narrated by a jovial "prisoner" named Will—is very good, informative, and engaging. You'll find out why prison kitchens came with a cat, why the bathtubs had a severe case of ring-around-the-tub, how they got prisoners

to sit still for their mug shots (and why these photos often included the prisoners' hands), and why the prison was renovated in the "panopticon" style in the late 19th century.

Cost and Hours: £4.50, April-Sept Wed-Sun 10:00-17:00, closed Tue and Oct-March, last entry one hour before closing, audioguide-£0.50, Clwyd Street, tel. 01824/708-281, www.ruthingaol.co.uk.

Nantclwyd y Dre

This Elizabethan-era "oldest timbered townhouse in Wales"—a white-and-brown half-timbered house between the castle and the market square—underwent an award-winning £600,000 renovation (funded partly by the EU) to convert it into a museum. Seven decorated rooms give visitors a peek into the history of the house, which was built in 1435.

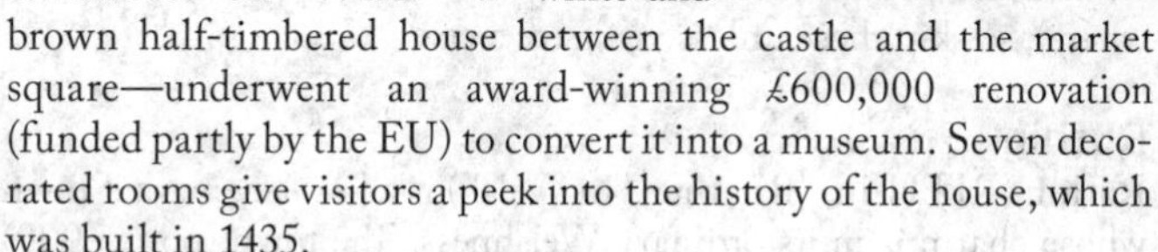

Cost and Hours: £4.50, April-Sept Fri-Sun 10:30-17:00, possibly open Mon-Tue mid-July-Aug, otherwise closed Mon-Thu and Oct-March, last entry 45 minutes before closing, Castle Street, tel. 01824/709-822, www.denbighshire.gov.uk.

Walks

For a scenic and interesting one-hour walk, try the Offa's Dyke Path to Moel Famau (the "Jubilee Tower," a 200-year-old war memorial on a peak overlooking stark moorlands). The trailhead is a 10-minute drive east of Ruthin on the A-494.

▲▲Welsh Choir

The Côr Rhuthun mixed choir usually rehearses weekly at the Pwllglas Village Hall (Thu at 20:00 except Aug, call or email in advance to confirm practice; located three miles south of Ruthin in the village of Pwllglas—follow the A-494 out of town in the direction of Blas; mobile 07724/112-984, www.corrhuthun.co.uk, cor@corrhuthun.co.uk).

Sleeping in Ruthin: **$$$ Manorhaus,** filling a Georgian building, is Ruthin's classiest sleeping option. Its eight rooms are impeccably appointed with artsy-contemporary decor, and the halls serve as gallery space for local artists. Guests enjoy use of the sauna, steam room, library, and mini cinema in the cellar. In fact, you could have a vacation and never leave the place. It's run by Christopher (who played piano for years in London's West End theaters) and Gavin (an architect and former mayor of Ruthin)—together, it seems, they've brought Ruthin a splash of fun and style (Sb-£75-

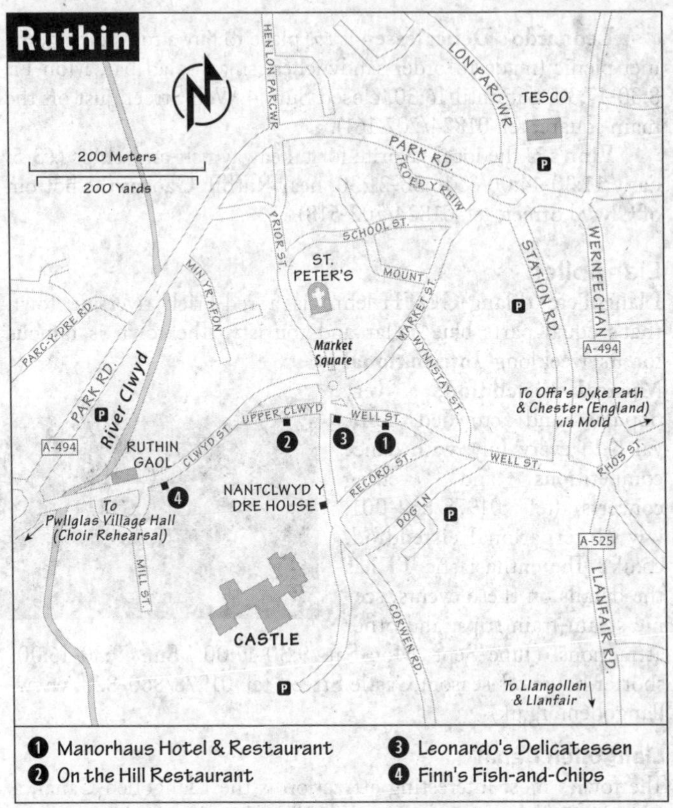

125, standard Db-£80-120, superior Db-£150, pricier Db suite-£180, check website for deals, no children under 9, recommended restaurant, Well Street, tel. 01824/704-830, www.manorhaus.com, post@manorhaus.com). Drivers can find cheaper sleeps by keeping an eye out for rustic hostel-like "bunkhouses" that dot the North Wales countryside.

Eating in Ruthin: **On the Hill** serves hearty £12-18 lunches and £12-22 dinners—mostly made with fresh, local ingredients—to an enthusiastic crowd. The Old World decor complements the good cuisine (lunch served Tue-Sat 12:00-14:00, dinner served Mon-Sat 18:30-21:00, Sun 17:00-21:00, 1 Upper Clwyd Street, tel. 01824/707-736).

Manorhaus is the town splurge in a recommended hotel (described above), with updated Welsh and British dinners served in a mod art-gallery space. Eating here—especially when in the care of Christopher or Gavin—is an evening in itself (£25 for two courses, £30 for three courses, dinner served daily 18:30-21:00, reservations recommended, Well Street, tel. 01824/704-830).

Leonardo's Delicatessen is *the* place to buy a top-notch gourmet picnic (made-to-order sandwiches, small salad bar, Mon-Fri 8:30-17:30, Sat until 16:30, closed Sun, 4 Well Street, just off the main square, tel. 01824/707-161).

Finn's is the local favorite for takeaway fish-and-chips (£3-5, daily 11:30-14:00 & 16:30-21:30, near Ruthin Gaol at the bottom of Clwyd Street, tel. 01824/702-518).

Llangollen

Llangollen (thlang-GOTH-lehn) is a red-brick riverside town that's equal parts blue collar and touristy. The town is famous for its weeklong **International Musical Eisteddfod,** a very popular and crowded festival held every July, with dance competitions and evening concerts (tel. 01978/862-001, www.international-eisteddfod.co.uk). The enthusiastic **TI** has the details on these events, scenic steam-train trips, and other attractions (June-Sept Mon-Sat 9:30-17:00, Sun 9:30-16:00, shorter hours off-season, Castle Street, tel. 01978/860-828, www.llangollen.org.uk).

Llangollen Canal

The town's most interesting attraction is the Llangollen Canal, a narrow, shallow waterway up the hill and across the bridge from the town center. You can stroll along the canal or take a boat ride from Llangollen Wharf.

Options include a 45-minute horse-drawn boat that goes for a spin around the wharf (£6.50, daily Easter-Oct, 2/hour 11:00-16:30 in July-Aug, shorter hours and less frequent rest of the year—call or check online to confirm schedule; tel. 01978/860-702, www.horsedrawnboats.co.uk); a two-hour motorized canal-boat trip that goes across the remarkable Pontcysyllte Aqueduct (£13.50, Easter-Oct daily at 12:15 and 13:45, sometimes also at 10:00 or 11:30, smart to book ahead); or, on weekends, a two-hour horse-drawn boat that floats down to Horseshoe Falls (£12, Easter-Oct Sat-Sun at 11:30, may also run on some weekdays—check with TI).

Plas Newydd

This is the home of two 18th-century upper-class women who ran off together and lived here as a couple for 50 years. Known as the "Ladies of Llangollen," Lady Eleanor Butler and Sarah Ponsonby escaped from their families and settled here in 1778, causing a sensation in Georgian society. The rich and famous beat

a path to their door, including the Duke of Wellington, Josiah Wedgwood, William Wordsworth, Lord Byron, and Sir Walter Scott. While historians say it's not possible to confirm whether they were lesbians, the pair slept in the same bed, cut their hair short, and liked to wear "mannish" riding habits. They were avid collectors of fine woodwork, which they incorporated into both the exterior and interior of their "cottage." Along with these ornate wood carvings, you'll see some of their personal belongings.

Cost and Hours: £6, April-Sept Wed-Mon 10:00-17:00, closed Tue and Oct-March, gardens open all year, 10-minute walk from TI on Hill Street, tel. 01978/862-834, www.denbighshire.gov.uk/visitor.

Valle Crucis Abbey

This lovely 13th-century Cistercian abbey makes for a nice walking destination (£3.50, April-Oct daily 10:00-17:00, closed but free access to grounds Nov-March, tel. 01978/860-326, www.llangollen.com/valle.html). A cross that's even older than the abbey, Eliseg's Pillar, is nearby.

Welsh Choir

The men's choir practices traditional Welsh songs weekly on Friday nights (19:30 at the Hand Hotel on Bridge Street, 21:30 pub sing-along afterward, hotel tel. 01978/860-303).

Sleeping in Llangollen: **$$ Glasgwm B&B** rents four spacious rooms in a Victorian townhouse—it's tidy, updated, and centrally located (Sb-£43, Db-£70-80, price depends on size of room, evening meals available by advance request, packed lunches-£5.50, free parking, Abbey Road, tel. 01978/861-975, www.glasgwm-llangollen.co.uk, glasgwm@llangollen.co.uk, friendly John and Heather).

$$$ Manorhaus is a luxurious boutique option in Llangollen, with six rooms and suites, run by the same owners of the recommended Manorhaus hotel in Ruthin (standard Db-£80-120, superior Db-£150, Db suite-£180, robes and slippers, restaurant, Hill Street, tel. 01978/860-775, www.manorhaus.com, post@manorhaus.com).

Llangollen Connections: To reach **Conwy,** you can take bus #94 to Ruabon and then transfer to a train (5/day, 2 hours total) or take bus #X6 to Llandudno Junction and transfer to a bus for Conwy (2/day, 2 hours).

North Wales Connections

Two major transfer points out of (or into) North Wales are Crewe and Chester. Figure out your complete connection at www.nationalrail.co.uk.

From Crewe by Train to: London's Euston Station (3/hour direct, 2 hours), Bristol, near **Bath** (2/hour, 2.5-3 hours, 1 transfer), **Cardiff** (1/hour direct, 3 hours), **Holyhead** (hourly, 2-2.5 hours, most with 1 transfer), **Blackpool** (hourly, 1.5-2.5 hours, 1 transfer), **Keswick** in the Lake District (hourly, 1.5-2.5 hours to Penrith, some with 1 transfer; then bus to Keswick, 45 minutes), **Birmingham** (4/hour direct, 1-1.5 hours), **Glasgow** (hourly, 3-3.5 hours, some with transfer).

From Chester by Train to: London's Euston Station (1-2/hour, 2-2.5 hours, some with transfer), **Liverpool** (4/hour direct, 45 minutes), points in North Wales via **Llandudno Junction** (2-3/hour, 1 hour).

FERRY CONNECTIONS BETWEEN NORTH WALES AND IRELAND

Two companies make the crossing between Holyhead (in North Wales, beyond Caernarfon) and Dublin. **Stena Line** sails from Holyhead to Dublin (4/day including 2 at night, 3.5 hours, British tel. 0844-770-7070, www.stenaline.co.uk). **Irish Ferries** also sails to Dublin (roughly 4/day—2 slow, 2 fast; slow boat takes 3-4 hours and includes 1 night sailing, fast boat takes 2 hours; reserve online for best fares; Britain tel. 0818-300-400, www.irishferries.com).

Sleeping near Holyhead Dock: On the island of Anglesey, the fine **$$ Monravon B&B** has five rooms a 15-minute uphill walk from the dock (Sb-£35, Db-£55, family deals, includes continental breakfast, cooked breakfast-£4, Porth-Y-Felin Road, tel. 01407/762-944, www.monravon.co.uk, monravon@yahoo.co.uk, John and Joan).

Sleeping En Route to Holyhead, Between Liverpool and Conwy: **$$ Celyn Villa B&B** is a lovely mid-19th-century house on the mainland, with three rooms with views of the Dee estuary (Sb-£50, Db-£70, family room-£85, 10 percent discount if you stay 2 or more nights, 2-night minimum July-Aug, dinner available, off the A-55 between Chester and Conwy in Holywell, Carmel Road, tel. 01352/710-853, www.celynvilla.co.uk, celynvilla@gmail.com, Paulene and Les).

ROUTE TIPS FOR DRIVERS

From North Wales to Liverpool (40 miles): From Ruthin or the A-55, follow signs to the town of *Mold,* then *Queensferry,* then *Manchester M-56,* then *Liverpool M-53,* which tunnels under the River Mersey (£1.70).

SCOTLAND

SCOTLAND

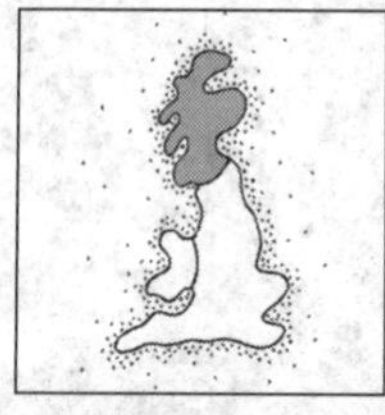

One of the three countries that make up Great Britain, rugged, feisty, colorful Scotland stands apart. Whether it's the laid-back, less-organized nature of the people, the stony architecture, the unmanicured landscape, or simply the haggis, go-its-own-way Scotland is distinctive.

Scotland encompasses about a third of Britain's geographical area (30,400 square miles), but has less than a tenth of its population (about 5.3 million). This sparsely populated chunk of land stretches to Norwegian latitudes. Its Shetland Islands, at about 60°N (similar to Anchorage, Alaska), are the northernmost point in Britain. You may see Scotland referred to as "Caledonia" (its ancient Roman name) or "Alba" (its Gaelic name). Scotland's fortunes were long tied to the sea; all of its leading cities are located along firths (estuaries), where major rivers connect to ocean waters.

The southern part of Scotland, called the Lowlands, is relatively flat and urbanized. The northern area—the Highlands—features a wild, severely undulating terrain, punctuated by lochs (lakes) and fringed by sea lochs (inlets) and islands.

The Highland Boundary Fault that divides Scotland geologically also divides it culturally. Historically, there were two distinct identities: rougher Highlanders in the northern wilderness and the more refined Lowlanders in the southern flatlands and cities. Highlanders represented the stereotypical image of "true Scots," speaking Gaelic, wearing kilts, and playing bagpipes, while Lowlanders spoke languages of Saxon origin and wore trousers. After the Scottish Reformation, the Lowlanders embraced Protestantism, while the Highlanders stuck to Catholicism. Although this Lowlands/Highlands division has faded over time, some Scots still cling to it.

The Lowlands are dominated by a

Scotland

Orkney Islands
Durness
John O'Groats
Thurso
Wick
Lewis
OUTER HEBRIDES
Harris
Ullapool
50 Kilometers
50 Miles
Isle of Skye
Applecross
North Atlantic
Portree
Inverness
CULLODEN
CLAVA CAIRNS
INNER HEBRIDES
Mallaig
Loch Ness
HIGHLANDS
Fort William
Ben Nevis
BALMORAL
Aberdeen
Ballater
Glencoe
Pitlochry
North Sea
Mull
Iona
Oban
Dundee
Stirling
Loch Lomond
St. Andrews
FALKIRK WHEEL
Glasgow
Edinburgh
Arran
LOWLANDS
Irish Sea
Ayr
Jedburgh
NORTHERN IRELAND
Cairnryan
Dumfries
Newcastle
Belfast
ENGLAND

pair of rival cities: Edinburgh (on the east coast's Firth of Forth) and Glasgow (on the west coast's Firth of Clyde) mark the endpoints of Scotland's 75-mile-long "Central Belt," where three-quarters of the country's population resides. Edinburgh, the old royal capital, teems with Scottish history and is the country's best tourist attraction. Glasgow, once a gloomy industrial city, is becoming a hip, laid-back city of art, music, and architecture. In addition to these two cities, the Lowlands' highlights include the medieval university town and golf mecca of St. Andrews, the small city of Stirling (with its castle and many nearby historic sites), and selected countryside stopovers.

The Highlands provide your best look at traditional Scotland. The sights are subtle, but the vivid traditional culture and friendly people are engaging. The Highlands are more rocky and harsh than other parts of the British Isles. Most of the "Munros"—Scotland's 282 peaks over 3,000 feet—are concentrated in the Highlands. It's no wonder that many of the exterior scenes of Hogwarts' grounds in the *Harry Potter* movies were filmed in this moody, spooky landscape (see page 994). Keep an eye out for shaggy Highland cattle (adorable "hairy coos," with their bangs falling in their eyes); bring bug spray in summer to thwart the tiny mosquitoes called midges, which can make life miserable; and plan your trip around trying to attend a Highland games (see sidebar on page 892).

Generally, the Highlands are hungry for the tourist dollar, and everything overtly Scottish is exploited to the kilt; you need to spend some time here to get to know the area's true character. You can get a feel for the Highlands with a quick drive to Oban, through Glencoe, then up the Caledonian Canal to Inverness. With more time, the Isles of Iona, Staffa, and Mull (an easy day trip from Oban) and countless brooding countryside castles will flesh out your Highlands experience.

At these northern latitudes, cold and drizzly weather isn't uncommon—even in midsummer. The blazing sun can quickly be covered over by black clouds and howling wind. Your B&B host will warn you to prepare for "four seasons in one day." Because Scots feel personally responsible for bad weather, they tend to be overly optimistic about forecasts. Take any Scottish promise of "sun by the afternoon" with a grain of salt—and bring your raincoat, just in case.

The major theme of Scottish history is the drive for independence, especially from England. (Scotland's rabble-rousing national motto is *Nemo me impune lacessit*—"No one provokes me with impunity.") Like Wales, Scotland is a country of ragtag Celts sharing an island with wealthy and powerful Anglo-Saxons. Scotland's Celtic culture is a result of its remoteness—the invading Romans were never able to conquer this rough-and-tumble people, and even built Hadrian's Wall to lock off this distant corner of their empire. The Anglo-Saxons, and their descendants the English, fared little better than the Romans did. Even King Edward I—who so successfully dominated Wales—was unable to hold on to Scotland for long, largely thanks to the relentlessly rebellious William Wallace a.k.a. "Braveheart" (see page 718).

Failing to conquer Scotland by the blade, England eventually absorbed it politically. In 1603, England's Queen Elizabeth I died without an heir, so her closest royal relative—Scotland's King James VI—took the throne, becoming King James I of England. It took another century or so of battles, both military and diplomatic, but the Act of Union in 1707 definitively (and controversially) unified the Kingdom of Great Britain. Meanwhile, the English parliament overthrew the grandson of James I when he became a Catholic, replacing him with a line of Protestant monarchs. In 1745, Bonnie Prince Charlie attempted to reclaim the throne on behalf of the deposed Stuarts, but his army was slaughtered at the Battle of Culloden (see page 947). This cemented English rule over Scotland, and is seen by many Scots as the last gasp of the traditional Highlands clan system. Bagpipes, kilts, the Gaelic language, and other symbols of the Highlands were briefly outlawed.

Scotland has been joined—however unwillingly—to England ever since, and the Scots have often felt oppressed by their English countrymen (see sidebar in this chapter). During the Highland Clearances in the 18th and 19th centuries, landowners (mostly English) decided that vast tracks of land were more profitable as grazing land for sheep than as farmland for people. Many Highlanders were forced to abandon their traditional homes and lifestyles and seek employment elsewhere, moving to the cities to work in Industrial Revolution-era factories. Large numbers ended up in North America, especially parts of eastern Canada, such as Prince Edward Island and Nova Scotia (literally, "New Scotland").

Americans and Canadians of Scottish descent enjoy coming "home" to Scotland. If you're Scottish, your surname will tell you which clan your ancestors likely belonged to. The prefix "Mac" (or "Mc") means "son of"—so "MacDonald" means the same thing as "Donaldson." Tourist shops everywhere are happy to help you track down your clan's tartan (distinctive plaid pattern). For more on how these "clan tartans" don't go back as far as you might think, see the sidebar on page 691.

Scotland shares a monarchy with the rest of the United Kingdom, though to Scots, Queen Elizabeth II is just "Queen Elizabeth"; the first Queen Elizabeth ruled England, but not Scotland. (In this book, I use Great Britain's numbering.) Scotland is not a sovereign state, but it is a "nation" in that it has its own traditions, ethnic identity, languages (Gaelic and Scots), and football league. To some extent, it even has its own government.

Recently, Scotland has enjoyed its greatest measure of political autonomy in centuries—a trend called "devolution." In 1999, the Scottish parliament convened in Edinburgh for the first time in almost 300 years; in 2004, it moved into its brand-new building near the foot of the Royal Mile. Though the Scottish parliament's powers are limited (most major decisions are still made in London), the Scots are enjoying the refreshing breeze of increased self-governance. In a 2014 independence referendum, the Scots favored staying in the United Kingdom by a margin of 10 percent. The question of independence will likely remain a pivotal issue in Scotland for many years to come.

Scotland even has its own currency...sort of. Scots use the same coins as England, Wales, and Northern Ireland, but Scotland also prints its own bills (featuring Scottish rather than English people and landmarks). Just to confuse tourists, three different banks print Scottish pound notes, each with a different design. In the Lowlands (around Edinburgh and Glasgow), you'll receive both Scottish and English pounds from ATMs and in change. But in the Highlands, you'll almost never see English pounds. Bank of England notes are legal and widely used; Northern Ireland bank notes are legal but less common.

The Scottish flag—a diagonal X-shaped white cross on a blue field—represents the cross of Scotland's patron saint, the Apostle Andrew (who was crucified on an X-shaped cross). You may not realize it, but you see the Scottish flag every time you look at the Union Jack: England's flag (the red St. George's cross on a white field) superimposed on Scotland's (a blue field with a white diagonal cross). The diagonal red cross (St. Patrick's cross) over Scotland's white one represents Northern Ireland. (Wales gets no love on the Union Jack.)

Here in "English-speaking" Scotland, you may still encounter a language barrier. First is the lovely lilting Scottish accent—which many linguists consider to be a separate language, called "Scots." You may already know several Scots words: lad, lassie, wee, bonnie, glen, loch, aye. On menus, you'll see neeps and tatties (turnips and potatoes). And in place names, you'll see ben (mountain), brae (hill), firth (estuary), and kyle (strait). Second is Gaelic (pronounced "gallic" here; Ireland's closely-related Celtic language is pronounced "gaylic")—the ancient Celtic language of the Scots. While only one percent of the population speaks Gaelic, it's making a comeback—particularly in the remote and traditional Highlands.

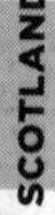

British, Scottish, and English

Scotland and England have been tied together for more than 300 years, since the Act of Union in 1707. For a century and a half afterward, Scottish nationalists rioted for independence in Edinburgh's streets and led rebellions ("uprisings") in the Highlands. In this controversial union, history is clearly seen through two very different filters.

If you tour a British-oriented sight, such as Edinburgh's National War Museum Scotland, you'll find things told in a "happy union" way, which ignores the long history of Scottish resistance—from the ancient Picts through the time of Robert the Bruce. The official line: In 1706-1707, it was clear to England and certain parties in Scotland (especially landowners from the Lowlands) that it was in their mutual interest to dissolve the Scottish government and fold it into Britain, to be ruled from London.

But talk to a cabbie or your B&B host, and you may get a different spin. Scottish independence is still a hot-button issue. Since 2007, the Scottish National Party (SNP) has owned the largest majority in the Scottish Parliament. During a landmark referendum in September 2014, the Scots voted to remain part of the union—but many polls, right up until election day, suggested that things could easily have gone the other way.

The rift shows itself in sports, too. While the English may refer to a British team in international competition as "English," the Scots are careful to call it "British." If a Scottish athlete does well, the English call him "British." If he screws up... he's a clumsy Scot.

While soccer is as popular here as anywhere, golf is Scotland's other national sport. But in Scotland, it's not necessarily considered an exclusively upper-class pursuit; you can generally play a round at a basic course for about £15. While Scotland's best scenery is along the west coast, its best golfing is on the east coast—home to many of its most prestigious golf courses. Most of these are links courses, which use natural sand from the beaches for the bunkers. For tourists, these links are more authentic, more challenging, and more fun than the regular-style courses (with artificial landforms) farther inland. If you're a golfer, St. Andrews—on the east coast—is a pilgrimage worth making.

Scottish cuisine is down-to-earth, often with an emphasis on local produce. Both seafood and "land food" (beef, chicken, lamb, and venison) are common. One Scottish mainstay—eaten more

SCOTLAND

Haggis and Other Traditional Scottish Dishes

Scotland's most unique dish, **haggis,** began as a peasant food. Waste-conscious cooks wrapped the heart, liver, and lungs of a sheep in its stomach lining, packed in some oats and spices, and then boiled the lot to create a hearty, if slightly palatable, meal. Traditionally served with "neeps and tatties" (turnips and potatoes), haggis was forever immortalized thanks to Robbie Burns' *Address to a Haggis.*

Today haggis has been refined almost to the point of high cuisine. You're likely to find it on many menus, including at breakfast. You can dress it up with anything from a fine whisky cream sauce to your basic HP brown sauce. To appreciating this iconic Scottish dish, think of how it tastes—not what it's made of.

The king of Scottish **black puddings** (blood sausage) is made in the Hebrides Islands. Called Stornoway, it's so famous that the European Union has granted it protected status to prevent imitators from using its name. A mix of beef suet, oatmeal, onion, and blood, the sausage is usually served as part of a full Scottish breakfast, but it also appears on the menus of top-class restaurants.

Be on the lookout for other traditional Scottish taste treats. **Cullen skink** is Scotland's answer to chowder: a hearty, creamy fish soup, often made with smoked haddock. A **bridie** (or Forfar bridie) is a savory meat pie similar to a Cornish pasty, but generally lighter (no potatoes). A **Scotch pie—**small, double-crusted, and filled with minced meat, is a good picnic food; it's a common snack at soccer matches and outdoor events. **Crowdie** is a dairy spread that falls somewhere between cream cheese and cottage cheese.

And for dessert, **cranachan** is similar to a trifle, made with whipped cream, honey, fruit (usually raspberries), and whisky-soaked oats. Another popular dessert is the **Tipsy Laird,** served at "Burns Suppers" on January 25, the annual celebration of national poet Robert Burns. It's essentially the same as a trifle but with whisky or brandy and Scottish raspberries.

by tourists than by Scots these days—is the famous haggis, tastier than it sounds and worth trying...even before you've tucked into the whisky. Also look for cullen skink, a satisfying chowder-like cream soup with smoked fish (see sidebar).

The "Scottish Breakfast" is similar to the English version, but they often add a potato scone (like a flavorless, soggy potato pancake) and haggis (best when served with poached eggs and HP brown sauce).

Breakfast, lunch, or dinner, the Scots love their whisky—and touring one of the country's many distilleries is a sightseeing treat. The Scots are fiercely competitive with the Irish when it comes to this peaty spirit. Scottish "whisky" is typically distilled twice, whereas Irish "whiskey" adds a third distillation (and an extra *e*). Some distilleries roast their barley over peat fires, giving many Scottish whiskies a smokier flavor than their Irish cousins. Also note that what we call "scotch"—short for "scotch whisky"—is just "whisky" here. I've listed a few of the most convenient and interesting distilleries to visit, but if you're a whisky connoisseur, make a point of tracking down and touring your favorite.

Outside of the main cities, Scotland's sights are subtle, but its misty glens, brooding countryside castles, and warm culture are plenty engaging. Whether toasting with beer, whisky, or Scotland's favorite soft drink Irn-Bru, enjoy meeting the Scottish people. It's easy to fall in love with the irrepressible spirit and beautiful landscape of this faraway corner of Britain.

EDINBURGH

Edinburgh is the historical, cultural, and political capital of Scotland. For nearly a thousand years, Scotland's kings, parliaments, writers, thinkers, and bankers have called Edinburgh home. Today, it remains Scotland's most sophisticated city.

Edinburgh (ED'n-burah—only tourists pronounce it like "Pittsburgh") is Scotland's showpiece and one of Europe's most entertaining cities. It's a place of stunning vistas—nestled among craggy bluffs and studded with a prickly skyline of spires, towers, domes, and steeples. Proud statues of famous Scots dot the urban landscape. The buildings are a harmonious yellow-gray, all built from the same local sandstone.

Culturally, Edinburgh has always been the place where Lowland culture (urban and English) met Highland style (rustic and Gaelic). Tourists will find no end of traditional Scottish clichés: whisky tastings, kilt shops, bagpipe-playing buskers, and gimmicky tours featuring Scotland's bloody history and ghost stories.

Edinburgh is two cities in one. The Old Town stretches along the Royal Mile, from the grand castle on top to the palace on the bottom. Along this colorful labyrinth of cobbled streets and narrow lanes, medieval skyscrapers stand shoulder to shoulder, hiding peaceful courtyards.

A few hundred yards north of the Old Town lies the New Town. It's a magnificent planned neighborhood from the 1700s. Here, you'll enjoy upscale shops, broad boulevards, straight streets, square squares, circular circuses, and Georgian mansions decked out in Greek-style columns and statues.

Today's Edinburgh is big in banking, scientific research, and scholarship at its four universities. Since 1999, when Scotland regained a measure of self-rule, Edinburgh reassumed its place as home of the Scottish Parliament. The city hums with life. Students and professionals pack the pubs and art galleries. It's especially lively in August, when the Edinburgh Festival takes over the town. Historic, monumental, fun, and well organized, Edinburgh is a tourist's delight.

PLANNING YOUR TIME

While the major sights can be seen in a day, I'd give Edinburgh two days and three nights.

Day 1: Tour the castle, then consider catching a city bus tour for a one-hour loop (departing from a block below the castle at the Hub/Tolbooth Church; you could munch a sandwich from the top deck if you're into multitasking). Back near the castle, take my self-guided Royal Mile walk, stopping in at shops and museums that interest you (Gladstone's Land is tops). At the bottom of the Mile, consider visiting the Scottish Parliament, the Palace of Holyroodhouse, or both. If the weather's good, you could hike back to your B&B along the Salisbury Crags.

Day 2: Visit the National Museum of Scotland. After lunch (several great choices nearby, on Forrest Road), stroll through the Princes Street Gardens and the Scottish National Gallery. Then follow my self-guided walk through the New Town, visiting the Scottish National Portrait Gallery and the Georgian House—or squeeze in a quick tour of the good ship *Britannia* (check last entry time before you head out).

Evenings: Options include various "haunted Edinburgh" walks, literary pub crawls, or live music in pubs. Sadly, full-blown traditional folk performances are just about extinct, surviving only in excruciatingly schmaltzy variety shows put on for tour-bus groups. Perhaps the most authentic evening out is just settling down in a pub to sample the whisky and local beers while meeting the locals...and attempting to understand them through their thick Scottish accents (see "Nightlife in Edinburgh," page 764).

Orientation to Edinburgh

A VERBAL MAP

With 490,000 people (835,000 in the metro area), Edinburgh is Scotland's second-biggest city (after Glasgow). But the tourist's Edinburgh is compact: Old Town, New Town, and the Dalkeith Road B&B area.

Edinburgh's **Old Town** stretches across a ridgeline slung between two bluffs. From west to east, this "Royal Mile" runs from the Castle Rock—which is visible from anywhere—to the base of the 822-foot dormant volcano called Arthur's Seat. For visitors, this east-west axis is the center of the action. Just south of the Royal Mile are the university and the National Museum of Scotland; farther to the south is a handy B&B neighborhood that lines up along **Dalkeith Road.** North of the Royal Mile ridge is the **New Town,** a neighborhood of grid-planned streets and elegant Georgian buildings.

In the center of it all—in a drained lake bed between the Old and New Towns—sit the Princes Street Gardens park and Waverley Bridge, where you'll find the Waverley train station, TI, Princes Mall, bus info office (starting point for most city bus tours), Scottish National Gallery, and a covered dance-and-music pavilion.

TOURIST INFORMATION

The crowded TI is as central as can be, on the rooftop of the Princes Mall and Waverley train station (Mon-Sat 9:00-18:00, Sun 10:00-18:00, July-Aug daily until 19:00, tel. 0131-473-3868, www.visitscotland.com). While the staff is helpful, be warned that much of their information is skewed by tourism payola (and booking seats on bus tours seems to be a big priority). There's also a TI at the airport (tel. 0131-344-3120).

For more information than what's included in the TI's free map, buy the excellent *Collins Discovering Edinburgh* map (which comes with opinionated commentary and locates almost every major sight). If you're interested in evening music, ask for the free monthly entertainment *Gig Guide* or buy the more comprehensive entertainment listing, *The List.* Also consider buying Historic Scotland's Explorer Pass, which can save you some money if you visit the castles at both Edinburgh and Stirling (for details, see page 993).

ARRIVAL IN EDINBURGH

By Train: Arriving by train at Waverley Station puts you in the city center and below the TI. Taxis queue almost trackside (near platform 11); the ramp they come and go on leads to Waverley Bridge. From the station, follow *Way Out–1–Princes Street* signs and ride up several escalators to Princes Street. From here, the TI is to your left, and the city bus stop is two blocks to your right (for bus directions from here to my recommended B&Bs, see "Sleeping in Edinburgh," later).

By Bus: Scottish Citylink, Megabus, and National Express buses use the bus station (with luggage lockers) in the New Town, two blocks north of the train station on St. Andrew Square.

By Plane: Edinburgh's slingshot of an airport is located eight miles northwest of the center (tel. 0844-481-8989, www.edinburghairport.com).

Taxis between the airport and city center are pricey (£20-25,

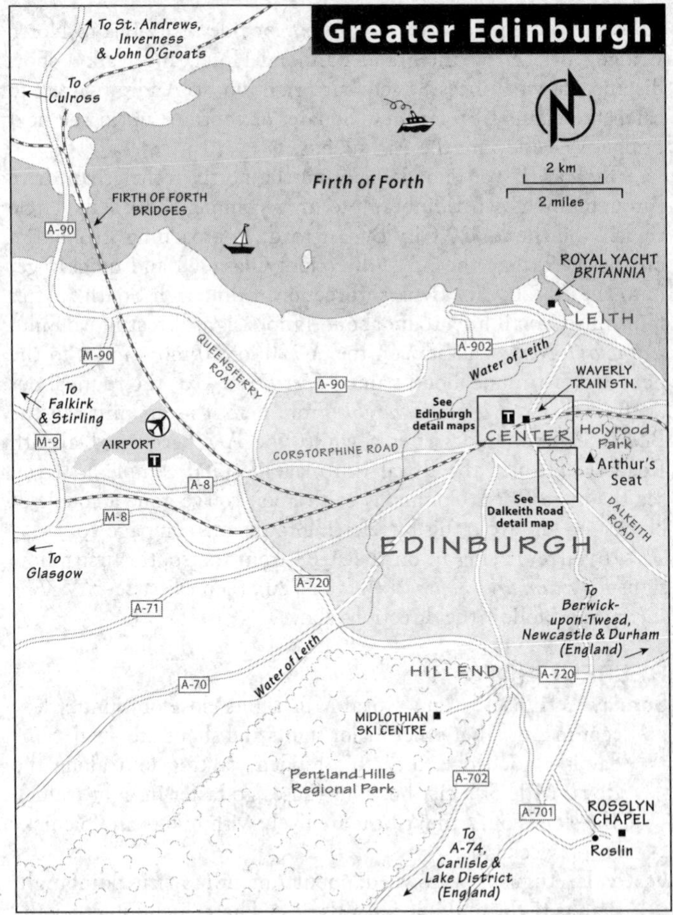

20 minutes to downtown or Dalkeith Road). Fortunately, the airport is well connected to central Edinburgh by tram and bus. Just follow signs outside; the tram tracks are straight ahead, and the bus stop is to the right, along the main road in front of the terminal. **Trams** make several stops in town, including along Princes Street and at St. Andrew Square (£5, 6/hour, 35 minutes, early morning until 23:30, www.edinburghtrams.com). The Lothian **Airlink bus #100** drops you at Waverley Bridge (£4.50, £7.50 round-trip, 6/hour, 30 minutes, buses run all day and 2/hour through the night, tel. 0131/555-6363, www.flybybus.com). Whether you take the tram or bus to the center, to continue on to my recommended B&Bs near Dalkeith Road, you can either take a taxi (about £7) or hop on a city bus (£1.50; see "Sleeping in Edinburgh," later).

To get from the Dalkeith Road B&Bs *to* the Airlink or tram

stops downtown, you can take a taxi...or ride a city bus to North Bridge, turn left at the grand Balmoral Hotel, and walk a short distance down Princes Street. Turn right up St. Andrew Street to catch the tram at St. Andrew Square, or continue up to the next bridge, Waverley, for the Airlink bus.

By Car: If you're arriving from the north, rather than drive through downtown Edinburgh to my recommended B&Bs, circle the city on the A-720 City Bypass road. Approaching Edinburgh on the M-9, take the M-8 (direction: Glasgow) and quickly get onto the A-720 City Bypass (direction: Edinburgh South). After four miles, you'll hit a roundabout. Ignore signs directing you into *Edinburgh North* and stay on the A-720 for 10 more miles to the next and last roundabout, named *Sheriffhall.* Exit the roundabout at the first left *(A-7 Edinburgh).* From here it's four miles to the B&B neighborhood. After a while, the A-7 becomes Dalkeith Road (you'll pass the Royal Infirmary hospital complex). If you see the huge Royal Commonwealth Pool, you've gone a couple of blocks too far (avoid this by referring to the map on page 768).

If you're driving in on the A-68 from the south, first follow signs for *Edinburgh South & West* (A-720), then exit at *A-7(N)/Edinburgh* and follow the directions above.

HELPFUL HINTS

Sunday Activities: Many Royal Mile sights close on Sunday (except in Aug), but other major sights and shops are open. Sunday is a good day to catch a guided walking tour along the Royal Mile or a city bus tour (buses go faster in light traffic). The slopes of Arthur's Seat are lively with hikers and picnickers on weekends.

Festivals: August is a crowded, popular month to visit Edinburgh, thanks to the multiple festivals hosted here, including the official **Edinburgh International Festival,** the **Fringe Festival,** and the **Military Tattoo.** Book ahead for hotels, events, and restaurant dinners if you'll be visiting in August, and expect to pay significantly more for your room. Many museums and shops have extended hours in August. For more festival details, see page 756.

Internet Access: Virtually all B&Bs and coffee shops offer free Wi-Fi, and all local public transit has fast, free Wi-Fi on board.

Baggage Storage: At the train station, you'll find pricey high-security luggage storage near platform 2 (£6/3 hours, £10/24 hours, daily 7:00-23:00). There are also lockers at the bus station on St. Andrew Square, just two blocks north of the train station.

Laundry: The **Ace Cleaning Centre** launderette is located near my recommended Dalkeith Road B&Bs, where they'll collect and drop off your laundry for a small extra fee (self-serve or full-serve, Mon-Fri 8:00-20:00, Sat 9:00-17:00, Sun 10:00-16:00, along bus route to city center at 13 South Clerk Street, opposite Queens Hall, tel. 0131/667-0549).

Bike Rental: The laid-back crew at **Cycle Scotland** offers bike tours and happily recommends good bike routes (£15/3 hours, £20/day, daily 10:00-18:00, just off Royal Mile at 29 Blackfriars Street, mobile 07796-886-899, www.cyclescotland.co.uk).

Car Rental: These places have offices both in the town center and at the airport: **Avis** (24 East London Street, tel. 0844-544-6059, airport tel. 0844-544-6004), **Europcar** (Waverley Station, near platform 2, tel. 0871-384-3453, airport tel. 0871-384-3406), **Hertz** (10 Picardy Place, tel. 0843-309-3026, airport tel. 0843-309-3025), and **Budget** (24 East London Street, tel. 0844-544-9064, airport tel. 0844-544-4605). Some downtown offices close or have reduced hours on Sunday, but the airport locations tend to be open daily. If you plan to rent a car, pick it up on your way out of Edinburgh—you won't need it in town.

Dress for the Weather: Weather blows in and out—bring your sweater and be prepared for rain. Locals say the bad weather is one of the disadvantages of living so close to England.

Updates to This Book: For the latest, see www.ricksteves.com/update.

GETTING AROUND EDINBURGH

Many of Edinburgh's sights are within walking distance of one another, but **buses** come in handy—especially if you're staying at a B&B in the Dalkeith Road area. Double-decker buses come with fine views upstairs. It's easy once you get the hang of it: Buses come by frequently (screens at bus stops show wait times) and have free, fast Wi-Fi on board. The only hassle is that you must pay with exact change (£1.50/ride, £4/all-day pass). As you board, tell your driver where you're going (or just say "single ticket") and drop your change into the box. Ping the bell as you near your stop. Buses run from about 6:00 (9:00 on Sun) to 23:00. You can pick up a route map at the TI or at the transit office at Old Town end of Waverley Bridge (tel. 0131/555-6363, www.lothianbuses.com). Edinburgh's single **tram** line (also £1.50/ride) is designed more for locals than tourists; it's most useful for reaching the airport (described earlier).

The 1,300 **taxis** cruising Edinburgh's streets are easy to flag down (£2.10 to start, then about £2.20/mile, rates go up after 18:00 and on weekends; a ride between downtown and the B&B neighborhood costs about £7). They can turn on a dime, so hail them in either direction.

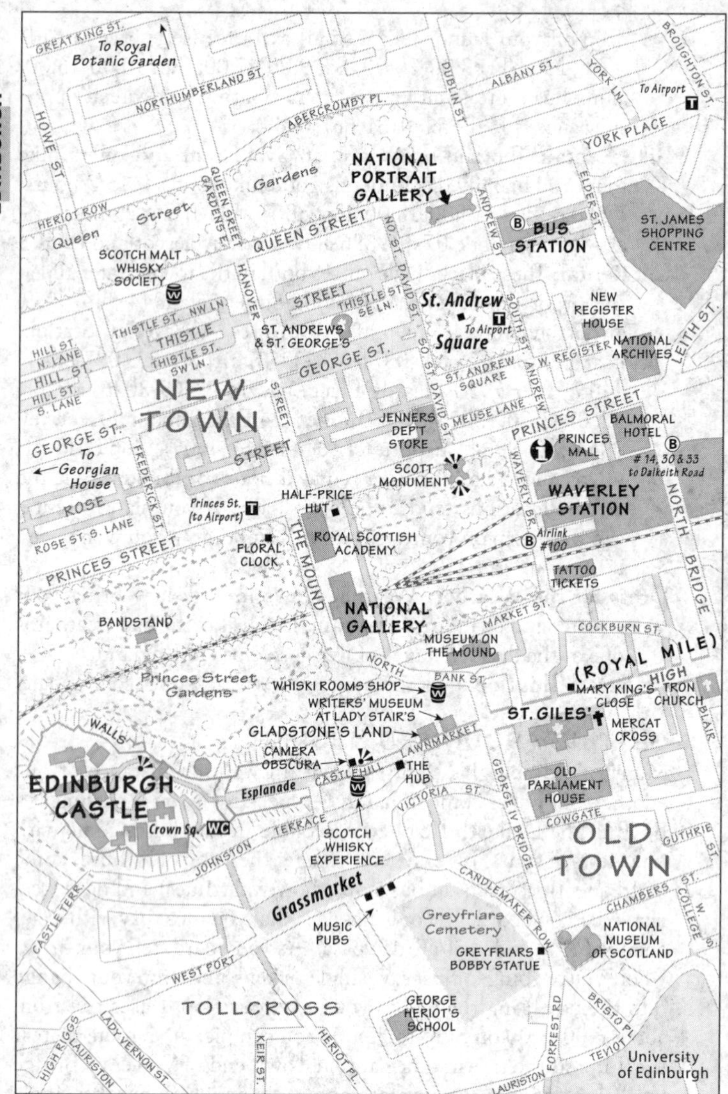

Tours in Edinburgh

Royal Mile Walking Tours

Walking tours are an Edinburgh specialty; you'll see groups trailing entertaining guides all over town. Below I've listed good all-purpose walks; for **literary pub crawls** and **ghost tours,** see "Nightlife in Edinburgh" on page 764.

Edinburgh Tour Guides offers a good historical walk (with-

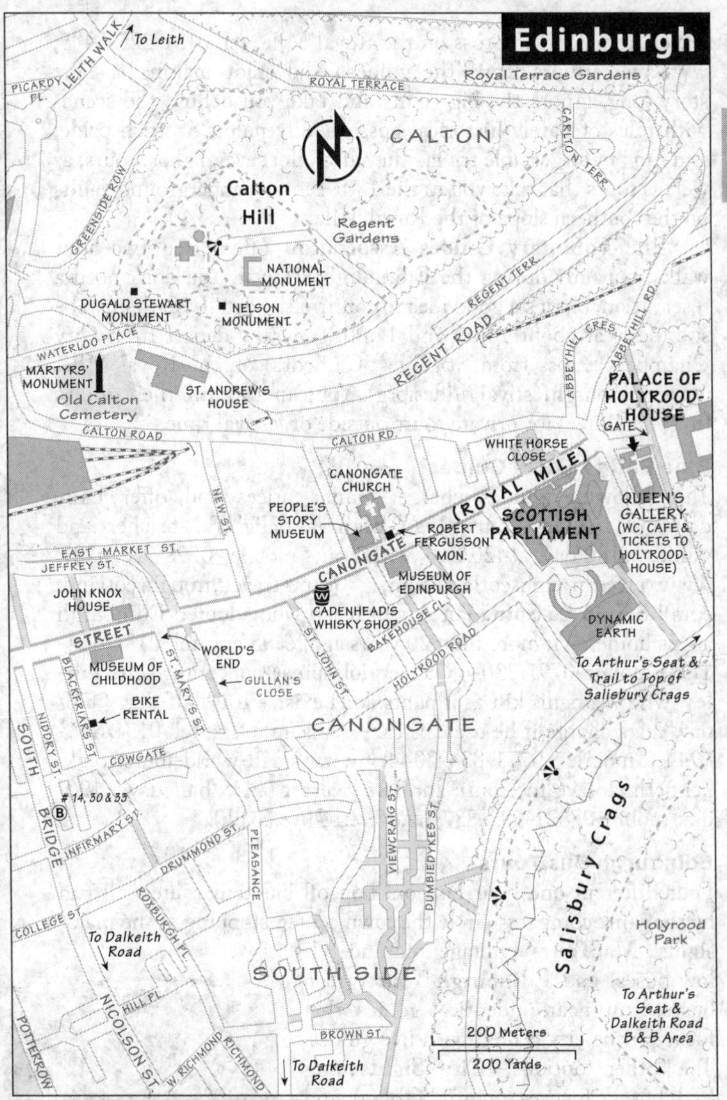

out all the ghosts and goblins). Their Royal Mile tour is a gentle two-hour downhill stroll from the castle to the palace (£15; daily at 9:30 and 19:00; meet outside Gladstone's Land, near the top of the Royal Mile—see map on page 695, must reserve ahead, mobile 0785-888-0072, www.edinburghtourguides.com, info@edinburghtourguides.com).

Mercat Tours offers a 1.5-hour "Secrets of the Royal Mile" walk that's more entertaining than intellectual (£12; £17 more for optional 45-minute guided Edinburgh Castle visit; daily at 13:30, leaves from Mercat Cross on the Royal Mile, tel. 0131/225-5445, www.mercattours.com). The guides, who enjoy making a short story long, ignore the big sights and take you behind the scenes with piles of barely historical gossip, bully-pulpit Scottish pride, and fun but forgettable trivia. They also offer several ghost tours, as well as tours that take you to the 18th-century underground vaults on the southern slope of the Royal Mile.

The **Voluntary Guides Association** offers free two-hour walks, but only during the Edinburgh Festival. You don't need a reservation, but it's a good idea to confirm the details on their website (daily at about 10:00 and 14:00, generally depart from City Chambers across from St. Giles' Cathedral on the Royal Mile, www.edinburghfestivalguides.org). You can also hire their guides (for a small fee) for private tours outside of festival time.

Blue Badge Local Guides

The following guides charge similar prices and offer half-day and full-day tours: **Jean Blair** (a delightful teacher and guide, £180/day, £420/day with car, mobile 0798-957-0287, www.travelthroughscotland.com, jean@travelthroughscotland.com); **Sergio La Spina** (an Argentinean who adopted Edinburgh as his hometown more than 20 years ago, £195/day, tel. 0131/664-1731, mobile 0797-330-6579, sergiolaspina@aol.com); **Ken Hanley** (who wears his kilt as if pants don't exist, £100/half-day, £175/day, extra charge if he uses his car—seats up to six, tel. 0131/666-1944, mobile 0771-034-2044, www.small-world-tours.co.uk, kennethhanley@me.com); and **Liz Everett** (£145/half-day, £190/day, mobile 07821-683-837, liz.everett@live.co.uk).

Edinburgh Bus Tours

Four different one-hour hop-on, hop-off bus tour routes, all run by the same company, circle the town center, stopping at the major sights. **MacTours** (vintage red-and-yellow buses) and **Edinburgh Tour** (green buses) run nearly identical routes that focus on the city center, with live guides. The other options—**City Sightseeing** (red buses, focuses on Old Town) and **Majestic Tour** (blue-and-yellow buses, includes a stop at the *Britannia* and Royal Botanic Garden)—have recorded commentary. You can pay for just one tour (£14/24 hours), but most people pay a few pounds more for a ticket covering all four buses (£20). Each of the four lines runs all day long (April-Oct roughly 9:30-19:00, shorter off-season; every 10-15 minutes, buy tickets on board, tel. 0131/220-0770, www.edinburghtour.com).

On sunny days the buses go topless, but come with increased traffic noise and exhaust fumes. For £50, the Royal Edinburgh Ticket covers two days of unlimited travel on all four tour buses, as well as admission (and line-skipping privileges) at Edinburgh Castle, the Palace of Holyroodhouse, and the *Britannia*. This could save you a few pounds if you plan to visit all these sights and to use a tour bus both days (www.royaledinburghticket.co.uk).

Weekend Tour Packages for Students

Andy Steves (Rick's son) runs **Weekend Student Adventures** (WSA Europe), offering three-day and longer guided and unguided packages—including accommodations, sightseeing, and unique local experiences—for student travelers in top European cities, including Edinburgh (guided trips from €199, see www.wsaeurope.com).

DAY TRIPS FROM EDINBURGH

Many companies run a variety of day trips to regional sights, as well as multiday and themed itineraries. (Several of the private guides listed earlier have cars, too.)

By far the most popular tour is the all-day **Highlands trip.** The standard Highlands tour gives those with limited time a chance to experience the wonders of Scotland's wild and legend-soaked Highlands in a single long day (about £40-50, roughly 8:00-20:30). Itineraries vary but you'll generally visit the vast and brutal Rannoch Moor; Glencoe, still evocative with memories of the clan massacre; views of Britain's highest mountain, Ben Nevis; Fort Augustus on Loch Ness (some tours have a 1.5-hour stop here with an optional boat ride); and pause for a 45-minute tea or pub break in Pitlochry. You also learn a bit about Edinburgh as you drive in and out. To save time, look for a tour that gives you a short glimpse of Loch Ness rather than driving its entire length or doing a boat trip. (Once you've seen a little of it, you've seen the whole shebang.)

Larger outfits, typically using bigger buses, include **Timberbush Highland Tours** (tel. 0131/226-6066, www.timberbushtours.com) and **Gray Line** (tel. 0131/555-5558, www.graylinescotland.com). Other companies pride themselves on keeping group sizes small, with 16-seat minibuses; these include **Rabbie's Trail Burners** (tel. 0131/226-3133, www.rabbies.com) and **Heart of Scotland Tours: *The Wee Red Bus*** (10 percent Rick Steves discount on full-priced day tours—mention when booking, occasionally canceled off-season if too few sign up—leave a contact number, tel. 0131/228-2888, www.heartofscotlandtours.co.uk, run by Nick Roche). For young backpackers, **Haggis Adventures** runs overnight trips of up to 10 days (office at 60 High Street, tel. 0131/557-9393, www.haggisadventures.com).

Edinburgh at a Glance

▲▲▲**Royal Mile** Historic road—good for walking—stretching from the castle down to the palace, lined with museums, pubs, and shops. **Hours:** Always open, but best during business hours, with walking tours daily. See page 690.

▲▲▲**Edinburgh Castle** Iconic hilltop fort and royal residence complete with crown jewels, Romanesque chapel, memorial, and fine military museum. **Hours:** Daily April-Sept 9:30-18:00, Oct-March 9:30-17:00. See page 712.

▲▲▲**National Museum of Scotland** Intriguing well-displayed artifacts from prehistoric times to the 20th century. **Hours:** Daily 10:00-17:00. See page 737.

▲▲**Gladstone's Land** Seventeenth-century Royal Mile merchant's residence. **Hours:** Daily July-Aug 10:00-18:30, April-June and Sept-Oct 10:00-17:00, closed Nov-March. See page 723.

▲▲**St. Giles' Cathedral** Preaching grounds of Calvinist John Knox, with spectacular organ, Neo-Gothic chapel, and distinctive crown spire. **Hours:** May-Sept Mon-Fri 9:00-19:00, Sat 9:00-17:00; Oct-April Mon-Sat 9:00-17:00; Sun 13:00-17:00 year-round. See page 725.

▲▲**Scottish Parliament Building** Striking headquarters for parliament, which returned to Scotland in 1999. **Hours:** Sept-June (when parliament is in session)—Mon and Fri-Sat 10:00-17:00, Tue-Thu 9:00-18:30; July-Aug and holidays (when parliament is in recess)—Mon-Sat 10:00-17:00; closed Sun year-round. See page 734.

▲▲**Palace of Holyroodhouse** The Queen's splendid home away from home, with lavish rooms, 12th-century abbey, and gallery with rotating exhibits. **Hours:** Daily April-Oct 9:30-18:00, Nov-March until 16:30, closed during royal visits. See page 735.

▲▲**Scottish National Gallery** Choice sampling of European masters and Scotland's finest. **Hours:** Daily 10:00-17:00, Thu until 19:00; longer hours in Aug: Sun-Wed 10:00-18:00, Thu-Sat 10:00-19:00. See page 741.

▲▲**Scottish National Portrait Gallery** Beautifully displayed *Who's Who* of Scottish history. **Hours:** Daily 10:00-17:00, Thu until 19:00. See page 746.

▲▲**Georgian House** Intimate peek at upper-crust life in the late 1700s. **Hours:** Daily April-Oct 10:00-17:00, July-Aug until 18:00, March and Nov 11:00-16:00; may be open Thu-Sun in Dec, otherwise closed Dec-Feb. See page 749.

▲▲**Royal Yacht *Britannia*** Ship for the royal family with a history of distinguished passengers, a 15-minute trip out of town. **Hours:** Daily April-Sept 9:30-16:30, Oct 9:30-16:00, Nov-March 10:00-15:30 (these are last-entry times). See page 749.

▲**Scotch Whisky Experience** Gimmicky but fun and educational introduction to Scotland's most famous beverage. **Hours:** Generally daily 10:00-18:00. See page 723.

▲**The Real Mary King's Close** Tour of underground street and houses last occupied in the 17th century, viewable by guided tour. **Hours:** April-Oct daily 10:00-22:00; Nov-March Sun-Thu until 17:00, Fri-Sat until 21:00 (these are last-tour times). See page 732.

▲**Museum of Childhood** Five stories of historic fun. **Hours:** Mon-Sat 10:00-17:00, Sun 12:00-17:00. See page 732.

▲**People's Story Museum** Everyday life from the 18th to 20th century. **Hours:** Mon-Sat 10:00-17:00, closed Sun except during Festival 12:00-17:00. See page 733.

▲**Museum of Edinburgh** Historic mementos, from the original National Covenant inscribed on animal skin to early golf balls. **Hours:** Mon-Sat 10:00-17:00, closed Sun except during Festival 12:00-17:00. See page 733.

▲**Rosslyn Chapel** Small 15th-century church chock-full of intriguing carvings. **Hours:** Mon-Sat 9:30-18:00, until 17:00 Oct-March, Sun 12:00-16:45 year-round. See page 751.

At **Discreet Scotland,** Matthew Wight and his partners specialize in tours of greater Edinburgh and Scotland in spacious SUVs—good for families (£360/9 hours, mobile 0798-941-6990, www.discreetscotland.com).

Edinburgh Walks

I've outlined two walks in Edinburgh: along the Royal Mile, and through the New Town. Many of the sights we'll pass on these walks are described in more detail later, under "Sights in Edinburgh."

THE ROYAL MILE

The Royal Mile is one of Europe's most interesting historic walks—it's worth ▲▲▲. The following self-guided stroll is also available as a 🎧 downloadable Rick Steves audio tour; see page 13.

Overview

Start at Edinburgh Castle at the top and amble down to the Palace of Holyroodhouse. Along the way, the street changes names—Castlehill, Lawnmarket, High Street, and Canongate—but it's a straight downhill shot totaling just over one mile. And nearly every step is packed with shops, cafés, and lanes leading to tiny squares.

The city of Edinburgh was born on the easily defended rock at the top where the castle stands today. Celtic tribes (and maybe the Romans) once occupied this site. As the town grew, it spilled downhill along the sloping ridge that became the Royal Mile. Because this strip of land is so narrow, there was no place to build but up. So in medieval times, it was densely packed with multistory "tenements"—large edifices under one roof that housed a number of tenants.

As you walk, you'll be tracing the growth of the city—its birth atop Castle Hill, its Old Town heyday in the 1600s, its expansion in the 1700s into the Georgian New Town (leaving the old quarter an overcrowded, disease-ridden Victorian slum), and on to the 21st century at the modern Scottish parliament building (2004).

In parts, the Royal Mile feels like one long Scottish shopping mall, selling all manner of kitschy souvenirs (known locally as "tartan tat"), shortbread, and whisky. But the streets are also packed with history, and if you push past the postcard racks into one of the many side alleys, you can still find a few surviving rough edges of the old city. Despite the drizzle, be sure to look up—spires, carv-

The Kilt

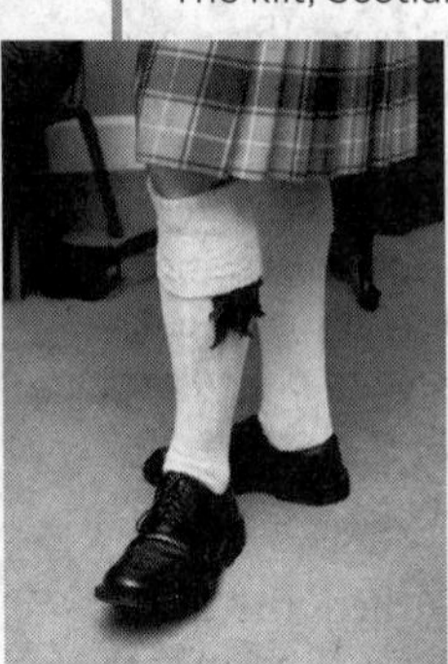

The kilt, Scotland's national dress, is intimately tied in with the country's history. The six-foot-by-nine-foot bolt of fabric originated in the 1500s as a multipurpose robe, toga, tent, poncho, and ground cloth. A wearer would lay it on the ground to scrunch up pleats, then wrap it around the waist and belt it. Extra fabric was thrown over the shoulder or tucked into the belt, creating both a rakish sash and a rucksack-like pouch.

The kilt was standard Highlands dress and became a patriotic statement during conflicts with England. After the tragic-for-Scotland Battle of Culloden in 1746, the British government wanted to end the Scottish clan system. Wearing the kilt, speaking Gaelic, and playing the bagpipes were all outlawed.

In 1782, kilts were permitted again, but had taken on an unrefined connotation, so many Scots no longer wanted to wear one. This changed in 1822 when King George IV visited Edinburgh, wearing a kilt to send the message that he was king of Scotland. Scottish aristocrats were charmed by the king's pageantry, and the kilt was in vogue once more.

During the king's visit, Sir Walter Scott organized a Highland festival that also helped change the image of traditional Scottish culture, giving it a newfound respectability. A generation later, Queen Victoria raised the image of Scottish culture even higher. She loved Scotland and wallpapered her palace at Balmoral with tartan patterns.

The colors and patterns of the original kilts were determined by what dyes were available and who wove them. Because members of one clan tended to live in the same areas, they often wore similar patterns—but the colors were muted, and the patterns weren't necessarily designed to represent a single clan. The "clan tartans" you'll see in Scottish souvenir shops—with a specific brightly-colored design for each family—started as a scam by fabric salesmen in Victorian times. Since then, tartanry has been embraced as if it were historic. (By the way, Scots use these key terms differently than Americans do: "Tartan" is the pattern itself, while "plaid" is the piece of cloth worn over the shoulder with a kilt.)

As Highlanders moved to cities and took jobs in factories, the smaller kilt, or philibeg, replaced the traditional kilt, which could become dangerously snagged by modern machinery. Half the weight of old-style kilts, the practical philibeg is more like a wraparound skirt.

Other kilt-related gear includes the sporran, the leather pouch worn around the waist, and the *sgian dubh* ("black knife"), the short blade worn in the top of the sock. If you're in the market for a kilt, see page 762.

ings, and towering Gothic "skyscrapers" give this city its unique urban identity.

This walk covers the Royal Mile's landmarks, but skips the many museums and indoor attractions along the way. These and other sights are described in walking order under "Sights in Edinburgh" on page 712. You can stay focused on the walk (which takes about 1.5 hours, without entering sights), then return later to visit the various indoor attractions; or review the sight descriptions beforehand and pop into those that interest you as you pass them.

• *We'll start at the Castle Esplanade, the big parking lot at the entrance to...*

❶ Edinburgh Castle

Edinburgh was born on the bluff—a big rock—where the castle now stands. Since before recorded history, people have lived on this strategic, easily defended perch.

The **castle** is an imposing symbol of Scottish independence. Flanking the entryway are statues of the fierce warriors who battled English invaders, William Wallace (on the right) and Robert the Bruce (left). Between them is the Scottish motto, *Nemo me impune lacessit*—roughly, "No one messes with me and gets away with it." (For a self-guided tour of Edinburgh Castle, see page 712.)

The esplanade—built as a military parade ground (1816)—is now the site of the annual Military Tattoo. This spectacular massing of regimental bands fills the square nightly for most of August. Fans watch from temporary bleacher seats to see kilt-wearing bagpipers marching against the spectacular backdrop of the castle. TV crews broadcast the spectacle to all corners of the globe.

When the bleachers aren't up, there are fine views in both directions from the esplanade. Facing north, you'll see the body of water called the Firth of Forth, and Fife beyond that. (The Firth of Forth is the estuary where the Forth River flows into the North Sea.) Still facing north, find the lacy spire of the Scott Memorial and two Neoclassical buildings housing art galleries. Beyond them, the stately buildings of Edinburgh's New Town rise. (For a self-guided walk of the New Town, see page 705.) Panning to the right, find the Nelson Monument and some faux Greek ruins atop Calton Hill (see page 755).

The city's many bluffs, crags, and ridges were built up by volcanoes, then carved down by glaciers—a city formed in "fire and ice," as the locals say. So, during the Ice Age, as a river of glaciers swept in from the west (behind today's castle), it ran into the super-hard volcanic basalt of Castle Rock and flowed around it, cutting valleys on either side and leaving a tail that became the Royal Mile you're about to walk.

At the bottom of the esplanade, where the square hits the road, look left to find a plaque on the wall above the tiny **witches' well** (now a planter). This memorializes 300 women who were accused of witchcraft and burned here. Below was the Nor' Loch, the swampy lake where those accused of witchcraft (mostly women) were tested: Bound up, they were dropped into the lake. If they sank and drowned, they were innocent. If they floated, they were guilty, and were burned here in front of the castle, providing the city folk a nice afternoon out. The plaque shows two witches: one good and one bad. Tickle the serpent's snout to sympathize with the witches. (I just made that up.)

• *Start walking down the Royal Mile. The first block is a street called...*

❷ Castlehill

You're immediately in the tourist hubbub. The big tank-like building on your left was the Old Town's **reservoir.** You'll see the wellheads it served all along this walk. While it once held 1.5 million gallons of water, today it's filled with the touristy Tartan Weaving Mill and Exhibition. While it's interesting to see the mill at work, you'll have to twist your way down through several floors of tartanry and Chinese-produced Scottish kitsch to reach it at the bottom level.

The black-and-white tower ahead on the left has entertained visitors since the 1850s with its **camera obscura,** a darkened room where a mirror and a series of lenses capture live images of the city surroundings outside. (Giggle at the funny mirrors as you walk fatly by). Across the street, filling the old Castlehill Primary School, is a gimmicky-if-intoxicating whisky-sampling exhibit called the **Scotch Whisky Experience** (a.k.a. "Malt Disney"). Both of these are described later, under "Sights in Edinburgh."

• *Just ahead, in front of the church with the tall lacy spire, is the old market square known as...*

❸ Lawnmarket

During the Royal Mile's heyday in the 1600s, this intersection was bigger and served as a market for fabric (especially "lawn," a linen-like cloth). The market would fill this space with bustle, hustle, and lots of commerce. The round white hump in the middle of the roundabout is all that remains of the official weighing beam called the Butter Tron—where all goods sold were weighed for honesty and tax purposes.

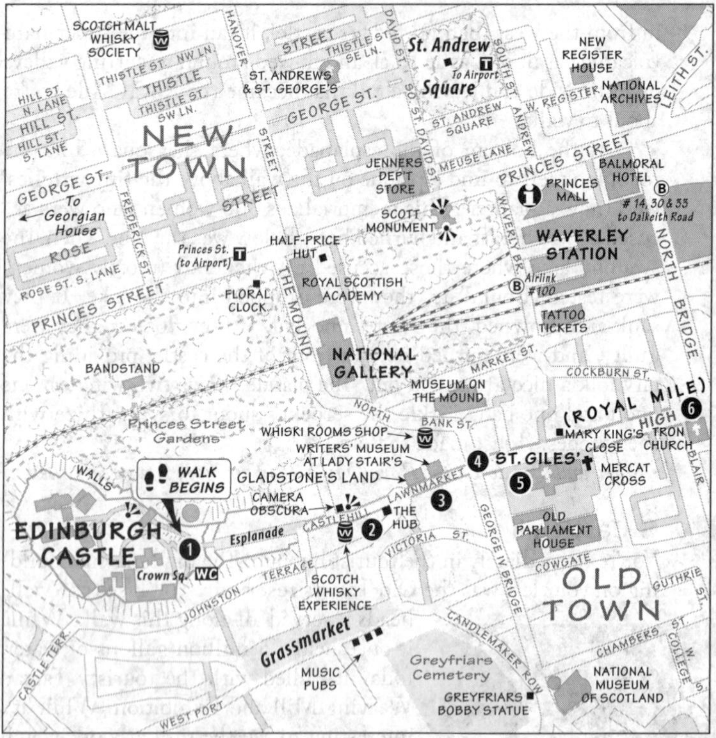

Towering above Lawnmarket, with the tallest spire in the city, is the former **Tolbooth Church.** This impressive Neo-Gothic structure (1844) is now home to the Hub, Edinburgh's festival ticket and information center. The world-famous Edinburgh Festival fills the month of August with cultural action. The various festivals feature classical music, traditional and fringe theater (especially comedy), art, books, and more. Drop inside the building to get festival info (see also page 756). This is a handy stop for its WC, café, and free Wi-Fi.

In the 1600s, this—along with the next stretch, called High

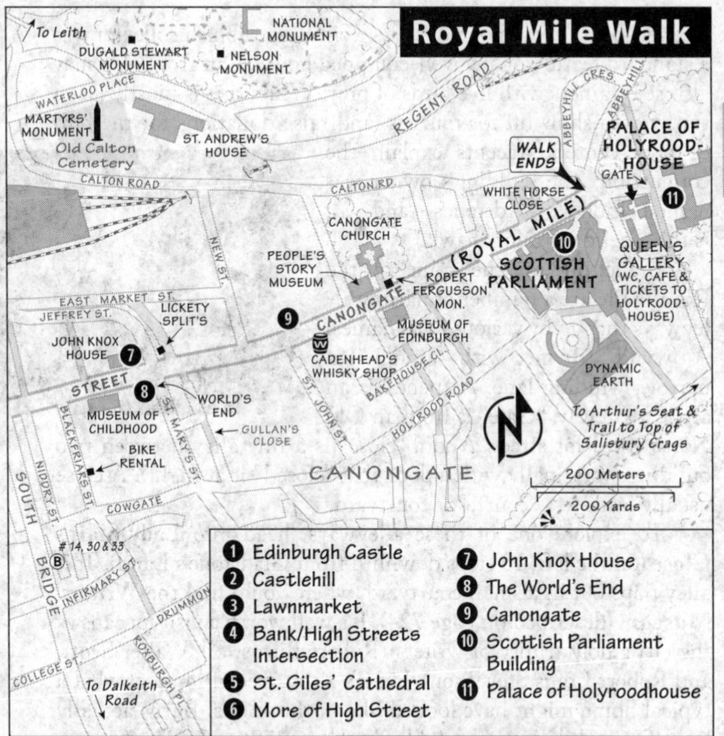

Street—was the city's main street. At that time, Edinburgh was bursting with breweries, printing presses, and banks. Tens of thousands of citizens were squeezed into the narrow confines of the Old Town. Here on this ridge, they built **tenements** (multiple-unit residences) similar to the more recent ones you see today. These tenements, rising up 10 stories and more, were some of the tallest domestic buildings in Europe. The living arrangements shocked class-conscious English visitors to Edinburgh because the tenements were occupied by rich and poor alike—usually the poor in the cellars and attics, and the rich in the middle floors.

• *Continue a half-block down the Mile.*

Gladstone's Land (at #477b, on the left), a surviving original tenement, was acquired by a wealthy merchant in 1617. Stand in front of the building and look up at this centuries-old skyscraper. This design was standard for its time: a shop or shops on the ground floor, with columns and an arcade, and residences on the floors above. Because window glass was expensive, the lower halves of window openings were made of cheaper wood, which swung out like shutters for ventilation—and were convenient for tossing out garbage. (For more on Gladstone's, see page 723). Notice the snoozing pig by the front door. Just like every house has a vacuum cleaner today, in the good old days a snorting rubbish collector was a standard feature of any well-equipped house. Out front, you may also see trainers with live birds of prey. While this is mostly just a fun way to show off for tourists (and raise donations for the bird of prey center), docents explain the connection: The building's owner was named Thomas Gledstanes—and *gled* is the Gaelic word for "hawk."

Branching off the spine of the Royal Mile are a number of narrow alleyways that go by various local names. A "wynd" (rhymes with "kind") is a narrow, winding lane. A "pend" is an arched gateway. "Gate" is from an Old Norse word for street. And a "close" is a tiny alley between two buildings (originally with a door that "closed" it at night). A close usually leads to a "court," or courtyard.

To explore one of these alleyways, head into **Lady Stair's Close** (on the left, 10 steps downhill from Gladstone's Land). This alley pops out in a small courtyard, where you'll find the **Writers' Museum** (described on page 724). It's well worth a visit for fans of the city's holy trinity of writers (Robert Burns, Sir Walter Scott, and Robert Louis Stevenson), but it's also a free glimpse of what a typical home might have looked like in the 1600s. Burns actually lived for a while in this neighborhood, in 1786, when he first arrived in Edinburgh.

Opposite Gladstone's Land (at #322), another close leads to **Riddle's Court.** Wander through here and imagine Edinburgh in the 17th and 18th centuries, when tourists came here to marvel at its skyscrapers. Some 40,000 people were jammed into the few blocks between here and the World's End pub (which we'll reach soon). Visualize the labyrinthine maze of the old city, with people scurrying through these back alleyways, buying and selling, and popping into taverns.

No city in Europe was as densely populated—or perhaps as filthy. Without modern hygiene, it was a living hell of smoke, stench, and noise, with the constant threat of fire, collapse, and disease. The dirt streets were soiled with sewage from bedpans emptied out windows. By the 1700s, the Old Town was rife with poverty and cholera outbreaks. The smoky home fires rising from tenements and the infamous smell (or "reek" in Scottish) that wafted across the city gave it a nickname that sticks today: "Auld Reekie."

• *Return to the Royal Mile and continue down it a few steps to take in some sights at the...*

❹ Bank/High Streets Intersection

A number of sights cluster here, where Lawnmarket changes its name to High Street and intersects with Bank Street and George IV Bridge.

Begin with **Deacon Brodie's Tavern.** Read the "Doctor Jekyll and Mr. Hyde" story of this pub's notorious namesake on the wall facing Bank Street. Then, to see his spooky split personality, check out both sides of the hanging signpost. Brodie—a pillar of the community by day but a burglar by night—epitomizes the divided personality of 1700s Edinburgh. It was a rich, productive city—home to great philosophers and scientists, who actively contributed to the Enlightenment. Meanwhile, the Old Town was riddled with crime and squalor. The city was scandalized when a respected surgeon—driven by a passion for medical research and needing corpses—was accused of colluding with two lowlifes, named Burke and Hare, to acquire freshly murdered corpses for dissection. (In the next century, in the late 1800s, novelist Robert Louis Stevenson would capture the dichotomy of Edinburgh's rich-poor society in his *Strange Case of Dr. Jekyll and Mr. Hyde.*)

In the late 1700s, Edinburgh's upper class moved out of the Old Town into a planned community called the New Town (a quarter-mile north of here). Eventually, most tenements were torn down and replaced with newer **Victorian buildings.** You'll see some at this intersection.

Look left down Bank Street to the green-domed **Bank of Scotland.** This was the headquarters of the bank, which had practiced modern capitalist financing since 1695. The building now houses the Museum on the Mound, a free exhibit on banking history (see page 725), and it's also the Scottish headquarters for Lloyds Banking Group—which swallowed up the Bank of Scotland after the financial crisis of 2008.

If you detour left down Bank Street toward the bank, you'll find the recommended **Whiski Rooms Shop.** If you head in the opposite direction, down George IV Bridge, you'll reach some recommended eateries (The Elephant House and The Outsider), as well as the excellent **National Museum of Scotland,** the famous Greyfriars Bobby statue, restaurant-lined Forrest Road, and photogenic Victoria Street, which leads to the pub-lined Grassmarket square (all described later in this chapter).

Otherwise, continue along the Royal Mile. As you walk, be

careful crossing the streets along the Mile. Edinburgh drivers—especially cabbies—have a reputation for being impatient with jaywalking tourists. Notice and heed the pedestrian crossing signals, which don't always turn at the same time as the car signals.

Across the street from Deacon Brodie's Tavern is a seated green statue of hometown boy **David Hume** (1711-1776)—one of the most influential thinkers not only of Scotland, but in all of Western philosophy. The atheistic Hume was one of the towering figures of the Scottish Enlightenment of the mid-1700s. Thinkers and scientists were using the experimental method to challenge and investigate everything, including religion. Hume questioned cause and effect in thought puzzles such as this: We can see that when one billiard ball strikes another, the second one moves, but how do we know the collision "caused" the movement? Notice his shiny toe: People on their way to trial (in the high court just behind the statue) or students on their way to exams (in the nearby university) rub it for good luck.

Follow David Hume's gaze to the opposite corner, where a **brass H** in the pavement marks the site of the last public execution in Edinburgh in 1864. Deacon Brodie himself would have been hung about here (in 1788, on a gallows whose design he had helped to improve—smart guy).

• *From the brass H, continue down the Royal Mile, pausing just before the church square at a stone wellhead with the pyramid cap.*

All along the Royal Mile, **wellheads** like this (from 1835) provided townsfolk with water in the days before buildings had plumbing. This neighborhood well was served by the reservoir up at the castle. Imagine long lines of people in need of water standing here, gossiping and sharing the news. Eventually buildings were retrofitted with water pipes—the ones you see running along building exteriors.

• *Ahead of you (past the Victorian statue of some duke), embedded in the pavement near the street, is a big heart.*

The **Heart of Midlothian** marks the spot of the city's 15th-century municipal building and jail. In times past, in a nearby open space, criminals were hanged, traitors were decapitated, and witches were burned. Citizens hated the rough justice doled out here. Locals still spit on the heart in the pavement. Go ahead...do as the locals do—land one right in the heart of the heart. By the way,

Edinburgh has two soccer teams—Heart of Midlothian (known as "Hearts") and Hibernian ("Hibs"). If you're a Hibs fan, spit again.

• *Make your way to the entrance of the church.*

❺ St. Giles' Cathedral

This is the flagship of the Church of Scotland (Scotland's largest denomination)—called the "Mother Church of Presbyterianism." The interior serves as a kind of Scottish Westminster Abbey, filled with monuments, statues, plaques, and stained-glass windows dedicated to great Scots and moments in history.

A church has stood on this spot since 854, though this structure is an architectural hodgepodge, dating mostly from the 15th through 19th century. In the 16th century, St. Giles' was a kind of national stage on which the drama of the Reformation was played out. The reformer John Knox (1514-1572) was the preacher here. His fiery sermons helped turn once-Catholic Edinburgh into a bastion of Protestantism. During the Scottish Reformation, St. Giles' was transformed from a Catholic cathedral to a Presbyterian church. The spacious interior is well worth a visit, and described in my self-guided tour on page 727.

• *Facing the church entrance, curl around its right side, into a parking lot.*

Sights Around St. Giles'

The grand building across the parking lot from St. Giles' is the **Old Parliament House.** Since the 13th century, the king had ruled a rubber-stamp parliament of nobles and bishops. But the Protestant Reformation promoted democracy, and the parliament gained real power. From the early 1600s until 1707, this building evolved to become the seat of a true parliament of elected officials. That came to an end in 1707, when Scotland signed an Act of Union, joining what's known today as the United Kingdom and giving up their right to self-rule. (More on that later in the walk.) If you're curious to peek inside, head through the door at #11 (free, described on page 731).

The great reformer **John Knox** is buried—with appropriate austerity—under parking lot spot #23. The statue among the cars shows King Charles II riding to a toga party back in 1685.

• *Continue on through the parking lot, around the back end of the church.*

Every Scottish burgh (town licensed by the king to trade) had three standard features: a "tolbooth" (basically a town hall, with a courthouse, meeting room, and jail); a "tron" (official weighing

scale); and a "mercat" (or market) cross. The **mercat cross** standing just behind St. Giles' Cathedral has a slender column decorated with a unicorn holding a flag with the cross of St. Andrew. Royal proclamations have been read at this mercat cross since the 14th century. In 1952, a town crier heralded the news that Britain had a new queen—three days after the actual event (traditionally the time it took for a horse to speed here from London). Today, Mercat Cross is the meeting point for many of Edinburgh's walking tours—both historic and ghostly.

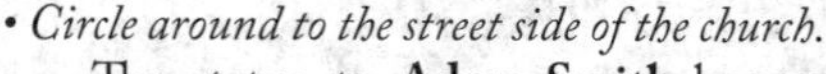

• *Circle around to the street side of the church.*

The statue to **Adam Smith** honors the Edinburgh author of the pioneering *Wealth of Nations* (1776), in which he laid out the economics of free market capitalism. Smith theorized that an "invisible hand" wisely guides the unregulated free market. Stand in front of Smith and imagine the intellectual energy of Edinburgh in the mid-1700s, when it was Europe's most enlightened city. Adam Smith was right in the center of it. He and David Hume were good friends. James Boswell, the famed biographer of Samuel Johnson, took classes from Smith. James Watt, inventor of the steam engine, was another proud Scotsman of the age. With great intellectuals like these, Edinburgh helped create the modern world. The poet Robert Burns, geologist James Hutton (who's considered the father of modern geology), and the publishers of the first *Encyclopedia Britannica* all lived in Edinburgh. Steeped in the inquisitive mindset of the Enlightenment, they applied cool rationality and a secular approach to their respective fields.

• *Head on down the Royal Mile.*

❻ More of High Street

A few steps downhill, at #188 (on the right), is the **Police Information Center.** This place provides a pleasant police presence (say that three times) and a little local law-and-order history to boot. Ask the officer on duty about the impact of modern technology and budget austerity on police work today. Seriously—drop in and discuss whatever law-and-order issue piques your curiosity (free, open daily 10:00-17:30, Aug until 21:30).

Continuing down this stretch of the Royal Mile, which is traffic-free most of the day (notice the bollards that raise and lower for permitted traffic), you'll see the Fringe Festival office (at #180), street musicians, and another wellhead (with horse "sippies," dating from 1675).

Notice those **three red boxes.** In the 20th century, people used these to make telephone calls to each other. (Imagine that!) These cast-iron booths are produced for all of Britain here in Scotland. As phone booths are decommissioned, some are finding new use as tiny shops, ATMs, and even showing up in residential neighborhoods as nostalgic garden decorations.

At the next intersection, on the left is **Cockburn Street** (pronounced "COE-burn"). This was cut through High Street's dense wall of medieval skyscrapers in the 1860s to give easy access to the Georgian New Town and the train station. Notice how the sliced buildings were thoughtfully capped with facades that fit the aesthetic look of the Royal Mile. In the Middle Ages, only tiny lanes (like Fleshmarket Close just uphill from Cockburn Street) interrupted the long line of Royal Mile buildings. These days, Cockburn Street has a reputation for its eclectic independent shops and string of trendy bars and eateries.

• *When you reach the* ***Tron Church*** *(17th century, currently housing a shopping center), you're at the intersection of* ***North and South Bridge streets.*** *These major streets lead left to Waverley Station and right to the Dalkeith Road B&Bs. Several handy bus lines run along here.*

This is the halfway point of this walk. Stand on the corner diagonally across from the church. Look up to the top of the Royal Mile at the Hub and its 240-foot spire. Notwithstanding its turret and 16th-century charm, the **Radisson Blu Hotel** just across the street is entirely new construction (1990), built to fit in. The city is protecting its historic look. The **Inn on the Mile** next door was once a fancy bank with a lavish interior. As modern banks are moving away from city centers, sumptuous buildings like these are being converted into ornate pubs and restaurants.

In the next block downhill are three **characteristic pubs,** side by side, that offer free traditional Scottish and folk music in the evenings. Notice the chimneys. Tenement buildings shared stairways and entries, but held individual apartments, each with its own chimney. Take a look back at the spire of St. Giles' Cathedral—inspired by the Scottish crown and the thistle, Scotland's national flower.

• *Go down High Street another block, passing near the* ***Museum of Childhood*** *(on the right, at #42, and worth a stop;* *see page 732**) and a fragrant* ***fudge shop*** *a few doors down, where you can sample various flavors (tempting you to buy a slab).*

Directly across the street, just below another wellhead, is the...

❼ John Knox House

Remember that Knox was a towering figure in Edinburgh's history, converting Scotland to a Calvinist style of Protestantism. His religious bent was "Presbyterianism," in which parishes are governed by elected officials rather than appointed bishops. This more democratic brand of Christianity also spurred Scotland toward political democracy. If you're interested in Knox or the Reformation, this sight is worth a visit (see page 732). Full disclosure: It's not certain that Knox ever actually lived here. Attached to the Knox House is the Scottish Storytelling Centre, where locals with the gift of gab perform regularly; check the posted schedule.

• *A few steps farther down High Street, at the intersection with St. Mary's and Jeffrey streets, you'll reach...*

❽ The World's End

For centuries, a wall stood here, marking the end of the burgh of Edinburgh. For residents within the protective walls of the city, this must have felt like the "world's end," indeed. The area beyond was called Canongate, a monastic community associated with Holyrood Abbey. At the intersection, find the brass bricks in the street that trace the gate (demolished in 1764). Look to the right down St. Mary's Street about 200 yards to see a surviving bit of that old wall, known as the **Flodden Wall.** In the 1513 Battle of Flodden, the Scottish king James IV made the disastrous decision to invade northern England. James and 10,000 of his Scotsmen were killed. Fearing a brutal English counterattack, Edinburgh scrambled to reinforce its broken-down city wall.

The pub on the corner, **No. 1 High Street,** is a centrally-located venue for live traditional music—pop in and see what's on tonight. Several other interesting shops are within a few steps of this spot. To the left, down Jeffrey Street, you'll see Scotland's top tattoo parlor, and a supplier for a different kind of tattoo (the Scottish Regimental Store). Across the street from those is the recommended **Lickety Splits,** a fine candy (or "sweets") shop and art gallery.

• *Continue down the Royal Mile—leaving old Edinburgh—as High Street changes names to...*

❾ Canongate

About 10 steps down Canongate, look left down Cranston Street (past the train tracks) to a good view of the Calton Cemetery up on **Calton Hill.** The obelisk, called Martyrs' Monument, remembers a group of 18th-century patriots exiled by London to Australia for their reform politics.

The round building to the left is the grave of philosopher David Hume. And the big turreted building to the right was the jail master's house. Today, the main reason to go up Calton Hill is for the fine views (described on page 755).

The giant blocky building that dominates the lower slope of the hill is **St. Andrew's House,** headquarters of the Scottish Government—including the office of the first minister of Scotland. According to locals, the building has also been an important base for MI6, Britain's version of the CIA. Wait a minute—isn't James Bond Scottish? Hmmm...

• *A couple of hundred yards farther along the Royal Mile (on the right at #172) you reach* ***Cadenhead's,*** *a serious place to sample and buy whisky (see page 760). About 30 yards farther along, you'll pass two worthwhile and free museums, the* ***People's Story Museum*** *(on the left, in the old tollhouse at #163) and* ***Museum of Edinburgh*** *(on the right, at #142; for more on both, see page 733). But our next stop is the church just across from the Museum of Edinburgh.*

The 1688 **Canongate Kirk** (Church)—located not far from the royal residence of Holyroodhouse—is where Queen Elizabeth II and her family worship whenever they're in town. (So don't sit in the front pew, marked with her crown.) The gilded emblem at the top of the roof, high above the door, has the antlers of a stag from the royal estate of Balmoral. The Queen's granddaughter married here in 2011.

The church is open only when volunteers have signed up to welcome visitors. Chat them up and borrow the description of the place. Then step inside the lofty blue and red interior, renovated with royal money; the church is filled with light and the flags of various Scottish regiments. In the narthex, peruse the photos of royal family events here, and find the list of priests and ministers of this parish—it goes back to 1143 (with a clear break with the Reformation in 1561).

Outside, turn right as you leave the church and walk up into the graveyard. The large gated grave (abutting the back of the People's Story Museum) is the affectionately-tended tomb of **Adam Smith,** the father of capitalism.

Just outside the churchyard, the statue on the sidewalk is of the poet **Robert Fergusson.** One of the first to write verse in the Scots language, he so inspired Robert Burns that Burns paid for Fergusson's tombstone in the Canongate churchyard and composed his epitaph.

Now look across the street at the **gabled house** next to the Museum of Edinburgh. Scan the facade to see shells put there in the 17th century to defend against the evil power of witches yet to be drowned.

• *Walk about 300 yards farther along. In the distance you can see the Palace of Holyroodhouse (the end of this walk) and soon, on the right, you'll come to the modern Scottish parliament building.*

Just opposite the parliament building is **White Horse Close** (on the left, in the white arcade). Step into this 17th-century courtyard. It was from here that the Edinburgh stagecoach left for London. Eight days later, the horse-drawn carriage would pull into its destination: Scotland Yard. Note that bus #35 leaves in two directions from here—downhill for the Royal Yacht *Britannia,* and uphill along the Royal Mile (as far as South Bridge) and on to the National Museum of Scotland.

• *Now walk up around the corner to the flagpoles (flying the flags of Europe, Britain, and Scotland) in front of the...*

⑩ Scottish Parliament Building

Finally, after centuries of history, we reach the 21st century. And finally, after three centuries of London rule, Scotland has a parliament building...in Scotland. When Scotland united with England in 1707, its parliament was dissolved. But in 1999, the Scottish parliament was reestablished, and in 2004, it moved into this striking new home. Notice how the eco-friendly building, by the Catalan architect Enric Miralles, mixes wild angles, lots of light, bold windows, oak, and native stone into a startling complex. (People from Catalunya—another would-be breakaway nation—have an affinity for Scotland.) From the front of the parliament building, look in the distance at the rocky Salisbury Crags, with people hiking the traverse up to the dramatic next summit called Arthur's Seat. Now look at the building in relation to the craggy cliffs. The architect envisioned the building as if it were rising right from the base of Arthur's Seat, almost bursting from the rock.

Since it celebrates Scottish democracy, the architecture is not a statement of authority. There are no statues of old heroes. There's not even a grand entry. You feel like you're entering an office park. Given its neighborhood, the media often calls the Scottish Parliament "Holyrood" for short (similar to calling the US Congress "Capitol Hill"). For details on touring the building and seeing parliament in action, see page 734.

• *Across the street is the **Queen's Gallery,** where she shares part of her* *amazing personal art collection in excellent revolving exhibits (see page 736). Finally, walk to the end of the road (Abbey Strand), and step up to the impressive wrought-iron gate of the Queen's palace. Look up at the stag with its holy cross, or "holy rood," on its forehead, and peer into the palace grounds. (The ticket office and palace entryway, a fine café, and a handy WC are just through the arch on the right.)*

⓫ Palace of Holyroodhouse

Since the 16th century, this palace has marked the end of the Royal Mile. An abbey—part of a 12th-century Augustinian monastery—originally stood in its place. While most of that old building is gone, you can see the surviving nave behind the palace on the left. According to one legend, it was named "holy rood" for a piece of the cross, brought here as a relic by Queen (and later Saint) Margaret. (Another version of the story is that King David I, Margaret's son, saw the image of a cross upon a stag's head while hunting here and took it as a sign that he should build an abbey on the site.) Because Scotland's royalty preferred living at Holyroodhouse to the blustery castle on the rock, the palace grew over time. If the Queen's not visiting, the palace welcomes visitors (see page 735 for details).

• *Your walk—from the castle to the palace, with so much Scottish history packed in between—is complete. And, if your appetite is whetted for more, don't worry; you've just scratched the surface. Enjoy the rest of Edinburgh.*

BONNIE WEE NEW TOWN WALK

Many visitors, mesmerized by the Royal Mile, never venture to the New Town. And that's a shame. With some of the city's finest Georgian architecture (from its 18th-century boom period), the New Town has a completely different character than the Old Town. This self-guided walk—worth ▲▲—gives you a quick orientation. "Part 1" takes about 45 minutes and helps you get your bearings; "Part 2" is more lightly narrated and connects you to one of the New Town's best sights, the Georgian House, in another 30 minutes.

Part 1: Into the New Town

• *Begin on Waverley Bridge, spanning the gully between the Old and New towns; to get there from the Royal Mile, just head down the curved Cockburn Street near the Tron Church (or cut down any of the "close"*

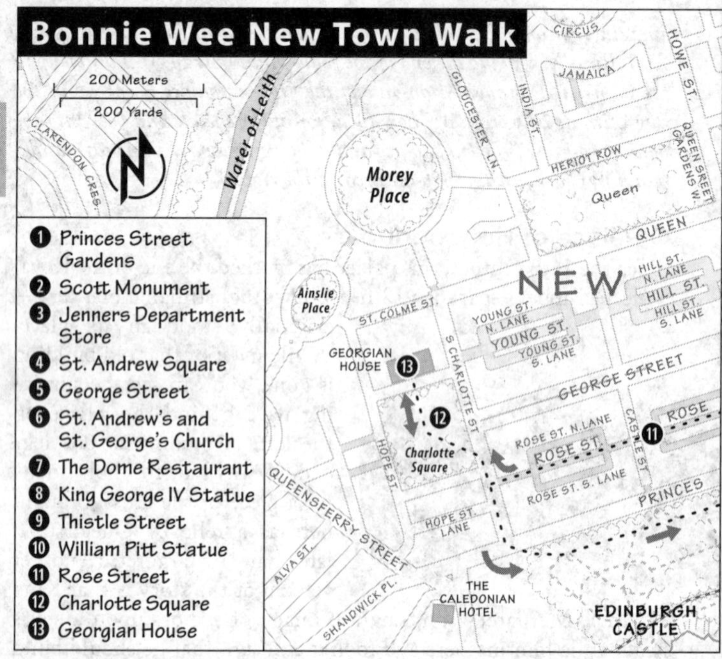

lanes opposite St. Giles' Cathedral). Stand on the bridge overlooking the train tracks, facing the castle.

View from Waverley Bridge: From this vantage point, you can enjoy fine views of medieval Edinburgh, with its 10-story-plus "skyscrapers." It's easy to imagine how miserably crowded this area was, prompting the expansion of the city during the Georgian period. Pick out landmarks along the Royal Mile, most notably the open-work steeple of St. Giles'.

A big lake called the **Nor' Loch** once was to the north (nor') of the Old Town; now it's a valley between Edinburgh's two towns. The lake was drained around 1800 as part of the expansion. Before that, the lake was the town's water reservoir...and its sewer. Much has been written about the town's infamous stink (a.k.a. the "flowers of Edinburgh"). The town's nickname, "Auld Reekie," referred to both the smoke of its industry and the stench of its squalor.

The long-gone loch was also a handy place for drowning witches. With their thumbs tied to their ankles, they'd be lashed to dunking stools. Those who survived the ordeal were considered "aided by the devil" and burned as witches. If they died, they were innocent and given a good Christian burial. Edinburgh was Europe's witch-burning mecca—any perceived "sign," including a small birthmark, could condemn you. Scotland burned more witches per capita than any other country—17,000 souls between 1479 and 1722.

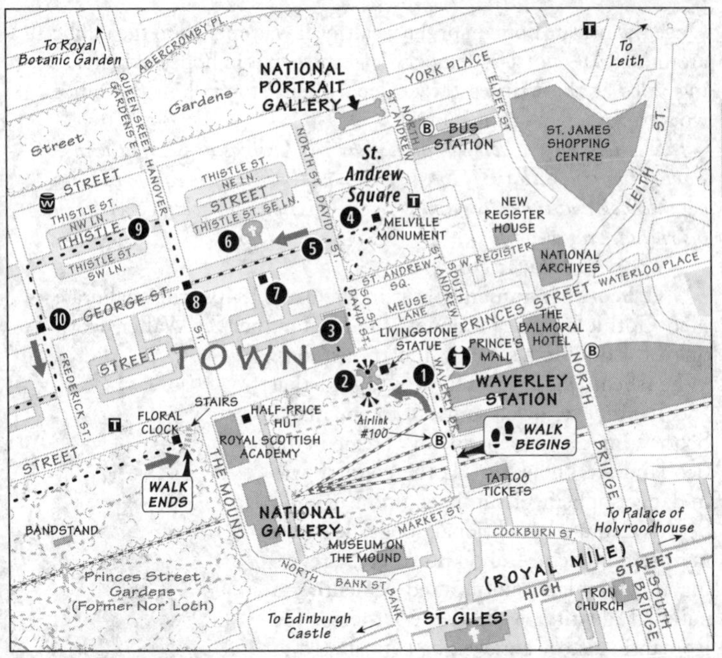

Visually trace the train tracks as they disappear into a tunnel below the **Scottish National Gallery** (with lesser-known paintings by great European artists; you can visit at the end of Part 1 of this walk—see page 741). The two fine Neoclassical buildings of the National Gallery date from the 1840s and sit upon a mound that's called, well, **The Mound.** When the New Town was built, tons of rubble from the excavations were piled here (1781-1830), forming a dirt bridge that connected the new development with the Old Town to allay merchant concerns about being cut off from the future heart of the city.

Turning 180 degrees (and facing the ramps down into the train station), notice the huge turreted building with the clock tower. **The Balmoral** was one of the city's two grand hotels during its glory days (its opposite bookend, The Caledonian, sits at the far end of the former lakebed—near the end of this walk). Aristocrats arriving by train could use a hidden entrance to go from the platform directly up to their plush digs. (Today The Balmoral is known mostly as the place where J. K. Rowling completed the final Harry Potter book.)

• *Now walk across the bridge toward the New Town. Before the corner, enter the gated gardens on the left, and head toward the big, pointy monument. You're at the edge of...*

❶ **Princes Street Gardens:** This grassy park, filling the former lakebed, offers a wonderful escape from the bustle of the city.

Once the private domain of the wealthy, it was opened to the public around 1870—not as a democratic gesture, but in hopes of increasing sales at the Princes Street department stores. Join the office workers for a picnic lunch break.

• *Take a seat on the bench indicated by the Livingstone (Dr. Livingstone, I presume?) statue. (The Victorian explorer is well-equipped with a guidebook, but is hardly packing light—his lion skin doesn't even fit in his rucksack carry-on.)*

Look up at the towering...

❷ **Scott Monument:** Built in the early 1840s, this elaborate Neo-Gothic monument honors the great author Sir Walter Scott, one of Edinburgh's many illustrious sons. When Scott died in 1832, it was said that "Scotland never owed so much to one man." Scott almost singlehandedly created the Scotland we know. Just as the country was in danger of being assimilated into England, Scott celebrated traditional songs, legends, myths, architecture, and kilts, thereby reviving the Highland culture and cementing a national identity. And, as the father of the Romantic historical novel, he contributed to Western literature in general. The 200-foot monument shelters a marble statue of Scott and his favorite pet, Maida, a deerhound who was one of 30 canines this dog lover owned during his lifetime. They're surrounded by busts of 16 great Scottish poets and 64 characters from his books. Climbing the tight, stony spiral staircase of 287 steps earns you a peek at a tiny museum midway, a fine city view at the top, and intimate encounters going up and down (£4; daily 10:00-19:00, until 16:00 Oct-March, tel. 0131/529-4068). For more on Scott, see page 726.

• *Exit the gate near Livingstone and head across busy Princes Street to the venerable...*

❸ **Jenners Department Store:** As you wait for the light to change (and wait...and wait...), notice how statues of women support the building—just as real women support the business. The arrival of new fashions here was such a big deal in the old days that they'd announce it by flying flags on the Nelson Monument atop Calton Hill.

Step inside and head upstairs into the grand skylit

atrium. The central space—filled with a towering tree at Christmas—is classic Industrial Age architecture. The Queen's coat of arms high on the wall indicates she shops here.

• *From the atrium, turn right and exit onto South St. David Street. Turn left and follow this street uphill one block up to...*

❹ **St. Andrew Square:** This green space is dedicated to the patron saint of Scotland. In the early 19th century, there were no shops around here—just fine residences; this was a private garden for the fancy people living here. Now open to the public, the square is a popular lunch hangout for workers. The Melville Monument honors a power-monger member of parliament who, for four decades (around 1800), was nicknamed the "uncrowned king of Scotland."

At the far corner of the park is the city's bus station, and beside it, the St. James Shopping Centre. And one block to the left is the excellent **Scottish National Portrait Gallery,** which introduces you to all of the biggest names in Scottish history (for a self-guided tour, see page 746).

• *Follow the Melville Monument's gaze straight ahead out of the park. Cross the street and stand at the top of...*

❺ **George Street:** This is the main drag of Edinburgh's grid-planned New Town. Laid out in 1776, when King George III was busy putting down a revolution in a troublesome overseas colony, the New Town was a model of urban planning in its day. The architectural style is "Georgian"—British for "Neoclassical." And the street plan came with an unambiguous message: to celebrate the union of Scotland with England into the United Kingdom. (This was particularly important, since Scotland was just two decades removed from the failed Jacobite uprising of Bonnie Prince Charlie.)

St. Andrew Square (patron saint of Scotland) and Charlotte Square (George III's queen) bookend the New Town, with its three main streets named for the royal family of the time (George, Queen, and Princes). Thistle and Rose streets—which we'll see on Part 2 of this walk—are named for the national flowers of Scotland and England.

The plan for the New Town was the masterstroke of the 23-year-old urban designer James Craig. George Street—20 feet wider than the others (so a four-horse carriage could make a U-turn)—was the main drag. Running down the high spine of the area, it afforded grand unobstructed views (thanks to the parks on either side) of the River Forth in one direction and the Old Town in the other. As you stroll down the street, you'll notice that Craig's grid is a series of axes designed to connect monuments new and old; later architects made certain to continue this harmony. For example, notice that the Scott Monument lines up perfectly with this first intersection.

• *Halfway down the first block of George Street, on the right, is...*

❻ **St. Andrew's and St. George's Church:** Designed as part of the New Town plan in the 1780s, the church is a product of the Scottish Enlightenment. It has an elliptical plan (the first in Britain) so that all can focus on the pulpit. If it's open, step inside. A fine leaflet tells the story of the church, and a handy cafeteria downstairs serves cheap and cheery lunches.

Directly across the street from the church is another temple, this one devoted to money. This former bank building (now housing the recommended restaurant ❼ **The Dome**) has a pediment filled with figures demonstrating various ways to make money, which they do with all the nobility of classical gods. Consider scurrying across the street and ducking inside to view the stunning domed atrium.

Continue down George Street to the intersection with a ❽ statue commemorating the visit by **King George IV.** Notice the particularly fine axis formed by this cross-street: the National Gallery lines up perfectly with the Royal Mile's skyscrapers and the former Tolbooth Church, creating a Gotham City collage.

• *Part 1 of our walk is finished; by now you've gotten your New Town bearings. If you were to turn left and head down Hanover Street, in a block you'd run into the Scottish National Gallery; the street behind it curves back up to the Royal Mile.*

But to see more of the New Town—including the Georgian House, offering an insightful look inside one of these fine 18th-century homes—stick with me for a few more long blocks through the rest of the New Town.

Part 2: Zigzag Through New Town to the Georgian House

You could continue straight down George Street—lined with ritzy hotels and glitzy bars—to Charlotte Square and the Georgian House. But we'll detour just a bit, zigzagging through side streets to see the various personalities that inhabit this rigid grid.

• *Turn right on Hanover Street; after just one (short) block, cross over and go down...*

❾ **Thistle Street:** Of the many streets in the New Town, this has perhaps the most vivid Scottish character. And that's fitting, as it's named after Scotland's national flower. At the beginning and end of the street, also notice that Craig's street plan included tranquil cul-de-sacs within the larger blocks. Thistle Street seems sleepy, but holds characteristic shops—especially fashionable clothing boutiques—and enticing restaurants (several are recommended later, under "Shopping in Edinburgh" and "Eating in Edinburgh"). For example, halfway down the street on the left, Howie Nicholsby's shop 21st Century Kilt updates traditional Scottish menswear.

You'll pop out at Frederick Street. Turning left, you'll see a ⑩ statue of **William Pitt,** prime minister under King George III. (Pitt's father gave his name to the American city of Pittsburgh—which Scots pronounce as "Pitts-burrah"...I assume.)

• *For an interesting contrast, we'll continue down another side street. Pass the statue of Pitt (heading toward Edinburgh Castle) and turn right onto...*

⑪ **Rose Street:** As a rose is to a thistle, and as England is to Scotland, so is brash, boisterous Rose Street to sedate, thoughtful Thistle Street. This stretch of Rose Street feels more commercialized, jammed with chain stores; the second block is packed with pubs and restaurants. As you walk, keep an eye out for the cobbled Tudor rose embedded in the brick sidewalk. When you cross the aptly-named Castle Street, linger over the grand views to Edinburgh Castle. It's almost as if they planned it this way... just for the views.

• *Popping out at the far end of Rose Street, across the street and to your right is...*

⑫ **Charlotte Square:** The building of the New Town started cheap with St. Andrew Square, but finished well with this stately space. In 1791, the Edinburgh town council asked the prestigious Scottish architect Robert Adam to pump up the design for Charlotte Square. The council hoped that Adam's plan would answer criticism that the New Town buildings lacked innovation or ambi-

tion—and they got what they wanted. Adam's design, which raised the standard of New Town architecture to "international class," created Edinburgh's finest Georgian square.

• *Along the right side of Charlotte Square, at #7 (just left of the pointy pediment), you can pay a visit to the* ⓭ ***Georgian House,*** *which gives you a great peek behind all of these harmonious Neoclassical facades* *(see page 749)**.*

When you're done touring the house, you can head back through the New Town grid, perhaps taking some different streets than the way you came. Or, for a restful return to our starting point, consider this...

Return Through Princes Street Gardens: From Charlotte Square, drop down to busy Princes Street (noticing The Caledonian hotel—the grand twin sister of The Balmoral at the start of our walk). But rather than walking along the busy bus-and-tram-lined shopping drag, head into **Princes Street Gardens** instead. With the castle looming overhead, you'll pass a playground, a fanciful Victorian fountain, more monuments to great Scots, war memorials, and a bandstand (which hosts Scottish country dancing—see page 765—as well as occasional big-name acts). Finally you'll reach a staircase up to the Scottish National Gallery; notice the oldest **floral clock** in the world on your left as you climb up.

• *Our walk is over. From here, you can tour the gallery; head up Bank Street just behind it to reach the Royal Mile; hop on a bus along Princes Street to your next stop (or B&B); or continue through another stretch of the Princes Street Gardens to the Scott Monument and our starting point.*

Sights in Edinburgh

▲▲▲EDINBURGH CASTLE

The fortified birthplace of the city 1,300 years ago, this imposing symbol of Edinburgh sits proudly on a rock high above you. The home of Scotland's kings and queens for centuries, the castle has witnessed royal births, medieval pageantry, and bloody sieges. Today it's a complex of various buildings, some dating from the 12th century, linked by cobbled roads that survive from its more recent use as a military garrison. The castle—with expansive views, plenty of history, and the stunning crown jewels of Scotland—is a fascinating and multifaceted sight that deserves several hours of your time.

Cost and Hours: £16.50, daily April-Sept 9:30-18:00, Oct-

March 9:30-17:00, last entry one hour before closing, tel. 0131/225-9846, www.edinburghcastle.gov.uk.

Avoiding Lines: The castle is usually least crowded after 14:00 or so; if planning a morning visit, the earlier the better. To avoid ticket lines (worst in Aug), book online and print your ticket at home. You can also pick up your prebooked ticket at machines just inside the entrance or at the Visitor Information desk a few steps uphill on the right. You can also skip the ticket line with a Historic Scotland Explorer Pass (see page 993 for details).

Getting There: Simply walk up the Royal Mile (if arriving by bus from the Dalkeith Road B&B area, get off at South Bridge and huff up the Mile for about 15 minutes). Taxis get you closer, dropping you a block below the esplanade at the Hub/Tolbooth Church.

Tours: Thirty-minute introductory **guided tours** are free with admission (2-4/hour, depart from Argyle Battery, see clock for next departure; fewer off-season). The informative **audioguide** provides four hours of descriptions, including the National War Museum Scotland (£3 if you purchase with your ticket; £3.50 if you rent it once inside).

Services: The clean WC at the entry routinely wins "British Loo of the Year" awards. For lunch, you have two choices. **The Redcoat Café**—located within Edinburgh Castle—is a big, bright, efficient cafeteria with great views (£6-10 quick, healthy meals). Punctuate the two parts of your castle visit (the castle itself and the impressive National War Museum) with a smart break here. The **Tea Rooms,** at the top of the hill directly across from the crown jewels, serves £10-15 sit-down meals in its tight space.

➲ Self-Guided Tour

From the ❶ **entry gate,** start winding your way uphill toward the main sights—the crown jewels and the Royal Palace—located near the summit. Since the castle was protected on three sides by sheer cliffs, the main defense had to be here at the entrance. During the castle's heyday in the 1500s, a 100-foot tower loomed overhead, facing the city.

• *Passing through the portcullis gate, you reach the...*

❷ **Argyle (Six-Gun) Battery, with View:** These front-loading

Edinburgh Castle

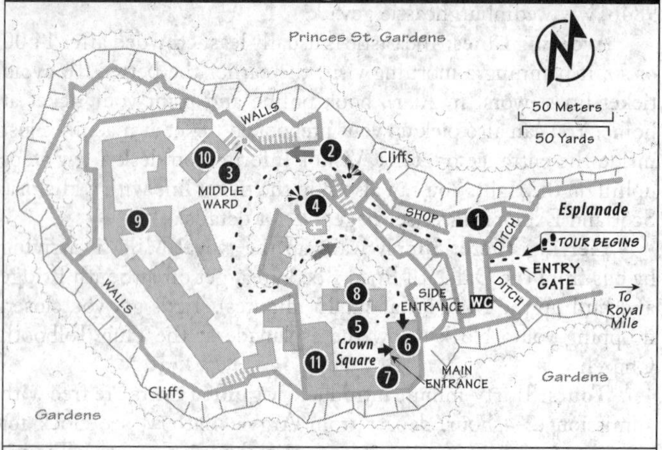

Princes St. Gardens
WALLS
Cliffs
MIDDLE WARD
SHOP
Esplanade
DITCH
TOUR BEGINS
ENTRY GATE
SIDE ENTRANCE
WC
To Royal Mile
Crown Square
MAIN ENTRANCE
Gardens
Cliffs
Gardens
50 Meters
50 Yards

Tour

1. Entry Gate & Tickets
2. Argyle Battery
3. One O'Clock Gun
4. St. Margaret's Chapel, Mons Meg & Dog Cemetery
5. Crown Square
6. Scottish Crown Jewels (Honours of Scotland)
7. Royal Apartments
8. Scottish National War Memorial
9. National War Museum Scotland

Eateries

10. Redcoat Café
11. Tea Rooms

cast-iron cannons are from the Napoleonic era (c. 1800), when the castle was still a force to be reckoned with.

From here, look north across the valley to the grid of the New Town. The valley sits where the Nor' Loch once was; this lake was drained and filled in when the New Town was built in the late 1700s, its swamps replaced with gardens. Later the land provided sites for the Greek-temple-esque Scottish National Gallery and Waverley Station. Looking farther north, you can make out the port town of Leith with its high-rises and cranes, the Firth of Forth, the island of Inchkeith, and—in the far, far distance (to the east)—the cone-like mountain of North Berwick Law, a former volcano.

Now look down. The sheer north precipice looks impregnable. But on the night of March 14, 1314, 30 armed men silently scaled this rock face. They were loyal to Robert the Bruce and determined to recapture the castle, which had fallen into English hands. They caught the English by surprise, took the castle, and—three months later—Bruce defeated the English at the Battle of Bannockburn.

• *A little farther along, near the café, is the...*

❸ **One O'Clock Gun:** Crowds gather for the 13:00 gun blast, a tradition that gives ships in the bay something to set their navigational devices by. Before the gun, sailors set their clocks with help from the Nelson Monument—that's the tall pillar in the distance on Calton Hill. The monument has a "time ball" affixed to the cross on top, which drops precisely at the top of the hour. But on foggy days, ships couldn't see the ball, so the cannon shot was instituted instead (1861). The tradition stuck, every day at 13:00. (Locals joke that the frugal Scots don't fire it at high noon, as that would cost 11 extra rounds a day.)

• *Continue uphill, winding to the left and passing through Foog's Gate. At the very top of the hill, on your left, is...*

❹ **St. Margaret's Chapel:** This tiny stone chapel is Edinburgh's oldest building (around 1120) and sits atop its highest point (440 feet). It represents the birth of the city.

In 1057, Malcolm III murdered King Macbeth (of Shakespeare fame) and assumed the Scottish throne. Later, he married Princess Margaret, and the family settled atop this hill. Their marriage united Malcolm's Highland Scots with Margaret's Lowland Anglo-Saxons—the cultural mix that would define Edinburgh.

Step inside the tiny unadorned church—a testament to Margaret's reputed piety. The style is Romanesque. The nave is wonderfully simple, with classic Norman zigzags decorating the round arch that separates the tiny nave from the sacristy. You'll see a facsimile of St. Margaret's 11th-century gospel book. The small (modern) stained-glass windows feature St. Margaret herself, St. Columba and St. Ninian (who brought Christianity to Scotland via Iona), St. Andrew (Scotland's patron saint), and William Wallace (the defender of Scotland). These days, the place is popular for weddings. (As it seats only 20, it's particularly popular with brides' parents.)

Margaret died at the castle in 1093, and her son King David I built this chapel in her honor (she was sainted in 1250). David expanded the castle and also founded Holyrood Abbey, across town. These two structures were soon linked by a Royal Mile of buildings, and Edinburgh was born.

Mons Meg, in front of the church, is a huge and once-upon-a-time frightening 15th-century siege cannon that fired 330-pound stones nearly two miles. Imagine. It was a gift from Philip the Good, duke of Burgundy, to his great-niece's husband King James II of Scotland.

Nearby, belly up to the banister and look down to find the **Dog Cemetery,** a tiny patch of grass with a sweet little line of doggie tombstones, marking the graves of soldiers' faithful canines in arms.

• *Continue on, curving downhill into...*

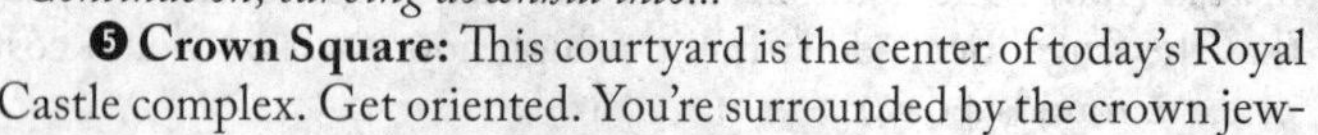

❺ **Crown Square:** This courtyard is the center of today's Royal Castle complex. Get oriented. You're surrounded by the crown jewels, the Royal Palace (with its Great Hall), and the Scottish National War Memorial.

The castle has evolved over the centuries, and Crown Square is relatively "new." After the time of Malcolm and Margaret, the castle was greatly expanded by David II (1324-1371), complete with tall towers, a Great Hall, dungeon, cellars, and so on. This served as the grand royal residence for two centuries. Then, in 1571-1573, the Protestant citizens of Edinburgh laid siege to the castle and its Catholic/monarchist holdouts, eventually blasting it to smithereens. (You can tour the paltry remains of the medieval castle in nearby **David's Tower.**) The palace was rebuilt nearby—around what is today's Crown Square.

• *We'll tour the buildings around Crown Square. First up: the crown jewels. The main year-round entry to the jewels is on Crown Square. In summer, there's a second option that avoids the long line: Head to the left as you face the main entrance and find another entry (near the WCs). This route takes you through the Honours of Scotland exhibition—an interesting, Disney-esque series of displays (which often moves at a shuffle) telling the story of the crown jewels and how they survived the harrowing centuries, but without any actual artifacts.*

❻ **Scottish Crown Jewels (Honours of Scotland):** For centuries, Scotland's monarchs were crowned in elaborate rituals involving three wondrous objects: a jewel-studded crown, scepter, and sword. These objects—along with the ceremonial Stone of Scone (pronounced "skoon")—are known as the "Honours of Scotland." Scotland's crown jewels may not be as impressive as England's, but they're treasured by locals as a symbol of Scottish nationalism. They're also older than England's; while Oliver Cromwell destroyed England's jewels, the Scots managed to hide theirs.

History of the Jewels: The Honours of Scotland exhibit that leads up to the Crown Room traces the evolution of the jewels, the ceremony, and the often turbulent journey of this precious regalia. Here's the SparkNotes version:

In 1306, Robert the Bruce was crowned with a "circlet of gold" in a ceremony at Scone—a town 40 miles north of Edinburgh, which Scotland's earliest kings had claimed as their capital. Around 1500, King James IV added two new items to the coronation ceremony—a scepter (a gift from the pope) and a huge sword (a gift from another pope). In 1540, James V had the original crown augmented by an Edinburgh goldsmith, giving it the imperial-crown shape it has today.

These Honours were used to crown every monarch: nine-month-old Mary, Queen of Scots (she cried); her one-year-old son James VI (future king of England); and Charles I and II. But the days of divine-right rulers were numbered.

In 1649, the parliament had Charles I (king of both England and Scotland) beheaded. Soon Cromwell's rabid English antiroyalists were marching on Edinburgh. Quick! Legend says two women scooped up the crown and sword, hid them in their skirts and belongings, and buried them in a church far to the northeast until the coast was clear.

When the monarchy was restored, the regalia were used to crown Scotland's last king, Charles II (1660). Then, in 1707, the Treaty of Union with England ended Scotland's independence. The Honours came out for a ceremony to bless the treaty, and were then locked away in a strongbox in the castle. There they lay for over a century, until Sir Walter Scott—the writer and great champion of Scottish tradition—forced a detailed search of the castle in 1818. The box was found...and there the Honours were, perfectly preserved. Within a few years, they were put on display, as they have been ever since.

The crown's most recent official appearance was in 1999, when it was taken across town to the grand opening of the reinstated parliament, marking a new chapter in the Scottish nation. As it represents the monarchy, the crown is present whenever a new session of parliament opens. (And if Scotland ever secedes, you can be sure that crown will be in the front row.)

The Honours: Finally, you enter the Crown Room to see the regalia itself. The four-foot steel **sword** was made in Italy under orders of Pope Julius II (the man who also commissioned Michelangelo's Sistine Chapel and St. Peter's Basilica). The **scepter** is made of silver, covered with gold, and topped with a rock crystal and a

William Wallace (c. 1270-1305)

In 1286, Scotland's king died without an heir, plunging the prosperous country into a generation of chaos. As Scottish nobles bickered over naming a successor, the English King Edward I—nicknamed "Longshanks" because of his height—invaded and assumed power (1296). He placed a figurehead on the throne, forced Scottish nobles to sign a pledge of allegiance to England (the "Ragman's Roll"), moved the British parliament north to York, and took the highly symbolic Stone of Scone to London, where it would remain for centuries.

WILLIAM WALLACE.

A year later, the Scots rose up against Edward, led by William Wallace (popularized in the film *Braveheart*). A mix of history and legend portrays Wallace as the son of a poor-but-knightly family that refused to sign the Ragman's Roll. Exceptionally tall and strong, he learned Latin and French from two uncles, who were priests. In his teenage years, his father and older brother were killed by the English. Later, he killed an English sheriff to avenge the death of his wife, Marion. Wallace's rage inspired his fellow Scots to revolt.

In the summer of 1297, Wallace and his guerrillas scored a series of stunning victories over the English. On September 11, a well-equipped English army of 10,000 soldiers and 300 horsemen began crossing Stirling Bridge. Wallace's men attacked, and in the chaos, the bridge collapsed, splitting the English ranks in two. The ragtag Scots drove the confused English into the river. The Battle of Stirling Bridge was a rout, and Wallace was knighted and appointed guardian of Scotland.

All through the winter, King Edward's men chased Wallace, continually frustrated by the Scots' hit-and-run tactics. Finally, at the Battle of Falkirk (1298), they drew Wallace's men out onto the open battlefield. The English with their horses and archers easily destroyed the spear-carrying Scots. Wallace resigned in disgrace and went on the lam, while his successors negotiated truces with the English, finally surrendering unconditionally in 1304. Wallace alone held out.

In 1305, the English tracked him down and took him to London, where he was convicted of treason and mocked with a crown of oak leaves as the "king of outlaws." On August 23, they stripped him naked and dragged him to the execution site. There he was strangled to near death, castrated, and dismembered. His head was stuck on a spike atop London Bridge, while his body parts were sent on tour to spook would-be rebels. But Wallace's martyrdom only served to inspire his countrymen, and the torch of independence was picked up by Robert the Bruce (see page 721). Despite the *Braveheart* movie, Robert the Bruce, not Wallace, was considered the original "Braveheart." (For the full story, see page 847.)

pearl. The gem- and pearl-encrusted **crown** has an imperial arch topped with a cross. Legend says the band of gold in the center is the original crown that once adorned the head of Robert the Bruce.

The **Stone of Scone** (a.k.a. the "Stone of Destiny") sits plain and strong next to the jewels. It's a rough-hewn gray slab of sandstone, about 26 by 17 by 10 inches. As far back as the ninth century, Scotland's kings were crowned atop this stone, when it stood at the medieval capital of Scone. But in 1296, the invading army of Edward I of England carried the stone off to Westminster Abbey. For the next seven centuries, English (and subsequently British) kings and queens were crowned sitting on a coronation chair with the Stone of Scone tucked in a compartment underneath.

In 1950, four Scottish students broke into Westminster Abbey on Christmas Day and smuggled the stone back to Scotland in an act of foolhardy patriotism. But what could they do with it? After three months, they abandoned the stone, draped in Scotland's national flag. It was returned to Westminster Abbey, where (in 1953) Queen Elizabeth II was crowned atop it. In 1996, in recognition of increased Scottish autonomy, Elizabeth agreed to let the stone go home, on one condition: that it be returned to Westminster Abbey for all British coronations. One day, the next monarch of the United Kingdom—Prince Charles is first in line—will sit atop it, reenacting a coronation ritual that dates back a thousand years.

• *Exit the crown jewel display, heading down the stairs. But just before exiting into the courtyard, turn left through a door that leads into the...*

❼ **Royal Apartments:** Scottish royalty lived in the Royal Palace only when safety or protocol required it (they preferred the Palace of Holyroodhouse at the bottom of the Royal Mile). Here you can see several historic but unimpressive rooms. The first one, labeled **Queen Mary's Chamber,** is where Mary, Queen of Scots (1542-1587), gave birth to James VI of Scotland, who later became King James I of England. Nearby **Laich Hall** (Lower Hall) was the dining room of the royal family.

The **Great Hall** (through a separate entrance on Crown Square) was built by James IV to host the castle's official banquets and meetings. It's still used for such purposes today. Most of the interior—its fireplace, carved walls, pikes, and armor—is Victorian. But the well-constructed wood ceiling

is original. This hammer-beam roof (constructed like the hull of a ship) is self-supporting. The complex system of braces and arches distributes the weight of the roof outward to the walls, so there's no need for supporting pillars or long cross beams. Before leaving, look for the big iron-barred peephole above the fireplace on the right. This allowed the king to spy on his subjects while they partied.

• *Across the Crown Square courtyard is the...*

❽ **Scottish National War Memorial:** This commemorates the 149,000 Scottish soldiers lost in World War I, the 58,000 who died in World War II, and the nearly 800 (and counting) lost in British battles since. This is a somber spot (stow your camera and phone). Paid for by public donations, each bay is dedicated to a particular Scottish regiment. The main shrine, featuring a green Italian-marble memorial that contains the original WWI rolls of honor, sits on an exposed chunk of the castle rock. Above you, the archangel Michael is busy slaying a dragon. The bronze frieze accurately shows the attire of various wings of Scotland's military. The stained glass starts with Cain and Abel on the left, and finishes with a celebration of peace on the right. To appreciate how important this place is, consider that Scottish soldiers died at twice the rate of other British soldiers in World War I.

• *Our final stop is worth the five-minute walk to get there. Backtrack to the café (and One O'Clock Gun), then head downhill to the...*

❾ **National War Museum Scotland:** This thoughtful museum covers four centuries of Scottish military history. Instead of the usual musty, dusty displays of endless armor, there's a compelling mix of videos, uniforms, weapons, medals, mementos, and eloquent excerpts from soldiers' letters.

Here you'll learn the story of how the fierce and courageous Scottish warrior changed from being a symbol of resistance against Britain to being a champion of that same empire. Along the way, these military men received many decorations for valor and did more than their

Robert the Bruce (1274-1329)

In 1314, Robert the Bruce's men attacked Edinburgh's Royal Castle, recapturing it from the English. It was just one of many intense battles between the oppressive English and the plucky Scots during the Wars of Independence.

In this era, Scotland had to overcome not only its English foes but also its own divisiveness—and no one was more divided than Robert the Bruce. As earl of Carrick, he was born with blood ties to England and a long-standing family claim to the Scottish throne.

When England's King Edward I ("Longshanks") conquered Scotland in 1296, the Bruce family welcomed it, hoping Edward would defeat their rivals and put Bruce's father on the throne. They dutifully signed the "Ragman's Roll" of allegiance—and then Edward chose someone else as king.

Twentysomething Robert the Bruce (the "the" comes from his original family name of "de Bruce") then joined William Wallace's revolt against the English. Legend has it that it was he who knighted Wallace after the victory at Stirling Bridge. When Wallace fell from favor, Bruce became a guardian of Scotland (caretaker ruler in the absence of a king) and continued fighting the English. But when Edward's armies again got the upper hand in 1302, Robert—along with Scotland's other nobles—diplomatically surrendered and again pledged loyalty.

In 1306, Robert the Bruce murdered his chief rival and boldly claimed to be king of Scotland. Few nobles supported him. Edward crushed the revolt and kidnapped Bruce's wife, the Church excommunicated him, and Bruce went into hiding on a distant North Sea island. He was now the king of nothing. Legend says he gained inspiration by watching a spider patiently build its web.

The following year, Bruce returned to Scotland and wove alliances with both nobles and the Church, slowly gaining acceptance as Scotland's king by a populace chafing under English rule. On June 24, 1314, he decisively defeated the English (now led by Edward's weak son, Edward II) at the Battle of Bannockburn. After a generation of turmoil (1286-1314), England was finally driven from Scotland, and the country was united under Robert I, king of Scotland.

As king, Robert the Bruce's priority was to stabilize the monarchy and establish clear lines of succession. His descendants would rule Scotland for the next 400 years, and even today, Bruce blood runs through the veins of Queen Elizabeth II, Prince Charles, princes William and Harry, and wee George and Charlotte.

share of dying in battle. But even when fighting alongside—rather than against—England, Scottish regiments still promoted their romantic kilted-warrior image.

Queen Victoria fueled this ideal throughout the 19th century. She was infatuated with the Scottish Highlands and the culture's untamed, rustic mystique. Highland soldiers, especially officers, went to great personal expense to sport all their elaborate regalia, and the kilted men fought best to the tune of their beloved bagpipes. For centuries the stirring drone of bagpipes accompanied Highland soldiers into battle—raising their spirits and announcing to the enemy that they were about to meet a fierce and mighty foe.

This museum shows the human side of war as well as the cleverness of government-sponsored ad campaigns that kept the lads enlisting. Two centuries of recruiting posters make the same pitch that still works today: a hefty signing bonus, steady pay, and job security with the promise of a manly and adventurous life—all spiked with a mix of pride and patriotism.

Stepping outside the museum, you're surrounded by cannons that no longer fire, stony walls that tell an amazing story, dramatic views of this grand city, and the clatter of tourists (rather than soldiers) on cobbles. Consider for a moment all the bloody history and valiant struggles, along with British power and Scottish pride, that have shaped the city over which you are perched.

• *The statue in the courtyard in front of the War Museum is* ***Earl Haig****—the Scotsman who commanded the British Army through the horrifying WWI trench warfare of Flanders Fields.*

From here, there's only one way out—the same way you came in.

SIGHTS ON AND NEAR THE ROYAL MILE

Camera Obscura

A big deal when it was built in 1853, this observatory topped with a mirror reflected images onto a disc before the wide eyes of people who had never seen a photograph or a captured image. Today, you can climb 100 steps for an entertaining 20-minute demonstration (3/hour). At the top, enjoy the best view anywhere of the Royal Mile. Then work your way down through five floors of illusions, holograms, and early photos. This is a big hit with kids, but very overpriced. (It's less impressive on cloudy days.)

Cost and Hours: £14, daily July-Aug 9:00-21:00, April-June and Sept-Oct 9:30-18:00, Nov-March 10:00-17:00, last demo one hour before closing, tel. 0131/225-4239, www.camera-obscura.co.uk.

▲The Scotch Whisky Experience

This gimmicky attraction—consisting of a "Malt Disney" whisky-barrel ride through the whisky production process followed by an explanation of Scotland's four main whisky regions—seems designed only to distill £14 out of your pocket. It does succeed in providing an entertaining yet informative orientation to the creation of Scottish fire-water (things get pretty psychedelic when you hit the yeast stage). The 50-minute experience includes sampling a wee dram and the chance to stand amid the world's largest Scotch whisky collection (almost 3,500 bottles). At the end, you'll find yourself in the bar with a fascinating wall of unusually shaped whisky bottles. Serious connoisseurs should stick with the more substantial shops in town (for ideas, see page 760), but this place can be worthwhile for beginners—particularly those who won't take a more serious Scotland distillery tour elsewhere. (See sidebar for more on whisky and whisky tastings).

Cost and Hours: £14 "silver tour" includes one sample, £24.50 "gold tour" includes four samples—one from each main region, generally daily 10:00-18:00, tel. 0131/220-0441, www.scotchwhiskyexperience.co.uk.

▲▲Gladstone's Land

This is a typical 16th- to 17th-century merchant's "land," or tenement building. These multistory structures—in which merchants ran their shops on the ground floor and lived upstairs—were typical of the time (the word "tenement" didn't have the slum connotation then that it has today). At six stories, this one was still just half the height of the tallest "Gothic skyscrapers." Gladstone's Land comes complete with an almost-lived-in, furnished interior. The downstairs cloth shop and upstairs kitchen and living quarters are brought to life by talkative guides. Keep this place in mind as you stroll the rest of the Mile, imagining other houses as if they still looked like this on the inside. (For a comparison of life in the Old Town versus the New Town, also visit the Georgian House, described later.)

Cost and Hours: £6.50, daily July-Aug 10:00-18:30, April-

Whisky 101

Whisky is high on the experience list of most visitors to Scotland—even for teetotalers. Whether at a distillery, a shop, or a pub, be sure to try a few drams. (From the Gaelic word for "drink," a dram isn't necessarily a fixed amount—it's simply a small slug.) While touring a distillery is a ▲▲▲ Scottish experience, many fine whisky shops (including Cadenhead's in Edinburgh) offer guided tastings and a chance to have a small bottle filled from the cask of your choice.

Types of Whisky

Scotch whiskies come in two broad types: **"single malt,"** meaning that the bottle comes from a single batch made by a single distiller; and **"blends,"** which master blenders mix and match from various whiskies into a perfect punch of booze. While single malts get the most attention, blended whiskies represent 90 percent of all whisky sales. They tend to be light and mild—making them an easier way to tiptoe into the whisky scene.

There are more than 100 distilleries in Scotland, each one proud of its unique qualities. The **Lowlands,** around Edinburgh, produce light and refreshing whiskies—more likely to be taken as

June and Sept-Oct 10:00-17:00, closed Nov-March, no photos, tel. 0844-493-2120, www.nts.org.uk.

Writers' Museum at Lady Stair's House

This aristocrat's house, built in 1622, is filled with well-described manuscripts and knickknacks of Scotland's three greatest literary figures: Robert Burns, Robert Louis Stevenson, and Sir Walter Scott. If you'd like to see Scott's pipe and Burns' snuffboxes, you'll love this little museum. You'll wind up steep staircases through a maze of rooms as you peruse first editions and keepsakes of these celebrated writers. Edinburgh's high society gathered in homes like this in the 1780s to hear the great poet Robbie Burns read his work—it's meant to be read aloud rather than to oneself. In the Burns room, you can hear his poetry—worth a few minutes for anyone, and essential for fans.

Cost and Hours: Free, Mon-Sat 10:00-17:00, closed Sun except during Festival 12:00-17:00, tel. 0131/529-4901, www.edinburghmuseums.org.uk.

an aperitif. Whiskies from the **Highlands** and **Islands** range from floral and sweet (vanilla or honey) to smoky (peaty) and robust. **Speyside,** southeast of Inverness, is home to half of all Scottish distilleries. Mellow and fruity, Speyside whiskies can be the most accessible for beginners. The **Isle of Islay** is just the opposite, specializing in the peatiest, smokiest whiskies—not for novices. Only a few producers remain to distill the smoky and pungent **Campbeltown** whiskies in the southwest Highlands, near Islay.

Tasting Whisky

Tasting whisky is like tasting wine; you'll use all your senses. First, swirl the whisky in the glass and observe its color and "legs"—the trail left by the liquid as it runs back down the side of the glass (quick, thin legs indicate light, young whisky; slow, thick legs mean it's heavier and older one). Then take a deep sniff—do you smell smoke and peat? And finally, taste it (sip!). Adding a few drops of water is said to "open up the taste"—look for a little glass of water with a dropper standing by, and try tasting your whisky before and after.

A whisky's flavor is most influenced by three things: whether the malt is peat-smoked; the shape of the stills; and the composition of the casks. Even local climate can play a role; some island distilleries tout the salty notes of their whiskies, as the sea air permeates their casks.

Museum on the Mound

Located in the basement of the grand Bank of Scotland building, this exhibit tells the story of the bank, which was founded in 1695 (making it only a year younger than the Bank of England, and the longest operating bank in the world). Featuring displays on cash production, safe technology, and bank robberies, this museum struggles mightily to make banking interesting (the case holding £1 million is cool). It's worth popping in if you have extra time or find the subject appealing.

Cost and Hours: Free, Tue-Fri 10:00-17:00, Sat-Sun from 13:00, closed Mon, down Bank Street from the Royal Mile—follow the street around to the left and enter through the gate, tel. 0131/243-5464, www.museumonthemound.com.

▲▲St. Giles' Cathedral

This is Scotland's most important church. Its ornate spire—the Scottish crown steeple from 1495—is a proud part of Edinburgh's skyline. The fascinating interior contains nearly 200 memorials honoring distinguished Scots through the ages.

Scotland's Literary Greats

Edinburgh was home to Scotland's three greatest literary figures, pictured here: Robert Burns (left), Robert Louis Stevenson (center), and Sir Walter Scott (right).

Robert Burns (1759-1796), known as "Rabbie" in Scotland and quite possibly the most famous and beloved Scot of all time, moved to Edinburgh after achieving overnight celebrity with his first volume of poetry (staying in a house on the spot where Deacon Brodie's Tavern now stands). Even though he wrote in the rough Scots dialect and dared to attack social rank, he was a favorite of Edinburgh's high society, who'd gather in fine homes to hear him recite his works. For more on Burns, see the sidebar, later.

One hundred years later, **Robert Louis Stevenson** (1850-1894) also stirred the Scottish soul with his pen. An avid traveler who always packed his notepad, Stevenson created settings that are vivid and filled with wonder. Traveling through Scotland, Europe, and around the world, he distilled his adventures into Romantic classics, including *Kidnapped* and *Treasure Island* (as well as *The Strange Case of Dr. Jekyll and Mr. Hyde*). Stevenson, who was married in San Francisco and spent his last years in the South

Cost and Hours: Free but donations encouraged; May-Sept Mon-Fri 9:00-19:00, Sat 9:00-17:00; Oct-April Mon-Sat 9:00-17:00; Sun 13:00-17:00 year-round; audioguide-£3, tel. 0131/225-9442, www.stgilescathedral.org.uk.

Concerts: St. Giles' busy concert schedule includes organ recitals and visiting choirs (frequent free events at 12:15, concerts Sun at 18:00 and sometimes Wed at 20:00, see schedule or ask for *Music at St. Giles* pamphlet at welcome desk or gift shop).

➲ **Self-Guided Tour:** Today's facade is 19th-century Neo-

Pacific, wrote, "Youth is the time to travel—both in mind and in body—to try the manners of different nations." He said, "I travel not to go anywhere...but to simply go." Travel was his inspiration and his success.

Sir Walter Scott (1771-1832) wrote the *Waverley* novels, including *Ivanhoe* and *Rob Roy.* He's considered the father of the Romantic historical novel. Through his writing, he generated a worldwide interest in Scotland, and reawakened his fellow countrymen's pride in their heritage. His novels helped revive interest in Highland culture—the Gaelic language, kilts, songs, legends, myths, the clan system—and created a national identity. An avid patriot, he wrote, "Every Scottish man has a pedigree. It is a national prerogative, as unalienable as his pride and his poverty." Scott is so revered in Edinburgh that his towering Neo-Gothic monument dominates the city center. With his favorite hound by his side, Sir Walter Scott overlooks the city that he inspired, and that inspired him.

The best way to learn about and experience these literary greats is to visit the Writers' Museum at Lady Stair's House (see page 724) and to take Edinburgh's Literary Pub Tour (see page 764).

While just three writers dominate your Edinburgh sightseeing, consider also the other great writers with Edinburgh connections: J. K. Rowling (who captures the "Gothic" spirit of Edinburgh with her Harry Potter series); current resident Ian Rankin (with his "tartan noir" novels); J. M. Barrie (who attended University of Edinburgh and later created Peter Pan); Sir Arthur Conan Doyle (who was born in Edinburgh, went to medical school here, and is best known for inventing Sherlock Holmes); and James Boswell (who lived 50 yards away from the Writers' Museum, in James Court, and is revered for his biography of Samuel Johnson).

Gothic, but most of what you'll see inside is from the 14th and 15th centuries. Engage the cathedral guides in conversation; you'll be glad you did.

Just inside the entrance, turn around to see the modern stained-glass ❶ **Robert Burns window,** which celebrates Scotland's favorite poet (see sidebar). It was made in 1985 by the Icelandic artist Leifur Breidfjord. The green of the lower level symbolizes the natural world—God's creation. The middle zone with the circle shows the brotherhood of man—Burns was a great internationalist. The top is a rosy red sunburst of creativity, reminding Scots of Burns' famous line, "My love is like a red, red rose"—part of a song near and dear to every Scottish heart.

To the right of the Burns window is a fine ❷ **Pre-Raphaelite window.** Like most in the church, it's a memorial to an important patron (in this case, John Marshall). From here stretches a great swath of war memorials.

As you walk along the north wall, find ❸ **John Knox's statue** (standing like a six-foot-tall bronze chess piece). Look into his eyes for 10 seconds from 10 inches away, and think of the Reformation struggles of the 16th century. Knox, the great religious reformer and founder of austere Scottish Presbyterianism, first preached here in 1559. His insistence that every person should be able to personally read the word of God—notice that he's pointing to a book—gave Scotland an educational system 300 years ahead of the rest of Europe (for more on Knox, see "The Scottish Reformation" on page 863). Thanks partly to Knox, it was Scottish minds that led the way in math, science, medicine, and engineering. Voltaire called Scotland "the intellectual capital of Europe."

Knox preached Calvinism. Consider that the Dutch and the Scots both embraced this creed of hard work, frugality, and strict ethics. This helps explain why the Scots are so different from the English (and why the Dutch and the Scots—both famous for their thriftiness and industriousness—are so much alike).

The oldest parts of the cathedral—the ❹ **four massive central pillars**—are Norman and date from the 12th century. They supported a mostly wooden superstructure that was lost when an invading English force burned it in 1385. The Scots rebuilt it bigger and better than ever, and in 1495 its famous crown spire was completed.

During the Reformation—when Knox preached here (1559-1572)—the place was simplified and whitewashed. Before this, when the emphasis was on holy services provided by priests, there were lots of little niches. With the new focus on sermons rather than rituals, the grand pulpit took center stage.

Knox preached against anything that separated you from God, including stained glass (considered the poor man's Bible, as illiterate Christians could learn from its pictures). Knox had the church's fancy medieval glass windows replaced with clear glass, but 19th-

St. Giles' Cathedral

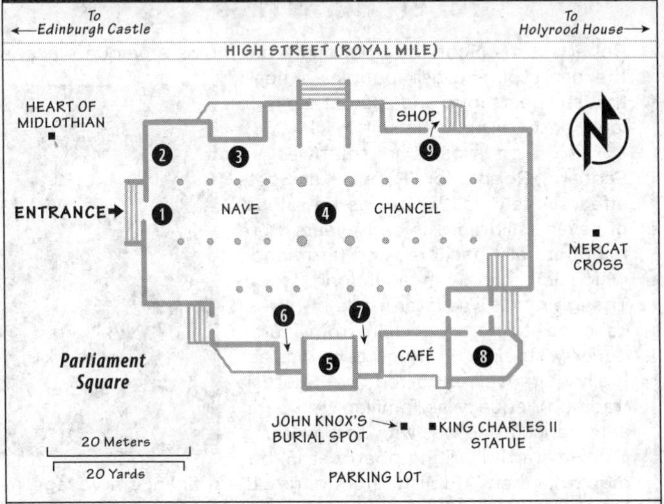

To Edinburgh Castle
To Holyrood House
HIGH STREET (ROYAL MILE)
HEART OF MIDLOTHIAN
SHOP
ENTRANCE
NAVE
CHANCEL
MERCAT CROSS
Parliament Square
CAFÉ
JOHN KNOX'S BURIAL SPOT
KING CHARLES II STATUE
20 Meters
20 Yards
PARKING LOT

1. Robert Burns Window
2. Pre-Raphaelite Window
3. John Knox Statue
4. Four Central Pillars
5. Organ
6. Stained-Glass Window
7. National Covenant
8. Chapel of the Knights of the Thistle
9. Down to Café & WC

century Victorians took them out and installed the brilliantly colored ones you see today.

Cross over to the ❺ **organ** (1992, Austrian-built, one of Europe's finest) and take in its sheer might.

Immediately to the right of the organ (as you're facing it) is a tiny chapel for silence and prayer. The dramatic ❻ **stained-glass window** above shows the commotion that surrounded Knox when he preached. The bearded fiery-eyed Knox had a huge impact on this community. Notice how there were no pews back then. The church was so packed, people even looked through clear windows from across the street. With his hand on the holy book, Knox seems to conduct divine electricity to the Scottish faithful.

To the left of the organ as you face it, in the next alcove, is a copy of the ❼ **National Covenant** (if it's not here, it may be in the chapel described next). It was signed in blood in 1638 by Scottish heroes who refused to compromise their religion for the king's. Most who signed were martyred (their monument is nearby in

Robert Burns (1759-1796)

Robert Burns, Scotland's national poet, holds a unique place in the heart of Scottish people—a heart that still beats loud and proud thanks, in large part, to Burns himself.

Born on a farm in southwestern Scotland, Robbie (or "Rabbie," as Scots affectionately call him), was the oldest of seven children. His early years were full of literally backbreaking farm labor, which left him with a lifelong stoop. Though much was later made of his ascendance to literary acclaim from a rural, poverty-stricken upbringing, he was actually quite well educated (per Scottish tradition), equally as familiar with Latin and French as he was with hard work.

He started writing poetry at 15, but didn't have any published until age 28—to finance a voyage to the West Indies (which promised better farming opportunities). When that first volume, *Poems, Chiefly in the Scottish Dialect,* became a sudden and overwhelming success, he reconsidered his emigration. Instead, he left his farm for Edinburgh, living just off the Royal Mile. He spent a year and a half in the city, schmoozing with literary elites, who celebrated this "heaven taught" farmer from the hinterlands as Scotland's "ploughman poet."

His poetry, written primarily in the Scots dialect, drew on his substantial familiarity with both Scottish tradition and Western literature. By using the language of the common man to create works of beauty and sophistication, he found himself wildly popular among both rural folk and high society. Hearty poems such as "To a Mouse," "To a Louse," and "The Holy Fair" exalted the virtues of physical labor, romantic love, friendship, natural beauty, and drink—all of which he also pursued with vigor in real life. This further endeared him to most Scots, though considerably less so to Church fathers, who were particularly displeased with his love

Grassmarket). You can see the original National Covenant in the Edinburgh Museum, described later.

Head toward the east (back) end of the church, and turn right to see the ❽ Neo-Gothic **Chapel of the Knights of the Thistle** (entry may be possible only with escorted tour—next tour time posted at entrance, £2 donation requested). The interior is filled with intricate wood carving. Built in two years (1910-1911), entirely with Scottish materials and labor, it is the private chapel of the Knights of the Thistle, the only Scottish chivalric order. It's used about once a year for the knights to gather (and, if one dies, to inaugurate a new member). Scotland recognizes its leading citi-

life (of Burns' dozen children, nine were by his eventual wife, the others by various servants and barmaids).

After achieving fame and wealth, Burns never lost touch with the concerns of the Scottish people, championing such radical ideas as social equality and economic justice. Burns bravely and loudly supported the French and American revolutions, which inspired one of his most beloved poems, "A Man's a Man for A' That," and even an ode to George Washington—all while other writers were being shipped off to Australia for similar beliefs. While his social causes cost him some aristocratic friends, it cemented his popularity among the masses, and not just within Scotland (he became, and remains, especially beloved in Russia).

Intent on preserving Scotland's rich musical and lyrical traditions, Burns traveled the countryside collecting traditional Scottish ballads. If it weren't for Burns, we'd have to come up with a different song to sing on New Year's Eve—he's the one who found, reworked, and popularized "Auld Lang Syne." His championing of Scottish culture came at a critical time: England had recently and finally crushed Scotland's last hopes of independence, and the Highland clan system was nearing its end. Burns lent the Scots dialect a new prestige, and the scrappy Scottish people a reinvigorated identity. (The official Burns website, www.robertburns.org, features a full collection of his works.)

Burns died at 37 of a heart condition likely exacerbated by so much hard labor (all the carousing probably hadn't helped, either). By that time, his fortune was largely spent, but his celebrity was going strong—around 10,000 people attended his burial. Even the Church eventually overcame its disapproval, installing a window in his honor at St. Giles' Cathedral. In 2009, his nation voted Burns "Greatest Ever Scot" in a TV poll. And every January 25 (the poet's birthday), on Burns Night, Scots gather to recite his songs and poems, tuck into some haggis ("chieftain o' the puddin' race," according to Burns), and raise their whisky to friendship, and Scotland.

zens by bestowing a membership upon them. The Queen presides over the ritual from her fancy stall, marked by her Scottish coat of arms—a heraldic zoo of symbolism. Are there bagpipes in heaven? Find the tooting stone angel at the top of a window to the left of the altar, and the wooden one to the right of the doorway you came in.

❾ **Downstairs** (enter stairs near the chapel entry) is an inviting recommended café, along with handy public toilets.

Old Parliament House

The building now holds the civil law courts, so you'll need to go through security first. Step in to see the grand hall with its fine

1639 hammer-beam ceiling and stained glass. This space housed the Scottish parliament until the Act of Union in 1707. The biggest stained-glass window depicts the initiation of the first Scottish High Court in 1532. The building is busy with wigged and robed lawyers hard at work in the old library (peek through the door) or pacing the hall deep in discussion. The cleverly-named Writz Café, in the basement, is literally their supreme court's restaurant (cheap, Mon-Fri 9:00-14:00, closed Sat-Sun).

Cost and Hours: Free, public welcome Mon-Fri 9:00-16:30, closed Sat-Sun, no photos, borrow info sheet next to security, enter behind St. Giles' Cathedral at door #11; open-to-the-public trials are just across the street at the High Court—the doorman has the day's docket.

▲The Real Mary King's Close

For an unusual peek at Edinburgh's gritty, plague-ridden past, join a costumed performer on an hour-long trip through an excavated underground street and buildings on the northern slope of the Royal Mile. Tours cover the standard goofy, crowd-pleasing ghost stories, but also provide authentic and historical insight into a part of town entombed by later construction. It's best to book ahead (online up to the day before, or by phone or in person for a same-day booking)—even though tours leave every 15 minutes, groups are small and the sight is popular.

Cost and Hours: £14; April-Oct daily 10:00-22:00, Nov-March Sun-Thu until 17:00, Fri-Sat until 21:00; these are last tour times, across from St. Giles' at 2 Warriston's Close—but enter through well-marked door facing High Street, tel. 0845-070-6244, www.realmarykingsclose.com.

▲Museum of Childhood

This five-story playground of historical toys and games is rich in nostalgia and history. Each well-signed gallery is as jovial as a Norman Rockwell painting, highlighting the delights and simplicity of childhood. The museum does a fair job of representing culturally relevant oddities, such as ancient Egyptian, Peruvian, and voodoo dolls, and displays early versions of toys it's probably best didn't make the final cut (such as a grim snake-centered precursor to the popular board game Chutes and Ladders).

Cost and Hours: Free, Mon-Sat 10:00-17:00, Sun 12:00-17:00, 42 High Street.

John Knox House

Intriguing for Reformation buffs, this fine medieval house dates back to 1470 and offers a well-explained look at the life of the great 16th-century reformer. Although most contend he never actually lived here, preservationists called it "Knox's house" to save it from

the wrecking ball in the 1840s. Regardless, the place has good information on Knox and his intellectual sparring partner, Mary, Queen of Scots. Imagine the Protestant firebrand John Knox and the devout Catholic Mary sitting face to face in old rooms like these, discussing the most intimate matters of their spiritual lives as they decided the course of Scotland's religious future. The sparsely furnished house contains some period furniture and exhibits on printing—an essential tool for early reformers. On the top floor there's a fun photo op with a dress-up cape, hat, and feather pen. Mind your head.

Cost and Hours: £5, Mon-Sat 10:00-18:00, closed Sun except in July-Aug 12:00-18:00, 43 High Street, tel. 0131/556-9579, www.tracscotland.org.

▲People's Story Museum

This engaging exhibit traces the working and social lives of ordinary people through the 18th, 19th, and 20th centuries. You'll see tools, products, and objects related to important Edinburgh trades (printing, brewing), a wartime kitchen, and a circa-1989 trip to the movies. On the top floor, a dated but endearing 22-minute film offers insight into the ways people have lived in this city for generations. On the ground floor, peek into the former jail, an original part of the historic building (the Canongate Tolbooth, built in 1591).

Cost and Hours: Free, Mon-Sat 10:00-17:00, closed Sun except during Festival 12:00-17:00, 163 Canongate, tel. 0131/529-4057, www.edinburghmuseums.org.uk.

▲Museum of Edinburgh

Another old house full of old stuff, this one is worth a stop for a look at its early Edinburgh history (and its handy ground-floor WC). Near the entrance, be sure to see the original copy of the National Covenant—written in 1638 on animal skin. Scottish leaders signed this, refusing to adopt the king's religion—and were killed because of it. Exploring the rest of the collection, keep an eye out for Robert Louis Stevenson's antique golf ball, James Craig's architectural plans for the Georgian New Town, an interactive kids' area with dress-up clothes, a sprawling top-floor exhibit on Edinburgh-born Earl Haig (who led the British Western Front efforts in World War I), and locally made glass and ceramics.

Cost and Hours: Free, same hours as People's Story Museum (listed above), 142 Canongate, tel. 0131/529-4143, www.edinburghmuseums.org.uk.

▲▲Scottish Parliament Building

Scotland's parliament originated in 1293 and was dissolved when Scotland united with England in 1707. But after the Scottish electorate and the British parliament gave their consent, in 1997 it was decided that there should again be "a Scottish parliament guided by justice, wisdom, integrity, and compassion." Formally reconvened by Queen Elizabeth II in 1999, the Scottish parliament now enjoys self-rule in many areas (except for matters of defense, foreign policy, immigration, and taxation). The current government, run by the Scottish Nationalist Party (SNP), is pushing for even more independence.

The innovative building, opened in 2004, brought together all the functions of the fledgling parliament in one complex. It's a people-oriented structure (conceived by Catalan architect Enric Miralles; for more on the building, see page 704). Signs are written in both English and Gaelic (the Scots' Celtic tongue).

For a peek at the building and a lesson in how the Scottish parliament works, drop in, pass through security, and find the visitors' desk. You're welcome in the public parts of the building, including a small ground-floor exhibit on the parliament's history and function and, up several flights of stairs, a viewing gallery overlooking the impressive Debating Chambers.

Cost and Hours: Free; Sept-June (when parliament is in session) Mon and Fri-Sat 10:00-17:00, Tue-Thu 9:00-18:30; July-Aug and holidays (when parliament is in recess) Mon-Sat 10:00-17:00; closed Sun year-round; www.scottish.parliament.uk. For a complete list of recess dates or to book tickets for debates, check their website or call their visitors services line at tel. 0131/348-5200.

Tours: Free worthwhile hour-long tours are offered by proud locals (2/hour, except when parliament is in session). While you can try just dropping in, these tours can book up—call or check online for times and reserve a spot.

Seeing Parliament in Session: You can call or sign up online to witness the Scottish parliament's hugely popular debates (usually Tue-Thu 14:00-18:00). On Thursdays from 12:00-12:30 the First Minister is on the hot seat and has to field questions from members across all parties.

▲▲Palace of Holyroodhouse

Built on the site of the abbey/monastery founded in 1128 by King David I, this palace was the true home, birthplace, and coronation spot of Scotland's Stuart kings in their heyday (James IV; Mary, Queen of Scots; and Charles I). It's particularly memorable as the site of some dramatic moments from the short reign of Mary, Queen of Scots—including the murder of her personal secretary, David Rizzio, by agents of her jealous husband. Today, it's one of Queen Elizabeth II's official residences. She usually manages her Scottish affairs here during Holyrood Week, from late June to early July (and generally stays at Balmoral in August). Holyrood is open to the public outside of the Queen's visits. Touring the interior offers a more polished contrast to Edinburgh Castle, and is particularly worth considering if you don't plan to go to Balmoral. The one-way audioguide route leads you through the fine apartments and tells some of the notable stories that played out here.

Cost: £11.60, includes quality one-hour audioguide; £16.40 combo-ticket includes the Queen's Gallery; £20 combo-ticket adds guided tour of palace gardens—summer only, ask for schedule when buying tickets; tickets sold in Queen's Gallery to the right of the castle entrance (see next listing).

Hours: Daily April-Oct 9:30-18:00, Nov-March until 16:30, last entry 1.5 hours before closing, tel. 0131/556-5100, www.royalcollection.org.uk. It's still a working palace, so it's closed when the Queen or other VIPs are in residence.

Visiting the Palace: The building, rich in history and decor, is filled with elegantly furnished Victorian rooms and a few darker, older rooms with glass cases of historic bits and Scottish pieces that locals find fascinating. Bring the palace to life with the audioguide. The tour route leads you into the grassy inner courtyard, then up to the royal apartments: dining rooms, *Downton Abbey*-style drawing rooms, and royal bedchambers. Along the way, you'll learn the story behind the 96 portraits of Scottish leaders (some real, others imaginary) that line the Great Gallery; why the king never slept in his official "state bed"; why the exiled Comte d'Artois took refuge in the palace; and how the current Queen puts her Scottish subjects at ease when she receives them here. Finally you'll twist up a tight spiral staircase to the private chambers of Mary, Queen of Scots, where conspirators stormed in and stabbed her secretary 56 times.

After exiting the palace, you're free to stroll through the evocative **ruined abbey** (destroyed by the English during the time of Mary, Queen of Scots, in the 16th century) and the **palace gardens** (closed Oct-April except some weekends). Some 8,000 guests—including many honored ladies sporting fancy hats—gather here every July when the Queen hosts a magnificent tea party. (She gets help pouring.)

Nearby: Hikers, note that the wonderful trail up Arthur's Seat starts just across the street from the gardens (see page 753 for details).

Queen's Gallery

This small museum features rotating exhibits of artwork from the royal collection. For more than five centuries, the royal family has amassed a wealth of art treasures. While the Queen keeps most in her many private palaces, she shares an impressive load of it here, with exhibits changing about every six months. Though the gallery occupies just a few rooms, its displays can be exquisite. The entry fee includes an excellent audioguide, written and read by the curator.

Cost and Hours: £6.60, £16.40 combo-ticket includes Palace of Holyroodhouse, daily 9:30-18:00, until 16:30 Nov-March, last entry one hour before closing, café, on the palace grounds, to the right of the palace entrance, www.royalcollection.org.uk. Buses #35 and #36 stop outside and can save you a walk to or from Princes Street/North Bridge.

Our Dynamic Earth

Located about a five-minute walk from the Palace of Holyroodhouse, this immense exhibit tells the story of our planet, filling several underground floors under a vast white Gore-Tex tent. It's pitched, appropriately, at the base of the Salisbury Crags. The exhibit is designed for younger kids and does the same thing an American science exhibit would do—but with a charming Scottish

accent. You'll learn about the Scottish geologists who pioneered the discipline, then step into a "time machine" to watch the years rewind, from cave dwellers to dinosaurs to the Big Bang. After viewing several short films on stars, tectonic plates, ice caps, and worldwide weather (in a "4-D" exhibit), you're free to wander past salty pools and a re-created rain forest.

Cost and Hours: £12.50, kids-£8, daily 10:00-17:30, until 18:00 July-Aug, closed Mon-Tue Nov-March, last entry 1.5 hours before closing, on Holyrood Road, between the palace and mountain, tel. 0131/550-7800, www.dynamicearth.co.uk.

SIGHTS SOUTH OF THE ROYAL MILE

▲▲▲National Museum of Scotland

This huge museum has amassed more historic artifacts than every other place I've seen in Scotland combined. It's all wonderfully displayed, with fine descriptions offering a best-anywhere hike through the history of Scotland.

Cost and Hours: Free, daily 10:00-17:00; free one-hour "Highlights" tours daily at 11:00 and 13:00, themed tours at 15:00—confirm tour schedule at info desk or on TV screens; two long blocks south of St. Giles' Cathedral and the Royal Mile, on Chambers Street off George IV Bridge, tel. 0131/247-4422, www.nms.ac.uk.

Eating: On the museum's fifth floor, the dressy and upscale **Tower restaurant** serves good food with a castle view (£19 lunch/early bird special, £16 afternoon tea, £35 three-course dinner special, fancy £18-32 meals; daily 10:00-23:00—later than the museum itself, tel. 0131/225-3003).

➲ **Self-Guided Tour:** The place gives you two museums in one. One wing houses a popular natural history collection, with everything from kid-friendly T. rex skeletons to Egyptian mummies. But we'll focus on the other wing, which sweeps you through Scottish history covering Roman and Viking times, Edinburgh's witch-burning craze and clan massacres, the struggle for Scottish independence, the Industrial Revolution, and right up to Scotland in the 21st century.

Get oriented on level 1, in the impressive glass-roofed Grand

Gallery. This part of the building houses the natural history collection.

• *To reach the Scottish history wing, exit the Grand Gallery at the far right end, under the clock.*

On the way, you'll pass the newly-renovated science and technology wing, where you might see Dolly the sheep—the world's first cloned mammal—born in Edinburgh and now stuffed and on display. Continue into Hawthornden Court (level 1), where our tour begins. (It's possible to detour downstairs from here to level -1 for Scotland's prehistoric origins—geologic formation, Celts, Romans, Vikings.)

• *Enter the door marked...*

Kingdom of the Scots (c. 1300-1700): From its very start, Scotland was determined to be free. You're greeted with proud quotes from what's been called the Scottish Declaration of Independence—the Declaration of Arbroath, a defiant letter written to the pope in 1320. As early as the ninth century, Scotland's patron saint, Andrew (see the small statue in the next room), had—according to legend—miraculously intervened to help the Picts and Scots of Scotland remain free by defeating the Angles of England. Andrew's X-shaped cross still decorates the Scottish flag today.

Turning right, enter the first room on your right, with imposing swords and other objects related to Scotland's most famous patriots—William Wallace and Robert the Bruce. Bruce's descendants, the Stuarts, went on to rule Scotland for the next 300 years. Eventually, James VI of Scotland (see his baby cradle) came to rule England as well (as King James I of England).

In the next room, a big guillotine recalls the harsh justice meted out to criminals, witches, and "Covenanters" (17th-century political activists who opposed interference of the Stuart kings in affairs of the Presbyterian Church of Scotland). Nearby, also check out the tomb (a copy) of Mary, Queen of Scots, the 16th-century Stuart monarch who opposed the Presbyterian Church of Scotland. Educated and raised in Renaissance France, Mary brought refinement to the Scottish throne. After she was imprisoned and then executed by Elizabeth I of England in 1587, her supporters rallied each other by invoking her memory. Pendants and coins with her portrait stoked the irrepressible Scottish spirit. Near the replica of Mary's tomb are tiny cameos, pieces of jewelry, and coins with her image.

Browse the rest of level 1 to see everyday objects from that age: carved panels, cookware, and clothes.

• *Backtrack to Hawthornden Court and take the elevator to level 3.*

Scotland Transformed (1700s): You'll see artifacts related to Bonnie Prince Charlie and the Jacobite rebellions as well as the ornate Act of Union document, signed in 1707 by the Scottish parliament. This act voluntarily united Scotland with England under the single parliament of Great Britain. For some Scots, this move was an inevitable step in connecting to the wider world, but for others it symbolized the end of Scotland's existence.

Union with England brought stability and investment to Scotland. In this same era, the advances of the Industrial Revolution were making a big impact on Scottish life. Mechanized textile looms (on display) replaced hand craftsmanship. The huge Newcomen steam-engine water pump helped the mining industry to develop sites with tricky drainage. (The museum puts the device in motion a few times a day.) Nearby is a model of a coal mine (or "colliery"); coal-rich Scotland exploited this natural resource to fuel its textile factories.

How the parsimonious Scots financed these new large-scale enterprises is explained in an exhibit on the Bank of Scotland. Powered by the Scottish work ethic and the new opportunities that came from the Industrial Revolution, the country came into relative prosperity. Education and medicine thrived. With the dawn of the modern age came leisure time, the concept of "healthful sports," and golf—a popular Scottish pastime. On display are some early golf balls, which date from about 1820, made of leather and stuffed with feathers.

• *Return to the elevator and journey up to level 5.*

Industry and Empire (1800s): Turn right and do a counterclockwise spin around this floor to survey Scottish life in the 19th century. Industry had transformed the country. Highland farmers left their land to find work in Lowland factories and foundries. Modern inventions—the phonograph, the steam-powered train—revolutionized everyday life. In Glasgow, architect Charles Rennie Mackintosh helped to define Scottish Art Nouveau. Scotland was at the forefront of literature (Robert Burns, Sir Walter Scott, Robert Louis Stevenson, the first printing of the Encyclopedia Britannica), science (Lord Kelvin, James Watt, Alexander Graham Bell... he was born here, anyway!), and world exploration (David Livingstone in Africa, Sir Alexander Mackenzie in Canada).

• *Climb the stairs to level 6.*

Scotland: A Changing Nation (1900s): Turn left and do a clockwise spin through this floor to bring the story to the present day. The two world wars decimated the population of this already-wee nation. In addition, hundreds of thousands emigrated, especially to Canada (where one in eight Canadians has Scottish origins). The small country has made a big mark on the world: You'll learn how Scots have gone global in the world of entertainment (early boy band Bay City Rollers, funk masters Average White Band, and the Proclaimers, who swore they'd walk a thousand miles to fall down at your door), to an impressive variety of films (gritty *Trainspotting,* fanciful *Harry Potter* blockbusters), to actor-comedians Billy Connolly and Craig Ferguson. The exhibit takes a sober look at the recent trend of devolution from the United Kingdom, especially the 1999 opening of Scotland's own parliament and the landmark 2014 referendum on Scottish independence. Finally, in the Sports Hall of Fame, you'll see the pioneers of modern golf (Tom Morris, from St. Andrews), auto racing (Jackie Stewart and Jim Clark), and a signed baseball by Glasgow-born Bobby (1951 home run) Thomson.

• *Finish your visit on level 7, the rooftop.*

Garden Terrace: Don't miss the great views of Edinburgh from this well-described roof garden, growing grasses and heathers from every corner of Scotland. When you're done, simply ride the elevator down to level 1 and the exit.

Greyfriars Bobby Statue and Greyfriars Cemetery

This famous **statue** of Edinburgh's favorite dog is across the street from the National Museum of Scotland. Every business nearby, it seems, is named for this Victorian Skye terrier, who is reputed to have stood by his master's grave in Greyfriars Cemetery for 14 years. The story was immortalized in a 1960s Disney flick, but recent research suggests that 19th-century businessmen bribed a stray to hang out in the cemetery to attract sightseers. If it was a ruse, it still works.

Just behind Bobby is the entrance to his namesake **cemetery.** Stepping through the gate, you'll see the pink-marble grave of Bobby himself. The well-tended cemetery is an evocative place to stroll, and a nice escape from the city's bustle. Harry Potter fans could turn it into a scavenger hunt: J. K. Rowling sketched out her saga just around the corner at The Elephant House Café—and a few of the cemetery's weather-beaten headstones bear familiar names, including McGonagall and Thomas Riddell. Beyond the cemetery fence are the frilly Gothic spires of posh George Heriot's School, said to have inspired Hogwarts. And just a few short blocks to the east is a street called... Potterrow.

Grassmarket

Once Edinburgh's site for hangings (residents rented out their windows—above the rudely-named "Last Drop" pub—for the view), today Grassmarket is a people-friendly piazza. It was originally the city's garage, a depot for horses and cows (hence the name). It's rowdy here at night—a popular place for "hen dos" and "stag dos" (bachelorette and bachelor parties). In the early evening, the Literary Pub Tour departs from here (see page 764). Some great shopping streets branch off from Grassmarket: Victoria Street, built in the Victorian Age, is lined with colorful little shops and eateries; angling off in the other direction, Candlemaker's Row has one of central Edinburgh's most creative arrays of design shops (and leads, in just a couple of minutes' walk, up to Greyfriars Bobby and the National Museum; for more shopping tips in this area, see page 760).

Hiding in the blur of traffic is a monument to the "Covenanters." These strict 17th-century Scottish Protestants were killed for refusing to accept the king's Episcopalian prayer book. To this day, Scots celebrate their national church's emphatically democratic government. Rather than big-shot bishops (as in the Anglican or Roman Catholic Church), they have a low-key "moderator" who's elected each year.

MUSEUMS IN THE NEW TOWN

These sights are linked by the "Bonnie Wee New Town Walk" on page 705.

▲▲Scottish National Gallery

This delightful small museum has Scotland's best collection of paintings. In a short visit, you can admire well-described works by Old Masters (Raphael, Rembrandt, Rubens), Impressionists (Monet, Degas, Gauguin), and a few underrated Scottish painters. (Scottish art is better at the National Portrait Gallery, described next.) Although there are no iconic masterpieces, it's a surprisingly enjoyable collection that's truly world-class.

Cost and Hours: Free; daily 10:00-17:00, Thu until 19:00; longer hours in Aug: Sun-Wed until 18:00, Thu-Sat until 19:00; the Mound (between Princes and Market streets), tel. 0131/624-6200, www.nationalgalleries.org.

Expect Changes: The gallery often loans artwork, including its finest paintings. Ask one of the friendly tartan-sporting attendants or at the info desk downstairs (near the WCs and gallery shop) if you can't find a particular item.

Next Door: The skippable **Royal Scottish Academy** hosts temporary art exhibits and is connected to the Scottish National Gallery at the Gardens level (underneath the gallery) by the Weston Link building (same hours as gallery, fine café and restaurant).

➲ **Self-Guided Tour:** Start at the gallery entrance (at the north end of the building). Climb the stairs to the upper level (north end), and take a left. You'll run right into...

Van der Goes—*The Trinity Panels* (c. 1473-1479): For more than five centuries, these panels have stood on this spot in Ed-

inburgh—first in a church, then (when the church was leveled to build Waverley train station) in this museum. The panels likely flanked a central scene of the Virgin Mary that was destroyed by Protestant vandals during the Reformation.

In the left panel is the Trinity: God the Father, in a rich red robe, cradles a spindly just-crucified Christ, while the dove of the Holy Spirit hovers between them. On the right, the church's director (the man who commissioned the painting from the well-known Flemish painter) kneels and looks on while an angel plays a hymn on the church organ. In typically medieval fashion, the details are meticulous—expressive faces, intricate folds in the robes, Christ's pallid skin, observant angels. The donor's face is a remarkable portrait, with realistic skin tone and a five-o'clock shadow. But the painting lacks true 3-D realism—God's gold throne is overly exaggerated, and Christ's cardboard-cutout body hovers weightlessly.

The flip side of the panels depicts Scotland's king and queen, who are best known to history as the parents of the boy kneeling alongside them. (You can ask the guard to open the panels.) He grew up to become James IV, the Renaissance king who made Edinburgh a cultural capital.

• *Go back across the top of the skylight, to a room where the next two paintings hang facing each other.*

Botticelli—*The Virgin Adoring the Sleeping Christ Child* (c. 1490): Mary looks down at her baby, peacefully sleeping in a flower-filled garden. It's easy to appreciate Botticelli's masterful style: the precisely-drawn outlines, the Virgin's pristine skin, the translucent glow. Botticelli creates a serene world in which no shadows are cast. The scene is painted on canvas—unusual at a time when wood panels were the norm. For the Virgin's rich cloak, Botticelli used ground-up lapis lazuli (a very pricey semiprecious stone), and her hem is decorated with gold leaf.

Renaissance-era art lovers would instantly catch the symbolism. Mary wears a wispy halo and blue cloak that recalls the sky blue of heaven. The roses without thorns and enclosed garden are both symbols of virginity, while the violet flowers (at bottom) represent humility. Darker symbolism hints at what's to come. The strawberries (lower right) signify Christ's blood, soon to be shed, while the roses—though thornless now—will become the Crown of Thorns. For now, Mary can adore her sleeping, blissful baby in a peaceful garden. But in a few decades she'll be kneeling again to weep over the dead, crucified Messiah.

Raphael—*Holy Family with a Palm Tree* (1506-1507): Mary, Joseph, and the Christ Child fit snugly within a round frame (a tondo), their pose symbolizing geometric perfection and the perfect family unit. Joseph kneels to offer Jesus flowers. Mary curves toward him. Baby Jesus dangles in between, linking the family together. Raphael also connects the figures through eye contact: Mary eyes Joseph, who locks onto Jesus, who gazes precociously back. Like in a cameo, we see the faces incised in profile, while their bodies bulge out toward us.

• *Back downstairs at ground level is the main gallery space. Circle around the collection chronologically, watching for works by Bellini, Titian, Velázquez, and El Greco. In Room 7, look for...*

Rubens—*Feast of Herod* (c. 1635-1638): All eyes turn to watch the dramatic culmination of the story of John the Baptist. Salome (standing in center) presents John's severed head on a platter to a horrified King Herod, who clutches the tablecloth and buries his hand in his beard to stifle a gag. Meanwhile, Herod's wife—who cooked up the nasty plot—pokes spitefully at John's head with a fork. A dog tugs at Herod's foot like a nasty conscience. The canvas—big, colorful, full of motion and drama—is totally Baroque. Some have suggested that the features of Herod's wife and Salome are those of Rubens' wife and ex-wives, and the head is Rubens himself.

• *Next, in Room 8, look for...*

Rembrandt—*Self-Portrait, Aged 51* (c. 1657): It's 1657, and 51-year-old Rembrandt has just declared bankruptcy. Besides financial hardship and the auctioning-off of his personal belongings, he's also facing social stigma and behind-the-back ridicule. Once Holland's most renowned painter, he's begun a slow decline into poverty and obscurity.

His face says it all. Holding a steady gaze, he stares with matter-of-fact acceptance, with his lips pursed. He's dressed in dark clothes against a dark background, with the only spot of light shining on the worry lines of his forehead. Get close enough to the canvas to see the thick paste of paint he used for the wrinkles around his eyes—a study in aging.

• *In Room 11, find...*

Gainsborough—*The Honorable Mrs. Graham* (1775-1777): The slender, elegant, lavishly-dressed woman was the teenage bride of a wealthy Scottish landowner. She leans on a column, ostrich feather in hand, staring off to the side (Thoughtfully? Determinedly? Haughtily?). Her faultless face and smooth neck stand out from the elaborately-ruffled dress and background foliage. This 18th-century woman wears a silvery dress that echoes 17th-century style—Gainsborough's way of showing how, though she was young, she was classy. Thomas ("Blue Boy") Gainsborough—the product of a clothes-making father and a flower-painting mother—uses aspects of both in this lush portrait. The ruby brooch on her bodice marks the center of this harmonious composition.

• *Climb the stairs to the upper level (south end, opposite from where you entered) and turn right for the Impressionists and Post-Impressionists.*

Impressionist Collection: The gallery has a smattering of (mostly smaller-scale) works from all the main artists of the Impressionist and Post-Impressionist eras. You'll see Degas' ballet scenes, Renoir's pastel-colored family scenes, Van Gogh's peasants, and Seurat's pointillism.

• *Keep an eye out for these three paintings (if you can't find them, ask an attendant).*

Monet's *Poplars on the Epte* (1891) was part of the artist's famous "series" paintings. He set up several canvases in a floating studio near his home in Giverny. He'd start on one canvas in the morning (to catch the morning light), then move to the next as the light changed. This particular canvas captures a perfect summer day, showing both the poplars on the riverbank and their mirror image in the still water. The subject matter begins to dissolve into a pure pattern of color, anticipating abstract art.

Gauguin's *Vision of the Sermon* (1888) shows French peasant women imagining the miraculous event they've just heard preached about in church—when Jacob wrestles with an angel. The painting is a watershed in art history, as Gauguin throws out the rules of "realism" that had reigned since the Renaissance. The colors are surreal, there are no shadows, the figures are arranged almost randomly, and there's no attempt to make the wrestlers appear distant. The diagonal tree branch is the only thing separating the everyday world from the miraculous. Later, when Gauguin moved to Tahiti (see his *Three Tahitians* nearby), he painted a similar world, where the everyday and magical coexist with symbolic power.

Sargent's *Lady Agnew of Lochnaw* (1892) is the work that launched the career of this American-born portrait artist. Lady Agnew—the young wife of a wealthy old Scotsman—lounges back languidly and gazes out self-assuredly. The Impressionistic smudges of paint on her dress and the chair contrast with her clear skin and luminous eyeballs. Her relaxed pose (one arm hanging down the side) contrasts with her intensity: head tilted slightly down while she gazes up, a corner of her mouth askew, and an eyebrow cocked seductively.

• *End your visit downstairs on the lower level, home to the...*

Scottish Collection: Though Scotland has produced few "name" painters, this small wing lets you sample some of the best. It's all in one room, designed to be toured chronologically (clockwise). At the end of the first (upper) concourse, look for paintings by **Allan Ramsay.** The son of the well-known poet of the same name, Ramsay painted portraits of curly-wigged men of the Enlightenment era (the philosopher David Hume, King George III) as well as likenesses of his two wives. Ramsay's portrait of the duke of Argyll—founder of the Royal Bank of Scotland—appears on the front of notes printed by this bank.

Downstairs, **Sir Henry Raeburn** chronicled the next generation: Sir Walter Scott, the proud kilt-wearing Alastair Macdonell, and the ice-skating Reverend Robert Walker, minister of the Canongate Church.

Sir David Wilkie's forte was small-scale scenes of everyday life. *The Letter of Introduction* (1813) captures Wilkie's own experience of trying to impress skeptical art patrons in London; even the dog is sniffing the Scotsman out. *Distraining for Rent* (1815) shows the plight of a poor farmer about to lose his farm—a common occurrence during 19th-century industrialization.

Pause and swoon before **William Dyce**'s *Francesca da Rimini* (1837). The star-crossed lovers—a young wife and her husband's kid brother—can't help but indulge their passion. The husband later finds out and kills her; at the far left, you see his ominous hand.

Finally, take in **William McTaggart**'s impressionistic landscape scenes from the late 1800s for a glimpse of the unique light, powerful clouds, and natural wonder of the Highlands.

▲▲Scottish National Portrait Gallery

Put a face on Scotland's history by enjoying these portraits of famous Scots from the earliest times until today. From its Neo-Gothic facade to a grand entry hall featuring a *Who's Who* of Scotland, to galleries highlighting the great Scots of each age, this impressive museum will fascinate anyone interested in Scottish culture. The gallery also hosts temporary exhibits highlighting the work of more contemporary Scots. Because of its purely Scottish focus, many travelers prefer this to the (pan-European) main branch of the National Gallery.

Cost and Hours: Free, daily 10:00-17:00, Thu until 19:00—occasional live music at 18:00, good cafeteria serving healthy £5-7 meals, 1 Queen Street, tel. 0131/624-6490, www.nationalgalleries.org.

Visiting the Gallery: In the stirring **entrance hall** you'll find busts of great Scots and a full-body statue of Robbie "Rabbie" Burns, as well as (up above) a glorious frieze showing a parade of important historical figures and murals depicting important events in Scottish history. (These are better viewed from the first floor and its mezzanine—described later). We'll start on the **second floor,** right into the thick of the struggle between Scotland and England over who should rule this land.

Reformation to Revolution (gallery 1): The collection starts with a portrait of **Mary, Queen of Scots** (1542-1587), her cross and rosary prominent. This controversial ruler set off two centuries of strife. Mary was born with both Stuart blood (the ruling family of Scotland) and the Tudor blood of England's monarchs (Queen Elizabeth I was her cousin). Catholic and French-educated, Mary felt alienated from her own increasingly Protestant homeland. Her tense conversations with the reformer John Knox must have been epic. Then came a series of scandals: She married unpopular Lord Darnley, then (possibly) cheated on him, causing Darnley to (possibly) murder her lover, causing Mary to (possibly) murder Darnley, then (possibly) run off with another man, and (possibly) plot against Queen Elizabeth.

Amid all that drama, Mary was forced by her own people to relinquish her throne to her infant son, **James VI.** Find his portraits as a child and as a grown-up. James grew up to rule Scotland, and when Queen Elizabeth (the Virgin Queen) died without an heir, he also became king of England (James I). But James' son, **Charles I,** after a bitter civil war, was arrested and executed in 1649: See the large *Execution of Charles I* painting high on the far wall, his blood-dripping head displayed to the crowd; nearby is a portrait of Charles in happier times, as a 12-year-old boy. His son, Charles II, restored the Stuarts to power. He was then succeeded by his Catholic brother James VII of Scotland (II of England), who was sent into exile in France. There the Stuarts stewed, planning a return to power, waiting for someone to lead them in what would come to be known as the Jacobite Rebellions.

The Jacobite Cause (gallery 4): The biggest painting in the room is *The Baptism of Prince Charles Edward Stuart.* Born in 1720, this heir to the thrones of Great Britain and Ireland is better known to history as "Bonnie Prince Charlie." (See his bonnie features in various portraits nearby, as a child, young man, and grown man.) Charismatic Charles convinced France to invade Scotland and put him back on the throne there. In 1745, he entered Edinburgh in triumph. But he was defeated at the tide-turning Battle of Culloden (1746). The Stuart cause died forever, and Bonnie Prince Charlie went into exile, eventually dying drunk and wasted in Rome, far from the land he nearly ruled.

Citizens of the World (galleries 5-6): The two biggest paintings here are of King George III and Queen Charlotte (namesakes of the New Town's main street and square). In the late 18th century, Scotland was doing just fine being ruled from England. Paintings here show the confidence of this age, when the New Town of Edinburgh was designed and built. In the 1760s, Edinburgh was the center of Europe's Enlightenment, powered by philosophers such as David Hume (find his portrait, by Allan Ramsay, who also painted the likeness of George III) and his economist friend Adam Smith (depicted in a cameo medallion).

The Age of Improvement (gallery 7): The faces portrayed here belonged to a new society whose hard work and public spirit achieved progress with a Scottish accent. Social equality and the Industrial Revolution "transformed" Scotland—you'll see portraits of the great poet Robert Burns, the son of a farmer (Burns was heralded as a "heaven-taught ploughman" when his poems were first published) and the inventor of the steam engine, James Watt.

Playing for Scotland (gallery 10): Lighten things up with a swing through old-time sports in Scotland, including early golf, curling, Highland Games (including "putting the stone"—similar to shot put), fox hunting, and croquet.

• *Now head back down to the first floor for a good look at the...*

Central Atrium (first floor): Great Scots! The atrium is decorated in a parade of late-19th-century Romantic Historicism. The **frieze** (working counterclockwise) is a visual encyclopedia, from an ax-wielding Stone Age man and a druid, to the early legendary monarchs (Macbeth), to warriors William Wallace and Robert the Bruce, to many kings (James I, II, III, and so on), to great thinkers, inventors, and artists (Allan Ramsay, Flora MacDonald, David

Hume, Adam Smith, James Boswell, James Watt), the three greatest Scottish writers (Robert Burns, Sir Walter Scott, Robert Louis Stevenson), and culminating with the historian Thomas Carlyle, who was the driving spirit (powered by the fortune of a local newspaper baron) behind creating this portrait gallery.

Best viewed from the first-floor mezzanine are the large-scale **murals** depicting great events in Scottish history, including the landing of St. Margaret at Queensferry in 1068, the Battle of Stirling Bridge in 1297, the Battle of Bannockburn in 1314, and the marriage procession of James IV and Margaret Tudor through the streets of Edinburgh in 1509.

• *Also on this floor is...*

Gallery 11: Artwork rotates in and out, but it always highlights Scots who are making an impact in the world today. You may see Annie Lennox, Ian Rankin, or distinguished Scottish scientists such as physicist Peter Higgs (theorizer of the Higgs boson, the so-called God particle). One constant is the stirring *Three Oncologists,* a ghostly painting depicting the anxiety and terror of cancer and the dedication of those working so hard to conquer it.

▲▲Georgian House

This refurbished Neoclassical house, set on Charlotte Square, is a trip back to 1796. It recounts the era when a newly gentrified and well-educated Edinburgh was nicknamed the "Athens of the North." Begin on the second floor, where you'll watch an interesting 16-minute video dramatizing the upstairs-downstairs lifestyles of the aristocrats and servants who lived here. Try on some Georgian outfits, then head downstairs to tour period rooms and even peek into the fully-stocked medicine cabinet. A volunteer guide shares stories and trivia: You'll learn why Georgian bigwigs had to sit behind a screen while enjoying a fire. A walk down George Street after your visit here can be fun for the imagination.

Cost and Hours: £7, daily April-Oct 10:00-17:00—July-Aug until 18:00, March and Nov 11:00-16:00, may be open Thu-Sun in Dec, otherwise closed Dec-Feb, last entry 45 minutes before closing, 7 Charlotte Square, tel. 0131/226-3318, www.nts.org.uk.

SIGHTS NEAR EDINBURGH

▲▲Royal Yacht *Britannia*

This much-revered vessel, which transported Britain's royal family for more than 40 years on 900 voyages (an average of once around the world per year) before being retired in 1997, is permanently

moored in Edinburgh's port of Leith. Queen Elizabeth II said of the ship, "This is the only place I can truly relax." Today it's open to the curious public, who have access to its many decks—from engine rooms to drawing rooms—and offers a fascinating time-warp to the late-20th-century lifestyles of the rich and royal. It's worth the half-hour bus or taxi ride from the center; figure on spending about 2.5 hours total on the outing.

Cost and Hours: £14, includes 1.5-hour audioguide, daily April-Sept 9:30-16:30, Oct 9:30-16:00, Nov-March 10:00-15:30, these are last entry times, tearoom; at the Ocean Terminal Shopping Mall, on Ocean Drive in Leith; tel. 0131/555-5566, www.royalyachtbritannia.co.uk.

Getting There: From central Edinburgh, catch Lothian bus #11 or #22 from Princes Street (just above Waverley Station), or #35 from the bottom of the Royal Mile (alongside the parliament building) to Ocean Terminal. The Majestic Tour hop-on, hop-off bus stops here as well. Drivers can park free in the blue parking garage. Take the shopping center elevator to level E, then follow the signs.

Visiting the Ship: First, explore the **museum,** filled with engrossing royal-family-afloat history. You'll see lots of family photos that evoke the fine times the Windsors enjoyed on the *Britannia*, as well as some nautical equipment and uniforms. Then, armed with your audioguide, you're welcome aboard.

This was the last in a line of royal yachts that stretches back to 1660. With all its royal functions, the ship required a crew of more than 200. Begin in the captain's bridge, which feels like it's been preserved from the day it was launched in 1953. Then head down a deck to see the officers' quarters, then the garage, where a Rolls Royce was hoisted aboard to use in places where the local transportation wasn't up to royal standards. The Veranda Deck at the back of the ship was the favorite place for outdoor entertainment. Ronald Reagan, Boris Yeltsin, Bill Clinton, and Nelson Mandela all sipped champagne here. The Sun Lounge, just off the back Veranda Deck, was the Queen's favorite, with Burmese teak and the same phone system she was used to in Buckingham Palace. When she wasn't entertaining, the Queen liked it quiet. The crew wore sneakers, communicated in hand signals, and (at least near the

Queen's quarters) had to be finished with all their work by 8:00 in the morning.

Take a peek into the adjoining his-and-hers bedrooms of the Queen and the Duke of Edinburgh (check out the spartan twin beds), and the honeymoon suite where Prince Charles and Lady Di began their wedded bliss.

Heading down another deck, walk through the officers' lounge (and learn about the rowdy games they played) and past the galleys (including custom cabinetry for the fine china and silver) on your way to the biggest room on the yacht, the state dining room. Now decorated with gifts given by the ship's many noteworthy guests, this space enabled the Queen to entertain a good-size crowd. The drawing room, while rather simple (the Queen specifically requested "country house comfort"), was perfect for casual relaxing among royals. Princess Diana played the piano, which is bolted to the deck. Note the contrast to the decidedly less plush crew's quarters, mail room, sick bay, laundry, and engine room.

▲Rosslyn Chapel

This small but fascinating countryside church, about a 20-minute drive outside of Edinburgh, is a riot of carved iconography. The patterned ceiling and walls have left scholars guessing about its symbolism for centuries.

Cost and Hours: £9, Mon-Sat 9:30-18:00, until 17:00 Oct-March, Sun 12:00-16:45 year-round, no photos allowed, located in Roslin Village, www.rosslynchapel.org.uk.

Getting There: Ride Lothian bus #37 from Princes Street (stop PJ) or North Bridge (1-2/hour, 45 minutes). By car, take the A-701 to Penicuik/Peebles, and follow signs for *Roslin;* once you're in the village, you'll see signs for the chapel.

Background: After it was featured in the climax of Dan Brown's 2003 bestseller *The Da Vinci Code,* the number of visitors to Rosslyn Chapel more than quadrupled. But the chapel's allure existed well before the books, and will endure long after they move from bargain bin to landfill. Founded in 1446 as the private mausoleum of the St. Clair family—who wanted to be buried close to God—the church's interior is carved with a stunning mishmash of Christian, pagan, family, Templar, Masonic, and other symbolism.

After the Scottish Reformation, Catholic churches like this fell into disrepair. But in the 18th and 19th centuries, Romantics such as Robert Burns and Sir Walter Scott discovered these evocative old ruins, putting Rosslyn Chapel back on the map. Even Queen Victoria visited, and gently suggested that the chapel be restored to its original state. Today, after more than a century of refits and refurbishments, the chapel transports visitors back to a distant and mysterious age.

Visiting the Chapel: From the ticket desk and visitors center, head to the chapel itself. Ask about docent lectures (usually at the top of the hour). If you have time to kill, pick up the good laminated descriptions for a clockwise tour of the carvings. In the crypt—where the stonemasons worked—you can see faint architectural drawings engraved in the wall, used to help them plot out their master design.

Elsewhere, look for these fun details: In the corner to the left of the altar, find the angels playing instruments—including one with bagpipes. Nearby, you'll see a person dancing with a skeleton. This "dance of death" theme—common in the Middle Ages—is a reminder of mortality: We'll all die eventually, so we might as well whoop it up while we're here. On the other side of the nave are carvings of the seven deadly sins and the seven acts of mercy. One inscription reads: "Wine is strong. Kings are stronger. Women are stronger still. But truth conquers all."

Flanking the altar are two carved columns that come with a legend: The more standard-issue column, on the left, was executed by a master mason, who soon after (perhaps disappointed in his lack of originality) went on a sabbatical to gain inspiration. While he was gone, his ambitious apprentice carved the beautiful corkscrew-shaped column on the right. Upon returning, the master flew into an envious rage and murdered the apprentice with his carving hammer.

Scattered throughout the church, you'll also see the family's symbol, the "engrailed cross" (with serrated edges). Keep an eye out for the more than one hundred "green men"—chubby faces with leaves and vines growing out of their orifices, symbolizing nature. This paradise/Garden of Eden theme is enhanced by a smattering of exotic animals (monkey, elephant, camel, dragon, and a lion fighting a unicorn) and some exotic foliage: aloe vera, trillium, and corn. That last one (framing a window to the right of the altar) is a mystery: It was carved well before Columbus sailed the ocean blue, at a time when corn was unknown in Europe. Several theories have been suggested—some far-fetched (the father of the man who built the chapel explored the New World before Columbus), and others more plausible (the St. Clairs were of Norse descent, and the Vikings are known to have traveled to the Americas well before Columbus). Other simply say it's not corn at all—it's stalks of wheat. After all these centuries, Rosslyn Chapel's mysteries still inspire the imaginations of historians, novelists, and tourists alike.

Royal Botanic Garden

Britain's second-oldest botanical garden (after Oxford) was established in 1670 for medicinal herbs, and this 70-acre refuge is now one of Europe's best.

Cost and Hours: Gardens—free, greenhouse—£5, daily March-Sept 10:00-18:00, until 17:00 Feb and Oct, until 16:00 Nov-Jan, greenhouse closes one hour earlier, café, a mile north of the city center at Inverleith Row, tel. 0131/552-7171, www.rbge.org.uk.

Getting There: It's a 10-minute bus ride from the city center: Take bus #8 from North Bridge, or #23 or #27 from George IV Bridge (near the National Museum) or The Mound. The Majestic Tour hop-on, hop-off bus also stops here.

Scottish National Gallery of Modern Art

This museum, set in a beautiful parkland, houses Scottish and international paintings and sculpture from 1900 to the present, including works by Matisse, Duchamp, Picasso, and Warhol. The grounds include a pleasant outdoor sculpture park and a café.

Cost and Hours: Free, daily 10:00-17:00, Aug until 18:00—until 19:00 Thu-Sat, 75 Belford Road, tel. 0131/624-6336, www.nationalgalleries.org.

Getting There: It's about a 20-minute walk west from the city center. Public transportation options aren't good, but a shuttle bus runs hourly between this museum and the Scottish National Gallery (£1 donation requested, confirm times on website).

URBAN HIKES

▲▲Holyrood Park: Arthur's Seat and the Salisbury Crags

Rising up from the heart of Edinburgh, Holyrood Park is a lush green mountain squeezed between the parliament/Holyroodhouse (at the bottom of the Royal Mile) and the Dalkeith Road B&B neighborhood. For an exhilarating hike, connect these two zones with a moderately strenuous 30-minute walk along the Salisbury Crags—reddish cliffs with sweeping views over the city. Or, for a more serious climb, make the ascent to the summit of Arthur's Seat, the 822-foot-tall remains of an extinct volcano. You can run up like they did in *Chariots of Fire,* or just stroll—at the summit, you'll be rewarded with commanding views of the town and surroundings.

On May Day, be on the summit at dawn and wash your face in the morning dew to commemorate the Celtic holiday of Beltane, the celebration of spring. (Morning dew is supposedly very good for your complexion.)

You can do this hike either from the bottom of the Royal Mile or from the B&B neighborhood.

From the Royal Mile: Begin in the parking lot below the Palace of Holyroodhouse. Facing the cliff, you'll see two trailheads. For the easier hike along the base of the **Salisbury Crags,** take the trail to the right. At the far end, you can descend into the Dalkeith Road area or—if you're up for more hiking—continue steeply up the switchbacked trail to the Arthur's Seat summit. If you know you'll want to ascend **Arthur's Seat** from the start, take the wider path on the left from the Holyroodhouse parking lot (easier grade, through the abbey ruins and "Hunter's Bog").

From the Dalkeith Road B&B Neighborhood: If you're sleeping in this area, enjoy a pre-breakfast or late-evening hike starting from the other side (in June, the sun comes up early, and it stays light until nearly midnight). From the Commonwealth Pool, take Holyrood Park Road, bear left at the first roundabout, then turn right at the second roundabout (onto Queen's Drive). Soon you'll see the trailhead, and make your choice: Bear right up the steeper "Piper's Walk" to **Arthur's Seat** (about a 20-minute hike from here, up a steeply switchbacked trail). Or bear left for an easier ascent up the "Radial Road" to the **Salisbury Crags,** which you can follow—with great views over town—all the way to Holyroodhouse Palace.

By Car: If you have a car, you can drive up most of the way to Arthur's Seat from behind (follow the one-way street from the palace, park safely and for free by the little lake, and hike up).

▲Calton Hill

For an easy walk with fine views over all of Edinburgh, head up to Calton Hill—the monument-studded bluff that rises up from the eastern end of the New Town. From the Waverley Station area, simply head east on Princes Street (which becomes Waterloo Place).

About five minutes after passing North Bridge, watch on the right for the gated entrance to the **Old Calton Cemetery**—worth a quick walk-through for its stirring monuments to great Scots. The can't-miss-it round monument honors the philosopher David Hume; just next to that is a memorial topped by Abraham Lincoln, honoring Scottish-American troops who were killed in combat. The obelisk honors political martyrs.

The views from the cemetery are good, but for even better ones, head back out to the main road and continue a few more minutes on Waterloo Place. Across the street, steps lead up into **Calton Hill.** Explore. Informational plaques identify the key landmarks. At the summit of the hill is the giant unfinished replica of the Parthenon, honoring those lost in the Napoleonic Wars. Donations to finish it never materialized, leaving it with the nickname "Edinburgh's Disgrace." Nearby, the old observatory is filled with an avant-garde art gallery, and the back of the hillside boasts sweeping views over the Firth of Forth and Edinburgh's sprawl. Back toward the Old Town, the tallest tower celebrates Admiral Horatio Nelson—the same honoree of the giant pillar on London's Trafalgar Square. The best views are around the smaller, circular Dugald Stewart Monument, with postcard panoramas overlooking the spires of the Old Town and the New Town.

More Hikes

You can hike along the river (called the Water of Leith) through Edinburgh. Locals favor the stretch between Roseburn and Dean Village, but the 1.5-mile walk from Dean Village to the Royal Botanic Garden is also good. For more information on these and other hikes, ask at the TI.

ACTIVITIES

Several enjoyable activities cluster near the B&B area around Dalkeith Road. For details, check their websites.

The **Royal Commonwealth Pool** is an indoor fitness and activity complex with a 50-meter pool, gym/fitness studio, and kids' soft play zone (daily, tel. 0131/667-7211, www.edinburghleisure.co.uk).

The **Prestonfield Golf Club**, also an easy walk from the B&Bs, has golfers feeling like they're in a country estate (dress code, 6 Priestfield Road North, tel. 0131/667-9665, www.prestonfieldgolf.com).

Farther out at **Midlothian Snowsports Centre** (a little south of town in Hillend; better for drivers), try brush-skiing—skiing without any pesky snow. It feels like snow-skiing on a slushy day, even though you're schussing over what seems like a million toothbrushes. Beware: Doctors are used to treating an ailment called "Hillend Thumb"—thumbs dislocated when people fall here and get tangled in the brush. Locals say that skiing here is like falling on a carrot grater (open evenings only—call to confirm hours, bus #4 or #15, tel. 0131/445-4433, www.midlothian.gov.uk).

Festivals in Edinburgh

Every summer, Edinburgh's annual festivals turn the city into a carnival of the arts. The season begins in June with the international film festival (www.edfilmfest.org.uk); then the jazz and blues festival in July (www.edinburghjazzfestival.com).

In August a riot of overlapping festivals known collectively as the **Edinburgh Festival** rages simultaneously—international, fringe, book, and art, as well as the Military Tattoo. There are enough music, dance, drama, and multicultural events to make even the most jaded traveler giddy with excitement. Every day is jammed with formal and spontaneous fun. Many city sights run on extended hours. It's a glorious time to be in Edinburgh...*if* you have (and can afford) a room.

If you'll be in town in August, book your room and tickets for major events (especially the Tattoo) as far ahead as you can lock in dates. Plan carefully to ensure you'll have time for festival activities as well as sightseeing. Check online to confirm dates; the best overall website is www.edinburghfestivals.co.uk. Several publications—including the festival's official schedule, the *Edinburgh Festivals Guide Daily, The List, Fringe Program,* and *Daily Diary*—list and evaluate festival events.

The official, more formal **Edinburgh International Festival** is the original. Major events sell out well in advance (ticket office at the Hub, in the former Tolbooth Church near the top of the Royal Mile, tel. 0131/473-2000, www.hubtickets.co.uk or www.eif.co.uk).

The less formal **Fringe Festival,** featuring edgy comedy and theater, is huge—with 2,000 shows—and has eclipsed the original festival in popularity (ticket/info office just below St. Giles' Cathedral on the Royal Mile, 180 High Street, bookings tel. 0131/226-0000, www.edfringe.com). Tickets may be available at the door, and half-price tickets for some events are sold on the day of the show at the Half-Price Hut, located at the Mound near the Scottish National Gallery.

The **Military Tattoo** is a massing of bands, drums, and bagpipes, with groups from all over the former British Empire and beyond. Displaying military finesse with a stirring lone-piper finale, this grand spectacle fills the Castle Esplanade (nightly except Sunday: Aug 5-27 in 2016, Aug 4-26 in 2017; performances Mon-Fri at 21:00, Sat at 19:30 and 22:30, £25-63, booking starts in Dec, Fri-Sat shows sell out first, all seats generally sold out by early summer, some scattered same-day tickets may be available; office open Mon-Fri 10:00-16:30, closed Sat-Sun, during Tattoo open until show time and closed Sun; 32 Market Street, behind Waverley Station, tel. 0131/225-1188, www.edintattoo.co.uk). Some performances are filmed by the BBC and later broadcast as a big national television special.

The **Festival of Politics,** adding yet another dimension to Edinburgh's festival action, is held in August in the Scottish parliament building. It's a busy weekend of discussions and lectures on environmentalism, globalization, terrorism, gender, and other issues (www.festivalofpolitics.org.uk).

Other summer festivals cover books (mid-late Aug, www.edbookfest.co.uk) and art (late July-Aug, www.edinburghartfestival.com).

Shopping in Edinburgh

Edinburgh is bursting with Scottish clichés for sale: kilts, shortbread, whisky...if they can slap a tartan on it, they'll sell it. Locals dismiss the touristy trinket shops, which are most concentrated along the Royal Mile, as "tartan tat." Your challenge is finding something a wee bit more authentic. If you want to be sure you are taking home local merchandise, check if the labels read: "Made in Scotland." "Designed in Scotland" actually means "Made in China." Shops are usually open 10:00-18:00 (later on Thu).

SHOPPING STREETS AND NEIGHBORHOODS

Near the Royal Mile

The Royal Mile is intensely touristy, mostly lined with interchangeable shops selling made-in-China souvenirs. (While they seem different, most of the shops along the Royal Mile are actually owned by the same family.) I've listed a few worthwhile spots along here later, under "What to Shop For." But in general, the two connecting streets listed next—an easy stroll from the top of the Royal Mile—offer more originality.

Victoria Street, which climbs steeply downhill from the Royal Mile (near the Hub/Tolbooth Church) to Grassmarket, has a fine concentration of creative shops. You'll see I. J. Mellis Cheesemonger (#30A, described later), The Red Door Gallery (fun and hip design—from prints to jewelry, #42), Walker Slater (designer tweed, #16 and #44, described later), Calezat (quality textiles), and more.

Candlemaker Row, exiting Grassmarket opposite Victoria Street, continues the fun lineup, but amps up the creative design. First, where the street meets Grassmarket, look for a pair of funky shops: Fabhatrix hat shop—with everything from dapper men's

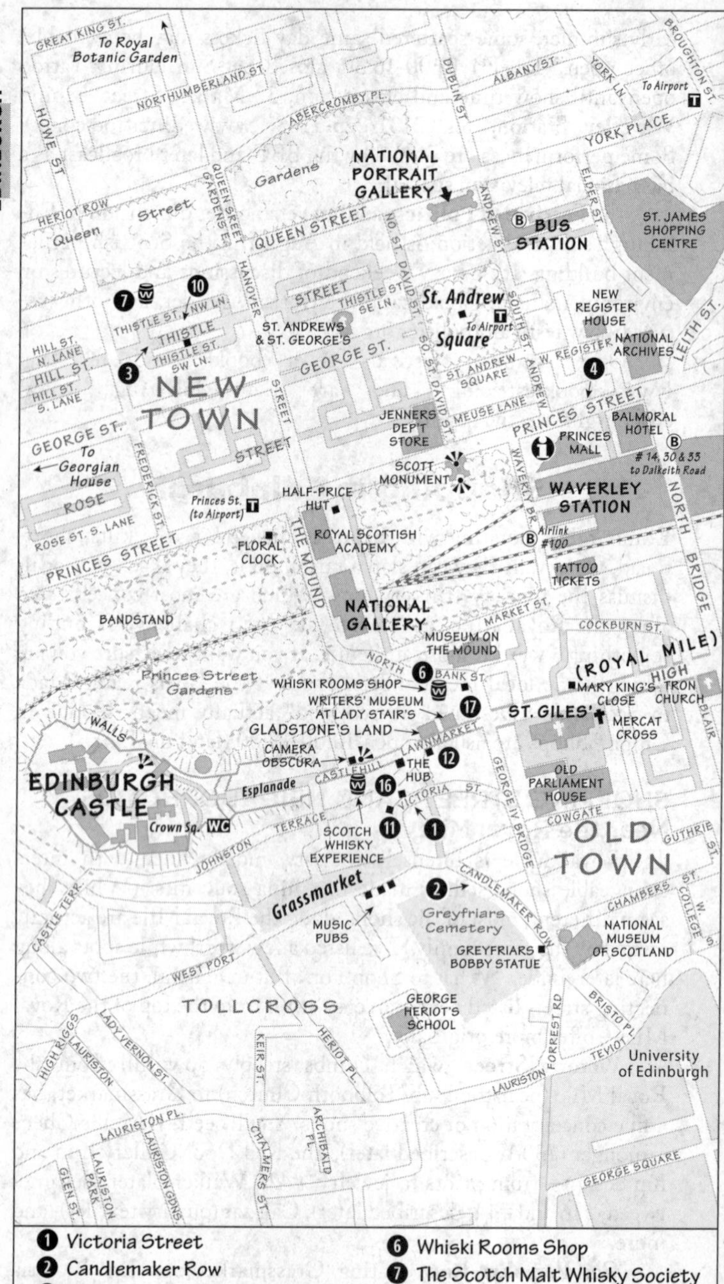

1 Victoria Street
2 Candlemaker Row
3 Thistle Street
4 Princes Street
5 Cadenhead's Whisky Shop
6 Whiski Rooms Shop
7 The Scotch Malt Whisky Society
8 Nicolson Kiltmakers
9 The Scottish Regimental Store

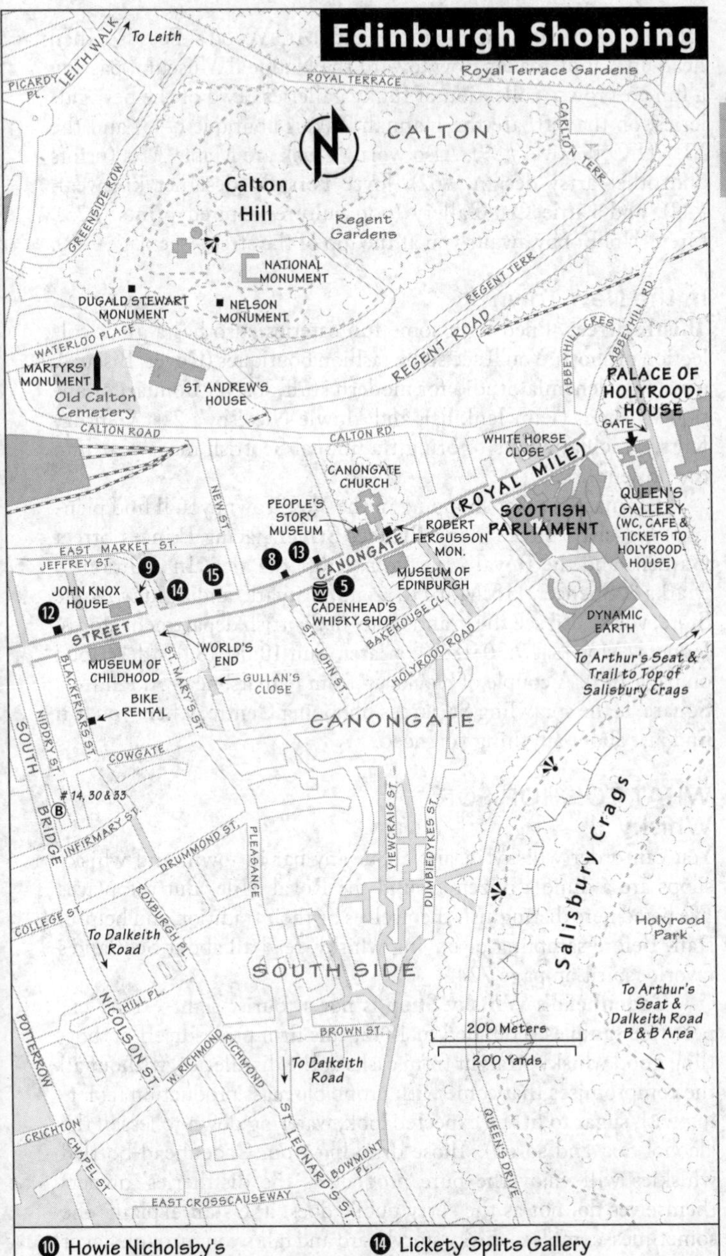

Edinburgh Shopping
To Leith
LEITH WALK
PICARDY PL.
ROYAL TERRACE
Royal Terrace Gardens
CALTON
CARLTON TERR.
Calton Hill
Regent Gardens
GREENSIDE ROW
NATIONAL MONUMENT
DUGALD STEWART MONUMENT
NELSON MONUMENT
REGENT TERR.
REGENT ROAD
WATERLOO PLACE
ABBEYHILL CRES.
ABBEYHILL RD.
MARTYRS' MONUMENT
Old Calton Cemetery
ST. ANDREW'S HOUSE
PALACE OF HOLYROOD-HOUSE
CALTON ROAD
CALTON RD.
WHITE HORSE CLOSE
GATE
CANONGATE CHURCH
(ROYAL MILE)
NEW ST.
PEOPLE'S STORY MUSEUM
ROBERT FERGUSSON MON.
SCOTTISH PARLIAMENT
QUEEN'S GALLERY (WC, CAFE & TICKETS TO HOLYROOD-HOUSE)
EAST MARKET ST.
JEFFREY ST.
CANONGATE
MUSEUM OF EDINBURGH
JOHN KNOX HOUSE
CADENHEAD'S WHISKY SHOP
BAKEHOUSE CL.
DYNAMIC EARTH
STREET
ST. JOHN ST.
HOLYROOD ROAD
WORLD'S END
To Arthur's Seat & Trail to Top of Salisbury Crags
MUSEUM OF CHILDHOOD
BLACKFRIARS ST.
ST. MARY'S ST.
GULLAN'S CLOSE
BIKE RENTAL
CANONGATE
NIDDRY ST.
SOUTH BRIDGE
COWGATE
14, 30 & 33
INFIRMARY ST.
DRUMMOND ST.
PLEASANCE
VIEWCRAIG ST.
DUMBIEDYKES ST.
Salisbury Crags
Holyrood Park
COLLEGE ST.
To Dalkeith Road
BOXBURGH PL.
SOUTH SIDE
To Arthur's Seat & Dalkeith Road B & B Area
HILL PL.
NICOLSON ST.
POTTERROW
BROWN ST.
200 Meters
200 Yards
W. RICHMOND
RICHMOND
To Dalkeith Road
QUEEN'S DRIVE
CRICHTON
CHAPEL ST.
ST. LEONARD'S ST.
BOWMONT PL.
EAST CROSSCAUSEWAY
10 Howie Nicholsby's 21st Century Kilts
11 Walker Slater Tweed
12 Ness Clothing (2)
13 Jewelry Shops
14 Lickety Splits Gallery
15 Cranachan & Crowdie Scottish Products
16 I.J. Mellis Cheesemonger
17 Coda Music

caps to outrageous fascinators—and Mr. Wood's Fossils. Then head up Candlemaker Row toward the National Museum, passing a fun-to-browse collection of funky galleries. Two of the best galleries, on the left, are the Hannah Zakari boutique (#43) and the PI-KU Collective (#39). Also worth a look are Maple Arts (prints and other artsy design, #62), Joyce Forsyth (designer knitwear, #42), and Little Ox Gallery (pop culture-inspired prints, #23). Greyfriars Bobby awaits you at the top of the street (see page 740).

In the New Town

Thistle Street, lined with some fun eateries, also has a great collection of shops. You'll see some fashion boutiques (Covet, Biscuit), jewelry (Alchemia Studio for modern stuff, Joseph Bonnar for antiques), shoes (Pam Jenkins), and Howie Nicolsby's 21st Century Kilts, which attempts to bring traditional Scottish menswear into the present day.

For mass-market shopping in the New Town, you'll find plenty of big chain stores along **Princes Street,** facing Princes Street Gardens and the Royal Mile from across the glen. In addition to Marks & Spencer, H&M, BHS, Zara, Primark, and a glitzy Apple Store, you'll also see the granddaddy of Scottish department stores, Jenners (Mon-Sat 9:30-18:30 or later, Sun 10:00-18:00; described on page 709). A couple of blocks up from Jenners, near St. Andrew Square, is the sprawling St. James Shopping Centre, where you can find just about anything you need.

WHAT TO SHOP FOR

Whisky

You can order whisky in just about any bar in town, and whisky shops are a dime a dozen around the Royal Mile. But the places I've listed here distinguish themselves by their tradition and helpful staff. Before sampling or buying whisky, read all about Scotland's favorite spirit on page 724.

Cadenhead's Whisky Shop is not a tourist sight—don't expect free samples. Founded in 1842, this firm prides itself on bottling good whisky straight from casks at the distilleries, without all the compromises that come with profitable mass production (coloring with sugar to fit the expected look, watering down to lessen the alcohol tax, and so on). Those drinking from Cadenhead-bottled whiskies will enjoy the pure product as the distilleries' owners themselves do, not as the sorry public does. The staff explains the sometimes-complex whisky storyboard and talks you through flavor profiles. Buy the right bottle to enjoy in your hotel room night after night (prices start around £14 for about 7 ounces)—unlike wine, whisky has a long shelf life after it's opened. The bottles are extremely durable; ask them to demonstrate (but get a second cap and twist off carefully, as they can break; Mon-Sat 10:30-17:30, closed Sun, 172 Canongate, tel. 0131/556-5864, www.wmcadenhead.com). They host whisky tastings a couple of times a month (posted in the shop)—a hit with aficionados.

Whiski Rooms Shop, just off the Royal Mile, comes with a knowledgeable, friendly staff that happily assists novices and experts alike to select the right bottle. Their adjacent bar usually has about 300 open bottles: Serious purchasers can get a sample. Even better, try one of their tastings. You have two options: You can order a flight in the bar, which comes with written information about each whisky you're sampling (12 options for £15-22, available anytime the bar is open). Or you can pay a few pounds more for a guided tasting (£20 introductory tasting, £38 premium tasting with the really good stuff, chocolate and cheese pairings also available; takes about one hour, reserve ahead). If you're doing a flight or a tasting, you'll get a small discount voucher for buying a bottle in the store (shop open daily 10:00-19:00, bar until 24:00, both open later in Aug, 4 North Bank Street, tel. 0131/225-1532, www.whiskirooms.com). There's a second location of the bar (but not the shop) farther down the Royal Mile, tucked in the row of pubs at 119 High Street.

Near the Dalkeith Road B&Bs: Perhaps the most accessible place to learn about local whiskies is conveniently located in the B&B neighborhood. **WoodWinters** is a nondescript shop with a passion both for traditional spirits and for the latest innovations in Edinburgh's booze scene. It's well-stocked with 300 whiskies and gins (a recently en vogue alternative to Scotch), as well as wines and local craft beers. Manager Rob invites curious browsers to sample a wee dram; he loves to introduce customers to something new (Mon-Wed and Sat 10:00-19:00, Tue-Fri 10:00-20:00, Sun 13:00-17:00, 91 Newington Road, www.woodwinters.com, tel. 0131/667-2760). For location, see the map on page 768.

In the New Town: **The Scotch Malt Whisky Society,** formerly a private club, recently opened its doors to the general public. While this place's shrouded-in-mystery pretense will be lost on novices, aficionados enjoy signing in at the front desk downstairs, then heading up to a bright contemporary whisky bar with anonymous numbered bottles of single malts from all over Scotland. In this "blind tasting" approach, you have to read each number's exacting description in the binder to make your choice...or enlist the help of the bartender (£5-36 glasses, Mon-Sat 11:00-23:00, closed

Sun, bar serves light dishes, on-site restaurant, 28 Queen Street, tel. 0131/220-2044, www.smws.com).

Kilts and Other Traditional Scottish Gear

Many of the kilt outfitters you'll see along the Royal Mile are selling cheap knock-offs, made with printed rather than woven tartan material. If you want a serious kilt—or would enjoy window-shopping for one—try one of the places below. These have a few off-the-rack options, but to get a kilt in your specific tartan and size, they'll probably take your measurements, custom-make it, and ship it to you. For a good-quality outfit (kilt, jacket, and accessories), plan on spending in the neighborhood of £1,000.

Nicolson Kiltmakers has a respect for tradition and quality. Owner Gordon enlists and trains local craftspeople who specialize in traditionally manufactured kilts and accessories. He

prides himself on keeping the old ways alive (in the face of deeply discounted "tartan tat") and actively cultivates the next generation of kiltmakers (daily 9:30-17:30, 189 Canongate, tel. 0131/558-2887, www.nicolsonkiltmakers.co.uk).

The Scottish Regimental Store, run by Nigel, is the official outfitter for military regiments. They sell top-of-the-line formal kiltwear, as well as medals and pins that can be a more affordable souvenir (Mon-Sat 10:30-17:00, closed Sun, 9 Jeffrey Street, tel. 0131/557-0249, www.scottishregimentalstore.co.uk).

Howie Nicholsby's 21st Century Kilts, in the New Town, brings this traditional craft into the present day. It's fun to peruse his photos of both kilted celebrities (from Alan Cumming to Vin Diesel) and wedding albums—which make you wish you were Scottish, engaged, and wealthy enough to hire Howie to outfit your bridal party (closed Sun-Mon, 48 Thistle Street, tel. 0131/220-9450, www.21stcenturykilts.com).

Tweed and Other Fashionwear

Several places around town sell the famous Harris Tweed (the authentic stuff is handwoven on the Isle of Harris). But these shops put a modern spin on a Scottish classic.

Walker Slater is the place to go for top-quality tweed at top prices. They have two locations tucked down

Victoria Street, just below the Royal Mile: menswear (at #16) and womenswear (#44). At both places, you'll find a rich interior and a wide variety of gorgeous jackets, scarves, bags, and more. This place feels elegant and exclusive (Mon-Sat 10:00-18:00, later on Thu, Sat until 17:00, usually closed Sun, www.walkerslater.com).

Ness, a women's clothing store, gives Scottish tweed a playful, colorful, contemporary spin. You'll find bags, scarves, and knitwear at two Royal Mile locations: across from the Hub at 367 High Street, and farther down, across from St. Giles' at 60 High Street (both open daily, www.ness.com).

Jewelry

Jewelry with Celtic designs, mostly made from sterling silver, is a popular and affordable souvenir. While you'll see these sold around town, two convenient shops face each other near the bottom of the Royal Mile: **Hamilton and Young,** which has a line of *Outlander*-inspired designs (173 Canongate), and **Celtic Design** (156 Canongate).

Food and Treats

Lickety Splits Gallery is part art, part candy, and all character. Naomi, who specializes in everything sweet, stocks her shelves with traditional candies and local crafts, including several map-based items ideal for globetrotters. Naomi also loves to share fascinating historical tidbits on the origins of Scotland's favorite childhood treats—from lucky tatties, soor plooms, and Edinburgh rock to parma violets, humbugs, and fizzy fangs... not to mention the epic scandal over how Chelsea Whoppers became Tootsie Rolls. Candy lovers can mix and match a little bag of goodies to go (Mon-Sat 11:00-17:30, Sun 12:00-16:00—but likely closed Sun in winter, 6 Jeffrey Street, mobile 07415-985-913).

Cranachan & Crowdie collects products (mostly edibles, some crafts) from more than 200 small independent producers all over Scotland. The selection goes well beyond the mass-produced clichés, and American Beth and Scottish Fiona love to explain the story behind each item (daily 11:00-18:00, on the Royal Mile at 263 Canongate, tel. 07951/587-420).

I. J. Mellis Cheesemonger, tucked down Victoria Street just off the top of the Royal Mile, stocks a wide variety of Scottish, English, and international cheeses. They're as knowledgeable about cheese as they are generous with samples (Mon-Sat 9:30-18:00,

Thu-Fri until 19:00, Sun 11:00-17:00, 30A Victoria Street, tel. 0131/226-6215).

Music

Coda, specializing in folk music—both old and new—sits just a few steps below the Royal Mile. This is the place to learn more about Celtic roots music (daily 9:30-17:30, 12 Bank Street, tel. 0131/622-7246).

Nightlife in Edinburgh

▲▲Literary Pub Tour

This two-hour walk is interesting even if you think Sir Walter Scott won an Oscar for playing General Patton. You'll follow the witty dialogue of two actors as they debate whether the great literature of Scotland was high art or the creative recreation of fun-loving louts fueled by a passion for whisky. You'll wander from the Grassmarket over the Old Town and New Town, with stops in three pubs as your guides share their takes on Scotland's literary greats. The tour meets at The Beehive pub on Grassmarket (£14, book online and save £2, May-Sept nightly at 19:30, April and Oct Thu-Sun, Jan-March Fri and Sun, Nov-Dec Fri only, www.edinburghliterarypubtour.co.uk).

▲Ghost Walks

A variety of companies lead spooky walks around town, providing an entertaining and affordable night out (offered nightly, most around 19:00 and 21:00, easy socializing for solo travelers). These two options are the most established.

The theatrical and creatively-staged **The Cadies & Witchery Tours,** the most established outfit, offers two different 1.25-hour walks: "Ghosts and Gore" (April-Aug only, in daylight and following a flatter route) and "Murder and Mystery" (year-round, after dark, hillier, more surprises and scares). The cost for either tour is the same (£9, includes book of stories, leaves from top of Royal Mile, outside the Witchery Restaurant, near Castle Esplanade, reservations required, tel. 0131/225-6745, www.witcherytours.com).

Auld Reekie Tours offers a scary array of walks daily and nightly (£9-12, 45-90 minutes, leaves from front steps of the Tron Church building on Cockburn Street, tel. 0131/557-4700, www.auldreekietours.com). Auld Reekie focuses on the paranormal, witch covens, and pagan temples, taking groups into the "haunted vaults" under the old bridges "where it was so dark, so crowded, and so squalid that the people there knew each other not by how they looked, but by how they sounded, felt, and smelt." If you want more, there's plenty of it (complete with screaming Gothic "jumpers").

Scottish Folk Evenings

A variety of £35-40 dinner shows, generally for tour groups intent on photographing old cultural clichés, are held in the huge halls of expensive hotels. (Prices are bloated to include 20 percent commissions.) Your "traditional" meal is followed by a full slate of swirling kilts, blaring bagpipes, and Scottish folk dancing with an old-time music hall emcee. If you like Lawrence Welk, you're in for a treat. But for most travelers, these are painfully cheesy. You can sometimes see the show without dinner for about two-thirds the price. The TI has fliers on all the latest venues.

Prestonfield House, a luxurious venue near the Dalkeith Road B&Bs, offers its kitschy "Taste of Scotland" folk evening with or without dinner Sunday to Friday. For £49, you get the show with two drinks and a wad of haggis; £62 buys you the same, plus a three-course meal and a half-bottle of wine (be there at 18:45, dinner at 19:00, show runs 20:00-22:00, April-Oct only). It's in the stables of "the handsomest house in Edinburgh," which is now home to the recommended Rhubarb Restaurant (Priestfield Road, a 10-minute walk from Dalkeith Road B&Bs, tel. 0131/225-7800, www.scottishshow.co.uk).

For something more lowbrow—and arguably more authentic—in summer, you can watch the **Princes Street Gardens Dancers** perform a range of Scottish country dancing. The volunteer troupe will demonstrate each dance, then invite spectators to give it a try (£4, June-July Mon 19:30-21:30, at Ross Bandstand in Princes Street Gardens—in the glen just below Edinburgh Castle, tel. 0131/228-8616, www.princesstreetgardensdancing.org.uk). The same group offers summer programs in other parts of town (see website for details).

Theater

Even outside festival time, Edinburgh is a fine place for lively and affordable theater. Pick up *The List* for a complete rundown of what's on (sold at newsstands, may be free at the TI; also online at www.list.co.uk).

▲▲Live Music in Pubs

While traditional music venues have been eclipsed by beer-focused student bars, Edinburgh still has a few good pubs that can deliver a traditional folk-music fix. The monthly *Gig Guide* (free at TI, accommodations, and various pubs, www.gigguide.co.uk) lists several places each night that have live music, divided by genre (pop, rock, world, and folk).

South of the Royal Mile: **Sandy Bell's** is a tight little pub with live folk music nightly from 21:30 (just outside the tourist zone, a few minutes' walk from the Greyfriars Bobby statue and the National Museum of Scotland at 25 Forrest Road, tel. 0131/225-2751). Food is very simple (toasted sandwiches and soup), drinks are cheap, tables are small, and the vibe is local. They also have weekend afternoon sessions (Sat at 14:00, Sun at 16:00).

Captain's Bar is a cozy music-focused pub with live sessions of folk and traditional music nightly around 21:00 (4 South College Street, http://captainsedinburgh.webs.com).

The Royal Oak is another good—if small—place for a dose of Celtic music (just off South Bridge opposite Chambers Road at 1 Infirmary Street, tel. 0131/557-2976).

The **Grassmarket** neighborhood (below the castle) bustles with live music and rowdy people spilling out of the pubs and into what was (once upon a time) a busy market square. While it used to be a mecca for Scottish folk music, today it's more youthful with a heavy-drinking, rockin' feel. It's fun to just wander through this area late at night and check out the scene. Thanks to the music and crowds, you'll know where to go...and where not to. Have a beer and follow your ear to places like **Biddy Mulligans** or **White Hart Inn** (both on Grassmarket). **Finnegans Wake,** on Victoria Street (which leads down to Grassmarket), also has live folk and rock each night.

On the Royal Mile: Three characteristic pubs within a few steps of each other on High Street (opposite Radisson Hotel) offer a fun setting, classic pub architecture and ambience, and live music for the cost of a beer: **Whiski Bar** (trad and folk nightly at 22:00), **Royal Mile** (nightly at 22:00, pop and folk music, trad most likely on Thu), and **Mitre Bar** (Fri-Sun at 21:00 or 21:30).

Just a block away (on South Bridge) is **Whistlebinkies Live Music Bar.** While they rarely do folk or Scottish trad, this is the most serious of the music pubs, with an actual stage and several acts nightly (schedule posted outside the door makes the genre clear: rock, pop, jazz, or blues, music starts at 19:00 or earlier, young crowd, fun energy, no cover, tel. 0131/557-5114). **No. 1 High Street** is an accessible little pub with a love of folk and traditional music and free performances many nights from 21:00 (Scottish trad on Tue-Wed, bluegrass on Thu). Drop by during your sightseeing as you walk the lower part of the Royal Mile, and ask what's on tonight (across from World's End, 1 High Street, tel. 0131/556-5758).

In the New Town: All the beer drinkers seem to head for the pedestrianized Rose Street, famous for having the most pubs per square inch anywhere in Scotland—and plenty of live music.

Pubs near Dalkeith Road B&Bs

The pubs in the Dalkeith Road B&B area don't typically have live music, but some are fun evening hangouts. **Leslie's Pub,** sitting between a working-class and an upper-class neighborhood, has two sides. Originally the gang would go in on the right to gather around the great hardwood bar, glittering with a century of *Cheers* ambience. Meanwhile, the more delicate folks would slip in on the left, with its discreet doors, plush snugs (cozy private booths), and ornate ordering windows. Since 1896, this Victorian classic has been appreciated for both its real ales and its huge selection of fine whiskies (listed on a lengthy menu). Dive into the whisky mosh pit on the right, and let them show you how whisky can become "a very good friend." (Leslie's is at 49 Ratcliffe Terrace, daily 11:00-24:00, tel. 0131/667-7205.)

Other good pubs in this area include **The Old Bell** (uphill from Leslie's, popular and cozy, with big TV screens), **The Salisbury Arms** (bigger, more sprawling, feels upscale), and **Reverie Bar** (bright open space with frequent live music); all three are described later, under "Eating in Edinburgh."

Sleeping in Edinburgh

Book ahead, especially in August, when the annual Festival fills Edinburgh. Conventions, rugby matches, school holidays, and weekends can make finding a room tough at almost any time of year. For the best prices, book direct.

B&Bs NEAR DALKEITH ROAD

South of town near the Royal Commonwealth Pool, these B&Bs—just off Dalkeith Road—are nearly all top-end, sporting three or four stars. While pricey, they come with uniformly friendly hosts and great cooked breakfasts, and are a good value for people with enough money. At these not-quite-interchangeable places, character is provided by the personality quirks of the hosts.

Most listings are on quiet streets and within a few minutes' walk of a bus stop, and most can provide triples or even quads for families.

Prices listed are for most of peak season; if there's a range, prices slide up with summer demand. During the Festival in August, prices are higher; B&Bs also do not accept bookings for one-night stays during this time. In winter, when demand is light,

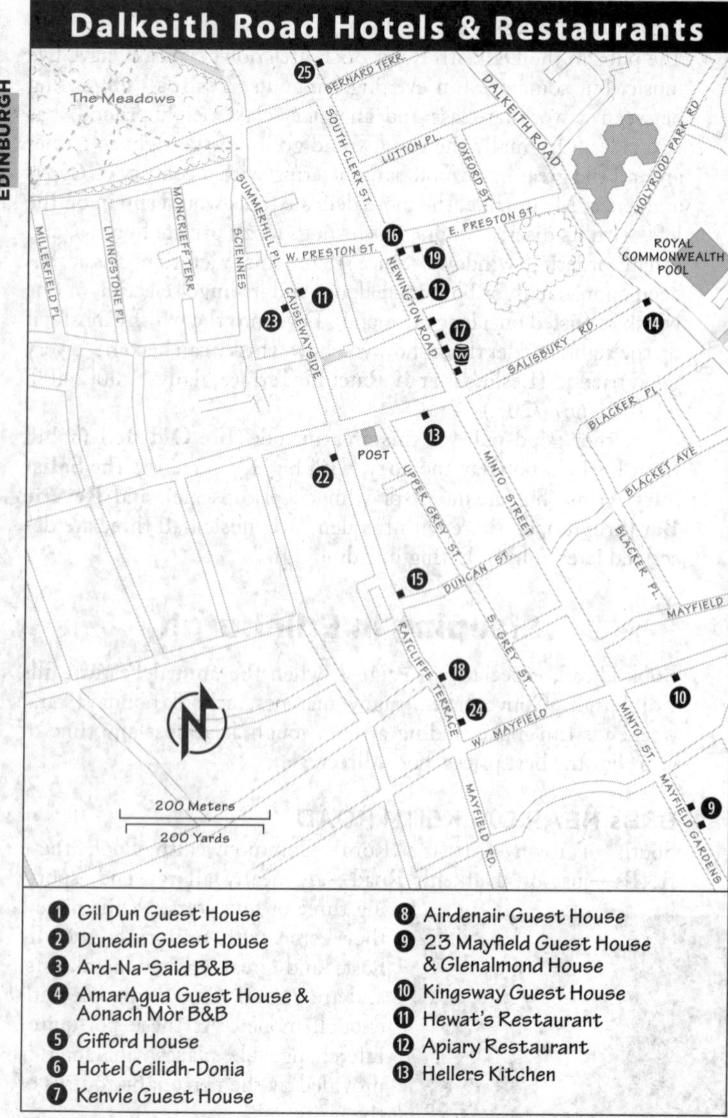

prices get really soft. Expect a 3-5 percent fee on top of these prices for using your credit card.

Near the B&Bs, you'll find plenty of great eateries (see "Eating in Edinburgh," later) and some good classic pubs (see "Nightlife in Edinburgh," earlier). A few places have their own private parking; others offer access to easy, free street parking (ask when booking—or better yet, don't rent a car for your time in Edinburgh). The

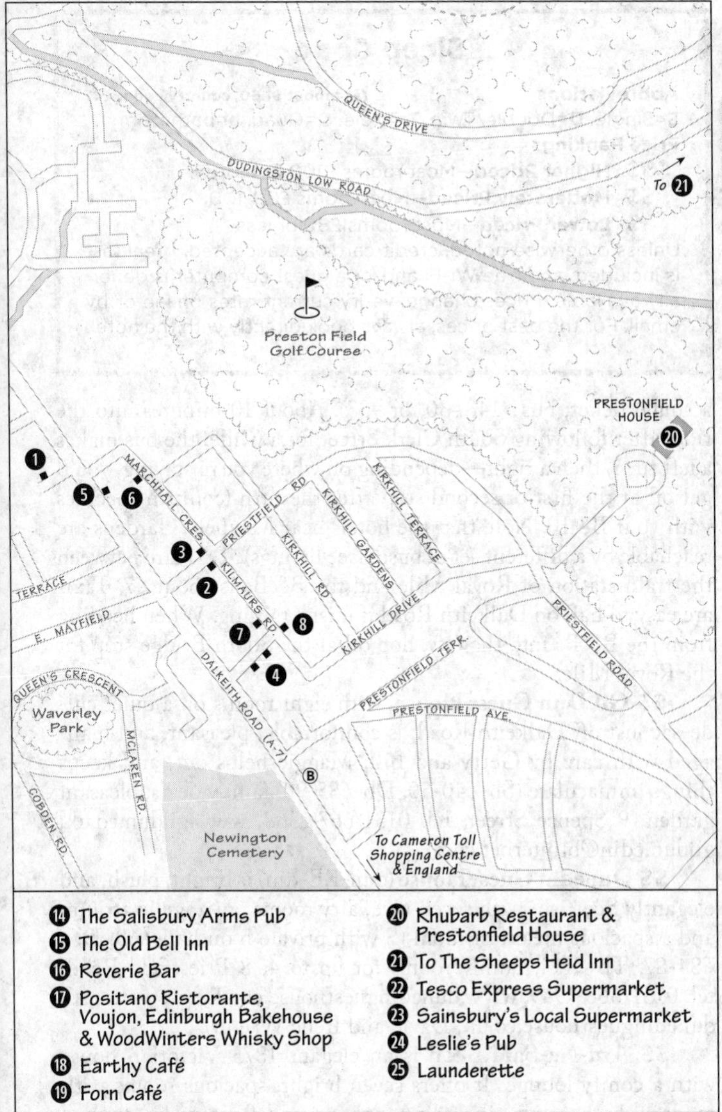

nearest launderette is Ace Cleaning Centre (which picks up and drops off; see page 682).

Getting There: This comfortable, safe neighborhood is a ten-minute bus ride from the Royal Mile. From the train station, the nearest place to catch the bus is around the corner on North Bridge: Exit the station onto Princes Street, turn right, cross the street, and walk up the bridge to the bus stop in front of the Marks & Spencer department store (£1.50, use exact change, tell the driver you want

Sleep Code

Abbreviations **(£1=about $1.60, country code: 44)**
S=Single, **D**=Double/Twin, **T**=Triple, **Q**=Quad, **b**=bathroom
Price Rankings
$$$ Higher Priced—Most rooms £100 or more
$$ Moderately Priced—Most rooms £80-100
$ Lower Priced—Most rooms £80 or less
Unless otherwise noted, credit cards are accepted, breakfast is included, and free Wi-Fi and/or a guest computer is generally available. Prices change; verify current rates online or by email. For the best prices, always book directly with the hotel.

a single ticket; bus #14, #30, or #33). About 10 minutes into the ride, after following South Clerk Street for a while, the bus makes a left turn, then a right—depending on where you're staying, you'll get off at the first or second stop after the turn (confirm specifics with your B&B). Note that the hotels near Mayfield Gardens are reachable by a different set of buses (see listings). Taxi fare between the train station or Royal Mile and the B&Bs is about £7. Taxis are easy to hail on Dalkeith Road if it isn't raining. When heading from the B&Bs into the city, hop off at the South Bridge stop for the Royal Mile.

$$ Gil Dun Guest House, with eight rooms on a quiet cul-de-sac just off Dalkeith Road, is comfortable, pleasant, and managed with care by Gerry and Bill; Maggie helps out, and keeps things immaculate (Sb-£40-50, Db-£85-90, family deals, pleasant garden, 9 Spence Street, tel. 0131/667-1368, www.gildun.co.uk, gildun.edin@btinternet.com).

$$ Dunedin Guest House (dun-EE-din) is bright, plush, and elegantly Scottish, with seven nice, airy rooms, an angelic atrium, and a spacious breakfast room (S with private b on hall-£60, Db-£84-87, Tb-£114, family rooms for up to 4, 8 Priestfield Road, tel. 0131/668-1949, www.dunedinguesthouse.co.uk, reservations@dunedinguesthouse.co.uk, David and Irene Wright).

$$ Ard-Na-Said B&B is an elegant 1875 Victorian house with a comfy lounge. It offers seven bright, spacious rooms with modern bathrooms—including one ground-floor room with a pleasant patio (Sb-£35-55, Db-£65-95, huge four-poster Db-£70-110, Tb-£90-120, prices depend on size of room and season, free parking, 5 Priestfield Road, tel. 0131/667-8754, www.ardnasaid.co.uk, enquiries@ardnasaid.co.uk, Jim and Olive Lyons).

$$ AmarAgua Guest House is an inviting Victorian home away from home, with five welcoming rooms and a Japanese garden. It's given a little extra sparkle by its energetic proprietors, former entertainers Dawn-Ann and Tony Costa (Db-£70-85, Tb-

£103-112, more for fancy four-poster rooms, 2-night minimum, 10 Kilmaurs Terrace, tel. 0131/667-6775, www.amaragua.co.uk, reservations@amaragua.co.uk).

$$ Gifford House, on busy Dalkeith Road, is a bright, flowery, creaky-floor retreat with six peaceful rooms—some with ornate cornices, super-king-size beds, and views of Arthur's Seat (Sb-£70-80, Db-£80-90, Tb-£114-120, Qb-£130-140, street parking, 103 Dalkeith Road, tel. 0131/667-4688, www.giffordhouseedinburgh.com, giffordhouse@btinternet.com, David and Margaret).

$$ Aonach Mòr B&B's eight decent rooms have views of either nearby Arthur's Seat or walled gardens (Db-£95, 10 percent Rick Steves discount if you book by email, 14 Kilmaurs Terrace, tel. 0131/667-8694, www.aonachmor.com, info@aonachmor.com, Callum and Jen).

$$ Hotel Ceilidh-Donia, bigger and more impersonal than the others listed here, rents 17 contemporary rooms with a pleasant back deck, a quiet bar, and a variety of breakfast choices (Sb-£50-66, Db-£70-120, 14 Marchhall Crescent, tel. 0131/667-2743, www.hotelceilidh-donia.co.uk, reservations@hotelceilidh-donia.co.uk).

$ Kenvie Guest House, expertly run by Dorothy Vidler, may be closing in 2017 (D-£66-70, Db-£74-80, these prices with cash and this book—mention it when you reserve, family deals, 16 Kilmaurs Road, tel. 0131/668-1964, www.kenvie.co.uk, dorothy@kenvie.co.uk).

$ Airdenair Guest House has five straightforward rooms on the second floor with a lofty above-it-all feeling. While getting a bit long in the tooth, it's a decent budget option (Sb-£40-45, Db-£70-80, Tb-£85-95, less off-season, 29 Kilmaurs Road, tel. 0131/668-2336, www.airdenair.com, jill@airdenair.com, Jill and Doug McLennan).

Guesthouses on or near Mayfield Gardens

These places are just a couple of blocks from the Dalkeith Road options, along the busy Newington Road thoroughfare. To reach them, you could take the buses listed for Dalkeith Road earlier, but it's easier to hop on bus #3, #7, #8, #29, #31, #37, or #49. Note: Some of these buses depart from the second bus stop, a bit farther along North Bridge.

$$$ At **23 Mayfield Guest House,** Ross (and Grandma Mary) rent eight splurge-worthy, thoughtfully appointed rooms complete with high-tech bathrooms and a hot tub in the garden. Little extras—such as locally sourced gourmet breakfasts, an inviting guest lounge outfitted with leatherbound Sir Arthur Conan Doyle books, an "honesty bar," and classic black-and-white movie screenings—make you feel like royalty (Sb-£79-110, Db-£80-140, bigger Db-£90-160, price depends on room size, family room for up to 4, Rick Steves discount with cash, swap library, free parking, 23 Mayfield Gardens, tel. 0131/667-5806, www.23mayfield.co.uk, info@23mayfield.co.uk). They also rent two apartments (details on website).

$$ Kingsway Guest House, with seven stylish rooms, is owned by conscientious, delightful Gary and Lizzie, who have thought of all the little touches—from a cozy leather-sofa lounge to the latest advice on neighborhood eats (Sb-£50-70, Db-£65-90, Tb-£80-120, Qb-£90-130, ask for Rick Steves discount when you book directly with the B&B and pay cash, free parking, 5 East Mayfield, tel. 0131/667-5029, www.edinburgh-guesthouse.com, booking@kingswayguesthouse.com).

$$ Glenalmond House, run by Jimmy and Fiona Mackie, has nine elegantly decorated rooms, modern bathrooms, and high prices (Db-£80-100, bigger four-poster Db-up to £130, Tb-£80-130, Qb-£120-169, ask for Rick Steves discount when you book by email or phone and pay cash, discount for longer stays, free parking, 25 Mayfield Gardens, tel. 0131/668-2392, www.glenalmondhouse.com, enquiries@glenalmondhouse.com).

BIG, MODERN HOTELS

The first listing's a splurge. The rest are cheaper than most of the city's other chain hotels, and offer more comfort than character. In each case, I'd skip the institutional breakfast and eat out. To locate these hotels, see the maps on page 775. You'll generally pay about £10 a day to park near these hotels.

$$$ Macdonald Holyrood Hotel is a four-star splurge, with 156 rooms up the street from the parliament building and Holyroodhouse Palace. With its classy marble-and-wood decor, fitness center, and pool, it's hard to leave. On a gray winter day in Edinburgh, this could be worth it (rates vary with demand, Db-£110-160, £50 more for recently-renovated "feature" rooms, breakfast costs extra, check for specials online, family deals, air-con, elevator, valet parking-£25, near bottom of Royal Mile, across from Dynamic Earth, 81 Holyrood Road, tel. 0131/528-8000, www.macdonaldhotels.co.uk).

$$$ The Inn on the Mile is your trendy central option, filling a renovated old bank building right in the heart of the Royal Mile (at North Bridge/South Bridge). The nine bright and stylish rooms are an afterthought to the busy upmarket pub, which is where you'll check in. If you don't mind some noise (from the pub and the busy street) and climbing lots of stairs, it's a handy home base (Db-£80-200 depending on season, breakfast-£9, air-con, 82 High Street, tel. 0131/556-9940, www.theinnonthemile.co.uk).

$$$ ***Handy But Impersonal Chain Hotels:*** Several cookie-cutter chain hotels sit close to the Royal Mile. These are more convenient for sightseeing than the B&Bs, but have far less character and warmth. Each hotel has complex "dynamic pricing" that fluctuates wildly with demand; to comparison-shop, check each one's website for the prevailing rate during your stay: **Motel One Edinburgh Royal,** part of a stylish German budget hotel chain, is between the train station and the Royal Mile; it feels upscale and trendy for its price range (208 rooms, pay more for a park view or less for a windowless "budget" room with skylight, elevator, 18 Market Street, tel. 0131/220-0730, www.motel-one.com, edinburgh-royal@motel-one.com; second location in the New Town/shopping zone at 134 Princes Street). **The Inn Place,** part of a small chain, fills the former headquarters of *The Scotsman* newspaper—a few steep steps below the Royal Mile—with 27 characterless, minimalist rooms at reasonable prices (best deals on weekdays, 20 Cockburn Street, tel. 0131/526-3780, www.theinnplaceedinburgh.co.uk).

Jurys Inn has 186 bright rooms on a quiet street just off the Royal Mile, a short walk from the station (some views, 43 Jeffrey Street, tel. 0131/200-3300, www.jurysinns.com). **Ibis Hotel Edinburgh Centre** has two convenient branches near the Tron Church, smack in the middle of the Royal Mile (99 rooms just behind the church at 6 Hunter Square, tel. 0131/240-7000, h2039@accor.com; 259 rooms in a bigger, less appealing branch around the corner along the busy South Bridge at #77, tel. 0131/292-0000, h8484@accor.com). **Holiday Inn Express Edinburgh Royal Mile** rents 78 rooms with stark modern efficiency just off the Royal Mile down St. Mary's Street (300 Cowgate, tel. 0131/524-8400, www.hiexpressedinburgh.co.uk; another Holiday Inn is at 16 Picardy Place, tel. 0131/558-2300, www.hieedinburgh.co.uk). **Travelodge Central** fills a hulking building just below the Royal Mile with 193 no-nonsense rooms (33 St. Mary's Street, tel. 0871-984-8484, www.travelodge.co.uk; four additional locations in the New Town).

HOSTELS

$ Edinburgh Central Youth Hostel rents 300 beds in rooms accommodating one to eight people (all with private bathrooms and lockers). Guests can eat cheaply in the cafeteria or cook for the cost of groceries in the members' kitchen (£20-30/bunk depending on season, private rooms available, 15-minute downhill walk from Waverley Station—head down Leith Walk, pass through two roundabouts, hostel is on your left—or take Lothian bus #22 or #25 to Elm Rowe, 9 Haddington Place off Leith Walk, tel. 0131/524-2090, www.syha.org.uk).

$ Smart City Hostel rents 620 bunks in austere industrial-strength dorms, each with its own private bathroom. But it can get crazy with raucous weekend stag and hen parties. Bar 50 in

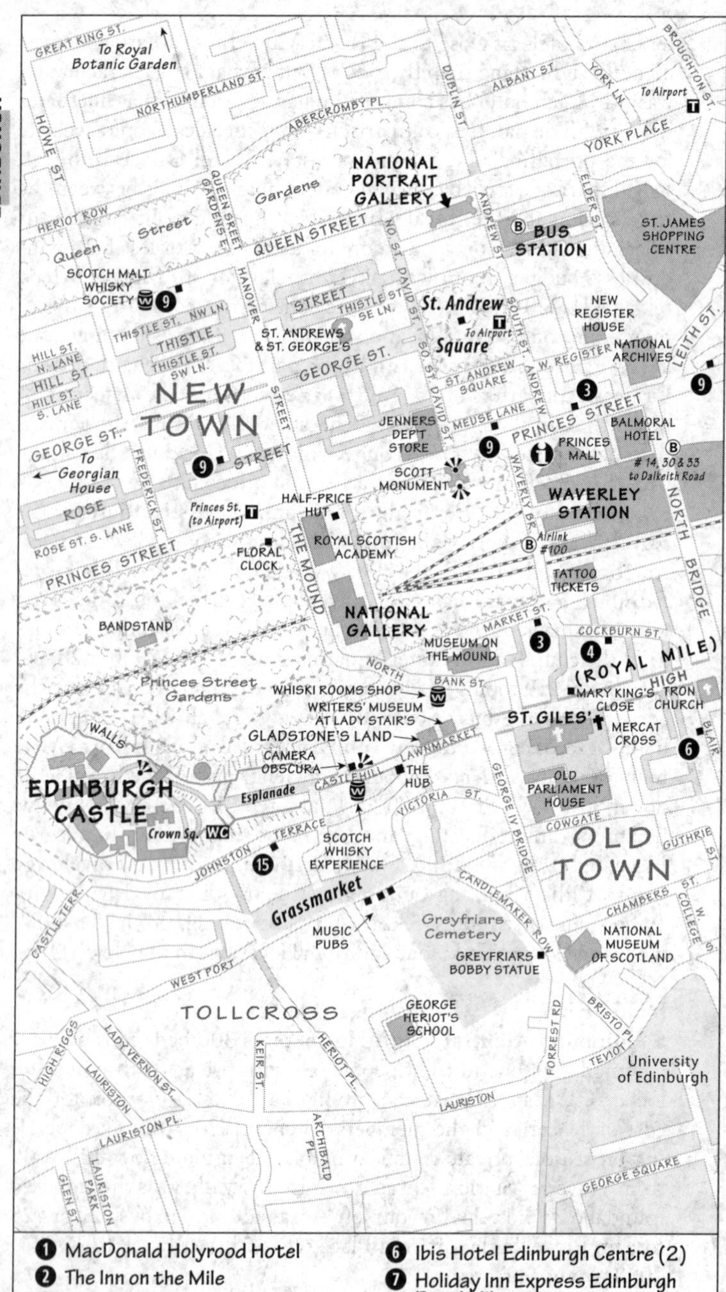
To Royal Botanic Garden
NATIONAL PORTRAIT GALLERY
BUS STATION
ST. JAMES SHOPPING CENTRE
To Airport
SCOTCH MALT WHISKY SOCIETY
St. Andrew Square
To Airport
NEW REGISTER HOUSE
NATIONAL ARCHIVES
ST. ANDREWS & ST. GEORGE'S
NEW TOWN
JENNERS DEPT STORE
BALMORAL HOTEL
PRINCES MALL
14, 30 & 33 to Dalkeith Road
To Georgian House
SCOTT MONUMENT
WAVERLEY STATION
HALF-PRICE HUT
Princes St. (to Airport)
ROYAL SCOTTISH ACADEMY
Airlink #100
FLORAL CLOCK
TATTOO TICKETS
BANDSTAND
NATIONAL GALLERY
MUSEUM ON THE MOUND
(ROYAL MILE)
Princes Street Gardens
WHISKI ROOMS SHOP
MARY KING'S CLOSE
TRON CHURCH
WRITERS' MUSEUM AT LADY STAIR'S
ST. GILES'
MERCAT CROSS
GLADSTONE'S LAND
CAMERA OBSCURA
THE HUB
EDINBURGH CASTLE
Esplanade
OLD PARLIAMENT HOUSE
Crown Sq.
SCOTCH WHISKY EXPERIENCE
OLD TOWN
Grassmarket
MUSIC PUBS
Greyfriars Cemetery
NATIONAL MUSEUM OF SCOTLAND
GREYFRIARS BOBBY STATUE
TOLLCROSS
GEORGE HERIOT'S SCHOOL
University of Edinburgh
GREAT KING ST.
NORTHUMBERLAND ST.
ABERCROMBY PL.
DUBLIN ST.
ALBANY ST.
YORK LN.
BROUGHTON ST.
YORK PLACE
HOWE ST.
HERIOT ROW
QUEEN STREET GARDENS E.
Queen Street Gardens
QUEEN STREET
NO. ST. DAVID ST.
ANDREW ST.
ELDER ST.
HANOVER
THISTLE ST. NW LN.
THISTLE
THISTLE ST. SW LN.
STREET
THISTLE ST. SE LN.
SO. ST. DAVID ST.
SOUTH ST. ANDREW
LEITH ST.
HILL ST. N. LANE
HILL ST.
HILL ST. S. LANE
GEORGE ST.
ST. ANDREW SQUARE
W. REGISTER
MEUSE LANE
PRINCES STREET
STREET
FREDERICK ST.
ROSE
ROSE ST. S. LANE
PRINCES STREET
THE MOUND
WAVERLEY BR.
NORTH BRIDGE
MARKET ST.
COCKBURN ST.
NORTH BANK ST.
HIGH
BLAIR
WALLS
LAWNMARKET
CASTLEHILL
VICTORIA ST.
GEORGE IV BRIDGE
COWGATE
GUTHRIE ST.
JOHNSTON TERRACE
CANDLEMAKER ROW
CHAMBERS ST.
W. COLLEGE ST.
CASTLE TERR.
WEST PORT
FORREST RD
BRISTO PL.
TEVIOT
HIGH RIGGS
LADY LAWSON ST.
LAURISTON
KEIR ST.
HERIOT PL.
LAURISTON
LAURISTON PL.
ARCHIBALD PL.
GLEN ST.
LAURISTON PARK
GEORGE SQUARE
❶ MacDonald Holyrood Hotel
❷ The Inn on the Mile
❸ Motel One Edinburgh Royal (2)
❹ The Inn Place
❺ Jurys Inn
❻ Ibis Hotel Edinburgh Centre (2)
❼ Holiday Inn Express Edinburgh Royal Mile
❽ Travelodge Central
❾ Travelodges (4)

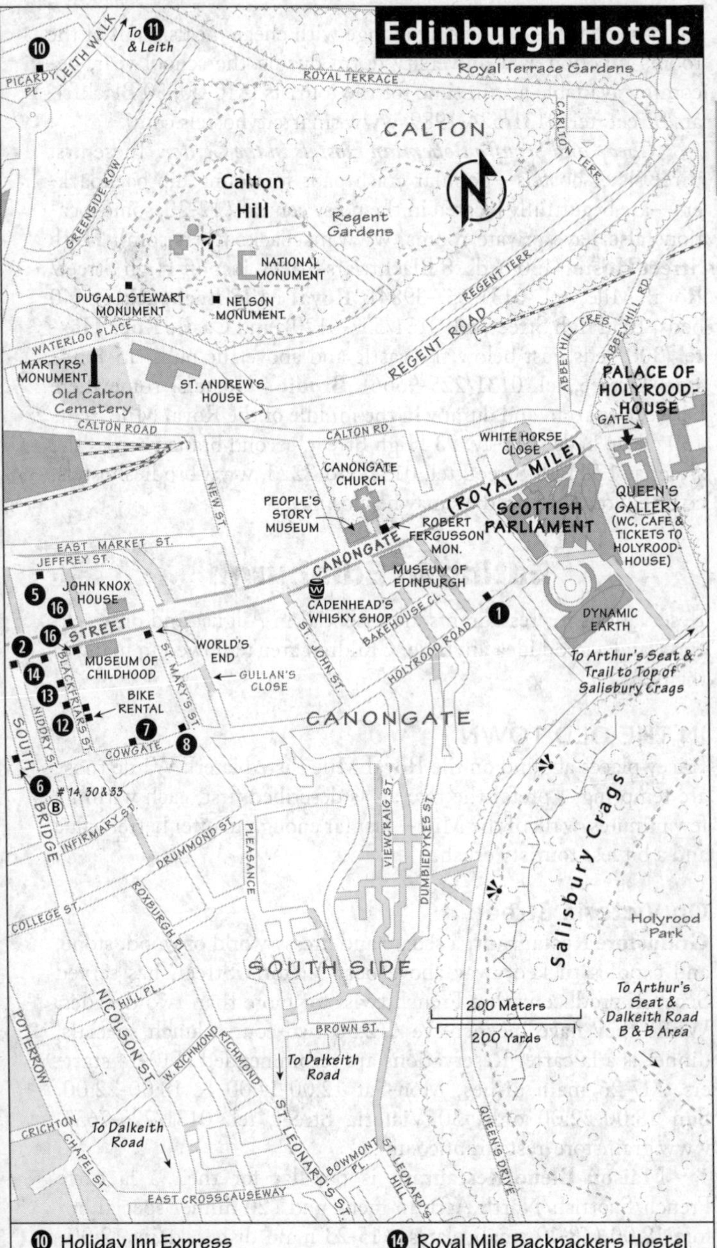
Edinburgh Hotels
To 11 & Leith
LEITH WALK
PICARDY PL.
ROYAL TERRACE
Royal Terrace Gardens
CALTON
CARLTON TERR.
GREENSIDE ROW
Calton Hill
Regent Gardens
NATIONAL MONUMENT
DUGALD STEWART MONUMENT
NELSON MONUMENT
REGENT TERR.
REGENT ROAD
WATERLOO PLACE
MARTYRS' MONUMENT
Old Calton Cemetery
ST. ANDREW'S HOUSE
ABBEYHILL CRES.
ABBEYHILL RD.
PALACE OF HOLYROOD-HOUSE
GATE
CALTON ROAD
CALTON RD.
WHITE HORSE CLOSE
CANONGATE CHURCH
(ROYAL MILE)
NEW ST.
PEOPLE'S STORY MUSEUM
ROBERT FERGUSSON MON.
SCOTTISH PARLIAMENT
QUEEN'S GALLERY (WC, CAFE & TICKETS TO HOLYROOD-HOUSE)
EAST MARKET ST.
JEFFREY ST.
CANONGATE
MUSEUM OF EDINBURGH
JOHN KNOX HOUSE
CADENHEAD'S WHISKY SHOP
BAKEHOUSE CL.
DYNAMIC EARTH
STREET
WORLD'S END
ST. JOHN ST.
HOLYROOD ROAD
To Arthur's Seat & Trail to Top of Salisbury Crags
MUSEUM OF CHILDHOOD
ST. MARY'S ST.
GULLAN'S CLOSE
BLACKFRIARS ST.
BIKE RENTAL
CANONGATE
NIDDRY ST.
COWGATE
SOUTH BRIDGE
14, 30 & 33
INFIRMARY ST.
DRUMMOND ST.
PLEASANCE
VIEWCRAIG ST.
DUMBIEDYKES ST.
Salisbury Crags
COLLEGE ST.
ROXBURGH PL.
Holyrood Park
SOUTH SIDE
HILL PL.
NICOLSON ST.
200 Meters
200 Yards
To Arthur's Seat & Dalkeith Road B & B Area
POTTERROW
W. RICHMOND
RICHMOND
BROWN ST.
To Dalkeith Road
ST. LEONARD'S ST.
CRICHTON
To Dalkeith Road
CHAPEL ST.
BOWMONT PL.
ST. LEONARD'S HILL
QUEEN'S DRIVE
EAST CROSSCAUSEWAY
10 Holiday Inn Express Edinburgh City Centre
11 To Edinburgh Central Youth Hostel
12 Smart City Hostel
13 High Street Hostel
14 Royal Mile Backpackers Hostel
15 Castle Rock Hostel
16 Brodie's Hostels (2)

the basement has an inviting lounge with cheap meals. Half of the rooms function as a university dorm during the school year, becoming available just in time for the tourists (£10-20, 50 Blackfriars Street, tel. 0131/524-1989, www.smartcityhostels.com).

Cheap and Scruffy Bohemian Hostels in the Center: These first three sister hostels—popular crash pads for young hip backpackers—are beautifully located in the noisy center (£12-20, some locations also have private rooms, www.macbackpackers.com): **High Street Hostel** (130 beds, 8 Blackfriars Street, just off High Street/Royal Mile, tel. 0131/557-3984); **Royal Mile Backpackers** (40 beds, 105 High Street, tel. 0131/557-6120); and **Castle Rock Hostel** (300 beds, just below the castle and above the pubs, 15 Johnston Terrace, tel. 0131/225-9666). **Brodie's Hostels,** somewhere between spartan and dumpy in the middle of the Royal Mile, rents 130 cheap beds (£13-17, 93 High Street, second branch across the street at 12 High Street, tel. 0131/556-2223, www.brodieshostels.co.uk). Note that Brodie's may be closing.

Eating in Edinburgh

Reservations for restaurants are essential in August and on weekends, and a good idea anytime. Children aren't allowed in many of the pubs.

IN THE OLD TOWN

Pricey places abound on the Royal Mile (listed later). While those are tempting, I prefer the two areas described first, each within a few minutes' walk of the Mile—just far enough to offer better value and a bit less touristy crush.

On Victoria Street

Grainstore Restaurant, a sedate and dressy world of wood, stone, and candles tucked away above busy Victoria Street, has served Scottish produce with a French twist for more than two decades. While they have inexpensive £12.50 two-course lunch specials, dinner is à la carte. Reservations are recommended (£10-14 starters, £17-26 main dishes, Mon-Sat 12:00-14:00 & 18:00-22:00, Sun 18:00-22:00 only, 30 Victoria Street, tel. 0131/225-7635, www.grainstore-restaurant.co.uk).

Maison Bleue Restaurant is popular for their à la carte French/Scottish/North African menu and £20 dinner special before 19:00 (£8-10 small plates, £15-23 main dishes, daily 12:00-22:00, 36 Victoria Street, tel. 0131/226-1900).

Oink carves from a freshly roasted pig each afternoon for sandwiches that come in £4 "oink" or £5 "grunter" sizes. Watch the pig shrink in the front window throughout the day (daily 11:00-18:00

or whenever they run out of meat, cash only, 34 Victoria Street, tel. 01890/761-355). There's another location at the bottom end of the Royal Mile, near the parliament building (at 82 Canongate).

Near the National Museum

These restaurants, located along George IV Bridge and Forrest Road (near the National Museum), are happily removed from the Royal Mile melee.

The Elephant House, two blocks out of the touristy zone, is a comfy neighborhood coffee shop where relaxed patrons browse newspapers in the stay-awhile back room, listen to soft rock, enjoy the castle and cemetery vistas, and sip coffee or munch a light meal. During the day, you'll pick up food at the counter and grab your own seat; after 17:00, the café switches to table service. It's easy to imagine J. K. Rowling spending long afternoons here writing the first Harry Potter book (£5-6 lunches, £8 dinner plates, traditional meat pies, vegetarian options, great desserts, daily 8:00-22:00, 2 blocks south of Royal Mile near National Museum of Scotland at 21 George IV Bridge, tel. 0131/220-5355).

The Outsider, also without a hint of Royal Mile tourism, is a sleek spot serving creative and trendy cuisine (good fish and grilled meats and vegetables) in a minimalist, stylish, hardwood, candlelit castle-view setting. It's noisy with enthusiasm, and the service is crisp and youthful. Reserve for dinner (£7 specials until 17:00, £15-18 main dishes, always a vegetarian course, good wines by the glass, daily 12:00-23:00, 30 yards up from The Elephant House at 15 George IV Bridge, tel. 0131/226-3131).

Just Past the National Museum, on Forrest Road: After passing the Greyfriars Bobby statue and the National Museum, fork left onto Forrest Road. As this is approaching the university campus, here you'll find a few more creative places that skew to a youthful clientele, with virtually no tourists.

Union of Genius is a creative soup kitchen with a strong identity. They cook up six delicious soups each morning at their main location in Leith, then deliver them to this shop by bicycle (for environmental reasons). These are supplemented with good salads and fresh-baked breads (various combos run £4-6). Everything is delicious, with fun foodie twists. Can't decide? Go for the "flight," with three small cups of soup and three types of bread. Line up at the counter, then either take your soup to go, or squeeze into a seat at the two small shared tables (Mon-Fri 8:30-16:00, Sat 12:00-16:00, closed Sun, 8 Forrest Road, tel. 0131/226-4436).

Next door, **Mums** is a kitschy diner serving up comfort food just like mum used to make. The menu runs to huge portions or heavy, greasy Scottish/British standards—bangers (sausages), meat pies, burgers, and artery-clogging breakfasts (served until 12:00)—

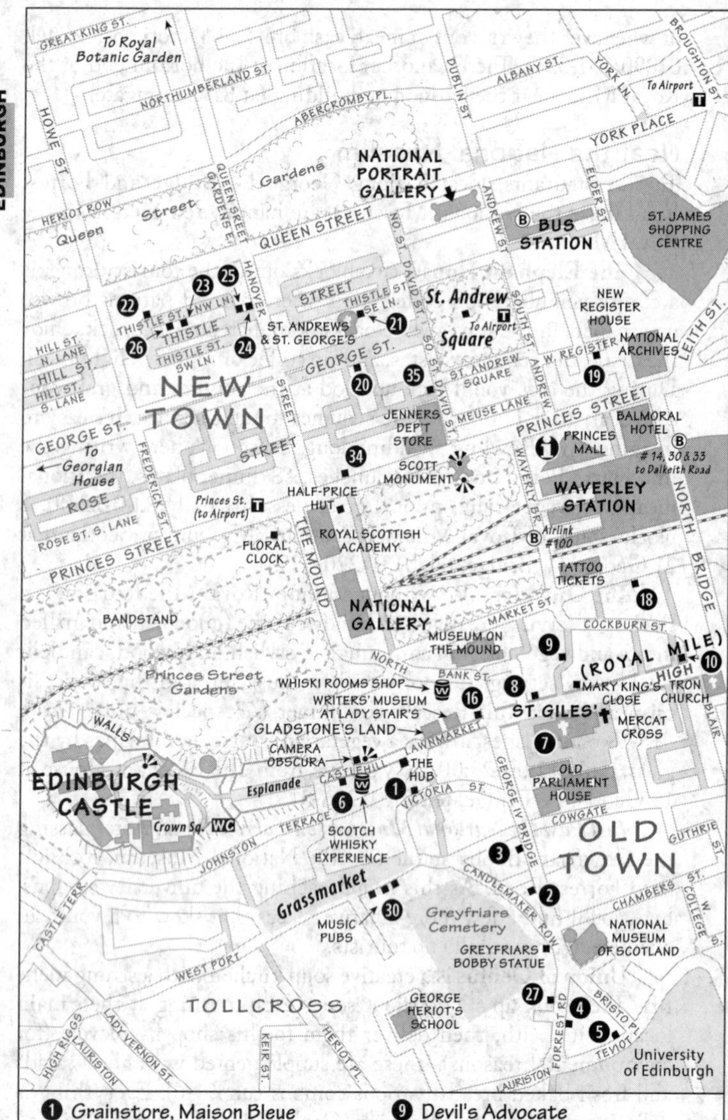

1. Grainstore, Maison Bleue & Oink
2. The Elephant House
3. The Outsider Restaurant
4. Union of Genius, Mums, and Frisky
5. Ting Thai Caravan
6. The Witchery by the Castle
7. St. Giles' Cathedral Café
8. Angels with Bagpipes
9. Devil's Advocate
10. The Baked Potato Shop
11. Edinburgh Larder
12. Mimi's Bakehouse Picnic Parlour
13. Wedgwood Restaurant
14. David Bann Restaurant
15. Clarinda's Tea Room
16. Deacon Brodie's Tavern
17. The World's End Pub
18. The Doric

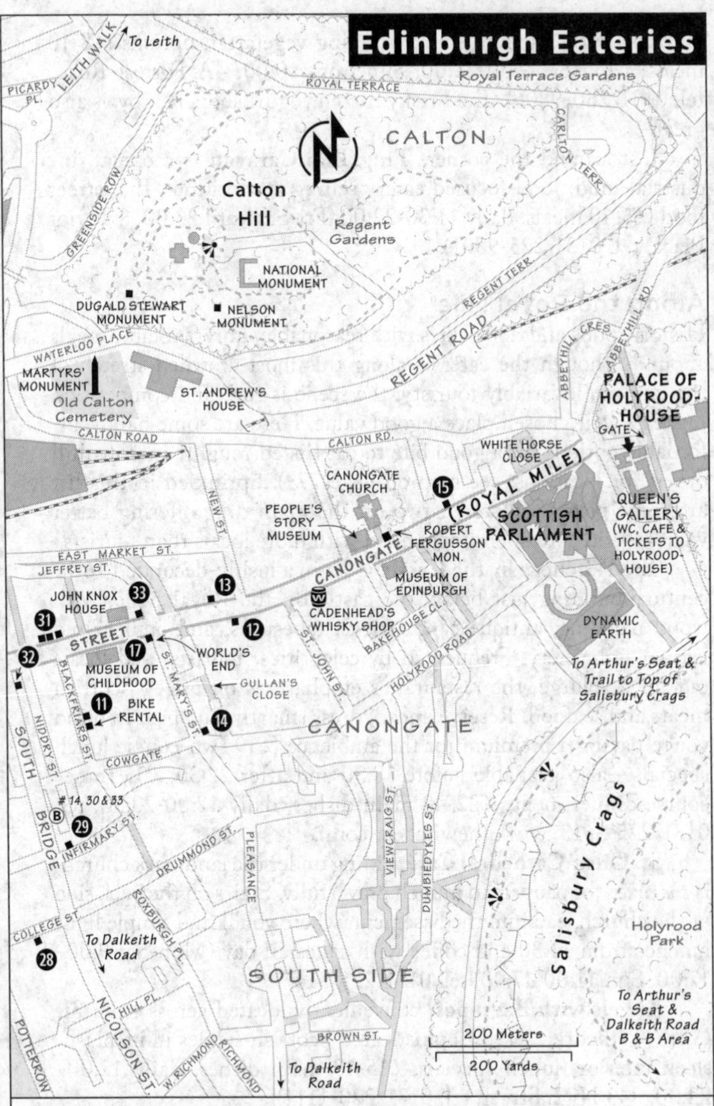

19 Café Royal
20 The Dome Restaurant
21 St. Andrew's & St. George's Church Undercroft Café
22 Le Café St. Honoré & The Bon Vivant Rest.
23 Fishers in the City
24 Henderson's of Edinburgh
25 Henderson's Vegan
26 El Cartel
27 Sandy Bell's Pub
28 Captain's Bar
29 The Royal Oak Pub
30 Biddy Mulligans, White Hart Inn & Finnegans Wake
31 Whiski Bar, Royal Mile & Mitre Bar
32 Whistlebinkies Bar
33 No. 1 High Street Pub
34 Marks & Spencer Food Hall
35 Sainsbury's Supermarket

all done with a foodie spin, including vegetarian options (£8-10 meals, Mon-Sat 9:00-22:00, Sun from 10:00, 4A Forrest Road, tel. 0131/260-9806). The **Frisky** frozen yogurt shop, nearby, is also great.

Just around the corner, **Ting Thai Caravan** is a casual, industrial-mod, food-focused eatery selling adventurous Thai street food (£5-10 meals, daily 11:30-22:00, Fri-Sat until 23:00, 8 Teviot Place, tel. 0131/225-9801).

Along the Royal Mile

Historic pubs and doily cafés with reasonable, unremarkable meals abound. Though the eateries along this most-crowded stretch of the city are invariably touristy, the scene is fun, and competition makes a well-chosen place a good value. Here are some handy, affordable options for a good bite to eat (listed roughly in downhill order; for locations, see map on page 779). Sprinkled in this list are some places a block or two off the main drag offering better values—and correspondingly filled with more locals than tourists.

The Witchery by the Castle is set in a lushly-decorated 16th-century building just below the castle on the Royal Mile, with wood paneling, antique candlesticks, tapestries, and opulent red leather upholstery. Frequented by celebrities, tourists, and locals out for a splurge, the restaurant's emphasis is on pricey Scottish meats and seafood. Reserve ahead, dress smartly, and bear in mind you're paying a premium for the ambience (£19 two-course lunch specials—also available before 18:30 and after 22:30, £35 three-course dinner menu, £22-42 main dishes, daily 12:00-23:30, tel. 0131/225-5613, www.thewitchery.com).

St. Giles' Cathedral Café, hiding under the landmark church, is *the* place for paupers to munch prayerfully. Stairs on the back side of the church lead into the basement, where you'll find simple light lunches from 11:30 and coffee with cakes all day (Mon-Sat 9:00-17:00, Sun 11:00-17:00, tel. 0131/225-5147).

Angels with Bagpipes, conveniently located across from St. Giles' Cathedral, serves sophisticated Scottish staples in its plush, sleek interior (lunch specials, £15-18 main dishes, daily 12:00-22:00, 343 High Street, tel. 0131/220-1111).

Devil's Advocate is a popular new gastropub that hides down the narrow lane called Advocates Close, directly across the Royal Mile from St. Giles'. With an old cellar setting—exposed stone and heavy beams—done up in modern style, it feels like a mix of old and new Edinburgh. Creative whisky cocktails kick off a menu that dares to be adventurous, but with a respect for Scottish tradition (£13-15 meals, daily 12:00-22:00, later for drinks, 8 Advocates Close, tel. 0131/225-4465).

The Baked Potato Shop is a handy spot to grab a hot, cheap, fast meal along the Royal Mile. They sell "the hottest tattie in town": baked potatoes with a wide variety of vegetarian fillings. It's best for takeaway, but they do have a few cramped seats (£5-7 meals, Mon-Sat 9:00-19:00, in summer until 21:00 or later, 56 Cockburn Street, tel. 0131/225-7572).

Edinburgh Larder promises "a taste of the country" in the center of the city. They focus on high-quality locally-sourced ingredients, available from a display case or as part of an enticing menu of breakfast and lunch dishes. It's a convivial space with rustic tables filled by local families (£5 soups, £7-9 sandwich plates, Mon-Fri 8:00-17:00, Sat-Sun from 9:00, 15 Blackfriars Street, tel. 0131/556-6922).

Mimi's Bakehouse Picnic Parlour, a handy Royal Mile outpost of a prizewinning bakery, serves up baked goods—try the scones—and sandwiches in their cute and modern shop (also £5 takeaway lunches, Mon-Fri 8:00-18:00, Sat-Sun from 10:00, 250 Canongate, tel. 0131/556-6632).

Wedgwood Restaurant is romantic, contemporary, chic, and as gourmet as possible with no pretense. Paul Wedgwood cooks while his wife Lisa serves with appetizing charm. The cuisine: creative, modern Scottish with an international twist and a whiff of Asia. The pigeon and haggis starter is scrumptious. Paul and Lisa believe in making the meal the event of the evening—don't come here to eat and run. I like the ground level with the Royal Mile view, but the busy kitchen ambience in the basement is also fine (£9-10 starters, £18-24 main courses, fine wine by the glass, daily 12:00-15:00 & 18:00-22:00, reservations advised, 267 Canongate on Royal Mile, tel. 0131/558-8737, www.wedgwoodtherestaurant.co.uk).

David Bann, just a three-minute walk off the Royal Mile, is a worthwhile stop for well-heeled vegetarians in need of a break from the morning fry-up. While vegetarian as can be, this place doesn't have even a hint of hippie. It's upscale (it has a cocktail bar), sleek, minimalist, and stylish (gorgeously presented dishes), serious about quality, and organic—they serve polenta, tartlets, soups, and light meals. Reserve ahead (£11-13 main dishes, decadent desserts, Mon-Fri 12:00-22:00, Sat-Sun from 11:00, vegan options, 56 St. Mary's Street, tel. 0131/556-5888).

Clarinda's Tea Room, near the bottom of the Royal Mile, is a charming and girlish time warp—a fine and tasty place to relax after touring the Mile or the Palace of Holyroodhouse. Stop in for a £6 quiche, salad, or soup lunch. It's also great for sandwiches and tea and cake anytime (Mon-Sat 8:45-16:45, Sun 9:30-16:45, 69 Canongate, tel. 0131/557-1888).

Historic Pubs along the Mile: To drink a pint or grab some forgettable pub grub in historic surroundings, consider one of the landmark pubs described on my self-guided walk: **Deacon Brodie's Tavern,** at a dead-center location on the Royal Mile (a sloppy pub on the ground floor with a sloppy restaurant upstairs) or **The World's End Pub,** farther down the Mile at Canongate (a colorful old place dishing up hearty meals from a creative menu in a fun, dark, and noisy space, 4 High Street). Both serve £8-12 pub meals and are open long hours daily. **The Doric,** less in-your-face but a notch up in quality, sits between the Royal Mile and the train station. Choose between the atmospheric pub or the classy upstairs bistro (£10-16 pub grub, daily 12:00-late, 15 Market Street, tel. 0131/225-1084).

IN THE NEW TOWN

While most of your sightseeing will be along the Royal Mile, it's important that your Edinburgh experience stretches beyond this happy tourist gauntlet. Just a few minutes away, in the Georgian part of town, you'll find a bustling world of office workers, students, and pensioners doing their thing. And at midday, that includes eating. Simply hiking over to one of these places will give you a good helping of modern Edinburgh. All these eateries are within a few minutes' walk of the TI and main Waverley Bridge tour-bus depot.

Elegant Spaces near Princes Street

For a staid glimpse at grand old Edinburgh, these are good choices.

Café Royal is a movie producer's dream pub—the perfect *fin de siècle* setting for a coffee, beer, or light meal. (In fact, parts of *Chariots of Fire* were filmed here.) Drop in, if only to admire the 1880 tiles featuring famous inventors (daily 12:00-14:30 & 17:00-21:30, bar food available all day, two blocks from Princes Mall on 19 West Register Street, tel. 0131/556-1884). There are two eateries here: the noisy pub (£10-15 main dishes) and the dressier restaurant, specializing in oysters, fish, and game (£17-22 plates, reserve for dinner—it's quite small and understandably popular).

The Dome Restaurant, in what was a fancy bank, serves modern international cuisine around a classy bar and under the elegant 19th-century skylight dome. With soft jazz and chic, white-tablecloth ambience, it feels a world apart. Come here not for the food, but for the opulent atmosphere (£13-15 plates until 17:00, £14-23 dinners until 21:45, daily 12:00-23:00, reserve for dinner, open for a drink any time under the dome; the adjacent, more intimate Club Room serves food Mon-Wed 10:00-17:00, Thu-Sat until late, closed Sun; 14 George Street, tel. 0131/624-8634).

Quick and Cheap Eats

St. Andrew's and St. George's Church Undercroft Café, in the basement of a fine old church, is the cheapest place in town for lunch—under £5 for a sandwich and soup. Your tiny bill helps support the Church of Scotland (Mon-Fri lunch only, closed Sat-Sun, at 13 George Street, just off St. Andrew Square, tel. 0131/225-3847).

Supermarkets: **Marks & Spencer Food Hall** offers an assortment of tasty hot foods, prepared sandwiches, fresh bakery items, a wide selection of wines and beverages, and plastic utensils at the checkout queue. It's just a block from the Scott Monument and the picnic-perfect Princes Street Gardens (Mon-Sat 8:00-19:00, Thu until 20:00, Sun 11:00-18:00, Princes Street 54—separate stairway next to main M&S entrance leads directly to food hall, tel. 0131/225-2301). **Sainsbury's** supermarket, a block off Princes Street, also offers grab-and-go items for a quick lunch (Mon-Sat 7:00-22:00, Sun 9:00-20:00, on corner of Rose Street on St. Andrew Square, across the street from Jenners, the classy department store).

Hip Eateries on and near Thistle Street

For something a little more modern and food-focused, head a few more minutes deeper into the New Town to find Thistle Street. This strip and its surrounding lanes are packed with more enticing eateries than the rest of the New Town put together. Browse the options here, but tune into these favorites.

Le Café St. Honoré, tucked away like a secret bit of old Paris, is a charming place with friendly service and walls lined by tempting wine bottles. It serves French-Scottish cuisine in tight Old World cut-glass elegance to a dressy crowd (£18 two-course and £24 three-course lunch and dinner specials, daily 12:00-14:00 plus Mon-Fri 17:15-22:00 and Sat-Sun 18:00-22:00, reservations smart—ask to sit upstairs, down Thistle Street from Hanover Street, 34 Northwest Thistle Street Lane, tel. 0131/226-2211, www.cafesthonore.com).

The Bon Vivant is woody, youthful, and candlelit, with a rotating menu of eclectic Mediterranean/Asian dishes and a companion wine shop serving 50 wines by the glass. They have fun £2 tapas plates and heartier £15-17 dishes, served either in the bar up front or in the restaurant in back (daily 12:00-22:00, 55 Thistle Street, tel. 0131/225-3275, www.bonvivantedinburgh.co.uk).

Fishers in the City is a bright, modern, high-energy, casual fish restaurant (£16-21 main dishes, daily 12:00-22:00, 58 Thistle Street, reservations smart, tel. 0131/225-5109, www.fishersrestaurantgroup.co.uk).

Henderson's of Edinburgh has fed a generation of New Town vegetarians hearty cuisine and salads. Even carnivores love this place for its delectable salads and desserts. Henderson's has two separate eateries: Their main restaurant, facing Hanover Street, is self-service by day but has table service after 17:00. Each evening after 19:00, they have pleasant live music—generally guitar or jazz (£12 meals, Mon-Wed 8:00-22:00, Thu-Sat until 23:00, closed Sun except in Aug, between Queen and George streets at 94 Hanover Street, tel. 0131/225-2131). Just around the corner on Thistle Street, **Henderson's Vegan** has a strictly vegan menu and feels a bit more casual (£9-10 plates, daily 12:00-21:30, tel. 0131/225-2605).

El Cartel is a youthful place serving up good tacos and other Mexican dishes in a cramped, edgy atmosphere (£5-8 small plates, daily 12:00-22:00, 64 Thistle Street).

IN THE B&B NEIGHBORHOOD, NEAR DALKEITH ROAD

Nearly all of these places (except for The Sheeps Heid Inn) are within a 10-minute walk of my recommended B&Bs. Reserve on weekends and during the Festival. For locations, see the map on page 768. For a cozy drink after dinner, visit the recommended pubs in the area (see "Nightlife in Edinburgh," earlier).

Sit-Down Restaurants

Hewat's Restaurant, welcoming and popular, is the neighborhood hit. Sample Scottish cuisine or their popular steak dishes in this elegantly whimsical dining space (Mon-Sat dinner only, closed Sun, early-bird specials before 19:00; weeknights: £19/2 courses, £23/3 courses; weekends: £12-17 à la carte dishes; 19 Causewayside, tel. 0131/466-6660, www.hewatsedinburgh.com).

Apiary brings a bit of hipster flair to this otherwise-stodgy neighborhood, with an inviting casual interior and a hit-or-miss, eclectic menu that mingles various international flavors (£10 lunch deals, £15 early-bird specials, £11-15 dinners, daily 10:00-15:30 & 17:30-22:00, 33 Newington Road, tel. 0131/668-4999, www.apiaryrestaurant.co.uk).

Hellers Kitchen is a casual blond-wood space specializing in dishes using local produce and fresh-baked breads. Check the big chalkboard to see what's on (£5-7 light bites and sandwiches, £9-13 main dishes, Mon-Sat 9:00-21:00, Sun 10:00-15:30, next to post office at 15 Salisbury Road, tel. 0131/667-4654).

Pub Grub

The Salisbury Arms Pub, with a nice garden terrace, serves upscale, pleasing traditional classics with yuppie flair in a space that exudes more Martha Stewart and Pottery Barn than traditional public house (£11-17 main dishes, evening specials, food served daily 12:00-22:00, across from the pool at 58 Dalkeith Road, tel. 0131/667-4518).

The Old Bell Inn, with an old-time sports-bar ambience—

fishing, golf, horses—serves £9-11 pub meals. This is a classic "snug pub"—all dark woods and brass beer taps, littered with evocative knickknacks. It comes with sidewalk seating and a mixed-age crowd (food served daily until 22:00, 233 Causewayside, tel. 0131/668-1573).

Reverie Bar is just your basic fun traditional pub with a focus on food rather than drinking. The big windows let in a lot of light, and there's free live music many nights from 21:30 (every other Sun-jazz, Mon-quiz night, Tue-traditional/folk; £11-14 main dishes, food served daily 12:00-15:00 & 17:00-21:00, real ales, 1 Newington Road, tel. 0131/667-8870).

Ethnic Options

Positano Ristorante has a spirited Italian ambience, as manager Donato injects a love of life and food into his little restaurant. The moment you step through the door, you know you're in for good, classic Italian cuisine (£9-11 pizzas and pastas, £14-17 plates, daily 12:00-14:00 & 17:00-23:00, 85 Newington Road, tel. 0131/662-9977).

Voujon Restaurant serves a fusion menu of Bengali and Indian cuisines. Vegetarians appreciate the expansive yet inexpensive offerings for £8 (£10-17 main dishes, daily 12:00-14:00 & 17:30-23:30, 107 Newington Road, tel. 0131/667-5046, www.voujonedinburgh.co.uk).

Fast Eats

At **Edinburgh Bakehouse,** award-winning baker James Lynch makes £1-2 fresh breads, sweets, and meat pies from scratch in this laid-back, nondescript shop. Locals line up for his morning rolls—which earned him the title "baker of the year." Stop by to see the friendly staff and open kitchen in action and judge for yourself (cash only, daily 7:00-18:00, 101 Newington Road).

Earthy is an organic farm-fresh café and grocery store with a proudly granola attitude. In the café, step up to the counter and take your pick of freshly-prepared salads, sandwiches, and baked goods (£6-7). Sit in the industrial-mod interior, with rustic picnic benches, or out in the ragtag back garden. In the well-stocked store, assemble a pricey but top-quality picnic, or just grab some snacks for your B&B room (Mon-Fri 9:00-18:00, Sat 9:00-17:00, Sun 10:00-17:00, store open a bit later, 33 Ratcliffe Terrace, tel. 0131/667-2967).

Forn, a simple but classy Catalan-themed café, has the best espresso drinks in this neighborhood, as well as baked goods and light meals (Tue-Sat 10:00-18:00, Sun 11:00-17:00, closed Mon, 1 East Preston Street, tel. 0131/667-4098).

Groceries: The nearest grocery stores are **Tesco Express** (daily

10:00-22:00, 158 Causewayside) and **Sainsbury's Local** (daily 6:30-23:00, 80 Causewayside). Cameron Toll Shopping Centre, about a half-mile south on your way out of town, houses a **Sainsbury's** superstore for more substantial supplies and gasoline.

Memorable Meals Farther Out

Rhubarb Restaurant specializes in Old World elegance. It's in "Edinburgh's most handsome house"—an over-the-top riot of antiques, velvet, tassels, and fringes. The plush dark-rhubarb color theme reminds visitors that this was the place where rhubarb was first grown in Britain. It's a 10-minute walk past the other recommended eateries behind Arthur's Seat, in a huge estate with big shaggy Highland cattle enjoying their salads al fresco. At night, it's a candlelit wonder. While most spend a wad here (£18-35 plates), they offer a £20 two-course lunch and a £35 three-course dinner. Reserve in advance and dress up if you can (daily 12:00-14:00 & 18:00-22:00, £23 afternoon tea served daily 14:00-19:00, in Prestonfield House, Priestfield Road, tel. 0131/662-2303, www.prestonfield.com). For details on their schmaltzy Scottish folk evening, see "Nightlife in Edinburgh," earlier.

The Sheeps Heid Inn, Edinburgh's oldest and most inviting public house, is equally notable for its history, date-night appeal, and hearty portions of affordable classy dishes. Though it requires a cab ride, it is worth the fare to dine in this dreamy setting in the presence of past queens and kings—or, if you prefer, outside in the classic garden courtyard (£11-18 main dishes, Mon-Sat 11:00-23:00 or 24:00, Sun 12:00-23:00, 43 The Causeway, tel. 0131/661-7974, www.thesheepheidedinburgh.co.uk).

Edinburgh Connections

BY TRAIN OR BUS

From Edinburgh by Train to: Glasgow (4/hour, 50 minutes), **St. Andrews** (train to Leuchars, 1-2/hour, 1 hour, then 10-minute bus into St. Andrews), **Stirling** (roughly 2/hour, 1 hour), **Inverness** (every 1-2 hours, 3.5-4 hours, some with change in Perth), **Oban** (5/day, 4.5 hours, change in Glasgow), **York** (2/hour, 2.5 hours), **London** (1-2/hour, 4.5 hours), **Durham** (hourly direct, 2 hours, more with changes, less frequent in winter), **Keswick/Lake District** (8-10/day to Penrith—some via Carlisle, 1.75 hours, then 40-minute bus ride to Keswick). **Train info:** Tel. 0345-748-4950, www.nationalrail.co.uk.

By Bus: Edinburgh's bus station is in the New Town, just off St. Andrew Square, two blocks north of the train station. Direct buses go to **Glasgow** (bus #900, 4/hour, 1-1.5 hours depending on traffic) and **Inverness** (about hourly, 4-5 hours). To reach other destinations in the Highlands—including **Oban, Fort William, or Glencoe**—you'll have to transfer. It's usually fastest to take the train to Glasgow and change to a bus there. For details, see "Getting Around the Highlands" on page 878. For bus info, stop by the station or call Scottish Citylink (tel. 0871-266-3333, www.citylink.co.uk). Additional long-distance routes may be operated by National Express (www.nationalexpress.com) or Megabus (www.megabus.com).

ROUTE TIPS FOR DRIVERS HEADING SOUTH

It's 100 miles south from Edinburgh to Hadrian's Wall; to Durham, it's another 50 miles.

To Hadrian's Wall: From Edinburgh, Dalkeith Road leads south and eventually becomes the A-68 (handy Cameron Toll supermarket with cheap gas is on the left as you leave Edinburgh Town, 10 minutes south of Edinburgh; gas and parking behind store). The A-68 road takes you to Hadrian's Wall in 2.5 hours. You'll pass Jedburgh and its abbey after one hour. (For one last shot of Scotland shopping, there's a coach tour's delight just before Jedburgh, with kilt makers, woolens, and a sheepskin shop.) Across from Jedburgh's lovely abbey is a free parking lot, a good visitors center, and pay toilets. The England/Scotland border is a fun, quick stop (great view, ice cream, and tea caravan). Just after the turn for Colwell, turn right onto the A-6079, and roller-coaster four miles down to Low Brunton. Then turn right onto the B-6318, and stay on it by turning left at Chollerford, following the Roman wall westward.

To Durham: If you're heading straight to Durham, you can take the scenic coastal route on the A-1 (a few more miles than the A-68, but similar time), which takes you near Holy Island and Bamburgh Castle.

GLASGOW

Glasgow (GLAS-goh)—astride the River Clyde—is a surprising city. In its heyday, Glasgow was one of Europe's biggest cities and the second-largest in Britain, right behind London. A century ago it had 1.2 million people, twice the size (and with twice the importance) of today. It was an industrial powerhouse producing 25 percent of the world's oceangoing ships. But in the mid-20th century, tough times hit Glasgow, giving it a rough edge and a run-down image.

At the city's low point during the Margaret Thatcher years (1980s), its leaders embarked on a systematic rejuvenation designed to again make Glasgow appealing to businesses, tourists...and locals. Today the city feels revitalized and goes out of its way to offer a warm welcome. Glaswegians (rhymes with "Norwegians") are the chattiest people in Scotland—and have the most entertaining (and impenetrable) accent.

Many travelers give Glasgow a miss, but that's a shame: I consider it Scotland's single-most underrated destination. Glasgow is a workaday Scottish city as well as a cosmopolitan destination, with an unpretentious friendliness, an energetic dining and nightlife scene, top-notch museums (most of them free), and a unique flair for art and design. It's also a pilgrimage site for architecture buffs, thanks to a cityscape packed with Victorian facades, early 20th-century touches, and bold and glassy new construction. Most beloved are the works by hometown boy Charles Rennie Mackintosh, the visionary—and now very trendy—architect who left his mark all over Glasgow at the turn of the 20th century.

Many more tourists visit Edinburgh, a short train trip away. But for a more complete look at urban Scotland, be sure to stop off in Glasgow. Edinburgh may have the royal aura, but Glasgow's down-to-earth appeal is captivating. In Glasgow, there's no upper-crust history, and no one puts on airs. In Edinburgh, people identify with the quality of the school they attended; in Glasgow, it's their soccer team allegiance. One Glaswegian told me, "The people of Glasgow have a better time at a funeral than the people of Edinburgh have at a wedding." In this newly energized city, friendly locals do their best to introduce you to the fun-loving, laid-back Glaswegian way of life.

PLANNING YOUR TIME

While many visitors blitz Glasgow as a day trip from Edinburgh (and a first day in Glasgow is certainly more exciting than a fourth day in Edinburgh)—or even from Stirling—the city can easily fill two days of sightseeing.

On a quick visit, follow my "Get to Know Glasgow" self-guided walk of the city center, tying together the most important sights in the city's core. If your time is short, the interiors most worth considering are the Tenement House and the Piping Centre.

With additional time, your options open up. Follow my West End walk to get a taste of Glasgow's most appealing residential zone, which has the city's best restaurants as well as a number of appealing sights. Fans of Art Nouveau and Charles Rennie Mackintosh can lace together a busy day's worth of sightseeing (the TI has a brochure laying it out). At a minimum, those interested in Mackintosh should visit the Mackintosh House at the Hunterian Gallery (in the West End), the Glasgow School of Art (which he designed), and the Mackintosh exhibit at the Kelvingrove Museum. (The first two are by tour only—call ahead to confirm the schedule.)

Regardless of how long you're staying, consider the two-hour hop-on, hop-off bus tour, which is convenient for getting the bigger picture and reaching three important sights away from the center (the Cathedral Precinct, the Riverside Museum, and the Kelvingrove Museum).

Day Trip from Edinburgh: For a full day, catch the 9:30 train to Glasgow (morning trains every 15 minutes; discount for same-day round-trip if leaving after 9:15 or on weekend); it arrives at Queen Street Train Station before 10:30. To fill your Glasgow

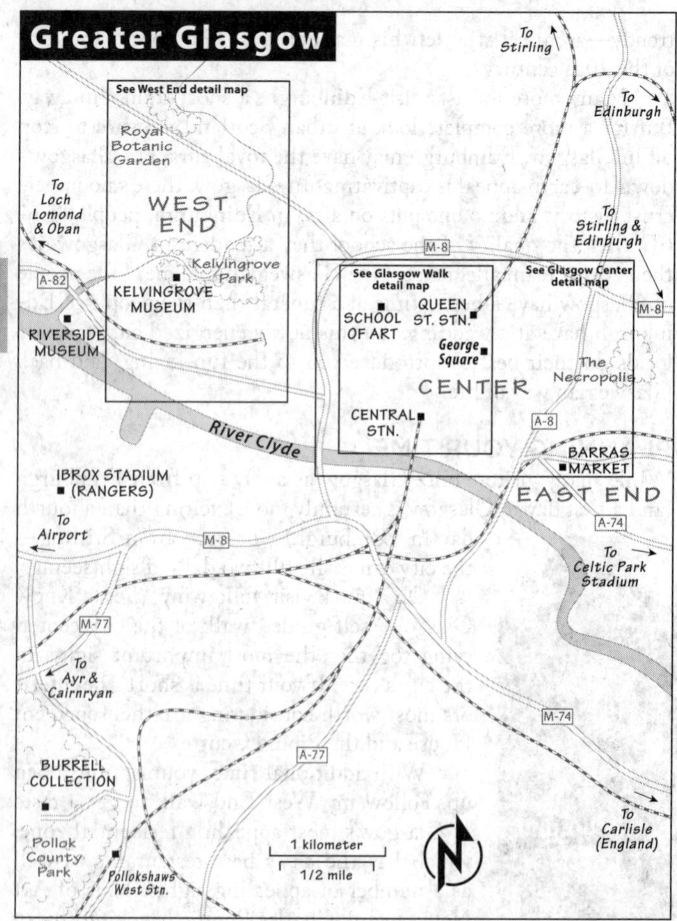

hours smartly, I'd do the entire hop-on, hop-off bus tour circuit (two hours), then follow my self-guided walk through downtown (finishing with the Tenement House). If you have time left, head to the West End for dinner or follow my self-guided West End Walk. Then hop the subway back to Queen Street Station (use the Buchanan Street stop) and catch the 21:00 train back to Edinburgh (evening trains depart every 30 minutes).

Orientation to Glasgow

Although it's often thought of as a "second city," Glasgow is actually Scotland's biggest (pop. 600,000, swelling to 1.2 million within Greater Glasgow—that's one out of every five Scots).

The tourist's Glasgow has two parts: The businesslike down-

When the Great Ships of the World Were "Clyde-Built"

Glasgow's River Clyde shipyards were the mightiest in the world, famed for building the largest moving manmade objects on earth. The shipyards, once 50 strong, have dwindled to just three. Yet a few giant cranes still stand to remind locals and visitors that from 1880 to 1950, a quarter of the world's ships were built here and "Clyde-built" meant reliability and quality. For 200 years, shipbuilding was Glasgow's top employer—as many as 100,000 workers at its peak, producing a new ship every two days. The glamorous Cunard ships were built here—from the *Lusitania* in 1906 (infamously sunk by a German U-boat in World War I, which almost brought the US into the war) to the *Queen Elizabeth II* in 1967. People still talk about the day when over 200,000 Glaswegians gathered for the launch, the Queen herself smashed the Champagne bottle on the prow, and the magnificent ship slid into the harbor. To learn lots more about shipbuilding in Glasgow, visit the excellent Riverside Museum (described under "Sights in Glasgow").

town (train stations, commercial zone, and main shopping drag) and the residential West End (B&Bs, restaurants, and nightlife). Both areas have great sights, and both are covered in this chapter by self-guided walks.

Glasgow's **downtown** is a tight grid of boxy office buildings and shopping malls, making it feel more like a midsized American city than a big Scottish one—like Cincinnati or Pittsburgh, but with shorter skyscrapers made of Victorian sandstone rather than glass and steel. The walkable city center has two main drags, both lined with shops and crawling with shoppers: Sauchiehall Street (pronounced "Suckyhall," running west to east) and Buchanan Street (running north to south). These two pedestrian malls—part of a shopping zone nicknamed the Golden Zed—make a big zig and zag through the heart of town (the third street of the Zed, Argyle Street, is busy with traffic and less appealing).

The **West End** is Glasgow's poshest suburb, with big homes and upscale apartment buildings, lots of green space, and the city's best B&Bs, shops, and restaurants. The area has three pockets of interest: near the Hillhead subway stop, with a lively restaurant scene and the Botanic Gardens; the University of Glasgow campus, with its stately buildings and fine museums; and, just downhill through a sprawling park, the area around the Kelvingrove Museum, with a lively nearby strip of trendy bars and restaurants (Finnieston).

TOURIST INFORMATION

The TI is next to the Glasgow Royal Concert Hall, where Buchanan Street swings left and becomes Sauchiehall (facing the concert hall's steps, it's to your left). While their main function seems to be booking day trips for various tour companies, they will answer questions and also hand out a good free map and brochures on Glasgow and the rest of Scotland (Mon-Sat 9:00-18:00, Sun 10:00-17:00, until 16:00 Oct-April, www.visitscotland.com).

Mackintosh Trail Ticket: This ticket, sold at the TI, covers entry to all Charles Rennie Mackintosh sights and public transportation to those outside the city limits (£10/day, www.crmsociety.com).

ARRIVAL IN GLASGOW

By Train: Glasgow, a major Scottish transportation hub, has two main train stations, which are just a few blocks apart in the heart of town: **Central Station** (with a grand, genteel interior under a vast steel-and-glass Industrial Age roof) and **Queen Street Station** (more functional, with better connections to Edinburgh and closer to the TI—take the exit marked *Buchanan Street* to reach the main shopping drag; the TI is at the top of the street and to the left). Both stations have pay WCs and pricey baggage storage. If going between the stations to change trains, you can walk five minutes or take the free roundabout "RailLink" bus #398. Trainspotters may enjoy the guided behind-the-scenes tours of Central Station, including a spooky abandoned Victorian train platform (book ahead, www.glasgowcentraltours.co.uk).

By Bus: Buchanan bus station is at Killermont Street, two blocks up the hill behind Queen Street train station.

By Car: Glasgow's downtown streets are steep, mostly one-way, and congested with buses and pedestrians. It may well be the most stressful place to drive in Scotland. Parking downtown is also a hassle: Metered street parking is very expensive (£3/hour) and limited to two hours during the day; garages are even more expensive (figure £22 for 24 hours). Ideally, do Glasgow without a car—for example, tour Edinburgh and Glasgow by public transit, then pick up your rental car on your way out of town. If you are stuck with a car in Glasgow, try to sleep in the West End, where driving and parking are easier (and commuting into downtown for sightseeing is a snap on the subway and buses).

The M-8 motorway, which slices through downtown Glasgow, is the easiest way in and out of the city. Ask your hotel for directions to and from the M-8, and connect with other highways from there.

By Air: For information on Glasgow's two airports, see "Glasgow Connections," at the end of this chapter.

HELPFUL HINTS

Safety: The city center, which is packed with ambitious career types during the day, can feel deserted at night. While the area between Argyle Street and the River Clyde has been cleaned up in recent years, parts can still feel sketchy. As in any big city, use common sense and don't wander down dark deserted alleys. The Golden Zed shopping drag, the Merchant City area (east of the train stations), and the West End all bustle with crowded restaurants well into the evening and feel well-populated in the wee hours.

If you've picked up a football (soccer) jersey or scarf as a souvenir, don't wear it in Glasgow; passions run very high, and most drunken brawls in town are between supporters of Glasgow's two rival soccer clubs: Celtic in green and Rangers in blue and red. (For more on the soccer rivalry, see page 796.)

Sightseeing: Almost every sight in Glasgow is free, but request £2-3 donations (www.glasgowmuseums.com). One exception is the Glasgow School of Art, but even there all proceeds go back to the school.

Sunday Travel: Bus and train schedules are dramatically reduced on Sundays—most routes have only half the departure times they have during the week. And trains run less frequently in the off-season; so if you want to get to the Highlands by bus on a Sunday in winter, forget it.

Internet Access: Wi-Fi is readily available in Glasgow; the main shopping drag is a big free hotspot. Many pubs and coffee shops offer free Wi-Fi as well.

Laundry: Majestic Launderette will pick up your dirty clothes at your B&B or hotel, then return them clean (call to arrange, figure around £12-15/load); they also have a self-service launderette near the Kelvingrove Museum in the West End (self-serve or full-serve, Mon-Fri 8:00-18:00, Sat 8:00-16:00, Sun 10:00-16:00, 1110 Argyle Street, tel. 0141/334-3433).

Local Guides: Joan Dobbie, a native Glaswegian and registered Scottish Tourist Guide, will give you the insider's take on Glasgow's sights (£120/half-day, £140/day, tel. 01355/236-749, mobile 07773-555-151, joan.leo@lineone.net). **Colin Mairs** is youthful, knowledgeable, and fun to be with (£100/half-day, £150/day, mobile 07716-232-001, www.ExcursionScotland.com, ExcursionScotland@gmail.com).

Highlands Day Trips: Most of the same companies that do Highlands side-trips from Edinburgh also operate trips from Glasgow. If you'd like to spend an efficient day away from the city, skim the descriptions and listings on page 685, and then check each company's website or browse the brochures at the TI for details.

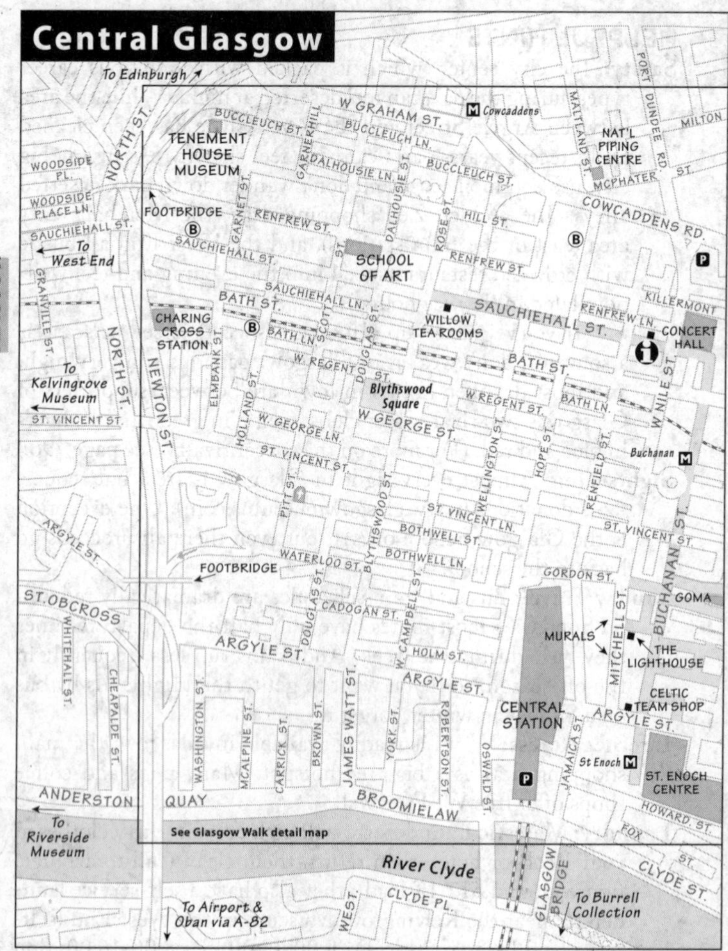

GETTING AROUND GLASGOW

By City Bus: Most city-center routes are operated by First Bus Company (£2/ride, £4.50 for all-day ticket on First buses, buy tickets from driver, exact change required). Buses run every few minutes down Glasgow's main thoroughfares (such as Sauchiehall Street) to the downtown core (train stations).

By Hop-On, Hop-Off Bus Tour: This tour connects Glasgow's far-flung historic sights in a two-hour loop and lets you hop on and off as you like for two days. Buses are frequent (every 10-20 minutes) and punctual, and alternate between live guides and recorded narration (both are equally good). The route covers the city very well, and the guide does a fine job of describing activities at each stop. While the first stop is on George Square, you

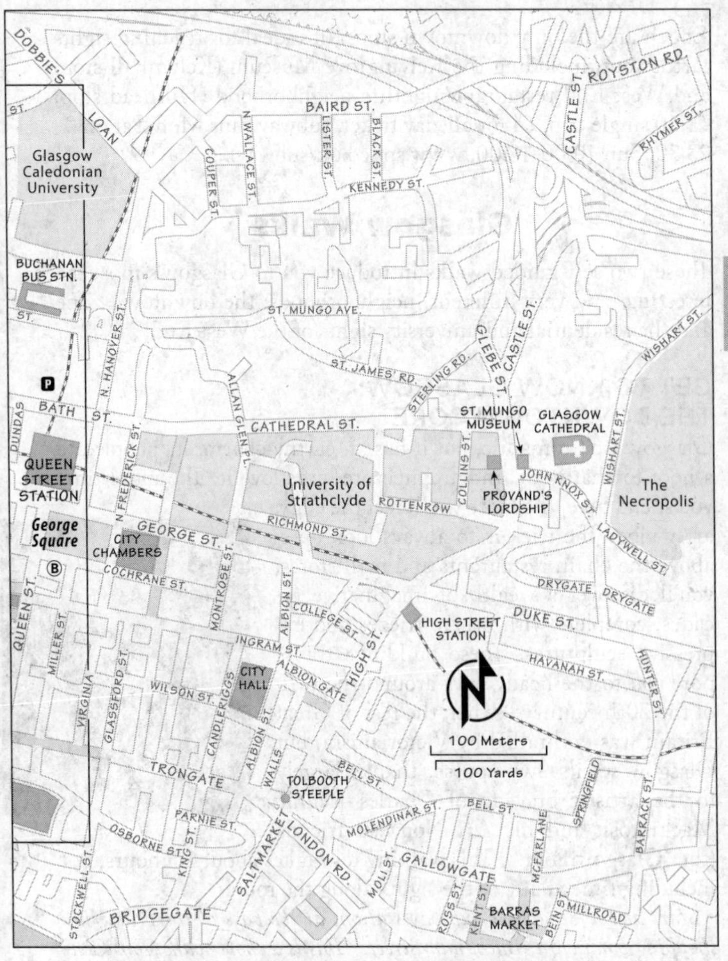

can hop on and pay the driver anywhere along the route (£13, tel. 0141/204-0444, www.citysightseeingglasgow.co.uk).

By Taxi: Taxis are affordable, plentiful, and often come with nice, chatty cabbies—all speaking in the impenetrable Glaswegian accent. Just smile and nod. Most taxi rides within the downtown area cost about £6; to the West End is about £8. Use taxis or public transport to connect Glasgow's more remote sights; splurge for a taxi (for safety) any time you're traveling late at night.

By Subway: Glasgow's cute little single-line subway system, nicknamed The Clockwork Orange, makes a six-mile circle that has 15 stops. While simple today, when it opened in 1896 it was the bee's knees (it's the world's third-oldest subway system, after those in London and Budapest). Though the subway is essentially useless for connecting city-center sightseeing (Buchanan Street and St.

Enoch are the only downtown stops), it's ideal for reaching sights farther out, including the Kelvingrove Museum (Kelvinhall stop) and West End restaurant/nightlife neighborhood (Hillhead stop; £1.60 single trip, £4 for all-day ticket, subway runs Mon-Sat 6:30-23:30, Sun 10:00-18:00, www.spt.co.uk/subway).

Glasgow Walks

These two self-guided walks introduce you to Glasgow's most interesting (and very different) neighborhoods: the downtown zone and the residential and university sights of the West End.

GET TO KNOW GLASGOW: THE DOWNTOWN CORE

Glasgow isn't romantic, but it has an earthy charm, its people are a hoot to chat with, and architecture buffs love it. The more time you spend here, the more you'll feel the edgy, artsy vibe. The trick is to always look up—above the chain restaurants and mall stores, you'll discover a wealth of imaginative facades, complete with ornate friezes and expressive sculptures. These buildings transport you to the heady days around the turn of the 20th century—when the rest of Great Britain was enthralled by Victorianism, but Glasgow set its own course, thanks largely to the artistic bravado of Charles Rennie Mackintosh and his Art Nouveau friends (the "Glasgow Four"). This walking tour takes about 1.5 hours, not including time at any of the sights along the route.

• *Start at the St. Enoch subway station, at the base of the pedestrian shopping boulevard, Buchanan Street. (This is a short walk from Central Station, a longer walk or quick cab ride from Queen Street Station.) Take a moment to get oriented.*

❶ Argyle Street and Nearby

The "Golden Zed" is the nickname for a Z-shaped pedestrian boulevard made of three streets: Sauchiehall, Buchanan, and Argyle. Always coming up with marketing slogans to goose the shopping metabolism of the city, this district (with the top shops in town) is also called the "Style Mile."

Of the three streets, Argyle (the busy cross street) is the least appealing, and Buchanan (the pedestrian mall straight ahead) is the best. But before heading up Buchanan, take a quick detour down Argyle to see a couple of slices of Glasgow life.

From the subway station, cross the busy street, then turn left along Argyle. A few doors down (on the right, at #154), notice the **Celtic Shop.** This shop is extreme green. That's the color of Glasgow's dominant (for now) soccer team. It's hard for outsiders to fathom the intensity of the rivalry between Glasgow's Celtic and Rangers. Celtic, founded by an Irish Catholic priest to raise money for poor Irish immigrants in the East End, is—naturally—green and favored by Catholics. (For reasons no one can explain, the Celtic team name is pronounced "sell-tic"—like it is in Boston. In all other cases, such as when referring to music, language, or culture, this word is pronounced "kell-tic.") Rangers, with team colors of the Union Jack (red, white, and blue), are more likely to be supported by Unionist and Protestant families. Today Celtic is in the major league and Rangers (wracked by scandals) have fallen into a lower division. Wander into the shop (minimizing or hiding any red or blue you might be wearing). Check out the energy in the photos and shots of the stadium filled with 60,000 fans. You're in a world where red and blue don't exist.

Now head a few steps down the alley (Mitchell Street) just past the Celtic Shop. While it seems a bit seedy, it should be safe...but look out for giant magnifying glasses and taxis held aloft by balloons. City officials have cleverly co-opted street artists by sanctioning huge, fun, and edgy **graffiti murals** like these. (You'll see even more if you side-trip down alleys along the Style Mile.)

• *Now backtrack to the base of...*

❷ Buchanan Street

Buchanan Street has a friendly Ramblas-style vibe with an abundance of street musicians. As you stroll uphill, keep an eye out for a few big landmarks: **Frasers** (#45, on the left) is a vast and venerable department store, considered the "Harrods of Glasgow." The **Argyll Arcade** (#30, opposite Frasers), dating from 1827, is the oldest arcade in town. It's filled mostly with jewelry and comes with security guards dressed in Victorian-era garb. Eager couples—whether they're engaged or about to be—can be heard to say, "Let's take a shortcut through here." **Princes Square** (at #48, just past Argyll Arcade) is a classic old building dressed with a modern steel peacock and foliage. Step inside to see the delightfully modernized Art Nouveau atrium.

At #97 (50 yards up, on the left) is one of two Mackintosh-designed **Willow Tea Rooms** (other location described later in this walk).

• *Just past the tearooms, turn down the alley on the right, called Exchange Place. You'll pass the recommended Rogano restaurant on your right before emerging onto...*

❸ Royal Exchange Square

The centerpiece of this square—which marks the entrance to the shopping zone called Merchant City—is a stately, Neoclassical, bank-like building. This was once the **private mansion** of one of the tobacco lords, the super-rich businessmen who reigned here through the 1700s, stomping through the city with gold-tipped canes. During the port's heyday, these entrepreneurs helped Glasgow become Europe's sixth-biggest city—number two in the British Empire.

Today the mansion houses the **Glasgow Gallery of Modern Art,** nicknamed GoMA. Circle around the building to the main entry (at the equestrian statue of the Duke of Wellington, often creatively decorated as Glasgow's favorite cone-head), and step back to take in the full Neoclassical facade. On the pediment, notice the funky mirrored mosaic celebrating the miracles of St. Mungo—an example of how Glasgow refuses to take itself too seriously. The temporary exhibits inside GoMA are generally forgettable, but the museum does have an unusual charter: It displays only the work of living artists (free, £2 suggested donation, Mon-Wed and Sat 10:00-17:00, Thu 10:00-20:00, Fri and Sun 11:00-17:00).

• *Facing the fanciful GoMA facade, turn right up Queen Street. Within a block, you'll reach...*

❹ George Square

This square, the centerpiece of Glasgow, is filled with statues and lined with notable buildings, such as the Queen Street train station and the Glasgow City Chambers (the big Neoclassical building standing like a secular church to the east, open by tour, generally Mon-Fri 10:30 and 14:30, free). In front of the City Chambers stands a monument to Glaswegians killed fighting in the World Wars. The square is decorated

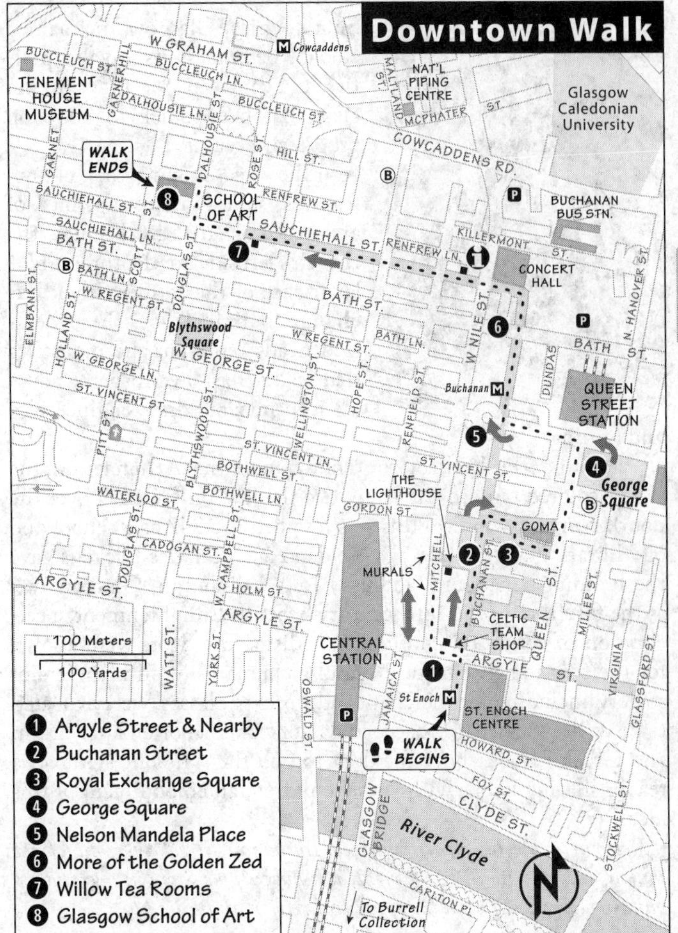

with a *Who's Who* of statues depicting great Glaswegians. Find James Watt (who perfected the steam engine that helped power Europe into the Industrial Age), as well as Scotland's two top poets: Robert Burns and Sir Walter Scott (capping the tallest pillar in the center). The two equestrian statues are of Prince Albert and a surprisingly skinny Queen Victoria—a rare image of her in her more svelte youth.

• *Just past skinny Vic and Robert Peel, turn left onto West George Street, and cross Buchanan Street to the tall church in the middle of...*

❺ Nelson Mandela Place

This is the first public space named for Nelson Mandela—honoring the man who, while still in prison, helped bring down apartheid in

South Africa. Glasgow, nicknamed Red Clyde Side for its socialist politics and empathy for the working class, has been quick to jump on progressive causes.

The area around this church features some interesting bits of architectural detail. Facing the church's left side are the three circular friezes of the former **Stock Exchange** (built in 1875). These idealized heads represent the industries that made Glasgow prosperous during its prime: building, engineering, and mining.

Around the back of the church find the **Athenaeum,** the sandy-colored building at #8 (notice the low-profile label over the door). Now a law office, this was founded in 1847 as a school and city library during Glasgow's Golden Age. (Charles Dickens gave the building's inaugural address.) Like Edinburgh, Glasgow was at the forefront of the 18th-century Scottish Enlightenment, a celebration of education and intellectualism. The Scots were known for their extremely practical brand of humanism; all members of society, including the merchant and working classes, were expected to be well-educated. (Tobacco lords, for example, often knew Latin and Greek.) Look above the door to find the symbolic statue of a reader sharing books with young children, an embodiment of this ideal.

• *Return to the big pedestrianized Buchanan Street in front of the church. Just downhill, to the right, is a huge Apple Store in a grand old building. But we'll head the opposite direction and start up...*

❻ Buchanan Street to Sauchiehall Street (More of the Golden Zed)

A short distance uphill is the glass entry to Glasgow's subway (from here you could ride directly to the Hillhead stop for the West End restaurant district; see "Eating in Glasgow," later). Soon after, on the right, you'll pass the Buchanan Galleries, an indoor mall that sprawls through several city blocks (offering a refuge in rainy weather).

At the top of Buchanan Street stands the **Glasgow Royal Concert Hall.** Its steps are a favorite perch where local office workers munch lunch and enjoy the street scene.

The statue is of **Donald Dewar,** who served as Scotland's first ever "First Minister" after the Scottish Parliament reconvened in 1999 (previously they'd been serving in London—as part of the British Parliament—since 1707).

*• From here, the Golden Zed zags left, Buchanan Street becomes Sauchiehall Street—look for the **TI** on your right—and the shopping gets cheaper and less elegant. While there's little of note to see, it's still a pleasant stroll. Walk a few blocks and enjoy the people-watching. Just before the end of the pedestrian zone, on the left side (at #217), is the...*

❼ Willow Tea Rooms

Tearooms were hugely popular during the industrial boom of the late 19th century. As Glasgow grew, more people moved to the suburbs, meaning that office workers couldn't easily return home for lunch. And during this age of Victorian morals, the temperance movement was trying to discourage the consumption of alcohol. Tearooms were designed to be an appealing alternative to eating in pubs.

These tearooms are also an Art Nouveau masterpiece by Charles Rennie Mackintosh. Visitors are welcome to browse. Mackintosh made his living from design commissions, including multiple tearooms for businesswoman Kate Cranston. Mackintosh designed everything here—down to the furniture, lighting, and cutlery. He took his theme for the café from the name of the street it's on—*saugh* is Scots for willow.

In the design of these tearooms, there was a meeting of the (very modern) minds. In addition to giving office workers an alternative to pubs, Cranston also wanted a place where women could gather while unescorted—in a time when traveling solo could give a woman a less-than-desirable reputation. An ardent women's rights supporter, Cranston requested that the rooms be bathed in white, the suffragettes' signature color.

On the ground floor, peruse the Mackintosh-inspired jewelry and the exhibit about his design in back. Then climb the stairs to find 20 tables run like a diner from a corner kitchen, serving simple meals to middle-class people—just as this place has since it opened in 1903. Be sure to look for the almost-hidden Room de Luxe dining room (upstairs). While most features of the Room de Luxe are reproductions (such as the chairs and the doors, which were too fragile to survive), it appears just as it did in Mackintosh's day (for details, see listing on page 825).

• From here it's a five-minute mostly-uphill walk to the must-see Mackintosh sight in the town center. Leaving the pedestrian zone, continue

Charles Rennie Mackintosh (1868-1928)

Charles Rennie Mackintosh brought an exuberant Art Nouveau influence to the architecture of his hometown. His designs challenged the city planners of this otherwise practical, working-class port city to create beauty in the buildings they commissioned.

As a student traveling in Italy, Mackintosh ignored the paintings inside museums and set up his easel to paint the exteriors of churches and buildings instead. He rejected the architectural traditions of ancient Greece and Rome. In Venice and Ravenna, he fell under the spell of Byzantine design, and in Siena he saw a unified medieval city design he would try to import—but with a Scottish flavor and palette—to Glasgow.

When Mackintosh was at the Glasgow School of Art, the Industrial Age dominated life. Factories belched black soot as they burned coal and forged steel. Mackintosh and his artist friends drew inspiration from nature and created some of the first Art Nouveau buildings, paintings, drawings, and furniture. His first commission came in 1893, to design an extension to the Glasgow Herald building. More work followed, including the Glasgow School of Art and the Willow Tea Rooms.

A radical thinker, Mackintosh shared credit with his artist

two more blocks on Sauchiehall, and make a right onto Dalhousie Street; the big, blond sandstone building on the left at the top of the hill is the...

❽ Glasgow School of Art

When he was just 28 years old—and still a no-name junior draftsman for a big architectural firm—Charles Rennie Mackintosh won the contest to create a new home for the Glasgow School of Art. He threw himself into the project, designing every detail of the building, inside and out.

While at first glance the School of Art seems to merge in with all the other red sandstone in Glasgow, its unique details begin to pop out on closer inspection. Mackintosh blended the zeitgeist for curvy, organic Art Nouveau with his wife, Margaret MacDonald (who specialized in glass and metalwork). He once famously said, "I have the talent...Margaret has the genius." The two teamed up with another husband-and-wife duo—Herbert MacNair and Margaret's sister, Frances MacDonald—to define a new strain of Scottish Art Nouveau, called the "Glasgow Style." These influential couples were known as "the Glasgow Four."

Mackintosh's works show a strong Japanese influence, particularly in his use of black-and-white contrast to highlight the idealized forms of nature. He also drew inspiration from the Arts and Crafts movement, with an eye to simplicity, clean lines, respect for tradition, and an emphasis on precise craftsmanship over mass production. While some of his designs appear to be repeated, no two motifs are exactly alike—just as nothing is exactly the same in nature.

Mackintosh insisted on designing every element of his commissions—even the furniture, curtains, and cutlery. As a furniture and woodwork designer, Mackintosh preferred to use cheaper materials, then paint them with several thick coats, hiding seams and imperfections and making the piece feel carved rather than built. His projects often went past deadline and over budget, but resulted in unusually harmonious spaces.

Mackintosh inspired other artists, such as painter Gustav Klimt and Bauhaus founder Walter Gropius, but his vision was not appreciated in his own time as much as it is now. He died with only £88 to his name. Now, a century after Scotland's greatest architect set pencil to paper, his hometown is at last celebrating his unique vision.

own taste for the clean black lines of Japanese minimalism. He also threw in some features evocative of the Romantic "Scottish Baronial" style of medieval Highland castles (unadorned sandstone, towers and turrets, and slit-like windows). And at the same time, the architect—not long out of school himself—ensured that the building served the needs of his patrons, the students. For example, notice the huge north-side windows (today facing a glassy green building); these were designed to bathe the painting studio in an even natural light all day long.

Mackintosh—who loved the hands-on ideology of the Arts and Crafts movement but was also a practical Scot—brought all the most recent technologies to this work. Those protruding wrought-iron brackets that hover outside the multipaned windows were invented during the Industrial Revolution and reinforce the big, fragile glass windows. Remember that this work was the Art Nouveau original, and that Frank Lloyd Wright, the Art Deco Chrysler

Building, and everything that resembles it came well after Charles Rennie Mack's time.

The interior is even more impressive. Unfortunately, the building was badly damaged by a fire in May 2014. It likely won't open again until 2018 or 2019 at the earliest. But you can still get a taste of Mackintosh's genius inside the school's **Reid Building,** the glassy green structure across the street. Inside is a shop highlighting students' works and a small free exhibition about Mackintosh, his masterpiece (including an impressive model of the School of Art), and his contemporaries (shop, exhibition, and tour desk open daily 10:00-16:30).

Tours: To learn more, sign up for a one-hour guided tour (likely £10). These include the exterior of the School of Art (with a clear explanation of its architecture and symbolism), a brief walk through the modern Reid Building, and a guided visit to a small but impressive collection of original furniture designed by Mackintosh and his wife and collaborator, Margaret MacDonald. Usually three or four tours run each day, but the schedule is in flux due to the fire damage and tours can book up, so it's best to check the school's website (www.gsa.ac.uk/tours), call ahead (tel. 0141/353-4526), or email (tours@gsa.ac.uk) to find out your options and book ahead. (Or just drop by and ask.) The tour fees help fund the conservation of Mackintosh's work, and as a bonus, you get to meet and enjoy the accent of a smart young Glasgow art student. Serious admirers can ask about the 2.25-hour Mackintosh-themed city walking tours given by students (£20, 4/week).

• *Our walk is finished, but two additional sights lie within a five-minute stroll (in different directions). The remarkably preserved* ***Tenement House*** *offers a fascinating glimpse into Glasgow lifestyles in the early 1900s. And the* ***National Piping Centre*** *is ideal for those who want to go beyond the clichés and gain a better appreciation for the history and musicality of Scotland's favorite instrument. Both are described on page 810, and either one is a good place to pass the time while you're waiting for your tour of the School of Art.*

WEST END WALK

Glasgow's West End—just a quick subway, bus, or taxi ride from downtown—is the city's top residential neighborhood. As in so many British cities, the western part of town—upwind of industrial pollution—was the most desirable. This area has great restaurants and nightlife (see "Eating in Glasgow," later), fine accommodations (see "Sleeping in Glasgow," later), and some lesser-known but worthwhile museums. This lightly-narrated walk provides a framework for exploring the West End. It begins at the Hillhead subway stop, meanders through dining and residential zones, explores some grand old university buildings (and related museums),

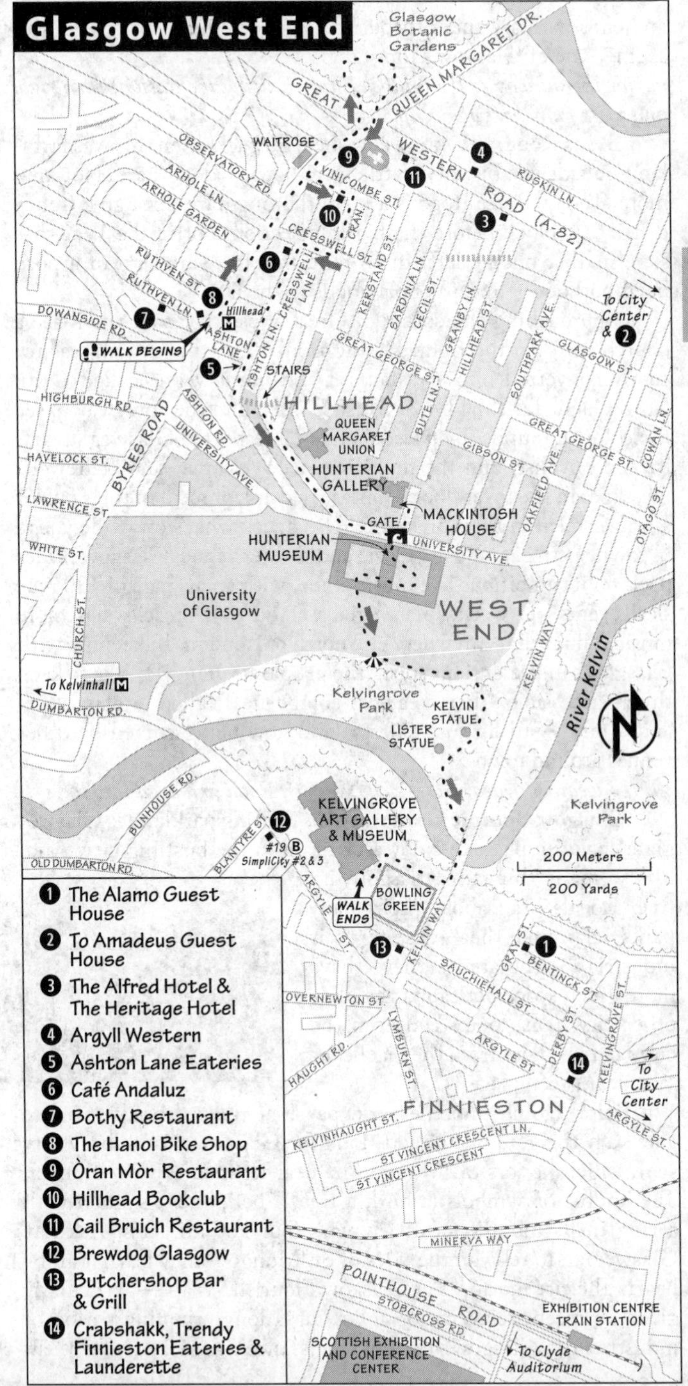
Glasgow West End
Glasgow Botanic Gardens
GREAT WESTERN ROAD (A-82)
QUEEN MARGARET DR.
WAITROSE
OBSERVATORY RD.
VINICOMBE ST.
ARHOLE LN.
ARHOLE GARDEN
CRESSWELL ST.
CRAN.
RUTHVEN ST.
RUTHVEN LN.
DOWANSIDE RD.
Hillhead
ASHTON LANE
WALK BEGINS
ASHTON LN.
CRESSWELL LANE
KERSTAND ST.
SARDINIA LN.
CECIL ST.
GRANBY LN.
HILLHEAD ST.
SOUTHPARK AVE.
RUSKIN LN.
To City Center & 2
GLASGOW ST.
GREAT GEORGE ST.
STAIRS
HILLHEAD
HIGHBURGH RD.
ASHTON RD.
BYRES ROAD
UNIVERSITY AVE.
QUEEN MARGARET UNION
BUTE LN.
GIBSON ST.
COWAN LN.
HAVELOCK ST.
HUNTERIAN GALLERY
LAWRENCE ST.
MACKINTOSH HOUSE
GATE
OAKFIELD AVE.
OTAGO ST.
HUNTERIAN MUSEUM
WHITE ST.
University of Glasgow
WEST END
CHURCH ST.
KELVIN WAY
River Kelvin
To Kelvinhall
DUMBARTON RD.
Kelvingrove Park
KELVIN STATUE
LISTER STATUE
BUNHOUSE RD.
KELVINGROVE ART GALLERY & MUSEUM
Kelvingrove Park
BLANTYRE ST.
#19
SimpliCity #2 & 3
OLD DUMBARTON RD.
200 Meters
200 Yards
ARGYLE ST.
WALK ENDS
BOWLING GREEN
GRAY ST.
BENTINCK ST.
SAUCHIEHALL ST.
OVERNEWTON ST.
LYMBURN ST.
DERBY ST.
KELVINGROVE ST.
HAUGHT RD.
ARGYLE ST.
To City Center
FINNIESTON
KELVINHAUGHT ST.
ST VINCENT CRESCENT LN.
ST VINCENT CRESCENT
MINERVA WAY
POINTHOUSE ROAD
STOBCROSS RD.
EXHIBITION CENTRE TRAIN STATION
SCOTTISH EXHIBITION AND CONFERENCE CENTER
To Clyde Auditorium
1 The Alamo Guest House
2 To Amadeus Guest House
3 The Alfred Hotel & The Heritage Hotel
4 Argyll Western
5 Ashton Lane Eateries
6 Café Andaluz
7 Bothy Restaurant
8 The Hanoi Bike Shop
9 Òran Mòr Restaurant
10 Hillhead Bookclub
11 Cail Bruich Restaurant
12 Brewdog Glasgow
13 Butchershop Bar & Grill
14 Crabshakk, Trendy Finnieston Eateries & Launderette

and ends with a wander through the park to the Kelvingrove Museum—one of Glasgow's top sights.

• *Ride the subway to the Hillhead stop. Exiting the station, turn right and walk four short blocks up...*

Byres Road: A *byre* is a cow shed. So back when this was farmland outside the big city, cattle were housed along here. Not anymore: Today, Byres Road is a main thoroughfare through a trendy district. A block before the big intersection, notice the **Waitrose** supermarket on the left. In Britain, this is a sure sign of a posh neighborhood—like a Whole Foods in the US.

Approaching the corner of Great Western Road, you'll see a church spire on the right. Dating from 1862, this church was recently converted into a restaurant and music venue called **Òran Mòr** (Gaelic for "The Great Music"). Step into the entryway to see the colorful murals (by Alasdair Gray, a respected Glaswegian artist and novelist) and the multilingual "Welcome" and "Farewell" messages in the foyer floor. Consider a drink or meal in their pub or a pricier meal in their brasserie. Also check what's on while you're in town, as this is a prime music and theater venue. Glasgow prides itself on its ambitious live music scene, with an average of 130 musical events per week; Glaswegians claim that the city has more music venues than anywhere else north of London. In keeping with Glasgow's unpretentious spirit, the people at Òran Mòr like to keep things accessible. They created a combo-deal called "a play, a pie, and a pint"—all for just £10-15 (and now being copied by other venues around town).

• *If the weather's good, cross Great Western Road and head into the...*

Glasgow Botanic Gardens: This inviting parkland is Glaswegians' favorite place to enjoy a break from the bustling city. And, like so many things in Glasgow, it's free. Locals brag about their many parks, claiming that—despite their industrial reputation—they have more green space per capita than any other city in Europe. And even the city's name comes from the Gaelic for "the dear green place."

Before going into the park, pause at the red-brick entrance gate. On the gate on the left, look for Glasgow's quite busy **city seal,** which honors St. Mungo, the near-legendary town founder. The jumble of symbols (a bird, a tree, a bell, and a salmon with a ring in its mouth) recall Mungo's four key miracles. Ask any Glaswegian to tell you the tales of St. Mungo—they learn it all by heart. The city motto, "Let Glasgow Flourish," is apt—particularly given its recent rejuvenation following a long crippling period of industrial rot. Glasgow's current renaissance was kicked off with an ambitious 1989 garden festival in a disused former shipyard. Now the city is one of Europe's trendiest success stories. Let Glasgow flourish, indeed.

Head farther into the park. If the sun's out, it'll be jammed with people enjoying some rare rays. Young lads wait all winter for the day when they can cry, "Sun's oot, taps aff!" and pull off their shirts to make the most of it.

In addition to the finely landscaped gardens, the park has two inviting greenhouse pavilions—both free and open to the public. The big white one on the right is the most elegant, with classical statues scattered among the palm fronds (but beware the killer plants, to the left as you enter). When the clouds roll in and the weather turns rotten—which is more the status quo—these warm, dry areas become quite popular.

When you're done in the park, head back out the way you came in. Back out on the street, before crossing Great Western Road, go right a few steps to find the blue **police call box.** Once an icon of British life, these were little neighborhood mini offices where bobbies could store paperwork and equipment, use the telephone, and catch up with each other. These days, some of the call boxes are being repurposed as coffee shops, ice-cream stands, and time machines. (They're surprisingly spacious inside.)

• *Cross back over Great Western Road and backtrack (past the Òran Mòr church/restaurant) one block down Byres Road. Turn left down Vinicombe Street (across from the Waitrose). Now we'll explore...*

Back-Streets West End: Peek inside the **Hillhead Bookclub**—a former cinema that's been converted into a hipster bar/restaurant serving affordable food (described later, under "Eating in Glasgow"). Just after that, turn right and walk (on Crawnworth Street) along the row of red-sandstone **tenements.** While that word has negative connotations stateside, here a "tenement" is simply an apartment building. And judging from the grand size, bulging bay windows, and prime location of these, it's safe to say they're far from undesirable. Many are occupied by a single family, while others are subdivided into five or six rooms for students (the university is right around the corner). Across the street from this tenement row (at #12) is a **baths club**—a private swim-

ming pool, like an exclusive health club back home. Historically, most people couldn't afford bathing facilities in their homes, so they came to central locations like this one to get clean every few days (or weeks). Today, it's the wealthy—not the poor—who come to places like this.

After the baths, turn right down Cresswell Street. A half-block down on the right, turn left down **Cresswell Lane**—an inviting, traffic-free, brick-floored shopping and dining zone. While the Golden Zed downtown is packed with chain stores, this is where you'll find charming one-off boutiques.

Browse your way to the end of the lane, cross the street, and head down the similar but even more appealing **Ashton Lane.** Scout this street and pick a place to return for dinner tonight—you can't go wrong. Fancy a film? Halfway down the street on the right, the Grosvenor Cinema shows both blockbusters and art-house fare (see listing on page 820).

• *When you reach the end of the lane, take a very sharp left up the stairs (with the beer garden for Brel on your left). At the top of the stairs, turn right along the road. You're now walking through the modern part of the...*

University of Glasgow Campus: Founded in 1451, this is Scotland's second-oldest university (after St. Andrews). Its 24,000 students sprawl through the West End. Unlike the fancy "old university" buildings, this area is gloomy and concrete. The hulking building on your left is the Queen Margaret Union, with a music venue that has hosted several big-name bands before they were famous—from Nirvana to Franz Ferdinand. (If you think Franz Ferdinand is an Austrian archduke rather than a Scottish alternative rock band...you've been out of college too long.)

Eventually you'll reach a wide cross street, University Avenue. Turn left up this street and walk two more blocks uphill. At the traffic light, the **Hunterian Gallery and Mackintosh House** are just up the hill on your left, and the **Hunterian Museum** is across the street on the right. Both are free, well worth a visit, and described on pages 814 and 816.

• *First, stop in at the Hunterian Gallery to sign up for the next (free) tour of the Mackintosh House. Spend any waiting time exploring the gallery's fine art collection—or, with a longer wait, jump ahead to the Hunterian Museum and come back to the Mackintosh House later.*

When you're done here, cross Uni-

versity Avenue. Instead of going through the main gate, go to the left end of the building facing the street to find a more interesting decorative gate.

University of Glasgow Main Building: Take a good look at the gate, which is decorated with the names of illustrious alums. Pick out the great Scots you're familiar with: James Watt, King James II, Adam Smith, Lord Kelvin, William Hunter (the namesake of the university's museums), and Donald Dewar, a driving force behind devolution who became Scotland's first "First Minister" in 1999.

Go through the gate and face the main university building. Stretching to the left is Graduation Hall, where commencement takes place. Head straight into the building, ride the elevator to floor 4, and take a walk through the **Hunterian Museum.**

After you visit the Hunterian Museum, find the grand staircase down (in the room with the Antonine Wall exhibit). You'll emerge into one of the twin quads enclosed by the enormous ensemble of university buildings. Veer right to find your way into the atmospheric Neo-Gothic **cloisters** that support the wing separating the two quads. These are modeled after the Gothic cloisters in the lower chapel of Glasgow Cathedral, across town. On the other side, you'll pop out into the adjoining quad. Enjoy pretending you're a student for a few minutes, then head out the door at the bottom of the quad.

Leaving the university complex, head for the tall flagpole. The turreted building just below is the Kelvingrove Museum, where this walk ends. (If you get turned around in the park, just head for those spires.) To the right, off in the distance, you'll see two silvery modern structures. Both are concert halls, part of an ambitious rejuvenation project along Glasgow's River Clyde waterfront.

• *From the flagpole, turn left and head to the end of the big building. Head down the stairs leading through the woods on your right (marked* James Watt Building*). When you reach the busy road, turn right along it for a short distance, then—as soon as you can—angle to the right back into the green space of...*

Kelvingrove Park: Another of Glasgow's favorite parks, this originated in the Victorian period, when there was a renewed focus on trying to get people out into green spaces. One of the first things you'll come to is a big statue of **Lord Kelvin** (1824-1907). Born William Thomson, he chose to take the name of the River Kelvin, which runs through Glasgow (and gives its name to many other things here, including the museum we're headed to). One of the most respected scientists of his time, Kelvin was a pioneer in the field of thermodynamics, and gave his name (or, actually, the river's) to a new absolute unit of temperature measurement designed to replace Celsius and Fahrenheit.

Just past Kelvin, bear left at the statue of **Joseph Lister** (1827-1912, of "Listerine" fame—he pioneered the use of antiseptics to remove infection-causing germs from the surgical environment), and take the bridge across the River Kelvin. Once across the bridge, turn right toward the museum. You'll walk along a pleasant bowling green that was built for the Commonwealth Games that Glasgow hosted in 2014. They needed lots of people to play here to help "season" the new court, so for a time it was free and open to anyone—creating a surge of popular interest in this very old and genteel sport.

Now's the time to explore the **Kelvingrove Museum,** described on page 816.

• *When you're finished at the museum, exit out the back end, toward the busy road. Several recommended restaurants are ahead and to the left, in the Finnieston neighborhood (see page 828). Or, if you'd like to hop on the subway, just turn right along Argyle Street and walk five minutes to the Kelvinhall station.*

Sights in Glasgow

JUST NORTH OF THE GLASGOW SCHOOL OF ART

Both of these sights are close to the end of my "Get to Know Glasgow" walk, earlier.

▲▲Tenement House

Here's a chance to drop into a perfectly-preserved 1930s-era middle-class residence. The National Trust for Scotland bought this otherwise ordinary row home, located in a residential neighborhood, because of the peculiar tendencies of Miss Agnes Toward (1886-1975). For five decades, she kept her home essentially unchanged. The kitchen calendar is still set for 1935, and canisters of licorice powder (a laxative) still sit on the bathroom shelf. It's a time-warp experience, where Glaswegian old-timers enjoy coming to reminisce about how they grew up.

Cost and Hours: £6.50, £3 guidebook, March-Oct daily 13:00-17:00, closed Nov-Feb, no photos allowed, 145 Buccleuch

Street (pronounced "ba-KLOO") down off the top of Garnethill, tel. 0141/333-0183, www.nts.org.uk.

Visiting the House: Buy your ticket on the main floor and poke around the little museum. You'll learn that in Glasgow, a "tenement" isn't a slum—it's simply an apartment house. In fact, tenements like these were typical for every class except the richest. Then head upstairs to the apartment, which is staffed by caring volunteers. Ring the doorbell to be let in. Ask them why the bed is in the kitchen, why the rooms still smell like natural gas, or why there are studs on the bannisters. As you look through the rooms laced with Victorian trinkets—such as the ceramic dogs on the living room's fireplace mantle—consider how different they are from Mackintosh's stark minimalist designs from the same period.

▲National Piping Centre

If you consider bagpipes a tacky Scottish cliché, think again. At this small but insightful museum, you'll get a scholarly lesson in the proud and fascinating history of the bagpipe. For those with a healthy attention span for history or musical instruments—ideally both—it's fascinating. On Thursdays and Fridays (usually 10:00-17:00), a piper is on hand to perform, answer questions, and show you around the collection. At other times, if it's quiet, ask the ticket-sellers to tell you more—some are bagpipe students at the music school across the street. The center also offers a shop, lessons, a restaurant, and accommodations.

Cost and Hours: £4.50, includes audioguide, Mon-Thu 9:00-19:00, Fri 9:00-17:00, Sat 9:00-15:00, closed Sun, 30 McPhater Street, tel. 0141/353-5551, www.thepipingcentre.co.uk.

Visiting the Museum: The collection is basically one big room packed with well-described exhibits, including several historic bagpipes. You'll learn that bagpipes from as far away as Italy, Spain, and Bohemia predated Scottish ones; that Lowlands bagpipes were traditionally bellows-blown rather than lung-powered; and why bagpipes started being used to inspire Scottish soldiers on the battlefield. At the back of the room, look for the hand-engraved backward printing plates for bagpipe sheet music (which didn't exist until the 19th century). The thoughtful, beautifully-produced audioguide—which mixes a knowledgeable commentary with sound bites of bagpipes being played and brief interviews with performers—feels like a 40-minute audio-documentary on the BBC. The 15-minute film shown at the end of the room sums up the collection helpfully. They also have a practice set of bagpipes in case you want to try your hand. The chanter fingering is easy if you play the recorder, but keeping the bag inflated is exhausting.

CATHEDRAL PRECINCT, WITH A HINT OF MEDIEVAL GLASGOW

Very little remains of medieval Glasgow, but a visit to the cathedral and the area around it is a visit to the birthplace of the city. The first church was built here in the seventh century. Today's towering cathedral is mostly 13th century—the only great Scottish church to survive the Reformation intact. In front you'll see an attention-grabbing statue of **David Livingstone** (1813-1873). Livingstone—the Scottish missionary/explorer/cartographer who discovered a huge waterfall in Africa and named it in honor of his queen, Victoria—was born eight miles from here.

Nearby, the Provand's Lordship is Glasgow's only secular building dating from the Middle Ages. The St. Mungo Museum of Religious Life and Art, built on the site of the old Bishop's Castle, is a unique exhibit covering the spectrum of religions. And the Necropolis, blanketing the hill behind the cathedral, provides an atmospheric walk through a world of stately Victorian tombstones. From there you can scan the city and look down on the brewery where Tennent's Lager (a longtime Glasgow favorite) has been made since 1885.

The four main sights, including the cathedral, are within close range of each other. As you face the cathedral, the St. Mungo Museum is on your right (with handy public WCs), the Provand's Lordship is across the street from St. Mungo, and the Necropolis is behind the cathedral and toward the right.

To reach these sights from Buchanan Street, turn east on Bath Street, which soon becomes Cathedral Street, and walk about 15 minutes (or hop a bus along the main drag—try bus #38, or #57, confirm with driver that the bus stops at the cathedral). To head to the Kelvingrove Museum after your visit, from the cathedral, walk two blocks up Castle Street and catch bus #19 (on the cathedral side).

▲Glasgow Cathedral

This blackened Gothic cathedral is a rare example of an intact pre-Reformation Scottish cathedral. (It was once known as "the Pink Church" for the tone of its stone. But with Industrial Age soot and modern pollution, it blackened. Cleaning would damage the integrity of the stone structure, so it was left black.) While the zealous Reformation forces of John Knox ripped out the stained glass and the ornate chapels of the Catholic age, they left the church standing.

Cost and Hours: Free, £3 suggested donation; Mon-Sat 9:30-17:30, Sun 13:00-17:00; until 16:30 Oct-March, ask about free guided tours, near junction of Castle and Cathedral Streets, tel. 0141/552-8198, www.glasgowcathedral.org.uk.

Visiting the Cathedral: Inside, look up to see the wooden barrel-vaulted ceiling, and take in the beautifully decorated section over the choir ("quire"). The choir screen is the only pre-Reformation screen surviving in Scotland. It divided the common people from the priests and big shots of the day, who got to worship closer to the religious action. Standing at the choir, turn around to look down the nave at the west wall, and notice how the right wall lists. (Don't worry; it's been listing—and still standing—for 800 years.) The cathedral's glass dates mostly from the 19th century. One window on the right side of the choir, celebrating the 14 trades of Glasgow, dates from 1951.

Step into the lower church (down stairs on right as you face the choir), where the central altar sits upon St. Mungo's tomb. Mungo was the seventh-century Scottish monk and mythical founder of Glasgow who established the first wooden church on this spot and gave Glasgow its name. Notice the ceiling bosses (decorative caps where the ribs come together) with their colorfully carved demons, dragons, and skulls.

▲Necropolis

From the cathedral, a lane leads over the "bridge of sighs" into the park filled with grand tombstones. Glasgow's huge burial hill has a wistful, ramshackle appeal. A stroll among the tombstones of the eminent Glaswegians of the 19th century gives a glimpse of Victorian Glasgow and a feeling for the confidence and wealth of the second city of the British Empire in its glory days.

With the Industrial Age (in the early 1800s), Glasgow's population tripled to 200,000. The existing churchyards were jammed and unhygienic. The city needed a beautiful place in which to bury its beautiful citizens, so this grand necropolis was established. Because Presbyterians are more into simplicity, the statuary is simpler than in a Catholic cemetery. Wandering among the disintegrating memorials to once-important people, I thought about how, someday, everyone's tombstone will fall over and no one will care.

The highest pillar in the graveyard is a memorial to John Knox. The Great Reformer (who's actually buried in Edinburgh) looks down at the cathedral he wanted to strip of all art, and even tear down. (The Glaswegians rallied to follow Knox, but saved the church.) If the cemetery's main black gates are closed, see if you can get in and out through a gate off the street to the right.

▲St. Mungo Museum of Religious Life and Art

This interesting museum, just in front of the cathedral, aims to promote religious understanding. Built in 1990 on the site of the old Bishop's Castle, it provides a handy summary of major and minor world religions, showing how each faith handles various rites of passage across the human lifespan: birth, puberty, marriage, death, and everything in between and after. Start with the 10-minute video overview on the first floor, and finish with a great view from the top floor of the cathedral and Necropolis.

Cost and Hours: Free, £3 suggested donation, Tue-Thu and Sat 10:00-17:00, Fri and Sun 11:00-17:00, closed Mon, free WCs downstairs, cheap ground-floor café, 2 Castle Street, tel. 0141/276-1625, www.glasgowmuseums.com.

Provand's Lordship

With low beams and medieval decor, this creaky home—supposedly the "oldest house in Glasgow"—is the only secular building surviving in Glasgow from the Middle Ages. It displays the *Lifestyles of the Rich and Famous*...circa 1471. The interior, while sparse and stony, shows off a few pieces of furniture from the 16th, 17th, and 18th centuries. Out back, explore the St. Nicholas Garden, which was once part of a hospital that dispensed herbal remedies. The plaques in each section show the part of the body each plant is used to treat.

Cost and Hours: Free, small donation requested, Tue-Thu and Sat 10:00-17:00, Fri and Sun 11:00-17:00, closed Mon, across the street from St. Mungo Museum at 3 Castle Street, tel. 0141/552-8819, www.glasgowmuseums.com.

THE WEST END

These sights are linked by my West End Walk on page 804.

▲Hunterian Gallery and Mackintosh House

Here's a sightseeing twofer: an art gallery offering a good look at some Scottish artists relatively unknown outside their homeland,

and the chance to take a guided tour through the reconstructed home of Charles Rennie Mackintosh, decorated exactly the way he liked it. For Charles Rennie Mack fans—or anyone fascinated by the worlds artists create for themselves to live in—it's worth ▲▲▲, and arguably provides a more intimate look at Mackintosh than does any other sight in town.

Cost and Hours: Gallery—free, Tue-Sat 10:00-17:00, Sun 11:00-16:00, closed Mon, across University Avenue from the main Hunterian Museum, tel. 0141/330-4221, www.gla.ac.uk/hunterian. Mackintosh House—entry only with free tour, departs every 30 minutes during gallery hours, last tour departs 30 minutes before closing.

Visiting the Museum: First, check in at the reception desk to sign up for a tour of the Mackintosh House. Spend your waiting time visiting the gallery, or, with a longer wait, head across the street to the Hunterian Museum (described later).

You'll take a 30-minute blitz tour through the **Mackintosh House.** In 1906, Mackintosh and his wife, Margaret MacDonald, moved into the end unit of a Victorian row house. Mackintosh gutted the place and redesigned it to his own liking—bathing the interior in his trademark style, a mix of curving organic lines and rigid proto-Art Deco functionalism. They moved out in 1914, and the house was demolished in the 1960s—but the university wisely documented the layout and carefully removed and preserved all of Mackintosh's original furnishings. In 1981, when respect for Mackintosh was on the rise, they built this replica house and reinstalled everything just as Mackintosh had designed it. On the tour, you'll see the entryway, dining room, drawing room, and bedroom—each one offering fascinating glimpses into the minds of these great artists. You'll see original furniture and decorations by Mackintosh and MacDonald, providing keen insight into their creative process. And in the top-floor exhibition, you'll see some Mackintosh works from other commissions.

The Hunterian's **art gallery** is manageable and worth exploring. One highlight is the modern Scottish art (1850-1960), focusing on two groups: the "Glasgow Boys," who traveled to France to study during the waning days of Realism (1880s), and, a generation later, the Scottish Colourists, who found a completely different inspiration in circa-1910 France—bright, bold, with an almost Picasso-like exuberance. The gallery also has an extensive collection of portraits by American artist James Whistler—Whistler's wife was of Scottish descent, as was Whistler's mother. (Hey, that has a nice ring to it.) The painter always found great support in Scotland, and his heir donated his estate to the University of Glasgow.

▲Hunterian Museum

The oldest public museum in Scotland was founded by William Hunter (1718-1783), a medical researcher. Today his natural science collection is housed in a huge and gorgeous space inside the university's showcase building. Everything is well presented and well explained. You'll see a perceptive exhibit on the Antonine Wall, built in A.D. 142 to seal off the Picts from the Roman Empire (and the lesser-known cousin of Hadrian's Wall). The eclectic collection also includes musical instruments, a display on the Glasgow-built *Lusitania,* and a fine collection of fossils, including the aquatic dinosaur called plesiosaur (possibly a distant ancestor of the Loch Ness monster). But most people can't get enough of the endless examples of deformities—two-headed animals, babies in jars, and so on. Ever the curious medical researcher, Hunter collected these for study, and today they still intrigue, titillate, and nauseate visitors to his museum.

Cost and Hours: Free, Tue-Sat 10:00-17:00, Sun 11:00-16:00, closed Mon, Gilbert Scott Building, University Avenue, tel. 0141/330-4221, www.gla.ac.uk/hunterian.

▲▲Kelvingrove Art Gallery and Museum

This "Scottish Smithsonian" displays everything from a stuffed elephant to fine artwork by the great masters. The well-described contents are impressively displayed in a grand 100-year-old Spanish Baroque-style building. The Kelvingrove claims to be one of the most-visited museums in Britain—presumably because of all the field-trip groups you'll see here. Watching all the excited Scottish kids—their imaginations ablaze—is as much fun as the collection itself.

Cost and Hours: Free, £3 suggested donation, Mon-Thu and Sat 10:00-17:00, Fri and Sun 11:00-17:00, free tours at 11:00 and 14:30, Argyle Street, tel. 0141/276-9599, www.glasgowmuseums.com.

Getting There: My self-guided West End Walk leads you here from the Hillhead subway stop, or you can ride the **subway** to the Kelvinhall stop. When you exit, turn left and walk five minutes. **Buses** #2 and #3 run from Hope Street downtown to the museum. It's also on **the hop-on, hop-off bus** route. No matter how you arrive, just look for the huge, turreted red-brick building.

Organ Concerts: At the top of the main hall, the huge pipe organ booms with a daily 30-minute recital at 13:00 (15:00 on Sunday).

Visiting the Museum: Built to house the city collection in 1902, the museum is divided into two sections.

The "Life" section, in the West Court, features a menagerie of stuffed animals (including a giraffe, kangaroo, ostrich, and moose) with a WWII-era Spitfire fighter plane hovering overhead. Branching off are halls with exhibits ranging from Ancient Egypt to "Scotland's First People" to weaponry ("Conflict and Consequence").

The more serene "Expression" section, in the East Court, focuses on artwork, including Dutch, Flemish, French, and local artists (from Mackintosh to the late-Realist "Glasgow Boys"). Upstairs, near the main hall, you'll find the museum's most famous painting, Salvador Dalí's *Christ of St. John of the Cross,* which brought visitors to tears when it was first displayed here in the 1950s. This section also has exhibits on "Scottish Identity in Art," letting you tour the country's scenic wonders and history on canvas.

AWAY FROM THE CENTER

▲▲Riverside Museum

Located along the River Clyde, this high-tech, extremely kid-friendly museum—nostalgic and modern at the same time—is dedicated to all things transportation-related. It was named the European museum of the year in 2013, and visiting here is a must for anyone interested in transportation and how it has shaped society.

Cost and Hours: Free, £3 suggested donation, Mon-Thu and Sat 10:00-17:00, Fri and Sun 11:00-17:00, ground-floor café with £6-9 meals, upstairs coffee shop with basic drinks and snacks, 100 Pointhouse Place, tel. 0141/287-2720, www.glasgowmuseums.com.

Getting There: It's on the riverfront promenade, two miles west of the city center. **Bus** #100 runs between the museum and George Square (2/hour, last departure from George Square at 15:02, operated by McColl's), or you can take a **taxi** (£6-8, 10-minute ride from downtown). The museum is also included on the **hop-on, hop-off sightseeing bus** route (described earlier, under "Getting Around Glasgow").

Visiting the Museum: Most of the collection is strewn across one huge wide-open floor. Upon entering, visit the info desk (to the right as you enter, near the shop) to ask about today's free tours and activities—or just listen for announcements. Also pick up a map from the info desk, as the museum's open floor plan can feel a bit like a traffic jam at rush hour.

Diving in, explore the vast collection: stagecoaches, locomotives, double-decker trolleys, and an entire wall stacked with vintage automobiles. Learn about the opening of Glasgow's old-timey subway (Europe's third oldest). Explore the collections of old toys and prams, and watch a film about 1930s cinema. Stroll the re-creation of a circa-1900 street, with video clips of local seniors in time-warp shops reminiscing (like about the time the little girl noticed her daddy was selling things to the pawn shop to pay the rent). A highlight is the shipping section, commemorating Glasgow's shipbuilding era. On the giant screen, exhilarating newsreels show that proud moment when "the band plays, the minister prays, the lady sponsor gives the name, the crowds cheer, and seconds later a new ship takes to the water for the first time."

Don't miss the much smaller upstairs section, with great views over the River Clyde, additional exhibits about ships built here in Glasgow, and what may or may not be the world's oldest bicycle. The description explains that two different inventors have tried to take credit for the bike—and both of them are Scottish.

Nearby: Be sure to head to the River Clyde directly behind the museum (just step out the back door). The ***Glenlee,*** one of five remaining tall ships built in Glasgow in the 19th century, invites visitors to come aboard (free, daily 10:00-17:00, Nov-Feb until 16:00, tel. 01413/573-699, www.thetallship.com). Good exhibits illustrate what it was like to live and work aboard the ship. Explore the officers' living quarters, then head below deck to the café and more exhibits. Below that, the cargo hold has kids' activities and offers the chance to peek into the engine room.

▲Burrell Collection

This eclectic art collection of a wealthy local shipping magnate includes sculpture (from Roman to Rodin), stained glass, tapestries, furniture, Asian and Islamic works, and halls of paintings—starring Cézanne, Renoir, Degas, and a Rembrandt self-portrait. It's

Shopping in Glasgow

Downtown, the **Golden Zed**—a.k.a. "Style Mile"—has all the predictable chain stores, with a few Scottish souvenir stands mixed in. For more on this, see the start of my self-guided "Get to Know Glasgow" Walk.

The West End also has some appealing shops. Many are concentrated on **Cresswell Lane** (covered in my self-guided West End Walk). Browsing here, you'll find an eclectic assortment of gifty shops, art galleries, design shops, hair salons, record stores, home-decor shops, and lots of vintage. Be sure to poke into De Courcy's Arcade, a two-part warren of tiny offbeat shops.

three miles outside the city center: Plan to make an afternoon of it, and leave time to walk around the surrounding park, where Highland cattle graze.

Cost and Hours: Free, Mon-Thu and Sat 10:00-17:00, Fri and Sun 11:00-17:00, Pollok Country Park, 2060 Pollokshaws Road, tel. 0141/287-2550, www.glasgowmuseums.com.

Getting There: From downtown, take **bus** #57 to Pollokshaws Road, or take a **train** to the Pollokshaws West train station; the entrance is a 10-minute walk from the bus stop and the train station. By **car,** follow the M-8 to exit at Junction 22 onto the M-77, then take the first exit and follow brown signs.

Nightlife in Glasgow

Glasgow has a youthful vibe, and its nightlife scene is renowned. The city is full of live music acts and venues. Walking through the city center, you'll pass at least one club or bar on every block. For the latest, *The Skinny* is Glasgow's information-packed alternative weekly (www.theskinny.co.uk). Or check out *The List* (www.list.co.uk) or the *Gig Guide* (www.gigguide.co.uk). All three are also available in print form around town.

DOWNTOWN

Glasgow's central business and shopping district is pretty sleepy after hours, but there are a few pockets of activity—each with its own personality. **Bath Street**'s bars and clubs are focused on young professionals as well as students; the recommended Pot Still is a perfect place to sample Scotch whisky (see page 826). Nearby, running just below the Glasgow School of Art, **Sauchiehall Street** is younger, artsier, and more student-oriented. The recently revitalized **Merchant City** zone, stretching just east of the Buchanan Street shopping drag, has a slightly older crowd and a popular gay scene.

IN THE WEST END

There's no shortage of after-hours fun in the West End.

In Hillhead: For a mainstream vibe with easy pickings, ride the subway to Hillhead and look around. **Òran Mòr** (a former church) and **Hillhead Bookclub** (a former cinema) are popular live music venues; check their websites for what's on (see listings on page 827). **Ashton Lane** and surrounding streets is another lively zone where you'll find engaging bars and music venues. **The Grosvenor Cinema,** right on Ashton Lane in the heart of the bustling West End restaurant scene, is a particularly inviting movie theater, with cushy leather seats in two theaters showing films big and small (most movies £10) and lots of special events. Bring in a drink from the cozy bar, or grab some Italian food at the upstairs restaurant (21 Ashton Lane, www.grosvenorcinema.co.uk, tel. 0845-166-6002).

In Finnieston: Glasgow's most up-and-coming hipster quarter, just below the Kelvingrove Museum, is packed with trendy bars and restaurants (for some recommendations, see page 828). But it also has an old-school selection of **Gaelic pubs.** If you're intrigued by Scotland's Gaelic-language culture, you don't need to travel deep into the Highlands to experience it. Finnieston's Argyle Street has a handful of spit-and-sawdust Gaelic pubs, some of which have live music in the evenings: check out **The Islay Inn** (at #1256), **The Park Bar** (at #1202), and **The Ben Nevis** (#1147).

Sleeping in Glasgow

For accommodations, choose between downtown (bustling by day, nearly deserted at night, close proximity to main shopping zone and some major sights, very expensive parking and one-way streets that cause headaches for drivers) and the West End (neighborhoody, best variety of restaurants, easier parking, easy access to West End sights and parks but a bus or subway ride from the center and train station).

DOWNTOWN

These accommodations are scattered around the city center. I've focused my listings on affordable chain hotels (prices vary from day to day—I've listed an average peak-season price for a standard double) and the best of the few independent hotels in this area. For locations, see the map on page 822. Glasgow also has all of the pre-

Sleep Code

Abbreviations **(£1=about $1.60, country code: 44)**
S=Single, **D**=Double/Twin, **T**=Triple, **Q**=Quad, **b**=bathroom
Price Rankings
$$$ Higher Priced—Most rooms £80 or more
$$ Moderately Priced—Most rooms £60-80
$ Lower Priced—Most rooms £60 or less
Unless otherwise noted, credit cards are accepted, and free Wi-Fi and/or a guest computer is generally available. Prices change; verify current rates online or by email. For the best prices, always book directly with the hotel.

dictable chains—**Premier Inn, Travelodge, Novotel, Mercure, Jurys Inn**—check online for deals.

$$$ Grasshoppers is a cheerful, above-it-all retreat on the sixth floor of a building overlooking Central Station. The 29 rooms are tight, with small "efficiency" bathrooms, but the welcome is warm, and there's 24-hour access to fresh cupcakes, shortbread, and ice cream (Db-£85-125 depending on demand, optional buffet dinner-£17, elevator, 87 Union Street, tel. 0141/222-2666, www.grasshoppersglasgow.com, info@grasshoppersglasgow.com).

$$$ Pipers' Tryst has eight simple rooms done up in good tartan style above a restaurant in the National Piping Centre (described on page 811). It's in a grand, old former church building overlooking a busy intersection, across the street from the downtown business, shopping, and entertainment district. The location is handy, if not romantic, and it's practically a pilgrimage for fans of bagpipes (Db-£89, includes continental breakfast, 30 McPhater Street, tel. 0141/353-5551, www.thepipingcentre.co.uk, hotel@thepipingcentre.co.uk).

$$ Adelaides Guest House rents eight clean and cheerful rooms in a multitasking church building that also houses a theater and nursery school. Ted and Lisa run the place with warmth and quirky humor (S-£40, Sb-£55, Db-£75, family deals, includes continental breakfast, cooked breakfast-£6, 209 Bath Street, tel. 0141/248-4970, www.adelaides.co.uk, reservations@adelaides.co.uk).

$$ Z Hotel, part of a small "compact luxury" chain, offers 104 sleek, efficiency-priced, yet still very stylish rooms. It's welcoming and handy to Queen Street Station, just a few steps off George's Square (Db-£58-90 depending on size—cheapest rooms don't have windows, breakfast-£8, air-con, elevator, free wine-and-cheese buffet each afternoon, 36 North Frederick Street, tel. 0141/212-4550, www.thezhotels.com).

$$ Ibis Glasgow, part of the modern hotel chain, has 141

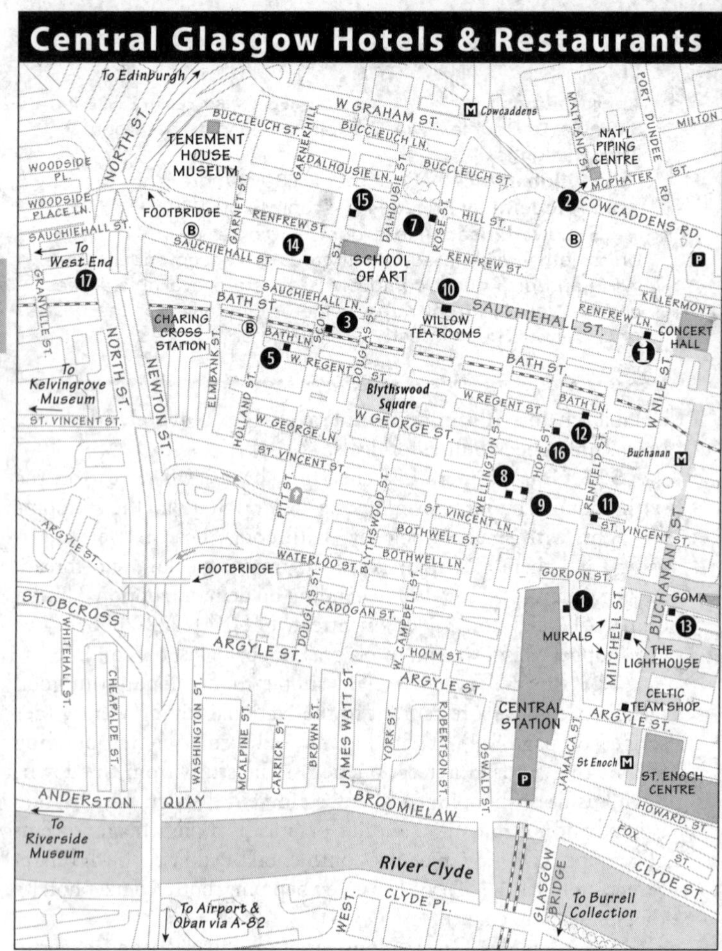

cookie-cutter rooms with blond wood and predictable comfort (Sb/Db-£58 on weeknights, £85 on weekends, £125 "event rate" during festivals and in Aug, breakfast-£9, elevator, restaurant, hiding behind a big Novotel at 220 West Regent Street, tel. 0141/225-6000, www.ibishotel.com, h3139@accor.com).

$$ Babbity Bowster, named for a traditional Scottish dance, is a pub and restaurant renting five simple, mod rooms up top. It's located in the trendy Merchant City on the eastern fringe of downtown, near several clubs and restaurants (Sb-£50, Db-£65, no breakfast, lots of stairs and no elevator, 10-minute walk from Central Station, 16 Blackfriars Street, tel. 0141/552-5055, www.babbitybowster.com, babbity@btinternet.com). The ground-floor pub serves £5-9 pub grub (daily 12:00-22:00); the first-floor res-

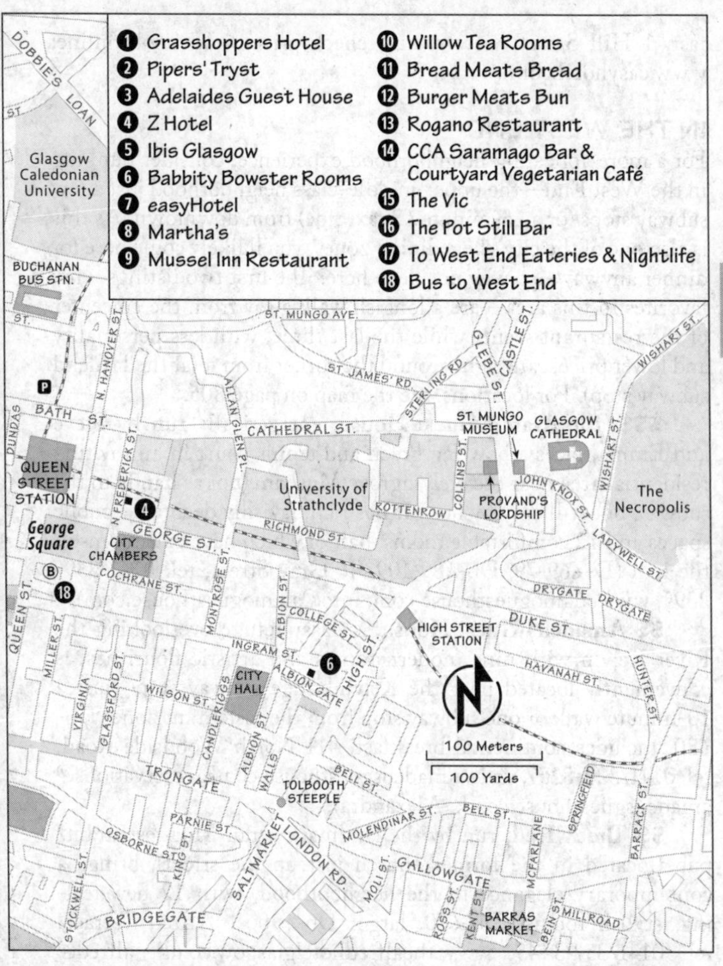

taurant, run by a French chef, offers £14-17 main dishes (Fri-Sat only 18:30-21:30, closed Sun-Thu).

$ easyHotel is part of the no-frills hotel chain. Its 124 miniscule bedrooms have super-tight bathrooms that feel popped out of a plastic mold. Like its easyJet airline parent company, its pricing is variable and à la carte. Book a room online (for the best deals—often Db-£25-39—book well in advance; the smallest windowless rooms are cheapest). Then pick and choose which services you want to pay for (Wi-Fi, TV remote control, room cleaning during your stay)—each comes with an additional fee. Stay here only if you want to save money and don't intend to hang out in your room. It's located on the northern edge of downtown, not far from the Glasgow School of Art and downtown shopping zone (no breakfast, 1 Hill Street; view rooms, check prices, and book online: www.easyhotel.com).

IN THE WEST END

For a more appealing neighborhood experience, consider bunking in the West End—the upper-middle-class neighborhood just a few subway stops (or a 15-minute £8 taxi ride) from downtown. As this is also one of the city's best dining zones, you'll likely come here for dinner anyway—so why not sleep here? The first two listings—my favorites in this area—are a longish walk away from the epicenter of the restaurant scene, while the last three, with less personality and lower prices, are right around the corner from it (at the Hillend subway stop). For locations, see the map on page 805.

$$$ The Alamo Guest House, energetically run by Steve and Emma, faces a bowling green and tennis court in an inviting residential area near the Kelvingrove Museum (not as handy to the subway, but still easy by bus). It has rich, lavishly decorated public spaces and 12 comfortable rooms, half of which have bathrooms in the hall (D-£69-79, Db-£89-109, 46 Gray Street, tel. 0141/339-2395, www.alamoguesthouse.com, info@alamoguesthouse.com).

$$ Amadeus Guest House, a classy refuge overlooking the River Kelvin with nine modern rooms and artistic flourishes, is conveniently located near the Kelvinbridge subway stop—just a 10-minute walk or one subway stop from the restaurant zone (Db-£80, includes continental breakfast, 411 North Woodside Road, tel. 0141/339-8257, www.amadeusguesthouse.co.uk, reservations@amadeusguesthouse.co.uk, Alexandra).

$$ The Alfred, run by the landmark Òran Mòr restaurant/pub (located in the former church just up the street), brings a contemporary elegance to the neighborhood, with 12 new-feeling, stylish rooms (Db-£70, larger Db-£90, 1 Alfred Terrace, tel. 0141/357-3445, www.thealfredhotelglasgow.co.uk, alfred@thealfredhotelglasgow.co.uk).

$$ Argyll Western, with 17 sleek and tartaned Scottish-themed rooms, feels modern, efficient, and a bit impersonal (Db-£70, breakfast-£5, 6 Buckingham Terrace, tel. 0141/339-2339, www.argyllwestern.co.uk, info@argyllwestern.co.uk).

$$ The Heritage Hotel is a lesser value—it's modern but characterless, and the 27 rooms are worn. But the location is convenient and the rates are reasonable (Db-£60, 4 Alfred Terrace, tel. 0141/339-6955, www.theheritagehotel.net, bookings@heritagehotel.fsbusiness.co.uk).

Eating in Glasgow

DOWNTOWN

Martha's is a dream come true for hungry, hurried sightseers (and local office workers) in search of a healthy and satisfying lunch. They serve a seasonal menu of fresh, flavorful wraps, rice boxes, soups, and other great meals made with Scottish ingredients but with eclectic, exotic, international flavors (Indian, Thai, Mexican, and so on). It's understandably popular: Just line up (it moves fast), order at the counter, and then find a table or take your food to go (£5-6 meals, Mon-Fri 7:30-18:00, Sat 9:00-16:00, closed Sun, 142A St. Vincent Street, tel. 0141/248-9771).

Mussel Inn offers light, good-value fish dinners and seafood plates in an airy, informal environment. The restaurant is a cooperative, owned and run by shellfish farmers. Their £10 "kilo pot" of Scottish mussels is popular with locals and big enough to share (£8 "lunchtime quickie" deals, £15-19 dinners, daily 12:00-14:30 & 17:00-22:00, except no afternoon closure Sat-Sun, 157 Hope Street, tel. 0141/572-1405).

The **Willow Tea Rooms,** designed by Charles Rennie Mackintosh, has a diner-type eatery and a classy Room de Luxe (described on page 801). The cheap and cheery menu covers both dining areas (£6-9 meals, £13 afternoon tea, Mon-Sat 9:00-17:00, Sun from 10:30, 217 Sauchiehall Street, tel. 0141/332-0521, www.willowtearooms.co.uk).

Bread Meats Bread is your place for trendy, satisfying, decadent burgers, sandwiches, and fries. The tight interior and few sidewalk tables are always hopping, and the greasy comfort food hits the spot (£7-10 sandwiches, Mon-Sat 11:00-22:00, Sun 11:00-20:00, 104 St. Vincent Street, tel. 0141/249-9898). **Burger Meats Bun,** a few blocks away, is an even younger-feeling cellar restaurant with what Glaswegians would call "dead excellent burgers" (£8-10 burgers and chicken sandwiches, daily 12:30-21:30, 48A West Regent Street, tel. 0141/353-6712).

Rogano is a time-warp Glasgow institution that retains much of the same classy Art Deco interior it had when it opened in 1935. You half-expect to see Bacall and Bogart at the next table. The restaurant has three parts: The bar in front has outdoor seating (£7 lunch sandwiches, £10-13 meals). The fancy dining room at the back of the main floor smacks of the officers' mess on the *Queen Mary,* which was built here on the Clyde during the same period (£20-31 meals with a focus on seafood, £15 afternoon tea). A more casual yet still dressy bistro in the cellar is filled with 1930s-Hollywood glamour (£11-14 meals; daily 12:00-21:30, fancy restaurant closed 16:00-18:00, 11 Exchange Place—just before giant archway from Buchanan Street, reservations smart, tel. 0141/248-4055, www.roganoglasgow.com).

Cheap Eats near the Glasgow School of Art: **CCA Saramago Bar and Courtyard Vegetarian Café,** located on the first floor of Glasgow's edgy contemporary art museum, charges art-student prices for its designer, animal-free food. An 18th-century facade, discovered when the site was excavated to build the gallery, looms over the atrium restaurant (£3-5 small plates, £6-7 sandwiches and salads, £9-11 main courses, food served daily 12:00-22:00, free Wi-Fi, 350 Sauchiehall Street, tel. 0141/332-7959). To find a student hangout within the Glasgow School of Art itself, face the modern Reid Building and hook around the left side to find the easy-to-miss entrance to **The Vic**—a funky bar/café with £4-7 starving-artist fare from an eclectic, international menu (Mon-Sat 12:00-22:00, closed Sun).

And More: Dozens of restaurants line the main commercial areas of town: Sauchiehall Street, Buchanan Street, and the Merchant City area. Many are similar, with trendy interiors, Euro disco-pop soundtracks, and dinner for about £15-20 per person.

For Your Whisky: **The Pot Still** is an award-winning malt whisky bar from 1835 that boasts a formidable array of more than 600 choices. You'll see locals of all ages sitting in its leathery interior, watching football (soccer) and discussing their drinks. They have whisky aged in sherry casks, whisky preferred by wine drinkers, and whisky from every region of Scotland. Give the friendly bartenders a little background on your beverage tastes, and they'll narrow down a good choice for you from their long list (whisky runs £3-75 per glass, average price £4-5, £2.50 pasties and pies, daily 11:00-24:00, 154 Hope Street, tel. 0141/333-0980).

IN THE WEST END

This hip, lively residential neighborhood/university district is worth exploring, particularly in the evening. The restaurant scene focuses on two areas (at opposite ends of my West End Walk): near the Hillhead subway stop and, farther down, in the Finnieston neighborhood below the Kelvingrove Museum. For locations, see the map on page 805.

Near Hillhead

There's a fun concentration of restaurants in the streets that fan out from the Hillhead subway stop (pay £8 for a taxi here from downtown). Most have tables out front to let you watch the parade of people, and also convivial gardens in the back. Before choosing a place, take a stroll and scout the whole scene, focusing on the streets noted below.

Along Ashton Lane: The top choice along here is **Ubiquitous Chip,** a beloved local landmark with various pubs and restaurants sprawling through a deceptively large building. The pricey restaurant fills a garden atrium (£23-28 main courses), but it's less expensive to opt for the upstairs brasserie, which overlooks that genteel scene, or the nondescript pub (£10-17 meals; daily 11:00-24:00, 12 Ashton Lane, tel. 0141/334-5007, www.ubiquitouschip.co.uk). You can also check out the eclectic Ashton Lane lineup, including **Ketchup** (American-style diner), **Brel** (Belgian beer bar), **Vodka Wódka** (Polish vodka bar), **The Wee Curry Shop** (Indian), and **Jinty McGuinty's** (Irish pub and beer garden). The recommended **Grosvenor Cinema** also has its own upstairs café, overlooking the Ashton Lane bustle.

On Cresswell Lane: Of the eateries along here, one favorite is **Café Andaluz,** which offers £5-7 tapas and sangria behind lacy wooden screens as the waitstaff clicks past on the cool tiles (Mon-Sat 12:00-23:00, Sun 12:30-22:30, 2 Cresswell Lane, tel. 0141/339-1111).

Along Ruthven Lane: Down this characteristic little lane, across Byres Road from the subway station, are two fine options: one Scottish and one Vietnamese, both with inside and outside seating. **Bothy Restaurant** offers tasty, traditional Scottish fayre in an inviting garden courtyard or a rustic-contemporary interior (£12-20 main dishes, daily 12:00-22:00, 11 Ruthven Lane, tel. 0141/334-4040). **The Hanoi Bike Shop,** a rare-in-Scotland Vietnamese "street food" restaurant, serves Asian tapas that are healthy and tasty, using local produce. With tight seating and friendly service, the place has a nice energy (small plates for around £6 each, £8-9 bigger plates, daily 12:00-23:00, 8 Ruthven Lane, tel. 0141/334-7165).

Dining/Nightlife Venues Farther North, near Great Western Road: **Òran Mòr,** a converted 1862 church overlooking a busy intersection, is one of Glasgow's most popular hangouts. It's a five-minute walk from the recommended restaurants (at the intersection of Byres and Great Western roads). In addition to hosting an outdoor beer garden, atmospheric bar (£7-10 pub grub, £4-5 lighter fare), and a pair of upscale-feeling restaurants (£25 meals), the building's former nave hosts a nightclub featuring everything from rock shows to traditional Scottish music nights—check the schedule on their website (bar open daily 9:00-very late; pub food served Mon-Sat 9:00-21:00, Sun 10:00-22:00; restaurants have slightly different hours, top of Byres Road at 731 Great Western Road, tel. 0141/357-6200, www.oran-mor.co.uk). **Hillhead Bookclub** is a historic cinema building cleared out to make room for fun, disco, pub grub, and lots of booze. It's a youthful and quirky art-school scene, with lots of beers on tap, creative cocktails, retro computer games, ping-pong, and theme evenings (£5-7 lunches, £8-10 dinners, Mon-Fri 11:00-24:00, Sat-Sun from 10:00, just off Byres Road at 17 Vinicombe Street, tel. 0141/576-1700).

Upscale Option: For a well-regarded upscale choice in this area, try **Cail Bruich**—serving award-winning classic Scottish dishes with an updated spin in an unpretentious setting. Reservations are smart (£16-21 lunches, £19-25 dinners, lunch Wed-Sun 12:00-14:00, dinner nightly 17:30-21:30, 725 Great Western Road, tel. 0141/334-6265, www.cailbruich.co.uk).

In Finnieston

This very trendy, up-and-coming neighborhood—with the most hipster charm in this very hipster city—stretches east from in front of the Kelvingrove Museum. It's a 15-minute downhill walk from the area described above, or you can ride the subway to the Kelvinhall stop and walk 10 minutes from there. I've listed these roughly in the order you'll reach them as you walk east from the Kelvingrove.

Brewdog Glasgow is a great place to sample Scottish microbrews—from their own brewery in Aberdeen, as well as guest brews—in an industrial-mod setting reminiscent of American brewpubs. Also American-style, they serve many of their beers cold—unlike the room temp of most British brews (also £8-9 burgers and pub grub, Mon-Sat 12:00-24:00, Sun from 12:30, directly across the street from Kelvingrove Museum at 1397 Argyle Street, tel. 0141/334-7175, www.brewdog.com).

Butchershop Bar & Grill is a casual, rustic, American-style steak house, but featuring Scottish products—focusing on dry-aged Scottish steaks (£12-16 main courses, £18-29 steaks, lunch and early-bird deals, daily 12:00-22:00, 1055 Sauchiehall Street, tel. 0141/339-2999, www.butchershopglasgow.com).

Trendy Finnieston Eateries on and near Argyle Street: **Crabshakk,** specializing in fresh seafood, is a foodie favorite, with a very tight bar-and-mezzanine seating area and tables spilling out onto the sidewalk. It's casual but still respectable, and worth reserving ahead (£8-16 meals plus seafood splurges, Tue-Sun 12:00-22:00, closed Mon, 1114 Argyle Street, tel. 0141/334-6127, www.crabshakk.com). Crabshakk anchors a strip of copycat funky/foodie eateries. Survey the choices along here (which change from week to week), but pay special attention to these three: **The Gannet** has £5-8 small plates and £15-20 meals, emphasizing Scottish ingredients with a modern spin (Tue-Sun 12:00-14:00 & 17:00-21:30, closed Mon, 1155 Argyle Street, tel. 0141/204-2081, www.thegannetgla.com). **Kelvingrove Café and Cocktails** is an unpretentious, rustic-chic bar serving creative £8-10 cocktails and £10-13 Scottish comfort food (daily 10:00-24:00, 1161 Argyle Street, tel. 0141/221-8988, www.kelvingrovecafe.com). **Ox and Finch,** a block up toward the main drag, is another good choice, serving £5-8 small plates in a more upscale, rustic wood-meets-industrial atmosphere (daily 12:00-22:00, 920 Sauchiehall Street, tel. 0141/339-8627, www.oxandfinch.com). Several other fun bars and eateries are in this area—browsing is a delight.

Glasgow Connections

Traveline Scotland has a journey planner that's linked to all of Scotland's train and bus schedule info. Go online (www.travelinescotland.com), call them at tel. 0871-200-2233, or use the individual websites listed below. If you're connecting with Edinburgh, note that the train is faster but the bus is cheaper.

BY TRAIN

From Glasgow's Queen Street Station by Train to: Oban (6/day, fewer on Sun, 3 hours), **Inverness** (11/day, 3 hours, 4 direct, others change in Perth), **Edinburgh** (4/hour, 50 minutes), **Stirling** (3/hour, 30-45 minutes).

From Glasgow's Central Station by Train to: Keswick in England's Lake District (roughly hourly, 1.5 hours to Penrith, then catch a bus to Keswick, 45 minutes—see page 517), **Cairnryan** and ferry to Belfast (take train to Ayr, 2/hour, 1 hour; then ride bus to Cairnryan, 1 hour), **Liverpool** (1-2/hour, 3.5-4 hours, change in Wigan or Preston), **Durham** (2/hour, 3 hours, may require change in Edinburgh), **York** (2/hour, 3.5 hours, may require change in Edinburgh), **London** (1-2/hour, 4.5-5 hours direct). Train info: Tel. 0345-748-4950, www.nationalrail.co.uk.

BY BUS

Glasgow's Buchanan bus station is a hub for reaching the Highlands. If you're coming from Edinburgh, you can take the bus to Glasgow and transfer here. Or, for a speedier connection, zip to Glasgow on the train, then walk a few short blocks to the bus station. (Ideally, try to arrive at Glasgow's Queen Street Station, which is closer to the bus station.) For more details on these connections, see "Getting Around the Highlands" on page 878.

From Glasgow by Bus to: Edinburgh (bus #900, 4/hour, 1-1.5 hours depending on traffic), **Oban** (buses #976 and #977; 5/day, 3 hours), **Fort William** (buses #914, #915, and #916; 8/day, 3 hours), **Glencoe** (buses #914, #915, and #916; 8/day, 2.5 hours), **Inverness** (express bus #G10, 5/day, 3.5 hours, additional options with transfer in Perth). Bus info: Tel. 0871-266-3333, www.citylink.co.uk.

BY PLANE

Glasgow International Airport: Located eight miles west of the city, this airport (code: GLA) has currency-exchange desks, a TI, Internet access, luggage storage, and ATMs (tel. 0844-481-5555, www.glasgowairport.com). Taxis connect downtown to the airport for about £20. Your hotel can likely arrange a private taxi service for £14. Bus #500 zips to central Glasgow (daily at least 4/hour 5:00-23:00, then hourly through the night, £6.50/one-way, £9/round-trip, 15-20 minutes to both train stations, 25 minutes to the bus station, catch at bus stop #1).

Prestwick Airport: A hub for Ryanair (as well as the US military, which refuels planes here), this airport (code: PIK) is about 30 miles southwest of the city center (tel. 0871-223-0700, ext. 1006, www.gpia.co.uk). The best connection is by train, which runs between the airport and Central Station (Mon-Sat 3/hour, 50 minutes, half-price with Ryanair ticket). Stagecoach buses link the airport with Buchanan Bus Station (£10, daily 4/hour plus a few nighttime buses, 45-60 minutes, check schedules at www.travelinescotland.com). If you're wondering about the Elvis Presley Bar, this airport is said to be the only piece of Britain that Elvis ever set foot on. (Elvis' manager, the Dutch-born Colonel Tom Parker, had a legal problem with British immigration.)

ROUTE TIPS FOR DRIVERS

From England's Lake District to Glasgow: From Keswick, take the A-66 for 18 miles to the M-6 and speed north nonstop (via Penrith and Carlisle), crossing Hadrian's Wall into Scotland. The road becomes the M-74 just north of Carlisle. To slip through Glasgow quickly, leave the M-74 at Junction 4 onto the M-73, following signs to *M-8/Glasgow.* Leave the M-73 at Junction 2, exiting onto the M-8. Stay on the M-8 west through Glasgow, exit at Junction 30, cross Erskine Bridge, and turn left on the A-82, following signs to *Crianlarich* and *Loch Lomond.* (For a scenic drive through Glasgow, take exit 17 off the M-8 and stay on the A-82 toward Dumbarton.)

STIRLING AND NEARBY

Stirling • William Wallace Monument • Bannockburn • Falkirk • Culross • Doune

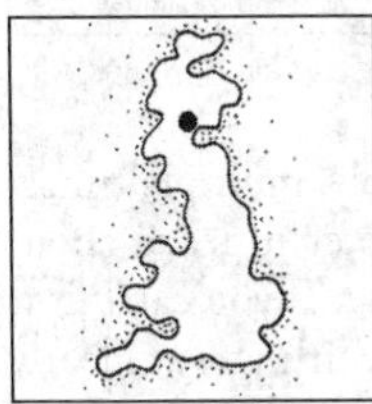

The historic city of Stirling is the crossroads of Scotland: Equidistant from Edinburgh and Glasgow (less than an hour from both), and rising above a plain where the Lowlands meet the Highlands, it's no surprise that Stirling has hosted many of the biggest names (and biggest battles) of Scottish history. Everyone from Mary, Queen of Scots to Bonnie Prince Charlie has passed through the gates of its stately, strategic castle.

From those cliff-capping ramparts, you can see where each of the three pivotal battles of Scotland's 13th- and 14th-century Wars of Independence took place: the Battle of Stirling Bridge, where against all odds, the courageous William Wallace defeated the English army; the Battle of Falkirk, where Wallace was toppled by a vengeful English king; and the Battle of Bannockburn, when—in the wake of Wallace's defeat—Robert the Bruce rallied to kick out the English once and for all (well, at least for a few generations). The William Wallace Monument and Bannockburn Visitors Centre—on the outskirts of Stirling, in opposite directions—are practically pilgrimage sites for patriotic Scots.

Stirling itself is sleepy, but it's an ideal home base for a variety of side-trips. In Falkirk, take a spin in a fascinating Ferris wheel for boats, and ogle the gigantic horse heads called The Kelpies. Sitting on the nearby estuary known as the Firth of Forth—on the way to Edinburgh or St. Andrews—is the gorgeously-preserved time-warp village of Culross. To the north, fans of Monty Python and *Outlander* flock to Doune Castle.

PLANNING YOUR TIME

You'll likely pass near Stirling (and, quite possibly, multiple times) as you travel through Scotland. Skim this chapter to learn about your options and select the stops that interest you. If you can't fit it all in on a pass-through, spend the night. Just as Stirling was ideally situated for monarchs and armies of the past, it's handy for present-day visitors seeking a home base: It's much smaller, and arguably even more conveniently located, than Edinburgh or Glasgow, and it has a variety of good accommodations. You'd need a solid three days to see all of the big sights within an hour's drive of Stirling—but most people are (and should be) more selective.

Stirling

Every Scot knows the city of Stirling (pop. 41,000) deep in their bones. This patriotic heart of Scotland is like Bunker Hill, Gettysburg, and the Alamo, all rolled into one. Stirling perches on a ridge overlooking Scotland's most history-drenched plain: a flat expanse—cut through by the twisting River Forth and the meandering stream called Bannockburn—that divides the Lowlands from the Highlands. And capping that ridge is Stirling's formidable castle, the seat of the final kings of Scotland.

From a traveler's perspective, Stirling is

a pleasant mini-Edinburgh, with a steep spine leading up to that grand castle. It's busy with tourists by day, but sleepy at night. The town and its castle lack personality—but both are striking and strategic.

Orientation to Stirling

Stirling's old town is situated along a long, narrow, steep hill. At its base are the train and bus stations and a thriving (but characterless) commercial district; at its apex is the castle. The old town feels like a steeper, shorter, less touristy, and far less characteristic version of Edinburgh's Royal Mile.

Tourist Information: The TI is a five-minute walk below the castle, just inside the gates of the Old Town Jail (daily 10:00-17:00, free Wi-Fi, St. Johns Street, tel. 01786/475-019).

Getting Around: While you can walk to Stirling Castle and other in-town sights, it's a long hike to the William Wallace Monument and Bannockburn Heritage Centre; instead, take a frequent public bus or a taxi (about £5-10 to either sight).

Sightseeing Deal: This area's three big historical sights—Stirling Castle, the William Wallace Monument, and Bannockburn Heritage Centre—offer a 10 percent discount if you show a ticket from any of the others.

Sights in Stirling

▲▲STIRLING CASTLE

"He who holds Stirling, holds Scotland." These fateful words have been proven, more often than not, to be true. Stirling Castle's prized position—perched on a volcanic crag overlooking a bridge over the River Forth, the primary passage between the Lowlands and the Highlands—has long been the key to Scotland. This castle was the preferred home of Scottish kings and queens in the Middle Ages; today it's one of the most historic—and most popular—castles in Scotland. Although it was recently renovated and lacks soul, it still has plenty to offer: spectacular views over a gentle countryside, tales of the dynamic Stuart monarchs, and several exhibits that try to bring the place to life.

Cost and Hours: £14.50, daily April-Sept 9:30-18:00, Oct-March 9:30-17:00, last entry 45 minutes before closing, Regimental

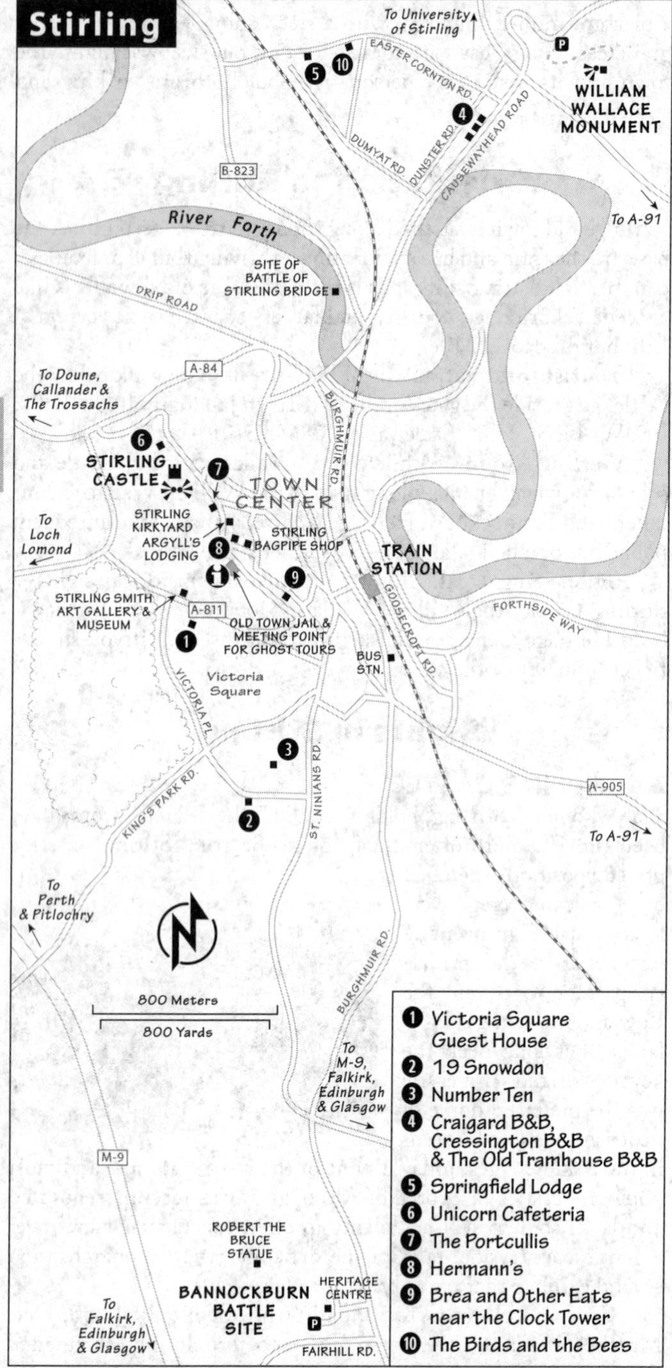
Stirling
To University of Stirling
EASTER CORNTON RD.
WILLIAM WALLACE MONUMENT
DUMYAT RD.
DUNSTER RD.
CAUSEWAYHEAD ROAD
B-823
To A-91
River Forth
SITE OF BATTLE OF STIRLING BRIDGE
DRIP ROAD
A-84
To Doune, Callander & The Trossachs
BURGHMUIR RD.
STIRLING CASTLE
TOWN CENTER
To Loch Lomond
STIRLING KIRKYARD
ARGYLL'S LODGING
STIRLING BAGPIPE SHOP
TRAIN STATION
STIRLING SMITH ART GALLERY & MUSEUM
A-811
OLD TOWN JAIL & MEETING POINT FOR GHOST TOURS
GOOSECROFT RD.
FORTHSIDE WAY
BUS STN.
Victoria Square
VICTORIA PL.
KING'S PARK RD.
ST. NINIANS RD.
A-905
To A-91
To Perth & Pitlochry
BURGHMUIR RD.
800 Meters
800 Yards
To M-9, Falkirk, Edinburgh & Glasgow
M-9
ROBERT THE BRUCE STATUE
BANNOCKBURN BATTLE SITE
HERITAGE CENTRE
To Falkirk, Edinburgh & Glasgow
FAIRHILL RD.
1 Victoria Square Guest House
2 19 Snowdon
3 Number Ten
4 Craigard B&B, Cressington B&B & The Old Tramhouse B&B
5 Springfield Lodge
6 Unicorn Cafeteria
7 The Portcullis
8 Hermann's
9 Brea and Other Eats near the Clock Tower
10 The Birds and the Bees

Museum closes one hour before castle, good café, tel. 01786/450-000, www.stirlingcastle.gov.uk.

Crowd-Beating Tips: Skip the ticket line by purchasing tickets online or using a Historic Scotland Explorer Pass (see page 993).

Tours: The included 30-minute **guided tour** helps you get your bearings—both to the castle and to Scottish history (generally hourly 10:00-16:00, likely more often in peak season and less off-season, departs from well outside the Fort Major's House). Docents posted throughout can tell you more, and you can rent a £3 **audioguide.**

Getting There: Stirling Castle sits at the very tip of a steep old town. Drivers should follow the *Stirling Castle* signs uphill through town to the esplanade, and park at the £4 lot just outside the castle gate. To save a little money, you can leave your car at the Castleview Park-and-Ride off the A-84 and hop on the shuttle bus (2/hour, none on Sun, 15-minute ride, drops you near the TI—walk up from there). Without a car, you can hike the 20-minute uphill route from the train or bus station to the castle, or take a taxi (about £5).

Background: The first castle was built here in the 12th century by King David I (1083-1153). But Stirling Castle's glory days were in the 16th century, when it became the primary residence of the Stuart monarchs, who turned it into a showpiece of Scotland—and a symbol of one-upmanship against England. (At the castle, you may also see the dynasty's name spelled the old way, "Stewart.")

James IV (1473-1513) married the sister of England's King Henry VIII, thereby knitting together the royal families of Scotland (the Stuarts) and England (the Tudors). James V (1512-1542) further expanded the castle. And the France-raised Mary, Queen of Scots (1542-1587) struggled against the rise of Protestantism in her realm. But when Mary's son, King James VI (1566-1625), was crowned King James I of England, he took his royal court with him—never to return to Stirling.

During the Jacobite rebellions of the 18th century, the military took over the castle—bulking it up and destroying its delicate beauty. Even after the Scottish threat had subsided, it remained a British garrison, home base of the Argyll and Sutherland regiments. (It still flies the Union Jack of the United Kingdom.) Finally, in 1964, work began to renovate the castle—an ambitious project that wrapped up just a few years ago. Today, while Stirling Castle is fully restored and gleaming, it feels new and fairly empty—with almost no historic artifacts.

➲ Self-Guided Tour

Begin on the esplanade, just outside the castle entrance, with its grand views.

The Esplanade: The castle's esplanade, a military parade ground in the 19th century, is a tour-bus parking lot in the 21st century. As you survey this site, remember that Stirling Castle bore witness to some of the most important moments in Scottish history. To the right as you face the castle, **King Robert the Bruce** looks toward the plain called Bannockburn, where he defeated the English army in 1314. Squint off to the horizon on Robert's left to spot the pointy stone monument capping the hill called Abbey Craig. This is the **William Wallace Monument,** marking the spot where the Scottish warrior surveyed the battlefield before his victory in the Battle of Stirling Bridge (1297). (Another major battle—one that Scots don't like to talk about as much—also took place nearby: Wallace's defeat at the Battle of Falkirk, in 1298.)

These great Scots helped usher in several centuries of home rule. In 1315, Robert the Bruce's daughter married into an on-the-rise noble clan called the Stuarts, who had distinguished themselves fighting at Bannockburn. When their son Robert became King Robert II of Scotland in 1371, he kicked off the Stuart dynasty. Over the next few generations, their headquarters—Stirling Castle—flourished. The fortified grand entry showed all who approached that James IV (r. 1488-1513) was a great ruler with a powerful castle.

• *Head through the first gate into Guardroom Square, where you can buy your ticket, ask about tour times, and consider renting the audioguide. Then continue up through the inner gate.*

Gardens and Battlements: Once through the gate, follow the passage to the left into a delightful grassy courtyard called the **Queen Anne Garden.** This was the royal family's playground in the 1600s. Imagine doing a little lawn bowling with the queen here.

In the casemates lining the garden is the **Castle Exhibition.** Its "Come Face to Face with 1,000 Years of History" exhibit provides an entertaining and worthwhile introduction to the castle. You'll meet each of the people who left their mark here, from the first Stuart kings to William Wallace and Robert the Bruce. Mind your head. The video leaves you thinking that reenactors of Jacobite struggles are even more spirited than our Civil War reenactors.

Leaving the garden the way you came, make a sharp U-turn up the ramp to the top of the **battlements.** From up here, this castle's strategic position is evident: Defenders had a 360-degree view of enemy armies approaching from miles away. These battlements were built in 1710, long after the castle's Stuart glory days, in response to the Jacobite rebellions (from the Latin word for "James"). By this time, the successes of William Wallace and Robert the Bruce were a distant memory; through the 1707 Act of Union, Scotland had become welded to England. Bonnie Prince Charlie—descendant of those original Stuart "King Jameses" who built this castle—was staging a series of uprisings to try to reclaim the throne of Great Britain for the Stuart line, frightening England enough to further fortify the castle. And sure enough, Bonnie Prince Charlie found himself—ironically—laying siege to the fortress that his own ancestors had built: Facing the main gate (with its two round towers), notice the pockmarks from Jacobite cannonballs in 1746.

• *Now head back down to the ramp and pass through that main gate, into the...*

Outer Close: As you enter this courtyard, straight ahead is James IV's yellow **Great Hall.** That brilliant hue—which historians believe is similar to the original color of the building—is known as "king's gold." While today the vivid color makes the building stick out from the rest of the castle, keep in mind that most of the buildings were built of sandstone—so their original color likely matched this yellow quite well. (Scanning the old gray walls all around, you can still see a few yellow patches that are less weathered.)

To the left as you face James IV's yellow hall is his son **James V's royal palace,** lined with finely-carved Renaissance statues. In 1540, King James V, inspired by French Renaissance châteaux he'd seen, had the castle covered with about 200 statues and busts to "proclaim the peace, prosperity and justice of his reign" and to validate his rule. Imagine the impression all these classical gods and goddesses made on visitors. The message: James' rule was a Golden Age for Scotland.

The **guided tours** of the castle depart from just to your right, near the well. Beyond that is the Grand Battery, with its cannons and rampart views and, underneath that, the Great Kitchens. We'll see both at the end of this tour.

• *Hike up the ramp between James V's palace and the Great Hall (under the crenellated sky bridge connecting them). You'll emerge into the...*

Inner Close: Standing at the center of Stirling Castle, you're surrounded by Scottish history. This courtyard was the core of the 12th-century castle. From there, additional buildings were added—each by a different monarch. While all are historic, they are entirely rebuilt and none have the patina of age. Facing downhill, you'll see the Great Hall. The Chapel Royal—where Mary, Queen of Scots was crowned in 1543—is to your left. The royal palace (containing the Royal Apartments) is to your right—notice the "I5" monogram above the windows (for the king who built it: James, or Iacobus in Latin, V). The Stirling Heads Gallery is above that. And behind you is the Regimental Museum.

• *We'll visit each of these in turn. First, at the far-left end of the gallery with the coffee stand, step into...*

The Great Hall: This is the largest secular space in medieval Scotland. Dating from 1503, this was a grand setting for the great banquets of Scotland's Renaissance kings. One such party, to which all of the crowned heads of Europe were invited, reportedly went on for three full days. This was also where kings and queens would hold court, earning it the nickname "the parliament." The impressive hammerbeam roof is a modern reconstruction, modeled on the early 16th-century roof at Edinburgh Castle. It's made of 400 local oak trees, joined by wooden pegs. If you flipped it over, it'd float.

• *At the far end of the hall, walk across the sky bridge into James V's palace. Here you can explore...*

The Royal Apartments: Six ground-floor apartments are colorfully done up as they might have looked in the mid-16th century, when James V and his queen, Mary of Guise, lived here. Costumed performers play the role of palace attendants, happy to chat with you about medieval life. You'll begin in the King's Inner Hall, where he received guests. Notice the 60 carved and colorfully-painted oak medallions on the ceiling in the king's presence chamber. The medallions are carved with the faces of Scottish and European royalty. These are copies, painstakingly reconstructed after expert research. You'll soon see the originals up close in the Stirling Heads Gallery.

Continue into the other rooms: the King's Bedchamber, with a four-poster bed supporting a less-than-luxurious rope mattress;

and then the Queen's Bedchamber, the Inner Hall, and the Outer Hall, offering a more vivid example of what these rich spaces would have looked like.

• *From the queen's apartments, you'll exit into the top corner of the Inner Close. Directly to your left, up the stairs, is...*

The Stirling Heads Gallery: This is, for me, the castle's highlight—a chance to see the originals of the elaborately carved and painted portrait medallions that decorated the ceiling of the king's presence chamber. Each one is thoughtfully displayed and lovingly explained.

• *If you were to leave this gallery through the exit, you'd wind up back down in the Queen Anne Garden. Instead, backtrack and exit the way you came in to return to the Inner Close, and visit the two remaining sights.*

The Chapel Royal: One of the first Protestant churches built in Scotland, the Chapel Royal was constructed in 1594 by James VI for the baptism of his first son, Prince Henry. The faint painted frieze high up survives from Charles I's coronation visit to Scotland in 1633. Clearly the holiness of the chapel ended in the 1800s when the army moved in.

Regimental Museum: At the top of the Inner Close, in the King's Old Building, is the excellent **Argyll and Sutherland Highlanders Museum.** Another highlight of the castle, it's barely mentioned in castle promotional material because it's run by a different organization. With lots of tartans, tassels, and swords, it shows how the spirit of Scotland was absorbed by Britain. The two regiments, established in the 1790s to defend Britain in the Napoleonic age and combined in the 1880s, have served with distinction in British military campaigns for more than two centuries. Their pride shows here in the building that's their headquarters, where they've been stationed since 1881. The "In the Trenches" exhibit is a powerful look at World War I, with accounts from the battlefield. Up the spiral stairs, the exhibit continues through World War II and conflicts in the Middle East to the present day.

• *When you're ready to move on, consider the following scenic route back to the castle exit.*

Rampart Walk to the Kitchen: The skinny lane between church and museum leads to the secluded Douglas Gardens at the rock's highest point. From here you can walk the ramparts downhill to the Grand Battery, with its cannon rampart at the Outer Close. The Outer Close was the service zone, with a well and the kitchen (below the cannon rampart). The great banquets of James VI didn't happen all by themselves, as you'll appreciate when you explore the fine medieval kitchen exhibit (where mannequin cooks oversee medieval recipes); to find it, head down the ramp and look for the *Great Kitchens* sign.

• *Your castle visit ends here, but your castle ticket includes Argyll's Lodging, a fortified noble mansion. Or, for a scenic route down into town, consider a detour through an old cemetery (both described next).*

MORE SIGHTS IN STIRLING

Old Kirkyard Stroll

Stirling has a particularly evocative old cemetery in the kirkyard (churchyard) just below the castle. For a soulful stroll, go down the stairs where the esplanade meets the parking lot (near the statue of the Scotsman fighting in the South African War). From here, you can wander through the tombstones—Celtic crosses, Victorian statues, and faded headstones—from centuries gone by. The rocky crag in the middle of the graveyard is a fine viewpoint. Work your way over to the Church of the Holy Rude, where you can reenter the town. From here, Argyll's Lodging and the castle parking lot are just to the left, and the TI and Old Town Jail are just to the right.

Argyll's Lodging

Just below the castle esplanade is this 17th-century nobleman's fortified mansion. European aristocrats wanted to live near power—making this location, where the Earl of Argyll's family resided for about a century, prime real estate. You'll get oriented with a historical display on the first floor, then see the kitchens, dining room, drawing room, and bedchambers. Pick up the descriptions in each room, or ask the docents if you have any questions. Argyll's Landing is less sterile than the castle and worth a few minutes.

Cost and Hours: Included in castle ticket, daily 12:45-17:30.

▲Historic and Haunted Walks

These entertaining and informative walking tours around Stirling are led by a local actor/historian. By day, the walks focus on the history of this royal burgh (£8, July-Aug Wed-Sun at 14:00 and 16:00, May-June and Sept Sat-Sun at 14:00 and 16:00, meets at Cowane's Hospital near the old church). By night, the guide plays the role of the "Happy Hangman," and spends most of the tour leading you through the old kirkyard's evocative cemetery (£6, July-Aug Tue-Sat at 20:30, Sept-June Fri-Sat at 20:00, meet in front of TI, www.stirlingghostwalk.com). Either walk takes about 1.25 hours and enhances your appreciation of Stirling beyond its famous castle.

Old Town Jail

Stirling's historic jail was built during the Victorian Age, when the purpose of imprisonment was shifting from punishment to rehabilitation. And today, theatrical 30-minute tours of the old building offer an insightful look at this page in history. Your hardworking guide changes costumes several times throughout the tour, giving you the perspectives of the old-school hangman, the idealistic new warden, and various prisoners. You'll see some of the old cells and end at the top of the tower, offering perhaps the best 360-degree views in town of the surrounding countryside. As this is a relatively new attraction, details may change; confirm before you go.

Cost and Hours: £5, likely July-Sept only, tours every 30 minutes daily 10:15-16:15, St. John Street, www.destinationstirling.com.

▲Stirling Bagpipes

This fun little shop, just a block below the castle on Broad Street, is worth a visit for those curious about this uniquely Scottish instrument. Owner Alan refurbishes old bagpipes here, but also makes new ones from scratch, in a workshop on the premises. The pleasantly cluttered shop, which is a bit of a neighborhood hangout, is littered with bagpipe components—chanters, drones, bags, covers, and cords. If he's not too busy, Alan can answer your questions and tell you more about bagpipes. He'll explain how the most expensive parts of the bagpipe are the "sticks"—the chanter and drones, carved from blackwood—while the bag and cover are cheap. A serious set costs £700...beginners should instead consider a £40 starter kit that includes a practice chanter (like a recorder) with a book of sheet music and a CD. Alan hopes to open a wee museum next door to show off his collection of historic bagpipes.

Cost and Hours: Free, Mon-Tue and Thu-Sat 10:00-18:00, closed Wed and Sun, 8 Broad Street, tel. 01786/448-886, www.stirlingbagpipes.com.

Nearby: On the wide street in front of the shop, look for Stirling's **mercat cross.** A standard feature of any Scottish town, this was the place where townsfolk would gather for the market, and where royal proclamations and executions took place. Today the commercial metabolism of this once-thriving street is at a low ebb. Locals joke that every 100 years, the shopping bustle moves one block farther down the road. These days, it's squeezed into the modern shopping mall between the old town and the river.

Stirling Smith Art Gallery and Museum

Tucked at the edge of the grid-planned Victorian Age neighborhood just below the castle, this endearing and eclectic museum is a hodgepodge of artifacts from Stirling's past: art gallery (where you can meet historical figures with connections to this proud little town), pewter collection, local history exhibits, items from world cultures, a steam-powered carriage, the mutton bone shard removed in the world's first documented tracheotomy (1853), and a 19th-century executioner's cloak and ax. The museum's prized piece is what they claim is the world's oldest surviving soccer ball—a 16th-century stitched-up pig's bladder that restorers found stuck in the rafters of Stirling Castle (presumably kicked up there in a spirited soccer game and forgotten). The building is surrounded by a garden filled with public art.

Cost and Hours: Free, Tue-Sat 10:30-17:00, Sun 14:00-17:00, closed Mon, Dumbarton Road, tel. 01786/471-917, www.smithartgalleryandmuseum.co.uk.

Sleeping in Stirling

IN THE VICTORIAN TOWN, SOUTH OF THE CASTLE

When Stirling expanded beyond its old walls during the Victorian Age, a modern grid-planned town sprouted just to the south. Today, this posh-feeling area holds a few B&Bs that are within a (long) walk of Stirling's old town and castle. These are all in large, spacious homes with easy parking.

$$$ Victoria Square Guest House has seven plush rooms in a beautiful location facing a big, grassy park. While the prices are high, it's neat as a pin, and Kari and Phil keep things running smoothly. Of my listings, it's the closest to the old town—about a 10-minute walk to the lower part of town, or 20 minutes up to the castle (Db-£110-140, 12 Victoria Square, tel. 01786/473-920, www.victoriasquareguesthouse.com, info@vsgh.co.uk).

$$ 19 Snowdon is a roomy, modern-feeling home with two simply furnished rooms and a fine garden out back (D with private b on the hall-£85, Db-£95, 19 Snowdon Terrace, tel. 01786/396-522, www.stirlingguesthouse.co.uk, janet.storrar@stirlingguesthouse.co.uk, Janet).

$ Number Ten rents three traditional rooms in an older but Scottish-feeling home (with tartan carpets and a nice garden) a bit farther from the town center (Db-£75, 10 Gladstone Place, tel. 01786/472-681, www.cameron-10.co.uk, cameron-10@tinyonline.co.uk, Carol and Donald Cameron).

ALONG CAUSEWAYHEAD ROAD, NORTH OF THE CASTLE

More than a dozen B&Bs offering slightly lower prices line Causewayhead Road, a busy thoroughfare that connects Stirling to the William Wallace Monument. From here, it's a long walk into town (or the Wallace Monument), but the location is handy for drivers

Sleep Code

Abbreviations **(£1=about $1.60, country code: 44)**
S=Single, **D**=Double/Twin, **T**=Triple, **Q**=Quad, **b**=bathroom
Price Rankings
$$$ Higher Priced—Most rooms £100 or more
$$ Moderately Priced—Most rooms £80-100
$ Lower Priced—Most rooms £80 or less
Unless otherwise noted, credit cards are accepted, breakfast is included, and free Wi-Fi and/or a guest computer is generally available. Prices change; verify current rates online or by email. For the best prices, always book directly with the hotel.

(each place has free parking). While this modern residential area lacks charm, it's convenient.

$ Craigard B&B has three small, modern, tidy, and proper rooms that offer good value (Db-£70, 40 Causewayhead Road, tel. 01786/460-540, mobile 0784-040-1551, www.craigardstirling.co.uk, craigard@hotmail.co.uk, Liz).

$ Cressington B&B has four bright, simple rooms—modern, but with classy touches (Db-£65, 34 Causewayhead Road, tel. 01786/462-435, Janie and Allan Neill).

$ The Old Tramhouse is the frilliest of the bunch, with four rooms that are elegantly decorated with a delicate charm (Db-£60-80, 42 Causewayhead Road, tel. 01786/449-774, mobile 0759-054-0604, www.theoldtramhouse.com, enquiries@theoldtramhouse.com, Alison Cowie).

$ Springfield Lodge sits at the back end of the residential zone that lines up along Causewayhead Road. It's across the street from farm fields, giving it a countryside feeling. The four neat rooms fill a spacious modern house (Db-£75-80, Easter Cornton Road—near the recommended Birds and Bees pub, tel. 01786/474-332, mobile 0795-469-2412, www.springfieldlodgebandb.co.uk, springfieldlodgebandb@gmail.com).

Eating in Stirling

Stirling isn't a place to go looking for high cuisine; eateries here tend to be satisfying but functional. All of these are open daily unless otherwise noted.

UP NEAR THE CASTLE

The **Unicorn Cafeteria,** within the castle itself, is excellent, going beyond basic cafeteria fare with tasty £6-10 meals and sandwiches (same hours as castle). Just below the Esplanade, **The Portcullis** is a pub that aches with history, from its dark, wood-grained bar area to its stony courtyard. The food, like the setting, is old-school (£5-7 light fare, £10-15 meals). For something more distinctive, head a few more steps down Broad Street to **Hermann's.** A bit more dressy, it serves a mix of Scottish and Austrian food (though thankfully, not on the same plate)—perfect for those times when you've got a hankering for haggis, but your travel partner wants Wiener schnitzel (£11-14 lunch specials, £19-22 dinner specials, £12-19 main courses à la carte, top of Broad Street, tel. 01786/450-632, www.hermanns-restaurant.co.uk).

LOWER DOWN IN THE TOWN

Lots of interchangeable eateries cluster around the clock tower at the bottom of town. King Street, below the tower, has a few options (including good Indian fare at **Maharaja**), while several more choices abound on Baker Street, above and to the right of the tower. Along here—tucked between several mostly chain pubs and ethnic eateries (Thai, Italian, Indian)—is **Brea,** a popular all-around eatery with an unpretentious vibe and an eclectic crowd-pleasing menu (£10 pizzas and burgers, £14-17 main courses, closed for lunch Mon, 5 Baker Street, tel. 01786/446-277).

COUNTRY PUB

The Birds and the Bees is a countryside pub a short walk through a residential neighborhood from the Causewayhead Road B&Bs. It's a sprawling complex; the interior has dark wood and country-kitschy decor (such as cowhide cushions), and there are also several outdoor seating areas in good weather (£10-14 pub grub, Easter Cornton Road, tel. 01786/473-663).

Stirling Connections

From Stirling by Train to: Edinburgh (roughly 2/hour, 1 hour), **Glasgow** (3/hour, 30-45 minutes), **Inverness** (every 1-2 hours, 3 hours, some transfer in Perth). Train info: Tel. 0345-748-4950, www.nationalrail.co.uk.

Near Stirling

The William Wallace Monument is just outside of town. Sights within side-trip distance include The Kelpies horse-head sculptures, the Falkirk Wheel boat "elevator," the stuck-in-time village of Culross, and Doune Castle.

JUST OUTSIDE OF STIRLING

▲William Wallace Monument

Commemorating the Scottish hero better known to Americans as "Braveheart," this sandstone tower—built during a wave of Scottish nationalism in the mid-19th century—marks the Abbey Craig hill on the outskirts of Stirling. This is where, in 1297, Wallace gathered forces and secured his largest-scale victory against England's King Edward I at the Battle of Stirling Bridge. The victory was a huge boost to the Scottish cause, but England came back to beat the Scots the next year. (For more about William Wallace, see page 718.)

Cost and Hours: £9.50, daily July-Aug 10:00-18:00, April-June and Sept-Oct 10:00-17:00, Nov-March 10:30-16:00, last entry 45 minutes before closing, café at visitors center, vending machines up top, tel. 01786/472-140, www.nationalwallacemonument.com. Skip the £2 audioguide, which repeats posted information.

Getting There: It's two miles northeast of Stirling on the A-8, signposted from the city center. Frequent public buses go from the Stirling bus station to the roundabout below the monument (10-15-minute ride)—from there, it's about a 15-minute hike up to the visitors center, then an additional hike up to the monument. Taxis cost about £6-8 one-way. From the visitors center parking lot, you'll need to hike (a very steep 15 minutes) or take a shuttle bus up the hill to the monument itself (depart every 10-15 minutes).

Visiting the Monument: Buy your ticket at the visitors center. Then hike or ride the shuttle bus up to the monument's base. Gazing up, think about how this fanciful structure, like Bavaria's famous Neuschwanstein Castle, was created in the 19th century and designed to evoke (and romanticize) earlier architectural styles—in this case, medieval Scottish castles. The crown-shaped top—reminiscent of St. Giles on the Royal Mile in Edinburgh—and the dynamic sculpture of William Wallace are patriotic to the max.

Entering, show your ticket and head up the very tight stone spiral staircases (claustrophobes be warned). You'll ascend a total of 246 steps, stopping at three levels partway up to catch your breath and see museum displays. The first level, the Hall of Arms, tells the story of William Wallace and the Battle of Stirling Bridge, including a dramatized post-battle debrief between Wallace and his right-hand man, Andrew de Moray (who would later die from his injuries). Next up is the Hall of Heroes, adorned with busts of great Scots—suggesting the debt this nation owes to Wallace. In the middle of the room, ogle Wallace's five-and-a-half-foot-long broadsword (and try to imagine drawing it from a scabbard on your back at a dead run). But it's not just hero worship: A thoughtful video presentation considers the role of Wallace in both Scottish and English history, and raises the point that one person's freedom fighter is another person's terrorist. The third level's exhibits are about the monument itself: when, why, and how it was built.

Finally you reach the top of the tower, with stunning views over Stirling, its castle, the River Forth (which twists back on itself in an almost 360-degree curve), and Stirling Bridge—a stone version that replaced the original wooden one. Looking out from the same vantage point as Wallace, imagine how the famous battle played out. But if you find yourself picturing *Braveheart*—with berserker Scots, their faces painted blue, running across a field to take on the English cavalry—you have the wrong idea. While that portrayal was cinematically powerful, in reality the battle took place on a bridge in a narrow valley (see sidebar).

▲Bannockburn Heritage Centre

On the southern outskirts of Stirling is the Bannockburn Heritage Centre, commemorating what many Scots view as their nation's most significant military victory over the invading English: the Battle of Bannockburn, won by a Scottish army led by Robert the Bruce against England's King Edward II in 1314. The high-tech experience, with 3-D screens and a re-creation of the battle, basically reduces Bannockburn to a video game. But for those interested in the history, it's a good way to really understand, blow by blow, what happened here. While Bannockburn's website recommends reservations, they're rarely needed (except on very busy weekends); just sign up for the next available slot when you arrive, and pass any waiting time (never more than an hour) by exploring the exhibit, grabbing a snack in the café, or walking out to the monument.

Debunking *Braveheart*

The 1995 multiple-Oscar-winner movie *Braveheart* informs many travelers' impressions of William Wallace and the battles near Stirling. But Mel Gibson's much-assailed Scottish accent may very well be the most authentic thing about the film.

In the 1297 Battle of Stirling Bridge, William Wallace and his ragtag Scottish forces hid out in the forest overlooking the bottleneck bridge, waiting until the perfect moment to ambush the English. Thanks to the tight quarters and the element of surprise, the Scots won an unlikely victory.

Braveheart serves up an entirely different version of events: armies lining up across an open field, with blue-faced kilted Highlanders charging at top speed toward heavily armored English troops. The filmmakers left out the bridge entirely, calling it simply "The Battle of Stirling." And the blue face paint? Never happened. A millennium before William Wallace, the ancient Romans did encounter war-painted fighters in Scotland, whom they called the Picts ("painted ones"). But painting faces in the late 13th century would be like WWII soldiers suiting up in chain mail.

Braveheart takes many other liberties with history. William Wallace was *not* the rugged-born Highlander depicted in the movie—he was born in Elderslie, in the Lowlands. Wallace did *not* vengefully kill Andrew de Moray for deserting him at Falkirk (Moray fought valiantly by Wallace's side at Stirling, and died from battle wounds). Robert the Bruce did *not* betray Wallace to the English. And William Wallace most certainly did *not* impregnate the future King Edward II's French bride...who was 10 years old and still living in France at the time of Wallace's death.

Also, the modern concept of national "Freee-dooooom!" was essentially unknown during the divine-right Middle Ages. Wallace wasn't fighting for "democracy" or "liberty"; he simply wanted to trade one authoritarian, aristocratic ruler (from London) for another (from Scotland).

Even the film's title is false: No Scottish person ever referred to Wallace as "Braveheart," which was actually the nickname of one of the film's villains, Robert the Bruce. After Robert's death, his heart was taken on a crusade to the Holy Land by his friend Sir James Douglas. During one battle, Douglas threw the heart at an oncoming army and shouted, "Lead on, brave heart, I will follow thee!"

Scottish people have mixed feelings about *Braveheart.* They appreciate the boost it gave to their underdog nation's profile—and to its tourist industry—juuust enough that they're willing to overlook the film's historical gaffes. For travelers, it can be enjoyable to watch *Braveheart* to prep for your trip...as entertainment. Then go to Stirling and get the real story. (For a fact-based account of Wallace's life, see the sidebar on page 718.)

Cost and Hours: £11.50, daily 10:00-17:30, Nov-Feb until 17:00, café, tel. 0844/493-2139, www.battleofbannockburn.com

Getting There: It's two miles south of Stirling on the A-872, off the M-80/M-9. For nondrivers, it's an easy bus ride from the Stirling bus station (a short walk south from the train station; several buses run on this route, 8/hour, 9-15 minutes).

Background: In simple terms, Robert the Bruce—who was first and foremost a politician—found himself out of political options after years of failed diplomatic attempts to make peace with the strong-arming English. William Wallace's execution left a vacuum in military leadership, and eventually Robert stepped in, waging a successful guerrilla campaign that came to a head as young Edward's army marched to Stirling. Although the Scots were greatly outnumbered, their strategy and use of terrain at Bannockburn—with its impossibly twisty stream presenting a natural barrier for the invading army—allowed them to soundly beat the English and drive Edward out of Scotland...for the time being. (For more about Robert the Bruce, see page 721.) This victory is so legendary among the Scots that the country's unofficial national anthem, "Flower of Scotland"—written 600 years after the battle—focuses on this one event: Robert the Bruce's ragtag squad "stood against him, proud Edward's army, and sent him homeward to think again." (The definitive version of this song was recorded in 1974 by the Scottish folk group The Corries. Look locally for a Corries CD—or buy the song online—and you might soon find yourself singing along at a pub.)

Visiting Bannockburn: Your visit is like preparing for, then playing, an intricate and computerized version of the war game Risk. For the main event, in the "battle room," you'll huddle around a large model of the terrain around Bannockburn and watch a virtual re-creation of troop movements. When buying your ticket, you'll have two choices: "Battle Show," a basic 15-minute recap of the battle; or "Battle Game," a 45-minute simulation where you actually get to take charge of one of the armies and direct their movements...before finding out how things actually turned out. Unless you're into strategy games, the "Battle Show" is plenty for most.

You'll begin by watching two short films to set the stage, then head into the main exhibition area, where giant screens show life-size soldiers at pivotal moments in the battle. Behind the screens you can interact with figures from both sides: Move your hand to get them to talk. Because there are no real artifacts on display, most of the exhibit is preparation for your time in the battle room. At the appointed time, report for battle. You'll come away with a very detailed tactical understanding of battle that shaped this important moment in Scottish and English history.

Leaving the center, hike out into the field behind, where you can see a **monument** to those lost in the fight. Nearby, on a plinth, stands an equestrian statue of **Robert the Bruce**—surveying the place where he lived his most important moment.

FALKIRK

Two engaging landmarks sit just outside the town of Falkirk, about 12 miles south of Stirling. Taken together, The Kelpies and the Falkirk Wheel offer a welcome change of pace from Scottish countryside kitsch. These flank Falkirk's otherwise unexciting town center, about a five-mile, 20-minute drive apart (depending on traffic; it's a riddle of roundabouts); ask for a flier illustrating directions between them at either site.

▲The Kelpies

Unveiled in 2014 and standing over a hundred feet tall ("the largest equine sculptures in the world"), these two giant steel horse heads have quickly become a symbol of this town and region. They may seem whimsical, but they're rooted in a mix of mythology and real history: Kelpies are magical, waterborne, shape-shifting sprites of Scottish lore, who often took the form of a horse. And historically, horses—the ancestors of today's Budweiser Clydesdales—were used as beasts of burden to power Scotland's industrial output. These statues stand over old canals where hardworking horses towed heavily laden barges. But if you prefer, you can just forget all that and ogle the dramatic energy-charged statues (particularly thrilling to Denver Broncos fans). A café nearby sells drinks and light meals, and a visitors center shows how the heads were built. You can take a 45-minute guided tour through the inside of one of the great beasts to see how they're supported by a sleek steel skeleton: 300 tons of steel apiece, sitting upon a foundation of 1,200 tons of steel-reinforced concrete, and gleaming with 990 steel panels.

Cost and Hours: Always open and free to view (£2 to park at the horse heads, free to park elsewhere); visitors center open daily 10:00-17:00. Tours—£6.95, daily at the bottom of every hour

10:30-16:30, fewer tours Oct-March, tel. 01324/506-850, www.thehelix.co.uk.

Getting There: The Kelpies are in a park called The Helix, just off the M-9 motorway—you'll spot them as you zip past. For a closer look, exit the M-9 for the A-905 (Falkirk/Grangemouth), then follow *Falkirk/A-904* and brown *Helix Park & Kelpies* signs.

▲▲Falkirk Wheel

At the opposite end of Falkirk stands this remarkable modern incarnation of Scottish technical know-how. You can watch the beautiful slow-motion contraption as it spins—like a nautical Ferris wheel—to efficiently shuttle ships between two canals separated by 80 vertical feet. With a visitors center, boat trips, hands-on kids' activity zone, and other amusements, the Falkirk Wheel makes engineering fun.

Cost and Hours: Wheel is free to view, visitors center open Mon-Fri 10:00-17:30, Sat-Sun until 18:30, shorter hours Nov-mid-March, park open until 20:00, tel. 0870-050-0208, www.thefalkirkwheel.co.uk.

Getting There: Exit the M-876 motorway for *A-883/Falkirk/Denny,* then follow brown *The Falkirk Wheel* signs. You'll park in a huge free lot, then stroll about 10 minutes along a canal and across a bridge to reach the visitors center and wheel.

Background: Scotland was a big player in the Industrial Revolution, thanks partly to its network of shipping canals (including the famous Caledonian Canal—see page 958). Using dozens of locks to lift barges up across Scotland's hilly spine, these canals were effective...but excruciatingly slow.

The 115-foot-tall Falkirk Wheel, opened in 2002, is a modern take on this classic engineering challenge: Linking the Forth and Clyde Canal below with the aqueduct of the Union Canal, 80 feet above. Rather than using rising and lowering water, the Wheel simply picks boats up and—ever so slowly—takes them where they need to go, like a giant waterborne elevator. In the 1930s, it took half a day to ascend or descend through 11 locks; now it takes only five minutes.

The Falkirk Wheel is the critical connection in the Millennium Link project, an ambitious £78 million initiative to restore the long-neglected Forth and Clyde and Union canals connecting Edinburgh and Glasgow. Today this 70-mile-long aquatic connection between Scotland's leading cities is a leisurely traffic jam of pleasure craft, and canalside communities have been rejuvenated.

Visiting the Wheel: Twice an hour, the Wheel springs (silently) to life: Gates rise up to seal off each of the water-filled gondolas, and then the entire structure slowly rotates a half-turn to swap the positions of the lower and upper boats—each of which stays comfortably upright. The towering structure is not only functional, but beautiful: The wheel's elegantly sweeping shape—with graceful cogs and pointed tips that slice into the water as they spin—was inspired by the Celtic double-headed ax. Or maybe it's a propeller, evoking Glasgow's shipbuilding heritage.

The big, slick **visitors center** has food, souvenirs, free WCs, and a few (not enough) exhibits explaining the Wheel. The Falkirk **TI,** just steps away, has similar hours and free Wi-Fi. Kids love exploring the **activity zone** that sprawls across the lake from the visitors center, with plenty of hands-on activities illustrating how human ingenuity has solved the problem of moving water from place to place (from the lock to the Archimedes screw to the piston pump). Around the far side of the basin, you can rent electric **boats** and canoes, or go **"waterwalking"** (stroll—or stumble—in inflated plastic balls across the water's surface).

Cruises: While it's fun just to watch the wheel in action, for a complete experience consider taking a one-hour boat trip. These begin at the basin in front of the visitors center, and include a ride up and down the wheel with a short boat trip on either end—all narrated by your skipper (£8.95, about hourly in summer, call visitors center or check website to confirm schedule and book ahead).

▲CULROSS

This time-warp of a village, sitting across the Firth of Forth from Edinburgh (about a 30-minute drive from Stirling), is a perfectly-preserved artifact from the 17th and 18th centuries. If you're looking to let your pulse slow, stroll through a steep and sleepy hamlet, and tour a creaky old manor house, Culross is your place. Filmmakers often use Culross to evoke Scottish villages of yore (you've seen it in everything from *Captain America: The First Avenger* to *Outlander*). While not worth a long detour, it's a workable stop for drivers connecting Edinburgh to either the Stirling area or St. Andrews (free parking lots flank the town center—an easy, 5-minute waterfront stroll away).

The story of Culross (which locals pronounce KOO-russ) is the story of Sir George Bruce, who, in the late 16th century, figured out a way to build coal mines beneath the waters of the Firth of Forth. The hardworking town flourished, Bruce built a fine mansion, and the town was granted coveted "royal burgh" status by the king. But several decades later, with Bruce's death and the flooding of the mines, the town's fortunes tumbled—halting its development and trapping it as if in amber for centuries. Rescued and rehabilitated by the National Trust for Scotland, today the entire village feels like one big open-air folk museum.

The main sightseeing attraction here is the misnamed **Culross "Palace,"** the big-but-creaky half-timbered home of George Bruce (£10.50, June-Aug daily 12:00-17:00, April-May and Sept closed Tue-Wed, shorter hours in Oct and closed Nov-March, tel. 01383/880-359, www.nts.org.uk/culross). Buy your ticket at the office under the town hall's clock tower, pick up the included audioguide, then head a few doors down to the ochre-colored palace. Following a 10-minute orientation film, you'll walk through several creaky floors to see how a small town's big shots lived four centuries ago. Docents in each room are happy to answer questions. You'll see the great hall, the "principal stranger's bedchamber" (guest room for VIPs), George Bruce's bedroom and stone strong room (where he stored precious—and flammable—financial documents), and the highlight, the painted chamber. The wood slats of its barrel-arched ceiling are painted with whimsical scenes illustrating Scottish virtues and pitfalls. You can also poke around the densely planted, lovingly tended garden out back. (Plants are sold at a table in the front courtyard.)

Your ticket also includes a 45-minute **guided walk** through the town itself (3/day, check website for schedule).

The only other real sight, a steep hike up the cobbled lanes to the top of town, is the partially-ruined **abbey.** While there are far more evocative ruins in Scotland, it's fun to poke into the stony, mysterious-feeling interior of this church. But the stroll up the town's cobbled streets past pastel houses, with their carefully tended flower boxes, is even better than the church itself.

IN DOUNE

The village of Doune (pronounced "doon") is just a 15-minute drive north of Stirling. While there's not much to see in town, on its outskirts is a pair of attractions: a castle and a distillery. In the village of Doune itself, notice the town seal: a pair of crossed pistols. Aside from its castle and whisky, the town is known for its historic pistol factory. Locals speculate that the first shot of the American Revolution was fired with a Doune pistol.

Getting There: Bus #1 runs from Stirling to Doune (Main Street), from which it's a 10-minute walk to the castle or a 20-minute walk to the distillery (both sit along the River Teith, but in different directions). Drivers head to Doune, then follow castle signs on pretty back roads from there.

Doune Castle

Doune Castle is worth considering for its pop-culture connections: Most recently, Doune stands in for Castle Leoch in the TV series *Outlander.* But well before that, parts of *Monty Python and the Holy Grail* were filmed here. And, while the castle may underwhelm *Outlander* fans (only some exterior scenes were shot here, and currently there's only one paltry display about the show on site), Python fans—and anyone who appreciates British comedy—will be tickled by the included audioguide, narrated by Python troupe member Terry Jones and featuring sound clips from the film. (If you're not into *Python* or *Outlander,* Scotland has better castles to visit.)

Cost and Hours: £5.50, daily April-Sept 9:30-17:30, Oct-March 10:00-16:00, tel. 01786/841-742.

Visiting the Castle: Buy your ticket and pick up the 45-minute audioguide, which explains that the castle's most important resident was not Claire Randall or the Knights Who Say Ni, but Robert Stewart, the Duke of Albany (1340-1420)—a man so influential he was called the "uncrowned king of Scotland." You'll see the cellars, ogle the empty-feeling courtyard, then scramble through the two tall towers and the great hall that connects them. The castle rooms are almost entirely empty, but they're brought to life by the audioguide. You'll walk into the kitchen's ox-sized fireplace to peer up the gigantic chimney, and visit the guest room's privy to peer down the medieval toilet. You'll finish your visit at the top of the main tower, with 360-degree views that allow you to fart in just about anyone's general direction.

Deanston Distillery

This big, attractive, red-brick industrial complex (formerly a cotton mill) sits facing the river just outside of Doune. While Deanston has been long respected for its fruity, slightly-spicy Highland single-malt whisky, the 2012 movie *The Angels' Share,* filmed partly at this distillery, helped put it on the map for tourists. The complex boasts a slick visitors center that's open for tours. On the 50-minute visit, you'll see the equipment used to make the whisky and enjoy a sample. (For more on whisky and the distillation process, see page 724.) A bit more corporate-feeling than some of my favorite Scottish distilleries, Deanston has the advantage of being handy to Stirling.

Cost and Hours: £8-10 depending on number of tastings, tours depart at the top of each hour daily 10:00-16:00 (last tour), best to call ahead to reserve, tel. 01786/843-010, www.deanstonmalt.com.

ST. ANDREWS

St. Andrews is synonymous with golf. But there's much more to this charming town than its famous links. Dramatically situated at the edge of a sandy bay, St. Andrews is the home of Scotland's most important university—think of it as the Scottish Cambridge. And centuries ago, the town was the religious capital of the country.

In its long history, St. Andrews has seen two boom periods. First, in the early Middle Ages, the relics of St. Andrew made the town cathedral one of the most important pilgrimage sites in Christendom. The faithful flocked here from all over Europe, leaving the town with a medieval all-roads-lead-to-the-cathedral street plan that survives today. But after the Scottish Reformation, the cathedral rotted away and the town became a forgotten backwater. A new wave of visitors arrived in the mid-19th century, when a visionary mayor (with the on-the-nose name Provost Playfair) began to promote the town's connection with the newly in-vogue game of golf. Most buildings in town date from this Victorian era.

Today St. Andrews remains a popular spot for students, golf devotees (from amateurs to professional golfers to celebrities), and occasionally Britain's favorite royal couple, Will and Kate (college sweethearts, U. of St. A. class of '05). With vast sandy beaches, golfing opportunities for pros and novices alike, playgrounds of castle and cathedral ruins, and a fun-loving student vibe, St. Andrews is an appealing place to take a vacation from your busy vacation.

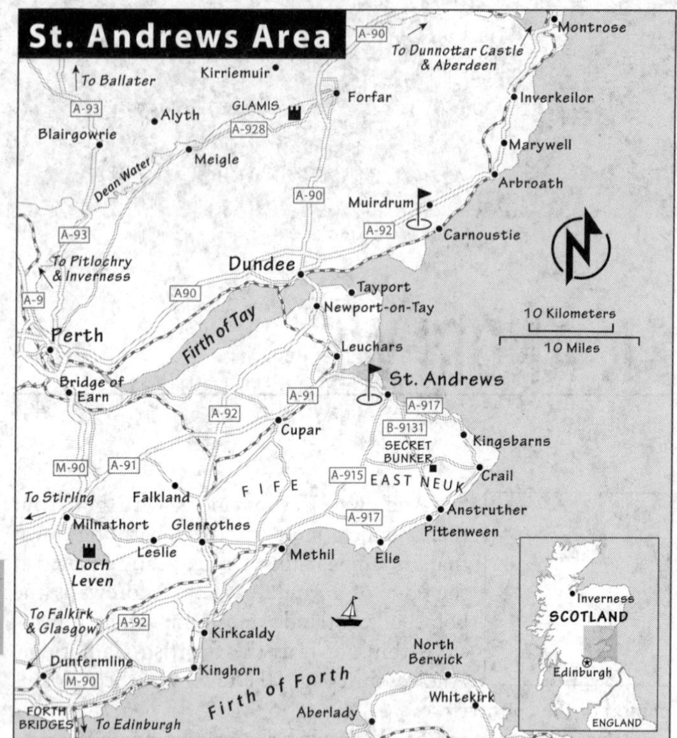

PLANNING YOUR TIME

St. Andrews, hugging the east coast of Scotland, is a bit off the main tourist track. But it's well-connected by train to Edinburgh (via bus from nearby Leuchars), making it a worthwhile day trip from the capital. Better yet, spend a night (or more, if you're a golfer) to enjoy this university town after dark.

If you're not here to golf, this is a good way to spend a day: Follow my self-guided walk, which connects the golf course, the university quad, the castle, and the cathedral. Dip into the Golf Museum, watch the golfers on the Old Course, play a round at "the Himalayas" putting green, or walk along the West Sands beach.

Orientation to St. Andrews

St. Andrews (pop. 16,000, plus several-thousand more students during term) is situated at the tip of a peninsula next to a broad bay. The town retains its old medieval street plan: Three main streets (North, Market, and South) converge at the cathedral, which overlooks the sea at the tip of town. The middle street—Market Street—has the TI and many handy shops and eateries. North of

North Street, the seafront street called The Scores connects the cathedral with the golf scene, which huddles along the West Sands beach at the base of the old town. St. Andrews is compact: You can stroll across town—from the cathedral to the historic golf course—in about 15 minutes.

TOURIST INFORMATION

St. Andrews' helpful TI is on Market Street, about two blocks in front of the cathedral (July-Aug Mon-Sat 9:15-18:00, Sun 10:00-17:00; April-June and Sept-mid-Oct Mon-Sat 9:15-17:00, Sun 11:00-16:00; mid-Oct-March Mon-Sat 9:15-17:00, closed Sun; free Wi-Fi, 70 Market Street, tel. 01334/472-021, www.visitfife.com or www.visitscotland.com).

ARRIVAL IN ST. ANDREWS

By Train and Bus: The nearest train station is in the village of Leuchars, five miles away. From there, a 10-minute bus ride takes you right into St. Andrews (buy ticket from driver, buses meet most trains—see schedule at bus shelter for next bus to St. Andrews; while waiting, read the historical info under the nearby flagpole). St. Andrews' bus station is near the base of Market Street—a short walk from most B&Bs and the TI. A taxi from Leuchars into St. Andrews costs about £14.

By Car: For a short stay, drivers can simply head into the town center and park anywhere along the street. Easy-to-use meters dispense stickers (£1/hour, coins only, 2-hour limit, monitored Mon-Sat 9:00-17:00). For longer stays, you can park for free along certain streets near the center (such as the small lot near the B&B neighborhood around Murray Place, and along The Scores), or use one of the long-stay lots near the entrance to town.

HELPFUL HINTS

Golf Events: Every five years, St. Andrews is swamped with about 100,000 visitors when it hosts the **British Open** (called simply "The Open" around here; the next one—celebrating The Open's 150th anniversary—is in 2021). The town also fills up every year in early October for the **Alfred Dunhill Links Championship.** Unless you're a golf pilgrim, avoid the town at these times (as room rates skyrocket).

School Term: The University of St. Andrews has two terms: spring semester ("Candlemas"), from mid-February through May; and fall semester ("Martinmas"), from mid-September until December. St. Andrews has a totally different vibe in the summer, when most students leave and are replaced by upper-crust golfers and tourists.

Sand Surfing and Adventure Activities: Non-golfers who want

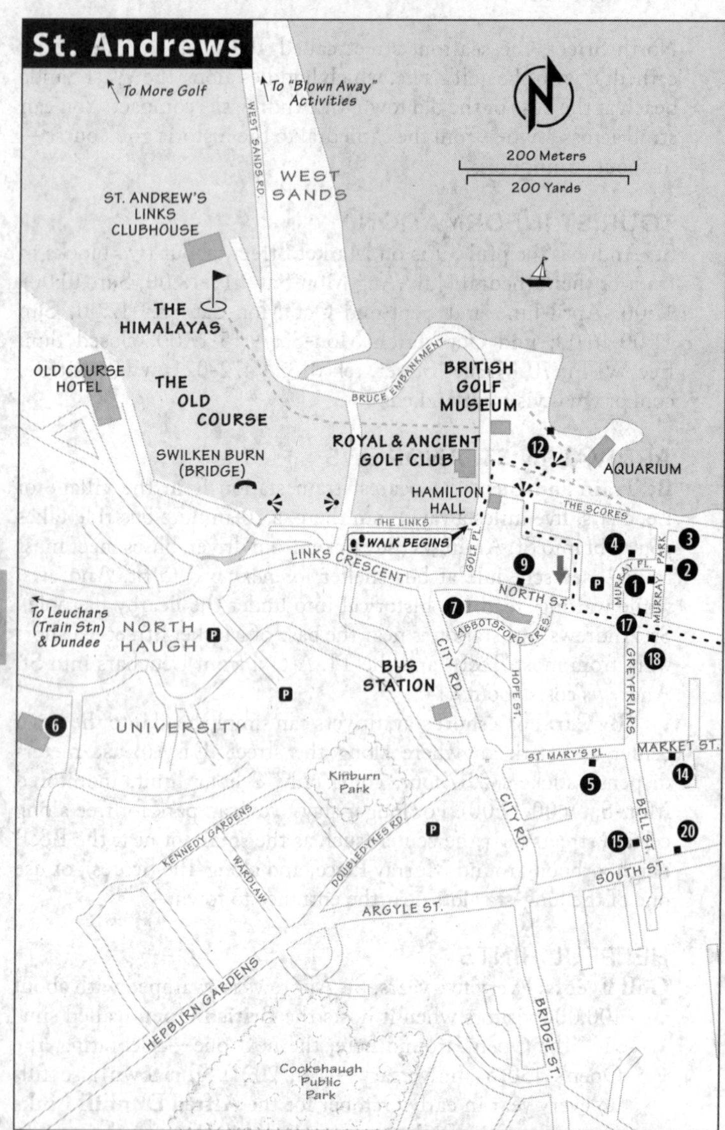

to stay busy while their travel partners play the Old Course may enjoy some of the adventure activities offered by **Blown Away**—including "land yachting" (zipping across the beach in wind-powered go-carts), kayaking, and paddle boarding.

1. Hoppity House B&B
2. Cameron House & Glenderran Guest House
3. Montague Guest House & Lorimer House
4. Doune Guest House
5. St. Andrews Tourist Hostel & The Grill House Restaurant
6. Agnes Blackadder Hall
7. McIntosh Hall
8. Forgan's Restaurant
9. Playfair's Restaurant
10. The Glass House Restaurant
11. The Doll's House Restaurant
12. The Seafood Restaurant
13. Cromars Fish & Chips
14. Tailend Fish & Chips
15. Aikmans Pub
16. The Central Pub
17. Greyfriars Pub
18. Taste Coffee
19. Luvians Bottle Shop
20. I.J. Mellis Cheesemonger
21. Fisher and Donaldson Pastries
22. B. Jannettas Ice Cream
23. Groceries (2)

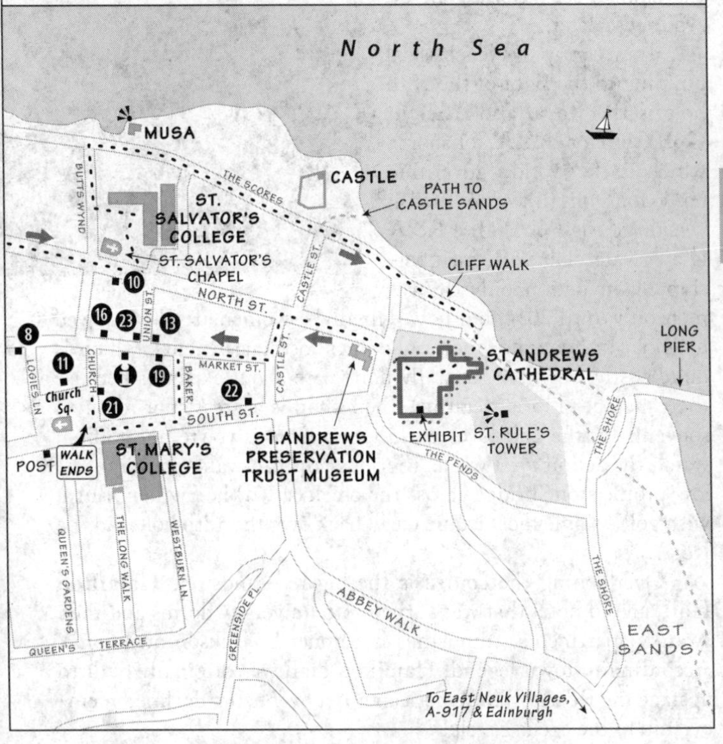

Brothers Guy and Jamie McKenzie set up shop at the northern tip of West Sands beach (sporadic hours—typically Mon-Fri only—so call first, tel. 07784/121-125, www.blownaway.co.uk, ahoy@blownaway.co.uk).

St. Andrews Walk

This walk links all of St. Andrews' must-see sights and takes you down hidden medieval streets. Allow a couple of hours, or more if you detour for the sights along the way.

• *Start at the base of the seaside street called The Scores, overlooking the famous golf course. (There are benches with nice views by the Links Golf Shop for those with a sandwich to munch.)*

▲The Old Course

You're looking at the mecca of golf. The 18th hole of the world's first golf course is a few yards away, on your left (for info on playing the course, see "Golfing in St. Andrews," later).

The gray Neoclassical building to the right of the 18th hole is the **Royal and Ancient Golf Club** (or "R&A" for short), which is the world's governing body for golf (like the British version of the PGA). The R&A is a private club with membership by invitation only; it was men-only until 2014, but now—finally!—women are also allowed to join. (In Scotland, men-only clubs lose tax benefits, which is quite costly, but they generally don't care about expenses because their membership is wealthy.) Their shop is a great spot to buy a souvenir for the golf lover back home. Even if you're not golfing, watch the action for a while. (Serious fans can walk around to the low-profile stone bridge across the creek called the Swilken Burn, with golf's single most iconic view: back over the 18th hole and the R&A.)

Overlooking the course is the big red-sandstone **Hamilton Hall,** an old hotel that was turned into university dorms and then swanky apartments (rumor has it Samuel L. Jackson owns one). According to town legend, Hamilton Hall was originally built to upstage the R&A by an American upset over being declined membership to the exclusive club.

Between Hamilton Hall and the beach is the low-profile **British Golf Museum** (described on page 871).

• *Now turn your back to the golf course and walk through the park (along the street called The Scores) a few steps to the obelisk.*

Beach Viewpoint

The broad two-mile-long sandy beach that stretches below the golf course is the **West Sands.** It's a wonderful place for a relaxing and/

or invigorating walk. Or do a slo-mo jog, humming the theme to *Chariots of Fire*—this is the beach on which the characters run in the movie's famous opening scene.

Walk to the benches on the bluff for a good look at the **cliffs** on your right. The sea below was once called "Witches' Lake" because of all the women and men pushed off the cliff on suspicion of witchcraft.

The big obelisk is a **martyrs' monument,** commemorating all those who died for their Protestant beliefs during the Scottish Reformation. (We'll learn more about that chapter of St. Andrews history farther along this walk.)

The Victorian bandstand **gazebo** (between here and the Old Course) recalls the town's genteel heyday as a seaside resort, when the train line ran all the way to town.

Just opposite the obelisk, across The Scores and next to Alexander's Restaurant, walk down the tiny **Gillespie Wynd alleyway.** It winds through the back gardens of the city's stone houses. Notice how the medieval platting gave each landowner a little bit of street front and a long back garden. St. Andrews' street plan typifies that of a medieval pilgrimage town: All main roads lead to the cathedral; only tiny lanes, hidden alleys, and twisting "wynds" (rhymes with "minds") such as this one connect the main east-west streets.

• *The wynd pops you out onto North Street. Make like a pilgrim and head left toward the cathedral—look for its ruined facade in the distance. We'll eventually end up at the cathedral, but we'll take a few interesting detours along the way.*

Walk about 100 yards to the small cinema, from where you'll see the church tower with the red clock face (our next stop). It's on the corner of North Street and Butts Wynd. For some reason, this street sign often goes missing.

St. Salvator's College

The tower with the red clock marks the entrance to St. Salvator's College. If you're a student, be careful not to stand on the **initials PH** in the pink cobbles in front of the gate. These mark the spot where St. Andrews alum and professor Patrick Hamilton—the Scottish Reformation's most famous martyr—was burned at the stake. According to student legend, as he suffered in the flames, Hamilton threatened that any students who stood on this spot would fail their exams. (And you thought you had dramatic professors.)

Now enter the grounds by walking through the arch under the

tower. (If the entrance is closed, you can go halfway down Butts Wynd and enter, or at least look, through the gate to the green square.) This grassy square, known to students as **Sally's Quad,** is the heart of the university. As most of the university's classrooms, offices, and libraries are spread out across the medieval town, this quad is the one focal point for student gatherings. It's where graduation is held every July, where the free-for-all food fight of Raisin Monday takes place in November (see sidebar on page 864), and where almost the entire student body gathered to celebrate the wedding day of their famous alumni couple—Prince William and Kate—complete with military flybys.

On the outside wall of St. Salvator's Chapel, under the arcade, are **display cases** holding notices and university information; if you're here in spring, you might see students nervously clustered here, looking to see if they've passed their exams.

Go through the simple wooden door and into the **chapel.** Dating from 1450, this is the town's most beautiful medieval church. It's a Gothic gem, with a wooden ceiling, 19th-century stained glass, a glorious organ, and what's supposedly the pulpit of reformer John Knox.

Stroll around Sally's Quad counterclockwise. If you're feeling curious, push a few doors (some seemingly off-limits university buildings, many marked by blue doors, are actually open to the public). On the east (far) side, stop to check out the crazy faces on the heads above the second-floor windows. Find the **university's shield** over the door marked *School 6.* The diamonds are from the coat of arms of the bishop who issued the first university charter in 1411; the crescent moon is a shout-out to Pope Benedict XIII, who gave the OK in 1413 to found the university (his given name was Peter de Luna); the lion is from the Scottish coat of arms; and the X-shaped cross is a stylized version of the Scottish flag (a.k.a. St. Andrew's Cross). On the next building to the left, facing the chapel, is St. Andrew himself (above door of building labeled *Upper & Lower College Halls*).

• *Exit the square at the west end—opposite the university shield—and turn right into Butts Wynd. (If the gate's closed, backtrack out the main gate and hang a right into Butts Wynd.) When the alley ends, you're back at The Scores. Across the street and a few steps to the right is the...*

Museum of the University of St. Andrews (MUSA)

This free museum is worth a quick stop. The first room has some well-explained medieval artifacts. Find the copy of the earliest-known map of the town, made in 1580—back when the town walls led directly to the countryside and the cathedral was intact. Notice that the street plan within the town walls has remained the same—but no golf course. The next room has some exhibits on student

The Scottish Reformation

It's easy to forget that during the 16th-century English Reformation—when King Henry VIII split with the Vatican and formed the Anglican Church (so he could get an officially-recognized divorce)—Scotland was still its own independent nation. Like much of northern Europe, Scotland eventually chose a Protestant path, but it was more gradual and grassroots than Henry VIII's top-down, destroy-the-abbeys approach. While the English Reformation resulted in the Church of England (a.k.a. the Anglican Church, called "Episcopal" outside of England), with the monarch at its head, the Scottish Reformation created the Church of Scotland, which had groups of elected leaders (called "presbyteries" in church jargon).

One of the leaders of the Scottish Reformation was John Knox (1514-1572), who studied under the great Swiss reformer John Calvin. Returning to Scotland, Knox hopped from pulpit to pulpit, and his feverish sermons incited riots of "born-again" iconoclasts who dismantled or destroyed Catholic churches and abbeys (including St. Andrew's Cathedral). Knox's newly minted Church of Scotland gradually spread from the Lowlands to the Highlands. The southern and eastern part of Scotland, around St. Andrews—just across the North Sea from the Protestant countries of northern Europe—embraced the Church of Scotland long before the more remote and Catholic-oriented part of the country to the north and west. Today about 40 percent of Scots claim affiliation with the Church of Scotland, compared with 20 percent who are Catholic (still mostly in the western Highlands). Glasgow and western Scotland are more Catholic partly because of the Irish immigrants who settled there after fleeing the potato famine in the 1840s.

life, including the "silver arrow competition" (which determines the best archer on campus from year to year) and several of the traditions explained in the "Student Life in St. Andrews" sidebar. The next room displays scientific equipment, great books tied to the school, and an exhibit on the Scottish Reformation. The final room has special exhibits. For a great view of the West Sands, climb to the rooftop terrace.

Cost and Hours: Free; April-Oct Mon-Sat 10:00-17:00, Sun 12:00-16:00; Nov-March Thu-Sun 12:00-16:00, closed Mon-Wed; 7 The Scores, tel. 01334/461-660, www.st-andrews.ac.uk/musa.

• *Leaving the museum, walk left toward the castle. The turreted stone buildings along here (including one fine example next door to the museum) are built in the Neo-Gothic Scottish Baronial style, and most are academic departments. About 100 yards farther along, the grand building on the right is St. Salvator's Hall, the most prestigious of the university residences and former dorm of Prince William.*

Just past St. Salvator's Hall on the left are the remains of...

Student Life in St. Andrews

St. Andrews is first and foremost a university town. Scotland's most prestigious university, founded in 1411, is the third-oldest in the English-speaking world after Oxford and Cambridge. While U. of St. A. is sometimes called "England's northernmost university" due to the high concentration of English students—as numerous as the Scottish ones—a quarter of the 6,000 undergrads and 1,000 grad students hail from overseas.

Some Scots resent the preponderance of upper-crust English students (disparagingly dubbed "Yahs" for the snooty way they say "yes"). However, these southerners pay the bills—they are on the hook for tuition, unlike Scots and most EU citizens. And no one seems to mind that the school's most famous graduates, Prince William and Kate Middleton (class of '05), are the definition of upper-class. Soon after "Wills" started studying art history here, the number of female art history majors skyrocketed. (He later switched to geography.)

As with any venerable university, St. Andrews has its share of quirky customs. Most students own traditional red academic "gowns" (woolen robes) to wear on special occasions, such as graduation. In medieval times, however, they were the daily uniform—supposedly so students could be easily identified in brothels and pubs. (In a leap of faith, divinity students—apparently beyond temptation—wear black.) The way the robe is worn indicates the student's status: First-year students (called "bejants") wear them normally, on the shoulders; second-years ("semi-bejants") wear them slightly off the shoulders; third-years ("tertians") wear them off one shoulder (right for "scientists," left for "artists"); and fourth-years ("magistrands") wear them off both shoulders.

The best time to see these robes is during the Pier Walk on Sundays during the university term. After church services (around noon), gown-clad students parade out to the end of the lonesome pier beyond the cathedral ruins. The tradition dates so far back that no one's sure how it started (probably to bid farewell to a visiting dignitary). Today, students just enjoy being a part of the visual spectacle of a long line of red robes flapping in the North Sea wind.

Another age-old custom is a social-mentoring system in which underclassmen choose an "academic family." On Raisin Monday, in mid-November, students give treats to their upperclassmen "parents"—traditionally raisins, but these days more often indulgences like wine and lingerie. Then the "parents" dress up their "children" in outrageous costumes and parade them through town. The underclassmen are obliged to carry around "receipts" for their gifts—written on unlikely or unwieldy objects like plastic dinosaurs, microwave ovens, or even refrigerators—and to sing the school song in Latin on demand. This oddball scenario invariably degenerates into a free-for-all food fight on Sally's Quad.

St. Andrews Castle

Overlooking the sea, the castle is an evocative empty shell—another casualty of the Scottish Reformation. With a small museum and good descriptions peppered around a mostly empty shell, it offers a quick king-of-the-castle experience in a striking setting.

Cost and Hours: £5.50, £8 combo-ticket includes cathedral exhibit, daily April-Sept 9:30-17:30, Oct-March 10:00-16:00, tel. 01334/477-196, www.historic-scotland.gov.uk.

Visiting the Castle: Your visit starts with a colorful kid-friendly exhibit about the history of the castle. Built by a bishop to entertain visiting diplomats in the late 12th century, the castle was home to the powerful bishops, archbishops, and cardinals of St. Andrews. In 1546, the cardinal burned a Protestant preacher at the stake in front of the castle. In retribution, Protestant reformers took the castle and killed the cardinal. In 1547, the French came to attack the castle on behalf of their Catholic ally, Mary, Queen of Scots. During the ensuing siege, a young Protestant refugee named John Knox was captured and sent to France to row on a galley ship. Eventually he traveled to Switzerland and met the Swiss Protestant ringleader, John Calvin. Knox brought Calvin's ideas back home and became Scotland's greatest reformer.

Next, head outside to explore. The most interesting parts are underground: the "bottle dungeon," where prisoners were sent, never to return (peer down into it in the Sea Tower); and the tight "mine" and even tighter "counter-mine" tunnels (follow the signs, crawling is required to reach it all; go in as far as your claustrophobia allows). This shows how the besieging pro-Catholic Scottish government of the day dug a mine to take (or "undermine") the castle—but were followed at every turn by the Protestant counterminers.

Nearby: Just below the castle is a small beach called the **Castle Sands,** where university students take a traditional and chilly morning dip on May 1. Supposedly, doing this May Day swim is the only way to reverse the curse of having stepped on Patrick Hamilton's initials (explained earlier).

• *Leaving the castle, turn left and continue along the bluff on The Scores, which soon becomes a pedestrian lane leading directly to the gate to the cathedral graveyard. Enter it to stand amid the tombstone-strewn ruins of...*

▲St. Andrew's Cathedral

Between the Great Schism and the Reformation (roughly the 14th-16th centuries), St. Andrews was the ecclesiastical capital of Scotland—and this was its showpiece church. Today the site features the remains of the cathedral and cloister (with walls and spires pecked away by centuries of scavengers), a graveyard, and a small exhibit and climbable tower.

Cost and Hours: Cathedral ruins—free, exhibit and tower—£4.50, £8 combo-ticket includes castle; daily April-Sept 9:30-17:30, Oct-March 10:00-16:00, tel. 01334/472-563, www.historic-scotland.gov.uk.

Background: It was the relics of the Apostle Andrew that first put this town on the map and gave it its name. There are numerous legends associated with the relics. According to one version, in the fourth century, St. Rule was directed in a dream to bring the relics northward from Constantinople. When the ship wrecked offshore from here, it was clear that this was a sacred place. Andrew's bones (an upper arm, a kneecap, some fingers, and a tooth) were kept on this site, and starting in 1160, the cathedral was built and pilgrims began to arrive. Since St. Andrew had a direct connection to Jesus, his relics were believed to possess special properties, making them worthy of pilgrimages on par with St. James' relics in Santiago de Compostela, Spain (of Camino de Santiago fame). St. Andrew became Scotland's patron saint; in fact, the white "X" on the blue Scottish flag evokes the diagonal cross on which St. Andrew was crucified (he chose this type of cross because he felt unworthy to die as Jesus had).

➲ **Self-Guided Tour:** You can stroll around the cathedral **ruins**—the best part of the complex—for free. First walk between the two ruined but still-towering ends of the church, which used to be the apse (at the sea end, where you entered) and the main entry (at the town end). Visually trace the gigantic footprint of the former church in the ground, including the bases of columns—like giant sawed-off tree trunks. Plaques identify where elements of the church once stood.

Looking at the one wall that's still standing, you can see the architectural changes that were made over the 150 years the cathedral was built—from the rounded Romanesque windows at the front to the more highly decorated, pointed Gothic arches near the back. Mentally rebuild the church, and try to imagine it in its former majesty when it played host to pilgrims from all over Europe.

The church wasn't destroyed all at once, like all those ruined abbeys in England (demolished in a huff by Henry VIII when he broke with the pope). Instead, because the Scottish Reformation was more gradual, this church was slowly picked apart over time. First just the decorations were removed from inside the cathedral. Then the roof was pulled down to make use of its lead. Without a roof, the cathedral fell further and further into disrepair, and was quarried by locals for its handy precut stones (which you'll still find in the walls of many old St. Andrews homes). The elements—a big storm in the 1270s and a fire in 1378—also contributed to the cathedral's demise.

The surrounding **graveyard,** dating from the post-Reformation Protestant era, is much more recent than the cathedral. In this golf-obsessed town, the game even infiltrates the cemeteries: Many notable golfers from St. Andrews are buried here (such as Young Tom—or "Tommy"—Morris, four-time British Open winner).

Go through the surviving wall into the former **cloister,** marked by a gigantic grassy square in the center. You can still see the cleats up on the wall, which once supported beams. Imagine the cloister back in its heyday, its passages filled with strolling monks.

At the end of the cloister is a small **exhibit** (entry fee required), with a relatively dull collection of old tombs and other carved-stone relics that have been unearthed on this site. Your ticket also includes entry to the surviving **tower of St. Rule's Church** (the rectangular tower beyond the cathedral ruins that was built to hold the precious relics of St. Andrew about a thousand years ago). If you feel like hiking up the 157 very claustrophobic steps for the view over St. Andrews' rooftops, it's worth the price. Up top, you can also look out to sea to find the pier where students traditionally walk out in their robes (see sidebar on page 864).

• *Leave the cathedral grounds on the town side of the cathedral. Angling right, head down North Street. Just ahead, on the left, is the adorable...*

▲St. Andrews Preservation Trust Museum and Garden

Filling a 17th-century fishing family's house that was protected from developers, this museum is a time capsule of an earlier, simpler era. The house itself seems built for Smurfs, but once housed 20 family members. The ground floor features replicas of a grocer's shop and a "chemist's" (pharmacy), using original fittings from actual stores. Upstairs are temporary exhibits. Out back is a tranquil garden (dedicated to the memory of a beloved professor) with "great-grandma's washhouse," featuring an exhibit about the history of soap and washing. Lovingly presented, this quaint, humble house provides a nice contrast to the big-money scene around the golf course at the other end of town.

Cost and Hours: Free but donation requested, generally open early June-early Oct daily 14:00-17:00, closed off-season, 12 North Street, tel. 01334/477-629, www.standrewspreservationtrust.org.

• *From the museum, hang a left around the next corner to South Castle Street. Soon you'll reach...*

Market Street

At the top of Market Street—one of the most atmospheric old streets in town—look for the tiny white house on your left, with the cute curved staircase. What's that chase scene on the roof?

Now turn right down Market Street (which leads directly to the town's center, but we'll take a curvier route). Notice how the streets and even the buildings are smaller at this oldest end of town, as if the whole city is shrinking as the streets close in on the cathedral. Homeowners along Market Street are particularly proud of their address, and recently pooled their money to spiff up the cobbles and sidewalks.

Passing an antique bookstore on your right, take a left onto Baker Lane, a.k.a. Baxter Wynd. You'll pass a tiny and inviting public garden on your right before landing on South Street.

• *Turn right and head down South Street. After 50 yards, cross the street and enter a gate marked by a cute gray facade and a university insignia.*

St. Mary's College

This is the home of the university's School of Divinity (theology). If the gate's open, find the peaceful quad with its gnarled tree that was purportedly planted by Mary, Queen of Scots. To get a feel of student life from centuries past, try poking your nose into one of the old classrooms.

• *Back on South Street, continue to your left. Some of the plainest buildings on this stretch of the street have the most interesting history—several of them were built to fund the Crusades. Turn right on Church Street. You can end this walk at charming Church Square—perhaps while enjoying a decadent pastry from the recommended Fisher and Donaldson bakery (closed Sun).*

But if you want to do more exploring, continue a few more yards down Church Street to Market Street, and turn right to find the TI, grocery stores, and the recommended Luvians Bottle Shop (whisky).

Golfing in St. Andrews

St. Andrews is the Cooperstown of golf. While St. Andrews lays claim to founding the sport (the first record of golf being played

here was in 1553), nobody knows exactly where and when people first hit a ball with a stick for fun. In the Middle Ages, St. Andrews traded with the Dutch; some historians believe they picked up a golf-like Dutch game on ice, and translated it to the bonnie rolling hills of Scotland's east coast. Since the grassy beachfront strip just outside St. Andrews was too poor to support crops, it was used for playing the game—and, centuries later, it still is. Why do golf courses have 18 holes? Because that's how many fit at the Old Course in St. Andrews, golf's single most famous site. While you putt-er around the course, keep in mind this favorite Scottish say-it-aloud joke: "Balls," said the queen. "If I had two, I'd be king." The king laughed—he had to.

The Old Course

The Old Course hosts the British Open every five years (next in 2021). At other times it's open to the public for golfing. The famous Royal and Ancient Golf Club (R&A) doesn't actually own the course, which is public and managed by the St. Andrews Links Trust. Drop by their clubhouse, overlooking the beach near the Old Course (open long hours daily, www.standrews.com). They have a well-stocked shop, a restaurant, and a rooftop garden with nice views over the Old Course.

Teeing Off at the Old Course: Playing at golf's pinnacle course is pricey (£170/person, less off-season), but open to the public—subject to lottery drawings for tee times and reserved spots by club members. You can play the Old Course only if you have a handicap of 24 (men) or 36 (women and juniors); bring along your certificate or card. If you don't know your handicap—or don't know what "handicap" means—then you're not good enough to play here (they want to keep the game moving). If you play, you'll do nine holes out, then nine more back in—however, all but four share the same greens.

Reserving a Tee Time: To ensure a specific tee time at the Old Course, you'll have to reserve a year ahead. You can fill out the form at www.standrews.com during a brief window between late

August and mid-September for tee times the following year. By late October, they'll confirm your date. Otherwise, some tee times are determined each day by a lottery called the "daily ballot." You can put your name in for this—on their website, in person, or by calling 01334/466-666—by 14:00 two days before (2 players minimum, 4 players max). They post the results online at 16:00. Note that no advance reservations are taken on Saturdays or in September, and the courses are closed on Sundays—which is traditionally the day reserved for townspeople to stroll.

Singleton Strategies: Single golfers aren't eligible to reserve or ballot. If you're golfing solo, you could try to team up with someone (try asking your B&B for tips). Or there's a Hail-Mary, last-minute strategy for the very determined: Each day, a few single golfers fill gaps in the schedule on a first-come, first-served basis. You have to show up in person at the starter's hut (with the small practice putting green, in front of the R&A). The starter generally arrives at 6:00 (yes, that's in the morning); die-hard golfers start lining up several hours before (be prepared to doze in the drizzle). This is a very long shot: You may get lucky...or you may get up early for nothing. The best advice is to swing by the starter's hut the day before, when they should have a sense of how likely a spot is to open up and can advise you on how early to arrive.

Other Courses: The trust manages six other courses (including two right next to the Old Course—the New Course and the Jubilee Course), plus the modern cliff-top Castle Course just outside the city. These are cheaper, and it's much easier to get a tee time (£75 for New and Jubilee, £120 for Castle Course, £15-45 for others). It's usually possible to get a tee time for the same day or next day (if you want a guaranteed reservation, make it at least 2 weeks in advance). The Castle Course has great views overlooking the town, but even more wind to blow your ball around.

Club Rental: You can rent decent-quality clubs around town for about £30. The **Auchterlonies** shop has a good reputation (on Golf Place—a few doors down from the R&A, tel. 01334/473-253, www.auchterlonies.com); you can also rent clubs from the Old Course links clubhouse for a few pounds more.

▲The Himalayas

Named for its dramatically hilly terrain, "The Himalayas" is basically a very classy (but still relaxed) game of minigolf. Technically the "Ladies' Putting Green," this cute little patch of undulating grass presents the perfect opportunity for nongolfers (female or male) to say they've played the links at St. Andrews—for less than the cost of a Coke. It's remarkable how the contour of the land can present even more challenging obstacles than the tunnels, gates, and distractions of a corny miniature golf course back home. Flat shoes are required (no high heels). You'll see it on the left as you walk toward the clubhouse from the R&A.

Cost and Hours: £3 for 18 holes. The putting green is open to nonmembers (tourists like you) Mon-Tue and Fri 10:30-16:45, Wed 10:30-12:00 & 16:00-18:30, Thu 11:00-18:30, Sat 10:30-18:00, and Sun 12:00-18:00, tel. 01334/475-196.

British Golf Museum

This exhibit, which started as a small collection in the R&A across the street, is the best place in Britain to learn about the Scots' favorite sport. It's fascinating for golf lovers.

Cost and Hours: £7, includes informative book about the history of golf; April-Oct Mon-Sat 9:30-17:00, Sun 10:00-17:00; Nov-March daily 10:00-16:00; last entry 45 minutes before closing; café upstairs; Bruce Embankment, in the blocky modern building squatting behind the R&A by the Old Course, tel. 01334/460-046, www.britishgolfmuseum.co.uk.

Visiting the Museum: The compact one-way exhibit reverently presents a meticulous survey of the game's history. At the entrance, a constant two-hour loop film shows highlights of the British Open from 1923 to the present. From here, follow the counterclockwise route to learn about the evolution of golf—from the monarchs who loved and hated golf (including the king who outlawed it because it was distracting men from church and archery practice), to Tom Morris and Bobby Jones, all the way up to the "Golden Bear" and a randy Tiger. Along the way, you'll see plenty of old clubs, balls, medals, and trophies, and learn about how the earliest "feathery" balls and wooden clubs were made. Touchscreens invite you to learn more, and you'll also see a "hall of fame" with items donated by today's biggest golfers. Finally you'll have a chance to dress up in some old-school golfing duds and try out some of that antique equipment for yourself.

Sleeping in St. Andrews

Owing partly to the high-roller golf tourists flowing through the town, St. Andrews' accommodations are quite expensive. I've listed high-season rates (June-Sept); most of these places are cheaper off-season. During graduation week in June, hotels often require a four-night stay and book up quickly. All of the ones I've listed, except the hostel and the dorms, are on the streets called Murray

Sleep Code

Abbreviations **(£1=about $1.60, country code: 44)**

S=Single, **D**=Double/Twin, **T**=Triple, **Q**=Quad, **b**=bathroom

Price Rankings

$$ Higher Priced—Most rooms £70 or more

$ Lower Priced—Most rooms less than £70

Unless otherwise noted, credit cards are accepted, breakfast is included, and free Wi-Fi and/or a guest computer is generally available. Prices change; verify current rates online or by email. For the best prices, always book directly with the hotel.

Park and Murray Place, between North Street and The Scores in the old town. If you need to find a room on the fly, head for this same neighborhood, which has far more options than just the ones I've listed below.

$$ Hoppity House is a bright and contemporary place, with attention to detail and built-in furniture that makes good use of space. You may find a stuffed namesake bunny or two hiding out among its six rooms. Helpful Gordon and Heather are fun to talk with and generous with travel tips (Sb-£45-65, Db-£75-90, deluxe Db-£90-110, price depends on size, family room, fridges in rooms, 4 Murray Park, tel. 01334/461-116, mobile 07701-099-100, www.hoppityhouse.co.uk, enquiries@hoppityhouse.co.uk).

$$ Cameron House has five old-fashioned, paisley, masculine-feeling rooms around a beautiful stained-glass atrium (S/Sb-£48, Db-£96, 11 Murray Park, tel. 01334/472-306, www.cameronhouse-sta.co.uk, info@cameronhouse-sta.co.uk, Donna).

$$ Montague Guest House has richly furnished public spaces—with a cozy leather-couches lounge—and eight straightforward rooms (Sb-£60, Db-£80-100 depending on size, 21 Murray Park, tel. 01334/479-287, www.montaguehouse.com, info@montagueguesthouse.com, Andrew and Gillian).

$$ Doune Guest House is golfer-friendly, with seven comfortable rooms (S-£49, Db-£98, cash only, 5 Murray Place, tel. 01334/475-195, www.dounehouse.com, info@dounehouse.com).

$$ Lorimer House has five comfortable, tastefully decorated rooms, including one on the ground floor (Db-£100, deluxe Db-£120, 19 Murray Park, tel. 01334/476-599, www.lorimerhouse.com, info@lorimerhouse.com, Mick and Chris Cordner).

$$ Glenderran Guest House offers five plush rooms (including two true singles) and a few nice breakfast extras (Sb-£60, Db-£115, same-day laundry-£10/load, 9 Murray Park, tel. 01334/477-951, www.glenderran.com, info@glenderran.com, Ray and Maggie).

Hostel: **$ St. Andrews Tourist Hostel** has 44 beds in colorful

4- to 8-bed rooms about a block from the base of Market Street. The high-ceilinged lounge is a comfy place for a break, and the friendly staff is happy to recommend their favorite pubs (bunk in dorm room-£20, St. Mary's Place, tel. 01334/479-911, www.standrewshostel.com).

UNIVERSITY ACCOMMODATIONS

In the summer (early June-Aug), some of the University of St. Andrews' student-housing buildings are tidied up and rented out to tourists. I've listed the most convenient options below (website for both: www.discoverstandrews.com; pay when reserving). Both of these include breakfast and Wi-Fi. Because true single rooms are rare in St. Andrews' B&Bs, these dorms are a good option for solo travelers.

$$ Agnes Blackadder Hall has double beds and private bathrooms; it's more comfortable, but also more expensive and less central (Sb-£55, Db-£75, family Qb-£109, North Haugh, tel. 01334/467-000, agnes.blackadder@st-andrews.ac.uk).

$ McIntosh Hall is cheaper and more central, but it only has twin beds and shared bathrooms (S-£40, D-£65, Abbotsford Crescent, tel. 01334/467-035, mchall@st-andrews.ac.uk).

Eating in St. Andrews

Forgan's is tempting and popular, tucked back in a huge space behind Market Street in what feels like a former warehouse. It's done up country-kitschy, with a rollicking energy, and serves up hearty food (£9-13 meals, Mon-Fri 12:00-22:00, Sat-Sun 10:00-22:00, 110 Market Street, tel. 01334/466-973, www.forgansstandrews.co.uk). On Friday and Saturday nights after 22:30, they have live *ceilidh* (traditional Scottish) music, and everyone joins in the dancing; consider reserving a booth for a late dinner, then stick around for the show.

Playfair's, a restaurant and steakhouse downstairs in the Ardgowan Hotel between the B&B neighborhood and the Old Course, has a cozy/classy interior and outdoor seating at rustic tables set just below the busy street (£6-8 lunches, £10-14 dinners, daily 12:00-late, off-season weekdays open for dinner only, 2 Playfair Terrace on North Street, tel. 01334/472-970).

The Glass House serves pizza, pasta, and salads in a two-story glass building with an open-style layout (£8 lunches, £9-12 dinners, early-bird specials, daily 12:00-22:00, second-floor outdoor patio, near the castle on 80 North Street, tel. 01334/473-673). The same company operates a couple other restaurants in town, with similar hours, prices, and early-bird deals, but each with its own personality: **The Grill House** offers Mexican-style food in a vibrantly colored space (St. Mary's Place, tel. 01334/470-500), while **The Doll's House** serves up cuisine with a French flair; its sidewalk seating out front is across from Holy Trinity Church (3 Church Square, tel. 01334/477-422). Comparing their early-dinner specials may help you choose (http://dollshousestandrews.co.uk).

The Seafood Restaurant is St. Andrews' favorite splurge. Situated in a modern glassy building overlooking the beach near the Old Course, it's like dining in an aquarium. The place serves locally-caught seafood to a room full of tables that wrap around the busy open kitchen. Dinner reservations are recommended; at both lunch and dinner you'll choose from a set-price menu—no à la carte (lunch: £22/2 courses, £28/3 courses; dinner: £40/2 courses, £50/3 courses; daily 12:00-14:30 & 18:00-21:30, The Scores, tel. 01334/479-475, www.theseafoodrestaurant.com).

On Market Street: In the area around the TI, you'll find a concentration of good restaurants—pubs, grill houses, coffee shops, Asian food, fish-and-chips (see later), and more...take your pick. Also on Market Street, you can stock up for a picnic at **Tesco** or **Sainsbury's Local.**

Fish-and-Chips: **Cromars** is a local favorite for takeaway fish-and-chips, centrally located on Market Street near the TI. At the counter, you can order yours to go, or—in good weather—enjoy it at the sidewalk tables (£6-10 fish-and-chips and burgers); farther in is a small sit-down restaurant with slightly higher prices and more choices (£9-14 main dishes; both open daily 10:30 until late, at the corner of Union and Market, tel. 01334/475-555). **Tailend,** owned by the same people, is a few blocks up Market Street. They also have a takeaway counter up front (£6-8 fish-and-chips) and a nicer sit-down area in the back (£12-15 main courses, £8-10 burgers, daily 11:30-late, 130 Market Street, tel. 01334/474-070).

Pubs: There's no shortage in this college town. These aren't "gastropubs," but they all serve straightforward pub fare (all open long hours daily). **Aikmans,** run by Barbara and Malcolm (two graduates from the university who couldn't bring themselves to leave), features a cozy wood-table ambience, a focus on ales, live music (traditional Scottish music occasionally, other live music Fri-Sat) and simple soups, sandwiches, and snacks (£3-6 basic grub, 32 Bell Street, tel. 01334/477-425). **The Central,** right along Market Street, is a St. Andrews standby, with old lamps and lots of brass (£5-7 sandwiches, £9-13 pub grub, 77 Market Street, tel. 01334/478-296). **Greyfriars,** with forgettable food, is in a classy modern hotel near the Murray Park B&Bs (£5-6 light meals, £8-13 main dishes, 129 North Street, tel. 01334/474-906).

Coffee: **Taste,** a little café just across the street from the B&B neighborhood, has the best coffee in town and a laid-back, borderline-funky ambience that feels like a big-city coffeehouse back home. It also serves cakes and light food (daily 7:00-22:00, 148 North Street, tel. 01334/477-959).

Whisky Shop: **Luvians Bottle Shop**—run by three brothers (**Lu**igi, **Vi**ncenzo, and **An**tonio)—is a friendly place to talk, taste, and purchase whisky. Distilleries bottle unique single-cask vintages exclusively for this shop to celebrate the British Open every five years (ask about the 21-year-old Springbank they received in 2015 to commemorate the tournament). With nearly 50 bottles open for tastings, a map of Scotland's whisky regions, and helpful team members, this is a handy spot to learn about whisky. They also sell a wide range of microbrews and offer guided tastings, such as the "Grand Tour" of Scottish whiskies for £15 per person (must arrange in advance, see website for details; daily 10:00-22:00 except Sun opens at 12:30, 66 Market Street, tel. 01334/477-752, www.luvians.com).

Cheese: **I. J. Mellis Cheesemonger,** the excellent Edinburgh cheese shop with a delectable array of Scottish, English, and international cheeses, has a branch on South Street (Mon-Sat 9:00-19:00, Sun 10:00-17:00, 149 South Street, tel. 01334/471-410).

Dessert: **Fisher and Donaldson** is beloved for its rich, affordable pastries and chocolates. Listen as the straw-hatted bakers chat with their regular customers, then try their Coffee Tower—like a giant cream puff filled with rich, lightly coffee-flavored cream—or their number-one seller, the fudge doughnut (Mon-Fri 6:00-17:15, Sat until 17:00, closed Sun, just around the corner from the TI at 13 Church Street, tel. 01334/472-201). **B. Jannettas,** which has been around for more than a century, features a creative range of 52 tasty ice-cream flavors (daily 9:00-22:00, 31 South Street, tel. 01334/473-285, www.jannettas.co.uk).

St. Andrews Connections

Trains don't go into St. Andrews—instead, use the Leuchars station (5 miles from St. Andrews, connected by buses coordinated to meet most trains, 2-4/hour, see "Arrival in St. Andrews" on page 857). The TI has useful train schedules, which also list bus departure times from St. Andrews.

From Leuchars by Train to: Edinburgh (1-2/hour, 1 hour), **Glasgow** (2/hour, 2 hours, transfer in Haymarket), **Inverness** (roughly hourly, 3.25-4 hours, 1-2 changes). Trains run less frequently on Sundays. Train info: Tel. 0345-748-4950, www.nationalrail.co.uk.

OBAN AND THE INNER HEBRIDES

Oban • Isles of Mull, Iona, and Staffa • Near Oban (Inveraray and Kilmartin Glen)

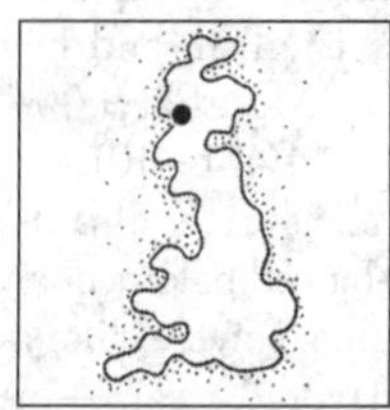

For a taste of Scotland's west coast, the port town of Oban is equal parts endearing and functional. This busy little ferry-and-train terminal has no important sights, but makes up the difference in character, in scenery (with its low-impact panorama of overlapping islets and bobbing boats), and with one of Scotland's best distillery tours. But Oban is also convenient: It's midway between the Lowland cities (Glasgow and Edinburgh) and the Highland riches of the north. And it's the "gateway to the isles," with handy ferry service to the Hebrides Islands.

If time is tight and serious island-hopping is beyond the scope of your itinerary, Oban is ideally situated for a busy and memorable full-day side-trip to three of the most worthwhile Inner Hebrides: big, rugged Mull; pristine little Iona, where buoyant clouds float over its historic abbey; and Staffa, a remote, grassy islet that's home to the famous basalt columns of Fingal's Cave…but inhabited only by sea birds. Sit back, let someone else do the driving, and enjoy a tour of the Inner Hebrides.

This chapter also includes a few additional sights near Oban, handy for those connecting the dots: the most scenic route between Glasgow and Oban (along the bonnie, bonnie banks of Loch Lomond and through the town of Inveraray, with its fine castle); and the faint remains of Kilmartin Glen, the prehistoric homeland of the Scottish people.

PLANNING YOUR TIME

If you're on a speedy blitz tour of Scotland, Oban is a strategic and pleasant place to spend the night. But you'll need two nights to enjoy Oban's main attraction: the side-trip to Mull, Iona, and

Staffa. There are few actual sights in Oban itself, beyond the distillery tour, but—thanks to its manageable size, scenic waterfront setting, and great restaurants—the town is an enjoyable place to linger.

Oban

Oban (pronounced OH-bin) is a low-key resort. Its winding promenade is lined by gravel beaches, ice-cream stands, fish-and-chip joints, a tourable distillery, and a surprising diversity of good restaurants. Everything in Oban is close together, and the town seems eager to please its many visitors: Wool and tweed are perpetually on sale, and posters announce a variety of day tours to Scotland's wild and wildlife-strewn western islands. When the rain clears, sun-starved Scots sit on benches along the Esplanade, leaning back to catch some rays. Wind, boats, gulls, layers of islands, and the promise of a wide-open Atlantic beyond give Oban a rugged charm.

Orientation to Oban

Oban, with about 10,000 people, is where the train system of Scotland meets the ferry system serving the Hebrides islands. As "gateway to the isles," its center is not a square or market, but its harbor. Oban's business action, just a couple of streets deep, stretches along the harbor and its promenade.

TOURIST INFORMATION

Oban's TI, located at the North Pier, sells bus and ferry tickets and is well-stocked with brochures (flexible hours, generally July-Aug Mon-Sat 9:00-19:00, Sun 10:00-17:00; April-June Mon-Sat 9:00-17:30, Sun 10:00-17:00; Sept-Oct daily 10:00-17:00; Nov-March Mon-Sat 10:00-17:00, Sun 11:00-15:00; 3 North Pier, tel. 01631/563-122, www.oban.org.uk).

HELPFUL HINTS

Internet Access: There's free Wi-Fi all over town, including at the TI and many cafés.

Bookstore: Waterstones, a huge bookstore overlooking the har-

Getting Around the Highlands

By Car: The Highlands are made for joyriding. There are a lot of miles, but they're scenic, the roads are good, and the traffic is light. Drivers enjoy flexibility and plenty of tempting stopovers. Be careful, but don't be too timid about passing; otherwise, diesel fumes and large trucks might be your main memory of driving in Scotland. The farther north you go, the more away-from-it-all you'll feel, with few signs of civilization. Even on a sunny weekend, you can go miles without seeing another car. Don't wait too long to gas up—village gas stations are few and far between, and can close unexpectedly. Get used to single-lane roads: While you can make good time when they're empty (as they often are), don't let your guard down, and slow down on blind corners—you never know when an oncoming car (or a roadblocking sheep) is right around the bend. If you do encounter an oncoming vehicle, unspoken rules of the road dictate that the driver closest to a pullout will use it—even if they have to back up. A little "thank-you" wave (or even just an index finger raised off the steering wheel) is the customary end to these encounters.

By Public Transportation: Glasgow is the gateway to this region (so you'll most likely have to transfer there if coming from Edinburgh). The **train** zips from Glasgow to Fort William and Oban in the west; and up to Stirling and Inverness in the east. For more remote destinations (such as Glencoe), the bus is better.

Most of the **buses** you'll need are operated by Scottish Citylink. You can pay the driver in cash when you board. But in peak season—when these buses fill up—it's smart to buy tickets in advance: Book online at www.citylink.co.uk, call 0871-216-3333, or stop by a bus station or TI. Booking the day before generally guarantees a seat; otherwise, you may get bumped to the next departure.

Glasgow's Buchanan Station is the main Lowlands hub for

borfront, offers maps and a fine collection of books on Scotland (long hours daily, 12 George Street, tel. 0843/290-8529).

Baggage Storage: The train station has luggage lockers, but is open limited hours (Mon-Sat 5:00-20:30, Sun 10:45-18:00)—confirm the closing time before committing (£3-5 depending on bag size).

Laundry: You'll find **Oban Quality Laundry** tucked a block behind the main drag on Stevenson Street (same-day drop-off service-£8-12/load, no self-service, Mon-Fri 9:00-17:00, Sat 9:00-13:00, closed Sun, tel. 01631/563-554).

Supermarket: Tesco is a five-minute walk from the train station (Mon-Sat 6:00-24:00, Sun 8:00-20:00, WC in front by registers, inexpensive cafeteria; walk through Argyll Square

reaching Highlands destinations. From Edinburgh, it's best to transfer in Glasgow (fastest by train, also possible by bus)—though there are direct buses from Edinburgh to Inverness, where you can connect to Highlands buses. Once in the Highlands, Inverness and Fort William serve as the main bus hubs.

Note that bus frequency can be substantially reduced on Sundays and in the off-season (Oct-mid-May). Unless otherwise noted, I've listed bus information for summer weekdays. Always carefully confirm schedules locally.

These buses are particularly useful for connecting the sights in this book:

Buses **#976** and **#977** connect Glasgow with Oban (5/day, 3 hours).

Buses **#914, #915,** and **#916** go from Glasgow to Fort William, stopping at Glencoe (8/day, 2.5 hours to Glencoe, 3 hours total to Fort William).

Bus **#918** goes from Oban to Fort William, stopping en route at Ballachulish near Glencoe (3/day, 1 hour to Ballachulish, 1.5 hours total to Fort William).

Bus **#44**—operated by Stagecoach, not Scottish Citylink—is a cheaper alternative for connecting Glencoe to Fort William (hourly Mon-Sat, none Sun, www.stagecoachbus.com).

Buses **#19** and **#919** connect Fort William with Inverness (7-9/day, 2 hours).

Buses **#M90** (express, 4 hours) and **#M91** (many stops, 5 hours) run from Edinburgh to Inverness; these depart about hourly, alternating between express and slow.

Bus **#G10** is an express connecting Inverness and Glasgow (5/day, 3.5 hours; many additional connections possible with change in Perth).

and look for entrance to large parking lot on right, Lochside Street).

Bike Rental: Oban Cycles is on the main drag (Tue-Sat 10:00-17:00, closed Sun-Mon, 87 George Street, tel. 01631/566-033).

Bus Station: The "station" is just a pullout marked by a stubby clock tower at the roundabout in front of the train station. In peak season, it's wise to prebook bus tickets the day before—either at the TI or at the West Coast Motors office (see next).

Bus and Island Tour Tickets: West Coast Motors, a block from the train station in the bright-red building along the harbor at 1 Queens Park Place, has two parts. The travel shop, on the left side, sells bus tickets (Mon-Fri 9:00-17:00, closed Sat-Sun—on those days, go to the other side). On the right side,

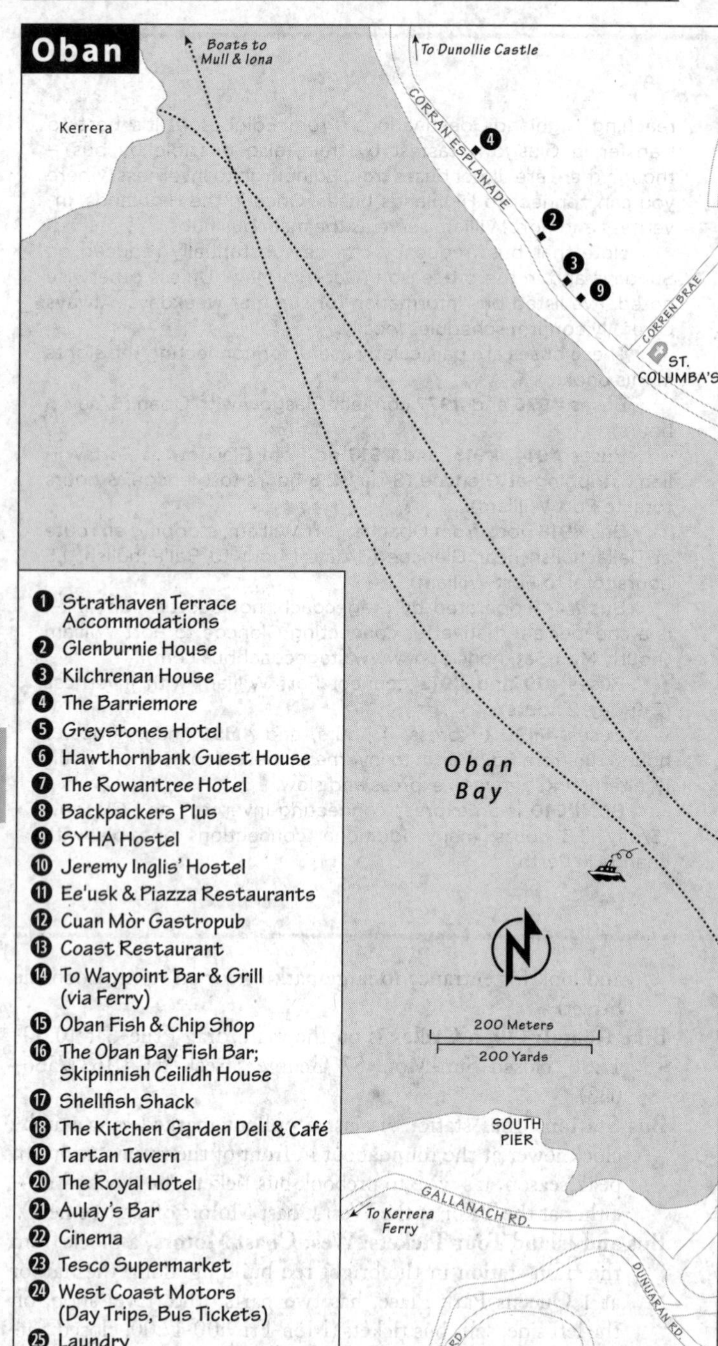
Oban
Boats to Mull & Iona
To Dunollie Castle
Kerrera
CORRAN ESPLANADE
CORREN BRAE
ST. COLUMBA'S
Oban Bay
200 Meters
200 Yards
SOUTH PIER
GALLANACH RD.
To Kerrera Ferry
DUNUARAN RD.
VILLA RD.
1 Strathaven Terrace Accommodations
2 Glenburnie House
3 Kilchrenan House
4 The Barriemore
5 Greystones Hotel
6 Hawthornbank Guest House
7 The Rowantree Hotel
8 Backpackers Plus
9 SYHA Hostel
10 Jeremy Inglis' Hostel
11 Ee'usk & Piazza Restaurants
12 Cuan Mòr Gastropub
13 Coast Restaurant
14 To Waypoint Bar & Grill (via Ferry)
15 Oban Fish & Chip Shop
16 The Oban Bay Fish Bar; Skipinnish Ceilidh House
17 Shellfish Shack
18 The Kitchen Garden Deli & Café
19 Tartan Tavern
20 The Royal Hotel
21 Aulay's Bar
22 Cinema
23 Tesco Supermarket
24 West Coast Motors (Day Trips, Bus Tickets)
25 Laundry
26 Bike Rental

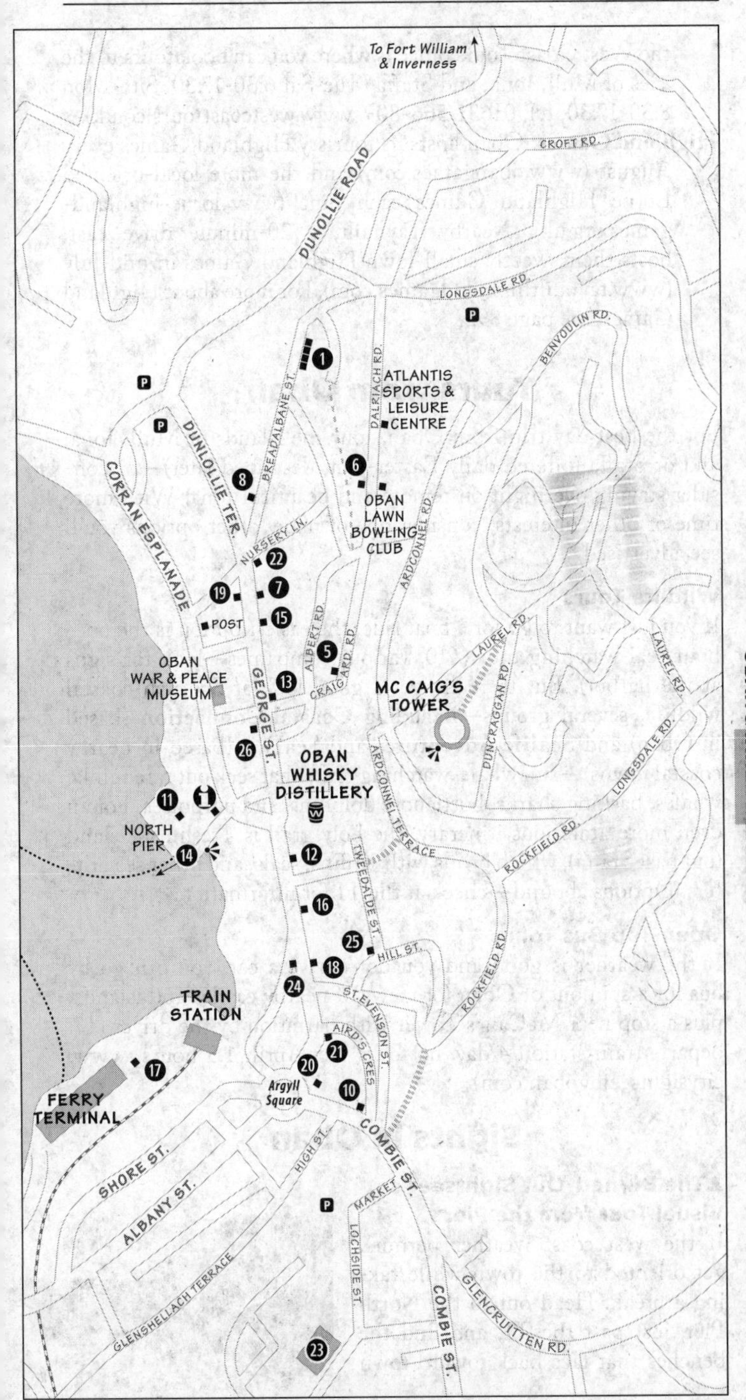
To Fort William & Inverness
CROFT RD.
DUNOLLIE ROAD
LONGSDALE RD.
BENVOULIN RD.
ATLANTIS SPORTS & LEISURE CENTRE
DALRIACH RD.
BREADALBANE ST.
DUNOLLIE TER.
CORRAN ESPLANADE
OBAN LAWN BOWLING CLUB
NURSERY LN.
ARDCONNEL RD.
POST
ALBERT RD.
CRAIGARD RD.
LAUREL RD.
OBAN WAR & PEACE MUSEUM
GEORGE ST.
MC CAIG'S TOWER
DUNCRAGGAN RD.
LONGSDALE RD.
OBAN WHISKY DISTILLERY
ARDCONNEL TERRACE
NORTH PIER
ROCKFIELD RD.
TWEEDALDE ST.
HILL ST.
TRAIN STATION
ST. EVENSON ST.
AIRD'S CRES
FERRY TERMINAL
Argyll Square
COMBIE ST.
HIGH ST.
SHORE ST.
ALBANY ST.
MARKET
LOCHSIDE ST.
GLENCRUITTEN RD.
GLENSHELLACH TERRACE
COMBIE ST.

the West Coast Tours office is where you can book tours to the isles of Mull, Iona, and Staffa (Tue-Sat 6:30-17:30, Sun-Mon 8:30-17:30, tel. 01631/566-809, www.westcoasttours.co.uk).

Highland Games: Oban hosts its touristy Highland Games every August (www.obangames.com) and the more local-oriented Lorne Highland Games each June (www.lorne-highland-games.org.uk). Nearby Taynuilt, a 20-minute drive east, hosts their sweetly small-town Highland Games in mid-July (www.taynuilthighlandgames.com). For more about Highland Games, see page 892.

Tours from Oban

For the best day trip from Oban, tour the islands of Mull, Iona, and/or Staffa (offered daily Easter-Oct, described later)—or consider staying overnight on remote and beautiful Iona. With more time or other interests, consider one of many other options you'll see advertised.

Wildlife Tours

If you just want to go for a boat ride, the easiest option is the one-hour seal-watching tour (£10, various companies—look for signs at the harbor). But to really get a good look at Scottish coastal wildlife, several groups—including **Coastal Connection** (based in Oban) and **Sealife Adventures** and **SeaFari** (based in nearby coastal towns)—run whale-watching tours that seek out rare minke whales, basking sharks, bottlenose dolphins, and porpoises. For an even more ambitious itinerary, the holy grail is Treshnish Island (out past Staffa), which brims with puffins, seals, and other sea critters. Options abound—check at the TI for information.

Open-Top Bus Tours

If the weather is good and you don't have a car, you can go by bus for a spin out of Oban for views of nearby castles and islands, plus a stop near McCaig's Tower with narration by the driver (£7, departs train station 4/day, no tours Oct-April, 1.5 hours, www.citysightseeingoban.com).

Sights in Oban

▲The Burned-Out Sightseer's Visual Tour from the Pier

If the west coast weather permits, get oriented to the town while taking a break: Head out to the North Pier, just past the TI, and find the benches that face back toward town (in front of the recommended Piazza restaurant). Take a seat and get to know Oban.

Scan the harborfront from left to right, surveying the mix of grand Victorian sandstone buildings and humbler modern storefronts. At the far-right end of town is the ferry terminal and—very likely—a lumbering ferry loading or unloading. Oban has always been on the way to something, and today is no different. The townscape seems dominated by Caledonian-MacBrayne, Scotland's biggest ferry company. CalMac's 30 ships serve 24 destinations and transport over 4 million passengers a year. The town's port has long been a lifeline to the islands.

Hiding near the ferry terminal is the train station. With the arrival of the train in 1880, Oban became the unofficial capital of Scotland's west coast and a destination for tourists. The Caledonian Hotel, the original terminus hotel that once served those train travelers, dominates the harborfront.

Tourism aside, herring was the first big industry. A dozen boats still fish commercially—you'll see them tucked around the ferry terminal. The tourist board, in an attempt to entice tourists to linger longer, is trying to rebrand Oban as a "seafood capital" rather than just the "gateway to the isles." As the ocean's supply has become depleted, most local fish is farmed. There's still plenty of shellfish.

After fishing, big industries here historically included tobacco (imported from the American colonies), then whisky. At the left end of the embankment, find the building marked *Oban Whisky Distillery.* It's rare to find a distillery in the middle of a town, but Oban grew up around this one. With the success of its whisky, the town enjoyed an invigorating confidence, optimism, and, in 1811, a royal charter. Touring the distillery is the best activity in Oban.

Above the distillery, you can't miss the odd mini-Colosseum. This is McCaig's Tower, an employ-the-workers-and-build-me-a-fine-memorial project undertaken by an Oban tycoon in 1900. McCaig died before completing the structure, so his complete vision for it remains a mystery. (This is an example of a "folly"—that uniquely British notion of an idiosyncratic structure erected by a colorful aristocrat.) While the building itself is nothing to see up close, a 10-minute hike through a Victorian residential neighborhood leads you to a peaceful garden and a commanding view.

Now turn and look out to sea, and imagine this: At the height of the Cold War, Oban played a critical role when the world's first two-way transatlantic telephone cable was laid from Gallanach Bay to Newfoundland in 1956—a milestone in global communication. This technology later provided the White House and the Kremlin with the "hotline" that was created after the Cuban Missile Crisis to avoid a nuclear conflagration.

▲▲West Highland Malt Scotch Whisky Distillery Tours

The 200-year-old Oban Whisky Distillery produces more than 25,000 liters a week and exports much of that to the US. The distillery offers serious and fragrant one-hour tours explaining the process from start to finish, with two smooth samples of their signature product: Oban whisky is moderately smoky and characterized by notes of sea salt, citrus, and honey. You'll also receive a whisky glass and a discount coupon for the shop. This is the handiest whisky tour you'll encounter—just a block off the harbor—and one of the best. The exhibition that precedes the tour gives a quick whisky-centric history of Oban and Scotland. Then your guide will walk you through each step of the process: malting, mashing, fermentation, distillation, and maturation. Photos are not allowed inside—supposedly because a spark from your camera could ignite the alcohol fumes. (Or maybe it has more to do with interdistillery competition.) For more on whisky, including how to taste it, see page 724.

Cost and Hours: Tours cost £8, are limited to 16 people, depart every 20-30 minutes, and fill up quickly. Because the hours tend to change frequently—and it's best to prebook in any case—check their website or call ahead for the specific schedule. But it's generally open July-Sept Mon-Fri 9:30-19:30, Sat-Sun 9:30-17:00; March-June and Oct-Nov daily 9:30-17:30; Dec-Feb daily 12:30-16:00; last tour 1.25 hours before closing, Stafford Street, tel. 01631/572-004, www.discovering-distilleries.com.

Serious Tasting: Connoisseurs can ask about their "exclusive tour," which adds a visit to the warehouse and four premium tastings in the manager's office (£40, 2 hours, likely July-Sept, Mon, Wed, and Fri at 16:00 only, reserve ahead).

Oban War & Peace Museum

Opened in 1995 on the 50th anniversary of Victory in Europe Day, this charming little museum focuses on Oban's experience during World War II. But it covers more than just war and peace. Photos show Oban through the years, and a 15-minute looped video gives a simple tour around the region. Volunteer staffers love to chat about the exhibit—or anything else on your mind.

Cost and Hours: Free; May-Oct Mon-Sat 10:00-18:00, Sun until 16:00; March-April and Nov daily until 16:00; closed Dec-Feb; Corran Esplanade, next to Regent Hotel on the promenade, tel. 01631/570-007, www.obanmuseum.org.uk.

Dunollie Castle and Museum

In a park just a mile up the coast, this spartan, stocky castle with 10-foot walls is a delightful stroll from the town center. The ruins offer a commanding, windy view of the harbor—a strategic spot back in the days when transport was mainly by water. For more than a thousand years, clan chiefs ruled this region from this ancestral home of Clan MacDougall, but the castle was abandoned in 1746. The adjacent house, which dates from 1745, shows off the MacDougall clan's family heritage—much of it naval; docents explain the charming, if humble, exhibits.

While the castle and museum are, frankly, not much, the local pride in the display and the walk from town make the visit fun. To get there, stroll out of town along the harborfront promenade. Cross the street at the war memorial (with inviting seaview benches). A gate leads to a little lane lined with historic and nature boards along the way to the castle.

Cost and Hours: £5, April-Oct Mon-Sat 10:00-16:00, Sun 13:00-16:00, closed Nov-March, tel. 01631/570-550, www.dunollie.org.

ACTIVITIES IN OBAN

Atlantis Leisure Centre

This industrial-type sports center is a good place to get some exercise on a rainy day or let the kids run wild for a few hours. It has a rock-climbing wall, tennis courts, indoor "soft play centre" (for kids under 5), and an indoor swimming pool with a big water slide. The outdoor playground is free and open all the time.

Cost and Hours: Pool only-£4/adult, £2.50/child, no rental towels or suits, fees for other activities; open Mon-Fri 7:00-21:30, Sat-Sun 9:00-18:30; call or check online for open-swim pool hours, on the north end of Dalriach Road, tel. 01631/566-800, www.atlantisleisure.co.uk.

Oban Lawn Bowling Club

The club has welcomed visitors since 1869. This elegant green is the scene of a wonderfully British spectacle of old men tiptoeing wishfully after their balls. It's fun to watch, and—if there's no match scheduled and the weather's dry—anyone can rent shoes and balls and actually play.

Cost and Hours: £5/person; informal hours, but generally daily 10:00-16:00 & 17:00 to "however long the weather lasts"; just south of sports center on Dalriach Road, tel. 01631/570-808, www.obanbowlingclub.com.

ISLANDS NEAR OBAN

The isles of Mull, Iona, and Staffa are farther out, require a full day to visit, and are described later in this chapter. For a quicker glimpse at the Inner Hebrides, consider these two options.

Isle of Kerrera

Functioning like a giant breakwater, the Isle of Kerrera (KEH-reh-rah) makes Oban possible. Just offshore from Oban, this stark but very green island offers a quick, easy opportunity to get that romantic island experience. While it has no proper roads, it offers nice hikes, a ruined castle, and a few sheep farms. You may see the Kerrera ferry filled with sheep heading for Oban's livestock market.

Getting There: You have two options for reaching the island. Easiest is a boat operated by the recommended Waypoint Bar & Grill, which goes from Oban's North Pier to the Kerrera Marina (£5 round-trip, free if you spend at least £5 at the restaurant, less frequent off-season). The other boat departs from two miles south of town (follow the coast road past the ferry terminal); from here, the boat goes to the middle of the island (passengers only, £4.50 round-trip, bikes free, 5-minute trip, Easter-Oct runs about 2/hour 8:00-18:00 with a break 12:30-14:00, fewer boats Sun and off-season, tel. 01631/563-665, if no answer contact Oban TI for info; www.kerrera-ferry.co.uk).

Sleeping on Kerrera: Your only option is the **$ Kerrera Bunkhouse,** a refurbished 18th-century stable that can sleep up to eight people in four compartments (£15/person, £100 for the entire bunkhouse, includes bedding but not towels, cheaper for 2 nights or more, open year-round but must book ahead, kitchen, tel. 01631/566-367, www.kerrerabunkhouse.co.uk, info@kerrerabunkhouse.co.uk, Martin and Aideen). They also run a tea garden that serves meals (Easter-Sept daily 10:30-16:30, closed Oct-Easter).

Isle of Seil

Enjoy a drive, a walk, some solitude, and the sea. Drive 12 miles south of Oban on the A-816 to the B-844 to the Isle of Seil (pronounced "seal"), connected to the mainland by a bridge (which, locals like to brag, "crosses the Atlantic"...well, maybe a small part of it).

Just over the bridge on the Isle of Seil is a pub called **Tigh-an-Truish** ("House of Trousers"). After the Jacobite rebellions, a new law forbade the wearing of kilts on the mainland. Highlanders on the island used this pub to change from kilts to trousers before they made the crossing. The pub serves great meals and good seafood dishes to those either in kilts or pants (pub likely open daily—call ahead, tel. 01852/300-242).

Seven miles across the island, on a tiny second island and facing the open Atlantic, is **Easdale,** a historic, touristy, windblown little slate-mining town—with a slate-town museum and an egomaniac's incredibly tacky "Highland Arts" shop (shuttle ferry goes the 300 yards). An overpriced direct ferry runs from Easdale to Iona; but, at twice the cost of the Mull-Iona trip, the same time on the island, and very little time with a local guide, it's hardly worth it. For a better connection to Iona, see page 896.

Nightlife in Oban

Little Oban has a few options for entertaining its many visitors. At the TI, pick up the *What's On* leaflet or check www.obanwhatson.co.uk. Fun low-key activities may include open-mic, disco, or quiz theme nights in pubs; occasional Scottish folk shows; coffee meetings; and—if you're lucky—duck races. On Wednesday nights, the Oban Pipe Band plays in the square by the train station. Here are a few other ways to entertain yourself while in town.

Live Music: On many summer nights, you can drop into **Skipinnish Ceilidh House** on the main drag for Highland music, song, and dancing. The owners—professional musicians Angus and Andrew—invest in talented musicians and put on a good show, featuring live bands, songs sung in Gaelic, Highland dancing, and great Scottish storytelling. For many, the best part is the chance to learn some *ceilidh* (KAY-lee) dancing. These group dances are a lot of fun—wallflowers and bad dancers are warmly welcomed, and the staff is happy to give you pointers (£10 music session, cheaper if prebooked online, pricier for concerts with visiting big-name *ceilidh* bands, music 2-3 nights/week mid-June-mid-Sept usually starting around 20:30, check website for schedule, 34 George Street, tel. 01631/569-599, www.skipinnishceilidhhouse.com). Various pubs and hotels in town have live traditional music in the summer; as specifics change from year to year, ask your B&B host or the TI for the latest (try the **Tartan Tavern,** a block off the waterfront at 3 Albany Terrace; or **The Royal Hotel,** just above the train station on Argyll Square).

Cinema: The Phoenix Cinema closed down for two years and then was saved by the community. It's now volunteer-run and booming (140 George Street, www.obanphoenix.com).

Characteristic Pub: Aulay's Bar, with decor that shows off Oban's maritime heritage, has two sides, each with a different personality. Having a drink here invariably comes with a good "blether" (conversation), and the gang is local (basic £6 pub grub, daily 11:00-24:00, 8 Airds Crescent, just around the corner from the train station and ferry terminal).

Sleeping in Oban

SIMPLE, AFFORDABLE B&Bs ON STRATHAVEN TERRACE

Oban's B&Bs offer a better value than its hotels. The following fine but interchangeable B&Bs line up on a quiet flowery street that's nicely located two blocks off the harbor, three blocks from the center, and a 10-minute walk from the train station. By car, as you enter town from the north, turn left immediately after King's Knoll Hotel and take your first right onto Breadalbane Street. ("Strathaven Terrace" is actually just the name for this row of houses on Breadalbane Street.) The alley behind the buildings has tight, free parking for all of these places. None of these B&Bs accepts credit cards.

$$ Gramarvin Guest House has four crisp and cheery rooms, one with a private bathroom in the hall (Db-£65-70, Tb-£98-105, at #5, tel. 01631/564-622, www.gramarvin.co.uk, mary@gramarvin.co.uk, Mary).

$$ Raniven Guest House has five simple, tastefully decorated rooms and gracious, fun-loving hosts Moyra and Stuart (Sb-£35-40, Db-£65-70, at #1, tel. 01631/562-713, www.ranivenoban.com, bookings@ranivenoban.com).

$$ Sandvilla B&B rents five fine rooms (Db-£60-70, at #4, tel. 01631/564-483, www.holidayoban.co.uk, sandvilla@holidayoban.co.uk, Josephine and Robert).

GUESTHOUSES AND SMALL HOTELS

These options are a step up from the B&Bs—in terms of both amenities and price. All have tight, free parking.

Along the Embankment

These are along the Esplanade, which stretches north of town above a cobble beach (with beautiful bay views); they are a 10-minute walk from the center.

$$$ Glenburnie House, a stately Victorian home, has an elegant breakfast room overlooking the bay. Its 12 spacious, comfortable, classy rooms feel like plush living rooms. There's a nice lounge and a tiny sunroom with a stuffed "hairy coo" head (Sb-£60, Db-£90-120, price depends on size and view, closed mid-Nov-March, the Esplanade, tel. 01631/562-089, www.glenburnie.co.uk, stay@glenburnie.co.uk, Graeme).

$$$ Kilchrenan House, the turreted former retreat of a textile magnate, has 14 large rooms, most with bay views. The

Sleep Code

Abbreviations **(£1=about $1.60, country code: 44)**
S=Single, **D**=Double/Twin, **T**=Triple, **Q**=Quad, **b**=bathroom

Price Rankings

$$$ Higher Priced—Most rooms £70 or more
$$ Moderately Priced—Most rooms £30-70
$ Lower Priced—Most rooms £30 or less

Unless otherwise noted, credit cards are accepted at hotels and hostels—but not B&Bs, breakfast is included, and free Wi-Fi and/or a guest computer is generally available. Prices change; verify current rates online or by email. For the best prices, always book directly with the hotel.

stunning rooms #5, #9, and #15 are worth the few extra pounds, while the "standard" rooms in the newer annex are a good value (Sb-£55, Db-£70-105, price depends on size and views, 2-night minimum, welcome drink of whisky or sherry, different "breakfast special" every day, family rooms, closed Nov-Feb, a few houses past the cathedral on the Esplanade, tel. 01631/562-663, www.kilchrenanhouse.co.uk, info@kilchrenanhouse.co.uk, Colin and Frances).

$$$ The Barriemore, at the very end of Oban's grand waterfront Esplanade, comes with a nice patio, front sitting area, and 14 well-appointed rooms. Some front-facing rooms have views; rooms in the modern addition in the back are cheaper (Sb-£65-75, Db-£90-110, Tb-£100-125, two ground-floor double minisuites with views-£130-165, less off-season, price depends on view, the Esplanade, tel. 01631/566-356, www.barriemore-hotel.co.uk, reception@barriemore-hotel.co.uk, Sue, Jan, and Mark).

Above the Town Center

These places perch a block above the main waterfront zone—a quick (but uphill) walk from all of the action. Many rooms come with views and are priced accordingly.

$$$ Greystones is the town's most enticing splurge. It fills a big, stately, turreted mansion at the top of town with five spacious rooms that mix Victorian charm and sleek gray-and-white minimalism. Built as the private home for the director of Kimberley Diamond Mine, it later became a maternity hospital, and today Mark and Suzanne have turned it into a stylish and restful retreat. The lounge and breakfast room offer stunning views over Oban and the offshore isles (Db-£120-165 depending on size and view, closed Nov-mid-Feb, 13 Dalriach Road, tel. 01631/358-653, www.greystonesoban.co.uk, stay@greystonesoban.co.uk).

$$$ Hawthornbank Guest House fills a big Victorian sandstone house with seven traditional-feeling rooms. Half of the rooms face bay views, and the other half overlook the town's lawn bowling green (Db-£65-95 depending on size and view, Dalriach Road, tel. 01631/562-041, www.hawthornbank.co.uk, hawthornbank@btinternet.com).

In the Town Center

$$$ The Rowantree Hotel is a group-friendly place with 24 good rooms reminiscent of a budget hotel in the US (with thin walls). They often have rooms when other places are full, and the location is very central—right on Oban's main drag (Sb-£60-90, Db-£100-130, includes breakfast—or skip breakfast to save a few pounds, cheaper off-season, easy parking, George Street, tel. 01631/562-954, www.rowantreehoteloban.co.uk).

HOSTELS

$ Backpackers Plus is central, laid-back, and fun. It fills part of a renovated old church with a sprawling public living room, 47 beds, and a staff generous with travel tips (bed in dorm room-£16, includes breakfast, great shared kitchen, £5 laundry service for guests only, 10-minute walk from station, on Breadalbane Street, tel. 01631/567-189, www.backpackersplus.com, info@backpackersplus.com, Peter). They have two other locations nearby with private rooms (D-£49, Db-£58).

$ The official **SYHA hostel,** on the scenic waterfront Esplanade, is in a grand building with 98 beds and smashing views of the harbor and islands from the lounges and dining rooms. While institutional, this place is quite nice (all rooms en suite, private rooms available, bed in dorm room-£22, bunk-bed Db-£46, Tb-£74, Qb-£96, price varies with demand, also has family rooms and 8-bed apartment with kitchen, £3/night more for nonmembers, breakfast and dinner extra, pay laundry, kitchen, tel. 01631/562-025, www.syha.org.uk, oban@syha.org.uk).

$ Jeremy Inglis' Hostel has 37 beds located two blocks from the TI and train station. This loosely-run place feels more like a commune than a youth hostel...and it's cheap (bed in dorm room-£18, S-£29, D-£36, cash only, includes linens, breakfast comes with Jeremy's homemade jam, kitchen, no curfew, second floor at 21 Airds Crescent, tel. 01631/565-065, jeremyinglis@mctavishs.freeserve.co.uk).

Eating in Oban

Oban brags that it is the "seafood capital of Scotland," and indeed it's sit-down restaurants (listed first) are surprisingly high quality for such a small town. For something more casual, consider a fish-and-chips joint.

SIT-DOWN RESTAURANTS

These fill up in summer, especially on weekends. To ensure getting a table, you'll want to book ahead. The first four are generally open daily from about 12:00-21:00, with an afternoon closure (from 14:00 or 15:00 to 17:00).

Ee'usk (a phonetic rendering of *iasg*, Scottish Gaelic for "fish") is a popular, stylish, family-run place on the waterfront. It has a casual-chic atmosphere, a bright and glassy interior, sweeping views on three sides, and fish dishes favored by both natives and tourists. Reservations are recommended every day in summer and on weekends off-season (£9-12 lunches, £14-22 dinners, no kids under age 12 at dinner, North Pier, tel. 01631/565-666, www.eeusk.com, MacLeod family).

Cuan Mòr is a popular casual restaurant that combines traditional Scottish with modern flair—both in its crowd-pleasing cuisine and in its furnishings, made of wood, stone, and metal scavenged from the beaches of Scotland's west coast (£6 lunches, £9-14 main courses, no afternoon closure, brewery in back, 60 George Street, tel. 01631/565-078).

Coast proudly serves fresh local fish, meat, and veggies in a mod pine-and-candlelight atmosphere. As everything is prepared and presented with care by husband-and-wife team Richard and Nicola—who try to combine traditional Scottish elements in innovative new ways—come here only if you have time for a slow meal (£11 lunches, £16-20 dinners, £15 two-course and £18 three-course specials, closed Sun for lunch, 104 George Street, tel. 01631/569-900).

Piazza, next door to Ee'usk and also run by the MacLeods, has similar decor but dishes up serviceable Italian cuisine and offers a more family-friendly ambience. They have some outdoor seats and big windows facing the sea (£8-12 pizzas and pastas, smart to reserve ahead July-Aug, tel. 01631/563-628, www.piazzaoban.com).

A Ferry Ride Across the Harbor: **Waypoint Bar & Grill,** just across the bay from Oban, is a laid-back patio at the Kerrera Marina with a no-nonsense menu of grilled seafood. It's not fancy, but the food is fresh and inexpensive, and on a nice day the open-air waterside setting is unbeatable (£6-11 lunches, £10-18 dinners, £24 seafood platter, May-Sept daily 11:00-23:00, closed Oct-April,

Scottish Highland Games

Throughout the summer, Highland communities host traditional festivals of local sport and culture. These Highland Games (sometimes called Highland Gatherings) combine the best elements of a track meet and a county fair. They range from huge and glitzy (such as Braemar's world-famous games, which the Queen attends, or the Cowal Highland Gathering, Scotland's biggest) to humble and endearingly small-town. Some of the more modern games come with loud pop music and corporate sponsorship, but still manage to celebrate the Highland spirit.

Most Highland Games take place between mid-June and late August (usually on Saturdays, but occasionally on weekdays). The games are typically a one-day affair, kicking off around noon and winding down in the late afternoon. At smaller games, you'll pay a nominal admission fee (typically around £5-7). Events are rain or shine (so bring layers) and take place in a big park ringed by a running track, with the heavy events and Highland dancing stage at opposite ends of the infield. Surrounding the whole scene are junk-food stands, a few test-your-skill carnival games, and local charities raising funds by selling hamburgers, fried sausage sandwiches, baked goods, and bottles of beer and Irn-Bru. The emcee's running commentary is a delightful opportunity to just sit back and enjoy a lilting Scottish accent.

The day's events typically kick off with a **pipe band** parading through town—often led by the local clan chieftain—and ending with a lap around the field. Then the sporting events begin.

In the **heavy events**—or feats of Highland strength—brawny kilted athletes test their ability to hurl various objects of awkward shapes and sizes as far as possible. In the weight throw, competitors spin like ballerinas before releasing a 28- or 56-pound ball on a chain. The hammer throw involves a similar technique with a 26-pound ball on a long stick, and the stone put (with a 20- to 25-pound ball) has been adopted in American sports as the shot put. In the "weight over the bar" event, Highlanders swing a 56-pound weight over a horizontal bar that begins at 10 feet high, and ends at closer to 15 feet. (That's like tossing a 5-year-old child over a double-decker bus.) And, of course, there's the caber toss: Pick up a giant log (the caber), get a running start, and release it end-over-end with enough force to (ideally) make the caber flip all the way over and land at the 12 o'clock position. (Most competitors wind up closer to 6.)

Meanwhile, the **track events** run circles around the muscle: the 90-meter dash, the 1,600-meter, and so on. The hill race adds a Scottish spin: Combine a several-mile footrace with the ascent of a nearby summit. The hill racers begin with a lap in the stadium before disappearing for about an hour. Keep an eye on nearby hillsides to pick out their colorful jerseys bobbing up and down a distant peak. This custom supposedly began when an 11th-century king staged a competition to select his personal letter carrier. After about an hour—when you've forgotten all about them—the hill racers start trickling back into the stadium to cross the finish line.

The **Highland dancing** is a highlight. Accompanied by a lone piper, the dancers (in groups of two to four) toe their routines with intense concentration. Dancers remain always on the balls of their feet, requiring excellent balance and stamina. While some men participate, most competitors are female—from wee lassies barely out of nappies, all the way to poised professionals. Common steps are the Highland fling (in which the goal is to keep the feet as close as possible to one spot), sword dances (in which the dancers step gingerly over crossed swords on the stage), and a variety of national dances.

Other events further enliven the festivities. The pipe band periodically assembles to play a few tunes, often while marching around the track (giving the runners a break). Larger games may have a massing of multiple pipe bands, or bagpipe and drumming competitions. You may also see re-enactments of medieval battles, herd dog demonstrations, or dog shows (grooming and obedience). Haggis hurling—a relatively new event in which participants stand on a whisky barrel and attempt to throw a cooked haggis as far as possible—has caught on recently. And many small-town events end with the grand finale of a town-wide tug-of-war, during which everybody gets bruised, muddy, and hysterical.

If you're traveling to Scotland in the summer, before locking in your itinerary, check online schedules to see if you'll be near any Highland Games. Rather than target the big famous gatherings, I make a point of visiting the smaller clan games. One helpful website—listing dates for most but not all of the games around Scotland—is www.shga.co.uk. For many travelers to Scotland, attending a Highland Games can be a trip-capping highlight. And, of course, many communities in the US and Canada also host their own Highland Games.

reservations smart, tel. 01631/565-888, www.waypointbarandgrill.com). A free-for-customers ferry to the marina leaves from Oban's North Pier—look for the sign near the Piazza restaurant (departs hourly at :10 past each hour, 10-minute trip).

FISH-AND-CHIP JOINTS

There are plenty of good fish-and-chips places in Oban, but these two are the town favorites. Each has a front counter serving food to go (for a few pounds less) and good seating with table service farther inside.

Oban Fish and Chip Shop, run by husband-and-wife team George and Lillian (with Lewis and Sammy working the fryer), serves praiseworthy haddock and mussels among other tasty options in a cheery blue cabana-like dining room. Consider venturing away from basic fish-and-chips into a world of more creative seafood dishes (£7 haddock-and-chips to go, £9-16 main courses to eat in, sit-down restaurant closes at 21:00, takeaway available later, 116 George Street, tel. 01631/567-000).

At **The Oban Bay Fish Bar,** which is also family-run, Renato serves all things from the sea (plus an assortment of Scottish classics) battered and fried. Choose between the casual restaurant or takeaway counter, where you can give fried haggis a try (£8-10 meals, cheaper for takeaway, daily 12:00-23:00, on the harborfront at 34 George Street, below Skipinnish, tel. 01631/565-855).

LUNCH

The green **shellfish shack** at the ferry dock regularly gets fresh deliveries from local fishermen and is the best spot to pick up a seafood sandwich or a snack. They sell smaller bites (such as cold sandwiches) for £3-6, as well as some bigger cold platters and a few £7 hot dishes (often free samples, picnic tables nearby, daily from 10:00 until the boat unloads from Mull around 17:45).

The Kitchen Garden is fine for soup, salad, or sandwiches. It's a deli and gourmet-foods store with a charming café upstairs (£4 sandwiches to go, £5-8 dishes upstairs, Mon-Sat 9:00-17:30, Sun 10:00-16:30, closed Sun Jan-mid-Feb, 14 George Street, tel. 01631/566-332).

Oban Connections

By Train from Oban: Trains link Oban to the nearest transportation hub in **Glasgow** (6/day, fewer on Sun, 3 hours); to get to **Edinburgh,** you'll have to transfer in Glasgow (5/day, 4.5 hours). To reach **Fort William** (a transit hub for the Highlands), you'll take the same Glasgow-bound train, but transfer in Crianlarich (3/day, 4 hours)—the direct bus is easier (see next). Oban's small train station has a ticket window and lockers (both open Mon-Sat 5:00-20:30, Sun 10:45-18:00, train info tel. 0345-748-4950, www.nationalrail.co.uk).

By Bus: Bus #918 passes through Ballachulish—a half-mile from **Glencoe**—on its way to **Fort William** (3/day, 1 hour to Ballachulish, 1.5 hours total to Fort William). Take this bus to Fort William, then transfer to bus #919 to reach **Inverness** (4 hours, 20-minute layover in Fort William). A different bus (#976 or #977) connects Oban with **Glasgow** (5/day, 3 hours), from where you can easily connect by bus or train to **Edinburgh** (figure 4.5 hours). Buses arrive and depart from a roundabout, marked by a stubby clock tower, just before the entrance to the train station (tel. 0871-266-3333, www.citylink.co.uk). You can buy bus tickets at the West Coast Motors shop near the bus stop or at the TI across the harbor. Book in advance during peak times.

By Boat: Ferries fan out from Oban to the **southern Hebrides** (see information on the islands of Iona and Mull, later). Caledonian MacBrayne Ferry info: Tel. 01631/566-688, free booking tel. 0800-066-5000, www.calmac.co.uk.

ROUTE TIPS FOR DRIVERS

From Glasgow to Oban via Loch Lomond and Inveraray: For details on the most scenic route from Glasgow to Oban, see "Near Oban" at the end of this chapter.

From Oban to Glencoe and Fort William: It's an easy one-hour drive from Oban to Glencoe. From Oban, follow the coastal A-828 toward Fort William. After about 20 miles—as you leave the village of Appin—you'll see the photogenic **Castle Stalker** marooned on a lonely island (you can pull over at the Wildlife Hub's huge parking lot for decent distant views of the castle). At North Ballachulish, you'll reach a bridge spanning Loch Leven; rather than crossing the bridge, turn off and follow the A-82 into the Glencoe Valley for about 15 minutes. (For tips on the best views and hikes in Glencoe, see the next chapter.) After exploring the valley, make a U-turn and return through Glencoe village. To continue on to Fort William, backtrack to the bridge at North Ballachulish (great view from bridge) and cross it, following the A-82 north.

For a scenic shortcut directly back to Glasgow or Edinburgh, continue south on the A-82 after Glencoe via Rannoch Moor and Tyndrum. Crianlarich is where the road splits and you'll either continue on the A-82 toward Loch Lomond and Glasgow or pick up the A-85 and follow signs for Stirling, then Edinburgh.

Isles of Mull, Iona, and Staffa

For the easiest one-day look at a good sample of the dramatic and historic Inner Hebrides (HEB-rid-eez) islands, take a tour from Oban to Mull, Iona, and Staffa. Though this trip is spectacular when it's sunny, it's worthwhile in any weather (but if rain or rough seas are expected, I'd skip the Staffa option).

GETTING AROUND THE ISLANDS

Here's the game plan: Take a ferry from Oban to Mull (45 minutes), ride a West Coast Motors tour bus across Mull (1.25 hours), then board a quick ferry from Mull to Iona. The total round-trip travel time is 5.5 hours—all of it incredibly scenic—plus about two hours of free time on Iona. With two extra hours and an extra £23, you can add a side-trip to Staffa (yet another boat trip—about 35 minutes each way—plus an hour free on that island). Buy your strip of tickets—one for each leg—at the West Coast Motors office in Oban (£40 for Mull/Iona tour, £63 for Mull/Iona/Staffa tour—£55 "early bird" option described later; April-Oct only—no tours Nov-March, book one day ahead in July-Sept if possible, bus tickets can sell out during busy summer weekends). You can also buy individual tickets for each leg, if you plan to spend extra time (or an overnight) on Iona.

Mull/Iona Tour: You'll leave in the morning from the Oban pier on the huge Oban-Mull **ferry** run by Caledonian MacBrayne (boats depart Mon-Fri at 9:45, Sat at 9:30, Sun at 9:50, board at least 20 minutes before departure). As the schedule can change from year to year, confirm your departure time carefully in Oban. The best inside seats on the ferry—with the biggest windows—are in the sofa lounge on the "observation deck" (level 4) at the back end of the boat. (Follow signs for the toilets, and look for the big staircase to the top floor; this floor also has its own small snack bar with hot drinks and basic sandwiches.) On board, if it's a clear day, ask a local or a crew member to point out Ben Nevis, the tallest mountain in Great Britain. The ferry has a fine cafeteria with hot meals and sandwiches packaged for picnicking, and a bookshop. Five minutes before landing on Mull, you'll see the striking 13th-century Duart Castle on the left.

Walk-on passengers disembark from deck 3, across from the bookshop (port side). Upon arrival in Mull, find your **bus** for the

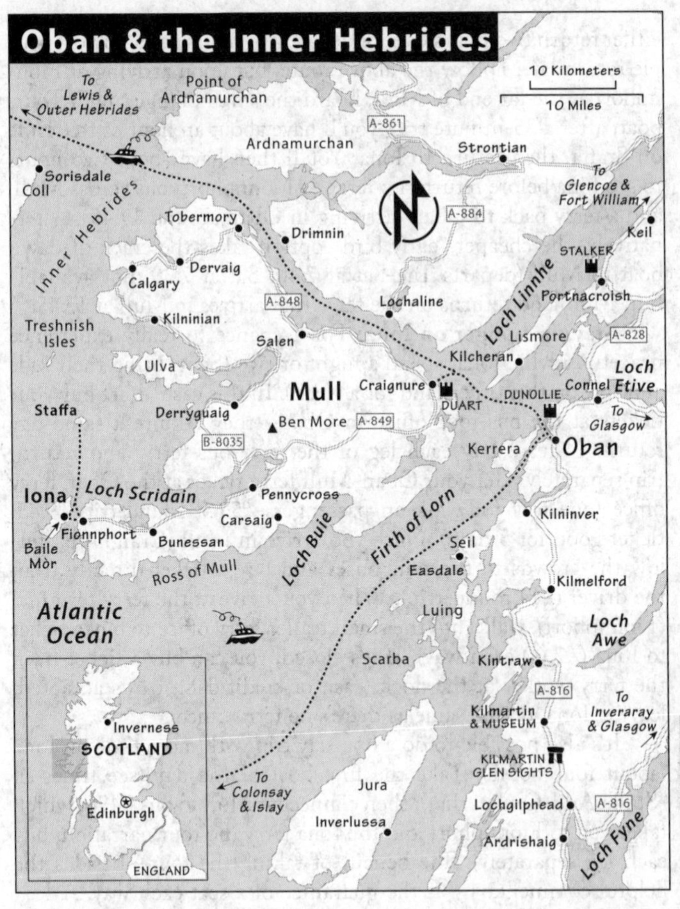

entertaining and informative ride across the Isle of Mull. The right (driver's) side offers better sea views during the second half of the journey to Fionnphort, while the left side has fine views of Mull's rolling wilderness. The driver spends the entire ride chattering away about life on Mull, slowing to point out wildlife, and sharing adages like, "If there's no flowers on the gorse, snogging's gone out of fashion." These hardworking locals make historical trivia fascinating—or at least fun. Your destination is Mull's westernmost ferry terminal, called Fionnphort, where you'll board a small rocking **ferry** for the brief ride to Iona. Unless you stay overnight, you'll have only about two hours to roam freely around the island before taking the ferry-bus-ferry ride in reverse back to Oban. The return boat arrives in Oban around 17:45.

Staffa Add-On: If you add Staffa, the basic structure is the same as described above. But to fit in the extra island, you'll need to either return two hours later or depart two hours earlier. Most people return late: Follow the above route, but upon arriving at Fionnphort at the far end of Mull, board the small orange Staffa Tours boat; after a 35-minute trip, you'll have about an hour of free time on Staffa, then return to Iona. You'll then have about two hours to see Iona before returning: ferry to Fionnphort, bus across Mull, and a ferry back to Oban (arriving in Oban around 19:45). Alternatively, the cheaper "early bird" option takes the crack-of-dawn boat to Mull (departs Tue-Sat at 7:40, Sat at 7:30, not available Sun-Mon) and returns on the ferry that arrives in Mull at 17:45.

Staying Longer on Iona: For a chance to really experience peaceful, idyllic Iona, spend a night or two (Scots bring their kids and stay on this tiny island for a week). In this case, don't buy your tickets at the bus-tour office in Oban—they require a same-day return. Instead, buy each leg of the ferry-bus-ferry (and return) trip separately. Get your Oban-Mull ferry ticket at the Oban ferry office (one-way for walk-on passengers-£5.65, round-trip-£9.45, ticket good for 5 days). Once you arrive in Mull (Craignure), follow the crowds to the tour buses and buy a ticket directly from the driver (£14 round-trip). When you arrive at the ferry terminal (Fionnphort), walk into the small trailer ferry office to buy a ticket to Iona (£2.60 each way). If it's closed, you can buy a ticket from the ferry worker at the dock (cash or credit/debit cards accepted; leaving Iona, do the same as there's no ferry office).

It's also possible to do a one-day trip with more time on Iona (about four hours). Take the first boat of the day (see times in "Staffa Add-On," earlier), then connect at Mull to bus #496, which takes you to Fionnphort and the Iona ferry (no tour narration, buy each leg separately). The benefit of taking the tour—besides the helpful commentary—is the guarantee of a seat each way. Ask at the bus tour office for details.

Driving: Don't bother trying to do this one-day trip by car—the Oban-Mull ferry crossing is very expensive (£69 round-trip for the car, plus passengers); because of tight ferry timings, you'll wind up basically following the tour buses anyway—and you'll miss all of the commentary. Driving on Mull comes with narrow single-track roads (with frequent pullouts or "passing places") clogged with sheep. Drive on Mull only if you have extra time to slow down and explore.

Mull

The Isle of Mull, the second-largest of the Inner Hebrides (after Skye), has nearly 300 scenic miles of coastline and castles and a 3,169-foot-high mountain, one of Scotland's Munros. Called Ben More ("Big Mountain" in Gaelic), it was once much bigger. At

10,000 feet tall, it made up the entire island of Mull—until a volcano erupted. Things are calmer now, and similarly, Mull has a noticeably laid-back population. My bus driver reported that there are no deaths from stress, and only a few from boredom.

With steep fog-covered hillsides topped by cairns (piles of stones, sometimes indicating graves) and ancient stone circles, Mull has a gloomy, otherworldly charm. Bring plenty of rain protection and wear layers in case the sun peeks through the clouds. As my driver said, Mull is a place of cold, wet, windy winters and mild, wet, windy summers.

On the far side of Mull, the caravan of tour buses unloads at Fionnphort, a tiny ferry town. The ferry to the island of Iona takes about 200 walk-on passengers. Confirm the return time with your bus driver, then hustle to the dock to make the first trip over (otherwise it's a 30-minute wait; on very busy days, those who dillydally may not fit on the first ferry). At the dock, there's a small ferry-passenger building with a meager snack bar and a pay WC; a more enticing seafood bar is across the street. After the 10-minute ride, you wash ashore on sleepy Iona (free WC on this side), and the ferry mobs that crowded you on the boat seem to disappear up the main road and into Iona's back lanes.

The **About Mull Tours and Taxi** service can also get you around Mull (tel. 01681/700-507 or mobile 0788-777-4550, www.aboutmull.co.uk). They also do day tours of Mull, focusing on local history and wildlife (half-day tours also available, shorter Mull tours can drop you off at Iona ferry dock at 15:00 for a quick Iona visit and pick you up at 18:00, minimum 2 people, must book ahead).

Iona

The tiny island of Iona, just 3 miles by 1.5 miles, is famous as the birthplace of Christianity in Scotland. You'll have about two hours here on your own before you retrace your steps (your bus driver will tell you which return ferry to take back to Mull).

A pristine quality of light and a thoughtful peace pervades the stark, (nearly) car-free island

and its tiny community. With buoyant clouds bouncing playfully off distant bluffs, sparkling-white crescents of sand, and lone tourists camped thoughtfully atop huge rocks just looking out to sea, Iona is a place that's perfect for meditation. To experience Iona, it's important to get out and take a little hike; you can follow some or all of my self-guided walk outlined below. And you can easily climb a peak—nothing's higher than 300 feet above the sea.

Orientation to Iona

The ferry arrives at the island's only real village, Baile Mòr, with shops, a restaurant/pub, a few accommodations, and no bank (get cash back with a purchase at the grocery store). The only taxi on Iona is **Iona Taxi** (tel. 07810-325-990, www.ionataxi.co.uk). Up the road from the ferry dock is a little **Spar** grocery (Mon-Sat 9:00-17:00, Sun from 11:00, shorter hours and closed Sun Oct-April, free island maps). Iona's official website (www.isle-of-iona.net) has good information about the island.

Iona Walk

Here's a basic self-guided route for exploring Iona. With the standard two hours on Iona that a day trip allows, you likely won't have time for everything. Either do a thorough visit to the abbey (with a guided tour and/or audioguide) and then a light stroll; or do the entire walk described below, but skip the abbey (unless you have time for a quick visit on your way back).

From the ferry dock, head directly up the single paved road that passes through the village and up a small hill to visit the **Nunnery Ruins,** one of Britain's best-preserved medieval nunneries (free).

Immediately after the nunnery, turn right on North Road to reach the chapel and abbey. You'll curve up through the fields—passing the parish church and Heritage Centre on your left (see later)—before the road swings right.

Soon, on the right, you'll see **St. Oran's Chapel,** in the graveyard of the Iona Abbey. This chapel is the oldest church building on the island. Inside you'll find a few grave slabs carved in the distinctive Iona School style, which was developed by local stone-carvers in the 14th century. On these tall, skinny headstones, look for the depictions of medieval warrior aristocrats with huge swords. Many more of these carvings have been moved to the abbey, where you can see them in its cloister and museum.

It's free to see the graveyard and chapel; the **Iona Abbey** itself has an admission fee, but it's worth the cost just to sit in the

History of Iona

St. Columba (521-597), an Irish scholar, soldier, priest, and founder of monasteries, got into a small war over the possession of an illegally-copied psalm book. Victorious but sickened by the bloodshed, Columba left Ireland, vowing never to return. According to legend, the first bit of land out of sight of his homeland was Iona. He stopped here in 563 and established an abbey.

Columba's monastic community flourished, and Iona became the center of Celtic Christianity. Missionaries from Iona spread the gospel throughout Scotland and northern England, while scholarly monks established Iona as a center of art and learning. The *Book of Kells*—perhaps the finest piece of art from "Dark Ages" Europe—was probably made on Iona in the eighth century. The island was so important that it was the legendary burial place for ancient Scottish clan chieftains and kings (including Macbeth of Shakespeare fame), and even some Scandinavian monarchs.

Slowly, the importance of Iona ebbed. Vikings massacred 68 monks in 806. Fearing more raids, the monks evacuated most of Iona's treasures to Ireland (including the *Book of Kells,* which is now in Dublin). Much later, with the Reformation, the abbey was abandoned and most of its finely carved crosses were destroyed. In the 17th century, locals used the abbey only as a handy quarry for other building projects.

Iona's population peaked at about 500 in the 1830s. In the 1840s, a potato famine hit, and in the 1850s, a third of the islanders emigrated to Canada or Australia. By 1900, the population was down to 210, and today it's only around 200.

But in our generation, a new religious community has given the abbey fresh life. The Iona Community is an ecumenical gathering of men and women who seek new ways of living the Gospel in today's world, with a focus on worship, peace and justice issues, and reconciliation (http://iona.org.uk).

stillness of its lovely, peaceful interior courtyard. (For details, see "Sights on Iona," later.)

Just beyond and across the road from the abbey is the **Iona Community's Welcome Centre** (free WCs), which runs the abbey with Historic Scotland and hosts modern-day pilgrims who come here to experience the birthplace of Scottish Christianity. (If you're staying longer, you could attend a worship service at the abbey—check the schedule here; tel. 01681/700-404, www.iona.org.uk.)

Its gift shop is packed with books on the island's important role in Christian history.

Continue past the abbey and welcome center on North Road. A 10-minute walk brings you to the footpath for **Dùn Ì,** a steep but short climb with good views of the abbey looking back toward Mull.

Returning to the main road, walk another 20-25 minutes to the end of the paved road, where you'll arrive at a gate leading through a sheep- and cow-strewn pasture to Iona's pristine white-sand **North Beach.** Dip your toes in the Atlantic and ponder what this Caribbean-like alcove is doing in Scotland. Be sure to allow at least 40 minutes to return to the ferry dock.

Sights on Iona

▲Iona Abbey

This mostly-rebuilt church marks the site of Christianity's arrival in Scotland. You'll see Celtic crosses, the original shrine of St. Columba, a big church slathered with medieval carvings, a tranquil cloister, and an excellent museum with surviving fragments of this site's fascinating layers of history.

Cost and Hours: £7.10, not covered by bus tour ticket, daily April-Sept 9:30-17:30, Oct-March until 16:30, museum closes 30 minutes earlier, tel. 01681/700-512, www.historic-scotland.gov.uk.

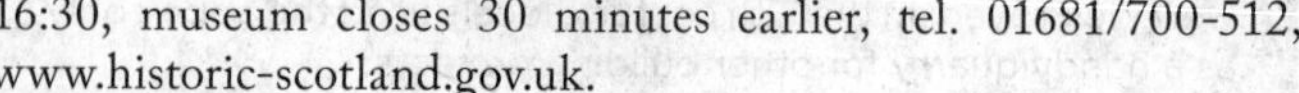

Visiting the Abbey: While the present abbey, nunnery, and graveyard go back to the 13th century, much of what you'll see was rebuilt in the 20th century. Be sure to read the "History of Iona" sidebar to prepare for your visit.

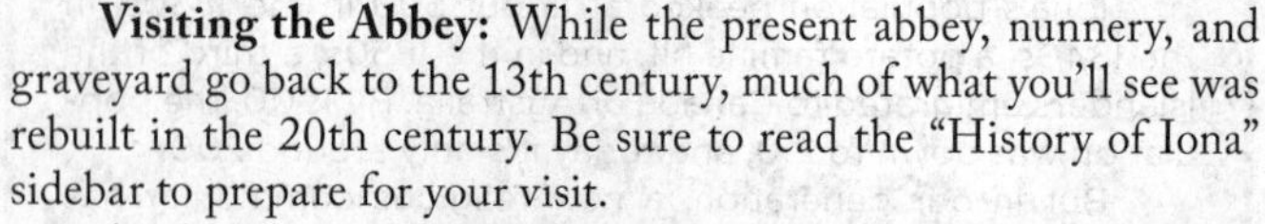

At the entrance building, pick up your included audioguide, and ask about the good 30-minute guided tours (4/day and well worthwhile). Then head toward the church. You'll pass two faded **Celtic crosses** (and the base of a third); the originals are in the museum at the end of your visit. Some experts believe that Celtic crosses—with their distinctive shape so tied to Christianity on the British Isles—originated right here on Iona.

Facing the entrance to the church, you'll see the original **shrine to St. Columba** on your left—a magnet for pilgrims.

Head inside the **church.** It feels like an active church—with hymnals neatly stacked in the pews—because it is, thanks to the Iona Community (across the street and explained in the "Welcome to Iona Walk"). While much of this space has been rebuilt, take a moment to look around and you'll find some original decorations. Plenty of original medieval stone carving (especially the capitals of many columns) still survives. To see a particularly striking example, stand near the pulpit in the middle of the church and look back to the entrance. Partway up the left span of the pointed arch framing the transept, look for the eternally screaming face. While interpretations vary, this may have been a reminder for the priest not to leave out the fire-and-brimstone parts of his message. Some of the newer features of the church—including the base of the baptismal font near the entrance, and the main altar—are carved from locally-quarried Iona marble: white with green streaks. In the right/south transept is the tomb of George Campbell—the Eighth Duke of Argyll, who donated this property in 1900, allowing it to be restored.

When you're ready to continue, find the poorly-marked door into the **cloister.** (As you face the altar, it's about halfway down the nave on the left, before the transept.) This space is filled with harmonious light, additional finely carved capitals (these are modern re-creations), and—displayed along the walls—several more of the tall, narrow tombstones like the ones displayed in St. Oran's Chapel. On these, look for a couple of favorite motifs: the long, intimidating sword (indicating a warrior of the Highland clans) and the ship with billowing sails (a powerful symbol of this seafaring culture).

Around the far side of the cloister is the shop. But before leaving, don't overlook the easy-to-miss **museum.** (To find it, head outside and walk around the left side of the abbey complex, toward the sea.) This modern, well-presented space exhibits a remarkable collection of original stonework from the abbey—including what's left of the three Celtic crosses out front—all eloquently described.

Take some time to linger and make sure you've seen all you want to see. Then go in peace.

Heritage Centre

This little museum, tucked behind the parish church between the nunnery ruins and the abbey (watch for signs), is small but well done, with displays on local and natural history and a tiny tearoom.

Cost and Hours: £2.50, Mon-Sat 10:30-16:30, closed Sun and Nov-mid-April, www.ionaheritage.co.uk.

Sleeping and Eating on Iona

These are listed roughly in the order you'll reach them as you climb the main road from the ferry dock. The two hotels listed here have some seaview rooms (with small windows) and closed in winter (Nov-March). At each one, the price drops for longer stays (more than 4-5 nights). Both also have restaurants. In addition to my suggestions listed below, there are many B&Bs, apartments, and a hostel (for options, see www.isle-of-iona.net/accommodation).

$$$ Argyll Hotel, built in 1867, proudly overlooks the waterfront, with 17 cottage-like rooms and pleasingly creaky hallways lined with bookshelves. Of the two hotels, it feels classier (Sb-£70, D-£85, Db-£99, larger Db-£150, luxury seaview Db-£170, extra bed for kids-£16, reserve far in advance for July-Aug, comfortable lounge and sunroom, tel. 01681/700-334, www.argyllhoteliona.co.uk, reception@argyllhoteliona.co.uk). Its dining room is open to the public for lunch (£6-8, daily 12:15-14:00, tea served until 16:30) and dinner (£12-20, 18:00-20:00).

$$$ St. Columba Hotel, a bit higher up in town and situated in the middle of a peaceful garden with picnic tables, has 27 institutional rooms and spacious lodge-like common spaces—such as a big, cushy seaview lounge (Sb-£74-88, Db-£127-155, huge view Db-£190, extra bed for kids-£15, closed Nov-March, next door to abbey on road up from dock, tel. 01681/700-304, www.stcolumba-hotel.co.uk, info@stcolumba-hotel.co.uk). Their fine 21-table restaurant, overlooking the water, is open to the public for lunch (£8-12, daily 12:15-14:30), tea (14:00-17:00), and dinner (£13-17, 18:30-20:00).

$$ Calva B&B, a five-minute walk past the abbey, has three spacious rooms (Db-£70, second house on left past the abbey, look for sign in window and gnomes on porch, tel. 01681/700-340; friendly Janetta, Ken, and Jack the bearded collie).

Staffa

Those more interested in nature than in church history will enjoy the trip to the wildly scenic Isle of Staffa. Completely uninhabited (except for seabirds), Staffa is a knob of rock draped with a vibrant green carpet of turf. Remote and quiet, it feels like a Hebrides nature preserve.

Most day trips give you an hour on Staffa—barely enough time to see its two claims to fame: The basalt columns of Fingal's Cave and (in summer) a colony of puffins. To squeeze in both, be ready to hop off the boat and climb the staircase. Partway up to the left, you can walk around to the cave (about 7 minutes). Or continue up to the top, then turn right and walk across the spine of the grassy island (about 10-15 minutes) to the cove where the puffins gather. (Your captain should point out both options, and let you know how active the puffins have been.)

▲▲Fingal's Cave

Staffa's shore is covered with bizarre, mostly-hexagonal basalt columns that stick up at various heights. It's as if the earth were offering God his choice of thousands of six-sided cigarettes. (The island's name likely came from the Old Norse word for "stave"—the building timbers these columns resemble.) This is the other end of Northern Ireland's popular Giant's Causeway. You'll walk along the uneven surface of these columns, curling around the far side of the island, until you can actually step inside the gaping mouth of a cave—where floor-to-ceiling columns and crashing waves combine to create a powerful experience. Listening to the water and air flowing through this otherworldly space inspired Felix Mendelssohn to compose his overture, *The Hebrides.*

While you're ogling the cave, consider this: Geologists claim these unique formations were created by volcanic eruptions more than 60 million years ago. As the surface of the lava flow quickly cooled, it contracted and crystallized into columns (resembling the caked mud at the bottom of a dried-up lakebed, but with deeper cracks). As the rock later settled and eroded, the columns broke off into the many stair-like steps that now honeycomb Staffa.

Of course, in actuality, these formations resulted from a heated rivalry between a Scottish giant named Fingal, who lived on Staffa, and an Ulster warrior named Finn MacCool, who lived across the sea on Ireland's Antrim Coast. Knowing that the giant was coming to spy on him, Finn had his wife dress him as a sleeping infant. The giant, shocked at the infant's size, fled back to Scotland in terror of whomever had sired this giant baby. Breathing a sigh of relief, Finn tore off the baby clothes and prudently knocked down the bridge.

▲▲Puffins

A large colony of Atlantic puffins settles on Staffa each spring and summer during mating season (generally early May through early August). Puffins—with their stout little bodies, penguin-like black-and-white colorings, beady black eyes, and brightly-colored beaks and feet—live most of their lives on the open ocean, coming to land only to breed. Puffins mate for life and typically lay just one egg each year, which the male and female take turns caring for. To feed their young, puffins plunge as deep as 200 feet below the sea's surface to catch sand eels and other small fish.

The puffins tend to scatter when the boat arrives. But after the boat pulls out and its passengers hike across the island, the very tame puffins' curiosity gets the better of them. First you'll see them flutter up from the offshore rocks, with their distinctive bobbing flight. They'll zip and whirl around, and finally they'll start to land on the lip of the cove. Sit quietly, move slowly, and be patient, and soon they'll get close. (If any seagulls are nearby, shoo them away—puffins are undaunted by humans, who do them no harm, but they're terrified of predator seagulls.)

In the waters around Staffa—on your way to and from the other islands—also keep an eye out for a variety of **marine life,** including seals, dolphins, porpoises, and the occasional minke whale, fin whale, or basking shark (a gigantic fish that hinges open its enormous jaw to drift-net plankton).

Near Oban

The following sights are worth considering for drivers. The first section outlines the best driving route from Glasgow to Oban, including the appealing pit stop at Inveraray. And the second section covers one of Scotland's most important prehistoric sites, Kilmartin Glen.

BETWEEN GLASGOW AND OBAN

The drive from Glasgow (or Edinburgh) to Oban provides dreamy vistas and your first look at the dramatic landscapes of the Highlands.

Driving Tour from Glasgow to Inveraray

Here's a loosely-narrated route: Leaving Glasgow on the A-82, you'll soon be driving along the west bank of **Loch Lomond.** The first picnic turnout has the best lake views, benches, a park, and a playground. Twenty-four miles long and speckled with islands, Loch Lomond is Great Britain's biggest lake by surface area, and second in volume only to Loch Ness. Thanks largely to its easy proximity to Glasgow (about 15 miles away), this scenic lake is a favorite retreat for Scots as well as foreign tourists. The southernmost of the Munros, Ben Lomond (3,196 feet), looms over the eastern bank.

Loch Lomond's biggest claim to fame is its role in a beloved folk song: "Ye'll take the high road, and I'll take the low road, and I'll be in Scotland afore ye... For me and my true love will never meet again, on the bonnie, bonnie banks of Loch Lomond." As you'll now be humming that all day (you're welcome), here's one interpretation of the song's poignant meaning: Celtic culture believes that fairies return the souls of the deceased to their homeland through the soil. After the disastrous Scottish loss at the Battle of Culloden, Jacobite ringleaders were arrested and taken for trial in faraway London. In some cases, accused pairs were given a choice: One of you will die, and the other will live. The song is a bittersweet reassurance, sung from the condemned to the survivor, that the soon-to-be-deceased will take the spiritual "low road" back to his Scottish homeland—where his soul will be reunited with the living, who will return on the physical "high road" (over land).

Halfway up the loch, at Tarbet, the road forks; keep left to stay on the A-83 (toward *Campbeltown*). You'll pass the village of Arrochar, then drive along the banks of Loch Long. The scenery crescendos as you pull away from the loch and twist up over the mountains and through a pine forest, getting your first glimpse of bald Highlands mountains—it's clear that you've just crossed the Highland Boundary Fault. Enjoy the waterfalls, and notice that the road signs are now in English as well as Gaelic. As you climb into more rugged territory—up the valley called Glen Croe—be mindful that the roads connecting the Lowlands with the Highlands (like the one down in the glen below) were originally a military project designed to facilitate government quelling of the Highland clans.

At the summit, watch for the large parking lot with picnic tables on your left (signed for *Argyll Forest Park*). Stretch your legs at what's aptly named the **Rest-and-Be-Thankful Pass.** The colorful name comes from the 1880s, when second- and third-class coach passengers got out and pushed the coach and first-class passengers up the hill.

Twisting down the far side of the pass, you'll drive through Glen Kinglas, and soon reach **Loch Fyne,** a saltwater "sea loch" famous for its shellfish (keep an eye out for oyster farms and seafood restaurants). In fact, Loch Fyne is the namesake of a popular UK restaurant chain.

Looping around Loch Fyne, you reach...

▲Inveraray

Nearly everybody stops at this lovely, seemingly made-for-tourists castle town on Loch Fyne. Park near the pier and browse the wide selection of eateries and tourist shops (**TI** open daily, on Front Street, tel. 01499/302-063; public WCs at end of nearby pier).

As you approach town, keep an eye on the right (when crossing the bridge) for the dramatic **Inveraray Castle.** This stronghold of one of the more notorious branches of the Campbell clan is scenic from afar and, if you can spare the time, fun to tour—it's worth ▲ (£10, April-Oct daily 10:00-17:45, closed Nov-March, last entry 45 minutes before closing, café, free parking—watch for signs from main road, tel. 01499/302-203, www.inveraray-castle.com). This residence of the Dukes of Argyll comes with a dramatic turreted exterior (one of Scotland's most striking) and a lavishly-decorated interior that feels spacious and neatly tended. Public-television fans may recognize this as "Duneagle Castle" (a.k.a. Uncle Shrimpy's pad) from one of the *Downton Abbey* Christmas specials—big photos of the Grantham and MacClare clans decorate the genteel rooms. Roam from room to room, reading the laminated descriptions and asking questions of the gregarious docents. The highlight is the Armory Hall that fills the main atrium, where swords and rifles are painstakingly arrayed in starburst patterns. As with many such castles, the aristocratic clan still lives here (*private* signs mark rooms where the family resides). The kids attend school in London, but spend a few months here each year; in the winter, the castle is closed to the public and they have the run of the place.

After touring the interior, do a loop through the finely manicured gardens.

Once in town, the main "sight" is the **Inveraray Jail,** an overpriced, corny, but mildly-educational former jail converted into a museum. This "living 19th-century prison" includes a courtroom where mannequins argue the fate of the accused. Then you'll head outside and explore the various cells of the outer courtyard. The playful guards may lock you up for a photo op while they explain how Scotland reformed its prison system in 1839—you'll see both "before" and "after" cells in this complex (£9, open daily, tel. 01499/302-381, www.inverarayjail.co.uk).

Leaving Inveraray: To continue **directly to Oban** (about an hour), leave Inveraray through the gate at the woolen mill and get on the A-819, which takes you through Glen Aray and along Loch Awe. A left turn on the A-85 takes you into Oban. If you have time to kill—and a healthy interest in prehistoric sites—going to Oban by way of **Kilmartin Glen** (described next) adds about 45 minutes of driving. To get there, head straight up Inveraray's main street and get on the waterfront A-83 (marked for *Campbeltown*); after a half-hour, in Lochgilphead, turn right onto the A-816, which takes you through Kilmartin Glen and all the way up to Oban. (To avoid backtracking, be ready to stop at the prehistoric sites lining the A-816 between Lochgilphead and Kilmartin village.)

SOUTH OF OBAN

Kilmartin Glen

Scotland isn't as rich with prehistoric sites as South England is, but the ones in Kilmartin Glen, while faint, are some of Scotland's most accessible—and most important. This wide valley, clearly imbued with spiritual and/or strategic power, contains reminders of several millennia-worth of inhabitants. Today it's a playground for those who enjoy tromping through grassy fields while daydreaming about who moved these giant stones here so many centuries ago. This isn't worth a long detour, unless you're fascinated by prehistoric sites.

Four to five thousand years ago, Kilmartin Glen was inhabited by Neolithic people who left behind fragments of their giant stony monuments. And 1,500 years ago, this was the seat of the kings of the Scoti, who migrated here from Ireland around A.D. 500, giving rise to Scotland's own branch of Celtic culture. From this grassy valley, the Scoti kings ruled their em-

The Irish Connection

The Romans called the people living in what is now Ireland the "Scoti" (meaning pirates). When the Scoti crossed the narrow Irish Sea and invaded the land of the Picts 1,500 years ago, that region became known as Scoti-land. Ireland and Scotland were never fully conquered by the Romans, and they retained similar clannish Celtic traits. Both share the same Gaelic branch of the linguistic tree.

On clear summer days, you can actually see Ireland—just 17 miles away—from the Scottish coastline. The closest bit to Scotland is the boomerang-shaped Rathlin Island, part of Northern Ireland. Rathlin is where Scottish leader Robert the Bruce retreated in 1307 after defeat at the hands of the English. Legend has it that he hid in a cave on the island, where he observed a spider patiently rebuilding its web each time a breeze knocked it down. Inspired by the spider's perseverance, Bruce gathered his Scottish forces once more and finally defeated the English at the decisive battle of Bannockburn (see page 846).

Flush with confidence from his victory, Robert the Bruce decided to open a second front against the English...in Ireland. In 1315, he sent his brother Edward over to enlist their Celtic Irish cousins in an effort to thwart the English. After securing Ireland, Edward hoped to move on and enlist the Welsh, thus cornering England with their pan-Celtic nation. But Edward's timing was bad: Ireland was in the midst of famine. His Scottish troops had to live off the land and began to take food and supplies from the starving Irish. Some of Ireland's crops may have been intentionally destroyed to keep it from being used as a colonial "breadbasket" to feed English troops. The Scots quickly wore out their welcome, and Edward the Bruce was eventually killed in battle near Dundalk in 1318.

It's interesting to imagine how things might be different today if Scotland and Ireland had been permanently welded together as a nation 700 years ago. You'll notice the strong Scottish influence in Northern Ireland when you ask a local a question and he answers, "Aye, a wee bit." And in Glasgow—on Scotland's west coast, closest to Ireland—an Ireland-like division between royalist Protestants and republican Catholics survives today in the form of soccer team allegiances. In big Scottish cities (like Glasgow and Edinburgh), you'll even see "orange parades" of protesters marching in solidarity with their Protestant Northern Irish cousins. The Irish—always quick to defuse tension with humor—joke that the Scots are just Irish people who couldn't swim home.

pire, called Dalriada (also sometimes written Dál Riata), which encompassed much of Scotland's west coast, the Inner Hebrides, and the northern part of Ireland. The Scoti spoke Gaelic and were Christian; as they overtook the rest of the Highlands—eventually absorbing their rival Picts—theirs became a dominant culture, which is still evident in pockets of present-day Scotland. Today, Kilmartin Glen is scattered with burial cairns, standing stones, and a hill called Dunadd—the fortress of the Scoti kings.

Visiting Kilmartin Glen: Sites are scattered throughout the valley, including some key locations along or just off the A-816 south of Kilmartin village. If you're coming from Inveraray, you'll pass these *before* you reach the village and museum itself. Each one is explained by good informational signs.

The bulbous hill called **Dunadd** sits just west of the A-816, about four miles north of Lochgilphead and four miles south of Kilmartin village (watch for blue, low-profile *Dunadd Fort* signs). A fort stood here since the time of Christ, but it was the Scoti kings—who made it their primary castle from the sixth to ninth centuries—that put Dunadd on the map. Park in the big lot at its base and hike through the faint outlines of terraces to the top, where you can enjoy sweeping views over all of Kilmartin Glen; this southern stretch is a marshland called "The Great Moss" (Moine Mhor). Look for carvings in the rock: early Celtic writing, the image of a boar, and a footprint (carved into a stone crisscrossed with fissures). This "footprint of fealty" (a replica) recalls the inauguration ceremony in which the king would place his foot into the footprint, symbolizing the marriage between the ruler and the land.

About two miles farther north on the A-816, brown *Dunchraigaig* signs mark a parking lot where you can cross the road to the 4,000-year-old, 100-foot-in-diameter **Dunchraigaig Cairn**—the burial place for 10 Neolithic VIPs. Circle around to find the opening, where you can still crawl into a small recess. This is one of at least five such cairns that together created a mile-and-a-half-long "linear cemetery" up the middle of Kilmartin Glen. From this cairn, you can walk five minutes to several more prehistoric structures: Follow signs through the gate, and walk to a farm field with **Ballymeanoch**—an avenue of two stone rows (with six surviving stones), a disheveled old cairn, and a stone circle.

About one more mile north on the A-816, just off the intersection with the B-8025 (toward *Tayvallich*), is the small Kilmartin Burn parking lot. From here, cross the stream to a field where the five **Nether Largie Standing Stones** have stood in a neat north-south line for 3,200 years. Were these stones designed as an astronomical observatory? Burial rituals or other religious ceremonies? Sporting events? Or just a handy place for sheep to scratch themselves? From here, you can hike the rest of the way through the field to the Nether Largie South Cairn and the Temple Wood Stone Circles, described next (which don't have their own parking).

For a quick look at those two, just beyond the Tayvallich turnoff on the A-816, turn left on the tiny road toward Slockavullin (over the stone bridge). You'll pass (in the field on your left) the **Nether Largie South Cairn,** then spot (on your right) the striking **Temple Wood Stone Circles.** The larger, older of these circles dates to more than 5,000 years ago, and both were added onto and modified over the millennia.

To get the big picture, head for the **Kilmartin House Museum,** in the center of Kilmartin village. The cute stone house has a ticket desk, bookshop, and café; the museum—with modern exhibits explaining this area's powerful history—fills the basement of the adjacent modern building (though a new home for the exhibit is in the works). The modest-but-modern museum features handy explanations, a few original artifacts, and lots of re-creations (£5, daily except closed Christmas-Feb, tel. 01546/510-278, www.kilmartin.org). From the museum, you can look out across the fields to see **Glebe Cairn,** one of the five cairns of the "linear cemetery." Another one, the **Nether Largie North Cairn,** was reconstructed in the 1970s and can actually be entered (a half-mile south of the museum; ask for directions at museum).

Many, many more prehistoric sites fill Kilmartin Glen (more than 800 within a six-mile radius); the museum sells in-depth guidebooks for the curious and can point you in the right direction for what you're interested in.

GLENCOE AND FORT WILLIAM

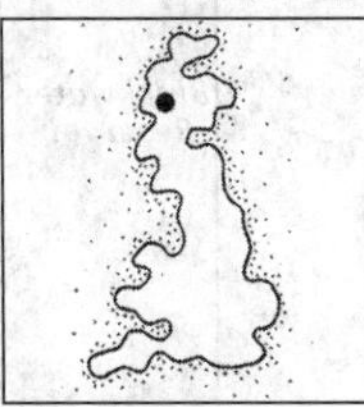

Scotland is a land of great natural wonders. And some of the most spectacular—and most accessible—are in the valley called Glencoe, just an hour north of Oban and on the way to Fort William, Loch Ness, or Inverness. The evocative "Weeping Glen" of Glencoe aches with both history and natural beauty. Beyond that, Fort William anchors the southern end of the Caledonian Canal, offering a springboard to more Highlands scenery. This is where Britain's highest peak, Ben Nevis, keeps its head in the clouds.

PLANNING YOUR TIME

On an quick visit, this area warrants just a few hours between Oban and Inverness: Wander through Glencoe village, tour its modest museum, then drive up Glencoe valley for views before continuing on your way. But if you have time to linger in the Highlands, Glencoe is an ideal place to do it. Settle in for a night (or more) to make time for a more leisurely drive and to squeeze in a hike or two—I give an overview of the best options, from easy strolls to challenging ascents.

Beyond Glencoe, Fort William—a touristy and overrated transportation hub—is skippable, but can be a handy lunch stop.

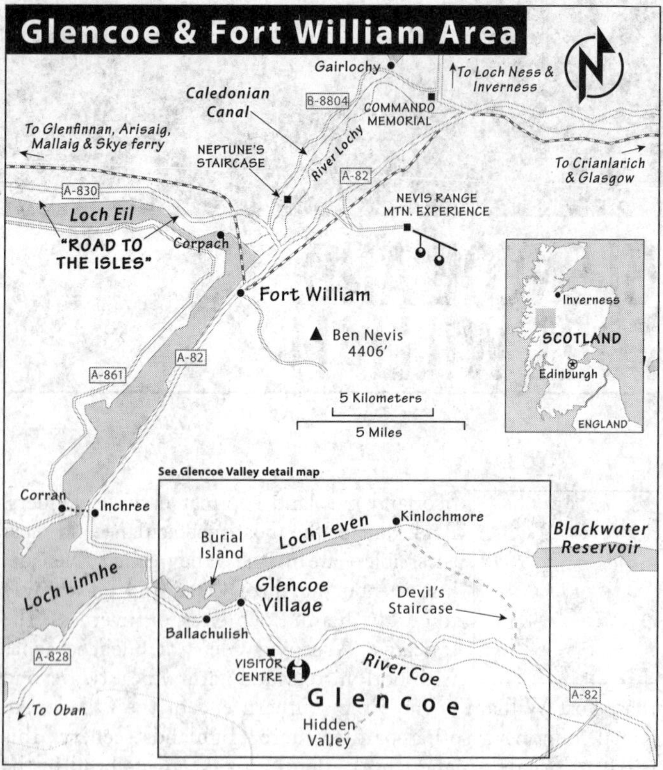

Glencoe & Fort William Area

Gairlochy
To Loch Ness & Inverness
Caledonian Canal
B-8804
COMMANDO MEMORIAL
To Glenfinnan, Arisaig, Mallaig & Skye ferry
NEPTUNE'S STAIRCASE
River Lochy
A-82
To Crianlarich & Glasgow
A-830
Loch Eil
NEVIS RANGE MTN. EXPERIENCE
"ROAD TO THE ISLES"
Corpach
Fort William
Inverness
Ben Nevis 4406′
SCOTLAND
A-82
Edinburgh
A-861
5 Kilometers
5 Miles
ENGLAND
See Glencoe Valley detail map
Corran
Inchree
Kinlochmore
Loch Leven
Blackwater Reservoir
Burial Island
Loch Linnhe
Glencoe Village
Devil's Staircase
Ballachulish
A-828
VISITOR CENTRE
River Coe
Glencoe
A-82
To Oban
Hidden Valley

Glencoe

This valley is the essence of the wild, powerful, and stark beauty of the Highlands. Along with its scenery, Glencoe offers a good dose of bloody clan history: In 1692, government Redcoats (led by a local Campbell commander) came to the valley and were sheltered and fed for 12 days by the MacDonalds—whose leader had been late in swearing an oath to the British monarch. Then, on the morning of February 13, the soldiers were ordered to rise up early and kill their sleeping hosts, violating the rules of Highland hospitality and earning the valley the nickname "The Weeping Glen." Thirty-eight men were killed outright; hundreds more fled through a blizzard, and some 40 additional villagers (mostly women and children) died from exposure. It's fitting that such an

epic, dramatic incident should be set in this equally epic, dramatic valley, where the cliffsides seem to weep (with running streams) when it rains.

Aside from its tragic history, this place has captured the imaginations of both hikers and artists. Movies filmed here include everything from *Monty Python and the Holy Grail* and *Highlander* to *Harry Potter and the Prisoner of Azkaban* and the James Bond film *Skyfall.* When filmmakers want a stunning, rugged backdrop; when hikers want a scenic challenge; and when Scots want to remember their hard-fought past...they all think of Glencoe.

Orientation to Glencoe

The valley of Glencoe is just off the main A-828/A-82 road between Oban and points north (such as Fort William and Inverness). If you're coming from the north, the signage can be tricky—at the roundabout south of Fort William, follow signs to *Crianlarich* and *A-82.* The most appealing town here is the sleepy one-street village of Glencoe, worth a stop for its folk museum and its status as the gateway to the valley. The town's hub of activity is its grocery store, which has an ATM (daily 8:00-19:00, until 20:00 Fri-Sat). The slightly larger and more modern town of Ballachulish (a half-mile away) has more services, including a nice Co-op grocery store (daily 7:00-22:00).

In the loch just outside Glencoe (near Ballachulish), notice the burial island—where the souls of those who "take the low road" are piped home. (For an explanation of "Ye'll take the high road, and I'll take the low road," see page 907.) The next island is the Island of Discussion—where those in dispute went until they found agreement.

TOURIST INFORMATION

Your best source of information (especially for walks and hikes) is the **Glencoe Visitor Centre,** described later. The nearest **TI** is well-signed in Ballachulish; it's buried inside a huge café and gift shop (daily Easter-Oct 9:00-17:00, Nov-Easter 10:00-16:00, tel. 01855/811-866, www.glencoetourism.co.uk). For more information on the area, see www.discoverglencoe.com.

Bike Rental: At **Crank It Up Gear,** Davy rents road and mountain bikes and can offer plenty of suggestions for where to pedal in the area (£15/half-day, £20/all day, just off the main street to the left near the start of town, 20 Lorn Drive, mobile 07746-860-023, www.crankitupgear.com).

Sights in Glencoe

Glencoe Village

Glencoe village is just a line of houses sitting beneath the brooding mountains. The only real sight in town is the folk museum (described below). But walking the main street gives a good glimpse of village Scotland. From the free parking lot at the entrance to town, go for a stroll. You'll pass lots of little B&Bs renting two or three rooms, the stony Episcopal church, the folk museum, the town's grocery store, and the village hall.

At the far end of the village, on the left just before the bridge, a Celtic cross **World War I** memorial stands on a little hill. Even this wee village lost 11 souls during that war—a reminder of Scotland's disproportionate contribution to Britain's war effort. You'll see memorials like this (usually either a Celtic cross or a soldier with bowed head) in virtually every town in Scotland.

If you were to cross the little bridge, you'd head up into Glencoe's wooded parklands, with some easy hikes (described later). But for one more landmark, turn right just before the bridge and walk about five minutes. Standing on a craggy bluff on your right is another memorial—this one to the **Glencoe Massacre,** which still haunts the memories of people here and throughout Scotland.

Glencoe and North Lorn Folk Museum

This gathering of thatched-roof, early 18th-century croft houses are jammed with local history, creating a huggable museum filled with humble exhibits gleaned from the town's old closets and attics. When one house was being rethatched, its owner found a cache of 200-year-old swords and pistols hidden there from the government Redcoats

after the disastrous Battle of Culloden. You'll also see antique toys, boxes from old food products, sports paraphernalia, a cabinet of curiosities, and plenty of information on the MacDonald clan. Be sure to look for the museum's little door that leads out back, where additional smaller buildings are filled with everyday items (furniture, farm tools, and so on), and exhibits on the Glencoe Massacre and Highland doctors.

Cost and Hours: £3, call ahead for hours—generally Easter-Oct Mon-Sat 10:00-16:30, closed Sun and off-season, sometimes closed at lunchtime, tel. 01855/811-664, www.glencoemuseum.com.

Glencoe Visitor Centre

This modern facility, a mile past Glencoe village up the A-82 into the dramatic valley, is designed to resemble a *clachan,* or traditional Highland settlement. The information desk inside the shop at the ranger desk is your single best resource for advice (and maps or guidebooks) about local walks and hikes (several of which are outlined later in this chapter). At the back of the complex, you'll find a viewpoint with a handy 3-D model of the hills for orientation. There's also a pricey £6.50 exhibition about the surrounding landscape, the region's history, wildlife, mountaineering, and conservation. It's worth the time to watch the more-interesting-than-it-sounds two-minute video on geology and the 14-minute film on the Glencoe Massacre, which thoughtfully traces the events leading up to the tragedy rather than simply recycling romanticized legends.

Cost and Hours: Free; April-Oct daily 9:30-17:30; Nov-March Thu-Sun 10:00-16:00, closed Mon-Wed; last entry 45 minutes before closing, free Wi-Fi, café, tel. 01855/811-307, www.glencoe-nts.org.uk.

Glencoe Valley Driving Tour

If you have a car, spend an hour or so following the A-82 through the valley, past the Glencoe Visitor Centre, into the desolate moor beyond, and back again. You'll enjoy grand views, dramatic craggy hills, and, if you're lucky, a chance to hear a bagpiper in the wind: Roadside Highland buskers often set up here on good-weather summer weekends. (If you play the recorder—and the piper's not swarmed with other tourists), ask to finger a tune while he does the hard work.)

Here's a lightly narrated explanation of the route. Along the way, I've pointed out sometimes easy-to-miss trailheads, in case you're up for a hike (hikes described in the next section).

➲ **Self-Guided Driving Tour:** Leaving Glencoe village on

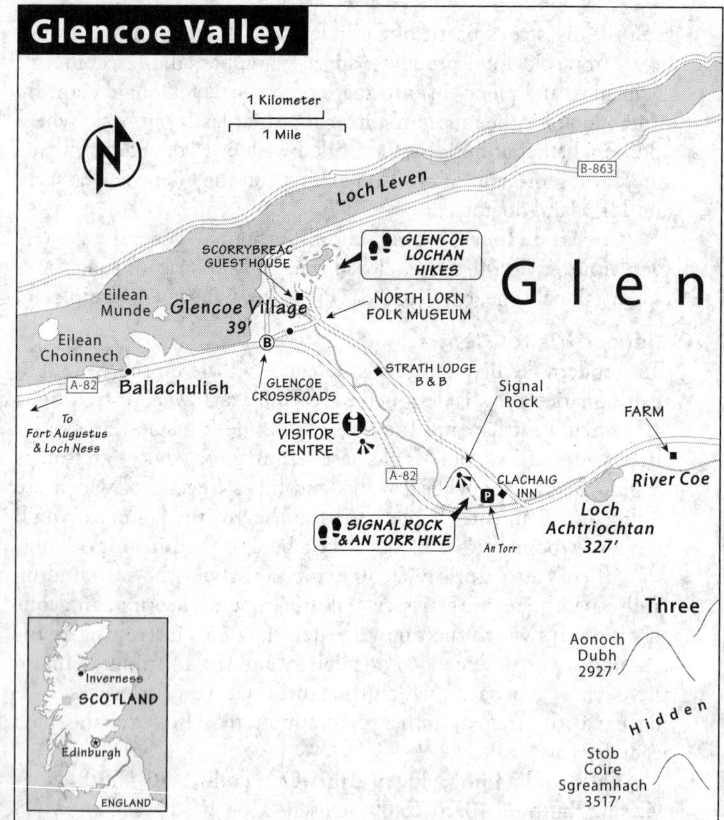

the A-82, it's just a mile to the **Glencoe Visitor Centre** (on the right, described earlier). Soon after, the road pulls out of the forested hills and gives you unobstructed views of the U-shaped valley.

About a mile after the visitors center on the left is a parking lot for **Signal Rock and An Torr,** a popular place for low-impact forested hikes. Just beyond, also on the left, is a single-track road leading to the **Clachaig Inn,** a classic hikers' pub (described on page 925). The hillsides above the inn were the setting for Hagrid's hut in the third Harry Potter movie (though nothing remains from filming).

Continuing along the A-82, you'll hit a straight stretch, passing a lake (Loch Achtriochtan), and then a small farm, both on the right. After the farm, the valley narrows a bit as you cut through Glencoe Pass. On the right, you'll pass two small parking lots. Pull into the second one for perhaps the best viewpoint of the entire valley, with point-blank views of the steep ridge-like mountains known as the **Three Sisters.** This is also the starting point for

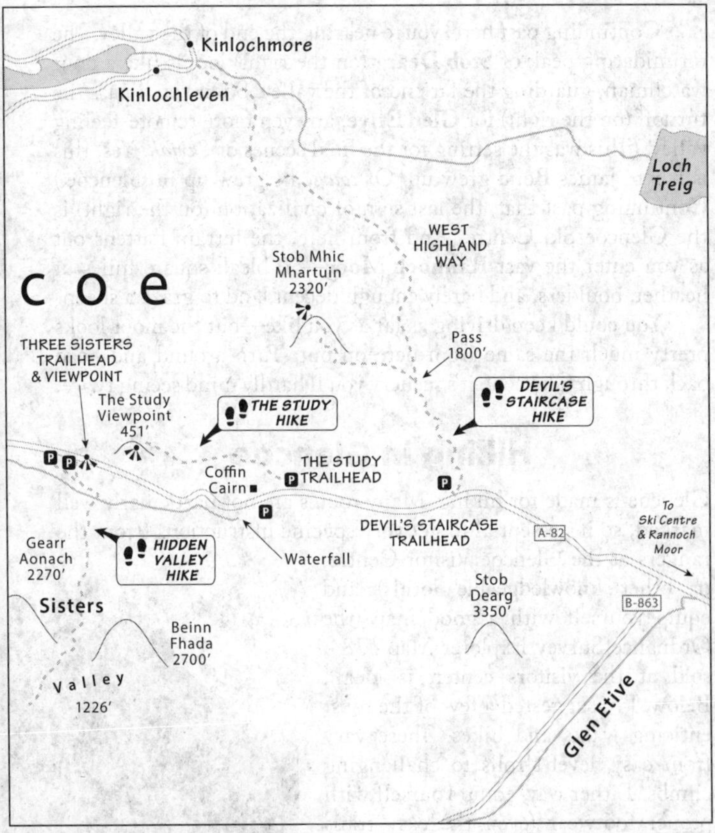

Kinlochmore
Kinlochleven
Loch Treig
WEST HIGHLAND WAY
Stob Mhic Mhartuin 2320′
coe
Pass 1800′
THREE SISTERS TRAILHEAD & VIEWPOINT
The Study Viewpoint 451′
THE STUDY HIKE
DEVIL'S STAIRCASE HIKE
Coffin Cairn
THE STUDY TRAILHEAD
DEVIL'S STAIRCASE TRAILHEAD
A-82
To Ski Centre & Rannoch Moor
Gearr Aonach 2270′
HIDDEN VALLEY HIKE
Waterfall
Stob Dearg 3350′
B-863
Sisters
Beinn Fhada 2700′
Valley 1226′
Glen Etive

the challenging **Hidden Valley hike,** which leads between the first and second sisters.

As you continue, keep an eye out for partially-ruined stone buildings—the remains of pillboxes built during World War II in anticipation of a possible Nazi invasion. After another mile or so—through some glorious waterfall scenery—watch on the left for the **Coffin Cairn,** which looks like a stone igloo (parking is just across the road if you want a cairn-and-waterfalls photo op). Just after the cairn, look on the left for pull-out parking for the **hike to The Study,** a viewpoint overlooking the road you just drove down (described later).

After this pull-out, you'll hit a straightaway for about a mile, followed by an S-curve. Just at the end of the curve, look for the pull-out parking on the left, just before the stand of pine trees. This is the trailhead for the **Devil's Staircase** hike, high into the hills.

Continuing past here, you're nearing the end of the valley. The intimidating peak of **Stob Dearg** (on the right) looms like a dour watchman, guarding the far end of the valley. Soon you'll pass the turnoff (on the right) for **Glen Etive**, an even more remote-feeling valley. (This was the setting for the final scenes of *Skyfall*. Yes, this is where James Bond grew up. Of *course* he grew up in Glencoe.) Continuing past that, the last sign of civilization (on the right) is the Glencoe Ski Centre. And from here, the terrain flattens out as you enter the vast **Rannoch Moor**—50 bleak square miles of heather, boulders, and barely enough decent land to graze a sheep.

You could keep driving as far as you like—but the moor looks pretty much the same from here on out. Turn around and head back through Glencoe...it's scenery you'll hardly mind seeing twice.

Hiking in Glencoe

Glencoe is made for hiking. Many routes are not particularly well marked, so it's essential to get very specific instructions (from the rangers at the Glencoe Visitor Centre, or other knowledgeable locals) and equip yourself with a good map (the Ordnance Survey Explorer Map #384, sold at the visitors center, is ideal). Below, I've suggested a few of the most enticing walks and hikes. These vary from easy, level strolls to challenging climbs. Either way, equip yourself with proper footwear (even the easy trails can get swamped in wet weather) and rain gear—you never know when a storm will blow in.

I've listed these roughly in order of how close they are to Glencoe village, and given a rough sense of difficulty for each. Some of them (including the first two) are more forested, but the ones out in the open—which really let you feel immersed in the wonders of Glencoe—are even better.

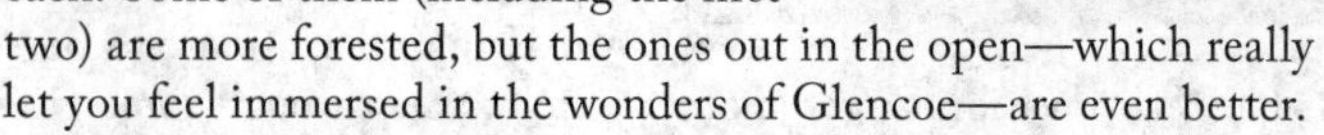

While you can walk to the first two areas from Glencoe village, the rest are best for drivers. Some of these trailheads are tricky to find; remember, I've designed the driving commentary in the previous section to help you find the hikes off the A-82.

Glencoe Lochan (Easy)

Perched on the forested hill above Glencoe village is an improbable slice of the Canadian Rockies. A century ago, this was the personal playground of Lord Strathcona, a local boy done good when he moved to Canada and eventually became a big Canadian Pacific Railway magnate. In 1894, he returned home with his Canadian wife and built the Glencoe House (which was recently restored into an exclusive top-of-the-top hotel, with suites starting around £500 a night). His wife was homesick for the Rockies, so he had the grounds landscaped to represent the lakes, trees, and mountains of her home country. They even carved out a manmade lake (Glencoe Lochan), which looks like a slice of Canada tucked under a craggy Scottish backdrop. (She was still homesick—they eventually returned to Canada.)

Today, the house and immediate surroundings are off-limits, but the rest of the area is open for exploration. Head to the end of Glencoe village, cross the bridge, and continue straight up (following signs for *Glencoe Lochan*)—it's a 20-minute uphill walk, or five-minute drive, from the village center. Once there, a helpful orientation panel in the parking lot suggests three different color-coded one-mile walking loops—mostly around that beautiful lake, which reflects the hillsides of Glencoe.

From this area, a good trail network called the **Orbital Recreational Track** follows the river through the forest up the valley, all the way to the Clachaig Inn (about 45 minutes one-way). This links you to the Signal Rock and An Torr areas (described next). Eventually they hope to extend this trail system across the valley and back to the Glencoe Visitor Centre, which would allow a handy loop hike around the valley floor.

Signal Rock and An Torr (Easy to Moderate)

This forested area has nicely-tended trails and gives you a better chance of spotting wildlife than the more desolate hikes described later. To explore this area, park at the well-marked lot just off of the A-82 and go for a walk. A well-described panel at the trailhead narrates three options: easy yellow route to the Clachaig Inn; longer blue route to Signal Rock; and strenuous black route along the hillsides of An Torr. The Signal Rock route brings you to a panoramic point overlooking the valley—so named because a fire could be lit here to alert others in case of danger.

Hidden Valley (Challenging)

Three miles east of Glencoe village, this aptly-named glen is tucked between two of the dramatic Three Sisters mountains. Also called the Lost Valley (Coire Gabhail in Gaelic), this was supposedly where the MacDonalds hid stolen cattle from their rivals, the Campbells (who later massacred them). This is the most challenging of the hikes I describe—it's strenuous and has stretches with uneven footing. Expect to scramble a bit over rocks and to cross a river on stepping stones (which may be underwater after a heavy rain). As the rocks can be slippery when wet, skip this hike in bad weather. Figure about two and a half to three hours round-trip (with an ascent of more than 1,000 feet).

Begin at the second parking lot at Glencoe Pass (on the right when coming from Glencoe), with views of the Three Sisters. You're aiming to head between the first and second Sisters (counting from the left). Hike down into the valley between the road and the mountains. Bear left, head down a metal staircase, and cross the bridge over the river. (Don't cross the bridge to the right of the parking lots—a common mistake.) Once across, you'll start the treacherous ascent up a narrow gorge. Some scrambling is required, and at one point a railing helps you find your way. The next tricky part is where you cross the river. You're looking for a pebbly beach and a large boulder; stepping stones lead across the river, and you'll see the path resume on the other side. But if the water level is high, the stones may be covered—though still passable with good shoes and steady footing. (Don't attempt to scramble over the treacherous slopes on the side of the river with the loose rocks called scree.) Once across the stepping stones, keep on the trail into the valley.

Much Easier Alternative: If you'd simply enjoy the feeling of walking deep in Glencoe valley—with peaks and waterfalls overhead—you can start down from the parking lot toward the Hidden Valley trail, and then simply stroll the old road along the valley floor as far as you want in either direction.

The Study (Easy to Moderate)

For a relatively easy, mostly level hike through the valley with a nice viewpoint at the end, consider walking to the flat rock called "The Study" and back. It takes about 45-60 minutes round-trip. The walk essentially parallels the main highway, but on the old road a bit higher up. You'll park just beyond the Three Sisters and the Coffin Cairn. From there, cut through the field of stone and marshy turf to the old road—basically two gravel tire ruts—and follow them to your left. You'll hike above the modern road, passing several modest waterfalls, until you reach a big, flat rock with stunning views of the Three Sisters, and the valley beyond. (Fellow hikers have marked the spot with a pile of stones.)

The Devil's Staircase (Strenuous but Straightforward)

About eight miles east of Glencoe village, near the end of the valley, you can hike this brief stretch of the West Highland Way. It was built by General Wade, the British strategist who came to Scotland after the 1715 Jacobite rebellion to help secure government rule here. Designed to connect Glencoe valley to the lochside town of Kinlochmore to the north, it's named for its challenging switchbacks. Most hikers simply ascend to the pass at the top (an 800-foot gain), then come back down to Glencoe. It's challenging, but easier to follow and with more comfortable footing than the Hidden Valley hike. Figure about 45-60 minutes up, and 30 minutes back down (add 45-60 minutes for the optional ascent to the summit of 2,320-foot Stob Mhic Mhartuin).

From the parking lot, a green sign points the way. It's a steep but straightforward hike up on switchback trails until you reach the pass—marked by a cairn (pile of stones). From here, you can head back down into the valley. Or, if you have stamina left, consider continuing higher—head up to the peak on the left, called **Stob Mhic Mhartuin.** The 30-40-minute hike to the top (an additional gain of 500 feet) earns you even grander views over the entire valley.

For an even longer hike, it is possible to carry on down the other side of the staircase to **Kinlochmore** (about 2 hours descent)—but your car will still be in Glencoe. Consider this: Leave your car in Glencoe village. Take a taxi to the trailhead. Hike across to Kinlochmore. Then take the hourly Stagecoach bus #44 back to Glencoe and your car.

Sleeping in Glencoe

Glencoe is an extremely low-key place to spend the night between Oban or Glasgow and the northern destinations. You'll join two kinds of guests: one-nighters just passing through, and outdoorsy types settling in for several days of hiking.

HUMBLE PLACES IN GLENCOE VILLAGE

The following B&Bs are along the main road through the middle of the village, and all are cash-only.

$$ Grianan B&B, across from the grocery store, comes with a homey feeling and two large rooms sharing a bath (D-£50, great for families, also rents self-catering cottage, tel. 01855/811-322, donaldyoung@hotmail.co.uk, Jane and Donald).

$$ Morven Cottage offers two rooms, a breakfast room overlooking the gardens, owners with plenty of character, and a son who was an extra in a Harry Potter movie (Db-£54, can accommodate double/twin/family, dogs welcome, tel. 01855/811-544, www.morvenbnb.com, Freddie and Bob).

$$ Dunire Guest House is a bit bigger—and pricier—than most, with five modern rooms (Db-£66-68, tel. 01855/811-305, www.dunireglencoe.co.uk, dunire.glencoe@hotmail.co.uk, Ann).

$$ Ghlasdrum B&B, next to the police station and set back from the A-82, has four large and modern rooms, a cozy dining

Sleep Code

Abbreviations **(£1=about $1.60, country code: 44)**

S=Single, **D**=Double/Twin, **T**=Triple, **Q**=Quad, **b**=bathroom

Price Rankings

$$$ Higher Priced—Most rooms £70 or more

$$ Moderately Priced—Most rooms £30-70

$ Lower Priced—Most rooms £30 or less

Unless otherwise noted, credit cards are accepted at hotels and hostels—but not B&Bs, breakfast is included, and free Wi-Fi and/or a guest computer is generally available. Prices change; verify current rates online or by email. For the best prices, always book directly with the hotel.

room with a fireplace, and the nicest bathrooms (Sb-£40, Db-£60, tel. 01855/811-593, maureen@ken110.orangehome.co.uk, Maureen and Ken).

$$ Tulachgorm B&B has two comfortable rooms sharing a bathroom in a modern house with fine mountain views (D-£50, tel. 01855/811-391, mellow Ann Blake and friendly border collie Jo).

OUTSIDE OF TOWN

These three options—offering more comforts than the simple places listed earlier—are on or near the back road that runs through the forest parallel to the main A-82. Each offers seclusion with good proximity to both the village and the valley (but are best-suited for drivers). To reach them, take the road up through the middle of Glencoe village and cross the bridge. For the Scorrybreac Guest House, head straight up the hill and follow signs. For the other two, turn right just after the bridge and follow the river; first you'll pass the Strath Lodge, and then—after driving about three miles past campgrounds and hostels—you'll reach the Clachaig Inn on the right.

$$$ Strath Lodge, energetically run by Ann and Dan (who are generous with hiking tips), brings a fresh perspective to Glencoe's otherwise stodgy accommodations scene. Their four rooms, upstairs in their modern, light-filled, lodge-like home, are partway down the road to the Clachaig Inn (standard Db-£82, superior Db-£97, tel. 01855/811-337, mobile 07775-826-080, www.strathlodgeglencoe.com, stay@strathlodgeglencoe.com).

$$$ Scorrybreac Guest House enjoys a privileged position just across the road from the restored Glencoe House (now a luxury hotel). From here, walks around the Glencoe Lochan wooded lake park are easy, and it's about a 10-minute walk down into the village. Emma and Graham rent five modern, nondescript rooms (Db-£68-88 depending on size, pay Wi-Fi, family rooms, tel. 01855/811-354, www.scorrybreacglencoe.com, scorrybreac@btinternet.com).

$$$ Clachaig Inn, which runs three popular pubs on site, also rents 23 rooms, all with private bath. It works well for hikers seeking a comfy mountain inn (Db-£104, recommended pub, tel. 01855/811-252, 3 miles from Glencoe, www.clachaig.com).

Eating in Glencoe

Choices around Glencoe are slim—this isn't the place for fine dining. But four options offer decent food a short walk or drive away. For evening fun, take a walk or ask your B&B host where to find music and dancing.

In Glencoe: The only real restaurant is **The Glencoe Gathering & Inn,** with lovely dining areas and a large outdoor deck. Choose between the quirky, fun pub, specializing in seafood with a Scottish twist, or the fancier restaurant (£9-16 main courses, food served daily 12:00-21:00, at junction of A-82 and Glencoe village, tel. 01855/811-265).

The **Glencoe Café,** also in the village, is just right for soups and sandwiches, and Justine's homemade baked goods—especially the carrot loaf—are irresistible (£4 soups, £8.50 soup and *panini* lunch combo, daily 10:00-17:00, last order at 16:00, free Wi-Fi).

Near Glencoe: **Clachaig Inn,** set in a stunning valley a few miles from Glencoe village, serves food all day long to a clientele that's half locals and half tourists. This unpretentious and very popular social hub features billiards, live music, £8-12 pub grub, and a wide range of whiskies and hand-pulled ales. There are three areas sharing the same menu: The upscale-chic Bidean Lounge, the spit-and-sawdust, pub-around-an-open-fire Boots Bar, and the adjoining former beer cellar aptly called The Snug (all open daily for lunch and dinner, music Sat from 21:00, see hotel listing earlier for driving directions, tel. 01855/811-252).

In Ballachulish: **Laroch Bar & Bistro,** in the next village over from Glencoe (toward Oban), is trying to bring some modern class to this sleepy corner of Scotland. Choose between the fancier bistro or the cozy bar with lighter fare (£15-20 meals, daily 12:00-22:00, tel. 01855/811-940, www.thelarochrestaurantandbar.co.uk). Drive into Ballachulish village, and you'll see it on the left.

Glencoe Connections

Buses don't actually drive down the main road through Glencoe village, though some (most notably those going between Glasgow and Fort William) stop near Glencoe village at a place called **"Glencoe Crossroads"**—a short walk into the village center. Other buses (such as those between Oban and Fort William) stop at the nearby town of **Ballachulish,** which is just a half-mile away (or a £3 taxi ride). Tell the bus driver where you're going ("Glencoe village") and ask to be let off as close as possible.

From **Glencoe Crossroads,** you can catch bus #914, #915, or #916 (8/day) to **Fort William** (30 minutes) or **Glasgow** (2.5 hours).

From **Ballachulish,** you can take bus #918 (3/day) to **Fort William** (30 minutes) or **Oban** (1 hour). Bus info: Tel. 0871-266-3333, www.citylink.co.uk.

There's another, cheaper option for reaching **Fort William** from either Glencoe Crossroads or Ballachulish: Stagecoach bus #44 runs hourly in each direction (Mon-Sat, no buses Sun, www.stagecoachbus.com).

To reach **Inverness,** transfer in Fort William. To reach **Edinburgh,** transfer in Glasgow.

Fort William

Fort William—after Inverness, the second-biggest town in the Highlands (pop. 10,000)—is Glencoe's opposite. While Glencoe is a humble one-street village, appealing to hikers and nature-lovers, Fort William's glammed-up main drag feels like one big Scottish shopping mall (with souvenir stands and outdoor stores touting perpetual "70 percent off" sales). The town is clogged with a United Nations of tourists trying to get out of the rain. Big bus tours drive through Glencoe...but they sleep in Fort William.

While Glencoe touches the Scottish soul of the Highlands, Fort William was a steely and intimidating headquarters of the counter-insurgency movement—in many ways designed to crush that same Highland spirit. After the English Civil War (early 1650s), Oliver Cromwell built a fort here to control his rebellious Scottish subjects. This was beefed up (and named for King William III) in 1690. And following the Jacobite uprising in 1715, King George I dispatched General George Wade to coordinate and fortify the crown's Highland defenses against further Jacobite dissenters. Fort William was the first of a chain of intimidating bastions (along with Fort Augustus on Loch Ness, and Fort George near Inverness) stretching the length of the Great Glen. But Fort William's namesake fortress is long gone, leaving nothing tangible to help today's visitors imagine its militaristic past.

Orientation to Fort William

Given its strategic position—between Glencoe and Oban in the south and Inverness in the east—you're likely to pass through Fort William at some point during your Highlands explorations. And, while "just passing through" is the perfect plan here, Fort William can provide a good opportunity to stock up on whatever you need (last supermarket before Inverness), grab lunch, and get any questions answered at the TI.

Arrival in Fort William: You'll find pay parking lots flanking the main pedestrian zone, High Street—one is squeezed between town and the loch, and the other is tucked up behind the main drag. The train and bus stations sit side-by-side just north of the old town center, an easy walk away.

Tourist Information: The TI is on the car-free main drag (generally July-Aug daily 9:30-18:30; Easter-June Mon-Sat 9:00-17:00, Sun 10:00-17:00; shorter hours off-season; free Wi-Fi, 15 High Street, tel. 01397/701-801). Free public WCs are up the street, next to the parking lot.

Sights in Fort William

West Highland Museum

Fort William's only real sight is its humble but well-presented museum. It's a fine opportunity to escape the elements, and—if you take the time to linger over the exhibits—genuinely insightful about local history and Highland life.

Cost and Hours: Free, £3 suggested donation, guidebook-£1, Mon-Sat 10:00-17:00, Nov-Dec and March until 16:00, closed Sun—but may be open Sun in July-Aug, closed Jan-Feb, on Cameron Square, tel. 01397/702-169, www.westhighlandmuseum.org.uk.

Visiting the Museum: Follow the suggested one-way route through exhibits on two floors. You'll begin by learning about the WWII green beret commandos, who were trained in secrecy near here (see "Commando Memorial" listing, later). Then you'll see the historic Governor's Room, decorated with the original paneling from the room in which the order for the Glencoe Massacre was signed. The ground floor also holds exhibits on natural history (lots of stuffed birds and other critters), mountaineering (old equipment), and archaeology (stone and metal tools).

Upstairs, you'll see a selection of old tartans and a salacious exhibit about Queen Victoria and John Brown (her Scottish servant...and, possibly, suitor). The good Jacobite exhibit gives a concise timeline of that complicated history, from Charles I to Bonnie Prince Charlie, and displays a selection of items emblazoned with the prince's bonnie face—including a clandestine portrait that you can only see by looking in a cylindrical mirror. Finally, the Highland Life exhibit collects a hodgepodge of tools, musical instruments (some fine old harps that were later replaced by the much louder bagpipes as the battlefield instrument of choice), and other bric-a-brac.

NEAR FORT WILLIAM

Ben Nevis

From Fort William, take a peek at Britain's highest peak, Ben Nevis (4,406 feet). Thousands walk to its summit each year. On a clear day, you can admire it from a distance. Scotland's only mountain cable cars—at the **Nevis Range Mountain Experience**—can take you to a not-very-lofty 2,150-foot perch on the slopes of Aonach Mòr for a closer look (£12, 15-minute ride, generally open daily but closed in high winds and mid-Nov-mid-Dec—call ahead, signposted on the A-82 north of Fort William, tel. 01397/705-825, www.nevisrange.co.uk).

▲Commando Memorial

This powerful bronze ensemble of three stoic WWII commandos, standing in an evocative mountain setting, is one of Britain's most beloved war memorials. During World War II, Winston Churchill decided that Britain needed an elite military corps. He created the British Commandos, famous for wearing green berets (an accessory—and name—later borrowed by elite fighting forces in the US and other countries). The British Commandos trained in the Lochaber region near Fort William, in the windy shadow of Ben Nevis. Many later died in combat, and this memorial—built in 1952—remembers those fallen British heroes.

Nearby is the Garden of Remembrance, honoring British Commandos who died in more recent conflicts, from the Falkland Islands to Afghanistan. It's also a popular place to spread Scottish military ashes. Taken together, these sights are a touching reminder that the US is not alone in its distant wars. Every nation has its share of honored heroes willing to sacrifice for what they believe to be the greater good.

Getting There: The memorial is about nine miles outside of Fort William, on the way to Inverness (just outside Spean Bridge); see "Route Tips for Drivers" on page 930.

Sleeping in Fort William

These two B&Bs are on Union Road, a five-minute walk up the hill above High Street. Each place has three rooms, one of which has a private bathroom in the hall.

$$ Glenmorven Guest House is a friendly, flower-bedecked, family-run place at the end of the road. The hospitality, special extras, and views of Loch Linnhe are worth the walk (Db-£65-70, laundry service, welcome whisky, lots of stairs up from the road, tel. 01397/703-236, www.glenmorven.co.uk, glenmorvenguesthouse@gmail.com, Anne and Colin Jamieson).

$$ Gowan Brae B&B ("Hill of the Big Daisy") is a hobbit-cute house with an antique-filled dining room and three rooms with loch or garden views (Db-£70, £60 in off-season, tel. 01397/704-399, www.gowanbrae.co.uk, gowan_brae@btinternet.com, Jim and Ann Clark).

Eating in Fort William

These places are on traffic-free High Street, near the start of town. All (except Deli Craft) are open daily for lunch; The Grog & Gruel also does dinner.

Deli Craft has good made-to-order deli sandwiches and other prepared foods—a handy place to assemble a tasty, healthy picnic (closed Sun, 61 High Street, tel. 01397/698-100).

Hot Roast Company sells beef, turkey, ham, or pork sandwiches, topped with some tasty extras, along with soup, salad, and coleslaw (£4 takeaway, a bit more for sit-down service, 127 High Street, tel. 01397/700-606).

The Grog & Gruel serves real ales, good £6-12 pub grub, and Tex-Mex and Cajun dishes, with some unusual choices such as burgers made from boar, haggis, or Highland venison (66 High Street, tel. 01397/705-078).

Fort William Connections

Fort William is a major transit hub for the Highlands, so you'll likely change buses here at some point during your trip.

From Fort William by Bus to: Glencoe (all Glasgow-bound buses—#914, #915, and #916; 8/day, 30 minutes; also Stagecoach bus #44, hourly Mon-Sat, none Sun), **Ballachulish** near Glencoe (Oban-bound bus #918, 3/day, 30 minutes; also Stagecoach bus #44, hourly Mon-Sat, none Sun), **Oban** (bus #918, 3/day, 1.5 hours), **Inverness** (buses #19 and #919, 7-9/day, 2 hours), **Glasgow** (buses #914, #915, and #916; 8/day, 3 hours). To reach **Edinburgh,** take the bus to Glasgow, then transfer to a train or bus (figure 5 hours total). Bus info: Citylink—tel. 0871-266-3333, www.citylink.co.uk; Stagecoach—www.stagecoachbus.com.

ROUTE TIPS FOR DRIVERS

From Fort William to Loch Ness and Inverness: Head north out of Fort William on the A-82. After about eight miles, in the village of Spean Bridge, take the left fork (staying on the A-82). About a mile later, on the left, keep an eye out for the **Commando Memorial** (described earlier and worth a quick stop). From here, the A-82 sweeps north and follows the Caledonian Canal, passing through **Fort Augustus** (a good lunch stop, with its worthwhile Caledonian Canal Visitor Centre), and then follows the north side of Loch Ness on its way to Inverness. Along the way, the A-82 passes **Urquhart Castle** and two **Loch Ness Monster exhibits** in Drumnadrochit (described in the Inverness and Loch Ness chapter).

From Oban to Fort William via Glencoe: See page 895 in the Oban chapter.

INVERNESS AND LOCH NESS

Inverness • Loch Ness • Culloden Battlefield • Clava Cairns

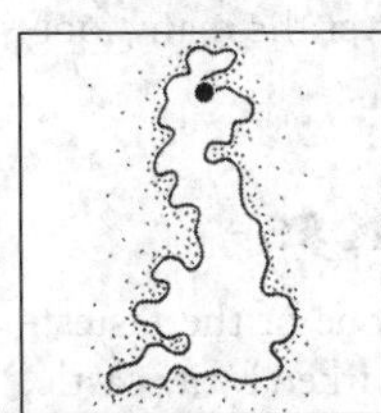

Inverness, the Highlands' de facto capital, is an almost-unavoidable stop on the Scottish tourist circuit. Fortunately, it's also a pleasant town and an ideal springboard for some of the country's most famous sights. Hear the music of the Highlands in Inverness and the echo of muskets at Culloden, where government troops drove Bonnie Prince Charlie into exile and conquered his Jacobite supporters. Ponder the mysteries of Scotland's murky prehistoric past at Clava Cairns, and get to know Macbeth's descendants at Cawdor Castle. Just to the southwest of Inverness, explore the locks and lochs of the Caledonian Canal while playing hide-and-seek with the Loch Ness monster.

PLANNING YOUR TIME

Though it has little in the way of sights, Inverness does have a workaday charm and is a handy spot to spend a night or two between other Highland destinations. One night here gives you time to take a quick tour of nearby attractions. With two nights, you can find a full day's worth of sightseeing nearby.

Note that Loch Ness is between Inverness and Oban or Glencoe. If you're heading to or from one of those places, it makes sense to see Loch Ness en route, rather than as a side trip from Inverness.

GETTING AROUND THE HIGHLANDS

With a car, the day trips around Inverness are easy. Without a car, you can get to Inverness by train (better from Edinburgh, Stirling, or Glasgow) or by bus (better from Oban and Glencoe), then side-trip to Loch Ness, Culloden, and other nearby sights by public bus or with a package tour.

Inverness

Inverness is situated on the River Ness at the base of a castle (the town's courthouse, not a tourist attraction). Inverness' charm is its normalcy—it's a nice midsize Scottish city that gives you a palatable taste of the "urban" Highlands and a contrast to cutesy tourist towns. It has a disheveled ruddy-cheeked grittiness and is well located for enjoying the surrounding countryside sights. Check out the bustling, pedestrianized downtown, or meander the picnic-friendly riverside paths and islands—best at sunset, when the light hits the castle and couples hold hands while strolling along the water and over the many footbridges.

Orientation to Inverness

Inverness, with about 67,000 people, has been one of the fastest-growing areas of Scotland for the last decade. Marked by its castle, Inverness clusters along the River Ness. Where the main road crosses the river at Ness Bridge, you'll find the TI; within a few blocks (away from the river) are the train and bus stations and an appealing pedestrian shopping zone. Most of my recommended B&Bs huddle atop a gentle hill behind the castle (a 10-minute uphill walk, or a £5 taxi ride, from the city center).

Tourist Information: At the centrally located TI, you can pick up activity and day-trip brochures, the self-guided *City Centre Trail* walking-tour leaflet, and the *What's On* weekly events sheet for the latest theater and music (all free). The office also has a bulletin board with timely local event information (June-Sept Mon-Sat 8:45-18:30, Sun 9:30-18:00; Oct-May Mon-Sat 9:00-17:00, Sun 10:00-17:00—except Dec-Feb until 15:00; free Wi-Fi, free WCs nearby, Castle Wynd, tel. 01463/252-401, www.inverness-scotland.com).

HELPFUL HINTS

Charity Shops: Inverness is home to several pop-up charity shops. Occupying vacant rental spaces, these are staffed by volunteers who are happy to talk about their philanthropy. You can pick up a memorable knickknack, adjust your wardrobe for the weather, and learn about local causes.

Festivals and Events: The summer is busy with special events, which can make it tricky to find a room. Book far ahead during these times, including the **Etape Loch Ness** bike race (early June), **Highland Games** (late June), **Belladrum Tartan Heart Festival** (music, late July), **Black Isle Show** (farm exhibits, early Aug), and **Loch Ness Marathon** (late Sept). The big **RockNess Music Festival** has been on hiatus due to budget cuts, but may return (www.rockness.co.uk).

For a real Highland treat, catch a **shinty match** (a combination of field hockey, hurling, and American football—but without pads). Inverness Shinty Club plays at Bught Park, along Ness Walk (the TI or your B&B can tell you if there are any matches on, or check www.spanglefish.com/invernessshintyclub).

Bookstore: Leakey's Bookshop, located in a converted church built in 1649, is the place to browse through teetering towers of musty old books and vintage maps, warm up by the wood-burning stove, and climb the spiral staircase to the loft for views over the stacks (Mon-Sat 10:00-17:30, closed Sun, in Greyfriar's Hall on Church Street, tel. 01463/239-947, Charles Leakey).

Baggage Storage: The train station has lockers (open Mon-Sat 6:40-20:30, Sun from 10:40), or you can leave your bag at the bus station's ticket desk (small fee, daily 7:45-18:15).

Laundry: New City Launderette is just across the Ness Bridge from the TI (self-service-£5-6/load, same-day full-service-about £10-12/load, priced by weight, Mon-Sat 8:00-18:00, until 20:00 Mon-Fri June-Oct, Sun 10:00-16:00 year-round, last load one hour before closing, 17 Young Street, tel. 01463/242-507). **Thirty Degrees Laundry** on Church Street is another option (full-service only-£10/load, drop off first thing in the morning for same-day service, Mon-Sat 8:30-17:30, closed Sun, 84 Church Street, tel. 01463/710-380).

Tours in Inverness

Walking Tours

Cameron—a.k.a. "the man in the kilt"—at **Happy Tours** offers history walks by day, and "Crime and Punishment" tours by night. These one-hour walks are cheeky and peppered with his political

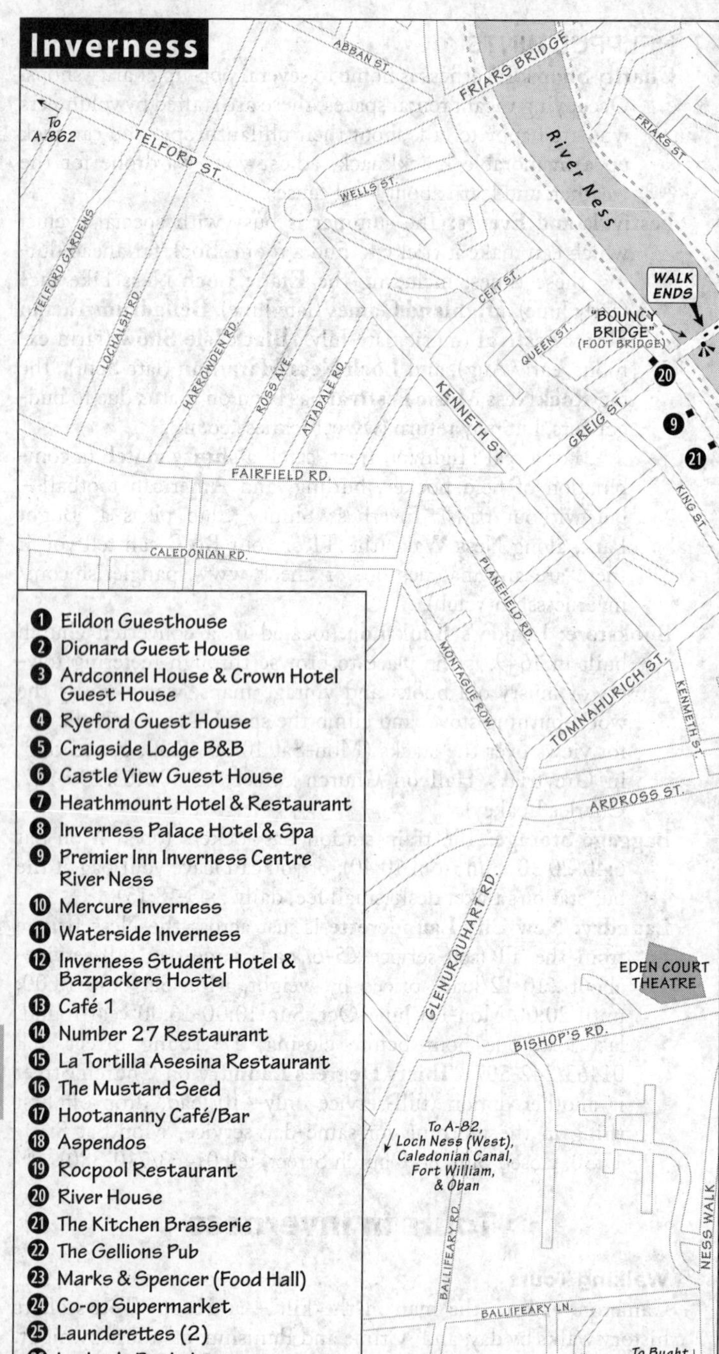
Inverness
To A-862
TELFORD ST.
ABBAN ST.
FRIARS BRIDGE
River Ness
FRIARS ST.
WELLS ST.
TELFORD GARDENS
LOCHALSH RD.
HARROWDEN RD.
ROSS AVE.
ATTADALE RD.
CELT ST.
QUEEN ST.
WALK ENDS
"BOUNCY BRIDGE" (FOOT BRIDGE)
KENNETH ST.
GREIG ST.
FAIRFIELD RD.
KING ST.
CALEDONIAN RD.
PLANEFIELD RD.
MONTAGUE ROW
TOMNAHURICH ST.
KENNETH ST.
ARDROSS ST.
GLENURQUHART RD.
EDEN COURT THEATRE
BISHOP'S RD.
To A-82, Loch Ness (West), Caledonian Canal, Fort William, & Oban
BALLIFEARY RD.
NESS WALK
BALLIFEARY LN.
To Bught Park
1 Eildon Guesthouse
2 Dionard Guest House
3 Ardconnel House & Crown Hotel Guest House
4 Ryeford Guest House
5 Craigside Lodge B&B
6 Castle View Guest House
7 Heathmount Hotel & Restaurant
8 Inverness Palace Hotel & Spa
9 Premier Inn Inverness Centre River Ness
10 Mercure Inverness
11 Waterside Inverness
12 Inverness Student Hotel & Bazpackers Hostel
13 Café 1
14 Number 27 Restaurant
15 La Tortilla Asesina Restaurant
16 The Mustard Seed
17 Hootananny Café/Bar
18 Aspendos
19 Rocpool Restaurant
20 River House
21 The Kitchen Brasserie
22 The Gellions Pub
23 Marks & Spencer (Food Hall)
24 Co-op Supermarket
25 Launderettes (2)
26 Leakey's Bookshop

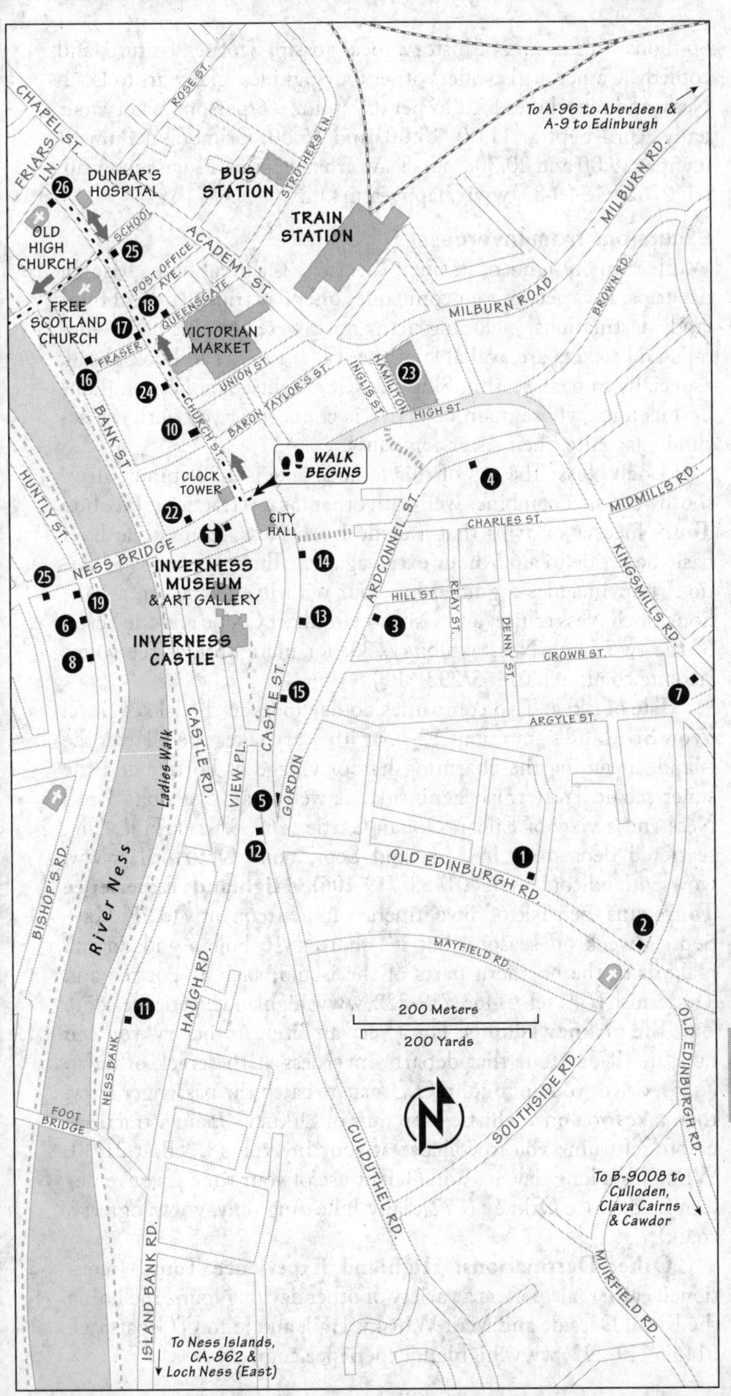
To A-96 to Aberdeen & A-9 to Edinburgh
CHAPEL ST.
FRIARS LN.
ROSE ST.
DUNBAR'S HOSPITAL
BUS STATION
STROTHERS LN.
TRAIN STATION
MILBURN RD.
OLD HIGH CHURCH
SCHOOL
ACADEMY ST.
POST OFFICE AVE.
QUEENSGATE
FREE SCOTLAND CHURCH
VICTORIAN MARKET
MILBURN ROAD
BROWN RD.
FRASER
UNION ST.
BARON TAYLOR'S ST.
INGLIS ST.
HAMILTON
HIGH ST.
BANK ST.
CHURCH ST.
WALK BEGINS
CLOCK TOWER
CITY HALL
MIDMILLS RD.
CHARLES ST.
HUNTLY ST.
NESS BRIDGE
INVERNESS MUSEUM & ART GALLERY
ARDCONNEL ST.
HILL ST.
REAY ST.
DENNY ST.
KINGSMILLS RD.
INVERNESS CASTLE
CROWN ST.
CASTLE ST.
ARGYLE ST.
Ladies Walk
CASTLE RD.
VIEW PL.
GORDON
OLD EDINBURGH RD.
BISHOP'S RD.
River Ness
MAYFIELD RD.
HAUGH RD.
200 Meters
200 Yards
NESS BANK
FOOT BRIDGE
SOUTHSIDE RD.
CULDUTHEL RD.
OLD EDINBURGH RD.
To B-9008 to Culloden, Clava Cairns & Cawdor
MURFIELD RD.
ISLAND BANK RD.
To Ness Islands, CA-862 & Loch Ness (East)

opinions—a fun mix of history, local gossip, Scottish culture, and comedy. Cameron also offers other tours, guides bike tours to Loch Ness, and rents bikes for £15 per day (tours-£6/person; history tour daily April-Sept at 11:00, 13:00, and 15:00; Crime and Punishment at 19:00 and 20:30; tours leave from steps of TI, just show up, tel. 07828/154-683, www.happy-tours.biz).

Excursions from Inverness

While thin on sights of its own, Inverness is a great home base for day trips. A variety of tour companies offer day trips to other Highlands destinations, including many not covered by this book—details and tickets are available at the TI. It's smart to book ahead, especially in peak season. Skip the City Sightseeing hop-on, hop-off bus tour (whose main objective is connecting you with cruises run by Jacobite, their sister company).

Loch Ness: The top of this famous lake is a 20-minute drive southwest, so it combines well with other local attractions. **Jacobite Tours** focuses on trips that include Loch Ness, from a one-hour basic boat ride to a 6.5-hour extravaganza. Their 3.5-hour "Sensation" tour includes a guided bus tour with live narration, a half-hour Loch Ness cruise, and visits to Urquhart Castle and the better of the two Loch Ness exhibits (£33, for more options see www.jacobite.co.uk, tel. 01463/233-999).

Isle of Skye: Two companies do day tours to the Isle of Skye. **Wow Scotland**'s ambitious 12-hour itinerary takes you all over the island, including the charming harbor village of Portree and the super-scenic Trotternish Peninsula, as well as a drive along Loch Ness and a view of Eilean Donan Castle (£69, 3/week June-Aug, scattered departures in May and Sept, none Oct-April, www.wowscotland.com, tel. 01463/719-106). **Highland Experience Tours** runs their Isle of Skye itinerary more frequently (daily May-Sept, 4/week off-season), but it's shorter (10 hours) and doesn't make it to the northern parts of the island, such as Portree and Trotternish (£49, tel. 01463/719-222, www.highlandexperience.com).

The Orkney Islands: For a very ambitious itinerary, you can take an all-day tour that departs Inverness at the crack of dawn (7:15), drives you up to John O'Groats to catch the passenger ferry, then takes you on a whistle-stop tour of Orkney's main attractions before returning you to collapse at your Inverness B&B at 21:00. While it's a long day, it's an efficient use of your time if you're determined to see Orkney (£72, daily June-Aug only, www.jogferry.co.uk).

Other Destinations: Highland Experience Tours (mentioned earlier) also offers a variety of other daylong tours, including the Royal Deeside and Malt Whisky Trail, and John O'Groats (tel. 01463/719-222, www.highlandexperience.com).

Inverness Walk

Humble Inverness has meager conventional sights, but its fun history and quirky charm become clear as you take this short self-guided walk.

• *Start at the clock tower and TI.*

Clock Tower and TI: Notice the **Gaelic language** on directional and street signs all around you. While nobody speaks Gaelic as a first language (and few Scottish people speak it at all), this old Celtic language symbolizes the strength of Scottish Highland culture.

The **clock tower** looming 130 feet above you is all that remains of a tollbooth building erected in 1791. This is the highest spire in town, and for generations was a collection point for local taxes. Here, four streets—Church, Castle, Bridge, and High—come together, integrating God, defense, and trade—everything necessary for a fine city.

About 800 years ago, a castle was built on the bluff overhead and the town of Inverness coalesced right about here. For centuries, this backwater town's economy was based on cottage industries. Artisans who made things also sold them. In 1854, the train arrived, injecting energy and money from Edinburgh and Glasgow, and the Victorian boom hit. With the Industrial Age came wholesalers, distributors, mass production, and affluence. Much of the city was built during this era, in Neo-Gothic style—over-the-top and fanciful, like the City Hall (from 1882, kitty-corner to the clock tower). With the Victorian Age also came tourism.

Look for the **Bible quotes** chiseled into the wall across the street from the City Hall. A civic leader, tired of his council members being drunkards, edited these Bible verses for maximum impact, especially the bottom two.

Hiding just up the hill (behind the eyesore concrete home of the Inverness Museum and Art Gallery) is **Inverness Castle.** Although the castle is closed to the public, it's worth hiking up there at some point during your visit to enjoy some of the best views of Inverness. The courthouse in the castle doesn't see a lot of action. In the last 30 years, there have been only two murders to prosecute. As locals like to say, "no guns, no problems." While hunters can own a gun, gun ownership in Scotland is complicated and tightly regulated.

By the way, every day and night in peak season, Cameron ("the man in the kilt" who gave me the material for this walk) gives entertaining hour-long guided walks that begin from the TI near here (see "Tours in Inverness," earlier).

• *Walk a few steps uphill toward the Scottish hamburger restaurant that caught on big-time in the US.*

Mercat Cross and Old Town Center: Standing in front of the City Hall is a well-worn mercat cross, which designated the market in centuries past. This is where the townspeople gathered to hear important proclamations, share news, watch hangings, gossip, and so on. The scant remains of a prehistoric stone at the base of the cross are what's left of Inverness' "Stone of Destiny." According to tradition, whenever someone moved away from Inverness, they'd take a tiny bit of home with them in the form of a chip of this stone—so it's been chipped and pecked almost to oblivion.

The yellow **Caledonian** building faces McDonald's at the base of High Street. (Caledonia was the ancient Roman name for Scotland.) It was built in 1847, complete with Corinthian columns and a Greek-style pediment, as the leading bank in town back when banks were designed to hold the money of the rich and powerful... and intimidate working blokes. Notice how nicely pedestrianized High Street welcomes people and seagulls...but not cars.

• *Next we'll head up Church Street, which begins between the clock tower and The Caledonian.*

Church Street: The street art you'll trip over at the start of Church Street is called ***Earthquake***—a reminder of the quake that hit Inverness in 1816. As the slabs explain, the town's motto is "Open Heartedness, Insight, and Perseverance."

Stroll down Church Street. Look up above the modern storefronts to see Old World facades. **Union Street** (the second corner on the right)—stately, symmetrical, and Neoclassical—was the fanciest street in the Highlands when it was built in the 19th century. Its buildings had indoor toilets. That was big news.

Midway down the next block of Church Street (on the right), an alley marked by an ugly white canopy leads to the **Victorian Market.** Explore this gallery of shops under an iron-and-glass domed roof dating from 1876 (closed Sun). The first section seems abandoned, but delve deeper to find some more active areas, where local shops mix with tacky "tartan tat" souvenir stands. If you're seriously into bagpipes, look for **Cabar Fèidh,** where American expat Brian sells CDs and sheet music, and repairs and maintains the precious instruments of local musicians.

Go back out of the market the way you came in and continue down Church Street. At the next corner you come to **Hootananny,** famous locally for its live music (pop in to see what's on tonight). Just past that is **Abertarff House,** the oldest house in Inverness. It was the talk of the town in 1593 for its "turnpike" (spiral staircase) connecting the floors.

Continue about a block farther along Church Street. The lane on the left leads to the **"Bouncy Bridge"** (where we'll finish this walk). Opposite that lane (on the right) is **Dunbar's Hospital,** with four-foot-thick walls. In 1668, Alexander Dunbar was a wealthy landowner who built this as a poor folks' home. You can almost read the auld script in his coat of arms above the door.

A few steps up Church Street, walk through the iron gate on the left and into the churchyard (we're focusing on the shorter church on the right—ignore the bigger one on the left). Looking at the WWI and WWII memorials on the church's wall, it's clear which war hit Scotland harder. While no one famous is buried here, many tombstones go back to the 1700s. Being careful not to step on a rabbit, head for the bluff overlooking the river.

Old High Church: There are a lot of churches in Inverness (46 Protestant, two Catholic, and two Gaelic-language), but these days, most are used for other purposes. This one, dating from the 11th century, is the most historic (but is generally closed). It was built on what was likely the site of a pagan holy ground. Early Christians called upon St. Michael to take the fire out of pagan spirits, so it only made sense that the first Christians would build their church here and dedicate the spot as St. Michael's Mount.

In the sixth century, the Irish evangelist monk St. Columba brought Christianity to northern England, the Scottish islands (at Iona), and the Scottish Highlands (in Inverness). He stood here amongst the pagans and preached to King Brude and the Picts.

Study the bell tower from the 1600s. The small door to nowhere (one floor up) indicates that back before the castle offered protection, this tower was the place of last refuge for townsfolk under attack. They'd gather inside and pull up the ladder. The church became a prison for Jacobites after the Battle of Culloden, and executions were carried out in the churchyard.

Every night at 20:00, the bell in the tower rings 100 times. It has rung like this since 1730 to remind townsfolk that it's dangerous to be out after dinner.

• *From here, you can circle back to the lane leading to the "Bouncy Bridge" and then hike out onto the bridge. Or you can just survey the countryside from this bluff.*

The River Ness: Emptying out of Loch Ness and flowing seven miles to the sea (a mile from here), this is one of the shortest rivers in the country. While it's shallow (you can almost walk across it), there are plenty of fish in it. A 64-pound salmon was once pulled out of the river right here. In the 19th century, Inverness was smaller, and across the river stretched nothing but open fields. Then, with the Victorian boom, the suspension footbridge (a.k.a. "Bouncy Bridge") was built in 1881 to connect new construction across the river with the town.

• *Your tour is over. Inverness is yours to explore.*

Sights in Inverness

Inverness Museum and Art Gallery

This free, likable town museum is worth poking around on a rainy day to get a taste of Inverness and the Highlands. The ground-floor exhibits on geology and archaeology peel back the layers of Highland history: Bronze and Iron ages, Picts (including some carved stones), Scots, Vikings, and Normans. Upstairs you'll find the "social history" exhibit (everything from Scottish nationalism to hunting and fishing) and temporary art exhibits.

Cost and Hours: Free, April-Oct Tue-Sat 10:00-17:00, shorter hours off-season, closed Sun-Mon year-round, cheap café, in the ugly modern building behind the TI on the way up to the castle, tel. 01463/237-114, www.highlifehighland.com.

Inverness Castle

Inverness' biggest non-sight has nice views from its front lawn, but the building itself isn't worth visiting. A wooden fortress that stood on this spot was replaced by a stone structure in the 15th century. In 1715, that castle was named Fort George to assert English control over the area. In 1745, it was destroyed by Bonnie Prince Charlie's Jacobite army and remained a ruin until the 1830s, when the present castle was built. The statue (from 1899) outside depicts Flora MacDonald, who helped Bonnie Prince Charlie escape from the English (see page 948). The castle was built as the courthouse, and when trials are in session, loutish-looking men hang out here, waiting for their bewigged barristers to arrive.

River Walks

As with most European cities, where there's a river, there's a walk. Inverness, with both the River Ness and the Caledonian Canal, does not disappoint. Consider an early-morning stroll along the Ness Bank to capture the castle at sunrise, or a post-dinner jaunt to Bught Park for a local shinty match (see "Helpful Hints—Festivals and Events," earlier). The forested islands in the middle of the River Ness—about a ten-minute walk south of the center—are a popular escape from the otherwise busy city.

Here's a good plan for your Inverness riverside constitutional: From the Ness Bridge, head along the riverbank under the castle (along the path called "Ladies Walk"). As you work your way up the river, you'll see the architecturally-bold Eden Court Theatre (across the river), pass a white pedestrian bridge, see a WWI memorial, and peek into the gardens of several fine old Victorian sandstone riverfront homes. Nearing the tree-covered islands, watch for fly-fishers in hip waders on the pebbly banks. Reaching the first skinny little island, take the bridge with the wavy wrought-iron railing and head down the path along the middle of the island. Notice that this is part of the Great Glen Way, a footpath that stretches from here all the way to Fort William (79 miles). Enjoy this little nature break, with gurgling rapids—and possibly a few midges. Reaching the bigger bridge, cross it and enjoy strolling through tall forests. After two more green-railinged bridges, traverse yet another island and find one last white-iron bridge that takes you across to the opposite bank. You'll pop out at the corner of Bught Park, the site of shinty practices and games—are any going on today?

From here, you can simply head back into town on this bank. If you'd like to explore more, you could continue farther south. It's not as idyllic or as pedestrian-friendly, but in this zone you'll find minigolf, a skate park, the Highland Archive building, the free Botanic Gardens (daily 10:00-17:00, until 16:00 Nov-March), and the huge Active Inverness leisure center, loaded with amusements including a swimming pool with adventure slides, a climbing wall, a sauna and steam area, and a gymnasium (www.invernessleisure.co.uk).

Continuing west from these leisure areas, you'll eventually hit the Caledonian Canal; to the south, this parallels the River Ness, and to the north is where it meets Beauly Firth, then Moray Firth and the North Sea. From the Tomnahurich Bridge, paths on either bank allow you to walk along the Great Glen Way until you're ready to turn around.

Nightlife in Inverness

Scottish Folk Music

While you can find traditional folk music sessions in pubs and hotel bars anywhere in town, two places are well established as *the* music pubs. Neither charges a cover for the music, unless a bigger-name band is playing.

The Gellions has live folk and Scottish music nightly (from 21:30 or 22:00). Just across the street from the TI, it has local ales on tap and brags it's the oldest bar in town (14 Bridge Street, tel. 01463/233-648, www.gellions.co.uk).

Hootananny is an energetic place with several floors of live rock, blues, or folk music, and drinking fun nightly. Music in the main bar usually begins about 21:30 (traditional music sessions Sun-Wed, bands on weekends). On weekends only, upstairs is the Mad Hatter's nightclub, complete with a "chill-out room" (bar open 12:00-24:00, 67 Church Street, tel. 01463/233-651, www.hootananny.co.uk). They also serve good traditional Scottish food (see listing in "Eating in Inverness," later).

Sleeping in Inverness

B&Bs ON AND NEAR ARDCONNEL STREET AND OLD EDINBURGH ROAD

These B&Bs are popular; book ahead for June through August (and during the peak times listed in "Helpful Hints," earlier), and be aware that some require a two-night minimum during busy times. The places I list are all a 10-minute walk from the train station and town center. To get to the B&Bs, either catch a taxi (£5) or walk: From the train and bus stations, go left on Academy Street. At the first stoplight (the second if you're coming from the bus station), veer right onto Inglis Street in the pedestrian zone. Go up the Market Brae steps. At the top, turn right onto Ardconnel Street toward the B&Bs and hostels.

$$ Eildon Guesthouse, set on a quiet corner, offers five tranquil rooms with spacious baths at an excellent value. The cute-as-a-button 1890s countryside brick home exudes warmth and serenity from the moment you open the gate (Db-£80, Tb-£115, family rooms, in-room fridges, parking, 29 Old Edinburgh Road, tel. 01463/231-969, eildonguesthouse@yahoo.co.uk, www.eildonguesthouse.co.uk, Jacqueline).

$$ Dionard Guest House, wrapped in a fine hedged-in garden just up Old Edinburgh Road from Ardconnel Street, has

Sleep Code

Abbreviations **(£1=about $1.60, country code: 44)**
S=Single, **D**=Double/Twin, **T**=Triple, **Q**=Quad, **b**=bathroom

Price Rankings

$$$ Higher Priced—Most rooms £90 or more
$$ Moderately Priced—Most rooms £60-90
$ Lower Priced—Most rooms £60 or less

Unless otherwise noted, credit cards are accepted at hotels and hostels—but not B&Bs, breakfast is included, and free Wi-Fi and/or a guest computer is generally available. Prices change; verify current rates online or by email. For the best prices, always book directly with the hotel.

cheerful common spaces and six pleasant slightly-faded rooms, including two on the ground floor (Db-£70-90 depending on size, in-room fridges, 39 Old Edinburgh Road, tel. 01463/233-557, www.dionardguesthouse.co.uk, enquiries@dionardguesthouse.co.uk, Brian and Doris—but they may be selling soon).

$$ Ardconnel House is a classic traditional place offering a nice, large guest lounge along with six spacious and comfortable rooms (Sb-£50, Db-£80, family room-£95, no children under 10, slightly cheaper off-season or for 3 or more nights, 21 Ardconnel Street, tel. 01463/240-455, www.ardconnel-inverness.co.uk, ardconnel@gmail.com, John and Elizabeth).

$$ Ryeford Guest House is a decent value, with six flowery rooms and piles of teddy bears (Sb-£47, Db-£74, Tb-£111, vegetarian breakfast available, small twin room #1 in back has fine garden view, Wi-Fi in front lounge, above Market Brae steps, go left on Ardconnel Terrace to #21, tel. 01463/242-871, www.scotland-inverness.co.uk/ryeford, joananderson@uwclub.net, Joan and George Anderson).

$$ Craigside Lodge B&B has five large rooms with tasteful modern flair. Guests share an inviting sunroom and a cozy lounge with a great city view (Sb-£45, Db-£75, just above Castle Street at 4 Gordon Terrace, tel. 01463/231-576, www.craigsideguesthouse.co.uk, enquiries@craigsideguesthouse.co.uk, Paul and Mandy).

$ Crown Hotel Guest House has six clean, bright rooms and an enjoyable breakfast room (Sb-£40, Db-£60, family room, lounge, 19 Ardconnel Street, tel. 01463/231-135, www.crownhotel-inverness.co.uk, reservations@crownhotel-inverness.co.uk, friendly Catriona—pronounced "Katrina"—Barbour).

Across the River: **$$ Castle View Guest House** sits right along the River Ness at the Ness Bridge—and, true to its name, it owns smashing views of the castle. Its eight rooms (half with views) are colorfully furnished, and the place feels a bit more urban than the traditional B&Bs listed earlier (Db-£80-90, 2a Ness Walk, tel. 01463/241-443, www.castleviewguesthouseinverness.com, enquiries@castleviewguesthouseinverness.com).

HOTELS

The following hotels may have rooms when my recommended B&Bs are full.

$$$ Heathmount Hotel's understated facade hides a chic retreat for comfort-seeking travelers. Its eight elegant rooms come with unique decoration, parking, and fancy extras (Sb-£90-110, Db-£105-160, rates depend on size, Kingsmill Road, tel. 01463/235-877, info@heathounthotel.com, www.heathmounthotel.com). Their restaurant is also recommended; see "Eating in Inverness."

$$$ Inverness Palace Hotel & Spa, a Best Western, is a fancy splurge with a pool, a gym, and 88 overpriced rooms. It's located right on the River Ness, across from the castle (rack rates: Db-£209-229, but you can often get a much better rate—even half-price—if you book a package deal on their website, even cheaper last-minute rooms, river/castle view rooms about £40 more than rest, breakfast extra, elevator, free parking, 8 Ness Walk, tel. 01463/223-243, www.invernesspalacehotel.co.uk, palace@miltonhotels.com).

$$$ Premier Inn Inverness Centre River Ness, along the River Ness, offers 99 predictable rooms. What the hotel lacks in charm and glitz it makes up for in affordable rates and location (Db-£60-120, £29 rooms not uncommon if booked online well in advance, air-con, elevator, parking-£10/day, 19-21 Huntly Street, tel. 01463/246-490, www.premierinn.com).

$$$ Mercure Inverness, right in the town center, has 118 rooms and feels less commercial than other chain hotels (Db-£125-175, much cheaper if booked in advance online, elevator, gym, parking-£4/day, entrance is at Church Street, tel. 0844/815-9006, www.mercureinverness.co.uk, sales.mercureinverness@jupiterhotels.co.uk).

$$$ Waterside Inverness, in a nice location along the River Ness, has 35 crisp, recently updated rooms and a river-view restaurant (Sb-£75, Db-£140, superior Db-£170, Qb-£190, call or check website for deals as low as Db-£85, 19 Ness Bank, tel. 01463/233-065, www.thewatersideinverness.co.uk, info@thewatersideinverness.co.uk).

HOSTELS ON CULDUTHEL ROAD

For funky and cheap dorm beds near the center and the recommended Castle Street restaurants, consider these friendly side-by-side hostels, geared toward younger travelers. They're about a 12-minute walk from the train station.

$ Inverness Student Hotel has 57 beds in nine rooms and

a laid-back lounge with a bay window overlooking the River Ness. The knowledgeable friendly staff welcomes any traveler over 18. Dorms are a bit grungy, but each bunk has its own playful name (bunk in dorm room-£17-18, price depends on season, breakfast-£2, free tea and coffee, pay laundry service, kitchen, 8 Culduthel Road, tel. 01463/236-556, www.invernessstudenthotel.com, info@invernessstudenthotel.com).

$ Bazpackers Hostel, a stone's throw from the castle, has a quieter, more private feel and 20 beds in basic dorms (bunk in dorm room-£17-19, D-£44, cheaper Oct-May, linens provided, reception open 7:30-23:00 but available 24 hours, no curfew, pay laundry service, 4 Culduthel Road, tel. 01463/717-663, www.bazpackershostel.co.uk). They also rent a small apartment nearby (£100, sleeps up to 4).

Eating in Inverness

You'll find a lot of traditional Highland fare—game, fish, lamb, and beef. Reservations are smart at most of these places, especially on summer weekends.

NEAR THE B&Bs, ON OR NEAR CASTLE STREET

The first three eateries line Castle Street, facing the back of the castle.

Café 1 serves up high-quality modern Scottish and international cuisine with trendy, chic bistro flair. This popular place fills up on weekends, so it's smart to call ahead (£13-22 main courses, lunch and early-bird dinner specials until 18:45, open Mon-Fri 12:00-14:30 & 17:00-21:30, Sat from 12:30 & 18:00, closed Sun, 75 Castle Street, tel. 01463/226-200, www.cafe1.net).

Number 27 has a straightforward crowd-pleasing menu that offers something for everyone—burgers, pastas, and more. The food is surprisingly elegant for this price range (£9-16 main courses, £5-9 lunches, daily 12:00-21:00, generous portions, local ales on tap, noisy bar up front not separated from restaurant in back, 27 Castle Street, tel. 01463/241-999).

La Tortilla Asesina has Spanish tapas, including spicy king prawns (the house specialty). It's an appealing, colorfully tiled, and vivacious dining option that feels like Spain (£3-7 cold and hot tapas—three make a meal, handy combination lunches, daily 12:00-22:00, 99 Castle Street, tel. 01463/709-809).

The recommended **Heathmount Hotel** serves good food in their quiet dining room (£9-18 meals, Mon-Fri 12:00-14:30 & 17:00-22:00, Sat-Sun 12:30-21:30, 5-minute walk down Argyle Street to Kingsmills Road, tel. 01463/235-877).

IN THE TOWN CENTER

The Mustard Seed serves Scottish food with a modern twist in an old church with a river view. It's pricey, but worth considering for a nice lively-at-lunch, mellow-at-dinner meal. Ask for a seat on the balcony if the weather is cooperating. Reservations are essential on weekends (£9 lunch specials, £13 early-bird specials before 19:00, £15-20 dinners, daily 12:00-15:00 & 17:30-22:00, on the corner of Bank and Fraser Streets, 16 Fraser Street, tel. 01463/220-220, www.mustardseedrestaurant.co.uk).

Hootananny mixes an energetic pub and live music with Scottish staples like lamb stovies (stew) and cullen skink (fish chowder). It's got a great join-in-the-fun vibe at night (£6-8 lunches, £9-10 dinners, food served Mon-Sat 12:00-15:00 & 17:00-20:30, Sun 17:00-21:30 only; see "Nightlife in Inverness," earlier).

Aspendos serves up freshly prepared, delicious Turkish dishes in a spacious, exuberantly decorated dining room (£12-15 main courses, daily 12:00-22:00, 26 Queensgate, tel. 01463/711-950).

Picnic: The **Marks & Spencer** Food Hall is best (you can't miss it—on the main pedestrian mall near the Market Brae steps at the corner of the big Eastgate Shopping Centre; Mon-Sat 8:00-18:00, Thu until 20:00, Sun 11:00-17:00, tel. 01463/224-844). There's a simpler **Co-op** market a few blocks away (daily 6:00-22:00, 59 Church Street).

ACROSS THE RIVER

Rocpool Restaurant is a hit with locals and good for a splurge. Owner/chef Steven Devlin serves creative modern European food in a sleek—and often crowded—chocolate/pistachio dining room. Reserve ahead or be sorry (£16 lunch specials, £18 early-bird weekday special until 18:45, £13-24 dinners; open Mon-Sat 12:00-14:30 & 17:45-22:00, closed Sun; across Ness Bridge from TI at 1 Ness Walk, tel. 01463/717-274, www.rocpoolrestaurant.com).

River House, a classy, sophisticated, but unstuffy riverside place, is the brainchild of Cornishman Alfie—who prides himself on melding the seafood know-how of both Cornwall and Scotland with a bit of Mediterranean flair. Reserve ahead for this small popular splurge (£18-21 main courses, Mon-Sat 17:30-21:30, Fri-Sat also 12:00-14:00, closed Mon off-season and Sun year-round, 1 Greig Street, tel. 01463/222-033, www.riverhouseinverness.co.uk).

The Kitchen Brasserie is the sister restaurant of The Mustard Seed (directly across the river). Equally good and popular, they serve fantastic homemade comfort food—pizza, pasta, and burgers—in an ultra-modern townhouse (£8 lunch specials, £13 early-bird special until 19:00, £10-16 dinners, daily 12:00-15:00 & 17:00-22:00, 15 Huntly Street, tel. 01463/259-119, www.kitchenrestaurant.co.uk).

Inverness Connections

From Inverness by Train to: Edinburgh (every 1-2 hours, 3.5-4 hours, some with change in Perth), **Glasgow** (11/day, 3 hours, 4 direct, others change in Perth). The Calendonian Sleeper provides overnight service to **London** (www.sleeper.scot). Train info: tel. 0345-748-4950, www.nationalrail.co.uk.

By Bus: For destinations in western Scotland, you'll first head for **Fort William** (bus #19 or #919, 7-9/day, 2 hours). For connections onward to **Oban** (figure 4 hours total) or **Glencoe** (3 hours total), see "Fort William Connections" on page 929. Inverness is also connected by direct bus to **Edinburgh** (about hourly, 4-hour express #M90 or 5-hour #M91 with many stops) and **Glasgow** (express bus #G10, 5/day, 3.5 hours, additional options with Perth transfer). These buses are run by Scottish Citylink; for schedules, see www.citylink.co.uk. Tickets are sold in advance online, by phone at tel. 0871-266-3333, or in person at the Inverness bus station (daily 7:45-18:15, baggage storage, 2 blocks from train station on Margaret Street, tel. 01463/233-371). For bus travel to England, check National Express (www.nationalexpress.com) or Megabus (http://uk.megabus.com).

ROUTE TIPS FOR DRIVERS

Inverness to Edinburgh (160 miles, 3.25 hours): Leaving Inverness, follow signs to the A-9 (south, toward Perth). If you haven't seen the Culloden Battlefield yet (described later), it's an easy detour: Just as you leave Inverness, head four miles east off the A-9 on the B-9006. Back on the A-9, it's a wonderfully speedy, scenic highway (A-9, M-90, A-90) all the way to Edinburgh.

To Oban or Glencoe: See page 929.

Near Inverness

Inverness puts you in the heart of the Highlands, within easy striking distance of a gaggle of famous and worthwhile sights: Commune with the Scottish soul at the historic Culloden Battlefield, where British history reached a turning point. Wonder at three mysterious Neolithic cairns, which remind visitors that Scotland's history goes back even before Braveheart. And enjoy a homey country castle at Cawdor. Loch Ness—with its elusive monster—is another popular and easy day trip.

CULLODEN BATTLEFIELD

Jacobite troops under Bonnie Prince Charlie were defeated at Culloden (kuh-LAW-dehn) by supporters of the Hanover dynasty (King George II's family) in 1746. Sort of the "Scottish Alamo," this last major land battle fought on British soil spelled the end of Jacobite resistance and the beginning of the clan chiefs' fall from power. Wandering the desolate, solemn battlefield, you sense that something terrible occurred here. Locals still bring white roses and speak of "The '45" (as Bonnie Prince Charlie's entire campaign is called) as if it just happened. The battlefield at Culloden and its high-tech visitors center together are worth ▲▲▲.

Orientation to Culloden

Cost and Hours: £11, £5 guidebook, daily April-Oct 9:00-17:30, June-Aug until 18:00, Nov-Dec and Feb-March 10:00-16:00, closed Jan, café, tel. 01463/796-090, www.nts.org.uk/culloden.

Tours: The good included **audioguide** leads you through the outdoor areas, using GPS to inform you about important sites on the battlefield (pick up before 17:00 at end of indoor exhibit, earlier off-season).

Getting There: It's a 15-minute **drive** east of Inverness. Follow signs to *Aberdeen*, then *Culloden Moor*—the B-9006 takes you right there (well-signed on the right-hand side). Parking is £2. Public **buses** leave from Inverness' Queensgate Street and drop you off in front of the entrance (£5 round-trip ticket, bus #8C or #8A, roughly hourly—none on Sun, 40 minutes, ask at TI for route/schedule updates). A **taxi** costs around £10-15 one-way.

Length of This Tour: Allow 2-2.5 hours.

Background

The Battle of Culloden (April 16, 1746) marks the steep decline of the Scottish Highland clans and the start of years of repression of Scottish culture by the English. It was the culmination of a year's worth of battles, and at the center of it all was the charismatic, enigmatic Bonnie Prince Charlie (1720-1788).

Charles Edward Stuart, from his first breath, was raised with a single purpose—to restore his family to the British throne. His grandfather was King James II (VII of Scotland), deposed in 1688 by the English Parliament for his tyranny and pro-Catholic bias. The Stuarts remained in exile in France and Italy until 1745, when young Charlie crossed the Channel from France to retake the throne in the name of his father (James VIII and III to his supporters). He landed on the west coast of Scotland and rallied support for the Jacobite cause. Though Charles was not Scottish-born, he was the rightful heir directly down the line from Mary, Queen of Scots—and so many Scots joined the Stuart family's rebellion out of resentment at being ruled by a foreign king (English royalty of German descent—though they were distantly related to Mary, Queen of Scots, too).

Bagpipes droned, and "Bonnie" (handsome) Charlie led an army of 2,000 tartan-wearing Gaelic-speaking Highlanders across Scotland, seizing Edinburgh. They picked up other supporters of the Stuarts from the Lowlands and from England. Now 6,000 strong, they marched south toward London—quickly advancing as far as Derby, just 125 miles from the capital—and King George II made plans to flee the country. But anticipated support for the Jacobites failed to materialize in the numbers they were hoping for (both in England and from France). The Jacobites had so far been victorious in their battles against the Hanoverian government forces, but the odds now turned against them. Charles retreated to the Scottish Highlands, where many of his men knew the terrain and might gain an advantage when outnumbered. The English government troops followed closely on his heels.

Against the advice of his best military strategist, Charles' army faced the Hanoverian forces at Culloden Moor on flat barren terrain that was unsuited to the Highlanders' guerrilla tactics. The Jacobites—many of them brandishing only broadswords, targes (wooden shields covered in leather and studs), and dirks (long daggers)—were mowed down by King George's cannons and horsemen. In less than an hour, the government forces routed the Jacobite army, but that was just the start. They spent the next weeks methodically hunting down ringleaders and sympathizers (and many others in the Highlands who had nothing to do with the battle), ruthlessly killing, imprisoning, and banishing thousands.

Charles fled with a £30,000 price on his head (an equivalent of millions of today's pounds). He escaped to the Isle of Skye, hidden by a woman named Flora MacDonald (her grave is on the Isle of Skye, and her statue is outside Inverness Castle). Flora dressed Charles in women's clothes and passed him off as her maid. Later, Flora was arrested and thrown in the Tower of London before being released and treated like a celebrity.

Charles escaped to France. He spent the rest of his life wandering Europe trying to drum up support to retake the throne. He drifted through short-lived romantic affairs and alcohol, and died in obscurity, without an heir, in Rome.

Though usually depicted as a battle of the Scottish versus the English, in truth Culloden was a civil war between two opposing dynasties: Stuart (Charlie) and Hanover (George). In fact, about one-fifth of the government's troops were Scottish (joined by many Germans, Swiss, and Dutch), and several redcoat deserters fought along with the Jacobites. However, as the history has faded into lore, the battle has come to be remembered as a Scottish-versus-English standoff—or, in the parlance of the Scots, the Highlanders versus the Strangers.

The Battle of Culloden was the end of 60 years of Jacobite rebellions, the last major battle fought on British soil, and the final stand of the Highlanders. From then on, clan chiefs were deposed; kilts, tartans, and bagpipes were outlawed; and farmers were cleared off their ancestral land, replaced by more-profitable sheep. Scottish culture would never recover from the events of the campaign called "The '45."

Self-Guided Tour

Culloden's visitors center, opened in 2008, is a state-of-the-art £10 million facility. The ribbon was cut by two young local men, each descended from soldiers who fought in the battle (one from either side). On the way up to the door, look under your feet at the memorial stones for fallen soldiers and clans, mostly purchased by their American and Canadian descendants. Your tour takes you through two sections: the exhibit and the actual battlefield.

The Exhibit

The initial part of the exhibit provides you with some background. As you pass the ticket desk, note the **family tree** of Bonnie Prince Charlie ("Charles Edward Stuart") and George II, who were distant cousins. Next is the first of the exhibit's shadowy-figure **touchscreens,** which connect you with historical figures who give you details from both the Hanoverian and Jacobite perspectives. A **map** shows the other power struggles happening in and around Europe, putting this fight for political control of Britain in a wider context. This battle was no small regional skirmish, but rather a key part of a larger struggle between Britain and its neighbors, primarily France, for control over trade and colonial

power. In the display case are **medals** from the early 1700s, made by both sides as propaganda.

From here, your path through this building is cleverly designed to echo the course of the Jacobite army. Your short march gets under way as Charlie sails from France to Scotland, then finagles the support of Highland clan chiefs. As he heads south with his army to take London, you, too, are walking south. Along the way, maps show the movement of troops, and wall panels cover the buildup to the attack, as seen from both sides. Note the clever division of information: To the left and in red is the story of the "government" (a.k.a. Hanoverians/Whigs/English, led by the Duke of Cumberland); to the right, in blue, is the Jacobites' perspective (Prince Charlie and his Highlander/French supporters).

But you, like Charlie, don't make it to London—in the dark room at the end, you can hear Jacobite commanders arguing over whether to retreat back to Scotland. Pessimistic about their chances of receiving more French support, they decide to U-turn, and so do you. Heading back up north, you'll get some insight into some of the strategizing that went on behind the scenes.

By the time you reach the end of the hall, it's the night before the battle. Round another bend into a dark passage, and listen to the voices of the anxious troops. While the English slept soundly in their tents (recovering from celebrating the Duke's 25th birthday), the scrappy and exhausted Jacobite Highlanders struggled through the night to reach the battlefield (abandoning their plan of a surprise night attack at Nairn and instead retreating back toward Inverness).

At last the two sides meet. As you wait outside the theater for the next showing, study the chart depicting how the forces were arranged on the battlefield. Once inside the theater, you'll soon be surrounded by the views and sounds of a windswept moor. An impressive four-minute **360° movie** projects the reenacted battle with you right in the center of the action (the violence is realistic; young kids should probably sit this one out). If it hasn't hit you already, the movie drives home just how outmatched the Jacobites were.

Leave the movie, then enter the last room. Here you'll find **period weapons,** including ammunition and artifacts found on the battlefield, as well as **historical depictions** of the battle. You'll also find a section describing the detective work required to piece together the story from historical evidence. On the far end is a huge map with narration explaining the combat you've just experienced while giving you a bird's-eye view of the field through which you're about to roam.

The Battlefield

Collect your free **audioguide** and go outside. From the back wall of the visitors center, survey the battlefield. In the foreground is a cottage used as a makeshift hospital during the conflict. To the east/right (south of the River Nairn) is the site that Lord George Murray originally chose for the action. In the end, he failed to convince Prince Charlie of its superiority, and the battle was held here—with disastrous consequences. Although not far from Culloden, the River Nairn site was miles away tactically, and things might have turned out differently for the Jacobites had the battle taken place there instead.

Bear left up the path, toward the battlefield. Your GPS guide knows where you are, and the attendant will give you directions on where to start. As you walk along the path, stop each time you hear the "ping" sound (if you keep going, you'll confuse the guide). The basic audioguide has 10 stops—including the Jacobite front line, the Hanoverian front line, and more—and takes a minimum of 30 minutes, which is enough for most people. At the third stop, you have the option of detouring along a larger loop (6 extra stops, mostly focusing on the Jacobite line—figure another 30 minutes minimum) before rejoining the basic route. Each stop has additional information on everything from the Brown Bess musket to who was standing on what front line—how long this part of the tour takes depends on how much you want to hear. Notice how uneven and boggy the ground is in parts, and imagine trying to run across this hummocky terrain with all your gear, toward almost-certain death.

INVERNESS & LOCH NESS

As you pass by the **mass graves,** marked by small headstones, realize that entire clans fought, died, and were buried together. (The fallen were identified by the clan badge on their caps.) The Mackintosh grave alone was 77 yards long.

When you've finished your walking tour, reenter the hall, return your audioguide, then catch the last part of the exhibit, which covers the aftermath of the battle. As you leave the building, hang a left to see the wall of **protruding bricks,** each representing a soldier who died. The handful of Hanoverian casualties are on the left (about 50); the rest of the long wall's raised bricks represent the multitude of dead Jacobites (about 1,500).

If you're having trouble grasping the significance of this battle, play a game of "What if?" If Bonnie Prince Charlie had persevered on this campaign and taken the throne, he likely wouldn't have plunged Britain into the Seven Years' War with France (his ally). And increased taxes on either side of that war led directly to the French and American revolutions. So if the Jacobites had won...the American colonies might still be part of the British Empire today.

CLAVA CAIRNS

Scotland is littered with reminders of prehistoric peoples—especially in Orkney and along the coast of the Moray Firth—but the Clava Cairns, worth ▲, are among the best-preserved, most interesting, and easiest to reach. You'll find them nestled in the spooky countryside just beyond Culloden Battlefield. These "Balnauran of Clava" are Neolithic burial chambers dating from 3,000 to 4,000 years ago. Although they appear to be just some giant piles of rocks in a sparsely forested clearing, a closer look will help you appreciate the prehistoric logic behind them. (The site is well-explained by informative plaques.) There are three structures: a central "ring cairn" with an open space in the center but no access to it, flanked by two "passage cairns," which were once covered. The entrance shaft in each passage cairn lines up with the setting sun at the winter solstice. Each cairn is surrounded by a stone circle, and the entire ensemble is framed by evocative trees—injecting this site with even more mystery.

Cost and Hours: Free, always open.

Getting There: Just after passing Culloden Battlefield on the B-9006 (coming from Inverness), signs on the right point to *Clava Cairns.* Follow this twisty road to the free parking lot by the stones. You can also walk from Culloden Battlefield, but it's three miles round-trip and not very appealing (mostly along roads; the Inverness TI has maps). Skip the cairns if you don't have a car or if the weather is bad.

CAWDOR CASTLE

Homey, intimate, and worth ▲, this castle is still the residence of the Dowager (read: widow) Countess of Cawdor, a local aristocratic branch of the Campbell family. The castle's claim to fame is its connection to Shakespeare's *Macbeth,* in which the three witches correctly predict that the protagonist will be granted the title "Thane of Cawdor." The castle is not used as a setting in the play—which takes place in Inverness, 300 years before this castle was built—but Shakespeare's dozen or so references to "Cawdor" are enough for the marketing machine to kick in. Today, virtually nothing tangibly ties Cawdor to the Bard or to the real-life Macbeth. But even if you ignore the Shakespeare lore, the castle is worth a visit.

Cost and Hours: £10.50, good £5 guidebook explains the family and the rooms, May-Sept daily 10:00-17:30, closed Oct-April, tel. 01667/404-401, www.cawdorcastle.com.

Getting There: It's on the B-9090, just off the A-96, about 15 miles east of Inverness (6 miles beyond Culloden and the Clava Cairns). In recent years, public transportation to the castle has been nonexistent—but ask at the Inverness TI just in case it has resumed.

Visiting the Castle: The chatty, friendly docents (including Jean at the front desk, who can say "welcome" and "mind your head" in 60 different languages) give the castle an air of intimacy—most are residents of the neighboring village of Cawdor and act as though they're old friends with the Dowager Countess (many probably are). Entertaining posted explanations—written by the countess' late husband, the sixth Earl of Cawdor—bring the castle to life and make you wish you'd known the old chap. While many of today's castles are still residences for the aristocracy, Cawdor feels even more lived-in than the norm—you can imagine the Dowager

Countess stretching out in front of the fireplace with a good book. Notice her geraniums in every room.

Stops on the tour include a tapestry-laden bedroom and a "tartan passage" speckled with modern paintings. In another bedroom (just before the stairs back down) is a tiny pencil sketch by Salvador Dalí. Inside the base of the tower, near the end of the tour, is the castle's proud symbol: a holly tree dating from 1372. According to the beloved legend, a donkey leaned against this tree to mark the spot where the castle was to be built—which it was, around the tree. (The tree is no longer alive, but its withered trunk is still propped up in the same position. No word on the donkey.)

The **gardens,** included with the ticket, are also worth exploring, with some 18th-century linden trees, a hedge maze (not open to the public), and several surprising species (including sequoia and redwood). In May and June, the laburnum arbors drip with yellow blossoms.

The nine-hole **golf course** on the castle grounds is bigger than pitch-and-putt and fun even for nongolfers (£12.50/person).

Nearby: The close but remote-feeling **village of Cawdor**—with a few houses, a village shop, and a tavern—is also worth a look if you've got time to kill.

Loch Ness

I'll admit it: I had my zoom lens out and my eyes on the water. The local tourist industry thrives on the legend of the Loch Ness monster. It's a thrilling thought, and there have been several seemingly reliable "sightings" (by monks, police officers, and sonar imaging). But even if you ignore the monster stories, the loch is impressive: 23 miles long, less than a mile wide, 754 feet deep, and containing more water than all of the freshwater bodies of England and Wales combined. It's essentially the vast chasm of a fault line, filled with water. Whoa. I'm thankful the loch is in Scotland—where property laws make it extremely difficult to buy or build along its banks—and not in California.

Getting There: The Loch Ness sights are a 20-minute drive southwest of Inverness. To drive the full length of Loch Ness takes about 45 minutes. Fort William-bound buses #19 and #919 make stops at Urquhart Castle and Drumnadrochit (7-9/day, 35-40 minutes).

Inverness & Loch Ness

To Ullapool
To John O'Groats & Thurso (Orkney ferry)
A-835
Garve
Cromarty Firth
B-9163
Black Isle
A-832
To Forres & Aberdeen
Dingwall
Fort George
Nairn
Fortrose
Contin
A-9
A-96
Moray Firth
A-835
Littlemill
Culloden Battlefield
Cawdor Castle
A-939
Beauly Firth
Beauly
A-862
Inverness
B-9006
Clava Cairns
B-851
A-82
Daviot
Findhorn
Struy
HIGHLANDS
A-831
Dores
Moy
Loch Ness Monster Exhibits
Tomatin
Drumnadrochit
Urquart Castle
To Speyside Whisky Trail
A-9
Loch Ness
Telford Bridge
10 Kilometers
A-95
10 Miles
Invermoriston
Aviemore
A-82
Inverness
Scotland
Cairngorm Mountains
Caledonian Canal Visitors Centre
River Spey
Fort Augustus
Edinburgh
To Fort William, Glencoe & Oban
To Pitlochry & Edinburgh

Sights on Loch Ness

Loch Ness Monster Exhibits

In July of 1933, a couple swore that they saw a giant sea monster shimmy across the road in front of their car by Loch Ness. Within days, ancient legends about giant monsters in the lake (dating as far back as the sixth century) were revived—and suddenly everyone was spotting "Nessie" poke its head above the waters of Loch Ness. Further sightings and photographic "evidence" have bolstered the claim that there's something mysterious living in this unthinkably deep and murky lake. (Most sightings take place in the deepest part of the loch, near Urquhart Castle.) Most witnesses describe a waterbound di-

nosaur (resembling the real, but extinct, plesiosaur). Others cling to the slightly more plausible theory of a gigantic eel. And skeptics figure the sightings can be explained by a combination of reflections, boat wakes, and mass hysteria. The most famous photo of the beast (dubbed the "Surgeon's Photo") was later discredited—the "monster's" head was actually attached to a toy submarine. But that hasn't stopped various cryptozoologists from seeking photographic, sonar, and other proof.

And that suits the thriving local tourist industry just fine. The Nessie commercialization is so tacky that there are two different monster exhibits within 100 yards of each other, both in the town of Drumnadrochit. Each has a tour-bus parking lot and more square footage devoted to their kitschy shops than to the exhibits. The overpriced exhibits are actually quite interesting—even though they're tourist traps, they'll appease that small part of you that knows the *real* reason you wanted to see Loch Ness.

Loch Ness Centre & Exhibition: This exhibit—the better option of the two, and worth ▲—is headed by a naturalist who has spent many years researching lake ecology and scientific phenomena. With video presentations and special effects, this exhibit explains the geological and historical environment that bred the monster story, as well as the various searches that have been conducted. Refreshingly, it retains an air of healthy skepticism instead of breathless monster-chasing. It also has some artifacts related to the search, such as a hippo-foot ashtray used to fake monster footprints and the *Viperfish*—a harpoon-equipped submarine used in a 1969 Nessie search (£7.45, daily Easter-Oct 9:30-17:45, July-Aug until 18:45, Nov-Easter 10:00-16:15, last entry 45 minutes before closing, in the big stone mansion right on the main road to Inverness, tel. 01456/450-573, www.lochness.com).

Nessieland Castle Monster Centre: The other exhibit (up a side road closer to the town center, affiliated with a hotel) is less serious. It's basically a tacky high-school-quality photo report and a 30-minute *We Believe in the Loch Ness Monster* movie, which features credible-sounding locals explaining what they saw and a review of modern Nessie searches. (The most convincing reason for locals to believe: Look at the hordes of tourists around you.) It also has small exhibits on the area's history and on other "monsters" and hoaxes around the world (£6, daily May-Sept 9:00-19:00, Oct-April 9:00-17:00, tel. 01456/450-342, www.nessieland.co.uk).

▲Urquhart Castle

The ruins at Urquhart (UR-kurt), just up the loch from the Nessie exhibits, are gloriously situated with a view of virtually the entire lake.

Cost and Hours: £8.50, guidebook-£4, daily April-Sept

The Caledonian Canal

Two hundred million years ago, two tectonic plates collided, creating the landmass we know as Scotland and leaving a crevice of thin lakes slashing diagonally across the country. This Great Glen Fault, from Inverness to Oban, is easily visible on any map.

200 years ago, British engineer Thomas Telford connected the lakes with a series of canals so ships could avoid the long trip around the north of the country. The Caledonian Canal runs 62 miles from Scotland's east to west coasts; 22 miles of it is manmade. Telford's great feat of engineering took 19 years to complete, opening in 1822 at a cost of one million pounds. But bad timing made the canal a disaster commercially. Napoleon's defeat in 1815 meant that ships could sail the open seas more freely. And by the time the canal opened, commercial ships were too big for its 15-foot depths. Just a couple of decades after the Caledonian Canal opened, trains made the canal almost useless...except for Romantic Age tourism. From the time of Queen Victoria (who cruised the canal in 1873), the canal has been a popular tourist attraction. To this day the canal is a hit with vacationers, recreational boaters, and lock-keepers who compete for the best-kept lock.

The scenic drive from Inverness along the canal is entertaining, with Drumnadrochit (Nessie centers), Urquhart Castle, Fort Augustus (five locks), and Fort William (under Ben Nevis, with the eight-lock "Neptune's Staircase"). As you cross Scotland, you'll follow Telford's work—22 miles of canals and locks between three lochs, raising ships from sea level to 51 feet (Ness), 93 feet (Lochy), and 106 feet (Oich).

While Neptune's Staircase, a series of eight locks near Fort William, has been cleverly named to sound intriguing, the best lock stop is midway, at Fort Augustus, where the canal hits the south end of Loch Ness. In Fort Augustus, the **Caledonian Canal Visitor Centre,** three locks above the main road, gives a good rundown on Telford's work (see page 960). Stroll past several shops and eateries to the top for a fine view.

Seven miles north, in the town of **Invermoriston,** is another Telford structure: a stone bridge, dating from 1805, which spans the Morriston Falls as part of the original road. Look for a small parking lot just before the junction at A-82 and A-887, on your right as you drive from Fort Augustus. Carefully cross the A-82 and walk three minutes back the way you came. The bridge, which took eight years to build and is still in use, is on your right.

9:30-18:00, Oct 9:30-17:00, Nov-March 9:30-16:30, last entry 45 minutes before closing, café, tel. 01456/450-551, www.historic-scotland.gov.uk.

Visiting the Castle: The visitors center has a tiny exhibit with interesting castle artifacts and a good eight-minute film taking you on a sweep through a thousand years of tumultuous history—from St. Columba's visit to the castle's final destruction in 1692. The castle itself, while dramatically situated and fun to climb through, is a relatively empty shell. After its owners (who supported the crown) blew it up to keep the Jacobites from taking it, the largest medieval castle in Scotland (and the most important in the Highlands) wasn't considered worth rebuilding or defending, and was abandoned. Well-placed descriptive signs help you piece together this once-mighty fortress. As you walk toward the ruins, take a close look at the trebuchet (a working replica of one of the most destructive weapons of English King Edward I), and ponder how this giant slingshot helped Edward grab almost every castle in the country away from the native Scots.

Loch Ness Cruises

Cruises on Loch Ness are as popular as they are pointless. The lake is scenic, but far from Scotland's prettiest—and the time-consuming boat trips show you little more than what you'll see from the road. As it seems that Loch Ness cruises are a mandatory part of every "Highlands Highlights" day tour, there are several options, leaving from the top, bottom, and middle of the loch. The basic one-hour loop costs around £14 and includes views of Urquhart Castle and lots of legends and romantic history (Jacobite is the dominant outfit of the many cruise companies, www.jacobite.co.uk). I'd rather spend my time and money at Fort Augustus or Urquhart Castle.

▲Fort Augustus

Perhaps the most idyllic stop along the Caledonian Canal is the little lochside town of Fort Augustus. It was founded in the 1700s—before there was a canal here—as part of a series of garrisons and military roads built by the English to quell the Highland clansmen, even as the Stuarts kept trying to take the throne in London. Before then, there were no developed roads in the Highlands—and without roads, it's hard to keep indigenous people down.

From 1725 to 1733, the English built 250 miles of hard roads and 40 bridges to open up the region; Fort Augustus was a central Highlands garrison at the southern tip of Loch Ness, designed to awe clansmen. It was named for William Augustus, Duke of Cumberland—notorious for his role in destroying the clan way of life in the Highlands. (When there's no media and no photographs to get in the way, ethnic cleansing has little effect on one's reputation.)

Fort Augustus makes for a delightful stop if you're driving through the area. Parking is easy. There are plenty of B&Bs, charming eateries, and an inviting park along the town's five locks. You can still see the capstans, surviving from the days when the locks were cranked open by hand.

The fine little **Caledonian Canal Visitor Centre** nicely tells the story of the canal's construction (free, daily Easter-Oct, tel. 01320/366-493).

Eating in Fort Augustus: You can eat reasonably at eateries along the canal. Try **The Little Neuk,** a good café serving filled rolls and homemade soups. **The Lock Inn** and **The Bothy** are pubs with decent food, and the **Canalside Chip Shop** offers fish and chips. The only real grocery store in town is the gas station, next to the TI, which is a five-minute walk north from the canal just after crossing the River Oich (also housing the post office, a WC, and an ATM).

BRITAIN: PAST AND PRESENT

To fully appreciate the many fascinating sights you'll encounter in your travels, learn the basics of the sweeping story of this land and its people. (Generally speaking, the fascinating stories you'll hear from tour guides are not true...and the boring ones are.)

Regardless of the revolution we had nearly 240 years ago, many American travelers feel that they "go home" to Britain. This most popular tourist destination has a strange influence and power over us. The more you know of Britain's roots, the better you'll get in touch with your own.

This chapter starts with a once-over of Britain's illustrious history. It's speckled throughout with more in-depth information about current issues and this great country's future. For more information about Scottish history, see the Scotland chapter; for Welsh history see the Wales chapter.

British History

ORIGINS (2000 B.C.–A.D. 500)

When Julius Caesar landed on the misty and mysterious isle of Britain in 55 B.C., England entered the history books. He was met by primitive Celtic tribes whose druid priests made human sacrifices and worshipped trees. (Those Celts were themselves immigrants, who had earlier conquered the even more mysterious people who built Stonehenge.) The Romans eventually settled in England (A.D. 43) and set about building towns and roads and establishing their capital at Londinium (today's London).

But the Celtic natives—consisting of Gaels, Picts, and Scots—were not easily subdued. Around A.D. 60, Boadicea, a queen of the Isle's indigenous people, defied the Romans and burned Londinium before the revolt was squelched. Some decades later, the Romans built Hadrian's Wall near the Scottish border as protection against their troublesome northern neighbors. Even today, the Celtic language and influence are strongest in these far reaches of Britain.

Londinium became a bustling Roman river-and-sea trading port. The Romans built the original London Bridge and a city wall, encompassing one square mile, which set the city boundaries for 1,500 years. By A.D. 200, London was a thriving Latin-speaking capital of Roman-dominated England.

DARK AGES (500-1000)

As Rome fell, so fell Roman Britain—a victim of invaders and internal troubles. Barbarian tribes from Germany, Denmark, and northern Holland, called Angles, Saxons, and Jutes, swept through the southern part of the island, establishing Angle-land. These were the days of the real King Arthur, possibly a Christianized Roman general who fought valiantly—but in vain—against invading barbarians.

In 793, England was hit with the first of two centuries of savage invasions by barbarians from Norway, called the Vikings or Norsemen. King Alfred the Great (849-899) liberated London from Danish Vikings, reunited England, reestablished Christianity, and fostered learning. Nevertheless, for most of this 500-year period, the island was plunged into a dark age—wars, plagues, and poverty—lit only by the dim candle of a few learned Christian monks and missionaries trying to convert the barbarians. Today, visitors see little from this Anglo-Saxon period.

WARS WITH FRANCE, WARS OF THE ROSES (1000-1500)

Modern England began with yet another invasion. In 1066, William the Conqueror and his Norman troops crossed the English Channel from France. William crowned himself king in Westminster Abbey (where all subsequent coronations would take place). He began building the Tower of London, as well as Windsor Castle, which would become the residence of many monarchs to come.

Over the succeeding centuries, French-speaking kings would rule England, and English-speaking kings invaded France as the two budding nations define their modern borders. Richard the Lionheart (1157-1199) ruled as a French-speaking king who spent most of his energy on distant Crusades. This was the time of the legendary (and possibly real) Robin Hood, a bandit who robbed from the rich and gave to the poor—a populace that felt neglected by its francophone rulers. In 1215, King John (Richard's brother), under pressure from England's barons, was forced to sign the Magna Carta, establishing the principle that even kings must follow the rule of law.

London asserted itself as England's trade center. London Bridge—the famous stone version, topped with houses—was built (1209), and Old St. Paul's Cathedral was finished (1314).

Then followed two centuries of wars, chiefly the Hundred Years' War with France (1337-1443), in which France's Joan of Arc rallied the French to drive English forces back across the Channel. In 1348, the Black Death (bubonic plague) killed half of London's population.

In the 1400s, noble families duked it out for the crown. The York and Lancaster families fought the Wars of the Roses, so-called because of the white and red flowers the combatants chose as their symbols. Rife with battles and intrigues, and with kings, nobles, and ladies imprisoned and executed in the Tower, it's a wonder the country survived its rulers.

THE TUDOR RENAISSANCE (1500s)

England was finally united by the "third-party" Tudor family. Henry VIII, a Tudor, was England's Renaissance king. Powerful, charismatic, handsome, athletic, highly sexed, a poet, a scholar, and a musician, Henry VIII thrust England onto the world stage. He was also arrogant, cruel, gluttonous, and paranoid. He went through six wives in 40 years, divorcing, imprisoning, or executing them when they no longer suited his needs. (To keep track of each one's fate, British kids learn this rhyme: "Divorced, beheaded, died; divorced, beheaded, survived.")

When the Pope refused to grant Henry a divorce so he could marry his mistress Anne Boleyn, Henry "divorced" England from the Catholic Church. He established the Protestant Church of England (the Anglican Church), thus setting in motion a century of bitter Protestant/Catholic squabbles. Henry's own daughter, "Bloody" Mary, was a staunch Catholic who presided over the burning of hundreds of prominent Protestants. (For more on Henry VIII, see the sidebar on page 106.)

After Mary came another of Henry's daughters (by Anne Boleyn)—Queen Elizabeth I. She reigned for 45 years, making England a great trading and naval power (defeating the Spanish Armada) and treading diplomatically over the Protestant/Catholic divide. Elizabeth presided over a cultural renaissance known (not surprisingly) as the "Elizabethan Age." Playwright William Shakespeare moved from Stratford-upon-Avon to London, beginning a remarkable career as the earth's greatest playwright. Sir Francis Drake circumnavigated the globe. Sir Walter Raleigh explored the Americas, and Sir Francis Bacon pioneered the scientific method. London's population swelled.

But Elizabeth—the "Virgin Queen"—never married or produced an heir. So the English Parliament invited Scotland's King

James (Elizabeth's first cousin twice removed) to inherit the English throne. The two nations have been tied together ever since, however fitfully.

KINGS VS. PARLIAMENT (1600s)

The enduring quarrel between England's kings and Parliament's nobles finally erupted into the Civil War (1642). The war pitted (roughly speaking) the Protestant Puritan Parliament against the Catholic aristocracy. Parliament forces under Oliver Cromwell defeated—and beheaded—King Charles I. After Cromwell died, Parliament invited Charles' son to take the throne—the "restoration of the monarchy." To emphasize the point, Cromwell's corpse was subsequently exhumed and posthumously beheaded.

This turbulent era was followed by back-to-back disasters—the Great Plague of 1665 (which killed 100,000) and the Great Fire of 1666 (which incinerated London). London was completely rebuilt in stone, centered on New St. Paul's Cathedral built by Christopher Wren. With a population over 200,000, London was now Europe's largest city. At home, Isaac Newton watched an apple fall from a tree, leading him to the mysterious force of gravity.

In the war between kings and Parliament, Parliament finally got the last word when it deposed Catholic James II and imported the Dutch monarchs William and Mary in 1688, guaranteeing a Protestant succession.

COLONIAL EXPANSION (1700s)

Britain grew as a naval superpower, colonizing and trading with all parts of the globe. Eventually, Britannia ruled the waves, exploiting the wealth of India, Africa, and Australia. (And America...at least until they lost its most important colony when those ungrateful Yanks revolted in 1776 in the "American War.") Throughout the century, the country was ruled by the German Hanover family, including four kings named George.

The "Georgian Era" was one of great wealth. London's population was now half a million, and one in seven Brits lived in London. The nation's first daily newspapers hit the streets. The cultural scene was refined: painters (like William Hogarth, Joshua Reynolds, and Thomas Gainsborough), theater (with actors like David Garrick), music (Handel's *Messiah*), and literature (Samuel Johnson's dictionary). Scientist James Watt's steam engines laid the groundwork for a coming Industrial Revolution.

In 1789, the French Revolution erupted, sparking decades of war between France and Britain. Britain finally prevailed in the early 1800s, when Admiral Horatio Nelson defeated Napoleon's fleet at the Battle of Trafalgar and the Duke of Wellington stomped

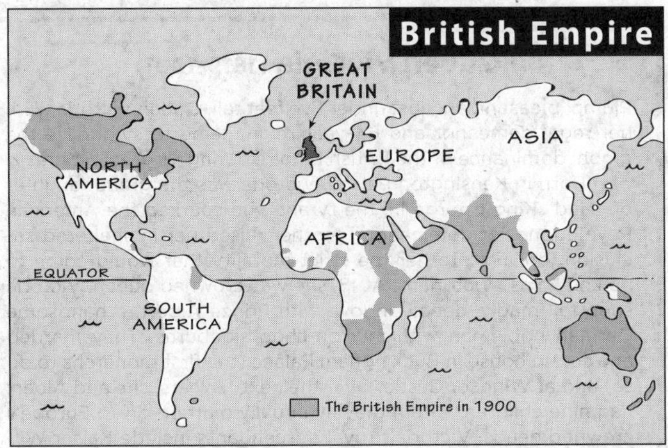

Napoleon at Waterloo. (Nelson and Wellington are memorialized by many arches, columns, and squares throughout England.)

By war's end, Britain had emerged as Europe's top power.

VICTORIAN GENTILITY AND THE INDUSTRIAL REVOLUTION (1800s)

Britain reigned supreme, steaming into the Industrial Age with her mills, factories, coal mines, gas lights, and trains. By century's end, there was electricity, telephones, and the first Underground.

In 1837, eighteen-year-old Victoria became queen. She ruled for 64 years, presiding over an era of unprecedented wealth, peace, and middle-class ("Victorian") values. Britain was at its zenith of power, with a colonial empire that covered one-fifth of the world.

Meanwhile, there was another side to Britain's era of superiority and industrial might. A generation of Romantic poets (William Wordsworth, John Keats, Percy Shelley, and Lord Byron) longed for the innocence of nature. Jane Austen and the Brontë sisters wrote romantic tales about the landed gentry. Painters like J. M. W. Turner and William Constable immersed themselves in nature to paint moody landscapes.

The gritty modern world was emerging. Popular novelist Charles Dickens brought literature to the masses, educating them about Britain's harsh social and economic realities. Rudyard Kipling critiqued the colonial system. Charles Darwin questioned the very nature of humanity when he articulated the principles of natural selection and evolution. Jack the Ripper, a serial killer of prostitutes, terrorized east London and was never caught. Not even by Sherlock Holmes—a fictional detective living at 221B Baker Street who solved fictional crimes that the real Scotland Yard couldn't.

Queen Victoria (1819-1901)

Plump, pleasant, and just under five feet tall, Queen Victoria, with her regal demeanor and 64-year reign, came to symbolize the global dominance of the British Empire during its greatest era.

Born in Kensington Palace, Victoria was the granddaughter of "Mad" King George III, the tyrant who sparked the American Revolution. Her domineering mother raised her in sheltered seclusion, drilling into her the strict morality that would come to be known as "Victorian." At 18, she was crowned queen. Victoria soon fell madly, deeply in love with Prince Albert, a handsome German nobleman with mutton-chop sideburns. They married and set up house in Buckingham Palace (the first monarchs to do so) and at Windsor Castle. Over the next 17 years, she and Albert had nine children, whom they eventually married off to Europe's crowned heads. Victoria's royal descendants include Kaiser Wilhelm II of Germany (who started World War I); the current monarchs of Spain, Norway, Sweden, and Denmark; and England's Queen Elizabeth II, who is Victoria's great-great-granddaughter.

Victoria and Albert promoted the arts and sciences, organizing a world's fair in Hyde Park (1851) that showed off London as *the* global capital. Just as important, they were role models for an entire nation; this loving couple influenced several generations with their wholesome middle-class values. Though Victoria is often depicted as dour and stuffy—she supposedly coined the phrase, "We are not amused"—in private she was warm, easy to laugh, plainspoken, thrifty, and modest, with a talent for sketching and journal writing.

In 1861, Victoria's happy domestic life ended. Her mother's death was soon followed by the sudden loss of her beloved Albert to typhoid fever. A devastated Victoria dressed in black for the funeral—and for her remaining 40 years never again wore any other color. She hunkered down at Windsor with her family. Critics complained she was an absentee monarch. Rumors swirled that her kilt-wearing servant, John Brown, was not only her close friend but also her lover. For two decades, she rarely appeared in public.

Over time, Victoria emerged from mourning to assume her role as one of history's first constitutional monarchs. She had

WORLD WARS AND RECOVERY (20th CENTURY)

The 20th century was not kind to Britain. Two world wars and economic struggles whittled Britain down from a world empire to an island chain struggling to compete in a global economy.

In World War I, Britain joined France and other allies to battle Germany in trench warfare. A million British men died. Meanwhile, after decades of rebellion, Ireland finally gained its independence—except for the Protestant-leaning Northern Ireland, which remained tied to Britain. This division of the Emerald Isle

inherited a crown with little real power. But beyond her ribbon-cutting ceremonial duties, Victoria influenced events behind the scenes. She studiously learned politics from powerful mentors (especially Prince Albert and two influential prime ministers) and kept well-informed on what Parliament was doing. Thanks to Victoria's personal modesty and honesty, the British public never came to disdain the monarchy, as happened in other countries.

Victoria gracefully oversaw the peaceful transfer of power from the nobles to the people. The secret ballot was introduced during her reign, and ordinary workers acquired voting rights (though this applied only to men—Victoria opposed women's suffrage). The traditional Whigs and Tories morphed into today's Liberal and Conservative parties. Victoria personally promoted progressive charities, and even paid for her own crown.

Most of all, Victoria became the symbol of the British Empire, which she saw as a way to protect and civilize poorer peoples. Britain enjoyed peace at home, while its colonial possessions included India, Australia, Canada, and much of Africa. Because it was always daytime someplace under Victoria's rule, it was often said that "the sun never sets on the British Empire."

The Victorian era saw great changes. The Industrial Revolution was in full swing. When Victoria was born, there were no trains. By 1842, when she took her first train trip (with much fanfare), railroads crisscrossed Europe. The telegraph, telephone, and newspapers further laced the world together. The popular arts flourished—it was the era of Dickens novels, Tennyson poems, Sherlock Holmes stories, Gilbert and Sullivan operettas, and Pre-Raphaelite paintings. Economically, Britain saw the rise of the middle class. Middle-class morality dominated—family, hard work, honor, duty, and sexual modesty.

By the end of her reign, Victoria was wildly popular, both for her personality and as a focus for British patriotism. At her Golden Jubilee (1887), she paraded past adoring throngs to Westminster Abbey. For her Diamond Jubilee (1897), she did the same at St. Paul's Cathedral. Cities, lakes, and military medals were named for her. When she passed away in 1901, it was literally the end of an era.

would result in decades of bitter strife, protests, and terrorist attacks known as "The Troubles."

In the 1920s, London was home to a flourishing literary scene, including T. S. Eliot (American-turned-British), Virginia Woolf, and E. M. Forster. In 1936, the country was rocked and scandalized when King Edward VIII abdicated to marry a divorced American commoner, Wallis Simpson. He was succeeded by his brother, George VI—"Bertie" of *The King's Speech* fame, and father of Queen Elizabeth II.

In World War II, the Nazi Blitz (aerial bombing campaign) reduced much of London to rubble, sending residents into Tube stations for shelter and the government into a fortified bunker (now the Churchill War Rooms). Britain was rallied through its darkest hour by two leaders: Prime Minister Winston Churchill, a remarkable orator, and King George VI, who overcame a persistent stutter. Amid the chaos of war, the colonial empire began to dwindle to almost nothing, and Britain emerged from the war as a shell of its former superpower self.

The postwar recovery began, aided by the United States. Many cheap concrete (ugly) buildings rose from the rubble.

Culturally, Britain remained world-class. Oxford professor J. R. R. Tolkien wrote *The Lord of the Rings* and his friend C. S. Lewis wrote *The Chronicles of Narnia.* In the 1960s, "Swinging London" became a center for rock music, film, theater, youth culture, and Austin Powers-style joie de vivre. America was conquered by a "British Invasion" of rock bands (The Beatles, The Rolling Stones, and The Who, followed later by Led Zeppelin, Elton John, David Bowie, and others), and James Bond ruled the box office.

The 1970s brought massive unemployment, labor strikes, and recession. A conservative reaction followed in the 1980s and '90s, led by Prime Minister Margaret Thatcher—the "Iron Lady." As proponents of traditional Victorian values—community, family, hard work, thrift, and trickle-down economics—the Conservatives took a Reaganesque approach to Britain's serious social and economic problems. They cut government subsidies to old-fashioned heavy industries (closing many factories, earning working-class ire), as they tried to nudge Britain toward a more modern economy.

In 1981, the world was captivated by the spectacle of Prince Charles marrying Lady Diana in St. Paul's Cathedral. Their children, Princes William and Harry, grew up in the media spotlight, and when Diana died in a car crash (1997), the nation—and the world—mourned.

The 1990s saw Britain finally emerging from decades of economic stagnation and social turmoil. An energized nation prepared for the new millennium.

EARLY 2000s

London celebrated the millennium with a new Ferris wheel (the London Eye), the Millennium Bridge, and the Millennium Dome exhibition (now "The O2"). In 2002, Queen Elizabeth II celebrated her 50-year Jubilee.

After two decades of Conservative politics, Britain was now ruled by a Labour (left-of-center) government under Prime Minister Tony Blair. Labour began shoring up a social-service system (health care, education, minimum wage) undercut by years of Conservative rule. But Blair's popularity was undermined when he joined the US invasion of Iraq. On the morning of July 7 ("7/7") in 2005, London's commuters were rocked by four terrorist bombs that killed dozens across the city. In subsequent years, Britain has had numerous terrorist plots that either caused destruction or were foiled by police.

Thankfully, one hot spot—Northern Ireland, plagued for decades by the "Troubles"—was healed. In the spring of 2007, the previously unthinkable happened when leaders of the ultra-nationalist party sat down with those of the ultra-unionist party. An agreement was reached and, after almost 40 years, the British Army withdrew.

In 2008, Britain suffered mightily in the global recession. The economy shrank more than 6 percent and faced a huge budget deficit. British voters turned for answers to the Conservative party under David Cameron, who was elected prime minister in 2010. Cameron's approach was "austerity"—cut government spending, raise the national sales tax, eliminate half a million public-sector jobs, and slash spending on unemployment benefits, public housing, police, and funding for the arts and the BBC. The question of whether these policies worked or hurt the economy has been a topic of great debate.

In 2012, in a one-two punch of festivity, the Brits hosted two huge events: the London Olympics and the Queen's Diamond Jubilee. The flurry of investment has left the country looking better than ever. This was just the latest of decades of renovation that have turned former urban wastelands and industrial waterfronts into hip, thriving people zones.

Britain Today

The Britain you visit today is vibrant and alive. It's smaller, and no longer the superpower it once was, but it's still a cultural and economic powerhouse.

WHAT'S SO GREAT ABOUT BRITAIN?

Think of it. At its peak in the mid-1800s, Britain owned one-fifth of the world and accounted for more than half the planet's industrial output. Today, the Empire is down to the Isle of Britain itself and a few token scraps (the Falklands, Gibraltar, Northern Ireland) and a loose association of former colonies (Canada, Australia) called the "British Commonwealth."

Geographically, the Isle of Britain is small—smaller than the state of Oregon—and its highest mountain (Ben Nevis in Scotland at 4,406 feet) is little more than a foothill by US standards. The population is a fifth that of the United States.

Get It Right

Americans tend to use "England," "Britain," and the "United Kingdom" (or "UK") interchangeably, but they're not quite the same.

- **England** is the country occupying the center and southeast part of the island.
- **Britain** is the name of the island.
- **Great Britain** is the political union of the island's three countries: England, Scotland, and Wales.
- The **United Kingdom** (UK) adds a fourth country, Northern Ireland.
- The **British Isles** (not a political entity) also includes the independent Republic of Ireland.
- The **British Commonwealth** is a loose association of possessions and former colonies (including Canada, Australia, and India) that profess at least symbolic loyalty to the Crown.

You can call the modern nation either the United Kingdom ("the UK"), "Great Britain," or simply "Britain."

It's small, but Britain is still Great.

Economically, Great Britain's industrial production is about 5 percent of the world's total. Ethnically, it's become quite diverse. It's a mix of Celtic (the natives of Scotland, Ireland, Wales, and Cornwall), Anglo-Saxon (the former "barbarians" from Dark Age times), the conquering Normans, and the many recent immigrants from around the world.

The Britain you visit today remains a global superpower of heritage, culture, and tradition. It's a major exporter of actors, movies, and theater; of rock and classical music; and of writers, painters, and sculptors. It's the perfect place for you to visit and make your own history.

CURRENT ISSUES AND THE POLITICAL LANDSCAPE

Britain is ruled by the House of Commons, with some guidance from the mostly figurehead Queen and House of Lords. Just as the United States Congress is dominated by Democrats and Republicans, Britain's Parliament has traditionally been dominated by two parties: left-leaning Labour and right-leaning Conservative ("Tories"). But other parties also attract votes (e.g., the center-left Liberal Democrats, or "Lib Dems"), and whoever rules must occasionally form some kind of coalition to remain strong.

Strangely, Britain's "constitution" is not one single document; the government's structures and policies are based on centuries of tradition, statutes, and doctrine, and much of it is not actually in writing. While this might seem potentially troublesome—if not dangerous—the British body politic takes pride in its ethos of civility and mutual respect, which has long made this arrangement work.

The prime minister is the chief executive but is not elected directly by voters; rather, he or she assumes power as the head of the party that wins a majority in parliamentary elections. While historically the prime minister could dissolve Parliament at will to make way for new elections, a law passed in 2011 now requires parliamentary elections to be held every five years.

In the May 2015 general election, Conservatives led by David Cameron won a working majority of seats in Parliament. The Labour Party led by Ed Miliband lost seats (and now holds its lowest total since 1987). The Scottish National Party became the third-largest party in the House of Commons, securing 56 of Scotland's 59 seats—taking many of these from the Labour Party.

The biggest issue in Britain today is the economy. The 2008 global downturn hurt Britain enormously, and it's been a long slog back. The dividing lines are similar to those in the States: should government nurture the economy through spending on social programs (Labour's platform), or cut programs and taxes to allow businesses to thrive (as Conservatives say)?

Wealth inequality is also a hot button. The 2008 downturn sharpened unemployment and slashed programs for the working class. This has resulted in protests and riots that pit poor young men against the police.

Like the US, Britain has suffered a number of terrorist threats and attacks. The question remains how to balance security with privacy concerns. The British have surveillance cameras everywhere—you'll frequently see signs warning you that you're being recorded. As Brits trade their privacy for security, many wonder if they've given up too much.

The terrorist threats have highlighted issues relating to Britain's large immigrant population (nearly 4 million). Brits are stunned that many terrorists (like the notorious "Jihadi John" of ISIS) speak the king's English and are born and raised in Britain. And some radical Islamic clerics seem to be preaching jihad in the mosque down the street. It raises the larger question: How well is the nation assimilating its many immigrants?

The large Muslim population is just one thread in the tapestry of today's Britain. While 9 out of 10 Brits are white, the country has large minority groups, mainly from Britain's former colonies: India, Pakistan, Bangladesh, Africa, the Caribbean, and many other places. Despite the tensions between some groups, for the most part Britain is relatively integrated, with minorities represented in most (if not all) walks of life.

Throughout the British Isles, you'll also see many Eastern Europeans (mostly Poles, Slovaks, and Lithuanians) working in restaurants, cafés, and B&Bs. These transplants—who started arriving after their home countries joined the EU in 2004—can make a lot more money working here than back home. Their presence has stirred controversy: While most of Britain has absorbed this new set of immigrants gracefully—and many British small-business owners have found them to be polite, hardworking, and affordable—a few Brits complain that the new arrivals are taking their jobs, diluting English culture, and receiving overgenerous financial aid.

Disagreements over migrant workers point to a larger issue: Britain's role in the European Union. Labour embraces the EU. Conservatives want to renegotiate the country's membership, or leave the EU altogether. A public referendum on whether Britain will remain in the EU is scheduled for June 2016, after this book goes to print. In February 2016, EU leaders agreed to give Great Britain special status if its people vote to stay in the 28-member union. The other EU member countries vowed to ensure a measure of British sovereignty, allow the pound to remain the national currency, and safeguard Great Britain's financial services industry. The British government would also be allowed to limit child-tax credits and other financial benefits to migrant workers from EU countries, among other changes.

A similar controversy brews over whether Scotland should be granted independence from rule from London. Nationalists insist a free Scotland would be rich (on oil reserves) and free from the "shackles" of London-based problems. Opponents insist it's the union of British peoples (and the strong pound) that make the country strong. Although Scottish voters rejected an independence referendum in 2014, the Scottish Nationalist Party has become a significant third-party kingmaker in British national elections.

Among social issues, binge-drinking is a serious problem. Since 2003, pubs can stay open past the traditional 23:00 closing time. An unintended consequence is that (according to one study) one in three British men and one in five British women routinely drinks to excess, carousing at pubs and sometimes in the streets.

Then there's the eternal question of the royals. Is having a monarch (who's politically irrelevant) and a royal family (who fill the tabloids with their scandals and foibles) worth it? In decades past, many Brits wanted to toss the whole lot of them. But the recent marriage of the popular William and Kate and the birth of their two cute kids have boosted royal esteem. According to pollsters, four out of five Brits want to keep their Queen and let the tradition live on.

Prime Minister David Cameron

David Cameron succeeded Gordon Brown as prime minister in May 2010, and lives at 10 Downing Street with his wife, Samantha, and their young children. Elected at age 43, Cameron was the youngest PM in two centuries. He heads the Conservative Party (the "Tories"), but has never quite fit the stodgy Conservative image. Rumors still swirl of wild parties and illicit drugs in his student days at Oxford. He's known as "Dave" to his friends, and he developed a habit of riding his bike to work. Cameron rose quickly through the political ranks: He worked to reelect Conservative PM John Major (1992), assisted the finance minister at 11 Downing Street (1992-1994), and was himself elected to Parliament in 2001, becoming head of the Conservative Party in 2005.

In 2010, Cameron's Conservative Party came to power, but it was hardly a sweeping Conservative mandate: Three parties split the vote, forcing Cameron's Conservatives to form a coalition with the (more left-leaning) Liberal Democrat Party. The Labour Party, which had held power in Britain for 13 years under Gordon Brown and Tony Blair, was the coalition's chief opposition.

Politically, Cameron is a moderate Conservative who is more pragmatic than ideological. Socially, he's "liberal" in the classical sense, advocating for personal freedoms—gay rights, decriminalization of drugs, allowing hunting and smoking, and ensuring citizens' privacy against government intrusion. Fiscally, he rails against big-government waste. His fiscal policies have emphasized austerity and belt-tightening in order to get the budget under control. The immediate result was a double-dip recession, but now Britain's economy is on the upswing. His most right-of-center stance is his support for distancing Britain from the euro and the European Union; he's negotiated new terms with the EU and scheduled a vote on Britain's EU membership for June 2016 (after this book goes to print).

Despite his personal appeal, Cameron can't quite shake the Conservatives' image as the party of the upper class. Cameron was born rich, married rich, and has worked within the corporate culture. His colleagues form an old boys' network from his days at Eton, England's most exclusive prep school. Fellow politician (and mayor of London until mid-2016) Boris Johnson is not only an old Oxford frat buddy but also a distant cousin. Cameron's reputation has been tarnished by his links to discredited media mogul Rupert Murdoch, and some have questioned his handling of riots in London and other urban centers in the summer of 2011.

As the Conservatives try to unite the country to solve Britain's economic and cultural problems, it remains to be seen whether David Cameron has brought a fresh enough approach to #10. Thanks to a successful reelection campaign in 2015, the people of Britain voted to give Cameron's party one more chance to deliver.

Royal Families: Past and Present

Royal Lineage

802-1066	Saxon and Danish kings
1066-1154	Norman invasion (William the Conqueror), Norman kings
1154-1399	Plantagenet (kings with French roots)
1399-1461	Lancaster
1462-1485	York
1485-1603	Tudor (Henry VIII, Elizabeth I)
1603-1649	Stuart (civil war and beheading of Charles I)
1649-1653	Commonwealth, no royal head of state
1653-1659	Protectorate, with Cromwell as Lord Protector
1660-1714	Restoration of Stuart dynasty
1714-1901	Hanover (four Georges, William IV, Victoria)
1901-1910	Saxe-Coburg (Edward VII)
1910-present	Windsor (George V, Edward VIII, George VI, Elizabeth II)

The Royal Family Today

It seems you can't pick up a British newspaper without some mention of the latest event, scandal, or oddity involving the royal family. Here is the cast of characters:

Queen Elizabeth II wears the traditional crown of her great-great grandmother Victoria, who ruled for 63 years, 7 months, and 2 days. In September 2015, Queen Elizabeth officially overtook Victoria as England's longest-reigning monarch. Elizabeth's husband is Prince Philip, who's not considered king.

Their son, Prince Charles (the Prince of Wales), is next in line to become king—and already holds the title as the longest "heir in waiting." But it's Prince Charles' sons who generate the tabloid buzz. The older son, Prince William (b. 1982), is a graduate of Scotland's St. Andrews University and served as a search-and-rescue helicopter pilot with the Royal Air Force. In 2011, when William married Catherine "Kate" Middleton, the TV audience was estimated at one-quarter of the world's population—more than two billion people. Kate—a commoner William met at university—is now the Duchess of Cambridge and will eventually become Britain's queen. Their son, Prince George Alexander Louis, born in 2013—and voted the most powerful and influential person in London by a poll in the *Evening Standard* two months later—will ultimately succeed William as sovereign. (A conveniently-timed change in the law ensured that William and Kate's firstborn would inherit the throne, regardless of gender.) In 2015, the royal couple welcomed the arrival of their second child, daughter Princess Charlotte Elizabeth Diana.

William's brother, redheaded Prince Harry (b. 1984), has mostly shaken his earlier reputation as a bad boy: He's proved his mettle as a career soldier, completing a tour in Afghanistan, doing charity work in Africa, and serving as an Apache aircraft commander with the Army Air Corps. Nonetheless, Harry's romances and high-wire party antics are popular tabloid topics.

For years, their parents' love life was also fodder for the British press: Charles' 1981 marriage to Princess Di, their bitter divorce, Diana's dramatic death in 1997, and the ongoing drama with Charles' longtime girlfriend—and now wife—Camilla Parker Bowles. Camilla, trying to gain the respect of the Queen and the public, doesn't call herself a princess—she uses the title Duchess of Cornwall. (And even when Charles becomes king, she will not be Queen Camilla—instead she plans to call herself the "Princess Consort.")

Charles' siblings are occasionally in the news: Princess Anne, Prince Andrew (who married and divorced Sarah "Fergie" Ferguson), and Prince Edward (who married Di look-alike Sophie Rhys-Jones).

Royal Sightseeing

You can see the trappings of royalty at Buckingham Palace (the Queen's London residence) with its Changing of the Guard; Kensington Palace—with a wing that's home to Will, Kate, and kids, and a cottage that serves as Harry's bachelor pad; Clarence House, the London home of Prince Charles and Camilla; Althorp Estate (80 miles from London), the childhood home and burial place of Princess Diana; Windsor Castle, a royal country home near London; and the crown jewels in the Tower of London.

Your best chances to actually see the Queen are on three public occasions: State Opening of Parliament (next in May 2016), Remembrance Sunday (early November, at the Cenotaph), or Trooping the Colour (one Saturday in mid-June, parading down Whitehall and at Buckingham Palace).

Otherwise, check the "Latest news and diary" section of www.royal.gov.uk, where you can search for future royal events.

BRITISH TV

Although it has its share of lowbrow reality programming, much British television is still so good—and so British—that it deserves a mention as a sightseeing treat. After a hard day of castle climbing, watch the telly over tea in your B&B.

For many years there were only five free channels, but now nearly every British television can receive a couple dozen. BBC television is government-regulated and commercial-free. Broadcasting of its eight channels (and of the five BBC radio stations) is funded by a mandatory £145.50-per-year-per-household television and radio license (hmmm, 60 cents per day to escape commercials and public-broadcasting pledge drives...not bad). Channels 3, 4, and 5 are privately owned, are a little more lowbrow, and have commercials—but those "adverts" are often clever and sophisticated, providing a fun look at British life. About 60 percent of households pay for cable or satellite television.

Whereas California "accents" fill US airwaves 24 hours a day, homogenizing the way our country speaks, Britain protects and promotes its regional accents by its choice of TV and radio announcers. See if you can tell where each is from (or ask a local for help).

Commercial-free British TV, while looser than it used to be, is still careful about what it airs and when. But after the 21:00 "watershed" hour, when children are expected to be in bed, some nudity and profanity are allowed, and may cause you to spill your tea.

American programs (such as *Game of Thrones, CSI, Friends, Frasier, How I Met Your Mother, The Simpsons, Family Guy,* and trash-talk shows) are very popular. But the visiting viewer should be sure to tune the TV to more typically British shows, including a dose of British situation- and political-comedy fun, and the top-notch BBC evening news. British comedies have tickled the American funny bone for years, from sketch comedy *(Monty Python's Flying Circus)* to sitcoms (*Are You Being Served?, Fawlty Towers, Red Dwarf, Absolutely Fabulous,* and *The Office*). Quiz shows and reality shows are taken very seriously here (*American Idol, America's Got Talent, Dancing with the Stars, Who Wants to Be a Millionaire?,* and *The X Factor* are all based on British shows). Jonathan Ross is the Jimmy Fallon of Britain for sometimes-edgy late-night talk. Other popular late-night "chat show" hosts include Graham Norton and Alan Carr. For a tear-filled slice-of-life taste of British soaps dealing in all the controversial issues, see the popular and remarkably long-running *Emmerdale, Coronation Street,* or *EastEnders.* The costume drama *Downton Abbey,* the long-running sci-fi serial *Doctor Who,* the small-town dramedy *Doc Martin,* and the modern-day crime series *Sherlock* have all become hits on both sides of the Atlantic.

NOTABLE BRITS OF TODAY AND TOMORROW

Only history can judge which British names will stand the test of time, but these days big names in the UK include politicians (David Cameron, Boris Johnson, Jeremy Corbyn), actors (Helen Mirren, Emma Thompson, Helena Bonham Carter, Jude Law, Stephen Fry, Ricky Gervais, Robert Pattinson, Daniel Radcliffe, Kate Winslet, Benedict Cumberbatch, Colin Firth), musicians (Adele, Chris Martin of Coldplay, James Arthur, Emeli Sandé, One Direction, Ed Sheeran, Sam Smith), writers (J. K. Rowling, E. L. James, Hilary Mantel, Tom Stoppard, Nick Hornby, Ian McEwan, Zadie Smith), artists (Damien Hirst, Rachel Whiteread, Tracey Emin, Anish Kapoor), athletes (David Beckham, Bradley Wiggins, Andy Murray), entrepreneurs (Sir Richard Branson, Lord Alan Sugar)... and, of course, William, Kate, and their children, George and Charlotte.

Architecture in Britain

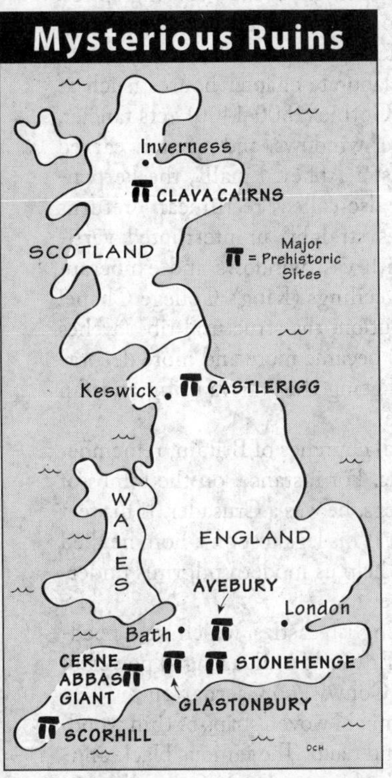

From Stonehenge to Big Ben, travelers are storming castle walls, climbing spiral staircases, and snapping the pictures of 5,000 years of architecture. Let's sort it out.

The oldest ruins—mysterious and prehistoric—date from before Roman times back to 3000 B.C. The earliest sites, such as Stonehenge and Avebury, were built during the Stone and Bronze ages. The remains from these periods are made of huge stones or mounds of earth, even man-made hills, and were created as celestial calendars and for worship or burial. Britain is crisscrossed with imaginary lines said to connect these mysterious sights (ley lines). Iron Age people (600 B.C.–A.D. 50) left desolate stone forts. The Romans thrived in Britain from A.D. 50 to 400, building cities, walls, and roads. Evidence of Roman greatness can be seen in lavish villas with ornate mosaic floors, temples uncovered beneath great English churches, and

Roman stones in medieval city walls. Roman roads sliced across the island in straight lines. Today, unusually straight rural roads are very likely laid directly on these ancient roads.

As Rome crumbled in the fifth century, so did Roman Britain. Little architecture survives from Dark Ages England, the Saxon period from 500 to 1000. Architecturally, the light was switched on with the Norman Conquest in 1066. As William earned his title "the Conqueror," his French architects built churches and castles in the European Romanesque style.

English Romanesque is called Norman (1066-1200). Norman churches had round arches, thick walls, and small windows; Durham Cathedral and the Chapel of St. John in the Tower of London are prime examples. The Tower of London, with its square keep, small windows, and spiral stone stairways, is a typical Norman castle. You can see plenty of Norman castles around England—all built to secure the conquest of these invaders from Normandy.

Gothic architecture (1200-1600) replaced the heavy Norman style with light vertical buildings, pointed arches, soaring spires, and bigger windows. English Gothic is divided into three stages. Early English Gothic (1200-1300) features tall, simple spires; beautifully carved capitals; and elaborate chapter houses (such as the Wells Cathedral). Decorated Gothic (1300-1400) gets fancier, with more elaborate tracery, bigger windows, and ornately carved pinnacles, as you see at Westminster Abbey. Finally, the Perpendicular Gothic style (1400-1600, also called "rectilinear") returns to square towers and emphasizes straight, uninterrupted vertical lines from ceiling to floor, with vast windows and exuberant decoration, including fan-vaulted ceilings (King's College Chapel at Cambridge). Through this evolution, the structural ribs (arches meeting at the top of the ceilings) became more and more decorative and fanciful (the most fancy being the star vaulting and fan vaulting of the Perpendicular style).

As you tour the great medieval churches of Britain, remember that almost everything is symbolic. For instance, on the tombs of knights, if the figure has crossed legs, he was a Crusader. If his feet rest on a dog, he died at home; but if his legs rest on a lion, he died in battle. Local guides and books help us modern pilgrims understand at least a little of what we see.

Wales is particularly rich in English castles, which were needed to subdue the stubborn Welsh. Edward I built a ring of powerful castles in North Wales, including Conwy and Caernarfon.

Gothic houses were a simple mix of woven strips of thin wood, rubble, and plaster called wattle and daub. The famous black-and-white Tudor (or "half-timbered") look came simply from filling in heavy oak frames with wattle and daub.

The Tudor period (1485-1560) was a time of relative peace

(the Wars of the Roses were finally over), prosperity, and renaissance. But when Henry VIII broke with the Catholic Church and disbanded its monasteries, scores of Britain's greatest churches were left as gutted shells. These hauntingly beautiful abbey ruins (Glastonbury, Tintern in Wales, Whitby, Rievaulx, Battle, St. Augustine's in Canterbury, St. Mary's in York, and lots more), surrounded by lush lawns, are now pleasant city parks.

Although few churches were built during the Tudor period, this was a time of house and mansion construction. Heating a home was becoming popular and affordable, and Tudor buildings featured small square windows and many chimneys. In towns, where land was scarce, many Tudor houses grew up and out, getting wider with each overhanging floor.

The Elizabethan and Jacobean periods (1560-1620) were followed by the English Renaissance style (1620-1720). English architects mixed Gothic and classical styles, then Baroque and classical styles. Although the ornate Baroque never really grabbed Britain, the classical style of the Italian architect Andrea Palladio did. Inigo Jones (1573-1652), Christopher Wren (1632-1723), and those they inspired plastered Britain with enough columns, domes, and symmetry to please a Caesar. The Great Fire of London (1666) cleared the way for an ambitious young Wren to put his mark on London forever with a grand rebuilding scheme, including the great St. Paul's Cathedral and more than 50 other churches.

The celebrants of the Boston Tea Party remember Britain's Georgian period (1720-1840) for its lousy German kings. But in architectural terms, "Georgian" is English for "Neoclassical." Its architecture was rich and showed off by being very classical. Grand ornamental doorways, fine cast-ironwork on balconies and railings, Chippendale furniture, and white-on-blue Wedgwood ceramics graced rich homes everywhere. John Wood Sr. and Jr. led the way, giving the trendsetting city of Bath its crescents and circles of aristocratic Georgian row houses.

The Industrial Revolution shaped the Victorian period (1840-1890) with glass, steel, and iron. Britain had a huge new erector set (so did France's Mr. Eiffel). This was also a Romantic period, reviving the "more Christian" Gothic style. London's Houses of Parliament are Neo-Gothic—they're just 140 years old but look 700, except for the telltale modern precision and craftsmanship. Whereas Gothic was stone or concrete, Neo-Gothic was often red brick. These were Britain's glory days, and there was more building in this period than in all previous ages combined.

The architecture of the mid-20th century obeyed the formula "form follows function"—it worried more about your needs than your eyes. But more recently, the dull "international style" has been nudged aside by a more playful style, thanks to cutting-edge

Typical Church Architecture

History comes to life when you visit a centuries-old church. Even if you wouldn't know your apse from a hole in the ground, learning a few simple terms will enrich your experience. Note that not every church has every feature, and that a "cathedral" isn't a type of church architecture, but rather a designation for a church that's a governing center for a local bishop.

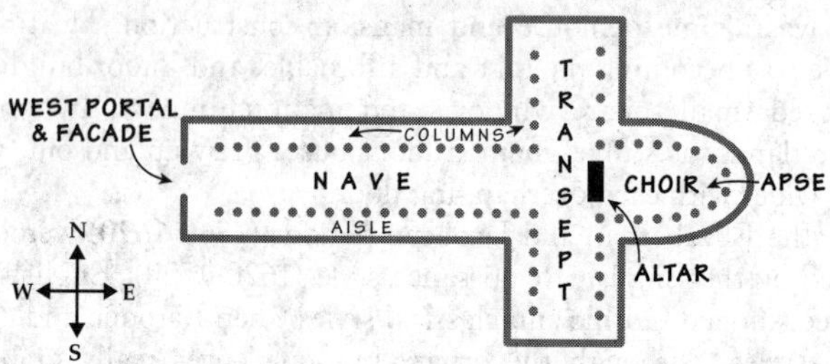

Aisles: The long, generally low-ceilinged arcades that flank the nave.

Altar: The raised area with a ceremonial table (often adorned with candles or a crucifix), where the priest prepares and serves the bread and wine for Communion.

Apse: The space beyond the altar, often bordered with small chapels.

Barrel Vault: A continuous round-arched ceiling that resembles an extended upside-down U.

Choir ("quire" in British English): A cozy area, often screened off, located within the church nave and near the high altar where services are sung in a more intimate setting.

Cloister: Covered hallways bordering a square or rectangular open-air courtyard, traditionally where monks and nuns got fresh air.

Facade: The exterior surface of the church's main (west) entrance, viewable from outside and usually highly decorated.

Groin Vault: An arched ceiling formed where two equal barrel vaults meet at right angles. Less common usage: term for a medieval jock strap.

Narthex: The area (portico or foyer) between the main entry and the nave.

Nave: The long central section of the church (running west to east, from the entrance to the altar) where the congregation sits or stands through the service.

Transept: In a traditional cross-shaped floor plan, the transept is one of the two parts forming the "arms" of the cross. The transepts run north-south, perpendicularly crossing the east-west nave.

West Portal: The main entry to the church (on the west end, opposite the main altar).

Typical Castle Architecture

Castles were fortified residences for medieval nobles. Castles come in all shapes and sizes, but knowing a few general terms will help you understand them.

Barbican: A fortified gatehouse, sometimes a stand-alone building located outside the main walls.

Crenellation: A gap-toothed pattern of stones atop the parapet.

Drawbridge: A bridge that could be raised or lowered using counterweights or a chain and winch.

Great Hall: The largest room in the castle, serving as throne room, conference center, and dining hall.

Hoardings (or Gallery or Brattice): Wooden huts built onto the upper parts of the stone walls. They served as watch towers, living quarters, and fighting platforms.

The Keep (or Donjon): A high, strong stone tower in the center of the castle complex; the lord's home and refuge of last resort.

Loopholes (or Embrasures): Narrow wall slits through which soldiers could shoot arrows.

Machicolation: A stone ledge jutting out from the wall, with holes through which soldiers could drop rocks or boiling oil onto wall-scaling enemies below.

Moat: A ditch encircling the wall, often filled with water.

Motte-and-Bailey: A form of early English castle, with a small hilltop fort (motte) and an enclosed fortified yard (bailey).

Parapet: Outer railing of the wall walk.

Portcullis: A heavy iron grille that could be lowered across the entrance.

Postern Gate: A small unfortified side or rear entrance from which to launch attacks or escape.

Towers: Tall structures with crenellated tops or conical roofs serving as lookouts, chapels, living quarters, or dungeons.

Turret: A small lookout tower rising up from the top of the wall.

Wall Walk (or Allure): A pathway atop the wall where guards could patrol and where soldiers stood to fire at the enemy.

The Yard (or Bailey): An open courtyard inside the castle walls.

architects such as Lord Norman Foster and Renzo Piano. In the last several years, London has added several creative buildings to its skyline: the City Hall (nicknamed "The Armadillo"), 30 St. Mary Axe ("The Gherkin"), 20 Fenchurch ("The Walkie-Talkie"), and the tallest building in the European Union, the pointy Shard London Bridge (called...um, "The Shard").

Even as it sets trends for the 21st century, Britain treasures its heritage and takes great pains to build tastefully in historic districts and to preserve its many "listed" (government-protected) buildings. With a booming tourist trade, these quaint reminders of its past—and ours—are becoming a valuable part of the British economy.

For more about British history, consider Europe 101: History and Art for the Traveler *by Rick Steves and Gene Openshaw, available at www.ricksteves.com.*

PRACTICALITIES

This chapter covers the practical skills of European travel: how to get tourist information, pay for things, sightsee efficiently, find good-value accommodations, eat affordably but well, use technology wisely, and get between destinations smoothly. To round out your knowledge, check out "Resources."

Tourist Information

Before your trip, start with the Visit Britain website, which contains a wealth of knowledge on destinations, activities, accommodations, and transport in Great Britain. Families will especially appreciate the "Britain for Kids & Families" travel suggestions. Maps, airport transfers, sightseeing tours, and theater tickets can be purchased online (www.visitbritain.com, www.visitbritainshop.com/usa for purchases). Also try these official tourism board websites: www.visitengland.com, www.visitwales.com, and www.visitscotland.com.

In Britain, a good first stop is generally the tourist information office (abbreviated **TI** in this book and locally as **TIC,** for "tourist information centre"). In London, the **City of London Information Centre,** near St. Paul's Cathedral, is helpful (see page 26).

Be aware that TIs are in business to help you enjoy spending money in their town. (Once upon a time, they were actually information services, but today some have become promoters masquerading as TIs.) While this corrupts much of their advice—and you can get plenty of information online—I still make a point to swing by the local TI upon arrival in a new town.

Even if they are overly commercial, TIs continue to be good places to confirm opening times, pick up a city map, and get information on public transit (including bus and train schedules), walking tours, special events, and nightlife. Prepare a list of questions and a proposed plan to double-check. Due to funding constraints, some of Britain's TIs are struggling; village TIs may be staffed by volunteers who need to charge you for maps and informational brochures.

Many TIs have information on the entire country or at least the region, so try to pick up maps for destinations you'll be visiting later in your trip. If you're arriving in town after the TI closes, call ahead or pick up a map in a neighboring town.

For all the help TIs offer, steer clear of their room-finding services (bloated prices, booking fees, no opinions, and commissions that come from the pocket of your B&B host).

Travel Tips

Emergency and Medical Help: In Great Britain, dial 999 or 112 for police help or a medical emergency. If you get sick, do as the locals do: Go to a pharmacy and see a "chemist" (pharmacist) for advice. Or ask at your hotel for help—they know of the nearest medical and emergency services. In London, St. Thomas' Hospital, across the river from Big Ben, has a fine reputation.

Theft or Loss: To replace a passport, you'll need to go in person to a US embassy. If your credit and debit cards disappear, cancel and replace them (see "Damage Control for Lost Cards" on page 989). File a police report, either on the spot or within a day or two; you'll need it to submit an insurance claim for lost or stolen rail passes or travel gear, and it can help with replacing your passport or credit and debit cards. For more information, see www.ricksteves.com/help. To minimize the effects of loss, back up your digital photos and other files frequently.

Time Zones: Britain, which is one hour earlier than most of continental Europe, is five/eight hours ahead of the East/West Coasts of the US. The exceptions are the beginning and end of Daylight Saving Time: Britain and Europe "spring forward" the last Sunday in March (two weeks after most of North America), and "fall back" the last Sunday in October (one week before North America). For a handy online time converter, see www.timeanddate.com/worldclock.

Business Hours: Most stores are open Monday through Saturday (roughly 9:00 or 10:00 to 17:00 or 18:00). In cities, some stores stay open later on Wednesday or Thursday (until 19:00 or 20:00). Some big-city department stores are open later throughout the week (Mon-Sat until about 21:00). Sundays have the same pros and cons as they do for travelers in the US: Sightseeing attractions are generally open, many street markets are lively with shoppers, banks and many shops are closed, public transportation options are fewer (for example, no bus service to or from smaller towns), and there's no rush hour. Friday and Saturday evenings are lively; Sunday evenings are quiet.

Watt's Up? Britain's electrical system is 220 volts, instead of North America's 110 volts. Most newer electronics (such as laptops, battery chargers, and hair dryers) convert automatically, so you won't need a converter, but you will need an adapter plug with three square prongs, sold inexpensively at travel stores in the US. Avoid bringing older appliances that don't automatically convert voltage; instead, ask to borrow one from your B&B or buy a cheap replacement in Britain. Low-cost hair dryers and other small appliances are sold at Superdrug and Boots (ask your hotelier for the closest branch). Or pop into a department store.

Discounts: Discounts (called "concessions" or "concs" in Britain) are not listed in this book. However, many sights, buses, and trains offer discounts to youths (up to age 18), students (with proper identification cards, www.isic.org), families, seniors (loosely defined as retirees or those willing to call themselves seniors), and groups of 10 or more. Always ask. Some discounts are available only for citizens of the European Union (EU).

Money

This section offers advice on how to pay for purchases on your trip (including getting cash from ATMs and paying with plastic), dealing with lost or stolen cards, VAT (sales tax) refunds, and tipping.

WHAT TO BRING

Bring both a credit card and a debit card. You'll use the debit card at cash machines (ATMs) to withdraw local cash for most pur-

Exchange Rate

1 British pound (£1) = about $1.60

While the euro (€) is now the currency of most of Europe, Britain is sticking with its pound sterling. The British pound (£), also called a "quid," is broken into 100 pence (p). Pence means "cents." You'll find coins ranging from 1p to £2 and bills from £5 to £50.

To convert prices from pounds to dollars, add about 60 percent: £20 = about $32, £50 = about $80. Check www.oanda.com for the latest exchange rates.

chases, and the credit card to pay for larger items. Some travelers carry a third card, in case one gets demagnetized or eaten by a temperamental machine.

For an emergency stash, bring several hundred dollars in hard cash in $20 bills. If you need to exchange the bills, go to a bank; avoid using currency-exchange booths because of their lousy rates and/or outrageous (and often hard-to-spot) fees.

CASH

Cash is just as desirable in Britain as it is at home. Small businesses (B&Bs, mom-and-pop cafés, shops, etc.) prefer that you pay your bills with cash. Some vendors will charge you extra for using a credit card, some won't accept foreign credit cards, and some won't take any credit cards at all. Cash is the best—and sometimes only—way to pay for cheap food, bus fare, taxis, and local guides.

Scotland and Northern Ireland issue their own currency in pounds, worth the same as an English pound. English, Scottish, and Northern Ireland's Ulster pound notes are technically interchangeable in each region, although Scottish and Ulster pounds are considered "undesirable" and sometimes not accepted in England. Banks in any of the three regions will convert your Scottish or Ulster pounds into English pounds for no charge. Don't worry about the coins, which are the same throughout the UK.

Throughout Europe, ATMs are the standard way for travelers to get cash. They work just like they do at home. To withdraw money from an ATM (known as a "cashpoint" in Britain), you'll need a debit card (ideally with a Visa or MasterCard logo for maximum usability), plus a PIN code (numeric and four digits). For increased security, shield the keypad when entering your PIN code, and don't use an ATM if anything on the front of the machine looks loose or damaged (a sign that someone may have attached a "skimming" device to capture account information). Try to withdraw large sums of money to reduce the number of per-transaction bank fees you'll pay.

When possible, use ATMs located outside banks—a thief is less likely to target a cash machine near surveillance cameras, and if your card is munched by a machine, you can go inside for help. Stay away from "independent" ATMs such as Travelex, Euronet, YourCash, Cardpoint, and Cashzone, which charge huge commissions, have terrible exchange rates, and may try to trick users with "dynamic currency conversion" (described at the end of "Credit and Debit Cards," next). Although you can use a credit card to withdraw cash at an ATM, this comes with high bank fees and only makes sense in an emergency.

While traveling, if you want to monitor your accounts online to detect any unauthorized transactions, be sure to use a secure connection (see page 1014).

Even in jolly olde Britain, pickpockets target tourists. To safeguard your cash, wear a money belt—a pouch with a strap that you buckle around your waist like a belt and tuck under your clothes. Keep your cash, credit cards, and passport secure in your money belt, and carry only a day's spending money in your front pocket.

CREDIT AND DEBIT CARDS

For purchases, Visa and MasterCard are more commonly accepted than American Express. Just like at home, credit or debit cards work easily at larger hotels, restaurants, and shops. I typically use my debit card to withdraw cash to pay for most purchases. I use my credit card sparingly: to book hotel reservations, to buy advance tickets for events or sights, to cover major expenses (such as car rentals or plane tickets), and to pay for things online or near the end of my trip (to avoid another visit to the ATM). While you could instead use a debit card for these purchases, a credit card offers a greater degree of fraud protection.

Ask Your Credit- or Debit-Card Company: Before your trip, contact the company that issued your debit or credit cards.

- Confirm that your **card will work overseas,** and alert them that you'll be using it in Europe; otherwise, they may deny transactions if they perceive unusual spending patterns.
- Ask for the specifics on transaction **fees.** When you use your credit or debit card—either for purchases or ATM withdrawals—you'll typically be charged additional "international transaction" fees of up to 3 percent (1 percent is normal) plus $5 per transaction. If your card's fees seem high, consider getting a different card just for your trip: Capital One (www.capitalone.com) and most credit unions have low-to-no international fees.
- Verify your daily ATM **withdrawal limit,** and if necessary, ask your bank to adjust it. I prefer a high limit that allows me to take out more cash at each ATM stop and save on bank fees; some travelers prefer to set a lower limit in case their card is stolen. Note

that foreign banks also set maximum withdrawal limits for their ATMs (£300 is usually the maximum).

• Get your bank's emergency **phone number** in the US (but not its 800 number, which isn't accessible from overseas) to call collect if you have a problem.

• Ask for your credit card's **PIN** in case you need to make an emergency cash withdrawal or encounter Europe's chip-and-PIN system; the bank won't tell you your PIN over the phone, so allow time for it to be mailed to you.

Magnetic-Stripe versus Chip-and-PIN Credit Cards: Europeans are increasingly using chip-and-PIN credit cards embedded with an electronic security chip and requiring a four-digit PIN. Your American-style card (with just the old-fashioned magnetic stripe) will work fine in most places. But it might not work at unattended payment machines, such as those at train and subway stations, toll plazas, parking garages, bike-rental kiosks, and gas pumps. If you have problems, try entering your card's PIN, look for a machine that takes cash, or find a clerk who can process the transaction manually.

Major US banks are beginning to offer credit cards with chips. Many of these are not true chip-and-PIN cards, but instead are chip-and-signature cards, for which your signature verifies your identity. These cards should work for live transactions and at most payment machines, but won't work for offline transactions such as at unattended gas pumps. If you're concerned, ask if your bank offers a true chip-and-PIN card. Andrews Federal Credit Union (www.andrewsfcu.org) and the State Department Federal Credit Union (www.sdfcu.org) offer these cards and are open to all US residents.

No matter what kind of card you have, it pays to carry pounds; you can always use an ATM to withdraw cash with your magnetic-stripe debit card.

Dynamic Currency Conversion: If merchants or hoteliers offer to convert your purchase price into dollars (called dynamic currency conversion, or DCC), refuse this "service." You'll pay even more in fees for the expensive convenience of seeing your charge in dollars. If your receipt shows the total in dollars only, ask for the transaction to be processed in the local currency. If the clerk refuses, pay in cash—or mark the receipt "local currency not offered" and dispute the DCC charges with your bank.

Some ATMs and retailers try to confuse customers by presenting DCC in misleading terms. If an ATM offers to "lock in" or "guarantee" your conversion rate, choose "proceed without conversion." Other prompts might state, "You can be charged in dollars: Press YES for dollars, NO for GBP." Always choose the local currency in these situations.

DAMAGE CONTROL FOR LOST CARDS

If you lose your credit, debit, or ATM card, you can stop people from using your card by reporting the loss immediately to the respective global customer-assistance centers. Call these 24-hour US numbers collect: Visa (tel. 303/967-1096), MasterCard (tel. 636/722-7111), and American Express (tel. 336/393-1111). In Britain, to make a collect call to the US, dial 0-800-89-0011. Press zero or stay on the line for an operator. European toll-free numbers (listed by country) can be found at the websites for Visa and MasterCard. Diner's Club has offices in Britain (tel. 0845-862-2937) and the US (tel. 514/877-1577; call collect).

Try to have this information ready: full card number, whether you are the primary or secondary cardholder, the cardholder's name exactly as printed on the card, billing address, home phone number, circumstances of the loss or theft, and identification verification (your birth date, your mother's maiden name, or your Social Security number—memorize this, don't carry a copy). If you are the secondary cardholder, you'll also need to provide the primary cardholder's identification-verification details. You can generally receive a temporary card within two or three business days in Europe (see www.ricksteves.com/help for more).

If you report your loss within two days, you typically won't be responsible for any unauthorized transactions on your account, although many banks charge a liability fee of $50.

TIPPING

Tipping in Britain isn't as automatic and generous as it is in the US. For special service, tips are appreciated, but not expected. As in the US, the proper amount depends on your resources, tipping philosophy, and the circumstances, but some general guidelines apply.

Restaurants: If a service charge is included in the bill, it's not necessary to tip. Otherwise, it's appropriate to tip about 10-12.5 percent. (For more information, see page 1004).

Taxis: For a typical ride, round up your fare a bit (for instance, if the fare is £4.50, pay £5). If the cabbie hauls your bags and zips you to the airport to help you catch your flight, you might want to toss in a little more. But if you feel like you're being driven in circles or otherwise ripped off, skip the tip.

Services: In general, if someone in the service industry does a super job for you, a tip of a pound or so is appropriate...but not required. If you're not sure whether (or how much) to tip for a service, ask a local for advice.

GETTING A VAT REFUND

Wrapped into the purchase price of your British souvenirs is a Value-Added Tax (VAT) of about 20 percent. You're entitled to get most of that tax back if you purchase more than £30 (about $48) worth of goods at a store that participates in the VAT-refund scheme (although individual stores can require that you spend more—Harrods, for example, won't process a refund unless you spend £50). Typically, you must ring up the minimum at a single retailer—you can't add up your purchases from various shops to reach the required amount.

Getting your refund is straightforward and, if you buy a substantial amount of souvenirs, well worth the hassle. If you're lucky, the merchant will subtract the tax when you make your purchase. (Note that if the store ships the goods to your US home, VAT is not assessed on your purchase.) You'll need to:

Get the paperwork. Have the merchant completely fill out the necessary refund document (either an official VAT customs form or the shop or refund company's own version of it). You'll have to present your passport at the store. Get the paperwork done before you leave the shop to ensure you'll have everything you need (including your original sales receipt).

Get your stamp at the border or airport. Process your VAT document at your last stop in the European Union (such as at the airport) with the customs agent who deals with VAT refunds. Arrive an additional hour early before you need to check in for your flight to allow time to find the local customs office—and to stand in line. It's best to keep your purchases in your carry-on. If they're too large or dangerous to carry on (such as knives), pack them in your checked bags and alert the check-in agent. You'll be sent (with your tagged bag) to a customs desk outside security; someone will examine your bag, stamp your paperwork, and put your bag on the belt. You're not supposed to use your purchased goods before you leave. If you show up at customs wearing your new Wellingtons, officials might look the other way—or deny you a refund.

Collect your refund. You'll need to return your stamped document to the retailer or its representative. Many merchants work with a service that has offices at major airports, ports, or border crossings (at Heathrow, Travelex counters and customs desks are located before and after security in terminals 2-5). These services, which extract a 4 percent fee, can refund your money immediately in cash or credit your card (within two billing cycles). If the retailer handles VAT refunds directly, it's up to you to contact the merchant for your refund. You can mail the documents from home, or more quickly from your point of departure (using an envelope you've prepared in advance or one that's been provided by the merchant). You'll then have to wait—it can take months.

CUSTOMS FOR AMERICAN SHOPPERS

You are allowed to take home $800 worth of items per person duty-free once every 31 days. As for food, you can take home many processed and packaged foods: vacuum-packed cheeses, dried herbs, jams, baked goods, candy, chocolate, oil, vinegar, mustard, and honey. Fresh fruits and vegetables and most meats are not allowed, with exceptions for some canned items. As for alcohol, you can bring in one liter duty-free (it can be packed securely in your checked luggage, along with any other liquid-containing items).

To bring alcohol (or liquid-packed foods) in your carry-on bag on your flight home, buy it at a duty-free shop at the airport. You'll increase your odds of getting it onto a connecting flight if it's packaged in a "STEB"—a secure, tamper-evident bag. But stay away from liquids in opaque, ceramic, or metallic containers, which usually cannot be successfully screened (STEB or no STEB).

For details on allowable goods, customs rules, and duty rates, visit www.cbp.gov.

Sightseeing

Sightseeing can be hard work. Use these tips to make your visits to Britain's finest sights meaningful, fun, efficient, and painless.

PLAN AHEAD

Set up an itinerary that allows you to fit in all your must-see sights. For a one-stop look at opening hours, see the "At a Glance" sidebars for London, Bath, Near Bath, the Cotswolds, Liverpool, the Lake District, York, and Edinburgh. Most sights keep stable hours, but you can easily confirm the latest by checking with the TI or visiting museum websites.

Don't put off visiting a must-see sight—you never know when a place will close unexpectedly for a holiday, strike, or royal audience. Many museums are closed or have reduced hours at least a few days a year, especially on holidays such as Christmas, New Year's, and Bank Holiday Mondays in May and August. A list of holidays is on page 1042; check online for possible museum closures during your trip. Off-season, many museums have shorter hours.

Going at the right time helps avoid crowds. This book offers tips on the best times to see specific sights. Try visiting popular sights very early or very late. Evening visits are usually peaceful, with fewer crowds. For tips on sights or events that should be booked in advance, see page 12.

Study up. To get the most out of the self-guided tours and sight descriptions in this book, read them before you visit. The British Museum rocks if you understand the significance of the Rosetta Stone.

AT SIGHTS

Here's what you can typically expect:

Entering: Be warned that you may not be allowed to enter if you arrive 30 to 60 minutes before closing time. And guards start ushering people out well before the actual closing time, so don't save the best for last.

Some important sights have a security check where you must open your bag or send it through a metal detector. Some sights require you to check daypacks and coats. (If you'd rather not check your daypack, try carrying it tucked under your arm like a purse as you enter.)

At ticket desks, you may see references to "Gift Aid"—a tax-deduction scheme that benefits museums, but this only concerns UK taxpayers.

Photography: If the museum's photo policy isn't clearly posted, ask a guard. Generally, taking photos without a flash or tripod is allowed. Some sights ban photos altogether.

Temporary Exhibits: Museums may show special exhibits in addition to their permanent collection. An extra fee, which may not be optional, might be assessed for these shows.

Expect Changes: Artwork can be on tour, on loan, out sick, or shifted at the whim of the curator. Pick up a floor plan as you enter, and ask museum staff if you can't find a particular item.

Audioguides and Apps: Many sights rent audioguides, which generally offer excellent recorded descriptions (about £4). If you bring your own earbuds, you can enjoy better sound and avoid holding the device to your ear. To save money, bring a Y-jack and share one audioguide with your travel partner. Increasingly, museums and sights offer apps—often free—that you can download to your mobile device (check their websites). I've produced free downloadable audio tours for major sights in this book, including London's British Museum, British Library, and St. Paul's Cathedral; my Westminster and Historic London: "The City" walks; and Edinburgh's Royal Mile—look for the 🎧 symbol in this book. For more on my audio tours, see page 13.

Guided tours are most likely to occur during peak season (usually £3-8 and widely ranging in quality). Some sights also run short introductory videos featuring their highlights and history. These are generally well worth your time and a great place to start your visit.

Services: Important sights and cathedrals may have an on-site café or cafeteria (usually a handy place to rejuvenate during a long visit—try a cheap "cream tea" to pick up your energy in midafternoon, like Brits do). The WCs at sights are free and generally nearly always clean.

Before Leaving: At the gift shop, scan the postcard rack or thumb through a guidebook to be sure that you haven't overlooked something that you'd like to see.

Every sight or museum offers more than what is covered in this book. Use the information in this book as an introduction—not the final word.

SIGHTSEEING MEMBERSHIPS

Many sights in Britain are managed by English Heritage, the National Trust, Cadw (a Welsh organization), or Historic Scotland; the sights don't overlap. Each organization has a combo-deal that can save some money for busy sightseers.

Membership in **English Heritage** includes free entry to more than 400 sights in England and discounted or free admission to about 100 more sights in Scotland and Wales. For most travelers, the **Overseas Visitor Pass** is a better choice than the pricier one-year membership (Visitor Pass: £30/9 days, £35/16 days, discounts for couples and families; Membership: £50 for one person, £88 for two; discounts for families, seniors, and students; children under 19 free; tel. 0370/333-1181, www.english-heritage.org.uk).

Membership in the **National Trust** is best suited for garden-and-estate enthusiasts, ideally those traveling by car. It covers more than 350 historic houses, manors, and gardens throughout Great Britain. From the US, it's easy to join online through the Royal Oak Foundation, the National Trust's American affiliate (one-year membership: $65 for one person, $95 for two, family and student memberships, www.royal-oak.org). For more on National Trust properties, see www.nationaltrust.org.uk.

Cadw's Explorer Pass covers many sights in Wales (3-day pass: £17.50 for one person, £27 for two, £37 for a family; 7-day pass available; buy at castle ticket desks, www.cadw.wales.gov.uk).

Historic Scotland's Explorer Pass covers its 78 properties, including Edinburgh Castle, Stirling Castle, and Urquhart Castle (£30/3 days out of any 5, £40/7 days out of any 14, www.historic-scotland.gov.uk/explorer). The pass allows you to skip the ticket-buying lines at these castles.

Factors to Consider: An advantage to these deals is that you'll feel free to dip into lesser sights without considering the separate cost of admission. But remember that your kids already get in free or cheaply at most places, and people over 60 get discounted prices at many sights. If you're traveling by car and can get to the remote sights, you're more likely to get your money's worth out of a pass or membership, especially during peak season (Easter-Oct), when all the sights are open.

Harry Potter Sights

Harry Potter's story is set in a magical, largely fictional Britain, but you can visit many real locations used in the film series. Other settings, like Diagon Alley, exist only at Leavesden Film Studios (north of London; see page 133).

London

Harry first realizes his wizard powers in *The Sorcerer's Stone* (2001) when talking with a snake at the **London Zoo**'s Reptile House. Later, Harry shops for school supplies in the glass-roofed **Leadenhall Market.**

In *The Chamber of Secrets* (2002), Harry catches the train to Hogwarts wizarding school at **King's Cross Station** from the fictional Platform 9-3/4 (between the real tracks 8 and 9).

In *The Prisoner of Azkaban* (2004), a three-decker bus dumps Harry at the Leaky Cauldron pub, shot on rough-looking Stoney Street at the southeast edge of **Borough Market.**

When the Order takes to the night sky on broomsticks in *The Order of the Phoenix* (2007), they pass over plenty of

Sleeping

I favor hotels and restaurants that are handy to your sightseeing activities. In Britain, small bed-and-breakfast places (B&Bs) generally provide the best value, though I also include some bigger hotels. Rather than list accommodations scattered throughout a town, I choose places in my favorite neighborhoods. My recommendations run the gamut, from dorm beds to fancy rooms with all of the comforts. Outside of pricey London, you can expect to find good doubles for £80-120 ($125-190), including cooked breakfasts and tax.

A major feature of the Sleeping sections in this book is my extensive and opinionated listing of good-value rooms. I like places that are clean, central, relatively quiet at night, reasonably priced, friendly, small enough to have a hands-on owner and stable staff, run with a respect

identifiable landmarks, including the **London Eye, Big Ben,** and **Buckingham Palace.** The **Millennium Bridge** collapses into the Thames in the dramatic finale to *The Half-Blood Prince* (2009). The real government offices of **Whitehall** serve as exteriors for the Ministry of Magic.

Elsewhere in England

Near Bath: In *The Sorcerer's Stone,* Harry is chosen for Gryffindor's Quidditch team in the halls of the 13th-century **Lacock Abbey.** Harry attends Professor Snape's class in one of the abbey's peeling-plaster rooms.

Northeast England: In *The Sorcerer's Stone,* Harry walks with his white owl, Hedwig, through a snowy courtyard in Durham's Cathedral.

Scotland

In *The Prisoner of Azkaban,* **Loch Shiel, Loch Eilt,** and **Loch Morar** (near Fort William) were the stand-ins for the Great Lake. **Steal Falls,** at the base of Ben Nevis, is the locale for the Triwizard Tournament in *The Goblet of Fire.*

Glencoe was the main location for outdoor filming in *The Prisoner of Azkaban* and *The Half-Blood Prince,* and many shots of the Hogwarts grounds were filmed in the Fort William and Glencoe areas.

for British traditions, and not listed in other guidebooks. (For me, meeting six out of these eight criteria means it's a keeper.) I'm more impressed by a convenient location and a fun-loving philosophy than flat-screen TVs and a pricey laundry service.

Britain has a rating system for hotels and B&Bs. Its stars are supposed to imply quality, but I find they mean only that the place is paying dues to the tourist board. Rating systems often have little to do with value.

Book your accommodations well in advance, especially if you want to stay at one of my top listings or if you'll be traveling during busy times. See page 1042 for a list of major holidays and festivals; for tips on making reservations, see page 1000.

Some people make reservations as they travel, calling hotels and B&Bs a few days to a week before their arrival. If you'd rather travel without any reservations at all, you'll have greater success snaring rooms if you arrive at your destination early in the day. If you anticipate crowds (weekends are worst) on the day you want to check in, call hotels at about 9:00 or 10:00, when the receptionist knows who'll be checking out and which rooms will be available.

RATES AND DEALS

I've described my recommended accommodations using a Sleep Code (see sidebar). The prices I list are for one-night stays in peak season, include a hearty breakfast unless otherwise noted, and assume you're booking directly with the B&B or hotel (not through a TI or online hotel-booking engine). Booking services extract a commission from the hotel, which logically closes the door on special deals. Book directly with the hotel.

My recommended accommodations generally have a website (often with a built-in booking form) and an email address; you can expect a response within a day (and often sooner).

If you're on a budget, it's smart to contact several hotels to ask for their best price. Comparison-shop and make your choice. While B&B prices tend to be fairly predictable, larger hotels often use "dynamic pricing," a computer-generated system that predicts the demand for particular days and sets prices accordingly: High-demand days can be more than double the price of low-demand days. This makes it impossible for a guidebook to list anything more accurate than a wide range of prices. I regret this trend. While you can assume that hotels listed in this book are good, it's difficult to say which ones are the better value unless you email to confirm the price.

As you look over the listings, you'll notice that some accommodations promise special prices to Rick Steves readers. To get these rates, you must book directly with the hotel (that is, not through a booking site like TripAdvisor or Booking.com), mention this book when you reserve, and then show the book upon arrival. Rick Steves discounts apply to readers with ebooks as well as printed books. Because I trust hotels to honor this, please let me know if you don't receive a listed discount. Note, though, that discounts understandably may not be applied to promotional rates.

A hotel's official "rack rates" (the highest rates they charge) can be misleading, because special promo deals are often available online.

Staying in B&Bs and small hotels can save money over sleeping in big hotels. Chain hotels can be even cheaper, but they don't include breakfast. When comparing prices between chain hotels and B&Bs, remember you're getting two breakfasts (about a £25 value) for each double room at a B&B. When establishing prices, confirm if the charge is per person or per room (if a price is too good to be true, it's probably per person). In this book, however, all room prices are listed per room, not per person.

In general, prices can soften if you do any of the following: Offer to pay cash, stay at least three nights, or mention this book. You can also try asking for a cheaper room or a discount, or offer to skip breakfast.

Sleep Code

(£1 = about $1.60)

Price Rankings

To help you easily sort through my listings, I've divided the accommodations into three categories based on the highest price for a basic double room with bath during high season:

$$$ Higher Priced
$$ Moderately Priced
$ Lower Priced

I always rate hostels as $, whether or not they have double rooms, because they have the cheapest beds in town.

Prices can change without notice; verify the hotel's current rates online or by email. For the best prices, always book directly with the hotel.

Abbreviations

To pack maximum information into minimum space, I use the following code to describe accommodations in this book. Prices are listed per room, not per person. When a price range is given for a type of room (such as double rooms listing for £80-120), it means the price fluctuates with the season, size of room, or length of stay; expect to pay the upper end for peak-season stays.

S = Single room (or price for one person in a double)
D = Double or twin room. "Double beds" can be two twins sheeted together and are usually big enough for nonromantic couples.
T = Triple (generally a double bed with a single)
Q = Quad (usually two double beds; adding an extra child's bed to a T is usually cheaper)
b = Private bathroom with toilet and shower or tub

According to this code, a couple staying at a "Db-£90" hotel would pay a total of £90 (about $145) per night for a double room with a private bathroom. Unless otherwise noted, breakfast is included and credit cards are accepted. For most places, the rates I list include the 20 percent VAT tax—but it's smart to ask when you book your room.

There's almost always Wi-Fi and/or a guest computer available, and it's generally free.

TYPES OF ACCOMMODATIONS

B&Bs and Small Hotels

B&Bs and small hotels are generally family-run places with fewer amenities but more character than a conventional hotel. They range from large inns with 15 to 20 rooms to small homes renting out a spare bedroom. Places named "guesthouse" or "B&B" typically have eight or fewer rooms. The philosophy of the management determines the character of a place more than its size and facilities offered. I avoid places run as a business by absentee owners. My top listings are run by people who enjoy welcoming the world to their breakfast table.

Compared to hotels, B&Bs and guesthouses give you double the cultural intimacy for half the price. While you may lose some of the conveniences of a hotel—such as fancy lobbies, in-room phones, and frequent bedsheet changes—I happily make the trade-off for the personal touches, whether it's joining my hosts for afternoon tea or relaxing by a common fireplace at the end of the day. If you have a reasonable but limited budget, skip hotels and go the B&B way.

Many B&Bs take credit cards, but may add the card service fee to your bill (about 3 percent). If you do need to pay cash for your room, plan ahead to have enough on hand when you check out.

B&Bs and small hotels come with their own etiquette and quirks. Keep in mind that owners are at the whim of their guests—if you're getting up early, so are they; and if you check in late, they'll wait up for you. Most B&Bs either have set check-in times (usually twice a day, in the morning and late afternoon), or will want to know when to expect you (call or email ahead to let them know).

B&B proprietors are selective about the guests they invite in for the night. Many do not welcome children. If you'll be staying for more than one night, you are a "desirable." In popular weekend-getaway spots, you're unlikely to find a place to take you for Saturday night only. If my listings are full, ask for guidance. Mentioning this book can help. Owners usually work together and can call up an ally to land you a bed.

Many B&B owners are also pet owners. If you're allergic, ask about resident pets when you reserve.

Small places usually serve a hearty fried breakfast of eggs and much more (for details on breakfast, see the Eating section, later). Because your B&B or small-hotel owner is often also the cook, breakfast hours are usually abbreviated (typically about an hour—make sure you know when it is before you turn in for the night). It's an unwritten rule that guests shouldn't show up at the very end of the breakfast period and expect a full cooked breakfast. If you do arrive late (or if you need to leave before breakfast is served), most establishments are happy to let you help yourself to cereal, fruit or juice, and coffee.

B&Bs and small hotels often come with thin walls and doors,

The Good and Bad of Online Reviews

User-generated travel review websites—such as TripAdvisor, Booking.com, and Yelp—have quickly become a huge player in the travel industry. These sites give you access to actual reports—good and bad—from travelers who have experienced the hotel, restaurant, tour, or attraction.

My hotelier friends in Europe are in awe of these sites' influence. Small hoteliers who want to stay in business have no choice but to work with review sites—which often charge fees for good placement or photos, and tack on commissions if users book through the site instead of directly with the hotel.

While these sites work hard to weed out bogus users, my hunch is that a significant percentage of reviews are posted by friends or enemies of the business being reviewed. I've even seen hotels "bribe" guests (for example, offer a free breakfast) in exchange for a positive review. Also, review sites are uncurated and can become an echo chamber, with one or two flashy businesses camped out atop the ratings, while better, more affordable, and more authentic alternatives sit ignored farther down the list. (For example, I find review sites' restaurant recommendations skew to very touristy, obvious options.) And you can't always give credence to the negative reviews: Different people have different expectations.

Remember that a user-generated review is based on the experience of one person. That person likely stayed at one hotel and ate at a few restaurants, and doesn't have much of a basis for comparison. A guidebook is the work of a trained researcher who has exhaustively visited many alternatives to assess their relative value. I recently checked out some top-rated TripAdvisor listings in various towns; when stacked up against their competitors, some are gems, while just as many are duds.

Both types of information have their place, and in many ways, they're complementary. If a hotel or restaurant is well-reviewed in a guidebook or two, and also gets good ratings on one of these sites, it's likely a winner.

and sometimes creaky floorboards, which can make for a noisy night. If you're a light sleeper, bring earplugs. And please be quiet in the halls and in your rooms at night...those of us getting up early will thank you for it.

In the Room: Every B&B offers "tea service" in the room—an electric kettle, cups, tea bags, coffee packets, and a pack of biscuits.

Your bedroom probably won't include a phone, but nearly every B&B has free Wi-Fi (if they don't, I'll generally note it in the listing). However, the signal may not reach to all of the floors; you may need to sit in the lounge to access it.

Treat these lovingly maintained homes as you would a friend's

Making Hotel Reservations

Reserve your rooms several weeks in advance—or as soon as you've pinned down your travel dates. Note that some national holidays merit your making reservations far in advance (see page 1042).

Requesting a Reservation: It's easiest to book your room through the hotel's website. (For the best rates, always use the hotel's official site and not a booking agency's site.) If there's no reservation form, or for complicated requests, send an email (see sample request).

The hotelier wants to know:

- the number and type of rooms you need
- the number of nights you'll stay
- your date of arrival
- your date of departure
- any special needs (such as bathroom in the room or down the hall, twin beds vs. double bed)

Mention any discounts—for Rick Steves readers or otherwise—when you make the reservation.

Confirming a Reservation: Most places will request a credit-card number to hold your room. If they don't have a secure online reservation form—look for the *https*—you can email your card number (I do), but it's safer to share that confidential info via a phone call or two emails (splitting your number between them).

Canceling a Reservation: If you must cancel, it's courteous—and smart—to do so with as much notice as possible, especially for smaller family-run places. Be warned that cancellation policies

house. Be careful maneuvering your bag up narrow staircases with fragile walls and banisters. And once in the room, use the luggage rack: Putting bags on the bed can damage nice comforters.

Electrical outlets have switches that turn the current on or off; if your appliance isn't working, flip the switch at the outlet.

You're also likely to encounter unusual bathroom fixtures. The "pump toilet" has a flushing handle or button that doesn't kick in unless you push it just right: too hard or too soft, and it won't go. (Be decisive but not ruthless.)

Most B&B baths have an instant water heater. This looks like an electronic box under the shower head with dials and buttons: One control adjusts the heat, while another turns the flow off and on (let the water run for a bit to moderate the temperature before you hop in). If the hot water doesn't work, you may need to flip a red switch (often located just outside the bathroom). If the shower looks mysterious, ask your B&B host for help...*before* you take your clothes off.

Americans sometimes assume they'll get new towels each day.

From: rick@ricksteves.com
Sent: Today
To: info@hotelcentral.com
Subject: Reservation request for 19-22 July

Dear Hotel Central,

I would like to reserve a room for 2 people for 3 nights, arriving 19 July and departing 22 July. If possible, I would like a quiet room with a double bed and private bathroom inside the room.

Please let me know if you have a room available and the price.

Thank you!
Rick Steves

can be strict; read the fine print or ask about these before you book. Internet deals may require prepayment, with no refunds for cancellations.

Reconfirming a Reservation: Always call or email to reconfirm your room reservation a few days in advance. For B&Bs or very small hotels, I call again on my day of arrival to tell my host what time I expect to get there (especially important if arriving late—after 17:00).

Phoning: For tips on calling hotels overseas, see page 1016.

The British don't, and neither should you. Hang towels up to dry and reuse.

Hotels

Many of my recommended hotels have three or more floors of rooms and steep stairs. Older properties often do not have elevators. If stairs are an issue, ask for a ground-floor room or choose a hotel with a lift (elevator). Air-conditioning isn't a given (I've noted which of my listings have it), but most places have fans. On hot summer nights, you'll want your window open—and in a big city, street noise is a fact of life. Bring earplugs or request a room on the back side or on an upper floor.

A "twin" room has two single beds; a "double" has one double bed. If you'll take either, let the hotel know, or you might be needlessly turned away. Most hotels offer family deals, which means that parents with young children can get a room with an extra child's bed or a discount for larger rooms. Teenagers are generally charged as adults.

An "en suite" room has a bathroom (toilet and shower/tub) attached to the room; a room with a "private bathroom" can mean that the bathroom is all yours, but it's across the hall. If you want your own bathroom inside the room, request "en suite."

If money's tight, ask for a room with a shared bathroom. You'll almost always have a sink in your room, and as more rooms go "en suite," the hallway bathroom is shared with fewer guests.

Note that to be called a "hotel," a place technically must have certain amenities, including a 24-hour reception (though this rule is loosely applied). TVs are standard in rooms, but may come with limited channels (no cable). Note that all of Britain's accommodations are now non-smoking.

Modern Hotel Chains: Chain hotels—common in bigger cities all over Great Britain—can be a great value (£60-100, depending on location; more expensive in London). These hotels are about as cozy as a Motel 6, but they come with private showers/WCs, elevators, good security, and often an attached restaurant. Branches are often located near the train station, on major highways, or outside the city center.

While most chain hotels have 24-hour reception, the service lacks a personal touch (at some, you'll check in at a self-service kiosk). Breakfast and Wi-Fi generally cost extra. For about the same price you may be able to get a basic room at a funkier and friendlier budget hotel or B&B in a more enjoyable neighborhood. But the chain hotel option is worth considering, especially for families, as kids often stay for free.

Room rates change from day to day with volume and vary depending on how far ahead you book. The best deals generally must be prepaid a few weeks ahead and may not be refundable—read the fine print carefully.

The biggest chains are **Premier Inn** (www.premierinn.com, toll reservations tel. 0871-527-9222) and **Travelodge** (www.travelodge.co.uk, toll reservations tel. 0871-984-8484). Both have attractive deals for prepaid or advance bookings. Other chains operating in Britain include the Irish **Jurys Inn** (www.jurysinns.com) and the French-owned **Ibis** (www.ibishotel.com). Couples can consider **Holiday Inn Express,** which generally allow only two people per room. It's like a Holiday Inn lite, with cheaper prices and no restaurant (make sure Express is part of the name or you'll be paying more for a regular Holiday Inn, www.hiexpress.co.uk).

At the Hotel: If you're arriving in the morning, your room probably won't be ready. Drop your bag safely at the hotel and dive right into sightseeing.

If you suspect night noise will be a problem (if, for instance, your room is over a noisy pub), ask for a quieter room in the back or on an upper floor. To guard against theft in your room, keep valuables out of sight. Some rooms come with a safe, and other hotels have safes at the front desk. I've never bothered using one.

Hoteliers can be a great help and source of advice. Most know their city well, and can assist you with everything from public transit and airport connections to finding a good restaurant, the nearest launderette, or a Wi-Fi hotspot.

Even at the best places, mechanical breakdowns occur: Air-conditioning malfunctions, sinks leak, hot water turns cold, and toilets gurgle and smell. Report your concerns clearly and calmly at the front desk. For more complicated problems, don't expect instant results.

Checkout can pose problems if surprise charges pop up on your bill. If you settle up your bill the afternoon before you leave, you'll have time to discuss and address any points of contention (before 19:00, when the night shift usually arrives).

Above all, keep a positive attitude. Remember, you're on vacation. If your hotel is a disappointment, spend more time out enjoying the city you came to see.

Hostels

Britain has hundreds of hostels of all shapes and sizes. Choose your hostel selectively. Hostels can be historic castles or depressing tenements, serene and comfy or overrun by noisy school groups. A hostel provides cheap beds where you sleep alongside strangers for about £20-30 (about $30-50) per night. Travelers of any age are welcome if they don't mind dorm-style accommodations and meeting other travelers. Cheap meals are sometimes available. Many hostels offer kitchen facilities, guest computers, Wi-Fi, and a self-service laundry. Most hostels provide all bedding, including sheets. Family and private rooms may be available on request.

Independent hostels tend to be easygoing, colorful, and informal (no membership required); www.hostelworld.com is the standard way backpackers search and book hostels, but also try www.hostels.com and www.hostelz.com. For London independent hostel listings, try www.hostellondon.com.

Official hostels are part of Hostelling International (HI) and share an online booking site (www.hihostels.com). In Britain, these official hostels are run by the YHA (www.yha.org.uk). For Scotland, also consult www.hostel-scotland.co.uk. Official hostels typically require that you either have a membership card or pay extra per night.

Apartments

Renting an apartment (or "flat") can be a fun and cost-effective way to go local. Usually equipped with a modest kitchen and living room, apartments can be a good option for families and groups on a budget, and anyone looking for more space and the option of cooking your own meals.

Websites such as Booking.com, Airbnb, VRBO, and FlipKey let you browse properties and correspond directly with property owners or managers. To find out more about an apartment's location, plot the address on Google Maps and virtually "explore" the neighborhood using the Street View feature.

Apartment prices vary depending on size, amenities, and location. Some places have a minimum-stay requirement (typically 4-5 nights). Read the contract carefully so you are aware of additional fees (a one-time cleaning fee is standard) and cancellation policies, which are usually less flexible than at a hotel (for example, a nonrefundable 50 percent deposit).

In most cases, you'll need to let the owner or property manager know your arrival time so they can meet you for check-in. Or they may give you a door code for self check-in.

Other Options: If a whole apartment is overkill, Airbnb and Roomorama also list rooms in private homes. Beds range from air-mattress-in-living-room basic to plush-B&B-suite posh. If you want a place to sleep that's free, Couchsurfing.org is a vagabond's alternative to Airbnb. It lists millions of outgoing members, who host fellow "surfers" in their homes.

Eating

These days, the stereotype of "bad food in Britain" is woefully dated. Britain has caught up with the foodie revolution, and I find it's easy to eat very well here.

British cooking has embraced international influences and good-quality ingredients, making "modern British" food quite delicious. While some dreary pub food still exists, you'll generally find the cuisine scene here innovative and delicious (but expensive). Basic pubs are more likely to dish up homemade creative dishes than microwaved pies, soggy fries, and mushy peas. Even traditional pub grub has gone upmarket, with gastropubs that serve locally-sourced meats and fresh vegetables.

All of Britain is smoke-free. Expect restaurants and pubs to be nonsmoking indoors, with smokers occupying patios and doorways outside.

When restaurant-hunting, choose a spot filled with locals, not tourists. Venturing even a block or two off the main drag leads to higher-quality food for a better price. Locals eat better at lower-rent locales.

Tipping: At pubs and places where you order at the counter, you don't have to tip. Regular customers ordering a round sometimes say, "Add one for yourself" as a tip for drinks ordered at the bar—but this isn't expected.

At restaurants and fancy pubs with waitstaff, tip about 10-12.5 percent. Most restaurants in London now add a 12.5 percent "optional" tip onto the bill: Tip only what you think the service warrants, and be careful not to tip double.

BREAKFAST (FRY-UP)

The traditional fry-up or full English/Scottish/Welsh breakfast—generally included in the cost of your room—is famous as a hearty way to start the day. Also known as a "heart attack on a plate," your standard fry-up is a heated plate with eggs, Canadian-style bacon and/or sausage, a grilled tomato, sautéed mushrooms, baked beans, and sometimes potatoes, kippers (herring), or fried bread (sizzled in a greasy skillet). Toast comes in a rack (to cool quickly and crisply) with butter and marmalade. Expect regional variations: You'll get black pudding (a blood sausage) in northern England, and in Scotland you may be offered a dense potato scone. The meal is typically topped off with tea or coffee. At a B&B or hotel, it may start with juice and cereal or porridge. Many progressive B&B owners offer vegetarian, organic, gluten-free, or other creative variations on the traditional breakfast.

Much as the full breakfast fry-up is a traditional way to start the morning, these days most hotels serve a healthier continental breakfast—with a buffet of everything you'd expect, such as yogurt, cereal, scrambled eggs, fruit, and veggies.

LUNCH AND DINNER ON A BUDGET

Even in pricey cities, plenty of inexpensive choices are available: pub grub, daily lunch and early-bird dinner specials, ethnic restaurants, cafeterias, fast food, picnics, greasy-spoon cafés, cheap chain restaurants, and pizza.

I've found that portions are huge, and **sharing plates** is generally just fine. Ordering two drinks, a soup or side salad, and splitting a £10 meat pie can make a good filling meal. If you're on a limited budget, share a main course in a more expensive place for a nicer eating experience.

Pub grub is the most atmospheric budget option. You'll usually get hearty lunches and dinners priced reasonably at £8-12 under ancient timbers (see "Pubs," later). Gastropubs, with better food, are more expensive.

Classier restaurants have some affordable deals. Lunch is usually cheaper than dinner; a top-end £25-for-dinner-type restaurant often serves the same quality two-course lunch deals for about half the price.

Many restaurants have **early-bird** or **pretheater specials** of two or three courses, often for a significant savings. Some places offer these on weekdays only; others have them every day. They are usually available only before 18:30 or 19:00. If you're bargain hunting and willing to eat a bit earlier, inquire or check websites for details.

Ethnic restaurants add spice to Britain's cuisine scene. Eating Indian, Bangladeshi, Chinese, or Thai is cheap (even cheaper if you do takeout). Middle Eastern stands sell gyro sandwiches, falafel, and *shwarmas* (grilled meat in pita bread). An Indian samosa (greasy, flaky meat-and-vegetable pie) costs about £2 and makes a very cheap, if small, meal. (For more, see "Indian Cuisine," later.) You'll find all-you-can-eat Chinese and Thai places serving £6 meals and offering even cheaper takeaway boxes. While you can't "split" a buffet, you can split a takeaway box. Stuff the box full, and you and your partner can eat in a park for under £2 each.

Fish-and-chips are a heavy, greasy, but tasty British classic. Every town has at least one "chippy" selling a takeaway box of fish-and-chips in a cardboard box or (more traditionally) wrapped in paper for about £4-7. You can dip your fries in ketchup, American-style, or "go English" and drizzle the whole thing with malt vinegar and fresh lemon.

Most large **museums** (and many historic **churches**) have handy moderately-priced cafeterias with forgettably decent food.

Picnicking saves time and money. Fine park benches and polite pigeons abound in most towns and city neighborhoods. You can easily get prepared food to go. The modern chain eateries on nearly every corner often have simple seating but are designed for takeout. Bakeries serve a wonderful array of fresh sandwiches and pasties (savory meat pies).

Open-air markets and supermarkets sell produce in small quantities. The corner grocery store has fruit, drinks, fresh bread, tasty British cheese, meat, and local specialties. Supermarkets often have good deli sections, even offering Indian dishes, and sometimes salad bars. Decent packaged sandwiches (£3-4) are sold everywhere. Munch a relaxed "meal on wheels" picnic during your open-top bus tour or river cruise to save 30 precious, minutes for sightseeing.

PUBS

Pubs are a fundamental part of the British social scene, and whether you're a teetotaler or a beer guzzler, they should be a part of your travel here. "Pub" is short for "public house." It's an extended common room where, if you don't mind the stickiness, you can feel the pulse of Britain. Smart travelers use pubs to eat, drink, get out of the rain, watch sporting events, and make new friends. Unfortunately, many city pubs have been afflicted with an excess of brass, ferns, and video slot machines. The most traditional atmospheric pubs are in the countryside and in smaller towns.

It's interesting to consider the role pubs filled for Britain's working class in more modest times: For workers with humble domestic quarters and no money for a vacation, a beer at the corner pub was the closest they'd get to a comfortable living room, a place to entertain, and a getaway. And locals could meet people from far away in a pub—today, that's you!

Though hours vary, pubs generally serve beer daily from 11:00 to 23:00, though many are open later, particularly on Friday and Saturday. (Children are served food and soft drinks in pubs, but you must be 18 to order a beer.) As it nears closing time, you'll hear shouts of "Last orders." Then comes the 10-minute warning bell. Finally, they'll call "Time!" to pick up your glass, finished or not, when the pub closes.

A cup of darts is free for the asking. People go to a public house to be social. They want to talk. Get vocal with a local. This is easiest at the bar, where people assume you're in the mood to talk (rather than at a table, where you're allowed a bit of privacy). The pub is the next best thing to having relatives in town. Cheers!

Pub Grub: For £8-12, you'll get a basic budget hot lunch or dinner in friendly surroundings. In high-priced London, this is your best indoor eating value. (For something more refined, try a **gastropub,** which serves higher-quality meals for £12-18.) The *Good Pub Guide* is an excellent resource (www.thegoodpubguide.co.uk). Pubs that are attached to restaurants, advertise their food, and are crowded with locals, are more likely to have fresh food and a chef—and less likely to sell only lousy microwaved snacks.

Pubs generally serve traditional dishes, such as fish-and-chips, roast beef with Yorkshire pudding (batter-baked in the oven), and assorted meat pies, such as steak-and-kidney pie or shepherd's pie (stewed lamb topped with mashed potatoes) with cooked vegetables. Side dishes include salads, vegetables, and—invariably—"chips" (French fries). "Crisps" are potato chips. A "jacket potato" (baked potato stuffed with fillings of your choice) can almost be a meal in itself. A "ploughman's lunch" is a "traditional British meal" of bread, cheese, and sweet pickles that nearly every tourist tries... once. These days, you'll likely find more pasta, curried dishes, and quiche on the menu than traditional fare.

Meals are usually served from 12:00 to 14:00 and again from 18:00 to 20:00—with a break in the middle (rather than serving straight through the day). Since they make more money selling beer, many pubs stop food service early in the evening—especially on weekends. There's generally no table service. Order at the bar, then take a seat. Either they'll bring the food when it's ready or you'll pick it up at the bar. Pay at the bar (sometimes when you order, sometimes after you eat). Don't tip unless it's a place with full table service. Servings are hearty and service is quick. If you're on a tight budget, it's OK to share a meal. A beer, cider, or dram of whisky adds another couple of pounds. Free tap water is always available. For a list of recommended historic pubs in London, see page 172. For details on ordering beer and other drinks, see the "Beverages" section, later.

GOOD CHAIN RESTAURANTS

I know—you're going to Britain to enjoy characteristic little hole-in-the-wall pubs, so mass-produced food is the furthest thing from your mind. But several excellent chains with branches across the UK keep long hours and can be a nice break from pub grub. My favorites are Pret, Wasabi, and Eat.

Pret (a.k.a. Pret à Manger) is perhaps the most pervasive of these modern convenience eateries. Some are takeout-only, and others have seating ranging from simple stools to restaurant-quality tables. The service is fast, the price is great, and the food is healthy and fresh. Their slogan: "Made today. Gone today. No 'sell-by' date, no nightlife."

Côte Brasserie is a contemporary French chain serving good-value French cuisine in reliably pleasant settings (£10-14 main dishes, early dinner specials).

Byron Hamburgers, an upscale hamburger-chain with hip interiors, is worth seeking out if you need a burger fix. While British burgers tend to be a bit overcooked by American standards, Byron's are your best bet (£7-10 burgers).

Wagamama Noodle Bar, serving up pan-Asian cuisine (udon noodles, fried rice, and curry dishes), is a noisy, organic slurpathon.

Portions are huge and splittable. There's one in almost every midsize city in Britain, usually located in sprawling halls filled with long shared tables and busy servers who scrawl your order on the placemat.

Loch Fyne Fish Restaurant is a Scottish chain that raises its own oysters and mussels. Its branches offer an inviting, lively atmosphere with a fine fishy energy and no pretense (£12-20 main dishes, early-bird specials).

Marks & Spencer department stores have a new feature: inviting deli sections with cheery sit-down eating (along with their popular sandwiches-to-go section).

Thai Square is a dependable Thai option with a nice atmosphere (£9-13 salads, noodle dishes, and curries; £14-19 meat dishes; £10 daily lunch box specials). Most branches are in London.

Masala Zone is a London chain providing a good predictable alternative to the many one-off hole-in-the-wall Indian joints around town. Try a curry-and-rice dish, a *thali* (platter with several small dishes), or their street food specials. Each branch has its own personality (£9-14 meals).

Ask and **Pizza Express** serve quality pasta and pizza in a pleasant sit-down atmosphere that's family-friendly. **Jamie's Italian** (from celebrity chef Jamie Oliver) is hipper and pricier.

Japanese: Three popular chains serve fresh and inexpensive Japanese food. **Itsu** and **Wasabi** are two bright and competitive chains that let you assemble your own plate in a fun and efficient way, while **Yo! Sushi** lets you pick your dish off a conveyor belt and pay according to the color of your plate. If you're in the mood for sushi, all are great.

Carry-Out Chains: While the following may have some seating, they're best as easy places to grab prepackaged food on the run.

Major supermarket chains have smaller offshoot branches that specialize in sandwiches, salads, and other prepared foods to go. These can be a picnicker's dream come true. Some shops are stand-alone, while others are located inside a larger store. The most prevalent—and best—is **M&S Simply Food** (an offshoot of Marks & Spencer; there's one in every major train station). **Sainsbury's Local** grocery stores also offer decent prepared food; **Tesco Express** and **Tesco Metro** run a distant third.

Some "cheap and cheery" chains provide office workers with good healthful sandwiches, salads, and pastries to go. These include **Apostróphe, Pod,** and **Eat** (with slightly higher-quality food and higher prices).

INDIAN CUISINE

Eating Indian food is "going local" in cosmopolitan multiethnic Britain. You'll find Indian restaurants in most cities and even in small towns. Take the opportunity to sample food from Britain's former colony. Indian cuisine is as varied as the country itself. In general, it uses more exotic spices than British or American cuisine—some hot, some sweet. Indian food is very vegetarian-friendly, offering many meatless dishes.

For a simple meal that costs about £10-12, order one dish with rice and naan (Indian flatbread). Generally one order is plenty for two people to share. Many Indian restaurants offer a fixed-price combination that offers more variety, and is simpler and cheaper than ordering à la carte. For about £20, you can make a mix-and-match platter out of several shareable dishes, including dal (simmered lentils) as a starter, one or two meat or vegetable dishes with sauce (for example, chicken curry, chicken *tikka masala* in a creamy tomato sauce, grilled fish tandoori, chickpea *chana masala*, or a spicy vindaloo dish), *raita* (a cooling yogurt that's added to spicy dishes), rice, naan, and an Indian beer (wine and Indian food don't really mix) or chai (cardamom/cinnamon-spiced tea, usually served with milk). An easy way to taste a variety of dishes is to order a thali—a sampler plate, generally served on a metal tray, with small servings of various specialties.

AFTERNOON TEA

Once the sole province of genteel ladies in fancy hats, afternoon tea has become more democratic in the 21st century. These days, people of leisure punctuate their day with an afternoon tea at a tearoom. Tearooms, which often serve appealing light meals, are usually open for lunch and close at about 17:00, just before dinner.

The cheapest "tea" on the menu is generally a "cream tea"; the most expensive is the "champagne tea." **Cream tea** is simply a pot of tea and a homemade scone or two with jam and thick clotted cream. (For maximum pinkie-waving taste per calorie, slice your scone thin like a miniature loaf of bread.) **Afternoon tea**—what many Americans would call "high tea"—is a pot of tea, small finger foods (such as sandwiches with the crusts cut off), scones, an assortment of small pastries, jam, and thick clotted cream. **Champagne tea** includes all of the goodies, plus a glass of bubbly. **High tea** to Brits generally means a more substantial late afternoon or early evening meal, often served with meat or eggs.

DESSERTS (SWEETS)

To the British, the traditional word for dessert is "pudding," although it's also referred to as "sweets" these days. Sponge cake, cream, fruitcake, and meringue are key players.

Trifle is the best-known British concoction, consisting of sponge cake soaked in brandy or sherry (or orange juice for children), then covered with jam and/or fruit and custard cream.

British Chocolate

My chocoholic readers are enthusiastic about British chocolates. As with other dairy products, chocolate seems richer and creamier here than it does in the US, so even the basics like Mars, Kit Kat (which was actually invented in York—see page 552), and Twix have a different taste. Some favorites include Cadbury Gold bars (filled with liquid caramel), Cadbury Crunchie bars, Nestlé's Lion bars (layered wafers covered in caramel and chocolate), Cadbury's Boost bars (a shortcake biscuit with caramel in milk chocolate), Cadbury Flake (crumbly folds of melt-in-your-mouth chocolate), Aero bars (with "aerated" chocolate filling), and Galaxy chocolate bars (especially the ones with hazelnuts). Thornton shops (in larger train stations) sell a box of sweets called the Continental Assortment, which comes with a tasting guide. (The highlight is the mocha white-chocolate truffle.) British M&Ms, called Smarties, are better than American ones. Many Brits feel that the ultimate treat is a box of either Nestlé Quality Street or Cadbury Roses—assortments of filled chocolates in colorful wrappers. (But don't mention the Kraft takeover of Cadbury—many Brits believe the American company changed the recipe for their beloved Dairy Milk bars, and they're not happy about it.) At ice-cream vans, look for the traditional "99p"—a vanilla soft-serve cone with a small Flake bar stuck right into the middle.

Whipped cream can sometimes put the final touch on this "light" treat.

The British version of custard is a smooth yellow liquid. Cream tops most everything that custard does not. There's single cream for coffee. Double cream is really thick. Whipped cream is familiar, and clotted cream is the consistency of whipped butter.

Fool is a dessert with sweetened pureed fruit (such as rhubarb, gooseberries, or black currants) mixed with cream or custard and chilled. Elderflower is a popular flavoring for sorbet.

Flapjacks here aren't pancakes, but are dense sweet oatmeal cakes (a little like a cross between a granola bar and a brownie). They come with toppings such as toffee and chocolate.

Scones are tops, and many inns and restaurants have their secret recipes. Whether made with fruit or topped with clotted cream, scones take the cake.

BEVERAGES

Beer: The British take great pride in their beer. Many locals think that drinking beer cold and carbonated, as Americans do, ruins the taste. Most pubs will have **lagers** (cold, refreshing, American-style beer), **ales** (amber-colored cellar-temperature beer), **bitters** (hop-flavored ale, perhaps the most typical British beer), and **stouts** (dark and somewhat bitter, like Guinness).

At pubs, long-handled pulls (or taps) are used to pull the traditional rich-flavored "real ales" up from the cellar. These are the connoisseur's favorites and often come with fun names. Served straight from the brewer's cask at cellar temperature, real ales finish fermenting naturally and are not pasteurized or filtered, so they must be consumed within two or three days after the cask is tapped. Naturally carbonated, real ales have less gassiness and head; they vary from sweet to bitter, often with a hoppy or nutty flavor.

Short-handled pulls mean colder, fizzier, mass-produced, and less interesting keg beers. Mild beers are sweeter, with a creamy malt flavoring. Irish cream ale is a smooth, sweet experience. Try the draft cider (sweet or dry)...carefully.

Order your beer at the bar and pay as you go, with no need to tip. An average beer costs £3. Part of the experience is standing before a line of hand pulls and wondering which beer to choose.

As dictated by British law, draft beer and cider are served by the pint (20-ounce imperial size) or the half-pint (9.6 ounces). (It's almost feminine for a man to order just a half; I order mine with quiche.) In 2011, the government sanctioned an in-between serving size—the schooner, or two-thirds pint (it's become a popular size for higher alcohol-content craft beers). Proper British ladies like a **shandy** (half beer and half 7-Up).

Whisky: While bar-hopping tourists generally think in terms of beer, many pubs are just as enthusiastic about serving whisky. If you are unfamiliar with whisky (what Americans call "Scotch" and the Irish call "whiskey"), it's a great conversation starter. Many pubs have dozens of whiskies available. Lists describe their personalities (peaty, heavy iodine finish, and so on), which are much easier to discern than most wine flavors.

A glass of basic whisky generally costs around £2.50. Let a local teach you how to drink it "neat," then add a little water. Make a friend, buy a few drams, and learn by drinking. Keep experimenting until you discover the right taste for you.

Consider going beyond the single-malt whisky rut. Like microbrews, small-batch innovative Scottish spirits are trendy right now. Blends can be surprisingly creative—even for someone who thinks they're knowledgeable about whisky—and non-whisky alternatives are pushing boundaries. For example, you'll find gin that's aged in whisky casks, taking off the piney edge and infusing a bit of that distinctive whisky flavor.

Distilleries throughout Scotland offer tours, but you'll often only learn about that one type of whisky. At a good whisky shop, the knowledgeable staff offer guided tastings (for a fee and typically arranged in advance), explaining four or five whiskies to help you develop your palate. If you don't care for a heavy, smoky whisky, ask for something milder. Some shops have several bottles open and will let you try a few wee drams to narrow down your options. I've listed both distillery tours and whisky shops in this book. Be aware: If they're providing samples, they're hoping you'll buy a bottle at the end.

For more about whisky, see the "Whisky 101" sidebar on page 724.

Other Alcoholic Drinks: Many pubs also have a good selection of wines by the glass, a fully stocked bar for the gentleman's "G and T" (gin and tonic), and the increasingly popular bottles of alcohol-plus-sugar (such as Bacardi Breezers) for the younger working-class set. **Pimm's** is a refreshing and fruity summer cocktail, traditionally popular during Wimbledon. It's an upper-class drink—a rough bloke might insult a pub by claiming it sells more Pimm's than beer.

Non-Alcoholic Drinks: Teetotalers can order from a wide variety of soft drinks—both the predictable American sodas and other more interesting bottled drinks, such as ginger beer (similar to ginger ale but with more bite), root beers, or other flavors (Fentimans brews some unusual options that are stocked in many pubs). Note that in Britain, "lemonade" is lemon-lime soda (like 7-Up).

Staying Connected

Staying connected in Europe gets easier and cheaper every year. The simplest solution is to bring your own device—mobile phone, tablet, or laptop—and use it just as you would at home (following the tips below, such as connecting to free Wi-Fi whenever possible). Another option is to buy a European SIM card for your mobile phone—either your US phone or one you buy in Europe. Or you can travel without a mobile device and use European landlines and computers to connect. Each of these options is described below, and you'll find even more details at www.ricksteves.com/phoning.

USING YOUR OWN MOBILE DEVICE IN EUROPE

Without an international plan, typical rates from major service providers (AT&T, Verizon, etc.) for using your device abroad are about $1.50/minute for voice calls, 50 cents to send text messages, 5 cents to receive them, and $20 to download one megabyte of data. But at these rates, costs can add up quickly. Here are some budget tips and options.

Use free Wi-Fi whenever possible. Unless you have an unlimited-data plan, you're best off saving most of your online tasks for Wi-Fi. You can access the Internet, send texts, and even make voice calls over Wi-Fi.

Tips on Internet Security

Using the Internet while traveling brings added security risks, whether you're getting online with your own device or at a public terminal using a shared network.

First, make sure that your device is running the latest version of its operating system and security software. Next, ensure that your device is password- or passcode-protected so thieves can't access your information if your device is stolen. For extra security, set passwords on apps that access key info (such as email or Facebook).

On the road, use only legitimate Wi-Fi hotspots. Ask the hotel or café staff for the specific name of their Wi-Fi network, and make sure you log on to that exact one. Hackers sometimes create a bogus hotspot with a similar or vague name (such as "Hotel Europa Free Wi-Fi"). The best Wi-Fi networks require entering a password.

Be especially cautious when checking your online banking, credit-card statements, or other personal-finance accounts. Internet security experts advise against accessing these sites while traveling. Even if you're using your own mobile device at a password-protected hotspot, any hacker who's logged on to the same network may be able to see what you're doing. If you do need to log on to a banking website, use a hard-wired connection (such as an Ethernet cable in your hotel room) or a cellular network, which is safer than Wi-Fi.

Never share your credit-card number (or any other sensitive information) online unless you know that the site is secure. A secure site displays a little padlock icon, and the URL begins with *https* (instead of the usual *http*).

Many cafés (including Starbucks and McDonald's) have hotspots for customers; look for signs offering it and ask for the Wi-Fi password when you buy something. You'll also often find Wi-Fi at TIs, city squares, major museums, public-transit hubs, airports, and aboard trains and buses. In Britain, another option is to sign up for Wi-Fi access through a company such as BT (one hour-£4, one day-£10, www.btwifi.co.uk) or The Cloud (free though sometimes slow, www.thecloud.net/free-wifi).

Sign up for an international plan. Most providers offer a global calling plan that cuts the per-minute cost of phone calls and texts, and a flat-fee data plan that includes a certain amount of megabytes. Your normal plan may already include international coverage (T-Mobile's does).

Before your trip, call your provider or check online to confirm that your phone will work in Europe, and research your provider's international rates. A day or two before you leave, activate the plan by calling your provider or logging on to your mobile phone account. Remember to cancel your plan (if necessary) when your trip's over.

Minimize the use of your cellular network. When you can't find Wi-Fi, you can use your cellular network—convenient but slower and potentially expensive—to connect to the Internet, text, or make voice calls. When you're done, avoid further charges by manually switching off "data roaming" or "cellular data" (in your device's Settings menu; if you don't know how to switch it off, ask your service provider or Google it). Another way to make sure you're not accidentally using data roaming is to put your device in "airplane" or "flight" mode (which also disables phone calls and texts, as well as data), and then turn on Wi-Fi as needed.

Don't use your cellular network for bandwidth-gobbling tasks, such as Skyping, downloading apps, and watching YouTube—save these for when you're on Wi-Fi. Using a navigation app such as Google Maps can take lots of data, so use this sparingly.

Limit automatic updates. By default, your device is constantly checking for a data connection and updating apps. It's smart to disable these features so they'll only update when you're on Wi-Fi, and to change your device's email settings from "auto-retrieve" to "manual" (or from "push" to "fetch").

It's also a good idea to keep track of your data usage. On your device's menu, look for "cellular data usage" or "mobile data" and reset the counter at the start of your trip.

Use Skype or other calling/messaging apps for cheaper calls and texts. Certain apps let you make voice or video calls or send texts over the Internet for free or cheap. If you're bringing a tablet or laptop, you can also use them for voice calls and texts. All you have to do is log on to a Wi-Fi network, then contact any of your friends or family members who are also online and signed into the same service. You can make voice and video calls using Skype, Viber, FaceTime, and Google+ Hangouts. If the connection is bad, try making an audio-only call.

You can also make voice calls from your device to telephones worldwide for just a few cents per minute using Skype, Viber, or Hangouts if you prebuy credit.

To text for free over Wi-Fi, try apps like Google+ Hangouts, WhatsApp, Viber, and Facebook Messenger. Apple's iMessage connects with other Apple users, but make sure you're on Wi-Fi to avoid data charges.

USING A EUROPEAN SIM CARD IN A MOBILE PHONE

This option works well for those who want to make a lot of voice calls at cheap local rates. Either buy a phone in Europe (as little as $40 from mobile-phone shops anywhere), or bring an "unlocked"

How to Dial

Many Americans are intimidated by dialing European phone numbers. You needn't be. It's simple, once you break the code.

Dialing Rules

Here are the rules for dialing, along with examples of how to call one of my recommended hotels in London (tel. 020/7730-8191). The 020 is London's area code.

Dialing Internationally to Britain

Whether you're phoning from a US landline, your own mobile phone, a Skype account, or a number in another European country (e.g., France to Britain), you're making an international call. Here's how to do it:

1. Dial the **international access code** (011 if calling from a US or Canadian phone; 00 if calling from any European phone number outside of Britain). If dialing from a mobile phone, you can enter a + in place of the international access code (press and hold the 0 key).
2. Dial the **country code** (44 for Britain).
3. Dial the **phone number** (drop the initial 0).

Examples:

- To call my recommended hotel from a **US or Canadian phone,** dial 011, then 44, then 20/7730-8191.
- To call from **any European phone number** (outside of Britain), dial 00, then 44, then 20/7730-8191.
- To call from any **mobile phone** (except a British one), dial +, then 44, then 20/7730-8191.

Dialing Within Britain

To make a domestic call (either from a British mobile phone or landline), you'll generally dial both the area code (including the initial 0) and the local number. If you're calling within the same area code, you could drop the area code and just dial the local number. But because area codes can vary in length, and mobile phones utilize their own sets of prefixes, I keep things simple by

US phone (check with your carrier about unlocking it). With an unlocked phone, you can replace the original SIM card (the microchip that stores info about the phone) with one that will work with a European provider.

In Europe, buy a European SIM card. Inserted into your phone, this card gives you a European phone number—and European rates. SIM cards are sold at mobile-phone shops, department-store electronics counters, some newsstands, and even at vending machines. Costing about $5-10, they usually include about that much prepaid calling credit, with no contract and no commitment. You can still use your phone's Wi-Fi function to get online. To

always dialing the full phone number, including the area code or prefix.

Example: To call my recommended hotel from any British landline or mobile phone, dial 020/7730-8191. If dialing from within the same 020 area code, you can just enter 7730-8191.

Calling from any European Country to the US

To call the US or Canada from Europe (either from a mobile phone or landline), dial 00 (Europe's international access code), 1 (US/Canada country code), and the phone number, including the area code. If calling from a mobile phone, you can enter a + instead of 00.

Example: To call my office in Edmonds, Washington, from anywhere in Europe, I dial 00-1-425-771-8303; or from a mobile phone, +-1-425-771-8303.

More Dialing Tips

British Phone Numbers: Numbers beginning with 074, 075, 076, 077, 078, and 079 are mobile numbers, which are more expensive to call than a landline. For directory assistance, dial 118-500, but it's expensive (£3.99/call and £1.39/minute)—find the number online instead.

Toll and Toll-Free Calls: "Freephone" numbers, starting 0800 or 0808, are free for all callers, whether dialed from a mobile phone or a landline. Numbers beginning with 084, 087, or 03 are toll numbers that can be dialed from British landlines or mobile phones, with per-minute prices that vary depending on who you're calling and which phone company carries the call (some as expensive as £0.45/minute). Numbers beginning with 09 are pricey toll calls, but you shouldn't encounter these unless you're calling chat lines. If you have questions about a prefix, call 100 for free help.

More Resources: The "Phoning Cheat Sheet" shows how to dial per country, or you can check www.countrycallingcodes.com or www.howtocallabroad.com.

get a SIM card that also includes data costs (including roaming), figure on paying $15-30 for one month of data within the country you bought it. This can be cheaper than data roaming through your home provider. To get the best rates, buy a new SIM card whenever you arrive in a new country.

I like to buy SIM cards at a mobile-phone shop where there's a clerk to help explain the options and brands. Lebara and Lycamobile operate in multiple European countries, and are reliable and economical. Ask the clerk to help you insert your SIM card, set it up, and show you how to use it. In some countries you'll be required to register the SIM card with your passport as an antiter-

The British Accent

In the olden days, a British person's accent indicated his or her social standing. Eliza Doolittle had the right idea—elocution could make or break you. Wealthier families would send their kids to fancy private schools to learn proper pronunciation. But these days, in a sort of reverse snobbery that has gripped the nation, accents are back. Politicians, newscasters, and movie stars are favoring deep accents over the Queen's English. While it's hard for American ears to pick out all the variations, most Brits can determine where a person is from based on their accent...not just the region, but often the village, and even the part of a town.

rorism measure (which may mean you can't use the phone for the first hour or two).

When you run out of credit, you can top it up at newsstands, tobacco shops, mobile-phone stores, or many other businesses (look for your SIM card's logo in the window), or online.

USING LANDLINES AND COMPUTERS IN EUROPE

It's easy to travel in Europe without a mobile device. You can check email or browse websites using public computers and Internet cafés, and make calls from your hotel room and/or public phones.

Phones in your **hotel room** can be inexpensive for local calls and calls made with cheap international phone cards (sold at newsstands, street kiosks, and train stations). You'll get a prepaid card with a toll-free number and a scratch-to-reveal PIN code; to make a call, dial the toll-free number, follow the prompts, enter the code, then dial your number.

Most hotels charge a fee for placing local and "toll-free" calls, as well as long-distance or international calls—ask for the rates before you dial. Since you're never charged for receiving calls, it's better to have someone from the US call you in your room.

Phones are rare in rooms at **B&Bs,** but if your room has one (or if you ask to use your host's phone), the advice above applies.

Public pay phones are getting harder to find, and they're expensive. To use one, you'll pay with a major credit card (which you insert into the phone—minimum charge for a credit-card call is £1.20) or coins (have a bunch handy; minimum fee is £0.60). Only unused coins will be returned, so put in biggies with caution.

Cheap **call shops,** often located in train-station neighborhoods, advertise low international rates. Before making your call, be completely clear on the rates (e.g., if there's a charge per unit, find out how long a unit is).

It's always possible to find **public computers:** at your hotel

Phoning Cheat Sheet

Just smile and dial, using these rules.

Calling a European number

- **From a mobile phone** (whether you're in the US or in Europe): Dial + (press and hold 0), then country code and number*
- **From a US/Canadian number:** Dial 011, then country code and number*
- **From a different European country** (e.g., German number to French number): Dial 00, then country code and number*
- **Within the same European country** (e.g., German number to another German number): Dial the number as printed, including initial 0 if there is one

** Drop initial 0 (if present) from phone number in all countries except Italy*

Calling the US or Canada from Europe

Dial 00, then 1 (country code for US/Canada), then area code and number; on mobile phones, enter + in place of 00

Country	Country Code	Country	Country Code
Austria	43	Italy	39 [2]
Belgium	32	Latvia	371
Bosnia-Herzegovina	387	Montenegro	382
Croatia	385	Morocco	212
Czech Republic	420	Netherlands	31
Denmark	45	Norway	47
Estonia	372	Poland	48
Finland	358	Portugal	351
France	33	Russia	7 [3]
Germany	49	Slovakia	421
Gibraltar	350	Slovenia	386
Great Britain & N. Ireland	44	Spain	34
Greece	30	Sweden	46
Hungary	36 [1]	Switzerland	41
Ireland	353	Turkey	90

[1] For long-distance calls within Hungary, dial 06, then the area code and number.

[2] When making international calls to Italy, do not drop the initial 0 from the phone number.

[3] For long-distance calls within Russia, dial 8, then the area code and number. To call the US or Canada from Russia, dial 8, then 10, then 1, then the area code and number.

(many have one in their lobby for guests to use), or at an Internet café or library (ask your hotelier or the TI for the nearest location). When typing on a European keyboard, use the "Alt Gr" key to the right of the space bar to insert the extra symbol that appears on some keys. If you can't locate a special character (such as @), simply copy it from a Web page and paste it into your email message.

MAIL

You can mail one package per day to yourself worth up to $200 duty-free from Europe to the US (mark it "personal purchases"). If you're sending a gift to someone, mark it "unsolicited gift." For details, visit www.cbp.gov and search for "Know Before You Go."

The British postal service works fine, but for quick transatlantic delivery (in either direction), consider services such as DHL (www.dhl.com).

Transportation

If you're debating between using public transportation or renting a car, consider these factors: Cars are best for three or more traveling together (especially families with small kids), those packing heavy, and those delving into the countryside—a tempting plan for this region. Trains and buses are best for solo travelers, blitz tourists, city-to-city travelers, and those who don't want to drive. While a car gives you more freedom, trains and buses zip you effortlessly and scenically from city to city, usually dropping you in the center, often near a TI. Cars are an expensive headache in places like London, but necessary for remote destinations not well-served by public transport.

In Britain, my choice is to connect big cities by train and to explore rural areas (the Cotswolds, North Wales, the Lake District, and the Scottish Highlands) footloose and fancy-free by rental car. The mix works quite efficiently (e.g., London, Bath, York, and Edinburgh by train, with a rental car for the rest).

BY TRAIN

Britain's great train system (15,000 departures from 2,400 stations daily) is the most expensive per mile in all of Europe. For the greatest savings, book online in advance and leave after rush hour (after 9:30).

Since Britain's railways have been privatized, it can be tricky to track down all your options; a single train route can be operated by multiple companies. However, one website covers all train lines (www.nationalrail.co.uk), and another covers all bus and train routes (www.traveline.org.uk—for information, not ticket

Public Transportation Routes in Britain
Rail
Eurostar
Bus
(8H)
Ferry with crossing time
Orkney Islands
Gill
Scrabster
John o' Groats
Thurso
Lewis
Elgin
Skye
Portree
Inverness
Culloden
Kyle
Loch Ness
Aviemore
Aberdeen
Mallaig
SCOTLAND
Fort William
Pitlochry
Dundee
Mull
Perth
Leuchars
Iona
Oban
St. Andrews
Stirling
Edinburgh
50 Kilometers
50 Miles
Berwick
Glasgow
Holy Island
(2H)
Cairnryan
(2-3H)
Hexham
Larne
Newcastle
To Amsterdam (15H)
Stranraer
Carlisle
Durham
Belfast
Penrith
North Sea
Keswick
Whitby
NORTHERN IRELAND
Danby
Windermere
North York Moors
Scarborough
Isle of Man
(8H)
ENGLAND
Irish Sea
York
Blackpool
Leeds
Hull
To Zeebrugge (10H)
Preston
Grimsby
Dublin
(7H)
Liverpool
Manchester
Holyhead
Conwy
(2-3H)
Chester
Bangor
Lincoln
Caernarfon
Betws-y-Coed
Stoke
Peter-borough
King's Lynn
Bed.
Derby
Norwich
REPUBLIC OF IRELAND
Pwllheli
Blaenau Ffest.
Telford
Wolv.
Harlech
Birmingham
Ely
Coventry
Ironbridge Gorge
Cambridge
Aberystwyth
Warwick
(3.5H)
Stratford
Harwich
Rosslare
WALES
Cheltenham
Moreton
To Hoek van Holland (6H)
Carmarthen
Stow
Oxford
Fishguard
Newport
London
Ebbs-fleet
Swansea
Reading
Canterbury
Cardiff
Bath
STONE-HENGE
Woking
Dover
Bristol
Ashford
(1.5H)
Wells
West-bury
Salisbury
Glastonbury
Brighton
Calais
Exeter
Newhaven
EUROSTAR (2.5H)
Atlantic Ocean
Dartmoor
Southampton
Portsmouth
To Dieppe (4H)
Truro
St. Ives
Plymouth
To Paris & Brussels
English Channel
Penzance
Falmouth
To St-Malo (11H)
To Ouistreham (6H)
To Roscoff (6H)
FRANCE

sales). Another good resource, which also has schedules for trains throughout Europe, is German Rail's timetable (www.bahn.com).

While not generally required, reservations are free and can normally be made well in advance. They are an especially good idea for long journeys or for travel on Sundays or holidays. Make reservations at any train station, by phone, or online when you buy your ticket. With a point-to-point ticket, you can reserve as late as two hours before train time, but rail-pass holders should book seats at least 24 hours in advance (see below for more on rail passes). You must reserve in advance for Caledonian Sleeper overnight trains between London and Scotland (www.sleeper.scot).

For information on the high-speed Eurostar train through the "Chunnel" to Paris or Brussels, see page 195.

Buying Train Tickets in Advance: The best fares go to those who book their trips well in advance of their journey. Savings can be significant. For a London-York round-trip (standard class), the full fare is about £112; if you book online at least a day ahead, off-peak and advance-purchase discounts can combine for a rate closer to £50. An advance fare for the same ticket booked a couple of months out can cost as little as £30.

The cheapest fares (minimum 7-day advance purchase) sell out fast. Especially in summer, it's often necessary to book six to eight weeks ahead. Keep in mind that "return" (round-trip) fares are not always cheaper than buying two "single" (one-way) tickets—thankfully National Rail's website will automatically display this option if it's the lowest fare. Cheap advance tickets often come with the toughest refund restrictions, so be sure to nail down your travel plans before you reserve.

To book ahead, go in person to any station, book online at www.nationalrail.co.uk, or call 0345-748-4950 (from the US, dial 011-44-20-7278-5240, phone answered 24 hours) to find out the schedule and best fare for your journey; you'll then be referred to the appropriate vendor—depending on the particular rail company—to book your ticket. If you order online, be sure you know what you want; it's tough to reach a person who can change your online reservation. You'll pick up your ticket at the station, or you may be able to print it at home.

A company called **Megabus** (through their subsidiary Megatrain) sells some discounted train tickets well in advance on a few specific routes, though their focus is mainly on selling bus tickets (info tel. 0871-266-3333, www.megatrain.com).

Buying Train Tickets as You Travel: If you'd rather have the flexibility of booking tickets as you go, you can save a few pounds by buying a round-trip ticket, called a "return ticket" (a same-day round-trip, called a "day return," is particularly cheap); buying before 18:00 the day before you depart; traveling after the morning

Sample Train Journey

Here is a typical example of a personalized train schedule printed out at a British train station (also online at www.nationalrail.co.uk). At the Llandudno Junction station in North Wales, I told the clerk I wanted to leave after 15:00 for Moreton-in-Marsh in the Cotswolds. Even though the trip involved two transfers, this schedule allowed me to easily navigate the rails.

Leaving	From	Platform	To	Arriving	Platform	Duration
15:27	Llandudno Junction [LLJ]	1	Hereford [HFD]	18:12	2	2h 45m
	Arriva Trains Wales service from Holyhead to Cardiff Central					
18:48	Hereford [HFD]	3	Worcester Foregate Street [WOF]	19:26	2	0h 38m
	London Midland service from Hereford to Birmingham New Street					
19:56	Hereford [HFD]	3	Worcester Foregate Street [WOF]	19:26	2	0h 38m
	Great Western Railway service from Great Malvern to London Paddington					

Often the conductor on your previous train can tell you which platform your next train will depart from, but it's wise to confirm. Scrolling overhead screens on the platforms often show arrivals, departures, and intermediate stops; some list train departures by their final destination only. If you are traveling to an intermediate stop and aren't sure which platform you need, ask any conductor or at the info desk. For example, after checking with the conductor, I know that I'll need to look for *Oxford* to catch the train for Moreton-in-Marsh.

Britain's train system can experience delays, so don't schedule your connections too tightly if you need to reach your destination at a specific time.

rush hour (this usually means after 9:30 Mon-Fri); and going standard class instead of first class.

Senior, Youth, Partner, and Family Deals: To get a third off the price of most point-to-point rail tickets, seniors can buy a Senior Railcard (ages 60 and up), younger travelers can buy a 16-25 Railcard (ages 16-25, or full-time students 26 and older), and two people traveling together can buy a Two Together Railcard (ages 16 and over). A Family and Friends Railcard gives adults about 33 percent off for most trips and 60 percent off for their kids ages 5 to 15 (maximum 4 adults and 4 kids). Each Railcard costs £30; see www.railcard.co.uk. These cards are valid for a year on almost all trains, including special runs such as the Heathrow Express, but are not valid on the Eurostar to Paris or Brussels (fill out application at

Rail Passes

Prices listed are for 2015 and are subject to change. For the latest prices, details, and train schedules (and easy online ordering), see www.ricksteves.com/rail.

"Standard" is the polite British term for "second" class. "Senior" refers to those age 60 and up. No senior discounts for standard class. "Youth" means under age 26. For each adult or senior BritRail or BritRail England pass you buy, one child (5–15) can travel free with you (ask for the "**Family Pass,**" not available with all passes). Additional kids pay the normal half-adult rate. Kids under 5 travel free.

Note: Overnight journeys begun on the final night of your pass can be completed the day after your pass expires—only BritRail allows this trick. A bunk in a twin sleeper costs $75.

BRITRAIL CONSECUTIVE PASS

	Adult 1st Class	Adult Standard	Senior 1st Class	Youth 1st Class	Youth Standard
3 consec. days	$333	$220	$283	$266	$176
4 consec. days	414	273	352	331	219
8 consec. days	590	396	501	472	317
15 consec. days	871	590	740	697	472
22 consec. days	1107	737	941	885	590
1 month	1311	871	1114	1049	687

BRITRAIL FLEXIPASS

	Adult 1st Class	Adult Standard	Senior 1st Class	Youth 1st Class	Youth Standard
3 days in 1 month	$414	$280	$350	$331	$224
4 days in 1 month	509	350	431	407	280
8 days in 1 month	748	502	635	598	401
15 days in 1 month	1117	755	948	894	604

Map key:

Approximate point-to-point one-way standard-class fares in US dollars by rail (solid line) and bus (dashed line). First class costs 50 percent more. Add up fares for your itinerary to see whether a railpass will save you money.

BRITRAIL ENGLAND CONSECUTIVE PASS

	Adult 1st Class	Adult Standard	Senior 1st Class	Youth 1st Class	Youth Standard
3 consec. days	$263	$185	$223	$210	$148
4 consec. days	333	220	283	266	176
8 consec. days	467	315	397	373	252
15 consec. days	702	467	597	562	373
22 consec. days	889	590	755	711	472
1 month	1047	702	890	838	562

Covers travel only in England, not Scotland, Wales, or Ireland.

BRITRAIL ENGLAND FLEXIPASS

Type of Pass	Adult 1st Class	Adult Standard	Senior 1st Class	Youth 1st Class	Youth Standard
3 days in 2 months	$333	$227	$283	$266	$182
4 days in 2 months	414	280	352	331	224
8 days in 2 months	597	403	507	477	323
15 days in 2 months	896	607	761	717	486

Covers travel only in England, not Scotland, Wales, or Ireland.

BRITRAIL LONDON PLUS PASS

	Adult 1st Class	Adult Standard
3 days out of 1 month	$286	$204
4 days out of 1 month	331	249
8 days out of 1 month	469	345

Covers much of SE England (see London Plus Coverage Map, online). Includes the Heathrow, Stansted, or Gatwick Express,on counted travel days, which can be used up to 6 months from the date you validate the pass in Britain (but not before pass is validated for the 8- or 15-day travel window). Many trains are standard class only. The 7 p.m. rule for night trains does not apply. Kids 5–15 half price; under 5 free.

BRITRAIL SOUTH WEST CONSECUTIVE PASS

	Adult 1st Class	Adult Standard	Senior 1st Class	Youth 1st Class	Youth Standard
3 consec. days	$238	$157	$203	$191	$126
4 consec. days	291	192	248	233	154
8 consec. days	414	281	352	332	225
15 consec. days	615	414	523	492	332
22 consec. days	774	520	658	619	416
1 month	915	615	777	732	492

BRITRAIL SOUTH WEST FLEXI PASS

	Adult 1st Class	Adult Standard	Senior 1st Class	Youth 1st Class	Youth Standard
3 days in 2 months	$291	$203	$248	$233	$163
4 days in 2 months	362	245	307	289	196
8 days in 2 months	527	351	448	422	281
15 days in 2 months	784	527	667	627	422

Covers most trains in SW England operated by First Great Western (but not east of Portsmouth), South West Trains, and Heathrow Express (see coverage map online); not other operators. Includes Newport-Cardiff-Swansea main line trains in Wales. Many trains offer Standard class only.

station, brochures on racks in info center, need to show passport; passport-type photo needed for 16-25 Railcard).

Rail Passes: A rail pass offers hop-on flexibility and no need to lock in reservations, except for overnight sleeper cars. The BritRail pass comes in "consecutive day" and "flexi" versions, with price breaks for youths, seniors, off-season travelers, and groups of three of more. Most allow one child under 16 to travel free with a paying adult. If you're exploring the backcountry with a BritRail pass, standard class is a good choice since many of the smaller train lines don't even offer first-class cars.

Other BritRail options include England-only passes, Scotland-only passes, Britain/Ireland passes, "London Plus" passes (good for travel in most of southeast England but not in London itself), and South West passes (good for the Cotswolds, Bath, Dorset, Devon, Cornwall, plus part of South Wales). These BritRail passes, as well as Eurail passes, get you a discount on the Eurostar train that zips you to continental Europe under the English Channel.

BritRail passes cannot be purchased locally; you must buy your pass through an agent before leaving the US. Seat and sleeper reservations can be made in advance when you buy your pass, or you can make reservations at the station before you travel.

For more detailed advice on figuring out the smartest rail pass options for your train trip, visit the "Trains & Rail Passes" section of my website at www.ricksteves.com/rail.

BY BUS

Although buses are about a third slower than trains, they're also a lot cheaper. And buses go many places that trains don't. Most long-haul domestic buses are operated by **National Express** (tel. 0871-781-8181, www.nationalexpress.com); their international departures are called **Eurolines** (www.eurolines.co.uk). Note that Brits distinguish between "buses" (for in-city travel with lots of stops) and "coaches" (long-distance cross-country runs)—though for simplicity in this book, I call both "buses."

A smaller company called **Megabus** undersells National Express with deeply discounted promotional fares—the farther ahead you buy, the less you pay (some trips for just £1.50, tel. 0141/352-4444, http://uk.megabus.com). While Megabus can be much cheaper than National Express, they tend to be slower than their competitor and their routes mainly connect cities, not smaller towns. They also sell discounted train tickets on selected routes.

Most long-haul domestic routes in Scotland are operated by **Scottish Citylink.** In peak season, it's worth booking your seat on popular routes at least a day in advance (at the bus station or

TI, online at www.citylink.co.uk, or by calling 0871-216-3333). At slower times, you can just hop on the bus and pay the driver.

Try to avoid bus travel on Friday and Sunday evenings, when weekend travelers are more likely to make buses sell out.

To ensure getting a ticket—and to save money with special promotions—book your ticket in advance online or over the phone. The cheapest prepurchased tickets can usually be changed (for a £5 fee), but not refunded. Check if the ticket is only "amendable" or also "refundable" when you buy.

Round-trip bus tickets usually cost less than two one-way fares. Budget travelers can save a wad with a bus pass. National Express sells **Brit Xplorer bus passes** for unlimited travel on consecutive days (£79/7 days, £139/14 days, £219/28 days, sold over the counter, non-UK passport required, tel. 0871-781-8178, www.nationalexpress.com). Check their website to learn about online deals; senior/youth/family cards and fares; and discounts for advance booking.

If you're focusing on Scotland, consider Citylink's **Explore Scotland pass,** which allows flexibility within specific time spans (£41/3 days in 5-day period, £62/5 days in 10-day period, £93/8 days in 16-day period, tel. 0871-266-3333, www.citylink.co.uk). For details on bus connections in the Scottish Highlands—where buses are the most useful—see page 878.

If you want to take a bus from your last destination to the nearest airport, you'll find that National Express often offers **airport buses.** Bus stations are normally at or near train stations (in London, the main bus station is a block southwest of Victoria Station).

RENTING A CAR

Rental companies in Britain require you to be at least 21 years old. Drivers under the age of 25 may incur a young-driver surcharge (depending on the class of car rented), and some rental companies will not rent to anyone 75 or older. If you're considered too young or old, look into leasing (covered later), which has less-stringent age restrictions.

Research car rentals before you go. It's cheaper to arrange most car rentals from the US. Consider several companies to compare rates. Most of the major US rental agencies (including Avis, Budget, Enterprise, Hertz, and Thrifty) have offices throughout Europe. Also consider the two major Europe-based agencies, Europcar and Sixt. It can be cheaper to use a consolidator, such as Auto Europe/Kemwel (www.autoeurope.com) or Europe by Car (www.europebycar.com), which compares rates at several companies to get you the best deal—but because you're working with a

British Radio

Local radio broadcasts can be a treat for drivers sightseeing in Britain. Many British radio stations broadcast nationwide; your car radio automatically detects the local frequency a station plays on and displays its name.

The BBC has five nationwide stations, which you can pick up in most of the country. These government-subsidized stations have no ads.

BBC Radio 1: Pop music, with youthful DJs spinning top-40 hits and interviewing big-name bands.

BBC Radio 2: The highest-rated station nationwide, aimed at a more mature audience, with adult contemporary, retro pop, and other "middle of the road" music.

BBC Radio 3: Mostly classical music, with some jazz and world music.

BBC Radio 4: All talk—current events, entertaining chat shows, special-interest topics such as cooking and gardening, and lots of radio plays.

middleman, it's especially important to ask in advance about add-on fees and restrictions.

Always read the fine print carefully for add-on charges—such as one-way drop-off fees, airport surcharges, or mandatory insurance policies—that aren't included in the "total price." You may need to query rental agents pointedly to find out your actual cost.

For the best deal, rent by the week with unlimited mileage. I normally rent the smallest, least expensive model with a stick shift (generally cheaper than automatic). Almost all rentals are manual by default, so if you need an automatic, request one in advance. An automatic makes sense for most American drivers: With a manual transmission in Britain, you'll be sitting on the right side of the car and shifting with your left hand...while driving on the left side of the road. When selecting a car, don't be tempted by a larger model, as it won't be as maneuverable on narrow, winding roads.

Figure on paying roughly $230 for a one-week rental. Allow extra for supplemental insurance, fuel, tolls, and parking. For trips of three weeks or more, leasing can save you money on insurance and taxes.

Picking Up Your Car: Big companies have offices in most cities, but small local rental companies can be cheaper. If you pick up the car in a smaller city or at an airport (rather than downtown), you'll more likely survive your first day on the road. Be aware that Brits call it "hiring a car," and directional signs at airports and train stations will read *Car Hire.*

Compare pickup costs (downtown can be less expensive than

BBC Radio 5 Live: Sporting events as well as news and sports-talk programs.

You'll encounter regional variations of BBC stations, such as BBC London, Radio York, BBC Scotland, and BBC Gaelic. At the top of the hour, many BBC stations broadcast the famous "pips" (indicating Greenwich Mean Time) and a short roundup of the day's news.

Beyond the BBC offerings, several private stations broadcast music and other content with "adverts" (commercials). Some are nationwide, including **XFM** (alternative rock), **Classic FM** (classical), **Absolute Radio** (pop), and **Capital FM** (pop).

Traffic Alerts: Ask your rental-car company about turning on automatic traffic alerts that play on the car radio. Once these are enabled (look for the letters *TA* or *TP* on the radio readout), traffic reports for the area you are driving in will periodically interrupt programming.

the airport) and explore drop-off options. For a trip covering both Britain and Ireland, you're better off with two separate car rentals. Always check the hours of the location you choose: Many rental offices close from midday Saturday until Monday morning and, in smaller towns, at lunchtime.

When selecting a location, don't trust the agency's description of "downtown" or "city center." In some cases, a "downtown" branch can be on the outskirts of the city—a long, costly taxi ride from the center. Before choosing, plug the addresses into a mapping website. You may find that the "train station" location is handier. But returning a car at a big-city train station or downtown agency can be tricky; get precise details on the car drop-off location and hours, and allow ample time to find it.

When you pick up the rental car, check it thoroughly and make sure any damage is noted on your rental agreement. Find out how your car's lights, turn signals, wipers, radio, and fuel cap function, and know what kind of fuel the car takes (diesel vs. unleaded). When you return the car, make sure the agent verifies its condition with you. Some drivers take pictures of the returned vehicle as proof of its condition.

The AA: The services of Britain's Automobile Association are included with most rentals (www.theaa.com), but check for this when booking to be sure you understand its towing and emergency road-service benefits.

Navigation Options

When renting a car in Europe, for a digital navigator you can use the mapping app that's already on your cellular-connected device, or download a mapping app that's designed to be used offline. As an alternative, you could rent a GPS device—known as a "satnav" in Britain—or bring your own GPS device from home. And of course, you can always refer to paper maps.

To use your mobile device for pulling up maps or routes on the fly, for turn-by-turn directions, or for traffic updates, you'll need to go online—so it's smart to get an international data plan (see page 1014). But just using GPS to locate your position on a map doesn't require an Internet connection (and therefore doesn't require Wi-Fi or cellular data). This means that once you have the map in your phone, you can navigate with it all day long without incurring data-roaming charges.

Using Your Device's Mapping App: The mapping app you use at home (such as Google Maps or Apple Maps) will work just as well for navigating Europe.

The most economical approach is to download information while you're on Wi-Fi (at your hotel, before setting out for the day). Google Maps' "save map to use offline" feature is useful for this, allowing you to view a map when you're offline (though you can't search for an address or get directions). Apple Maps doesn't offer a save-for-offline feature, though it does automatically cache (save) certain data. So if you bring up the maps you need or plan your route while on Wi-Fi in the morning, the Apple Maps app may end up caching those maps and not using data roaming much during the day.

No matter which app you use, view the maps in standard view (not satellite view) to limit data use. And consider bringing a car charger: Even offline, mapping services gobble up battery life.

Using a Third-Party Offline Mapping App: A number of well-designed apps allow you much of the convenience of online maps without any costly cellular data demands. City Maps 2Go is popular; OffMaps and Navfree also offer good, zoomable offline maps—similar to Google Maps—for much of Europe. You need to be online to download the app, but once that's done, the maps are accessible anywhere (note that you won't get turn-by-turn directions, which require a data connection).

Using GPS: Some drivers prefer using a dedicated GPS unit—not only to avoid using cellular data, but because a standalone GPS can be easier to operate (important if you're driving solo). The downside: It's expensive—around $10-30 per day. Your car's GPS unit may only come loaded with maps for its home country—if you need additional maps, ask. If you have a portable GPS device at home, you can take that instead, but you'll need to buy and download European maps before your trip. This option is far less expensive than renting.

Using Paper Maps: Several good road atlases cover all of Britain. Ordnance Survey, Collins, AA, and Bartholomew editions are all available at tourist information offices, gas stations, and bookstores. The tourist-oriented Collins Touring maps do a good job of highlighting the many roadside attractions you might otherwise drive right past. Before you buy a map, look at it to be sure it has the level of detail you want.

Car Insurance Options

When you rent a car, you are liable for a very high deductible, sometimes equal to the entire value of the car. Limit your financial risk with one of these three options: Buy Collision Damage Waiver (CDW) coverage with a low or zero deductible from the car-rental company, get coverage through your credit card (free, if your card automatically includes zero-deductible coverage), or get collision insurance as part of a larger travel-insurance policy.

Basic **CDW** includes a very high deductible (typically $1,000-1,500). Though each rental company has its own variation, basic CDW costs $15-35 a day (figure roughly 30 percent extra) and reduces your liability, but does not eliminate it. When you reserve or pick up the car, you'll be offered the chance to "buy down" the basic deductible to zero (for an additional $10-30/day; this is sometimes called "super CDW" or "zero-deductible coverage").

If you opt for **credit-card coverage,** there's a catch. You'll technically have to decline all coverage offered by the car-rental company, which means they can place a hold on your card (which can be up to the full value of the car). In case of damage, it can be time-consuming to resolve the charges with your credit-card company. Before you decide on this option, quiz your credit-card company about how it works.

If you're already purchasing a **travel-insurance policy** for your trip, adding collision coverage is an option. For example, Travel Guard (www.travelguard.com) sells affordable renter's collision insurance as an add-on to its other policies; it's valid everywhere in Europe except the Republic of Ireland, and some Italian car-rental companies refuse to honor it, as it doesn't cover you in case of theft.

For more on car-rental insurance, see www.ricksteves.com/cdw.

Leasing

For trips of three weeks or more, consider leasing (which automatically includes zero-deductible collision and theft insurance). By technically buying and then selling back the car, you save lots of money on tax and insurance. Leasing provides you a brand-new car with unlimited mileage and a 24-hour emergency assistance program. You can lease for as little as 21 days to as long as five and a half months. Car leases must be arranged from the US. One of many companies offering affordable lease packages is Europe by Car (www.europebycar.com/lease).

Driving in Britain

Driving in Britain is wonderful—once you remember to stay on the left and after you've mastered the roundabouts. Every year, however, I get a few notes from traveling readers advising me that, for them, trying to drive in Britain was a nerve-racking and regrettable mistake. If you want to get a little slack on the roads, drop by a gas station or auto shop and buy a green *P* (probationary driver with license) sign to put in your car window (don't get the red *L* sign, which means you're a learner driver without a license and thus prohibited from driving on motorways).

Many Yankee drivers find the hardest part isn't driving on the left, but steering from the right. Your instinct is to put yourself on the left side of your lane, which means you may spend your first day or two constantly drifting into the left shoulder. It can help to remember that the driver always stays close to the center line.

Road Rules: Be aware of typical European road rules; for example, many countries require headlights to be turned on at all times, and it's generally illegal to drive while using your mobile phone without a hands-free device. In Britain, you're not allowed to turn left on a red light unless a sign or signal specifically authorizes it, and on motorways it's illegal to pass drivers on the left. Ask your car-rental company about these rules, read the Department for Transport's *Highway Code* (www.gov.uk/highway-code), or check the US State Department website (www.travel.state.gov, search for your country in the "Learn about your destination" box, then click on "Travel and Transportation").

Speed Limits: Speed limits are in miles per hour: 30 mph in town, 70 mph on the motorways, and 50 or 60 mph elsewhere (though, as back home, many British drivers consider these limits advisory). The national sign for 60 mph is a white circle with a black slash. Motorways have electronic speed limit signs; posted speeds can change depending on traffic or the weather. Follow them accordingly.

Note that road-surveillance cameras strictly enforce speed limits. Any driver (including foreigners renting cars) photographed speeding will get a nasty bill in the mail. (Cameras—in foreboding gray boxes—flash on rear license plates to respect the privacy of anyone sharing the front seat with someone he or she shouldn't.) Signs (an image of an old-fashioned camera) alert you when you're entering a zone that may be monitored by these "camera cops." Heed them.

Roundabouts: Don't let a roundabout spook you. After all, you routinely merge into much faster traffic on American highways back home. Traffic flows clockwise, and cars already in the roundabout have the right-of-way; entering traffic yields (look to your right as you merge). You'll probably encounter "double-roundabouts"—figure-eights where you'll slingshot from one roundabout directly into another. Just go with the flow and track signs carefully. When approaching an especially complex roundabout, you'll first pass a diagram showing the layout and the various exits. And in many cases, the pavement is painted to indicate the lane you should be in for a particular road or town.

Freeways (Motorways): The shortest distance between any two points is usually the motorway (what we'd call a "freeway"). In Britain, the smaller the number, the bigger the road. For example, the M-4 is a freeway, while the B-4494 is a country road.

Motorway road signs can be confusing, too few, and too late. Miss a motorway exit and you can lose 30 minutes. Study your map before taking off. Know the cities you'll be lacing together, since road numbers are inconsistent. British road signs are never marked with compass directions (e.g., *A-30 West*); instead, you need to know what major town or city you're heading for *(A-30 Penzance)*. The driving directions in this book are intended to be used with a good map. Get a road atlas, easily purchased at gas stations in Britain, or download digital maps before your trip (see page 1030).

Unless you're passing, always drive in the "slow" lane on motorways (the lane farthest to the left). The British are very disci-

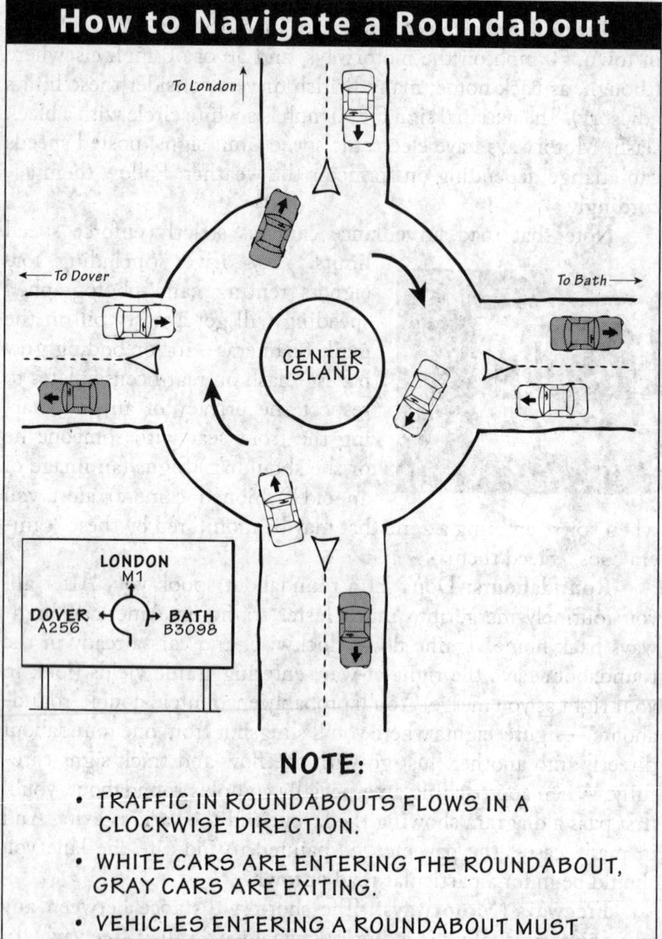

plined about this; ignoring this rule could get you a ticket (or into a road-rage incident). Remember to pass on the right, not the left.

Rest areas are called "services" and often have a number of useful amenities, such as restaurants, cafeterias, gas stations, shops, and motels.

Fuel: Gas (petrol) costs about $10 per gallon and is self-serve. Pump first and then pay. Diesel rental cars are common; make sure you know what kind of fuel your car takes before you fill up. Unleaded pumps are usually green. Note that self-service gas pumps often accept only cash or a chip-and-PIN credit card (see page 987).

Driving in Cities: Whenever possible, avoid driving in cities. Be warned that London assesses a congestion charge. Most cities have modern ring roads to skirt the congestion. Follow signs to the parking lots outside the city core—most are a 5- to 10-minute walk to the center—and avoid what can be an unpleasant grid of one-way streets (as in Bath) or roads that are restricted to public transportation during the day.

Driving in Rural Areas: Outside the big cities and except for the motorways, British roads tend to be narrow. In towns, you may have to cross over the center line just to get past parked cars. Adjust your perceptions of personal space: It's not "my side of the road" or "your side of the road," it's just "the road"—and it's shared as a cooperative adventure. If the road's wide enough, traffic in both directions can pass parked cars simultaneously, but frequently you'll have to take turns—follow the locals' lead and drive defensively.

Narrow country lanes are often lined with stone walls or woody hedges—and no shoulders. Some are barely wide enough for one car. Go slowly, and if you encounter an oncoming car, look for the nearest pullout (or "passing place")—the driver who's closest to one is expected to use it, even if it means backing up to reach it. If another car pulls over and blinks its headlights, that means, "Go ahead; I'll wait to let you pass." British drivers—arguably the most courteous on the planet—are quick to offer a friendly wave to thank you for letting them pass (and they appreciate it if you reciprocate). Pull over frequently—to let faster locals pass and to check the map.

Parking: Pay attention to pavement markings to figure out where to park. One yellow line marked on the pavement means no parking Monday through Saturday during work hours. Double yellow lines mean no parking at any time. Broken yellow lines mean short stops are OK, but you should always look for explicit signs or ask a passerby. White lines mean you're free to park.

In some towns, drivers will see signs for "disc zone" parking. This is free, time-limited parking. But to use it, you must obtain a clock parking disc from a shop and display it on the dashboard (set the clock to show your time of arrival). Return within the signed time limit to avoid being ticketed.

Rather than look for street parking, I generally pull into the most central and handy pay-and-display parking lot I can find. To pay and display, feed change into a machine, receive a timed ticket, and display it on the dashboard or stick it to the driver's-side win-

Driving in Great Britain
m = miles
h = hours
Note: Your times may vary based on traffic, sheep, construction & road conditions.
SCOTLAND
ENGLAND
WALES
To Durness 70m • 2.25h
To John o'Groats 120m • 2.5h
Ullapool
Portree
Skye
Kyle of Lochalsh
Inverness
Loch Ness (Urquhart Castle)
Aberdeen
Glencoe
Mull
Fionnport
Craignure
Oban
Pitlochry
Stirling
St. Andrews
Edinburgh
Glasgow
Holy Island
Cairnryan
Hadrian's Wall (Housesteads Fort)
Durham
Keswick (N. Lake Dist.)
Windermere (S. Lake Dist.)
Whitby
Blackpool
Preston
York
Holyhead
Conwy
Liverpool
Caernarfon
Ruthin
Betws-y-Coed
Ironbridge
Coventry
Warwick
Stratford
Cambridge
Cotswolds (Stow)
Tintern
Cardiff
Oxford
London
Bath
Avebury
Wells
Glastonbury
Canterbury
Salisbury
Dover
To Land's End 100m • 2h
Dartmoor Nat'l Park
Corfe Castle
Portsmouth
Brighton

dow. Rates are reasonable by US standards, and locals love to share stickers that have time remaining. If you stand by the machine, someone on their way out with time left on their sticker will probably give it to you.

Some parking garages (a.k.a. "car parks") are totally automated and record your car's license plate with a camera when you enter. You'll need to enter the first few letters or digits of your license plate number (which the Brits call a "number plate" or just "vehicle registration") at the payment machine when you pay before exiting.

Most parking payment machines in larger towns accept credit cards with a chip, but it's smart to keep coins handy for machines and parking meters that don't.

FLIGHTS

The best comparison search engine for both international and intra-European flights is www.kayak.com. For inexpensive flights within Europe, try www.skyscanner.com or www.hipmunk.com; for inexpensive international flights, try www.vayama.com.

Flying to Europe: Start looking for international flights four to five months before your trip, especially for peak-season travel. Off-season tickets can be purchased a month or so in advance. Depending on your itinerary, it can be efficient to fly into one city and out of another. If your flight requires a connection in Europe, see my hints on navigating Europe's top hub airports at www.ricksteves.com/hub-airports.

Flying Within Europe: Several cheap no-frills airlines affordably connect Britain with other destinations in the British Isles and throughout Europe. If you're considering a train ride that's more than five hours long, a flight may save you both time and money. When comparing your options, factor in the time it takes to get to the airport and how early you'll need to arrive to check in.

Well-known cheapo airlines include easyJet (www.easyjet.com) and Ryanair (www.ryanair.com). **EasyJet** flies from London (Gatwick, Luton, Stansted, and Southend), Liverpool, Edinburgh, Glasgow, and Inverness. **Ryanair** flies from London (mostly from Stansted Airport, as well as Gatwick and Luton), Liverpool, Edinburgh, and Glasgow. Other airlines to consider include **CityJet** (based at London City Airport, www.cityjet.com), **Monarch** (specializes in connecting to Mediterranean resorts, www.monarch.co.uk), **Thomson** (similar to Monarch, www.thomsonfly.com), **Flybe** (www.flybe.com), and **Brussels Airlines** (with frequent connections from Heathrow, Bristol, Birmingham, and Manchester to its Brussels hub, www.brusselsairlines.com).

Be aware of the potential drawbacks of flying with a discount airline: nonrefundable and nonchangeable tickets, minimal or nonexistent customer service, pricey and time-consuming treks to secondary airports, and stingy baggage allowances with steep overage fees. If you're traveling with lots of luggage, a cheap flight can quickly become a bad deal. To avoid unpleasant surprises, read the small print before you book. These days you can also fly within Europe on major airlines affordably—and without all the aggressive restrictions—for around $100 a flight.

Flying to the US and Canada: Because security is extra tight for flights to the US, be sure to give yourself plenty of time at the airport. It's also important to charge your electronic devices before you board because security checks may require you to turn them on (see www.tsa.gov for the latest rules).

Resources

RESOURCES FROM RICK STEVES

Rick Steves Great Britain is one of many books in my series on European travel, which includes country and regional guidebooks (including Scotland, England, and Ireland), city guidebooks (London, Paris, Rome, Florence, etc.), Snapshot guides (excerpted chapters from my country guides), Pocket Guides (full-color little books on big cities, including London), and my budget-travel skills handbook, *Rick Steves Europe Through the Back Door.* Most of my titles are available as ebooks. My phrase books—for Italian, French, German, Spanish, and Portuguese—are practical and budget-oriented. My other books include *Europe 101* (a crash course on art and history designed for travelers); *Mediterranean Cruise Ports* and *Northern European Cruise Ports* (how to make the most of your time in port); and *Travel as a Political Act* (a travelogue sprinkled with tips for bringing home a global perspective). A more complete list of my titles appears near the end of this book.

Video: My public television series, *Rick Steves' Europe,* covers Europe from top to bottom with over 100 half-hour episodes. To watch full episodes online for free, see www.ricksteves.com/tv. Or to raise your travel I.Q. with video versions of our popular classes (including my talks on travel skills, packing smart, European art for travelers, travel as a political act, and individual talks covering most European countries), see www.ricksteves.com/travel-talks.

Audio: My weekly public radio show, *Travel with Rick Steves,* features interviews with travel experts from around the world. A complete archive of 10 years of programs (over 400 in all) is available at www.ricksteves.com/radio. I've also produced self-guided **audio tours** of some of the top sights in London and Edinburgh. Most of this audio content is available for free through my **Rick Steves Audio Europe app,** an extensive online library organized by destination. For more on my app, see page 13.

Maps: The black-and-white maps in this book are concise

and simple, designed to help you locate recommended places and get to local TIs, where you can pick up more in-depth maps of cities and regions (usually free). Better maps are sold at newsstands and bookstores. The *Rick Steves Britain, Ireland & London City Map* is useful for planning ($9, www.ricksteves.com). Map apps for your smartphone or tablet are also handy (see "Navigation Options," earlier).

APPENDIX

Useful Contacts

Emergencies

Police and Ambulance: Tel. 999

Embassies and Consulates

In London

US Consulate and Embassy: Tel. 020/7499-9000 (all services), no walk-in passport services; for emergency 36-hour passport service, email LondonEmergencyPPT@state.gov or call all-services number, 24 Grosvenor Square, Tube: Bond Street, http://london.usembassy.gov

Canadian High Commission: Tel. 020/7004-6000, passport services available Mon-Fri 9:30-13:00, Canada House, Trafalgar Square, Tube: Charing Cross, www.unitedkingdom.gc.ca

In Edinburgh

US Consulate: Tel. 0131/556-8315; after-hours tel. 020/7499-9000, no walk-in passport services; 3 Regent Terrace, Mon-Fri 8:30-17:00, closed Sat-Sun, http://edinburgh.usconsulate.gov

Canadian Consulate: Mobile 0770-235-9916 (business hours);

after hours call the Canadian High Commission (contact info on previous page)

Directory Assistance

Operator Assistance: Tel. 100 (free)
Directory Assistance: Toll tel. 118-500 (£0.59/minute, plus £0.23/minute connection charge from fixed lines)
International Directory Assistance: Toll tel. 118-505 (£3.99/call and £1.39/minute)

Holidays and Festivals

This list includes national holidays observed throughout Britain plus selected festivals. Many sights and banks close on national holidays—keep this in mind when planning your itinerary. Throughout Britain, hotels get booked up during Easter week; over Early May, Spring, and Summer Bank Holidays; and during Christmas, Boxing Day, and New Year's Day. On Christmas, virtually everything shuts down, even the Tube in London. Museums also generally close December 24 and 26.

Many British towns have holiday festivals in late November and early December, with markets, music, and entertainment in the Christmas spirit (for instance, Keswick's Victorian Fayre).

Throughout the summer, communities small and large across Scotland host their annual Highland Games (like a combination track meet/county fair)—a wonderful way to get in touch with local culture and traditions. For more on the Highland Games, see page 892.

Before planning a trip around a festival, make sure to verify its dates by checking the festival website or the Visit Britain website (www.visitbritain.com).

Here are some major holidays:

Jan 1	New Year's Day
Jan 2	New Year's Holiday (closures)
Jan 25	Burns Night, Scotland (poetry readings, haggis)
Mid-Feb	London Fashion Week (www.londonfashionweek.co.uk)
Mid-Feb	Jorvik Viking Festival, York (costumed warriors, battles; www.jorvik-viking-festival.co.uk)
Early March	Literature Festival, Bath (www.bathlitfest.org.uk)
Easter Sunday	March 27 in 2016, April 16 in 2017

Easter Monday	March 28 in 2016, April 17 in 2017
Early May	Bank Holiday: May 2 in 2016, May 1 in 2017
Early-mid-May	Jazz Festival, Keswick (www.keswickjazzfestival.co.uk)
Late May	Chelsea Flower Show, London (www.rhs.org.uk/chelsea)
Late May	Bank Holiday: May 30 in 2016, May 29 in 2017
Late May-early June	International Music Festival, Bath (www.bathmusicfest.org.uk)
Late May-early June	Fringe Festival, Bath (alternative music, dance, and theater; www.bathfringe.co.uk)
June	Edinburgh International Film Festival (www.edfilmfest.org.uk)
Early June	Beer Festival, Keswick (music, shows; www.keswickbeerfestival.co.uk)
Early-mid June	Trooping the Colour, London (military bands and pageantry, Queen's birthday parade; www.trooping-the-colour.co.uk)
Mid-June	Royal Highland Show, Edinburgh (Scottish-flavored county fair, www.royalhighlandshow.org)
Late June	Royal Ascot Horse Race, Ascot (near Windsor; www.ascot.co.uk)
Mid-late June	Golowan (Midsummer) Festival, Penzance (www.golowan.org)
Late June-early July	Wimbledon Tennis Championship, London (www.wimbledon.org)
July	Edinburgh Jazz and Blues Festival (www.edinburghjazzfestival.com)
Mid-July	Early Music Festival, York (www.ncem.co.uk)
Late July-early Aug	Cambridge Folk Festival (www.cambridgefolkfestival.co.uk)
Aug	Edinburgh Military Tattoo (massing of military bands, www.edintattoo.co.uk)
Aug	Edinburgh Fringe Festival (offbeat theater and comedy, www.edfringe.com)
Aug	Edinburgh International Festival (music, dance, shows; www.eif.co.uk)
Late Aug	Notting Hill Carnival, London (costumes, Caribbean music, www.thenottinghillcarnival.com)
Late Aug	Bank Holiday: Aug 29 in 2016, Aug 28 in 2017 (England and Wales only)

Late Aug-late Oct	Illuminations, Blackpool (waterfront light festival, www.visitblackpool.com/illuminations)
Mid-Sept	London Fashion Week (www.londonfashionweek.co.uk)
Late Sept	Jane Austen Festival, Bath (www.janeausten.co.uk)
Late Sept	York Food and Drink Festival (www.yorkfoodfestival.com)
Nov 5	Bonfire Night, or Guy Fawkes Night, Britain (fireworks, bonfires, effigy-burning of 1605 traitor Guy Fawkes)
Dec 1	St. Andrew's Day Bank Holiday (Scotland)
Dec 24-26	Christmas holidays

Recommended Books and Films

To learn more about Britain past and present, check out a few of these books and films.

Nonfiction

All Creatures Great and Small (James Herriot, 1972). Herriot's beloved semi-autobiographical tales of life as a Yorkshire veterinarian were made into a long-running BBC series (1978-1990).

The Anglo Files: A Field Guide to the British (Sarah Lyall, 2008). A *New York Times* reporter in London wittily recounts the eccentricities of life in the UK.

Cider with Rosie (Laurie Lee, 1959). This semi-autobiographical boyhood novel set in a Cotswolds village just after World War I has been adapted for TV three times, including by the BBC in 2015.

Crowded with Genius (James Buchan, 2003). This account of Edinburgh's role in the Scottish Enlightenment details the city's transformation from squalid backwater to marvelous European capital.

Dead Wake (Erik Larson, 2015). Larson gives an evocative account of the doomed 1915 voyage of British luxury liner *Lusitania*, sunk by a German U-boat during World War I.

Edinburgh: Picturesque Notes (Robert Louis Stevenson, 1879). One of the city's most famous residents takes readers on a tour of his hometown.

The Emperor's New Kilt (Jan-Andrew Henderson, 2000). Henderson deconstructs the myths surrounding the tartan-clad Scots.

England: 1000 Things You Need To Know (Nicolas Hobbes, 2009).

Hobbes presents a fun peep into the facts, fables, and foibles of English life.

Fever Pitch (Nick Hornby, 1992). Hornby's memoir illuminates the British obsession with soccer.

A History of Britain (Simon Schama, 2000-2002). The respected historian presents a comprehensive, thoroughly-readable three-volume collection.

A History of Modern Britain (Andrew Marr, 2007). This searching look at the transformations in British life over the last few decades accompanies a BBC documentary series of the same name.

A History of Wales (John Davies, revised 2007). This insightful history tells the story of Wales from the Ice Age to the present.

How England Made the English: From Hedgerows to Heathrow (Harry Mount, 2012). Mount offers a witty, engaging look at the symbiotic relationship between the English landscape and English culture.

How the Scots Invented the Modern World (Arthur Herman, 2001). The author explains the disproportionately large influence the Scottish Enlightenment had on the rest of Europe.

The Kingdom by the Sea: A Journey Around the Coast of Great Britain (Paul Theroux, 1983). After 11 years as an American expatriate in London, travel writer Theroux takes a witty tour of his adopted homeland.

A Land (Jacquetta Hawkes, 1951). This postwar bestseller is a sweeping, poetic natural history of the British landscape and imagination.

The Last Lion (William Manchester, final book completed by Paul Reid; 1983, 1988, and 2012). This superb three-volume biography recounts the amazing life of Winston Churchill from 1874 to 1965.

Literary Trails (Christina Hardyment, 2000). Hardyment reunites famous authors with the environments that inspired them.

The Matter of Wales (Jan Morris, 1985). The half-English, half-Welsh author reveals the mysteries and joys of life in Wales.

My Love Affair with England (Susan Allen Toth, 1994). Toth brings England vividly to life in a captivating traveler's memoir recalling the country's charms and eccentricities.

Notes from a Small Island (Bill Bryson, 1995). In this irreverent and delightful memoir, US expat Bryson writes about his travels through Britain—his home for two decades.

This Little Britain: How One Small Country Changed the Modern World (Harry Bingham, 2007). Bingham offers an informative, entertaining review of Great Britain's contributions to world history.

A Traveller's History of England (Christopher Daniell, revised 2005).

A British archaeologist and historian provides a comprehensive yet succinct overview of English history.

A Traveller's History of Scotland (Andrew Fisher, revised 2009). Fisher probes Scotland's turbulent history, beginning with the Celts.

With Wings Like Eagles (Michael Korda, 2009). An English-born writer gives a historical analysis of Britain's pivotal WWII air battles versus the German Luftwaffe.

Fiction

For the classics of British drama and fiction, read anything—and everything—by William Shakespeare, Charles Dickens, Jane Austen, and the Brontës.

Atonement (Ian McEwan, 2001). This disquieting family saga set in upper-class England at the start of World War II dramatizes the consequences of a childhood lie. The 2007 motion picture starring James McAvoy and Keira Knightley is also excellent.

Behind the Scenes at the Museum (Kate Atkinson, 1995). Starting at her conception, this book's quirky narrator recounts the highs and lows of life in a middle-class English family.

Brideshead Revisited (Evelyn Waugh, 1945). This celebrated novel examines the intense entanglement of a young man with an aristocratic family.

Bridget Jones's Diary (Helen Fielding, 1996). A year in the life of a single, 30-something woman in London is humorously chronicled in diary form (also a motion picture).

Complete Poems and Songs of Robert Burns (Robert Burns, 2012, featuring work from 1774–1796). This collection showcases the work of a Scottish icon who wrote in the Scots language, including that New Year's classic "Auld Lang Syne."

The Heart of Midlothian (Sir Walter Scott, 1818). This novel from one of Great Britain's most renowned authors showcases the life-and-death drama of lynchings and criminal justice in 1730s Scotland. Other great reads by Sir Walter include *Waverley* (1814, described later), *Rob Roy* (1818), and *Ivanhoe* (1819).

Here Be Dragons (Sharon Kay Penman, 1985). The author melds history and fiction to bring 13th-century Wales vividly to life (first in a trilogy).

High Fidelity (Nick Hornby, 1995). This humorous novel traces the romantic misadventures and musical musings of a 30-something record-store owner. Another good read is Hornby's 1998 coming-of-age story, *About a Boy.* (Both books were also made into films.)

Knots and Crosses (Ian Rankin, 1987). The Scottish writer's first Inspector Rebus mystery plumbs Edinburgh's seamy underbelly.

Macbeth (William Shakespeare, 1606). Shakespeare's "Scottish Play" depicts a guilt-wracked general who assassinates the king to take the throne.

Mapp and Lucia (E. F. Benson, 1931). A rural village in the 1930s becomes a social battlefield. In *Lucia in London* (1927), the protagonist attempts social climbing in the big city.

A Morbid Taste for Bones (Ellis Peters, 1977). Brother Cadfael, a Benedictine monk-detective, tries to solve a murder in 12th-century Shropshire (first book in a series; also adapted for British TV in 1996).

The Murder at the Vicarage (Agatha Christie, 1930). The prolific mystery writer's inquisitive Miss Marple character is first introduced in this book.

Outlander (Diana Gabaldon, 1991). This genre-defying series kicks off with the heroine time-traveling from the Scotland of 1945 to 1743. A popular TV adaptation began airing in 2014.

The Paying Guests (Sarah Waters, 2014). This realistic and suspenseful tale of love, obsession, and murder plays out amid the shifting culture of post-WWII upper-class London.

The Pillars of the Earth (Ken Follett, 1990). This epic set in a fictional town in 12th-century England chronicles the birth of Gothic architecture.

The Prime of Miss Jean Brodie (Muriel Spark, 1961). The story of an unconventional young teacher who plays favorites with her students is a modern classic of Scottish literature.

Pygmalion (George Bernard Shaw, 1913). This stage play, on which the famous film *My Fair Lady* is based, tells the story of a young Cockney girl groomed for high society.

Rebecca (Daphne du Maurier, 1938). This mysterious tale set on the Cornish Coast examines upper-class English lives and their secrets.

Restoration (Rose Tremain, 1989). This evocative historical novel takes readers to the heights and depths of 17th-century English society.

The Strange Case of Dr. Jekyll and Mr. Hyde (Robert Louis Stevenson, 1886). This famous Gothic yarn by a Scottish author chronicles a fearful case of transformation in London, exploring Victorian ideas about conflict between good and evil.

SS-GB (Len Deighton, 1979). In a Nazi-occupied Great Britain, a Scotland Yard detective finds there's more to a murder than meets the eye.

A Study in Scarlet (Sir Arthur Conan Doyle, 1888). The mystery novel that introduced the world to detective Sherlock Holmes and his trusty sidekick, Dr. Watson.

The Sunne in Splendour (Sharon Kay Penman, 2008). Penman's big entertaining book paints King Richard III as a rather decent chap (one in a series of historical novels).

Sunset Song (Lewis Grassic Gibbon, 1932). Farm girl Chris Guthrie is rudely confronted by adolescence, modernity, and war in this lauded Scottish classic, the first book in the trilogy "A Scots Quair."

The Warden (Anthony Trollope, 1855). The first novel in the "Chronicles of Barsetshire" series addresses moral dilemmas in the 19th-century Anglican church.

Waverley (Sir Walter Scott, 1814). Idealistic young soldier Edward Waverley gets ensnared by the intrigues of the 1745 Jacobite uprising, which aimed to bring back the Stuart dynasty.

White Teeth (Zadie Smith, 2000). The postwar lives of two army buddies—a native Englishman and a Bengali Muslim—are chronicled in this acclaimed debut novel.

Wolf Hall and *Bring Up the Bodies* (Hilary Mantel, 2010/2012). At the intrigue-laced Tudor court of Henry VIII, Thomas Cromwell becomes the king's right-hand man. The superb 2015 BBC miniseries *Wolf Hall* is based on both books.

Film and TV

Alfie (1966). In 1960s London, a womanizer (Michael Caine) eventually must face up to his boorish behavior (also a 2004 remake with Jude Law). Other "swinging London" films include *Blow-up* (1966) and *Georgy Girl* (1966).

Austin Powers: International Man of Mystery (1997). Mike Myers stars in this loony send-up of mid-century English culture, the first film in a three-part series.

Battle of Britain (1969). An all-star cast and marvelous aerial combat scenes tell the story of Britain's "finest hour" of World War II.

Bend It Like Beckham (2003). A teenage girl of Punjabi descent plays soccer against her traditional parents' wishes in this lighthearted comedy-drama.

Billy Elliot (2000). A young boy pursues his dream to dance ballet amid a coal miners' strike in working-class northern England.

Blackadder (1983-1989). This wickedly funny BBC sitcom starring Rowan Atkinson skewers various periods of English history in the course of four series (also several TV specials).

Braveheart (1995). Mel Gibson stars in this Academy Award-winning adventure about the Scots overthrowing English rule in the 13th century.

Call the Midwife (2012-). London's poor East End comes to gritty, poignant life in this BBC drama tracing the lives of a team of nurse midwives in the late 1950s and early 1960s.

Chariots of Fire (1981). This Academy Award winner traces the lives of two British track stars competing in the 1924 Paris Olympics.

Doc Martin (2004-). A brilliant but socially inept London surgeon finds new challenges and opportunities when he opens a practice in a seaside village in Cornwall.

Downton Abbey (2010-2015). This popular aristocratic soap opera explores the travails of the Crawley family and their servants in early 20th-century Yorkshire (shot at Highclere Castle, about 70 miles west of London).

The Elephant Man (1980). A severely disfigured man reveals his sensitive soul in this stark portrayal of Victorian London.

Elizabeth (1998). Cate Blanchett portrays Queen Elizabeth I as she learns the royal ropes during the early years of her reign. Blanchett reprises her role in the sequel, *Elizabeth: The Golden Age* (2007).

Elizabeth I (2005). In this BBC/HBO miniseries, the inimitable Helen Mirren chronicles the queen's later years with a focus on her court's intrigue and her yearning for love.

Foyle's War (2002-2015). This fine BBC series follows detective Christopher Foyle as he solves crimes in southern England during and shortly after World War II.

Goodbye, Mr. Chips (1939). The headmaster of a boys' boarding school in Victorian-era England recalls his life in this romantic drama.

Gosford Park (2001). This intriguing film is part comedy, part murder mystery, and part critique of England's class stratification in the 1930s.

A Hard Day's Night (1964). The Beatles star in their debut film, a comedy depicting several days in the life of the band.

Highlander (1986). An immortal swordsman remembers his life in 16th-century Scotland while preparing for a pivotal battle in the present day.

A History of Scotland (2010). This BBC series presented by Neil Oliver offers a succinct, lightly dramatized retelling of Scottish history.

Hope and Glory (1987). John Boorman directed this semi-autobiographical story of a boy growing up during World War II's London blitz.

How Green Was My Valley (1941). Director John Ford's Academy Award winner chronicles the lives of a 19th-century Welsh coal-mining family.

Howards End (1992). This Academy Award winner, based on the E. M. Forster novel, captures the stifling societal pressure underneath the gracious manners in turn-of-the-century England.

The Imitation Game (2014). Cryptanalyst Alan Turing (Benedict

Cumberbatch) is recruited by British intelligence agency MI6 to help crack the Nazis' Enigma code during World War II.

James Bond films (1962-). These classic films follow a dashing officer in Britain's Secret Intelligence Service, who likes his martinis "shaken, not stirred."

Jane Eyre (2011). Charlotte Brontë's 1847 gothic romance has been made into a movie at least nine times, most recently this one starring Mia Wasikowska and Michael Fassbender.

The King's Speech (2010). Colin Firth stars as the stuttering King George VI on the eve of World War II.

Lark Rise to Candleford (2008-2011). Based on Flora Thompson's memoirs, this evocative series chronicles life in a poor Victorian-era hamlet and its neighboring, more hoity market town.

A Man for All Seasons (1966). Lord Chancellor Sir Thomas More incurs the wrath of Henry VIII when he refuses to help annul the king's marriage to Catherine of Aragon.

Mr. Bean (1990-1995). Rubber-faced comedian Rowan Atkinson's iconic character bumbles through life barely uttering a word in this zany sitcom (that also spawned two motion pictures).

Monarch of the Glen (2000). Set on Loch Laggan, this TV series features stunning Highland scenery and the eccentric family of a modern-day laird.

Monty Python and the Holy Grail (1975). This surreal take on Arthurian legend is a classic of British comedy.

Mrs. Brown (1997). A widowed Queen Victoria (Dame Judy Dench) forges a very close friendship with her Scottish servant, John Brown (Billy Connolly).

My Fair Lady (1964). Audrey Hepburn stars as a poor Cockney flower seller who is transformed into a lady of high society by an arrogant professor.

Notting Hill (1999). Hugh Grant and Julia Roberts star in this romantic comedy set in the London neighborhood of...you guessed it.

Persuasion (1995). Set in 19th-century England, this Jane Austen tale of status was partially filmed in Bath.

Poldark (2015-). In this hit BBC series, Ross Poldark returns to Cornwall after fighting in the Revolutionary War to find his estate, tin mines, and relationship in ruins.

Pride and Prejudice (1995). Of the many versions of Jane Austen's classic, this BBC miniseries starring Colin Firth is the winner.

The Queen (2006). Helen Mirren expertly channels Elizabeth II at her Scottish Balmoral estate in the days after Princess Diana's death. Its prequel, *The Deal* (2003), probes the relationship between Tony Blair and Gordon Brown.

The Remains of the Day (1993). Anthony Hopkins stars as a butler doggedly loyal to his misguided, politically-naive master in 1930s England.

Rob Roy (1995). The Scottish rebel struggles against feudal landlords in 18th-century Scotland.

Sammy and Rosie Get Laid (1987). An unconventional middle-class couple's promiscuous adventures expose racial tensions in multiethnic London.

Sense and Sensibility (1995). Star Emma Thompson wrote the screenplay for this adaptation of Jane Austen's 1811 novel of the Dashwood sisters, who seek financial security through marriage.

Shakespeare in Love (1999). Tudor-era London comes to life in this clever romantic film set in the original Globe Theatre.

Sherlock (2010-). Holmes (Benedict Cumberbatch) and Watson (Martin Freeman) are excellent in this BBC update of the detective's story, set in present-day London.

Sherlock Holmes (2009). Robert Downey Jr. tackles the role of the world's most famous detective.

Sweeney Todd (2007). Johnny Depp stars as a wrongfully imprisoned barber who seeks revenge in this gritty Victorian-era musical.

To Sir, with Love (1967). Sidney Poitier grapples with social and racial issues in an inner-city school in London's East End.

The Tudors (2007-2010). Showtime's racy, lavish series is a gripping loosely-accurate chronicle of the marriages of Henry VIII.

Upstairs, Downstairs (1971-1975). This TV series follows an aristocratic family and their servants in their new home at 165 Eaton Place.

Waterloo Bridge (1940). This Academy Award-nominated romantic drama recalls the lost love between a ballerina (Vivien Leigh) and a WWI army officer.

Wolf Hall (2015). This excellent BBC historical miniseries details the exploits of Thomas Cromwell, the chief minister to King Henry VIII.

FOR KIDS

A Bear Called Paddington (Michael Bond, 1958). A bear from Peru winds up in a London train station, where he's found and adopted by a human family.

An Illustrated Treasury of Scottish Folk and Fairy Tales (Theresa Breslin, 2012). Kelpies, dragons, brownies, and other inhabitants of the Scottish Isles come to life in this lovely volume of traditional lore.

Brave (2012). This Disney flick follows an independent young Scottish princess as she fights to take control of her own fate.

The Chronicles of Narnia books (C.S. Lewis, 1950-1956) and movies (2005-). Four siblings escape from WWII London into a magical world. The first of the seven novels, *The Lion, the Witch & the Wardrobe,* was also a BBC miniseries (1988).

Harry Potter books (J. K. Rowling, 1997-2007) and films (2001-2011). After discovering he's a wizard, a young boy in England gets whisked off to a magical world of witchcraft and wizardry. There he finds great friendships as well as grave evils, which he alone can destroy. (See page 994 for a list of *Harry Potter* sights in Great Britain.)

Kidnapped (Robert Louis Stevenson, 1886). This fantastic adventure story is based on events in 18th-century Scotland.

A Little Princess (1939). In this film adaptation of the classic novel, Shirley Temple plays a girl whose fortunes fall and rise again in a Victorian London boarding school.

Mary Poppins (1964). Though filmed on a set in California, this beloved musical starring Julie Andrews and Dick Van Dyke is set in Edwardian London.

This Is Britain (Miroslav Sasek, 1962, updated 2008). Vivid illustrations bring the British Isles to life in this classic picture book.

Peter Pan (2003). The latest in a long line of films adapting the classic 1902 novel *Peter and Wendy,* this live-action version flies real English children to Neverland.

The Secret Garden (Frances Hodgson Burnett, 1911). Orphaned Mary discovers nature and love in a gloomy Yorkshire mansion on the edge of a moor in this beloved classic, which has been adapted for stage and screen.

The Story of Britain from the Norman Conquest to the European Union (Patrick Dillon, 2011). Studious older children will get a healthy dose of history from this elegant, illustrated volume.

Wallace & Gromit TV series and films (1990-2012). Absent-minded inventor Wallace and his dog Gromit may live in northwest England, but these unique characters are beloved by children around Great Britain and the rest of the world.

Winnie-the-Pooh and *The House at Pooh Corner* (A. A. Milne, 1926-1928). This two-volume classic children's tale, set in England, revolves around a bear and his friends in the Hundred Acre Wood. The success of Milne's books has led to numerous book, film, and TV adaptations.

Young Sherlock Holmes (1985). A young Sherlock and his sidekick, Watson, work to solve the mystery of a series of nonsensical suicides. The film includes some scenes that may be frightening for younger children.

Conversions and Climate

NUMBERS AND STUMBLERS

- Some British people write a few of their numbers differently than we do: 1 = 1, 4 = 4, 7 = 7.
- In Europe, dates appear as day/month/year, so Christmas 2017 is 25/12/17.
- What Americans call the second floor of a building is the first floor in Britain.
- On escalators and moving sidewalks, Brits keep the left "lane" open for passing. Keep to the right.
- To avoid the British version of giving someone "the finger," don't hold up the first two fingers of your hand with your palm facing you. (It looks like a reversed victory sign.)
- And please...don't call your waist pack a "fanny" pack (see the British-Yankee Vocabulary list at the end of this appendix).

METRIC CONVERSIONS

Britain uses the metric system for nearly everything. Weight and volume are typically calculated in metric: A kilogram is 2.2 pounds, and one liter is about a quart (almost four to a gallon). Temperatures are generally given in Celsius, although some newspapers also list them in Fahrenheit.

1 foot = 0.3 meter
1 yard = 0.9 meter
1 mile = 1.6 kilometers
1 centimeter = 0.4 inch
1 meter = 39.4 inches
1 kilometer = 0.62 mile
1 square yard = 0.8 square meter
1 square mile = 2.6 square kilometers
1 ounce = 28 grams
1 quart = 0.95 liter
1 kilogram = 2.2 pounds
32°F = 0°C

IMPERIAL WEIGHTS AND MEASURES

Britain hasn't completely gone metric. Driving distances and speed limits are measured in miles. Beer is sold as pints (though milk can be measured in pints or liters), and a person's weight is measured in stone (a 168-pound person weighs 12 stone).

1 stone = 14 pounds
1 British pint = 1.2 US pints
1 imperial gallon = 1.2 US gallons or about 4.5 liters

CLOTHING SIZES

When shopping for clothing, use these US-to-Britain comparisons as general guidelines (but note that no conversion is perfect).

- Women's dresses and blouses: Add 4 (US women's size 10 = UK size 14)

- Men's suits, jackets, and shirts: US and UK sizes are the same
- Women's shoes: Subtract 2½ (US size 8 = UK size 5½)
- Men's shoes: Subtract about ½ (US size 9 = UK size 8½)

BRITAIN'S CLIMATE

First line, average daily high; second line, average low; third line, average days without rain. For more detailed weather statistics for destinations in this book (and elsewhere), check www.wunderground.com.

J	F	M	A	M	J	J	A	S	O	N	D
LONDON											
43°	44°	50°	56°	62°	69°	71°	71°	65°	58°	50°	45°
36°	36°	38°	42°	47°	53°	56°	56°	52°	46°	42°	38°
16	15	20	18	19	19	19	20	17	18	15	16
CARDIFF (SOUTH WALES)											
45°	45°	50°	56°	61°	68°	69°	69°	64°	58°	51°	46°
35°	35°	38°	41°	46°	51°	54°	55°	51°	46°	41°	37°
13	14	18	17	18	17	17	16	14	15	13	13
YORK											
43°	44°	49°	55°	61°	67°	70°	69°	64°	57°	49°	45°
33°	34°	36°	40°	44°	50°	54°	53°	50°	44°	39°	36°
14	13	18	17	18	16	16	17	16	16	13	14
EDINBURGH											
42°	43°	46°	51°	56°	62°	65°	64°	60°	54°	48°	44°
34°	34°	36°	39°	43°	49°	52°	52°	49°	44°	39°	36°
14	13	13	16	16	17	15	14	15	14	14	13

Fahrenheit and Celsius Conversion

Britain uses both Celsius and Fahrenheit to take its temperature. For a rough conversion from Celsius to Fahrenheit, double the number and add 30. For weather, remember that 28°C is 82°F—perfect. For health, 37°C is just right. At a launderette, 30°C is cold, 40°C is warm (usually the default setting), 60°C is hot, and 95°C is boiling.

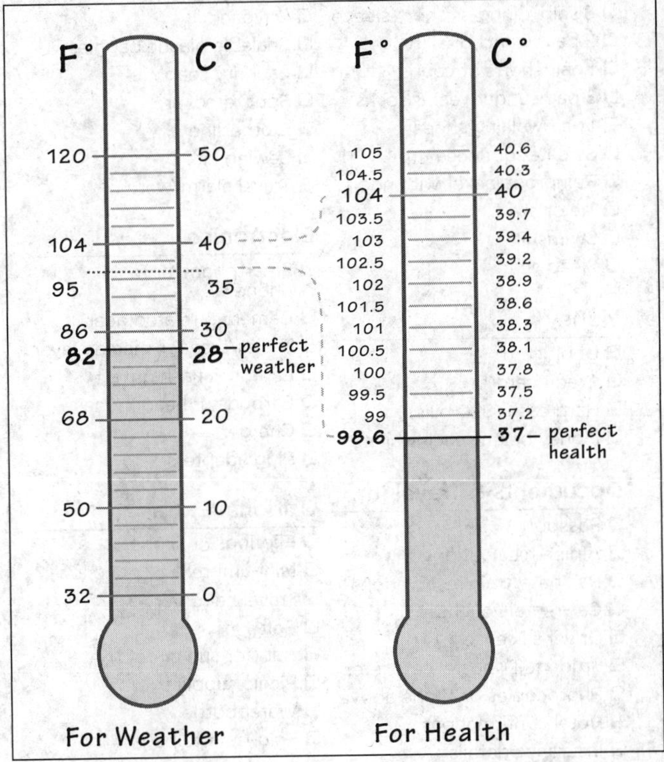

Packing Checklist

Whether you're traveling for five days or five weeks, you won't need more than this. Pack light to enjoy the sweet freedom of true mobility.

Clothing

- ❑ 5 shirts: long- & short-sleeve
- ❑ 2 pairs pants or skirt
- ❑ 1 pair shorts or capris
- ❑ 5 pairs underwear & socks
- ❑ 1 pair walking shoes
- ❑ Sweater or fleece top
- ❑ Rainproof jacket with hood
- ❑ Tie or scarf
- ❑ Swimsuit
- ❑ Sleepwear

Money

- ❑ Debit card
- ❑ Credit card(s)
- ❑ Hard cash ($20 bills)
- ❑ Money belt or neck wallet

Documents & Travel Info

- ❑ Passport
- ❑ Airline reservations
- ❑ Rail pass/train reservations
- ❑ Car-rental voucher
- ❑ Driver's license
- ❑ Student ID, hostel card, etc.
- ❑ Photocopies of all the above
- ❑ Hotel confirmations
- ❑ Insurance details
- ❑ Guidebooks & maps
- ❑ Notepad & pen
- ❑ Journal

Toiletries Kit

- ❑ Toiletries
- ❑ Medicines & vitamins
- ❑ First-aid kit
- ❑ Glasses/contacts/sunglasses (with prescriptions)
- ❑ Earplugs
- ❑ Packet of tissues (for WC)

Miscellaneous

- ❑ Daypack
- ❑ Sealable plastic baggies
- ❑ Laundry soap
- ❑ Spot remover
- ❑ Clothesline
- ❑ Sewing kit
- ❑ Travel alarm/watch

Electronics

- ❑ Smartphone or mobile phone
- ❑ Camera & related gear
- ❑ Tablet/ereader/media player
- ❑ Laptop & flash drive
- ❑ Earbuds or headphones
- ❑ Chargers
- ❑ Plug adapters

Optional Extras

- ❑ Flipflops or slippers
- ❑ Mini-umbrella or poncho
- ❑ Travel hairdryer
- ❑ Belt
- ❑ Hat (for sun or cold)
- ❑ Picnic supplies
- ❑ Water bottle
- ❑ Fold-up tote bag
- ❑ Small flashlight
- ❑ Small binoculars
- ❑ Insect repellent
- ❑ Small towel or washcloth
- ❑ Inflatable pillow
- ❑ Some duct tape (for repairs)
- ❑ Tiny lock
- ❑ Address list (to mail postcards)
- ❑ Postcards/photos from home
- ❑ Extra passport photos
- ❑ Good book

BRITISH-YANKEE VOCABULARY

For a longer list, plus a dry-witted primer on British culture, see *The Septic's Companion* (Chris Rae). Note that instead of asking, "Can I help you?" many Brits offer a more casual, "You alright?" or "You OK there?"

advert: advertisement
afters: dessert
Antipodean: an Australian or New Zealander
aubergine: eggplant
banger: sausage
bangers and mash: sausage and mashed potatoes
Bank Holiday: legal holiday
bap: small roll, roll sandwich
bespoke: custom-made
billion: a thousand of our billions (a million million)
biro: ballpoint pen
biscuit: cookie
black pudding: sausage made with onions, pork fat, oatmeal, and pig blood
bloody: damn
blow off: fart
bobby: policeman ("the Bill" is more common)
Bob's your uncle: there you go (with a shrug), naturally
boffin: nerd, geek
bollocks: all-purpose expletive (a figurative use of testicles)
bolshy: argumentative
bomb: success or failure
bonnet: car hood
boot: car trunk
braces: suspenders
bridle way: path for walkers, bikers, and horse riders
brilliant: cool
brolly: umbrella
bubble and squeak: cabbage and potatoes fried together
bum: butt
candy floss: cotton candy
caravan: trailer
car-boot sale: temporary flea market, often for charity
car park: parking lot
cashpoint: ATM
casualty: emergency room
cat's eyes: road reflectors
ceilidh (KAY-lee): informal evening of song and folk fun (Scottish and Irish)
cheap and cheerful: budget but adequate
cheap and nasty: cheap and bad quality
cheers: good-bye or thanks; also a toast
chemist: pharmacist
chicory: endive
Chinese whispers: playing "telephone"
chippie: fish-and-chips shop; carpenter
chips: French fries
chock-a-block: jam-packed
chuffed: pleased
chunter: mutter
cider: alcoholic apple cider
clearway: road where you can't stop
coach: long-distance bus
concession: discounted admission
concs (pronounced "conks"): short for "concession"
coronation chicken: curried chicken salad
cos: romaine lettuce
cot: baby crib
cotton buds: Q-tips
courgette: zucchini
craic (pronounced "crack"):

APPENDIX

fun, good conversation (Irish/Scottish and spreading to England)
crisps: potato chips
cuppa: cup of tea
dear: expensive
dicey: iffy, risky
digestives: round graham cookies
dinner: lunch or dinner
diversion: detour
dogsbody: menial worker
donkey's years: ages, long time
draughts: checkers
draw: marijuana
dual carriageway: divided highway (four lanes)
dummy: pacifier
elevenses: coffee-and-biscuits break before lunch
elvers: baby eels
face flannel: washcloth
fag: cigarette
fagged: exhausted
faggot: sausage
fancy: to like, to be attracted to (a person)
fanny: vagina
fell: hill or high plain (Lake District)
first floor: second floor
fiver: £5 bill
fizzy drink: pop or soda
flutter: a bet
football: soccer
force: waterfall (Lake District)
fortnight: two weeks (shortened from "fourteen nights")
fringe: hair bangs
Frogs: French people
fruit machine: slot machine
full Monty: whole shebang, everything
gallery: balcony
gammon: ham
gangway: aisle
gaol: jail (same pronunciation)
gateau (or gateaux): cake
gear lever: stick shift
geezer: "dude"
give way: yield
goods wagon: freight truck
gormless: stupid
goujons: breaded and fried fish or chicken sticks
green fingers: green thumbs
half eight: 8:30 (not 7:30)
hard cheese: bad luck
heath: open treeless land
hen night (or **hen do**)**:** bachelorette party
holiday: vacation
homely: homey or cozy
hoover: vacuum cleaner
ice lolly: Popsicle
interval: intermission
ironmonger: hardware store
ish: more or less
jacket potato: baked potato
jelly: Jell-O
jiggery-pokery: nonsense
Joe Bloggs: John Q. Public
jumble (sale): rummage sale
jumper: sweater
just a tick: just a second
kipper: smoked herring
knackered: exhausted (Cockney: cream crackered)
knickers: ladies' panties
knocking shop: brothel
knock up: wake up or visit (old-fashioned)
ladybird: ladybug
lady fingers: flat, spongy cookie
lady's finger: okra
lager: light, fizzy beer
left luggage: baggage check
lemonade: lemon-lime pop like 7-Up, fizzy

lemon squash: lemonade, not fizzy
let: rent
licenced: restaurant authorized to sell alcohol
lift: elevator
listed: protected historic building
loo: toilet or bathroom
lorry: truck
mack: mackintosh raincoat
mangetout: snow peas
marrow: summer squash
mate: buddy (boy or girl)
mean: stingy
mental: wild, memorable
mews: former stables converted to two-story rowhouses
mobile (MOH-bile): cell phone
moggie: cat
motorway: freeway
naff: tacky or trashy
nappy: diaper
natter: talk on and on
newsagent: corner store
nought: zero
noughts & crosses: tic-tac-toe
off-licence: liquor store
on offer: for sale
OTT: over the top, excessive
panto, pantomime: fairy-tale play performed at Christmas (silly but fun)
pants: (noun) underwear, briefs; (adj.) terrible, ridiculous
pasty (PASS-tee): crusted savory (usually meat) pie from Cornwall
pavement: sidewalk
pear-shaped: messed up, gone wrong
petrol: gas
piccalilli: mustard-pickle relish
pillar box: mailbox
pissed (rude), **paralytic, bevvied, wellied, popped up, merry, trollied, ratted, rat-arsed, pissed as a newt:** drunk
pitch: playing field
plaster: Band-Aid
plonk: cheap, bad wine
plonker: one who drinks bad wine (a mild insult)
prat: idiot
publican: pub owner
public school: private "prep" school (e.g., Eton)
pudding: dessert in general
pukka: first-class
pull, to be on the: on the prowl
punter: customer, especially in gambling
put a sock in it: shut up
queue: line
queue up: line up
quid: pound (£1)
randy: horny
rasher: slice of bacon
redundant, made: laid off
Remembrance Day: Veterans' Day
return ticket: round trip
revising; doing revisions: studying for exams
ring up: call (telephone)
roundabout: traffic circle
rubber: eraser
rubbish: bad
satnav: satellite navigation, GPS
sausage roll: sausage wrapped in a flaky pastry
Scotch egg: hard-boiled egg wrapped in sausage meat
Scouser: a person from Liverpool
self-catering: accommodation with kitchen

Sellotape: Scotch tape
services: freeway rest area
serviette: napkin
setee: couch
shag: intercourse (cruder than in the US)
shambolic: chaotic
shandy: lager and 7-Up
silencer: car muffler
single ticket: one-way ticket
skip: Dumpster
sleeping policeman: speed bumps
smalls: underwear
snap: photo (snapshot)
snogging: kissing, making out
sod: mildly offensive insult
sod it, sod off: screw it, screw off
sod's law: Murphy's law
soda: soda water (not pop)
soldiers (food): toast sticks for dipping
solicitor: lawyer
spanner: wrench
spend a penny: urinate
spotted dick: raisin cake with custard
stag night (or **stag do**): bachelor party
starkers: buck naked
starters: appetizers
state school: public school
sticking plaster: Band-Aid
sticky tape: Scotch tape
stone: 14 pounds (weight)
stroppy: bad-tempered
subway: underground walkway
sultanas: golden raisins
surgical spirit: rubbing alcohol
suspenders: garters
suss out: figure out
swede: rutabaga
ta: thank you
take the mickey/take the piss: tease
tatty: worn out or tacky
taxi rank: taxi stand
telly: TV
tenement: stone apartment house (not necessarily a slum)
tenner: £10 bill
theatre: live stage
tick: a check mark
tight as a fish's bum: cheapskate (watertight)
tights: panty hose
tin: can
tip: public dump
tipper lorry: dump truck
toad in the hole: sausage dipped in batter and fried
top hole: first rate
top up: refill (a drink, mobile-phone credit, petrol tank, etc.)
torch: flashlight
towel, press-on: panty liner
towpath: path along a river
trainers: sneakers
treacle: golden syrup
Tube: subway
twee: quaint, cutesy
twitcher: bird-watcher
Underground: subway
verge: grassy edge of road
verger: church official
way out: exit
wee (verb): urinate
Wellingtons, wellies: rubber boots
whacked: exhausted
whinge (rhymes with hinge): whine
wind up: tease, irritate
witter on: gab and gab
wonky: weird, askew
yob: hooligan
zebra crossing: crosswalk
zed: the letter Z

INDEX

INDEX

F

INDEX

M

INDEX

INDEX

Q

R

INDEX

MAP INDEX

Our website enhances this book and turns

Explore Europe

At ricksteves.com you can browse through thousands of articles, videos, photos and radio interviews, plus find a wealth of money-saving travel tips for planning your dream trip. And with our mobile-friendly website, you can easily access all this great travel information anywhere you go.

TV Shows

Preview the places you'll visit by watching entire half-hour episodes of Rick Steves' Europe (choose from all 100 shows) on-demand, for free.

Rick's Free Travel App

AUDIO EUROPE

Get your FREE **Rick Steves Audio Europe**™ app to enjoy…

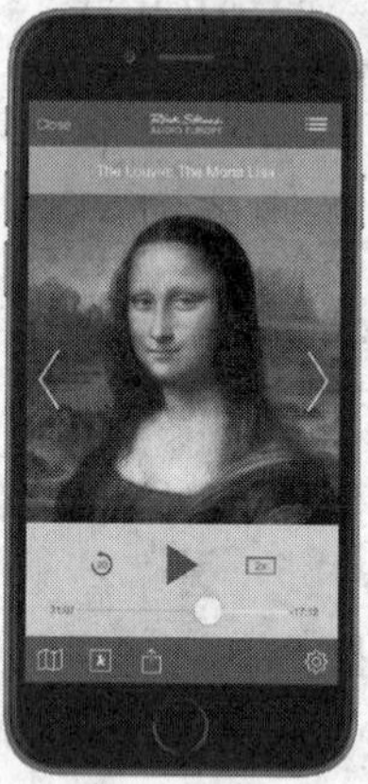

- Dozens of self-guided tours of Europe's top museums, sights and historic walks
- Hundreds of tracks filled with cultural insights and sightseeing tips from Rick's radio interviews
- All organized into handy geographic playlists
- For iPhone, iPad, iPod Touch, Android

With Rick whispering in your ear, Europe gets even better.

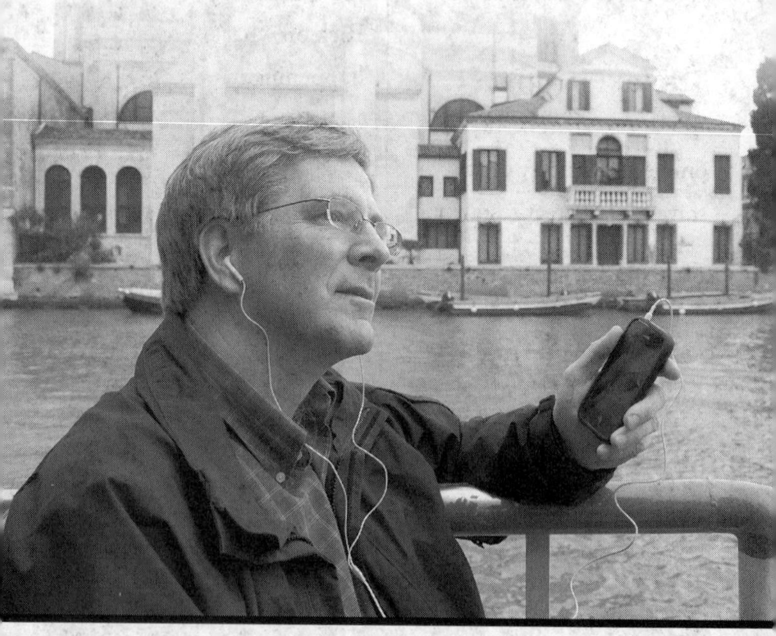

Find out more at ricksteves.com

Save time and energy

This guidebook is your independent-travel toolkit. But for all it delivers, it's still up to you to devote the time and energy it takes to manage the preparation and logistics that are essential for a happy trip. If that's a hassle, there's a solution.

Rick Steves Tours

A Rick Steves tour takes you to Europe's most interesting places with great

with minimum stress

guides and small groups of 28 or less. We follow Rick's favorite itineraries, ride in comfy buses, stay in family-run hotels, and bring you intimately close to the Europe you've traveled so far to see. Most importantly, we take away the logistical headaches so you can focus on the fun.

Join the fun

This year we'll take 18,000 free-spirited travelers—nearly half of them repeat customers—along with us on 40 different itineraries, from Ireland to Italy to Istanbul. Is a Rick Steves tour the right fit for your travel dreams? Find out at ricksteves.com, where you can also get Rick's latest tour catalog and free Tour Experience DVD.

Europe is best experienced with happy travel partners. We hope you can join us.

See our itineraries at ricksteves.com

Rick Steves

BEST OF GUIDES

Best of France
Best of Germany
Best of Ireland
Best of Italy
Best of Spain

EUROPE GUIDES

Best of Europe
Eastern Europe
Europe Through the Back Door
Mediterranean Cruise Ports
Northern European Cruise Ports

COUNTRY GUIDES

Croatia & Slovenia
England
France
Germany
Great Britain
Ireland
Italy
Portugal
Scandinavia
Scotland
Spain
Switzerland

CITY & REGIONAL GUIDES

Amsterdam & the Netherlands
Belgium: Bruges, Brussels, Antwerp & Gher
Barcelona
Budapest
Florence & Tuscany
Greece: Athens & the Peloponnese
Istanbul
London
Paris
Prague & the Czech Republic
Provence & the French Riviera
Rome
Venice
Vienna, Salzburg & Tirol

SNAPSHOT GUIDES

Basque Country: Spain & France
Berlin
Copenhagen & the Best of Denmark
Dublin
Dubrovnik
Edinburgh
Hill Towns of Central Italy
Italy's Cinque Terre
Krakow, Warsaw & Gdansk
Lisbon

Nearly all Rick Steves guides are available as ebooks. Check with your favorite bookseller.

Rick Steves guidebooks are published by Avalon Travel, an imprint of Perseus Books, a Hachette Book Group compa

Maximize your travel skills with a good guidebook.

Loire Valley
Madrid & Toledo
Milan & the Italian Lakes District
Naples & the Amalfi Coast
Northern Ireland
Norway
Sevilla, Granada & Southern Spain
St. Petersburg, Helsinki & Tallinn
Stockholm

POCKET GUIDES

Amsterdam
Athens
Barcelona
Florence
London
Munich & Salzburg
Paris
Prague
Rome
Venice
Vienna

TRAVEL CULTURE

Europe 101
European Christmas
European Easter
Postcards from Europe
Travel as a Political Act

***RICK STEVES' EUROPE* DVDs**

12 New Shows 2015-2016
Austria & the Alps
The Complete Collection 2000-2016
Eastern Europe
England & Wales
European Christmas
European Travel Skills & Specials
France
Germany, BeNeLux & More
Greece, Turkey & Portugal
The Holy Land: Israelis & Palestinians Today
Iran
Ireland & Scotland
Italy's Cities
Italy's Countryside
Scandinavia
Spain
Travel Extras

PHRASE BOOKS & DICTIONARIES

French
French, Italian & German
German
Italian
Portuguese
Spanish

PLANNING MAPS

Britain, Ireland & London
Europe
France & Paris
Germany, Austria & Switzerland
Ireland
Italy
Spain & Portugal

RickSteves.com   @RickSteves

Rick Steves books are available at bookstores and through online booksellers.

Credits

RESEARCHERS

To help update this book, Rick relied on...

Tom Griffin

After growing up in Wisconsin, Tom first headed east—living in London, Paris, and Germany—before reversing direction to end up on the West Coast. A former newspaper reporter, magazine editor, and ESL teacher, he now researches and edits guidebooks for Rick Steves' Europe. He lives in Seattle with his wife, Julie.

Robyn Stencil

Robyn credits the origin of her love affair with England to the Thames, supporting her motto "where there's a river, there's a run." Her ideal British adventure involves the call of gulls, plenty of flat whites, and friendly people from rocky coastline to green hills. When she's not researching, guiding, or pursuing the perfect burger, Robyn calls Seattle home, where she works as a tour operations specialist for Rick Steves' Europe.

Contributors

Cameron Hewitt

Born in Denver and raised in central Ohio, Cameron settled in Seattle in 2000. Ever since, he has spent three months each year in Europe, contributing to guidebooks, tours, radio and television shows, and other media for Rick Steves' Europe, where he serves as content manager. Cameron married his high school sweetheart (and favorite travel partner), Shawna, and enjoys taking pictures, trying new restaurants, and planning his next trip.

Gene Openshaw

Gene has co-authored a dozen *Rick Steves* books and contributes to many others. For this book, he wrote material on Europe's art, history, and contemporary culture. When not traveling, Gene enjoys composing music, recovering from his 1973 trip to Europe with Rick, and living everyday life with his daughter.

ACKNOWLEDGMENTS

Thanks to Roy and Jodi Nicholls for their research help, to Sarah Murdoch for writing the original version of the southern England chapters, to Jennifer Hauseman for the original version of the Glasgow chapter, to Colin Mairs for his help in Glasgow and throughout Scotland, and to friends listed in this book, who put the "Great" in Great Britain.

Avalon Travel
An imprint of Perseus Books
A Hachette Book Group company
1700 Fourth Street
Berkeley, CA 94710

Printed in Canada by Friesens
Second printing April 2017

ISBN 978-1-63121-297-0
ISSN: 1090-6843

For the latest on Rick's lectures, guidebooks, tours, public radio show, and public television series, contact Rick Steves' Europe, 130 Fourth Avenue North, Edmonds, WA 98020, 425/771-8303, www.ricksteves.com, rick@ricksteves.com.

Rick Steves' Europe
Special Publications Manager: Risa Laib
Managing Editor: Jennifer Madison Davis
Editors: Glenn Eriksen, Tom Griffin, Katherine Gustafson, Suzanne Kotz, Cathy Lu, John Pierce, Carrie Shepherd
Editorial & Production Assistant: Jessica Shaw
Editorial Intern: Grace Swanson
Contributors: Cameron Hewitt, Gene Openshaw
Researchers: Tom Griffin, Robyn Stencil
Graphic Content Director: Sandra Hundacker
Maps & Graphics: David C. Hoerlein, Lauren Mills, Mary Rostad

Avalon Travel
Senior Editor and Series Manager: Madhu Prasher
Editor: Jamie Andrade
Associate Editor: Sierra Machado
Copy Editor: Maggie Ryan
Proofreader: Patty Mon
Indexer: Stephen Callahan
Cover Design: Kimberly Glyder Design
Maps & Graphics: Kat Bennett, Mike Morgenfeld

Front Cover: The Cathedral of St. Andrews East Tower © Dominic Arizona Bonuccelli
Title Page: Beefeater © Dominic Arizona Bonuccelli
Front Matter Color: Glasgow, Scotland © Jennifer Hauseman
Additional Photography: Dominic Arizona Bonuccelli, Cutty Sark Trust (p. 128), Rich Earl, Barb Geisler, Tom Griffin, Jennifer Hauseman, Cameron Hewitt, David C. Hoerlein, Cathy Lu, Darbi Macy, Lauren Mills, Sarah Murdoch, Pat O'Connor, Gene Openshaw, Rhonda Pelikan, Jennifer Schutte, Sarah Slauson, Rick Steves, Gretchen Strauch, Bruce VanDeventer, Wikimedia Commons (PD-Art/PD-US).

Want more Britain?

Maximize the experience with Rick Steves as your guide

Guidebooks
London, England, and Scotland guides make side-trips smooth and affordable

Planning Maps
Use the map that's in sync with your guidebook

Rick's TV Shows
Preview where you're going with 9 shows on Britain

Free! Rick's Audio Europe™ App
Covering all the big sights and walks in London and more

Small Group Tours
Rick offers 4 great itineraries through Britain

For all the details, visit ricksteves.com